NOW ALL ROADS LEAD TO FRANCE

The Last Years of Edward Thomas

Matthew Hollis

WINDSOR
PARAGON

First published 2011
by Faber and Faber
This Large Print edition published 2012
by AudioGO Ltd
by arrangement with
Faber and Faber Ltd

Hardcover   ISBN: 978 1 445 82597 7
Softcover   ISBN: 978 1 445 82598 4

British Library Cataloguing in Publication Data available

Printed and bound in Great Britain by
MPG Books Group Limited

for Mum

and I rose up, and knew that I was tired, and continued my journey

EDWARD THOMAS, *Light and Twilight*

CONTENTS

ILLUSTRATIONS

MAPS

Edward Thomas spent the day before he died under particularly heavy bombardment. The shell that fell two yards from where he stood should have killed him, but instead it was a rare dud. Back at billet, the men teased him on his lucky escape; someone remarked that a fellow with Thomas's luck should be safe wherever he went. The next morning was the first of the Arras offensive. Easter Monday dawned cold and wintry. The infantry in the trenches fixed their bayonets and tightened their grip around their rifles; behind them, the artillery made their final preparations to the loading and the fusing of the shells. Thomas had started late to the Observation Post; he had not rung through his arrival when the bombardment began. The Allied assault was so immense that some Germans were captured half-dressed; others did not have time to put on their boots and fled barefoot through the mud and snow. British troops sang and danced in what only a few hours before had been no-man's-land. Edward Thomas left the dugout behind his post and leaned into the opening to take a moment to fill his pipe. A shell passed so close to him that the blast of air stopped his heart. He fell without a mark on his body.

I

STEEP

1913

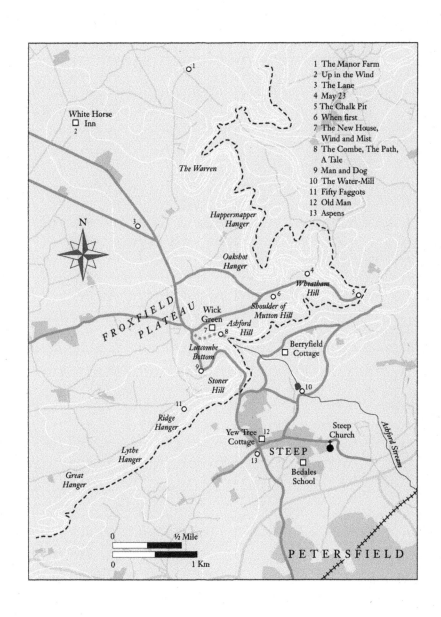

1 The Manor Farm
2 Up in the Wind
3 The Lane
4 May 23
5 The Chalk Pit
6 When first
7 The New House,
   Wind and Mist
8 The Combe, The Path,
   A Tale
9 Man and Dog
10 The Water-Mill
11 Fifty Faggots
12 Old Man
13 Aspens

White Horse
Inn
2

The Warren

Happersnapper
Hanger

Oakshot
Hanger

N

Wheatham
Hill

When first 6

Shoulder of
Mutton Hill

FROXFIELD PLATEAU

Wick
Green

Ashford
Hill

Berryfield
Cottage

Luscombe
Bottom

Stoner
Hill

Ridge
Hanger

Lythe
Hanger

Great
Hanger

Yew Tree
Cottage

STEEP

Steep
Church

Ashford Stream

Bedales
School

0   ½ Mile

0   1 Km

PETERSFIELD

WINTER

There has been opened at 35, Devonshire-street, Theobalds-road, a 'Poetry Bookshop', where you can see any and every volume of modern poetry. It will be an impressive and, perhaps, an instructive sight.

EDWARD THOMAS, *Daily Chronicle*, 14 January 1913

At the cramped premises off Theobald's Road in Bloomsbury, Harold Monro was preparing for the opening of his new bookshop. Before the turn of the year, Monro had announced that on 1 January 1913 he would open a poetry bookshop 'in the heart of London, five minutes' walk from the British Museum'. It would be devoted to the sale of verse in all its forms—books, pamphlets, rhyme sheets and magazines—and would be both a venue for poetry readings and the base for an intrepid publishing programme. 'Let us hope that we shall succeed in reviving, at least, the best traits and qualities of so estimable an institution as the pleasant and intimate bookshop of the past.' To Monro that revival meant something particular: wooden settles, a coal fire, unvarnished oak bookcases, a selection of literary reviews lain out on the shop table and, completing the scene, Monro's cat Pinknose curled up beside the hearth.[1]

The premises stood on a poorly lit, narrow street between the faded charm of the eighteenth-century Queen Square and the din of the tramways thundering up Theobald's Road. The shop occupied a small ground-floor room, twelve feet across and lit from the street by a fine five-panelled window; in the back was an office from where Monro ran his publishing empire. Upstairs was a dignified drawing room where the twice-weekly poetry readings were initially held, and two floors of bedrooms lay above, available to guests at a price of 'a sonnet and a shilling'—or three and sixpence a week in hard cash. Much of the surrounding area had been slum-cleared at the turn of the century when Kingsway was carved through from Bloomsbury Square to the Strand, but not Devonshire Street, which survived in squalor, cluttered by dustbins and vaulting cats. Public houses pinned the street at either end, while along its modest 150 yards traded two undertakers and, by report, a brothel. Many of the buildings were served by a single outside tap, and it was not unknown for passers-by to be hit with fish bones and other scraps cast out from an upstairs window, or chased down the street by boys with catapults. This was the setting for the Poetry Bookshop, in the heart of what one visitor called a 'murderous slum'.[2]

On 8 January 1913, a week later than planned, the Bookshop officially opened its doors. Poets, journalists, critics, readers, patrons: they came in their dozens, until barely a foot of standing room was left unclaimed. That afternoon and the one that followed, three hundred people crammed into the little shop, filling the staircase and the first-floor drawing room; for the capital's poets it was an occasion not to be missed. Wilfrid Gibson, the most popular young poet of the decade, was already resident in the attic rooms and had only to walk downstairs, while the wooden-legged, self-declared 'super-tramp', W. H. Davies, had hobbled in all the way from Kent. Lascelles ('he said it like tassels') Abercrombie had been invited to open the proceedings, but speculated that to ask a man of his years might seem tactless to the elders (he was about to turn thirty-two); W. B. Yeats diplomatically suggested that perhaps the honour should not befall a poet of any description. But Monro was adamant, and turned to the fifty-year-old Henry Newbolt, then Chair of Poetry at the Royal Society of Literature, to perform the ceremony. At Newbolt's side was Edward Marsh, Secretary to the First Lord of the Admiralty Winston Churchill and editor of an anthology launched that day that would become one of the best-selling poetry series of the century. Among its contributors was the twenty-five-year-old Rupert Brooke, who was in Cornwall that afternoon recovering from the strain of his fraught personal life but who would give a reading at the Bookshop before the month was out. F. S. Flint, a dynamic young civil servant and poet who spoke nine languages, took a place on the busy staircase and told the stranger beside him that he could tell by his shoes that he was an American. The shoes belonged to Robert Frost, newly arrived in London, who confessed that he should not have been there at all:

> One dark morning, early in the New Year, or maybe it was late in December, I found myself passing before the window of a shop where a clerk was arranging volumes of current poetry. A notice announced the opening, that night, of Harold Monro's Poetry Bookshop. I went

7

in and asked if I might return for the evening. The assistant told me the guests were 'Invited'. But I might try.[3]

Frost, aged thirty-eight, was a literary unknown without a book to his name and he had come to England to see that changed. Through the Poetry Bookshop he would make an introduction with another American who had achieved the very thing that Frost desired. Ezra Pound was a precocious young poet and editor who, at twenty-seven, had published four collections of his own; he would become closely involved in Frost's drive to publication and would make many appearances in the Bookshop himself. In the time ahead, almost every poet worth their salt would become part of the story of the Poetry Bookshop. T. S. Eliot would be a caller, Wilfred Owen a tenant in the attic rooms. Robert Graves, Charlotte Mew, Frances Cornford, Richard Aldington and Eleanor Farjeon would have books published under the shop's imprint. Others saw print through the shop's journal, *Poetry and Drama*: Thomas Hardy, D. H. Lawrence, Robert Bridges, Rabindranath Tagore, Amy Lowell, F. T. Marinetti and Walter de la Mare among them. Others again gave public readings: Yeats recited to a sell-out audience, Wilfrid Gibson performed in a droning monotone; W. H. Davies suffered nerves (cured when he was encouraged to think of the whisky afterwards), Sturge Moore forgot his lines; Ford Madox Hueffer read hurriedly, Rupert Brooke inaudibly, and Ralph Hodgson, who could not tolerate so much as a mention of his own work, simply refused to read at all, while simply no one could silence the actorly John Drinkwater.

The Poetry Bookshop would withstand all weathers: poor sales, infighting, alcoholism, a world war, competition, relocation, expansion and contraction, even romance between the poets and employees. 'All the poets have joined together to hire a big house near the British Museum,' reported the visiting sculptor Gaudier-Brzeska, 'where they live and work, and have underneath it a shop where they sell poetry by the pound.' For the next two decades, the Bookshop would be exactly what Rupert Brooke pronounced it to be when it opened that January in 1913: the centre of the New Poetry.[4]

*   *   *

In 1913, a new direction in poetry was desperately needed. The heyday of Victorian poetry was long over. Matthew Arnold had died in 1888, Robert Browning a year later, and the Laureate Alfred, Lord Tennyson had followed three years after that; the brother and sister Rossettis either side of this eminent trio. Swinburne and Meredith lived on but their best work was behind them, while the curtain had fallen on the risqué *fin-de-siècle* and their leading lights: Aubrey Beardsley, Oscar Wilde and Ernest Dowson had all died as the century turned. The Edwardian decade that followed had left behind a strandline of conservative imperialist verse: Henry Newbolt likening the Englishman at war to a public school-boy at cricket ('Play up! Play up! And play the game!'), while Rudyard Kipling wrote of the Empire's inheritance as 'the white man's burden'. It was 'tub-thumping stuff', Siegfried Sassoon told Rupert Brooke, offensive to some, plain silly to others. But the poet who most typified

9

the inadequacy of the age was the laureate Alfred Austin, a poet considered so terrible that he was better loved for the parodies of his verse rather than anything he wrote. In a hasty ode to the botched 1896 Jameson Raid in the Transvaal (a raid so shambolic that instead of cutting the telegraph wires to mask their position Jameson's company cut a wire fence by mistake), Austin attempted to honour his subject with a dignity reminiscent of Tennyson's 'The Charge of the Light Brigade', but instead he managed only this:

> So we forded and galloped forward
> As hard as our beasts could pelt,
> First eastward, then trending nor'ward,
> Right over the rolling veldt,

Bad as they were, these verses might have been quietly forgotten had it not been for an unkind satirist who parodied them yet more succinctly— 'They went across the veldt, | As hard as they could pelt'—a couplet that stuck in the public's craw, forever attributed to Austin, though he never actually wrote it. The mockery of the laureate might have been vindictive (it would worsen), but it was not without purpose; as Ezra Pound put it, 'Parody is, I suppose, the best criticism—it sifts the durable from the apparent.' The treatment doled out to Austin characterised a wider discrediting of Edwardian literature, and when Henry James said of H. G. Wells that he had 'so much talent with so little art' he said as much about Edwardian fiction in general as he did about Wells himself. Expectations were high for a promising new generation of novelists. Katherine Mansfield had

10

recently published her debut *In a German Pension*, while Virginia Woolf was finishing hers (*The Voyage Out*) and James Joyce was preparing *Dubliners*. D. H. Lawrence, whose *Sons and Lovers* would publish that year, said much about the moment when he likened it to an awakening from a night of oppressive dreams:

> And now our lungs are full of new air, and our eyes see it is morning, but we have not forgotten the terror of the night. We dreamed we were falling through space into nothingness, and the anguish of it leaves us rather eager. But we are awake again, our lungs are full of new air, our eyes of morning.[5]

These were unsettling times in England. The cost of living was soaring, and trade union membership had rocketed in recent years; the political left anticipated strikes, even riots as the Liberal government and the conservative courts undermined the legal standing and protection of the unions. Suffragettes were taking up direct action, breaking shop windows, starting letterbox fires, defacing public artworks, chaining themselves to railings; some went on hunger strike in prison and were subjected to brutal force-feeding. Women did not have the vote, nor did men who were without property. Irish Home Rule dominated debate at Westminster: the predominantly Catholic South urgently wanted to see it implemented, while the mainly Protestant North just as vehemently wished to block any measure of independence. Civil war loomed across the water, the British army feared mutiny, while the unofficial and rival armies of the Irish Volunteers

11

and the Ulster Volunteer Force were now drilling and gun running. The agricultural labour force was demoralised and impoverished, and England's 'green and pleasant lands' were rarely seen by the industrial classes locked into long and dangerous hours in the factories; the venerated 'all red line' of telegraph cables that linked Britain's Empire across the globe seemed a profitable market only for the rich. So did the telephone, the aeroplane, the radio, the motor car, the electric light bulb, the high-speed train, the cinema and other recent developments. The United States and the newly unified Germany had overtaken Britain as industrial powers. These were difficult days for Britain, uncertain hours for a fading empire, watching nervously the growing danger of Germany's own imperial aims.

*   *   *

At the end of the Edwardian era, literary attitudes were also in revolt. According to the *Times Literary Supplement*, 'public taste decreed that you should attend Fabian summer schools with vegetarians and suffragettes, and sit at the feet of Nietzsche, Ibsen, and Mr Bernard Shaw'. True enough, many of the poets who emerged from university at the turn of the century did so with leanings that were Fabian, Socialist or Liberal; but more importantly, they were writing in new ways, downplaying Victorian rhetoric and laying claim to anything, however 'unpoetic', that might lend their work realism. By 1911 that search for realism had introduced a coarseness which resonated with public taste but not with the gatekeepers of English literature. When Rupert Brooke published *Poems* that year (the only collection that appeared in his lifetime), its graphic treatment of a seasick, lovesick 'Channel Passage' included the lines, 'Retchings twist and tie me, | Old meat, good meals, brown gobbets, up I throw', which were generally considered vulgar, below decency or, at best, what the *Times Literary Supplement* described as 'swagger and brutality'. But it was John Masefield's poem *The Everlasting Mercy*, published first in the *English Review* in 1911, that had the greatest effect of all. The 1,700-line poem recounted the exploits of a bawdy, boozy village poacher; a braggart who boasts, 'I drunk, I fought, I poached, I whored, | I did despite unto the Lord', and who is confronted setting a trap:

> Now when he sees me set my snare,
> He tells me 'Get to hell from there.
> This field is mine,' he says, 'by right;
> If you poach here, there'll be a fight.
> Out now,' he says, 'and leave your wire;
> It's mine.'
>   'It ain't.'
>   'You put.'
>   'You liar.'
>
> 'You closhy put.'
>   'You bloody liar.'[6]

Modest as it might seem by today's standards, this was far from polite Edwardian fare and the poem thrilled the new audiences; as Edmund Blunden later reflected, it 'energised poetry and the reading of it, no matter what extremes of feeling it then aroused or now fails to arouse'. Gutsy, galloping, vernacular, here was verse story-telling that readers hungered for—as Harold Monro put it, 'that the general public could appreciate without straining its intelligence'.[7]

If Masefield and Brooke were the figureheads of this poetic revival, they were not yet the poets' poets. That distinction fell to two men: Thomas Hardy and W. B. Yeats. But they were an older generation and of secure reputation with a dozen volumes of verse between them, whose passions were seen by some to lie elsewhere. Hardy was by then in his seventies, and it was his novels that the public seemed likely to remember. Irishman William Butler Yeats was still in his forties, but his work with the Abbey Theatre was considered by many in the poetry world as a waste of his considerable talents, while his aloof manner by common agreement made him unapproachable. Neither man seemed likely to direct a revolution in verse; that challenge would fall to a younger division of writers, 'the two newest and most forward movements in English poetry', said Harold Monro: the Georgians and the Imagists.[8]

*   *   *

In the summer of 1911, with George V newly enthroned, Harold Monro addressed his friend Arthur Sabin over lunch with uncharacteristic excitement. 'We are living in a new Georgian era—and, by Jove, Arthur, we are the new Georgian poets'. Within eighteen months, he would publish a book from his Devonshire Street headquarters that captured the new mood exactly; but the idea for it would not come from him.[9]

Rupert Brooke was a frequent guest at Edward

14

Marsh's apartments in Gray's Inn, London, and one night in September 1912 he and Marsh sat up late, discussing how best to shake the public of their ignorance of contemporary poetry. There and then, they counted a dozen poets worth publishing, and put the idea of an anthology to Monro. Five hundred copies were printed: half received on 16 December 1912, the remainder on Christmas Eve; all were sold by Christmas Day. A reprint was hurried through, then another and another. By the end of its first year, the book was in its ninth printing and was on its way to 15,000 sales. The name of this remarkable anthology was *Georgian Poetry*.

At its simplest, the Georgian Poets were those who appeared in the five volumes that Edward Marsh would edit over the next decade; but these writers were brethren by more than publication alone. The Georgians looked to the local, the commonplace and the day-to-day, mistrusting grandiosity, philosophical enquiry or spiritual cant. Many held an attachment to the traditions of English Romantic verse; they looked to Wordsworth in their connection to the land rather than to John Donne and the Metaphysical pursuit of the soul. The style was innocent, intimate and direct; lyric in form, rhythmic in drive, it dovetailed short sketches of the natural world with longer meditations on the condition of the human heart. It was not a poetry of public politics and represented no particular ideology or constituency, but attempted instead to convey rapture in the modest miracles of life: in a daffodil, a bird's song or the breeze that stroked the branches of an oak tree. It employed whimsy in place of calculation, charm

15

rather than conviction, and attempted the lightness of a pianist playing with one hand; its subject matter would be as everyday as a country lane or a village fence post.

To its critics, this was an approach that could only equate to 'minor' verse and 'littleness', and some thought them in love with littleness; Richard Aldington: 'They took a little trip for a week-end to a little cottage where they wrote a little poem on a little scheme'; Robert Graves: 'Georgianism became principally concerned with Nature and love and leisure and old age and childhood and animals and sleep and other uncontroversial subjects.' Sentiment came easily to the Georgian poets, rigour less so. Their rhythm could be flip, their diction vague, their imagery imprecise. 'Unless a man write with his whole nature concentrated upon his subject he is unlikely to take hold of another man,' wrote Edward Thomas in a book published in 1913; and the Georgians did not concentrate nearly hard enough. The desire for realism lost intensity, becoming homely, hearthside and lazily affectionate. What in the mouth of John Masefield or Rupert Brooke had in 1911 seemed like the gritty tang of a rough cider became instead the comfort of a hot drink at bedtime; T. S. Eliot: 'The Georgians caress everything that they touch.' More likely than not, the Georgian poem about a songbird or a wild animal would embalm the little creature that it had intended to 'free' in the imagination of the reader; worse still, what it captured was rarely some essence of the animal but more frequently the poet's dubious decoration. But still they ventured, using their notebooks as butterfly nets to capture and take home their subjects for examination. 'We go to it as would-be poets or as solitaries, vagabonds, lovers,' wrote Edward Thomas temporarily adopting a Georgian guise, 'to escape foul air, noise, hard hats, black uniforms, multitudes, confusion, incompleteness, elaborate means without clear ends—to escape ourselves.'[10]

*   *   *

'We are at the beginning of another "Georgian period",' wrote Edward Marsh proudly in 1912, 'which may take rank in due time with the several great poetic ages of the past.' Humbug, thought Ezra Pound, who was busily ensuring that the Georgians were not going to have the new dawn entirely to themselves. Under his direction there would be an alternative to these country verses that was more angular, more radical, more revolutionary: Imagism.[11]

It was in a tea shop in Kensington in 1912 that Pound first informed Richard Aldington and Hilda Doolittle that they were 'Imagists', which entailed agreement upon three principles:

1 Direct treatment of the 'thing', whether subjective or objective.
2 To use absolutely no word that does not contribute to the presentation.
3 As regarding rhythm: to compose in the sequence of the musical phrase, not in sequence of a metronome.

Direct treatment, a pared language, a relatively free verse: these were sharp distinctions from the gentle Georgians. No sing-song rhythms or cloying subject matter, no abstractions, no ornament, no superfluous word; this was language stripped down to the bone, harder and saner, 'austere, direct, free from emotional slither.' Pound's two-line 'In a Station of the Metro' from 1913:

The apparition   of these faces   in the crowd   :
Petals   on a wet, black   bough   .[12]

Modern, forward-facing, trim, these were poems for their age, influenced by French Symbolism and pictorial Cubism, in which a single, carefully chosen image could do more, it was proposed, than any detailed description that the Georgians might concoct. If the Georgians were to be regional in their outlook, Imagists would be citizens of the world, Aldington explained, and they chose their meeting place accordingly, gathering in a restaurant called The Eiffel Tower in London's Soho under the watchful direction of a young Cambridge graduate, T. E. Hulme, and the fiery, Idaho-born Ezra Pound. A roving talent scout, Pound sent off the work of Aldington, Doolittle (whom he rechristened 'H.D.') and others to Harriet Monroe (no connection to Harold Monro) for her Chicago-based magazine *Poetry*, and he would counter *Georgian Poetry* with the most declamatory anthology of its kind for the Poetry Bookshop in 1914, *Des Imagistes*.

It seems unthinkable that Ezra Pound could ever have cast in his lot with the rustic Georgians, but it almost happened. In 1912 Edward Marsh wrote to Pound to ask if he could include two of his pieces in the first *Georgian Poetry*, but Pound declined. He declined not out of an aversion to Georgianism:

18

he withheld one poem because he felt it did not represent any modern trend and the other because it was due out imminently in a book of his own. Was there anything among his earlier works that Marsh might take, asked Pound. There was not, but they agreed to have the question revisited if the anthology went into a second volume. By the time it came to assembling the next edition a feud had opened between the bitterly opposed camps of Georgians and Imagists.

*　　*　　*

These were intoxicating days in the capital. London was, wrote Ford Madox Hueffer, 'unrivalled in its powers of assimilation—the great, easy-going, tolerant, lovable, old dressing-gown of a place that it was then, but was never more to be'. For poets, the Bookshop on Devonshire Street would be at the centre of operations, and on its opening on 8 January 1913 many of the era's shaping forces were making their introductions. Robert Frost may not have been invited but he had found his way to the right place at the right time. 'I was only too childishly happy in being allowed . . . for a moment in a company in which I hadn't to be ashamed of having written verse,' he recalled. But there was someone else in the Poetry Bookshop that day who was not known to the American. This person would open more doors for him than F. S. Flint, be a more influential critic than Ezra Pound and be a better friend than Wilfrid Gibson; he would influence the reputation of almost every writer present and would become, in Frost's words, 'the only brother I ever had'.[13]

Though they did not meet that day, also in the room was Edward Thomas.

*   *   *

Edward Thomas had travelled to the Poetry Bookshop from his parents' home in Balham, London. He had spent the past two months living in East Grinstead, West Sussex, completing the only novel he would finish. But Sussex was not his family home: that lay fifty miles to the west at Steep in Hampshire, and he had come away to escape it. His spirits were desperately low. Thirty-four years of age, a married father of three, Thomas was, in his mind, little more than a literary hack, writing all the hours that he could manage to bring home a modest income. The relentless, ungratifying work left him exhausted and bitter, while the din of family life served only to worsen his mood. In poor spirits he treated his family cruelly, scolding the children and reprimanding his wife, and the more he did so, the worse his spirits became. The only way he knew to break the cycle was to leave; sometimes his absences lasted days, at other times he would be gone for months. At these moments, even to drag himself home for a weekend was more than he could manage, and though the children missed him and his wife yearned, he convinced himself that they could only be happy without him. Away from his family he could begin to lift himself again and carry on.

However turbulent his home life, Thomas's literary work could not afford to skip a beat. In weekly visits to London he would petition editors for commissions and take the opportunity to catch up with friends, among them Harold Monro, who had been a guest at the family home that autumn when Thomas had teased that although Monro sold poets he was really no better than a poet himself. Thomas rarely spoke or wrote in a style that brought his audience to outright laughter, but he had a subtle wit that was so dry it could be mistaken for waspishness. He could sting, certainly, and was frequently stung, but only rarely would he allow a poison to creep into his comments, and even then only out of desperation. He was rarely motivated by jealousy or egotism, he lacked vanity and was spared the arrogance of some of his peers, so when Thomas told Monro that he would attend the opening of his bookshop on the condition that he was guaranteed protection against assault by any of the poets, Monro knew precisely how to take the remark. The guarantee was sought only partly in jest, for Thomas was a professional reviewer of verse and his brilliant, uncompromising articles were the making of many young reputations and the breaking of others; as a letter in *The Times* put it, 'He was the man with the keys to the Paradise of English Poetry', and those he damned could be unforgiving. A fortnight after he died in 1917, de la Mare wrote:

Edward Thomas must have been a critic of rhymes in his nursery. How much generous help and encouragement many living poets owe to his counsel only themselves could say. To his candour, too. For the true cause, he believed, is better served by an uncompromising 'Trespassers will be prosecuted' than by an amiable 'All are welcome'.

Trespassers came in many forms—the pompous, the incompetent, the insincere, the unskilled, the tone-deaf—and those he suspected of inadequacy he pursued without mercy. Thomas despised the substandard wherever he encountered it: in the anointed, in his peers, but most especially he despised it in himself. For when he was not sharpening his mind on the reviewing he did for a living, he was blunting it again through the commissions that were beneath his talents: endless and often aimless prose measured out by the page to fulfil his contractual obligations. The homes of the writers, lepidoptery, superstitions, civic guides, topography, lumbering biographies, histories of castles: these were just some of the efforts that he put his name to, work that left him empty and exhausted, and bitter at the abuse of his powers.[14]

By 1913 Edward Thomas had published twenty prose books under his own name and had edited or introduced a dozen more. Over seventy of his articles had been printed in periodicals and well in excess of 1,500 signed book reviews while many more were published anonymously. In 1912–13 he had published three biographies, a gathering of Norse tales and almost fifty signed reviews of works ranging from Chaucer to his contemporaries. He was working on a travel book tracing the Icknield Way, a country tale told by a townsman, an autobiographical novel and several smaller pieces for the literary journals. For all this, Thomas might expect to earn up to £250 a year, a salary a little over that of a schoolmaster's. Financially, he was comfortable enough to feed a family of five in a rented cottage; sometimes there was a little left over to hire some help about the home, at other times he took in paying guests to subsidise the household income. But he always honoured his promises, whether or not he was paid for keeping them.[15]

Thomas left the opening of the Poetry Bookshop that evening to meet Mervyn, his twelve-year-old son, at Victoria station and catch the seven o'clock train back to his parents' house in Balham. Bronwen, his ten-year-old daughter, waited for him there, but his youngest, Myfanwy, aged just two and a half, was carrying a cold and a boil and remained at East Grinstead, where the family had joined Edward for Christmas, cared for by Helen, the woman he had married thirteen years ago, who loved him with a passion that he could no longer return.

*　　　*　　　*

By all accounts Edward Thomas was a striking man who turned heads wherever he went. At six foot he was tall for the times, slim, loose-limbed and vigorous. He had thick, rather long fair hair, lightened by his time spent outdoors, a narrow face with strong cheekbones, rounding at a firm chin, and steady grey-blue eyes so sharp that he once observed the difference in the two eyes of a dog from a moving bus. His expression was grave and detached, but his smile, when it came, could be coy, whimsical or proud. He rarely laughed. A short clay pipe was never far from his lips or the palm of his left hand. He spoke in a clear baritone, though often he kept his own counsel, and preferred the company of an individual to a group. He had a

23

countryman's stride, and never put his long legs under a table but always sat square on. He dressed in a suit of tawny tweed, which was old, sunned and slightly loose, and which, he liked to say, smelt of dog whenever it was damp. His jacket pockets were impossibly deep, and from these he would pull maps, apples and clay pipes in a procession as apparently endless as the scarves from a magician's hand. It was said that the melancholy that was stamped upon him seemed only to make his beauty more apparent.[16]

*　　　*　　　*

Thomas had been plagued by depression from before his university days at Oxford. There, he fought to shake it out of himself: he tried drink and opium, took up rowing and rowdiness, but could not hold the bleak moods back. When the dark thoughts overran him, he told himself that he valued life too much to take it away, or that he was too sedentary to go through with ending it; but in recent years he had become harder to console. In advertising his sorrows, as he put it, he had punished his family, decimated his friends and broken down his self-respect. 'Things have been very wrong,' he told his old friend Jesse Berridge in February 1913. 'My health is now definitely bad— not mere depression—and I don't know how it will develop.'[17]

Towards his wife Helen he was cruel at these times. Hard silences, harsh words, quiet fury, despair. She learned not to pursue him into his agony but to leave him be, and continue with her daily chores. She would chatter across the silences until she ran out of chatter or he of patience, and either the silence resumed or it would be broken by his angry departure from the house. She became expert at identifying his mood from his demeanour returning home: his hundred-yard stare, his pale and haggard expression, his hunch at the shoulders, his lips tightly shut as if to hold in an unkind word. Often he worked or walked late in the evening and if she waited up with his supper he would rage at her for doing so. He hated her fussing and her pretence that all was well, but the loathing he felt toward his own cowardice was stronger. Unable to do what he believed he should and put an end to his suffering, he was left to berate himself bitterly: 'I'm the man who always comes home to his supper.' Mealtimes could pass in silence: the children too frightened to talk, Thomas grief-stricken by his effect upon them. He would provoke them and they would cry and he would depart again, leaving Helen afraid that he might not return, and afraid of his mood when he did.[18]

Some years before, at Berryfield Cottage in Steep, Thomas had written this:

I sat thinking about ways of killing myself. My revolver has only one bullet left. I couldn't hang myself: and though I imagined myself cutting my throat with a razor on Wheatham I had not the energy to go. Then I went out and thought what effects my suicide would have. I don't think I mind them. My acquaintances—I no longer have friends—would talk a day or two (when they met) and try to explain and of course see suggestions in the past. W. H. Davies would suffer a little; Helen and

25

the children—less in reality than they do now, from my accursed tempers and moodiness. It is dislike of the effort to kill myself and fear that I could not carry it through if I half did it that keeps me alive. Only that. For I hate my work, my reviewing: my best I feel is negligible: I have no vitality, no originality, no love. I do harm. Love is dead and lust almost dead.[19]

In the winter of 1908 he made an attempt on his life that he documented in a short story, which, layered against Helen's account, his diary and his notes, forms a picture of events on that November day. He had turned on Bronwen because she dared disturb his melancholy; and now she was wailing, and her cries struck him to the core; he could stand it no longer. He went to the drawer where he kept an old revolver, the barrel of which was brown with rust and whose chambers had become so stiff that they would not turn without the encouragement of both hands. Time was when he had thought of throwing the gun away; but now he was grateful for it and the one remaining ball cartridge which would still, he fancied, force its way along the rusty barrel. He turned toward the front door. His wife had watched him at the drawer; she knew what he kept there. Desperate to distract him, she pleaded that he might take his daughter along; but he rebuked them both. He felt sure of what he was to do: he said he felt 'called to death'. He crossed the wheat fields in front of the house and began to climb Shoulder of Mutton Hill. Hurriedly, Helen gathered the children and led them away from the cottage down to the stream so that they could paddle and push their boats on the water without needing her attentions; she was out of her mind with worry. From the hill he stared at the house, hoping perhaps to see his daughter run into the garden and compel him to go back. He gazed down upon the elder hedgerow that flanked the house, and then lifted his eyes to the Downs and the hazy sun, searching to find a reason to turn around. Nothing responded to him and he responded to nothing. He wished for a place to hide, away from family and self-disgust, somewhere far off enough that the sound of a gunshot would not travel home, and finally he found it, surrounded by beech trees, cut off from the path and flanked by the hill. He pushed the cartridge home and turned the chamber into place, and took a final glance across the woods. Someone was walking in the hills above him, calling a name that he could not determine. He felt a sudden sense of shame, and raised the gun quickly to his chest. His finger fluttered on the trigger; too lightly to fire. He closed his eyes and imagined that he had succeeded, imagined his discovery by the walker, who would marvel at the calm confidence of the act. He opened his eyes. He was shaking with cold. He turned for home. Neither husband nor wife would speak of the episode, though both would write of it. 'Shall I make the tea?' said Helen as he took off his boots. 'Please,' is what he said.[20]

'How nice it would be to be dead if only we could know we were dead,' he had written to Gordon Bottomley in the weeks before the attempt. 'That is what I hate, the not being able to turn around in the grave & say It is over.'[21]

*   *   *

27

Helen Noble first laid eyes on Edward Thomas in the summer of 1894 when the sixteen-year-old youth began calling on her father at their home near Wandsworth Common. James Ashcroft Noble mentored Thomas and helped in finding him a publisher for the book he published at the age of eighteen, *The Woodland Life*. Thomas was by then already a precocious essayist, but was still impressionable enough to be guided by Mr Noble in his discovery of Keats and Shelley. But Mrs Noble took less kindly to Thomas's appearances at their Wandsworth home and less kindly still to her husband's attempts to encourage a friendship with their daughter. Not that the bohemian Helen needed any encouragement in the company of the athletic, handsome young man who climbed high into elm trees to steal her a heron's egg and who sent her a chaffinch's nest prised from an apple tree because she said she had never before seen one. A year older than Edward, Helen was a confident, even forward girl who took it upon herself to call on the Thomas household while Edward was out in order to introduce herself to his parents. The move incensed Helen's mother, who felt that her daughter's behaviour was wholly unbecoming, and when Mr Noble died in 1896 she forbade Helen any sight of Edward. In the bitter fights that followed, Helen left home for a post as a nursery governess in Broadstairs, Kent, where she looked after a young girl called Hope Webb and from where she wrote long, affectionate letters to Edward. By the time he went up to Lincoln College, Oxford, in the autumn of 1897 they had become lovers. Helen was still a governess but now in London, and it was here that the young couple would meet for walks on Wandsworth Common or to browse the salacious paperbacks on the booksellers' row at Holywell Street.[22]

When Helen fell pregnant while Edward was an undergraduate their relationship underwent a sea-change. It became one of temperance, described by Thomas as a happiness 'so mild and cool' that it resembled a 'saintliness'. They married secretly at Fulham Register Office on 19 June 1899 and kept their union from their parents. Mrs Noble's discovery of their secret brought about the final estrangement in the turbulent relationship between mother and daughter, though Helen was at least now welcomed in the household of Mr and Mrs Thomas and allowed to move in there while Edward completed his degree.[23]

Philip Mervyn Thomas was born while Edward was still at university. The prospect of having to earn a living for his new family put a strain on the young man which he would never fully overcome. Distracted and depressed, Edward missed out on the First in History for which he was headed, thereby ruling out the academic career that he had seen as the answer to his financial plight. He desired a literary life for himself but feared the poverty it would inflict upon his family. His father pushed him towards what he saw as a more reputable career in the civil service; but Edward instead began a series of speculative calls upon London's literary editors, among them Henry Nevinson of the *Daily Chronicle*, who remembered their unlikely interview.

He was tall, absurdly thin, and a face of

29

attractive distinction and ultra refinement was sicklied over with nervous melancholy and the ill condition of bad food or hunger. Almost too shy to speak, he sat down proudly and asked if I could give him work. I enquired what work he could do and he said 'None' . . . I asked whether he would like some reviewing on any subject, and on what. He replied that he knew nothing of any subject, and was quite sure he could not write, but certainly he did want work of some sort.[24]

From the *Chronicle* and the other papers for which he toiled he earned a meagre £52 in the twelve months after leaving Oxford University; he doubled that income the following year, but it was not nearly enough: he owed Lincoln College £60, and was summoned before the Oxford County Courts.

Helen and Edward's first home together in Earlsfield's Atheldene Road was a squalid south London terrace; it lasted them only four months. Then came rooms off Nightingale Lane in Balham for 11s. a week; they endured those for just eight months. Teaching posts promising £120 a year came and went but Thomas did not apply for a single one of them. The fights with his father worsened, and Edward forbade him to make job enquiries at Whitehall on his behalf even though the young couple were living hand to mouth. The penury, the squalor, the sleepless nights around the baby became too much to bear. Edward turned against city living. Day after day he took a bicycle or a train out of the capital to look for a country home. From one such journey he returned to tell Helen that he had found them a functional red-brick cottage a mile from Bearsted in Kent, not a pretty house and not cheap, but at least not London. From Kent, Edward earned what he could from his pen: calling on or corresponding with the London editors as he would do throughout his life, at times begging his way into work. His total savings in 1902 were 1s. 8½d., about enough to rent his cottage for a day. He suffered long fits of melancholy, and took extended walks in an attempt to keep his mood away from the cottage. But he could not save Helen from his anger. One morning she returned from the post office to report that no letters offering work had arrived for him that day. 'Why tell me what is written on your pale wretched face?' he lashed out at her. 'I am cursed, and you are cursed because of me. I hate the tears I see you've been crying. Your sympathy and your love are both hateful to me. Hate me, but for God's sake don't stand there, pale and suffering. Leave me, I tell you; get out and leave me.' For the only time in their life together, the unsinkable Helen lost her ability to cope. Pregnant for a second time, she wrote distressingly to her best friend, Janet Hooton, 'This alone is terrible as no one wants the wee thing; no one looks forward to its coming, and I least of anyone.'

> You ask why we don't want it? Because we are very poor; because it means more anxiety for Edward and more work for him. Home will become unendurable to him. Even now poverty, anxiety, physical weakness, disappointments and discouragements are making him bitter, hard and impatient, quick to violent anger, and subject to long

31

fits of depression . . . He is selling some of his dearest books to pay for baby clothes and doctors, etc. and as he packs them up I know how he is rebelling at fate, how hard life seems to him, how he regrets it all . . . He cannot love, Janet, he cannot respond to my love. How can he when all is so dark, and I, I have deprived him of it all, the joys of life and love and success. If he would only begin life again without me my heart would rejoice. I should be very happy, for his happiness is all I care for . . . I have prayed that I and my babe may die, but we shall not, tho this would free Edward.[25]

Helen's sister Irene could not bear to see her sibling in such despair, and for the only time in his life, Edward found himself openly challenged about his matrimonial behaviour. 'My spirit burned within me,' Irene recorded, 'and I felt I *must* say what was in my heart. I shall never forget how he took it,—admitting everything, extenuating nothing. His humility melted me, and I felt drawn to him in a way I had never before.' Edward's callous behaviour had once again slipped retribution.[26]

It was the commission of a book on Oxford that rescued them both; that, and a legacy that had come to Helen. The contract from A. & C. Black came with a £100 advance, £20 on signature: it was Thomas's first commission and it was a lifeline. Rachel Mary Bronwen was born in 1902, and the family, now four strong, moved closer into Bearsted village itself, to a half-timbered tall and narrow house on the village green. For a while the new setting and the new work helped to lift the family's spirits. Thomas even participated in village life. He learned to improve his woodworking skills from the neighbouring wheelwright, who taught him how to make a simple spade handle out of ash and the different uses to which a plane could be put. Thomas would in time take what he was learning to carve the furniture around which they would live. But he was also stealing yet more time away from domestic company he found harder and harder to abide. 'No one knows how difficult I find it to live with Helen,' he wrote in his diary in 1903, 'though I admire her, like her, perhaps love her.' Helen consoled herself that through a longer struggle they would win out. 'Deep in my heart I knew that he depended on me, and would need me when his horrible suffering was over.' She loved him as a wife and with 'the pride of a mother', and bided her time, and devoted herself to her children.[27]

At eighteen months, young Bronwen developed pneumonia and almost died; the house on the green was deemed insanitary and brought a move to a farmhouse in the Weald of Kent, a few miles south of Sevenoaks. Elses Farm was surrounded by oast houses, hayricks, stables and an orchard; nightingales flocked in the hedgerows. For the first time, Thomas came to watch the year's seasons in completion: to watch the team of horses turning the plough before seeding, or the raking of the bush harrows or the reaping of the crops. He rented a study-cottage a mile or more from the farm, and wore a footpath through the copse trekking back and forth; other times he took off for London. With two children to attend to on her own, his absences confined Helen to an isolated life, indoors away from the friends she had made in Bearsted.

Once more she found herself writing long, aching letters after him; his replies were sometimes warm, sometimes brusque, but mostly businesslike in their call on her to cash cheques or send whatever items or clothing he needed.[28]

By 1906, earning £250 a year, the poverty that Edward and Helen had known in their early years together seemed to be behind them at last, but it had come at a price to their relationship. 'What I really ought to do is live alone,' he told Jesse Berridge. 'But I can't find the courage to do the many things necessary for taking that step. It is really the kind H. and the children who make life almost *impossible*.'[29] Somehow they adapted to the outbursts and the absences. The wretchedness at home rose and tempered and rose again; the absences became longer. Edward was away when their third child, Helen Elizabeth Myfanwy ('Baba') was born, some eight years after Bronwen. By the time Edward Thomas met Robert Frost, it was clear to the American that he was all but living alone.[30]

The absences were crippling to Helen. She was warm and impulsive, a product of her father's free-thinking influence, but her untidy spontaneity made her a hopeless housekeeper and a poor cook to Edward's irritation. She felt acutely aware that she was not conventionally pretty—she wore round glasses on a round and rosy face—and was mortified by a sense that Edward's friends must have wondered what he saw in her, a woman who was neither as brilliant nor as beautiful as he; she believed that he kept her apart from his London life as though she were someone to be ashamed of. But she took pride in her body and her physicality, and lacked the sexual prudery of the time and was

34

indifferent to the opinion of others, outraging her closest friend by her premarital intimacy with Edward. She said she 'hated' the idea of the legal contract of marriage and saw herself as a semi-wild child of nature, 'a part of the stirring earth'; she looked to Edward to teach her the nouns for it all. It was her bohemianism that allowed her to 'manage' his disappearances emotionally; but it was these same unconventional attitudes that left her isolated and wounded when he left.[31]

*   *   *

Edward Thomas's doctors diagnosed him with neurasthenia, a term largely discredited today, but widely used then to describe any number of ill-defined conditions, including anxiety, lassitude, listlessness or a general emotional disturbance characterised by fatigue or irritability. For years his physicians prescribed one abstinence after another: from tobacco, from alcohol, a sugar-free diet. They tried brown bread and vegetarianism, even a prescription of fifteen minutes' daily exercise with dumb-bells for a man who would think nothing of walking twenty miles a day. But instead of helping in his recovery, Thomas felt that these doctors were merely 'unmaking' him. 'I have somehow lost my balance,' he confessed to a friend in 1911, 'and can never recover it by diet or rule or any deliberate means, but only by some miracles from within or without.' Exhaustion overtook him; he had written seven books that year and could no longer keep his despair at bay. Helen feared he was once again suicidal, and in desperation turned to his friends for help. But their response was not always

35

sympathetic. W. H. Hudson, the naturalist whom Thomas admired more than any living writer, said idly: 'I am sorry to hear that Thomas has broken down again—why will he work so incessantly and so furiously?'[32]

Psychology in England was in its primitive stages before the war, with psychosomatic disorders little understood. Thomas himself was not uncritical of his own condition, nor was he unappreciative of the energies that it produced within him. Aware that the depression was also a source of creativity, he had in the past been ambivalent about attempts to purge it. 'I wonder whether for a person like myself whose most intense moments were those of depression a cure that destroys the depression may not destroy the intensity,' he wrote in 1908, adding '—a *desperate* remedy?' But in 1912 he had finally met an individual who could help with a subtler understanding of his suffering.[33]

Godwin Baynes was every bit a new man for a new century. Tall, charismatic and athletic, he had studied medicine at Trinity College, Cambridge (where he had been a 'blue' for the university as a swimmer and oarsman), before training at Barts and at La Salpêtrière in Paris. Baynes was a war hero before the Great War, decorated by Enver Pasha for his work to establish a hospital for Balkan refugees in 1912; he had returned to England to open a practice for the poor in Bethnal Green, where many of Baynes's first clients were suffering from starvation and had little to offer by way of payment. The surgery attracted a constant stream of social visitors, both in and out of hours, and evening gatherings would include poetry readings or musical recitals. Baynes was at the centre of a whirl of leisured young socialites who liked nothing more than to spend their time on tennis courts, inventing parlour games or attending the theatre. His popularity would eventually exhaust him, and when it did he moved with his wife from London to Wisbech, Cambridgeshire, in the winter of 1913 in search of a quieter life. When the town council learned of his impending arrival, they met him from the train with a brass band.[34]

Godwin Baynes would study under Carl Jung and was a pioneer of an early form of psychoanalysis in England, and with Edward Thomas he made an experimental foray into the discipline. Their first session took place in April 1912, when Thomas spent ten days in Baynes's company at Broughton Gifford in Wiltshire. There the men walked and talked, and Thomas reported enthusiastically, 'The doctor is working magic with my disordered intellect.' Helen witnessed the progress from a distance; Baynes was indeed a magician, it seemed to her, and she implored Edward to grasp the opportunity given him. Thomas would stay with Baynes in the Bethnal Green surgery for a few days at a time, talking formally on a daily basis for an 'analytic hour' for a payment that was likely to have been 2s. 6d. a session (about the price of a poetry book). But of equal importance was the time spent together out of surgery, when Baynes had the foresight to treat Thomas as a friend and not only as a patient.[35]

No medical notes survive of their sessions together, but a notebook exists that Baynes kept while studying under Jung in 1920. In it he records a dream in which Thomas appeared before him.

The delicate poet who was killed in the war. He was my friend. In my early, eager innocence I tried amateurishly to cure his Neurasthenia by suggestion. I often reproached myself for taking a fee for my childish effort for of course I did not cure him.

He was a generous, witty comrade and in his soul he was saintly. He saw deeply into the hearts and souls of men for he too had known the clutch of the erotic complex and this was the source of his neurosis.

His face was Christ-like and it is his link with Christ the Lover of Man that brings his sorrowful, pitiful soul into his eyes.[36]

Baynes never expanded upon his insight into Thomas's neurosis, but possibly he alluded to a belief that since childhood Thomas had relied too deeply upon other people, notably his mother, to lift the gloom of unhappiness.

To find self-reliance, to determine his own path: these were the drives that Thomas took from his sessions with Baynes. How was he to live without paining others? Could he cast his own fortune after these lengthy years or would he continue down the same tormented path? And if he could effect a change, where should he look to in order to make it happen? Should he live without dependence upon others as the sessions with the doctor seemed to suggest, or should he hold out for the help of a rescuing hand? It was a question that was forming into the central and tumultuous struggle of his life. In 1906 Thomas had prophesied that amid his despondency an individual would one day emerge as his rescuer. 'I feel sure that my salvation depends on a person and that person cannot be Helen because she has come to resemble me too much.'[37]

Early in 1913 it seemed to Thomas that the prophecy might prove true, and that the long-hoped-for saviour could be the gifted, kindly Godwin Baynes.

Such a person would indeed emerge to help Edward Thomas out of his despair that year; but he would not be a doctor.

*　　　*　　　*

As the SS *Parisian* skirted the dark headlands of Donegal and Antrim, Robert and Elinor Frost and their four children must have wondered what this new episode in their lives would bring. They had sailed from Boston nine days before, barely a fortnight after making a decision to sail at all. Seasick and wearied, landfall had been a welcome sight, and at sunrise on 2 September 1912 the *Parisian*—which months before had sailed to the aid of the stricken *Titanic*—entered the Clyde estuary and brought its tired passengers safely to disembarkation at Glasgow docks. In Frost's pocket was $1,100 raised, after mortgage, from the sale of the family's simple, two-storey white clapboard farmhouse and thirty acres of land outside of the small New Hampshire town of Derry. In addition, he was due an annual annuity of $800 from his grandfather's estate, minus the $120 they had spent on their passage: it would be enough to last them a year or even two, but they had no home in New England to which they could return and the gamble simply had to pay off. 'We could risk it,' said Frost.[38]

Robert Frost felt he had made little of his life up until then. A failed poultry farmer and poet who had been all but ignored by American editors, he chose now to be as far away as possible from his prying relatives in Lawrence, Massachusetts, and out of the grasp of his teaching job at Plymouth, New Hampshire, which was making too much use of his time, he thought. In the summer of 1912 the family gathered in the kitchen of their Derry farm to discuss a change of scene: west, across a continent to Vancouver where Frost's friend and lifelong correspondent John Bartlett was living, or east, across an ocean to England, where Frost's wife Elinor had long spoken of a wish to live 'under thatch'. Frost's daughter, Lesley, recorded the moment.

> We were standing around my mother who was ironing in the kitchen when my father said, 'Well, let's toss for it,' and he took a nickel from his pocket. 'Heads England, tails Vancouver.' Heads it was! All that had been contemplated was fresh scenery, peace to write, the excitement of change.[39]

A fortnight later, on 23 August 1912, the Frosts were sailing to England. But England was not, contrary to the advice he had been given, cheaper than America, and an exchange rate of almost five dollars to the pound ensured that Frost would have to look beyond London and its expensive rents for a home. To do so he walked not into a property agent as might be expected, but into the offices of the popular journal *T.P.'s Weekly* after reading a column on country walks, which to Frost's mind suggested a knowledge of neighbouring rural locations. The column's editor, a retired policeman, not only advised the American of several possibilities but went so far as to guide him personally, accompanying him on the twenty-one-mile train ride north-west of London to Beaconsfield, where the Frosts would find their first English home in a new-built bungalow. Frost bought second-hand furniture locally, and from London he made arrangements for the delivery of the family's possessions: the rugs, some kitchenware, his typewriter and, for reassembly, Elinor's rocking chair and his stout, adjustable Morris chair on which he wrote by laying a wooden board across its stout arms. It would be, as he informed a friend, 'a lesson to you in plain living', homely enough for now, although little more, he would reflect, than camping. For the time being, Beaconsfield seemed a suitably literary stop for Frost's ambitions. G. K. Chesterton lived just four streets away, but he was merely the most recent of many esteemed residents that had also included Thomas Gray, buried at nearby Stoke Poges, and most alluring of all, the cottage in nearby Chalfont St Giles where Milton finished *Paradise Lost*. Frost had found himself a home amid what he called 'the great tradition of English lyric poetry'.[40]

*   *   *

Shorter and stockier than Thomas, and almost as physically restless, Frost had fair hair which the wind would blow into untidy tufts. His blue eyes lit up when he was teasing his friends. He spoke with a New England drawl, and was frequently blunt and quick to anger, an anger that unlike Thomas's

41

could become physical. But his humour pervaded all his talk, sarcastic one moment, kindly another. Goader, teaser, talker, thinker, Frost was cubbish, mischievous and driven. He once said that he would like his epitaph to read that he had a lover's quarrel with the world.[41]

Frost's father, William Frost, had married the Scottish-born mathematics teacher Isabelle Moodie in 1874, who bore him a son and a daughter. But William Frost was no family man: a gambler and drinker who carried a revolver on San Francisco's semi-feral streets: in his son's words, 'a bad boy who never stopped being one'. William Frost died of tuberculosis when Robert was just eleven and his mother Isabelle moved the children back to the ancestral family home of Lawrence, Massachusetts. It was in high school that the shy seventeen-year-old Frost met the equally retiring Elinor White, the woman he would marry. By then he had begun writing his first poems, publishing a handful of verses and articles in the high-school bulletin for which he was chief editor. (He published Elinor's poetry too, though it has been suggested that she stopped writing when this stoked jealousy in Robert.) He entered Dartmouth College and Harvard University but failed to stay the course at either; he suffered from a mysterious recurring illness (he feared tuberculosis), and when Elinor became pregnant with their second child he saw no virtue in continuing his study. First born had been a boy, Elliot, who became a constant companion as soon as he was able to walk, following Frost about the farm as he saw to his daily chores. But Elliot was overcome by fever in the summer of 1900, and was prescribed ineffectual homeopathic treatment by Isabelle's doctor. As their son's condition worsened, Robert and Elinor called in their own doctor, who examined the boy and gravely announced that he had been summoned too late: Elliot had an acute case of cholera infantum and would not survive the night. Elliot died that evening; he had not reached his fourth birthday. A wild grief came between the parents. Frost reproached himself for failing to summon help sooner, saying first that his neglect was tantamount to murder, then crying out that this was a wrathful God's vengeance upon him; but to Elinor his was merely the selfish and hubristic anguish of a man unable to see that the loss was not his own but Elliot's.[42]

A farm in west Derry, New Hampshire, offered a fresh start for Robert, Elinor and their surviving daughter, Lesley. The family moved in October 1900, and grew to include a son, Carol, and two more daughters. But the trials were not behind them. In 1907, Robert caught pneumonia, possibly brought on by a drunken night lost in snowy woods, and Elinor nursed him to recovery while heavily pregnant with their sixth and, as it would turn out, final child: a baby girl who died the day after she was born. The pain of Elliot's death had been enormous, but to lose a second child was unthinkable and unbearable, and strain entered the marriage like never before. Robert succumbed to bouts of severe depression, Elinor to exhaustion. Lesley Frost recalled one terrible night when she was woken by her father and told to follow him down through the cold house to the kitchen. There she found her mother, weeping with her head in hands, and noticed for the first time that her father

43

was holding a revolver. Robert told the distraught child to choose between them, a mother or a father, as only one of them would make it through to morning.[43]

No wonder the Frosts sought a change in fortunes, and though the probity of Lesley's recollection has been questioned, it nonetheless marked a turning point in the family story. In the autumn of 1906 Frost began teaching in Derry and was by all accounts an effective if rather indolent teacher. ('Anything here anyone wants to keep?' he asked his class of the assignment they had just given in, and when they shook their heads in unison, Frost binned the lot, saying that if they did not value them enough to keep then he did not value them enough to read.) Teaching was a financial necessity in those Derry years, for Frost admitted that any one of his apple trees earned more a year standing stock-still with its roots in the ground than he did uprooted and rushing around, and he vowed to write better verse and find an audience for it. Although he was already writing the poems that would fill his first two books, he had published only a handful of them. By the winter of 1911 he was focussed on the idea of a literary career, and told a friend that 'the forward movement is to begin next year'. In 1912 he made the commitment to his poetry that he had long put off. 'I am going to be justified of my poetry before the end,' he commented. 'I have hung off long enough. I wasn't going to pass forty without having it out with myself on this score.'[44]

*   *   *

From his study 700 feet up on the East Hampshire Hangers, Thomas could make out sixty miles of South Downs at one glance. Beneath him, the hillside dropped southward into a dark coombe of beech and yew trees; along the ridge lay the Shoulder of Mutton, so called for the lamb-chop shape of its grassy clearing amid the yew line. To the north lay the hangers of Oakshott, Happersnapper, Roundhills, Reston and the Warren, each descending rapidly north-east from the plateau into farmland. To the south and west, Ashford Hill and Lutcombe Bottom pinned a second, curling ridge that passed through Strawberry Hanger, Lythe Hanger, Great Hanger and Cold Hill. Thick, broad-leafed woods plunged down from the plateau, more beech and yew, some small-leafed limes, some larch wound with clematis or ivy and carpeted with wild garlic and the celandines that prospered in the wetter lands each February. Woodpeckers drummed through the canopy, roe deer and fox ran the floor below. The village at the foot of the scarp was named Steep (Old English *stēap* or steep place) after the sheer escarpment at the western end of the Weald (OE *weald*, woodland); the clay and flint plateau above it was Froxfield (the frogs' field or stream). Connecting the two was Stoner Hill, a cart road impassable in heavy weather, in places sinking fifteen feet below the fields under the pounding of the carriers and the rain. While trade men trekked this hard hill, Thomas and his children followed a cut through the woods down through Ashford Hanger along a path that led to school.[45]

Thomas's heart would quicken whenever he looked upon Shoulder of Mutton Hill, but it would

45

not quicken for the house that lay on top of it. Wick Green on Cockshott Lane should have been a dream home, but it never became so. Since 1906 the Thomases had rented at Berryfield Cottage a mile along the Ashford stream from Steep, but when the estate was broken up for sale Thomas had no means of purchasing the cottage there. In September 1908 a friend came to the rescue: a William Morris disciple named Geoffrey Lupton offered to build the Thomases a house at the head of Ashford Gorge to the highest standards: hand-made bricks and tiles, solid oak doors and timbers and floors, finished with wrought-iron fittings cast from Lupton's own smithy and a recessed terrace that Helen had petitioned for. Nothing could fault its aspect or those sixty miles of South Downs views, but the house was hard, cold even in summer and frequently enveloped in the foggy mists that would crawl out of the coombe below and swallow everything about them. Worse than the mist and the cold was the wind, which roared over the hills or rushed up from the valley with a terrible moan. On some days it seemed to govern the house and its inhabitants, and Thomas readily submitted to its rule, feeling that it bound together somehow his past and the past of the world within it. He said that it carried upon its back old griefs and new griefs yet to come, foretold of terrible times and made a new house old. On the high slope, the wind was his subject and his master; it seemed to bully at his spirits and was locked into the house with him on the day he first closed the front door. It was in the gable room beneath this wind that Myfanwy was born, and he did not know which sound caused in him the more despair: her cries or the wind's howl.

All around were the hard, stone soils, and the flint that was 'the one crop that never failed'. It was a cold, biting, bitten-at place. The grey mind of the wind, he wrote, looked down upon his own grey mind.[46]

* * *

The day after the opening of the Poetry Bookshop in January, Thomas had returned to Steep, where a New Year's greetings card lay in wait. It was an introductory correspondence with a young, naive socialite who would become his confidante. This was Eleanor Farjeon, thirty-one years of age, who had sent him a goodwill message emblazoned with a sailing ship, which he took, teasingly, as an invitation from her to what he called 'lessons in navigation' at their upcoming social gathering in Broughton Gifford, Wiltshire. It was a coquettish, even flirtatious response by Thomas: he was familiar with the social set and hardly needed any help in negotiating the subtleties that accompanied these occasions. Yet beneath his surface he yearned for all the navigation he could get. Edward and Eleanor had met at a tea gathering before Christmas, and he would not have mistaken her for anything other than an impressionable character. She was a quiet, shy, bespectacled woman, her dark hair fixed carelessly in a bun, who thought herself unnoticeably plain and who, in her own description, was as emotionally immature as a girl of eighteen. From an early age she felt more at home in a library than in polite society and as a child she retreated into familial relationships and a passion for books. Her father was a Jewish Victorian novelist who had escaped East End impoverishment, her mother the daughter of an actor, and she had a trio of talented brothers; but Eleanor would be outdone by none of them. From the age of seven she was pounding out stories on her father's typewriter; by the time she met Thomas she had already published two volumes of poems. It was said of her that when she wrote she smiled; and it would not be long before she would fall in love with Edward Thomas, the writer and the man.[47]

*   *   *

On 14 January, a warm if mischievous review of *Georgian Poetry* appeared in the *Daily Chronicle*, written by Edward Thomas, in which he praised the initiative of a bookshop that, he believed, promised not only a new access to readers but discernment in an age in which anyone with five pounds to spare could have a book of poems printed. 'It brings out with great cleverness many sides of the modern love of the simple and primitive, as seen in children, peasants, savages, early men, animals, and Nature in general.' Thomas wove an acerbic wit through many of his reviews. He wrote once to Monro, 'I can't pretend to take myself seriously as a writer about poetry when even the ½d. newspapers are forsaking me. And your Review does seem certain to give that false appearance of seriousness to what I might say.' He enjoyed playing with false appearances in his articles, and in his praising of the primitive love of children, peasants, savages and early men he was giving a gentle send-up to Georgian sensibilities. In a second review of the anthology, the same mocking tone appeared when

48

he suggested that the volume was an exemplary selection of poetry from the years 1911 and 1912: 'Compare it with a similar book of poetry from 1901 and 1902 and its novelty is apparent,'— adding, 'There is, by the way, no anthology of 1901 and 1902.' But his humour did not always come across entirely as he intended, and on this occasion he wrote to Monro to explain: 'I was alarmed to see how chilly my notice of the Georgian Anthology appeared in the Chronicle. But I had to ask the editor to cut out the passage where I made a mistaken reference to Poetry and Drama and he cut out too much.' Dry or chilly, his review at least carried the stamp of independence that would mark his work throughout his life; by contrast, a notice in *Poetry and Drama* (published at the Bookshop) by Henry Newbolt (guest of honour at the Bookshop) would stake the unlikely claim that these poems would astonish and delight the reader in equal measure and 'prove the coming of a new breath of poetic emotion'.[48]

Thomas had long since refused unpaid review work, and had once declined an invitation from Monro to review *'con amore'*, in part fearing the journal in question, *Poetry Review*, would become 'a sort of home for incurables'. But in January 1913 he had made an exception to help launch the new journal from the Bookshop, *Poetry and Drama*, and his first contribution would cause a sensation. Ella Wheeler Wilcox was probably the most widely read poet of the day; her *One Hundred Poems*, just published in London by Gay and Hancock, would breeze through 100,000 sales in only a decade and a half. Wilcox employed a popular rather than literary language, a homespun, hearthside philosophy, and a wobbly sense of rhythm ribboned with a chiming end-rhyme. Those familiar with Thomas's incisive reviews could not have expected him to like Wilcox's work, and sure enough he did not; but what made such an impact upon readers of the piece was not his consternation but the tone that he employed in communicating that consternation. Thomas wrote the review ironically. In a meticulous sacking, he feigned praise in order to make a series of irresponsible claims that he knew Wilcox's poetry could not hope to meet. He lauded, for example, her subtle appreciation of the Japanese people and then quoted her description of 'Brave little people of large aims.' Of her stance towards life he asked, 'How many times does she repeat the lesson contained in this? "Don't look for the flam as you go through life." Well she knows that you cannot have too much of a good thing.' Wilcox said familiar things cheerily and repeatedly, Thomas wrote, and what was her greatest triumph? To possess a talent that the common man or woman could aspire to. 'Her glory is the more bright that it has been attained with the help only of a metrical skill commonly possessed by minor poets, a light sympathy with all sorts of ideas, and without principle or sense of beauty.'[49]

A light sympathy with all sorts of ideas; it was a piece of critical surgery as withering as it was precise, and at London's literary gatherings Thomas's review was hailed triumphantly. Not only had he exposed the most popular poet of the day as an impostor, said his peers, but more importantly he had landed a blow against the kind of popular Victorian literature that had come to swamp contemporary bookshelves. It was an achievement of which Thomas himself was unusually pleased. Rarely before had he congratulated himself on his work, but now he referred to himself proudly as 'the poisoner of Wilcox'. But for all the guile, for all the dry and witty pen strokes, the risk of adopting irony was self-evident: not everybody may pick up on the tone. Wilcox herself came to consider Thomas a great admirer, and her American publishers appeared to have been similarly caught out; so delighted were they by the review that they supplied Thomas with a complete set of her books. It was not the present, surely, the reviewer would have hoped for; but perhaps the publishers understood the article's tone full-well and were simply returning serve.[50]

*   *   *

Godwin Baynes had encouraged in Edward Thomas a process of self-interrogation, and in 1913 Thomas began to use his life story as subject for his writing more expressly than before. Towards the end of January, a short account of his early years appeared in the journal *T.P.'s Weekly* under the title 'How I Began'. At the same time he was completing an autobiographical novel, and would later that year begin work on a childhood memoir. Thomas had frequently projected himself onto his countryside characters, but not until now had he expressly made himself the subject of his writing in the first person, and for the first time, readers were offered an insight into his childhood.[51]

On what is now Lansdowne Gardens, nestled between London's South Lambeth and Wandsworth Roads, stands an imposing, four-storey, semi-detached Victorian villa that was the first London home to Philip Henry and Mary Elizabeth Thomas. It is built on the northern spoke of a fine residential circus completed by local builder John Snell in the middle of the nineteenth century. By the time Mr and Mrs Thomas rented their rooms, South Lambeth had become heavily built-up on the back of a wave of 1860s terraces that had filled in around the expansive villas of twenty years earlier. Residential building had swept over smallholdings, market gardens and farms along the line of the London and South Western Railway, and had recently overrun the isolation of Battersea and Clapham villages. It was here among these urbanising boroughs that on 3 March 1878 Edward Philip Thomas was born.[52]

Philip Henry Thomas had distinguished himself in the Civil Service Examination and been posted to the Board of Trade on a staff clerkship for light rail and tramways. He had moved to London in 1873 from Swindon, having left his home town in Tredegar, Ebbw Vale, thirty miles north of Cardiff. A self-made man, and the first from his family to make the social climb from skilled manual labour into the middle classes, he was a Welsh speaker whose preparation for the Civil Service Examination had given him command of French, German and Latin besides. He was a staunch liberal committed to free trade and Home Rule for Ireland, and an ardent follower of David Lloyd George, with whom he would walk across the park from the underground station at Westminster most mornings. At the Battersea Parliament he honed his skills in public speaking and was invited by the Liberal Party to stand as their candidate in the Clapham Division of the 1918 General Election where, according to a local newspaper, he 'put up a strong fight against odds' despite losing. To his family he was known as 'The Public Man' for the lectures he gave each Sunday in the nearby town hall for the Battersea Ethical Society. Baptised Anglican and brought up Methodist, Philip Thomas became an atheist after exploring many denominations, eventually settling in Positivist circles, where he spoke from the pulpit at the Church of Humanity in Holborn. Edward remembered his father taking him along to the hustings at Washington Music Hall in Battersea on Sunday evenings to hear Keir Hardie talk about the formation of an Independent Labour Party and Michael Davitt on the pressing need for Irish Home Rule.

> I have only one clear early glimpse of my father—darting out of the house in his slippers and chasing and catching a big boy who had bullied me. He was eloquent, confident, black-haired, brown-eyed, all that my mother was not. By glimpses I learnt with awe and astonishment that he had once been of my age.[53]

To his surprise, Edward learned that his father knew more about marbles than the best players at Edward's school. He would tell and retell the story of the Wiltshire moonrakers hanging in a chain over a bridge to fetch the moon out and had a repertoire of songs and comic speeches that would delight his children, together with a library of several hundred books in which young

Edward had his formative literary encounters. But he was a stern and aspirational man who pushed the young Edward relentlessly: first toward evening classes in Physics and Latin, later for St Paul's School in Hammersmith, and later still a career alongside him in the civil service. Years of pushing and badgering and bloody-mindedness left the relationship between father and son fraught and fractious; it deteriorated irrevocably when Edward, at university, found himself accused by his father of being a bad debtor, reading libidinous materials, drinking and smoking to excess. An 'open break' occurred, in Helen's words, fuelled by Philip Thomas's disgust at what he saw as a kind of dandyism in his son: an aesthetic whim to pursue literary dead-ends rather than provide as a husband and father should provide. When Edward finally found his way to writing verse, he would record his feelings for his father in contemptuous terms. 'I may come near loving you | When you are dead,' he wrote. 'But not so long as you live | Can I love you at all.'[54]

Of his mother, Edward could recall even less, although what he remembered he did so in idealised terms:

She is plainest to me not quite dressed, in white bodice and petticoat, her arms and shoulders rounded and creamy smooth . . . I liked the scent of her fresh warm skin and supposed it unique. Her straight nose and chin made a profile that for years formed my standard. No hair was so beautiful to me as hers was, light golden brown hair, long and rippling. Her singing at fall of night, especially if we were alone together, soothed and fascinated me, as though it had been divine, at once the mightiest and the softest sound in the world.[55]

As a physical description, these words would not have seemed out of place if Edward Thomas was writing of a lover, and certainly she appeared to offer him a perfection that he never found in Helen. Towards his mother's sister, Edward expressed a similar physical attraction, and it was in watching her sitting less than half dressed on a chair that he developed what he called his first 'conscious liking for the female body'. Mary Thomas dressed in long skirts with mysterious hidden pockets, and a wide black belt into which she tucked a half-hunter watch on a long gold chain. She made and mended Edward's clothes, cooked and comforted, and may have been prone to the melancholia that would wreak havoc upon him, as hinted at in Edward's description of her as 'diffident and sad and not clever', and Helen's as 'very retiring and shy and sad'. One of Edward's earliest memories was witnessing her rise distraught from the dining table to cry out, 'I am going to die', before her husband took her on his knee to soothe her. In her son's letters and prose, she remains a ghostly, sallow figure, attractive and remote, comforting yet forlorn, someone towards whom Thomas felt protection and love.[56]

When Edward was two, the Thomases moved to a late-Victorian end-of-terrace house just off Bolingbroke Grove, fifty yards from Wandsworth Common. The house was more modest than the last, but unlike their restrictive rooms in Lambeth, the family had its entire run. Edward lived here until the age of ten; his brothers Ernest, Theodore and Reginald were all born there. The family moved again, four streets to the north to a larger house at Shelgate Road where Edward's fourth and fifth brothers, Oscar and Julian, were born. This was the house that would remain the family home throughout Edward's time at university.[57]

Thomas liked best of all the map-making sessions at his Wandsworth board school, poring over the intricacies of the western coastline of the British Isles, or inking the mountainous uplands with a herring-bone marking. It was the journey to school rather than anything that happened within its walls that captured the young Edward's imagination: spinning tops or marbling or trading small objects with the other boys in the streets. Walking back in cold weather he would strike sparks from his iron-shod heels against the kerbstone. But it was the Common that was the principal site of Edward's childhood games. Though divided by a railway track and bordered on all sides by houses, it was a wild and inexhaustible place to Edward, with its hawthorn and gorse thickets, its towering elms and roaming foxes, its tumbledown slopes and irregular-shaped ponds. He fished with a worm and a cotton line, dropping sticklebacks and anything else he caught into a jam jar. Other times he would go further afield still, to Wimbledon Common, to gaze at the caged animals outside the corn chandler's, or to study the hapless fishermen on the River Wandle. The smell of the local paper mill caught on the evening breeze and stirred in the young boy 'a quiet sort of poetic delight'; it was the first time he had witnessed the allure of bright running water.[58]

At ten, his father moved him to a local private school, where he now studied alongside the sons of tradesmen. At eleven, he won a place at Battersea Grammar School, and he found he could learn quickly and easily, taking pleasure in coming top of his class. He took to Byron more than he took to his classmates, though more than either he took to keeping pigeons after watching a neighbouring boy's mastery of the birds. At the clap of this boy's hands they would ascend half a mile into the sky, returning at the lure of his carefully tuned whistle; Edward learned the boy's whistle, but was never able to gain such height from his own flock. He kept a dozen different breeds: homers, tumblers, dragoons and, pride of the roost, a pair of red-ruffled Jacobins from Wales. Endlessly he watched for signs of offspring; but no young ever came from the few eggs and he took away the duds to blow.

Philip Thomas's peripatetic search through different chapels and preachers took an early toll on Edward. He loathed Sunday school, and made no friends at the chapels, instead cultivating what he called a 'drug of boredom' that saw him through the sermons, largely oblivious to their teachings. But worse than this were the stiff Sunday clothes that set him apart from the other boys playing on the street. Edward longed for a sudden gust that would blow his hat clean from his head and into some puddle. He called it his 'Upastree', in a reference to the evergreen that was said to destroy all life for a fifteen-mile radius. Chapel and Sunday school became 'cruel ceremonious punishments' for the freedom of weekends; he retained what he called a 'profound quiet detestation' of Sunday for the rest of his life.[59]

At twelve, Thomas moved school again, to another private school in Wandsworth at his father's direction, where intense attention was given to manners and etiquette. Thomas's early interest in books dissipated, and he found encounters with Virgil and Shakespeare 'obscure and tedious'. He became engaged in party politics for the only time in his life, and stood as a Liberal candidate in his school elections (a Tory landslide): 'poetry was nothing to me compared with Home Rule'. Greater success lay in his athletic pursuits, for while Edward was no runner, he could out-walk any boy in the school. On sports day, it seemed he would leave his peers in his wake on the mile-walking race; but as he approached the finish line in the lead, he believed he could hear one of the boys running behind him, cheating surely, but closing on him nonetheless. He hated the feeling of being hunted down, and could not abide the prospect of being overtaken so close to the line, and so with a hundred yards to go, convinced that victory would be stolen away, he pulled up. It was better to throw the race than to be beaten; but his father did not agree, and accused him of cowardice and of lacking the courage to see the race home. He would carry the charge of cowardice throughout his life: it would haunt his friendship with Robert Frost and would even influence his thinking about the war.[60]

St Paul's in Hammersmith, at the age of fifteen, was an altogether different experience. Never before had he encountered boys like this, who discussed Maupassant's stories knowledgeably or had already secured a scholarship for Oxbridge. Lunchtimes he kept his own company, reading Richard Jefferies and not easily making friends. In

58

broken Latin, he wrote in his Algebra book 'I love birds more than books', and was ridiculed by the boy next to him, not for his sentimentality but for the shortcoming of his Latin. 'I felt unimportant, isolated, out of place, and only not despised because I was utterly unnoticed.' School reports painted a distant child, unengaged in the school community. 'I wish he seemed to take more interest in life generally' (July 1894). 'I wish he were a more sociable person' (December 1894). Eventually Mr Thomas became discouraged: Edward failed to win a scholarship to ease the crippling school fees, and in the Easter of 1895 he withdrew his son from the school.[61]

But of all images from his school days that stayed with him most deeply, it was perhaps the gift of his first school prize, a book called *The Key of Knowledge*, which to Thomas's eternal anguish, he lost.

It disappeared, I never had any idea how, before I had read far into it, and I never saw it again. From time to time down to the present day I have recalled the loss, and tried to recover first of all the book, later on the thread of its story, something that would dissipate from its charm the utter darkness of mystery. For example, fifteen years ago in Wiltshire, two strangers passed me and I heard one of them, a big public schoolboy, say to the other, a gamekeeper, 'What do you think is the key of knowledge?' and back came the old loss, the old regret and yearning, faint indeed, but real. There were times when I fancied that the book held the key to an otherwise inaccessible wisdom and happiness, and the robbery appeared satanically sinister.[62]

SPRING

In the spring of 1913 *The Icknield Way* appeared. Handsomely published by Constable at 7s. 6d. in green ribbed cloth with gilt edges, a folding map and illustrated endpapers, it was a book that promised a great deal of its author. 'Much has been written of travel, far less of the road': these were the enigmatic words with which Edward Thomas opened, so announcing the book's true subject— neither the departure nor the arrival nor even, in the familiar adage, the journey itself, but the *road*, 'the rough, tussocky sheaf of cartways', the lanes riddled with rabbit burrows, the ancient chalk path lined with pewits, stone curlews and wheatears.[1]

On a hot, dry summer's day in 1911, Thomas had joined the old highway at Thetford in Norfolk, crossing the chestnut-shaded clear water of the Thet, through a field of buttercups to the heavier waters of the Ouse, over the Nuns' Bridges and out in the Brecklands. The hard, straight lands of Cambridgeshire lay before him, then the hillier country of Hertfordshire, over the old Ermine Street at Royston, through Bedfordshire, climbing steeply over Telegraph Hill, and descending to cross the third of the ancient roads, Watling Street, beneath the Downs at Dunstable. There at dusk he fell in with a man who appeared to be following the same path, a man who might easily be mistaken for Thomas himself: 'a lean, indefinite man; half his life lay behind him like a corpse, so he said, and half was before him like a ghost'. Jealous of youth, disrespectful of seniority, the man, whom he called simply 'the philosopher', could not decide whether to feel happiness or melancholy at the sight of the Downs at dusk, and turned to his past in order to decide the matter, recounting an occasion when he had been digging all day in heavy flint soils like those of the Froxfield plateau. He said he had been turning clay at the very limit of his strength at just such a dusk as the men witnessed now when he overheard a woman singing through the woods on the hill road above him. Her song had been captivating: full of wild love and youthful spirit, marked by melody and a bewitching silence, hanging and swooping in the air as a kestrel might in flight, and it roused 'the philosopher' to lyricism.

Oh, for a horse to ride furiously, for a ship to sail, for the wings of an eagle, for the lance of a warrior or a standard streaming to conquest, for a man's strength to dare and endure, for a woman's beauty to surrender, for a singer's fountain of precious tones, for a poet's pen!

Thomas listened to the man's lament, himself uncertain whether to attribute the encounter half to happiness or half to melancholy, but never confessing to the reader that the other man was his own alter ago, in search of his own poet's pen. It was not the first time that Thomas had carved an image of himself into his writing, but from that moment on the other would become a doppelgänger to haunt his writing, and would loom larger and more sinister in works still to come.[2]

Thomas should have excelled in his subject along the Icknield Way: an expert map reader with a hawk's eye for detail and an innate internal compass, he ought to have loved his tracing of the old chalk highway that ran from East Anglia to the South West. But Thomas had been mentally and emotionally exhausted when he prepared the book in 1911, and it showed in the weight of his prose, in thick, heavy passages that at times threatened to congeal around the reader. So feverish was his need to produce work that year, and so feverish his moods, that he barely gave himself time enough to navigate the route, covering most of the ground in two cycle rides and an extended stint of research at the British Museum. A book that was to have been a delight became simply, in his words, 'another of those books made out of books founded on other books', and the critics agreed with him: 'The ordinary reader may gain the impression of a tired man struggling with blistered feet over hot, dusty roads, with so many miles a day to walk in order to write a book so many words in length, rather than a writer fresh and eager, entering upon his task with zest. A tired author too soon fatigues his reader.'[3]

One night of rain on his journey, recorded in three overbearing pages, the darkness overwhelmed him. That evening, Thomas had ridden downhill under a train of Lombardy poplars and ash into the Berkshire village of East Hendred. The rain that had been building all day began to thunder down in long, soaking strokes. He sheltered at the village inn and lay awake listening to the rain on the roof. Louder and louder it fell, hammering the gutters, roaring in the trees, flattening and pounding and exhausting. It was a terrible rain, he wrote, endless and somehow judgemental, extinguishing the flame of summer, a rain that would still be falling on him when he was in his grave, and that spoke to him now like 'a ghostly double'. He lifted his face to the window to counter the bitter words, but there was nothing out there but the darkness and the thick black rain. Briefly, the unremitting sound was broken by the call of a bird in the downpour, but the cry seemed so content that it served only to distance him further from nature. He was not a part of nature. The wonder of the world was drowning and returning to the darkness; the rain was taking away the gift of life he had never truly grasped. 'Blessed are the dead that the rain rains on.'[4]

*　　　*　　　*

On 15 March 1913 the first issue of Harold Monro's *Poetry and Drama* appeared, priced at 2s. 6d. and bearing an engraving of the Poetry Bookshop on its front cover with a map showing the shop's location on the back. Among its announcements was the award of a prize for the best poem of 1912, to Rupert Brooke's 'The Old Vicarage, Grantchester'. Edward Thomas had been among the judges, but he did not vote for Brooke. 'I have found it very hard to choose among your poets,' he admitted to Monro. 'I should like to give four names instead of one, but as I must not I have come to the conclusion I ought to name "The Stone" by W. W. Gibson.' If this were a surprise to Monro, it was a far greater one to Thomas, who had written disparaging reviews of Gibson for years, but he had admired this effort in long, looping iambic tetrameter in which a stonemason is asked by the woman he loves to cut a memorial for her dead lover. Brooke, who took the £30 prize by 'a decided majority of the votes', was becoming a familiar name in the Poetry Bookshop.

On 28 January he had become the first poet other than Monro to give a reading there, and had been harangued en route by the children of Devonshire Street on account of his long hair. For Brooke to have recited his own poetry would have seemed vulgar in those early days at the Bookshop, when the style of the day was the theatrical recitation of others' work. Anthologies and handbooks taught the student poet how to deport himself with an essential complement of twenty-six basic emotions, contempt, fear, pride, mirth, indecision, self-esteem, love and gratitude among them, or this communiqué on how to enact 'sorrow':

> Sometimes the face is buried in the hands; sometimes the hands will be firmly pressed together; often the whole body will lie prostrate, and sobs that are almost convulsive, will shake it. Sometimes the hands will be pressed to the forehead, or they may be extended in front of the body.

Brooke kept to passages from Donne and Swinburne and reported that thousands of devout women were present, 'and some clergymen'. But he was sending himself up; his audience that night had been six people.[5]

Edward Thomas had contributed not only his article on Ella Wheeler Wilcox to that first number but a review of W. B. Yeats, who had just issued a revised edition of his *Poems* of 1895. Faced with a new edition of older work, some reviewers might have taken the opportunity to make a summary assessment of a career to date, but not Thomas, who made instead a careful inspection

65

of Yeats's corrections down to his hyphens, and found the Irishman's revisions wanting. To Thomas the alterations that Yeats had made over the intervening years seemed overworked, inappropriate and even 'limp'; Thomas concluded that, 'He seems to have been revising in cold blood what was written in a mood now inaccessible.'[6]

That Thomas could be stern with Yeats was due in part to his admiration for a poet whose reputation he rightly felt was 'not only assured, but pre-eminent among the distinguished poets still in their prime'. Thomas was tough on the writers he most admired, partly to maintain his critical independence but partly also out of the disappointment he experienced when he believed a genuine talent was underachieving. Between 1902 and 1913, Thomas appraised the Irishman's work in fourteen signed reviews; in many he found Yeats's choice of subject matter lazily convenient—especially when it came to the fashionable Celtic revival—and once condemned him for 'moving about in a world where perfect dreams are as cheap as evening papers'.[7]

Yeats's craft as a writer, however, overcame reservations that Thomas held about his subject matter. His use of speech rhythms in particular caught Thomas's imagination from his earliest reviews. Quoting lines from 'The King's Threshold', Thomas observed that '"Speech delighted with its own music" is the best definition of Mr Yeats's verse.' Just as he would Frost's, Thomas could not praise highly enough Yeats's use of blank verse for the way it could communicate spoken language. 'We are now more than ever struck by the beauty of the ordinary speeches which, in their naturalness and real poetry, prove as much as Wordsworth's preface that the speech of poetry can be that of life.' It seems likely that Thomas and Yeats would have met in the small world of London poetry, but there is no evidence to that; yet even without a personal relationship Yeats bestowed upon Thomas a great gift. In reading Yeats, said Thomas, 'I seem to find, with astonishment, that verse is the natural speech of men, as singing is of birds'. That verse could be natural speech would become central to the beliefs and friendship that Edward Thomas would share with Robert Frost in 1914; but Thomas had made his comment on Yeats in 1904.[8]

* * *

Robert Frost had marked his arrival in England with a pale lyric about the pleasures of experiencing the English maritime ('For the breeze was a watery English breeze | Always fresh from one of the seas'), but it was the need to find a publisher for his existing poems that motivated him more than the new work. Over several evenings in the autumn of 1912, after the family had gone to bed each night, Frost began to lay out on the living-room floor in front of the fireplace what he called his 'stack' of loose manuscript poems brought over in his suitcase to Beaconsfield. He had begun with a hundred or more, three times the number that he would need for a book; and bit by bit, he filleted the manuscript, crumpling up the rejects and casting them onto the fire, until he was left with an assembly of thirty-two poems.

I have never written poetry every day as you know. It was just every so often that I would weed out this pile or do something to a poem. One evening I found myself sitting on the floor by the fireplace, burning what I could spare. These were poems of youth, written separately, between 1892–1912, not in a design to be together. They were all of the period when I thought I preferred nature to people, quite at the mercy of myself, not always happy. They represented a sort of clinical curve. I put the [unburned] poems in my pocket, and next day realized that they had a unity, could be a book.

The 'unity' was an account of five of his years on the Derry farm, and was what he called 'the unforced expression of a life I was forced to live'. He titled the manuscript after a line of Longfellow's, *A Boy's Will*, and set Lesley, his eldest, the task of typing a fair copy on the family's elderly Blickensderfer machine. Before the end of October, less than two months after setting foot in the country, Robert Frost had found a publisher willing to take him on.[9]

David Nutt's offices were at 6 Bloomsbury Street, on a bustling corner near the British Museum; but it was Marie Nutt who greeted Frost, an 'erratic, erotic, exotic' French widow, 'dressed all in black, as if she had just risen from the sea'. A novelist and suffragette who had been a vice-president of the National Political League since 1910, Mrs Nutt was a formidable character and wily businesswoman who offered to publish Frost provided that he subsidised the printing, an arrangement that was commonplace at the time.

Frost refused to contribute, but signed a contract in which he waived his rights to the royalty of the first 250 copies thereby ensuring that he would donate his first £3 2s. of earnings straight back to the publisher. Moreover, the tie-in clause insisted that the next three books should also come to David Nutt and should do so 'on the same terms'. It was, as Frost would later reflect, 'a fool's contract' that would cause considerable irritation to his future American publisher, Henry Holt & Co., but for now he was anxious not to let the opportunity for publication pass.[10]

Early in March 1913, a week before the planned publication of his debut *A Boy's Will*, Frost took a train from Beaconsfield into London for an appointment with Ezra Pound, who had given him his calling card addressed 10 Church Walk, Kensington, to which he added in hand 'at home sometimes'. (Frost: 'I didn't like that very well.') Pound received his guest in a purple silk gown, and asked to inspect a copy of Frost's book. Frost confessed that he was waiting to see a copy himself, but would gladly send one on when they arrived from the publisher. Patience was not one of Pound's known virtues and he insisted that the two of them pay a visit right then and there to the offices of David Nutt. On arrival, they were offered a single advance copy between them, which Pound snapped up; Frost, it is said, did not so much as manage to hold the book in his hands that day. The two men returned to Pound's Kensington flat, where Frost was told to pick a book for himself while his host settled into his reading. 'You don't mind OUR liking this, do you?' asked Pound. 'Oh no—' Frost said, 'go ahead and like it.' Pound shooed his guest from his home and began work on a review. 'Have just discovered another Amur'kn'', he noted proudly to Harriet Monroe in Chicago. 'We should print this notice at once as we ought to be first and some of the reviewers here are sure to make fuss enough to get quoted in N.Y.'[11]

Ezra Pound had come to London in 1908, aged twenty-two, with £3 in his pocket and knowing no one, but with one introduction particularly in mind: 'I thought Yeats knew more about poetry than anybody else.' He succeeded in gaining an invitation to Yeats's Monday salons at 18 Woburn Buildings, off Russell Square. 'This queer creature Ezra Pound, who has become really a great authority on the troubadours, has I think got closer to the right sort of music for poetry,' wrote Yeats to Lady Gregory at the time. 'However, he cannot sing, as he has no voice. It is like something on a very bad phonograph.' Yeats adopted Pound in a quasi-secretarial fashion, while Pound taught Yeats to fence, a moment recorded heroically by the Irishman ('I thought no more was needed | Youth to prolong | Than dumb-bell and foil | To keep the body young'), and mockingly by the American ('He would thrash around with the foils like a whale'). But strains in the relationship began to show when Pound exceeded his station in attempting silent 'improvements' to those poems by Yeats that he was preparing to send to *Poetry* in Chicago. By 1913, Pound had taken Yeats firmly in hand and did not shy from giving a few home truths. 'Although he is the greatest of living poets,' said Pound, '. . . his art has not broadened much in scope during the past decade.' Yeats knew it to be the case, and in January 1913 confessed to 'a fortnight of gloom over my work—I felt something was wrong with it. However on Monday night I got Sturge Moore in and last night Ezra Pound and we went at it line by line and now I know what is wrong and am in good spirits.' Yeats let it be known that between Sturge Moore and Pound, it was the latter who was the more insightful critic of the two (Pound: 'I should *hope* so!!!'), admitting that the young American had him return to 'the definite and concrete'. But he remained cautious in his opinion of Pound's own writing and told Lady Gregory, 'he is very uncertain, often very bad though very interesting sometimes. He spoils himself by too many experiments and has more sound principles than taste.' He found Pound's rhythms erratic ('devil's metres') and he took a dwindling interest in the American's verse. Pound responded in kind, downgrading his respect for the Irishman, saying Yeats was 'a bit woolly at the edges', then that 'Yeats on VERY rare occasions would make an intelligent remark', and finally that he had become 'merely celtic'.[12]

Pound, in Frost's eyes, was ever 'the stormy petrel', but he was also the gatekeeper for the introduction that Frost wanted more than any other, to Yeats himself, and at the end of March 1913 the invitation he so badly sought finally arrived. Yeats's Monday gatherings had been a fixture for almost twenty years when Frost joined the circle, and were remembered affectionately by some, scathingly by others. John Masefield had been among the guests charmed by the gothic candles (electricity was shunned), a flickering coal fire, the Jack Yeats paintings, the Blake etchings and the wooden lectern where the works

71

of Chaucer lay casually but deliberately open. But to others, the effect was artificial and even facile. Douglas Goldring, an editor from the *English Review*, recalled an evening where a young poet curled at Yeats's feet pressed him to sing one of his lyrics to a traditional Irish air. Yeats, who despite his comments on Pound was himself tone-deaf, duly obliged, and what followed was, in Goldring's memory, 'a sort of dirge-like incantation, calculated to send any unhappy giggler into hysterics'. As the tuneless wail gathered strength, the young editor tried to stifle his mirth, but eventually the settle on which he was seated began to shake under his merriment until Yeats flashed him a look from behind his pince-nez that brought all laughter to an end.[13]

Frost's first evening at Woburn Buildings was wearing on without him having made any noticeable impression upon his host. During a lull in conversation, he seized his opportunity and proposed that in reading any poem he could always tell whether it had come quickly to the author or whether it had been a product of labour. Yeats was dubious, but Frost now had his attention and pressed on, saying that he could tell, for example, that Yeats's own 'The Song of Wandering Aengus' was very clearly the act of a single, fluent burst of inspiration. Not so, said Yeats, he had agonised over the poem, an agony which those present understood to refer to Maud Gonne; and as Yeats went on, ever deeper into his personal stories, Frost knew that the moment had passed and he left that first evening with the sense of opportunity squandered.

Elinor Frost despaired at Yeats's refusal to

help forward her husband's career. She watched the frustration build in Robert, aware of the significance that a good word from Yeats could bring. He had in fact praised Frost's work in conversation with Pound; 'If only he would say so publicly,' Elinor bemoaned to a friend, 'but he won't, he is too taken up with his own greatness.' When no endorsement came, Frost took matters into his own hands, informing one publisher that 'Ezra Pound acclaimed me publicly. Yeats has said in private that the book is the best thing American for some time.' The public endorsement never came and Frost would tire of Yeats, though not before he would tire of Ezra Pound.[14]

Frost's friendship with Pound lasted a mere four months. Pound would press him to join his exploration of *vers libre* (Frost: 'writing free verse is like playing tennis with the net down'), and in order to make his point rewrote a poem of Frost's, saying, 'You've done it in fifty words. I've shortened it to forty-eight.' 'And spoiled my metre, my idiom and my idea,' Frost protested. The tension spilled into knockabout comedy in the middle of the London restaurant in which the two men had lunch in 1913. Pound was then taking lessons in judo and insisted on demonstrating a hold upon his lunch date. Frost was told to rise from his chair, whereupon Pound grasped his wrist and proceeded to throw him over his back and on to the restaurant floor, where he lay dazed, surrounded by the surprised glances of restaurant onlookers. 'Wasn't ready for him at all,' said Frost. 'I was just as strong as he was.' Along with T. S. Eliot, Frost would one day help secure Pound's release from St Elizabeth's Hospital for the criminally insane, but for the time being their friendship was done. 'An incredible ass', wrote Frost of Pound in autumn of 1913, 'he hurts more than he helps the person he praises'.[15]

*   *   *

In the spring of 1913 Edward Thomas may not yet have known about Robert Frost but already he knew all he ever wanted to about Ezra Pound. When Thomas reviewed Pound's debut collection *Personae* in 1909, the young American was 'only just getting under sail', in Thomas's words, and he chose, as often he would with debutants, to ease the passage of that journey. 'He has very great things in him,' Thomas told his friend Gordon Bottomley before taking his support public. In the first of two reviews, Thomas described how the work 'bursts upon the mind' and offered an astute summary of verses that were not seduced by melody, golden words, fashion, rhetoric or Celticism. 'It is the old miracle that cannot be defined, nothing more than a subtle entanglement of words, so that they rise out of their graves and sing.' In a second notice in the *English Review* Thomas praised the promise of this 'admirable poet' who would, he believed, eventually be exposed as a 'great soul'. Edward Thomas should not have been alone in identifying the precocious talent on display in that book, but so contrary did his opinions run to prevailing tastes that his reviews got him into difficulties with London's literary circles.[16]

The Square Club was one of the many literary cliques that met in the capital in those pre-war years. One regular attendee was the adventure writer Edgar Jepson, and it is to him that we owe the colourful account of the moment when Square Club read with horror Thomas's reviews of Pound. 'You could not be a poet in those days unless they discovered and made you,' Jepson explained. 'They would not allow it.'

> Then E. T. fairly tore it: in a review *he praised the verse of Ezra Pound!*
>
> I shall never forget the meeting of the Square Club a few days after that monstrous action: the pale, shocked, contorted faces of the poet-makers, the men who discovered and made John Freeman; the nervous leaping into corners; the choked whispers; the jerky gestures; even between the courses the harsh sound of grinding teeth.
>
> Poor Edward Thomas! He did look so hot and bothered. His protest that he had acted in good faith, that at the time of the writing of the review he had really fancied that he liked the verse of Ezra Pound, drew from his colleagues only horrid rumblings. How *could* he have liked the verse of a man whom none of them had discovered, much less made? Why, none of them even knew him! The thoughtlessness! The betrayal! The shattering blow to English Literature.[17]

Never before had Edward Thomas suffered the bad opinion of his peers, and the effect on him was distressing. With his literary reputation under scrutiny, for the only time in his career Thomas renounced his opinion. 'Oh I do humble myself over Ezra Pound,' he wrote to Gordon Bottomley a few days later. 'He is & cannot ever be very good. Certainly he is not what I mesmerized myself—out of pure love of praising new poetry!—into saying he was & I am very much ashamed & only hope I shall never meet the man.' Alas, Thomas would not have his way on this either, and in September 1909 found himself seated beside Pound at a Square Club dinner. Pound's flamboyance and Thomas's introspection found no meeting point as the evening wore on, and Pound took little from the encounter except to say in a letter home that he had met the man who reviewed him to his advantage. Thomas, on the other hand, prickled with dislike for Pound. His literary opinion of the work had already been turned on its heels in private, and in a review of Pound's second book, *Exultations*, later the same year he would clarify his error in public. In it Thomas admitted to have been duped by Pound's pyrotechnics and suggested that behind the poems' dazzling façade there existed 'very nearly nothing at all': no expression from the heart, no memorable phrasing, in fact much that he had said about *Personae* but without the benefit of the doubt that he gave to a first book. Pound's style was obscure, thought Thomas, and pestered by variousness: 'still interesting—perhaps promising— certainly distressing'.[18]

In truth, the difference in Thomas's public attitude toward Pound's two books was not considerable, but the change in his private views was pronounced. Edward Thomas had let Pound get under his skin and it provoked in him a brutal self-examination. 'Ezra Pound's second book was a miserable thing and I was guilty of a savage recantation after meeting the man at a dinner,' he told Bottomley. 'It was very treacherous and my severity was due to self-contempt as much as to dislike of his work.' Thomas's response to Pound had been wildly temperamental: in the space of only a few months he had first admired the work then said that he had been mistaken, a mistake that he initially described as literary, then personal and then, finally, one born of self-contempt. There may be no truth in the suggestion that the writers of the Square Club influenced his change of mind, but there can be no doubt that Ezra Pound effected in Thomas a crisis of his own convictions. Thomas's erratic treatment of Pound is a clouding episode in a critical career of otherwise incorruptible value: a man who knew his own literary mind inside-out and was never afraid to tell it straight to his very closest friends.[19]

Pound had no notion of the anxieties he had stirred within Edward Thomas, but his dismissal of the man was absolute. 'He was a mild fellow with no vinegar in his veins.'[20]

*   *   *

A wild south-westerly brought thunder and downpour to London on Good Friday 1913. Thomas waited for the worst of it to pass before setting out on his bicycle from his parents' house in Balham at ten that morning. He headed south-west, weaving between puddles a yard wide and three inches deep through a city that seemed to him to be expanding hungrily. The fields that surrounded Garratt Green in his youth were being filled in by allotments and new houses, though here and there was evidence of the low clearings he remembered as a child. Watercress beds were still worked in the

River Wandle, though the mudbanks at the old Copper Mill no longer marked the town boundary that he recalled from childhood. His commission was a simple one: to take a bicycle ride from London to the Quantocks and write a 300-page account of the journey. Thomas's route would take him from Nightingale Lane in Balham, under the North Downs to Guildford, along the Hog's Back to Farnham towards Winchester, over Salisbury Plain and the Mendips to Glastonbury, before Bridgwater, the Quantocks and down to the sea. He would set out with one purpose in mind, to look for the arrival of spring in an early martin, some larch green or blackthorn white, a chiffchaff: any sign to show him that the new season had arrived, and he would complete the journey in a week.

The rain fell harder as he crossed the rail bridge at Haydons Road station, harder still as he turned onto Merton Road, until finally he was forced to take shelter from the downpour under the awning of a cheerless pet shop. Another traveller sheltered there, and with no sign of the weather relenting, Thomas watched as the other man, for want of something better to do, entered the shop for a scrawny cock chaffinch that hung in the window; he emerged awkwardly a few moments later with a paper bag in which the small bird was pounding away. As the rain subsided, the man mounted his bicycle but had not advanced more than a few hundred yards before he pulled to the side of the carriageway, and released the dingy bird, which flew straight up and into the lavender of a neighbouring garden. To the watching Thomas, the man performed this task with a self-conscious air, 'as if he knew how many great men had done it before'.

It was the first of many unsettling encounters with this strange character that Thomas would have en route.[21]

Somewhere beyond Morden, he caught up with him once more, sketching a gilt weathervane that had captured his attention and being jeered by a band of young men. In Salisbury he met him again, this time in a hotel lobby, with a growing ambivalence toward their encounters.

> This Other Man, as I shall call him, ate his supper in silence, and then adjusted himself in the armchair, stretching himself out so that all of him was horizontal except his head. He was smoking a cigarette dejectedly, for he had left his pipe behind at Romsey.

Wherever he went, Thomas browsed the tobacconists for the perfect pipe. He chose plain, bone-like clays, unglazed and uncoloured, short and straight, and liked to keep two or three about his person at all times. Most that he acquired were indifferent; many cracked at sudden exposure to the flame, others heated too quickly and could stick on the lip, or broke when tapping out the fur. But one or two survived the process by a heat gradually applied, and these became toughened and sweetened and aged with a fine old ivory hue. But the Other Man's eyes had glazed as Thomas explained all this to him, and when he had finished he asked instead whether Thomas had seen the weathervanes and pub signs at Albury, Butts Green, Dorking, Shalford, Leatherhead. Some Thomas had seen, certainly, though from the conversation they shared it was apparent that the two men had independently been travelling the very same route.[22]

Each day, Thomas travelled onward towards Somerset; each day, the Other Man caught up with him. The bells of George Herbert's Bemerton church were calling worshippers to prayer as Thomas cycled past in a rare moment of communion from which he was shaken by the sudden appearance of the Other Man, who overtook him on the road and turned to recite in an exaggerated fashion Herbert's sonnet 'Sin', followed by some improvised lines of his own, 'Good Lord, or whatever Gods there be, deliver us.' Thomas was disgusted at the Other Man's tone, which he found mocking and self-congratulatory, and was pleased to lose him at the next village.[23]

Again and again came the encounters with the Other Man, at by-roads, weirsides and village inns. Thomas scorned him for his aimless anecdotes, his health-food snacks of monkey nuts and brown bread (once his own diet), and took delight at seeing him bettered in an argument; it was some time before it dawned on Thomas that his companion might be a travel writer like himself. 'You are lucky to get money for doing what you like,' said Thomas:

'What I like!' he muttered, pushing his bicycle back uphill, past the goats by the ruin, and up the steps between walls that were lovely with humid moneywort, and saxifrage like filigree, and ivy-leaved toadflax. Apparently the effort loosened his tongue. He rambled on and on about himself, his past, his writing, his digestion; his main point being that he did not like writing. He had been attempting the

80

impossible task of reducing undigested notes about all sorts of details to a grammatical, continuous narrative. He abused notebooks violently. He said that they blinded him to nearly everything that would not go into the form of notes . . . 'Good God!' said he. But luckily we were by this time on the level. I mounted. He followed.[24]

Catkins wagged in the poplars on the narrow lane down to Kilve church, where Thomas approached the culmination of his journey. There, he had one final encounter with the Other Man, who explained he had come to establish whether Wordsworth was correct in suggesting that the church had no weathercock; Wordsworth was, and the Other Man departed, laughing as he rode. Thomas sat on the pebbles of Kilve beach, watching smoke from a fire on the Quantocks roll down toward the sea. A meadow pipit hauled itself twenty or thirty feet skyward, and swung down and away with a sweet blast of song. The next day he climbed the north slope of Cothelstone Hill in the Quantocks, and there he discovered on 28 March the first bluebells and cowslips that told him that he had found spring.[25]

'You mustn't give away the fact that the Other Man is rather a lie,' said Thomas to Jesse Berridge presenting him a copy of *In Pursuit of Spring*. (Berridge had ridden with Thomas on part of the journey, as had his brother Julian.) But the Other Man was not a lie, he was a projection of Thomas's alter ego, just as the figure of 'the philosopher' and the 'ghostly double' of the rain had been in *The Icknield Way*. Under the tutelage of his doctor

Godwin Baynes, Thomas was drawing even deeper into his inner matter, dredging up disturbance, doubt and even despair for what his publisher had expected to be a work of mild-mannered travel literature.[26]

*   *   *

Thomas worked hard in writing up *In Pursuit of Spring* from his parents' house in Balham and from Martin Freeman's in Maida Vale. He was pleased with his progress: his rhythm was fluent and for several weeks he wrote exhaustively, typing 4,000 words a day. On 6 May he felt he had progressed sufficiently to return home to Wick Green at Steep. His time in London had brought no review work, but he had at least secured a small commission from B. T. Batsford on the subject of 'ecstasy'. It seemed strange that Thomas should choose a moment of extended depression to address a rapturous subject, but it was not without reason. He hinted at his thinking when he told Gordon Bottomley that he was interested in any stories which communicated 'man's belief at various times that something can clear things up for him without immediate help of the intellect.' Thomas wanted the work to be a piece of personal salvage and naively hoped that in exposing himself to the subject matter he might somehow discover a cure for his own condition. But he found the work heavy going and could not settle to the task. By the end of July he was still struggling for a way into the material, and finally set it aside in the autumn. He would explain to Eleanor Farjeon at the time, 'I did a third, then soberly and finally decided it was mostly muck and so ill-arranged that it could not be rewritten.' His attempt to jump-start his prose into rapture had been a failure.[27]

*   *   *

Robert Frost may have been a novice on the publishing scene, but he was in no doubt as to what it was that sold books. For all the efforts of the Poetry Bookshop, works like Frost's were not sold through browsing but through the notices they received in the newspapers. So when a fortnight had passed since publication of *A Boy's Will* without any sign of attention, Frost became anxious. 'I am in mortal fear now, lest the reviewers should fail to take any notice of it.' When the notices did come they were not what he hoped. The first, in the *Athenaeum*, set the tone. 'Many of his verses do not rise above the ordinary, though here or there a happy line or phrase lingers gratefully in the memory.' The second, a round-up shared with no fewer than sixty-two titles in the *Times Literary Supplement*, was barely better. 'The writer is not afraid to voice the simplest of his thoughts and fancies . . . though the thought may be feebly or obscurely expressed.' More agitating still were two reviews from Pound which praised Frost's lack of pretension but went on to describe the poems as infelicitous and 'a little raw', referring sceptically to their 'utter sincerity' as if that were something to be suspicious of. Worse followed when Pound provocatively announced that Frost had 'been long scorned by "the great American editors"' (a phrase dripping with sarcasm from Pound's pen): 'It is the old story.' Frost winced to see his book being

83

used as an object with which to beat his country's editors, and was furious with Pound for usurping the review. Better notices followed, but few seemed to get beneath the skin of the poems, and fewer still were moved to outright praise.[28]

The book's reception was proving to be a struggle for Frost, who was feeling his first pangs for America. 'We are very, very homesick in this English mud. We can't hope to be happy long out of New England. I never knew how much of a Yankee I was till I had been out of New Hampshire a few months.' And yet perhaps all too aware of the bind of his contract with David Nutt, he noted ruefully, 'I seem in a fair way to become an Englishman.'[29]

*   *   *

Rupert Brooke also wished himself away from England. Distress in his romantic life had forced upon him the desire to be anywhere else, and by mid-May, he had finalised his plans for a voyage to the United States and the South Seas that would keep him abroad for more than a year. He had planned to visit Edward Thomas in Steep before sailing, but London's tireless social whirl gripped him too firmly once again. 'I'm sorry,' he wrote to Thomas. 'I wish I'd been able to come. Now, I'm off to America. I sail next Thursday. I shall stay—I don't know how long. Perhaps next March's primroses'll fetch me back.' The night before his departure, Brooke threw a party for himself in a dingy club off Regent's Street; Wilfrid Gibson came to see off his friend, as did the critic John Middleton Murry. 'You might charge me with some message for the continent of America and for Ella Wheeler,' Brooke told Thomas. 'And I could leave the muses of England in your keeping—I do that anyhow. Feed the brutes.'[30]

Thomas and Brooke had been on friendly terms since the summer of 1910, when Brooke was courting a pupil at Bedales School in the village of Steep. Thomas discreetly abetted the young couple by issuing invitations for them to rendezvous at Wick Green, but Brooke's attention wandered and he embarked on other relationships that led to misery, a stillborn child, an elopement to Germany and ultimately a nervous breakdown. Athletic, intelligent, mischievous and labelled by W. B. Yeats as 'the handsomest young man in England' (Winston Churchill concurred), Rupert Brooke captivated those whom he met throughout his short life. Thomas was not so easily seduced, though he enjoyed Brooke's company when he returned to stay later the same autumn, this time while Helen was away, leaving the two men to fend chaotically but cheerily for themselves in the kitchen. Between courses and breaks for tobacco, Brooke shared his poems with his host and left Hampshire recharged, setting all else aside to work on them. In age, the men were nine years apart, in temperament even further, and though Thomas grew to mistrust Brooke's flamboyance, he liked his early work well enough.

Poems, issued by Sidgwick & Jackson in December 1911, was the only collection that Brooke saw published. Gravelly and gutsy, it was a book that gave the equivalent of literary indigestion to many reviewers, some of whom felt that Brooke was wilfully out to shock and even repulse. Most did not hide their revulsion, focussing their rage upon 'A Channel Passage' and asking, as did the *Morning Post*, 'what possible excuse is there for a sonnet describing a rough Channel crossing with gusto worthy of a medical dictionary?' Reviewers lined up to agree: 'The appalling narrative of a cross-Channel voyage should never have been included in the volume' (*New Age*); 'His disgusting sonnet on love and sea-sickness ought never to have been printed' (*Times Literary Supplement*); 'better left unprinted, nay unwritten' (Dublin *Express*). Not for the first time, it would take Edward Thomas in a review for the *Daily Chronicle* to change the literary weather. Unlike his more conservative colleagues, Thomas understood Brooke's particular brand of revolt as 'a symptomatic quintessence of the rebellious attitude today'. Brooke was new, and he was representative, Thomas realised, and though he could identify naivety in the preparation of the work (Brooke had lazily reused the same image in three places, he pointed out), he knew that such mistakes were corrected with practice as a poet's artistry grew. And grow it surely would, Thomas announced, for Brooke would not be an inconsiderable poet; and in a brilliant and witty swipe at the critics, Thomas signed off in this way: 'Copies should be bought by everyone over forty who has never been under forty.'[31]

SUMMER

The English newspapers carried accounts of renewed troubles in the distant Balkans that June. With the ink barely dry on the first treaty, a second Balkan War had broken out that would take the death toll to 150,000 in the region. Austria–Hungary looked nervously on at her quarrelling neighbours, and in particular at Serbia, which had grown strong under the patronage of Russia. But the events seemed a long, long way from England. In 1913, nobody could foresee the distance these sparks would carry; certainly not Edward Thomas, who at that moment could barely see beyond his writing desk. He had written, rewritten and typed *In Pursuit of Spring* and might have felt some joy at finishing his most coherent prose book yet, but instead he was exhausted and felt himself at a crossroads, feeling that home was the worst place for him to be and yet unable to decide whether or not to decamp. Helen tried to keep out of his way, but the strain was terrible and she sparked his temper in remarking that he looked tired. 'Tired is not what I am,' he snapped. 'I'm sick of the whole of life—of myself chiefly, of you and the children . . . I despise myself for not putting an end to it.' He set off on a bicycle tour, but tiredness overtook him and forced him to turn back. Days later he tried again, this time reaching friends in Broughton Gifford. He felt no anger toward Helen and the children, only a need to be apart. He kept in touch with her and asked what she might like for her birthday, but his tone was considerate rather than affectionate, familiar rather than intimate. At nearby Dillybrook Farm, a white cock and a turkey cock were fighting in the yard when Thomas arrived. The white cock puffed out his neck feathers and jumped at the larger bird, but could not see him off, conceding ground until eventually the turkey began to tread him down and the white cock escaped only by clambering beneath him. Round and round the white cock circled before it retreated. The victorious turkey dragged his outstretched wing tips through the dirt, his breast feathers exaggerated to a dark sporran. It was a brutal display, but Thomas was not about to intervene in a conflict that did not concern him.[1]

To write even a page of anything new attempted the impossible, wearying both himself and the family, and he told Eleanor Farjeon of his 'little yet endless' tale. 'The point is I have to help myself and have been steadily spoiling myself for the job for I don't know how long,' he wrote.

> You see the central evil is selfconsciousness carried so far beyond selfishness as selfishness is beyond self denial, (not very scientific comparison) and now amounting to a disease, and all I have got to fight it with is the knowledge that in truth I am not the isolated selfconsidering brain which I have come to seem—the *knowledge* that I am something more, but not the belief that I can reopen the connection between that brain and the rest.[2]

Thomas had to help himself more; and part of that help lay in a restoration of a long-standing partnership with his literary agent in Covent

88

Garden, Charles Francis Cazenove. Thomas had grown impatient at his agent's inability to place the books he was having ideas for and had announced a parting of company the previous autumn. 'I must see what a change will do, if anything can be done at all,' he told Cazenove at the time. 'The combination between us was ceasing to be anything but a friendly one.' But Thomas was not entirely doing justice to a combination that had produced, in Cazenove's words, 'quite a respectable number of books through our intermediary', and the agent tactfully explained the difficulty. 'You want to write books of a certain kind, and to have a commission in each case before you write. As what you want to say is not of the obvious kind which publishers can grasp at once, and as you prefer not to write first and sell the book afterwards, your agent's work is necessarily—please don't think I'm grumbling at all—rather more difficult than is the case with most of the men for whom one acts.' Cazenove took his ten per cent share of the fees he negotiated, but often he would secure an offer from a publisher that Thomas would turn down, leaving him unpaid for his efforts. He was a shrewd and even-tempered agent, canny enough to attempt to charge Martin Secker £10 for the mere privilege of viewing Thomas's first 15,000 words (non-refundable if Secker did not take the book). Thomas's proposals to Cazenove could be wild or untimely: he once put forward a boxing anthology ('with a good title it might be attractive, don't you think?') and an anthology of 'worst poems', while he turned down offers for books on Wordsworth and Tennyson and Shelley (because of unacceptable terms) and blew the most lucrative deal he had ever been

89

offered when he dithered and disappointed over a proposal on Shakespeare. Now, less than a year after its dissolution, the partnership of Cazenove and Thomas was reinstated, and the agent busied himself on his client's behalf, beginning negotiation with Methuen for a book following in the footsteps of English authors that would posthumously become *A Literary Pilgrim in England.*[3]

*　　　*　　　*

The summer days of 1913 were not happy ones for Robert Frost. 'This getting reviewed for poetry over here is all sorts of a game,' he wrote. The early reception of *A Boy's Will* had been undeniably disappointing, and had confirmed his fear that the sophistication of his work might not be understood. He wrote to a colleague in America, 'At least I am sure I can count on you to give me credit for knowing what I am about. You are not going to make the mistake Pound makes of assuming that my simplicity is that of the untutored child. I am not undesigning.' That summer, driven by a desire to give weight to his design, Frost immersed himself more deeply than ever before in a study of prosody. From the mid-1890s he had mentioned ideas about speech and about sound, but he had yet to connect them. It had taken the sting of those early reviews and their charge of 'simplicity' to stir him into outlining a theory of his poetry. He would call it 'the sound of sense'.

I alone of English writers have consciously set myself to make music out of what I may call the sound of sense. Now it is possible

90

to have sense without the sound of sense (as in much prose that is supposed to pass muster but makes very dull reading) and the sound of sense without sense (as in Alice in Wonderland which makes anything but dull reading). The best place to get the abstract sound of sense is from voices behind a door that cuts off the words.[4]

Simply stated, Frost's belief was this: cadence is a natural part of human speech—it gives the speaking voice its intonation, its modulation and its rhythm. We use cadence to indicate and understand meaning in a way that goes deeper than the content of individual words into the arena of moods and atmospheres. So when, in Frost's favourite example, we hear voices behind a closed door we can broadly make out sense even if the words themselves are not clear. We can detect anger, affection, happiness and so forth because the cadence gives us a kind of sonic blueprint for the meaning and carries a communicative charge all of its own. This is the basis of 'the sound of sense' and its importance to poetry lies in the understanding that a line of verse can communicate tonally as well as through the literal definition of words. Patterns of sound and rhythm establish a tone or mood that the poem must work towards—or against—but to which it must never be indifferent. As Frost wrote, it is entirely possible to separate sense from the *sound* of sense: 'Jabberwocky', in his example, is full of the *sound* of sense without containing any real sense at all, whereas a set of travel directions, conversely, may be full of sense without anything resembling the sound of sense.

Eleanor Farjeon was walking with Frost and Thomas in Gloucestershire in 1914 when they encountered the idea in practice. Standing atop a cart two fields off, they saw a farmhand lifting up some kind of load with his pitchfork. Frost stopped and hollered a question to the man, 'What are you doing there, this fine afternoon?' The farmhand was too far away to have heard Frost's precise words, but he straightened up and hollered an answer that in turn was too distant for the individual words to be audible—and yet the meaning of the exchange was precisely clear. Frost turned to Thomas, Eleanor recalled: 'That's what I mean,' he said.[5]

Once the poet has grasped the sound of sense, Frost believed, the next task was to stretch the irregular rhythms of speech across the regulated rhythms of poetry:

> if one is to be a poet he must learn to get cadences by skillfully breaking the sounds of sense with all their irregularity of accent across the regular beat of the metre. Verse in which there is nothing but the beat of the metre furnished by the accents of the polysyllabic words we call doggerel. Verse is not that. Neither is it the sound of sense alone. It is a resultant from those two.[6]

Frost's beliefs had been forged in a culture that was quite different from that of his English peers. He had grown up with a sense that his country's history was being written by his contemporaries and was not simply handed down from forefathers or ancient textbooks. It was disparate, contested, dramatic and changing by the day in ways that seemed distinct from the tales of the Old World. The idea of the frontier was something that many Americans had experienced in the nineteenth century, and the isolation, self-determination and the pioneering sense of individualism that accompanied it. Frost may have paid little homage to Walt Whitman, but he shared his predecessor's manifest interest in the destiny of a new people. The British were not a new people: they had traditions, rules, they had things to lose; Americans, in contrast, had everything to gain. True, there were literary and moral influences that had travelled from England: the Romantics' sense of quest and their investment in the landscape had made a profound impact on Frost and his fellow American poets; so too had certain Puritan values based on self-reliance. But Frost and many of his countrymen would employ a language of progress that valued conversation above rhetoric in its drive to speak plainly: to communicate across vast distances, to be national through the personal. Like so many in his generation, Frost pursued what Whitman called the 'song of myself': an epic of individualism, self-discovery and ceaseless adventure. Writing when he did and from where he did, Frost stood at the confluence of two streams, traditional and modern: a meeting of English craft with American idioms and ideas, or what he once called, 'the old-fashioned way to be new'.[7]

That language should carry a sonic meaning was not a new idea: Frost understood that something in the vocal gesture of primitive humans conveyed a meaning long before the development of a framework of language. He was aware too that the idea had its antecedents in poetry and liked to paraphrase Carlyle's instruction to poets from 1840: 'See deep enough, and you see musically.' And he acknowledged the sonic skill of his contemporary, the poet Edwin Arlington Robinson whose plain address and musicality had not gone unnoticed by Frost ('we two were close akin up to a certain point of thinking'). What made Frost's approach different was that he believed that it was the rhythms of *speech*—as opposed to music or traditional metre—that should guide our ear when employing the sound of sense. It was a view entirely counter to the times in England—counter to the ornate Victorians and the minimalist Imagists, counter also to the musical Georgians—and was born out of a trenchant belief that 'words exist in the mouth, not in books'. Shakespeare, John Clare or William Wordsworth may have extolled similar practices before him, as had Longfellow or even Robinson, but Frost felt certain that his register was lower, more communal and ultimately more natural, stating, 'I dropped to an everyday level of diction that even Wordsworth kept above.'[8]

But in one claim at least Frost was mistaken: that he alone of English writers had consciously set out to make music from the sound of sense. As he was soon to discover, Edward Thomas had been thinking along the very same lines.

*   *   *

Behind his loquacity and sometimes bluff manner, Frost's assurance was fragile and prone to doubt. He confessed to F. S. Flint that he was suffering from a sense of uncertainty both towards his poems

94

and his ability, even to feeling foolish. But his outward crisis did not appear to tamper with the writer within, as between the winter and summer of 1913 Frost was writing many of the finest poems he would ever write.[9]

The meditative 'After Apple-Picking', with Frost's long two-pointed ladder sticking through a tree toward heaven, was probably underway before Frost came to England, but he had finished it in Beaconsfield earlier in the winter. The harrowing 'Home Burial', in which an estranged couple struggle to overcome the death of a child, was written over this time; Frost said that he based it upon grieving friends in Epping, New Hampshire, but it seemed unmistakable in its reflection of the Frosts' own tragedy with Elliot and even repeated the words that Elinor used at the time, 'the world's evil'. 'Mending Wall' would be written that summer after the drystone walls of Fife reminded him of those that hemmed his old farm at Derry. And he wrote the masterful 'Birches' tramping through the muddy front garden at Beaconsfield Bungalow. Like other pieces from that time, the composition was English but the setting was distinctly American, and recalled his childhood riding birch trees, taught to his own children. Frost's daughter Lesley, then aged six, wrote at the time of an outing into the woods to collect chestnuts: 'We started home and on the way home i climbed up a hi birch and came down with it and i stopped in the air about three feet and papa cout me.' (Frost went out of his way to have it known that every one of his poems from this period onward were 'based on actual experience'.) 'Birches' showed the complete grasp that Frost had on his art. It demonstrated his belief that the individual line was a unit of sense tied by 'sentence sounds', and showed the unerring skill with which he varied his rhythm to avoid monotony and maintain surprise. His exquisite use of image (bent tree trunks like girls who had thrown their hair forwards), his hearthside wit ('Earth's the right place for love: | I don't know where it's likely to go better') and the unshakeable strength of his opening and closing phrases were on as powerful display in this poem as they ever would be.[10]

Pinpointing the composition of these poems is not without its difficulty. Frost did not date his work, nor did he like to preserve drafts. ('A poet never takes notes. You never take notes in a love affair.') He maintained that there were very few drafts, in fact, and that the poems came naturally, as Keats once said, or not at all. 'I wrote whole poems of two hundred lines at a sitting,' he claimed: 'I believe I was not over two hours with "Home Burial". It stands in print as it was in the first draft.' Frost wished his work to be seen as the offerings of a natural and unforced writer, and took care not to present himself as 'writerly'. In part, he was manufacturing an image for himself, but he was also protecting a vital ingredient in his art. Frost was a great believer in surprise. He believed a poem required surprise in order for it to operate at its full potential, and wrote of the need for the poet to succumb to this. 'No tears in the writer, no tears in the reader. No surprise for the writer, no surprise for the reader.' He said that he never started a poem whose ending he already knew, for to have done so would, he believed, deny a fundamental purpose in poetry: that writing was an act of discovery. 'I write to find out what I didn't know I knew.' Other times he phrased the idea slightly differently, but always the same basic premise: surprise leading to discovery. It was a thrilling and courageous approach to poetry, and one that might suppose a high number of discarded drafts as the poet came to 'find out' what it is that their poem had to say. But not Frost, or so he maintained.[11]

In fact it was rarely wise to take at face value any story about Frost that was rendered by the man himself. He was, for example, a keeper of notebooks (forty-eight that we know about), and was not always effective in covering his tracks. Of 'Stopping by Woods on a Snowy Evening', he said that he was working late into the night and crossed to the window seeing that dawn had arrived, whereupon the poem 'just came': all he needed to do was cross the floor and write it down. But inspection of his surviving manuscripts tells a different story. Though much of the poem did indeed come swiftly to him, the second stanza nearly defeated him altogether: he made four passes at its first line before leaving it incomplete. This cubbish, and at times dissembling, writer understood full well the value of being the storyteller. He was at pains to point out that he was not, unlike his peers, contributing a penny toward the publication of his book, when in fact he was underwriting it through his royalties. He chose to present himself as a farmer, when really he had struggled even to keep chickens. In political language, Frost was a 'spinner' who took great care to put across the image of himself that he thought did his work the best service. 'You want to watch me,' he advised knowingly toward the end of his life. 'Check up on me some.'[12]

*   *   *

On 3 July 1913 W. B. Yeats read for the first time for Harold Monro's Poetry Bookshop. The event was a sell-out, the shop's first, and forty disappointed people had to be turned from the door. A shop assistant remembered the moment when Yeats took to the stage. 'A ripple of excitement ran through the packed audience, then a deep expectant hush as the poet stood silent for a moment framed in the candlelight against the dark curtain, a tall dark romantic figure with a dreamy inward look on his pale face. He began softly, almost chanting, "The Hosting of the Sidhe", his silvery voice gradually swelling up to the solemn finale. No one moved.' Edward Thomas did not attend. He was in Steep making the final arrangements for the move to the newly built workman's cottage yards from Bedales School in the village. For five years the Thomases had lived at Wick Green on the top of the Froxfield plateau but he prepared for the move to a smaller house by selling his books and gathering 'a vast collection of manuscripts' and letters for burning; he saved little. Yew Tree Cottage was made available for a minuscule rent of three shillings a week. The living room and kitchen were one room, and with no study for Thomas to work in, he arranged with Geoffrey Lupton to retain the Bee House in the garden at Wick Green indefinitely for a shilling a week. Thomas climbed the hill every day to the study, descending for lunch at noon before walking in the early afternoon via a route which would take him back to the study for the rest of the day until

98

supper at half past eight. When he was not walking, Thomas took pleasure in attending to the garden in the shadow of the ancient yew after which the cottage was named. He planted herbs by the door: rosemary, lavender, thyme and old man, propagated from cuttings given by Gordon Bottomley or carried with them from their cottages in Kent. Damson trees were trained over the brickwork, honeysuckle and traveller's joy woven about the trunks. He built a modest porch over the entrance and encouraged jasmine to climb freely. He wrote to Bottomley, 'We have moved & are now fairly fitted into our narrow quarters to everyone's satisfaction.' Not least to Helen's, who wrote to Janet Hooton,

We are in our cottage now, and we love it. It's awfully cosy and pretty and I love doing all the work . . . It is I who am making a home for Edward, the only time I've had it all in my own hands, and I believe it's going to be the happiest home we've had. I know I shall do my best, and my dear old boy is trying too . . . He's tried hard during these last two years to kill my love for him but it's just the same as it always was, it's my great treasure, the thing that keeps me going, that is my life, that and the children. In my heart I have memories so splendid that I am rich in happiness tho' I spend so very many days of utter misery. Sometimes I think he does not love me any more, and my soul gets into a panic of terror, and then out of the darkness comes some wonderful gleam that gives me new hope, new life, new being and I start again. And now in this cottage it's all going to be easier.[13]

The school holidays arrived, and Helen left for Switzerland with her sister Irene and the girls and Thomas took up an offer from Eleanor Farjeon for Mervyn and he to join her and friends aboard a houseboat on the Norfolk Broads. The holiday was a postponement from the previous year when the great floods of August 1912 had devastated the Anglian waterways, humbling bridges and washing away the roads that could bring help. Then, quanters and marshmen had rowed over the waterlogged fields and herded tonne bullocks into swimming downriver to safety, but now Ranworth Broad was a happy haven as the company assembled on a small houseboat called *The Fawn*. Slow meals were cooked and enjoyed on deck under the summer sunshine. Thomas was contented: he sang Welsh songs as he washed up after dinner, and larked around with dinner plates over his head in the position of a halo: 'Let us be Saints!' He talked easily on daily walks with Eleanor, chatting breezily with a passing carrier and filling his impossibly large pockets with the season's first apples. Mervyn slept on the cabin floor, and won a full bed when Eleanor's friends left a day early, giving the three of them a contented familial last day together on the water. With Mervyn present, Helen would have had no reason to fear the intimate living arrangements, and could she have seen the manner in which her husband relaxed into Eleanor's company she would have been pleased. In her absence, the friendship that was building between Edward and Eleanor was gaining strength: kindly, playful and for each of them liberating. But it would be, said Eleanor, the last week of happiness that Thomas experienced that year. The buoyancy of those summer weeks was only short lived and when the holiday was over she said the gloom that descended on him 'weighed him down till the end of the year'.[14]

* * *

Early in August, from the offices of the Poetry Bookshop, Robert Frost received an inviting postcard from Wilfrid Gibson. 'I'll be here at 7:30 on Wednesday evening and delighted to see you. Bring some poems.' Gibson had taken a room in the upper storey of the Bookshop, and it was here that he received Frost on the evening of 6 August. After W. B. Yeats and John Masefield, Wilfrid Gibson was the most popular poet of his day. He was an affable character, cherished for his kindness and his warmth (D. H. Lawrence: 'I think Gibson is one of the clearest and most lovable personalities I know'), and Frost took to his unpretentious style instantly. 'He's just one of the plain folks with none of the marks of the literary poseur about him—none of the wrongheadedness of the professional literary man.' The two became such fast friends that by November Frost had announced Gibson as the closest of his peers in England, and a finer poet than the man he had briefly befriended, Ezra Pound. But Gibson had a streak of vanity that would soon undo him in Frost's eyes, and he would later imply that the American had called unannounced to push his work upon him. Frost would come to detect a superior tone in Wilfrid Gibson that would later enrage him, but in the immediate months ahead their friendship would

101

blossom.[15]

Frost saw in Gibson's mature poetry a mirror of his own: the verse of a 'people's poet' who concerned himself with the lives of working folk and who, in Elkin Mathews, had found himself a publisher of repute from the start. Yet Gibson's first verses, published in his early twenties, had been cruelly exposed when he sent them out into the sharp-toothed world of literary London, where a young Edward Thomas, just six months older than Gibson and busily making his own name as a critic, lay in wait.

'He seems to us to be nearly a perfect minor poet—without the intellectual equipment for originality,' wrote Thomas in a damning first review in 1902. 'Minor' was not the insult that it might be mistaken for today (Thomas himself had once stated that the future of poetry was minor; adding, 'Anything, however small, may make a poem; nothing, however great, is certain to'), but in case there was any doubt about Gibson's particular kind of minority Thomas would clear up the matter in a later review: 'He is essentially a minor poet in the bad sense, for he is continually treating subjects poetically, writing about things instead of creating them.' Harsh though this sounds, Thomas had made a crucial point about not only Gibson's verse but all poetry: namely, that bad poems make the mistake of confusing poetic writing *about* a subject with the skill of making good poetry. Thomas would frequently charge Gibson with the crime of distorting subject matter to meet the needs of poetry and of possessing a wobbly sense of craft: 'It is utterly cheap senseless rhythm, and lack of value in words no artist would pass by.'[16]

Poor Wilfrid Gibson. By his own admission, he was never a master craftsman; he once told an assembly of Chicago professors that he did not know one form of versification from another. By the time he was producing his best verse Thomas had all but written him off. Gibson learned to strip back the ostentation that had bedevilled his earlier books, and while Thomas conceded this he nonetheless thought that Gibson was somehow in the wrong business. 'At the end of this book we have the feeling that after all, he has merely been embellishing what would have been more effective as pieces of rough prose, extracts from a diary, or even a newspaper. The verse has added nothing except unreality, perhaps, not even brevity.'[17]

Not everyone agreed with Thomas in his opinion of Gibson. In certain circles, Gibson was seen as a star in the making, if not one already made: a popular new writer giving voice to experiences and to people outside of the recent realm of poetry. A poet's standing will rarely stay fixed across time, but Gibson's has plummeted to such a degree as to make it seem incredible to modern readers just how popular he was in the years before and during the war. Yeats and Hardy were more widely read than Gibson, but they were of older generations, and among his own only John Masefield, in the wake of his vastly successful *The Everlasting Mercy*, enjoyed more popularity. In one single week in January 1913, 20,000 people saw Gibson's poetic-drama *Womenkind* performed in Glasgow, while a whirlwind reading tour of the north of England saw him feted at literary receptions and society dinners. Such was Gibson's elevation as a poet that when Frost and Thomas called unexpectedly one day in

103

1914, they were turned away by Geraldine Gibson because the great man was at work in his study and should not be disturbed. She was not alone in her assessment of her husband's talents: Robert Bridges told Marsh that he considered Gibson's work in *Georgian Poetry* to be 'very remarkable', to which Marsh responded 'I think he is the most careful artist of them all.' Few poets at that time had troubled to enquire into working lives as Gibson was doing then. His interest in the women's movement (his sister Elizabeth was active with the Women's Social and Political Union) undoubtedly influenced *Womenkind*, and saw two of his poems published by Sylvia Pankhurst's paper, *The Woman's Dreadnought*. It is curious that Thomas should be so ruthless with him; Thomas who, after all, was frequently found giving voice to people working across the landscape that he himself knew: the watercress man, the fieldhand, the landlady at the inn, the farmer, the alienated urban worker. He may have sensed an attempt to court popularity in Gibson that he mistrusted, even suspected a distasteful appropriation of their lives, real or imagined, for the purposes of poetry. Neither would have been traits of which Thomas would have approved, but nor would he have believed that they constituted cardinal sins. So what was at the root of Thomas's disdain?[18]

Gibson's lack of precision, and his lack of an inner editor, made for moments of laziness or generalisation that Thomas would not have been able to tolerate. His failure to deliver memorable speech in writing, his failure to fix an irresistible rhythm, his inability to communicate tonally, was to Thomas an unconscionable breach of his promise as a poet: without cadence, a poem could only act upon the intellect and could therefore only ever be partially successful. Gibson was an example of the noble failure that Thomas perceived in his own prose and would seek to rectify when given his chance in verse. Gibson's work had been a platform on which Thomas had honed the beliefs that would lead him to the deepest development of his own art. He had no title quite so neat as Frost's, and never would, but what he was expressing was the sound of sense.

AUTUMN

Edward Thomas idled away the last of the school holiday with Mervyn at London Zoo, where he watched the vultures flap lamely down from their perches after being stirred up by the keeper. He longed to be away from family life, far away, and explained to his agent that he felt he must consider an extended visit to Australia, New Zealand or Canada if he could find a publisher to underwrite the move: 'I am quite prepared to go.' Cazenove was quick to dissuade him that there would be a market for such a book, and the moment would pass, but a seed had been planted in Thomas's mind and in the months to come he would think very seriously about leaving England. Helen returned from Switzerland at the end of August, and shared just a few days with Edward in Steep before he headed to Bethnal Green to stay with Godwin Baynes. It would be his last visit to his doctor. Following such a promising start, Thomas had come to doubt the effectiveness of his treatment. His spirits were no longer improving and the charm of Baynes's attention was wearing thin; he was ready to dispense with the doctor's services. 'Godwin can't really help me,' he confessed to Eleanor Farjeon. 'When he first came to see me he made me feel that I was the most important person in the world to him. As I came to know his world I found he gave the same impression to everybody—and I don't like being one of a crowd.' It was a petulant but characteristic remark of Thomas's: as a child he had not liked the crowd of five brothers, as an adult he abhorred the scrum of Clapham Junction. His doctor treated him as an individual and as a friend, but he did the same with everyone he treated. Godwin Baynes, it seemed, would not after all be the 'saviour' of Edward Thomas.[1]

Thomas left Bethnal Green and crossed to London's Victoria station, where he took a train to the home of Vivian Locke Ellis at East Grinstead for a week's stay; by now, Eleanor noted, the grey mood had thoroughly set in. He had come to suspect that he might be suffering from the initial stages of diabetes, though he was never formally diagnosed. His mind was bitter and furtive, and began to disturb his sleep. Even with a good book and lighted candle at his bedside, Thomas struggled to stay awake for more than a few minutes after turning in, but lately he had taken to waking before dawn, restless and disturbed. 'Any memory can now decompose me,' he wrote, 'any face, any word, any event, out of the past has to be entertained for a minute or an hour, according to its will, not mine.' In this semi-waking condition, his senses would harangue him and cause him to distort his surroundings. The rain-soaked poplars at the window crackled with a sound like fire. A robin's song in the fir copse behind the house seemed to be a relentless and dreadful form of hypnotism. He lay trying to understand the significance of the discord—the flat birdsong and the quiet moan of the wind in the fir trees—and as he lay in the darkness, to his surprise, the moment began to cast itself in his mind in verse form, rhymed in order to help preserve it in his memory.

I was resolved not to omit the date; and so

much so that the first line had to be 'The seventh of September,' nor could I escape from this necessity. Then September was to be rhymed with. The word 'ember' occurred and stayed; no other would respond to all my calling. The third and fourth lines, it seemed, were bound to be something like—

> The sere and the ember
> Of the year and of me.

This gave me no satisfaction, but I was under a very strong compulsion. I could do no more; not a line would add itself to the wretched three; nor did they cease to return again and again to my head.

Gradually the lines dimmed in his head and the moan of the fir trees and the robin's song returned, and Thomas slipped back into sleep.[2]

Later that day, Thomas wrote to Walter de la Mare. 'In sleepless hours this morning I found myself (for the first time) trying hard to *rhyme* my mood and failing very badly indeed, in fact comically so, as I could not complete the first verse or get beyond the rhyme of ember and September. This must explain any future lenience towards the mob of gentlemen that rhyme with ease.' In time to come, Thomas would tell a friend that his poems had all been written since November 1914 ('I had done no verses before and did not expect to'); yet the three abandoned lines from that September night in 1913 show that Thomas was tuning in to the possibility of recording his experiences in verse before then.[3]

In fact Thomas had written verse in his late teens. His notebooks record a number of efforts through the spring and early summer of 1896, aged eighteen, which squeeze ornate words or insensible phrases into uncomfortable shapes, such as this triplet:

> I love thee thou'rt my own in hue
> I love thee oh the word was hard
> And thou wert very fair and good.

The language of these early lines was literary and already archaic for the times, and sat proudly beside his more natural prose entry of the same date:

> Happy whitethroats—singing ever and flitting thro' the brake together in sun and shadow[4]

Poems, as opposed to disembodied verses, begin to appear in his notebooks in 1897, when Thomas was a first-year undergraduate at Oxford, but these had ceased by 1898 after his inner editor found them pale, unmusical and imitative. They remained dormant until he was preparing his prose book *Beautiful Wales* in 1905 when, under cover of an anonymous translation ('reduced to its lowest terms by a translator'), he slipped in an effort of his own.

> She is dead, Eluned,
> Who was part of Spring,
> And of blue summer and red Autumn,
> And made the Winter beloved;
> She is dead, and these things come not again.

Even to his close friends the 'translation' had not been an obvious trick. When Gordon Bottomley had enquired after the original in Welsh, Thomas had looked sorrowfully at him and asked if he would be disappointed to learn there was no original in Welsh. Then who wrote it, Bottomley had asked, only to see in Thomas's kindly smile that the piece was clearly his own. Bottomley urged further such efforts of his friend, but Thomas had said then, 'I do not know how to do the trick again.' Yet the instinct to versify did not remain completely buried in Thomas. Under a deluge of book reviews, he wrote to Bottomley in 1905 that he dreamed of 'original writing', as he called it, 'but never get so far as to get out paper and pen for it'. In 1907, again to Bottomley, he admitted to interruptions in his thought that tantalisingly escaped him: 'things occur to me and I think for about the length of a lyric and then down and blank and something new—'. Thoughts 'the length of a lyric' then had been bubbling for many years before his night of insomnia at East Grinstead, but these thoughts came and went without ever being captured in poetry. For the time being at least, the 'trick' of announcing himself in verse form continued to elude Thomas.[5]

*   *   *

Frost had been waiting at Beaconsfield station for the train to London when he noticed some lines of verse in a discarded newspaper at his feet. 'Eve, with her basket, was | Deep in the bells and grass, | Wading in bells and grass | Up to her knees'. It had an appealing rhythm, dactylic and driven, and

110

the American read on. 'Picking a dish of sweet |
Berries and plums to eat, | Down in the bells and
grass | Under the trees.' The poem was 'Eve', a
lyric by the poet and Fleet Street veteran Ralph
Hodgson. Frost tore it out and put in his pocket,
and asked Gibson for an introduction; and in the
second week of September the poets met. Frost
gave Hodgson his verse in typescript, to which
Hodgson responded, 'it is like nothing I have seen
from your country, and I foresee a welcome for it
in ours.' It was a warm and supportive introduction
from Hodgson, but more important still would be
a second introduction that he set up a few weeks
later.

> My dear Frost,
> Shall you by chance be in town on Tuesday?
> If so you might turn up at St George's
> Restaurant, next to the Coliseum in St
> Martin's Lane close by Trafalgar Square—
> at about 4. Edward Thomas will be up and I
> think you'd both like to know each other.

Thomas and Frost were now within touching
distance.[6]

* * *

Thomas returned to Steep from East Grinstead,
and wrote to a friend about his financial anxieties
in the new cottage. 'It is cheaper here, not cheap
enough though for my income, to use a euphemism.
Am I just to wait and do work I can in a quietly
dispirited state? I get wonderfully near deciding
I shall not go on indefinitely, tho I don't see how

111

to round it off.' His spirits seemed as fractious now as they had ever been. It pained Helen terribly to see him this way, and she felt helpless in the face of it. As an untrammelled spirit, she believed that Edward was entitled to his moods, even to his harrowing behaviour towards her and the children; but there were moments when his despair seemed to pass into something deeper, and these were the times that she became truly frightened, as now, when he left once more stating business in London. On Sunday 5 October, en route to Walter de la Mare's, Thomas penned a hasty note to Eleanor Farjeon about their meeting the next day.

> Will you forgive me if I do not turn up tomorrow? I have an appointment of uncertain aim with an American just before and may not be able to come. In any case it would be 4.30 before I could come. So if it suits you you will wait there: if you dislike the uncertainty don't come but forgive me. You understand: I might not come at all.

The American was Robert Frost, but Thomas almost did not make it there at all.[7]

When Thomas arrived at de la Mare's south London home, his host found him wildly out of sorts, fitful and despairing. For the only time in his life, Thomas spoke openly to his friend of his desire for suicide. De la Mare listened to Thomas's anguish and did everything he could to talk his friend around; but he could not have been entirely confident of his success, for no sooner had Thomas left than de la Mare felt the need to write to his friend, no doubt repeating the advice

112

and friendship he had given in company. The letter was waiting for Thomas at his parents' the next morning. By then a desperate Thomas had been out early to make what he ominously called 'a certain purchase'; but as he read de la Mare's kindly, caring letter a change was effected in him. His hand was shaking, his writing uncharacteristically scrawny as he scribbled a hurried reply.

My dear de la Mare
I don't know how much I have to thank you before and can't nicely distinguish between post and propter but certain it is that this morning I hadn't more of my original design left than to make (I think largely for form's sake) a certain purchase. I wish I could have seen you again. I was a nuisance, I know. But I can at any rate write something better now than 'The Attempt'. Your letter when I found it here at 7 finally disarmed me. I feel a fool, a sort of wise fool,—not one of your best creations,—with not a shred of peacock about me,—but such as it is, it thanks you for its existence.

'The Attempt' was the name Thomas gave to the short story he had published in 1911 based upon the day he took his revolver into the woods at Steep, and now he told de la Mare that he had something better to write about. But as the morning progressed, Thomas's nerves began to steady and later that same day he wrote for a second time. 'Thank you for what you said last night. I think I have now changed my mind though I have the Saviour in my pocket. The final argument was my

113

mother who has received nearly all the other blows possible. I very much hope you did not take me quite as seriously as I did myself.'[8]

A certain purchase . . . the Saviour in my pocket; chilling words that seem likely to have meant one of two things: that about his person Thomas was carrying a weapon or he was carrying a poison, either one of which he intended to put to a terminal application. Thomas already owned a gun, but that lay in a drawer back in Steep with Helen. To have acquired another would not have taken a great deal of effort, though thankfully it would have required at least some. In 1913, a licence was necessary for the purchase of a pistol but that licence was readily available from any post office and needed only the payment of a fee; no licence was required at all for anyone intending to keep the pistol solely in their home. But the picture of Thomas queuing in a post office for what was in effect a suicide permit seems incredible, given his manic frame of mind. More likely, he had gone out for a toxin that he could self-administer. Horticultural poisons, a number of which carried arsenic in potentially fatal doses, were readily available over the counter in 1913 and required no permit, nor even special labelling if they were sold for agricultural use in such products as sheep-dip. From his years of medicinal use, Thomas also knew how to obtain opium in sufficient doses to poison himself that way if he wished to. Whatever the 'Saviour'—bullet or poison—it was in his pocket when he went on to meet the American in St George's Café at four o'clock that day.

*　　　*　　　*

114

Robert Frost recalled clearly the St George's Café at which Edward Thomas held court each Tuesday. He remembered its curious access off St Martin's Lane, 'through a little side door to the right, up two flights of brass-lined stairs, through a door with "Smoking" on it, to the chess room, where he presided over another gathering at tea.' So regular were Thomas's appearances there that he acquired from his peers the nickname 'The Iambic'. The room on the first floor was light yet cosy, with white overmantels to the fireplaces and an oak clock ticking from the papered wall; but mostly the poets met on the floor above that in a room that mingled the scent of coffee with, as one guest remembered, 'the reek of half a hundred pipes'. A dining guide from 1899 told that the clientele had changed very little over the years, describing 'a fair sprinkling of men, neither obtrusively smart nor obtrusively shabby', which might well have described Thomas's crowd when he made it his regular haunt sometime around 1906. 'Chessmen, draughts, and dominoes in action. A hum of men's talk,' recorded one visitor: a place where the actors gathered and nodded their recognition to the writers, the painters, the handful of travelling paper merchants that made the vegetarian café their home. Davies, de la Mare, Hodgson and the two Freemans, John and Martin, were Thomas's regulars; others including Edward Garnett and Harold Monro came and went. The informal conversation of the circle was captured by another visitor, who unbeknown to Thomas kept notes of their conversations at the café and other meeting spots in London in 1908–9. In what is in effect the only interview that Thomas ever gave (albeit

115

unwittingly), he emerges as fluent and relaxed in his conversation in the café, and moves smoothly between discussions on reviewing, on critics, on Oxford and Wales, and on his contemporary generation of poets. Thomas banters good-naturedly with Walter de la Mare, who says he does not think Masefield a genius; Thomas disagrees, and de la Mare says that every reviewer who used the word 'genius' ought to be fined for the benefit of a literary fund. Harry Hooton interrupts to say that he had seen a viper in Minsmere; a sure sign of spring, replies Thomas, and asks had Hooton pinched its tail and let it go, for that was the way to ensure that future generations were frightened of men. De la Mare confesses that he could not distinguish between a viper and an adder, but Thomas assures him, 'They are one and the same.' Thomas and de la Mare had met at the St George's Café most weeks since being introduced in 1907. It was at such moments in the company of de la Mare and in the reviewing of his poems that some of Thomas's formative theories on poetry had been forged. But the friendship would be gently demoted by Thomas in favour of the American's; by 1916 he would say of de la Mare, 'We rather fence with one another now, remembering we once got on very well.'[9]

Curiously, nothing at all survives of a meeting that was to mark the beginning of the most important friendship either Frost or Thomas would ever have. A few days later, Eleanor surprised Thomas with a singularly direct question. 'Haven't you ever written poetry, Edward?' Thomas let out a self-deprecating laugh. 'Me?' he said, 'I couldn't write a poem to save my life.'[10]

*　　　*　　　*

In October, Martin Secker published Thomas's critical biography of Walter Pater at 7s. 6d., with its dedication to Joseph Conrad. Twenty-one years his senior, Conrad was one of the very few people who ever overawed Thomas, making him prone to an uncharacteristic form of babbling. Time and again in Conrad's company he found he would blurt out commentaries that he instantly wished he could retract in case Conrad believed that he had meant them. Thomas's visits to Conrad in Kent were not infrequent: he was there when Myfanwy was born in Steep in August 1910 and he brought Mervyn with him on other occasions. Once, Conrad came across his son Boris fishing with Thomas using a line without a hook in a pond which had no fish in it. 'Thomas smiled with a shadowy irony, but he sat on, fishing.'[11]

Conrad was a great stylist, Thomas believed, more so than Walter Pater, who privileged the eye over the ear and suffered from a catastrophic failure of rhythm. As failures go, a lack of sound and rhythm might seem a curious charge to lay at the door of a prose writer, whose readers might reasonably look to other qualities besides. But Thomas was stating something more than the qualities of Walter Pater; he was beginning to make a statement about himself. In writing the book, Thomas had understood more clearly than before that the engine of writing should, he believed, first and foremost, be rhythm. 'An exquisite naturalness is hard to attain, when the writing, disturbed by protuberant words, has no continuous rhythm to

117

give it movement and coherence.' From the eye to the ear using naturally expressive rhythm: Thomas was naming the qualities he would look for from now on, and they were qualities that he would find only in verse.[12]

*   *   *

Following four months of wrangling, Cazenove finally delivered a deal with Methuen for *A Literary Pilgrim in England* that Thomas felt he could sign. At £80, it was a substantial advance and it would need to be, as it was among the last and the most grinding of the prose books that Thomas would write. Virginia Woolf would say that the book brought 'the very look of the fields and the roads before us', but hers was a lone voice of praise. The book turned out to be a lethargic ramble through the locales of twenty-nine of his favourite writers, infused with the weariness that he experienced when writing it, and conveying, in the words of a review at the time, a 'waywardness of direction'. His moods were very bad, full of anxiety and gloom, and he likened his spirits to a dull flat shore that no longer expected the tide to return. He felt entirely unprepared for a return to life in Steep with Helen and the children. 'The less I see the better of anyone who can't ignore that there is something there,' he told Eleanor. How the family were expected to ignore the depressive 'something there' was beyond any of them. For years Helen had absorbed the brutality of his moods rather than impose boundaries on his behaviour; she would recoil from his words white and wounded, refusing to rise to the shouting match that he appeared to seek. He told her once that these occasions were

118

moments of 'dreadful playacting' that overcame him, and he wanted her to know that the truer condition was one of love. She clung to those words every time he raised his voice at her, adamant that the 'real' Edward was the man who loved her and not the man of cruelty. But as she had done the previous winter, she now had to watch him pack his bag once more as he began to make arrangements to repair to East Grinstead, where the Ellises had once again made available to him 'the long small room' that was the stone outbuilding in their garden.[13]

Thomas left for East Grinstead early in November. Once again, he had seen to it that the atmosphere at Yew Tree Cottage was one of misery. 'We have been having a rotten time,' he confessed to a friend. 'I had a very persistent attack of depression which a series of quite tangible if not really enormous misfortunes seemed to be confirming beyond anything I had known before. This made me unbearable at home. In fact the sense of being the cause of so much worry and pain to Helen and the children made me daily worse (both to them and myself). So I decided to get away.' Family life had not always been like this. In the past, when the depression was at bay, Thomas at times had taken pleasure in domesticity. Picnics on the South Downs, walks together through the Hangers, descents of the Shoulder of Mutton with one or other of the children on his shoulders, songs at bath time in front of the fire: such moments were not unknown. But they had not been a feature of family life lately. For the next two and a half months Thomas would keep his distance and recover his nerves. But the children missed their father, no matter what his spirits. 'I hope you are

119

feeling better and happier,' wrote Bronwen from Steep. 'I must say good bye yet I do not want to, I wish I could be sent by post to you but I cannot. Good by Daddy Boy'; it had been her eleventh birthday just over a week before. For Thomas at least, the change in circumstance began to pay dividend, as almost overnight his volatile moods improved. He worked steadily on a study of John Keats, sitting down at his desk from half past six in the morning until five at night, though he found the work trying and mechanical, and doubted if he would muster the strength for any insight into the poems.[14]

On Tuesdays he continued to make his weekly visits to London, taking trains into town to catch up with friends at St George's Café or occasionally to meet with Helen. Two thousand copies of his 1911 book *Celtic Stories* had been ordered by the Australian government for their schools, and here at last was some literary news which cheered him. But not everyone was so receptive of his work: the critics had not been kind to *Walter Pater*, and Thomas revealed candidly that he feared for its chances. 'Pater will be a complete failure,' he forecast. 'It is universally condemned by the Patricians who have been whipped up as reviewers.' But he had at least finally completed the twenty-four 'proverbs' for younger readers, as he called them, which he posted to Cazenove, even though they lacked a title. 'I think they are mostly intelligible to quite young children but hope adults will want to look over the children's shoulders.' An expansion of popular sayings into miniature fictions, the 'proverbs' were Thomas's first and only venture into children's books, written across a decade but completed in a year when he was frequently away from his own children. Cazenove had been touting a proposal around the publishing houses for months, and had finally had them accepted by Heinemann in October. But it would be knocked back a few weeks later, after Thomas had unwisely begun to harangue the publisher and they returned the draft manuscript as a result. It would be a further two years before the book saw light of day, and only then paid for with a measly £10 from Gerald Duckworth; by this time it had found itself a name as *Four-and-Twenty Blackbirds*, and a dedication, to Eleanor Farjeon.[15]

In November Duckworth published the only novel that Thomas would complete, *The Happy-Go-Lucky Morgans*, priced at 6s. and dedicated to his parents. A semi-autobiographic tale about a Balham family of Welsh ancestry ('more Welsh than Balhamitish'), its story stretched across the commons of south London and the landscapes of Wiltshire and South Wales that Thomas experienced as a boy. It would not be a success. The novel won few readers and fewer plaudits for its thin plot and polite style. Thomas's friend W. H. Hudson went so far as to consider the book a mistake. 'I believe he has taken the wrong path and is wandering lost in the vast wilderness,' he wrote. 'He is essentially a poet, one would say of the Celtic variety . . . I should say that in his nature books and fiction he leaves all there's best and greatest in him unexpressed . . . I believe that if Thomas had the courage or the opportunity to follow his own genius he could do better things.' But the novel had fulfilled a purpose: it had been a staging post in a remarkable year of self-examining prose that Godwin Baynes had inspired.[16]

121

*   *   *

The Italian Futurist Filippo Marinetti gave a recital for the Poetry Bookshop in November, impersonating the sound of a machine gun in order to express the violence of modernity. 'London is vaguely alarmed and wondering whether to laugh or not,' reported Richard Aldington. Marinetti was so noisy that Yeats had to ask him to stop after his neighbours banged on the party walls during a private audience at Woburn Buildings. But Harold Monro at least was swept up by the possibility of adapting some tenets of his own and wrote in an editorial:

> The first principles of *our* Futurism are:
>   i. To forget God, Heaven, Hell, Personal Immortality, and to remember, always the earth.
>   ii. To lift the eyes from a sentimental contemplation of the past, and though dwelling in the present, nevertheless, always to *live* in the future of the earth.

There was barely a poet in Imagist or Georgian circles who would not have concurred with Monro's first principle in 1913: contemporary poets were more likely to inspect the ground beneath them than they were to look up at the heavens. But the second principle would not only separate the Georgians from the Imagists but, when he began to write verse himself, from Edward Thomas as well. Monro's second tenet would be a challenge that few, if any, Georgian poets would succeed in truly passing; but when Edward Thomas eventually turned to verse his best poems would have precisely that eerie feel of having been written in the present while living in the future of the earth.[17]

For all the unintended comedy of Marinetti's delivery, Futurism did have a watchful eye fixed upon developments in Europe. In the autumn of 1913, with parts of south-eastern Europe already at war, disputes between the fractious poets in London eerily echoed those concerns that were in debate nationally and internationally. Modernity, technology, rapid-fire, confrontation: this was Futurism; preservation, contemplation, timeless methods of communication: this was Georgianism. Across the continent, European economies were embracing new technologies and mechanised powers; many, including Germany, were taking full advantage of these developments to arm militarily against their neighbours. Britain may have held naval superiority but her standing army was barely a quarter the size of Germany's. The British government put her faith in her navy and in older emblems of national character and traditional methods of governance and trade, believing that its greatest enemies lay not on the European mainland but at home. Strikers, unionists, suffragettes, Irish republicans and the unemployed were just some of the rebellious groups that Westminster strove to quell, and may very well have failed to suppress had war not broken out in 1914.

*   *   *

Winter was moving in. Cold winds were bringing showers from the south-west as Robert Frost sat up late in Beaconsfield reflecting on his next move. In letters back to the States he was busily shaping his thoughts about the audience he wished to have for his work, and it was not the literary coterie that he sought. 'There is a kind of success called "of esteem",' he wrote, 'and it butters no parsnips.' That form of success meant approval by the critical few, he reasoned, and Frost yearned to reach beyond that.

> I want to be a poet for all sorts and kinds. I could never make a merit of being caviare to the crowd the way my quasi-friend Pound does. I want to reach out, and would if it were a thing I could do by taking thought.

But Frost did not yet have the literary platform beneath him that he needed, and what he sought, consciously now, was a reputation that he could carry back to America, one that would help him persuade publishers there that he could be a poet 'for all sorts and kinds' of readers. Only that way did a literary income lie, he reasoned. But he knew there was more still to do. Though homesick, he prepared to dig in for a little longer:

> Of course no amount of success can keep us here more than another year after this. My dream would be to get the thing started in London and then do the rest of it from a farm in New England where I could live cheap and get Yankier and Yankier. We may decide to go home this year.[18]

WINTER

Thomas would stay at East Grinstead until 15 January. There he had made what he called a 'cloistered tranquillity', in which he could work provided that he received no news from home. He had visited Steep at the end of November and found the stresses intolerable; he felt in no hurry to return. His work on a childhood memoir was underway in earnest, a book which he intended as an attempt to put on paper what he saw when he thought of himself up to the age of seventeen. And he was preparing a second autobiographical novel that, he promised Eleanor, would feature people 'totally unlike himself'—a gentle joke about the introspection in which he was now engaged.[1]

Thomas's spirits were improving with every day he spent away from Steep, and he found himself in receptive mood by the time W. H. Davies came to stay in December. Wherever Davies went and whoever he stayed with he was guaranteed to leave behind plenty for his hosts to talk about. Since the publication of *The Autobiography of a Super-Tramp* in 1908, he had been a curiosity to literary London, a much-courted accessory to any social function for his shocking travelling tales of vagrancy and prostitution. To Davies, such attentions were a flattery that both baffled and overwhelmed, but it also brought him a square meal which, at times, could not otherwise readily be relied upon. His friends worried that he was little more to these society hosts than a semi-exotic bird, caged for their pleasure, and some petitioned the government for financial help on his behalf to aid his independence, none more so than his closest literary friend, Edward Thomas, whom he met in 1905.

W. H. Davies was Welsh born, older than Thomas by seven years, and he lived a peripatetic, hand-to-mouth existence that his friend quietly admired. Thomas was drawn to the carefree existence that he associated with a tramp's life and as a boy had marvelled at a man he met on a Wiltshire riverbank, David 'Dad' Uzzell, for his knowledge of safe havens, sources of food and places to bed down for the night. By Davies's standards, 'Dad' was no tramp (he lived in a Victorian town house that he shared with his wife), but his freedom to obey his own hours and follow only nature's rules had been an intoxicating embodiment of a spirit that the teenage Thomas had found in the pages of Richard Jefferies. The homeless, roaming countryman would be a frequent visitor to Thomas's prose, as eventually to his verse, and was always a character of application and know-how, having a relationship to his earthy surroundings that Thomas could not help but envy. Davies's experience of destitution was a little different. He rarely slept in open fields and was more familiar with hostelries, missionaries, park benches and whorehouses. His right foot had been severed at the ankle when he went under the wheels of a railcar he had illegally jumped in Ottawa, and although dogs would sink their teeth into the wooden leg he had been given, he remained cheerful, explaining that all dogs had that prejudice and you could not blame them for it. Nor were children averse to having their fun: Bronwen, Thomas's eldest daughter, once teased poor Davies after he was barely mobile enough to escape an oncoming wooden cart: 'It would not matter if it ran over you, would it Sweet William, because you are made of wood!' On one occasion the leg did become broken, and Davies pressed upon Thomas the need to be discreet about obtaining a replacement. Thomas duly sketched a design for the local wheelwright without giving away its purpose, and received in return a bill for 'Curiosity Cricket Bat 5s. 0d.'.[2]

Davies published a debut volume that, thanks to an unscrupulous printer, cost him his life savings of £19 (it should have cost him £5, said Thomas); he sent it to literary reviewers asking for the price of the book or its return. Thomas reviewed it positively (Davies was destined for fame, he wrote) and encouraged him to write of his wild North American experiences, which he duly did, although a manuscript of *The Autobiography of a Super-Tramp* was rejected by publishers until A. C. Fifield said he would take it on if it were accompanied by an introduction from a known writer. It was Thomas who secured the foreword from George Bernard Shaw that all but guaranteed the book would sell.[3]

In Kent in 1905–6, Thomas offered Davies the tiny study-cottage he had taken a mile from his home at Elses Farm. Some days the two worked side by side, but Thomas soon gave over the space entirely to Davies, paid his rent and provided furniture and every comfort he could afford his friend. When the Thomases moved to Hampshire in 1906, Davies was encouraged to stay on subsidised by Thomas, but he seemed lonesome without his ally and chose to give up the cottage to move first to Sevenoaks and then back to London. Helen wrote

127

asking if the furniture they had provided might be passed on to a maid of hers; Davies replied that, not having known what to do with the furniture, he had chopped it up and burned it, and not knowing what to do with the tin utensils given to him he had buried them. He moved to London above a grocer's shop in Great Russell Street, and busied himself with furnishing it in the design that he thought would befit a metropolitan poet. He had heard that literary men burned peat, and he turned to Thomas for his advice on where he should store it within the confines of his cramped flat: Thomas suggested that if he burned a few books then there might be space on the vacated shelf to stack the peat as bookends. Davies never quite knew when he was being teased but he ordered the peat nonetheless and stored it in the only place he could think to accommodate it, on the hearth in front of the fire. He returned home one day to find a crowd had gathered around the grocer's shop and firemen dousing flames from the upstairs room where a spark from the fire had set the peat alight.[4]

Davies won friends quickly (Frost, December 1913: 'Davies is lovely') but lost them just as quickly (Frost, May 1914: 'simply assinine' [sic]). But for all his naivety, Davies was no simpleton, recalled Helen Thomas. He knew well enough what people took him for, and was a shrewd judge of character, neither duped by flattery nor humbled by those who thought themselves above him. Davies was a professional misfit who earned what he could from adopting the part of a shocked and shocking traveller in life's experiences. But his attempts at sensation remained always modest: he was so naturally shy that when he attended a party he rarely moved from the seat he first occupied in case he drew too much attention to himself in the process.[5]

*   *   *

The December issue of Harold Monro's *Poetry and Drama* showed that the journal was now more than finding its feet, attracting contributions from Thomas Hardy and Robert Bridges, who had become Poet Laureate following the death of Alfred Austin that summer. Frost sent a copy of the journal to a friend in the States, annotating it with humorous and biting descriptions of his peers, including his assessment of Monro as 'the gloomy spirit that edits this'. Never a professional critic, Frost was spared the potential embarrassment of having to comment openly on others' work; not so Edward Thomas, who when not in the invidious position of reviewing acquaintances in public was frequently pressed for his private comments by friends. Whatever the work and wherever it came from, Thomas was principled in his opinion. Literary criticism was at a low ebb in those years before the war, and was a profession characterised, he felt, by 'secondhand words and paralysed, inelectric phrases'. Reviews appeared regularly in the tabloid as well as broadsheet press, but informed insight was comparatively rare. 'There seem to be four principal kinds of reviews—', Thomas would announce in 1914, 'the interesting and good; the interesting, but bad; the uninteresting, but good; the uninteresting and bad. Most are of the last kind.' Thomas's ability— and crucially his willingness—to write frankly as well as incisively in his reviews made for reading that was both interesting and good, but it caused him considerable anguish. He once asked Jesse Berridge to forgive his 'diabolical frankness' after advising his friend that sonnets were not his strong suit at the very moment that Berridge was planning to publish a collection of them. He told Harold Monro that he might be wise sticking to prose as his verse-form was so decorous as to become an obstacle between his ideas and the reader. And poor Jack Haines would find out bluntly and simply that 'you do not express yourself in verse'. In all his critical dealings Thomas remained resolute to his commitment to use, 'as the trees and birds did, | A language not to be betrayed'.[6]

Eleanor Farjeon may not have been aware of quite how uncompromising Thomas could be when she sent him the fantasy novel that she had had privately bound. Though not yet an accomplished poet, she was no novice by 1913 with two full-length volumes under her belt, the first with the respectable Elkin Mathews. If Thomas felt a special affection for Eleanor he would not let it intrude upon the opinion that he gave of her *The Soul of Kol Nikon*, informing her that he had failed to finish the work after stumbling over her prose. '[I] am wondering if I ought to go on after the sentence where he "sank his hand in the moon-ray and drew forth a silver horn and offered it to Kol". For I find myself trying in vain to see or in some way to apprehend the action.' Thomas made clear that he found the work inauthentic, believing that Farjeon had suffocated her material by imposing too many authorial aspirations, while failing to draw out any artistic expression. 'Is this brutal?'

he asked her. 'Much reviewing prevents me from seeing books as men walking. I hit them and get quite a shock when I find I have hit a man: yet go on hitting books all the same. However I know that you don't want me to tell lies even to save my own soul and it's doubtful if I could do so by being a polite saint in the matter of Kol Nikon.' Though she put on a brave face, Thomas's dissection of her book could only have been devastating from a writer she admired, a critic she respected, and a man with whom she had now fallen in love.[7]

*   *   *

As Thomas completed his book on Keats early in December he saw it as the closing of another short chapter in his own life. He was beginning to feel that he was intruding upon his hosts in East Grinstead and would, in the new year, need to move on once more, though whether this meant to Hampshire was not yet clear. With work on *A Literary Pilgrim in England* having stalled he was thinking of new projects he might undertake and gave his agent a familiar sounding list of subjects: 'Shelley; next the Shakespeare, next the Living Poets'. None of these would come to pass. Thomas's moods had been lightening at East Grinstead, but as the prospect of departure approached he began to slump back into his usual patterns, and he wrote of 'a very persistent attack of depression'. His confidence in his writing was low, and he felt he was not earning enough to support his family. For the first time since university he thought seriously about an alternative career. He secured testimonials from his friends to help with his references before applying for a teaching job with London County Council. But no sooner had he submitted the application than he withdrew it, explaining that he would rather face a gamekeeper than stand before any class of students.[8]

With Edward more or less permanently away, Helen turned to Eleanor Farjeon for companionship that winter. As they sat up late at night, Eleanor unburdened her feelings for Edward. 'You know what I feel for him, don't you,' she asked tentatively, 'you know I love him?' 'Yes, Eleanor, I do.' Eleanor delicately offered to withdraw from the Thomases' lives altogether, but Helen would have none of it. She chose instead to see Eleanor's feelings as a mirror of her own, a confirmation of herself at a time of abandonment. 'If having you could make him any happier, I'd give him to you gladly,' said Helen. Her comments were kindly meant, but she would never have 'given' Edward to Eleanor or anyone else. For Helen had made a calculation: that so long as she retained Edward's fidelity then she would, she believed, retain him along with it. She felt sure that he would not develop a sexual attraction for Eleanor; that being so, Eleanor would be not only an ally to her but an asset, providing something that Helen could not: Eleanor would, in effect, look out for Edward when he was away in London, just as Helen did when he was in Steep.[9]

Helen and the children joined Thomas and the Ellises at East Grinstead that Christmas as they had the year before. For once, Thomas seemed comfortable surrounded by his family and friends. The children were delighted to be with their father, and Edward was able to take pleasure in their company. He managed even to be kindly toward

Helen in the few days she stayed before taking the children to her sister in Chiswick. On Boxing Day Thomas told Eleanor of the 'cheerfulness' of the Christmas they had all spent together. His head throbbed from the mulled wine of the day before, but his spirits seemed bright, even coquettish, as he thanked her for the hamper she had sent from London. 'If only you could have included some of yourselves in the box! For excellent as the elements are—Ellises, Coxes & Thomases—still, somehow, I don't know.' Thomas's comments must have seemed like a dalliance to the impressionable Eleanor, a flirtation of the kind that he had made during their week together on the Norfolk Broads and one that she found alluring and flattering. These were confusing times for Eleanor: she had admitted her love to Helen and herself, but she was far from breathing a word of it to Edward.[10]

*   *   *

Dear Frost (if you don't mind),
    I shall be glad to see you again and Flint for the first time on Monday next at St George's at 4. You remember the place in St Martin's Lane where we first met. Top floor. I think Davies and Hodgson will be there.
    Yours sincerely
    E Thomas.[11]

Three days before Christmas, Thomas and Frost met again at St George's Café. The meeting must have gone well, for Thomas would begin to invite Frost to stay with him at Balham whenever he was in London. Among their conversations that day

133

would have been the news that Frost's friend Wilfrid Gibson had moved out of the Poetry Bookshop for a cottage in Gloucestershire. Gibson had married Harold Monro's assistant Geraldine Townsend on 9 December, and Monro was not in the least bit pleased. In a momentary loss of perspective, he accused Gibson of wooing Geraldine in order to make use of her editorial experience in a publishing venture that Gibson was planning with Lascelles Abercrombie. Gibson was furious and he blasted his former landlord to anyone who would listen. 'Monro is a swine!' he told Edward Marsh. 'He's shown himself up in his true colours.' The newly-weds left London under a cloud and moved to a half-timbered rosy brick cottage at Greenway Cross in Dymock, Gloucestershire, less than two miles from the Abercrombies. It was known as the Old Nail-Shop after the trade that was once plied there, and it stood on a low track close to the course of the River Leadon. Robert Frost learned with interest of Gibson's new venture: he had never lived in a community of poets and now the calling seemed irresistible. 'There was the urge to be with those who spoke our language and understood our thoughts.' Gibson's enthusiasm for his new surroundings penetrated deep into Frost's homesickness for the life he had given up in New England. He took no pleasure from suburban Beaconsfield, while all the time his frustration with the narrow-mindedness of London's literary society was mounting.

I should have thought to escape such nonsense in the capital of the world. It is not a question with them of how much native poetry there is in you or of how much you get down on paper,

134

but of what method you have declared for. Your method must be their method or they won't accept you as a poet.

Frost would follow Gibson to Gloucestershire in 1914 and in so doing draw Edward Thomas with him. But he was not the only one preparing to turn his back on the city. Godwin Baynes had exchanged his practice in Bethnal Green for a new start in Wisbech. Though they had become all but estranged, the departure of his former doctor took from Thomas the one man who had tried to take a deeper interest in him. In his friendship and counsel, Baynes had not uncovered a cure for Thomas's chronic depression but he had opened the way for a more self-examined life. The bounty of autobiographical writings that Baynes had triggered were in full flow and would aid Thomas in his movement toward the most expressive output of his life, the poems. It was the closing of the only formal chapter of psychoanalysis that Edward Thomas would undergo, but the self-reflexive processes that it had triggered would emerge fully formed in the extraordinary year ahead.[12]

II

DYMOCK

1914

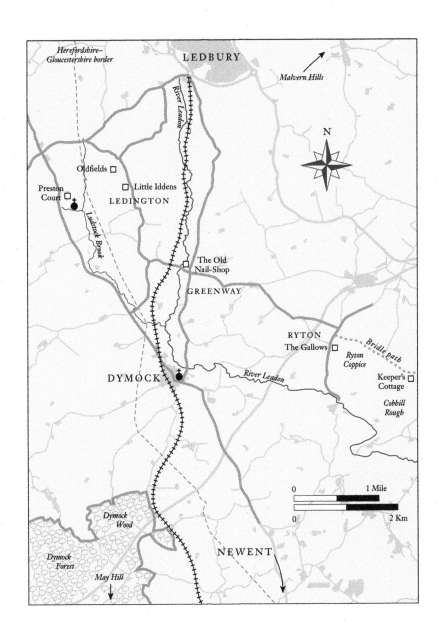

*Herefordshire–
Gloucestershire border*

LEDBURY

Malvern Hills

N

River Leadon

Oldfields □

□ Little Iddens

Preston
Court □

LEDINGTON

Luktock Brook

The Old
Nail-Shop □

GREENWAY

RYTON

The Gallows □

Bridle path

*Ryton
Coppice*

Keeper's □
Cottage

River Leadon

*Cobhill
Rough*

DYMOCK

*Dymock
Wood*

*Dymock
Forest*

May Hill

NEWENT

0   1 Mile

0   2 Km

WINTER

The Gallows in Ryton, east of Dymock, Gloucestershire, was perishingly cold as Lascelles Abercrombie put the finishing touches to a new dramatic poem. Ground frost lay for two weeks around the house that had no electricity, and sitting still to write five hundred lines of verse was no way to stay warm. But the work, a grand poem with a grand title, had fired his energies over the chill winter and brought almost daily enquiries from his neighbour, Wilfrid Gibson. 'The Olympians' was to be the crowning contribution to a publishing venture that the two men had planned since the later spring of 1913. Stirred by the success of *Georgian Poetry* and by Abercrombie's recent and profitable self-publication, Gibson had been persuaded that the home-produced anthology was a viable route to market if the content were good enough. He urged Rupert Brooke to come in on the project (Brooke: 'I'll "come in", right in, without knocking'), John Drinkwater too, and agreed with Abercrombie that the four-handed journal would promote the work of these men and no others. They settled on a title for their Gloucestershire venture, *New Numbers*.[1]

'I foresee the average number will read as follows,' wrote Brooke in an affectionate send-up of his partners in print:

1 Lascelles Abercrombie: 'Haman and Mordecai' pp. 1–78
2 John Drinkwater: 'The Sonority of God: An Ode' pp. 79–143

3 W. W. Gibson: 'Poor Bloody Bill: A Tale' pp. 144–87
4 Rupert Brooke: 'Oh, Dear! oh, Dear! A Sonnet' p. 188
5 Lascelles Abercrombie: 'Asshur-Bani-Pal and Og King of Bashan' pp. 189–254
6 John Drinkwater: 'William Morris: an Appreciation in verse' pp. 255–377
7 W. W. Gibson: 'Gas Stoves: No. 1. A Brave Poor Thing' pp. 377–594[2]

Brooke's spoof was entirely benign—of Abercrombie for his light pomposity, of Drinkwater's worthiness, of Gibson for his try-hard humility and a dig at his own histrionic style for good measure—although as it turned out, it would eerily resemble the contents of the first issue proper. Announced for January publication, *New Numbers* was quite literally a cottage industry: Abercrombie and Gibson steered the editorial work from the Gallows, while Catherine Abercrombie addressed the envelopes with a child on her knee and Wilfrid made himself pale by licking too many stamps. The journal was printed locally at the Crypt House Press in Gloucester, and mailed to subscribers from the post office in Dymock and initially to local booksellers as well, although this was stopped after Geraldine Gibson explained that the beastly bookshops 'take copies in sale or return and generally send them back rather the worse for wear'. To the editorial team's delight, the printing of five hundred copies had to be repeated when it sold out faster than anticipated.[3]

While Harold Monro noted 'the bad commercial organisation' of the journal, others gave the new imprint a helping hand. Writing anonymously in the *Times Literary Supplement*, Walter de la Mare was fulsome in his praise: 'so fine, so individual, and so various'. Edward Thomas, who in general was kinder to new projects than to repeat offenders, wrote in uncharacteristically glowing notices for the *New Weekly* and *Daily Chronicle* that the journal showed 'much that is best and newest in poetry': Brooke at his most brilliant, Drinkwater at his most lucid, and Abercrombie and Gibson at their most vivacious. Thomas would not be so forgiving of later issues, which in printing Brooke's 'The Soldier' would publish the war's most popular poem, but for now *New Numbers* was off to an undeniably good start.[4]

The journal was the seal on a literary community that Abercrombie had long sought. He had attempted to woo John Drinkwater to the area before he persuaded Wilfrid Gibson; Gordon Bottomley had once been targeted too. Yet it would be many years before the botanist and poet Jack Haines gave a collective name to the individuals who gathered in Gloucestershire in the year before the war. Abercrombie, Gibson, Drinkwater, Brooke, Frost and Thomas: christened 'the Dymock Poets' after the parish which, for a time in 1914, became a part of each of their lives.[5]

Dymock lay to the north-west corner of Gloucestershire, in an enclave that spilled untidily into Herefordshire a few miles from the market town of Ledbury. The vale took its name from the Leadon or 'broad stream' which winds south and east through Dymock before tumbling into the Severn west of Gloucester. The valley is bounded

143

to the north by the ancient Malvern Hills which rise for eight northerly miles toward the Iron Age fort at British Camp and their peak at Worcestershire Beacon. To the south of the valley lies a landmark more distinctive still, the whaleback Silurian sandstone dome of May Hill, with its crown of pine trees, its grassland slopes of birch and oak.

By the time the poets came to the region, Dymock was no longer the rich wool community that it once had been. Cider and perry were still produced from the red-loamed orchards, while the pressing of wild daffodils for hessian cloth brought a migrant labour force by rail each spring; but much else besides was in change or decline. Six blacksmiths and three wheelwrights had once made fittings for the railway and for the carriages and carts that serviced the rail tracks and fields; none survived by 1914, though the station continued as a well-kept branch line with neatly tended flower beds and horse-drawn carriages waiting outside. Labourers and mechanical reapers now worked alongside one another, the horse-drawn machines cutting the bulk of the corn while men took sickles and scythes to the field edge, working their take into string-bound stooks to dry. Threshing of the corn continued long into the winter months, sometimes for a hundred days without break, and took a team of six or seven men: two pitching the sheaves onto the threshing box, another feeding it into the drum, a fourth man bagging the grain as it was cast down the rear chute of the machine, while two or three others carried the filled bags to the granary. In this way a bay of sheaves, some eight yards by five yards and twenty feet high, could be threshed in a single day.

The poets who came to Dymock in those pre-war years were drawn to such ways of living. They came from the cities for an elemental life, for the earth beneath their boots or the breeze that stirred the wheat fields. They came to walk, to write, to cultivate a few crops for their kitchen table; they were moderately poor but not as poor as the labourers around them, and the little they earned from their pens was enough to keep themselves and their families.

First to arrive had been Lascelles Abercrombie, an articulate and kindly man, a dreamer who worked for his dream, whose buoyant spirits became subdued in later life by a sense of literary underachievement. He was a shy man, who laughed well, said Rupert Brooke, but it was the generosity of character that most stayed in the memory of his friends, as it did in Thomas's, who days before his own death in Arras wrote, 'I do not know his equal for keenness and warmth'. Abercrombie's instincts were typically Georgian in spirit: a move from the industrial north to the southern countryside to pursue an artistic life based on self-sufficiency on the land. In truth neither Abercrombie nor any of the Georgian poets could depend upon their farming skills to survive; with the exception of Ralph Hodgson, who later farmed in the United States, the most any of them could hope to cultivate was a modest vegetable patch. But it was the ideal that was important, and when the Abercrombies secured a cottage in Ryton, east of Dymock village, in April 1911, Lascelles believed his utopian dream could be realised.[6]

The Gallows were a pair of adjoining cottages connected by a narrow passageway which took

145

their name from the site where, centuries before, a poacher by the name of Jock of Dymock had been hanged for stealing the King's deer. (Jock, a pagan, strapped the antlers to his back and would charge at passers-by from the underground tunnels that joined the old Priest's House in the village with Wintour's Green and the Harrow where he lived.) The cottages stood above the lane, reached by sheer stone steps, sheltered by elms and flanked by a cherry orchard, close to the Redmarley hills and their dense covering of larch conifers. The smaller and older of the two cottages, where Abercrombie liked to work, was known as The Study. This side of the red-brick house was plastered and whitewashed, and had a rye-thatched roof three hundred years old in places, so steep, noted Frost (himself a future tenant), that the eaves descended to brush the sleeves of passers-by. Abercrombie worked in the downstairs room, while upstairs was the bedroom he shared with his wife Catherine and beside that, the children's room. The larger, newer cottage at the end of the passageway was built of red sandstone and connected to a kitchen, a pantry, a shed and three upstairs bedrooms.

Wilfrid Gibson would be among the first guests. 'This is a fairy-tale house,' he told Edward Marsh, who would make his own visit and describe, in turn to Rupert Brooke, a 'most delicious little house' with crimson ramblers and a stone courtyard where Abercrombie had rigged up a cold-water shower. Brooke travelled to see the cottage for himself, and it impressed him no less than it had the others. 'Abercrombie's is the most beautiful you can imagine: black-beamed & rose-covered. And a porch where one drinks great mugs of cider,

& looks at fields of poppies in the corn. A life that makes London a foolish affair.' But it was the lifestyle as much as the Gallows that appealed to the Abercrombies and their visitors. Under an awning permanently pitched beneath the elms they came to call the Seven Sisters, the Abercrombies cooked dinner in a cast-iron pot slung over an open fire in the company of Gibson or Drinkwater, reciting their latest poems in draft. 'I lay on a stoop of hay and listened,' Catherine Abercrombie remembered, 'and watched the stars wander through the elms, and thought I had found the why and wherefore of life.' Lascelles Abercrombie had found his measure in Gloucestershire. He found fulfilment writing by day, stepping out in the evening to take the air or to hear owls hooing in the woods.

> Here I am in a cottage in Gloucestershire, living the life (or very nearly) I have always wanted to live!—How did that happen? I scarcely know . . . the opening came, and without stopping to think, I broke away and ran.

These were happy days for Abercrombie, and Gibson, ever quick to chronicle events, mopped up the atmosphere in a poem dedicated to Lascelles and set beneath his elms beside a back-garden campfire. 'As, under the shelter of that ageless tree | In a rapt and dreaming circle we lay around | The crackling faggots, listening to the sound | Of old words moving in new harmony.'[7]

Abercrombie was an insightful and conscientious critic, who spent slavish hours at his copy. Thomas feared that the effort would one day break his spirit

147

('how long can he stand it?'), but Abercrombie, who published few prose books, had little choice as he depended upon his reviews almost exclusively for his living. By 1914 his financial predicament was causing concern among friends; once £200 a year, his income would tail off dramatically in 1914. A worried Catherine Abercrombie suggested her husband take harvesting work, but the situation was temporarily relieved when Edward Thomas and Walter de la Mare, supported by Edward Marsh and Robert Bridges, successfully appealed for the award of a relief bursary for struggling writers.[8]

Abercrombie's verse was held in high regard in 1914. It was often florid in design and grand in execution: long, sweeping monologues and dialogues which devoured politics, philosophy and the classics alike. For sheer intelligence alone, it cut a swathe through middlebrow Edwardian verse, not least in its ambitious desire to unite philosophy and drama en route to a new kind of dramatic verse. The staging of his poetry— part theatrical, part page—was comparatively experimental for the time, as was the blank verse in which Abercrombie trusted. But he, like many of his peers, suffered from a lack of editorial conversation. The Georgians were not pushed nearly hard enough by one another or by their publishers, who were in effect little more than paid printers; worse, they were not pushed hard enough by themselves. They settled too readily for comfort and consolatory tropes, and almost to an individual failed to develop fully their inner editor. They formed a coterie of gentlemen who cared for polite manners and polite verse, which helped them to work collegially and generously to secure financial

148

assistance for one another; by the same creed, they thought it ungallant to comment upon one another's work or were too grand to seek advice themselves. It would be no wonder when the quiet, respectful, straining-to-hear Georgians were blown clear by the deafening war.

Thomas had been among the first in his reviews to identify Abercrombie's promise. In 1908 he applauded the freshness of the irregular rhythms, the drama of the delivery and the ambition of the themes: inspection of any half-dozen lines, he wrote in an early review, 'would prove him a new poet, not a mere melodious gentle spirit'. By the time Abercrombie published his second book of poems in 1911, he was writing, thought Thomas, a 'tremendous unflagging rhapsody' of a kind that had not been seen since Shelley and Marlowe. By now he and Thomas had become friends. Thomas was three years older than Abercrombie and kept a benevolent eye on him; but friendship, with Thomas, was no guarantee of critical favour and as Thomas grew disappointed in Abercrombie's lack of advancement, their relationship would come under strain. Abercrombie had no ear for his verse and frequently wrote with 'no cumulative value', said Thomas. A long poem, 'Mary and the Bramble', had 'few charms', he declared, while Abercrombie's dramatic verse marked a squandering of talent that by 1914 Thomas felt the need to describe as 'intolerable'. Robert Frost did not share Thomas's disenchantment: 'Abercrombie (whom I mustn't praise too much for he is in the house with me) leaves them all behind in the sublime imaginative sort of thing,' he wrote. But Thomas could not agree and let it be known in

149

the way he always did: publicly, and in print. For Catherine Abercrombie, the reviews of her husband could be too much, and Thomas learned to keep his distance from Ryton at these times: '[I] shall hardly venture there as Mrs Abercrombie is a little hostile because I sometimes criticize Lascelles.'[9]

*   *   *

Edward Thomas had left East Grinstead for a month-long stay in a friend's town house in Hammersmith that January. He spent a weekend in Balham with Helen and the children, who stepped around him as delicately as they knew how, but the strain of reuniting in front of Edward's disapproving father was not easy on anyone. Edward had invited Frost to be a regular guest at the St George's gatherings, and in those early weeks of 1914 it seems likely from the sudden informality of their letters that Frost joined Thomas and others at one of the weekly four o'clock gatherings. Frost sent the first of many poems he would show Thomas over the time ahead (possibly 'The Housekeeper') about which Thomas commented that he liked the poem considerably except for the final line. But a critical commentary was not Thomas's only motivation for writing to Frost. Uncertain of a return to Steep, but certain that he would not be able to withstand London for long, he was on the hunt for another study and enquired of Frost whether he knew of cheap lodgings in Beaconsfield. Progress on the childhood memoir was haphazard, his drafting chaotic. He had slept under half a dozen different roofs in as many weeks, and had grown tired of the travelling, beginning, or so he feared, to treat his friends as little more than innkeepers. After three and a half months of living apart from his family, Thomas decided that there was nowhere else to turn but Steep.[10]

Never had the continuing marriage of Edward and Helen Thomas been in such doubt as it was that winter. In his earliest conversations with Frost, Thomas had been reminded of a partnership's commitments. Frost had experienced his own moments of doubt in the past: in depression or anger, or amid the recriminations that followed the loss of two children; but nothing now could turn the American from his family or his marriage, and it was, he felt, up to Thomas to reflect the same belief in his own situation. A union that had survived fourteen and a half years now appeared to be on the line. 'I set about trying to reconcile them,' said Frost.[11]

* * *

'I wish you were nearer so that we could see one another easily and our children,' Thomas confessed to Frost in February. He had eyed the distances on the map: it was a day's cycle ride from Steep to Beaconsfield, not entirely discouraging, but not as near as he would like. He had enjoyed reading 'The Code' in the journal that Frost had sent him ('your poem was really the only thing in "Poetry" I was glad to read'), and set about planning a visit for the following month. Frost enclosed some photographs from New England, and Thomas responded to the pictures by saying that he wished he could be sure that he might see the American's homeland with his own eyes: 'But you know already how I waver and on what wavering things I depend.'[12]

One of those waverings was money, and in the winter of 1913–14 it was reasonably tight. For Thomas, the business of publishing books had long become a financial necessity as he struggled to earn a living wage. He had proposed studies on Conrad and Masefield, to which his agent had tested the market and replied in disparaging terms that made Thomas's anger boil. Not for the first time he lost patience with his agent: '[£]37.10 for 60,000 words is impossible for a writer who can't serialise and is not immensely prolific,' he told Cazenove. 'It isn't merely that the money is so little but that to work at that price means to do bad work and that means that my reputation and my price get worse and worse.' It was a familiar trap, and it was closing around Thomas. He felt his writing was downwardly mobile, worthy of decreasing respect, and it was torturing him. The relief was palpable when, on 26 February, he was able to break the news to de la Mare that he was to receive a grant of £150 from the Royal Literary Fund, lobbied for in part by de la Mare himself.[13]

SPRING

Eleanor Farjeon was in Steep in March to join Helen in the celebration of Edward's thirty-sixth birthday; she gave him a gift of an apple tree. Getting to her feet at the end of the evening, she kissed Helen goodnight, and then Edward, before ascending the stairs to bed. It was a small gesture, but it was the first time Eleanor had openly displayed her affection for the man she felt so much for. As she began to undress in her bedroom, Helen entered quietly and embraced her as if she had given them both something more important than any fruit tree. It took courage to slip Edward's defences, Eleanor admitted, but through her courage she would leave behind her an atmosphere more tranquil than before. Edward and Helen busied themselves in the garden after she departed, sowing peas and beans, and digging in the potatoes, the artichokes and the apple tree. As they toiled, a harmony seemed to exist between them that had not been apparent in years.[1]

Frost celebrated his fortieth birthday on 26 March. Thomas had been at the Bungalow in Beaconsfield with him the day before: it was Thomas's first visit and it would be his last, for the Frosts were days away from moving. But closer as the men were drawing, they were not as yet the intense friends they would become. For the moment, that distinction belonged to the man who had tempted Frost to Gloucestershire, and the day after Thomas's departure Frost wrote, 'I have no friend here like Wilfrid Gibson'.[2]

153

Gibson wrote to say that he had found a cottage a mile and a half up the lane from his, in Ledington; to Frost, this sounded like the very move the family needed and he quickly closed out his arrangements. By the end of March the family had packed and were ready to leave, but first a birthday treat was in order. Having sold some poems to Harold Monro for *Poetry and Drama*, Frost cashed his payment in the form of a week's accommodation at the Poetry Bookshop, and moved the family into two rooms on Devonshire Street, across the landing from Jacob Epstein, as a base for the family's sightseeing. 'We mean to do the city for the youngsters', he reported, which meant the Tower of London and—well, for the moment he could not think of another sight that London might have to offer but he bought himself a guidebook and the family took in what they could, including the Albert Memorial in Hyde Park, whose bronze animals he would later say sparked his poem, 'The Cow in Apple Time'. Elinor and the children revelled in their week in London; Frost too, though his thoughts were squarely on Gloucestershire. 'I am going to be with my friends Gibson and Abercrombie, the English poets,' he wrote cheerily, and although the family had not yet seen the place that would become their most famous English home, they did at least have a name. Little Iddens.[3]

*   *   *

Wild daffodils were thick in the meadows when the Frosts arrived at their new cottage. The neighbouring fields were busy with lambing, and nearby in the elm trees a cuckoo sang throughout

154

that first month. Little Iddens was just two miles from Gibson's cottage on a road without motor cars, and the rent was cheap—at around 4s. a week, a fraction of the sum paid at Beaconsfield, although it was smaller than the Bungalow and was perishingly cold. The sixteenth-century frame of the cottage must have seemed to the Frosts every bit the quaint ideal of English rural living they had longed for. Though the roof was tiled and not 'under thatch', as Elinor had dreamed of, its exterior of whitewashed brick and dark timbers had buckled over the years, adding characterful protrusions to the brickwork above the latticed porch. A black wrought-iron wood stove offered little heat to the two downstairs rooms, while two bedrooms and a recessed alcove just large enough to take an overnight guest were to be found up a tight, sheer staircase.[4]

The cottage faced southward toward May Hill and opened onto a vegetable garden, shaded in places by a weeping ash and a bay tree. At its back was a walnut tree in a yard of cobbles that opened onto grass; from there a hand-pump supplied the water. A yew shaded the house on the roadside, an orchard flanked it on the other. Mealtimes (and bedtimes too, recalled Eleanor Farjeon) were at no particular fixed time and were simple affairs, usually cold rice, bread and fruit from the pantry. The children were told to help themselves whenever they felt hungry, just as they were told to go to bed whenever they felt tired. Gibson and Abercrombie were daily callers in those first weeks, and would gamely round up the Frosts for picnics; but they were far from the only guests. Jack Haines travelled from Gloucester to try and meet the American he had heard so much about, though apparently not what he looked like, by chance stopping Frost the better part of the way up from Greenway to Little Iddens to ask if he knew where the American poet lived. Haines was a solicitor by profession, but a poet by vocation, and his love for botany gave the two men much common ground for their walks into the Malvern Hills. It was Frost who urged Haines to make the acquaintance of Edward Thomas: 'You are to meet him when he is here for the month of August—and a mighty fine fellow you'll say he is.' But Thomas did not wait until then.[5]

Frost had been settled for just three weeks when Thomas made his first visit to Little Iddens. With Mervyn and Bronwen in tow (Helen remained in Steep with Myfanwy), Edward had spent ten days cycling in Wales, and the children were tired as they stowed their bicycles aboard the train that brought them to Dymock. The Frosts' cottage was too small to accommodate the three of them and Thomas rented rooms at the neighbouring farm, Oldfields. On the morning of 27 April he called on Frost just after seven thirty, before setting out to cross Ludstock Brook for Preston Church, in the first of what would be many such walks together in Gloucestershire that year. 'We can go almost anywhere we wish on wavering footpaths through the fields,' reported Frost. 'The fields are so small and the trees so numerous along the hedges that, as my friend Thomas says in the loveliest book on spring in England, you may think from a little distance that the country was solid woods.' *In Pursuit of Spring* had been published for only a fortnight when Thomas brought along a copy for Frost. The American was delighted with his gift and would go on, in a tale that has been frequently retold (though much misquoted), to thumb through the book and urge his friend to revisit his prose and write it out in verse form using just the same cadence; but that moment was still to come.[6]

In his notebooks Thomas recorded warm days beside the River Leadon, but few of the marvels that he and Frost were uncovering in the countryside. The daffodil fields, the woods of Dymock Forest, the Leadon Valley, the Malverns, May Hill, the medieval tempera and frescos at St Mary's, Kempley: all of these were as new to Thomas as they were to Frost. The more they walked the more their friendship deepened: Frost chuckling as Thomas havered over which route to take, Thomas grinning at another enquiry from Frost as to whether they had much further to go. 'I think Edward blamed most my laziness,' Frost told Haines. 'He would have liked me better if I had walked farther with him.' But walk they did, at times as many as twenty-five miles, though usually, for Frost's benefit, considerably fewer. They would spend days together in this way: walking and talking, about verse, about their home life or their peers, stopping now and again to examine the flora in the hedgerow, or to lean on a stile or gate. Frost delighted in his friend's knowledge of wild flowers and bird calls, while Thomas could listen all day to his companion speak about verse; and they found a meeting of minds on their ideas about poetry: on speech rhythms and sound-sense, on uncluttered diction, on cadence and the ear. To Frost, the thoroughness and insight of Thomas's knowledge was second to none; to Thomas, Frost's instincts were sharper and truer than any he had met.

Writer to reader, poet to critic, or at least that is how Thomas understood those first talks; but Frost had already seen a poet in Thomas and would set about convincing his friend that they were talking writer to writer. It was in this good-humoured and affectionate manner that their friendship found its spirit-level.[7]

That week in April Thomas made a call on Lascelles Abercrombie in Ryton, and if Thomas's reviews had created a tense atmosphere in the past it was temporarily forgotten. But not so at the Old Nail-Shop, where Thomas's years of pounding had been neither forgotten nor forgiven. 'Gibson and I are too conscious of what we used to think of one another,' Thomas confided on his return to Steep. 'I like his later work, but temperamentally.'[8]

Thomas had returned to Hampshire by the time W. H. Davies paid his 'respects' to Dymock in May. He booked himself in with Gibson at the Old Nail-Shop and in little time at all disgraced himself as only Davies could. Once there, he had volunteered conversation about the prostitutes it had been his good fortune to know, going so far as to reveal some prices that he had paid in the past fortnight, and according to Frost 'entirely disgusted the Gibsons with whom he was visiting'. Davies's hosts would take an unkindly form of revenge on a later visit. Under a heavy rainstorm, the Gibsons attempted to hurry Davies on his wooden leg the best part of two miles down to Ryton, cajoling him onward until he was breaking out in sweats. The reward for his endeavour, said Gibson as they strode, was an appointment with Abercrombie, the greatest poet in England. 'Huh,' puffed Davies, 'a good thing it's the greatest poet in England.'

Gibson let the sarcasm in Davies's tone pass and hurried in on arrival to tell Abercrombie the news that Davies thought him the nation's greatest poet. 'But that's what Davies thinks he is himself,' said Frost, when he heard the story. 'And that is what Gibson, or Gibson's wife, thinks Gibson is.' Already the poets were squabbling in their new Eden and Frost's displeasure was beginning to rise, no doubt increased by Davies's visits to Little Iddens, where the grateful Gibsons deposited him daily. There Davies appointed himself a tutor on nature to Lesley Frost who, at fifteen, was more than a match for the Welshman. *See now*, he said, gesturing, *That little green bird, what is it?* Lesley struggled to keep a straight face. *A sparrow*, she said, *And it isn't green, is it?* 'He really doesn't know nature at all,' Frost remarked dismissively of a poet whom he had initially admired. Nor was Davies found to be a better conversationalist when it came to prosody. 'Absolutely uncritical untechnical untheoretical', said Frost: the very qualities that Frost himself had been accused of.[9]

Davies's visit to Gloucestershire may not have been a success, but Thomas's had been. 'He and I tired the sun down with talking on the footpaths and stiles of Ledington and Ryton,' recalled Frost. It would be the first of many occasions of what the American liked to call their 'talks–walking'. 'The important thing to us is that we are near Gibson,' Frost had written in May, but by June the Frosts' personal compass was turning toward Thomas. 'Rob and I think everything of him,' wrote Elinor Frost. 'He is quite the most admirable and lovable man we have ever known.'[10]

*   *   *

The meadows may have been flush with spring, but in those first weeks in Dymock Robert Frost witnessed another aspect of rural life that lurked out of sight of the casual visitor. On his walks, he observed a poverty in the English fields that was quite unlike anything he had seen at home. In Gloucestershire, mothers cleared stones ahead of the plough for a shilling a day; he watched them work through a downpour, carrying flints the size of their fists in their aprons. Children worked as soon as they were physically able to bring in an extra sixpence a day. Families survived on a pound a week, some on as little as half that. But worse even than the physical and financial hardship, what riled Frost in particular was the sight of the English class system in action, where the fieldhand was at the lowest rung of a social structure that demanded cap-tipping and kowtowing. Bullied by farmers, hounded by gamekeepers, the rural worker's life was one where even a minor transgression could put you out of work or worse. It was humiliating and dehumanising, Frost thought. 'These people are allowed to call only a small part of their soul their own.'[11]

Agricultural workers were as poor in 1914 as they had been in 1880 when Thomas Hardy portrayed their hardship. To manage a household on one pound a week, in the words of a social study of the time, took 'wisdom and loving-kindness, and after that as much cleanliness and order as can be squeezed in'. Rent would comprise a third of spending, then clothing and finally food. Diets were poor. Bread formed the bulk of any spending on food, a few potatoes and a little meat or fish in the cities, a little cheese and bacon on the land. Whatever protein there was in the household went to keeping the breadwinner fit, as his ill health could leave the family destitute. An allotment of any kind could entirely change a family's fortune, for if you could grow potatoes then you could keep chickens on the skin peelings, which in turn brought you eggs. But mostly such smallholdings were fought off by ruthless landowners, fearing that allotments would not only drain energy but increase the independence of their farmhands. There was one other outlay without which no work could be undertaken, and that was boots. Footwear was an item that had to withstand all conditions: mud, flint, sun, walking, rain and frost. In the towns, careful families saved through a boot club to replace worn shoes, but rural workers had no insurance and no organisation that could have provided it. Their population was scattered, hard to unionise, poorly educated, and living entirely in tied cottages at the mercy of the farmer for their job, their wage and their home. At the Census of 1911, a teacher earned annually just over £175, an agricultural labourer under £50.[12]

* * *

Thomas had returned from Little Iddens with Bronwen and Mervyn to Steep on 2 May. He and Helen had spent most of April apart, and though they had seemed to be getting along better already he was preparing for another absence. The dry heat of April had given way to ten days of May rain, and on the 11th Thomas returned to Gloucestershire, this time to join Eleanor Farjeon

161

at an ancient (they suspected haunted) farmhouse at Kingham in the Cotswolds, which had been loaned to her for the month, accompanied by her brother Bertie and the woman that he would marry in October, Joan Thornycroft. Thomas worked on *A Literary Pilgrim in England* from 5 to 7.30 each morning before relaxing in the company of his friends, walking amiably with Eleanor, smoking endlessly with Bertie and casting admiringly after Joan Thornycroft, whom Eleanor believed was Thomas's very ideal of femininity. It must have troubled Eleanor to see Thomas look after another woman in that way, yet if she was uncertain of her place in his complex affections, then she might have taken comfort in the outcome of a parlour game they played one evening after dinner. Under the rules of the game, each player was asked to liken their mutual friends to a list of towns or flowers or other criteria that was similarly pleasant or benign. But Thomas interpreted the rules rather differently, awarding or withholding marks based on his friends' personal qualities: positive scores for such attributes as grit, minuses for vanity or similar. Eleanor scored highly among the eleven names rated by Thomas, though, tellingly, it was Godwin Baynes who outshone all others (he did not include his new friend Robert Frost or any of the poets known only to him). But tucked away in the middle of his list was something more revealing still: namely, what appeared to be Thomas's self-scorecard of his own qualities and failures. In it, he rated himself as highly adaptable and lacking in vanity or ostentation, but cursed with little fire or *joie de vivre*; and he described himself as one part Christian to nine parts Pagan.[13]

162

By the time he left Kingham, Thomas was planning a return to Gloucestershire provided he could sublet Yew Tree Cottage. This time he would bring Helen and the entire family with him for a month of living beside the Frosts. The summer was beginning to be mapped out, and August 1914, their date of choosing, looked set to be an unforgettable month.[14]

*　　　*　　　*

On 15 May 1914, little more than a year after the first, David Nutt published the second book of verse from Robert Frost. It had been advertised in their company catalogue as *Farm Servants and Other People*, but Frost had abandoned this in favour of the more generic *New Englanders*, then *New England Hill Folk*, until he remembered the property page of his old newspaper that carried the section-heading 'North of Boston', which gave the collection its title. One thousand octavo sheets were printed, as they had for *A Boy's Will*, with 350 or so copies bound in coarse green linen for distribution.[15]

Frost said that *North of Boston* took up the themes where *A Boy's Will* laid them down; but it was more confident, more firmly defined, darker and more gripping than its predecessor, and certainly more assured in its footfall. The beginnings of the book were made in Derry, where three of its poems were written; 'All the rest of North of Boston I wrote in England,' said Frost, 'on an inspiration compounded of homesickness and the delight of new friendships.'[16]

'Something there is that doesn't love a wall.' The book opened with a first line of intrigue and guile, in

163

a loose, variable blank verse that would send a pulse rippling through the collection. 'The Death of the Hired Man', 'Home Burial', 'After Apple-Picking' would follow in a volume bookended by two short lyrics, each set in italics to distinguish them from the main works. The first of these lyrics was an octave that would ever after be set as the preliminary verse of his *Collected Poems*, beginning 'I'm going out to clean the pasture spring,' and concluding 'I sha'n't be gone long.—You come too.' Inclusive, informal, inviting: Frost was making good on his promise to be a 'a poet for all sorts and kinds'.[17]

When Thomas wrote to Frost on 19 May, *North of Boston* had been out for four days although Thomas had yet to see it. Nonetheless, his mind was focussed on the discussions about prosody that the two men had shared that spring, and he gave Frost a friendly warning: 'You really should start doing a book on speech and literature, or you will find me mistaking your ideas for mine and doing it myself. You can't prevent me from making use of them: I do so daily & want to begin over again with them & wring all the necks of my rhetoric—the geese. However, my "Pater" would show you I had got onto the scent already.' Indeed he had. Walter Pater was once a stylist much admired by Thomas, but now found hard to read. In explaining Pater's limitation, as he saw it, Thomas summoned phrases that would define his very approach to writing, in tones he would subsequently find echoed in Frost. Of Pater, Thomas observed—

When his prose sounds well it is with a pure sonority of words that is seldom related to sense.

—in other words, it was the *sound* that powered and defined the sentence and not only the definition that might be found in a dictionary. Thomas had not met Frost when he wrote this in 1912, still less heard the phrase 'sound of sense', yet already he was employing the vocabulary of sounds, sonority of words and sense. Earlier still, in 1910, Thomas wrote of Robert Burns's verse, 'It is as near to the music as nonsense could be, and yet it is perfect sense.' It was a statement that entirely foreshadowed the beliefs that he shared with Frost.[18]

In fact Thomas had been mining this seam for many years. As early as 1901 he had written, 'The best lyrics seem to be the poet's natural speech', and in 1907 championed Sidney Lanier's comment that verse comprises 'such sounds and silences as can be co-ordinated by the ear . . . and exists by virtue of the simple time-relations between the units of sound'. Over a number of years he paid tributes to Yeats's deployment of speech rhythms; on occasion he even employed the same language as Frost, complaining in 1912 that Lafcadio Hearn lacked 'any natural sweet cadence', while admitting that there were powers at work in Swinburne's verse beyond his explanation, except to say that 'the sound and the sense of the first line seem to prepare for it all'.[19]

But it was with Walter Pater that Thomas had made his case most clearly, a writer, he said, who was incapable of hearing the rhythms of speech.

His very words are to be seen, not read aloud; for if read aloud they betray their artificiality

165

by a lack of natural expressive rhythm.

And he continued,

> Nothing so much as the writer's rhythm can give that intimate effect 'as if he had been talking'. Rhythm is of the essence of a sincere expressive style.

Natural expressive rhythm: in other words, cadence; *as if he had been talking*: speech sounds. And now Thomas combined them to lay down a charge and a challenge for living literature:

> It has to make words of such a spirit, and arrange them in such a manner, that they will do all that a speaker can do by innumerable gestures and their innumerable shades, by tone and pitch of voice, by speed, by pauses, by all that he is and all that he will become.[20]

Writing *Walter Pater* had allowed Thomas to identify the values he most admired in writing, but it had also illuminated the shortcomings in his own method. In the spring of 1912 he saw for the first time that his own processes of note-taking were destroying his natural expressive rhythm: 'Criticising Pater has helped the discovery. But it is too late now, in these anxious and busy times, to set about trying to write better than perhaps I was born to.' From his prose criticism of Walter Pater it seemed clear now that, consciously or not, Thomas was preparing a run at poetry. And now, in May 1914, he put to Frost the most important question he would ever lay before his friend: could he, Edward Thomas, possibly write poetry?

> I wonder whether you can imagine me taking
> to verse. If you can I might get over the feeling
> that it is impossible—which at once obliges
> your good nature to say 'I can'. In any case I
> must have my 'writer's melancholy' though
> I can quite agree with you that I might spare
> some of it to the deficient. On the other hand
> even with registered post, telegraph &c &
> all modern conveniences I doubt if I could
> transmit it.

Frost could certainly imagine his friend taking
to verse and had no doubts about his ability to
transmit it; he told him so.

> Edward Thomas had about lost patience with
> the minor poetry it was his business to review.
> It took me to tell him what his trouble was.
> He was suffering from a life of subordination
> to his inferiors. Right at that moment he was
> writing as good a poetry as anybody alive but
> in prose form where it didnt declare itself
> and gain him recognition. I referred to the
> paragraphs here and there in such a book as
> The Pursuit of Spring and pointed them out.
> Let him write them in verse form in exactly
> the same cadence and we would see. Thats all
> there was to it. His poetry declared itself in
> verse form and in the year before he died he
> took his place where he belonged among the
> English poets.[21]

The declaration of Thomas's verse was now less

than six months away, but it was not the only event that occupied his mind in the spring of 1914. Since their earliest meetings, Frost had spoken about New England with a passion that had stirred Thomas. The American had not hidden his desire to return home and in February had encouraged Thomas to think about joining him. Thomas had considered such a move once before when, in the spring of April 1912, in some despair, he had written to his agent lamenting the lack of work and speculated on a change of career and a relocation to the United States. Cazenove had talked him out of that voyage as he had the trip to Australia, but in the spring of 1914 Thomas and Frost were beginning to talk with increasing seriousness about a move by both of their families. The two would farm together, said Frost, and if farming did not work for any reason then there would always be the possibility of teaching. Thomas knew he was no farmer and had not struggled to see behind Frost's pretence to be one, and he doubted that he could ever be capable of teaching. But perhaps he might find a literary living in New England more or less as he did in the 'old' country. By the spring they had made an agreement that whenever Frost sailed back home he would take Mervyn with him in an advance party on the expectation that the rest of the Thomases would follow.[22]

*   *   *

North of Boston received an anonymous mention that May in the *Times Literary Supplement* in a disappointing notice that spoke of Frost's 'naïve individuality' and his 'little pictures from ordinary life'. To Frost it must have seemed that the pattern that had accompanied *A Boy's Will* looked likely to repeat itself. He was on his guard for what might follow, but he took comfort from the knowledge that his neighbours Lascelles Abercrombie and Wilfrid Gibson were also preparing reviews: friends, he reasoned, who had been party to his discussions on the sound of sense and could surely be relied upon to deepen readers' understanding of his art. Ezra Pound had also declared his intention to produce a review, but that worrying news was more than compensated by the knowledge that Edward Thomas was also to write about the book. From their week together in April, Frost knew that Thomas understood his thinking better than anyone and had shared in Frost's despair at the unsigned *TLS* review. Thomas suspected he knew its author to be Walter de la Mare, and he told Frost as much. Though he had yet to meet him, Frost now decided that he supposed de la Mare to be 'a bit of a British snob'.[23]

SUMMER

The prospect of further commissioned work must have filled Thomas with dread that first week in June. He was bone tired and working ever longer hours to meet his deadlines. The manuscript of *A Literary Pilgrim in England* dragged on, and he slaved away at criticism for the usual journals about books about which he did not care one jot. Half a dozen of his reviews and two articles were printed in June alone, and still he tried for further commissions. 'I am so plagued with work,' he confessed to Frost, 'burning my candle at 3 ends.' All the while the one book he did wish to write about was still to make an appearance through his letterbox. With no sign of a review copy of *North of Boston* from the publisher and no personal copy sent by Frost, Thomas contented himself in re-reading in typescript the poems that his friend had sent him, and told Gordon Bottomley eagerly, 'His getting back to pure speech rhythms is going to do good.' He bided his time by continuing his correspondence with Frost on sound-sense. 'Yes I quite see about using the "naked tones", not the mere words, of certain profoundly characteristic instinctive rhythms,' he concurred. 'And No, you don't bore me. Only I feel a fraud in that I have unconsciously rather imitated your interest in the matter.' There was no imitation, only a convergence of minds, but it was typical of Thomas's graceful manner to offer Frost the stronger hand.[1]

When Thomas left for London on 8 June *North of Boston* had just arrived. He devoured the book on the train, revisiting the familiar poems 'Home Burial' and 'The Housekeeper', and encountering for the first time the newer pieces that he had not seen in typescript. By the time he met up with Walter de la Mare on 9 June he had made up his mind about the singular importance of the work and he prepared to argue out the point with his friend. To Thomas's surprise de la Mare had not seen the book, which told him that he had been wrong to suppose his friend the author of the disparaging *TLS* review. He told Frost of his mistake, but the American's mind was made up about this Englishman who considered himself superior.

'There is not a bad one among them, not one I haven't enjoyed very much', Thomas wrote in a letter to Frost '—only the last line of each of those two leaves me with a shade of dissatisfaction. Which is a foolish thing for me to say without saying a great deal more.' Thomas would say more, a great deal more, and over the next few weeks he began to prepare the copy for the reviews that would do more than any other to influence the reception of Frost's book.[2]

It was not unusual at the time for professional critics to write more than one review of an individual book. When a second commission occurred, a less scrupulous writer might respond by reconstituting their original ideas in an unsigned notice; but not Thomas. When he reviewed a book a second time, he was fastidious in breaking new ground. Each review should be a development from the last, he believed, so that if he had discussed a writer's rhythm in one review, for example, he might address their use of rhyme in another, or if prosody first then influences next, and so on. With

171

imagination and diligence, he kept his copy fresh: it was not easy to distil your thoughts into one piece of writing only to be asked to do it again; but for *North of Boston*, Thomas chose to write three.

As Thomas prepared his copy, he set off to see Gordon Bottomley in his new home, The Sheiling at Silverdale, in Lancashire. He found his friend laid up by another in a line of crippling illnesses that had incapacitated him since childhood, wishing for a break in the sultry weather and yet, despite it all, uncomplaining and seemingly 'one of the happiest people in the world'. Thomas was ashamed of his own petulance in the face of such stoicism. In the past, they had taken a steamer boat on Lake Windermere (Thomas had refused to pause at Wordsworth's grave at St Oswald's Church), but with Bottomley now immobile, they sat together and watched the weather rumble in over Morecambe Bay. 'This has been a year of years for weather,' he wrote to Helen. 'I wish things were coming right. Still I have contrived to get more pleasure than almost ever before out of the weather. We have been happier too, in spite of all.'[3]

Bottomley had listened as Thomas recounted in detail his conversations with Frost about sound-sense. What Thomas told Bottomley that day stayed with his friend and would enter into his own writing practice. Bottomley summarised Thomas's words:

[W]hen a man writes verse so attentively and of custom that his skill becomes instinct and carries him beyond the domination of verse-mechanism, his own speech-tunes and phrasings in daily life will control his use of metrical pattern. The latter will become a

172

constant, felt rather than exhibited, and the actual words will go over it like a counterpoint: in the end the poet's own speaking voice and cadences will be heard, through his personal vocal rhythms.[4]

*　　　*　　　*

Thunder broke on 10 June; a torrential downpour followed. The cool nights gave way to hot days, which by the month's end were rocketing into the eighties. In the roasting heat, London was enjoying a musical summer like no other. The Grand Russian Season at the Royal Theatre, Drury Lane, was the talk of the town: the self-taught Russian bass Fyodor Chaliapin enthralled opera-goers with his performances of Mussorgsky, Prokofiev and Borodin. But it was the Diaghilev Ballet that truly won the capital's hearts thanks to the performances of its stars, Vaslav Nijinksky and Tamara Karsavina. On the night of 23 June, Richard Strauss's *The Legend of Joseph* had its English premiere conducted by the composer himself. Edward, Helen and Joan Thornycroft squeezed into the packed and stifling auditorium, and heard the audience give the performance an outstanding reception, although the *New York Times* in a cable dispatch reported the grumbling of the critics. Thomas too was doubtful, and referred to the evening as 'hot air', and not only in deference to the unseasonably fierce temperature.[5]

The next morning he rose early at his parents' house in Balham. The weather was glorious from 4.20 a.m., and by ten o'clock tiers of thin white cloud stepped high into the morning sky. Helen

173

and he hurried to be away, leaving the children with Edward's parents, and crossed London to Paddington in time to catch the 10.20 train to Malvern. At 11.44 the train drew up at Oxford; haymakers toiled beneath the hot sun; it was eighty degrees in the shade that day.

Then we stopped at Adlestrop, thro the willows cd be heard a chain of blackbirds songs at 12.45 & one thrush & no man seen, only a hiss of engine letting off steam. Stopping outside Campden by banks of long grass willow herb & meadowsweet, extraordinary silence between the two periods of travel—looking out on grey dry stones between metals & the shiny metals & over it all the elms willows & long grass—one man clears his throat—and a greater rustic silence. No house in view[.] Stop only for a minute till signal is up.[6]

It was midsummer. The weather in Dymock was hot and rainless; wild roses flowered in the hedgerow, and somewhere distant a blackcap sang. With the early evening sun at their shoulder, Edward and Helen and Robert and Elinor left Little Iddens and headed down the lane toward the Old Nail-Shop. Helen was meeting these new friends for the first time, and that evening there was a gathering that would do much to define the Gloucestershire poets. Rupert Brooke had returned to England from the South Seas on 6 June and was staying with the Gibsons, looking 'browner and older and better looking after his tour', thought Thomas; Abercrombie and Catherine

174

made the short walk from the Gallows. Never before or again would so many of the poets gather in Gloucestershire: only John Drinkwater was missing of the six who would one day be known as the Dymock Poets. Gibson recorded the moment in metric prose.

Do you remember the still summer evening
When, in the cosy cream-washed living-room
Of The Old Nailshop, we all talked and
    laughed—
Our neighbours from The Gallows, Catherine
And Lascelles Abercrombie; Rupert Brooke;
Elinor and Robert Frost, living a while
At Little Iddens, who'd brought over with
    them
Helen and Edward Thomas? In the lamplight
We talked and laughed; but, for the most part,
    listened
While Robert Frost kept on and on and on,
In his slow New England fashion, for our
    delight,
Holding us with shrewd turns and racy quips,
And the rare twinkle of his grave blue eyes?

We sat there in the lamplight, while the day
Died from rose-latticed casements, and the
    plovers
Called over the low meadows, till the owls
Answered them from the elms, we sat and
    talked—
Now, a quick flash from Abercrombie; now,
A murmured dry half-heard aside from
    Thomas;
Now, a clear laughing word from Brooke; and

then
Again Frost's rich and ripe philosophy,
That had the body and tang of good
    draught-cider,
And poured as clear a stream.

For once Gibson's craft is not on trial: we are simply grateful for his documentation. No other testimony allows us to imagine how these poets interacted: Frost, holding court, the tireless raconteur, Abercrombie's sharp interjections, Thomas's arid undercuts, Brooke irresistible in his wit and merriment; even Gibson himself is mirrored in the observational, workmanlike reportage. If ever these poets had a moment of unity it was at the Old Nail-Shop that evening of 24 June; and among the conversational topics that united them that evening might well have been a letter which would bring them closer still.[7]

When Thomas called at the Gallows two days later, he was shown a letter that Abercrombie had just received from Ezra Pound who, even by his irascible standards, had written in unusual temper. For reasons that were clear to neither Abercrombie nor Thomas, Pound's patience with the former had snapped, and now he demanded public satisfaction. 'Ezra Pound has tried to honour himself by challenging Abercrombie to a duel,' Thomas recounted. 'Pound merely said something like "Your stupidity now amounts to a public insult" and "My seconds will wait on you." Whether Abercrombie had trounced the Imagists I don't know but I fancy not. Ezra has long been antipathetic to his betters.' Pound's summons does not survive, although Thomas's recollection of its contents is confirmed by two others who also saw it. Privately, Pound had been scathing about *Georgian Poetry*, but he had at least reserved judgement on Abercrombie himself, whose work, he felt up until then, had risen above the decrepitude of the other contributions. But Abercrombie had subsequently drawn Pound's ire for reasons that escaped him. According to one version of the story, Abercrombie had called on young poets to return to Wordsworth and Milton; in another, he had publicly taken a veiled swipe at Imagism. Most likely, Pound's pique was stoked by little more than Abercrombie being the most identifiable figure of the Georgian school of poets, which was excuse enough for a quarrel. (Pound would remove a line of Eliot's from *The Waste Land* with the damning inscription, 'georgian'.) Imagists laughed that, hearing of Pound's skill with a rapier, Abercrombie had cold-called on Yeats to ask him to intervene only to have the front door answered by Pound himself and to flee terrified into the London streets. Georgians joked that Abercrombie had the upper hand because he had invoked his right as the challenged party to nominate the weapon of combat, and had wittily picked unsold copies of their respective books. No duel was ever fought, and whether or not Pound was serious about the encounter, he would not lower his sights from the Georgians. Abercrombie, once respectable in Pound's eyes, was singled out for ridicule as one of the 'literary hen-coops', and the Georgians 'the stupidest set of Blockheads to be found in any country'. Thomas had once praised the potential of Abercrombie and Pound evenly, but he no longer felt need to be impartial. 'What imbeciles the Imagists are,' he said.[8]

Eighteen months previously there had been no 'Georgians' and no 'Imagists', only individual poets writing individual poems. In the days before such sharp lines were drawn, Pound might have found his way into Edward Marsh's *Georgian Poetry*. Yet Harold Monro's decision to give each of these competing clans their own anthology under the imprint of the Poetry Bookshop appeared not, as he might have hoped, to have fostered diversity, but merely to have heightened intransigence.

*   *   *

After lunch on 27 June, Thomas left the literary squabble behind and took the train with Helen for Coventry to see the friends with whom their son would later lodge. As they returned home two days later, the papers carried news of an assassination in Sarajevo. The heir to the Austro-Hungarian throne had visited the Bosnian province; seven conspirators, Serbian nationalists, had lain in wait along the route. The first lost his nerve and let the royal car pass, a second threw a grenade that bounced off its target and detonated further down the street. As the cortège re-routed the attackers' moment appeared to have gone. Gavrilo Princip had abandoned his attempt, and had stopped on the corner of Franzjosefstrasse to buy a sandwich when the royal car came unexpectedly into view. The driver had taken a wrong turning; in trying to reverse, the engine stalled. Princip could not believe his luck. At nineteen, he was barely old enough to call himself a man, yet the shots he fired that day would trigger the greatest slaughter the world had ever known.

*   *   *

Heavy rains fell in July. Thomas spent the month at Steep behind his typewriter working on *A Literary Pilgrim in England* and assembling a flora anthology that publishers T. C. & E. C. Jack had agreed to commission. He asked Frost whether he might include 'A Tuft of Flowers', and by 17 July the anthology was finished. 'I like him more and more,' he told Bottomley, 'which is as it should be if I am to till New Hampshire at his side which appears more and more likely.' Frost came to Yew Tree Cottage for the weekend of 18–19 July: it was his first visit to Steep, and it gave the friends the chance to talk over the idea of America further. Thomas longed to be rid of the endless literary criticism; he had been covering twenty pages a day writing about sub-standard books and felt that he could not go on. 'I hate it all and find it more than difficult to keep up,' he told Eleanor Farjeon. 'So I am beginning to think of New Hampshire as the only possibility though really not thinking of it as quite possible either.' The only-possible-and-yet-impossible road: how often had Thomas found himself there, without options or self-determination, following a path that he did not fully understand but which at a deep level he believed to be inevitable. He was wavering in a way that Frost had already begun to mock; even so, the American's friendship was gratefully received: 'His wanting me is some encouragement,' said Thomas.[9]

Thomas published the first of two round-up reviews of John Drinkwater in which the most he could manage by way of compliment was to praise the writer's 'enthusiasm and eagerness'. In 1911 he had accused Drinkwater of facility, quipping that he dispensed with 'a fluency of words that leaves no more behind it than a five-minute shower on a hot day'. Drinkwater may have been the least accomplished of the Dymock poets ('Bell daffodils that are aglow | In Ryton Woods now, where they go | Who are my friends and makes good rhymes'), but his work for the Birmingham Repertory Theatre was the envy of Abercrombie and Gibson. He was a polite, polished and determined character who needed no invitation to share his work, as Catherine Abercrombie remembered of his arrival at Ryton, where 'he read some of his poems to us straight away, and how I wished he would not, as he turned himself into a fashionable parson, voice and all, and eyes to the ceiling, to do it—'. Thomas and Drinkwater never met, though Thomas had established all he thought he needed to know about the man from his writing. 'I had always heard ill of Drinkwater and rated him by his verses which was pretty hard on him.'[10]

*   *   *

Rupert Brooke was relishing his return to London. He dined at 10 Downing Street and at the Savoy, brushed up on the Russian Ballet season, breakfasted with Siegfried Sassoon, Paul Nash and W. H. Davies, lunched with D. H. Lawrence and with Henry James, and supped with W. B. Yeats, Bernard Shaw, J. M. Barrie and G. K. Chesterton: a not untypical week in the life of Rupert Brooke. On 28 July he read for the second and, as it turned out, last time at the Poetry Bookshop, reciting from his own work to an audience of sixty-five. He was nervous and confessed privately to one member of the audience how he dreaded the thought of having to perform. He sat on the corner of one of the Bookshop's oak tables, swinging a leg to and fro as he listened to the admirers who had gathered around him, 'beautiful as an annunciating angel' said one, but not to the American poet and critic Amy Lowell, who happened to be in town that night:

> I toiled up the narrow stairs of a little outhouse behind the Poetry Bookshop, and in an atmosphere of overwhelming sentimentality, listened to Mr Rupert Brooke whispering his poems. To himself, it seemed, as nobody else could hear him. It was all artificial and precious. One longed to shout, to chuck up one's hat in the street when one got outside.

Throughout the reading, an elderly lady in the front row raised and lowered her ear trumpet, straining to make out his voice until eventually she could take no more. 'Speak up, young man!' she hollered.[11]

Austrian authorities in Sarajevo responded brutally to the Archduke's assassination. Two hundred Bosnian Serbs were rounded up and hanged in the city's prisons, while authorities were believed to be turning a blind eye to a wave of pogroms in the countryside. But the ripples from Princip's shots had not yet carried beyond the region. The royal funeral in Vienna would focus weeks of internal manoeuvres among the country's political and military leaders. An Austrian invasion of Serbia needed the support of Germany if Russia were to be kept at bay. It registered little with the poets of London and Gloucestershire when at twelve noon on the day of Brooke's reading Austria declared war on Serbia.

*   *   *

It was Jack Haines who sent Robert Frost the unsigned notice in *The Nation* of *North of Boston* that both men recognised as the work of Abercrombie. The review was both warm and astute, and had applauded the attempt by Frost 'to capture and hold within metrical patterns the very tones of speech'. In making a direct reference to the sound of sense, Abercrombie scored a notable first (though rather ungallantly Frost said that he had provided Abercrombie his 'catchwords'). A second, anonymous write-up in the *Pall Mall Gazette* had noted 'the woof of familiar metres crossed constantly by the warp of instinctive cadences' in what was a perceptive analogy for the overlaying of variable speech rhythms upon the strictures of conventional blank verse. Other reviews were less fulsome, but at least Frost had an endorsement to look forward to from the second of his Gloucestershire neighbours, Wilfrid Gibson. Or so he thought; but the review in *The Bookman* that July was not at all what Frost had been hoping for. Gibson's opening remarks affected praise, but in acknowledging that some readers might entertain such descriptions as 'unsophisticated', 'simplicity' and 'artlessness' he cast an ambiguity that could not fail to get up Frost's hackles. In company with Gibson, as with Abercrombie, Frost had spent many hours talking about the sound of sense and

Gibson was well aware of the sophistication of the American's prosody. But the tone of the review worsened.

> I am inclined to wonder at times if, in his determination to avoid artifice, Mr Frost has not discarded too much. There are legitimate excitements, as well as illegitimate, in the enjoyment of verse; and in reading some of these poems I have missed the exhilaration of an impelling and controlling rhythm.

Gibson may have felt many things about *North of Boston*, but it seems unthinkable that he could have missed an impelling rhythm in this most skilfully rhythmic of books. Thomas, in his reviews of Gibson, repeatedly accused him of lacking any metrical art himself, which might go a little way to explain Gibson's remark, but to Frost the commentary from his friend must have seemed bizarre. What was Gibson up to? Was he trying to put Frost somehow in his place? Was he envious? Until that moment, Frost had declared Gibson his closest friend, but now that friendship would begin to deteriorate. In 1916 Frost said of Gibson that, 'No sooner had I got down into the country near him than I began defining my position with regard to him—and you know what that means. It means sheering off from him.'[12]

Frost believed that a good showing in England was essential to help him find publication at home. He now feared that after everything he had tried—uprooting his family from New Hampshire, the year in Beaconsfield, the move to Gloucestershire, the fruitless efforts to procure the favour of Pound and Yeats and lately Gibson—after all of that, his literary venture in England might still result in failure.

But his fortunes were about to change.

'This is one of the most revolutionary books of modern times,' Edward Thomas declared, 'but one of the quietest and least aggressive.' It was a bold and intriguing claim with which to open the review that appeared in the *Daily News* on 22 July: could a book really be both revolutionary *and* quiet? Thomas prepared to explain.

> These poems are revolutionary because they lack the exaggeration of rhetoric, and even at first sight appear to lack the poetic intensity of which rhetoric is an imitation. Their language is free from the poetical words and forms that are the chief material of secondary poets. The metre avoids not only the old-fashioned pomp and sweetness, but the later fashion also of discord and fuss. In fact, the medium is common speech.

For old-fashioned pomp read the Edwardian elders; for discord and fuss read the Imagists: even Thomas, it appeared, was not above mud slinging in the wake of recent events. But the comparison was not merely personal, for Thomas was making yet another statement about the kind of writing that he valued: neither the old florid styles nor the fashion for new artificialities, but simple common speech.[13]

The poems of *North of Boston* depended not upon objects of conventional beauty and yet they were beautiful, he wrote. The language rarely relied on rhetoric and yet it was memorable speech. And the style was as 'low' as the characters who spoke it, as unembellished as the blank verse that conducted it; it had the unpretentiousness of prose but was not prose; tellingly, said Thomas, 'It is poetry because it is better than prose.'

The book was not without failures, Thomas conceded. What began in mystery in places ended in obscurity, and here and there the accents required for reading seemed to remain just out of reach of the reader. But the successes such as 'The Death of the Hired Man' lifted Frost to a place of his own, 'above all other writers of verse in America'. Ezra Pound could not have liked that, not one little bit; but finally, here was a statement in which Frost could delight and could take back to his native country. 'It speaks,' wrote Thomas, 'and it is poetry.'

It is poetry because it is better than prose. It speaks, and it is poetry. Two phrases that stand out as much for what they tell us of Thomas as Frost.

In the summer of 1914 Thomas was still a prose writer and not yet a poet. For almost his entire adult life he had earned his living from prose, but clearly now, in this review and elsewhere, Thomas was retuning his ear toward a form of writing that is cadenced and memorable and that propels itself using the rhythms of speech.

In a second notice, for the monthly *English Review*, Thomas praised Frost's refusal to be seduced by the modern fashion for 'glory' words. Frost's book stood out from the crowd, he wrote, in its ability to make poetry without being poetical, which was an experiment reminiscent of Wordsworth's but with an important difference. Where Wordsworth contemplated, Frost

185

sympathised, exposing fewer of his own feelings and more of his subjects', so allowing him to write a form of eclogue that was both homely and racy, lyric and dramatic. In places the results were 'masterpieces of deep and mysterious tenderness': plain-spoken verse that might appear akin to prose in places, until spoken aloud when the emotion of the work rises out through the unmistakable rhythm of the poetry.[14]

A third review was to follow in the *New Weekly*, and Thomas found a still sharper way to focus his ideas about speech.

> Mr Frost has, in fact, gone back, as Whitman and as Wordsworth went back, through the paraphernalia of poetry into poetry again. With a confidence like genius, he has trusted his conviction that a man will not easily write better than he speaks when some matter has touched him deeply.

Thomas had isolated precisely what it was that allowed Frost's work to stand apart from the pack.[15]

In the space of three short reviews, Edward Thomas had concisely introduced and evaluated the importance of this new writer. In not one of the three reviews did he baffle the reader with discussions of prosody or technique, he did not even employ the words 'cadence', 'tone' or 'sound' that Frost himself used so much. Thomas had said simply that Frost was revolutionary because he wove everyday speech rhythms and common dictions across blank verse, and in so doing had taken readers much closer to the genuine matter of poetry than just about anyone before him. Frost was delighted by what he read. At last he felt understood, endorsed by a man whom other men listened to, and believed for the first time that his work might, after all, begin to earn him the reputation that he yearned for. Frost was in no doubt of the gift that Thomas had bestowed upon him, and would never lose sight of it. 'He gave me standing as a poet—', Frost acknowledged in 1921, 'he more than anyone else.'[16]

It was a debt that Frost feared he could never repay.

But he had already begun to repay it.

*　　*　　*

On 1 August the Thomases were in Steep making their final arrangements for their month's holiday in Gloucestershire. The family would travel in two parties: Edward and Mervyn would set off by bicycle on the 3rd, breaking the journey en route, while Helen and the two girls would leave Steep a day later by train. Peter Mrosovski, a pupil at Bedales who was boarding at Yew Tree Cottage, was put on the train to London for his summer holiday return home to Russia, leaving the Thomases to finalise their plans. But as 1 August wore on, something unexpected happened: Peter reappeared on their doorstep. The boy explained that he had got as far as Millwall docks to be told that Germany had declared war on Russia, and that there was no longer a safe passage home for him. Helen and Edward discussed the new situation: there would be room for Peter in Gloucestershire, and the boy could travel with Helen if he could

187

find no alternative route home. For the time being Thomas appeared more interested in the glorious weather than in the escalation of war, baking skies which he speculated idly might form 'a minor poem in prose'. He had that day delivered the typescript of *A Literary Pilgrim in England* to Cazenove and admitted to Eleanor Farjeon to feeling at a loose end. 'Who will want the thing now? I may as well write poetry. Did anyone ever begin at 36 in the shade?' The previous September he had begun but abandoned a poem in his waking hours at Ellis's East Grinstead house. Then, in May, he had asked Frost whether he could ever imagine him taking to verse. And now, on the eve of his holiday with Frost he was again prospecting for poetry.[17]

On 3 August, Edward and Mervyn set off from Steep in breezy, showering weather. They rode north-west, breaking their journey in Wiltshire as planned, and may well have learned the news that Germany had that day declared war on France. They were away early the next morning, into a headwind, and were quickly on the outskirts of Swindon. As a boy, Thomas had spent many of his holidays here and was familiar with the Great Western Railway's engineering works that dominated the town: some of his relatives had been employed there. Many times as a boy he had heard the factory hooter calling its workers. Each morning it hailed at 6.45, then again with a shorter blast at 7.20 and again at 7.25; if you were not in the factory by the fourth blast, you were late for work. But on the evening of 4 August, the twin brass domes of the hooter let out ten extended bellows that carried for miles.

Britain was at war.

Germany had violated Belgian borders early in the morning of 4 August. Twelve forts around Liège guarded the gateway to the Belgian plain; under heavy barrage, all of them would fall by 16 August. The Germans torched towns as they went, pushing a human wall of refugees ahead to protect them from retreating infantry fire. Six thousand five hundred Belgian and French civilians were mown down or massacred in the first month alone. The push toward Paris would end in a French stand at the Marne river in September. Germany pulled back to higher ground and dug in, the French followed suit, and so began the building of trenched fortifications that would eventually stretch five hundred miles from the English Channel to the border of Switzerland.

*   *   *

Thomas and Frost were sitting together on an orchard stile near Little Iddens when word came that the firing had started. They wondered whether they might be able to hear the guns from their corner of Gloucestershire.[18]

In London, Harold Monro had no doubts about the right course of action. A call from the War Office for motorcycle volunteers had appeared in that morning's *Daily Mirror* and he responded, only to be turned away on account of the difficulty of finding spare parts for his American motorcycle. When he returned the next day on a British-built bike, he was told that the vacancy had been filled.[19]

At Cley-next-the-Sea on the north coast of Norfolk, Rupert Brooke woke from a nightmare about impending war to find that it had begun. To his hosts, the Cornfords, he uttered not a word all day, but that evening Frances asked, 'But Rupert, *you* won't have to fight?' Said Brooke, 'We shall *all* have to fight.'[20]

At a teachers' conference in Stratford-upon-Avon, Lascelles Abercrombie and John Drinkwater were extolling the importance of Shakespeare when they learned the news. Godwin Baynes and his wife Rosalind were idling in a rowing boat on the River Ouse at St Ives; they tethered their boat and rushed to buy in food supplies.[21]

Rosalind's first cousin, Siegfried Sassoon, had walked into the Drill Hall at Lewes and enlisted the day before.[22]

Robert Graves, aged nineteen, was in his family's holiday home in North Wales; within days he would volunteer for the Royal Welch Fusiliers.

In Bagnères-de-Bigorre, in the south of France, a twenty-year-old man who would train alongside Edward Thomas was teaching when France was invaded; he climbed to the top of a hill and gazed both north to where he supposed the fighting might be, and south over the Pyrenees to the safety of Spain, wondering in which direction his future lay. His name was Wilfred Owen.[23]

*　　　*　　　*

'GREAT BRITAIN DECLARES WAR ON GERMANY', read the banner of the country's most popular paper, the *Daily Mirror*. The *Daily Telegraph* reported the deployment of 'enthusiastic troops', and *The Times* looked to a poem from Henry Newbolt to rally the national mood. By the following morning, the tone of the national press had become determined. 'England expects that every man will do his duty', wrote *Daily Express* while the *Daily Telegraph* urged upon its readers 'tears of pride' for the strength of the nation's stance. But the Manchester *Guardian*, which had hoped Britain would not be drawn into the conflict, warned that the country was facing 'the greatest calamity that anyone living has known'.[24]

Thomas loathed what he was reading in the newspapers: jingoistic clichés and nationalistic nonsense about the brave Brits and the evil Germans. How one nation could be painted so honourably and another so diabolically bewildered him: the Germans and Britons were not so different, men were men and felt fear equally whatever their uniform if you pointed a gun at them. He neither hated Germans nor loved Englishmen and wanted nothing to do with this campaign. 'I should like to avoid too much of this strain because it is not the strain of the men who are fighting or going to fight, but rather of morbid people in whom their balance and fusion of mind and body is impossible, and who admire frantically what is impossible to themselves.'[25]

The language of the press was provocative if not incendiary, but in Dymock, where Thomas was headed, the war seemed less immediate. Robert Frost had gone into Ledbury to stock up on tins of biscuits, boxes of soap, packets of cereal: preparations that seemed oddly siege-like and that did not go unnoticed in the town. Later that afternoon, Edward and Mervyn arrived along the Gloucester road having covered the 120 miles from

Hampshire without difficulty, but Helen's journey had been anything but straightforward. When she set off that morning, with the two girls and Peter Mrosovski in tow, the transport systems were already in chaos, and her train from Petersfield stopped at Oxford and would not continue any further. Laden with suitcases and children, and the pet dog Rags, Helen had prepared for a night on the station platform when finally a train arrived that would take them as far as Malvern. The taxi that took them onward stopped to ask directions from a policeman in Ledbury, who questioned them suspiciously about the late hour of their travel and the presence of a foreigner, though just a boy. There was a harvest moon above the Malvern Hills when the car pulled up at Oldfields; Edward was waiting for them at the gate and greeted them with his signature call, *Coo-ee*.[26]

Helen's midnight journey and Frost's conspicuous stock-up in Ledbury had attracted local attention. Stranger still, the Gibsons had staying with them a curious, thickly bearded poet from the Netherlands called van Doorn and the volume of unfamiliar accents aroused mistrust in the parish reminiscent of that which greeted Coleridge and Wordsworth in Nether Stowey during the Napoleonic War. Until then, the denizens of Dymock had been tolerated, if not welcomed, in the lanes and inns, as Thomas explained, 'But once it got about, in a certain part of Gloucestershire, that a Dutchman had been staying in one house, that an American family lived in another, that a party (including a Russian boy) had arrived by motor-car at a third in the middle of the night, all sorts of people joined in the hunt—the policeman, the retired clergyman, acting on the principle that "you never know what these naturalised Americans are," and the illiterate anonymous senders of reports that we sat up late at night.' A policeman came calling to follow up reports of those late-night sightings, even that Frost had been heard singing Germanic songs from the cellar at Little Iddens. Gibson was pressed over his Dutch visitor, and even Abercrombie, well known locally by now, came under suspicion for entertaining an artist with a rare physical disability. Thomas laughed off the intrusion as country gossip, Gibson too, but Frost did not; it riled him and according to Helen announced that if the policeman cared to call again then he, Frost, would personally shoot him. It would not be the last time that Frost had a run-in with the local constabulary.[27]

In the days that followed, calm was restored in the parish. Thomas and Frost renewed their talks–walking. Oldfields and Little Iddens were separated by three meadows, a gate, a brook and two stiles, so close that on a clear evening when the wind was low, it was possible to hear the voices of the children ringing from one place to the other. Each day, several times a day, Thomas walked between the cottages, through the rolling meadow beside Oldfields where a bay colt and an old mare ambled, down the sloping middle meadow and a tiny brook, there over a stile and up into the rougher grass of the Iddens meadow.[28]

Sometimes they tended to the garden, or took their families for a picnic outing. But best of all, they liked to slip the reins and walk out together on the Dymock fields. Scant rain fell to break the heat, but the rains of July had swelled the corn and the rooks cawed while the wheat fields were harvested beneath them. Wherever the men walked, half-attentive to footpaths, among the windfalls that the wasps had undermined, they moved in an instinctive sympathy. Their talk ranged over marriage and friendship, wildlife and the war. Sometimes there was no talk and a silence gathered about them; but often at a gate or stile it started up again or was prompted by the meeting of a stranger in the lanes: a word or two and they were off once more. Where they went they went without a map, setting their course by the sun or by the distant arc of May Hill crowning the view to the south; at dusk, the towering elms and Lombardy poplars or the light of a part-glimpsed cottage saw them home.[29]

On 6 August a full moon rose on an evening of heavy precipitation. The two friends were descending the Malverns when a rare lunar rising occurred, what Frost recorded as 'A very small moon-made prismatic bow'. What they witnessed, judging by Frost's description, was a moonbow that as it rose in the night sky became a lunar corona. Frost wrote of it later:

A wonder! Bow and rainbow as it bent,
Instead of moving with us as we went,
(To keep the pots of gold from being found)
It lifted from its dewy pediment
Its two mote-swimming many-colored ends,
And gathered them together in a ring.
And we stood in it softly circled round
From all division time or foe can bring
In a relation of elected friends.

To Thomas, it seemed like the first rainbow that ever was.[30]

The moods indoors were less agreeable. Helen found the conditions in Oldfields cramped and was less than taken by the company of her American neighbours. About Elinor Frost she was scathing: she found her careworn and defeated, a hopeless housekeeper who peeled potatoes in a dry bucket, and whose personality was nebulous and lacked the vigour of her husband's. Around Robert, Helen was uneasy, and found him erratic, bossy, given to illiberal and offensive remarks. The Thomas children became bored and Myfanwy injured herself falling from a swing, while Edward heard from Cazenove that *A Literary Pilgrim in England* was under-length by 10,000 words and would need enhancing. 'One thing and another leaves me very irritable indeed,' Edward told Eleanor Farjeon. To make matters worse, Mr Chandler, the owner of Oldfields, was called into service in Hereford, and Thomas suspected he and Frost might be left to complete the farmer's harvest. Worse still, with the country at war Thomas was aware that literary work of the kind that he depended on was certain to dry up. He told his old friend John Freeman that he felt more secluded than ever from the realities of events. 'I am working as much as I can by finding jobs for myself when even an unpatriotic person can't imagine it is of the least importance or money value,' he wrote. 'I get no work and discover no likelihood. Otherwise little is changed except in the newspapers. The harvest comes in.' Even with his landlord called into service, the war remained remote to Edward Thomas, and ten days after the outbreak of hostilities he admitted that he had not given first thought to serving his country.[31]

Eleanor Farjeon herself joined the party on 20 August, and settled in quickly at neighbouring Glyn Iddens as the guest of an elderly, kindly couple called Farmer, from where she recorded two of the more characterful episodes of those summer weeks. Mr Farmer's chuckling manners met Mrs Farmer's matronly ways ('Mother!' was his name for her, 'Father!' hers for him), and one evening they invited the poets to a lavish dinner replete with vats of the Farmers' home-made cider. When the moment in the evening came for the poets to rise to their feet, they found they had no legs beneath them. They attempted to rise and sank again, grinned and rose again in supportive pairs—Thomas and Frost, Abercrombie and Gibson—before weaving their ways home. On another occasion, an afternoon of stirring heat, Frost eyed his potato patch and announced that it was ready for digging; Thomas tugged his forelock mischievously and said yes sir, he would be about it the very next day. Sure enough when the morning came Thomas was at the vegetable patch; he was joined by Eleanor and, for a while at least, Frost's twelve-year-old son Carol. Under a hot sun, the 'hired' help rolled their sleeves and worked their rows in toil and sweat while Frost moved among them, directing here, smoking there. 'Wot abaht that little bit, mister,' said Thomas, a glint in his eye, straightening on his fork before turning back to the patch in hand.[32]

A new moon rose over Dymock on 21 August. In the days that followed, Frost and Thomas continued their pattern of talks–walking, and as they did so, something seemed to be shifting in Thomas's

196

mind. On 26 August the friends found themselves walking through the afternoon into the night. Thomas jotted in his notebook: 'a sky of dark rough horizontal masses in N.W. with a 1/3 moon bright and almost orange low down clear of cloud and I thought of men east-ward seeing it at the same moment. It seems foolish to have loved England up to now without knowing it could perhaps be ravaged and I could and perhaps would do nothing to prevent it.' A new sensibility was emerging in Edward Thomas. The war was three weeks old and for the first time he was imagining his countrymen abroad, sharing the same moon as he. He had no care for the politics of the conflict, but his mood was troubled by a different kind of awareness. He was weighing the worth of the land beneath his feet and the way of life that it supported. What would he do, if called upon, to protect it? Would he do anything at all?[33]

*   *   *

The walks with Frost had inspired Thomas to suggest a new line of work to his agent back in London. On 19 August, Thomas had asked Cazenove whether he could place a series of articles that recorded the impact of the war upon the working people he was meeting in the fields of Gloucestershire and Herefordshire. From conversations happened upon with labourers or drovers at a stile or gate or country inn, the pieces would form a foot-worn, first-hand, non-combatant's view of the campaign; they might even allow Thomas to feel that he was doing something for the war effort. Cazenove understood that the

197

country was in the grip of patriotism, and felt that any such pieces would require careful handling. He passed on Thomas's proposal to Austin Harrison at the *English Review*, who echoed the agent's anxiety. 'Nothing must be said which will stop recruiting,' Harrison had warned: this was his belief and that of his peers in the press, and no journal would risk appearing unpatriotic at the present time. Thomas was summoned to London on 27 August to give Harrison his assurances in person. He felt confident that he could strike a tone that did not seem unpatriotic, and made a gentleman's agreement with Harrison to that effect. Thomas would write three articles to appear over nine months and in return Harrison would offer £25 for 5,000 words. At a time when his livelihood looked doubtful, Thomas's proposal was a financial masterstroke.[34]

Thomas was not alone in struggling to find a satisfactory response to the war. Frost felt himself on similarly uncertain ground, if anything more persuaded than Thomas of the patriotic cause while knowing it not to be his own. 'You must think I have been and gone to war for the country that made me a poet,' he wrote to a friend in America on 20 August. 'My obligation is not quite as deep as that.' Nevertheless, were he younger, he said, and not the father of four then he might well make the cause his own. 'American or no American, I might decide that I ought to fight the Germans simply because I know I should be afraid to.' But in truth, what troubled him deep down was not the prospect of action or even the suffering of others but his own immediate prospects in literature. 'The war is an ill wind to me,' he admitted. 'It ends for the time being the thought of publishing any more books.

198

Our game is up.'[35]

In 1913, the number of books published was just one tenth of the output of today, but it was then a growth economy that had boomed by 25 per cent in five years. The war would have a devastating impact on the industry—a shortage of resources, labour and income would ensure that by 1918 the production of new editions was only a third of the number before the war; it would be the mid-1920s before the industry recovered. Overnight, editors were no longer commissioning book reviews, only articles that were expressly concerned with the conflict, and for Abercrombie and Thomas this posed a practical crisis. Abercrombie admitted to Marsh that his earnings to date were about half those of previous years, while expectations for the rest of 1914 were 'about £10'. At the same moment Thomas told Bottomley, 'I have of course no prospect of earning any sort of living while the war lasts.' Gibson did not rely upon review work and his income was less threatened: earnings from his verse alone matched Abercrombie's entire annual income. Publishers were swift to cut back on their commissioning and also on their staff, as Walter de la Mare found when he was released from his role as Reader at Heinemann. Frost did no such work, but he could see the ceiling being lowered on his *North of Boston*.[36]

If Frost could not see past his next publication, Rupert Brooke was experiencing a more physical response to the war. Something had shifted within him that August. To Gibson, he appeared listless and distracted, and confessed to his friend of feeling tearful and depressed. All he could focus on was the war. Part of him wanted to be left alone, quite alone, to live his life and follow his writing in peace: had he have wished to be a soldier he would have been one long ago. But the unrest within him grew until he came to understand the war as potentially the most important experience of his lifetime. 'Well, if Armageddon's *on*,' he said, 'I suppose one should be there.' Being there, he imagined at first, might mean accepting a placement as an international correspondent— many of his writer friends had put themselves down for that. But to go to war in that capacity was merely to offer curiosity when decent people were offering their lives, he believed: gesture was not enough. He wanted to feel that he might use his brain somehow, felt certain his skills must be needed in intelligence work; but so did many of the literary young men up and down the country and wherever he looked, Brooke found only waiting lists. Bitterly despondent, unable to vent his feelings, his moods became tortured and destructive. 'Half my heart is of England,' he wrote, 'the rest is looking for some home I haven't yet found.'[37]

The war, it was widely said, would be over by Christmas, and everywhere young men were rushing to do their bit in time. But doing your bit was harder than Brooke had supposed in those early days of the war. The professional army was well equipped for the needs of the short campaign that was believed to lie ahead; officers were not required, and applicants could be rejected on such irrelevancies as the condition of their teeth. Brooke explained: 'It's not so easy as you think—for a person who has no military training or knowledge, save the faint, almost prenatal, remembrance of some khaki drilling at Rugby—to get to the "front". I'm one of a band who have been offering themselves, with a vague persistence, to their country, in various quarters of London for some days, and being continually refused.'[38]

* * *

For Edward Thomas the summer in Dymock was over. On 2 September, the family packed their bags and left Oldfields. He told Gordon Bottomley that he had seen too little of Abercrombie, too much of Gibson and Frost daily. His three articles for the *English Review* had given him a watering hole in a commissioning desert, but he knew beyond those any further prospects for work were remote. For all his adult life he had lived by his prose but now he could see his livelihood disappearing. Perverse as it seemed to him, he would now entertain the thought of volunteering for financial reasons alone. A private earned only 1s. a day in 1915, but officers considerably more: a corporal upwards of 2s. 6d. daily, a sergeant in excess of 3s., a sergeant major 4s., with separation allowances of 12s. 6d. paid weekly to spouses (a family with four children would receive as much again), and responsibility allowances on top of that. It was nothing like the income that Thomas's writing had once generated, but it was more than it could generate now. Owlishly, Thomas watched the movements of his friends for the slightest guide. 'Hodgson is guarding Chelsea Gas Works. Rupert Brooke I hear has joined the army. The Blast poets I hear have not. If this war goes on I believe I shall find myself a sort of Englishman, tho neither poet nor soldier. If I

201

could earn anything worthwhile as a soldier I think I should go.'[39]

Thomas had once felt an ambivalence toward his 'Englishness'. 'I am 5/8 Welsh,' he had said when pressed by a Welshman on the subject in 1908, continuing, 'I have some Spanish blood and some blood from Wiltshire in my veins.' Thomas never spoke or understood Welsh and never lived in Wales, but from the age of four he holidayed with great-aunts in Newport, Caerleon and Swansea. At ten, he would sing the Irish nationalist song 'The Minstrel Boy', believing it to be about Wales, 'and as I sang the song I melted and trembled with a kind of gloomy pleasure in being about to die for Wales'. At twenty-one, he wrote of the country as a calling: 'It is like a homesickness, but stronger than any homesickness I ever felt—stronger than any passion.' For much of his life, perhaps until the war, Wales held an almost mystical draw for him, 'In spite of my accidentally Cockney nativity'. But as the summer of 1914 moved into autumn, Thomas had reached into a corner of himself that he had been barely aware of. The man who did not consider himself a patriot, who loathed nationalism, who believed his countrymen were the birds, was cultivating a new skin.[40]

On 3 September 1914 he put it this way to Jesse Berridge: 'I am slowly growing into a conscious Englishman.'[41]

AUTUMN

The temperature was eighty degrees in the shade as Mervyn Thomas and Peter Mrosovski set off from Dymock back to Steep at the beginning of September. Peter had stayed with the Thomases throughout their month in Gloucestershire, and as Edward headed north by train to begin his commission for the *English Review*, his bicycle was ridden home by the young Russian. The boys made good progress until Mervyn took a nail in his front tyre outside Swindon. They broke their journey at the Central Hotel in Swindon, sharing a bed to save money, and next morning carried the bikes on the train in a journey interrupted by troop manoeuvres on Salisbury Plain and a mass of soldiers at Winchester station. They made it home an hour before Helen and the girls at five o'clock on 3 September.[1]

Edward Thomas meanwhile was on his way north, recording the conversations of the people he met en route about the war. For a week he sought the views of working people in railway compartments and station platforms, in taverns and on trams, and in between took pleasure in the sights encountered along the way: a shipless sea north of Hartlepool, the bridges onto Newcastle's riverside streets below. But introducing himself to the British public was not the most comfortable of activities for this man who once described social intercourse as an intense form of solitude. He found his own conversation unnatural, his questions forced, stultifying to any spontaneity on the part of those he interviewed; even so the portrait he captured was filled with character.[2]

In the West Midlands, people poured into Birmingham library to learn more about the war. In the East Midlands, a thin man with a duck-bill nose berated another too overweight to serve: 'When the Kaiser reaches Coventry he'll see a lot like you.' At Sheffield, a Saturday football crowd were donating part of their wages. A young man, homesick for his Northumberland village, walked twenty-six miles into Newcastle to enlist. Elsewhere, people talked without inhibition. The Irish had responded manfully, said one man looking up from reading the *British Weekly*, and now it was for the English to follow suit. This unfortunate business had bound people together as nothing else could, said another. One man took a swing at someone who had called him German in his looks, but mostly the atmosphere was calm, the mood stoic and reflective.

Many were talking as much of work as war. Companies cut wages or lengthened their hours; some laid off their young unmarried men, knowing they had recourse to enlist: in Birmingham, these were jewellers whose labour was now less in demand, at Newcastle, the men of the collier ships whose markets had been Prussian. But elsewhere firms did well: bootmakers in Leicester, saddlers in Walsall, manufacturers of explosives at Elswick; the war firms prospered. Recruitment bands played cheerily in the streets with campaign tunes that carried across the rooftops. Publicans were busier than ever, and a man in khaki did not need to buy drinks. The roasting summer sun had produced a bumper harvest, and warmed the labourers and the recruits sleeping out of doors; park keepers struggled to keep control of their crowded parks.

Paris would fall, German communications would be cut, an Allied advance would send them back to where they came from: such was the talk of the taverns and the parks and the streets in the towns up and down England. The Germans were a savage lot, killers of children and of pensioners, and those who had settled in England should be turned out and those on the continent should be moved on. And as for the Kaiser himself, the mad bull, which English man or woman did not seek just five minutes alone with him, he who not so long ago was only too happy to kiss the cheek of King Edward? People struggled to explain the early German advances; some said the retreating Allies were luring them into a trap, some that the Germans must be good soldiers. The working classes were suffering disproportionately, said one man, but he was shouted down with cries of 'Socialist!' Someone in Coventry spoke against the grain to say, as Thomas would to his appalled father, that a German was not so very different from an Englishman, no better and no worse. Girls said the men should get themselves off the street corner and fight: it is not in our nature to fight, says one. It is in all our natures to fight, says another.[3]

In the countryside, the war seemed less tangible. Stories of German casualties or sinkings at sea were passed by word of mouth without any real means of confirming their accuracy. The town had its newspapers and its cheek-by-jowl talk, but the countryside was dispersed and isolated. The war was often most noticeable by the absences it created: many fieldhands had left their work and gone into the towns to enlist. On the coast, the fishermen had met many Germans and now plotted their country's defence, but inland some had never met one and had no idea how to react if they did: was it true that the Germans would cut off the hands of those they captured?[4]

Thomas wondered what all of this might pose for England. He asked what did it mean at a time like this to have a love of one's country, and met a man who seemed to provide an answer. To that man, wrote Thomas, 'England was a place where "one isn't forbidden to do what one wants to do or forced to do what somebody else wants", and that in spite of gamekeepers, for whoever met a landowner in a wood? I take this to be the foundation of patriotism.' It was significant that Thomas should invoke the symbol of the gamekeeper at a time of war. Since his youth, the gamekeeper had represented the privatisation of nature, to him, the possession of the living ground and the animals to which it gave a home, the miracle of the earth patrolled for the benefit of the few: 'Pride, stupidity, servility'. One who loves the world outside the gamekeeper's patrol, who loves tolerance and permission, who engages with the living land, that person might reasonably be considered a patriot. But other forms of patriotism were not so benign. Thomas condemned the kind of patriot who, out of ignorance or prejudice alone, scorned the lifestyles that he had not experienced for himself, the man who belittled the cultures of foreign lands or even of neighbouring counties. The Wiltshire man who said Hampshire was the place where they held the pig aloft to see the band go by; the Hampshire man who said that in Wiltshire they buried the donkey with its feet out of the ground so as to polish its shoes. These were neighbours who quarrelled at their every difference only to turn as one upon the outsider who interferes. 'A happy nation luxuriates in its differences and distinctions,' he wrote; the greater the differences, the greater the affection for those differences. There may be places that we find more pleasant, but there can be no word that stirs the emotion quite like that of 'home'. In a line that reads peculiarly modern, he concluded, 'England is a system of vast circumferences circling round the minute neighbouring points of home.'[5]

*   *   *

'The thing is going pretty well,' Brooke had said on the eve of the publication of the third *New Numbers* in July, 'about seven or eight hundred of each number, which pays expenses very easily, and leaves a good bit for division.' But that was before the outbreak of war, and surely the Dymock journal would now struggle to survive. In truth, the harmony of *New Numbers* had always been deceptive. Despite Drinkwater's insistence on a mutual appreciation of each other's work, Gibson and Abercrombie had shared an uneasiness toward his and Brooke's contributions to the journal, suspecting that Drinkwater might use it as a vehicle to print the work that he could not get published elsewhere while Brooke's offerings seemed wildly variable. 'They're very poor, aren't they?' Gibson lamented to Edward Marsh of Brooke's poems; Abercrombie agreed. D. H. Lawrence had poured scorn on the second issue that spring, and in particular on the two-act play in blank verse that Abercrombie had set in a country pub. 'Why, why, in God's name, is Abercrombie messing about with Yokels and Cider and runaway wives?' he demanded. 'I loathe his rather nasty efforts at cruelty . . . What is the matter with the man?—there's something wrong with his soul.' Thomas had let that issue pass uncontested, but about the third number he would not be restrained. Abercrombie's efforts were journalistic, Gibson's mercantile, Brooke was going to war anyway, while 'Drinkwater must be hopeless in this incarnation and I haven't heard of another.' Thomas's patience with these writers had finally run out, but his reservations were slight in comparison to the more personal attack launched by Robert Frost, who on 21 September wrote to Jack Haines.

> All Drinkwater is is a soaker. All one reads him for is to find out who he has been soaking in lately. Neither is Brooke worth bothering with (in this phase—if he ever was in any) . . .
> Abercrombie doesnt quite persuade me to accept his [?]convention that it doesnt matter if his people say unlikely things provided they say poetic things. And Gibson is sometimes so [?]even he makes me nervous.

Abercrombie confirmed privately that the next issue of the journal would be its last.[6]

*   *   *

In travelling the country for his *English Review* articles, Thomas had been given his first exposure to the impact of war. Times were as hard and they were uncertain, and he was no less affected than the men he had spoken to on his travels. 'I don't quite know what will happen,' he admitted to Jesse Berridge. 'The obvious thing is to join the Territorials but I can't leave other people to keep my family till I know I can't do it myself.' To Bottomley and to Farjeon he said the same. His thoughts began to loop in those first days of September. 'I don't know what may turn up.' 'My own plans are more uncertain.' It would be a good time for trying America, he told Bottomley, if only he could leave Helen and the children: but he could not. A good time for the Territorials, but he could not go there either. The walks with Frost in Gloucestershire had brought him a friendship like no other as well as a desire to protect the country he walked; he felt pushed in two sharply contrasting directions: to America with Frost or to the war in Europe. He returned to Steep on 10 September and set to work writing up the first of the three articles for the *English Review*. 'When it is done,' he said, 'I shall find out what sort of soldier they still want at Petersfield.'[7]

*   *   *

Frost had considered that the game was up for the publishing of his poetry in England. But on 2 September, the publishing house of Henry Holt in New York wrote to the London offices of David Nutt to say that a copy of *North of Boston* had been enthusiastically pressed upon them by Florence Holt, the wife of the company president, and that the poems were 'uncommonly interesting'.

209

In fact Mrs Holt had written directly to Frost in August from her home on Four Winds Farm, in Stowe, Vermont, taking care not to commit her husband's press, and yet still hoping that, even from Gloucestershire, the American might recognise the publishing name behind her letter ('you will not be displeased to know of our interest'). But Frost mistook the letter for that of an unknown New England farmer's wife and offered no reply. The opportunity might so easily have passed had Mrs Holt not tried again, this time through her husband's company. The Holt editors were cautious, and informed Mrs Nutt that 'we cannot see a paying market here for this particular volume', though they would be glad to inspect any next book that Frost produced. Mrs Nutt was not impressed: 'We consider that under present political circumstances American publishers ought to show some willingness to help English publishers who have had sufficient daring and intelligence to recognise the talent of one of their countrymen.' In the event, Mrs Nutt's letter crossed with a follow-up from Holt, who had written again to advise that they were prepared after all to gamble on a modest 150 copies of the sheets for binding in the US market. Between the efforts of two women, Mrs Holt and Mrs Nutt, Robert Frost was finally to be published in America.[8]

*   *   *

Back in London, yet another new character was about to become entangled in the story of the Poetry Bookshop. On 7 July, a twenty-five-year-old Harvard graduate, T. S. Eliot, had passed through London en route to summer school in Germany, only to find himself stranded when the course in Marburg was cancelled in the wake of the declaration of war. In the ensuing lock-down, students were told they could not leave the country for a fortnight, and it was not until 21 August that the American arrived back in London. Uncertain of his next move, he took rooms on Bedford Place not far from the Bookshop and was struck by the little corner of bohemia he had discovered. 'Shady Bloomsbury, the noisiest place in the world, a neighbourhood at present given over to artists, musicians, hackwriters, Americans, Russians, French, Belgians, Italians, Spaniards, and Japanese, formerly Germans also . . . a delightfully seedy part of town.' He swiftly won himself a scholarship to study at Oxford and went up to Merton College that autumn. But this bright young student was also a gifted poet whose first poems were about to reach the desk of Harold Monro.[9]

Like Pound and Frost, Eliot was a literary unknown when he arrived in London. A Harvard friend, Conrad Aiken, was living in the capital at the time and offered to circulate his friend's work ahead of his arrival. Eliot agreed and gave him a poem written in the summer of 1911 that had yet to see the light of day, 'The Love Song of J. Alfred Prufrock'. But Monro was not in the least interested in taking the poem for *Poetry and Drama* and according to Aiken returned to him saying that it was 'absolutely insane'. Undeterred, Aiken found a second occasion to present Eliot's work to the editor, possibly at a party following Brooke's Bookshop reading of 28 July, when he happened to have with him a copy of 'La Figlia

Che Piange' (Eliot: 'the first poem of mine that was ever put in to any respectable anthology and therefore must be completely inoffensive'). Monro gave this second piece similarly short shrift, handing it back to Aiken, remarking, 'O I can't be bothered with this'; but as Aiken walked home, he became concerned that Monro might have mistakenly thought that he had thrust his own work upon him, and wrote the next day to clear up any confusion, sending Eliot's poem together with an address at which to reach the American. 'Of course that too was rejected,' Aiken reported.[10]

Edward Thomas knew nothing of the unpublished T. S. Eliot, but he did know Conrad Aiken, who had just sent him his work. 'I am reading the third bard who wants my opinion since September,' he told Eleanor wearily that October. 'The first 2 I spoke the truth to and they didn't thank me. This one will be the same I fear.' Aiken was an unashamed self-promoter, something which would not have gone unnoted by Harold Monro and may well have contributed to the editor's reluctance to look properly at the material before him; even so, said Aiken, Monro passed over the work three times. 'I doubt if he ever received an idea clean at first go,' said Pound dismissively, 'or ever gripped it at once by the handle,' and he took from Eliot a copy of 'Prufrock' when they met for the first time that September. By the following summer, Pound had succeeded in getting the poem published in Harriet Monroe's *Poetry*. Eliot made the best of an awkward situation and attended his first event at the Bookshop that month ('lectures at 5 p.m. with wax candles'), but he was not settling well to literary London. His sympathies about the war were complicated by his time in Germany, and he found incredible the decision of an American friend at Oxford to become naturalised in order to seek a war commission. ('I certainly shall not go to that length.') There were few signs that autumn in 1914 that Eliot's residence would be a permanent one. 'I don't think that I should ever feel at home in England,' he wrote.[11]

*   *   *

Thomas had spent much of September travelling but longing to be back at home; yet no sooner was he in Steep then he felt ready to leave once again. On 5 October, he set off by bicycle for Wales, passing through Avebury, then Bristol and Swansea, the Brecon Beacons, arriving in Gloucestershire on the 14th after rainfall and punctures had hampered his journey. His destination was not Little Iddens for once but the Gallows, where the Frosts had moved early in September after their landlord asked for the cottage to be vacated for hired help and the Abercrombies had taken them in. The Frosts had stayed only five months on Ledington Hill, but now, with the move to Ryton, Elinor could at last fulfil her dream of living under thatch. Lascelles, Catherine and the Abercrombie children would live in one of the adjoining cottages, the Frosts in the other, though with Catherine pregnant with her third child, the Abercrombies spent much of the winter away, leaving the Frosts the run of the entire property. Frost would draft or set a clutch of poems at the Gallows, among them some lines to the elms behind the cottage, 'The Sound of Trees'; but by far the most important of the poems he would begin there was a piece that for the time being carried the working title 'Two Roads', which was to become 'The Road Not Taken'. Thomas found the Frosts off colour during that October visit: Elinor was tired, Robert nervy and barely eating. 'I don't know how the Frosts will get through the winter,' he told Eleanor Farjeon. 'He isn't a bit well and she is too hardworked.' They idled and talked under languid weather, and Thomas for once found himself longing to be not with Frost but at home. He told Helen he was sorry to be extending his time away, but was finding comfort from the soft still days, rising ahead of his hosts each morning to light the fires before heading out to pick apples from beneath a bent old tree in the fodder field. Thomas walked up into the woods above the path at Ryton; along the Leadon the trees carried yellow and ruddy leaves, and only the silver willows and the dark green elms held on to their summer colours. He wrote to Cazenove to propose an anthology 'about England, English places and English life', but his agent was doubtful, replying that the market was saturated with such books; five had been published in the past week alone. 'What I want to write,' Thomas persisted, 'is an account of the name of England and its meaning, especially its emotional meaning . . . to show what is meant when a man speaks of England and especially since the war.' It seemed that nothing now, not a week in Wales or talk with Frost about New Hampshire, could distract Thomas from the topic that truly captivated him in the autumn of 1914: England. He jotted in his notebook: 'The war national but as yet dark and chaotic in brain'. Poets had further to go, he thought, before the experience of war would find a valuable translation into poetry.[12]

* * *

A gloomy letter from Frost was awaiting Thomas when he returned to Steep. Ill health and poor spirits had gotten the better of the American. 'When I wrote like that you replied that you wished I were near enough to be kicked,' wrote Thomas. 'Well, I wish you were near enough to kick you, but have no faith in that kind of school.' It was the first time that Thomas was able to dictate the emotional temperature of their relationship, and it would not be the last; but for now, Thomas had anxieties of his own that he wished to share. 'I have just made myself ill with thinking hard for an hour,—going up to my study and sitting there,—that I ought to enlist next week in town.'[13]

As Thomas began six months of dithering about the probity of enlisting, Rupert Brooke was having his application fast tracked. Having failed to get into the army, he pressed Edward Marsh to exercise his influence with Winston Churchill, and was found an opening in a new naval unit, a volunteer reserve attached to HMS *Victory*. The company would be an assembly of 'more or less trained men'—'more' being the Royal Marines, 'less' being Brooke, who had received only the most preliminary of drills. But as a naval reservist, he had the chance to circumvent months of training camp. On 15 September he completed his application for a commission, and by the 27th he left Charing

Cross for camp on the Kent coast. On the night of 4 October, Brooke sailed from Dover in a convoy escorted by two destroyers, and by morning lay off the coast of Dunkirk, waiting for the tide to turn. They were heading for Antwerp and reached the outskirts of the city to find that it had been pounded almost to rubble by German shells. The Brigade's own station was heavily bombarded, and Brooke lost his spare clothes and some unfinished draft manuscripts in scrambling to safety. On 9 October, the city fell and a British retreat was ordered.

I marched through Antwerp, deserted, shelled, and burning, one night, and saw ruined houses, dead men and horses: and railway-trains with their lines taken up and twisted and flung down as if a child had been playing with a toy. And the whole heaven and earth was lit up by the glare from the great lakes and rivers of burning petrol, hills and spires of flame. That was like Hell, a Dantesque Hell, terrible.

But the Hell for the refugees was worse: hundreds of thousands, stricken and crying, moving into the night in two endless columns. What he witnessed would only harden his resolve about his decision to fight, and back in London he reported the slaughter directly to Winston Churchill. Friends found him harrowed and traumatised, quite changed with his cropped military haircut from the man they once knew. In July when he read at the Poetry Bookshop he had been called angelic, but now when he called on Monro the proprietor described him

216

as 'haggard and discouraged, and talking almost entirely about the war'. Within ten days, Brooke was back with his unit and waiting redeployment, but he was exhausted and succumbed to flu. As he made his recovery, he began a run of five sonnets, among which was one that would enter the national consciousness for what it appeared to say about self-sacrifice.

> If I should die, think only this of me:
> That there's some corner of a foreign field
> That is for ever England . . .

He gave the poem and the other four pieces to Wilfrid Gibson for *New Numbers*, but it was to be *The Times* that would make the sonnet famous when it reprinted the poem after his death. He wrote to Walter de la Mare of his horror at the thought of England invaded 'as of some virginity violated'; but beneath the bravado, Brooke was privately concerned at the scale of catastrophe the war implied. A letter in November hinted at his turmoil. 'It's a great life, fighting, while it lasts. The eye grows clearer and the heart. But it's a bloody thing, half the youth of Europe blown through pain to nothingness, in the incessant mechanical slaughter of these modern battles.'[14]

*   *   *

At the St George's Café, Edward Thomas was about to extend his quarrel with the war. Late in October, he took tea with Ralph Hodgson, who a year before had introduced Thomas to Frost in the very same space. Hodgson had been among

217

the first of their circle to enlist in August, and was serving as a warden at the Chelsea Gas Works when Thomas expressed his hesitations about the conflict. He would not believe that the German was a worse fellow than the Englishman, or that one countryman felt any less fearful about the war than the other. These were controversial views for Thomas to be exposing at this moment. The 'rape' of Belgium, as it was coming to be known, had stirred public anger, and Hodgson rounded on Thomas. Every Englishman had a duty to be patriotic and to do their bit, he said, and Thomas's views were an abomination. Hodgson became angrier, until he branded Thomas a 'Teuton', rose hastily and knocked aside a nearby chair before storming out of the Café in a fury, his British bulldog Mooster trotting loyally after him. Thomas was shaken by the exchange: rows with his father on the subject had been one thing, but this assault by a friend so rattled him that he wrote to Harold Monro to say that Hodgson's remarks had almost made him join up. 'Hodgson flung off today labelling me pro-German. I almost enlisted afterwards in repentance. I could almost face bayonets to bring him round, but not quite, tho I fear it would be the only measure.' The dispute had become so heated and so painful to each man they concluded it inadvisable to be in one another's company for the time being. 'He and I are not meeting till the war is over,' Thomas told Bottomley. 'I am not patriotic enough for his exuberant taste.' Edward Thomas and Ralph Hodgson would never speak again.[15]

*   *   *

Between 25 and 30 November, Edward Thomas returned to see Robert Frost at the Gallows, his sixth visit to Gloucestershire since April, and the last trip he would make there. En route, he took a train to London to collect volunteering papers from the Parliamentary Recruiting Committee. He was a long way from a decision to join up, but he knew that he would rather conduct any enlistment on his own terms than risk being 'pitchforked', as he put it, into service. It was curious that Thomas should think he might be pressed in that way: in November 1914 there was no conscription and would not be for another year and more. When Prime Minister Asquith introduced it in January 1916, married men continued to be exempt; it would not be until April 1916 that service was made universal for men under the age of forty-one, by which time Thomas had long since been at war. For the time being, it was not at all apparent how a course of action might become clearer to him: he lacked the impulse to fight that had pulled in Rupert Brooke and other men and realised that thinking endlessly as he had been doing was unlikely to produce an answer. On the train to London he had shared his dilemma with a young soldier sitting opposite him, and the men agreed that 'no man could face war if he could foresee his own part in the fighting. The difference between people is that they try or do not try in various degrees— often against their will—to foresee it.' He collected his volunteer's papers, though they would remain unsigned for now.[16]

Thomas arrived at the Gallows to find that the Abercrombies were still away, leaving the Frosts the continued run of the two cottages and Thomas the chance to settle in for a few days. As before, he would rise early to light the house fires in what would have been his working hours, but now he had no work, and this November visit was intended to be pure leisure. He and Frost would head out to walk as far as the weather would allow. Some days they swept south and west toward May Hill, others east to Ketford Mill, but wherever they walked they were frequently the guests of William Lygon, the seventh Earl Beauchamp. Lord Beauchamp's seat was the Madresfield Court at Malvern that Evelyn Waugh would make the setting for Brideshead, although his holdings extended to a thousand acres of wooded land that surrounded and included the Gallows. Abercrombie and select locals (possibly including Wilfrid Gibson) were granted access to the preserve—and to the neighbouring land owned by an industrialist, George Stacey Albright—for walking, picnics or blackberry picking; but unaccompanied children were not permitted and if caught were terrified into dumping their punnets by the surly head gamekeeper, a man named Bott who reported to Albright at Bromsberrow Place north-east of the Gallows, and may also have reported to Lord Beauchamp. Rarely without his shotgun, Bott was a prowler and a bully, and was not averse to waving his weapon at any adults he suspected to be trespassing.

One morning in late November, Thomas and Frost were strolling in the woods when they were intercepted by the keeper, who challenged their presence and told the men bluntly to clear out. As a resident of the Gallows, Frost believed he was extended the same courtesy as Abercrombie and so entitled to roam wherever he wished, and he told the keeper as much. Bott was unimpressed and some sharp words were exchanged, and when the poets emerged onto the road they were challenged once more by the keeper who, according to a notebook source, had lain in wait, 'snooping in the hedge, glowering'. Tempers flared and Bott called Frost 'a damned cottager' before raising his shotgun at the two men. Incensed, Frost was on the verge of accosting the man, but hesitated when he saw Thomas back off. Heated words continued to be had, with the adversaries goading then finally parting and the poets talking heatedly of the incident as they walked. Thomas said that the keeper's aggression was unacceptable and that something should be done. Frost's ire peaked as he listened to Thomas: something would indeed be done and done right now and if Thomas wanted to follow him he could see it being done. The men turned back, Frost angrily, Thomas hesitantly, but the gamekeeper was no longer on the road. His temper wild, Frost insisted on tracking the man down, which they did, to a small cottage at the edge of Grove Coppice along the bridle path that linked the Old Smithy at Ryton to Redmarley D'Abitot. Frost beat on the door, and left the startled keeper in no doubt as to what would befall him were he ever to threaten Frost or his children or bar them access to the preserve. Satisfied that the force of his point had been made, Frost repeated his warning for good measure, turned on his heel and prepared to leave. What happened next would be a defining moment in the friendship of Robert Frost and Edward Thomas, and would plague Thomas to his dying days.[17]

The keeper, recovering his wits, reached above the door for his twelve-bore shotgun and came outside, this time heading straight for Thomas, who until then had not been the keeper's target. The gun was raised again; instinctively Thomas backed off, and the gamekeeper saw the men from his property and back onto the bridle path, where they left under the keeper's watchful aim.

Unknown to the poets, there was a witness to the incident. Ted Hill, a boy of twelve, had been 'going down fro' grandmother's' in Ketford Mill and was on the way to nearby Gamage Hall to pick hops when he stopped in to see 'ole Bott', as he knew him. The boy was inside the cottage when the poets rapped on the door. Through the open doorway, he saw the whole exchange from beginning to end and remembered Frost's words for the rest of his life. 'He said "Come out over the fence," he said, "and I'll teach you a lesson". He said, "Come on, put 'em up."' When the keeper put up not his fists but his shotgun, the poets did not stay to complete the lesson: they 'went off a bit smartish like', said Hill.[18]

For Ted Hill the incident had little to do with notions of 'gentry', as Frost would claim, and everything to do with 'spying'. The countryside was rife with suspicion towards anything and anyone out of the ordinary. The post office at nearby Bromsberrow Heath, he said, was run by a blind man, German, a 'perfeck stranger', who was thought to be a spy. And that was the concern about Frost and Thomas, Hill recalled: they had arrived in the area at about the same time and on the eve of war, and they lived close by one another, and Frost spoke English strangely. They were suspicious all right and the keeper was doing his job as would have been expected, thought Hill; in fact, the strangers were very lucky not to have been filled with lead shot that day.

The poets walked back along the bridle path to the Gallows, Frost's anger cooling into a satisfaction with his own response; but not Thomas's, who wished that the incident had never arisen and that his mettle had not been tested in the presence of his friend. The next day the constable from Ryton arrived at the Gallows to inform Frost that a complaint had been made against him of threatening the keeper with bodily harm, and explained that while he was sure that it was nothing he was nonetheless obliged to investigate all such complaints, and issued the American with a summons to appear before the local magistrate. With Abercrombie still away, Frost turned for help to Wilfrid Gibson, but to the American's horror his neighbour refused to side with him against the gamekeeper. Like the Gallows, Gibson's cottage at Greenway Cross was in the gift of the Beauchamp estate, and he was not about to risk his tenancy over a dispute with a gamekeeper who, after all, was Albright's—and possibly also Lord Beauchamp's—man. Frost's fury would now turn on Gibson, but thankfully Abercrombie at least did come to his friend's aid, calling on Jack Haines in his role as a solicitor for legal guidance on how they might respond.

My dear Haines,
Frost, I hope, has by this [time] put before you his trouble with Albright's keeper. I am trying to get at Albright personally, but don't yet know what the result will be. And if he won't keep his keeper in order, I am determined to bring the law in if it *can* come

223

in. As to the affair in the wood, we can, of course, do nothing; but when the keeper takes to threatening Frost *in the road*, the affair is obviously intolerable and must be put a stop to. Preferably, as I say, by getting directly at Albright; for I still think there must be some misunderstanding. But I should like to know now whether the fellow's brutal behaviour does make him liable to a summons. I understand Frost has Thomas as a witness. Sorry to trouble you!

Yours in haste
Lascelles Abercrombie.[19]

Abercrombie understood well the different implications between an encounter in private woodland and one on the public highway, where neither Albright's nor Lord Beauchamp's jurisdiction extended. Haines must have urged caution and calm, and while his reply is lost, his advice effects a change in attitude from Abercrombie, who writes again a few days later.

My dear Haines,
Many thanks for your most sensible letter. My sole reason for writing to you was on account of the alleged insult in the road, which, if true, was clearly intolerable and to be put a stop to somehow or other. Thomas's description of it, however, scarcely bears out Frost's, and I now believe he had rather exaggerated the incident in a way which he is a trifle inclined to: I mean he is peculiarly sensitive to anything remotely resembling insult or deliberate annoyance to himself. This is not the first time he has been

224

aggrieved.—As to the wood incident, he had, of course, no right there. I have permission, but that does not imply permission to my friends. The strange thing was that the keeper, knowing where Frost was staying (so Frost says) should have been so unpleasant. If you can see Frost it would be a great advantage. I believe the secret of the whole thing is that Frost does not know how to talk to such folks as keepers. We are all very well and hope you and your family are too.

Yours sincerely
Lascelles Abercrombie
[*margin*] I have asked my sister to interview Albright.[20]

Abercrombie skilfully persuaded the landowner not only to drop the case against Frost, but may also have succeeded in having the gamekeeper re-educated in his ways. In Frost's re-telling, Lord Beauchamp sent him no less than a personal apology, accompanied by an instruction to the gamekeeper that if he wanted so much to fight he had better enlist.[21]

In the days that followed, Thomas and Frost did their best to make light of the incident. Frost wrote to Monro at the Poetry Bookshop in ebullient terms:

Think of me as engaged in a little war of my own down here with a bad game keeper who attacked me for going where he allowed the Gibsons to go as gentry. Me he called a 'damned cottager'. *Now* who will have the better claim of the title of People's Poet?

225

Thomas says it is the best testimonial I have had and I must get my publisher to use the game keeper in advertising me—that is, if I survive my war with the brute—and even if I don't.[22]

But the mood at the Gallows had become more uncertain. Frost was unaware of the degree to which Abercrombie and Haines and even Thomas mistrusted his handling of the episode. Whatever the motives for Gibson's behaviour, he understood, as Thomas did, the rules that governed English country affairs, and it was apparent to all that Frost did not. But Frost would not forgive Gibson for his lack of support, and made no effort to conceal it. 'I can't help looking on him as the worst snob I met in England and I can't help blaming the snob he is for the most unpleasant memory I carried away from England: I mean my humiliating fight with the gamekeeper. Gibson is a coward and a snob not to have saved me from that.' Frost's feelings for Gibson would never recover.[23]

Back at the Gallows, Thomas watched a storm picking up in the trees; he imagined he could hear the clothes on the line crackle like a wood fire rising. He turned over the day's events in his head. Had he acted cowardly? He felt certain of it and suspected Frost of thinking the same. Not once but twice had he failed to hold his ground, while his friend had no such difficulty standing his. Many times as a boy he had run the gauntlet of gamekeepers, sometimes slipping them, other times not and so taking their punishment; but they had never held any fear for him. Something had changed in him; something that amused him as a child now frightened him. The worst punishment that had befallen him as a boy had been to be dragged before his father; this time, with his father nowhere to answer for him, he had let Frost speak instead. His courage had been found wanting, at a time when men such as Rupert Brooke had found it in themselves to face genuine dangers.[24]

In the years that followed, Myfanwy Thomas would suggest that Frost was near to calling her father a coward for not squaring up to the gamekeeper. But Frost made no such suggestion; even had he believed it to be the case he would not have needed to express it. He knew that Thomas's profound self-examination would make that unnecessary. More likely the incident fuelled Frost's tendency to tease his friend for a timidity that he found 'funny and fascinating'. Thomas would not take a teasing well, and his feelings on the episode turned characteristically inward. 'I've thrown away a chance to fight a gamekeeper,' he would reflect, 'And I less often trespass.'[25]

The incident with the gamekeeper symbolised all that was rotten in the state of England's fields for Robert Frost.

We found that like as not the gamekeeper had his eye on us, squinting out from under his cap. One had to show a birth certificate to prove he wasn't a poacher and avoid arrest; and because one didn't have on knee breeches and a red coat they suspected the worse.

But it was an incident that Frost would overcome. In time, he would embrace it anecdotally, retelling the story with aplomb and making it fully his own as he would so many of the challenging episodes in his life, cheerily likening his treatment by Bott to that doled out by his English publisher. But for Edward Thomas, the encounter would leave him haunted. He would relive the moment again and again. In his verse and in his letters to Frost—in the week when he left for France, even in the week of his death—Thomas felt hunted by the fear and cowardice he had experienced in that stand-off with the gamekeeper. He felt mocked by events and probably by the most important friend of his life, and he vowed that he would never again let himself be faced down. When the call came again he would hold his nerve and face the gunmen.[26]

'That's why he went to war,' said Frost.[27]

*   *   *

The friends parted company at Newent station; Thomas returned to Steep a troubled man. But he was also a changed man. In the days that immediately followed his visit to Ryton, he would tackle the task of which Frost thought him wholly capable, if 'afeared'. A movement of gigantic, personal significance was underway. It had been surfacing before he met Frost, but it had taken the year's friendship for it to boil over. It would lift his spirits, deepen his tolerance, satisfy his life-long need to find self-worth. Never again would his chronic depression overwhelm him so utterly, never again would he think of himself as a mere hack. Not a different man, said Eleanor Farjeon, but the same man in another key.[28]

Edward Thomas was about to become a poet.

WINTER

Early in November 1914, sometime in the weeks before visiting Frost at the Gallows, Edward Thomas had called at the White Horse inn on the Froxfield plateau above Wick Green, known as the pub with no name ever since its sign went missing from the frame that leaned from the blackthorn hedgerow into the road. The inn was a regular haunt for Thomas, his favourite of those which surrounded Steep, standing on higher ground than any in Hampshire. It was set back from the road in a ring of beech trees, surrounded by gorse in which stone curlews made their home. Thomas liked to sit in the low-ceilinged tap room after walking, writing his notes or listening to the cadence of conversations in the bar. In May he had told Frost of the new start he intended to make in his writing, to 'wring all the necks of my rhetoric—the geese', and on that November day he echoed that same phrase in a few hasty notes scribbled down in his notebook, beside an entry dated 2 November 1914.[1]

I could wring the old girl's neck
That put it here
A public house! (Charcoal burner)
by bringing up and quite outdoing
The idea of London
Two woods around and never a road in sight
Trees roaring like a train without an end
But she's dead long ago
Only a motorist from far away
Or marketers in carts once a fortnight

229

Or a few fresh tramps ignorant
of the house turning.

Thomas was a perennial note taker: he depended
on his notebooks to refresh the details that
would vitalise his prose. In them he recorded the
landscape that he was moving through, a crook in
a river, a cottage gable, the variety of birds in the
hedgerow, whether the trees were elm or beech or
yew, the direction of weather. But on this day, the
jottings had a more conversational tone than usual,
phrases that resembled less his topographic style
and something more like the patterns of speech.
*I could wring the old girl's neck | That put it here |
A public house!* . . . twelve thin, disjointed lines
quickly scribbled down. Thomas did not return to
these notes immediately: he had commitments to
fulfil to the *English Review* and *Poetry and Drama*.
But on 16 November he did return, and began to
craft a 1,200-word prose sketch in an exercise book
to which he gave the title 'The White Horse'. The
sketch began:

Tall beeches overhang the inn, dwarfing and
half hiding it, for it lies back a field's breadth
from the by road. The field is divided from
the road by a hedge and only a path from one
corner and a cart track from the other which
meet under the beeches connect the inn with
the road. But for a signboard or rather the
post and empty iron frame of a signboard
close to the road behind the hedge a traveller
could not guess at an inn. The low dirty white
building looks like a farmhouse, with a lean-to,
a rick and a shed of black boarding at one side

. . .

The prose continued to describe the situation of the inn on the high plateau, and it introduced what it now became apparent was an individual speaker of the lines jotted in the field notebook: a girl who had been born in the isolated inn, but had departed and returned to find it an exposed, forsaken place, where the wind howled through the trees.

> 'I should like to wring the old girl's neck for coming away here.' So said the woman who fetched my beer when I found myself at the inn first. She was a daughter of the house, fresh from a long absence in service in London, a bright wildish slattern with a cockney accent and her hair half down. She spoke angrily. If she did not get away before long, she said, she would go mad with loneliness. She looked out sharply: all she could see there was nothing but the beeches and the tiny pond beneath them and the calves standing in it drinking, alternately grazing the water here and there thinking, and at last going out and standing still on the bank thinking.[2]

There is no reason to suppose that the piece was intended to be anything other than a short prose piece; but sometime between concluding the draft on 16 November and returning in early December from his visit to Frost, Thomas did something extraordinary that he had not systematically attempted in years. He began a poem.

231

'I cd wring the old thing's neck that put it
here!
    A public house! it may be public for
Squirrels and such like and ghosts of
charcoal burners
    Or highwaymen . . .'

The poem had opened with stride, confidence
and a command of tone. Instinctively it had found
its form in variable blank verse, in a loose iambic
pentameter that moved the poem calmly but surely
forward: I could *wring* the *old* thing's *neck* that *put*
it *here!* | A *pub*lic *house* it *may* be *pub*lic *for* . . .
Thomas continued,

            . . . 'But I call it a hermitage

He paused; this was possibly the first wrong step.
The hermitage was not necessary to the story of
the poem, he realised, or at least not necessary at
this point in the tale; he should let the speaker—
and more importantly, the reader—pause for
breath. Thomas took his pen and struck out the
line. He continued.

            . . . The wild girl laughed.

(or maybe simply 'She' laughed? No, the former
had the better scansion)

                    . . . 'But I
    Loathe it ~~and sort~~ since I came back from
Kennington
    And 'twas to see it. And for nothing else

232

no, not that,

> . . . since I came back from
> Kennington
> And gave my place up.'

not quite. Again,

> . . . gave up a good place.'

Yes, that was it. From the top, then, Thomas read back:

> 'I could wring the old thing's neck that put it here!
> A public house! it may be public for
> Squirrels and such like and ghosts of charcoal burners
> Or highwaymen.' The wild girl laughed. 'But I
> Loathe it since I came back from Kennington
> And gave up a good place.'

With these five and a half lines, the poem had its opening. He continued:

> . . . Her Cockney accent only

no, not *only*, that was an unwanted extra couple of syllables,

> . . . Her Cockney accent
> Made her seem wilder
> Made her and the place seem wilder as she

233

shrieked at me

too long, too harsh. He tried again, but found only
wrong turnings:

> ... seem wilder by calling

up
~~Through tassled tumbled hair~~
~~Pausing~~ there in her ~~scrubbing~~
~~And then subduing quite the idea of~~
To be subdued immediately by wildness
Only to be subdued at once by wildness
The idea of London here in this forest
parlour.
~~shade~~
~~Under the beech murmurs~~
~~beech tree mur~~
~~Under the~~

Maddeningly, the poem was getting away from
him. The start had been assured, but now he was
becoming disoriented by the many possible paths
that were opening up before him. Over the next few
hours the draft moved both forward and backward.
He would strike through every third or fourth line,
but still he made rapid progress, filling four pages
of the exercise book with 100 lines and more of
the poem with all the speed that his training in
journalism had lent him.[3]
Some sections snapped quickly into place;
others were more of a struggle. Three simple lines
about the ploughing up of charcoal took him a
dozen attempts to find his way, but find his way he
eventually did, until the draft began to peter once
more, this time toward the end, where it finished on

an inconsequential note.

> Once upon a time 'twas plain the inn and
> smithy
>   on
> Stood merely ~~over~~ the border of a waste
> ~~Through which the road meandered~~
>   horse or   ~~take~~
> Where ~~ever~~ cart could ~~make its~~ pick its own
> new course
> ~~Paths come on all sides to the inn~~
> On all sides, then as now, paths ran to the
> inn
> But not one road. And a farmtrack from a
> gate

As an ending this was hopeless and Thomas knew it. Instinctively he moved these lines into the first third of the poem, which left the draft to conclude with the serving girl stating that despite her complaining she intended to remain at the inn.

> You won't catch me going back to
> Kennington.
> I reckon I shall stay, ~~now the signs gone~~.
> But I do wish
> Twasn't so lonely and the wind wouldn't
> ~~roar~~ sound so.

This was better, but an ending was required that was more suggestive and more resonant still: something that might deepen or elevate the experience, that might open out the possibilities of the poem. To find it, Thomas would do something that was entirely his own: he went back to the initial

235

prose draft, to the calves grazing around the pond. In so doing he gave a clear illustration of how his mind was working at that moment: to use his prose as a well into which he might dip for poetry.

A second handwritten draft followed immediately, tidying up the sprawl of the first, and on Thursday 3 December, Thomas typed up the 115-line poem, making final amendments as he went. Here is the poem's opening and its closing:

UP IN THE WIND

'I could wring the old thing's neck that put it here!
A public-house! it may be public for birds,
Squirrels and such-like, ghosts of charcoal-burners
And highwaymen.' The wild girl laughed. 'But I
Hate it since I came back from Kennington.
I gave up a good place.' Her Cockney accent
Made her and the house seem wilder by calling up—
Only to be subdued at once by wildness—
The idea of London, there in that forest parlour,
Low and small among the towering beeches
And the one bulging butt that's like a font.
. . .
                         Between the open door
And the trees two calves were wading in the pond,
Grazing the water here and there and thinking,

236

'When first I came here I had hope': Edward Thomas at Steep, 1914

'It is really the kind H. and the children who make life almost *impossible*': conditions at home were frequently under strain. Clockwise: Helen (1914), Mervyn (1912), Myfanwy (1914) and Bronwen (1910)

'the centre of the New Poetry': the Poetry Bookshop, 35 Devonshire Street WC1, February 1913

'A young Apollo, golden-haired': Rupert Brooke, 1913

Dymock Poets, Birmingham Repertory Theatre, May 1914, left to right: John Drinkwater, Wilfrid Gibson, Edward Marsh, Lascelles Abercrombie, Geraldine Gibson, Catherine Abercrombie

‘I have come to the borders of sleep’:
Thomas chose to keep his verse secret
from his army colleagues by disguising
it as prose: he used capital letters
to indicate new lines and paragraph
breaks to mark stanzas ('Lights Out',
Royal Artillery Barracks, Trowbridge,
November 1916)

'She may be seeking me and no other':
Thomas was loved not only by Helen, but
by Eleanor Farjeon (above, 1913) and Edna
Clarke Hall (below, c.1894)

'pre-eminent among the distinguished poets still in their prime': W. B. Yeats, 1911 (left)

'the stormy petrel': Pound (right) was never far from the centre of the controversy

'Nights of storm, days of mist, without end': Wick Green was an unloved family home 1909–13, though Thomas retained happier memories of the Bee House in the garden which he kept on as a study until 1916

'greater friends than almost any two ever were practising the same art': Robert Frost and Edward Thomas forged a seemingly unbreakable friendship only for the war to tear it apart

'Fast beat my heart at sight of the tall slope.' View from the Shoulder of Mutton Hill, Steep, nearby Thomas's study at Wick Green. Berryfield Cottage, the family's first Hampshire home, lies to the right hidden by yew trees; the stone in the foreground is a memorial to Thomas, erected in 1937

'I'm bound away for ever': a harrowed-looking Thomas, one month before his departure for France, by Mervyn, High Beech, December 1916

Sipping and thinking, both happily, neither
long.
The water wrinkled, but they sipped and
thought,
As careless of the wind as it of us.
'Look at those calves. Hark at the trees
again.'[4]

If the opening owed something to his friend
Robert Frost in their conversational eclogue,
these final lines were utterly Thomas's. In laying
them down he had demonstrated to himself a key
notion: that his poem should use only words that
his speaker, the girl, might use, and should find
rhythms in the poem that rightly reflected her
rhythms of speech. Rigid iambic pentameter would
have sounded unnatural in the mouth of this wild-
eyed girl, but blank verse—extending or contracting
a line where need be—was the right expression for
the mixture of casual gossip and dramatic energy
with which the poem spoke.

His first poem had emerged in an unwieldy
manner from his prose, but it was, in an important
sense, better than his prose. The prose had done
everything asked of it: polite, unshowy lines pitched
at the level of a quietly spoken conversation; but
the poem had that and more besides: it had cadence
and it had drama. It was an extraordinary first
effort, full of character and good phrasing; tonally,
perhaps, it borrowed from his friend Robert Frost,
and by the standards of poetry it carried a prosaic
bagginess that he would have to shake off; but in
places it soared with an energy and confidence that
showed glimpses of the promise to come.

Thomas left his study at Wick Green and

descended through the December darkness of the Hangers to Yew Tree Cottage. The most severe of self-critics, he remained dissatisfied with the poem he had written and would omit it when the time came to prepare his book. But his lack of satisfaction would simply drive him on, and he would return to his study the following morning and make a start on an entirely new poem.

*   *   *

For the next four days Thomas climbed through the hanger woods to his study to begin a new poem with each new day. 'November', his second, was, like his first, developed from a rough prose paragraph that he had jotted down in his notebook days before, but it was a piece quite unlike the first in every other way. It emerged not in the blank verse of 'Up in the Wind', but was instead clasped in rhyming couplets, using a song phrasing of Thomas's own that overlaid a more familiar medieval calendric rhyme, 'Thirty days hath September'. With its fascination with the seasons and the weather, the poem signalled a subject matter that would become a hallmark of Thomas's verse.

> November's days are thirty:
> November's earth is dirty,
> Those thirty days, from first to last;
> And the prettiest things on ground are the paths . . .

It was an uncomplicated piece of natural observation, never entirely comfortable in its skin;

238

'a shade sententious', thought Thomas, and owing a debt to Shelley that few but Thomas would have noticed had he not pointed it out. At so early a stage in his verse, Thomas had an eye for detail that was stronger than his sense of the poem, and this one swung unevenly in and out of its guiding rhyme and metre; but he posted it nonetheless to Ryton to draw Frost's comments. The draft had included phrasings that seemed either too precious or too trivial to the American, and Thomas was grateful for the 'kick' to set him straight. 'The foot's seal and the wing's light word', Thomas had written frothily until Frost advised against it, and helped him settle upon a phrasing that was altogether sturdier. 'I am glad that you spotted "wing's light word",' wrote Thomas appreciatively. 'I knew it was wrong and also that many would like it.' Knowing that many would like it and yet that it was wrong: in only his second poem, Thomas had tackled a challenge that all poets must address some time in their development—namely, that popularity may need to be conceded for the sake of a better poem. It can take years for a young poet to learn the importance of that sacrifice, but it had taken Thomas just two poems in two days.[5]

Next morning, 5 December, Thomas climbed up through Ashford Hanger once again to the Bee House and settled in to compose a companion piece to 'November' which he called 'March'.

Now I know that Spring will come again,
Perhaps tomorrow: however late I've patience
After this night following on such a day.

If Frost's hand was apparent in the conversational

239

tone of 'Up in the Wind', and in the revised lines of 'November', in 'March' it took a more inspirational touch still. Thomas's search for a true spring had been the subject of the prose book he gave to Frost, *In Pursuit of Spring*, and now these first three lines seemed to reflect Frost's urging for Thomas to revisit those lines of prose, and to write them, as Frost put it, 'in verse form in exactly the same cadence'. In prose:

> All the thrushes of England sang at that hour, and against that background of myriads I heard two or three singing their frank, clear notes in a mad eagerness to have all done before dark; for already the blackbirds were chinking and shifting places along the hedgerows.

In verse:

> What did the thrushes know? Rain, snow, sleet, hail,
> Had kept them quiet as the primroses.
> They had but an hour to sing. On boughs they sang,
> On gates, on ground; they sang while they changed perches
> And while they fought, if they remembered to fight:
> So earnest were they to pack into that hour
> Their unwilling hoard of song . . .

What did the thrushes know? There, in those five words, is a phrasing that is already and entirely Thomas's own. The questioning, doubtful tone,

240

the restless enquiry, the fallibility of a poet's voice: these were already instinctively, distinctively, the voice of Edward Thomas. Some Georgian poets might promise to understand a bird and 'translate' it for the reader's benefit; others might even claim to become the bird itself and live the experience on behalf of the reader. But Edward Thomas was altogether more equivocal in his promise, knowing that as a human being he must always remain outside of the experience of the animal, as if knowledge itself was uncertain, guessed at, and yet still possible to catch for the careful listener, at least in the moment of birdsong. 'Something they knew—I also, while they sang': as close to the animal as we are ever likely to get, a vague sharing of we know not what through song—these were marks of Thomas.[6]

But if the ideology was tentative and subtle, the craft was gaining in confidence. Thomas had finished three of the final nine lines with the word 'silence': a bold use of repetition in a form where each word counts for so much. It was a courageous move that might be expected of a veteran poet; but Thomas was accelerating his apprenticeship. The past three days had brought impressive results, but on the fourth day Thomas would achieve something spectacular.

In the same exercise book in which he wrote his short prose 'The White Horse' is another from 17 November 1914, called 'Old Man's Beard'. The title may have been a rare slip from Thomas, for the plant he wrote of in the piece was not Old Man's Beard but old man, a southernwood shrub sometimes known as Lad's Love. The plant was a gift from Gordon Bottomley upon moving into

241

Wick Green in December 1909; by April 1910 it had grown to become 'a beautiful great bush' at Thomas's study window. When the family moved down the hill and into the cramped Yew Tree Cottage in 1913, Thomas took a cutting from the bush and planted it beside the front door of the new home.[7]

On 11 November 1914 Thomas had scribbled in his field notebook: '*Old Man* scent, I smell again and again not really liking it but venerating it because it holds the secret of something very long ago which I feel it may someday recall, but I have got no idea what.' The thought of writing about the redolent smell had been with him for some time (at least since a story from the summer of 1909 called 'The Old House'), but in November 1914 a prose draft followed the inscriptions in his notebook, just as it had with 'Up in the Wind'. 'Old Man's Beard' was less than 300 words in length and carried the feel of an accomplished prose poem, beginning with an image of Myfanwy taking in the scent, and concluding,

> No garden comes back to me, no hedge or path, no grey green bush called old man's beard or lad's love, no figure of mother or father or playmate, only a dark avenue without an end.

A little less than three weeks later, and Thomas roughed out a draft in verse.

> Old Man or Lad's Love.—in the name there's nothing
> To one that knows not Lad's Love or

Old Man.

The first two lines had snapped cleanly into place, but when it came to describe the herb itself Thomas unexpectedly fumbled his lines. Three or four times he went about the plant's description, finding the line and then losing it again. But mostly he moved forward with little correction. The intense crossing-out that had characterised the first poems, the transposing of sections, the striking-through of ideas: mostly these were absent now as the act of drafting itself was rapidly becoming more assured. Where the first three poems had laboured and lurched, 'Old Man' had grown into itself very quickly, demonstrating Thomas's growing confidence with blank verse, unafraid to swell or contract the line by two or three syllables where necessary. No sooner had he finished than Thomas brushed down the poem in a second, cleaner draft that was almost without correction. With 'Up in the Wind' he had struggled for an ending, but here it was largely in place from the outset, nudged gently into position with each working draft:

> . . . only a dark avenue without an end. [prose]
> Only a dark avenue: without end or name.
> [first draft]
> Only an avenue dark without end or name.
> [second draft]
> Only an avenue, dark, nameless, without end.
> [final draft][8]

'Old Man' was a poem of which Thomas was rightly proud, and one that caught the attention of editors. When in February 1917 Harriet Monroe took three of Thomas's poems for her Chicago *Poetry*, it was the piece she led off with, and when, a month later, Thomas was anthologised for the first time in England, this would be the first of eighteen poems printed in *An Annual of New Poetry*. It had taken a mere four poems for Thomas to find his voice.

*   *   *

On Monday 7 December, Thomas began his fifth poem in five days, 'The Signpost', which found a traveller standing at a junction unable to choose the path to take. Thomas had spoken of his indecision so often to his friends that to some—especially Frost—it had become an almost comic attribute of his character. But Thomas himself was less amused, and frequently felt anxiety towards the decisions he faced about his home life, about the way he earned his living and, recently, about the war. And now he was giving himself something else about which to decide: poetry. And the self-analysis was bursting through.

> I read the sign. Which way shall I go?
> A voice says: You would not have doubted so
> At twenty. Another voice gentle with scorn
> Says: At twenty you wished you had never been born.[9]

Once again, Thomas drew upon the method he had employed all week: beginning with a reaching back into his notebooks or his prose, then producing an incomplete first draft by hand in his exercise book, followed by a second in which he effectively

244

completed the poem, then a third draft, typed, in which minor changes of tense or phrase would be made as he tidied up the poem for presentation. The time frame from the first draft to the typed poem was usually a single day. The opening of this poem gave him more difficulties than he had experienced earlier in the week, and the fit of the form was not at all obvious to him: first he used rhyming couplets, then quatrains, then back to couplets. The first draft brought him eighteen lines, the second a further twelve, and by the end of the afternoon he had an accomplished draft.[10]

Throughout Thomas's prose are figures at a crossroads uncertain of their path ahead; here, in his verse, the speaker of the poem is left standing at the signpost paralysed by indecision. The need to make decisions and the fear of doing so would be an emblem of Thomas's thinking and writing over the next six months as he wavered about the war. And something else too: Thomas would send the poem to Frost the following week, and it would reinforce in Frost the line of thinking about his friend that resulted in the American's most famous poem of all, 'The Road Not Taken'. But that poem was still a year and a half away, and for now it was Thomas not Frost who was experiencing a creative explosion in a remarkable week of poetry.

*   *   *

'My works come pouring in on you now,' Thomas told Frost on 15 December. 'Tell me all you dare about them.' Less than a fortnight after completing his first poem, Thomas had not only sent his friend a batch of verses in Ryton, but had had a reply and had written in response to that reply. Thomas's industry was frantic, even manic: poems and letters about poems and replies to those letters about poems. There was little room for family or for worrying about money: the experience was all consuming. He confessed to Frost of feeling 'uncommonly cheerful mostly', pleased with some of the pieces, but something else besides. 'I find myself engrossed and conscious of a possible perfection as I never was in prose,' he said. 'Still, I won't begin thanking you just yet, tho if you like I will put it down now that you are the only begetter right enough.'[11]

*   *   *

In that first week of poetry, Thomas had established most of the themes that would characterise his verse in the two years ahead: the rhythms of speech and thought and song, the variable blank verse form, the use of country characters who would conduct his narratives, the elemental conditions of the weather and the seasons, the spaces in which the human and the natural worlds intersect, the power of memory and of childhood, the hesitation and doubt that he found so disabling in his own life. His writing would get clearer, more focussed and more memorable, but there would be few new themes introduced after that first week. One such new theme, however, would arrive in the next few days. It was a feature that had touched his prose in recent years and had been guided to the surface by Godwin Baynes; now it would feature in his verse. It saw Thomas at his most schizophrenic, at his darkest and most interesting: it was the projection

246

of his alter ego upon his writing.

'The Other', probably from the second week of December 1914, was one of four poems written that week for which no manuscripts survive; only a single typescript, retained by Robert Frost, ensured that the poem was preserved at all. Like 'March', 'The Other' seemed to take a helping hand from Frost's directive to look back at his prose such as *In Pursuit of Spring* and write it again in verse cadence. The 'Other Man' then had ridden with Thomas along his trail from London to Somerset, and it is likely that his appearance in that book recalled in Frost an episode in the American's past, when he encountered his own double on a snowy wood road in New Hampshire and 'felt as though I was going to meet my own image in a slanting mirror'. More chilling, more energised and more disturbing than any of its appearances in prose, 'The Other' had a distinct formal structure: ten stanzas of ten lines (Thomas added an eleventh verse in his note to Frost), in loose iambic tetrameter and a novel but rigid rhyme scheme which pinched and pushed at the reader's senses. Thomas knew instinctively how rhyme eased the transmission of a poem, but here he deliberately stacked the rhymes vertiginously in a way that made them tense and clipped, hunched at the shoulders of the poem, and so setting the reader's nerves jangling.[12]

'The forest ended,' the poem began, in the most beguiling of the openings that Thomas had found to date. Out into the clearing the 'I' emerges glad of the light, glad of the smell of mint and grass, and finds before him an inn. There, he is mistaken for another man, a double, identical in every way, who had slept there the night before. The 'I' is

247

gripped by a sense of fear and yet, urged on by some unarticulated desire, he chooses to pursue the man in the hope to 'outrun that other', with no clear notion of what he would do were he to catch him. Days pass without a sighting, the 'I' ever more driven to confrontation. In a tap room in a roadside inn, where the 'I' is taking rest, he hears above the pub chatter the voice of the Other Man asking for him, telling the bartender of a figure he knew had been following him, oppressing him, chasing him down; and with the tables turned suddenly, the once-persecuted now-persecuting 'I' slips silently from the inn. The 'I' continues to follow the 'Other', but at distance, careful not to be detected. And so it would go on: the 'Other' pursued, unable to rest; the 'I' pursuing, unable to give up the chase.

In 1911, in a pit of despair, Thomas had written to a friend about his doctors' decision to prescribe him a vegetarian diet. 'I hope it will cure my head, which is almost always wrong now—a sort of conspiracy going on in it which leaves me only a joint tenancy and a perpetual scare of the other tenant and wonder what he will do.' The 'joint tenancy' had been crippling at times for Thomas. More often than not, it took the form of a critical or mocking voice from within: an inner judge who was not afraid to voice his contempt of Thomas's behaviour, his decisions or his talents. Thomas had met him in *The South Country*, 'a tall, spare, shock-headed man' escaping the life of a town clerk for the country. He had met him again on the Icknield Way, 'a lean, indefinite man' lamenting a raft of lost opportunities. He had been a projection in *The Happy-Go-Lucky Morgans*, and elsewhere, in

248

a short story, 'a poet of a kind, who made a living out of prose'. He was the voice who mocked him in 'The Signpost', and now it appeared that he would be pursued into the realm of his verse.[13]

*   *   *

Thomas had sent his fortnight's work to Frost, but his friend was not the only recipient of his poems. With some boldness, he sent them also to Harold Monro at the Poetry Bookshop. 'I enclose some poems which I should like you to look at,' wrote Thomas on 15 December. 'If you think anything of them the writer, who wishes to be very strictly anonymous, would like to see a small book of these and others. I deliver myself into your hands.' That Thomas felt able to send his work to the leading poetry journal of the day a mere two weeks into his apprenticeship said much for the self-belief he had attained.[14]

After ten poems in two weeks, Thomas took a few days' break from writing verse. Christmas came and went, the family all together for once and enjoying one another's company ('in the modified Thomas style', he said). But even amid the opening of presents and the washing up of dinner plates, Thomas did not neglect his poetry for long. Set at the Elizabethan house at Prior's Dean on the Froxfield plateau north of Steep, 'The Manor Farm' was a transitional poem for Thomas that carried cadences of Frost's (Thomas: 'But earth would have her sleep out, spite of the sun'; Frost: 'But they would have the rabbit out of hiding'). But it contained moments in which Thomas was using a syntax that was quite his own: 'The air

249

raised not a straw,' he wrote, knowing that no other wording would work so precisely as this; a dignified, respectful syntax, mild in its formality, iambic for the memory's aid. There were false notes too: an awkward elision 'But 'twas not Winter', in no way needed for the metre, seemed an elevated, poetic stroke. But he was confident of his ending when challenged by a friend: 'I rather think I will stick to it,' he wrote, adding sagely, 'If one can feel what one has written and not what one *meant*...'[15]

On Christmas Day, Thomas wrote a song based on a traditional ballad, 'The Lincolnshire Poacher', which he now adapted to reflect his encounter with 'ole Bott' at Ryton only a month before:

Since then I've thrown away a chance to fight
    a gamekeeper;
And I less often trespass, and what I see or
    hear
Is mostly from the road or path by day: yet still
    I sing:
'Oh, 'tis my delight of a shiny night in the
    season of the year.'

From an early age, Thomas had loved the song form; given the opportunity in adult life he readily compiled an anthology of his favourite selections in *The Pocket Book of Poems and Songs for the Open Air*. He liked to sing to himself as he walked across the south country or to Myfanwy as she sat on his knee before bed. Thomas was a fine singer with a musical ear and a drive to explore musical phrasings that would distinguish him from Frost. His friend had a gift for hearing the speaking voice and for casting it into speech rhythms, but he was

250

no musician; and while the poems that Thomas wrote in song form may not have been among his finest efforts, he would frequently use the measures and the line breaks of ballad and of song form to vary his natural leaning towards blank verse.[16]

Two shorter poems followed, set in the coppice that surrounded the narrow Ashford stream at Lutcombe in Steep, each skilful in its use of repetition to tune the reader's ear to the circumstance of the poem. 'The Combe' was the more powerful of the two with its tone of foreboding and its harking back to the older, Celtic woodlands, and the badger, 'That most ancient Briton of English beasts', dug out and given to the hounds. Thomas had finished fifteen poems in the month of December—eclogues, blank verse, ballads, poems short and long—roughly one quarter of the number that he would need to compile a collection for the Poetry Bookshop. But on that front his verse now received its first setback. Harold Monro wrote to say that he did not have time to consider Thomas's work. Thomas—who had contributed, unpaid, the best of the articles that *Poetry and Drama* had published over the past two years, the figure whom many thought the leading critic of his day and the greatest catch that Monro had made for the journal, a man who had just broken into verse—for him, inexplicably, Monro could not spare the time to read his first poems. Thomas was stunned. 'I sent what I had to Monro asking for secrecy. He kept it 4 days and then said he hadn't had time to read it, so I took it back rather crestfallen, tho it is quite possible that he meant he hadn't been able to get anyone to help him to an opinion.'[17]

251

It would be only the first of a series of setbacks that Thomas would receive on the long road to the publication of his verse.

*   *   *

As December deepened, it became increasingly apparent to the British public that the war would not be over by Christmas. Edward Thomas was no more decided than before about enlistment and at the beginning of the month had even written to his literary agent to seek his thoughts. 'You startle me by saying you are not sure whether or not you should enlist,' Cazenove had replied. 'That is a matter which every man must settle with himself, but I should have thought your calls were elsewhere.' London was teeming with soldiers in the run-up to Christmas, and it startled Robert Frost to find several of them in the Poetry Bookshop when he called in one morning. A young man in uniform eyed him for a short while before approaching him and opening a discussion that kept the men engaged for some time. The soldier was Robert Graves, still only nineteen, who listened patiently as Frost mused briefly on whether or not he, as an American, should enlist in the British Army, before turning to the reception of his work by publishers in the United States. 'They say the germans [sic] have made the whole Atlantic unsafe', Frost had written that month. 'This raises questions for me.'

1) Do I dare to go home now?
2) Won't it be more dangerous to go every day we delay?

3) Won't it be impossible to get money across
to live on pretty soon?
4) Do I dare to stay?

The letter caught Frost's dilemma on the horns. And yet it was not everything that it appeared to be. In a letter from earlier that month, now lost, Robert Frost had written to Thomas to tell him of his 'few remaining weeks here', and though he did not yet have a timetable for a departure, the course of action was at least decided upon. When he left, Mervyn would go with him; this too was now decided upon. Thomas let his thoughts turn to his fourteen-year-old son and the life he would now experience on the other side of the Atlantic. 'I thought it might be god's idea to get Mervyn away from me for ever.'[18]

*   *   *

On New Year's Day 1915, Edward Thomas settled into a poem in which a man leaning on a rake was mistaken from a distance as possessing a third leg. Though the man in the poem was not of serving age, the image of maimed or paraplegic men on crutches was becoming a more familiar sight in the cities, one which Thomas would have seen in his visits to London and which seemed now to have entered his verse. The man wished the new year would come soon, as the public had wished for Christmas, but his words were muffled by the roar of the wind through the trees. Thomas would write many poems over the next two years in which the events of the war took place obliquely in the margins of the page: the missing cast of characters

253

who had been killed in France, the unattended garden tools, the rusty harrow, the older men missing their mates, the bereft wives. But he would never write of or from the trenches. In his poems of early January, the source of a river would be found 'drowning the sound of earth', a brook 'roaring with black hollow voices', while another, written on 8 January, found him asking himself whether the protection of beauty required a physical or even violent defence.[19]

As it happened, Thomas had just ensured that he himself would be incapable of any form of physical defence for some time to come. On 2 January, descending the Shoulder of Mutton, he sprained his ankle so severely that he would be unable to put any weight on it for several weeks. It was not until 6 January that he was able to make it out of bed and into the deck chair that Helen had brought into the bedroom. The sprain would leave him immobile for the month, and inconvenienced for much longer, and for the time being would kick any thought of enlistment into touch. But for his poetry it would be a tremendous blessing.

Laid up in his bedroom in Yew Tree Cottage, Thomas began to tell his friends openly for the first time about the poetry he had started writing. 'I have even begun to write verse,' he told Jesse Berridge, 'but don't tell a soul, as if it is to be published at all it must be anonymously.' He dug out a selection of poems to send to Eleanor Farjeon, and invited her to keep any that she liked provided she made typed copies, for he was sending his only typescripts. By 7 January he was able to sit in his deck chair for most of the day with his foot up, and by 10 January was finally able to make it downstairs. But he could only hop, and was in a filthy temper. Under the low ceilings of the cottage, he penned a claustrophobic trimeter in tight rhyming couplets about his desire to be out under the open skies. 'While I, I know that trees | Under that lofty sky | Are weeds, fields mud, and I would arise and go far | To where the lilies are.' *Arise and go*? Yeats's 'Lake Isle of Innisfree' had not been far from his thoughts, but the more interesting influence within these lines was still to be felt: the resonating 'I, I' that Robert Frost would echo when he wrote 'The Road Not Taken'.[20]

Eleanor Farjeon was reading all of Thomas's verse by January. She wrote with some comments about Thomas's use of rhythm, to which he replied, 'If I am consciously doing anything I am trying to get rid of the last rags of rhetoric and formality which left my prose so often with a dead rhythm only,' adding, 'If I can be honest and am still bad at rhythm it will be because I am bad in rhythm.' A few days later Eleanor wrote again, this time about his use of rhyme. Once again Thomas responded with frank insight, 'I don't believe rhyme is at all a *bad* trouble. I use it now more often than not and always fancy I leave the rhymed pieces as easy as the rest, but tho I am so young a versifier I don't pretend to be sure.' The ankle may have curtailed his movements but had offered him an uninterrupted run at his poems, and the result had been a literary dam burst. Confined to the cottage, between 4 and 23 January, Thomas completed sixteen poems in twenty days.[21]

*   *   *

255

As Edward Thomas read back through his field notebooks on 8 January, he came across this entry from his train ride to Dymock on 24 June 1914.

A glorious day from 4.20 a.m. & at 10 tiers above tiers of white cloud with dirtiest grey bars above the sea of slate and dull brick by Battersea Pk—then at Oxford tiers of pure white with loose longer masses above and gaps of dark clear blue above haymaking and elms.

'Then we stopped at Adlestrop', the notebook had continued, and quickly it had suggested to Thomas the easy, wistful tone that would become his most loved and best remembered poem; but its opening lines had been anything but effortless.

Yes I remember Adlestrop,
At least the name. One afternoon
          train
The express / slowed down there and drew up
Quite

He stopped and scored this out with a rapid repeated stroke, and underneath he started again, this time giving the poem its title and changing the variety of the train.

        Yes, I remember Adlestrop,
        At least the name. One afternoon
Of heat   The ~~steam~~ train slowed ~~down~~ and drew up
        There unexpectedly. 'Twas June.

He had reworked the third line and added a

fourth, and from there the three remaining stanzas followed rapidly with just two minor corrections along the way. But he remained unsatisfied with the first stanza and made two further attempts at tightening it. Of course the train had to be 'express' if it was to pull up 'unexpectedly', he reasoned, though about this word he also had doubts and tried 'Against its custom' before he hit upon exactly the word he wanted: 'unwontedly'.

ADLESTROP

Yes. I remember Adlestrop—
The name, because one afternoon
Of heat the express-train drew up there
Unwontedly. It was late June.

The steam hissed. Someone cleared his throat.
No one left and no one came
On the bare platform. What I saw
Was Adlestrop—only the name

And willows, willow-herb, and grass,
And meadowsweet, and haycocks dry,
No whit less still and lonely fair
Than the high cloudlets in the sky.

And for that minute a blackbird sang
Close by, and round him, mistier,
Farther and farther, all the birds
Of Oxfordshire and Gloucestershire.

Of all the poems that Edward Thomas would leave behind, it is these sixteen lines of loose tetrameter that are perhaps hardest to put a finger on. What is it that has gotten so under the skin of readers over the years? This gently chimed poem, cherished

257

among the nation's favourites, has none of the expressive rhythm that Thomas so championed in Frost, and none of his dramatic narrative. Perhaps it is something to do with the lazed, heat-filled atmosphere it evokes of that last summer before the war (its provenance a mere six weeks before the start of the conflict, its drafting less than six months later), or the inscrutable chorus of birdsong into which the poem dissolves. Most probably, it is not the pinpointing of any particular episode or event that stirs this poem to life, but something about the wordlessness of thought and memory, the power of recall, the notion that the senses are capable of remembrance, and that the mind can overcome things lost or misplaced to travel across space or time; what one of Thomas's greatest admirers, Ivor Gurney, would call, 'nebulously intangibly beautiful'. It would be published in the *New Statesman* three weeks after Edward Thomas's death.[22]

*   *   *

The month's outpouring of poetry had been extraordinary, but Thomas was keenly aware that these verses, however pleasing, were not a source of income, and as he looked over his finances for the month he realised that he had earned a sum total of two pounds in January. It came as a welcome relief when, on 24 February, he received a cheque from the *English Review* for £11 6s. 10d. He told John Freeman that he still wished to join Frost in America but wondered where the money might come from. And now he had in his pocket the literature on enlistment that he had collected from

258

the National Service League.

> It isn't glory that I want, but just to get rid
> of the thoughts I have had since I first felt I
> ought to do something, tho I never felt I
> could except under what seems a sort of
> alien compulsion. I hate all crowds. I hate
> uncertainty. So naturally I hate the idea of
> being in the army in any capacity.[23]

By the beginning of February, Frost's final travel
arrangements were falling into place, but not
Mervyn's, for whom an obstacle now arose. Having
left his enquiries rather late, Frost discovered that,
at fifteen, the boy was under-age by a year in the
eyes of US immigration. Frost urged Thomas to
make contact with the American Consulate in
London. 'Say who you are and who I am that he is
going with. Ask if he would better have a passport.
Say he may be staying a matter of a year or two and
leave it to the consul to mention ages if he likes
to. Hurry this up.' A gloom descended over the
Thomas household: they had depended upon Frost
to know the particularities of US immigration, and
now became anxious that at the eleventh hour he
would disappoint Mervyn and leave the boy behind.
Frost, meanwhile, was caught up in preparations for
the journey home. On 5 February, the family moved
out of the Gallows and into Oldfields in Ledington,
and gave away their furniture in return for a week's
board. The pull home to America away from the
European war was stronger now than ever, Frost
told Jack Haines. 'I can't help being glad I decided
to use the protection of our flag.'[24]

At Steep, Thomas was still immobile, and

continued dutifully typing his English anthology and speculating as to whether the cyclist corps might be the right place for him if he were to serve when he recovered. He wrote 'House and Man' (a poem that possibly provoked Frost's 'An Old Man's Winter Night'), but his ankle was too badly sprained to make one last journey to Dymock to see his friend depart. Frost had offered to put back their boat tickets if Thomas would return to Gloucestershire one last time, but Thomas was in no state to go, and Frost conceded that, 'we doubt if it would be wise to put off that evil day'. And so Frost came to Thomas, and at 10.15 on the morning of 6 February he and his family arrived in Hampshire to say their goodbyes. They stayed from Saturday until Tuesday morning, the poets sitting up late each evening in the cramped Yew Tree Cottage, talking into the small hours. So much had changed since they had first spoken this way a year ago. In Frost's words: 'Thomas and I had become so inseparable that we came to be looked on as some sort of literary Siamese twins in a literary scene, with a spiritual bond holding us together.' With the American's retreat home, that bond would now be tested to the full, in what must have been a private agony for Thomas. Frost had brought him inspiration and humour, kindness and sympathy and understanding; he had listened with patience to his complaints, he had encouraged him in his marriage and had guided his writing, roughed him up when called upon, and now Thomas would have to face all this by himself.[25]

After the Frosts departed, Thomas wrote a quiet, ruminative lyric in which he noticed the felling of a willow copse, appreciated only after it had gone:

Strange it could have hidden so near!
And now I see as I look
That the small winding brook,
A tributary's tributary, rises there.

On the morning of 11 February, the Thomases
rose at six. Father and son said a strained goodbye,
before the boy left with Helen, his travel documents
still unresolved, to be reunited with the Frosts at
Liverpool docks. Thomas wrote a hand-wringing
poem for Mervyn that day:

Parting today a double pain:
First because it was parting; next
Because the ill it ended vexed
And mocked me from the Past again . . .

In fifteen years, Thomas had struggled to find a
way to fully relate to his son. His own father had
been pushily aspirational, and Edward would
not make the same mistake with Mervyn; but he
would make a different one, detaching himself
to the point where his son was left uncertain of
his father's feelings. 'It means the end of any
chance of being anything to the boy,' Thomas told
Eleanor. 'But I only hope I haven't been nothing
to him for too long now.' Myfanwy, the youngest,
felt it too, and commented once, 'For most of my
life I have felt that he did not care for me.' Only
Bronwen seemed to break through the barriers
that he silently erected. She alone seemed capable
of pulling him out of himself, whether through her
delight in botany or her simple refusal to be downtrodden. It was to her that this uncollected lyric was

261

written, inked into her schoolgirl autograph album, probably in 1914 or early 1915:

> This is the constellation of the Lyre:
> Its music cannot ever tire,
> For it is silent. No man need fear it:
> Unless he wants to, he will not hear it.

But starting that day Thomas tried in his letters to make manifest his love for Mervyn, through paper and ink in a way he had not managed in the flesh.[26]

Frost had not left time to make his other farewells personally, and sent hasty notes to Harold Monro, promising to return just as soon as he had made some money, and to F. S. Flint, thanking him for his introductions, leaving just enough time for a departing swing at Wilfrid Gibson ('You and I wont believe Gibsons is a better kind of poetry than mine,' he wrote to Sidney Cox. 'Solway Ford is one of his best. It is a good poem. But it is oh terribly made up'), and on 13 February he and his family stood with Mervyn on the gangway of the SS *St Paul* at Liverpool, preparing to board the ship that would take them home. He idled a few moments away chatting about his poetry to a ticket inspector who, reported Frost, urged him to stay in England 'till our greatness ripened a little more'. 'If I don't go now I wont go at all,' Frost had protested, and suggested playfully that if he stayed any longer he would become a British subject and might even take a run at the Poet Laureateship. The inspector, apparently an admirer of Robert Bridges, had thought that was more than enough of that and ushered the family aboard. The *St Paul* sailed for New York City under the cover of darkness, joining a convoy that was shepherded out into the Irish Sea by two naval destroyers. Among the flotilla was the *Lusitania*, a Cunard liner, that in only a few months' time would be sunk by a German U-boat, taking almost 1,200 lives. It would be the worst tragedy of the campaign at sea, and would begin to effect a change in public opinion that would lead to America entering the war.[27]

*   *   *

Helen would not have shared her husband's enthusiasm to send her son away with the two Americans of whom she had formed such a low opinion. For her eldest child at fifteen to be crossing the Atlantic in a time of war—and for an indefinite stay—could only have caused her distress, even if the plan was now for the family to follow him out when the conflict was over. She left with Myfanwy for a fortnight's break at Hatch, while Thomas took Bronwen into London, where his father was quarrelsome and his mother beleaguered. From Steep, he wrote a coded and ponderous lyric that he entitled 'Home', possibly alluding to the difficulties at Balham but possibly also reflecting his own peripatetic state of recent years. Steep had often been a suggestion as much as a lived reality, for him; latterly, at least, it had not been the site of conflict that it once was, but it had hardly been a place of happiness. Where was his home exactly? In Hampshire? In London? Or would it be overseas with Frost?

All the while, Thomas's restless conscience continued to needle him about the war. On 24 February he wrote of an owl's cry 'telling me plain what I escaped | And others could not': namely, enlistment. Eleanor, meanwhile, was by now sending out scores of Edward's poems to journals under his direction. He asked her to use the pseudonym 'Edward Phillips', before changing his mind in favour of 'Edward Marendaz' from his mother's family, and then once again for the name that he was to stick with throughout his publishing of his poetry, 'Edward Eastaway', from his father's side. Thomas explained his desire for anonymity: 'I want to begin by doing without the advantages and disadvantages of being known,' he told John Freeman. 'I don't want to be asking for compliments from friends; also I don't feel at present that I could stand criticism.' When the poems were eventually returned by *Blackwood's Magazine* in March, Thomas took the news stoically. 'I suppose Blackwood just thought it looked very much like prose and was puzzled by the fact that it was got up like verse.' G. W. Blackwood had returned the pieces to Eleanor Farjeon, writing 'the poems are to me somewhat of a puzzle, and I do not think I could venture upon them. They are, however, exceedingly interesting, and I shall be very pleased indeed to consider anything else which Mr Eastaway may write at any time which he thinks likely to suit Maga.' What Thomas had received from *Blackwood's* was a note of encouragement, but he certainly was not relaying that to friends.[28]

*　　　*　　　*

The Atlantic crossing had been wretched: nine days of getting 'kicked about' in high seas, had brought seasickness and a vow by Robert Frost never to make the voyage again. Predictably, Mervyn's papers were not in order and for once Frost found himself in a situation of which he could not talk his way out. The boy was detained as an illegal alien and incarcerated at Ellis Island detention centre for the night. Frost had to ring around for help, and eventually connected with friends in New York City who were able to assist in the clearance of Mervyn's papers; but not before the boy had experienced life with, as Frost put it, 'the scum of the earth'. Elinor and the Frost children retired to a farm in Bethlehem, New Hampshire, where they would stay as paying guests until June, while Mervyn remained temporarily detained. It was not the triumphant return that Frost had hoped for, nor the arrival that Mervyn might have wished. 'The first sight of America was bad very bad and disposed us to sing Why did I cross the deep?' said Frost. But there was one piece of good news that awaited Frost when he stepped off the boat from England. On 20 February, while he was at sea, *North of Boston* had been published in New York City by Henry Holt and Company.[29]

Frost's journey may have been uncomfortable, but he and the family had at least arrived at their destination. On 28 February Rupert Brooke had set sail on a journey to the Dardanelles that he would not complete. His mood had been urgent and provocative. In January he had written to John Drinkwater in quarrelsome form from Dorset, where he was training with 'A' Company of the Hood Battalion, awaiting the orders that would take him towards Constantinople.

Not a bad place and time to die, Belgium, 1915? I want to kill my Prussian first. Better than coughing out a civilian soul amid bed-clothes and disinfectant and gulping medicines in 1950. The world'll be tame enough after the war, for those that see it. I had hopes that England'ld get on her legs again, achieve youth and merriment, and slough the things I loathe—capitalism and feminism and hermaphroditism and the rest. But on maturer consideration, pursued over muddy miles of Dorset, I think there'll not be much change. What there is for the better though. Certain sleepers have awoken in the heart. Come and die. It'll be great fun. And there's great health in the preparation. The theatre's no place, now.[30]

III

HIGH BEECH

1915–16

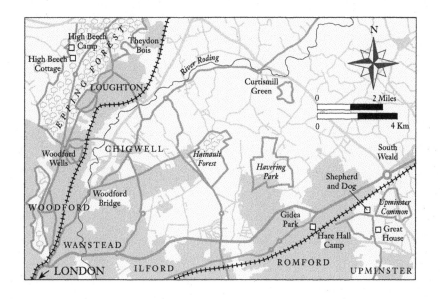

SPRING

Snow lay on the ground in Steep late into February. Stoner Hill was locked in ice, and conditions for walking, had Thomas been capable of it, were treacherous. He was still lame, but now at least able to manage short distances. On 3 March Eleanor came for the night against the wishes of her mother, who believed that her daughter was caught in an unrequited relationship with Edward and that her visits could only cause her pain. But Eleanor came regardless, and encouraged Thomas out on a short walk. Mostly, when Thomas went walking, he took with him a stick to regulate his stride or aid an ascent. But now he needed one simply for balance as he eased himself back onto his feet after two months laid up. He took pride in making and seasoning his own sticks, and she recalled how his eye would scour the hedgerows and the tree roots as he walked, looking for an arm of ash or hazel or his favoured oak. When Eleanor left the next day, so did Thomas. Moving more freely now than at any time for two months, he took flight from Steep once again, to London and Coventry, returning to Helen after a week away.[1]

Consciously now, Thomas was examining the transition of his writing from prose into poetry, and he grasped each opportunity that came his way to discuss it. He told John Freeman. 'What I have done so far have been like the quintessences of the best parts of my prose books—not much sharper or more intense, but I hope a little: since the first

271

take off they haven't been Frosty very much or so I imagine.' He was driven with a passion for writing that he had never experienced before. Some mornings Thomas could hardly wait to walk up the hill and light the fire in his study. His daily routine was now study–garden–study: rising at seven and climbing up to the Bee House, descending to Yew Tree Cottage at lunchtime, and returning to his study in the middle of the afternoon; bed at 11. He reached into his boyhood holidays in west Wales to write one of the comparatively few poems in which he drew on the Welsh countryside, relating a child's yearning (his brother's, he said cagily) for their mother. He wrote an accompanying poem which looked to his urban upbringing in London: once a place of suffocation for him, but now portrayed as a haven of sorts to the outsider. And in between these poems of Welsh country and English towns was sandwiched a short, unsettling lyric under whose arches the past and the future converged uneasily. He called it 'The Bridge', and wrote to John Freeman following a visit by his friend to Steep on 20 March: 'Do come down again and let us prove that we have some Englishness in common. You shan't label me Welsh whatever you do to escape my remarks.'[2]

His poems were reflecting the changing season, in particular the loosening of the frozen ground and the crops that Thomas was able now to sow in the garden of Yew Tree Cottage. He was trying out new forms when he could: short lyrics based on folk as well as verse metres, some of which struggled for effect. Meanwhile he continued to push Frost's poetry whenever he could, coaxing friends and nudging editors, but taking care to avoid the kind of divisive response that Pound had stirred up. He explained the delicacy of the situation to his friend Edward Garnett, a writer and critic who knew all about such sensitivities, having been instrumental in getting D. H. Lawrence's *Sons and Lovers* published in 1913. 'He had been at American editors 10 years in vain,' wrote Thomas:

> But may I suggest it might damage him there if you rubbed the Americans' noses in their own dirt? I know he thought so. Most English reviewers were blinded by theories they had as to what poetry should look like. They did not see how true he was, and how pure in his own style. I think the Hired Man, the Wood Pile, the Black Cottage and one or two others— such as Home Burial—masterpieces.

But Thomas could not extend the same compliments to Frost's former neighbours in Gloucestershire. 'I've not dipped into New Numbers yet,' he admitted three months after publication of its final issue. 'Drinkwater is hopeless. Gibson, for me, almost equally so. Abercrombie, I fancy, applies the lash, and I wonder whether he always did. I used to think he was naturally a spirited steed. I am always anxious to like him.'[3]

Thomas had listened attentively to Frost's criticisms of his poems, and made adjustments in the light of his friend's comments, but he was altogether more resistant to the comments of others. Hudson and Farjeon had commented with little effect on Thomas's early verses, and now Edward Garnett would encounter the same. When

273

Garnett responded to the selection given to him on 9 March, Thomas found the advice uncomfortable, and batted it back. He refused Garnett's suggestion to correct the last line of 'The Manor Farm' (W. H. Hudson had singled out the very same line for criticism) and let him know firmly that it was his favourite among the pieces sent. He refused to correct 'Tears' to make it, as Garnett had suggested, 'marketable'. He conceded faults elsewhere in the poems that he said he did not feel minded to correct, and even pointed out others that his friend had overlooked; Garnett must have wondered why he was asked for his comments in the first place. He had found Thomas's verse proximate, coarse and rhythmically untidy, and yet Thomas would seek his opinion once more, sending him what he called a further 'swamping' in April: 'You cannot imagine how eagerly I have run up this byeway and how anxious I am to be sure it is not a cul de sac.'[4]

Thomas shared his work with more of his friends to much the same effect. Vivian Locke Ellis, at whose house in East Grinstead he had spent his winters, told Thomas his rhythm was rough and not emphatic enough. Gordon Bottomley agreed that he was enslaved by his own prose rhythms. W. H. Davies took a quick look at a small unsigned selection and, to mutual embarrassment, pronounced confidently that this was unquestionably the work of Robert Frost. Thomas would be more careful in future about passing around his poems anonymously. Monro, Hudson, Garnett, Ellis, Bottomley, Davies: to a man, they had failed to see as Frost had seen the quality of their friend's work. Julian Thomas, Edward's youngest and closest brother, did at least appreciate the poems, and late in March read them out at home to their parents in Edward's absence, but the response there was hardly better. 'Father calls them pure piffle,' Julian recorded in his diary, 'and says no one will publish them.'[5]

* * *

That spring, Thomas wrote two poems that centred on the cold, unlovable house at Wick Green above Steep, but with money now so tight, Thomas reluctantly accepted what he dubbed a 'filthy job—a book on the Duke of Marlborough to be done in haste'. And done in haste it would be: six weeks of research, four weeks in the writing: some 75,000 words, up to 3,000 a day. Thomas loathed every minute of it: the mind-numbing research at the British Museum (he called this 'pap'), the weariness of the prose laid down at Steep ('undigested and useless') about a subject with whom he felt no affinity. 'The only good thing will be letting me deeper into the secret of how not to write.' As a publishing enterprise, it was at least mercifully quick: Chapman & Hall issued the book on 19 October 1915, a mere six months after Thomas had begun it. But it was an agony for Thomas. He had moved beyond prose now, and hated the chore of having to write to length. It would be the last prose book that he would produce and it was a relief to get back to writing lyric verse at Easter, among which was a penetrating quatrain that would typify the oblique way in which Thomas would write about the war.

IN MEMORIAM (EASTER, 1915)

The flowers left thick at nightfall in the wood
This Eastertide call into mind the men,
Now far from home, who, with their
    sweethearts, should
Have gathered them and will do never again.[6]

For such a short lyric it made for long and uncomfortable reading, full of disruptive sense and quarrelsome syntax, awkward to read aloud due to rhythms that he tied trickily to what he once praised in a review as 'thought moments' rather than those that belong to metre or speech. Nowhere would the reader be allowed to settle amid the careful knots that the poet had pulled so tightly: the skilful way the word 'thick' swats across the first line, knocking out what would otherwise be a neat line of iambic pentameter; the way 'This Eastertide' surprises the sense in the second; the clipped sub-clauses of the third line, each a set of gates to slow, enclose and hold up the understanding; and the final five words of the fourth line, quite deliberate in their staccato shaking of the rhythm. Here, at the end, the stressed line endings that have come before are dispensed with, and the effect is hesitant, uncertain, irresolvable. There is no choice but to read this poem over again, to go back to the start and refresh the eye, to keep the lines turning on the tongue and in the mind, so that they stay within the reader's thoughts as a memorial should. Nowhere does the poem mention war, and yet it is a powerful war poem.[7]

The short, Eastertide lyrics had followed 'Lob', a much lengthier piece that had attracted Frost's attention. 'The goodness is in Lob,' Frost had written of Thomas's longest poem to date, and perhaps his finest, thought Frost, written and worked over on 3 and 4 April 1915. It was his most confident performance yet: striding effortlessly across 150 lines of iambic pentameter and rhyming couplets, exploring English folklore and mythology through an archetypal countryman who had appeared in many guises throughout his prose and verse: mole-catcher, umbrella man, watercress man, sage. But the model was real as well as creative, based upon someone Thomas met fishing on a canal bank during his childhood holidays in Wiltshire, David 'Dad' Uzzell. 'I called [him] Dad, in the Wiltshire style, almost from the first day. I remember him first as a stiff straight man, broad-shouldered and bushy bearded, holding his rod out and watching his float very intently.' Uzzell knew the names of the birds and could imitate their calls, and identify most of the wild flowers that he and the teenage Thomas encountered on their wanderings between Swindon and Wootton Bassett. He lived simply with his wife in a modest terrace in Swindon, taking his living partly from his catches in the river or the fields outside the town. 'Every man who was ever any good had a little apple-face man or woman like this somewhere not very far back in his pedigree,' wrote Thomas in his 1913 book *The Country*; someone who stood, like the badger of the coombe, as that most ancient of Britons. 'He has been in England as long as dove and daw.'[8]

'I like the first half of Lob best: it offers something more like action with the different people coming in and giving the tones of speech,' continued Frost. 'But the long paragraph is a feat.

277

I never saw anything like you for English.' Gordon Bottomley responded warmly too, as did Eleanor Farjeon, but when Edward Garnett repeated his wish to see greater regularity in the verse, Thomas politely but firmly brushed his view aside. 'It would be the easiest thing in the world to clean it all up and trim it and have every line straightforward in sound and sense,' he replied, 'but it would not really improve it. I think you read too much with the eye perhaps.'[9]

*   *   *

Thomas had recovered sufficiently from his disappointment with Harold Monro to repeat his approach for publication. On 20 April he wrote once again to the Poetry Bookshop to say that he would very much like to bring out a small book of poems and that he would like Monro to be 'the publisher and keeper of the secret'—by which he meant the true identity of Edward Eastaway. He had sixty-one poems, ample for a sixty-four-page book, the preferred extent at the time. Fearing that Monro might ask about finance, Thomas made clear that he could not afford to subsidise the publication himself, but would send along a manuscript if the editor was interested. This time Monro was willing to take a look, and five days after his initial enquiry, Thomas packaged up a 'variety of verses' and posted them off to Devonshire Street.

I should like some to please you. Let me know if any do, but if any don't, please don't tell me what you *think* of them,—for this reason, that

I do not care a button what anybody thinks of them but I am at the same time excessively thin skinned[.] I should have said I don't want to know what anyone thinks of them whether favourable or not. But I am anxious to know if anyone really *likes* them or some or one of them . . . Can you manage to return these before the end of the week?[10]

To be both thin skinned and not caring a button would be a tightrope that Thomas would find difficulty in walking. Monro did get back to Thomas before the week's end, but with a decision to turn down the manuscript for publication. Monro's response is sadly lost, but piecing together Thomas's comments it appears as though the editor felt there was a gulf between 'conception and execution', hinting that he felt the poems were not the authentic voice of a writer whose prose he had come to know so well. Thomas wrote back:

Many thanks for saying it. I am sorry because I feel utterly sure they are me. I expect obstacles and I get them. It was chiefly to save myself what I think unnecessary pain that I asked for no explanations. One blow was better. I assume the verses expressed nothing clearly that you care about, as that is the only ground for not liking written work. But don't let us talk about it.[11]

Thomas insisted that he was not at all influenced by the views of Monro or anyone else, though he conceded such responses took a certain readjustment. In truth, he felt let down by

Monro's offhand rejection: it was the first he had experienced from a poetry publisher and it would leave a bitter taste; from that point on, Thomas cashed the contributors' payments that *Poetry and Drama* posted him, having worked for free until then. To Eleanor, he relayed only that he had sent Monro 'a lot of verses in hopes he would make a book of them. He won't. He doesn't like them at all.'[12]

Monro was not the only editor unwilling to take a chance on Edward Thomas. In the final two weeks of March alone, Eleanor sent out no fewer than thirteen of Thomas's poems to nine different journals: all were rejected. These journals—*The Nation*, *TLS*, *English Review*, *New Statesman* among them—were busy publications with a large postbag, and it is possible to see how an unknown, pseudonymous poet might have been overlooked. But Monro's postbag was not so overrun, and he knew the identity of the author and had (this time at least) taken the trouble to read the submission; so why might he have turned Thomas down?[13]

Edward Thomas's poems were unlike those of his Georgian peers. Their tone was more tentative and more complex than most of the period's poetry; they drew no special attention to themselves, and avoided showy sonnets or epic dramas and tended to resist the various formal symmetries of the time. The cadence of the speech rhythms and particularly of the 'thought moments' was strange to Georgian ears. The restlessness, the unresolved endings, the refusal to bow to nostalgia or to a moral convenience may have left contemporary readers unsatisfied, where today these are some of the very qualities that keep his work alive for modern readers. Thomas was a modern writer in still-modernising times, quite out of keeping with many Georgian sentiments. These lines on ecology, for example, sound eerily contemporary and contrast with Georgian ideas about preservation.

> Men help to maintain the country as they think it should be. According to their tastes they destroy or they work to preserve rights of way: while some blotch and blight the hills, others will have this hollow or that summit made a possession of the people for ever, or they save old houses or build new ones worthy to please the eyes of 1912 and 2012.[14]

Frost attempted to shed some kindly light on the poor reception of Thomas's poems to date. 'You are a poet or you are nothing. But you are not psychologist enough to know that no one not come at in just the right way will ever recognize you. *You* can't go to Garnett for yourself; *you* can't go to De la Mare. I told you and I keep telling you. But as long as your courage holds out you may as well go right ahead making a fool of yourself. All brave men are fools.'[15]

Harold Monro would recognise his error in turning down the poems of Edward Thomas. In November 1917 he hosted a tribute reading of Thomas's work at the Bookshop and so began his amends. In 1920 he wrote to Helen to ask if he might take on a collected edition of her husband's work. 'I wish I could fall in with your suggestion,' wrote Helen, 'but I can't. I very much wish that you had accepted the poems when Edward first showed them to you: I remember well his hurt at your refusal. But it can't be helped now, & it's man of you to acknowledge your mistake . . . I can't help wishing that Edward's poems had had the advantage that they would have had coming from the Poetry Bookshop. But it's too late now.'[16]

*   *   *

On 18 April Rupert Brooke was aboard the *Grantully Castle* anchored in the Aegean when a cutting from *The Times* reached him. It carried the story of a rousing sermon given by the Dean of St Paul's on Easter Sunday in which he concluded a reading from Isaiah with Brooke's poem 'The Soldier'. The Dean had commented from the pulpit that such 'enthusiasm of a pure and elevated patriotism had never found a nobler expression', a comment which *The Times* had reprinted along with the poem. A few days later, Brooke developed a swelling on his lip where a mosquito bite had become infected. He took to his bunk; pain flushed in his chest and back, while the abscess that had formed on his neck pumped the poisoned blood around his body. The battalion surgeon looked in on him with increasing frequency, transferring him to a French hospital ship anchored at Skyros, the *Duguay-Trouin*. On 22 April he was barely conscious, and on 23 April not at all. At 4.46 in the afternoon he died. When the *Grantully Castle* sailed for Gallipoli the next morning, it did so without Rupert Brooke's body. His friends had buried him in an olive grove on Skyros.[17]

Winston   Churchill   grasped   the   moment politically. 'He expected to die; he was willing to die for the dear England whose beauty and majesty he knew; and he advanced towards the brink in perfect serenity, with absolute conviction of the rightness of his country's cause, and a heart devoid of hate for fellow-men,' he wrote in *The Times*. 'He was all that one would wish England's noblest sons to be in days when no sacrifice but the most precious is acceptable.'[18]

'I was struck sad for Rupert. But he chose the right way,' Robert Frost wrote to Jack Haines in Gloucestershire. 'Your letter telling of his death came right on the heels of another from [J. C.] Smith saying how much the war had done to make him a better poet. The war saved him only to kill him.' In the other corner of the county, the grief among the *New Numbers* poets was palpable. 'O Eddie, it's too terrible! I cannot realize at all yet what it means,' said Gibson to Marsh, who in turn locked himself away at Greenway Cross for eight days to work on a prose tribute. Heartfelt, hopeless sentiments poured out in verse from Abercrombie, from Drinkwater and from Gibson. But the sharpest memoriam in verse had already been written, and came not from the Dymock Poets but from Brooke's long-standing companion, Frances Cornford, who in 1910 had characterised her friend as a young Apollo, 'Magnificently unprepared | For the long littleness of life'.[19]

Edward Thomas kept a cooler head, and made a typically canny assessment of his friend's literary standing in public. 'No poet of his age was so much esteemed or admired, or was watched more hopefully. His work could not be taken soberly, whether you like it or not. It was full of the thought,

283

the aspiration, the indignation of youth.' It was simply the glamour and flashiness of Brooke's personal life that Thomas mistrusted, and he wrote revealingly (accusingly?) of Brooke 'dying conspicuously'. In private, Thomas was even more incisive, admitting to Frost that he had written the obituary on Brooke

> not daring to say that those sonnets about him enlisting are probably not very personal but a nervous attempt to connect with himself the very widespread idea that self sacrifice is the highest self indulgence. You know. And I don't dispute it. Only I doubt if he knew it or would he have troubled to drag in the fact that enlisting cleared him of 'All the little emptiness of love'? Well, I daren't say so, not having enlisted or fought the keeper.

Were these sonnets, cherished by the public as expressions of the highest self-sacrifice, in fact to be understood in contradiction to the very values that won them fame? To have said so in print, at that moment, might have been more incendiary than Thomas wished to be, given the national mood; but it remains a profound loss to our understanding of Brooke that Thomas would never return to develop his thought.[20]

'Men never spoke ill of him,' said Thomas and nor would he. He knew the work to be immature— 'eloquent experiences of thoughts or fancies rather than pure poetry' he once said to Jack Haines—but it was the talent as yet unachieved in Brooke that made his passing such a loss to literature. When Frost pressed him for his assessment, Thomas said everything that needed to be said. 'I think he succeeded in being youthful and yet intelligible and interesting (not only pathologically) more than most poets since Shelley. But thought gave him (and me) indigestion. He couldn't mix his thought or the result of it with his feeling. He could only think about his feeling. Radically, I think he lacked power of expression. He was a rhetorician, dressing things up better than they needed. And I suspect he knew too well both what he was after and what he achieves.' Indeed he did; though Thomas had no way of knowing, Brooke had made his own assessment of the sonnets that won him fame: 'God they're in the rough, these five camp-children.'[21]

1914 and Other Poems was hurried into print in June 1915 and opened with the five sonnets that had made Brooke's name. Sidgwick & Jackson issued 1,000 copies in a hopeless underestimation of the book's appeal; they reprinted twice that month alone, three times in July and were in their tenth impression by November. Rupert Brooke's verse would sell a quarter of a million copies within a decade.

*   *   *

On 1 May RMS *Lusitania* embarked on her final voyage across the Atlantic, departing Pier 54 of New York harbour with almost two thousand passengers aboard. Five days later the liner's Captain, William Turner, received an intercept from the British Admiralty warning of U-boat activity in the area. He ordered a blackout and posted a double lookout on deck, but he did not zig-zag as liner captains were taught to do, nor did he increase speed in line with procedure. The *Lusitania* was thirty miles off the coast of the Old Head of Kinsale on 7 May when she crossed in front of *U-20*. At 14.10 a young lookout spotted a line of foam hurtling towards the ship's starboard side. The torpedo struck beneath the bridge; the liner went down in eighteen minutes. Only six of her forty-eight lifeboats were successfully lowered; some tipped as the crewmen lost their grip on the lowering-falls, spilling passengers into the sea, others overturned under the list of the ship or caught on the port-side rivets. Of the 1,198 deaths, 128 were Americans. The sinking had brought the first significant US casualties of the war, and sparked public outrage. 'I wonder if your papers made you realize that we are ready to fight over the Lusitania if Germany doesn't come to terms?' wrote Frost to Jack Haines. But America still had further to go before she was ready to enter the war, and did not feel sentimental over the invasion of Belgium as Britons did, Frost explained. 'No nation ever went to war from sentiment alone. I have said this before. We are out of this fight to stay out.'[22]

*   *   *

'The Lusitania seems to increase the distance between us,' wrote Thomas to Frost, still uncertain of which side of the Atlantic he would eventually find himself on.

> The war will have ended, many other things
> Have ended, maybe, that I can no more
> Foresee or more control than robin and wren.

286

Frost was the only person he could be 'idle' with, Thomas said, but the financial cost of emigrating seemed prohibitive and the uncertainty of employment intimidating. 'I could perhaps only risk it if I really made up my mind I would see editors as much as possible. I dread them as much as that keeper,' he told Frost. 'Like everything else that means an unusual and conscious step it looks impossible, like becoming a teacher or a soldier—I suppose I ought to write a long short story about a man who didn't enlist.'[23]

SUMMER

Zeppelins were coming to London, Thomas wrote to Frost on 1 June. The capital was bombed the night before and gripped now by the panic buying of gas masks. Air strikes were a new threat for the British people: they had begun along the east coast in January but had been sporadic and ineffectual; now the airships were coming for the cities, spreading terror as they went. Helen worried about her husband's visits to town, but Edward had not needed to travel to London since he began writing up *The Life of the Duke of Marlborough* in May. By 19 June, the book was finished. Thomas celebrated with a week's cycling that led him up to Jack Haines's house at Hucclecote in Gloucestershire, where he wrote a confessional lyric, opening:

> I built myself a house of glass:
> It took me years to make it:
> And I was proud. But now, alas,
> Would God someone would break it.

Thomas had found joy in childhood throwing stones 'over into the unknown depths of a great garden and hearing the glass-house break'. He longed for someone to break through the edifice that he had put around himself, an edifice designed, he said, to protect his humility. To Edward Garnett he explained that any 'superiority' that his friend detected was nothing more than a self-defence, prone to thickening into a 'callosity'. More than anything, he missed Frost's companionship, a

288

feeling that was only deepened by his walks that week with Haines around Dymock, when the two men had talked about Frost as they strode. Frost alone among his friends had taken him by the scruff of the neck and urged better things from him: he had been the one man willing to throw stones, to 'kick' the nonsense out of him. Helen and Eleanor were too much in awe of Thomas—or feared too much his rebuke—to take on such a bullish role, but not Frost, who had urged Thomas not to judge himself with such harshness. 'I can't help it,' had been Thomas's response, 'but I can help personally-conducted tours to the recesses.' It was a new realisation from Thomas: that he might now be able to control his descent into the worst areas of his depression.[1]

Haines and Thomas climbed May Hill together that visit, though not to the crown of fir trees that ringed the summit where he had walked the previous summer with Frost. He began 'Words', a poem set on the great hillside: 'Out of us all | That make rhymes, | Will you choose | . . . | Choose me, | You English words?' Everything now was revolving around Thomas's quarrel with himself: whether or not to write poetry, go to America, enlist. Money was tighter than ever. 'It is wretched to be willing to work, to think I know what I can do, and yet not to be sure of £150 a year,' he told Eleanor. 'If anybody said You go and join the Royal Garrison Artillery and they will give you a commission, I believe I should go next month.' Food prices were a quarter higher than when the war broke out, bread by as much as a half—'and work so much more than 25% scarcer'—and he began to watch more jealously than before as the few remaining bursaries and grants passed him by, some of them given to his friends. 'De la Mare has got £100 a year now from the Civil List, and he was making £400 at least,' he complained to Frost. 'I was annoyed especially as I am told I have no chance myself as being too young and not as well known as many others who will be applying. Let me admit also that I felt they might have let me sign the petition as I have probably reviewed him more than anyone else. That is frank.' Thomas was beginning to lose patience with friends that he had spent years supporting in his reviews—de la Mare in particular, Davies to an extent—friends who showed no sign of returning the encouragement when it came to his own poetry, let alone petitioning on his behalf for a Civil List pension as he had done over the years for others.[2]

America had never seemed so certain, Eleanor Farjeon recalled. Thomas had gone so far as to prepare his mother for the news that he might emigrate. In those early weeks of June his mind seemed all but made up. 'I am thinking about America as my only chance (apart from Paradise),' he wrote to Frost on 14 June, and to Eleanor he said much the same, that 'America is a chance and that I see no other'. In his correspondence he used and reused this word 'chance', as if America were both an opportunity but also a lottery outside his control. Departure to the States would use up what savings he had (enough to last for only four months) and would, he felt certain, sever his ties with the English newspaper editors for good. It would also mean pulling Bronwen out of Bedales, her fees having been subsidised by Helen's occasional teaching there, so the gamble was substantial: was he prepared, he asked himself, to wager his savings 'and leave the rest to chance'? What guarantees did he have? None that he could see. Some people, he acknowledged, would let their faith guide them in their decision, but not Thomas, who was adamant that he was alone when it came to such matters. 'It all comes of not believing. I will leave nothing to chance *knowingly.*'[3]

Thomas's vacillation was now bordering on comic, and even Helen teased him with a precision of wit not lost upon him. He explained to Frost, 'These last few days I have been looking at 2 alternatives, trying to enlist or coming out to America. Helen points out that I could try America and then enlist if it failed, but not the other way around.' But secretly, Thomas admitted that the venture might not necessarily include Helen. 'We shall certainly not all go to America,' he confessed to Bottomley. 'I should go alone if other things fail.' Would he really cross the Atlantic without his wife and daughters now, after the difficulties that they were beginning to overcome in their relationships? And in a time of war? When he had no income with which to support them? What about that other crossing, of the English Channel to join British soldiers in France? Was the war the more realistic outcome? 'Frankly I do not want to go,' he confessed, 'but hardly a day passes without my thinking I should. With no call, the problem is endless.'[4]

But the problem was not endless, for a poem of Frost's had arrived which would dramatically force Thomas's hand.

THE ROAD NOT TAKEN

Two roads diverged in a yellow wood,
And sorry I could not travel both
And be one traveler, long I stood
And looked down one as far as I could
To where it bent in the undergrowth;

Then took the other, as just as fair,
And having perhaps the better claim,
Because it was grassy and wanted wear;
Though as for that the passing there
Had worn them really about the same,

And both that morning equally lay
In leaves no step had trodden black.
Oh, I kept the first for another day!
Yet knowing how way leads on to way,
I doubted if I should ever come back.

I shall be telling this with a sigh
Somewhere ages and ages hence:
Two roads diverged in a wood, and I—
I took the one less traveled by,
And that has made all the difference.[5]

Noble, charismatic, wise: in the years since its composition, 'The Road Not Taken' has been understood by some as an emblem of individual choice and self-reliance, a moral tale in which the traveller takes responsibility for their own destiny. But it was never intended to be read as such by Frost, who was well aware of the playful ironies contained within it, and would go on to warn audiences, 'You have to be careful of that one;

it's a tricky poem—very tricky.' Frost knew that reading the poem as straight morality tale would pose a number of difficulties. For one: how can we evaluate the outcome of the road *not* taken? For another: had the poet chosen the road *more* travelled by, then that, presumably, would also have made all the difference. Choices might actually be equal, in other words, and Frost had set traps in the very heart of the poem intended to explode a more earnest reading. First he placed a mischievous admission about the wearing of the grass, that along each path 'the passing there | Had worn them really about the same', suggesting that neither was apparently more travelled by. And just in case the trap was missed he set another: 'both that morning equally lay | In leaves no step had trodden black', meaning that there was no discernible difference between the two paths at all. So when the poem culminates in a claim that he took the path less travelled by, it does so with its tongue in its cheek.[6]

'The Road Not Taken' is typical of Frost's skill with perspective and with mirrors: behind the neat, unfussy frontage is an experience of great depth and subtlety, and no small amount of wit. For the poem to appear wise to some and ironic to others is a credit to the sophisticated way in which Frost had become the poet 'for all sorts and kinds': no wonder it stands as such a beguiling poem in the minds of readers; no wonder it has been taken so much to heart. But the poem carried a more personal message besides, 'about a friend who had gone off to war', as he later recalled it, 'a person who, whichever road he went, would be sorry he didn't go the other'. That person was Edward Thomas.[7]

Begun, most likely, at the Gallows in the late

autumn of 1914, the poem was set in the woods of Dymock where Frost and Thomas had walked that season and on which Frost now based his mischievous tribute. *Two roads diverged in a yellow wood*: the much celebrated opening line may itself have been intended as a homage to Thomas, who had opened a 1911 story, 'Three roads meet in the midst of a little green'. (Thomas made Eleanor Farjeon a gift of that story in 1913; it is not beyond possibility that he did the same for Frost.) Many were the occasions when Thomas would guide Frost on the promise of rare wild flowers or birds' eggs, only for the walk to conclude in self-reproach when the path Thomas chose bore no such wonders. Amused at Thomas's inability to satisfy himself, Frost chided him, 'No matter which road you take, you'll always sigh, and wish you'd taken another.' But to Thomas, it was not the least bit funny. It pricked at his confidence, at his sense of fraudulence, reminding him he was neither a true writer nor a true naturalist, cowardly in his lack of direction. And now the one man who understood his indecisiveness most astutely was mocking him for it.[8]

Thomas took the 'tease' badly. He felt the poem to be a rebuke for his own inability to choose between the pursuit of poetry and a career in prose—worse, at his indecisive attitude toward the war, so often expressed to Frost. And he retorted with a sting. 'It's all very well for you poets in a yellow wood to say you choose, but you don't,' he protested. 'If you do, ergo I am no poet. I didn't choose my sex yet I was simpler then. And so I can't leave off going in after myself tho' some day I may. I didn't know after I left you at Newent

294

I was going to begin to write poetry.' Contrary to his understanding of the poem, Thomas was announcing himself as a fatalist, it was clear now. He did not believe in self-determination, or that the spirit could triumph over adversity; some things seemed unavoidable, inevitable. Had he *chosen* poetry he could not be a poet: as he had written in 'Words', it had in some sense to choose him. How free spirited his friend seemed in comparison. This American who tossed aside his teaching and sailed for England on a long-shot, knowing no one and without a place to go; who rode his literary fortunes and won his prize, then sailed again to make himself a new home. None of this was Thomas. 'It isn't in me.'[9]

It seems curious that Edward Thomas, the man who had understood Frost's writing better than anyone, could not see the poem for what it was. He puzzled at 'the simple words and unemphatic rhythms' which could not, he surmised, lead to great things. 'It staggered me to think that perhaps I had always missed what made poetry poetry if it was here,' he told the American. And he determinedly assured Frost that he had 'got the idea', when plainly he had not.[10]

Frost, a little stung, responded, 'Edward, Methinks you strikest too hard in so small a matter. A tap would have settled my poem. I wonder if it was because you were trying too much out of regard for me that you failed to see that the sigh was a mock sigh, hypocritical for the fun of the thing.' But Thomas saw no such fun: 'You have got me again over the Path not taken & no mistake . . . I doubt if you can get anybody to see the fun of the thing without showing them & advising them

295

which kind of laugh they are to turn on.' Frost had already discovered as much on reading the poem before a college audience, where it was 'taken pretty seriously', he admitted, despite 'doing my best to make it obvious by my manner that I was fooling . . . Mea culpa.'[11]

A strange but revealing exchange had occurred in which Thomas had exposed something deep within his poetry and his character. And what he had exposed was this: that choice was not, counter to his reading of Frost, an act of free will. Instead, some choices are prescribed, compelled, ingrained in circumstance or personality; some characters are 'called'.

He broke the news to Frost. 'Last week I had screwed myself up to the point of believing I should come out to America & lecture if anyone wanted me to. But I have altered my mind. I am going to enlist on Wednesday if the doctor will pass me.' Thomas made his will, granting Helen its sole execution. On Saturday 10 July he rose early and walked up through the Ashford Hanger to his study where he drafted 'The Brook', in which the poet watched his daughter paddling in the stream, when a butterfly settled on a hot stone, 'as if I were the last of men | And he the first of insects to have earth | And sun together and know their worth.' Thomas had made the same allusion in his prose piece written about his walks with Frost in Dymock, 'This England', of the urgent need to connect—to understand and fight for—the value of the landscape around him. 'Something, I felt, had to be done before I could look again composedly at English landscape,' he wrote then, 'at the elms and poplars about the houses, at the purple-headed wood-betony with two pairs of dark leaves on a stiff stem, who stood sentinel among the grasses or bracken by hedge-side or wood's-edge. What he stood sentinel for I did not know, any more than what I had got to do.' Now, finally, he knew what he had to do. Thomas was passed fit, and the same week, he sat down to lunch with his confidante, Eleanor Farjeon, and informed her that he had enlisted in the Artists Rifles, and that he was glad; he did not know why, but he was glad. Only days before it seemed certain that he would emigrate to America to join Frost, as the two men had planned. And yet suddenly, everything was different. Eleanor would later describe how, in volunteering, the 'self-torment had gone out of him'. And Helen: 'I had known that the struggle going on in his spirit would end like this.'[12]

* * *

Thomas explained himself to Frost in a letter. 'To find myself living near you and not working for editors would be better than anything I ever did and better than I dare expect,' but he could not leave now, he said, not before he had taken the King's shilling: he would have to wait out the war. 'The best way out is always through,' Frost had written in *North of Boston*, and now Thomas echoed his friend's words as he explained his enlistment: 'It is not my idea of pleasure,' he admitted, 'but I do want to go right through.' The pain in Thomas's letter was palpable. He wanted more than anything to keep alive the possibility that he might come to New England at some later time. 'There is no one to keep me here except my mother,' he confessed. And he told Frost of his first sonnet: 'A month or two [ago] I dreamt we were walking near Ledington but we lost one another in a strange place & I woke saying to myself "somehow someday I shall be here again" which I made the last line of some verses.'[13]

A DREAM

Over known fields with an old friend in dream
I walked, but came sudden to a strange
   stream.
Its dark waters were bursting out most bright
From a great mountain's heart into the light.
They ran a short course under the sun, then
   back
Into a pit they plunged, once more as black
As at their birth; and I stood thinking there
How white, had the day shone on them, they
   were,
Heaving and coiling. So by the roar and hiss
And by the mighty motion of the abyss
I was bemused, that I forgot my friend
And neither saw nor sought him till the end,
When I awoke from waters unto men
Saying: 'I shall be here some day again.'

The roar and hiss and the mighty motion of the abyss seemed unmistakably war torn, and amid the din his friend would be temporarily forgotten, neither seen nor sought until the episode was done. It had been the greatest friendship of his life, but it had been challenged first by a gamekeeper and now by the notion of a road not taken, and Thomas dreamed of forgetting his friend. Curious that he should choose this moment to explore a sonnet for the first time, a form frequently employed for love poetry, and one which he had long loathed. 'I have a dread of the sonnet,' he had written in 1902. 'It must contain 14 lines and a man must be a tremendous poet or a cold mathematician if he can accommodate his thoughts to such a condition. The result is—in my opinion—that many of the best sonnets are rhetoric only.' He wrote just seven, and a handful of double and treble sonnets; but here the form had fitted the moment exactly.[14]

Thomas's verse seemed naturally in tune with Frost in that week of his great decision. On 11 July he wrote the poem that Frost would describe as 'the loveliest of all', 'Aspens', after the whispering poplars on the crossroads at the Cricketers Inn, Steep; the next morning he wrote 'The Mill-Water', with its unmistakable tribute to Frost: 'The sound comes surging in upon the sense'. On 14 July Thomas took his army medical examination. He was seen along with six other men, stripped and measured together and made to hop around the room on each foot. He told the doctor nothing of the diabetes which he believed had begun to develop some time before 1914, and they did not spot it; he knew that had it been diagnosed it would have been grounds on which to reject him. And so he passed, and began the process of letting his friends know. At St George's Café that day, Edward Garnett was the first to receive the news, then Davies and Freeman. Jack Haines got the first letter, written that evening. 'I am enlisting. I passed the doctor today and go up on Monday to join the Artists Rifles and get turned (if possible) into an officer.' For Eleanor, he prepared a personal visit, calling at her mother's home on Fellows Road. 'I rose as he came into the room,' she wrote. 'He bent his head, and for the only time in our fours years of friendship we kissed spontaneously. He sat down saying, "Well, I've joined up."' But to Helen, he broke the news by telegram, and left her alone in Steep with her despair: '"No, no no," was all I could say; "not that".'[15]

*   *   *

On the morning of 19 July Thomas reported to 17 Dukes Road, near London's Euston station, to be attested Private 4229 in the 28th Battalion, The London Regiment (Artists Rifles). He swore his oath. 'I, Philip Edward Thomas, swear by Almighty God, that I will be faithful and bear true allegiance to His Majesty King George the Fifth, His Heirs, and Successors, and that I will, as in duty bound, honestly and faithfully defend His Majesty, His Heirs, and Successors, in Person, Crown and Dignity, against all enemies, according to the conditions of my service.' To swear before a god in whom he did not have faith, to a monarchy he had been brought up to believe was imperialist, and to defend their Person, Crown and Dignity (not *People, Country* and *Culture*): what was he agreeing to?[16]

Thomas reported for physical drill at Regent's Park the next morning, six full hours of it, but it was hardly the start that he had been hoping for, as his new army boots pressed painfully at the still-sore tendon on his right foot and he had to be put on sick leave for the remainder of the week. 'Silly to be in uniform and useless,' he told Eleanor ahead of an appointment with the doctor. 'I only hope he won't give me leisure to think why I joined. Several people *have* asked me, but I could not answer yet.' To Bottomley he could offer only the haziest of explanations, pleading that it was not a desperate resolution, nor one with a particular purpose, 'but the natural culmination of a long series of moods and thoughts'. Laid up and out of action on his first week, Thomas spent the time writing poetry from his parents' house in Balham where he had been billeted, spending six hours 'perspiring' over ten lines. He began to look over his dreaded Marlborough proofs and, more pleasantly, spent the weekend catching up with friends in and around London. He wrote regularly to Helen, but did not return at the weekend to be with her in Steep. By now she had come to be glad of one thing at least: that there was to be no move to the States; she put her store instead in the hope that the war would be over long before Edward would be sent overseas. But at that moment his mind was tuned to confrontation, and he wrote eight lines of verse that seemed to serve as a call to arms:

COCK-CROW

Out of the wood of thoughts that grows by
    night
To be cut down by the sharp axe of light,—
Out of the night, two cocks together crow,
Cleaving the darkness with a silver blow:
And bright before my eyes twin trumpeters
    stand,
Heralds of splendour, one at either hand,
Each facing each as in a coat of arms:
The milkers lace their boots up at the farms.

'Here then ends reviewing & I suppose verses, for a time,' he told Gordon Bottomley. Indeed it did: it would be four months until Thomas felt prepared to face another poem.[17]

*   *   *

Robert Frost had received the news from Edward Thomas of his enlistment. If there had been so much as a whiff of cowardice over the incident with the gamekeeper then it had been most certainly dispelled. From the farm in Franconia, New Hampshire, where he had moved in April, Frost wrote to Thomas in heroic terms. 'I am within a hair of being precisely as sorry and as glad as you are. You are doing it for the self-same reason I shall hope to do it for if my time ever comes and I am brave enough, namely, because there seems nothing else for a man to do.' Thomas would have chuckled affectionately at Frost's bluff and rhetoric, which seemed more closely aligned to the Frontier spirit than anything he would experience in the Home Counties training camps; but he would have appreciated the sentiment well enough. He was quite untroubled by the notions of masculinity that could entangle Frost at times, though he would have greatly valued the camaraderie which Frost now offered him. 'You have let me follow your thought in almost every twist and turn toward this conclusion,' Frost wrote. 'I know pretty well how far down you have gone and how far off sideways. And I think the better of you for it all. Only the very bravest could come to the sacrifice in this way.'[18]

On Monday 26 July Thomas returned from sick leave to try again at army life. For the next two weeks he wondered if his tendon would hold up to the strain of daily drill, but hold up it did. Typhoid inoculations and poor sleeping left him feverish and weary by the week's end, however, and he was grateful when Vivian Locke Ellis offered to drive him from London to Steep and back in his new motor car on the weekend of 7–8 August; Mrs Ellis came too, and stayed on with Helen to offer her company. It was as much as Thomas could manage to walk gingerly up to the hilltop study with Bronwen, who chatted in her indefatigable way: did he have his uniform yet? what was the drill like? and a dozen other questions about his new life in the army.

Thomas's billeting at his parents' at Rusham Road, Balham was, predictably, causing strain and he anxiously awaited a transfer to camp. 'My father is so rampant in his cheery patriotism that I become pro German every evening,' he reported to Frost. 'We can never so beat the Germans that they will cease to remember their victories. Pom-pom.' The Defence of the Realm Act had been introduced days before, and anyone now speaking well of the enemy could expect a fine, even for a comment made at a private dinner party; Edward must have wondered wryly whether his father might be close to invoking it. Mercifully, he believed that he would be in the Artists Rifles camp at Epping Forest within the fortnight, and once there, expected three to four months of training before deployment. But this was guesswork, he admitted, for he had no sense

303

of which regiment he might ultimately serve in or where his first commission might take him, and for the moment it did not much matter: 'one ceases to be curious'.[19]

By the fourth week he was recovered and beginning to enjoy life again. 'I am a real soldier now,' he told Frost on 10 August. 'I stand very nearly as straight as a lamp post and apparently get smaller every week in the waist and have to get new holes punched in my belt.' His day began at six each morning, polishing his buttons and belt, his boots and his badge, before leaving Balham and heading across London to Dukes Road for physical drill. He enjoyed the exercise: the running, the battlefield training, even the leap-frog that the recruits were put through daily; but he found the society strained, as he told Jack Haines. 'The drills and lectures and marches are quite interesting, but not the men— they are the worst yet, quite impossible to make friends of and everyday acquaintances, and mostly cockneys, business men, clerks etc.' The regiment was populated by those with intelligent newspaper opinions and an interest in clothes, he thought— public school, literary or professional men—in short, those quite like himself with whom he could not get along. 'It is a question now whether I should have been worse off say in the Welch Fusiliers with a mixture of clerks and shopmen and manual workers.'[20]

The Artists Rifles formed in the middle of the nineteenth century as a volunteer group of writers, painters, musicians and engravers; Minerva and Mars were their patrons. They founded their headquarters in Dukes Road in 1880, one of twenty-eight volunteer battalions that combined to form

304

the London Regiment. Dante Gabriel Rossetti had served with the Artists, as had Algernon Swinburne and William Morris. Paul Nash saw service there during the Great War, as would Wilfred Owen. Eventually, recruitment was limited by recommendation from serving members ('they let in anybody now who will pay 25/- a year subscription', Thomas complained), but for the time being it was a popular choice among university and public school graduates, who were frequently considered such capable officers that they were poached by other army units or chosen to set up Officers Training Corps. In excess of 10,000 officers were commissioned during the war after training with the Artists Rifles; the Royal Artillery alone took nearly a thousand. But they suffered appalling casualties: some 6,000 of the 15,000 serving Artists were killed, wounded or posted missing or captive.[21]

*   *   *

As Thomas settled into life with the Artists, Edward Garnett had left for duty with the Ambulance Corps on the Italian Front. T. E. Hulme was returning injured from the Western Front, while John Masefield was serving as a hospital orderly and Ralph Hodgson in the anti-aircraft squadron patrolling the east coast of England. Abercrombie, Gibson and Drinkwater were in civilian clothes; Rupert Brooke was dead. Jack Haines reported he would go mad if he enlisted, but expected that he would have to anyway. Walter de la Mare was forty-two and would be beyond even the age limit for conscription when it was introduced in 1916. W. H. Davies and

Gordon Bottomley were invalided. Harold Monro was 'in the country with his girl', said Thomas, apparently unaware of his efforts to enlist, while two other visitors to the Poetry Bookshop, Siegfried Sassoon and Robert Graves, were now serving in France. Wilfred Owen was still a civilian teacher, but he had now made his decision to enlist.[22]

Edward Thomas had felt that none of his friends besides Frost had seemed willing to help his poetry forward that summer, but Lascelles Abercrombie now would. He was prospecting for an anthology of contemporary verse that he was hoping to co-edit for Constable, and when Bottomley showed him the poems that Thomas had sent him, Abercrombie agreed at once that they should be included. *An Anthology of New Poetry* would come out in March 1917, a month before Thomas's death; it would be the only time that he saw a selection of his work in print. Across the Atlantic, Robert Frost was toasting news which testified to the new readership that he was winning. 'The Road Not Taken' appeared in the *Atlantic Monthly* in August 1915. But if he mentioned this to Thomas then that particular letter has gone astray.[23]

AUTUMN

As Edward Thomas walked through the streets of Balham with his daughter Bronwen, he began to feel the south London crowds pressing in on him. 'I stand it better with her,' he told Frost, 'but it is pretty bad—all the mean or villa streets that have filled the semi-rural places I knew 25 years ago.' It was a strange and strained existence he now lived: a thirty-seven-year-old man billeted with his parents, settled in neither army nor literary work, separated from his wife and children apart from the weekend reunions under the scrutiny of his father. But the training drills at least had become more adventurous: mapping on Hampstead Heath on 6 September, night operations on the 9th. Thomas was assigned guard duties—twenty-four hours on, twenty-four hours off—and given musket training, map-making lectures and a troop to march around the Heath weekly; 'It is all like being somebody else.' Tired from the drill work, numbed by the routine, Thomas felt his perspectives beginning to warp. 'The country is a little strange to me,' he confessed to Frost. 'It seems as if in my world there was no Autumn though they are picking hops in Kent. On Hampstead Heath the other day I watched the bees at the bramble flowers and green blackberries and they looked so unfamiliar and with a kind of ugliness, partly but not wholly due to the fact that the earth around was dirty London earth.' As if to restore some normality to his senses, he tried to coax these thoughts into blank verse in his head, but failed to finish them and the lines drifted

307

out of reach. The transfer to camp could not come soon enough.[1]

On 17 September Thomas made the move that he had longed for, by train from Liverpool Street station out to High Beech Camp near Loughton, Essex, on the fringe of Epping Forest. He was already familiar with the area's literary history (Alfred, Lord Tennyson had written 'In Memoriam' in the village at the same time that John Clare was at the neighbouring asylum), but he was less intimate with the countryside itself, and so had travelled up previously to acquaint himself with his new surroundings. Epping Forest he found a miniature paradise, crowded with oaks and beeches and bustling with wild flowers and deer, but the camp proved to be something quite else: noisy and draughty and ugly, he thought, badly arranged, dirty. It was also semi-deserted when he arrived, with half of the men on leave, and Thomas found himself hanging around restlessly, escaping for walks to nearby Loughton or Theydon Bois. He described the scene to Jack Haines. 'We are in huts, nearly a hundred of us in a big corrugated iron room formerly used for Sunday school treats etc to feed in. High Beech is a great pleasure resort, high in the middle of Epping Forest. The conditions are cramped and not over clean. The food is ill-cooked and ill-served, and has to be eaten in haste in a dark dirty room that the rain comes into. And the nights are cold.'[2]

Thomas did his best to settle in, in those first weeks at the end of September, but found the situation isolating and the routines stultifying. In fact, 'dismal' was the word Thomas used to describe his moods by the start of October. Whether it was the company or the discomfort or the solitude, he could not say, but he felt his spirits lowering once again. No one sought out his companionship in those early weeks, nor did he seek theirs: the Artists were not making a good impression. 'I suppose writers generally have been people who tasted far more things than they ever swallowed,' he wrote to Helen. There were exceptions, he continued: Shelley had been an activist, Tennyson a volunteer, 'And I—,' he wrote dryly, 'dig in the garden.' But worse than the company was the restriction on his movements, forbidding him to wander in Epping Forest or slip away back to London. It annoyed him to think that 'a foxhunting major' had the power to deny him leave on a whim. He could not take pleasure even in reading, as he explained to Walter de la Mare. 'I don't think about books or writing except on a sleepless night when I sometimes make a few lines and a half and don't bother to write them down.' The poems were slipping away from him in his fatigued state, and he was resentful of the aimless physical labour, digging channels in the heavy clay, spading it into the barrow, carting it away, all watched over by a bullying officer: 'The hardest work I ever did,' he told de la Mare, and a waste of time to boot, he felt, when that time might be better spent improving his leadership skills. 'Apparently any man who will stand up and get shot is useful however hurried his training,' he told Frost wearily, and shortly after that he succumbed to an injured knee that would lame him for two days. Finally, his despondency did tip into verse. 'Some day I shall think this a happy day, | And this mood by the name of melancholy | Shall no more blackened and obscured be,' he wrote gloomily, in

309

the first poem he had written since enlisting in the summer. And his mood was not a bit improved to learn that his younger brother Reggie had enlisted with the Artists, and would soon be joining him at camp.[3]

*   *   *

Despite the cutbacks that publishers made in their commissioning they were at least honouring their existing commitments; indeed they were doing so expeditiously, noted Thomas, before conditions worsened. 'My books come streaming out,' he told Bottomley, as no fewer than three appeared at once: the dreaded *Life of the Duke of Marlborough* from Chapman and Hall at a pricey 10s. 6d., while Duckworth issued *Four-and-Twenty Blackbirds* at 2s. 6d. and Oxford University Press published the anthology he had edited, *This England*. The trio received 'friendly useless reviews', he told Frost, but included in *This England* were two poems by Thomas himself under the name of 'Edward Eastaway', which he had inserted at the eleventh hour after the publisher asked him to fill two blank pages that had arisen in the typesetting. 'Haymaking' and 'The Manor Farm' became the first publication of his poems in book form, and joined the 'House and Man' and 'Interval', which had recently appeared in his friend James Guthrie's *Root and Branch* magazine, as among the first of his poems to have been published anywhere. Edward Marsh, however, had decided against the inclusion of either Thomas or Frost in his second volume of *Georgian Poetry*, not caring for Thomas's verse and imposing a new rule to exclude overseas writers from consideration. *Georgian Poetry 1913–1915* would go through 19,000 copies in nineteen impressions, but Thomas could hardly have cared less. His letters were becoming less literary and more focussed upon army life and war. 'The air here is full of rumours. Some say we are all going to leave the camp in a week to make way for 300 young officers. There is a remote chance that they may try to turn me into an instructor of some kind. I am rather loth to entertain the idea, partly because now I have taken the step the only way to satisfy my vanity is to become an officer and go out.' If anything, Thomas had more interest in the welfare of his family now that he was forcibly parted from them. He saw Bronwen whenever he had leave for London, and kept in close touch with Helen over Myfanwy, and in his letters to Frost he asked frequently after Mervyn, who was temporarily lodging with the family in Franconia. Edward and Helen now hoped the boy would return to England in December to take up the schooling they had arranged for him in Coventry. At long last, Thomas expressed an interest in and anxiety for the well-being of his son.[4]

*   *   *

Temperatures in camp dipped regularly below freezing in November. Icy rain gave way to snow, four inches of it on the 15th. Thomas had been promoted to lance corporal, the second tier of non-commissioned officer ranking just above private, in charge of a dozen men for five days a week. His duties involved helping the men with their

311

understanding of the lectures, and guiding them with the use of a compass and protractor to sketch the kind of topographic detail on their manoeuvres that could be put to military advantage; it was a good application of Thomas's eye for natural detail. Instructing the men was beginning to ease his long-standing fear of teaching, and he let Frost know that he would be better equipped to teach in an American summer school in future.[5]

When Helen wrote to say that she was suffering from influenza, Thomas took leave to look after her. It was to be a surprise, but the surprise backfired on him emotionally; he returned to find the house in a mess and Helen 'as much scared and surprised as pleased' to see him, and he felt the familiar depression overtake him. He descended to what he called 'the old level' that he had come to associate with Steep, and realised that his army work had been acting as a counterbalance to his spirits. 'Does one really get rid of things at all by steadily inhibiting them for a long time on end?' he asked Frost. 'Am I indulging in the pleasure of being someone else?' Thomas returned to London to find that he had been asked to report to a new camp not far from High Beech: Hare Hall, in Gidea Park, Romford.[6]

*   *   *

At Dukes Road, in Euston, where Edward Thomas had signed up, a new signatory had added his name to the Artists Rifles on 21 October. Wilfred Owen had failed in his bid for a university scholarship and had left England in 1914 to teach in France when the war had broken out. For another year he remained in France, nonchalant, he said, toward the horrors of the conflict despite having seen the mutilation at first hand on a visit to a war hospital. But by the summer of 1915 he was fully intent on enlisting, and returned to England that September to volunteer for the Artists Rifles. On 20 October he underwent his medical, receiving a typhoid injection that badly inflamed his arm, though not enough to prevent him taking his oath the next day, nor from attending a reading at the Poetry Bookshop that night. Owen had made visits to the Bookshop earlier in the year, but now over the next month he would become a regular caller, returning the following week when he listened to a gloomy recital by Harold Monro and exchanged a few words with the bookshop's owner. On 4 November 1915 Owen returned once more, this time in uniform. He remembered the sound of his new army boots clomping up the workshop stairs and the admiring looks of what he called the 'poetic ladies'; he recalled also the glance given to him by Monro, saddened to see yet another young poet enlisted. Owen had written only two dozen poems by then, and had just rented a room above a coffee house opposite the Bookshop at 5s. 6d. per week: 'a plain enough affair—candlelight—no bath'. But no sooner had he taken the room than he received his orders to report to Hare Hall training camp.[7]

Owen would get a chance to return when a week's instruction in London later that winter allowed him to take a room in the Poetry Bookshop itself. At the week's end, when Owen was packing for his return to camp, Harold Monro climbed the stairs to the attic rooms with the manuscript that Owen had given him. 'So we sit down,' Owen recorded excitedly, 'and I have the time of my life. For he was "very struck" with these sonnets. He went over things in detail and told me what was fresh and clever, and what was second-hand and banal; and what was Keatsian, and what "modern". He summed up their value as far above that of the Little Books of Georgian Verse.' Owen was a long way from the outpouring of verse that he would experience at Craiglockhart War Hospital on the outskirts of Edinburgh in the autumn of 1917. As Monro leafed through the poems, there was scant trace of the poet Owen would within two years become: it would take the savagery of the St Quentin trenches and the friendship of Siegfried Sassoon to instil that in him.[8]

On 15 November Wilfred Owen joined his company at Liverpool Street station and boarded the train that would take him to Gidea Park. On the same station platform were Edward Thomas and his brother Reggie, entering Hare Hall on the very same day.

'No one much wants to go into camp in low country Essex only 12 miles from London, and in winter,' Thomas wrote to Frost, 'but they say it is a particularly good camp. The huts etc. were prepared for the Sportsman's Battalion and filled up at unusual expense by some of the rich members of the Battalion.' The camp was designed and built by the architects and engineers who served in it to hold 1,400 men in forty long huts, with a canteen, hospital and sergeants' mess: twelve companies in three battalions in all. 'All very nicely set out here,' Owen reported mildly, as he and Thomas settled in.[9]

'I wonder would you recognize me with hair

cropped close and carrying a thin little swagger cane,' Thomas wrote to Frost, adding, 'I was never so well or in so balanced a mood'. And he wrote to his mother's sister in California in similar vein, telling her that he had enjoyed his training at almost every point, and had been shown nothing but kindness in camp. 'I really hope my turn will come and that I shall see what it really is and come out of it with my head and most of my limbs.'[10]

But if Thomas's spirits were buoyant, Frost's were not. Elinor's pregnancy had ended in miscarriage; in a reversal of form, it was the American who now wrote melancholically. 'I have reached the point this evening where no letter to or from you will take the place of seeing you. I am simply down on the floor kicking and thrashing with resentment against everything as it is. I like nothing, neither being here with you there and so hard to talk to nor being so ineffectual at my years to help myself or anyone else.' Frost doubted Thomas's revived spirits. In Dymock, they had felt able to run themselves down without reproach, but now Frost worried that an equilibrium might have become unbalanced. Behind his friend's reports of happiness, Frost suspected that there was a nihilism in Thomas that was fuelling his high spirits. Thomas had written that he did not look forward with any anxiety, but merely looked forward 'without a thought to something'. 'I don't want you to die,' Frost wrote. '(I confess I wanted you to face the possibility of death): I want you to come over here and begin all over the life we had in St Martin's Lane at Tyler's Green at White Leaved Dale and at Balham. Use should decide it for you. If you can be more useful living than dying I dont see that you have to go behind that. Dont be run away with by your nonsense.'[11]

Yet Thomas's moods were not quite as he presented them to his aunt or Frost. With others he was more variable, telling Eleanor that he continued to find companionship a problem, that he had always found communion difficult unless with someone like Frost. To Jack Haines he admitted that he knew his happiness might not lie in England: 'I can't see that there will be anything for me when the War is over, if I am alive and well, but to go to New Hampshire and start afresh.' But the routine was at least comfortable enough for him to find time once again to write verse. He was now wholly dependent upon Eleanor for typing and sent her two poems for putting into typescript. But he kept his writing entirely secret from his camp colleagues. His reservation is a matter of regret, for only a few huts away was Wilfred Owen, who likewise was keeping his early verses to himself. Had the two men declared their interest then they would surely have taken to one another's company. Thomas would have liked Owen for his gentle, unassuming presence, his passionate belief in the power of verse, his sharp intelligence and his knowledge of Wales. Owen would have flourished under Thomas's guidance, learned from his knowledge of literature and welcomed the kind of senior patronage that he would find in Siegfried Sassoon. Fifteen years the junior, it remains a tantalising thought that Owen might have learned about speech rhythms and sound-sense from Edward Thomas at such an impressionable age. Owen would go on to write some of the most graphic, shocking and energised poetry of the war, but who knows how it might have developed under Thomas's guiding eye. Owen was probably instructed in map-reading by Edward Thomas, but being at the time outside the professional literary world, he would not have recognised his tutor for the literary critic he was. It seems likely that two of the finest poets of the war may have seen each other or even spoken, before going about their army business none the wiser.[12]

*   *   *

Whatever the reason for the swings in Thomas's mood and for the differing reports that he gave, there may have been one new factor at play that he was largely concealing from his friends. In November, Thomas made a social call on a woman he had not seen in more than fifteen years. She lived only a few miles from Hare Hall Camp and was a poet and painter, trained at the Slade by Henry Tonks. She was a year younger than Thomas, beautiful, a mother of two; and she was desperately lonely. Her friendship with Edward would pose Helen Thomas a sterner test than was ever presented by Eleanor Farjeon. Her name was Edna Clarke Hall.

WINTER

Great House, near Upminster Common, a few miles from Hare Hall Camp, was a red-brick Georgian farmhouse with tall chimneys and a large bay window which opened outward onto a wild overrun garden. The house was surrounded by so many trees that on first appearance it seemed to have grown out of a coppice. Elm floorboards were laid throughout, and the house was furnished by curiosities that the owner had acquired over the years: a Clementi piano rescued from a local tavern, a delicate pearwood writing desk. The house was home to William and Edna Clarke Hall, but more so to Edna, as her husband was very rarely at home.

Edna Clarke Hall had exhibited her watercolours annually with Vanessa Bell's Friday Club since 1910; in April 1914 a successful solo exhibition at the Chenil Gallery in Chelsea showed fifty-six works and grossed £147 in sales. Shortly after, she temporarily set aside her paints to spend the next two years on verse. Her life in Essex was lonely. William Clarke Hall was a barrister and campaigner for children's rights who spent lengthy weeks in his chambers at Gray's Inn, leaving his wife feeling isolated in their country house. The couple had two boys of their own, but Edna could not forgive her husband's decision to apply his energies to the children of his charity work, some of whom were foundlings, abandoned by prostitutes. William would return at the weekends with an orphan in tow, sometimes leaving Edna to care for the child when he returned to London the next week. For

Edna, the longing and the hurt was intense. 'O why does a man engrose [sic] his mind in this cause of prostitutes leaving his wife sick to the heart in loneliness,' she wrote in her journal.[1]

On a cold day in November 1915, Edna returned to Great House from London, where she had spent a restless night in a strange hotel, recalling a face 'young and sad and full of exquisite gentleness'. The face belonged to Edward Thomas, and on recalling him instantly, she said, 'the little room became sacred with his incense'. Edna and Edward met around the turn of the century, when even then it was apparent to both that her marriage seemed to lack understanding. Thomas used to visit her then in the company of a solicitor friend who would discuss law with William, leaving Edna and Edward to one another's company. '*They* are *there*—', said Edward flirtatiously, '*we are here*—'. Each recorded a physical awareness of the other, and Thomas went so far as to tell Edna that Helen had become one of her admirers after he described her beauty to his wife, 'though I will swear that I have not done you justice in my descriptions'. Helen saw Edna for herself in the autumn of 1900, and was intimidated, she told Edna, by her presence. 'You came unexpectedly and you had your arms full of autumn branches and I felt very shy of you because of your beauty and your sweetness, because you had so much that because of my love for Edward I hoped to have.' There was an ease and an intimacy about Thomas's manner with Edna in those turn-of-the-century days, and in 1900 he told her, 'I live—if living it may be called—by my writing, "literature" we call it in Fleet St. (*derived from "litter", as we say "a litter of pigs" or "he made an awful litter"*).'[2]

Fifteen years had passed before Edna's dream of Edward in the 'strange hotel' in 1915. Edna herself takes up the story of what happened next.

But that day when I returned home Willie greeted me with 'who do you think came here yesterday?' My mind said 'Edward Thomas' but my lips questioned 'who?' 'M.__ P. __'! answered Willie and though I would give him welcome my 'O really' was a flimsy disguise to the disappointment to that sense of inner certainty which the name had contradicted— and then came from Willie—'who do you think came with him?' I held my answer which this time came leaping to my lips and well content to my 'tell me?' I heard the name from his
   'Edward Thomas.'
   And when he came again the next day I spoke of that—and he spoke of the clay as we sat by the open fire with the window on either side.

Edna's journals are littered with the word 'clay'. It was a medium she understood artistically, but its value here lies in the symbol that she associated with Thomas, as she described him, 'he clay if you will'. In her journal she wrote out his line from 'Wind and Mist'—'the clay first broke my heart and then my back'—before setting to verse their meeting that November day.

I spoke yesterday of that strange
Heralding on your return that came to me
You spoke to me of clay—

320

Thus sitting quiet, my son upon my knee
At open hearth where orchard wood did burn
We met again with words spoke casually
Of pshycie [sic] hours and heavy clay by turn
Your words gave weight to what I had to say
And mine did lightly penetrate your clay.[3]

Over his eight months stationed at Hare Hall
Camp, Thomas became a frequent caller, though
how frequent neither he nor Edna recorded. The
two would walk together in the fields and lanes
surrounding the house, gathering fallen wood
from the orchard with which they would feed the
open fire as they talked of their arts of poetry and
painting.

When in the barn studio he found a drawing
of our road dipping down he said that he had
often prayed they would never be asked to
march down there because of the mystery it
held for him, and then finding a watercolour—
trees and a woman and goat by the road side
he was filled with pleasure—'I am glad you
like that but why do you?' 'Because it is so
true.'
Thomas standing a little apart wrote
something. 'Are you still at your mapping?' I
asked. 'No' he said 'I was only making a note—
it is a bad habit I have.' and he smiled a little
saying it.[4]

Thomas's gentle understanding of Edna's domestic
plight, and their rangy, artistic conversations and
shared interests, were a lifeline to Edna that winter
of 1915. Throughout her journals she captured

many of his characteristic, gentle touches.

> There is a smile at the corner of those lips
> where pride with tenderness dwell—There is
> ease in the quiet manner and in the blue of
> those eyes like thoughts shy and perfect as a
> bird—elusive as the unknown bird he tells of
> in the earthly woodlands.
>
> > O genius of Edward Thomas
> > you are dearly loved—
> > give me your flowers.[5]

As 1915 drew to a close, Thomas seemed changed. He was happier—at least at camp, though lonely and missing the friendship of Robert Frost. His work as a map instructor had brought him a new confidence in his abilities to teach and impart his skills, and the routine of army life had given him a structure within which he could contain the darker urges of his depression. But his hesitations about the war itself continued to surface: he questioned the motivation of the conflict, despised its jingoism and profiteering, and could not abide the brutish xenophobia that it engendered by the 'the cross-eyed gents' who ran the newspapers. On 26 November he had jotted the first lines to a poem that would be his angriest response yet to the war; one month later, on Boxing Day 1915, he completed a draft in verse.

THIS IS NO CASE OF PETTY RIGHT OR WRONG

> This is no case of petty right or wrong
> That politicians or philosophers

Can judge. I hate not Germans, nor grow hot
With love of Englishmen, to please newspapers.
Beside my hate for one fat patriot
My hatred of the Kaiser is love true:—
A kind of god he is, banging a gong.
But I have not to choose between the two,
Or between justice and injustice. Dinned
With war and argument I read no more
Than in the storm smoking along the wind
Athwart the wood. Two witches' cauldrons roar.
From one the weather shall rise clear and gay;
Out of the other an England beautiful
And like her mother that died yesterday.
Little I know or care if, being dull,
I shall miss something that historians
Can rake out of the ashes when perchance
The phoenix broods serene above their ken.
But with the best and meanest Englishmen
I am one in crying, God save England, lest
We lose what never slaves and cattle blessed.
The ages made her that made us from the dust:
She is all we know and live by, and we trust
She is good and must endure, loving her so:
And as we love ourselves we hate her foe.[6]

Mervyn arrived home from America on Sunday 19 December, but he had missed his connecting train to Steep and so missed his father, who had had to be back in Hare Hall for 9.15 that evening. Edward managed to get home the following week and spent time walking with his son. He told Eleanor, 'Mervyn met me and I hardly knew him,'—he found his son easier in temper, as he himself had become, and he wrote to Frost that they took pleasure in one another's company. For the first time in almost a year the family were all together: Helen, Bronwen, Myfanwy, Edward and Mervyn, each one pleased to be spending their Christmas together at Steep.[7]

On New Year's Day, Thomas got away from camp and up to London, but he had a quarrelsome day. He saw his father, and this time the simmering disagreements about the war broke out fully into the open. 'He made me very sick,' Thomas recounted to Frost. 'He treats me so that I have a feeling of shame that I am alive. I couldn't sleep after it. Nothing much happened. We argued about the war and he showed that his real feeling when he is not trying to be nice and comfortable is one of contempt. I know what contempt is and partly what I suffered was from the reminder that I had probably made Helen feel exactly the same.' Over the weeks that followed Thomas composed the only poem about his father that he would write, a scornful, poisonous verse dripping with animosity.

> I may come near loving you
> When you are dead
> And there is nothing to do
> And much to be said.

Edward would not see that day; his father died in 1920. It would be some time before Helen would release the poem for publication; when she did, Walter de la Mare queried the openness of its punctuation with the poetry editor of its publishing house, T. S. Eliot, who replied, 'I do not find the slight ambiguity unpleasing.'[8]

Thomas returned to camp more drearily than ever before following the row with his father. 'I shall recover, but it makes a difference and I am inclined not to see him again for a time.' He called on Monro at the Poetry Bookshop, but found the proprietor in cantankerous form, delighting in opinions that were given, believed Thomas, simply for the sake of self-assertion. 'It will be a good thing if I don't see Monro again,' said Thomas, who seemed to be turning from anyone he could. But there was at least one piece of news that pleased him from his visit to the Poetry Bookshop: Ralph Hodgson, he learned, with whom he had quarrelled about the war, had 'sent his love to me, so I am forgiven'.[9]

*   *   *

If the row with his father overshadowed Thomas's first week back at camp, a move to a new company did little to improve his mood. The fastidiousness of their morning parade was a daily irritant. Although only a lance corporal, Thomas was the senior officer in the hut, which meant he had to take charge of its twenty men, organising cleaning duties, supervising mealtimes and calling the roll. He admitted to Eleanor that he was not really enjoying it and had been out of sorts since the row with his father. And to top it all, Thomas ran foul of the authorities after covering for one of his men, the artist Arnold Mason, and signing him present when he knew him to be stealing a few hours' extra leave; when Mason did not return until the next morning he and Thomas were each hauled up before the senior officers for 'serious talks', which Thomas suspected might impede his chances of a promotion to full corporal.[10]

Thomas began to draft 'Rain', set in the camp's

325

Hut 51 but drawing heavily on that evening in 1911 when he was caught in the blackening downpour along the Icknield Way. Thomas had continually drawn upon his field notebooks to aid his memory, but on this occasion he had lifted his published prose.

RAIN

Rain, midnight rain, nothing but the wild rain
On this bleak hut, and solitude, and me
Remembering again that I shall die
And neither hear the rain nor give it thanks
For washing me cleaner than I have been
Since I was born into this solitude.
Blessed are the dead that the rain rains upon:
But here I pray that none whom once I loved
Is dying tonight or lying still awake
Solitary, listening to the rain,
Either in pain or thus in sympathy
Helpless among the living and the dead,
Like a cold water among broken reeds,
Myriads of broken reeds all still and stiff,
Like me who have no love which this wild rain
Has not dissolved except the love of death,
If love it be towards what is perfect and
Cannot, the tempest tells me, disappoint.[11]

Thomas was indeed denied his promotion to corporal in retribution for his misdemeanour with Arnold Mason. The episode left him feeling inadequate, and not succeeding as he instinctively felt he should, while his teaching was bringing only mixed results. When the call for officers came in that month Thomas gave it serious consideration. 'I felt inclined to volunteer for France when 300 were asked for last week, and I still hope we may (all of us instructors) go if only for a time just to get me out of this camp to a different kind of mind.' And coming home from Hare Hall that weekend of 22 January, Thomas put to paper a sixty-four-line poem that he had begun to turn over in his head the week before, and which very clearly now pointed towards the next step in his journey:

> Now all roads lead to France
> And heavy is the tread
> Of the living; but the dead
> Returning lightly dance:
>
> Whatever the road bring
> To me or take from me,
> They keep me company
> With their pattering,
>
> Crowding the solitude
> Of the loops over the downs,
> Hushing the roar of towns
> And their brief multitude.[12]

As the winter deepened, something began to change in the poetry that Edward Thomas was writing. In January and February, and then again in March and April, a string of poems mined, or struggled to mine, the subject of love. By the early spring there were seven pieces, another by the middle of May. He had written little love poetry among his first hundred poems, and those he did compose were largely rhetorical or song-based verses that could hardly be described as confessional. But there was something different in the tone of the pieces that

327

winter and spring, something concentrated, even wilful. Was he simply deepening the range of his craft with the love lyric, or was he experiencing anguish at his separation from home and Helen? Or was he touched by a different proximity altogether: the return into his life of another woman who had stirred something deep within him?

The first of these lyrics, 'The clouds that are so light', seemed to speak knowingly of the interdependence of the observed and the observer, the muse and poet: 'Away from your shadow on me | Your beauty less would be'. It was a coquettish, even mysterious poem, which Edward sent to Helen, as was his habit, though her questioning of it revealed that she had deemed it not to be a piece about herself. Thomas was short tempered in his response. 'Fancy your thinking that I might have someone in view in those verses beginning "The clouds that are so light",' he wrote. 'Fancy your being pleased at the idea. Well, perhaps you wouldn't be, if there really were someone, in which case I would hardly write verses, I think.' The phrasing seemed peculiar, goading even, *if there really were someone*: why say what there was no need to say, why plant a seed of worry? Perhaps realising that he had overstepped the mark, Thomas tried a consolatory tone. 'Oh, you needn't think of another lady. There would have to be 2 to make a love affair and I am only one.' But this was still ambiguous: was there then 'another lady'? Did 'one' of the '2' wish for a love affair? Finally, Thomas struck a tone of reassurance. 'Nobody but you would ever be likely to respond as I wished. I don't like to think anybody but I could respond to you. If you turned to anybody else I should come to an end immediately.' Helen took huge comfort from the moments when Edward addressed her with affection. To her it harked back to more romantic days when the demand for love seemed mutual and dependent; it also gave her hope that the time ahead would be a better one. But what had Thomas stirred up?[13]

On past experience alone Helen had cause to worry. Thomas had spent the winter of 1907–8 in Minsmere on the Suffolk coast, preparing his biography of Richard Jefferies, with a family for whom Helen had been a governess when she was courting Edward. Hope Webb had been a favourite of Helen's then, and now, aged eighteen, she had grown into an attractive girl, as Thomas reported to Bottomley at the time. 'I got very fond of a girl of 17 [sic] with two long plaits of dark brown hair & the richest grey eyes, very wild & shy, to whom I could not say 10 words, nor she to me . . . But I liked her for her perfect wild youthfulness & remoteness from myself & now I think of her every day in vain acquiescent dissatisfaction, & shall perhaps never see her again, & shall be sad to hear she ever likes anyone else even tho she will never like me.' Over the Christmas holidays that year, Edward and Hope had taken walks along the coast, collected pebbles and shells (and a human skull for Walter de la Mare that had rolled out of the crumbling cliff-top graveyard); he had settled in to tactful criticism of her teenage verses. 'I had the sharpest pains and pleasures of satisfaction, longing and - - - -' Thomas broke off a letter to de la Mare at the time. When Hope returned to school in January 1908, Thomas stayed on in Suffolk and lent her books and wrote her letters, and urged her to keep their wanderings secret. 'I have become so deeply corrupted,' he told a friend at the time. 'My wife and family are quite forgotten among these delights.' Thomas experienced a kind of fretful giddiness and could not concentrate on his book; he sent her his *Pocket Book of Poems and Songs for the Open Air* and felt what he referred to at the time as 'a strong unreasoning liking' for the girl. It was at this point that he shared his feelings quite matter-of-factly with Helen.[14]

Helen responded in a string of letters, with each one expressing more anxiety than the last. 'If I was the Webbs, I'd be proud to think that you loved Hope,' she wrote with initial restraint, 'for they might see with half an eye that you are not the sort to enter her room at night, or kiss her behind the door—unless she wanted you to. Well never mind sweetheart, perhaps she loves you—in her way,—she's reading Jefferies, that's something isn't it?' But the next day her tone had become more concerned. 'Hope's written again to you, and you to her I suppose. I wonder (I do really so please tell me, I'm quite serious) what you want her to develop into, or what you want "it" to develop into. You are fond of her, but you can't make her fond of you without making it difficult for her. Is it to be the friendship of a middle aged man, a man of letters etc. etc. and of a simple schoolgirl, the sort of idyllic affair that your biographers will dote on—a passionless, innocent, intimate, uncleish, loverish affair that makes one wish in reading the biography that "I" had been the girl. Is it to be that sort? Or is she meant to slip unconsciously into something more, with sentiment in it, and heart openings, and in fact a love affair, or what? It puzzles me . . . Do tell me . . . I don't know if I'm any better for having written this letter, or if I'll cry myself to sleep.' Next Helen urged her husband to come to his senses: 'you will be careful won't you; she's so very young, so very ignorant, and you don't know her a bit, what she is at all, only that she's different from the others, dark haired and dark eyed'. And then Helen made a risky move: rather than repel Edward's feelings, she offered to bring them into their inner circle. 'I don't want anything else at all if you'll love me,' she wrote. 'I want you to love Hope if you'll love me, too. But I'm so different I don't see how you can.' What followed were a series of pounding love letters in which Helen stressed her understanding and his need for independence. 'The greatest thing I could do for you would be to slip away,' she had written on Valentine's Day 1908.[15]

Helen's departure would not be necessary. Thomas's exchanges with Hope were unsatisfying, as he knew they would be, for he understood full well that his interest in the girl was consolation against a depression that 'no doctor can cure me of'. Hope did not keep her own counsel, as Thomas had asked, but confided in her sister, who, knowing that Thomas was a married man and suspecting his intentions, passed chapter and verse onto her parents. Thomas was interviewed by her irate father, who demanded that no further contact with his daughter be had, and a humiliated Thomas bid his friends not to speak of it. Helen believed that Edward had taken a cruel pleasure in stoking her jealousy; but he had at least responded by inviting her to join him in Minsmere, which she did. The episode was concluded; Edward tried to curb his unkindness, Helen to improve the home life that she offered.

331

She had handled the episode deftly: encouraging his sense of independence, understanding his desires, praising his attractiveness and appealing subtly to the impeccability of his morals. Five years later she would manage the arrival of Eleanor Farjeon in a similar way, bringing her into the inner circle and supervising the feelings of all involved; but she was not able to extend the same influence with the older, wiser and more beautiful Edna Clarke Hall.[16]

The friendship of Edward and Edna progressed delicately, without scandal and without causing pain to anyone else. Edna was captivated by the return into her life of her former friend; the private journals she kept after his death are teeming with rich, physical and sometimes intimate descriptions of Thomas. She wrote out in full or in part no fewer than fifteen of his poems in her journals, and many of her own besides, as she explained to him in a letter after his death.

> Dear Edward, I fear it is your lot to bear upon your stalwart but ghostly shoulder the responsibility of many nerves and I must confess to you—so dear among the dead—that you have been an inspiration to me, and that many verses are written to you, but there are some *not* penned in your name—and it is these unnamed that may in the imagination of the few be yet so placed. I see you smile—you make no trouble of it? dear friend! then all is well.

Typical of Edna's many verses:

TO E. T.

Remote and still you stood a little space
With eyes scarce lowered 'gainst the rays that
    sought them
And warmly touched the lips that could have
    taught them
How beauty dwells in any sunlit place
And thus you stood the sunlight on your face.

But Thomas, in the next of the winter love poems, his first in February and among the most brutally honest of any in his collection, chose to make an announcement of a very different sort: a lyric which questioned his capacity to love at all, setting the grander claims of the love poets ('Those things that poets said') against his more muted personal experience.

> For certainly not thus,
> Then or thereafter, I
> Loved ever. Between us
> Decide, good Love, before I die.

> Only, that once I loved
> By this one argument
> Is very plainly proved:
> I loving not am different.

Who, if anyone, did Thomas now address? Was he working through his withdrawal from Helen or conveying a message to Edna that he was incapable of love? Or was he simply talking to nobody but himself? It seemed for whatever reason that in his verse he now felt the need to explore or explain himself romantically. And two days after the last poem, came another, this one untitled.

No one so much as you
Loves this my clay,
Or would lament as you
Its dying day.
You know me through and through
Though I have not told,
And though with what you know
You are not bold.

None ever was so fair
As I thought you:
Not a word can I bear
Spoken against you.

All that I ever did
For you seemed coarse
Compared with what I hid
Nor put in force.

My eyes scarce dare meet you
Lest they should prove
I but respond to you
And do not love.

We look and understand,
We cannot speak
Except in trifles and
Words the most weak.

For I at most accept
Your love, regretting
That is all: I have kept

Only a fretting

That I could not return
All that you gave
And could not ever burn
With the love you have,

Till sometimes it did seem
Better it were
Never to see you more
Than linger here

With only gratitude
Instead of love—
A pine in solitude
Cradling a dove.[17]

For the second time Helen found herself
questioning the inspiration behind Edward's new
poem. Thomas told her that these were verses to his
mother, and it is not beyond possibility they might
have begun that way in the mind of the author.
Thomas was on sick leave and had been staying at
Balham with his parents at the time, and the only
surviving manuscript shows that he had struck out
'London' as the place of composition (replacing
it with 'Going home on sick leave' to Steep); his
mother may well have been in his thoughts then,
not least because he had written the poisoned
verses to his father only three days before. But by
the conclusion of the poem the addressee seemed
not to be a mother at all but a person to whom the
'I' was incapable of returning affection: a lover, in
other words, or rather a former or potential lover;
Helen, perhaps, whom he was heading home to

335

see that day, or possibly there lies a clue planted knowingly or otherwise by its author—'clay', which had already become a kind of codeword that he shared with Edna Clarke Hall.

The love poems he wrote in the winter of 1916 do not point neatly to one person; nor should it be assumed that their author was in love in order to have written them (he had stressed that he was not). In response to this last poem, Thomas had been at pains to tell Helen that he was in fact incapable of loving:

> you know my usual belief is that I don't and can't love and haven't done for something near 20 years. You know too that you don't think my nature really compatible with love, being so clear and critical. You know how unlike I am to you, and you know that you love, so how can I?

He held no naive assumptions about the true subject of love poetry. In 1910 he had written:

> Love-poetry, like all other lyric poetry, is in a sense unintentionally overheard, and only by accident and in part understood, since it is written not for any one, far less for the public, but for the understanding spirit that is in the air round about or in the sky or somewhere.

That 'understanding spirit' might well have been Thomas himself, for it seems likely that these poems were written as much in address to himself as ever they were to another person. Why give your lover a mere poem, Thomas wrote once, when the gift

336

of love itself was on offer? 'The love-poem is not for the beloved, for it is not worthy, as it is the least thing that is given'. He understood that the most apparently intimate poem may be a performance. 'A poet writes always of his personal life,' said W. B. Yeats, but with a caveat: 'there is always phantasmagoria'. Thomas's poems are filled with a 'phantasmagoria' of fictive voices and imaginative episodes, and it would be an underestimation of his creative powers to read them as mere transcriptions of life events. Nevertheless, there were moments in his poetry when the distance between art and life seemed barely anything at all. 'I *am* the aspen,' Thomas wrote to Eleanor Farjeon when advising her how to understand his poem about the poplar trees beside the crossroads where he lived in Steep. And now yet another love poem followed on 14 February, Valentine's Day; the final stanza:

> She is to be kissed
> Only perhaps by me;
> She may be seeking
> Me and no other: she
> May not exist.

This, entitled 'The Unknown', is the most knowing and most playful of three February poems and may express most truly the flirtation with Edna: that it was to Thomas, and possibly to Edna, an unobtainable idea.[18]

Ever the martyr when it came to Edward's feelings, Helen said that she was glad that he had met Edna once again, that it was good for him to have someone there to talk to in the strange new life he had undertaken. The times at Great House

refreshed him, she knew, and she welcomed anything and anyone who brought warmth to his life. But privately she agonised about the one quality that she knew she could not bring him: beauty. In that sense alone, Eleanor Farjeon had not been a threat to their marriage, and Hope Webb had been but a girl; but Edna Clarke Hall had a beauty that took their relationship out of Helen's hands, and it was a source of anguish for her. 'Why wasn't I beautiful to Edward?' Helen asked Edna in 1919. 'Oh I did so long for your beauty not to take it from him, not take but give, to have hair & eyes & mouth & that something else . . .
I remember you so clearly standing for all I longed to have to give him.'[19]

*   *   *

Snowstorms and gales battered Hare Hall Camp in February. Three inches of snow fell on the 26th alone. Thomas evaded the measles that were rife in the camp, but he could not elude the chill that was doing the rounds, and was signed off on convalescent leave for the first week in February. He spent it in Balham, writing 'The Ash Grove', sending drafts of six stanzas to Helen and of seven to Eleanor, before paring it down to just four. In the meantime, he had been at work on a war sonnet which fizzled with anti-religious anger toward a 'stone-deaf and stone-blind' God sitting aloft the rampage of conflict. But it was the love poems which had captured his attention that month, and it was telling of the vulnerability that had crept in between Helen and Edward that when, in February, he sent her the poem about his father with its hurtful finale

338

'But not so long as you live | Can I love you at all',
Helen mistook them to be lines about herself. Once
again, Thomas was called upon to reassure. 'Fancy
your thinking those verses had anything to do with
you,' he insisted. 'Fancy your thinking, too, that I
should let you see them if they were. They are not to
a woman at all. You know precisely all that I know
of any woman I have cared a little for. They are as a
matter of fact to father. So now, unless you choose
to think I am deceiving you (which I don't think I
ever did), you can be at ease again.'[20]

There was a pause of almost three weeks until
Thomas wrote his next poem in early March,
though that too was a love poem, 'Celandine':

> She found the celandines of February
> Always before us all. Her nature and name
> Were like those flowers, and now immediately
> For a short swift eternity back she came,
> Beautiful, happy, simply as when she wore
> Her brightest bloom among the winter hues
> Of all the world; and I was happy too,
> Seeing the blossoms and the maiden who
> Had seen them with me Februarys before,
> Bending to them as in and out she trod
> And laughed, with locks sweeping the mossy
> sod.

Thomas had a special affection for the yellow
flower that he had seen each spring while walking
through Ashford Hanger. It took to the damp,
mossy banks there, and was to him every bit the
messenger of spring, appearing most commonly
in the first week of March, as it did now when he
wrote this poem, though less commonly with the

five petals that the flower in the poem bore.

> But this was a dream: the flowers were not true,
> Until I stooped to pluck from the grass there
> One of five petals and I smelt the juice
> Which made me sigh, remembering she was
>   no more,
> Gone like a never perfectly recalled air.

Within the stream of love poems that Thomas was writing that winter and spring, two themes seemed to have emerged quite clearly now: his belief in his inability to love and the illusory quality of love itself.[21]

As February deepened the snow came heavily. It settled into a thick, dirty coverage that prevented all walking. Cold and hemmed in, Thomas was in gloomy form. He told Jack Haines that his *Four-and-Twenty Blackbirds* had been little reviewed; 'As to a book of my verses I can't think of it now. I am in no hurry and I hardly think there would be any buyers for Eastaway or Thomas. I shall remain Eastaway for a time yet.' There was no news of any likely deployment that might take him away from Essex, and in fact very little news of the war itself, about which the men in camp rarely liked to say too much.[22]

Germany had begun an offensive in Verdun, north-eastern France, on 21 February. It was a bombardment on a scale never before witnessed: more than a million shells rained in on that day alone on French trenches that were first blown apart, then lit up by flame-throwers and finally mopped up by storm troopers. A hole was punched in French lines three miles deep, though continued resistance would ensure that the battle would rage for a further ten months. It would be the longest single campaign of the war, costing a quarter of a million lives.

SPRING

Since leaving England a year earlier, Frost had written to Thomas once a month or so, but the American's correspondence that winter had all but stopped and Thomas began a string of letters by highlighting the silence. 'It seems an age since I wrote and longer since I heard from you' (December); 'Again it is an immeasurable time since I heard from you' (January); 'I wish you would write' (January); 'What have I done that you shouldn't write to me for a month or more?' (February). Was there a problem, he wondered. Was Frost retreating in his friendship, sensing that Thomas's future in New England seemed uncertain? Finally, in February, Frost broke his silence and wrote to say that he had been detained delivering a talk for an audience in Lawrence, Massachusetts, but he said nothing of the poems that his friend had been sending. 'Your not mentioning them made me think I had missed fire,' wrote Thomas, 'I have written so many I suppose I am always missing fire.'[1]

Frost did indeed believe that Thomas's future looked uncertain. Once, the war had seemed a temporary interruption to his preparation for America, but now it began to fill his vision, deeper and further than before. 'You ask if I think it is going to be a long war,' Thomas told him. 'I don't think, but I do expect a lot of unexpected things and am not beginning really to look forward to any change. I hardly go beyond assuming that the war will end.' The inactivity was making Thomas restless. He could neither see an end to the conflict nor very clearly what his role in it would be. The camp measles, his chill, the numbing cold, a denied promotion and now the refusal of leave which meant he had to spend his thirty-eighth birthday in camp instead of at Steep. 'The long and short of it seems to be that I am what I was, in spite of my hopes last July,' he told Frost: the improvement in his spirit that had begun with his enlistment had reached a plateau. He continued to 'go in' on himself, as he had once put it to Frost, to ruminate and deflate. He managed at least to take walks around Epping Forest, sometimes in company, though usually alone, but found the countryside eerily quiet, the villages emptied of men, while those in camp simply waited and waited for orders. 'We don't know who or where or what we are.'[2]

If camp offered an artificial state, 'home' seemed a less and less authentic alternative. The word in itself sounded strange and strained, and Thomas sensed he was not alone in finding the captivity of camp something akin to an escape from family life. He wrote twenty-seven lines in which three men (possibly Thomas and the artists Paul Nash and John Wheatley) returned through the snow towards Hare Hall Camp, their 'home' and shelter for the time ahead: 'The word "home" raised a smile in us all three, | And one repeated it, smiling just so | That all knew what he meant and none would say.' Days later, he returned to the poem and added the final eight lines, in which thoughts of homesickness were dispelled: to admit as much would make life unendurable, 'else I should be | Another man, as often now I seem'.[3]

Thomas was feeling homeless and ill at ease with himself. He knew 'this captivity | Must somehow come to an end', but had no idea how to bring that about. The snow lingered into the first week of March, when conditions finally began to improve. 'The weather is changing at last. The snow has melted. The sun is very warm. The rooks in the camp trees are nesting. They wake us at 5.30.' Thomas recorded the 'thought moment' precisely in verse.

THAW

Over the land freckled with snow half-thawed
The speculating rooks at their nests cawed
And saw from elm-tops, delicate as flower of
    grass,
What we below could not see, Winter pass.

On 16 March he sat in the Shepherd and Dog public house, two miles from camp, writing to Frost while Arnold Mason quietly sketched him. News that his younger brother Reggie had been made a full corporal ahead of him hardly lifted his mood. 'These reminders that I am going to be passed over all the time don't please me.' But Edward made full corporal himself at the end of the month ('I wear 2 stripes or chevrons on my upper arm now— not on the skin, but the sleeve'), and was working daily with three other non-commissioned officers to teach the hundred-strong company to read and make maps, lecturing twice a day to thirty men at a time. He found himself getting ever more comfortable in his teaching, and told Eleanor that he wished for the time being to continue in this role rather than seek any kind of action abroad.[4]

Whatever the provenance of the winter love poems, the quartet of pieces he wrote that spring were very certainly written for his family. He once referred to them as 'household poems', one for each of his children, and one for Helen.[5]

The first, the shortest and the sweetest of the quartet, was for 'my elder daughter', and drew upon the Essex places that he would like to give her in return for the flowers that she brought him. For Mervyn he would write a poem 'to my son' in which reciprocity was more of a tussle. For 'my daughter the younger', he had nothing to give her but 'Steep and her own world'. And for Helen, 'I would give you back yourself, | . . . And myself, too, if I could find | Where it lay hidden and it proved kind.'[6]

*   *   *

On Easter Sunday from his hut at Hare Hall, Thomas drafted an identical pair of twelve-line lyrics each of which hinted at the passing of opportunity. One found two people walking, believing that happiness had eluded them, or perhaps simply accepting the limits of their situation.

> When we two walked in Lent
> We imagined that happiness
> Was something different
> And this was something less.

It was a poem that balanced yearning with the solace that came from survival, knowing that each had been able to 'live free' at least in the memory

345

of what had been shared. A second poem also drew upon walking.

LIKE THE TOUCH OF RAIN

Like the touch of rain she was
On a man's flesh and hair and eyes
When the joy of walking thus
Has taken him by surprise:

With the love of the storm he burns,
He sings, he laughs, well I know how,
But forgets when he returns
As I shall not forget her 'Go now.'

There for a moment the ink of the first draft ended, until Thomas returned later to add in pencil:

Those two words shut a door
Between me and the blessed rain
That was never shut before
And will not open again.

It would seem hasty or unwise to claim that any one person might have been the subject of this runic poem: Thomas himself had already made clear that even the most apparently intimate love poems might have taken more than one person (or even nobody at all) as their subject.

It is not only the present or past lover of one particular woman that can read and penetrate and enjoy love-poems, and this fact alone might show how vain it is to regard them as addressed merely to those whose names they

346

may bear.

And yet the timing of both poems and their references to walking would fit with the way in which he spent his hours with Edna Clarke Hall in Essex. Lent had begun on 8 March that year, when Thomas was in camp two miles from Edna, and they may well have walked together then, picking celandines just as Thomas had written. Of course, there was nothing in the poems to suggest that it had to apply to *that* Lent of 1916, and the companion might equally well have been Helen, if indeed the poem was not a pure fiction. But the stirring of the physical senses—touch, flesh, hair, eyes—the burning with the love of the storm— these might well have been features of Thomas's attraction to Edna, and were all details mentioned by Edna in her journals; even if it is doubtful if the situation ended with a dismissal, 'go now'. Whatever the feelings that might have captivated him that spring, it would appear, at least in his verse, as if he were aware of having survived something or having scrambled to safer ground. Whether that threat had been intimacy or something quite different, it seemed now as May came that he really was preparing to 'go now': from the frustration of camp life in Essex to a further field.[7]

Thomas never mentioned Edna to Robert Frost: after the men's talks about marriage and responsibility in 1914 he almost certainly would not have chosen to confide any feelings he might have had. In 1908 he had made the mistake of telling his friends of Hope Webb, only to be roundly humiliated and having to instruct them, blushingly, 'Don't talk about this.' The relative absence of

347

Edna's name in Thomas's correspondence is no surprise, especially when he was writing letters from camp that might very well have been prone to gossip or censorship. For Thomas, a private allure would have been enough: a companion, a muse, a subject of desire. He once wrote that the goal of love was not the possession of another person but the stimulation of desire for things both known and unknown: 'It is a desire of impossible things which the poet alternately assuages and rouses again by poetry.' This phantom love, if that is what it was—a world in which 'she may not exist', where 'flowers were not true', where dreams and clouds and shadows and storms leave us 'unillumined' or in 'helpless fretting'—this now, after happy months of flirtation and speculation, may have been coming to a close.[8]

*　　　*　　　*

Less than two years on from the experiment in semi-communal living in Gloucestershire, Dymock's poets were now scattered. Robert Frost was in America; Rupert Brooke in a grave in Skyros. Edward Thomas was in camp in Essex and John Drinkwater kept largely to Birmingham. Wilfrid Gibson had been rejected from army service on health grounds, and though he remained for the time being at the Old Nail-Shop in September he would leave for West Malvern. Lascelles Abercrombie had been rejected on the same grounds, but in March 1916 the founding and driving spirit of the Dymock Poets was preparing to leave the Gallows for good. Though his family would stay on in the cottage while he looked for a new home, he himself was preparing to move back north to the Mersey, where he was to undertake industrial work steel-testing in a munitions factory in Liverpool. With no poets at Little Iddens or Oldfields, and with Abercrombie now away from the Gallows, it was an unlikely time for a new poet to come calling in Dymock; but that is exactly what happened when a young writer and musician, dressed in his army khakis, wandered the parish lanes to find the poets he had heard about. At Ryton he met Catherine Abercrombie playing with her young boys in a field near the Gallows, and asked if she could direct him to the home of the poet Lascelles Abercrombie. He was Ivor Gurney, and he would be wounded on Good Friday 1917 at Vermand south of Arras, three days before Thomas's death nearby. In 1918 he would begin setting to music the first of nineteen of Thomas's poems and would remain fascinated with his work in post-war years of deteriorating mental health. Helen would visit Gurney in Dartford Asylum after the war, bringing maps of Gloucestershire on which he would trace out the paths that Thomas and the Dymock poets had walked.[9]

But if the Dymock community had floundered, the Poetry Bookshop continued to flourish. Yeats gave his second reading on 11 April, held at the Passmore Edwards Settlement on Tavistock Square to accommodate the interest from an audience of more than three hundred. Monro had the good sense to publish 'The Farmer's Bride' by Charlotte Mew, and a debut from Robert Graves, though he squandered the chance to publish Siegfried Sassoon, and found that D. H. Lawrence and Robert Frost had existing contractual arrangements when he enquired after books from them. A second volume of *Georgian Poetry* had appeared from the Bookshop that winter, though Thomas thought little of it. 'The new man Ledwidge isn't any good, is he?' he had told Frost after thumbing it through. Francis Ledwidge was an Irish republican who had joined the British army because it stood between Ireland and a common enemy; but when British soldiers executed the leaders of the Easter Rising in Dublin that April, he became a desperately conflicted man. He drank heavily, reported late for duty and was court-martialled for insubordination. Ledwidge was killed by a German shell in 1917 while road-building on the Western Front, but the events in Dublin seemed curiously not to register with Thomas, who had been schooled in Irish Home Rule by his father. He seemed cut off now from external events, able to see little beyond camp life. The events of the Easter Rising might have had a profound effect on the life of Edward Thomas had he not already joined the army. On the day after the Rising, Prime Minister Asquith caved to pressure from David Lloyd George and on 26 April introduced universal military service.[10]

Nightingales surrounded the camp in May. The warm evenings opened into hot days, and Thomas found himself able to take more frequent walks, sometimes in the company of his fellow map-reading instructors, sometimes alone. He was finding the life comfortable enough to consider, seriously now, professional work within the military. A Welsh army job had come to light, Thomas told Eleanor Farjeon, to provide reportage ('"Eye-witness" stuff') for the newspapers, which he supposed he could do, if with a little reluctance 'and not to suit Welsh taste', though in the event, nothing would come of this. He wrote a quatrain, twinned with 'In Memoriam (Easter, 1915)', alike in almost every part of its syntax, 'The Cherry Trees', and a few days later, at Hare Hall Camp, a poem which appeared to trace the walks that Thomas might have taken in the woods around Great House, Edna's Essex home.[11]

IT RAINS

It rains, and nothing stirs within the fence
Anywhere through the orchard's untrodden,
    dense
Forest of parsley. The great diamonds
Of rain on the grassblades there is none to
    break,
Or the fallen petals further down to shake.

And I am nearly as happy as possible
To search the wilderness in vain though well,
To think of two walking, kissing there,
Drenched, yet forgetting the kisses of the rain:
Sad, too, to think that never, never again,

Unless alone, so happy shall I walk
In the rain. When I turn away, on its fine stalk
Twilight has fined to naught, the parsley
    flower
Figures, suspended still and ghostly white,
The past hovering as it revisits the light.

In only two of Thomas's 142 collected poems do people kiss, here and in 'The Unknown', written three months apart, both in Essex, with Helen away and Edna close by. It is reasonable to suppose both poems are fantasies, projections of ideals and desires; even so, the settings on which they were based would appear to be real enough. Edward and Edna did take walks in the rain through the orchard around Great House where they collected firewood. One entry from Edna's journal reads, 'A night under the orchard trees again which seems to restore me to curious energy'; another, already quoted, records Edna and Edward feeding the fire 'At open hearth where orchard wood did burn'. But there is little in Edna's journals to expressly suggest that a kiss might have taken place. So intensely does she linger over the minute detail of their glances and touches that an event as noteworthy as this would probably have been written up more than once. In only one poem does she hint that this might have happened, a sextet linked to Thomas by the finest of threads only: the sunlight in which she recorded seeing him for the last time. 'And in the sun stood you; | Your kiss took me to heaven!'[12]

It remains fanciful stuff; and yet, something had gotten beneath Thomas's skin. On 13–14 May he followed 'It rains' with a sonnet whose love-worn speaker pronounced, 'I had not found my goal', finishing, 'But thinking of your eyes, dear, I become | Dumb: for they flamed, and it was me they burned.' And travelling from Essex to Hampshire in June he wrote a lingering, even lascivious poem, more corporeal than before, in which eyes met eyes, and gazed on cheeks and hair, culminating in the uncharacteristic claim, 'I know your lust | Is love.' The months in Essex had produced eight or nine intimate poems, but whoever or whatever had been in his thoughts, those musings would now cease and his thoughts would turn toward the war.[13]

* * *

On 1 May Frost sent Thomas a new poem, set in familiar blank verse and featuring a wounded soldier invalided home to his grateful wife, knowing that the sooner the recovery the sooner the return to action. The poem was not based upon Thomas biographically, but the gentle domestic drama between the soldier and wife seemed sympathetically in tune with Thomas's life in Steep, even down to the wife's attention to the face and hands of her beloved, an obsession of Helen's.

NOT TO KEEP

They sent him back to her. The letter came
Saying . . . And she could have him. And
    before
She could be sure there was no hidden ill
Under the formal writing, he was in her sight,
Living. They gave him back to her alive—
How else? They are not known to send the
    dead—
And not disfigured visibly. His face?
His hands? She had to look, to ask,
'What is it, dear?' And she had given all
And still she had all—*they* had—they the
    lucky!
Wasn't she glad now? Everything seemed won,
And all the rest for them permissible ease.
She had to ask, 'What was it, dear?'
                    'Enough,

Yet not enough. A bullet through and
    through.
High in the breast. Nothing but what good
    care
And medicine and rest, and you a week,
Can cure me of to go again.' The same
Grim giving to do over for them both.
She dared no more than ask him with her eyes
How was it with him for a second trial.
And with his eyes he asked her not to ask.
They had given him back to her, but not to
    keep.

'This last letter . . . with the poem "Not to Keep"
mends all,' Thomas wrote to Frost. Though the
letter has not survived, from the tone of the
poem alone Thomas must have felt understood
once more, no longer goaded by Frost, no longer
belittled, but cared for, empathised with. The next
day, Thomas wrote the poem that would most
keenly express the value of the friendship with
Frost that grew up in Gloucestershire that summer
of 1914.

THE SUN USED TO SHINE

The sun used to shine while we two walked
Slowly together, paused and started
Again, and sometimes mused, sometimes
    talked
As either pleased, and cheerfully parted

Each night. We never disagreed
Which gate to rest on. The to be
And the late past we gave small heed.

We turned from men or poetry

To rumours of the war remote
Only till both stood disinclined
For aught but the yellow flavorous coat
Of an apple wasps had undermined;

Or a sentry of dark betonies,
The stateliest of small flowers on earth,
At the forest verge; or crocuses
Pale purple as if they had their birth

In sunless Hades fields. The war
Came back to mind with the moonrise
Which soldiers in the east afar
Beheld then. Nevertheless, our eyes

Could as well imagine the Crusades
Or Caesar's battles. Everything
To faintness like those rumours fades—
Like the brook's water glittering

Under the moonlight—like those walks
Now—like us two that took them, and
The fallen apples, all the talks
And silences—like memory's sand

When the tide covers it late or soon,
And other men through other flowers
In those fields under the same moon
Go talking and have easy hours.[14]

An ease had been restored to the friendship of
Edward Thomas and Robert Frost. Frost shared
his recollections on his anxiety of reaching forty,

355

but Thomas was in resolute form. 'I find less to grumble at out loud than 10 years ago: I suppose I am more bent on making the best of what I have got instead of airing the fact that I deserve so much more.' Yet his visits to the theatre of late had made him feel old enough, at least as a writer. He had spent the afternoon of 20 May seeing a trio of plays by Brooke, Gibson and Bottomley, and found he had seen right through each piece, exposing the artificiality of the writing and the techniques employed; it was this that made him feel old, he told Frost. His literary friendships were receding for his new life at camp. Nobody recognised him now, he said. He had exchanged his tweeds for khaki, and acquaintances from his literary life had stood just a yard away from him at the theatre without a flicker of recognition. But two young artists in camp were becoming friends to Thomas in terms to which he could relate: a gifted young painter called Paul Nash was particularly skilled at finding birds' nests; another, John Wheatley (whose portrait of Thomas hangs in the National Gallery) was a 'perfect Welshman'. 'I am really lucky to have such a crowd of people always round & these 2 or 3 nearer,' he told Frost in a nod to his snowy walk back to camp with the men, 'you might guess from "Home" how much nearer'. There was a kindness about these men that extended into the senior ranks, he explained, and in particular their captain who hoped they would stay out of trouble, remember their Ps & Qs and generally do everything 'top-hole'. 'He is a kind huge man with no memory, very fond of the country. The other day in the fields he said "Company, attention! Oh, look at that rabbit."'[15]

Towards the end of May Thomas's ambivalence

to a war overseas seemed as pronounced as ever. Life at camp was convivial enough for him to have been considering permanent positions, and until now he had no interest in serving abroad. Woken by the camp bugle, he wrote lines that were a conscious response to Brooke's now famous war sonnets and their corner of a foreign field. '"No one cares less than I, | Nobody knows but God, | Whether I am destined to lie | Under a foreign clod"'. Nobody knew indeed, but Thomas himself was about to have a change of heart that would bring the foreign clod very much closer.[16]

* * *

The war was less than two years old—Thomas's own war almost a year—when he began a poem on 27 May with the working title of 'The Last Team'; by the time he had finished it, he had taken a step towards his decision to seek a commission on the front line. The poem he wrote may not have been a conventional war poem, but the war touched every part of it. It would be written into the storm and the fallen tree, into the missing man and in the mysterious lovers. It would bring together, as the war itself would, a confluence of class: labourer and poet, manual worker and man of leisure; archetypes and of course real men, who might meet again in France, where the furrow would become the trench.[17]

AS THE TEAM'S HEAD-BRASS

As the team's head-brass flashed out on the turn
The lovers disappeared into the wood.

357

I sat among the boughs of the fallen elm
That strewed an angle of the fallow, and
Watched the plough narrowing a yellow square
Of charlock. Every time the horses turned
Instead of treading me down, the ploughman
    leaned
Upon the handles to say or ask a word,
About the weather, next about the war.
Scraping the share he faced towards the wood,
And screwed along the furrow till the brass
    flashed
Once more.
            The blizzard felled the elm whose crest
I sat in, by a woodpecker's round hole,
The ploughman said. 'When will they take it
    away?'
'When the war's over.' So the talk began—
One minute and an interval of ten,
A minute more and the same interval.
'Have you been out?' 'No.' 'And don't want to,
    perhaps?'
'If I could only come back again, I should.
I could spare an arm. I shouldn't want to lose
A leg. If I should lose my head, why, so,
I should want nothing more.... Have many gone
From here?' 'Yes.' 'Many lost?' 'Yes: a good few.
Only two teams work on the farm this year.
One of my mates is dead. The second day
In France they killed him. It was back in March,
The very night of the blizzard, too. Now if
He had stayed here we should have moved the
    tree.'
'And I should not have sat here. Everything
Would have been different. For it would have
    been

Another world.' 'Ay, and a better, though
If we could see all all might seem good.' Then
The lovers came out of the wood again:
The horses started and for the last time
I watched the clods crumble and topple over
After the ploughshare and the stumbling team.[18]

'If we could see all', Thomas had written, 'all might seem good.' This skilfully awkward, monosyllabic line, with its mirrored 'all's turning to face one another in its middle, was arguably the most revealing 'thought moment' that Edward Thomas had written. The speaker idling on his elm tree had appeared unmoved by the war when the poem began. He had been flip when the ploughman had asked if he had been out to France, adopting a tone of Shakespearean foolery over the loss of limbs. But in the ellipsis he had understood something invaluable, and realised what was wrong with the scene in which he sat: that the world he enjoyed was contingent upon those who were willing to fight for it. It was somewhere around this time, said Eleanor Farjeon, that she pressed him on precisely why he chose to enlist. Thomas was said to pause, bend down to scoop a handful of soil from around his shoe, and say, 'Literally, for this.'[19]

If we could see all, then we could know the consequence and the value of our actions and so choose which paths to take. Thomas had agreed as much with the young soldier he met on the train the day he collected his enlistment papers: the difference between people was that some strained harder than others to foresee what they could of it. Many of Thomas's poems are about moments that cannot be seen or chosen. Poets in their yellow

359

wood might claim to choose but not Thomas: his roads were not of his making and do not yield up their destination readily.

Within eight weeks of writing this poem, Thomas had committed himself to service overseas. He recorded the moment in a letter to Frost, on 28 July 1916.

A new step I have taken makes a good moment for writing. I offered myself for Artillery and today I was accepted, which means I shall go very soon to an Artillery School and be out in France or who knows where in a few months. After months of panic and uncertainty I feel much happier again except that I don't take easily to the trigonometry needed for artillery calculations. I have done very nearly all that I could do here in the way of teaching, lecturing, and taking charge of men in and out of doors. My old acquaintances were mostly moving out. The speeding up of things left no chance of enjoying the walks we used to have. So I had to go.

In writing 'As the team's head-brass' he had made his decision to seek a commission at the front, and now it seemed possible to find the war in much that he wrote: the bugle call was echoed in the calls of moorhens, tall reeds resembled the criss-cross of bayonets, the eyes that had looked tenderly were now turned towards the battlefield. His mind was made up.

> I'm bound away for ever,
> Away somewhere, away for ever.[20]

SUMMER

Thomas knew little about the artillery work for which he applied that June. He would require a precise knowledge of trigonometry in order to prepare the necessary calculations of angle, depth and velocity that the heavy siege guns would need to knock out German trenches. It took him some weeks to convince the authorities of his capabilities, though to a friend he put the application more simply: 'I am delighted with the idea of change'. From the Civil List he learned that he was not to receive a pension but a single grant of £300 to aid his writing; the news of missing out on an annual income could only have increased his sense of living day by day: 'the only certain thing is that the unexpected will happen,' he told Frost.[1]

Thomas's relief that the two men were corresponding again was palpable; he told Haines, 'Frost by the way has begun to send me letters again and some verses, very good ones. He is cheerful again, and not yet easy. The War preys on him, and he can't be feeling quite at home.' Frost must have forgiven his old friend for his outburst over 'The Road Not Taken' to send his poems across the sea once more, and they met only praise from Thomas, 'An Old Man's Winter Night', 'Out, Out—' and 'Encounter' among them.[2]

Thomas fell sick with an indeterminate illness again in June. His health was a regular concern now: he was highly susceptible to chills, colds and infections in the cheek-by-jowl life at camp. His immune system may have been weakened by the

361

diabetes from which he was convinced he was suffering. According to his friend Jesse Berridge, Thomas was obsessed with a story he had heard that sufferers grew so hungry that they ate earth, and not without cause: sufferers were often starved as part of their treatment. Insulin was not medically available until 1921, and without a carefully regulated diet sufferers risked the onset of coma. But Thomas had refused to declare his illness to the army authorities; he ate the same food in camp as everyone else and seemed quite indifferent to the danger his diet might pose, and while weight loss in camp was not uncommon due to the plain fare and physical regime, it could also be a symptom of the illness. He had already told Frost that he was having to get new holes punched in his belt, so much was he shrinking in the waist; by 1916, photographs would picture him looking wiry and gaunt. He never suffered a serious episode (which may suggest Type I diabetes), and kept his suspicions almost entirely to himself, and with good reason, said Gordon Bottomley, for had Thomas declared his illness he would not have been sent to the front.[3]

Thomas's poems that summer reflected his desire to apply himself:

But now that there is something I could use
My youth and strength for, I deny the age,
The care and weakness that I know—refuse
To admit I am unworthy of the wage
Paid to a man who gives up eyes and breath
For what can neither ask nor heed his death.

Eleanor described the sentiment within these lines

as 'sick', but Thomas defended them, saying, 'I thought it was more than a shade heroic.' And the 'shades' were certainly darker now. But by the month's end he had penned a poem that beckoned its reader into the echoing forest that lay at the end of 'The Green Roads', a fragment of woodland six miles from his camp. He said that he could not imagine a wilder, quieter place than this; but the poem bore a sinister undercurrent of stolen memories and forgetting, of nettle towers and dead oak trees, the white feathers of a plucked goose. Thomas's meditative and formal powers had rarely been in a state of fuller accomplishment, nor his subject matter darker or more strange.[4]

*   *   *

On 24 June an Allied bombardment began nearby the River Somme in north-eastern France; the explosions were so ground-shaking that windows reverberated in London 160 miles away. The assault would last for a week on a scale so destructive that by the time the artillery had finished pounding German lines, the infantry should have been able to push unopposed into the space evacuated by the Germans. Or at least that was the hope. But the German trenches were dug far deeper than had been allowed for, and when thirteen divisions of the British army went over the top on 1 July, the enemy machine guns rose from their dugouts and mowed them down in their thousands: 19,000 British soldiers were killed and twice that number were wounded. It would be the costliest day the British army had ever known. In Franconia, Robert Frost monitored events from afar. 'I believe the forward movement has come,' he told Haines. 'They are off, and my heart's with them with all the love I bear England.' But the forward movement came at unprecedented cost. By November, the Somme campaign had floundered in the French mud with 420,000 British losses; three to every two Germans. The scale of the devastation would produce a reassessment of training and of tactics in the British army; but it would do something else besides: it would alter the initial mood of patriotism among the ranks for ever. The optimistic war that Rupert Brooke and others had cheered would now give way to a harrowing outpouring of verse from the men who had witnessed the horror of the slaughter.[5]

Robert Graves found himself in reserve north of Mametz Wood at the Somme that month. On 20 July his Royal Welch regiment were entrenched on a ridge beside a churchyard in Bazentin-le-Petit when the German bombardment came in. A fragment of shell punctured Graves's back beneath his shoulder blade and passed out through his chest, inches from his heart. He was ferried to a dressing station outside Mametz Wood where his death was announced to his colonel; his parents were informed and an obituary printed in *The Times*. But he had not died, and on 5 August *The Times* printed a correction that he was in fact recovering from his wounds in London's Highgate hospital. He would return to France briefly in 1917, but nerve damage largely kept him from further action at the front.[6]

Godwin Baynes had been in the comparative safety of a base hospital in Etaples, on the north-west French coast, when the Battle of the Somme began; but he would get much closer to the action. By August he was at the front, and was knocked down and bruised by a German shell at Delville Wood where he also caught trench fever. He was invalided to the Isle of Wight on 4 September and spent the remainder of the year there at Osborne House Convalescent Home for Officers, recovering from what on his army form was listed as 'debility', most likely shell-shock. It was a moment that turned out to save his life: the doctors that were sent to replace him were all killed when their hospital was bombed.[7]

Edward Thomas was clearing out his study at Steep that first day of the Somme offensive. With her husband fighting abroad, Mrs Lupton had asked Thomas to empty the Bee House in the garden of Wick Green so that she could take it back for her own use. For seven years it had been where Thomas worked and was the place where nearly all of his poetry had been written. 'I never thought it could happen,' he told John Freeman, of an ousting that would, as it turned out, be a severing of the final significant tie for Thomas in Hampshire. With Bronwen at school in London and Mervyn preparing to start an apprenticeship in the bus works at Walthamstow, Yew Tree Cottage was more spacious than it had been when they moved in the summer of 1913, though not spacious enough to accommodate a study or his many books, and once again Thomas prepared to sell off his stock to anyone who would take it. More importantly, Helen was now anxious and isolated. She wanted to move to Walthamstow, to make a home there for Mervyn which would also bring her nearer to Hare Hall Camp. Steep had lost its hold upon them all.[8]

*　　*　　*

365

Thomas had had two poems included in the arts journal *Form*: 'Lob' and 'Words', printed under the name Edward Eastaway. It was the third publication to have issued his work, although all had come either through personal connections or under his own editorship. By contrast, that July alone Frost had poems published in three separate journals, among them the harrowing 'Out, Out—' in *McClure's*, based on an incident in Bethlehem, New Hampshire, in 1910, when a family friend, a boy of sixteen, died following an accident involving a sawing machine. Frost had earned around £200 from poetry publications since leaving England, but for Thomas seeing his own poems in print was still something new, and yet he was not impressed by *Form*, which had run late by several months and seemed to him 'an ugly tasteless mess'. But James Guthrie was about to issue Thomas's first single-authored selection, *Six Poems*, which rolled off his Flansham press from 1916 in an elegant edition limited to one hundred copies. By now, Thomas had enough poems to fill two books of verse, and he began to turn his mind to exactly that: to seeing a volume of his poetry published.[9]

In London on 15 August he met Roger Ingpen, a brother-in-law of Walter de la Mare, whom he knew from his childhood days in Wandsworth. Ingpen had once brought Thomas a contract for *Richard Jefferies*, and was now running a modest London imprint called Selwyn and Blount ('I believe he is both Selwyn and Blount', wrote Thomas). Not since his disappointment with the Poetry Bookshop had Thomas approached a publisher, but when Ingpen asked to see a manuscript Thomas readily agreed.

Over the next two weeks, from his parents' house in Balham, Thomas prepared a typescript. He had finished 131 poems to date, and with eighteen of those reserved for the anthology that Abercrombie was preparing, Thomas was left with the task of omitting about half of the pieces he had written. By the start of September he had made his preliminary selection. He had not yet written the poem he would place first; but he knew exactly where he wished the book to finish, with 'Words', the poem he had composed after visiting May Hill with Jack Haines the day they spoke about Robert Frost. The final verse:

> Let me sometimes dance
> With you,
> Or climb
> Or stand perchance
> In ecstasy,
> Fixed and free
> In a rhyme,
> As poets do.[10]

*   *   *

It had been just over a year since Thomas enlisted and he told Frost that, 'I don't believe I often had as good times as I have had, one way and another, these past 13 months.' He wrote eight stanzas that seemed firmly to set the passing seasons behind him. The falling of the apples that August reminded him of the previous summer when the war began 'To turn young men to dung'; and in what might conceivably have been an enigmatic parting reference to Edna Clarke Hall, he wrote of a time 'when the lost one was here'.[11]

Thomas's departure would be a hard blow for Edna, who would sink into a terrible depression in the years to come. In Edward she had found a relationship of a kind that she believed she could never have with her husband: one that was careful, artistic and loving. It was sunset when she said her goodbye.

> These eyes looked upon him, and may not do
> so again
> These ears heard his voice, and may not do so
> again
> This hand has touched his, and may not do so
> again
> Yet with eyes of my new knowledge would I
> look upon him . . . I would again mark the
> gentleness and resolution of the contours
> of that face that had so haunted my
> imagination as I saw it last in light of the
> setting sun—he standing before me silent
> and unaware.[12]

Robert Frost replied to Thomas's news of his transfer to the artillery. 'My whole nature simply leaps at times to cross the ocean to see you for one good talk,' he wrote, though he knew that he might not find Thomas if he did. Thomas had explained that he might 'go out' at any moment: 'This waiting troubles me. I really want to be out.' And so Frost left open the offer that he hoped might still one day be taken up. 'What's mine is yours,' he wrote. 'Here are a house and forty odd acres of land you can think of as a home and a refuge when your war is over. We shall be waiting for you.'[13]

At Steep, Thomas lit a bonfire as he had once before and burned papers and letters, and those books that he had been unable to sell; the fire burned so hot that the embers smouldered for days. On 25 August he reported for duty at Handel Street, in Bloomsbury; he was now an Officer Cadet in the Royal Artillery.

AUTUMN

The Thomases were a family dispersed that autumn. Edward was stationed in Bloomsbury by day; by evening, billeted back at his parents in Balham. Mervyn was in Walthamstow and Bronwen with Helen's sister in Chiswick, while six-year-old Myfanwy stayed on at Yew Tree Cottage with John Freeman's family, who had now assumed the lease. Helen had taken advantage of the childminding and escaped to the Lake District with her sister for a few days' walking, but Edward was not best pleased to find the organisation of the house move left to him: 'Helen runs away so comfortably from affairs,' he grumbled to Frost. Thomas was in particularly nihilistic form. 'I am rather impatient to go out and be shot at,' he continued. 'That is all I want, to do something if I am discovered to be any use,' he wrote, having at last discovered that 'something' which he could use his 'youth and strength for'. The future seemed more unknowable than ever, he wrote, and hard to take quite seriously let alone depend upon. 'I have been saying to myself lately that I don't really care a fig what happens. But perhaps I do.—I am cut off. All the anchors are up. I have no friends now.'[1]

Edward Thomas sat in the sunlight of Brunswick Square in the grounds of the Foundling Hospital that September, watching the children play beneath the great London planes of Coram's Fields. Talk among the cadets was about anything but the war, and he wrote now that it formed a seal around them and him, of silence and of secrets that might only be broken with his death. The daily rhythm

370

was his only guiding drive, not love or country but the modest pleasures in such moments as he experienced watching the children in Brunswick Square. Many times in the past Thomas had imagined a world without him in it, or thought about the effect his absence might have on others, and now he asked himself the question in verse:

What will they do when I am gone? It is plain
That they will do without me as the rain
Can do without the flowers and the grass . . .

In the spring Thomas had complained mildly to Frost that 'nobody recognises me now'; at the time he had shrugged it off, but in the poem he wrote now he was pained to find that those who knew him had passed him in the street without recognition: 'I was naught to them. I turned about | To see them disappearing carelessly'. It was typical of Thomas to turn such a casual or benign episode into an assumed lack of self-worth, when in truth any one of his friends would have delighted at the encounter; instead, he wondered what would happen if he took away that friendship.[2]

Thomas was in a bleak mood: run down physically and with an infected hand, and possibly suffering from a lack of balance in his blood sugars. He told Frost, 'I am still poor and feeble and it is very nearly all I can do to keep on with the work here, tho it is not hard physically.' Not for the first time, Frost chuckled at the self-pity he detected in Thomas, and was certain it was time to kick some nonsense out of him once again. 'I began to think our positions were reversed—', he replied cheerily, 'you had got well-minded from having plunged

371

into things and I had got soul-sick from having plunged out of them. Your letter shows you can still undertalk me when you like. A little vaccination and a little cold and you are down where it makes me dizzy to look in after you. You are so good at black talk that I believe your record will stand unbroken for years to come. It's as if somebody should do the hundred yards in five seconds flat.' Frost was the only one ever able to send up Edward Thomas successfully, but for a moment he laid his mischief aside. 'I'm afraid Englishmen aren't liking Americans very much now,' he continued. 'Should I dare go back to England at this moment? I often long to.' But Thomas only smiled at the suggestion of Frost's return, 'It is one of the impossiblest things,' he wrote.[3]

*   *   *

By the third week of September, Thomas had sent off his typescript of poems to Roger Ingpen at Selwyn and Blount, and had received the orders that would take him gratefully out of London, to the Royal Artillery Barracks in Trowbridge, Wiltshire. There, he found that his weekends were his own, and delighted in two days' walking through the fields to Dillybrook Farm and to Bradford on Avon along the route he had cycled for *In Pursuit of Spring*. The camp was set up in tents, rather than the huts he had come to know in Essex, and he welcomed the chance to see the night sky once more, to be outdoors and to make new acquaintances. The barracks' trumpeter announced everything from reveille to lights out on a cracked horn and with no real proficiency, but Thomas

372

found he did not mind.

THE TRUMPET

Rise up, rise up,
And, as the trumpet blowing
Chases the dreams of men,
As the dawn glowing
The stars that left unlit
The land and water,
Rise up and scatter
The dew that covers
The print of last night's lovers—
Scatter it, scatter it!

While you are listening
To the clear horn,
Forget, men, everything
On this earth newborn,
Except that it is lovelier
Than any mysteries.
Open your eyes to the air
That has washed the eyes of the stars
Through all the dewy night:
Up with the light,
To the old wars;
Arise, arise![4]

Thomas's experience of the war was very different from that of the other soldier poets. Where Sassoon, Graves and others had rushed to enlist and then recoiled at the horror of their experience of the conflict, Thomas's war seemed to be running in reverse. Initially unmoved and unsympathetic, fervently anti-nationalist, the longer the war went on the more committed he appeared, ever keener to seek action at the front, and writing the conflict into his verses with increasing verve. But his attitude to the conflict essentially did not change, and even this apparently front-footed poem did not abandon its guile or its irony. It was a mark of Thomas's accomplishment as a poet that he could now set his form and his content in opposition: the form, strident, galloping, heroic, offering no room for detour or for doubt, as clear and assured as the bugle call itself, but the content suggesting other tones— the dark stars that failed to illuminate the earth below, the hounding of dreams, the need to disperse the impression of the lovers in the dew, the cry to forget the newborn life for a loyalty to older wars.

Thomas had written the poem he would place first in his collection, and yet in composing he did his best to conceal that it was a poem at all. The verses were scribbled down amid the arithmetic calculations that Thomas was making about the trajectory of shells, disguising it as prose with a code to distinguish the line breaks. 'You see I have written it with only capitals to mark the lines,' he told Eleanor, 'because people are all around me and I don't want them to know.' As she observed, the paper bore testament to how hard self-consciousness died in Thomas: he did not mind poets knowing he was a soldier, but he would not allow soldiers to learn he was a poet.[5]

*   *   *

Helen moved into a cottage in the village of High Beech on 8 October. It seemed a bitter-sweet irony that all the while that Edward had been in camp there Helen had lived in Steep, and now she moved to Essex two months after he had moved out. The setting was picturesque, as Thomas told Elinor Frost: high on a hill alone beside seven or eight miles of forest, amid small ponds and wide glades and 'oaks, hornbeams, beeches, bracken, hollies, and some heather'. But the cottage itself was squalid: a semi-detached nurseryman's house, 'ugly, cold and inconvenient', remembered Helen, 'dismal and poorly-planned', said Eleanor. Edward could not get leave on the weekend that Helen moved her possessions and she was left supervising hired help whom she suspected to be drunk. But together, Helen and the children made the best of it and soon Helen was keeping Leghorn chickens and netting crops to keep out rabbits. And it was only seven miles from Mervyn's work, to which he cycled in the dark at six each morning while owls were still about the roads.[6]

*   *   *

On 20 October Thomas sent Helen a set of the verses which he was preparing for Selwyn and Blount with an instruction to forward them by registered post to Frost in Franconia, having first made a careful copy of the contents so that he could replicate them at a later date. 'Don't send to Frost before I tell you that the thing is settled,' he urged, but the typescript never arrived in New England, and was believed to be lost at sea. Thomas himself was restless for news, and when Selwyn and Blount had not replied after a month, he wrote to Roger Ingpen to ask him to come to a decision. Late in November he received the news he wanted. 'I have an anthology[,] an upcoming volume of verses at last,' he told Jack Haines. 'The publisher is fixed—Selwyn and Blount. Frost is getting a duplicate to offer an American publisher. It has just gone.' And he had decided on a title for the volume. 'The book is to be simply "Poems",' he wrote to Bottomley, 'unless the publisher prefers "Lob & other Poems" or "The Trumpet & other Poems"'. He had been given only sixty-four pages by Selwyn and Blount but that was plenty, he said, 'I find I can get a lot into 64 pp.' Indeed he could: sixty-four poems, in fact.[7]

Poems was assembled from two typewriters—Thomas's in part but mostly Eleanor's—and a title page emblazoned in Thomas's own hand: 'Poems by Edward Eastaway'. The copies were drawn from typescripts that were not always the most recent drafts, and so required him to make one or two minor corrections: an added or amended word to the last lines of 'The Manor Farm' and 'The Green Roads', changes to articles in 'As the team's head-brass', and in 'Haymaking' a last-minute switch to have the reformer William Cobbett replace the poet William Cowper. 'November Sky' became 'November', and elsewhere Thomas gave no fewer than twenty-three poems their titles for the first time, now that he could put off that moment no longer. He carefully marked the folios to correspond with the contents page, where he made only small alterations to the running order, shuffling 'Lights Out' down to the third-last poem to stress its importance to the collection. 'The Trumpet', his ironic bugle call, would be first; 'The Sign-Post' from his indecisive traveller, second; 'Words', would remain the book's finale.[8]

'I just arranged my book in the nick of time,' Thomas told Frost on 29 November. 'For a letter came today warning me to expect a call to my "new unit". Which means probably going straight to a battery and not to any final school.' He told Frost that Roger Ingpen would wait to hear from him directly before passing the typescript for press, which spoke volumes about the store Thomas set in Frost's word.[9]

Frost, meanwhile, had seen his work in four journals that past month in the run-up to the publication of his latest book. In the early winter of 1916 *Mountain Interval* became Frost's third collection in little over three years. It was published by Henry Holt in New York, so becoming Frost's first original American edition. The poems in the book were leaner than those in *North of Boston*, frequently in blank verse, skilfully balancing neat dramatic dialogues against shorter lyrics. The collection opened with 'The Road Not Taken', typeset in italics to suggest a governing tone for the book, as was the concluding poem, 'The Sound of the Trees', ensuring that the collection was bookended by two of the poems from Ryton. In between, it moved through pieces that had been written before his time in England (such as 'An Old Man's Winter Night', 'Hyla Brook'), and those written after ('A Time to Talk', 'Out, Out—' and 'Snow'), and a fair showing of the pieces he had written or published in Beaconsfield ('A Patch of Old Snow' and 'Birches') or Gloucestershire ('Pea Brush', 'Putting in the Seed' and 'The Cow in Apple Time'). Thomas was no longer reviewing, and even if he had been Frost no longer would have needed his help. His reputation was growing so powerfully that he was offered a professorial position at Amherst College within a month of publication; from a single semester's teaching he would make around double the annual

377

salary that Thomas had made in his best days as a hack.[10]

Frost meditated on the upcoming American presidential elections that would return Woodrow Wilson to office by the narrowest of margins. Wilson had campaigned as the man who had successfully kept the country out of the war; now America was only months away from joining it. But Frost told Thomas he had 'stopped asseverating' from his safe-house across the Atlantic. As an American, he said, he did not believe he should enlist, but the very least he could do was not to attempt to empathise with those taking greater risks than he.

You rather shut me up by enlisting. Talk is almost too cheap when all your friends are facing bullets. I don't believe I ought to enlist (since I am of course an American), but if I can't enlist, at least I refuse to talk sympathy beyond a certain point.

Instead, he concentrated once again on an attempt to lure Thomas to America, this time with the suggestion of a three-week lecture tour. 'Does that sound so very unmilitary?' asked Frost. 'They ought to consider that you were literary before you were military.' But Thomas's attentions were almost entirely military. 'I might very well be in France before Christmas,' he replied. 'I hope so.' When a room-mate, the actor Granville Barker, left for duties on Coast Defence, Thomas told Eleanor, 'I suppose his friends have urged his country not to risk his life. I hope I shall always be as eager to risk mine as I have been these last few months.' In fact Thomas was also on the move, to Wanstrow in Somerset for a week's further training, where he was billeted with a squad of forty men for lectures and practical work by day (walks and writing by night) before being granted ten days of leave. On 20 November he travelled to Lancashire to see his old friend Gordon Bottomley in Silverdale. Bottomley recalled Thomas's composure, and the sense of ease and contentedness that had now come over him: 'a happy, tranquillising presence, with a steadfast, gentle outlook on new dangers and old troubles'. Thomas sang bawdy army songs with a quiet mischief that Bottomley found very funny, and the two men watched a storm coming in over the mountains 'painted by the wild air' of the Kirkstone Pass; it was magnificent, and Thomas told Bottomley that he was a fortunate man. *Fortunate*, said Bottomley, surprised, with *his* life of disability? Yes, replied Thomas, fortunate because no one, even in ill health, could deserve so much.[11]

Thomas returned from Silverdale to High Beech, where Eleanor Farjeon came to stay. She found him in the very opposite of the mood described by Gordon Bottomley: restless, waspish, argumentative, out of sorts, making no disguise of the fact that life in camp was more of a home to him than the little cottage. Eleanor watched him chop the wood stack, knowing that he would not be burning it with his family that winter.[12]

On 23 November Thomas had been given a commission as second lieutenant, Royal Garrison Artillery (Special Reserve), making the call to France imminent. From Trowbridge, he wrote 'Lights Out', a poem that he said 'sums up what I have often thought at that call'; though no reader could mistake its deeper undercurrent.[13]

379

LIGHTS OUT

I have come to the borders of sleep,
The unfathomable deep
Forest where all must lose
Their way, however straight,
Or winding, soon or late;
They cannot choose.

Many a road and track
That, since the dawn's first crack,
Up to the forest brink,
Deceived the travellers
Suddenly now blurs,
And in they sink.

Here love ends,
Despair, ambition ends,
All pleasure and all trouble,
Although most sweet or bitter,
Here ends in sleep that is sweeter
Than tasks most noble.

There is not any book
Or face of dearest look
That I would not turn from now
To go into the unknown
I must enter and leave alone
I know not how.

The tall forest towers;
Its cloudy foliage lowers
Ahead, shelf above shelf;
Its silence I hear and obey
That I may lose my way
And myself.[14]

WINTER

On 3 December Thomas transferred to Lydd, on the south coast of Kent, to complete the last sections of his training. There the Royal Artillery had their barracks in a camp that became known to the locals as 'Tin Town' for the cheap metal huts the army had erected. Lydd camp was a bare place even in good weather, but in winter it was desolate. Soon the wind and hail belted over the flats, chilling the shingle and caking the long rows of low huts in salt. It was blustery and bustling: two or three battalions a week passing through on their way to Codford in Wiltshire, the mustering point for their departure to France. But Thomas was glad of the setting, and appreciated the shingle flats, and the medieval village with its church tower commanding the marshes in all directions. And he was comforted to recognise at least one familiar face among the men who had been assigned to his hut.[1]

On 5 December the conciliatory Herbert Asquith had resigned as prime minster, replaced two days later by David Lloyd George. Robert Frost for one was pleased. 'Lloyd George is the great man and he belongs where he now takes his place,' he wrote, and he sent Thomas an unconvincing Shakespearean sonnet, 'Suggested by Talk of Peace at This Time', which, 'from a quiet place apart' in Franconia, hesitantly bid France onward until Truth be saved and Hell thwarted. The poem was neither published nor collected by Frost, though Thomas recognised the good intentions behind its

381

hesitation to command others to do what the poet himself would not. But the politicians had no such hesitation. On 12 December Germany attempted to consolidate her gains by offering a 'Peace Note' via the Vatican. The Note promised proposals that would 'serve as the basis for the restoration of a lasting peace', and for a week the Allies waited for a clarification. None was forthcoming, and on 19 December Lloyd George used his first prime ministerial address to kick the offering into the gutter. 'To enter, on the invitation of Germany, proclaiming herself victorious, without any knowledge of the proposals she proposes to make, into a conference is to put our heads into a noose with the rope end in the hands of Germany,' he pronounced. 'We shall put our trust rather in an unbroken army than in broken faith.' David Lloyd George, the man who once walked to Westminster every morning with Philip Henry Thomas, had committed Britain to a continuation of the conflict, ensuring that Edward Thomas would see the front.[2]

'This is only to tell you just a few facts,' Thomas wrote to Eleanor Farjeon on 7 December. 'One is that they asked for volunteers to go straight out to Batteries in France and I made sure of it by volunteering. Don't let Helen know.' Thomas seemed fully absorbed in army life now; his letters to Helen were businesslike, informing her of the latest chances of his going to France, and telling her not to begin to grumble if he were denied leave at Christmas, before signing off with a distant 'I hope all is well'. There was little else for him to say in those loitering weeks in Lydd, other than that he had surprised himself as an acting commander by 'not making too bad a hash of it'.[3]

382

By mid-December, *Poems* was almost 'fixed up'. 'One or two pieces' might have to be cut for length, thought Thomas, though in fact the publishers managed to retain them all. He expected not to see the proofs himself, and asked John Freeman and Eleanor Farjeon to supervise their production on his behalf. Mentally, he was tidying loose ends in preparation for France, and he told both Frost and Farjeon that he had put away his childish things. He now knew he would be posted to 244 Siege Battery: a captain, a lieutenant and five second lieutenants (of which he was one), and a company of around 150 men—a motley rabble in the words of their commanding officer, 'semi-trained and ill-disciplined, and quite unfit for active service'.[4]

On 22 December a camp order was issued forbidding weekend leave that extended into Christmas. Thomas let Helen know the disappointing news that this last Christmas before France would be spent apart. He could be posted at any time now, he told her, and to any place, adding that if she were to hear of anyone wanting to give him a Christmas present he could do with any of the following: an oilskin overcoat, arctic socks (two sizes too small for wearing inside his army boots), a periscope, a pocket sextant. To Helen the news was devastating: it made a thumping noise in her head. But then something happened that Helen could think of only as a 'miracle': the army changed its mind. Leave was granted after all, and Edward was able to go to High Beech. Helen and the children sang songs in delight; and if that were not enough, she received an unexpected gift of £20 from a fund to writers administered by Wilfrid and Viola Meynell, and travelled into London to buy

383

supplies for the family and a small Christmas tree for Myfanwy, who would go pale with surprise when she came into the room to find it on Christmas Day. Mervyn and Bronwen went down the lane to wait for their daddy, while Helen returned to prepare a turkey with Myfanwy. The approach of Edward's footsteps had been muffled by the snow, but the call of his 'Coo-ee' from the lane was unmistakable. He was 'so very glad' to be home.[5]

*   *   *

On 29 December, having returned to Lydd, Thomas wrote to Myfanwy telling her about the poem 'Out in the Dark' written on an evening over Christmas in which she had not wanted to enter the sitting room because it was gloomy. He told her that they were to shoot with real guns for the first time, and that France seemed ever closer. 'I do hope peace won't come just yet. I should not know what to do, especially if it came before I had really been a solider. I wonder if you want peace, and if you can remember when there was no war.' And then he sympathised with her visit to town to have a bad tooth taken out. 'I hope you don't dislike the dentist who took it away.' It was a care and kindness that Thomas would show more of in the weeks ahead.[6]

*   *   *

On 23 December Wilfrid Gibson left England for a tour of the United States. (Thomas to Frost: 'You have borrowed Gibson from us. Pray don't trouble to return him unless empty.') He was the last of the Dymock poets to leave Gloucestershire.

British soldiers had been drafted into the parish to help with hay-baling; children picked wool where it had snagged on the hedgerows and barbed wire for the war effort. German prisoners of war worked in the fields of Dymock in 1917, turning potatoes in the fields. Peggy Carless was a telegram girl for the Greenway Post Office. When a message was received she was sent out on her bicycle to deliver it. It was a job she had loved until then, riding the gentle lanes on her red bicycle, but now the telegrams she carried to families that she had grown up with told of the death of their sons. Over a hundred of Dymock's men left to fight; a third did not return.[7]

*   *   *

New Year's Day broke sunny and bright over Lydd. The rattle of practice fire had become as routine to the men as it had to the wildlife. Sixteen rounds of ammunition cracked no more than twenty yards from where Thomas was standing, and it deafened him for a moment only. A hundred yards further off, sheep barely scattered at the sound and a thrush continued to sing from a gorse bush. The men were getting to know the heavy weaponry with which they would be working; guns that weighed up to four and a half tons and took a team of a dozen draught horses to pull. A six-inch howitzer fired from Trafalgar Square could reach Crystal Palace six miles away; a sixty-pound field gun could fire a shrapnel or lyddite shell two miles further still, as far as Epping Forest.[8]

On the weekend of 6–7 January, Thomas was at High Beech for the last time before he left for

France. Friends arrived to say their goodbyes. Eleanor Farjeon was among them, and received her instructions to work with John Freeman in supervising Edward's typescript through the press. At the top of the stairs, Farjeon and Thomas kissed goodnight. 'Strong as it was,' she wrote, 'and for me so very deep, our friendship had remained undemonstrative from beginning to end.' She left on 9 January, while Helen cooked and Edward bathed Myfanwy in an old zinc tub in front of the open fire and sang the folk songs she so loved to hear:

> O Father, Father come build me a boat
> That on the ocean I may float
> And every flagship I chance to meet
> I will enquire for my William Sweet
> For a maid a maid I shall never be
> Till apples grow on an orange tree.

He read stories to Bronwen and studied maps with Mervyn and told each of them to be always kind to their mother while he was away. But between Edward and Helen the kindness was not so easily manageable. Helen remembered his sharpness and her provocation. He was terse as he reminded her about their life assurance and other documents he thought she might one day need, and they bickered about trivialities, Helen wanting a bookshelf put up on a wall that Edward said was too rotten to support it. The last day he might have had with Helen he spent in London instead. He had a dental check, lunch with Harry Hooton and invited his literary friends to present themselves, at St George's Café; in the event only two came, Roger Ingpen and W. H. Davies, and after Ingpen left, Davies and Thomas strolled up Charing Cross Road together in silence, the mood awkward even between these two oldest of friends. Thomas returned to High Beech and to Helen. With his luggage standing in the hall the enormity of the situation seemed too much to speak of. He pressed upon her the need, should he not return, for hired help to dig in the potatoes, and when that failed to ease the tension took out his prismatic compass and showed her how to take a bearing from it; when she cried he closed the casing and put the instrument away. Helen could no longer rein back her desperation and felt engulfed by an uncontrollable grief of a kind that would plague her in the years ahead. She would recount his tenderness in that moment. She wrote of his gentle ability to soothe and steady her, to give her both the emotional and the physical reassurance for which she so longed. He read to her and carried her to the bedroom in his greatcoat. 'Helen, Helen, Helen,' he had said, 'Remember that, whatever happens, all is well between us for ever and ever.' When the morning came, she stood at the gate and watched him disappear into the mist and snow. Edward for his part recorded nothing of the details, only this entry in his diary: 'Said goodbye to Helen, Mervyn and Baba.'[9]

Bronwen travelled with Edward into London and on to his parents' house at Balham. Each of Edward's five brothers came to dinner that night; next morning he said goodbye to them all and to Bronwen and returned to Lydd, where in his diary he scribbled a cluttered and probably unfinished poem of twelve lines regarding the hope behind the gloom of parting.

> The sorrow of true love is a great sorrow
> And true love parting blackens a bright
>   morrow:
> Yet almost they equal joys, since their despair
> Is but hope blinded by its tears, and clear
> Above the storm the heavens wait to be
>   seen.[10]

There was still some snow lying on the Kentish roads when Thomas wrote to his son from Lydd to wish him a happy birthday for the 15th: he sent the boy a book on slide-rulers, and said that he hoped to be home for the next one. He wrote to Helen to say that, for intelligence reasons, he would be able to tell her little of his whereabouts once in France and so outlined for her a code with which he might evade the censor. 'If I am at the Somme I shall say "I am pleased with my situation". If I am at Ypres I shall say "I am *fairly* pleased with my situation". If I am at Havre or somewhere far back in reserve, which may happen at first, I shall say "We are as safe as at Lydd".' He was dawdling in camp, waiting for the call to go to Codford, the final staging post before France, and told Frost that he was 'impatient to go'.[11]

On 15 January Thomas left Lydd beneath light snow and red sun and reached Codford on Salisbury Plain under cover of darkness. The camp where he was to be billeted for the next two weeks was bitterly cold and conditions were poor: though there was electric light and an open fire, the huts had bare boards and there was no officers' mess, leaving the men to club together to buy whatever they needed. It was here that the final mobilisation would take place: guns and stores were collected for transport, while final provisions were issued to the men: gas respirators, tin hats, field dressings. But spirits were high as the men marched through a frosty, clear, following day to Wylye, Stockton, Sherrington, singing as they went. These were days of light snow at night and hard frosts by morning and walks at dusk. Thomas considered little beyond what he would take to France. He had the works of Shakespeare, the Book of Common Prayer and Laurence Sterne's *Sentimental Journey* (he had smiled to overhear an officer at Ashford station asking for the poetry of Ella Wheeler Wilcox): 'It will probably be all I want,' he told Eleanor, though from Helen he asked for a few more home comforts: socks, waistcoat and slippers. Beyond that, he kept more intimate feelings at bay and even seemed remote as he signed off a letter to his mother, 'Yours ever Edward Thomas'.[12]

Thick snow descended in mid-January; Eleanor recalled that it held back the spring until April. At Codford, the camp locked in against the bitter cold for its final fortnight of training. Thomas gave lectures on map-reading and learned to ride a motor cycle; in the post came a cake from his mother and a volume of Shakespeare's Sonnets from Helen. 'No church parade for me,' Thomas noted in his diary for Sunday 21 January, and chose instead to walk for thirteen miles along iced roads and over frozen grass to Barford St Martin and Netherhampton, where he had lunch with the family of Henry Newbolt. He noted the ivied ash trees, the freezing drizzle, the view over the Downs, and a family of poachers that he stopped to watch roasting their catch over a

389

slow wood fire. The next morning at 10.30 he made the last of his personal visits, to see Jack Haines in Gloucester. He told Haines that he had taken to composing his poems in the early hours when it was too dark to read, before committing them to paper in daylight. They sat up into the early hours 'gossiping about Frost' and Haines gave Thomas the one book he had hoped to take to France more than any other, Frost's *Mountain Interval*. When Haines toasted his good future, Thomas smiled and said 'no one could tell what future was good future'.[13]

Though a poet and a botanist, it was in his capacity as a solicitor that Haines sat down with Thomas that weekend, having drawn up by hand a Memorandum of Agreement with Selwyn and Blount for Thomas's *Poems*. The clauses were familiar to Thomas; he had signed contracts for thirty books of his own and many besides that he had edited; but this would be the last. The six clauses were simple and standard. The work would be produced at the publisher's expense, indemnified by the author who would offer them English language rights throughout the world. In return, the publisher would pay Thomas a royalty of ten per cent on the published price after 250 copies, and fifteen per cent should the edition reprint its initial 500 copies; but the fact that the publishers would withhold payment on the first 250 copies meant that, in effect, Thomas would contribute £4 7s. 6d. to the expense of the book. All other sums from sales in any other territories—be they books, printed sheets or serial—would be equally divided between the author and the publisher. If the print run of 525 sold through, Thomas stood to earn £4 16s. 3d.[14]

On 23 January, on the train back from Gloucester,

Thomas read the whole of *Mountain Interval* except for one piece, the long poem 'Snow', which he kept back for another time. 'They are very good,' he told Eleanor, 'though never better or different from "North of Boston".' To Frost he wrote affectionately, 'I did admire, but much more it was getting close to you again that the reading meant. Probably it is that makes me more homesick than I have been for some time. Homesick or something.' Thomas missed the plain-speaking companionship that Frost had given him; he missed being able to be simply himself. He had heard girls in the train talk heartlessly of how 'facing realities' would be the making of so-and-so; but 'so-and-so can't face more than he was born to, I expect: nor I,' he wrote. 'So that I worry less and less about that gamekeeper.' His fatalism was on full display. The incident with the gamekeeper and the quarrel over 'The Road Not Taken': each had been instrumental in demonstrating what he understood as the inevitability of certain forces in life. By this, he did not mean preordination or destiny or any of the terms a church might appropriate, but something to do with the elemental conditions embedded in the natural world: the coursing of water, the power of wind, the gravity of rain—something pagan and ancient, as he once explained, 'When gods were young | This wind was old.' For so long, he had been plagued by indeterminacy, but the war was an irresistible force that overtook the uncertainty in Thomas, and for a moment he sounded more Frost-like than Frost. 'It is always better to do a thing than to "imagine" what it would be like to do it,' he wrote. 'Someday we can discuss the difference—that is if you have imagined [it] at all.'[15]

In the final days at Codford he walked as much

391

as he could, too far in fact, for trailing over the frosty Downs under a clear new moon, his new boots began to chafe his ankles and cause abrasions that would dog him throughout his time in France. As he rested his sore heels, he learned that the guns would ship out to France on 27 January, the battery embarking two days later. The loading of lorries began in earnest, attaching the guns to the four-wheel drives in biting, easterly winds. The rawness of his ankles was such that it kept him awake in the cold nights, and prevented him from walking far enough by day to fully warm up.

With two days to go before embarkation, Saturday broke with the sighting of a fox in the frost, and 'the sun like a bright coin between the knuckles of opposite hills'. A telegram had come to say that Myfanwy was staying with Arthur Ransome's wife Ivy at Hatch, which told him all that he needed to know of how things had gotten on top of Helen in his absence from Essex; in the time to come, she would place young Baba with friends while wrestling with her grief for Edward. Hatch was only thirteen miles from Codford, and Thomas swapped his boots for a colleague's and set off to see his daughter. Warm fires and cold ice for his feet awaited him at the Ransomes', where he spent the night. He mentioned nothing of it to Helen in his letters, only the journey back on Sunday, which he made through freezing rain on a hired bicycle in order to save his blistered feet. For once, he followed a sentimental path, returning along the hedgeless roads that previously he had taken with Mervyn towards the house of the man who had formally opened the Poetry Bookshop, Henry Newbolt. It must have seemed such a long time ago that he had attended that opening of the

Devonshire Street shop, gossiping about the literary world, of commissions and reviews, of new poets and of the squabbles of the poetry fraternity that seemed so minor now. How many things had changed for him since he chatted in that bookshop, unaware that the greatest friend he would ever have stood only a few feet away. That friendship, the birth of his own verse and the outbreak of war had led him here, to an isolated lane in a frozen dusk, on the last evening he would experience in England.[16]

IV

ARRAS

1917

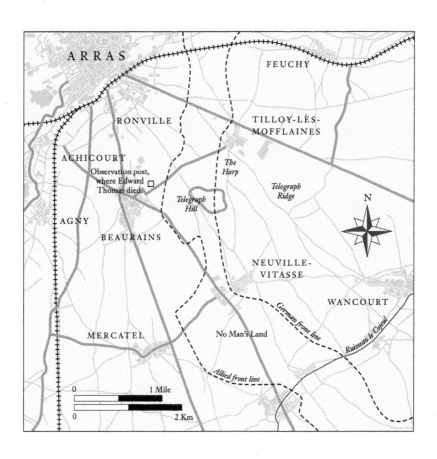

ARRAS

FEUCHY

RONVILLE

TILLOY-LÈS-
MOFFLAINES

ACHICOURT

Observation post,
where Edward
Thomas died.

The
Harp

Telegraph
Ridge

Telegraph
Hill

N

AGNY

BEAURAINS

NEUVILLE-
VITASSE

WANCOURT

German front line

Ruisseau le Cojeul

MERCATEL

No Man's Land

Allied front line

0   1 Mile

0   2 Km

Winter–Spring

The men of 244 Siege Battery rose in the winter cold at five o'clock; by half past six they were marching from Codford through the frost, singing 'Pack Up Your Troubles' in the darkness. Edward Thomas said to hear the men sing the rotten song with such gusto brought a tear to his eye. The train to Southampton was perishingly cold, but delivered them to the docks by half past nine that morning. The rest of the day would be spent waiting for dusk to fall so that they could sail under cover of darkness. Thomas sat in the South Western Hotel, listening to the sea captains talking of sailing routes to Australia, and writing to Helen as he would now do systematically—mostly, some five letters a week for the next two months. At seven o'clock that evening, they sailed on the *Mona's Queen*. It was 'a tumbling crossing' he noted, but the arrival at Le Havre at four the next morning was restful and unforgettable. Tall pale houses lit the quay. At sunrise they marched through fields full of cotton bales and falling snow. They arrived at camp at 9.45 a.m.; Thomas wrapped himself tightly in blankets from the officers' mess to stave off the worst of the chill. His single duty that day was the censoring of letters, which would be his almost daily activity from now on; for one so reticent in his own correspondence, he always encouraged his men not to be shy of familiar comments in theirs. He wrote to Eleanor Farjeon to ask after the progress of his book proofs and to make sure that she had not omitted the dedication, TO ROBERT FROST. He barely felt like reading, and was sure that writing verse was an impossibility. 'No more goodbyes now,' he told Eleanor. 'I shall begin to look ahead perhaps, if I ever do look ahead again. Long it is since I did so.' And to Helen, he wrote this: 'What do you think of "Armed Men in Tears" as the title of my next book?' Neither Edward nor Helen could have thought much of it as a title, but then he did not suppose it could be. For the question was in fact a code: Edward was letting Helen know that he thought he was on his way to Armentières, 200 miles north on the French–Belgian border.[1]

*   *   *

The battery spent almost a week in Le Havre. Thomas took the opportunity to purchase some soft low-topped boots in order to ease his chafed ankles, and on 4 February the orders came to leave the port and begin the move up to the front. For two hours the men were held at the station; singing broke out along the platform and some men joked 'All tickets' as they were boarded thirty-five to a carriage. For the next two days the train crawled through the snow-filled countryside of Picardy: first Buchy, then Alaincourt, then Amiens, arriving at Doullens at sunset. All the while, the clanking of the train was accompanied by the sound of the guns that seemed to draw ever closer.[2]

Spirits among the officers were good. Thomas cooked dinner for the six of them (the CO rarely joined them for dinner), while the talk was light and silly, and he wrote to Helen of 'a very merry evening'. Many evenings would pass off this way:

with wine, cooking and cheese, and the mess gramophone lifting tunes into the night air. 'We six are a rum company', he told Frost, amid an atmosphere that more closely resembled a superior class of picnic than an outpost seven miles from enemy lines. Thomas even had a manservant assigned to lay his dining table, collect his firewood, wash and darn his clothes. 'Very good, sir,' he would say, and, 'You gentlemen have to put up with the same as us,' and 'It's the same for everyone.' Sometimes it took the heavy firing through the nights to remind them just where they really were.[3]

For a week the battery moved up unhurriedly through snowy roads and frozen fields. Thomas would scout ahead in one of the advance lorries looking for a farmhouse or a barn in which to billet the men, noting, as he travelled, the details of his surroundings: the crookedness of a farmyard, a crumbling dovecote, an 'enemy plane like pale moth beautiful among shrapnel bursts'. He relayed the atmosphere to Eleanor: 'We have crept slowly, uncomfortably, but to me amusingly up to our fighting position, often cold, never certain of the next 24 hours, picknicking, pigging it, and arrived at last yesterday afternoon. We officers are in a farmhouse alongside a main road leading to a cathedral town 2 miles off. We are warm but have no other luxuries. We are part of the target of the German artillery 3 miles or so to the east of us; their shellholes are common behind us and the shells rattle our windows frequently, while friendly batteries shoot over our heads.' The cathedral town was Arras, capital of the Nord-Pas-de-Calais region, a citadel with a once-fine cathedral square that had narrowly avoided capture by the Germans in the autumn of 1914.

401

Thomas had billeted his men there on a road to the south of the city on 9 February. The next day, with little fuss, he recorded in his diary, 'One dead man under railway bridge', so neat and still in his sacking that Thomas at first did not realise he was dead.[4]

Each morning, Thomas's duty was to identify an observation post from which he might survey the placement and the condition of the German lines, and so determine the tactical situation of his own battery. Many of the best posts had long since been demolished by shell-fire: the church towers and chimneys of the surrounding villages, even the tall poplars so characteristic of the landscape; now the slightest ridge might be a valuable rampart, but by definition these areas had very little in the way of cover. Thomas was never more exposed than in his work looking out from the observation posts; a head too long poked above the rise or a glint from the sun on his field glasses might be all a sniper needed to lock on. Not a living thing came into view on the first day of his observation, only a 'snowy broken land with posts and wires and dead trees' and a shadow-line where he knew the German trench to be. But he told his parents that he was 'privately pleased' to have completed what he called 'his first day of the real thing'.[5]

By 11 February, the battery had settled into positions outside Arras, a mile from German lines. Snow lay thick on the ground in all directions, and silenced everything but the guns. It was desolate, beautiful, cold; white fields rolled into no-man's-land. The first death was reported in the sister battery and someone put on a recording of Gounod's 'Ave Maria'; it rang out over the snow and brought everyone to a standstill.[6]

A thaw came and exposed the year's first grass. Thomas watched hare and wild duck in the field south-east of the guns, but nowhere on the rolling hills did he see sheep or cattle, only barbed wire and the occasional telephone pole rising out of the snow. Here and there the ground was pocked with shell holes and all around villages lay in ruins, mostly abandoned, with only the most hardened inhabitants remaining. Thomas read the volume of Shakespeare's Sonnets that Helen had given him, but mostly he did not feel much like reading. 'Of course I can't write,' he told de la Mare, 'but then I don't want to or think about it.' No letters had yet arrived for the battery and men's moods were occasionally tetchy: his captain barked at him. 'You get on with your sonnets.' 'Awful fug,' thought Thomas.[7]

When finally the letters did come through, Thomas learned from Eleanor that the proofs for *Poems* had arrived from Selwyn and Blount and that they had corrected some minor slips. 'My proofs sound as if they would be perfect,' he wrote back. In fact the proofs were less than perfect. The compositor had been careless, centring the poems unevenly, separating some by two lines, others by one, and stretching the turned lines artificially to meet the right-hand margin as if they were prose. The thin leading beneath the titles lent the page a mean, cramped look. In short, it was a mess.[8]

*   *   *

Thomas was seconded to the headquarters of the Heavy Artillery Group on 21 February, three miles from his battery. His skills in map reading

403

were much needed at HQ to help assemble the reconnaissance photographs that the aeroplanes were bringing back, and for the next two weeks he would be loaned out from his battery, working on minor intelligence scraps, dispatches, administrating and answering telephones. Rather than enjoying the outdoors as he had with the 244th, he was now stuck inside the inner workings of the army, and Thomas was not pleased. 'Am I to stay on here and do nothing but have cold feet', he asked in his diary, adding, 'No thrushes, but chaffinches say "Chink" in the chestnut tree in the garden.' He puzzled at the lack of thrushes more than he did the deployment of the guns, and the fact that he had not heard a blackbird since his arrival in France.[9]

'You know that life is in so strange that I am only half myself,' he wrote to Frost on 23 February, 'and the half that knows England and you is obediently asleep for a time. Do you believe me? It seems I have sent it to sleep to make the life endurable— more than endurable, really enjoyable in a way.' Thomas had struggled to reconnect to Frost since leaving England. He said that he had read the remaining poem in *Mountain Interval*, 'Snow', and liked it, comparing it to Horace, but that was all the literary conversation he would manage. Rarely as he looked out over no-man's-land from his observation post did he think of human suffering; the German line was just 2,000 yards away but in his diary, he wrote: 'The shelling must have slaughtered many jackdaws but has made home for many more.' A few days later, 'Chaffinches and partridges, moles working on surface', adding, 'Does a mole ever get hit by a shell?' He had still seen only one dead body, and recorded only one Allied fatality. He had supervised the digging of the trenches, though the cold weather had largely spared him and his men the terrible mud. He had done 'a little firing', he told Bottomley, but essentially had not yet been fired at in return. He knew that must surely change. 'Why do Huns not retaliate on Arras guns?' he wrote on 24 February. 'Some day this will be one of the hottest places this side of Hell, if it is this side.' That evening, the officers took a long dinner: hors d'oeuvres, roast mutton, Christmas pudding, whisky, coffee, Maraschino chocolates; *Peer Gynt* played on the gramophone. Walking back to Arras in the dark, owls hunted on the Dainville road.[10]

*   *   *

Edward Thomas came under fire for the first time on 26 February. He had gone to Achicourt to inspect whether a gun position was visible to the Germans: it must have been, for machine-gun bullets whistled overhead accompanied by four shell bursts 150 yards away. Thomas wrote to Helen that the experience had made him feel 'shy', and yet eager to carry on as far as possible as though nothing had happened. 'This makes the heart beat but no more than if I were going to pay a call on a stranger,' he wrote. 'I try to console myself by reflecting that you cannot escape either by running or by standing still. There is no safe place and consequently why worry? And I don't worry.' But German fire was only the half of his danger that day. Returning back from Achicourt toward his siege battery, Thomas had just walked clear of the muzzle of his own eighteen-pounder when it opened up. 'I was within 3 yards of being shot by one of our own guns,' he told Bottomley; 'The order comes to fire and they fire,' to Helen, 'damn them.' It was not all Grieg and poetry, he now had to admit.[11]

He had professed his happiness to Frost, but he adopted no such disguise with Helen. The lack of exercise and the excess of food and perhaps his recent exposure to artillery were making him downcast. He asked after Mervyn, wondering whether the boy might join an Officer Training Corps, and then he paused, 'But I am depressed', he wrote:

it becomes harder for me to think about things at home and somehow, although this life does not absorb me, I think, yet, I can't think of anything else. I don't hanker after anything I don't miss anything. I am not even conscious of waiting. I am just quietly in exile, a sort of half or quarter man—at Romford I was half or *three* quarter man. Only sometimes I hear things I really care for, far off as if at the end of a telephone.

And he added, 'The fact is it is a sort of interval in reality, a protracted railway waiting room. Yet of course not always merely that.'[12]

*   *   *

For the next week, Edward Thomas continued his secondment to Group HQ three miles from his battery. He recorded 'idle cold hours indoors', sitting up late for dispatches and stifling tempers, while artillery fire rattled constantly through the streets where the operations were situated. 'I am fed up with sitting on my arse doing nothing that anybody couldn't do better,' he wrote furtively. His thirty-ninth birthday came and went without any post. 'I still don't hear from you,' he wrote to Frost, and relayed to his friend the recent skirmishes; how enemy planes were chased off with salvos of anti-aircraft fire, only to be followed by a barrage of German artillery as the planes reported back on positions. But at least the whistle of the raining shells told them all that it was not gas coming in. Thomas wrote that he no longer wanted anything consciously, 'except, I suppose, the end'. His moods had been dampening for days; he told Frost,

> I hear my book is coming out soon. Did the duplicate verses ever reach you? You have never said so. But don't think I mind. I should like to be a poet, just as I should like to live, but I know as much about my chances in either case, and I don't really trouble about either. Only I want to come back more or less complete.[13]

No sooner had Thomas mailed this off than another came in the post: Helen had forwarded a letter she had received from Frost, who had written to her believing it the quickest way to get news to him. 'I have found a publisher for his poems in America,' Frost declared. On the strength of the poems that had gotten through to Frost, he had convinced Holt of the merits of his friend's work, and to their credit Holt showed none of the caution that had marked their acquisition of Frost:

407

they agreed to follow Selwyn and Blount and issue Thomas's *Poems* on their side of the Atlantic. It was extraordinary news: the poet who had come so recently to his trade and who had met with one rejection after another from English editors was, with a little help from his friends, to have his debut published in both Britain and America. Frost offered to write a foreword for the book if Thomas were willing to 'throw off' his pseudonym and publish under his own name.[14]

'So you did find a publisher after all. I have just heard,' Thomas replied. And that was it: no thank you, no euphoria, and only a passing mention in his diary. 'Yesterday was cold and raw and I became very depressed and solitary by the evening,' he continued in his letter to Frost. 'Very soon, I expect to have no time or room left for depression.' The snow had set in once more, and there was nothing to see but the snow itself, nothing to hear but artillery. Occasionally he saw children in the devastated villages 'too poor or too helpless' to leave, he told his friend, 'but I probably am not going to describe any more except to make a living'. It was a telling comment for Thomas to make. In January he had written something tiny but of equal importance to Helen: 'Please put these letters in my drawer.' It seemed he intended to use his letters and his diary to write about the war after his return; his enlistment was something he intended to survive and the re-emergence of his gloom expressed not a death wish but a growing recognition that he might not live.[15]

'I can't *feel* that my chances of escape are very good,' he wrote to Walter de la Mare, who had just returned from his lecture tour of the States where he had met a reluctant Frost. This was the final letter that Thomas would write to his old friend, and it would be plaintive. In purple pencil, in a cramped and urgent hand, he described the cold and the dirt and the fatigue and the uncertainty.

> We might see the apple blossom but I doubt that. Nobody is very hopeful. I think myself that things may go on at this rate for more than a year. The rate may be changed, but not if the Hun can help it, and his retirement looks very inconvenient in every way. I wish you had said more about Frost. One is absolutely friendless here . . . You say it would be good if we could have a talk, but, you know, I fancy it would not do to have a real friend out here.[16]

*   *   *

At an exposed crossroads on the outskirts of Arras known as the 'Windy Corner', Thomas surveyed his most dangerous observation so far. There stood one of the few factory chimneys that had not been destroyed by shelling: two hundred feet high, it promised a key vantage point from which to observe the German lines; but it was horribly vulnerable and had been hit three times already by small fire, loosening parts of the brickwork. From reconnaissance, Thomas knew that iron rings inside the chimney served as a ladder, and that one of the rings was loose, but he did not know which one. Worse still, the funnel tapered, so that in climbing the inside of the chimney he would hang further out over the ground below with each rung he ascended. He tested the first rings and began to climb. A shell exploded close by and shook the chimney. Then another and another. Thomas's nerve failed him. 'It was impossible and I knew it,' he explained to Frost. 'As a matter of fact I had no light and no information about the method of getting up so that all the screwing up I had given myself would in any case have been futile. It was just another experience like the gamekeeper.'[17]

The incident with the keeper haunted him until the very end.

*   *   *

The following day was calm: the first thrush appeared, and from the orchard that was his billet Thomas watched a ploughman take his team of horses up and down the misty field; each time they climbed the ridge they came into view of German artillery, but not a shot was fired. The night brought heavy bombardment. Thomas had barely slept for the pounding; when he did, he dreamed almost for the first time since leaving England. In his dream he was at home again, but as he told Helen in a letter, 'I was a sort of visitor and I could not stay to tea.' It was a very feeble dream, he told her, but in his mind it clearly signified something more: 'You must not convince yourself you are merely waiting, you know.'[18]

*   *   *

On 20 March Thomas started out at four in the morning through the darkness toward the observation posts at Ronville. The trench where he would begin his observation was stiff with cold until the rain fell and loosened it into a terrible slurry. 'You have often heard of the mud out here, haven't you? Well, I have been in it. It is what you have heard. You nearly pull your leg off, and often your boot off, at each step in the worst places—the stiff soft clay sucks around the boot at each step.'[19]

A few hundred yards to the west of their position lay the strategic promontory of Telegraph Hill, overlooking the Allies along a ridge that linked it to the German lines. 'Telegraph hill quiet as if only rabbits lived there,' he recorded in his diary, but two German snipers lay patiently in wait for the slightest movement by an unwary infantryman. With his keen eyesight, he had already spotted them and would stay out of their sights that day, but he felt terribly exposed. The fact that for once he left his diary at camp, 'in case', as he put it, spoke of the danger he was prepared for. The first shelling went south into Beaurains, but it turned slowly northward to his position at Ronville. In came the fire—'horrible flap of 5.9 a little along the trench'— all day, all night. He slept leaning against the trench wall, in a cold, wet and seemingly endless night. He was finally relieved at eight o'clock the next morning, returning to billet as engineers were repairing the roads; the shell holes had filled with water and blood. He fell into an exhausted sleep that afternoon and did not wake until morning.[20]

*   *   *

'Nobody quite knows what is happening and whether it is really altogether favourable or not,' he wrote to a friend. The battery was still stationed in the orchard outside Arras, and still

411

they waited for the order to move up. His senses seemed sharply alive, exaggerated even, after his terrible night in the trench. His diary records: 'Beautiful was Arras yesterday coming down from Beaurains and seeing Town Hall ruin white in sun like a thick smoke beginning to curl. Sprinkle of snow today in sun.' That evening, the gramophone played Chopin's 'Berceuse'. For a second time, Thomas watched the plough going up over the crest towards Beaurains; once again, the German artillery let the farmer alone.[21]

'Isn't it wonderful how some men get hit and some don't,' he wrote to Mervyn. 'But it is the same with trees and houses, so that I don't see why it makes some people "believe in God".' But belief did have its virtues, he told his son. 'It is a good thing to believe. I think brave people all believe something and I daresay they are not so likely to be killed as those who don't believe and are not so brave.' And he mentioned Mervyn's new bicycle that his son had told him about: could he buy the old one from him on his return? Might Mervyn oil it for him and hang it on the kitchen wall at High Beech? 'I should like to ride out to Jesse's with you in the summer.'[22]

*   *   *

Thomas rose early on 24 March and set out for Beaurains, a devastated village on the lip of the front line. He had observed this 'ghastly' place many times from a distance, but now that he saw it up close it was, he said, a true vision of Hell. Never did he imagine it would be so bad. The broken brick and stone walls had formed 'dunes' of

412

rubble throughout the pulverised village; the trees were splintered and snapped and torn; only the tombstones in the graveyard still stood: they were all the evidence that a church had once stood there. Overhead, a British plane went down in a hail of flaming fragments. Thomas was pleased to retreat to what was to be the battery's new position: an ash copse in an old chalk quarry where hazel and birch had taken root, between the villages of Agny and Achicourt. He rested his back against the mossy chalk and watched a rabbit which had refused to be driven out. He marvelled at the animals' ability to survive. The chalk soils reminded him of the Froxfield plateau, just as the broken stone of Beaurains village had put him in mind of his old Steep cottage.[23]

*   *   *

The battery moved up on the 26th. The Service Corps lorries arrived to transport the equipment up to the chalk pit, leaving the men to make the journey on foot through the night. The darkness covered the troops' movement, and by daylight no shell-fire had come into the copse. Thomas supervised the bending and cutting of the birches which lay in their battery's line of fire, and for a few brief moments he and another officer looked for primroses. These were 'pleasant and even merry hours and moments', he noted, in particular for the kindness between the men, sharing their provisions from home, among them the Fortnum and Mason package that Eleanor had sent out. 'I keep feeling that I should enjoy it more if I knew I would survive it.'[24]

413

A new zero-line was established, and the battery began to dig in in earnest. 'Death looms, but however it comes it is unexpected, whether from appendicitis or bullet,' he wrote to his youngest brother. 'I have suffered more from January to March in other years than this.'[25]

*   *   *

Heavy snow fell on 2 April. 'Things are closely impending now and will have happened before you get this and you will know all about them, so I will not try to tell you what they are, especially as I could not get them past the censor,' he told Frost. 'And I hear nothing of you—yet you are no more like an American in a book than you were 2½ years ago. You are among the unchanged things that I can not or dare not think of except in flashes.' These would be the final words that Thomas wrote to Frost.[26]

*   *   *

On 4 April Helen Thomas wrote from High Beech to her dear friend Janet Hooton.

> I'm getting on all right tho' this terrible winter will stand out in my memory as a sort of nightmare. The intense cold and the long dark days in this strange place, and then on January 11th that terrible parting, not knowing when we should see each other again; knowing nothing but that for each of us it was so terrible that I did not know one could live through such agony . . . That awful fear is

414

always clutching at my heart, but I put it away time after time, and keep at my work and think of his home-coming.[27]

On Good Friday, Edward Thomas read over a clipping that Gordon Bottomley had sent him. *An Anthology of New Poetry*, co-edited by Lascelles Abercrombie, had been published in February, carrying eighteen of Thomas's poems under the name of Edward Eastaway. A review in the *Times Literary Supplement* had singled out his contribution. 'He is a real poet, with the truth in him.' A second, in the *New Statesman*, claimed to know (but did not reveal) the author's true identity: 'His poems are better than his prose, good though some of this has been. There are not enough of them here to give one an exact notion of his power and his limitations. But "The Wood", "Aspens", "The Brook", "Wind and Mist", and "For These" would, by themselves, be enough to show that he is worth fifty Frosts.'[28]

Robert Frost said this: 'His poetry is so very brave—so unconsciously brave. He didn't think of it for a moment as war poetry, though that is what it is. It ought to be called Roads to France.'[29]

Good Friday was the day that the United States entered the war.

*   *   *

On the weekend of 7–8 April the heavy guns of 244 Siege Battery stood wheel to wheel on the sunken road before the quarry that ran parallel to the front.

Saturday April 7 or 8—Arras

Dearest

Here I am in my valise on the floor of my dugout writing before sleeping. The artillery is like a stormy tide breaking on the shores of the full moon that rides high and clear among white cirrus clouds . . . Hardly anything came near the O.P. or even the village. I simply watched the shells changing the landscape. The pretty village among trees that I first saw two weeks ago is now just ruins among violated stark tree trunks. But the sun shone and larks and partridge and magpies and hedgesparrows made love and the trench was being made passable for the wounded that will be harvested in a day or two. Either the Bosh is beaten or he is going to surprise us . . . One officer has to be at the O.P. every day and every other night. So it will be all work now till further notice—days of ten times the ordinary work too. So goodnight and I hope you sleep no worse than I do . . .

Sunday. I slept jolly well and now it is sunshine and wind and we are in for a long day and I must post this when I can.

All and always yours Edwy[30]

Edward Thomas spent the day before he died under particularly heavy bombardment. The shell that fell two yards from where he stood should have killed him, but instead it was a rare dud. Back at billet, the men teased him on his lucky escape; someone remarked that a fellow with Thomas's luck should be safe wherever he went.

Myfanwy Thomas was embroidering a wild duck onto a postcard to send to her daddy when the telegraph boy drew up outside the house. Helen read the message in silence, while he waited for her reply. 'No answer,' she eventually said.[31]

Thomas's commanding officer wrote, 'We buried him in a little military cemetery a few hundred yards from the battery, the exact spot will be notified to you by the parson. As we stood by his grave the sun came and the guns round seemed to stop firing for a short time.'[32]

On the last pages of his war diary, Edward Thomas wrote, 'I never understood quite what was meant by God', and in pencil the following three lines,

> Where any turn may lead to Heaven
> Or any corner may hide Hell
> Roads shining like river up hill after rain.[33]

Robert Frost wrote to Helen in condolence. 'I want to see him to tell him something. I want to tell him, what I think he liked to hear from me, that he was a poet.'[34]

Helen lived for fifty years following Edward's death; she never remarried. The memoirs that she wrote of their life together would be cherished by readers, though little loved by Edward's friends at the time. Robert Frost for one railed against them. He thought Helen had made Edward look ridiculous in his innocence, emasculated in an 'undressing to the public'. Robert and Helen never reconciled their differences; in later years he removed a dedication to her from his *Selected Poems*.[1]

Mervyn was seventeen when his father died. They never overcame what he called the 'unhappy strangeness' between them. He had been unable to relate to his father's literary life, but through his apprenticeship they had begun to find a language they could share based on engineering or the servicing of an army motorbike. Mervyn would qualify as a draughtsman and would work as a technical editor and motor journalist; he served with the Kent Rifle Regiment in 1918 and with the REME Corps in the Middle East during the Second World War.[2]

Bronwen's adult life was marked by tragedy: she lost three husbands and suffered poor health, and though she trained to be a dress designer she never made a profession for herself. Myfanwy stayed with her aunt during Helen's long period of illness that followed Edward's death; she became a teacher after the Second World War. Both daughters brought up children through periods of absent fathers.

Robert Frost would face tragedy of his own.

In 1938 Elinor died, and without the woman that he had loved from his school days, he became grief stricken. His son Carol shot himself shortly after; he was the fourth child that Robert had buried. But Frost's poetry prospered. He won a Pulitzer prize for his fourth book of poems, the homely named *New Hampshire*, and sold a million poetry books in his lifetime; he spoke at the inauguration of President Kennedy. He wrote poems that touched upon Thomas and the war; a copy of *Mountain Interval* was among Edward's personal effects.[3]

Within a month of Thomas's death, Siegfried Sassoon and Wilfred Owen had both been invalided back to England. Sassoon had taken a sniper's bullet in the chest at Arras; that summer he would write a letter of 'wilful defiance', published in *The Times*, in which he accused the British government of deliberately prolonging the war. It took an intervention by Robert Graves to prevent a court-martial. Sassoon was dispatched to the care of W. H. R. Rivers at Craiglockhart War Hospital, where he met Owen suffering from shell-shock. Together they would write some of the most powerful poetry of the war before returning to action, Sassoon surviving his ordeal, Owen not.

Ezra Pound was furious at the way he thought Britain had served up her young men to slaughter: 'For an old bitch gone in the teeth, | For a botched civilization'. He moved to Italy where his anti-American and anti-Semitic broadcasts for Radio Rome saw him arraigned for treason by the United States; Frost was among the writers who secured his release from a Washington mental asylum in 1958. Richard Aldington fought in and survived

420

the conflict; T. E. Hulme was not so fortunate. T. S. Eliot was unsuccessful in his attempt to serve in the United States Navy.[4]

Thomas's agent, Charles Francis Cazenove, died after a short illness in 1915; Godwin Baynes moved to Zurich to study under Carl Jung.

Eleanor Farjeon became a leading author of children's books. Edna Clarke Hall returned to painting and exhibited widely in the 1920s and 30s; she lived to be one hundred.

Walter de la Mare was saddened to discover that Thomas felt let down by his friends. 'E. T. was probably feeling bitterly isolated,' Edward Garnett explained to him in 1920, 'I don't think I gauged the extent of this, myself, till later on.' De la Mare penned an affecting tribute: 'You would have grieved—'twixt joy and fear—| To know how my small loving son | Had wept for you, my dear.'[5]

Wilfrid Wilson Gibson published the most widely read book of war poetry by a non-combatant, but his popularity would not endure. In 1934 he wrote to Frost to say, 'I am one of those unlucky writers whose books have predeceased him'; he did not write a single line of verse for the final twelve years of his life. Ivor Gurney died in an asylum in Dartford in 1937; John Drinkwater died that year too. W. H. Davies married after the war; it was said that he conducted the ceremony in near panic.[6]

Lascelles Abercrombie came to see his life's work as 'unrealized ambition', and would reflect ruefully, 'I have lived in Gloucestershire, and I have known what it is to have Wilfrid Gibson and Robert Frost for my neighbours; and John Drinkwater, Rupert Brooke, Edward Thomas, Will Davies, Bob Trevelyan, Arthur Ransome have drunk my cider and talkt [sic] in my garden. I make no cider now, and I have no garden. But once I lived in Gloucestershire.'[7]

*   *   *

Georgian Poetry sold close to 70,000 copies across five volumes, but the poets it published began to distance themselves from it after the war. By the time the last in the series appeared in 1922 it had outstayed its welcome, and was meekly swept aside by the force of the new, modernising literature. T. S. Eliot's *The Waste Land* and James Joyce's *Ulysses* were published that year, and seemed infinitely more attuned to the disruptive and disturbing new world in which readers found themselves—what Eliot in 1923 called, 'the immense panorama of futility and anarchy which is contemporary history'. The truths and reliabilities of the old order had foundered in the war: nine million young men had gone to their graves in adherence to them. The Georgians would be all but forgotten in the decade ahead. The lease at the Poetry Bookshop expired in 1926, and Harold Monro moved to new premises opposite the British Museum. The original atmosphere never quite transferred, and when Monro died in 1932, the shop struggled on for three years before finally closing its doors.[8]

*   *   *

Poems, by Edward Thomas, was published in London by Selwyn and Blount in October 1917, and by Holt in New York City four months

422

later. Some, like W. H. Hudson, held to their opinions that Thomas's poetic gift 'was rather a small one'. But F. R. Leavis wrote in 1932 that it was a body of work of 'a very rare order'. W. H. Auden and C. Day Lewis said that Thomas was a poet they had 'little or no hope of ever equalling'. Dylan Thomas believed he had grown to be loved by so very many that we could hardly think of a time when he was not alive: 'It is as though we had always known his poems, and were only waiting for him to write them.' In preparing the *Oxford Book of Twentieth Century English Verse*, Philip Larkin would permit Edward Thomas as many poems as T. S. Eliot. Ted Hughes would put it most clearly of anyone. 'He is the father of us all.'9

From the Selwyn and Blount, 21 YORK BUILDINGS,
ADELPHI, LONDON, W.C.,
AUTUMN CATALOGUE 1918, R. E. INGPEN advertises:

Poems By EDWARD THOMAS

Second Edition
With a Portrait in Photogravure. Crown 8vo.
Boards. 3s. 6d. net.

'They are among the rarest fruits of these strange
years.'
Times Literary Supplement

'No other book of English verse, published within
my own time shows the same vivid spirit of love,
the same saturation with English country life and
tradition.'
The New Statesman

'The "Poems" are the last word in English poetry.'
Manchester Guardian

'Edward Thomas's *Poems* is a book that gives us the
essence of all that he spent his life in trying to say in
prose. It is a beautiful book.'
Daily News and Leader

'these poems are certainly the best thing he ever
did.'
The Nation

424

'He leaves us more than we deserved, something that will be treasured by posterity for ever.'
English Review

ACKNOWLEDGEMENTS

I am indebted to the Estate of Edward Thomas for permission to reproduce unpublished and copyrighted materials. 'Iris by Night', 'The Road Not Taken' and 'Not to Keep', The Poetry of Robert Frost, edited by Edward Connery Latham, © 1969 Henry Holt and Co.; reprinted by permission of Henry Holt and Co., LLC. Robert Frost letters to Edward Thomas from Selected Letters of Robert Frost, edited by Lawrance Thompson, © Lawrance Thompson and Henry Holt and Co; reprinted by permission of Henry Holt and Co., LLC.

I am grateful to the following institutions and individuals: Art Workers Guild (Monica Grose Hodge); Battersea Library, Wandsworth Heritage Service (Jane Allen, Felix Lancashire and Ruth MacLeod); Bodleian Library, Oxford (Colin Harris); British Postal Museum and Archive (Claire Woodforde); Cardiff University Library, Edward Thomas Collection (Alison Harvey and Peter Keelan); Dartmouth College, Rauner Special Collections Library (Andrea Bartelstein); Durham University Library, Claude Collier Abbott Collection (Mike Harkness); Fleet Architects (Richard Henson); Foundling Museum (Shelley Mullane); Gloucester Archives (Mick Heath); Imperial War Museum (Tony Richards and Alan Wakefield); Lincoln College Library, Oxford (Andrew Mussell); Met Office (Mark Beswick, Sandy Berridge); National Library of Wales, Aberystwyth (Martin Robson-Riley); New York Public Library, Berg Collection

(Steve Crook); State University of New York, University at Buffalo, Poetry Collection, Lockwood Memorial Library (James Maynard); University of British Columbia Library, Norman Colbeck Collection (Katherine Kalsbeek); University of Gloucestershire, Dymock Poets Archive (Lorna Scott); University of Texas at Austin, Harry Ransom Center (Molly Schwartzburg).

My thanks to Maggie Fergusson, Paula Johnson and Tom Ponsonby (also to James Meek) for a Royal Society of Literature Jerwood Award for Non-Fiction, and to the following publications: *A Winter Garland 2006* (Wordsworth Trust, 2006), *Branch Lines: Edward Thomas and Contemporary Poetry* (ed. Guy Cuthbertson and Lucy Newlyn, Enitharmon 2007); *Edward Thomas Fellowship Newsletter* (ed. Richard Emeny); *Dymock Poets and Friends* (ed. Jeff Cooper).

My special gratitude to Richard Emeny for his insight and advice, and to those who have aided me at the Edward Thomas Fellowship, in particular Chris Brown, Liz Emeny, Anne Harvey, Edward C. Thomas, Colin Thornton, Stephen Turner and Rosemary Vellender; at the Friends of the Dymock Poets especially Jeff Cooper, Linda Hart (and The Butterfly) and Roy Palmer; to Barbara Davis, Jean Eversham and Bob May in Dymock, to Kirsten and Paul Westaway and Goliath at Gamage Hall Farm, where some of this book was written; to Pippa Bush and Robert Moreland; to Jonathan Barker, Bill Barnett, Diana Baynes Jansen, Sabina ffrench Blake, Roland Chambers, Ron Costley, John Haffenden, Andrew Motion, Juliet Nicolson, Richard Purver, Keith Sands and Alison Thomas.

Thank you to Neil Belton and to Kate
428

Murray-Browne at Fabers for their expertise and passion, to Rachel Alexander, Kate Burton and Alex Holroyd, and to Shona Andrew, Robert Brown, Eleanor Crow, Patrick Fox, Hannah Griffiths, Paul Keegan, Gemma Lovett, Sarah Savitt and Kate Ward also. To Polly Clark, Antony Dunn, Clare Pollard and Owen Sheers.

My personal thanks to Mum and to Simon, and to Claire, James and Beowulf.

*   *   *

In suggesting amendments for this paperback edition, I am grateful to Jeff Cooper, Julia Copus, Robert Gomme, Linda Hart, John Jurica, Andrew Stevenson and Frances Whistler.

NOTES ON SOURCES

In researching Edward Thomas I have drawn only upon primary sources, though I would like to acknowledge below those titles which informed my reading or might be of interest to readers wishing to know more. Some of the primary sources I have seen have been examined by others before me, and inevitably I have made links that I went on to discover had already been made; in no way do I intend to be disrespectful to other researchers, and where their work has consciously informed mine I have acknowledged it to be the case. No writer on Thomas can be unaware of the contribution made to our reading of the poems by two scholars in particular: Edna Longley, whose *Poems and Last Poems* was published by Collins in 1973 (wholly revised as *The Annotated Collected Poems*, Tarset: Bloodaxe, 2008), and R. George Thomas, whose edition of *Collected Poems* was published by Oxford University Press in 1978 (reissued as *Collected Poems and War Diary*, London: Faber & Faber, 2004); both editors offer extensive original notes on the poems. William Cooke's research with the manuscripts also deserves special mention (*Edward Thomas: A Critical Biography*, London: Faber & Faber, 1970), while Matthew Spencer's work on the letters of Thomas and Frost has been invaluable in the preparation of this book.

Selections of Edward Thomas's prose can be found in Roland Gant (ed.), *The Prose of Edward Thomas* (London: Falcon Press, 1948) and *Edward Thomas on the Countryside* (London: Faber &

Faber, 1977), and Edna Longley (ed.), *A Language Not to Be Betrayed: Selected Prose* (Manchester: Carcanet, 1981), which also contains a selection of Thomas's reviews, as does Richard Emeny (ed.), *Edward Thomas on the Georgians* (Cheltenham: Cyder Press, 2004) and Trevor Johnson (ed.), *Edward Thomas on Thomas Hardy* (Cheltenham: Cyder Press, 2002). For bibliographic information I have consulted Robert P. Eckert, *Edward Thomas: A Biography and a Bibliography* (London: Dent, 1937), Richard Emeny, *Edward Thomas 1878–1917: Towards a Complete Checklist of His Publications* (ed. Jeff Cooper, Blackburn: White Sheep Press, 2004) and John Buchan, 'A Bibliography of Philip Edward Thomas, 1878–1917' (private collection, 2005). Students of Thomas's work might also like to know of Judy Kendall's edited volume *Edward Thomas's Poets* (Manchester: Carcanet, 2007) and of Guy Cuthbertson and Lucy Newlyn's forthcoming series of *Prose Writings* (Oxford University Press).

Memoirs by Eleanor Farjeon and Helen Thomas merit special mention. *Edward Thomas: the Last Four Years* is an invaluable account of Eleanor's friendship with Thomas; written forty years after events, it understandably contains some factual inconsistencies as well as a number of transcription and dating errors, and where my text departs from the published text it is because I have followed the original letters in Battersea Library (though I have included page numbers from the memoir for readers familiar with the work). Helen Thomas's *As it Was* and *World Without End* (collected in *Under Storm's Wing*) are a moving account of her life with Edward, written to help her come to terms with her grief;

yet as Myfanwy Thomas acknowledged, the works contained 'a fictional licence' (notably, the book's much-praised honeymoon sequence), and though they offer a moving insight into the marriage their perspective is also a partial and in places distorted one and I have been cautious in drawing upon them in depth here. Nevertheless I recommend both of these works to readers seeking a personal account of Thomas's life.

There exist a number of critical and biographical works not cited in my sources, chief among them: H. Coombes, *Edward Thomas* (London: Chatto & Windus, 1956), Jan Marsh, *Edward Thomas: A Poet for his Country* (London: Elek, 1978) and Stan Smith, *Edward Thomas*, Faber Student Guides (London: Faber & Faber, 1986).

In researching Robert Frost and others I have consulted many sources, both primary and secondary (see bibliography below), but the following deserve special and grateful acknowledgement. Two books on Robert Frost's English years by Lesley Lee Frances and John Walsh have been particularly valuable, while Lawrance Thompson's three-volume biography of Frost has been a frequent point of consultation.

The best introduction to the work of the Dymock Poets remains Linda Hart's *Once They Lived in Gloucestershire: A Dymock Poets Anthology* (Lechlade: Green Branch, 1995); Sean Street's *The Dymock Poets* (Bridgend: Seren, 1994) provides a critical account and many valuable articles can be found in *Dymock Poets and Friends* (ed. Jeff Cooper) and the *Edward Thomas Fellowship Newsletter* (ed. Richard Emeny and Guy Cuthbertson). For local history,

I have consulted Jennifer Davies, *Safe in Print: Memories of Donnington, Ryton and Broomsgreen* (published privately, 1994), George Dudfield, *Mud on My Boots: A View of Dymock Life 1909 to 1930* (Ledbury: published privately, 1988) and J. E. Gethyn-Jones, *Dymock Down the Ages* (published privately, 1959, 1966). Robert H. Ross, *The Georgian Revolt: Rise and Fall of a Poetical Ideal, 1910–22* (Carbondale: Southern Illinois University Press, 1965) provides a fine overview of the era. In addition to works on the Poetry Bookshop by Joy Grant and Dominic Hibberd, I have drawn on J. Howard Woolmer, *The Poetry Bookshop 1912–1935: A Bibliography* (Revere, Penn.: Woolmer Brotherson, 1988).

My background reading on the war includes Correlli Barnett, *The Great War* (London: Park Lane Press, 1979 and BBC, 2003), Cyril Falls, *Military Operations: France and Belgium, 1917* (London: Macmillan, 1940), Edward Gleichen, *Chronology of the Great War*, 3 vols (London: Constable, 1918–20), Michael Howard, *The First World War* (Oxford: Oxford University Press, 2002), Hew Strachan, *The First World War* (London: Simon & Schuster, 2003) and A. J. P. Taylor, *English History, 1914–45* (Oxford: Clarendon Press, 1965).

I—ARCHIVE SOURCES

Berg   Berg Collection, New York Public Library
BL   British Library
Bod.   Bodleian Library, University of Oxford
DCL   Dartmouth College Library, Hanover, New Hampshire

DPA   Dymock Poets Archive, University of
      Gloucestershire
DUL   Claude Collier Abbott Collection, Durham
      University Library
ETC   Edward Thomas Collection, Cardiff
      University Library
FF   Faber & Faber
GA   Gloucestershire Archives
IWM   Imperial War Museum
LCL   Lincoln College Library, University of
      Oxford
LML   Lockwood Memorial Library, State
      University of New York at Buffalo
NA   National Archives, Kew
NLW   National Library of Wales, University of
      Aberystwyth
UBC   Norman Colbeck Collection, University of
      British Columbia, Vancouver
UTA   Harry Ransom Center, University of Texas
      at Austin
WHS   Wandsworth Heritage Services, Battersea
      Library

Diaries, Notebooks, Manuscripts and Typescripts

ADW   A. Duncan Williams transcript, 1908–09
      (Bod. MS Eng. misc. c. 501)
BL 44990   autograph of 62 poems, 24 Dec. 1914–
      24 May 1915 (BL Add. Mss. 44990)
diary   Edward Thomas's diary, 12 Dec. 1900–20
      Oct. 1901 (NLW 22900B), 13 Sept. 1902–13
      June 1904 (NLW 22902B), 1908 (NLW
      22907B), 1915 (NLW 22912B)
Don d. 28   notebook of 67 fair copies, 25 June
      1915–24 Dec. 1916 (Bod. MS Don. d. 28)
ECH   Edna Clarke Hall, journals and papers: four

uncatalogued journals (here called ECH$_{1-4}$) Aug. 1917–23 July 1923, and a notebook of fair copies (poems) (private hands)

FNB   Field Note Books (Berg)

JT   typescript of 23 poems, once owned by Julian Thomas, Dec. 1914– (NLW 23077C)

JWH John Wilton Haines papers: 'Edward Thomas by J. W. Haines', GA (D10828/4/11) and 'E.T. 22 Jan. 1917', (GA D10828/4/4)

LML MS   notebook of 5 poems, 16 Nov.–7 Dec. 1914 (LML)

M$_{1-2}$ Mervyn Thomas, two notebooks of 27 poems, 14 Dec. 1914–4 May 1915 (NLW 22920A) and 27 poems, 4 March 1916–5 July 1916 (NLW 22921A)

MET   typescript of 17 poems, once owned by Mary Elizabeth Thomas (BL)

PTS   *Poems* (printer's) typescript (Bod. MS Eng. poet. d. 214)

RLW   Memories of Edward Thomas Collected by Rowland L. Watson, ETC (DPA)

WD   Edward Thomas's War Diary, private collection

II—PERIODICALS AND BROADSHEETS

Academy
American Literature (*AL*)
Atlantic Monthly (*AM*)
The Athenaeum
The Bookman
Clapham Observer (*CO*)
Claremont Quarterly (*CQ*)
The Criterion

Daily Chronicle (DC)
Daily Express (DE)
Daily Mirror (DM)
Daily News (DN)
The Dial
Dymock Poets and Friends (DPF)
Daily Telegraph (DT)
English Review (ER)
Edward Thomas Fellowship Newsletter (ETFN)
Everyman
Form
Guardian
Morning Post (MP)
The Nation
New Age (NA)
New Freewoman (NF)
New Numbers (NN)
New Statesman (NS)
New Weekly (NW)
New York Times (NYT)
Newsweek
Observer
Poetry (Chicago) *(PC)*
Poetry and Drama (PD)
Poetry Review (PR)
Poetry Wales (PW)
Root and Branch (RB)
The Spectator
The Times
Times Literary Supplement (TLS)
T.P.'s Weekly (TPW)
Virginia Quarterly Review (VQR)
Westminster Gazette (WG)
Week's Survey (WS)
Yale Review (YR)

III—PUBLISHED WORKS BY EDWARD THOMAS

ACP *Annotated Collected Poems* (ed. Edna Longley), Tarset: Bloodaxe, 2008

ACS *Algernon Charles Swinburne: A Critical Study*, London: Martin Secker, 1912

BW *Beautiful Wales*, London: A. & C. Black, 1905

CET *The Childhood of Edward Thomas: A Fragment of Autobiography*, London: Faber & Faber, 1938

Country *The Country*, London: B. T. Batsford, 1913

CP1920 *Collected Poems*, London: Selwyn and Blount, 1920

CP1928 *Collected Poems*, London: Ingpen and Grant, 1928

CP1949 *Collected Poems*, London: Faber and Faber, 1949

CP1978 *Collected Poems* (ed. R. George Thomas) Oxford: Clarendon, 1978

CS *Celtic Stories*, Oxford: Clarendon, 1911

FIL *The Flowers I Love: A Series of Twenty-Four Drawings in Colour* (ed.), London: T. C. & E. C. Jack, 1916

FIP *Feminine Influence on the Poets*, London: Martin Secker, 1910

FTB *Four-and-Twenty Blackbirds*, London: Duckworth 1915

GB *George Borrow*, London: Chapman & Hall, 1912

HE *The Heart of England*, London: J. M. Dent, 1906

HGLM *The Happy-Go-Lucky Morgans*, London:

438

Duckworth, 1913

HS   *Horae Solitariae*, London: Duckworth, 1902

IPS   *In Pursuit of Spring*, London: Thomas Nelson, 1914

IW   *The Icknield Way*, London: Constable, 1913

Keats *Keats*, London: T. C. & E. C. Jack, 1916

LDM *The Life of the Duke of Marlborough*, London: Chapman & Hall, 1915

LH   *Lafcadio Hearn*, London: Constable, 1912

LP   *Last Poems*, London: Selwyn and Blount, 1918

LPE *A Literary Pilgrim in England*, London: Methuen, 1917

LS   *The Last Sheaf*, London: Cape, 1928

LT   *Light and Twilight*, London: Duckworth, 1911

MM *Maurice Maeterlinck*, London: Methuen, 1911

NT   *Norse Tales*, Oxford: Clarendon, 1912

Oxford   *Oxford*, London: A. & C. Black, 1903

PB   *The Pocket Book of Poems and Songs for the Open Air* (ed.), London: E. Grant Richards, 1907

Poems   *Poems*, London: Selwyn and Blount, 1917

RJ   *Richard Jefferies*, London: Hutchinson, 1909

SC   *The South Country*, London: J. M. Dent, 1909

SP   *Six Poems*, Flansham: Pear Tree Press, 1916

TE   *This England: An Anthology from Her Writers* (ed.), London: Oxford University Press, 1915

WL   *The Woodland Life*, London: William Blackwood and Sons, 1897

WP   *Walter Pater: A Critical Study*, London: Martin Secker, 1913

IV—CORRESPONDENCE

Letters from Edward Thomas

–ADW   A. Duncan Williams, IWM; *Poems* (facsimile edn.), London: Imperial War Museum, 1997

–CB Clifford Bax, UTA; *Selected Letters* (ed. R. George Thomas), Oxford: Oxford University Press, 1995

–CFC   Charles Francis Cazenove, DUL

–EB Emily Bottomley, ETC; *Letters to Gordon Bottomley* (ed. R. George Thomas), London: Oxford University Press, 1968

–ECH   Edna Clarke Hall, Berg

–EF Eleanor Farjeon, WHS; *Farjeon*

–EG Edward Garnett, UTA; *Letters to Edward Garnett*, Edinburgh: Tragara, 1981

–EWF   Elinor White Frost, *Elected Friends: Robert Frost and Edward Thomas to one another* (ed. Matthew Spencer), New York: Handsel, 2003

–GB Gordon Bottomley, ETC; *Letters to Gordon Bottomley* (ed. R. George Thomas), London: Oxford University Press, 1968

–HEMT   Helen Elizabeth Myfanwy Thomas, ETC

–HH Harry Hooton, Colbeck Collection, University of British Columbia, Vancouver; Moore, *Selected Letters* (ed. R. George Thomas), London: Oxford University Press, 1995, R. George Thomas

–HM Harold Monro, LML; *Poetry Wales*, XIII, 4 (Spring 1978), 43–70

–HT Helen Thomas, ETC; *Letters to Helen* (ed.

R. George Thomas), Manchester: Carcanet, 2000

–IMacA   Ian MacAlister, WHS

–JB   Jesse Berridge, NLW; *Letters of Edward Thomas to Jesse Berridge* (ed. Anthony Berridge), London: Enitharmon, 1983

–JF   John Freeman, Berg, typescript in WHS

–JH   Janet Hooton, ETC; *Letters to Helen* (ed. R. George Thomas), Manchester: Carcanet, 2000

–JT   Julian Thomas, ETC; *Selected Letters* (ed. R. George Thomas), Oxford: Oxford University Press, 1995

–JWH   John Wilton Haines, GA

–MET   Mary Elizabeth Thomas, ETC

–MPT   Mervyn Philip Thomas, ETC

–MT Margaret Townsend, Bod. MS Eng. Lett. d. 281

–PHT   Philip Henry Thomas, ETC; *Letters to Helen* (ed. R. George Thomas), Manchester: Carcanet, 2000

–RF   Robert Frost, DCL; *Elected Friends: Robert Frost and Edward Thomas to one another* (ed. Matthew Spencer), New York: Handsel, 2003

–RMBT   Rachel Mary Bronwen Thomas, ETC

–WdlM   Walter de la Mare, Bod. MS Eng. Lett. c. 376

–WHH   W. H. Hudson, private collection; *ETFN*, LII (Aug. 2004), *Selected Letters* (ed. R. George Thomas), Oxford: Oxford University Press, 1995

Other Correspondence

CFC–   Charles Francis Cazenove to Edward Thomas (ET), DUL

DHL–   D. H. Lawrence to Edward Marsh (EM),
The Letters of D. H. Lawrence, vol. II, *June
1913–October 1916* (ed. G. Zytaruk and J. T.
Boulton), Cambridge: Cambridge University
Press, 1981

EG– Edward Garnett to Walter de la Mare
(WdlM), Whistler

EM– Edward Marsh to Rupert Brooke (RB),
Hassall, *Edward Marsh*

EP– Ezra Pound to Alice Corbin Henderson
(ACH), Harriet Monroe, *Poetry* (Chicago)
(*PC*), *Letters of Ezra Pound 1907–1941* (ed.
D. D. Paige), London: Faber & Faber, 1950

EWF–   Elinor White Frost to Margaret
Bartlett (MB), Leona White Harvey (LWH),
Selected Letters of Robert Frost (ed. Lawrance
Thompson), New York: Holt, Rinehart and
Winston, 1964

FH– Florence Holt to Robert Frost (RF),
Selected Letters of Robert Frost (ed. Lawrance
Thompson), New York: Holt, Rinehart and
Winston, 1964

FL– Franklin Lushington to Helen Thomas (HT),
ETC, WHS

GG– Geraldine Gibson to John Wilton Haines
(JWH), DPA

GWB–   G. W. Blackwood to Eleanor Farjeon
(EF), *Letters to Edward Garnett*, Edinburgh:
Tragara, 1981

HJ– Henry James to Mrs Humphry Ward (HW),
The Letters of Henry James (ed. Percy
Lubbock), vol. II, London: Macmillan, 1920

HT– Helen Thomas to Edna Clarke Hall (ECH),
private collection; Edward Thomas (ET),
ETC (NLW), *Letters to Helen* (ed. R. George

Thomas), Manchester: Carcanet, 2000; Janet
Hooton (JH), ETC, *Under Storm's Wing*;
Harold Monro (HM), LML, *Poetry Wales*,
XIII, 4 (Spring 1978)

IG– Ivor Gurney to Marion Scott (MS),
Collected Letters of Ivor Gurney (ed. R. K. R.
Thornton), Manchester: Carcanet, 1991

JWH– John Wilton Haines to Robert P. Eckert
(RPE), Bod. MS Eng. Lett. c. 281

LA– Lascelles Abercrombie to Edward Marsh
(EM), Berg, DPA; John Wilton Haines
(JWH), GA

MPT– Mervyn Philip Thomas to Edward
Thomas (ET), ETC

RB– Rupert Brooke to Edward Thomas (ET),
Letters of Rupert Brooke (ed. Geoffrey
Keynes), London: Faber & Faber, 1968
(*Letters*); Eileen Wellesley (EW), *Letters*;
Harold Monro (HM) [King's College Library,
Cambridge], Hibberd, *Harold Monro*; John
Drinkwater (JD), *Letters*; Jacques Raverat
(JR), *Letters*; Ka Cox (KC), Hassall, *Rupert
Brooke*; Leonard Bacon (LB), *Letters*; Noel
Olivier (NO), *Song of Love: The Letters of
Rupert Brooke and Noel Olivier* (ed. Pippa
Harris), London: Bloomsbury, 1991; Russell
Loines (RL), *Letters*; Ruth Mary Brooke
(RMB), *Letters*; Walter de la Mare (WdlM),
Whistler; Wilfrid Wilson Gibson, (WWG)
Letters

RF– Robert Frost to Edward Garnett (EG),
Selected Letters of Robert Frost (ed. Lawrance
Thompson), New York: Holt, Rinehart and
Winston, 1964 (*Selected Letters*); Ernest
Jewell (EJ), Sergeant, *The Trial by Existence*,

New York: Holt, Rinehart and Winston, 1960; Ernest Silver (ES), *Selected Letters*; Edward Thomas (ET), Berg, ETC, *Elected Friends: Robert Frost and Edward Thomas to one another* (ed. Matthew Spencer), New York: Handsel, 2003 (*Elected Friends*); F. S. Flint (FSF), UTA, Lawrance Thompson, *Robert Frost: The Early Years, 1874–1915*, New York: Holt, Rinehart and Winston, 1966, Walsh; Gertrude McQuesten (GMcQ), Boston University Library, Walsh; Grace Walcott Conkling (GWC), *Poetry Wales*, XIII, 4 (Spring 1978); Harold Monro (HM), *Selected Letters*; Harold Roy Brennan (HRB), *American Literature*, LIX, 1 (March 1987), 117; Helen Thomas (HT), DCL, *Elected Friends*; John T. Bartlett (JTB), *Selected Letters*; John Wilton Haines (JWH), private collection, *Selected Letters*; Lascelles Abercrombie (LA), *Selected Letters*; Louis Untermeyer (LU), *Letters of Robert Frost to Louis Untermeyer* (ed. Untermeyer), New York: Holt, Rinehart and Winston, 1963; R. P. T. Coffin (RPTC), *Selected Letters*; Sidney Cox (SC), *Selected Letters*; Susan Hayes Ward (SHW), *Selected Letters*; Thomas B. Mosher (TBM), *Selected Letters*; Wilbur E. Rowell (WER), *Selected Letters*

RH– Ralph Hodgson to Robert Frost (RF), DCL, *Selected Letters of Robert Frost* (ed. Lawrance Thompson), New York: Holt, Rinehart and Winston, 1964

RMBT– Rachel Mary Bronwen Thomas to Edward Thomas (ET), ETC

TSE– T. S. Eliot to Conrad Aiken (CA),

Eleanor Hinkley (EH), *Letters of T. S. Eliot*,
vol. I, *1898–1922* (ed. Valerie Eliot and Hugh
Haughton), revised edn, London: Faber
& Faber, 2009; Miss Grenside (MG), FF,
Rdlm163

WBY– W. B. Yeats to Lady Gregory (LG),
Letters of W. B. Yeats (ed. Allen Wade),
London: Rupert Hart-Davis, 1954

WHH– W. H. Hudson to Edward Garnett (EG),
Letters from W. H. Hudson to Edward Garnett,
London: Dent, 1925, *153 Letters from W.
H. Hudson* (ed. Edward Garnett), London:
Nonesuch Press, 1923

WO–Wilfred Owen to Susan Owen (SO), *Collected
Letters of Wilfred Owen* (ed. Harold Owen and
John Bell), London: Oxford University Press,
1967

WWG– Wilfrid Wilson Gibson to Edward Marsh
(EM), Berg; Robert Frost (RF), DCL

V—ADDITIONAL WORKS CITED

Abercrombie, Catherine, 'Memoirs of a Poet's
Wife', *The Listener*, 15 Nov. 1956

Abercrombie, Lascelles, *The Poems of Lascelles
Abercrombie*, London: Oxford University Press,
1930

Abercrombie, Lascelles and R. C. Trevelyan (eds.),
An Annual of New Poetry, London: Constable,
1917

Aiken, Conrad, *Ushant: An Essay*, New York: Duell,
Sloan and Pearce, 1952

Baynes Jansen, Diana, *Jung's Apprentice: A
Biography of Helton Godwin Baynes*, Einsiedeln:

Daimon Verlag, 2003

Berridge, Jesse, 'Edward: A Memoir', *Letters of Edward Thomas to Jesse Berridge* (ed. Anthony Berridge), London: Enitharmon, 1983

Blunden, Edmund, 'Poetry of the Present Reign', *John O'London's Weekly*, 27 April 1935

Bottomley, Gordon, 'A Note on Edward Thomas', *Welsh Review*, IV, 3 (Sept. 1945), 166–78

Brooke, Rupert, *Poems*, London: Sidgwick and Jackson, 1911

———, *1914 and Other Poems*, London: Sidgwick and Jackson, 1915

Browne, Maurice, *Recollections of Rupert Brooke*, Chicago: Alexander Greene, 1927

Carlyle, Thomas, *On Heroes, Hero-Worship and the Heroic in History*, London: James Fraser, 1841

Carpenter, Humphrey, *A Serious Character: A Life of Ezra Pound*, London: Faber & Faber, 1988

Cornford, Frances, *Poems*, London: Priory, 1910

Crane, Joan St C., *Robert Frost: A Descriptive Catalogue of Books and Manuscripts in the Clifton Waller Barrett Library, University of Virginia*, Charlottesville: Virginia University Press, 1974

Davies, Jennifer, *Safe in Print: Memories of Donnington, Ryton and Broomsgreen*, published privately, 1994

Davies, W. H., *The Autobiography of a Super-Tramp*, London: Jonathan Cape, 1908

———, *Later Days*, London: Jonathan Cape, 1925

Davies, W. H. et al., *In Memoriam: Edward Thomas*, London: Moreland Press, 1919

Day Lewis, C., 'The Poetry of Edward Thomas', *Essays by Divers Hands* (Transactions of the Royal Society of Literature of the United Kingdom), XXVIII (1956)

De la Mare, Walter, *Motley and Other Poems*, London: Constable, 1918

del Re, Arundel, 'Georgian Reminiscences', *Studies in English Literature*, English Seminar, University of Tokyo, 1932, 1934

Drinkwater, John, *Olton Pools*, London: Sidgwick and Jackson, 1917

————, *Loyalties*, London: Sidgwick and Jackson, 1919

————, *Discovery: Being the Second Book of an Autobiography, 1897–1913*, London: Ernest Benn, 1932

Dudfield, George, *Mud on My Boots: A View of Dymock Life 1909 to 1930*, Ledbury: published privately, 1988

Ede, H. S., *A Life of Gaudier-Brzeska*, London: Heinemann, 1930

Egremont, Max, *Siegfried Sassoon: A Biography*, London: Picador, 2005

Eliot, T. S., 'Verse Pleasant and Unpleasant', *The Egoist*, March 1918

————, *Poetry Speaks: A Twentieth-Century Anthology Read by the Poets* (cassette recording), ed. Peter Orr, Argo, 1982

————, *The Waste Land: A Facsimile and Transcript of the Original Drafts including the Annotations of Ezra Pound* (ed. Valerie Eliot), London: Faber & Faber, 1971

English Catalogue of Books, London: The Publishers' Circular, 1914–25

Farjeon, Eleanor, *Edward Thomas: The Last Four Years*, London: Oxford University Press, 1958

Fast Beat My Heart: Edward Thomas and Family at Steep (audiobook), Edward Thomas Fellowship, 2008

447

Feld, Rose C., 'Robert Frost Relieves His Mind', *New York Times Book Review*, 21 Oct. 1923

Fletcher, John Gould, *Life is My Song*, New York: Farrar and Rinehart, 1937

Ford, Ford Madox, *Return to Yesterday*, London: Gollancz, 1931

Francis, Lesley Lee, *The Frost Family's Adventure in Poetry: Sheer Morning Gladness at the Brim*, Columbia: Missouri University Press, 1994

Francis, Robert, *Robert Frost: A Time to Talk*, London: Robson, 1973

Frost, Lesley, *New Hampshire's Child: The Derry Journals of Lesley Frost* (ed. Arnold Grade and Lawrance Thompson), New York: SUNY Press, 1969

Frost, Robert, *A Boy's Will*, London: David Nutt, 1913

———, *North of Boston*, London: David Nutt, 1914

———, *Mountain Interval*, New York: Henry Holt, 1916

———, *New Hampshire*, New York: Henry Holt, 1921

———, *Collected Poems*, New York: Henry Holt, 1930

———, *A Further Range*, New York: Henry Holt 1936

———, *Family Letters of Robert and Elinor Frost* (ed. Arnold Grade), Albany: SUNY Press, 1972

———, *Notebooks of Robert Frost* (ed. Robert Faggen), Cambridge, Mass.: Harvard University Press, 2006

———, *Collected Prose of Robert Frost* (ed. Mark Richardson), Cambridge, Mass.: Harvard University Press, 2007

Gallup, Donald, *A Bibliography of Ezra Pound*,

London: Rupert Hart-Davis, 1969

Garnett, David, *The Golden Echo*, London: Chatto & Windus, 1953

Gawsworth, John, *Ten Contemporaries: Notes Towards Their Definitive Bibliography*, London: Ernest Benn, 1932

Gethyn-Jones, J. E., *Dymock Down the Ages*, revised edition, privately printed at Gloucester by Albert E. Smith (Printers) Ltd, 1966

Gibson, Ashley, *Postscript to Adventure*, London: J. M. Dent, 1930

Gibson, Wilfrid Wilson, *Battle*, London: Elkin Mathews, 1915

—— *Friends*, London: Elkin Mathews, 1916

—— *The Golden Room and Other Poems*, London: Macmillan, 1928

Gleichen, Edward Lord, *Chronology of the Great War*, 3 vols, London: Constable, 1918–20

Goldring, Douglas, *South Lodge: Reminiscences of Violet Hunt, Ford Madox Ford, and the English Review Circle*, London: Constable, 1943

Grant, Joy, *Harold Monro and the Poetry Bookshop*, London: Routledge and Kegan Paul, 1967

Graves, Robert, *Goodbye to All That*, London: Jonathan Cape, 1929; revised edn., London: Cassell, 1957

Graves, Robert and Laura Riding, *A Survey of Modernist Poetry*, London: Heinemann, 1927

——, *The Common Asphodel: Collected Essays on Poetry, 1922–1949*, London: Hamish Hamilton, 1949

Haines, John Wilton, 'The Dymock Poets', *Gloucestershire Countryside*, I, 9 (Oct. 1933), 131–3

Harvey, Anne (ed.), *Adlestrop Revisited: An*

Anthology Inspired by Edward Thomas's Poem, Stroud: Sutton, 1999

Hassall, Christopher, *Edward Marsh: A Biography*, London: Longman, 1959

————, *Rupert Brooke: A Biography*, London: Faber & Faber, 1964

Hibberd, Dominic, *Harold Monro: Poet of the Age*, Basingstoke: Palgrave, 2001

————, *Wilfred Owen: A New Biography*, London: Weidenfeld and Nicolson, 2002

Hodgson, Ralph, *Poets Remembered*, Cleveland, Ohio: Rowfant Club, 1967

Jefferies, Richard, *The Gamekeeper at Home* (1878) and *The Amateur Poacher* (1879), Oxford: Oxford University Press, 1978

Jepson, Edgar, *Memories of an Edwardian and Neo-Georgian*, London: Secker, 1938

Keynes, Geoffrey, *A Bibliography of Rupert Brooke*, London: Rupert Hart-Davis, 1959

Larkin, Philip (ed.), *The Oxford Book of Twentieth Century English Verse*, Oxford: Clarendon, 1973

Lathem, Edward Connery (ed.), *Interviews with Robert Frost*, New York: Holt, 1966

Lawrence, D. H., 'The Georgian Renaissance', *Rhythm*, II (March 1913)

Leavis, F. R., *New Bearings in English Poetry*, London: Chatto & Windus, 1932/Peregrine, 1963

Lowell, Amy, 'A Letter from London, 28 Aug. 1914', *Little Review*, I (Sept. 1914)

Marsh, Edward (ed.), *Georgian Poetry 1911–1912*, London: Poetry Bookshop, 1912

Masefield, John, *The Everlasting Mercy*, London: Sidgwick and Jackson, 1911

Mertins, Louis, *Life and Walks-Talking*, Norman: Oklahoma University Press, 1965

Monro, Harold, *Some Contemporary Poets*, London: Leonard Parsons, 1920

Moore, John, *The Life and Letters of Edward Thomas*, London: Heinemann, 1939

Motion, Andrew, *The Poetry of Edward Thomas*, London: Routledge & Kegan Paul, 1980

Nevinson, H. W., *Changes and Chances*, London: Nisbet & Co., 1923

Newham-David, Lieut.-Col., *Dinners and Diners: Where and How to Dine in London*, London: Grant Richards, 1899

Norman, Charles, *Ezra Pound*, London: Macmillan, 1960

Patry, Rose I., *Practical Handbook on Elocution*, London: Swan Sonnenshein, 1909

Pound, Ezra (ed.), *Des Imagistes: An Anthology*, London: Poetry Bookshop, 1914

———, *Lustra*, London: Elkin Mathews, 1916

———, *Hugh Selwyn Mauberley*, London: Ovid, 1920

———, *Literary Essays* (ed. T. S. Eliot), London: Faber & Faber, 1954

Reeves, Maud Pember, *Round About a Pound a Week*, London: G. Bell & Sons Ltd, 1913

Sassoon, Siegfried, *Siegfried's Journey 1916–1920*, London: Faber & Faber, 1945

Sergeant, Elizabeth Shepley, *Robert Frost: The Trial by Existence*, New York: Holt, Rinehart and Winston, 1960

Severn, Mark (Major Franklin Lushington), *The Gambardier*, London: Ernest Benn, 1930

Sitwell, Sir Osbert, *Laughter in the Next Room*, London: Macmillan, 1949

Sokol, B. J., 'The Publication of Robert Frost's First Books: Triumph and Fiasco', *Book Collector*,

XXVI, 2 (Summer 1977), 228–40

Stock, Noel, *The Life of Ezra Pound*, London: Routledge & Kegan Paul, 1970

Stonesifer, Richard J., *W. H. Davies: A Critical Biography*, London: Jonathan Cape, 1963

Sutton, William (ed.), *Newdick's Season of Frost: An Interrupted Biography of Robert Frost*, Albany: SUNY Press, 1976

Taylor, A. J. P., *English History, 1914–45*, Oxford: Clarendon Press, 1965

Thomas, Alison, *Portraits of Women: Gwen John and Her Forgotten Contemporaries*, Cambridge: Polity, 1994

Thomas, Dylan, *On the Air with Dylan Thomas: The Broadcasts* (ed. Ralph Maud), New York: New Directions, 1992

Thomas, Helen, *Under Storm's Wing*, Manchester: Carcanet, 1988

Thomas, Myfanwy, *One of These Fine Days: Memoirs*, Manchester: Carcanet, 1982

Thomas, R. George, *Edward Thomas: A Portrait*, Oxford: Clarendon, 1985

Thompson, Lawrance, *Robert Frost: The Early Years, 1874–1915*, New York: Holt, Rinehart and Winston, 1966

———, *Robert Frost: The Years of Triumph, 1915–1938*, New York: Holt, Rinehart and Winston, 1970

Thompson, Lawrance and R. H. Winnick, *Robert Frost: The Later Years, 1938–1963*, New York: Holt, Rinehart and Winston, 1976

Tomalin, Ruth, *W. H. Hudson: A Biography*, London: Faber & Faber, 1982

Voices and Visions: Robert Frost (videotape), Annenberg/CPB Collection, New York Center for Visual History, 1988

Walsh, John Evangelist, *Into My Own: The English Years of Robert Frost*, New York: Grove Weidenfeld, 1988

Whistler, Theresa, *The Life of Walter de la Mare*, London: Gerald Duckworth, 1993

Whiteman, W. M., *The Edward Thomas Country*, Southampton: Paul Cave, 1978/1988

Yeats, W. B., *The Wild Swans at Coole*, London: Macmillan, 1919

———, *Essays and Introductions*, New York: Macmillan, 1961

NOTES

I—STEEP

WINTER 1913

1. 35 Devonshire Street, Bloomsbury WC (now renamed 34–5 Boswell Street); Monro, *PR*, I, 11 (Nov. 1912), 498.
2. Browne, 37; also Sitwell, 35; del Re, 38; Grant, 61–5.
3. Sergeant, 105, 101.
4. Gaudier-Brzeska in Ede, 131; RB–HM, 11 June 1913, 126.
5. Sassoon in Hassall, *Rupert Brooke*, 451; Austin, 'Jameson's Raid', *The Times*, 11 Jan. 1896; EP–PC, 22 Oct. 1913, 13; HJ–HW, 24 Oct. 1912, 273–6; Lawrence, xvii–xx.
6. *TLS*, 11 Nov. 1920, 729; Brooke, 'A Channel Passage', *Poems*, 49; *TLS*, 29 Aug. 1912, 337; Masefield, 2–3.
7. Blunden, 111; Monro, 23.
8. Monro, *PD*, II, 6 (June 1914), 180.
9. A. K. Sabin in Grant, 93.
10. Aldington in Carpenter, 178; Graves and Riding, 118–19; *WP*, 215–16; Eliot, 'Verse Pleasant and Unpleasant', 43–4; *Country*, 55.
11. Marsh, v.
12. Flint, *PC*, I, 6 (March 1913), 199; Pound, *Literary Essays*, 3; Pound, *PR*, I, 2 (Feb. 1912); Pound, 'In a Station of the Metro', *PC*, II, 1 (April 1913), 12, and *Lustra*, 45 in variant form.

13. Ford, 419; RF–FSF, 21 Jan. 1913, Thompson, *Early Years*, 408; RF–EG, 29 April 1917, 217.
14. See ET–EB, Nov. 1912, 225; see ET–HM, 3 Jan. 1913, 54; Thomas Seccomb, *TLS*, 16 April 1917; Walter de la Mare, *WG*, 28 April 1917.
15. See *GB, LH, ACS, NT, IW, Country, HGLM*.
16. See Ashley Gibson, 10; see Hodgson in RLW, 59; see Bottomley, 168; see ECH, *c.* March 1919; see Walter de la Mare, *CP1920*; see Farjeon, 24; see JWH, 'Edward Thomas by J. W. Haines', 5; see Helen Thomas, 21–2; see Catherine Abercrombie.
17. See ET diary, 2 May 1901: 'I brood too much for suicide; the thought to kill myself kills itself by intensity. How many sedentary people do commit suicide?'; see ET–GB, 5 Dec. 1912, 225–6; ET–JB, 14 Feb. 1913, 70.
18. Helen Thomas, 143.
19. ET, loose notes, 9 Oct. 1907, in R. George Thomas, 141.
20. 'The Attempt', *LT*, 160–73; Helen Thomas, 113–14; ET diary, 29 Nov. 1908: 'Up, 7. Reading. After tried to shoot myself. Evening reading. Read Marlowe. To bed, 11.'
21. ET–GB, 6 Nov. 1908, 174–5.
22. See *WL*.
23. ET–HH, *c.*1898, Moore, 41.
24. Nevinson, 195.
25. 117 Atheldene Road, Earlsfield, London SW (2 Nov. 1900–12 Feb. 1901), see *HS*, 103–5; 7 Nightingale Parade, Nightingale Lane, Balham, London SW (12 Feb. 1901–Oct. 1901); Rose Acre, Bearsted, nr Maidstone, Kent (9 Oct. 1901–March 1903); see ET–JB, 6 May 1902, 29; Helen Thomas, 90–1; HT–JH, 7 June 1902.

26. Irene McArthur in RLW.
27. See *Oxford*; Ivy Cottage, The Green, Bearsted, nr Maidstone, Kent (March 1903–Feb. 1904); diary, 27 Oct. 1903; Helen Thomas, 99, 101; HT–ET, 10 Dec. 1903, 23.
28. Elses Farm, The Weald, nr Sevenoaks, Kent (May 1904–26 Oct. 1906); Helen Thomas, 103.
29. ET–JB, 8 Aug. 1905, 47; ET–GB, 30 June 1905, 87, and 24 Jan. 1906, 103; see 'Hawthornden', *LT*, 120–1.
30. Frost in Mertins, 135.
31. Helen Thomas, 42, 96.
32. ET–GB, 19 July 1908, 165; ET–HH, Dec. 1911, *Selected Letters*, 68–9; WHH–EG, 12 Nov. 1911, 118.
33. ET–GB, 21 May 1908, 163.
34. 30 Victoria Park Square, behind the Bethnal Green Museum (now Museum of Childhood).
35. ET–GB, 18 April 1912, 221.
36. Baynes Jansen, 137.
37. ET–GB, 26 Dec. 1906, 129.
38. Frost in Sergeant, 89.
39. See Frost, *Collected Prose*, 35–73; see Frost in Mertins, 102; Lesley Frost, quoted in D. Tatham, *A Poet Recognized: Notes about Robert Frost's First Trip to England*, privately printed, 1969, 9–10, reproduced in Walsh, 30–1.
40. RF–JTB, *c.*5 Nov. 1912, 99; RF–SHW, 15 Sept. 1912, 52; *Voices and Visions*.
41. See Farjeon, 88.
42. See Thompson, *Early Years*, 504–5n; see Sergeant, 7.
43. See Thompson, *Early Years*, 308–9, 340.
44. Sergeant, 71; RF–SHW, 4 Nov. 1907, 41, and 19 Dec. 1911, 43; Jack Haines in Mertins, 131;

Voices and Visions; RF–EJ, 6 May 1913, 108.

45. See ET, 'Wind and Mist', 1 April 1915, Abercrombie and Trevelyan, 42–4 and *LP*, 41–3; 'The Combe', 30 Dec. 1914, *Poems*, 19; *SC*, 148–9; 'The Path', 26 March 1915, *Poems*, 18.

46. See ET, 'When first', July or Oct. 1916, *Poems*, 22–3; Berryfield Cottage, Ashford Chase Estate, Steep (26 Oct. 1906–18 Dec. 1909); ET–GB, 15 March 1910, 199; Wick Green, Froxfield (18 Dec. 1909–22 July 1913); see ET, 'The New House', 19 March 1915, Abercrombie and Trevelyan, 41, *LP*, 34, 'Wind and Mist', *LP*, 41–3.

47. ET–EF, 10 Jan. 1913, 5.

48. ET, *DC*, 14 Jan. 1913; ET–HM, 26 Dec. 1911, 52; ET, *The Bookman*, March 1913; ET–HM, 15 Jan. 1913, 55; Newbolt, *PD*, I, 1 (March 1913), 46.

49. ET–HM, 23 Nov. 1911, 50; ET, *PD*, I, 1 (March 1913), 33–42.

50. ET–EF, 5 Dec. 1913, 46.

51. ET, 'How I Began', *LS*, 15–20; *HGLM*; *CET*.

52. 10 Upper Lansdowne Road North, Lambeth, SW (now renamed, 14 Lansdowne Gardens) (1878–80).

53. *CO*, 24 Dec. 1920; *CET*, 17.

54. See ET–PHT, undated [1899], 11; ET, 'I may come near loving you', 8 Feb. 1916, *CP1949*, 189.

55. *CET*, 18–19.

56. *CET*, 19; ET–EF, ?mid-June 1913, 13; Helen Thomas, 28; *CET*, 19.

57. 49 Wakehurst Road, Wandsworth, London SW (1880–8); 61 Shelgate Road, Wandsworth, London SW (1888–97).

58. *CET*, 44.
59. *CET*, 32–3.
60. *CET*, 103, 105, 115.
61. *CET*, 143–4.
62. *CET*, 26.

SPRING 1913

1. *IW*, 91.
2. *IW*, 137, 142.
3. *IW*, vi; *Athenaeum*, 26 April 1913, 454–5.
4. *IW*, 280–3.
5. ET–HM [Feb. 1913], 55, and 24 Feb. 1913, 56; Monro, *PD*, I, 1 (March 1913), 7; Patry, 221; RB–NO, 12 Feb. 1913, 243.
6. ET, *PD*, I, 1 (March 1913), 53–6.
7. ET, *DC*, 5 March 1909; ET, *DC*, 12 July 1902.
8. ET, *WS*, 18 June 1904; ET, *DC*, 1 Jan. 1907; ET, *WS*, 18 June 1904.
9. Frost, 'In England', Thompson, *Early Years*, 396; Sergeant, 97; RF–SHW, 13 May 1913, 73.
10. Frost in Mertins, 107; Frost in Robert Francis, 16; RF–LA, 21 Sept. 1915, 193.
11. Sergeant, 102; Thompson, *Early Years*, 411; EP–ACH, March 1913, 14; EP–*PC*, March 1913, 16.
12. See Pound, 'How I Began', *TPW*, 6 June 1913; Pound, *Paris Review*, 28 (1962); WBY–LG, 1909, 543; Yeats, 'A Song', *Wild Swans at Coole*, 22; Pound, *Paris Review*, 28 (1962); Pound, *PC*, I, 4 (Jan. 1913), 125; WBY–LG, 1 and 3 Jan. 1913 quoted in Carpenter, 192; Pound, 'The Later Years', *PC*, IV, 2 (May 1914), 65; Carpenter, 172.
13. RF–JTB, *c.*4 April 1913, 71; Goldring, 49.
14. EWF–MB, *c.*3 July 1914, 78; RF–TBM, 15 June

1913, 74.

15. Frost, Milton Academy, Massachusetts, 17 May 1935; Frost in Sergeant, 106; Frost interviewed by Richard Poirier, 'The Art of Poetry No. 2', *Paris Review*, 24 (Summer–Fall 1960), 16; RF–TBM, 24 Oct. 1913, 96.
16. ET–GB, 1 May 1909, 185; ET, *DC*, 7 June 1909; ET, *ER*, June 1909.
17. Jepson, 140–1.
18. ET–GB, 12 June 1909, 187; ET, *DC*, 23 Nov. 1909.
19. ET–GB, 14 Dec. 1909, 197.
20. Pound in Stonesifer, 239.
21. *IPS*, 44.
22. *IPS*, 119, 124–7.
23. *IPS*, 141.
24. *IPS*, 219–20.
25. Wordsworth, 'Anecdote for Fathers'; *IPS*, 282.
26. ET–JB, 3 May 1914, 74.
27. ET–GB, 7 May 1913, 228; see ET–JB *c.*25 July 1913; ET–EF, ?31 Oct. 1913; Farjeon, 43.
28. RF–JTB, *c.*4 April 1913, 70; *Athenaeum*, 5 April 1913, 379; *TLS*, 10 April 1913, 155; Ezra Pound, *PC*, II, 2 (May 1913), 72–4, and *NF*, I, 9 (Sept. 1913).
29. RF–SHW, 13 May 1913, 73.
30. RB–ET, *c.*15 May 1913, 459.
31. *MP*, 11 Dec. 1911; *NA*, 18 Jan. 1912; *TLS*, Dublin *Express* in Hassall, *Rupert Brooke*, 535–7; ET, *DC*, 9 April 1912.

SUMMER 1913

1. Helen Thomas, 142; see ET–GB, mid-June 1913, 229–30; see ET–HT, 23 June 1913, 68–70.

2. ET–EF [?midsummer 1913], 13.
3. ET–CFC, 14 Sept. 1912; CFC–ET, 16 Sept. 1912; ET–CFC, 18 June 1913; ET–CFC, 10 Nov. 1913.
4. RF–JTB, 6 Aug. 1913, 88; RF–TBM, 17 July 1913, 84; see RF–SHW, 4 Dec. 1894, 25 and RF–SHW, 8 July 1896, 27; RF–JTB, 4 July 1913, 79–80.
5. See Farjeon, 90.
6. RF–JTB, 4 July 1913, 80–1.
7. Frost, *Collected Prose*, 116.
8. Carlyle, 135; RF–RPTC, 24 Feb. 1938, 461; RF–SC, 19 Jan. 1914, 107–8; RF–TBM, 17 July 1913, 83.
9. See RF–FSF, 16 July 1913, UTA in Walsh, 125.
10. See Thompson, *Early Years*, 598n; Lesley Frost, II, 2; Lathem, 109; Frost, 'Birches', *AM*, Aug. 1915, and *Mountain Interval*, 29–30.
11. Frost interview with Cecil Day Lewis, BBC, 13 Sept. 1957, *CQ*, Spring 1958; Frost in Feld, 2; Frost, 'The Figure a Poem Makes', *Collected Prose*, 132.
12. See Frost, *Notebooks*; see Thompson, *Early Years*, 597; Frost, *Newsweek*, 11 Feb. 1963, 90–1.
13. Arundel del Re, 'Georgian Poets', New Zealand Broadcasting Service talk cited in Grant, 78; ET–JB [early June 1913], 71; ET–GB, 2 Aug. 1913, 230; HT–JH, 6 Aug. 1913, 200.
14. Farjeon, 24–7.
15. WWG–RF, 4 Aug. 1913, DCL, Walsh, 156; DHL–EM, 17 Dec. 1913, 119–20; RF–GMcQ [early Dec. 1913], 157; see Gibson, 'The First Meeting', in Thompson, *Early Years*, 439.
16. ET, *DC*, 15 Dec. 1902; *MM*, 28; ET, *DC*, 18 April 1908.

17. ET, *DC*, 9 March 1912.
18. See WWG–EM, 14 and 23 Jan. 1913; Bridges and Marsh see Hassall, *Edward Marsh*, 208.

AUTUMN 1913

1. ET–CFC, 9 Sept. 1913; ET in Farjeon, 12.
2. See Farjeon, 30; ET, 'Insomnia', *LS*, 39–43.
3. ET–WdlM, 'Sunday' [?7 Sept. 1913], 220v–221r; ET–WHH, 18 March 1915, 11.
4. ET, 'Notes mainly out of doors', IV, 28 April 1896, ETC, *CP1978*, 455–6.
5. *BW*, 82–3; Bottomley, 173; ET–GB, 30 June 1905, 87; ET–GB, 14 May 1907, 140.
6. See Thompson, *Early Years*, 441; RH–RF, 14 Sept. 1913, 92; RH–RF [*c*.1–5 Oct. 1913], DCL.
7. ET–HH, 24 Sept. 1913, *Selected Letters*, 86; ET–EF [post dated, 5 Oct. 1913], 37.
8. ET–WdlM, 6 Oct. 1913, 209r–v; ET–WdlM, [post dated, 6 Oct. 1913], 211r.
9. St George's Café, 37 St Martin's Lane, London; Frost in Mertins, 114; Ashley Gibson, 2; see Newham-David, 93; see Hodgson, 16; ADW, 1–22; ET–RF, 4 Nov. 1916, 156.
10. Farjeon, 41.
11. See ET–GB, 26 Aug. 1910, 207; see Moore, 137, 79.
12. *WP*, 220.
13. Virginia Woolf, *TLS*, Oct. 1917; A. H. Anderson, *Observer*, 25 Nov. 1917; ET–EF [*c*. Oct. 1913], 41, and 'Friday' [poss. 31 Oct. 1913], 43; see Helen Thomas, 137.
14. ET–IMacA, 18 Dec. 1913; RMBT–ET, 9 Nov. 1913; see *Keats*.
15. See *CS*; ET–CFC, 30 Nov. 1913; ET–CFC,

14 Nov. 1913; see *FTB*.

16. *HGLM*, 1; WHH–EG, *153 Letters*, 94.
17. F. T. Marinetti, *PD*, I, 3 (Sept. 1913), 263;
    Aldington, *NF*, I, 12 (Dec. 1913), 226; Harold
    Monro, *PD*, I, 3 (Sept. 1913), 262.
18. RF–JTB, *c.*5 Nov. 1913, 98; RF–ES, 8 Dec.
    1913, 103.

WINTER 1913/14

1. ET–EF, 5 Dec. 1913, 46.
2. See Davies, *Autobiography*, 162; see Ashley
   Gibson, 49–50; Helen Thomas, 217.
3. ET, *DC*, 21 Oct. 1905; ADW, 11.
4. Stidulph's Cottage, Egg Pie Lane, The
   Weald; see ADW, 11; 14 Great Russell Street,
   Bloomsbury WC (1916–22); see also Hodgson,
   14–15.
5. Frost's annotated copy of *PD*, I, 4 (Dec. 1913),
   421, enc. RF–JTB, *c.*15 Dec. 1913, 105; RF–SC,
   18 May 1914; 123; see Helen Thomas, 220; see
   Davies *Later Days*, 50.
6. See *PD*, I, 4 (Dec. 1913); RF–JTB, *c.*15 Dec.
   1913, 105; ET, 'Reviewing: An Unskilled
   Labour', *PD*, II, 5 (March 1914), 37; ET–JB, 27
   April 1902, 27; ET–JB, 7 Nov. 1902, 37; ET–HM,
   19 July 1911, 48–9; ET–JWH, 15 July 1915; ET, 'I
   never saw that land before', 5 May 1916, *LP*, 9.
7. ET–EF, 5 Dec. 1913, 46, and 8 Dec. 1913, 47–8.
8. ET–CFC, 18 Dec. 1913; ET–IMacA, 18 Dec.
   1913.
9. Farjeon, 52–3.
10. ET–EF, 26 Dec. 1913, 53.
11. ET–RF, 17 Dec. 1913, 3.
12. WWG to EM, 7 Nov. 1913; Frost in Mertins,

117; RF–GMcQ, Dec. 1913 in Walsh, 157–8.

II—DYMOCK

1. RB–RMB, 21 July 1913, 484.
2. RB–WWG, 23 July 1913, 486–7.
3. *NN*, I, 1 (Feb. 1914): Gibson, 'Bloodybush Edge'; Brooke, 'Sonnet', 'A Memory', 'One Day', 'Mutability'; Abercrombie, 'The Olympians'; Drinkwater, 'The Poet to His Mistress', 'The New Miracle', 'The Boundaries', 'A Town Window', 'Memory'; GG–JWH, 12 Jan. 1914.
4. HM, *PD*, II, 6 (June 1914), 178–9; WdlM, *TLS*, 19 March 1914; ET, *NW*, 21 March 1914, also *DC*, 19 April 1914.
5. Haines.
6. See RB–KC, 13 June 1914, 449; ET–GB, 4 April 1917, 283.
7. WWG–EM, 12 Dec. 1912; EM–RB, 18 Aug. 1913, 242; RB–RL, 6 July 1914, 598; Catherine Abercrombie; Lascelles Abercrombie in Gawsworth; Gibson, 'Trees', *Friends*, 19.
8. ET–GB, 12 Oct. 1909, 195; LA–EM, 5 Sept. 1914.
9. ET, *DC*, 29 Feb. 1908; ET, *DC*, 28 Dec. 1911; ET *DC*, 28 Dec. 1911; ET, *DC*, 9 Aug. 1911; ET, *DC*, 10 Jan. 1913; RF–TBM, 139; ET–GB, 28 Dec. 1914, 241.
10. 11 Luxemburg Gardens, Hammersmith, London; see ET–EF, 26 Jan. 1914, 59; see ET–RF, 30 Jan. 1914, 6; see ET–EF [Feb. 1914], 60; see ET–CB, 19 Feb. 1914, 90.
11. Frost in Mertins, 135.
12. ET–RF, 19 Feb. 1914, 7; *PC*, III, 5 (Feb. 1914),

169–71; ET–RF, 24 Feb. 1914, 8.
13. See ET–GB, 30 June 1905, 87; ET–CFC, 23
    Feb. 1914, Bod. MS Eng. Lett. d. 281.

SPRING 1914

1. See Farjeon, 61–2.
2. RF–SC, 26 March 1914, 121.
3. See Frost, 'The Fear', 'A Hundred Collars', *PD*,
   I, 4 (Dec. 1913), 406–15; RF–SC, 26 March
   1914, 121; see Sergeant, 146; RF–WER, 26
   March 1914, 120.
4. Little Iddens, Ledington (*c*.3 April–Sept. 1914);
   see RF–SC, 18 May 1914, 124; see EFW–LWH,
   c. 20 June 1914, 126; *Voices and Visions*; RF–
   SC, 26 March 1914, 121.
5. See ET, 'This England', *The Nation*, 7 Nov.
   1914, 170–1, *LS*, 216–17; see Farjeon, 89; see
   RF–JWH, 17 July 1915, 183; RF–JWH [*c*.1 July
   1914], 128.
6. See Farjeon, 69; see FNB 74; RF–SC, 18 May
   1914, 124.
7. See FNB 74; see ET–EF, 28 April 1914, 69; see
   ET, 'This England', *LS*, 215; RF–JWH, 20 Jan.
   1921, 263.
8. ET–GB, 22 May 1914, 233.
9. RF–SC, 18 May 1914, 123; RF–SC, [17 Sept.
   1914], 136; RF–SC, 18 May 1914, 123.
10. Frost, 'A Romantic Chasm', *Collected Prose*,
    158; RF–SC, 18 May 1914, 124; EWF–LWH
    [*c*.20 June 1914], 126.
11. RF–ES, 23 Feb. 1914, 118.
12. Reeves, 19.
13. See Farjeon, 66, 71.
14. See, ET–EF, 16 May 1914, 73.

465

15. See Frost, 'Preface to an Expanded *North of Boston*', *Collected Prose*, 196.
16. Frost, *North of Boston*, x; Frost in Feld, 2.
17. Frost, 'The Pasture', *North of Boston*, vii; RF–JTB, *c*.5 Nov. 1913, 98.
18. ET–RF, 19 May 1914, 9–10; RF–SC, Dec. 1914, 140; *WP*, 103; *FIP*, 293.
19. *DC*, 27 Aug. 1901; *The Bookman*, Oct. 1907; *LH*, 48; *ACS*, 174.
20. *WP*, 104, 218, 210.
21. ET–GB, 22 March 1912, 220; ET–RF, 19 May 1914, 10–11; RF–HRB, 19 Dec. 1925, *AL*, 59, 1 (March 1987), 117.
22. ET–CFC, 4 April 1912.
23. *TLS*, 28 May 1914, 262; RF–LU, 14 Nov. 1916, 45.

SUMMER 1914

1. ET–RF, 6 June 1914, 12; ET–GB, 29 May 1914, 234; ET–RF, 6 June 1914, 12.
2. ET–RF [10 June 1914], 14 (as 'possibly July 1, 1914').
3. ET–EF, 20 June 1914, 75; ET–HT, 17 June 1914, 73.
4. Bottomley, 175.
5. *NYT*, 24 June 1914; ET–EF [24 June 1914], 76.
6. FNB 75, 24 June 1914; for a detailed investigation into this journey see Harvey, 1–22.
7. ET–GB, 27 June 1914, 235; Gibson, 'The Golden Room', *AM*, Feb. 1926, and *Golden Room*, 172.
8. ET–GB, 27 June 1914, 235; ET–GB, 7 July 1914, 236; see Frost in Sergeant, 105, and Fletcher, 72; Eliot, *Waste Land*, 98; EP–*PC*,

12 Oct. 1915, 64; Pound in Carpenter, 179; ET–
GB, 22 May 1914, 233; see Jeff Cooper, *DPF*, 7
(2008), 32–9 for Abercrombie and Pound.

9. See *LPE, FIL*; ET–GB, 7 July 1914, 236; ET–
EF, 17 July 1914, 79.

10. ET, *The Bookman*, July 1914; ET, *DC*, 16 Dec.
1911; Drinkwater, 'Daffodils', *Olton Pools*, 27;
Catherine Abercrombie; ET–GB, 6 Nov. 1915,
256.

11. A. K. Sabin in Grant, 81; Lowell, 6; Arundel del
Re, 'The Poetry Bookshop', BBC talk 1962, in
Grant, 81 (some versions of this story assign the
heckler as Amy Lowell herself).

12. Abercrombie, *The Nation*, 13 June 1914,
423; RF–JWH [late June or early July 1914];
Gibson, *The Bookman*, July 1914; RF–FSF,
24 Aug. 1916; see Walsh, 172–7.

13. ET, *DN*, 22 July 1914.

14. ET, *ER*, Aug. 1914, 142–3.

15. ET, *NW*, 8 Aug. 1914, 249.

16. RF–GWC, 28 June 1921, 22–3.

17. ET–EF, 2 Aug. 1914, 81.

18. See Thompson and Winnick, 241.

19. See Hibberd, *Harold Monro*, 147.

20. RB in Hassall, *Rupert Brooke*, 457.

21. See Baynes Jansen, 97.

22. See Egremont, 63.

23. See WO–SO, 25 May 1917, 464.

24. *DM*, 4 Aug. 1914; *DT*, 4 Aug. 1914; *The Times*,
4 Aug. 1914; *DE*, 5 Aug. 1914; *DT*, 5 Aug. 1914;
Guardian, 5 Aug. 1914.

25. See ET, 'This is no case of petty right or wrong',
26 Dec. 1915, *LP*, 77; ET–MT, 23 Nov. 1914,
CP1978, 406.

26. See Helen Thomas, 229.

27. ET, 'It's a Long, Long Way', *ER*, Dec. 1914, 85–92, *LS*, 140; WWG–EM, 23 Aug. 1914; see Helen Thomas, 230.
28. See FNB 78, 19 Aug. 1914; see ET, 'This England', *LS*, 216–17.
29. See ET, 'The sun used to shine', 22 May 1916, *Poems*, 47–8.
30. Frost, 'Iris by Night', *VQR*, April 1936, *A Further Range*, 81–2; ET–EF, 22 May 1915, 141.
31. See Helen Thomas, 228–30; ET–EF, 14 Aug. 1914, 83; ET–JF, 14 Aug. 1914; see ET–EF, 14 Aug. 1914, 83.
32. See Farjeon, 90–5.
33. FNB 77, 26 Aug. 1914.
34. CFC–ET, 26 Aug. 1914.
35. RF–SC, 20 Aug. 1914, 131.
36. *English Catalogue of Books*, 1914, 1919; LA–EM, 5 Sept. 1914; ET–GB, 3 Sept. 1914, 238; see WWG–EM, 18 Nov. 1914.
37. Brooke, 'An Unusual Young Man', *NS*, 23 Aug. 1914, 638–40; RB–EW, 15–17 Aug. 1914, 608.
38. RB–EW, 15–17 Aug. 1914, 608.
39. See ET–GB, 3 Sept. 1914, 238; ET–WdlM, 30 Aug. 1914, 239. *Blast*, a new journal produced by Wyndham Lewis and Ezra Pound, had been launched in London in June 1914.
40. ADW, 8; *BW*, v; ET, 'Addenda to Autobiography', Berg; notebook, 31 Aug. 1899, UBC); ET–IMacA, 30 Aug. 1900, *Selected Letters*, 16; see ET, 'Home', *LP*, 39; see *SC*, 7.
41. ET–JB, 3 Sept. 1914, 74.

AUTUMN 1914

1. MPT–ET [*c*.3 Sept. 1914].
2. See ET–EF, 13 Sept. 1914, 96, and ET–GB, 21 Sept. 1914, 239; see ET–GB, 17 March 1904, 53.
3. ET, 'Tipperary', *ER*, Oct. 1914, *LS*, 113–34.
4. ET, 'It's a Long, Long Way', *ER*, Dec. 1914, *LS*, 135–49.
5. ET, 'England', *ER*, Oct. 1914, *LS*, 98; *HE*, 194; *LS*, 104–5; ET, 'England', *ER*, Oct. 1914; *LS*, 111.
6. RB–RL, 6 July 1914, 597; see Drinkwater, *Discovery*, 213; see EM–RB, 18 Aug. 1913, 242–3; WWG–EM, 9 March 1914 (see also 22 Dec. 1913 and 22 March 1914); DHL–EM, 24 May 1914, 176–7; ET–GB, 21 Sept. 1914, 239; RF–JWH, 21 Sept. 1914.
7. ET–JB, 3 Sept. 1914, 74. see ET–GB, 3 Sept. 1914, 238;. ET–EF, 4 Sept. 1914, 95; ET–EF, 13 Sept. 1914, 96.
8. FH–RF, 7 Aug. 1914, 131; Holt–Nutt letters, 2 and 12 Sept. 1914 in Frost, *Selected Letters*, 133–4.
9. TSE–EH, 8 Sept. 1914, 60.
10. Aiken, 258; Eliot, *Poetry Speaks*; Conrad Aiken to Joy Grant, 31 Oct. 1962 in Grant, 102; for a questioning of Aiken's account of events see Hibberd, *Harold Monro*, 153–4.
11. ET–EF, 21 Oct. 1914, 101; EP, *The Criterion*, XI (July 1932), 583; TSE–CA, 30 Sept. 1914, 64; TSE–EH, 14 Oct. 1914, 66–7.
12. ET–EF, 21 Oct. 1914, 101; ET–CFC, 16 Oct. 1914 (and CFC–ET of same date); ET–CFC, 10 Dec. 1914; FNB 79, Oct.–Dec. 1914.
13. ET–RF, 31 Oct. 1914, 29–30.

14. RB–JR, 24 Sept. 1914, 619; RB–LB, 11 Nov. 1914, 632; Monro, 'Personal Recollections of Rupert Brooke', *Everyman*, 24 July 1930, 803; Brooke, 'The Soldier', *NN*, I, 4 (Dec. 1914), 169, *1914 and Other Poems*, 15; RB–WdlM, 20 Nov. 1914, 238; RB–LB, 11 Nov. 1914, 633.
15. ET–HM [*c*. late Oct. 1914], 61. ET–GB, 30 Jan. 1915, 243; see Whistler, 238 for possible further encounter.
16. ET–WHH, 26 Nov. 1914; *Selected Letters*, 101.
17. Newdick notes of conversation with Frost, 26 July 1936 in Sutton, 298.
18. Ted Hill, *Voices and Visions*; Hill, interview with Rev. Reg Legge, Dymock 1982, private collection.
19. LA–JWH, 1 Dec. 1914.
20. LA–JWH, 4 Dec. 1914.
21. See Thompson, *Early Years*, 468.
22. RF–HM, Dec. 1914, 142.
23. RF–JWH, 2 April 1915.
24. See FNB 79, 27 Nov. 1914.
25. Myfanwy Thomas in Helen Thomas, 14; RF–GWC, 28 June 1921, 23; ET, 'An Old Song', *LP*, 69.
26. Frost in Mertins, 117; see RF–LA, 21 Sept. 1915, 193.
27. Frost in Newdick, Sutton, 298.
28. RF–GWC, 28 June 1921, 23; see Farjeon, 56.

WINTER 1914/15

1. ET–RF, 19 May 1914, 10.
2. FNB 79, facing 2 Nov. 1914 (reprinted in *CP1978*, 374); ET, 'The White Horse', LML (*CP1978*, 435–6, with variants).

3. ET, 'Up in the Wind', LML (*CP1978*, 437–41, for a differing transcription).
4. ET, 'Up in the Wind', 3 Dec. 1914, *CP1920,* 87.
5. FNB 79, 1 Dec. 1914 (*CP1978*, 379–80); ET, 'November', 4 Dec. 1914, *Poems*, 51; ET–EG, 13 March 1915, 25; ET–RF, 15 Dec. 1914, 38.
6. RF–HRB, 19 Dec. 1925, 117; *IPS*, 178; ET, 'March', 5 Dec. 1914, *LP*, 35.
7. ET–GB, 6 April 1910, 201.
8. FNB 79, 11 Nov. 1914 (*CP1978*, 381); ET, 'Old Man's Beard', 17 Nov. 1914, LML (*CP1978*, 443–4, for a differing transcription); ET, 'Old Man', 6 Dec. 1914, *LP*, 13.
9. ET, 'The Signpost', 7 Dec. 1914, *Poems*, 9.
10. FNB 79, *c.* Dec. 1914.
11. ET–RF, 15 Dec. 1914, 39.
12. RF–SHW, 10 Feb. 1912, 45.
13. ET–IMacA, in Moore, 172; *SC*, 73; *IW*, 137; ET, 'The Pilgrim', *LS*, 52.
14. ET–HM, 15 Dec. 1914, 63.
15. ET–EF, 26 Dec. 1914, 105; ET, 'The Manor Farm', 24 Dec. 1914, *Poems*, 12; Frost, 'Mending Wall', *North of Boston*, 11; ET–WHH, *Selected Letters*, 108.
16. ET, 'An Old Song', 25 Dec. 1914, *LP*, 69.
17. ET–EF [*c.*22 Dec. 1914], 104.
18. CFC–ET, 3 Dec. 1914; Frost–Graves meeting recorded by Robert Graves, 'The Truest Poet', *Sunday Times*, 3 Feb. 1963, 11 in Thompson, *Early Years*, 472; RF–SC, 14 Dec. 1914, 138–9; ET–RF, 15 Dec. 1914, 39.
19. ET, 'The New Year', 1 Jan. 1915, *LP*, 84; 'The Source', 4 Jan. 1915, Abercrombie and Trevelyan, 56, *LP*, 61;'The Penny Whistle', 5 Jan. 1915, *Poems*, 59; see 'Tears', 8 Jan. 1915,

10–11.

20. ET–JB, 6 Jan. 1915, 76; see ET–EF, 6 Jan. 1915, 109; ET, 'The Lofty Sky', 10 Jan. 1915, *RB*, II, 2 (Dec. 1917), 32, *LP*, 45–6.
21. ET–EF, 10 and 16 Jan. 1915, 110–11.
22. FNB 75, 24 June 1914; BL Add. Mss. 44990; ET, 'Adlestrop', 8 Jan. 1915, *NS*, 28 April 1917, 87, *Poems*, 40–1; see *The Bookworm*, BBC1, 13 Oct. 1995; IG–MS, Nov. 1917, 375.
23. ET–JF, 21 Jan. 1915.
24. RF–ET, *c.*1 Feb. 1915, 42; RF–JWH [*c.*2 Feb. 1915].
25. ET, 'House and Man', 3–4 Feb. 1915, *RB*, I, 4 (*c.*1915), 59, *LP*, 90 ('It was dark with forest boughs | That brushed the walls and made the mossy tiles'); Frost, 'An Old Man's Winter Night', *Mountain Interval*, 14 ('All out-of-doors looked darkly in at him | Through the thin frost, almost in separate stars, | That gathers on the pane in empty rooms'): RF–JWH, *c.*10 Feb. 1915; Frost in Mertins, 136.
26. ET, 'Parting', 11 Feb. 1915, *LP*, 57; ET–EF, 24 Jan. 1915, 114; Myfanwy Thomas, 42; ET, 'This is the constellation of the Lyre', ETC.
27. See RF–HM and RF–FSF, both *c.*13 Feb. 1915, 152; RF–SC, 2 Feb. 1915, 151; RF–LA, 15 March 1915, 157.
28. ET, 'The Owl', 24 Feb. 1915, *Poems*, 12–13; ET–JF, 21 Feb. 1915; ET–EF, 12 March 1915, 124; GWB–EF, 6 March 1915, 34n.
29. RF–LA, 15 March 1915, 157; RF–Frost children [Feb. 1915], in Frost, *Family Letters*, 3; RF–JWH, 14 March 1915.
30. RB–JD, 18–25 Jan. 1915, 655.

III—HIGH BEECH

SPRING 1915

1. See Farjeon, 121–2.
2. ET–JF, 8 March 1915; see ET–EF, 25 March 1915, Farjeon, 127–8; ET, 'The Child on the Cliffs', 11 March 1915, *LP*, 53; 'Good-night', 16 March 1915, *LP*, 54; 'The Bridge', 12 March 1915, *NS*, 28 April 1917, 87, *Poems*, 30; ET–JF, 23 March 1915.
3. See ET, 'Will you come?', 25 March 1915, *Poems*, 14; 'The Wasp Trap', 27 March 1915, *LP*, 55; 'A Tale', 28–31 March 1915, *LP*, 56; ET–EG, 17 March 1915, 27; ET–JF, 8 March 1915.
4. ET–EG, 13 March 1915, 25.
5. See ET–RF, 3 May 1915, 52; see ET–EF, 4 May 1915, 133; see ET–RF, 15 May 1915, 54; see Stonesifer, 116; see Tomalin, 213; Julian Thomas, diary entry 23 March 1915 in *CP1978*, 409–10.
6. ET–EF, 5 April 1915, 128; see diary 1915 for daily progress on *LDM*; ET–RF, 22 April 1915, 47; ET, 'In Memoriam (Easter 1915)', 6 April 1915, *Poems*, 26.
7. ET, *DC*, 18 Sept. 1902, see Motion, 61.
8. RF–ET, 17 April 1915, 43; see ET, 'Lob', 3–4 April 1915, *Poems*, 30–5; *CET*, 129–30; see Helen Thomas, 46–52; *Country*, 9.
9. RF–ET, 17 April 1915, 43; ET–EG, *c.* April 1915, 29.
10. See ET–HM, 20 April 1915, 64; ET–HM, 25 April 1915, 65.
11. See ET–RF, 15 May 1915, 54; ET–HM [*c.* May 1915], 65–6.

473

12. ET, 1915 diary, 41v; ET–EF, 4 May 1915, 133.
13. ET, 1915 diary, 2v.
14. *Country*, 59.
15. RF–ET, 17 April 1915, 43.
16. HT–HM [*c*.1920], 67.
17. *The Times*, 5 April 1915; see Hassall, *Rupert Brooke*, 502.
18. Churchill, *The Times*, 26 April 1915.
19. RF–JWH, 15 May 1915; WWG–EM, 'Saturday' [?late April 1915]; see Abercrombie, 'R. B.', *Poems*, 15; Drinkwater, 'Rupert Brooke', *Loyalties*, 26; Gibson ['The Going'], 'Rupert Brooke', *Friends*, 7, 11–13; Cornford, 'Youth', 5.
20. ET, 'Rupert Brooke', *ER*, June 1915; ET–RF, 14 June 1915, 61 (as '13 June 1915').
21. ET–RF, 3 May 1915, 51; ET–JWH, 5 May 1915; ET–RF, 19 Oct. 1916, 153–4; Hassall, *Rupert Brooke*, 481.
22. RF–JWH, 15 May 1915.
23. ET–RF, 15 May 1915; ET, 'Fifty Faggots', *NS*, 28 April 1917, 87, *Poems*, 26; ET–RF, 23 May 1915, 57.

SUMMER 1915

1. See ET–RF, 31 May 1915, 59 (as '1 June 1915'); ET, 'I built myself a house of glass', 25 June 1915, *LP*, 16; *CET*, 53; ET–EG, 24 June 1915, *ETFN*, 52 (Aug. 2004), 16 (*ACP*, 242); see ET–RF [10 June 1914], 15 (as 'probably July 1, 1914'); ET–EF, 18 June 1915, 147.
2. ET, 'Words', 26–28 June 1914, *Poems*, 61–3; ET–EF, post dated 8 June 1915, 146; see Hansard, HC Deb., 22 April 1915, 71, 378; ET–RF, 14 June 1915, 62 (as '13 June 1915');

ET–RF, 28 June 1915, 74 (probably 29 June, diary, 28v).

3. ET–RF, 14 June 1915, 63 (as '13 June 1915'); ET–EF, post dated 18 June 1915, 147; ET–RF, 15 June 1915, 67.
4. ET–RF, 18 June 1915, 69; ET–GB, 30 June 1915, 251; ET–RF, 15 June 1915, 66.
5. Frost, 'The Road Not Taken', *AM*, Aug. 1915, *Mountain Interval*, 9.
6. Frost at Bread Loaf Writers' Conference, 26 Aug. 1961, in Thompson, *Years of Triumph*, 546.
7. Frost at Bread Loaf Writers' Conference, 23 Aug. 1953 in Thompson, *Years of Triumph*, 546.
8. ET, 'The Stile', *LT*, 46; see Farjeon, 40; Frost, in reminiscence, 16 Aug. 1947 in Thompson, *Years of Triumph*, 88.
9. ET–RF, 14 June 1915, 63–4 (as '13 June 1915'); ET–RF, 22 July 1915, 82.
10. EF–RF, 14 June 1915, 62 (as '13 June 1915').
11. RF–ET, 26 June 1915, 70; ET–RF, 11 July 1915, 78; RF–ET, 26 June 1915, 70.
12. ET–RF, 11 July 1915, 78; ET, 'The Brook', 10 July 1915, Abercrombie and Trevelyan, 59, *LP*, 85; ET, 'This England', *LS*, 221; Farjeon, 152; Helen Thomas, 153.
13. ET–RF, 22 July 1915, 82; Frost, 'A Servant to Servants', *North of Boston*, 66; ET–RF, 22 July 1915, 82–3.
14. ET, 'A Dream', *c.* 8 July 1915, *LP*, 22, see FNB 80 after 23 May 1915 and after 2 June 1915 for dream and early draft; ET–JB, 7 Nov. 1902, 36.
15. RF–ET, 31 July 1915, 87 (cf. ECH₁: 'I become aware of the loveliness of "Aspens". I am not among those men "who like a different tree."' [30 March–2 April 1919]; ET, 'Aspens', 11 July

1915, Abercrombie and Trevelyan, 49, *LP*, 68; 'The Mill-Water', *LP*, 20; see Bottomley, 177; ET–JWH [14 July 1915]; Farjeon, 152; Helen Thomas, 153.
16. ET, Attestation form, 19 July 1915, NA.
17. ET–EF, 20 July 1915, 152–3; ET–GB, 21 July 1915, 253; see ET, 'Digging', 21 July 1915, *LP*, 18, and ET–EF, 21 July 1915, 153; ET, 'Cock-Crow', 23 July 1915, 61; ET–GB, 15 July 1915, 252 (as '14 July 1915').
18. RF–ET, 31 July 1915, 86.
19. ET–RF, ?10 Aug. 1915, 89 (as '9.viii.15'); ET–RF, 21 Aug. 1915, 91.
20. ET–RF, ?10 Aug. 1915, 88 (as '9.viii.15'); ET–JWH, 28 Aug. 1915; ET–RF, 28 Aug. 1915, 93.
21. ET–RF, 28 Aug. 1915, 93; Artists Rifles Association figures.
22. ET–RF, 21 Aug. 1915, 91.
23. Frost, 'The Road Not Taken', *AM*, Aug. 1916, *Mountain Interval*, 9.

AUTUMN 1915

1. ET–RF, 5 Sept. 1915, 96; ET–RF, 3 Sept. 1915, 95.
2. See ET–EF [30 Sept. 1915], 166; ET–JWH, 28 Sept. 1915.
3. ET–RF, 4 Oct. 1915, 97; ET–HT, 11 Oct. 1915, NLW (*ACP* 262); ET–RF, 4 Oct. 1915, 98; ET–WdlM [*c.*5 Oct. 1915]; ET–RF, 5 Oct. 1915, 99; ET, 'October', 15–16 Oct. 1915, *Poems*, 48–9.
4. ET–GB, 6 Nov. 1915, 256; ET–RF, 6 Nov. 1915, 103–4; ET, *TE*, 111–12; *RB*, I, 4 (*c.*1915), 59–60; ET–RF, 12 Oct. 1915, 101.
5. See ET–RF, 12 Nov. 1915, 105.

6. ET–RF, 13 Nov. 1915, 107.
7. WO–SO, 26 Oct. 1915, 361; WO–SO [?31 Oct. 1915], 365 (as '[2 November 1915]').
8. See WO–SO, post dated 28 Feb. 1916, 382; WO–SO [?4 March 1916], 383–4.
9. ET–RF, 12 Nov. 1915, 105; WO–SO [post dated 15 Nov. 1915], 366.
10. ET–RF, 13 Nov. 1915, 107; ET–MT, 21 Nov. 1915, 84.
11. RF–ET, 23 Nov. 1915, 108–9; ET–RF, 12 Nov. 1915, 106; RF–ET, 23 Nov. 1915, 108–9.
12. See ET–EF, post dated 18 Nov. 1915, 170; ET–JWH, 20 Nov. 1915.

WINTER 1915/16

1. See Alison Thomas, 115–16; ECH$_2$ [21–30 May 1919].
2. ECH$_2$ [c.16–24 Sept. 1919]; ET–ECH, c.16 Nov. 1900; HT–ECH, 24 Feb. 1919; ET–ECH, c.16 Nov. 1900, Berg.
3. ECH$_2$ [c.1–19 Jan. 1920].
4. ECH$_2$, 21 May 1919.
5. ECH$_1$ [15–21 March 1919].
6. ET–GB, 11 Feb. 1916; see FNB 80, 26 Nov. 1915 ('This is no case of little right or wrong'); ET, 'This is no case of petty right or wrong', 26 Dec. 1915, *SP*, 9; *LP*, 77.
7. ET–EF [post dated 30 Dec. 1915], 178.
8. ET–RF, 2 Jan. 1916, 115; ET, 'I may come near loving you', 8 Feb. 1916, *CP1949*, 189; TSE–MG, 30 May 1949.
9. ET–RF, 2 Jan. 1916, 114–15.
10. ET–EF [post dated 7 Jan. 1916], 180; ET–EF [15 Jan. 1916], 'probably July 21', 205; ET–RF,

16 Jan. 1916, 116.

11. ET, 'Rain', 7 Jan. 1916, *Poems*, 54–5.

12. ET–RF, 30 Jan. 1916, 119; ET, 'Roads', 22 Jan. 1916, Abercrombie and Trevelyan, 53–5, *LP*, 74–6.

13. ET, 'The clouds that are so light', 15 Jan. 1916, *Poems*, 36; ET–HT, *c.*24 Jan. 1916, LCL (*CP1978*, 408–9).

14. ET–GB, 7 Feb. 1908, 156; ET–WdlM, 19 Feb. 1908, 32r; ET–HH, 18 and 28 Jan. 1908, UBC.

15. HT–ET, 18, 19 Jan. and 5, 13 and 14 Feb. 1908.

16. ET–GB, 26 Feb. 1908, 156; ET–HH, 7 March 1908, UBC.

17. ECH$_4$; ECH$_3$ [19 Jan.–16 Feb. 1920]; ET, 'Those things that poets said', 9 Feb. 1916, *LP*, 66; ET, 'No one so much as you', 11 Feb. 1916, *CP1928*, 192–3.

18. ET–HT, 24 Feb. 1916, 81; *FIP*, 76; Yeats, *Essays and Introductions*, 509; ET, 'The Unknown', 14 Feb. 1916, Abercrombie and Trevelyan, 45–6, *LP*, 28–9.

19. HT–ECH, 12 Dec. 1919.

20. ET, 'February Afternoon', 7–8 Feb. 1916, *LP*, 17; ET–HT, 24 Feb. 1916, 81.

21. ET, 'Celandine', 4 March 1916, *LP*, 11.

22. ET–JWH, 24 Feb. 1916.

SPRING 1916

1. ET–RF, 6 Dec. 1915, 2 and 16 Jan. 1916, 21 Feb. 1916, 111–21; ET–RF, 5 March 1916, 123.

2. ET–RF, 5 March 1916, 123–5.

3. ET, '"Home"', 7–10 March 1915, *Poems*, 55–6.

4. ET–RF, 16 March 1916, 126; ET, 'Thaw', 10 March 1916, *Poems*, 16; ET–RF, 16 March 1916,

128; ET–RF, 21 May 1916, 133.

5. ET–GB, 24 April 1916, 266.

6. ET, 'If I should ever by chance', 29 March–6 April 1916, *Poems*, 19; 'If I were to own', 1–7 April 1916, *Poems*, 20–1; 'What shall I give?', 2–8 April 1916, *Poems*, 20; 'And you, Helen', 9 April 1916, 21–2.

7. ET, 'When we two walked', 23 April–1 May 1916, *Poems*, 25; 'Like the touch of rain', 23–30 April 1916, M_2, *Poems*, 17–18; *FIP*, 76–7.

8. ET–HH, 7 March 1908, UBC; see ET–GB, 20 Dec. 1915, 258; *FIP*, 91.

9. See Catherine Abercrombie; see Helen Thomas, 239–41.

10. ET–RF, 6 Dec. 1915, 112.

11. ET–EF, 8 May 1916, 195.

12. ET, 'It Rains', 11–13 May 1916, *Poems*, 28; ECH_2 [5–8 Sept. 1919]; ECH_3 [1–19 Jan. 1920]; ECH, 'The Kiss', ECH poems.

13. ET, 'Some eyes condemn', 13–14 May 1916, 36–7; 'After you speak', 3 June 1916, *Poems*, 24.

14. Frost, 'Not to Keep', *YR*, Jan. 1917, *New Hampshire*, 97; ET–RF, 21 May 1916, 131. ET, 'The sun used to shine', 22 May 1916, *Poems*, 47–8.

15. ET–RF, 21 May 1916, 131–2.

16. ET, 'No one cares less than I', 25–26 May 1916, *LP*, 73.

17. ET–EF, 4 June 1916, 144 (wrongly sequenced as '4 June 1915').

18. ET, 'As the team's head-brass', 27 May 1916, *Poems*, 15–16.

19. Farjeon, 154.

20. ET–RF, 28 July 1916, 230; ET, 'Bright clouds', 4–5 June 1916, *Poems*, 35–6; 'Early one

morning', 8–11 June 1916, *Poems*, 27–8.

SUMMER 1916

1. ET–JB, 12 June 1916, 80; ET–RF, 10 June 1916, 138.
2. ET–JWH, 13 June 1916.
3. See Berridge, 89; see Bottomley, 177; see ET–RF, 10 Aug. 1915, 88 (as '9 Aug. 1915').
4. ET, 'There was a time', 23 June 1916, *LP*, 71; ET–EF, 28 June 1916, 201–2.
5. RF–JWH, 4 July 1916, 205.
6. See Graves, 181–7; *The Times*, 5 Aug. 1915.
7. See Baynes Jansen, 104.
8. ET–JF, July 1916.
9. ET, 'Lob', 'Words', *Form*, I, 1, April 1916, 33–4; see Thompson, *Early Years*, 566–7; see RF–ET, 15 Aug. 1916, 141; ET–GB, 30 July 1916, 269; ET, *SP* : 'Sedge-Warblers', 'This is no case of petty right or wrong', 'Aspens', 'A Private', 'Cock-Crow', 'Beauty'.
10. ET–EWF, 27 Nov. 1916, 163.
11. ET–RF, 15 Aug. 1916, 145; ET, 'Gone, gone again', *c.*26–7 Aug. 1916, *NS*, 28 April 1917, 87, *Poems*, 46–7.
12. ECH$_1$ [30 March–2 April 1919].
13. RF–ET, 15 Aug. 1916, 142; ET–RF, 15 Aug. 1915, 144.

AUTUMN 1916

1. ET–RF, 9 Sept. 1916, 147; ET, 'There was a time', 23 June 1916, *LP*, 71.
2. See ET, 'That girl's clear eyes', 10 Sept. 1916, *LP*, 59; 'What will they do?', 15 Sept. 1916, *LP*,

25; ET–RF, 21 May 1916, 132.
3. ET–EF, 9 Sept. 1916, 146; RF–ET, 28 Sept. 1916, 150; ET–RF, 29 Nov. 1916, 164.
4. ET, 'The Trumpet', *c.*26–8 Sept. 1916, *Poems*, 9.
5. ET–EF [probably 27 Sept. 1916], 219, where it appears out of sequence; see Farjeon, 218.
6. ET–EWF, 27 Nov. 1916, 163; Helen Thomas, 162; Farjeon, 229; see ET–RF, 29 Nov. 1916, 165.
7. ET–HT, 20 Oct. 1916; ET–JWH, 29 Nov. 1916; ET–RF, 29 Nov. 1916, 165; ET–GB, *c.*1 Dec. 1916, 275.
8. PTS.
9. ET–RF, 29 Nov. 1916, 164; see ET–RF, 12 Jan. 1917, 172.
10. Frost, 'The Gum-Gatherer', *Independent*, Oct. 1916; 'The Bonfire', *Severn Arts*, Nov. 1916; 'An Encounter', *AM*, Nov. 1916; 'Snow', *PC*, IX, 2 (Nov. 1916); all collected in *Mountain Interval*.
11. RF–ET, 6 Nov. 1916, 158; ET–RF, 24 Nov. 1916, 160; ET–EF, 6 Nov. 1916, 218; Bottomley, 177–8.
12. See Farjeon, 229.
13. Official military record detailing confirmation of officer commission, 23 Nov. 1916, NA; ET–EF, 6 Nov. 1916, 218.
14. ET, 'Lights Out', Nov. 1916, *Poems*, 59–60.

WINTER 1916/17

1. See Severn, 115.
2. RF–ET, 7 Dec. 1916, 166–7; ET–RF, 31 Dec. 1916, 170; Lloyd George, *The Times*, 20 Dec. 1916.
3. ET–EF, 7 Dec. 1916, 231; ET–HT, 12 and

29 Dec. 1916.

4. ET–RF, 16 Dec. 1916, 169; see ET–EF, 16 Dec. 1916, 235; Severn, 119.
5. See ET–HT, 22 Dec. 1916; see Helen Thomas, 163–5; ET–EF, 27 Dec. 1916, 237.
6. ET–HEMT, 29 Dec. 1916.
7. ET–RF, 22 Jan. 1917, 173; see Dudfield, 12; see Jennifer Davies, 9; see Gethyn-Jones, 142.
8. See ET–HT, 1 Jan. 1917; see Severn, 12–17.
9. Farjeon, 241; Myfanwy Thomas in *Fast Beat My Heart*; W. H. Davies, *Voices*, 1919, in Stonesifer, 116; Helen Thomas, 167–73; WD, 1v.
10. ET, 'The sorrow of true love', 13 Jan. 1917, WD, 15r.
11. ET–MPT, 12 Jan. 1917; ET–HT, 14 Jan. 1917; ET–RF, 12 Jan. 1917, 172.
12. See WD, 2r; see ET–HT, 15 Jan. 1917; see Severn, 115; see ET–HT, 20 Jan. 1917; ET–EF, 17 Jan. 1917, 242; see ET–HT, 17 Jan. 1917; ET–MET, 17 Jan. 1917.
13. Farjeon, 243; WD, 3v; JWH, 'E.T. 22 Jan. 1917'.
14. Bod. MS Eng. Lett. c. 281.
15. ET–EF, 25 Jan. 1917, 244; ET, 'The Mountain Chapel', Dec. 1914, *LP*, 62–3; ET–RF, 22 Jan. 1917, 173–4.
16. WD, 4v; ET–HT, 28 Jan. 1917.

IV—ARRAS

WINTER–SPRING 1917

1. WD, 29 Jan. 1917, 5r; ET–EF, 31 Jan. 1917, 247; Farjeon, 247.
2. WD, 4 Feb. 1917, 6r.
3. ET–HT, 7 Feb. 1917; ET–RF, 11 Feb. 1917, 178;

WD, 8 Feb. 1917, 6v.

4. WD, 8 Feb. 1917, 6v; ET–EF, 10 Feb. 1917, 247; WD, 9 Feb. 1917, 7r.

5. WD, 9 Feb. 1917, 7r; ET–MET/PHT, 10 Feb. 1917, *Selected Letters*, 136.

6. See WD, 12 Feb. 1917, 7r.

7. ET–WdlM, 14 Feb. 1917; WD, 13 Feb. 1917, 7v.

8. ET–EF, 21 Feb. 1917, 251.

9. WD, 22 Feb. 1917, 8v.

10. ET–RF, 23 Feb. 1917, 179–80; WD, 23 Feb. 1917, 9r; WD, 25 Feb. 1917, 9r; ET–GB, 26 Feb. 1917, 277; WD, 24 Feb. 1917, 9r.

11. ET–HT, 27 Feb. 1917, *Selected Letters*, 142; ET–GB, 26 Feb. 1917, 277; ET–HT, 27 Feb. 1917.

12. ET–HT, 27 Feb. 1917, *Selected Letters*, 142–3.

13. WD, 9 March 1917, 10v; ET–RF, 6 March 1917, 182.

14. RF–HT, 6 Feb. 1917, 211.

15. ET–RF, 9 March 1917, 183–4 (as '8 March 1917'); ET–HT, 27 Jan. 1917.

16. ET–WdlM, 9 March 1917, 300r–301r.

17. See ET–MPT, 23 March 1917; see WD, 15 March 1917, 11v; ET–RF, 2 April 1917, 186–7.

18. ET–HT, 17 March 1917, 85–7.

19. ET–EF, 22 March 1917, 257.

20. WD, 20 March 1917, 12r.

21. ET–ADW, 22 March 1917; WD, 22 March 1917, 12v.

22. ET–MPT, 23 March 1917.

23. See ET–HT, 24 March 1917, 88.

24. ET–EF, 27 March 1917, 258.

25. ET–JT, 30 March 1917, 156.

26. ET–RF, 2 April 1917, 186–8.

27. HT–JH, 4 April 1917, 203–4.

28. *TLS*, 29 March 1917, 151; J. C. Squire

('Solomon Eagle'), *NS*, 31 March 1917, 617.

29. RF–EG, 29 April 1917, 217.
30. ET–HT, 7–8 April 1917, 96.
31. Helen Thomas, 300.
32. FL–HT, 10 April 1917.
33. WD, 14v; lines loose in WD.
34. RF–HT, 27 April 1917, 216.

*   *   *

1. RF–SC, 11 Oct. 1928, 351; see JWH–RPE, 22 Feb. 1934, 'In common with many of E.T.'s intimate friends, and certainly with some of the Thomas family, I was a good deal upset by Helen's two books when they were published.'
2. Mervyn Thomas in RLW, 16.
3. See Sokol, 228; see Frost, 'War Thoughts at Home' [Jan. 1918], *VQR*, Fall 2006, 113, 'To E.T.', *YR*, April 1920, *New Hampshires*, 83, 'A Soldier', *McCalls*, May 1927, *Collected Poems*; see Inventory of personal effects, 4 May 1917, NA.
4. Pound, *Hugh Selwyn Mauberley*, 13.
5. EG–WdlM, 29 April 1920, 230; de la Mare, 'To E. T.: 1917', *Motley*, 55.
6. See Gibson, *Battle*; WWG–RF, 3 Jan. 1934, DCL, Lesley Lee Francis, 190; Conrad Aiken in Stonesifer, 137.
7. Lascelles Abercrombie, v; Abercrombie in Gawsworth, 20–1.
8. Eliot, 'Ulysses, Order, and Myth', *The Dial*, 75 (Nov. 1923), 480–3; 38 Great Russell Street, London WC.
9. W. H. Hudson [1919] in Tomalin, 213; Leavis, 64; Day Lewis, 75; see Larkin; Dylan Thomas, 208; Ted Hughes speaking at Westminster Abbey, 11 Nov. 1985.

Collins

Collins
English
Dictionary

HarperCollins Publishers
Westerhill Road
Bishopbriggs
Glasgow
G64 2QT
Great Britain

Second Edition 2006

Previously published as
Collins Pocket Dictionary
© HarperCollins Publishers 2006

Produced exclusively for John Smith

Latest Reprint 2006

© William Collins Sons & Co. Ltd 1984
© HarperCollins Publishers 1992,
1996, 2000, 2004, 2006

ISBN 978-0-00-780164-0

Collins® and Bank of English® are
registered trademarks of
HarperCollins Publishers Limited

www.collins.co.uk

A catalogue record for this book is
available from the British Library

Computing support and typesetting
by Thomas Widmann

Printed in Italy by
Rotolito Lombarda S.p.A.

Acknowledgements
We would like to thank those authors
and publishers who kindly gave
permission for copyright material to
be used in the Collins Word Web. We
would also like to thank Times
Newspapers Ltd for providing
valuable data.

CONTENTS

EDITORIAL STAFF

EDITORS
Sandra Anderson
Jennifer Baird
Justin Crozier
Andrew Holmes
Elspeth Summers

WRITE FOR LIFE
Penny Hands

FOR THE PUBLISHERS
Elaine Higgleton
Lorna Sinclair Knight

William Collins' dream of knowledge for all began with the publication of his first book in 1819. A self-educated mill worker, he not only enriched millions of lives, but also founded a flourishing publishing house. Today, staying true to this spirit, Collins books are packed with inspiration, innovation, and practical expertise. They place you at the centre of a world of possibility and give you exactly what you need to explore it.

Language is the key to this exploration, and at the heart of Collins Dictionaries is language as it is really used. New words, phrases, and meanings spring up every day, and all of them are captured and analysed by the Collins Word Web. Constantly updated, and with over 2.5 billion entries, this living language resource is unique to our dictionaries.

Words are tools for life. And a Collins Dictionary makes them work for you.

Collins. Do more

FEATURES OF THE DICTIONARY

ducat [**duck**-it] *n* former European gold or silver coin.

duchess *n* **1** woman who holds the rank of duke. **2** wife or widow of a duke.

Regional Label ————— **duchesse** *n NZ* dressing table with a mirror.

duchy *n, pl* **duchies** territory of a duke or duchess.

Part of Speech ————— **duck**¹ *n* **1** water bird with short legs, webbed feet, and a broad blunt bill. **2** its flesh, used as food. **3** female of this bird. **4** *Cricket* score of nothing.

duckling *n* baby duck.

duck² *v* **1** move (the head or body) quickly downwards, to avoid being seen or to dodge a blow. **2** plunge suddenly under water. **3** *Informal* dodge (a duty or responsibility).

Entry Word ————— **duct** *n* **1** tube, pipe, or channel through which liquid or gas is conveyed. **2** bodily passage conveying secretions or excretions.

ductile *adj* (of a metal) able to be shaped into sheets or wires.

Register Label ————— **dud** *Informal* ♦ *n* **1** ineffectual person or thing. ♦ *adj* **2** bad or useless.

dude *n US informal* **1** man. **2** *Old-fashioned* dandy. **3** any person.

Idiom ————— **dudgeon** *n* **in high dudgeon** angry, resentful.

due *adj* **1** expected or scheduled to be present or arrive. **2** owed as a debt. **3** fitting, proper. ♦ *n* **4** something that is owed or required. ♦ *pl* **5** charges for membership of a club or organization.

Example ————— ♦ *adv* **6** directly or exactly, e.g. *due south*. **due to** attributable to or caused by.

> ☑ **WORD TIP**
> The use of *due to* as a compound preposition as in *the performance has been cancelled due to bad weather* was formerly considered incorrect, but is now acceptable.

Usage Help —————

FEATURES OF THE DICTIONARY

an earlier point in order to replay.

rewire *v* provide (a house, engine, etc.) with new wiring.

rewrite *v* **1** write again in a different way. ◆ *n* **2** something rewritten. — Sense Number

rhapsody *n, pl* **-dies 1** freely structured emotional piece of music. **2** expression of ecstatic enthusiasm. **rhapsodic** *adj* **rhapsodize** *v* speak or write with extravagant enthusiasm.

rhea [**ree**-a] *n* S American three-toed ostrich.

rhenium *n Chem* silvery-white metallic element with a high melting point. — Subject Label

rheostat *n* instrument for varying the resistance of an electrical circuit.

rhesus [**ree**-suss] *n* small long-tailed monkey of S Asia. **rhesus factor, Rh factor** antigen commonly found in human blood. — Pronunciation

rhetoric *n* **1** art of effective speaking or writing. **2** artificial or exaggerated language. **rhetorical** *adj* (of a question) not requiring an answer. — Related Word **rhetorically** *adv*

rheumatism *n* painful inflammation of joints or muscles. **rheumatic** *n, adj* (person) affected by rheumatism. **rheumatoid** *adj* of or like rheumatism.

Rh factor *n* see RHESUS. — Cross-reference

rhinestone *n* imitation diamond.

rhino *n* short for RHINOCEROS.

rhinoceros *n, pl* **-oses, -os** large thick-skinned animal with one or two horns on its nose.

> ☑ **SPELLING TIP**
> The pronunciation of **rhinoceros** probably misleads some people into making the mistake of adding a *u* before the final *s* (*rhinocerous*). — Spelling Help

rhizome *n* thick underground stem producing new plants.

rhodium *n Chem* hard metallic element.

ABBREVIATIONS USED IN THE DICTIONARY

AD	anno Domini	Meteorol	Meteorology
adj	adjective	Mil	Military
adv	adverb	n	noun
Anat	Anatomy	N	North
Archit	Architecture	Naut	Nautical
Astrol	Astrology	NZ	New Zealand
Aust	Australia(n)	Obs	Obsolete
BC	before Christ	Offens	Offensive
Biol	Biology	orig.	originally
Brit	British	Photog	Photography
Chem	Chemistry	pl	plural
C of E	Church of England	prep	preposition
conj	conjunction	pron	pronoun
E	East	Psychol	Psychology
e.g.	for example	®	Trademark
esp.	especially	RC	Roman Catholic
etc.	et cetera	S	South
fem	feminine	S Afr	South Africa(n)
foll.	followed	Scot	Scottish
Geom	Geometry	sing	singular
Hist	History	US	United States
interj	interjection	usu.	usually
Lit	Literary	v	verb
masc	masculine	W	West
Med	Medicine	Zool	Zoology

A a

a *adj* indefinite article, used before a noun being mentioned for the first time.

AA 1 Alcoholics Anonymous. **2** Automobile Association.

aardvark *n* S African anteater with long ears and snout.

AB able-bodied seaman.

aback *adv* **taken aback** startled or disconcerted.

abacus *n* beads on a wire frame, used for doing calculations.

abalone [ab-a-**lone**-ee] *n* edible sea creature with a shell lined with mother of pearl.

abandon *v* **1** desert or leave (one's wife, children, etc.). **2** give up (hope etc.) altogether. ♦ *n* **3** lack of inhibition. **abandoned** *adj* **1** deserted. **2** uninhibited. **abandonment** *n*

abase *v* humiliate or degrade (oneself). **abasement** *n*

abashed *adj* embarrassed and ashamed.

abate *v* make or become less strong. **abatement** *n*

abattoir [**ab**-a-twahr] *n* place where animals are killed for food.

abbess *n* nun in charge of a convent.

abbey *n* dwelling place of, or a church belonging to, a community of monks or nuns.

abbot *n* head of an abbey of monks.

abbreviate *v* shorten (a word) by leaving out some letters. **abbreviation** *n* shortened form of a word or words.

ABC¹ *n* **1** alphabet. **2** basics of a subject.

ABC² Australian Broadcasting Corporation.

abdicate *v* give up (the throne or a responsibility). **abdication** *n*

abdomen *n* part of the body containing the stomach and intestines. **abdominal** *adj*

abduct *v* carry off, kidnap. **abduction** *n* **abductor** *n*

aberration *n* **1** sudden change from what is normal, accurate, or correct. **2** brief lapse in control of one's thoughts or feelings. **aberrant** *adj* showing aberration.

abet *v* **abetting, abetted** help or encourage in wrongdoing. **abettor** *n*

abeyance *n* **in abeyance** not in use.

abhor *v* **-horring, -horred** detest utterly. **abhorrent** *adj* hateful, loathsome. **abhorrence** *n*

abide *v* **1** endure, put up with. **2** *Obs* stay or dwell, e.g. *abide with me*. **abide by** *v* obey (the law, rules, etc.). **abiding** *adj* lasting.

ability *n, pl* **-ties 1** competence, power. **2** talent.

abject *adj* **1** utterly miserable. **2** lacking all self-respect. **abjectly** *adv*

abjure *v* deny or renounce on oath.

ablative *n* case of nouns in Latin and other languages, indicating source, agent, or instrument of action.

ablaze *adj* burning fiercely.

able *adj* capable, competent. **ably** *adv* **able-bodied** *adj* strong and healthy.

ablutions *pl n* act of washing.

abnormal *adj* not normal or usual. **abnormally** *adv* **abnormality** *n*

aboard *adv, prep* on, in, onto, or into (a ship, train, or plane).

abode *n* home, dwelling.

abolish *v* do away with. **abolition** *n* **abolitionist** *n* person who wishes to do away with something, esp. slavery.

abominable *adj* detestable, very bad.
abominable snowman large apelike
creature said to live in the Himalayas.
abominably *adv*

abomination *n* someone or
something that is detestable.

aborigine [ab-or-**rij**-in-ee],
aboriginal *n* original inhabitant of a
country or region, esp. (A-) Australia.
aboriginal *adj*

abort *v* **1** have an abortion or perform
an abortion on. **2** have a miscarriage. **3**
end a plan or process before
completion. **abortive** *adj*
unsuccessful.

abortion *n* **1** operation to end a
pregnancy. **2** *Informal* something
grotesque. **abortionist** *n* person who
performs abortions, esp. illegally.

abound *v* be plentiful. **abounding** *adj*

about *prep* **1** concerning, on the
subject of. **2** in or near (a place). ♦ *adv*
3 nearly, approximately. **4** nearby.
about to shortly going to. **not about
to** determined not to. **about-turn** *n*
complete change of attitude.

above *adv, prep* **1** over or higher
(than). **2** greater (than). **3** superior
(to). **above board** in the open,
without dishonesty.

abracadabra *n* supposedly magic
word.

abrasion *n* scraped area on the skin.

abrasive *adj* **1** harsh and unpleasant in
manner. **2** tending to rub or scrape.
♦ *n* **3** substance for cleaning or
polishing by rubbing.

abreast *adv, adj* side by side. **abreast
of** up to date with.

abridge *v* shorten by using fewer
words. **abridgment, abridgement** *n*

abroad *adv* **1** to or in a foreign
country. **2** at large.

abrogate *v* cancel (a law or

agreement) formally. **abrogation** *n*

abrupt *adj* **1** sudden, unexpected. **2**
blunt and rude. **abruptly** *adv*
abruptness *n*

abs *pl n Informal* abdominal muscles.

abscess *n* inflamed swelling containing
pus.

☑ **SPELLING TIP**
There is a silent *c* in the middle of
abscess that's easy to forget.

abscond *v* leave secretly.

abseil [**ab**-sale] *v* go down a steep drop
by a rope fastened at the top and tied
around one's body.

absent *adj* **1** not present. **2** lacking. **3**
inattentive. ♦ *v* **4** stay away. **absently**
adv **absence** *n* **1** being away. **2** lack.
absentee *n* person who should be
present but is not. **absenteeism** *n*
persistent absence from work or
school. **absent-minded** *adj*
inattentive or forgetful.
absent-mindedly *adv*

absinthe *n* strong green
aniseed-flavoured liqueur.

absolute *adj* **1** complete, perfect. **2**
not limited, unconditional. **3** pure, e.g.
absolute alcohol. **absolutely** *adv* **1**
completely. ♦ *interj* **2** certainly, yes.
absolutism *n* government by a ruler
with unrestricted power.

absolve *v* declare to be free from
blame or sin. **absolution** *n*

absorb *v* **1** soak up (a liquid). **2** take in.
3 engage the interest of (someone).
absorption *n* **absorbent** *adj* able to
absorb liquid. **absorbency** *n*

abstain *v* **1** choose not to do
something. **2** choose not to vote.
abstainer *n* **abstention** *n* abstaining,
esp. from voting. **abstinence** *n*
abstaining, esp. from drinking alcohol.
abstinent *adj*

abstemious *adj* taking very little

alcohol or food. **abstemiousness** *n*

abstract *adj* **1** existing as a quality or idea rather than a material object. **2** theoretical. **3** (of art) using patterns of shapes and colours rather than realistic likenesses. ♦ *n* **4** summary. **5** abstract work of art. **6** abstract word or idea. ♦ *v* **7** summarize. **8** remove. **abstracted** *adj* lost in thought. **abstraction** *n*

abstruse *adj* not easy to understand.

absurd *adj* incongruous or ridiculous. **absurdly** *adv* **absurdity** *n*

abundant *adj* plentiful. **abundantly** *adv* **abundance** *n*

abuse *v* **1** use wrongly. **2** ill-treat violently. **3** speak harshly and rudely to. ♦ *n* **4** prolonged ill-treatment. **5** harsh and vulgar comments. **6** wrong use. **abuser** *n* **abusive** *adj* **abusively** *adv* **abusiveness** *n*

abut *v* **abutting, abutted** be next to or touching.

abysmal *adj* *Informal* extremely bad, awful. **abysmally** *adv*

abyss *n* very deep hole or chasm.

AC alternating current.

a/c account.

acacia [a-**kay**-sha] *n* tree or shrub with yellow or white flowers.

academy *n, pl* -**mies** **1** society to advance arts or sciences. **2** institution for training in a particular skill. **3** *Scot* secondary school. **academic** *adj* **1** of an academy or university. **2** of theoretical interest only. ♦ *n* **3** lecturer or researcher at a university. **academically** *adv* **academician** *n* member of an academy.

acanthus *n* prickly plant.

ACAS (in Britain) Advisory Conciliation and Arbitration Service.

ACC (in New Zealand) Accident Compensation Corporation.

accede *v* **1** consent or agree (to). **2** take up (an office or position).

accelerate *v* (cause to) move faster. **acceleration** *n* **accelerator** *n* pedal in a motor vehicle to increase speed.

☑ **SPELLING TIP**

The commonest misspelling of **accelerate** in the Bank of English has a double *l*. In fact, a double *c* is correct, but there should be only one *l*.

---

accent *n* **1** distinctive style of pronunciation of a local, national, or social group. **2** mark over a letter to show how it is pronounced. **3** stress on a syllable or musical note. ♦ *v* **4** place emphasis on.

accentuate *v* stress, emphasize. **accentuation** *n*

accept *v* **1** receive willingly. **2** agree to. **3** consider to be true. **acceptance** *n* **acceptable** *adj* **1** tolerable. **2** satisfactory. **acceptably** *adv* **acceptability** *n*

access *n* **1** means of or right to approach or enter. ♦ *v* **2** obtain (data) from a computer. **accessible** *adj* easy to reach. **accessibility** *n*

accession *n* taking up of an office or position.

accessory *n, pl* -**ries** **1** supplementary part or object. **2** person involved in a crime although not present when it is committed.

accident *n* **1** mishap, often causing injury. **2** event happening by chance. **accidental** *adj* **1** happening by chance or unintentionally. ♦ *n* **2** *Music* symbol indicating that a sharp, flat, or natural note is not a part of the key signature. **accidentally** *adv*

acclaim *v* **1** applaud, praise. ♦ *n* **2** enthusiastic approval. **acclamation** *n*

acclimatize *v* adapt to a new climate or environment. **acclimatization** *n*

accolade *n* **1** award, honour, or praise. **2** award of knighthood.

accommodate *v* **1** provide with lodgings. **2** have room for. **3** oblige, do a favour for. **4** adapt or adjust (to something). **accommodation** *n* house or room for living in. **accommodating** *adj* obliging.

☑ **SPELLING TIP**
The Bank of English shows that people usually remember that **accommodation** and **accommodate** have two *c*s, but they often forget that these words have two *m*s as well.

accompany *v* **-nying, -nied 1** go along with. **2** occur with. **3** provide a musical accompaniment for. **accompaniment** *n* **1** something that accompanies. **2** *Music* supporting part that goes with a solo. **accompanist** *n*

accomplice *n* person who helps another to commit a crime.

accomplish *v* **1** manage to do. **2** finish. **accomplishment** *n* **1** completion. **2** personal ability or skill. **accomplished** *adj* expert, proficient.

accord *n* **1** agreement, harmony. ♦ *v* **2** fit in with.

accordance *n* **in accordance with** conforming to or according to.

according *adv* **according to 1** as stated by. **2** in conformity with. **accordingly** *adv* **1** in an appropriate manner. **2** consequently.

accordion *n* portable musical instrument played by moving the two sides apart and together, and pressing a keyboard or buttons to produce the notes. **accordionist** *n*

accost *v* approach and speak to, often aggressively.

account *n* **1** report, description. **2** business arrangement making credit available. **3** record of money received and paid out with the resulting balance. **4** person's money held in a bank. **5** importance, value. ♦ *v* **6** judge to be. **on account of** because of. **accountable** *adj* responsible to someone or for something. **accountability** *n*

accounting *n* skill or practice of maintaining and auditing business accounts. **accountant** *n* person who maintains and audits business accounts. **accountancy** *n*

accoutrements *pl n* clothing and equipment for a particular activity.

accredited *adj* authorized, officially recognized.

accretion [ak-**kree**-shun] *n* **1** gradual growth. **2** something added.

accrue *v* **-cruing, -crued** increase gradually. **accrual** *n*

accumulate *v* gather together in increasing quantity. **accumulation** *n* **accumulative** *adj* **accumulator** *n Brit & Aust* rechargeable electric battery.

accurate *adj* exact, correct. **accurately** *adv* **accuracy** *n*

accursed *adj* **1** under a curse. **2** detestable.

accusative *n* grammatical case indicating the direct object.

accuse *v* charge with wrongdoing. **accused** *n* **accuser** *n* **accusing** *adj* **accusation** *n* **accusatory** *adj*

accustom *v* make used to. **accustomed** *adj* **1** usual. **2** used (to). **3** in the habit (of).

ace *n* **1** playing card with one symbol on it. **2** *Informal* expert. **3** *Tennis* unreturnable serve. ♦ *adj* **4** *Informal* excellent.

acerbic [ass-**sir**-bik] *adj* harsh or bitter. **acerbity** *n*

acetate [**ass**-it-tate] *n* **1** *Chem* salt or ester of acetic acid. **2** (also **acetate rayon**) synthetic textile fibre.

acetic [ass-**see**-tik] *adj* of or involving vinegar. **acetic acid** colourless liquid used to make vinegar.

acetone [**ass**-it-tone] *n* colourless liquid used as a solvent.

acetylene [ass-**set**-ill-eez] *n* colourless flammable gas used in welding metals.

ache *n* **1** dull continuous pain. ♦ *v* **2** be in or cause continuous dull pain.

achieve *v* gain by hard work or ability. **achievement** *n* something accomplished.

Achilles heel [ak-**kill**-eez] *n* small but fatal weakness.

Achilles tendon *n* cord connecting the calf muscle to the heel bone.

achromatic *adj* **1** colourless. **2** *Music* with no sharps or flats.

acid *n* **1** *Chem* one of a class of compounds, corrosive and sour when dissolved in water, that combine with a base to form a salt. **2** *Slang* LSD. ♦ *adj* **3** containing acid. **4** sour-tasting. **5** sharp or sour in manner. **acidic** *adj* **acidify** *v* **acidity** *n* **Acid (House)** *n* type of funk-based electronically edited disco music with hypnotic sound effects. **acid rain** rain containing acid from atmospheric pollution. **acid test** conclusive test of value.

acknowledge *v* **1** admit, recognize. **2** indicate recognition of (a person). **3** say one has received. **acknowledgment, acknowledgement** *n*

acme [**ak**-mee] *n* highest point of achievement or excellence.

acne [**ak**-nee] *n* pimply skin disease.

acolyte *n* **1** follower or attendant. **2** *Christianity* person who assists a priest.

aconite *n* **1** poisonous plant with hoodlike flowers. **2** poison obtained from this plant.

acorn *n* nut of the oak tree.

acoustic *adj* **1** of sound and hearing. **2** (of a musical instrument) not electronically amplified. **acoustics** *n* **1** science of sounds. ♦ *pl* **2** features of a room or building determining how sound is heard within it. **acoustically** *adv*

acquaint *v* make familiar, inform. **acquainted** *adj* **acquaintance** *n* **1** person known. **2** personal knowledge.

acquiesce [ak-wee-**ess**] *v* agree to what someone wants. **acquiescence** *n* **acquiescent** *adj*

acquire *v* gain, get. **acquisition** *n* **1** thing acquired. **2** act of getting.

acquisitive *adj* eager to gain material possessions. **acquisitiveness** *n*

acquit *v* **-quitting, -quitted 1** pronounce (someone) innocent. **2** behave in a particular way. **acquittal** *n*

acre *n* measure of land, 4840 square yards (4046.86 square metres). **acreage** [**ake**-er-rij] *n* land area in acres.

acrid [**ak**-rid] *adj* pungent, bitter.

acrimonious *adj* bitter in speech or manner. **acrimony** *n*

acrobat *n* person skilled in gymnastic feats requiring agility and balance. **acrobatic** *adj* **acrobatics** *pl n* acrobatic feats.

acronym *n* word formed from the initial letters of other words, such as NASA.

across *adv, prep* **1** from side to side (of). **2** on or to the other side (of). **across the board** applying equally to all.

acrostic *n* lines of writing in which the first or last letters of each line spell a word or saying.

acrylic *n, adj* (synthetic fibre, paint, etc.) made from acrylic acid. **acrylic acid** strong-smelling corrosive liquid.

act *n* **1** thing done. **2** law or decree. **3** section of a play or opera. **4** one of

several short performances in a show.
5 pretended attitude. ♦ *v* **6** do something. **7** behave in a particular way. **8** perform in a play, film, etc. **act of God** unpredictable natural event. **acting** *n* **1** art of an actor. ♦ *adj* **2** temporarily performing the duties of. **actor, actress** *n* person who acts in a play, film, etc.

ACT Australian Capital Territory.

actinium *n Chem* radioactive chemical element.

action *n* **1** process of doing something. **2** thing done. **3** lawsuit. **4** operating mechanism. **5** minor battle. **actionable** *adj* giving grounds for a lawsuit. **action replay** rerun of an event on a television tape.

active *adj* **1** moving, working. **2** busy, energetic. **3** *Grammar* (of a verb) in a form indicating that the subject is performing the action, e.g. *threw* in *Kim threw the ball*. **actively** *adv* **activity** *n* **1** state of being active. **2** *pl* **-ties**) leisure pursuit. **activate** *v* make active. **activation** *n* **activator** *n* **activist** *n* person who works energetically to achieve political or social goals. **activism** *n*

actual *adj* existing in reality. **actually** *adv* really, indeed. **actuality** *n*

actuary *n, pl* **-aries** statistician who calculates insurance risks. **actuarial** *adj*

actuate *v* start up (a device).

acuity [ak-**kew**-it-ee] *n* keenness of vision or thought.

acumen [**ak**-yew-men] *n* ability to make good judgments.

acupuncture *n* medical treatment involving the insertion of needles at various points on the body. **acupuncturist** *n*

acute *adj* **1** severe. **2** keen, shrewd. **3** sharp, sensitive. **4** (of an angle) less than 90°. ♦ *n* **5** accent (´) over a letter to indicate the quality or length of its sound, as in café. **acutely** *adv* **acuteness** *n*

ad *n Informal* advertisement.

AD anno Domini.

adage *n* wise saying, proverb.

adagio *n, pl* **-gios**, *adv Music* (piece to be played) slowly and gracefully.

adamant *adj* unshakable in determination or purpose. **adamantly** *adv*

Adam's apple *n* projecting lump of thyroid cartilage at the front of the throat.

adapt *v* alter for new use or new conditions. **adaptable** *adj* **adaptability** *n* **adaptation** *n* **1** thing produced by adapting something. **2** adapting. **adaptor, adapter** *n* device for connecting several electrical appliances to a single socket.

add *v* **1** combine (numbers or quantities). **2** join (to something). **3** say or write further.

addendum *n, pl* **-da 1** addition. **2** appendix to a book etc.

adder *n* small poisonous snake.

addict *n* **1** person who is unable to stop taking drugs. **2** *Informal* person devoted to something. **addicted** *adj* **addiction** *n* **addictive** *adj* causing addiction.

addition *n* **1** adding. **2** thing added. **in addition** besides, as well. **additional** *adj* **additionally** *adv* **additive** *n* something added, esp. to a foodstuff, to improve it or prevent deterioration.

addled *adj* confused or unable to think clearly.

address *n* **1** place where a person lives. **2** direction on a letter. **3** location. **4** formal public speech. ♦ *v* **5** mark the destination, as on an envelope. **6** make a speech. **7** give attention to (a problem, task, etc.). **addressee** *n* person addressed.

☑ **SPELLING TIP**

If you spell **address** wrongly, you probably miss out one *d*. Remember to double the *d* and the *s*.

adduce *v* mention something as evidence or proof.

adenoids [**ad**-in-oidz] *pl n* mass of tissue at the back of the throat. **adenoidal** *adj* having a nasal voice caused by swollen adenoids.

adept *adj, n* very skilful (person).

adequate *adj* 1 sufficient, enough. 2 not outstanding. **adequately** *adv* **adequacy** *n*

adhere *v* 1 stick (to). 2 be devoted (to). **adherence** *n* **adherent** *n* devotee, follower. **adhesion** *n* 1 sticking (to). 2 joining together of parts of the body that are normally separate, as after surgery.

adhesive *n* 1 substance used to stick things together. ♦ *adj* 2 able to stick to things.

ad hoc *adj, adv* Latin for a particular purpose only.

adieu [a-**dew**] *interj* Lit farewell, goodbye.

ad infinitum [ad in-fin-**eye**-tum] *adv* Latin endlessly.

adipose *adj* of or containing fat.

adj. adjective.

adjacent *adj* 1 near or next (to). 2 having a common boundary. 3 *Geom* (of a side in a right-angled triangle) lying between a specified angle and the right angle.

adjective *n* word that adds information about a noun or pronoun. **adjectival** *adj*

adjoin *v* be next to. **adjoining** *adj*

adjourn *v* 1 close (a court) at the end of a session. 2 postpone temporarily. 3 *Informal* go elsewhere. **adjournment** *n*

adjudge *v* declare (to be).

adjudicate *v* 1 give a formal decision on (a dispute). 2 judge (a competition). **adjudication** *n* **adjudicator** *n*

adjunct *n* subordinate or additional person or thing.

adjure *v* 1 command (to do). 2 appeal earnestly.

adjust *v* 1 adapt to new conditions. 2 alter slightly so as to be suitable. **adjustable** *adj* **adjuster** *n* **adjustment** *n*

adjutant [**aj**-oo-tant] *n* army officer in charge of routine administration.

ad-lib *v* -libbing, -libbed 1 improvise a speech etc. without preparation. ♦ *n* 2 improvised remark.

admin *n* Informal administration.

administer *v* 1 manage (business affairs). 2 organize and put into practice. 3 give (medicine or treatment).

administrate *v* manage (an organization). **administrator** *n*

administration *n* 1 management of an organization. 2 people who manage an organization. 3 government, e.g. *the Bush administration.*

administrative *adj* of the management of an organization.

admiral *n* highest naval rank. **Admiralty** *n* (in Britain) former government department in charge of the Royal Navy.

admire *v* regard with esteem and approval. **admirable** *adj* **admirably** *adv* **admiration** *n* **admirer** *n* **admiring** *adj* **admiringly** *adv*

admissible *adj* allowed to be brought in as evidence in court. **admissibility** *n*

admission *n* 1 permission to enter. 2 entrance fee. 3 confession.

admit v -mitting, -mitted **1** confess, acknowledge. **2** concede the truth of. **3** allow in. **admittance** n permission to enter. **admittedly** adv it must be agreed.

admixture n **1** mixture. **2** ingredient.

admonish v reprove sternly. **admonition** n

ad nauseam [ad **naw**-zee-am] adv Latin to a boring or sickening extent.

ado n Lit fuss, trouble.

adobe [ad-**oh**-bee] n sun-dried brick.

adolescence n period between puberty and adulthood. **adolescent** n, adj (person) between puberty and adulthood.

adopt v **1** take (someone else's child) as one's own. **2** take up (a plan or principle). **adoption** n **adoptive** adj related by adoption.

adore v **1** love intensely. **2** worship. **adorable** adj **adoration** n **adoring** adj **adoringly** adv

adorn v decorate, embellish. **adornment** n

adrenal [ad-**reen**-al] adj near the kidneys. **adrenal glands** glands covering the top of the kidneys.

adrenalin, adrenaline n hormone secreted by the adrenal glands in response to stress.

adrift adj, adv **1** drifting. **2** without a clear purpose.

adroit adj quick and skilful. **adroitly** adv **adroitness** n

adsorb v (of a gas or vapour) condense and form a thin film on a surface. **adsorption** n

adulation n uncritical admiration.

adult adj **1** fully grown, mature. ♦ n **2** adult person or animal. **adulthood** n

adulterate v spoil something by adding inferior material. **adulteration** n

adultery n, pl -teries sexual unfaithfulness of a husband or wife. **adulterer, adulteress** n **adulterous** adj

adv. adverb.

advance v **1** go or bring forward. **2** further (a cause). **3** propose (an idea). **4** lend (a sum of money). ♦ n **5** forward movement. **6** improvement. **7** loan. ♦ pl **8** approaches to a person with the hope of starting a romantic or sexual relationship. ♦ adj **9** done or happening before an event. **in advance** ahead. **advanced** adj **1** at a late stage in development. **2** not elementary. **advancement** n promotion.

advantage n **1** more favourable position or state. **2** benefit or profit. **3** Tennis point scored after deuce. **take advantage of 1** use (a person) unfairly. **2** use (an opportunity). **advantageous** adj **advantageously** adv

advent n **1** arrival. **2** (A-) season of four weeks before Christmas. **Adventist** n member of a Christian sect that believes in the imminent return of Christ (also **Seventh Day Adventist**).

adventitious adj added or appearing accidentally.

adventure n exciting and risky undertaking or exploit. **adventurer, adventuress** n **1** person who unscrupulously seeks money or power. **2** person who seeks adventures. **adventurous** adj

adverb n word that adds information about a verb, adjective, or other adverb. **adverbial** adj

adversary [**ad**-verse-er-ree] n, pl -saries opponent or enemy.

adverse adj **1** unfavourable. **2** antagonistic or hostile. **adversely** adv **adversity** n very difficult or hard circumstances.

advert n Informal advertisement.

advertise v **1** present or praise (goods or services) to the public in order to encourage sales. **2** make (a vacancy, event, etc.) known publicly. **advertisement** n public announcement to sell goods or publicize an event. **advertiser** n **advertising** adj, n

☑ **SPELLING TIP**
Some verbs can be spelt ending in either -ise or -ize, but **advertise** and **advise** always have an s.

advice n recommendation as to what to do. **advise** v **1** offer advice to. **2** notify (someone). **advisable** adj prudent, sensible. **advisability** n **advisory** adj giving advice. **advised** adj considered, thought-out, e.g. ill-advised. **advisedly** adv deliberately.

☑ **SPELLING TIP**
The Bank of English shows that people sometimes write **advise** with an s where they ought to write **advice** with a c. The verb is **advise** and the noun is **advice**.

adviser, advisor n person who offers advice, e.g. on careers to students or school pupils.
advocaat n liqueur with a raw egg base.
advocate v **1** propose or recommend. ♦ n **2** person who publicly supports a cause. **3** Scot & S Afr barrister. **advocacy** n
adze n tool with an arched blade at right angles to the handle.
aegis [**ee**-jiss] n sponsorship, protection.
aeolian harp [ee-**oh**-lee-an] n musical instrument that produces sounds when the wind passes over its strings.
aeon [**ee**-on] n immeasurably long period of time.

aerate v put gas into (a liquid), as when making a fizzy drink. **aeration** n
aerial adj **1** in, from, or operating in the air. **2** relating to aircraft. ♦ n **3** metal pole, wire, etc., for receiving or transmitting radio or TV signals. **aerial top dressing** spreading of fertilizer from an aeroplane onto remote areas.
aerobatics pl n stunt flying. **aerobatic** adj
aerobics n exercises designed to increase the amount of oxygen in the blood. **aerobic** adj
aerodrome n small airport.
aerodynamics n study of how air flows around moving solid objects. **aerodynamic** adj
aerofoil n part of an aircraft, such as the wing, designed to give lift.
aerogram n airmail letter on a single sheet of paper that seals to form an envelope.
aeronautics n study or practice of aircraft flight. **aeronautical** adj
aeroplane n powered flying vehicle with fixed wings.
aerosol n pressurized can from which a substance can be dispensed as a fine spray.
aerospace n earth's atmosphere and space beyond.
aesthetic [iss-**thet**-ik] adj relating to the appreciation of art and beauty. **aesthetics** n study of art, beauty, and good taste. **aesthetically** adv **aesthete** [**eess**-theet] n person who has or affects an extravagant love of art. **aestheticism** n
aether n same as ETHER.
aetiology [ee-tee-**ol**-a-jee] n same as ETIOLOGY.
afar adv **from afar** from or at a great distance.
affable adj friendly and easy to talk to.

affably adv **affability** n
affair n 1 event or happening. 2 sexual relationship outside marriage. 3 thing to be done or attended to. ♦ pl 4 personal or business interests. 5 matters of public interest.
affect[1] v 1 act on, influence. 2 move (someone) emotionally.
affect[2] v 1 put on a show of. 2 wear or use by preference. **affectation** n attitude or manner put on to impress. **affected** adj 1 displaying affectation. 2 pretended.
affection n fondness or love. **affectionate** adj loving. **affectionately** adv
affianced [af-**fie**-anst] adj Old-fashioned engaged to be married.
affidavit [af-fid-**dave**-it] n written statement made on oath.
affiliate v (of a group) link up with a larger group. **affiliation** n
affinity n, pl -**ties** 1 close connection or liking. 2 close resemblance. 3 chemical attraction.
affirm v 1 declare to be true. 2 uphold or confirm (an idea or belief). **affirmation** n **affirmative** n, adj (word or phrase) indicating agreement.
affix v 1 attach or fasten. ♦ n 2 word or syllable added to a word to change its meaning.
afflict v give pain or grief to. **affliction** n
affluent adj having plenty of money. **affluence** n wealth.
afford v 1 have enough money to buy. 2 be able to spare (the time etc.). 3 give or supply. **affordable** adj
afforest v plant trees on. **afforestation** n
affray n Brit, Aust & NZ law noisy fight, brawl.
affront v, n insult.
Afghan 1 adj 2 of Afghanistan or its language. **Afghan hound** large slim dog with long silky hair.
aficionado [af-fish-yo-**nah**-do] n, pl -**dos** enthusiastic fan of something or someone.
afield adv **far afield** far away.
aflame adj burning.
afloat adv, adj 1 floating. 2 at sea.
afoot adv, adj happening, in operation.
aforesaid, aforementioned adj referred to previously.
aforethought adj premeditated, e.g. with malice aforethought.
Afr. Africa(n).
afraid adj 1 frightened. 2 regretful.
afresh adv again, anew.
African adj 1 of Africa. ♦ n 2 person from Africa. **African violet** house plant with pink or purple flowers and hairy leaves.
Afrikaans n language used in S Africa, descended from Dutch.
Afrikaner n White S African whose mother tongue is Afrikaans.
Afro- combining form African, e.g. Afro-Caribbean.
aft adv at or towards the rear of a ship or aircraft.
after prep 1 following in time or place. 2 in pursuit of. 3 in imitation of. ♦ conj 4 at a later time than. ♦ adv 5 at a later time. **afters** pl n Brit informal dessert.
afterbirth n material expelled from the womb after childbirth.
aftercare n 1 support given to a person discharged from a hospital or prison. 2 regular care required to keep something in good condition.
aftereffect n result occurring some time after its cause.
afterglow n 1 glow left after a source of light has gone. 2 pleasant feeling left after an enjoyable experience.
afterlife n life after death.
aftermath n results of an event

considered together.

afternoon *n* time between noon and evening.

aftershave *n* lotion applied to the face after shaving.

afterthought *n* **1** idea occurring later. **2** something added later.

afterwards, afterward *adv* later.

Ag *Chem* silver.

again *adv* **1** once more. **2** in addition.

against *prep* **1** in opposition or contrast to. **2** in contact with. **3** as a protection from.

agape *adj* **1** (of the mouth) wide open. **2** (of a person) very surprised.

agaric *n* fungus with gills on the underside of the cap, such as a mushroom.

agate [**ag**-git] *n* semiprecious form of quartz with striped colouring.

age *n* **1** length of time a person or thing has existed. **2** time of life. **3** latter part of human life. **4** period of history. **5** long time. ♦ *v* **ageing** *or* **aging, aged** make or grow old. **aged** *adj* **1** [**ay**-jid] old. **2** [rhymes with **raged**] being at the age of. **ageing, aging** *n, adj* **ageless** *adj* **1** apparently never growing old. **2** seeming to have existed for ever. **age-old** *adj* very old.

agency *n, pl* **-cies 1** organization providing a service. **2** business or function of an agent. **3** *Old-fashioned* power or action by which something happens.

agenda *n* list of things to be dealt with, esp. at a meeting.

agent *n* **1** person acting on behalf of another. **2** person or thing producing an effect.

agent provocateur [**azh**-on prov-vok-at-**tur**] *n, pl* **agents provocateurs** [**azh**-on prov-vok-at-**tur**] person employed by the authorities to tempt people to commit illegal acts

and so be discredited or punished.

agglomeration *n* confused mass or cluster.

aggrandize *v* make greater in size, power, or rank. **aggrandizement** *n*

aggravate *v* **1** make worse. **2** *Chiefly informal* annoy. **aggravating** *adj* **aggravation** *n*

✓ **SPELLING TIP**

The biggest problem with spelling **aggravate** is not how many *g*s there are at the beginning, but that there is an *a* (not an *e*) in the middle.

aggregate *n* **1** total. **2** rock consisting of a mixture of minerals. **3** sand or gravel used to make concrete. ♦ *adj* **4** gathered into a mass. **5** total or final. ♦ *v* **6** combine into a whole. **aggregation** *n*

aggression *n* **1** hostile behaviour. **2** unprovoked attack. **aggressive** *adj* **1** showing aggression. **2** forceful. **aggressively** *adv* **aggressiveness** *n* **aggressor** *n*

✓ **SPELLING TIP**

The Bank of English shows that **aggressive** is quite a common word and that *agressive* is a common way of misspelling it.

aggrieved *adj* upset and angry.

aggro *n Brit, Aust & NZ slang* aggressive behaviour.

aghast *adj* overcome with amazement or horror.

agile *adj* **1** nimble, quick-moving. **2** mentally quick. **agility** *n*

agitate *v* **1** disturb or excite. **2** stir or shake (a liquid). **3** stir up public opinion for or against something. **agitation** *n* **agitator** *n*

aglow *adj* glowing.

AGM annual general meeting.

agnostic n **1** person who believes that it is impossible to know whether God exists. ♦ adj **2** of agnostics. **agnosticism** n

ago adv in the past.

agog adj eager or curious.

agony n, pl **-nies** extreme physical or mental pain. **agonize** v **1** worry greatly. **2** (cause to) suffer agony. **agonizing** adj **agony aunt** journalist who gives advice in an agony column. **agony column** newspaper or magazine feature offering advice on personal problems.

agoraphobia n fear of open spaces. **agoraphobic** n, adj

agrarian adj of land or agriculture.

agree v **agreeing, agreed 1** be of the same opinion. **2** consent. **3** reach a joint decision. **4** be consistent. **5** (foll. by with) be suitable to (one's health or digestion). **agreeable** adj **1** pleasant and enjoyable. **2** prepared to consent. **agreeably** adv **agreement** n **1** agreeing. **2** contract.

agriculture n raising of crops and livestock. **agricultural** adj **agriculturalist** n

agronomy [ag-**ron**-om-mee] n science of soil management and crop production. **agronomist** n

aground adv onto the bottom of shallow water.

ague [**aig**-yew] n Old-fashioned periodic fever with shivering.

ahead adv **1** in front. **2** forwards.

ahoy interj shout used at sea to attract attention.

AI 1 artificial insemination. **2** artificial intelligence.

aid v, n (give) assistance or support.

aide n assistant.

aide-de-camp [**aid**-de-**kom**] n, pl **aides-de-camp** [**aid**-de-**kom**] military officer serving as personal assistant to

a senior.

AIDS acquired immunodeficiency syndrome, a viral disease that destroys the body's ability to fight infection.

AIH artificial insemination by husband.

ail v **1** trouble, afflict. **2** be ill. **ailing** adj sickly **ailment** n illness.

aileron n movable flap on an aircraft wing which controls rolling.

aim v **1** point (a weapon or missile) or direct (a blow or remark) at a target. **2** propose or intend. ♦ n **3** aiming. **4** intention, purpose. **aimless** adj having no purpose. **aimlessly** adv

ain't Not standard **1** am not. **2** is not. **3** are not. **4** has not. **5** have not.

air n **1** mixture of gases forming the earth's atmosphere. **2** space above the ground, sky. **3** breeze. **4** quality or manner. **5** tune. ♦ pl **6** affected manners. ♦ v **7** make known publicly. **8** expose to air to dry or ventilate. **on the air** in the act of broadcasting on radio or television. **airless** adj stuffy. **air bag** vehicle safety device which inflates automatically in a crash to protect the driver or passenger when they are thrown forward. **airborne** adj **1** carried by air. **2** (of aircraft) flying. **airbrush** n atomizer spraying paint by compressed air. **airfield** n place where aircraft can land and take off. **air force** branch of the armed forces responsible for air warfare. **air gun** gun fired by compressed air. **air hostess** female flight attendant. **airlift** n **1** transport of troops or cargo by aircraft when other routes are blocked. ♦ v **2** transport by airlift. **airlock** n **1** air bubble blocking the flow of liquid in a pipe. **2** airtight chamber. **airmail** n **1** system of sending mail by aircraft. **2** mail sent in this way. **airman** n member of the air force. **air miles** miles of free air travel that can be earned by buying airline

tickets and various other products.
airplay n broadcast performances of a record on radio. **airport** n airfield for civilian aircraft, with facilities for aircraft maintenance and passengers. **air raid** attack by aircraft. **airship** n lighter-than-air self-propelled aircraft. **airspace** n atmosphere above a country, regarded as its territory. **airstrip** n cleared area where aircraft can take off and land. **airtight** adj sealed so that air cannot enter.

air conditioning n system that controls the temperature and humidity of the air in a building. **air conditioner**

aircraft n any machine that flies, such as an aeroplane. **aircraft carrier** warship for the launching and landing of aircraft.

airing n **1** exposure to air for drying or ventilation. **2** exposure to public debate.

airline n company providing scheduled flights for passengers and cargo. **airliner** n large passenger aircraft.

airworthy adj (of aircraft) fit to fly. **airworthiness** n

airy adj airier, airiest **1** well-ventilated. **2** light-hearted and casual. **airily** adv

aisle [rhymes with **mile**] n passageway separating seating areas in a church, theatre, etc., or row of shelves in a supermarket.

ajar adj, adv (of a door) partly open.

akimbo adv with arms akimbo with hands on hips and elbows outwards.

akin adj akin to similar, related.

alabaster n soft white translucent stone.

à la carte adj, adv (of a menu) having dishes individually priced.

alacrity n speed, eagerness.

à la mode adj fashionable.

alarm n **1** sudden fear caused by

awareness of danger. **2** warning sound. **3** device that gives this. **4** alarm clock. ♦ v **5** fill with fear. **alarming** adj **alarmist** n person who alarms others needlessly. **alarm clock** clock which sounds at a set time to wake someone up.

alas adv unfortunately, regrettably.

albatross n large sea bird with very long wings.

albeit conj even though.

albino n, pl -nos person or animal with white skin and hair and pink eyes.

album n **1** book with blank pages for keeping photographs or stamps in. **2** long-playing record.

albumen n egg white.

albumin, albumen n protein found in blood plasma, egg white, milk, and muscle.

alchemy n medieval form of chemistry concerned with trying to turn base metals into gold and to find the elixir of life. **alchemist** n

alcohol n **1** colourless flammable liquid present in intoxicating drinks. **2** intoxicating drinks generally. **alcoholic** adj **1** of alcohol. ♦ n **2** person addicted to alcohol. **alcoholism** n addiction to alcohol.

alcopop n Brit, Aust & S Afr informal alcoholic drink that tastes like a soft drink.

alcove n recess in the wall of a room.

aldehyde n one of a group of chemical compounds derived from alcohol by oxidation.

alder n tree related to the birch.

alderman n formerly, senior member of a local council.

ale n kind of beer.

alert adj **1** watchful, attentive. ♦ n **2** warning of danger. ♦ v **3** warn of danger. **4** make (someone) aware of (a fact). **on the alert** watchful.

alertness *n*

alfalfa *n* kind of plant used to feed livestock.

alfresco *adv, adj* in the open air.

algae [**al**-jee] *pl n* plants which live in or near water and have no true stems, leaves, or roots.

algebra *n* branch of mathematics using symbols to represent numbers. **algebraic** *adj*

ALGOL *n Computers* programming language for mathematical and scientific purposes.

algorithm *n* logical arithmetical or computational procedure for solving a problem.

alias *adv* **1** also known as. ♦ *n* **2** false name.

alibi *n* **1** plea of being somewhere else when a crime was committed. **2** *Informal* excuse.

alien *adj* **1** foreign. **2** repugnant (to). **3** from another world. ♦ *n* **4** foreigner. **5** being from another world. **alienate** *v* cause to become hostile. **alienation** *n*

alight[1] *v* **1** step out of (a vehicle). **2** land.

alight[2] *adj* **1** on fire. **2** lit up.

align [a-**line**] *v* **1** bring (a person or group) into agreement with the policy of another. **2** place in a line. **alignment** *n*

alike *adj* **1** like, similar. ♦ *adv* **2** in the same way.

alimentary *adj* of nutrition. **alimentary canal** food passage in the body.

alimony *n* allowance paid under a court order to a separated or divorced spouse.

A-line *adj* (of a skirt) slightly flared.

aliquot *Maths* ♦ *adj* **1** of or denoting an exact divisor of a number. ♦ *n* **2** exact divisor.

alive *adj* **1** living, in existence. **2** lively.

alive to aware of. **alive with** swarming with.

alkali [**alk**-a-lie] *n* substance which combines with acid and neutralizes it to form a salt. **alkaline** *adj* **alkalinity** *n* **alkaloid** *n* any of a group of organic compounds containing nitrogen.

all *adj* **1** whole quantity or number (of). ♦ *adv* **2** wholly, entirely. **3** (in the score of games) each. **give one's all** make the greatest possible effort. **all in** *adj* **1** exhausted. **2** (of wrestling) with no style forbidden. ♦ *adv* **3** with all expenses included. **all right** *adj* **1** adequate, satisfactory. **2** unharmed. ♦ *interj* **3** expression of approval or agreement. **all-rounder** *n* person with ability in many fields.

Allah *n* name of God in Islam.

allay *v* reduce (fear or anger).

allege *v* state without proof. **alleged** *adj* **allegedly** *adv* **allegation** *n* unproved accusation.

allegiance *n* loyalty to a person, country, or cause.

allegory *n, pl* **-ries** story with an underlying meaning as well as the literal one. **allegorical** *adj*

allegretto *n, pl* **-tos,** *adv Music* (piece to be played) fairly quickly or briskly.

allegro *n, pl* **-gros,** *adv Music* (piece to be played) in a brisk lively manner.

alleluia *interj* same as HALLELUJAH.

allergy *n, pl* **-gies** extreme sensitivity to a substance, which causes the body to react to it. **allergic** *adj* having or caused by an allergy. **allergen** *n* substance capable of causing an allergic reaction.

alleviate *v* lessen (pain or suffering). **alleviation** *n*

alley *n* **1** narrow street or path. **2** long narrow enclosure in which tenpin bowling or skittles is played.

alliance *n* **1** state of being allied. **2**

formal relationship between countries or groups for a shared purpose.

alligator *n* reptile of the crocodile family, found in the southern US and China.

alliteration *n* use of the same sound at the start of words occurring together, e.g. *moody music*. **alliterative** *adj*

allocate *v* assign to someone or for a particular purpose. **allocation** *n*

allot *v* **-lotting, -lotted** assign as a share or for a particular purpose. **allotment** *n* **1** distribution. **2** portion allotted. **3** small piece of public land rented to grow vegetables on.

allotrope *n* any of two or more physical forms in which an element can exist.

allow *v* **1** permit. **2** set aside. **3** acknowledge (a point or claim). **allow for** *v* take into account. **allowable** *adj* **allowance** *n* **1** amount of money given at regular intervals. **2** amount permitted. **make allowances for 1** treat or judge (someone) less severely because he or she has special problems. **2** take into account.

alloy *n* **1** mixture of two or more metals. ♦ *v* **2** mix (metals).

allspice *n* spice made from the berries of a tropical American tree.

allude *v* (foll. by *to*) refer indirectly to. **allusion** *n* indirect reference. **allusive** *adj*

allure *n* **1** attractiveness. ♦ *v* **2** entice or attract. **alluring** *adj*

alluvium *n* fertile soil deposited by flowing water. **alluvial** *adj*

ally *n, pl* **-lies 1** country, person, or group with an agreement to support another. ♦ *v* **-lying, -lied 2 ally oneself with** join as an ally. **allied** *adj*

alma mater *n* school, university, or college that one attended.

almanac *n* yearly calendar with detailed information on anniversaries, phases of the moon, etc.

almighty *adj* **1** having absolute power. **2** *Informal* very great. ♦ *n* **3 the Almighty** God.

almond *n* edible oval-shaped nut which grows on a small tree.

almoner *n Brit* formerly, a hospital social worker.

almost *adv* very nearly.

alms [**ahmz**] *pl n Old-fashioned* gifts to the poor.

aloe *n* **1** plant with fleshy spiny leaves. ♦ *pl* **2** bitter drug made from aloe leaves.

aloft *adv* **1** in the air. **2** in a ship's rigging.

alone *adj, adv* without anyone or anything else.

along *prep* **1** over part or all the length of. ♦ *adv* **2** forward. **3** in company with others. **alongside** *prep, adv* beside (something).

aloof *adj* distant or haughty in manner. **aloofness** *n*

alopecia [al-loh-**pee**-sha] *n* loss of hair.

aloud *adv* in an audible voice.

alpaca *n* **1** Peruvian llama. **2** wool or cloth made from its hair.

alpenstock *n* iron-tipped stick used by climbers.

alphabet *n* set of letters used in writing a language. **alphabetical** *adj* in the conventional order of the letters of an alphabet. **alphabetically** *adv* **alphabetize** *v* put in alphabetical order.

alpine *adj* **1** of high mountains. **2** (A-) of the Alps. ♦ *n* **3** mountain plant.

already *adv* **1** before the present time. **2** sooner than expected.

alright *adj, interj* all right.

Alsatian *n* large wolflike dog.

also *adv* in addition, too. **also-ran** *n* loser in a race, competition, or election.

alt. *combining form Informal* alternative *alt.rock.*

altar *n* **1** table used for Communion in Christian churches. **2** raised structure on which sacrifices are offered and religious rites are performed. **altarpiece** *n* work of art above and behind the altar in some Christian churches.

alter *v* make or become different. **alteration** *n*

altercation *n* heated argument.

alter ego *n* **1** second self. **2** very close friend.

alternate *v* **1** (cause to) occur by turns. ♦ *adj* **2** occurring by turns. **3** every second (one) of a series. **alternately** *adv* **alternation** *n* **alternator** *n* electric generator for producing alternating current. **alternating current** electric current that reverses direction at frequent regular intervals.

alternative *n* **1** one of two choices. ♦ *adj* **2** able to be done or used instead of something else. **3** (of medicine, lifestyle, etc.) not conventional. **alternatively** *adv*

although *conj* despite the fact that.

altimeter [al-**tim**-it-er] *n* instrument that measures altitude.

altitude *n* height above sea level.

alto *n, pl* **-tos** *Music* **1** short for CONTRALTO. **2** (singer with) the highest adult male voice. **3** instrument with the second-highest pitch in its group.

altogether *adv* **1** entirely. **2** on the whole. **3** in total.

altruism *n* unselfish concern for the welfare of others. **altruistic** *adj* **altruistically** *adv*

aluminium *n Chem* light silvery-white metal that does not rust.

alumnus [al-**lumm**-nuss] *n, pl* **-ni** [-nie] graduate of a college. **alumna** [al-**lumm**-na] *n fem, pl* **-nae** [-nee]

always *adv* **1** at all times. **2** for ever.

alyssum *n* garden plant with small yellow or white flowers.

am *v* see BE.

AM 1 amplitude modulation. **2** (in Britain) Member of the National Assembly for Wales.

a.m. ante meridiem: before noon.

amalgam *n* **1** blend or combination. **2** alloy of mercury and another metal.

amalgamate *v* combine or unite. **amalgamation** *n*

amandla [ah-**mand**-lah] *n S Afr* political slogan calling for power to the Black population.

amanuensis [am-man-yew-**en**-siss] *n, pl* **-ses** [-seez] person who writes from dictation.

amaranth *n* **1** imaginary flower that never fades. **2** lily-like plant with red, green, or purple flowers.

amaryllis *n* lily-like plant with large red, pink, or white flowers.

amass *v* collect or accumulate.

amateur *n* **1** person who engages in a sport or activity as a pastime rather than as a profession. **2** person unskilled in something. ♦ *adj* **3** not professional. **amateurish** *adj* lacking skill. **amateurishly** *adv*

amatory *adj* relating to romantic or sexual love.

amaze *v* surprise greatly, astound. **amazing** *adj* **amazingly** *adv* **amazement** *n*

Amazon *n* **1** strong and powerful woman. **2** legendary female warrior. **Amazonian** *adj*

ambassador *n* senior diplomat who represents his or her country in another country. **ambassadorial** *adj*

amber *n* **1** clear yellowish fossil resin. ♦ *adj* **2** brownish-yellow.

ambergris [**am**-ber-greece] *n* waxy substance secreted by the sperm whale, used in making perfumes.

ambidextrous adj able to use both hands with equal ease.

ambience n atmosphere of a place.

ambient adj surrounding.

ambiguous adj having more than one possible meaning. **ambiguously** adv **ambiguity** n

ambit n limits or boundary.

ambition n **1** desire for success. **2** something so desired, goal. **ambitious** adj **ambitiously** adv

ambivalence n state of waiting two conflicting emotions at the same time. **ambivalent** adj **ambivalently** adv

amble v **1** walk at a leisurely pace. ♦ n **2** leisurely walk or pace.

ambrosia n Myth food of the gods. **ambrosial** adj

ambulance n motor vehicle designed to carry sick or injured people.

ambush n **1** act of waiting in a concealed position to make a surprise attack. **2** attack from a concealed position. ♦ v **3** attack from a concealed position.

ameliorate [am-**meal**-yor-rate] v make (something) better. **amelioration** n

amen interj so be it: used at the end of a prayer.

amenable adj likely or willing to cooperate.

amend v make small changes to correct or improve (something). **amendment** n

amends pl n **make amends for** compensate for.

amenity n, pl -ties useful or enjoyable feature.

American adj **1** of the United States of America or the American continent. ♦ n **2** person from America or the American continent. **Americanism** n expression or custom characteristic of Americans.

amethyst [**am**-myth-ist] n bluish-violet variety of quartz used as a gemstone.

amiable adj friendly, pleasant-natured. **amiably** adv **amiability** n

amicable adj friendly. **amicably** adv

amid, amidst prep in the middle of, among. **amidships** adv at or towards the middle of a ship.

amino acid [am-**mean**-oh] n organic compound found in protein.

amiss adv **1** wrongly, badly. ♦ adj **2** wrong, faulty. **take something amiss** be offended by something.

amity n friendship.

ammeter n instrument for measuring electric current.

ammonia n **1** strong-smelling alkaline gas containing hydrogen and nitrogen. **2** solution of this in water.

ammonite n fossilized spiral shell of an extinct sea creature.

ammunition n **1** bullets, bombs, and shells that can be fired from or as a weapon. **2** facts that can be used in an argument.

amnesia n loss of memory. **amnesiac** adj, n

amnesty n, pl -ties general pardon for offences against a government.

amniocentesis n, pl -ses removal of some amniotic fluid to test for possible abnormalities in a fetus.

amniotic fluid n fluid surrounding a fetus in the womb.

amoeba [am-**mee**-ba] n, pl -bae, -bas microscopic single-celled animal able to change its shape.

amok [a-**muck**, a-**mock**] adv **run amok** run about in a violent frenzy.

among, amongst prep **1** in the midst of. **2** in the group or number of. **3** to each of, e.g. divide it among yourselves.

amoral [aim-**mor**-ral] adj without moral standards. **amorality** n

amorous adj feeling, showing, or

relating to sexual love. **amorously** adv

amorphous adj without distinct shape.

amortize v pay off (a debt) gradually by periodic transfers to a sinking fund.

amount n 1 extent or quantity. ♦ v 2 (foll. by to) be equal or add up to.

amour n (secret) love affair.

amp n 1 ampere. 2 Informal amplifier.

ampere [**am**-pair] n basic unit of electric current.

ampersand n the character (&), meaning and.

amphetamine [am-**fet**-am-mean] n drug used as a stimulant.

amphibian n 1 animal that lives on land but breeds in water. 2 vehicle that can travel on both land and water. **amphibious** adj living or operating both on land and in water.

amphitheatre n open oval or circular building with tiers of seats rising round an arena.

amphora [**am**-for-ra] n, pl -phorae two-handled ancient Greek or Roman jar.

ample adj 1 more than sufficient. 2 large. **amply** adv

amplifier n device used to amplify a current or sound signal.

amplify v -fying, -fied 1 increase the strength of (a current or sound signal). 2 explain in more detail. 3 increase the size or effect of. **amplification** n

amplitude n greatness of extent.

ampoule n small sealed glass vessel containing liquid for injection.

amputate v cut off (a limb or part of a limb) for medical reasons. **amputation** n

amuck adv same as AMOK.

amulet n something carried or worn as a protection against evil.

amuse v 1 cause to laugh or smile. 2 entertain or divert. **amusing** adj **amusement** n 1 state of being

amused. 2 something that amuses.

an adj form of a used before vowels, and sometimes before h.

anabolic steroid n synthetic steroid hormone used to stimulate muscle and bone growth.

anachronism [an-**nak**-kron-iz-zum] n person or thing placed in the wrong historical period or seeming to belong to another time. **anachronistic** adj

anaconda n large S American snake which kills by constriction.

anaemia [an-**neem**-ee-a] n deficiency in the number of red blood cells. **anaemic** adj 1 having anaemia. 2 pale and sickly. 3 lacking vitality.

anaesthetic [an-niss-**thet**-ik] n, adj (substance) causing loss of bodily feeling. **anaesthesia** [an-niss-**theez**-ee-a] n loss of bodily feeling. **anaesthetist** [an-**neess**-thet-ist] n doctor trained to administer anaesthetics. **anaesthetize** v

anagram n word or phrase made by rearranging the letters of another word or phrase.

anal [**ain**-al] adj of the anus.

analgesic [an-nal-**jeez**-ik] n, adj (drug) relieving pain. **analgesia** n absence of pain.

analogous adj similar in some respects.

analogue n 1 something that is similar in some respects to something else. ♦ adj 2 displaying information by means of a dial.

analogy n, pl -gies 1 similarity in some respects. 2 comparison made to show such a similarity. **analogical** adj

analysis n, pl -ses 1 separation of a whole into its parts for study and interpretation. 2 psychoanalysis. **analyse** v 1 make an analysis of (something). 2 psychoanalyse. **analyst** n person skilled in analysis. **analytical, analytic** adj

analytically *adv*

anarchism *n* doctrine advocating the abolition of government.

anarchist *n* **1** person who advocates the abolition of government. **2** person who causes disorder. **anarchistic** *adj*

anarchy [**an**-ark-ee] *n* **1** lawlessness and disorder. **2** lack of government in a state. **anarchic** *adj*

anathema [an-**nath**-im-a] *n* detested person or thing.

anatomy *n*, *pl* -**mies 1** science of the structure of the body. **2** physical structure. **3** person's body. **4** detailed analysis. **anatomical** *adj* **anatomically** *adv* **anatomist** *n* expert in anatomy.

ANC African National Congress.

ancestor *n* **1** person from whom one is descended. **2** forerunner. **ancestral** *adj* **ancestry** *n* lineage or descent.

anchor *n* **1** heavy hooked device attached to a boat by a cable and dropped overboard to fasten the ship to the sea bottom. **2** *v* **3** fasten with or as if with an anchor. **anchorage** *n* place where boats can be anchored. **anchorman, anchorwoman** *n* **1** broadcaster in a central studio who links up and presents items from outside camera units and other studios. **2** last person to compete in a relay team.

anchorite *n* religious recluse.

anchovy [**an**-chov-ee] *n*, *pl* -**vies** small strong-tasting fish.

ancient *adj* **1** dating from very long ago. **2** very old. **ancients** *pl n* people who lived very long ago.

ancillary *adj* **1** supporting the main work of an organization. **2** used as an extra or supplement.

and *conj* **1** in addition to. **2** as a consequence. **3** then, afterwards.

andante [an-**dan**-tay] *n*, *adv Music* (piece to be played) moderately slowly.

andiron *n* iron stand for supporting logs in a fireplace.

androgynous *adj* having both male and female characteristics.

android *n* robot resembling a human.

anecdote *n* short amusing account of an incident. **anecdotal** *adj*

anemometer *n* instrument for recording wind speed.

anemone [an-**nem**-on-ee] *n* plant with white, purple, or red flowers.

aneroid barometer *n* device for measuring air pressure, consisting of a partially evacuated chamber in which variations in pressure cause a pointer on the lid to move.

aneurysm, aneurism [**an**-new-riz-zum] *n* permanent swelling of a blood vessel.

anew *adv* **1** once more. **2** in a different way.

angel *n* **1** spiritual being believed to be an attendant or messenger of God. **2** person who is kind, pure, or beautiful. **angelic** *adj* **angelically** *adv*

angelica *n* **1** aromatic plant. **2** its candied stalks, used in cookery.

Angelus [**an**-jell-uss] *n* **1** (in the Roman Catholic Church) prayers recited in the morning, at midday, and in the evening. **2** bell signalling the times of these prayers.

anger *n* **1** fierce displeasure or extreme annoyance. ♦ *v* **2** make (someone) angry.

angina [an-**jine**-a] *n* heart disorder causing sudden severe chest pains (also **angina pectoris**).

angle[1] *n* **1** space between or shape formed by two lines or surfaces that meet. **2** divergence between these, measured in degrees. **3** corner. **4** point of view. ♦ *v* **5** bend or place (something) at an angle.

angle[2] *v* **1** fish with a hook and line. **2**

(foll. by *for*) try to get by hinting. **angling** *n*

angler *n* person who fishes with a hook and line.

Anglican *n, adj* (member) of the Church of England. **Anglicanism** *n*

anglicize *v* make or become English in outlook, form, etc.

Anglo- *combining form* **1** English, e.g. *Anglo-Scottish.* **2** British, e.g. *Anglo-American.*

Anglo-Saxon *n* **1** member of any of the W Germanic tribes that settled in England from the fifth century AD. **2** language of the Anglo-Saxons. ♦ *adj* **3** of the Anglo-Saxons or their language.

angophora *n* Australian tree related to the eucalyptus.

angora *n* **1** variety of goat, cat, or rabbit with long silky hair. **2** hair of the angora goat or rabbit. **3** cloth made from this hair.

Angostura Bitters *pl n* ® bitter tonic, used as a flavouring in alcoholic drinks.

angry *adj* **-grier, -griest 1** full of anger. **2** inflamed, e.g. *an angry wound.* **angrily** *adv*

angst *n* feeling of anxiety.

angstrom *n* unit of length used to measure wavelengths.

anguish *n* great mental pain. **anguished** *adj*

angular *adj* **1** (of a person) lean and bony. **2** having angles. **3** measured by an angle. **angularity** *n*

anhydrous *adj Chem* containing no water.

aniline *n* colourless oily liquid obtained from coal tar and used for making dyes, plastics, and explosives.

animal *n* **1** living creature with specialized sense organs and capable of voluntary motion, esp. one other than a human being. **2** quadruped. ♦ *adj* **3** of animals. **4** sensual, physical.

animate *v* **1** give life to. **2** make lively. **3** make a cartoon film of. ♦ *adj* **4** having life. **animated** *adj* **animation** *n* **1** technique of making cartoon films. **2** liveliness and enthusiasm. **animator** *n*

animism *n* belief that natural objects possess souls. **animist** *n, adj* **animistic** *adj*

animosity *n, pl* **-ties** hostility, hatred.

animus *n* hatred, animosity.

anion [**an**-eye-on] *n* ion with negative charge.

anise [**an**-niss] *n* plant with liquorice-flavoured seeds.

aniseed *n* liquorice-flavoured seeds of the anise plant.

ankle *n* joint between the foot and leg. **anklet** *n* ornamental chain worn round the ankle.

annals *pl n* yearly records of events.

anneal *v* toughen (metal or glass) by heating and slow cooling.

annelid *n* worm with a segmented body, such as an earthworm.

annex *v* **1** seize (territory). **2** take (something) without permission. **3** join or add (something) to something larger. **annexation** *n*

annexe *n* **1** extension to a building. **2** nearby building used as an extension.

annihilate *v* destroy utterly. **annihilation** *n*

anniversary *n, pl* **-ries 1** date on which something occurred in a previous year. **2** celebration of this.

anno Domini [an-no **dom**-in-eye] *adv Latin* (indicating years numbered from the supposed year of the birth of Christ) in the year of our Lord.

annotate *v* add notes to (a written work). **annotation** *n*

announce *v* **1** make known publicly. **2** proclaim. **announcement** *n* **announcer** *n* person who introduces radio or television programmes.

annoy v irritate or displease.
annoyance n

annual adj **1** happening once a year. **2**
lasting for a year. ♦ n **3** plant that
completes its life cycle in a year. **4**
book published once every year.
annually adv

annuity n, pl **-ties** fixed sum paid
every year.

annul v **-nulling, -nulled** declare
(something, esp. a marriage) invalid.
annulment n

annular [**an**-new-lar] adj ring-shaped.

Annunciation n Christianity angel
Gabriel's announcement to the Virgin
Mary of her conception of Christ.

anode n Electricity positive electrode in
a battery, valve, etc. **anodize** v coat
(metal) with a protective oxide film by
electrolysis.

anodyne n **1** something that relieves
pain or distress. ♦ adj **2** relieving pain
or distress.

anoint v smear with oil as a sign of
consecration.

anomaly [an-**nom**-a-lee] n, pl **-lies**
something that deviates from the
normal, irregularity. **anomalous** adj

anon adv Obs in a short time, soon.

anon. anonymous.

anonymous adj **1** by someone whose
name is unknown or withheld. **2**
having no known name.
anonymously adv **anonymity** n

anorak n light waterproof hooded
jacket.

anorexia n psychological disorder
characterized by fear of becoming fat
and refusal to eat (also **anorexia
nervosa**). **anorexic** adj, n

another adj, pron **1** one more. **2**
different (one).

answer n **1** reply to a question,
request, letter, etc. **2** solution to a
problem. **3** reaction or response. ♦ v **4**
give an answer (to). **5** be responsible
to (a person). **6** respond or react.
answerable adj (foll. by for or to)
responsible for or accountable to.
answering machine device for
answering a telephone automatically
and recording messages.

ant n small insect living in highly
organized colonies. **anteater** n **1**
mammal which feeds on ants by
means of a long snout. **2** same as
ECHIDNA. **3** same as NUMBAT. **ant hill**
mound built by ants around their nest.

antacid n substance that counteracts
acidity, esp. in the stomach.

antagonist n opponent or adversary.
antagonism n open opposition or
hostility. **antagonistic** adj
antagonize v arouse hostility in,
annoy.

Antarctic n **1** the Antarctic area
around the South Pole. ♦ adj **2** of this
region.

☑ SPELLING TIP

Almost one in every hundred
references to the **Antarctic** in the
Bank of English is written without its
first c as Antartic. Note there is a c
after the r.

---

ante n **1** player's stake in poker. ♦ v
-teing, -ted or **-teed 2** place (one's
stake) in poker.

ante- prefix before in time or position,
e.g. antedate; antechamber.

antecedent n **1** event or circumstance
happening or existing before another.
♦ adj **2** preceding, prior.

antedate v precede in time.

antediluvian adj **1** of the time before
the biblical Flood. **2** old-fashioned.

antelope n deerlike mammal with long
legs and horns.

antenatal adj during pregnancy,

before birth.

antenna n **1** pl **-nae** insect's feeler. **2** pl **-nas**) aerial.

anterior adj **1** to the front. **2** earlier.

anteroom n small room leading into a larger one, often used as a waiting room.

anthem n **1** song of loyalty, esp. to a country. **2** piece of choral music, usu. set to words from the Bible.

anther n part of a flower's stamen containing pollen.

anthology n, pl **-gies** collection of poems or other literary pieces by various authors. **anthologist** n

anthracite n hard coal burning slowly with little smoke or flame but intense heat.

anthrax n dangerous disease of cattle and sheep, communicable to humans.

anthropoid adj **1** like a human. ♦ n **2** ape, such as a chimpanzee, that resembles a human.

anthropology n study of human origins, institutions, and beliefs. **anthropological** adj **anthropologist** n

anthropomorphic adj attributing human form or personality to a god, animal, or object. **anthropomorphism** n

anti- prefix **1** against, opposed to, e.g. anti-war. **2** opposite to, e.g. anticlimax. **3** counteracting, e.g. antifreeze.

anti-aircraft adj for defence against aircraft attack.

antibiotic n **1** chemical substance capable of destroying bacteria. ♦ adj **2** of antibiotics.

antibody n, pl **-bodies** protein produced in the blood, which destroys bacteria.

anticipate v **1** foresee and act in advance of. **2** look forward to. **anticipation** n **anticipatory** adj

anticlimax n disappointing conclusion to a series of events.

anticlockwise adv, adj in the opposite direction to the rotation of the hands of a clock.

antics pl n absurd acts or postures.

anticyclone n area of moving air of high pressure in which the winds rotate outwards.

antidote n substance that counteracts a poison.

antifreeze n liquid added to water to lower its freezing point, used esp. in car radiators.

antigen [**an**-tee-jen] n substance, usu. a toxin, causing the blood to produce antibodies.

antihero n, pl **-roes** central character in a book, film, etc., who lacks the traditional heroic virtues.

antihistamine n drug used to treat allergies.

antimacassar n cloth put over a chair-back to prevent soiling.

antimony n Chem brittle silvery-white metallic element.

antipathy [an-**tip**-a-thee] n dislike, hostility. **antipathetic** adj

antiperspirant n substance used to reduce or prevent sweating.

antiphon n hymn sung in alternate parts by two groups of singers. **antiphonal** adj

antipodes [an-**tip**-pod-deez] pl n any two places diametrically opposite one another on the earth's surface. **the Antipodes** Australia and New Zealand. **antipodean** adj

antipyretic adj **1** reducing fever. ♦ n **2** drug that reduces fever.

antiquary n, pl **-quaries** student or collector of antiques or ancient works of art. **antiquarian** adj **1** of or relating to antiquities or rare books. ♦ n **2** antiquary.

antiquated adj out-of-date.

antique n 1 object of an earlier period, valued for its beauty, workmanship, or age. ♦ adj 2 made in an earlier period. 3 old-fashioned.

antiquity n 1 great age. 2 ancient times. **antiquities** pl n objects dating from ancient times.

antiracism n policy of challenging racism and promoting racial tolerance.

antirrhinum n two-lipped flower of various colours.

anti-Semitism n discrimination against Jews. **anti-Semitic** adj

antiseptic adj 1 preventing infection by killing germs. ♦ n 2 antiseptic substance.

antisocial adj 1 avoiding the company of other people. 2 (of behaviour) harmful to society.

antistatic adj reducing the effects of static electricity.

antithesis [an-**tith**-iss-iss] n, pl -ses [-seez] 1 exact opposite. 2 placing together of contrasting ideas or words to produce an effect of balance. **antithetical** adj

antitoxin n (serum containing) an antibody that acts against a toxin.

antitrust adj Aust & S Afr (of laws) opposing business monopolies.

antler n branched horn of male deer.

antonym n word that means the opposite of another.

anus [**ain**-uss] n opening at the end of the alimentary canal, through which faeces are discharged.

anvil n heavy iron block on which metals are hammered into particular shapes.

anxiety n, pl -ties state of being anxious.

anxious adj 1 worried and tense. 2 intensely desiring. **anxiously** adv

any adj, pron 1 one or some, no matter which. ♦ adv 2 at all, e.g. it isn't any worse. **anybody** pron anyone.

anyhow adv anyway. **anyone** pron 1 any person. 2 person of any importance. **anything** pron **anyway** adv 1 at any rate, nevertheless. 2 in any manner. **anywhere** adv in, at, or to any place.

Anzac n (in World War 1) a soldier serving with the Australian and New Zealand Army Corps. **Anzac Day** 25th April, a public holiday in Australia and New Zealand commemorating the Anzac landing at Gallipoli in 1915.

AOB (on the agenda for a meeting) any other business.

aorta [eh-**or**-ta] n main artery of the body, carrying oxygen-rich blood from the heart.

apace adv Lit swiftly.

apart adv 1 to or in pieces. 2 to or at a distance. 3 individual, distinct.

apartheid n former official government policy of racial segregation in S Africa.

apartment n 1 room in a building. 2 flat.

apathy n lack of interest or enthusiasm. **apathetic** adj

ape n 1 tailless monkey such as the chimpanzee or gorilla. 2 stupid, clumsy, or ugly man. ♦ v 3 imitate.

aperient [ap-**peer**-ee-ent] adj 1 having a mild laxative effect. ♦ n 2 mild laxative.

aperitif [ap-per-rit-**teef**] n alcoholic drink taken before a meal.

aperture n opening or hole.

apex n highest point.

APEX Brit, NZ & S Afr Advance Purchase Excursion: reduced fare for journeys booked a specified period in advance.

aphasia n disorder of the central nervous system that affects the ability to speak and understand words.

aphid [**eh**-fid], **aphis** [**eh**-fiss] *n* small insect which sucks the sap from plants.

aphorism *n* short clever saying expressing a general truth.

aphrodisiac [af-roh-**diz**-zee-ak] *n* **1** substance that arouses sexual desire. ♦ *adj* **2** arousing sexual desire.

apiary *n, pl* -**ries** place where bees are kept.

apiculture *n* breeding and care of bees.

apiece *adv* each.

aplomb *n* calm self-possession.

apocalypse *n* **1** end of the world. **2** event of great destruction. **the Apocalypse** book of Revelation, the last book of the New Testament. **apocalyptic** *adj*

Apocrypha [ap-**pok**-rif-fa] *pl n* **the Apocrypha** collective name for the 14 books of the Old Testament which are not accepted as part of the Hebrew scriptures.

apocryphal [ap-**pok**-rif-al] *adj* (of a story) of questionable authenticity.

apogee [**ap**-oh-jee] *n* **1** point of the moon's or a satellite's orbit that is farthest from the earth. **2** highest point.

apology *n, pl* -**gies** **1** expression of regret for wrongdoing. **2** (foll. by *for*) poor example (of). **apologetic** *adj* showing or expressing regret. **apologetically** *adv* **apologetics** *n* branch of theology concerned with the reasoned defence of Christianity. **apologist** *n* person who formally defends a cause. **apologize** *v* make an apology.

✔ **SPELLING TIP**
Remember that the correct way to spell **apology** is with one *p* and one *l*.

apoplexy *n Med* stroke. **apoplectic** *adj* **1** of apoplexy. **2** *Informal* furious.

apostasy [ap-**poss**-stass-ee] *n, pl* -**sies**

abandonment of one's religious faith or other belief. **apostate** *n, adj*

a posteriori [**eh** poss-steer-ee-**or**-rye] *adj* involving reasoning from effect to cause.

Apostle *n* **1** one of the twelve disciples chosen by Christ to preach his gospel. **2** (a-) ardent supporter of a cause or movement. **apostolic** *adj*

apostrophe [ap-**poss**-trof-fee] *n* **1** punctuation mark (') showing the omission of a letter or letters in a word, e.g. *don't*, or forming the possessive, e.g. *Jill's car*. **2** digression from a speech to address an imaginary or absent person or thing.

apothecary *n, pl* -**caries** *Obs* chemist.

apotheosis [ap-poth-ee-**oh**-siss] *n, pl* -**ses** [-seez] **1** perfect example. **2** elevation to the rank of a god.

appal *v* -**palling**, -**palled** dismay, terrify. **appalling** *adj* dreadful, terrible.

✔ **SPELLING TIP**
The verb **appal** has two *p*s, but only one *l*. If you extend it with an ending beginning with a vowel, you must add another *l*, as in **appalling**.

apparatus *n* equipment for a particular purpose.

apparel *n Old-fashioned* clothing.

apparent *adj* **1** readily seen, obvious. **2** seeming as opposed to real. **apparently** *adv*

✔ **SPELLING TIP**
It's quite common to spell **apparently** with three *a*s, but there should only be two - and then an *e*.

apparition *n* ghost or ghostlike figure.

appeal *v* **1** make an earnest request. **2** attract, please, or interest. **3** request a review of a lower court's decision by a higher court. ♦ *n* **4** earnest request. **5** attractiveness. **6** request for a review of a lower court's decision by a higher court. **appealing** *adj*

appear *v* **1** become visible or present. **2** seem. **3** be seen in public. **appearance** *n* **1** appearing. **2** outward aspect.

appease *v* **1** pacify (a person) by yielding to his or her demands. **2** satisfy or relieve (a feeling). **appeasement** *n*

appellant *n* person who makes an appeal to a higher court.

appellation *n Formal* name, title.

append *v* join on, add. **appendage** *n* thing joined on or added.

appendicitis *n* inflammation of the appendix.

appendix *n, pl* **-dices, -dixes 1** separate additional material at the end of a book. **2** *Anat* short closed tube attached to the large intestine.

☑ **WORD TIP**

Extra sections at the end of a book are *appendices*. The plural *appendixes* is used in medicine.

---

appertain *v* (foll. by *to*) **1** belong to. **2** be connected with.

appetite *n* **1** desire for food or drink. **2** liking or willingness. **appetizer** *n* thing eaten or drunk to stimulate the appetite. **appetizing** *adj* stimulating the appetite.

applaud *v* **1** show approval of by clapping one's hands. **2** approve strongly. **applause** *n* approval shown by clapping one's hands.

apple *n* round firm fleshy fruit that grows on trees. **in apple-pie order** *Informal* very tidy.

appliance *n* device with a specific function.

applicable *adj* relevant, appropriate.

applicability *n*

applicant *n* person who applies for something.

application *n* **1** formal request. **2** act of applying something to a particular use. **3** diligent effort. **4** act of putting something onto a surface.

appliqué [ap-**plee**-kay] *n* kind of decoration in which one material is cut out and attached to another.

apply *v* **-plying, -plied 1** make a formal request. **2** put to practical use. **3** put onto a surface. **4** be relevant or appropriate. **apply oneself** concentrate one's efforts. **applied** *adj* (of a skill, science, etc.) put to practical use.

appoint *v* **1** assign to a job or position. **2** fix or decide, e.g. *appoint a time*. **3** equip or furnish. **appointment** *n* **1** arrangement to meet a person. **2** act of placing someone in a job. **3** the job itself. ♦ *pl* **4** fixtures or fittings.

apportion *v* divide out in shares.

apposite *adj* suitable, apt. **apposition** *n* grammatical construction in which two nouns or phrases referring to the same thing are placed one after another without a conjunction, e.g. *my son the doctor*.

appraise *v* estimate the value or quality of. **appraisal** *n*

appreciate *v* **1** value highly. **2** be aware of and understand. **3** be grateful for. **4** rise in value. **appreciable** *adj* enough to be noticed. **appreciably** *adv* **appreciation** *n* **appreciative** *adj* feeling or showing appreciation.

apprehend *v* **1** arrest and take into custody. **2** grasp (something) mentally. **apprehension** *n* **1** dread, anxiety. **2** arrest. **3** understanding. **apprehensive** *adj* fearful or anxious.

apprentice *n* **1** someone working for a skilled person for a fixed period in order to learn his or her trade. ♦ *v* **2**

take or place (someone) as an apprentice. **apprenticeship** n

apprise v make aware (of).

appro n **on appro** Brit, Austral, NZ & S Afr informal on approval.

approach v **1** come near or nearer (to). **2** make a proposal or suggestion to. **3** begin to deal with (a matter). ♦ n **4** approaching or means of approaching. **5** approximation. **approachable** adj **approach road** smaller road leading into a major road.

approbation n approval.

appropriate adj **1** suitable, fitting. ♦ v **2** take for oneself. **3** put aside for a particular purpose. **appropriately** adv **appropriateness** n **appropriation** n

approve v **1** consider good or right. **2** authorize, agree to. **approval** n **1** consent. **2** favourable opinion. **on approval** (of goods) with an option to be returned without payment if unsatisfactory.

approx. approximate(ly).

approximate adj **1** almost but not quite exact. ♦ v (foll. by to) **2** come close to. **3** be almost the same as. **approximately** adv **approximation** n

appurtenances pl n minor or additional features.

Apr. April.

après-ski [ap-ray-**skee**] n social activities after a day's skiing.

apricot n **1** yellowish-orange juicy fruit like a small peach. ♦ adj **2** yellowish-orange.

April n fourth month of the year. **April fool** victim of a practical joke played on April 1 (**April Fools' Day**).

a priori [eh pry-**or**-rye] adj involving reasoning from cause to effect.

apron n **1** garment worn over the front of the body to protect the clothes. **2** area at an airport or hangar for

manoeuvring and loading aircraft. **3** part of a stage in front of the curtain.

apropos [ap-prop-**poh**] adj, adv appropriate(ly). **apropos of** with regard to.

apse n arched or domed recess, esp. in a church.

apt adj **1** having a specified tendency. **2** suitable. **3** quick to learn. **aptly** adv **aptness** n **aptitude** n natural ability.

aqualung n mouthpiece attached to air cylinders, worn for underwater swimming.

aquamarine n **1** greenish-blue gemstone. ♦ adj **2** greenish-blue.

aquaplane n **1** board on which a person stands to be towed by a motorboat. ♦ v **2** ride on an aquaplane. **3** (of a motor vehicle) skim uncontrollably on a thin film of water.

aquarium n, pl **aquariums, aquaria 1** tank in which fish and other underwater creatures are kept. **2** building containing such tanks.

aquatic adj **1** living in or near water. **2** done in or on water. **aquatics** pl n water sports.

aquatint n print like a watercolour, produced by etching copper.

aqua vitae [**ak**-wa **vee**-tie] n Obs brandy.

aqueduct n structure carrying water across a valley or river.

aqueous adj of, like, or containing water.

aquiline adj **1** (of a nose) curved like an eagle's beak. **2** of or like an eagle.

Arab n **1** member of a Semitic people originally from Arabia. ♦ adj **2** of the Arabs. **Arabic** n **1** language of the Arabs. ♦ adj **2** of Arabic, Arabs, or Arabia.

arabesque [ar-ab-**besk**] n **1** ballet position in which one leg is raised behind and the arms are extended. **2**

elaborate ornamental design.

arable *adj* suitable for growing crops on.

arachnid [ar-**rak**-nid] *n* eight-legged invertebrate, such as a spider, scorpion, tick, or mite.

Aran *adj* (of sweaters etc.) knitted in a complicated pattern traditional to the Aran Islands, usu. with natural unbleached wool.

arbiter *n* **1** person empowered to judge in a dispute. **2** person with influential opinions about something.

arbitrary *adj* based on personal choice or chance, rather than reason. **arbitrarily** *adv*

☑ **SPELLING TIP**

The spelling *arbitary* appears 22 times in the Bank of English. But the correct spelling, **arbitrary**, appears 1959 times: it has three *r*s.

---

arbitration *n* hearing and settling of a dispute by an impartial referee chosen by both sides. **arbitrate** *v* **arbitrator** *n*

arboreal *adj* of or living in trees.

arboretum [ahr-bore-**ee**-tum] *n, pl* **-ta** place where rare trees or shrubs are cultivated.

arboriculture *n* cultivation of trees or shrubs.

arbour *n* glade sheltered by trees.

arc *n* **1** part of a circle or other curve. **2** luminous discharge of electricity across a small gap between two electrodes. ◆ *v* **3** form an arc.

arcade *n* **1** covered passageway lined with shops. **2** set of arches and their supporting columns.

arcane *adj* mysterious and secret.

arch[1] *n* **1** curved structure supporting a bridge or roof. **2** something curved. **3** curved lower part of the foot. ◆ *v* **4** (cause to) form an arch. **archway** *n*

passageway under an arch.

arch[2] *adj* **1** superior, knowing. **2** coyly playful. **archly** *adv* **archness** *n*

arch- *combining form* chief, principal, e.g. *archenemy*.

archaeology *n* study of ancient cultures from their physical remains. **archaeological** *adj* **archaeologist** *n*

archaic [ark-**kay**-ik] *adj* **1** ancient. **2** out-of-date. **archaism** [**ark**-kay-iz-zum] *n* archaic word or phrase.

archangel [**ark**-ain-jell] *n* chief angel.

archbishop *n* chief bishop.

archdeacon *n* priest ranking just below a bishop.

archdiocese *n* diocese of an archbishop.

archer *n* person who shoots with a bow and arrow. **archery** *n*

archetype [**ark**-ee-type] *n* **1** perfect specimen. **2** original model. **archetypal** *adj*

archipelago [ark-ee-**pel**-a-go] *n, pl* **-gos 1** group of islands. **2** sea full of small islands.

architect *n* person qualified to design and supervise the construction of buildings. **architecture** *n* **1** style in which a building is designed and built. **2** designing and construction of buildings. **architectural** *adj*

architrave *n* Archit **1** beam that rests on columns. **2** moulding round a doorway or window.

archive [**ark**-ive] *n* **1** (often pl) collection of records or documents. **2** place where these are kept. **archival** *adj* **archivist** [**ark**-iv-ist] *n* person in charge of archives.

Arctic *n* **1 the Arctic** area around the North Pole. ◆ *adj* **2** of this region. **3** (a-) *Informal* very cold.

ardent *adj* **1** passionate. **2** eager, zealous. **ardently** *adv* **ardour** *n* **1**

passion. **2** enthusiasm, zeal.

arduous *adj* hard to accomplish, strenuous. **arduously** *adv*

are[1] *v see* BE.

are[2] *n* unit of measure, 100 square metres.

area *n* **1** part or region. **2** size of a two-dimensional surface. **3** subject field.

arena *n* **1** seated enclosure for sports events. **2** area of a Roman amphitheatre where gladiators fought. **3** sphere of intense activity.

aren't are not.

areola *n, pl* **-lae, -las** small circular area, such as the coloured ring around the human nipple.

argon *n Chem* inert gas found in the air.

argot [**ahr**-go] *n* slang or jargon.

argue *v* **-guing, -gued** **1** try to prove by giving reasons. **2** debate. **3** quarrel, dispute. **arguable** *adj* **arguably** *adv* **argument** *n* **1** quarrel. **2** discussion. **3** point presented for or against something. **argumentation** *n* process of reasoning methodically. **argumentative** *adj* given to arguing.

☑ **SPELLING TIP**

There's an *e* at the end of **argue**, but you should leave it out when you write **argument**. A lot of people get that wrong.

argy-bargy *n, pl* **-bargies** *Informal* squabbling argument.

aria [**ah**-ree-a] *n* elaborate song for solo voice, esp. one from an opera.

arid *adj* **1** parched, dry. **2** uninteresting. **aridity** *n*

aright *adv* rightly.

arise *v* **arising, arose, arisen** **1** come about. **2** come into notice. **3** get up.

aristocracy *n, pl* **-cies** highest social class. **aristocrat** *n* member of the aristocracy. **aristocratic** *adj*

arithmetic *n* **1** calculation by or of numbers. ♦ *adj* **2** of arithmetic. **arithmetical** *adj* **arithmetically** *adv*

ark *n* **1** *Old Testament* boat built by Noah, which survived the Flood. **2** (A-) *Judaism* chest containing the writings of Jewish Law.

arm[1] *n* **1** either of the upper limbs from the shoulder to the wrist. **2** sleeve of a garment. **3** side of a chair. **armful** *n* as much as can be held in the arms. **armchair** *n* upholstered chair with side supports for the arms. **armhole** *n* opening in a garment through which the arm passes. **armpit** *n* hollow under the arm at the shoulder.

arm[2] *v* **1** supply with weapons. **2** prepare (a bomb etc.) for use. **arms** *pl n* **1** weapons. **2** military exploits. **3** heraldic emblem.

armada *n* large number of warships.

armadillo *n, pl* **-los** small S American mammal covered in strong bony plates.

Armageddon *n* **1** *New Testament* final battle between good and evil at the end of the world. **2** catastrophic conflict.

armament *n* **1** military weapons. **2** preparation for war.

armature *n* revolving structure in an electric motor or generator, wound with coils carrying the current.

armistice [**arm**-miss-stiss] *n* agreed suspension of fighting.

armour *n* **1** metal clothing formerly worn to protect the body in battle. **2** metal plating of tanks, warships, etc. **armourer** *n* maker, repairer, or keeper of arms or armour. **armoury** *n* place where weapons are stored.

army *n, pl* **armies** **1** military land forces of a nation. **2** great number.

aroma *n* pleasant smell. **aromatic** *adj* **aromatherapy** *n* massage with fragrant oils to relieve tension.

arose v past tense of ARISE.

around prep, adv **1** on all sides (of). **2** from place to place (in). **3** somewhere in or near. **4** approximately.

arouse v **1** stimulate, make active. **2** awaken.

arpeggio [arp-**pej**-ee-oh] n, pl **-gios** Music notes of a chord played or sung in quick succession.

arr. 1 arranged (by). **2** arrival. **3** arrive(d).

arraign [ar-**rain**] v **1** bring (a prisoner) before a court to answer a charge. **2** accuse. **arraignment** n

arrange v **1** plan. **2** agree. **3** put in order. **4** adapt (music) for performance in a certain way. **arrangement** n

arrant adj utter, downright.

arras n tapestry wall-hanging.

array n **1** impressive display or collection. **2** orderly arrangement, esp. of troops. **3** Poetic rich clothing. ♦ v **4** arrange in order. **5** dress in rich clothing.

arrears pl n money owed. **in arrears** late in paying a debt.

arrest v **1** take (a person) into custody. **2** stop the movement or development of. **3** catch and hold (the attention). ♦ n **4** act of taking a person into custody. **5** slowing or stopping. **arresting** adj attracting attention, striking.

arrive v **1** reach a place or destination. **2** happen, come. **3** Informal be born. **4** Informal attain success. **arrival** n **1** arriving. **2** person or thing that has just arrived.

arrogant adj proud and overbearing. **arrogantly** adv **arrogance** n

arrogate v claim or seize without justification.

arrow n **1** pointed shaft shot from a bow. **2** arrow-shaped sign or symbol used to show direction. **arrowhead** n

pointed tip of an arrow.

arrowroot n nutritious starch obtained from the root of a W Indian plant.

arse n Vulgar slang buttocks or anus. **arsehole** n Vulgar slang **1** anus. **2** stupid or annoying person.

arsenal n place where arms and ammunition are made or stored.

arsenic n **1** toxic grey element. **2** highly poisonous compound of this. **arsenical** adj

arson n crime of intentionally setting property on fire. **arsonist** n

art n **1** creation of works of beauty, esp. paintings or sculpture. **2** works of art collectively. **3** skill. ♦ pl **4** nonscientific branches of knowledge. **artist** n **1** person who produces works of art, esp. paintings or sculpture. **2** person skilled at something. **3** artiste. **artiste** n professional entertainer such as a singer or dancer. **artistic** adj **artistically** adv **artistry** n artistic skill. **arty** adj **artier, artiest** Informal having an affected interest in art.

artefact n something made by human beings.

arteriosclerosis [art-ear-ee-oh-skler-**oh**-siss] n hardening of the arteries.

artery n, pl **-teries 1** one of the tubes carrying blood from the heart. **2** major road or means of communication. **arterial** adj **1** of an artery. **2** (of a route) major.

artesian well [art-**teez**-yan] n well bored vertically so that the water is forced to the surface by natural pressure.

Artex n ® Brit textured plaster-like covering for ceilings and walls.

artful adj cunning, wily. **artfully** adv **artfulness** n

arthritis n painful inflammation of a joint or joints. **arthritic** adj, n

arthropod n animal, such as a spider

or insect, with jointed limbs and a segmented body.

artichoke *n* flower head of a thistle-like plant, cooked as a vegetable.

article *n* **1** written piece in a magazine or newspaper. **2** item or object. **3** clause in a document. **4** *Grammar* any of the words *the, a,* or *an.*

articled *adj* bound (as an apprentice) by a written contract.

articulate *adj* **1** able to express oneself clearly and coherently. **2** (of speech) clear, distinct. **3** *Zool* having joints. ♦ *v* **4** speak or say clearly and coherently. **articulately** *adv* **articulated** *adj* jointed. **articulated vehicle** large vehicle in two separate sections joined by a pivoted bar. **articulation** *n*

artifice *n* **1** clever trick. **2** cleverness, skill. **artificer** [art-**tiff**-iss-er] *n* craftsman.

artificial *adj* **1** man-made, not occurring naturally. **2** made in imitation of something natural. **3** not sincere. **artificial insemination** introduction of semen into the womb by means other than sexual intercourse. **artificial intelligence** branch of computer science aiming to produce machines which can imitate intelligent human behaviour. **artificial respiration** method of restarting a person's breathing after it has stopped. **artificially** *adv* **artificiality** *n*

artillery *n* **1** large-calibre guns. **2** branch of the army who use these.

artisan *n* skilled worker, craftsman.

artless *adj* **1** free from deceit or cunning. **2** natural, unpretentious. **artlessly** *adv*

arum lily [**air**-rum] *n* plant with a white funnel-shaped leaf surrounding a spike of flowers.

arvie *n S Afr informal* afternoon.

as *conj* **1** while, when. **2** in the way that. **3** that which, e.g. *do as you are told.* **4** since, seeing that. **5** for instance. ♦ *adv, conj* **6** used to indicate amount or extent in comparisons, e.g. *he is as tall as you.* ♦ *prep* **7** in the role of, being, e.g. *as a mother, I am concerned.*

asafoetida *n* strong-smelling plant resin used as a spice in Eastern cookery.

a.s.a.p. as soon as possible.

asbestos *n* fibrous mineral which does not burn. **asbestosis** *n* lung disease caused by inhalation of asbestos fibre.

ascend *v* go or move up. **ascent** *n* **1** ascending. **2** upward slope. **ascendant** *adj* dominant or influential. ♦ *n* **in the ascendant** increasing in power or influence. **ascendancy** *n* condition of being dominant. **the Ascension** *Christianity* passing of Jesus Christ from earth into heaven.

ascertain *v* find out definitely. **ascertainable** *adj* **ascertainment** *n*

ascetic [ass-**set**-tik] *n, adj* (person) abstaining from worldly pleasures and comforts. **asceticism** *n*

ascorbic acid [ass-**core**-bik] *n* vitamin C.

ascribe *v* attribute, as to a particular origin. **ascription** *n*

aseptic [eh-**sep**-tik] *adj* free from harmful bacteria.

asexual [eh-**sex**-yew-al] *adj* without sex. **asexually** *adv*

ash[1] *n* **1** powdery substance left when something is burnt. ♦ *pl* **2** remains after burning, esp. of a human body after cremation. **the Ashes** cricket trophy competed for in test matches by England and Australia. **ashen** *adj* pale with shock. **ashtray** *n* receptacle for tobacco ash and cigarette butts. **Ash Wednesday** first day of Lent.

ash[2] *n* tree with grey bark.

ashamed *adj* feeling shame.

ashlar *n* square block of hewn stone

used in building.

ashore *adv* towards or on land.

ashram *n* religious retreat where a Hindu holy man lives.

Asian *adj* **1** of the continent of Asia or any of its peoples or languages. **2** *n* **3** person from Asia or a descendant of one. **4** person from the Indian subcontinent or a descendant of one. **Asian pear** apple-shaped pear with crisp juicy flesh.

> ✔ **WORD TIP**
> Use *Asian* for 'someone who comes from Asia'. *Asiatic* in this context can be offensive.

aside *adv* **1** to one side. **2** out of other people's hearing, e.g. *he took me aside to tell me his plans.* ♦ *n* **3** remark not meant to be heard by everyone present.

asinine *adj* stupid, idiotic.

ask *v* **1** say or write (something) in a form that requires an answer. **2** make a request or demand. **3** invite.

askance [ass-**kanss**] *adv* **look askance at 1** look at with an oblique glance. **2** regard with suspicion.

askew *adv, adj* to one side, crooked.

aslant *adv, prep* at a slant (to), slanting (across).

asleep *adj* **1** sleeping. **2** (of limbs) numb.

asp *n* small poisonous snake.

asparagus *n* plant whose shoots are cooked as a vegetable.

aspect *n* **1** feature or element. **2** position facing a particular direction. **3** appearance or look.

aspen *n* kind of poplar tree.

asperity *n* roughness of temper.

aspersion *n* **cast aspersions on** make derogatory remarks about.

asphalt *n* black hard tarlike substance

used for road surfaces etc.

asphodel *n* plant with clusters of yellow or white flowers.

asphyxia [ass-**fix**-ee-a] *n* suffocation. **asphyxiate** *v* suffocate. **asphyxiation** *n*

aspic *n* savoury jelly used to coat meat, eggs, fish, etc.

aspidistra *n* plant with long tapered leaves.

aspirate *Phonetics* ♦ *v* **1** pronounce with an *h* sound. ♦ *n* **2** *h* sound.

aspire *v* (foll. by *to*) yearn (for), hope (to do or be). **aspirant** *n* person who aspires. **aspiration** *n* strong desire or aim.

aspirin *n* **1** drug used to relieve pain and fever. **2** tablet of this.

ass *n* **1** donkey. **2** stupid person.

assagai *n* same as ASSEGAI.

assail *v* attack violently. **assailant** *n*

assassin *n* person who murders a prominent person. **assassinate** *v* murder (a prominent person). **assassination** *n*

assault *n* **1** violent attack. ♦ *v* **2** attack violently. **assault course** series of obstacles used in military training.

assay *n* **1** analysis of a substance, esp. a metal, to ascertain its purity. ♦ *v* **2** make such an analysis.

assegai [**ass**-a-guy] *n* slender spear used in S Africa.

assemble *v* **1** collect or congregate. **2** put together the parts of (a machine). **assemblage** *n* **1** collection or group. **2** assembling. **assembly** *n* **1** *pl* **-blies** assembled group. **2** assembling. **assembly line** sequence of machines and workers in a factory assembling a product.

assent *n* **1** agreement or consent. ♦ *v* **2** agree or consent.

assert *v* **1** declare forcefully. **2** insist upon (one's rights etc.). **assert**

oneself put oneself forward forcefully. **assertion** n **assertive** adj **assertively** adv

assess v 1 judge the worth or importance of. 2 estimate the value of (income or property) for taxation purposes. **assessment** n **assessor** n

asset n 1 valuable or useful person or thing. ♦ pl 2 property that a person or firm can sell, esp. to pay debts.

asseverate v declare solemnly.

assiduous adj hard-working. **assiduously** adv **assiduity** n

assign v 1 appoint (someone) to a job or task. 2 allot (a task). 3 attribute. **assignation** n 1 assigning. 2 secret arrangement to meet. **assignment** n 1 task assigned. 2 assigning.

assimilate v 1 learn and understand (information). 2 absorb or be absorbed or incorporated. **assimilable** adj **assimilation** n

assist v give help or support. **assistance** n **assistant** n 1 helper. ♦ adj 2 junior or deputy.

assizes pl n Brit court sessions formerly held in each county of England and Wales.

associate v 1 connect in the mind. 2 mix socially. ♦ n 3 partner in business. 4 friend or companion. ♦ adj 5 having partial rights or subordinate status, e.g. associate member. **association** n 1 society or club. 2 associating.

assonance n rhyming of vowel sounds but not consonants, as in time and light.

assorted adj consisting of various types mixed together. **assortment** n assorted mixture.

assuage [ass-**wage**] v relieve (pain, grief, thirst, etc.).

assume v 1 take to be true without proof. 2 take upon oneself, e.g. he assumed command. 3 pretend, e.g. I assumed indifference. **assumption** n 1

thing assumed. 2 assuming.

assure v 1 promise or guarantee. 2 convince. 3 make (something) certain. 4 insure against loss of life. **assured** adj 1 confident. 2 certain to happen. **assuredly** adv definitely. **assurance** n assuring or being assured.

✓ **WORD TIP**
When used in the context of business, assurance and insurance have the same meaning.

astatine n Chem radioactive nonmetallic element.

aster n plant with daisy-like flowers.

asterisk n 1 star-shaped symbol (*) used in printing or writing to indicate a footnote etc. ♦ v 2 mark with an asterisk.

astern adv 1 at or towards the stern of a ship. 2 backwards.

asteroid n any of the small planets that orbit the sun between Mars and Jupiter.

asthma [**ass**-ma] n illness causing difficulty in breathing. **asthmatic** adj, n

astigmatism [eh-**stig**-mat-tiz-zum] n inability of a lens, esp. of the eye, to focus properly.

astir adj Old-fashioned 1 out of bed. 2 in motion.

astonish v surprise greatly. **astonishment** n

astound v overwhelm with amazement. **astounding** adj

astrakhan n 1 dark curly fleece of lambs from Astrakhan in Russia. 2 fabric resembling this.

astral adj 1 of stars. 2 of the spirit world.

astray adv off the right path.

astride adv, prep with a leg on either side (of).

astringent adj 1 causing contraction of body tissue. 2 checking the flow of

blood from a cut. **3** severe or harsh.
♦ n **4** astringent substance.
astringency n

astrolabe n instrument formerly used to measure the altitude of stars and planets.

astrology n study of the alleged influence of the stars, planets, and moon on human affairs. **astrologer** n **astrological** adj

astronaut n person trained for travelling in space.

astronautics n science and technology of space flight. **astronautical** adj

astronomy n scientific study of heavenly bodies. **astronomer** n **astronomical** adj **1** very large. **2** of astronomy. **astronomically** adv

astrophysics n science of the physical and chemical properties of stars, planets, etc. **astrophysical** adj **astrophysicist** n

astute adj perceptive or shrewd. **astutely** adv **astuteness** n

asunder adv Obs or poetic into parts or pieces.

asylum n **1** refuge or sanctuary. **2** old name for a mental hospital.

asymmetry n lack of symmetry. **asymmetrical, asymmetric** adj

asymptote [**ass**-im-tote] n straight line closely approached but never met by a curve.

at prep indicating position in space or time, movement towards an object, etc., e.g. at midnight; throwing stones at windows.

atavism [**at**-a-viz-zum] n recurrence of a trait present in distant ancestors. **atavistic** adj

ate v past tense of EAT.

atheism [**aith**-ee-iz-zum] n belief that there is no God. **atheist** n **atheistic** adj

atherosclerosis n, pl -ses disease in which deposits of fat cause the walls of the arteries to thicken.

athlete n person trained in or good at athletics. **athletic** adj **1** physically fit or strong. **2** of an athlete or athletics. **athletics** pl n track-and-field sports such as running, jumping, throwing, etc. **athletically** adv **athleticism** n

athwart prep **1** across. ♦ adv **2** transversely.

atlas n book of maps.

atmosphere n **1** mass of gases surrounding a heavenly body, esp. the earth. **2** prevailing tone or mood (of a place etc.). **3** unit of pressure. **atmospheric** adj **atmospherics** pl n radio interference due to electrical disturbance in the atmosphere.

atoll n ring-shaped coral reef enclosing a lagoon.

atom n **1** smallest unit of matter which can take part in a chemical reaction. **2** very small amount. **atom bomb** same as ATOMIC BOMB.

atomic adj **1** of or using atomic bombs or atomic energy. **2** of atoms. **atomic bomb** bomb in which the energy is provided by nuclear fission. **atomic energy** nuclear energy. **atomic number** number of protons in the nucleus of an atom. **atomic weight** ratio of the mass per atom of an element to one twelfth of the mass of a carbon atom.

atomize v reduce to atoms or small particles.

atomizer n device for discharging a liquid in a fine spray.

atonal [eh-**tone**-al] adj (of music) not written in an established key.

atone v make amends (for sin or wrongdoing). **atonement** n

atop prep Lit on top of.

atrium n, pl atria **1** upper chamber of either half of the heart. **2** central hall extending through several storeys of a modern building. **3** main courtyard of an ancient Roman house.

atrocious *adj* **1** extremely cruel or wicked. **2** horrifying or shocking. **3** *Informal* very bad. **atrociously** *adv* **atrocity** *n* **1** wickedness. **2** *pl* **-ties**) act of cruelty.

atrophy [**at**-trof-fee] *n, pl* **-phies 1** wasting away of an organ or part. **2** *v* **-phying, -phied 3** (cause to) waste away.

attach *v* **1** join, fasten, or connect. **2** attribute or ascribe. **attached** *adj* (foll. by *to*) fond of. **attachment** *n*

attaché [at-**tash**-shay] *n* specialist attached to a diplomatic mission. **attaché case** flat rectangular briefcase for papers.

attack *v* **1** launch a physical assault (against). **2** criticize. **3** set about (a job or problem) with vigour. **4** affect adversely. ♦ *n* **5** act of attacking. **6** sudden bout of illness. **attacker** *n*

attain *v* **1** achieve or accomplish (a task or aim). **2** reach. **attainable** *adj* **attainment** *n* accomplishment.

attar *n* fragrant oil made from roses.

attempt *v* **1** try, make an effort. ♦ *n* **2** effort or endeavour.

attend *v* **1** be present at. **2** go regularly to a school, college, etc. **3** look after. **4** pay attention. **5** apply oneself (to). **attendance** *n* **1** attending. **2** number attending. **attendant** *n* **1** person who assists, guides, or provides a service. ♦ *adj* **2** accompanying. **attention** *n* **1** concentrated direction of the mind. **2** consideration. **3** care. **4** alert position in military drill. **attentive** *adj* **1** giving attention. **2** considerately helpful. **attentively** *adv* **attentiveness** *n*

attenuated *adj* **1** weakened. **2** thin and extended. **attenuation** *n*

attest *v* affirm the truth of, be proof of. **attestation** *n*

attic *n* space or room within the roof of a house.

attire *n* *Formal* fine or formal clothes.

attired *adj* dressed in a specified way.

attitude *n* **1** way of thinking and behaving. **2** posture of the body.

attorney *n* **1** person legally appointed to act for another. **2** *US & S Afr* lawyer.

attract *v* **1** arouse the interest or admiration of. **2** draw (something) closer by exerting a force on it. **attraction** *n* **1** power to attract. **2** something that attracts. **attractive** *adj* **attractively** *adv* **attractiveness** *n*

attribute *v* **1** (usu. foll. by *to*) regard as belonging to or produced by. ♦ *n* **2** quality or feature representative of a person or thing. **attributable** *adj* **attribution** *n* **attributive** *adj* *Grammar* (of an adjective) preceding the noun modified.

attrition *n* constant wearing down to weaken or destroy.

attune *v* adjust or accustom (a person or thing).

atypical [eh-**tip**-ik-al] *adj* not typical.

Au *Chem* gold.

aubergine [**oh**-bur-zheen] *n* *Brit* dark purple tropical fruit, cooked and eaten as a vegetable.

aubrietia [aw-**bree**-sha] *n* trailing plant with purple flowers.

auburn *adj* (of hair) reddish-brown.

auction *n* **1** public sale in which articles are sold to the highest bidder. ♦ *v* **2** sell by auction. **auctioneer** *n* person who conducts an auction.

audacious *adj* **1** recklessly bold or daring. **2** impudent. **audaciously** *adv* **audacity** *n*

audible *adj* loud enough to be heard. **audibly** *adv* **audibility** *n*

audience *n* **1** group of spectators or listeners. **2** formal interview.

audio *adj* **1** of sound or hearing. **2** of or

for the transmission or reproduction of sound. **audio typist** typist trained to type from a dictating machine. **audiovisual** adj (esp. of teaching aids) involving both sight and hearing.

audit n **1** official examination of business accounts. ♦ v **auditing, audited 2** examine (business accounts) officially. **auditor** n

audition n **1** test of a performer's ability for a particular role or job. ♦ v **2** test or be tested in an audition.

auditorium n, pl **-toriums, -toria** area of a concert hall or theatre where the audience sits.

auditory adj of or relating to hearing.

au fait [oh **fay**] adj French **1** fully informed. **2** expert.

Aug. August.

auger n tool for boring holes.

aught pron Obs anything whatever.

augment v increase or enlarge. **augmentation** n

au gratin [oh **grat**-tan] adj covered and cooked with breadcrumbs and sometimes cheese.

augur v be a sign of (future events). **augury** n **1** foretelling of the future. **2** pl **-ries**) omen.

august [aw-**gust**] adj dignified and imposing.

August n eighth month of the year.

auk n northern sea bird with short wings and black-and-white plumage.

aunt n **1** father's or mother's sister. **2** uncle's wife. **auntie, aunty** n, pl **aunties** Informal aunt. **Aunt Sally** Brit, NZ & S Afr **1** figure used in fairgrounds as a target. **2** target of abuse or criticism.

au pair n young foreign woman who does housework in return for board and lodging.

aura n distinctive air or quality of a person or thing.

aural adj of or using the ears or hearing.

aureole, aureola n halo.

au revoir [oh riv-**vwahr**] interj French goodbye.

auricle n **1** upper chamber of the heart. **2** outer part of the ear. **auricular** adj

aurochs n, pl **aurochs** recently extinct European wild ox.

aurora n, pl **-ras, -rae** bands of light sometimes seen in the sky in polar regions. **aurora australis** aurora seen near the South Pole. **aurora borealis** aurora seen near the North Pole.

auscultation n listening to the internal sounds of the body, usu. with a stethoscope, to help with diagnosis.

auspices [aw-spiss-siz] pl n **under the auspices of** with the support and approval of.

auspicious adj showing signs of future success, favourable. **auspiciously** adv

Aussie n, adj Informal Australian.

Aust. Australia(n).

austere adj **1** stern or severe. **2** ascetic or self-disciplined. **3** severely simple or plain. **austerely** adv **austerity** n

Australasian n, adj (person) from Australia, New Zealand, and neighbouring islands.

Australia Day n Aust public holiday on 26th January.

Australian n, adj (person) from Australia.

autarchy [aw-tar-kee] n absolute power or autocracy.

autarky [aw-tar-kee] n policy of economic self-sufficiency.

authentic adj known to be real, genuine. **authentically** adv **authenticity** n **authenticate** v establish as genuine. **authentication** n

author n **1** writer of a book etc. **2** originator or creator. **authorship** n

authority *n, pl* **-ties 1** power to command or control others. **2** (often pl) person or group having this power. **3** expert in a particular field.
authoritarian *n, adj* (person) insisting on strict obedience to authority.
authoritative *adj* **1** recognized as being reliable. **2** possessing authority.
authoritatively *adv* **authorize** *v* **1** give authority to. **2** give permission for. **authorization** *n*

autism *n Psychiatry* disorder, usu. of children, characterized by lack of response to people and limited ability to communicate. **autistic** *adj*

auto- *combining form* self-, e.g. *autobiography.*

autobiography *n, pl* **-phies** account of a person's life written by that person. **autobiographical** *adj* **autobiographically** *adv*

autocrat *n* **1** ruler with absolute authority. **2** dictatorial person.
autocratic *adj* **autocratically** *adv* **autocracy** *n* government by an autocrat.

autocross *n* motor-racing over a rough course.

Autocue *n* ® electronic television prompting device displaying a speaker's script, unseen by the audience.

autogiro, autogyro *n, pl* **-ros** self-propelled aircraft resembling a helicopter but with an unpowered rotor.

autograph *n* **1** handwritten signature of a (famous) person. ♦ *v* **2** write one's signature on or in.

automat *n US* vending machine.

automate *v* make (a manufacturing process) automatic. **automation** *n*

automatic *adj* **1** (of a device) operating mechanically by itself. **2** (of a process) performed by automatic equipment. **3** done without conscious thought. **4** (of a firearm) self-loading. ♦ *n* **5** self-loading firearm. **6** vehicle with automatic transmission. **automatically** *adv*

automaton *n* **1** robot. **2** person who acts mechanically.

automobile *n US* motor car.

autonomy *n* self-government. **autonomous** *adj*

autopsy *n, pl* **-sies** examination of a corpse to determine the cause of death.

autosuggestion *n* process in which a person unconsciously influences his or her own behaviour or beliefs.

autumn *n* season between summer and winter. **autumnal** *adj*

auxiliary *adj* **1** secondary or supplementary. **2** supporting. ♦ *n, pl* **-ries 3** person or thing that supplements or supports. **auxiliary verb** verb used to form the tense, voice, or mood of another, such as *will* in *I will go.*

avail *v* **1** be of use or advantage (to). ♦ *n* **2** use or advantage, esp. in *to no avail.* **avail oneself of** make use of.

available *adj* obtainable or accessible. **availability** *n*

avalanche *n* **1** mass of snow or ice falling down a mountain. **2** sudden overwhelming quantity of anything.

avant-garde [av-ong-**gard**] *n* **1** group of innovators, esp. in the arts. ♦ *adj* **2** innovative and progressive.

avarice [**av**-a-riss] *n* greed for wealth. **avaricious** *adj*

avast *interj Naut* stop.

avatar *n Hinduism* appearance of a god in animal or human form.

Ave. Avenue.

avenge *v* take revenge in retaliation for (harm done) or on behalf of (a person harmed). **avenger** *n*

avenue *n* **1** wide street. **2** road

between two rows of trees. **3** way of approach.

aver [av-**vur**] v **averring, averred** state to be true.

average n **1** typical or normal amount or quality. **2** result obtained by adding quantities together and dividing the total by the number of quantities. ♦ adj **3** usual or typical. **4** calculated as an average. ♦ v **5** calculate the average of. **6** amount to as an average.

averse adj (usu. foll. by to) disinclined or unwilling. **aversion** n **1** strong dislike. **2** person or thing disliked.

avert v **1** turn away. **2** ward off.

aviary n, pl **aviaries** large cage or enclosure for birds.

aviation n art of flying aircraft. **aviator** n

avid adj **1** keen or enthusiastic. **2** greedy (for). **avidly** adv **avidity** n

avocado n, pl **-dos** pear-shaped tropical fruit with a leathery green skin and yellowish-green flesh.

avocation n Old-fashioned **1** occupation. **2** hobby.

avocet n long-legged wading bird with a long slender upward-curving bill.

avoid v **1** prevent from happening. **2** refrain from. **3** keep away from. **avoidable** adj **avoidance** n

avoirdupois [av-er-de-**poise**] n system of weights based on pounds and ounces.

avow v **1** state or affirm. **2** admit openly. **avowal** n **avowed** adj **avowedly** adv

avuncular adj (of a man) friendly, helpful, and caring towards someone younger.

await v **1** wait for. **2** be in store for.

awake v **awaking, awoke, awoken 1** emerge or rouse from sleep. **2** (cause to) become alert. ♦ adj **3** not sleeping. **4** alert.

awaken v awake.

award v **1** give (something, such as a prize) formally. ♦ n **2** something awarded, such as a prize.

aware adj having knowledge, informed. **awareness** n

awash adv washed over by water.

away adv **1** from a place, e.g. go away. **2** to another place, e.g. put that gun away. **3** out of existence, e.g. fade away. **4** continuously, e.g. laughing away. ♦ adj **5** not present. **6** distant, e.g. two miles away. **7** Sport played on an opponent's ground.

awe n **1** wonder and respect mixed with dread. ♦ v **2** fill with awe. **awesome** adj **1** inspiring awe. **2** Slang excellent or outstanding. **awestruck** adj filled with awe.

awful adj **1** very bad or unpleasant. **2** Informal very great. **3** Obs inspiring awe. **awfully** adv **1** in an unpleasant way. **2** Informal very.

awhile adv for a brief time.

awkward adj **1** clumsy or ungainly. **2** embarrassed. **3** difficult to use or handle. **4** inconvenient. **awkwardly** adv **awkwardness** n

awl n pointed tool for piercing wood, leather, etc.

awning n canvas roof supported by a frame to give protection against the weather.

awoke v past tense of AWAKE. **awoken** v past participle of AWAKE.

AWOL adj Mil absent without leave.

awry [a-**rye**] adv, adj **1** with a twist to one side, askew. **2** amiss.

axe n **1** tool with a sharp blade for felling trees or chopping wood. **2** Informal dismissal from employment etc. ♦ v **3** Informal dismiss (employees), restrict (expenditure), or terminate (a project).

axil n angle where the stalk of a leaf

joins a stem.

axiom *n* **1** generally accepted principle. **2** self-evident statement. **axiomatic** *adj* self-evident.

axis *n, pl* **axes 1** (imaginary) line round which a body can rotate or about which an object or geometrical figure is symmetrical. **2** one of two fixed lines on a graph, against which quantities or positions are measured. **axial** *adj*

axle *n* shaft on which a wheel or pair of wheels turns.

axolotl *n* aquatic salamander of central America.

ayatollah *n* Islamic religious leader in Iran.

aye, ay *interj* **1** yes. ♦ *n* **2** affirmative vote or voter.

azalea [az-**zale**-ya] *n* garden shrub grown for its showy flowers.

azimuth *n* **1** arc of the sky between the zenith and the horizon. **2** horizontal angle of a bearing measured clockwise from the north.

azure *adj, n* (of) the colour of a clear blue sky.

B b

BA Bachelor of Arts.

baa *v* **baaing, baaed 1** make the characteristic bleating sound of a sheep. ♦ *n* **2** cry made by a sheep.

babble *v* **1** talk excitedly or foolishly. **2** (of streams) make a low murmuring sound. ♦ *n* **3** muddled or foolish speech.

babe *n* baby.

babel *n* confused mixture of noises or voices.

baboon *n* large monkey with a pointed face and a long tail.

baby *n, pl* **-bies 1** very young child or animal. **2** *Slang* sweetheart. ♦ *adj* **3** comparatively small of its type. **babyish** *adj* **baby-sit** *v* take care of a child while the parents are out. **baby-sitter** *n*

baccarat [**back**-a-rah] *n* card game involving gambling.

bacchanalia [back-a-**nail**-ee-a] *n* wild drunken party or orgy.

bach [**batch**] *NZ* ♦ *n* **1** small holiday cottage. ♦ *v* **2** look after oneself when one's spouse is away.

bachelor *n* **1** unmarried man. **2** person who holds the lowest university or college degree.

☑ SPELLING TIP

We find *batchelor* spelt with a *t* 14 times in the Bank of English. The correct spelling has no *t*: **bachelor**.

---

bacillus [bass-**ill**-luss] *n, pl* **-li** [-lie] rod-shaped bacterium.

back *n* **1** rear part of the human body, from the neck to the pelvis. **2** part or side of an object opposite the front. **3** part of anything less often seen or used. **4** *Ball games* defensive player or position. ♦ *v* **5** (cause to) move backwards. **6** provide money for (a person or enterprise). **7** bet on the success of. **8** (foll. by *onto*) have the back facing towards. ♦ *adj* **9** situated behind. **10** owing from an earlier date. ♦ *adv* **11** at, to, or towards the rear. **12** to or towards the original starting point or condition. **backer** *n* person who gives financial support. **backing** *n* **1** support. **2** musical accompaniment for a pop singer. **backward** *adj* **1** directed towards the rear. **2** retarded in physical, material, or intellectual development. **backwardness** *n* **backwards** *adv* **1** towards the rear. **2** with the back foremost. **3** in the reverse of the usual direction. **back up** *v* support. **backup** *n* **1** support or reinforcement. **2** reserve or substitute.

backbencher *n* Member of Parliament who does not hold office in the government or opposition.

backbiting *n* spiteful talk about an absent person.

backbone *n* **1** spinal column. **2** strength of character.

backchat *n* *Informal* impudent replies.

backcloth, backdrop *n* painted curtain at the back of a stage set.

backdate *v* make (a document) effective from a date earlier than its completion.

backfire *v* **1** (of a plan) fail to have the desired effect. **2** (of an engine) make a loud noise like an explosion.

backgammon *n* game played with counters and dice.

background *n* **1** events or circumstances that help to explain something. **2** person's social class, education, or experience. **3** part of a scene or picture furthest from the viewer.

backhand n Tennis etc. stroke played with the back of the hand facing the direction of the stroke. **backhanded** adj ambiguous or implying criticism, e.g. a backhanded compliment. **backhander** n Slang bribe.

backlash n sudden and adverse reaction.

backlog n accumulation of things to be dealt with.

backpack n large pack carried on the back.

backside n Informal buttocks.

backslide v relapse into former bad habits. **backslider** n

backstage adv, adj behind the stage in a theatre.

backstroke n swimming stroke performed on the back.

backtrack v 1 return by the same route by which one has come. 2 retract or reverse one's opinion or policy.

backwash n 1 water washed backwards by the motion of a boat. 2 repercussion.

backwater n isolated or backward place or condition.

backwoods pl n remote sparsely populated area.

bacon n salted or smoked pig meat.

bacteria pl n, sing -rium large group of microorganisms, many of which cause disease. **bacterial** adj **bacteriology** n study of bacteria. **bacteriologist** n

bad adj worse, worst 1 of poor quality. 2 lacking skill or talent. 3 harmful. 4 immoral or evil. 5 naughty or mischievous. 6 rotten or decayed. 7 unpleasant. **badly** adv **badness** n

bade v a past tense of BID.

badge n emblem worn to show membership, rank, etc.

badger n 1 nocturnal burrowing mammal of Europe, Asia, and N America with a black and white head. ♦ v 2 pester or harass.

badinage [**bad**-in-nahzh] n playful and witty conversation.

badminton n game played with rackets and a shuttlecock, which is hit back and forth over a high net.

Bafana bafana [bah-**fan**-na] pl n S Afr South African national soccer team.

baffle v 1 perplex or puzzle. ♦ n 2 device to limit or regulate the flow of fluid, light, or sound. **bafflement** n

bag n 1 flexible container with an opening at one end. 2 handbag or piece of luggage. 3 Offens ugly or bad-tempered woman. ♦ v bagging, bagged 5 put into a bag. 6 succeed in capturing, killing or scoring. **baggy** adj (of clothes) hanging loosely.

bagatelle n 1 something of little value. 2 board game in which balls are struck into holes.

bagel n hard ring-shaped bread roll.

baggage n suitcases packed for a journey.

bagpipes pl n musical wind instrument with reed pipes and an inflatable bag.

bail[1] n 1 Law money deposited with a court as security for a person's reappearance in court. 2 v 3 pay bail for (a person).

bail[2], **bale** v (foll. by out) 1 remove (water) from (a boat). 2 Informal help (a person or organization) out of a predicament. 3 make an emergency parachute jump from an aircraft.

bail[3] n Cricket either of two wooden bars across the tops of the stumps.

bailey n outermost wall or court of a castle.

bailiff n 1 sheriff's officer who serves writs and summonses. 2 landlord's agent.

bairn n Scot child.

bait n 1 piece of food on a hook or in a trap to attract fish or animals. 2 v 3 put a piece of food on or in (a hook or trap). 4 persecute or tease.

baize n woollen fabric used to cover billiard and card tables.

bake v 1 cook by dry heat as in an oven. 2 make or become hardened by heat. **baking powder** powdered mixture containing sodium bicarbonate, used as a raising agent in baking.

baker n person whose business is to make or sell bread, cakes, etc. **baker's dozen** thirteen. **bakery** n, pl -**eries** place where bread, cakes, etc. are baked or sold.

bakkie n S Afr small truck.

Balaclava, Balaclava helmet n close-fitting woollen hood that covers the ears and neck.

balalaika n guitar-like musical instrument with a triangular body.

balance n 1 state in which a weight or amount is evenly distributed. 2 amount that remains, e.g. the balance of what you owe. 3 weighing device. 4 difference between the credits and debits of an account. ♦ v 5 weigh in a balance. 6 make or remain steady. 7 consider or compare. 8 compare or equalize the money going into or coming out of an account.

balcony n, pl -**nies** 1 platform on the outside of a building with a rail along the outer edge. 2 upper tier of seats in a theatre or cinema.

bald adj 1 having little or no hair on the scalp. 2 plain or blunt. 3 (of a tyre) having a worn tread. **balding** adj becoming bald. **baldness** n

balderdash n stupid talk.

bale¹ n 1 large bundle of hay or goods tightly bound together. ♦ v 2 make or

put into bales.

bale² v same as BAIL².

baleful adj vindictive or menacing. **balefully** adv

balk, baulk v 1 be reluctant to (do something). 2 thwart or hinder.

Balkan adj of any of the countries of the Balkan Peninsula: Romania, Bulgaria, Albania, Greece, the former Yugoslavia, and the European part of Turkey.

ball¹ n 1 round or nearly round object, esp. one used in games. 2 single delivery of the ball in a game. 3 pl Vulgar slang 4 testicles. 5 nonsense. ♦ v 6 form into a ball. **ball bearings** steel balls between moving parts of a machine to reduce friction. **ball cock** device with a floating ball and a valve for regulating the flow of water. **ballpoint, ballpoint pen** n pen with a tiny ball bearing as a writing point.

ball² n formal social function for dancing. **ballroom** n

ballad n 1 narrative poem or song. 2 slow sentimental song.

ballast n substance, such as sand, used to stabilize a ship when it is not carrying cargo.

ballet n 1 classical style of expressive dancing based on conventional steps. 2 theatrical performance of this. **ballerina** n female ballet dancer.

ballistics n study of the flight of projectiles, such as bullets. **ballistic missile** missile guided automatically in flight but which falls freely at its target.

balloon n 1 inflatable rubber bag used as a plaything or decoration. 2 large bag inflated with air or gas, designed to float in the atmosphere with passengers in a basket underneath. ♦ v 3 fly in a balloon. 4 swell or increase rapidly in size. **balloonist** n

ballot n 1 method of voting. 2 actual vote or paper indicating a person's choice. ♦ v **-loting, -loted 3** vote or ask for a vote from.

ballyhoo n exaggerated fuss.

balm n **1** aromatic substance used for healing and soothing. **2** anything that comforts or soothes.

Balmain bug n edible Australian shellfish.

balmy adj **balmier, balmiest** (of weather) mild and pleasant.

baloney n Informal nonsense.

balsa [**bawl**-sa] n very light wood from a tropical American tree.

balsam n **1** soothing ointment. **2** flowering plant.

baluster n set of posts supporting a rail.

balustrade n ornamental rail supported by balusters.

bamboo n tall treelike tropical grass with hollow stems.

bamboozle v **1** Informal cheat or mislead. **2** confuse, puzzle.

ban v **banning, banned 1** prohibit or forbid officially. ♦ n **2** official prohibition.

banal [ban-**nahl**] adj ordinary and unoriginal. **banality** n

banana n yellow crescent-shaped fruit.

band[1] n **1** group of musicians playing together. **2** group of people having a common purpose. **bandsman** n **bandstand** n roofed outdoor platform for a band. **band together** v unite.

band[2] n **1** strip of some material, used to hold objects. **2** Physics range of frequencies or wavelengths between two limits.

bandage n **1** piece of material used to cover a wound or wrap an injured limb. ♦ v **2** cover with a bandage.

bandanna, bandana n large brightly coloured handkerchief or neckerchief.

B & B bed and breakfast.

bandicoot n ratlike Australian

marsupial.

bandit n robber, esp. a member of an armed gang. **banditry** n

bandolier n shoulder belt for holding cartridges.

bandwagon n **jump, climb on the bandwagon** join a party or movement that seems assured of success.

bandy adj **-dier, -diest 1** (also **bandy-legged**) having legs curved outwards at the knees. ♦ v **-dying, -died 2** exchange (words) in a heated manner. **3** use (a name, term, etc.) frequently.

bane n person or thing that causes misery or distress. **baneful** adj

bang n **1** short loud explosive noise. **2** hard blow or loud knock. ♦ v **3** hit or knock, esp. with a loud noise. **4** close (a door) noisily. ♦ adv **5** precisely. **6** with a sudden impact.

banger n **1** Informal Brit & Aust old decrepit car. **2** Slang sausage. **3** firework that explodes loudly.

bangle n bracelet worn round the arm or the ankle.

banish v **1** send (someone) into exile. **2** drive away. **banishment** n

banisters pl n railing supported by posts on a staircase.

banjo n, pl **-jos, -joes** guitar-like musical instrument with a circular body.

bank[1] n **1** institution offering services such as the safekeeping and lending of money. **2** any supply, store, or reserve. ♦ v **3** deposit (cash or cheques) in a bank. **banking** n **banknote** n piece of paper money. **bank on** v rely on.

bank[2] n **1** raised mass, esp. of earth. **2** sloping ground at the side of a river. ♦ v **3** form into a bank. **4** cause (an aircraft) or (of an aircraft) to tip to one side on turning.

bank[3] n arrangement of switches, keys,

oars, etc. in a row or in tiers.

banker n manager or owner of a bank.

bankrupt n **1** person declared by a court to be unable to pay his or her debts. ♦ adj **2** financially ruined. **3** v **4** make bankrupt. **bankruptcy** n

banksia n Australian evergreen tree or shrub.

banner n **1** long strip of cloth displaying a slogan, advertisement, etc. **2** placard carried in a demonstration or procession.

bannisters pl n same as BANISTERS.

banns pl n public declaration, esp. in a church, of an intended marriage.

banquet n elaborate formal dinner.

banshee n (in Irish folklore) female spirit whose wailing warns of a coming death.

bantam n small breed of chicken. **bantamweight** n boxer weighing up to 118lb (professional) or 54kg (amateur).

banter v **1** tease jokingly. ♦ n **2** teasing or joking conversation.

Bantu n **1** group of languages of Africa. **2** Offens Black speaker of a Bantu language.

baobab [**bay**-oh-bab] n African tree with a thick trunk and angular branches.

baptism n Christian religious ceremony in which a person is immersed in or sprinkled with water as a sign of being cleansed from sin and accepted into the Church. **baptismal** adj **baptize** v perform baptism on.

Baptist n member of a Protestant denomination that believes in adult baptism by immersion.

bar[1] n **1** rigid length of metal, wood, etc. **2** solid, usu. rectangular block, of any material. **3** anything that obstructs or prevents. **4** counter or room where drinks are served. **5** heating element in

an electric fire. **6** Music group of beats repeated throughout a piece of music. ♦ v barring, barred **7** secure with a bar. **8** obstruct. **9** ban or forbid. ♦ prep **10** (also barring) except for. **the Bar** barristers collectively. **barman, barmaid** n

bar[2] n unit of atmospheric pressure.

barb n **1** cutting remark. **2** point facing in the opposite direction to the main point of a fish-hook etc. **barbed** adj **barbed wire** strong wire with protruding sharp points.

barbarian n member of a primitive or uncivilized people. **barbaric** adj cruel or brutal. **barbarism** n condition of being backward or ignorant. **barbarity** n **1** state of being barbaric or barbarous. **2** pl -ties) vicious act. **barbarous** adj **1** uncivilized. **2** brutal or cruel.

barbecue n **1** grill on which food is cooked over hot charcoal, usu. outdoors. **2** outdoor party at which barbecued food is served. ♦ v **3** cook (food) on a barbecue.

barber n person who cuts men's hair and shaves beards.

barbiturate n drug used as a sedative.

bar code n arrangement of numbers and parallel lines on a package, which can be electronically scanned at a checkout to give the price of the goods.

bard n Lit poet.

bare adj **1** unclothed, naked. **2** without the natural or usual covering. **3** unembellished, simple. **4** just sufficient. ♦ v **5** uncover. **barely** adv only just. **bareness** n

bareback adj, adv (of horse-riding) without a saddle.

barefaced adj shameless or obvious.

bargain n **1** agreement establishing what each party will give, receive, or perform in a transaction. **2** something bought or offered at a low price. ♦ v **3** negotiate the terms of an agreement. **bargain for** v anticipate or take into account.

barge n **1** flat-bottomed boat used to transport freight. ♦ v **2** Informal push violently. **barge in, into** v interrupt rudely.

barista [bar-**ee**-sta] n person who makes and sells coffee in a coffee bar.

baritone n (singer with) the second lowest adult male voice.

barium n Chem soft white metallic element.

bark[1] n **1** loud harsh cry of a dog. ♦ v **2** (of a dog) make its typical cry. **3** shout in an angry tone.

bark[2] n tough outer layer of a tree.

barley n tall grasslike plant cultivated for grain.

barmy adj -mier, -miest Slang insane.

barn n large building on a farm used for storing grain.

barnacle n shellfish that lives attached to rocks, ship bottoms, etc.

barney n Informal noisy fight or argument.

barometer n instrument for measuring atmospheric pressure. **barometric** adj

baron n **1** member of the lowest rank of nobility. **2** powerful businessman. **baroness** n **baronial** adj

baronet n commoner who holds the lowest hereditary British title.

baroque [bar-**rock**] n **1** highly ornate style of art, architecture, or music from the late 16th to the early 18th century. ♦ adj **2** ornate in style.

barque [**bark**] n sailing ship, esp. one with three masts.

barra n Aust informal short for BARRAMUNDI.

barrack v criticize loudly or shout against (a team or speaker).

barracks pl n building used to

accommodate military personnel.

barracouta n large Pacific fish with a protruding lower jaw and strong teeth.

barracuda n tropical sea fish.

barrage [**bar**-rahzh] n **1** continuous delivery of questions, complaints, etc. **2** continuous artillery fire. **3** artificial barrier across a river to control the water level.

barramundi n edible Australian fish.

barrel n **1** cylindrical container with rounded sides and flat ends. **2** tube in a firearm through which the bullet is fired. **barrel organ** musical instrument played by turning a handle.

barren adj **1** (of a woman or female animal) incapable of producing offspring. **2** (of land) unable to support the growth of crops, fruit, etc. **barrenness** n

barricade n **1** barrier, esp. one erected hastily for defence. ♦ v **2** erect a barricade across (an entrance).

barrier n anything that prevents access, progress, or union.

barrister n Brit, Aust & NZ lawyer qualified to plead in a higher court.

barrow[1] n **1** wheelbarrow. **2** movable stall used by street traders.

barrow[2] n mound of earth over a prehistoric tomb.

barter v **1** trade (goods) in exchange for other goods. ♦ n **2** trade by the exchange of goods.

basalt [**bass**-awlt] n dark volcanic rock. **basaltic** adj

base[1] n **1** bottom or supporting part of anything. **2** fundamental part. **3** centre of operations, organization, or supply. **4** starting point. **5** v **6** (foll. by on or upon) use as a basis (for). **7** (foll. by at or in) to station or place. **baseless** adj

base[2] adj **1** dishonourable or immoral. **2** of inferior quality or value. **baseness** n

baseball n 1 team game in which runs are scored by hitting a ball with a bat then running round four bases. 2 ball used for this.

basement n partly or wholly underground storey of a building.

bash Informal ♦ v 1 hit violently or forcefully. ♦ n 2 heavy blow. 3 party.

bashful adj shy or modest. **bashfully** adv **bashfulness** n

basic adj 1 of or forming a base or basis. 2 elementary or simple. **basics** pl n fundamental principles, facts, etc. **basically** adv

BASIC n computer programming language that uses common English words.

basil n aromatic herb used in cooking.

basilica n rectangular church with a rounded end and two aisles.

basilisk n legendary serpent said to kill by its breath or glance.

basin n 1 round open container. 2 sink for washing the hands and face. 3 sheltered area of water where boats may be moored. 4 catchment area of a particular river.

basis n, pl -ses fundamental principles etc. from which something is started or developed.

bask v lie in or be exposed to something, esp. pleasant warmth.

basket n container made of interwoven strips of wood or cane. **basketwork** n

basketball n 1 team game in which points are scored by throwing the ball through a high horizontal hoop. 2 ball used for this.

Basque n, adj (member or language) of a people living in the W Pyrenees in France and Spain.

bas-relief n sculpture in which the figures project slightly from the background.

bass[1] [base] n 1 (singer with) the lowest adult male voice. 2 adj 3 of the lowest range of musical notes.

bass[2] n edible sea fish.

basset hound n smooth-haired dog with short legs and long ears.

bassoon n low-pitched woodwind instrument.

bastard n 1 Offens obnoxious or despicable person. 2 person born of parents not married to each other.

baste[1] v moisten (meat) during cooking with hot fat.

baste[2] v sew with loose temporary stitches.

bastion n 1 projecting part of a fortification. 2 thing or person regarded as defending a principle.

bat[1] n 1 any of various types of club used to hit the ball in certain sports. ♦ v batting, batted 2 strike with or as if with a bat. **batsman** n Cricket person who bats or specializes in batting.

bat[2] n nocturnal mouselike flying animal.

batch n group of people or things dealt with at the same time.

bated adj **with bated breath** in suspense or fear.

bath n 1 large container in which to wash the body. 2 act of washing in such a container. ♦ pl 3 public swimming pool. ♦ v 4 wash in a bath. **bathroom** n room with a bath, sink, and usu. a toilet.

Bath chair n wheelchair for an invalid.

bathe v 1 swim in open water for pleasure. 2 apply liquid to (the skin or a wound) in order to cleanse or soothe. 3 (foll. by in) fill (with), e.g. bathed in sunlight **bather** n

bathos [bay-thoss] n sudden ludicrous change in speech or writing from a serious subject to a trivial one.

batik [bat-**teek**] *n* **1** process of printing fabric using wax to cover areas not to be dyed. **2** fabric printed in this way.

batman *n* officer's servant in the armed forces.

baton *n* **1** thin stick used by the conductor of an orchestra. **2** short bar transferred in a relay race. **3** police officer's truncheon.

battalion *n* army unit consisting of three or more companies.

batten *n* strip of wood fixed to something, esp. to hold it in place. **batten down** *v* secure with battens.

batter¹ *v* hit repeatedly. **battering ram** large beam used to break down fortifications.

batter² *n* mixture of flour, eggs, and milk, used in cooking.

battery *n, pl* -**teries 1** device that produces electricity in a torch, radio, etc. **2** group of heavy guns operating as a single unit. ♦ *adj* **3** kept in series of cages for intensive rearing.

battle *n* **1** fight between large armed forces. **2** conflict or struggle. ♦ *v* **3** struggle.

battle-axe *n* **1** *Informal* domineering woman. **2** (formerly) large heavy axe.

battlement *n* wall with gaps along the top for firing through.

battleship *n* large heavily armoured warship.

batty *adj* -**tier, -tiest** *Slang* eccentric or crazy.

bauble *n* trinket of little value.

bauera *n* small evergreen Australian shrub.

baulk *v* same as BALK.

bauxite *n* claylike substance that is the chief source of aluminium.

bawdy *adj* **bawdier, bawdiest** (of writing etc.) containing humorous references to sex.

bawl *v* shout or weep noisily.

bay¹ *n* stretch of coastline that curves inwards.

bay² *n* **1** recess in a wall. **2** area set aside for a particular purpose, e.g. *loading bay.*

bay³ *v* **1** howl in deep prolonged tones.

bay⁴ *n* Mediterranean laurel tree. **bay leaf** its dried leaf, used in cooking.

bay⁵ *adj, n* reddish-brown (horse).

bayonet *n* **1** sharp blade that can be fixed to the end of a rifle. ♦ *v* -**neting, -neted 2** stab with a bayonet.

bazaar *n* **1** sale in aid of charity. **2** market area, esp. in Eastern countries.

bazooka *n* portable rocket launcher that fires an armour-piercing projectile.

BBC British Broadcasting Corporation.

BC before Christ.

BCG antituberculosis vaccine.

be *v, present sing 1st person* **am.** *2nd person* **are.** *3rd person* **is.** *present pl* **are.** *past sing 1st person* **was.** *2nd person* **were.** *3rd person* **was.** *past pl* **were.** *present participle* **being.** *past participle* **been 1** exist or live. **2** used as a linking between the subject of a sentence and its complement, e.g. *John is a musician.* **3** forms the progressive present tense, e.g. *the man is running.* **4** forms the passive voice of all transitive verbs, e.g. *a good film is being shown on television tonight.*

beach *n* **1** area of sand or pebbles on a shore. ♦ *v* **2** run or haul (a boat) onto a beach. **beachhead** *n* beach captured by an attacking army on which troops can be landed.

beacon *n* fire or light on a hill or tower, used as a warning.

bead *n* **1** small piece of plastic, wood, etc., pierced for threading on a string to form a necklace etc. **2** small drop of moisture. **beaded** *adj* **beading** *n* strip of moulding used for edging furniture. **beady** *adj* small, round, and glittering, e.g. *beady eyes*.

beagle *n* small hound with short legs and drooping ears.

beak¹ *n* **1** projecting horny jaws of a bird. **2** *Slang* nose. **beaky** *adj*

beak² *n Brit, Aust & NZ slang* judge, magistrate, or headmaster.

beaker *n* **1** large drinking cup. **2** lipped glass container used in laboratories.

beam *n* **1** broad smile. **2** ray of light. **3** narrow flow of electromagnetic radiation or particles. **4** long thick piece of wood, metal, etc., used in building. **5** *v* **6** smile broadly. **7** divert or aim (a radio signal, light, etc.) in a certain direction.

bean *n* seed or pod of various plants, eaten as a vegetable or used to make coffee etc.

beanie *n* close-fitting woollen hat.

bear¹ *v* **bearing, bore, borne 1** support or hold up. **2** bring, e.g. *to bear gifts*. **3** *passive* **born**) give birth to. **4** tolerate or endure. **5** hold in the mind. **bearable** *adj* **bear out** *v* show to be truthful.

bear² *n* large heavy mammal with a shaggy coat. **bearskin** *n* tall fur helmet worn by some British soldiers.

beard *n* hair growing on the lower parts of a man's face. **bearded** *adj*

bearer *n* person who carries, presents, or upholds something.

bearing *n* **1** relevance (to). **2** person's general social conduct. **3** part of a machine that supports another part, esp. one that reduces friction. ◆ *pl* **4** sense of one's own relative position.

beast *n* **1** large wild animal. **2** brutal or uncivilized person. **beastly** *adj* unpleasant or disagreeable.

beat *v* **beating, beat, beaten** *or* **beat 1** hit hard and repeatedly. **2** move (wings) up and down. **3** throb rhythmically. **4** stir or mix vigorously. **5** overcome or defeat. **6** *n* **7** regular

throb. **8** assigned route, as of a policeman. **9** basic rhythmic unit in a piece of music. **beat up** *v* injure (someone) by repeated blows or kicks.

beatify [bee-**at**-if-fie] *v* **-fying, -fied** *RC Church* declare (a dead person) to be among the blessed in heaven: the first step towards canonization. **beatific** *adj* displaying great happiness. **beatification** *n* **beatitude** *n* *Christianity* any of the blessings on the poor, meek, etc., in the Sermon on the Mount.

beau [**boh**] *n, pl* **beaux, beaus 1** boyfriend or admirer. **2** man greatly concerned with his appearance.

Beaufort scale *n* scale for measuring wind speeds.

beautician *n* person who gives beauty treatments professionally.

beautiful *adj* **1** very attractive to look at. **2** very pleasant. **beautifully** *adv*

beautify *v* **-fying, -fied** make beautiful. **beautification** *n*

beauty *n, pl* **-ties 1** combination of all the qualities of a person or thing that delight the senses and mind. **2** very attractive woman. **3** *Informal* something outstanding of its kind.

beaver *n* amphibious rodent with a big flat tail. **beaver away** *v* work industriously.

becalmed *adj* (of a sailing ship) motionless through lack of wind.

became *v* past tense of BECOME.

because *conj* on account of the fact that. **because of** on account of.

beck¹ *n* **at someone's beck and call** having to be constantly available to do as someone asks.

beck² *n N English* stream.

beckon *v* summon with a gesture.

become *v* **-coming, -came, -come 1** come to be. **2** (foll. by *of*) happen to. **3** suit. **becoming** *adj* **1** attractive or pleasing. **2** appropriate or proper.

bed n **1** piece of furniture on which to sleep. **2** garden plot. **3** bottom of a river, lake, or sea. **4** layer of rock. **go to bed with** have sexual intercourse with. **bed down** v go to or put into a place to sleep or rest. **bedpan** n shallow bowl used as a toilet by bedridden people. **bedridden** adj confined to bed because of illness or old age. **bedrock** n **1** solid rock beneath the surface soil. **2** basic facts or principles. **bedroom** n **bedsit, bedsitter** n furnished sitting room with a bed.

bedding n sheets and covers that are used on a bed.

bedevil v **-illing, -illed** harass, confuse, or torment.

bedlam n noisy confused situation.

bedraggled adj untidy, wet, or dirty.

bee n insect that makes wax and honey. **beehive** n structure in which bees live. **beeswax** n wax secreted by bees, used in polishes etc.

beech n tree with a smooth greyish bark.

beef n flesh of a cow, bull, or ox. **beefy** adj **1** like beef. **2** Informal strong and muscular. **beefburger** n flat grilled or fried cake of minced beef. **beefeater** n yeoman warder at the Tower of London.

been v past participle of BE.

beep n **1** high-pitched sound, like that of a car horn. ♦ v **2** (cause to) make this noise.

beer n alcoholic drink brewed from malt and hops. **beery** adj

beet n plant with an edible root and leaves. **beetroot** n type of beet plant with a dark red root.

beetle n insect with a hard wing cover on its back.

befall v Old-fashioned happen to (someone).

befit v be appropriate or suitable for. **befitting** adj

before conj, prep, adv indicating something earlier in time, in front of, or preferred to, e.g. before the war; brought before a judge; death before dishonour. **beforehand** adv in advance.

befriend v become friends with.

beg v **begging, begged 1** solicit (for money or food), esp. in the street. **2** ask formally or humbly.

began v past tense of BEGIN.

beget v **-getting, -got** or **-gat, -gotten** or **-got** Old-fashioned **1** cause or create. **2** father.

beggar n person who lives by begging **beggarly** adj

begin v **-ginning, -gan, -gun 1** start. **2** bring or come into being. **beginner** n person who has just started learning to do something. **beginning** n

begonia n tropical plant with waxy flowers.

begrudge v **1** envy (someone) the possession of something. **2** give or allow unwillingly.

beguile [big-**gile**] v **1** cheat or mislead. **2** charm or amuse. **beguiling** adj

begun v past participle of BEGIN.

behalf n **on behalf of** in the interest of or for the benefit of.

behave v **1** act or function in a particular way. **2** conduct (oneself) properly.

behaviour n manner of behaving.

behead v remove the head from.

beheld v past of BEHOLD.

behest n order or earnest request.

behind prep, adv **1** indicating position to the rear, lateness, responsibility, etc., e.g. behind the wall; behind schedule; the reasons behind her departure. ♦ n **2** Informal buttocks.

behold v **-holding, -held**

Old-fashioned look (at). **beholder** n

beholden adj indebted or obliged.

behove v *Old-fashioned* be necessary or fitting for.

beige adj pale brown.

being n **1** state or fact of existing. **2** something that exists or is thought to exist. **3** human being. ♦ v **4** present participle of BE.

belabour v attack verbally or physically.

belated adj late or too late. **belatedly** adv

belch v **1** expel wind from the stomach noisily through the mouth. **2** expel or be expelled forcefully, e.g. *smoke belched from the factory.* ♦ n **3** act of belching.

beleaguered adj **1** struggling against difficulties or criticism. **2** besieged by an enemy.

belfry n, pl **-fries** part of a tower where bells are hung.

belgium sausage n NZ large smooth bland sausage.

belie v show to be untrue.

belief n **1** faith or confidence. **2** opinion. **3** principle accepted as true, often without proof.

believe v **1** accept as true or real. **2** think, assume, or suppose. **believable** adj **believer** n **believe in** be convinced of the truth or existence of.

Belisha beacon [bill-**lee**-sha] n *Brit* flashing orange globe mounted on a post, marking a pedestrian crossing.

belittle v treat as having little value or importance.

bell n **1** hollow, usu. metal, cup-shaped instrument that emits a ringing sound when struck. **2** device that rings or buzzes as a signal.

belladonna n (drug obtained from) deadly nightshade.

bellbird n Australasian bird with bell-like call.

belle n beautiful woman, esp. the most attractive woman at a function.

bellicose adj warlike and aggressive.

belligerent adj **1** hostile and aggressive. **2** engaged in war. ♦ n **3** person or country engaged in war. **belligerence** n

bellow v **1** make a low deep cry like that of a bull. **2** shout in anger. ♦ n **3** loud deep roar.

bellows pl n instrument for pumping a stream of air into something.

belly n, pl **-lies 1** part of the body of a vertebrate which contains the intestines. **2** stomach. **3** front, lower, or inner part of something. ♦ v **-lying, -lied 4** (cause to) swell out. **bellyful** n *Slang* more than one can tolerate.

belong v **1** (foll. by *to*) be the property of. **2** (foll. by *to*) be a part or member of. **belongings** pl n personal possessions.

beloved adj **1** dearly loved. ♦ n **2** person dearly loved.

below prep, adv at or to a position lower than, under.

belt n **1** band of cloth, leather, etc., worn usu. around the waist. **2** long narrow area, e.g. *a belt of trees.* **3** circular strip of rubber that drives moving parts in a machine. ♦ v **4** fasten with a belt. **5** *Slang* hit very hard. **6** *Slang* move very fast.

bemoan v express sorrow or dissatisfaction about.

bemused adj puzzled or confused.

bench n **1** long seat. **2** long narrow work table. **the bench** judge or magistrate sitting in court, or judges and magistrates collectively. **benchmark** n criterion by which to measure something.

bend v **bending, bent 1** (cause to) form a curve. **2** (often foll. by *down*) etc. incline the body. **3** n **4** curved part. ♦ *pl* **5** *Informal* decompression sickness. **bendy** *adj*

beneath *adv, prep* **1** below. **2** not worthy of.

Benedictine *adj* of an order of Christian monks and nuns founded by Saint Benedict.

benediction *n* prayer for divine blessing.

benefactor, benefactress *n* someone who supports a person or institution by giving money. **benefaction** *n*

beneficent [bin-**eff**-iss-ent] *adj* charitable or generous. **beneficence** *n*

beneficial *adj* helpful or advantageous.

beneficiary *n, pl* **-ciaries** person who gains or benefits.

benefit *n* **1** something that improves or promotes. **2** advantage or sake, e.g. *I'm doing this for your benefit.* **3** payment made by a government to a poor, ill, or unemployed person. **4** *v* **-fiting, -fited 5** do or receive good.

benevolence *n* **1** inclination to do good. **2** act of kindness. **benevolent** *adj* **benevolently** *adv*

benighted *adj* ignorant or uncultured.

benign [bin-**nine**] *adj* **1** showing kindliness. **2** (of a tumour) not threatening to life. **benignly** *adv*

bent *v* **1** past of BEND. ♦ *adj* **2** curved. **3** *Slang* dishonest or corrupt. **4** *Brit & Aust offens slang* homosexual. ♦ *n* **5** personal inclination or aptitude. **bent on** determined to pursue (a course of action).

bento, bento box *n* thin lightweight box divided into compartments, which contain small separate dishes comprising a Japanese meal.

benzene *n* flammable poisonous liquid used as a solvent, insecticide, etc.

bequeath *v* dispose of (property) as in a will. **bequest** *n* legal gift of money

or property by someone who has died.

berate *v* scold harshly.

bereaved *adj* having recently lost a close friend or relative through death. **bereavement** *n*

bereft *adj* (foll. by *of*) deprived.

beret [**ber**-ray] *n* round flat close-fitting brimless cap.

berg¹ *n* iceberg.

berg² *n S Afr* mountain.

bergamot *n* small Asian tree, the fruit of which yields an oil used in perfumery.

beri-beri *n* disease caused by vitamin B deficiency.

berk *n Brit, Aust & NZ slang* stupid person.

berm *n NZ* narrow grass strip between the road and the footpath in a residential area.

berry *n, pl* **-ries** small soft stoneless fruit.

berserk *adj* **go berserk** become violent or destructive.

berth *n* **1** bunk in a ship or train. **2** place assigned to a ship at a mooring. ♦ *v* **3** dock (a ship).

beryl *n* hard transparent mineral.

beryllium *n Chem* toxic silvery-white metallic element.

beseech *v* **-seeching, -sought** *or* **-seeched** ask earnestly; beg.

beset *v* trouble or harass constantly.

beside *prep* **1** at, by, or to the side of. **2** as compared with. **beside oneself** overwhelmed or overwrought. **besides** *adv, prep* in addition.

besiege *v* **1** surround with military forces. **2** overwhelm, as with requests.

besotted *adj* infatuated.

besought *v* a past of BESEECH.

bespeak *v* indicate or suggest. **bespoke** *adj* (esp. of a suit) made to the customer's specifications.

best *adj* **1** most excellent of a particular

group etc. ♦ *adv* **2** in a manner surpassing all others. ♦ *n* **3** most outstanding or excellent person, thing, or group in a category. **best man** groom's attendant at a wedding. **bestseller** *n* book or other product that has sold in great numbers.

bestial *adj* **1** brutal or savage. **2** of or like a beast. **bestiality** *n*

bestir *v* cause (oneself) to become active.

bestow *v* present (a gift) or confer (an honour). **bestowal** *n*

bestride *v* have or put a leg on either side of.

bet *n* **1** the act of staking a sum of money or other stake on the outcome of an event. **2** stake risked. **3** *v* **betting, bet** *or* **betted 4** make or place (a bet). **5** *Informal* predict.

betel [**bee**-tl] *n* Asian climbing plant, the leaves and nuts of which can be chewed.

bête noire [bet **nwahr**] *n, pl* **bêtes noires** person or thing that one particularly dislikes.

betide *v* happen (to).

betoken *v* indicate or signify.

betray *v* **1** hand over or expose (one's nation, friend, etc.) treacherously to an enemy. **2** disclose (a secret or confidence) treacherously. **3** reveal unintentionally. **betrayal** *n* **betrayer** *n*

betrothed *adj* engaged to be married. **betrothal** *n*

better *adj* **1** more excellent than others. **2** improved or fully recovered in health. ♦ *adv* **3** in a more excellent manner. **4** in or to a greater degree. ♦ *pl n* **5** one's superiors. ♦ *v* **6** improve upon.

bettong *n* short-nosed rat kangaroo.

between *prep, adv* indicating position in the middle, alternatives, etc.

betwixt *prep, adv Old-fashioned* between.

bevel *n* **1** slanting edge. ♦ *v* **-elling, -elled 2** cut a bevel on (a piece of timber etc.).

beverage *n* drink.

bevy *n, pl* **bevies** flock or group.

bewail *v* express great sorrow over.

beware *v* be on one's guard (against).

bewilder *v* confuse utterly. **bewildering** *adj* **bewilderment** *n*

bewitch *v* **1** attract and fascinate. **2** cast a spell over. **bewitching** *adj*

beyond *prep* **1** at or to a point on the other side of. **2** outside the limits or scope of. ♦ *adv* **3** at or to the far side of something.

bi- *combining form* two or twice, e.g. *bifocal; biweekly.*

biannual *adj* occurring twice a year. **biannually** *adv*

bias *n* **1** mental tendency, esp. prejudice. **2** diagonal cut across the weave of a fabric. **3** *Bowls* bulge or weight on one side of a bowl that causes it to roll in a curve. ♦ *v* **-asing, -ased** *or* **-assing, -assed 4** cause to have a bias. **biased, biassed** *adj*

bib *n* **1** piece of cloth or plastic worn to protect a young child's clothes when eating. **2** upper front part of dungarees etc.

Bible *n* **1** sacred writings of the Christian religion. **2** (b-) book regarded as authoritative. **biblical** *adj*

bibliography *n, pl* **-phies 1** list of books on a subject. **2** list of sources used in a book etc. **bibliographer** *n*

bibliophile *n* person who collects or is fond of books.

bibulous *adj* addicted to alcohol.

bicarbonate *n* salt of carbonic acid. **bicarbonate of soda** powder used in baking or as medicine.

bicentenary 1 *n, pl* **-naries 2** 200th

anniversary.

biceps n muscle with two origins, esp. the muscle that flexes the forearm.

bicker v argue over petty matters.

bicycle n vehicle with two wheels, one behind the other, pedalled by the rider.

bid v bidding, bade, bidden 1 say (a greeting). 2 command. 3 past bid) offer (an amount) in an attempt to buy something. ♦ n 4 offer of a specified amount. 5 attempt. **bidder** n **biddable** adj obedient. **bidding** n command.

biddy-bid, biddy-biddy n, pl -bids, -biddies NZ low-growing plant with hooked burrs.

bide v bide one's time wait patiently for an opportunity.

bidet [bee-day] n low basin for washing the genital area.

biennial adj 1 occurring every two years. ♦ n 2 plant that completes its life cycle in two years.

bier n stand on which a corpse or coffin rests before burial.

bifocals pl n spectacles with lenses permitting near and distant vision.

big adj bigger, biggest 1 of considerable size, height, number, or capacity. 2 important through having power, wealth, etc. 3 elder. 4 generous. ♦ adv 5 on a grand scale. **bighead** n Informal conceited person. **big-headed** adj **big shot, bigwig** n Informal important person.

bigamy n crime of marrying a person while still legally married to someone else. **bigamist** n **bigamous** adj

bigot n person who is intolerant, esp. regarding religion or race. **bigoted** adj **bigotry** n

bijou [bee-zhoo] adj (of a house) small but elegant.

bike n Informal bicycle or motorcycle.

bikini n woman's brief two-piece

swimming costume.

bilateral adj affecting or undertaken by two parties.

bilberry n bluish-black edible berry.

bilby n, pl -bies Australian marsupial with long pointed ears and grey fur.

bile n bitter yellow fluid secreted by the liver.

bilge n 1 Informal nonsense. 2 ship's bottom.

bilingual adj involving or using two languages.

bilious adj sick, nauseous.

bill¹ n 1 statement of money owed for goods or services supplied. 2 draft of a proposed new law. 3 poster. 4 Chiefly US & Canadian piece of paper money. 5 list of events, such as a theatre programme. ♦ v 6 send or present a bill to. 7 advertise by posters.

bill² n bird's beak.

billabong n Aust stagnant pool in an intermittent stream.

billet v -leting, -leted 1 assign a lodging to (a soldier). ♦ n 2 accommodation for a soldier in civil lodgings.

billet-doux [bill-ee-doo] n, pl **billets-doux** love letter.

billhook n tool with a hooked blade, used for chopping etc.

billiards n game played on a table with balls and a cue.

billion n 1 one thousand million. 2 formerly, one million million. **billionth** adj

billow n 1 large sea wave. 2 v 3 rise up or swell out. **billowy, billowing** adj

billy, billycan n, pl -lies, -lycans metal can or pot for cooking on a camp fire.

biltong n S Afr strips of dried meat.

bimbo n Slang attractive but empty-headed young person, esp. a woman.

bin *n* container for rubbish or for storing grain, coal, etc.

binary *adj* **1** composed of two parts. **2** *Maths, computers* of or in a counting system with only two digits, 0 and 1.

bind *v* **binding, bound 1** make secure with or as if with a rope. **2** place (someone) under obligation. **3** enclose and fasten (the pages of a book) between covers. ♦ *n* **4** *Informal* annoying situation. **binder** *n* firm cover for holding loose sheets of paper together. **binding** *n* **1** anything that binds or fastens. **2** book cover.

bindi-eye *n* small Australian plant with burlike fruit.

bindweed *n* plant that twines around a support.

binge *n* *Informal* bout of excessive indulgence, esp. in drink.

bingo *n* gambling game in which numbers are called out and covered by the players on their individual cards.

binoculars *pl n* optical instrument consisting of two small telescopes joined together.

binomial *n, adj* (mathematical expression) consisting of two terms.

bio- *combining form* life or living organisms, e.g. *biology*.

biochemistry *n* study of the chemistry of living things. **biochemist** *n*

biodegradable *adj* capable of being decomposed by natural means.

biodiversity *n* existence of a wide variety of species in their natural environment.

biographer *n* person who writes an account of another person's life.

biography *n, pl* **-phies** account of a person's life by another person. **biographical** *adj*

biological *adj* of or relating to biology.

biology *n* study of living organisms.

biologist *n*

bionic *adj* having a part of the body that is operated electronically.

biopsy *n, pl* **-sies** examination of tissue from a living body.

biotechnology *n* use of microorganisms, such as cells or bacteria, in industry and technology.

bioterrorism *n* use of viruses, bacteria, etc., by terrorists. **bioterrorist** *n*

biped [**bye**-ped] *n* animal with two feet.

biplane *n* aeroplane with two sets of wings, one above the other.

birch *n* **1** tree with thin peeling bark. **2** birch rod or twigs used, esp. formerly, for flogging offenders.

bird *n* **1** creature with feathers and wings, most types of which can fly. **2** *Slang* young woman.

birdie *n* *Golf* score of one stroke under par for a hole.

biretta *n* stiff square cap worn by the Catholic clergy.

Biro *n* ® ballpoint pen.

birth *n* **1** process of bearing young; childbirth. **2** act of being born. **3** ancestry. **give birth to** bear (offspring). **birth control** any method of contraception. **birthday** *n* anniversary of the day of one's birth. **birthmark** *n* blemish on the skin formed before birth. **birthright** *n* privileges or possessions that someone is entitled to as soon as he or she is born.

biscuit *n* small flat dry sweet or plain cake.

bisect *v* divide into two equal parts.

bisexual *adj* sexually attracted to both men and women. **bisexuality** *n*

bishop *n* **1** clergyman who governs a diocese. **2** chessman which is moved diagonally. **bishopric** *n* diocese or office of a bishop.

bismuth *n Chem* pinkish-white metallic element.

bison *n, pl* **-son** large hairy animal of the cattle family, native to N America and Europe.

bistro *n, pl* **-tros** small restaurant.

bit¹ *n* small piece, portion, or quantity. **a bit** rather, somewhat. **bit by bit** gradually.

bit² *n* **1** metal mouthpiece on a bridle. **2** cutting or drilling part of a tool.

bit³ *v* past tense of BITE.

bit⁴ *n Maths, computers* single digit of binary notation, either 0 or 1.

bitch *n* **1** female dog, fox, or wolf. **2** *Offens* spiteful woman. ♦ *v* **3** *Informal* complain or grumble. **bitchy** *adj* **bitchiness** *n*

bite *v* **biting, bit, bitten 1** grip, tear, or puncture the skin, as with the teeth or jaws. **2** take firm hold of or act effectively upon. **3** *n* **4** act of biting. **5** wound or sting inflicted by biting. **6** snack. **biter** *n* **biting** *adj* **1** piercing or keen. **2** sarcastic.

bitter *adj* **1** having a sharp unpleasant taste. **2** showing or caused by hostility or resentment. **3** extremely cold. ♦ *n* **4** beer with a slightly bitter taste. ♦ *pl* **5** bitter-tasting alcoholic drink. **bitterly** *adv* **bitterness** *n*

bittern *n* wading marsh bird with a booming call.

bitumen *n* black sticky substance obtained from tar or petrol.

bivalve *n, adj* (marine mollusc) with two hinged segments to its shell.

bivouac *n* **1** temporary camp in the open air. ♦ *v* **-acking, -acked 2** camp in a bivouac.

bizarre *adj* odd or unusual.

blab *v* **blabbing, blabbed** reveal (secrets) indiscreetly.

black *adj* **1** of the darkest colour, like coal. **2** (B-) dark-skinned. **3** without

hope. **4** angry or resentful, e.g. *black looks.* **5** unpleasant in a macabre manner, e.g. *black comedy.* **6** *n* **7** darkest colour. **8** (B-) member of a dark-skinned race. **9** complete darkness. ♦ *v* **10** make black. **11** (of trade unionists) boycott (goods or people). **blackness** *n* **blacken** *v* **1** make or become black. **2** defame or slander. **black magic** magic used for evil purposes. **black market** illegal trade in goods or currencies. **black sheep** person who is regarded as a disgrace by his or her family. **black spot** place on a road where accidents frequently occur.

blackball *v* **1** exclude from a group. ♦ *n* **2** *NZ* hard boiled sweet with black-and-white stripes.

blackberry *n* small blackish edible fruit.

blackbird *n* common European thrush.

blackboard *n* hard black surface used for writing on with chalk.

blackboy *n* Australian plant with grasslike leaves and a spike of small white flowers.

blackbutt *n* Australian eucalyptus tree with hard wood used as timber.

blackcurrant *n* very small blackish edible fruit that grows in bunches.

blackfish *n* small dark Australian estuary fish.

blackguard [**blag**-gard] *n* unprincipled person.

blackhead *n* black-tipped plug of fatty matter clogging a skin pore.

blackleg *n* person who continues to work during a strike.

blacklist *n* list of people or organizations considered untrustworthy etc.

blackmail *n* **1** act of attempting to extort money by threats. ♦ *v* **2** (attempt to) obtain money by blackmail.

blackout *n* **1** extinguishing of all light

as a precaution against an air attack. **2** momentary loss of consciousness or memory. **black out** v **1** extinguish (lights). **2** lose consciousness or memory temporarily.

blacksmith n person who works iron with a furnace, anvil, etc.

black snake n venomous Australian snake.

black swan n black Australian swan with a red beak.

bladder n **1** sac in the body where urine is held. **2** hollow bag which may be filled with air or liquid.

blade n **1** cutting edge of a weapon or tool. **2** thin flattish part of a propeller, oar, etc. **3** leaf of grass.

blame v **1** consider (someone) responsible for. **2** n **3** responsibility for something that is wrong. **blameless** adj **blameworthy** adj deserving blame.

blanch v **1** become white or pale. **2** prepare (vegetables etc.) by plunging them in boiling water.

blancmange [blam-**monzh**] n jelly-like dessert made with milk.

bland adj dull and uninteresting. **blandly** adv

blandishments pl n flattery intended to coax or persuade.

blank adj **1** not written on. **2** showing no interest or expression. **3** n **4** empty space. **5** cartridge containing no bullet. **blankly** adv **blank verse** unrhymed verse.

blanket n **1** large thick cloth used as covering for a bed. **2** concealing cover, as of snow. **3** v **4** cover as with a blanket.

blare v **1** sound loudly and harshly. ♦ n **2** loud harsh noise.

blarney n flattering talk.

blasé [**blah**-zay] adj indifferent or bored through familiarity.

blaspheme v speak disrespectfully of (God or sacred things). **blasphemy** n **blasphemous** adj **blasphemer** n

blast n **1** explosion. **2** sudden strong gust of air or wind. **3** sudden loud sound, as of a trumpet. **4** v **5** blow up (a rock etc.) with explosives. **blastoff** n launching of a rocket.

blatant adj glaringly obvious. **blatantly** adv

blaze¹ n **1** strong fire or flame. **2** very bright light. **3** v **4** burn or shine brightly.

blaze² n mark made on a tree to indicate a route.

blazer n lightweight jacket, often in the colours of a school etc.

blazon v proclaim publicly.

bleach v **1** make or become white or colourless. ♦ n **2** bleaching agent.

bleak adj **1** exposed and barren. **2** offering little hope.

bleary adj **-rier, -riest** with eyes dimmed, as by tears or tiredness. **blearily** adv

bleat v **1** (of a sheep, goat, or calf) utter its plaintive cry. **2** n **3** cry of sheep, goats, and calves.

bleed v **bleeding, bled 1** lose or emit blood. **2** draw blood from (a person or animal). **3** Informal obtain money by extortion.

bleep n **1** short high-pitched sound made by an electrical device. ♦ v **2** make a bleeping sound. **bleeper** n small portable radio receiver that makes a bleeping signal.

blemish n **1** defect or stain. ♦ v **2** spoil or tarnish.

blench v shy away, as in fear.

blend v **1** mix or mingle (components or ingredients). **2** look good together. ♦ n **3** mixture. **blender** n electrical appliance for puréeing vegetables etc.

bless v **1** make holy by means of a

religious rite. **2** call upon God to protect. **3** endow with health, talent, etc. **blessed** *adj* holy. **blessing** *n* **1** invoking of divine aid. **2** approval. **3** happy event.

blether *Scot* ◆ *v* **1** talk, esp. foolishly or at length. ◆ *n* **2** conversation.

blew *v* past tense of BLOW¹.

blight *n* **1** person or thing that spoils or prevents growth. **2** withering plant disease. ◆ *v* **3** frustrate or disappoint.

blighter *n Informal* irritating person.

blimp *n* small airship.

blind *adj* **1** unable to see. **2** unable or unwilling to understand. **3** not determined by reason, e.g. *blind hatred.* ◆ *v* **4** deprive of sight. **5** deprive of good sense, reason, or judgment. ◆ *n* **6** covering for a window. **7** something that serves to conceal the truth. **blindly** *adv* **blindness** *n*

blindfold *v* **1** prevent (a person) from seeing by covering the eyes. ◆ *n* **2** piece of cloth used to cover the eyes.

blink *v* **1** close and immediately reopen (the eyes). **2** shine intermittently. ◆ *n* **3** act of blinking. **on the blink** *Slang* not working properly.

blinkers *pl n* leather flaps on a horse's bridle to prevent sideways vision.

blip *n* spot of light on a radar screen indicating the position of an object.

bliss *n* perfect happiness. **blissful** *adj* **blissfully** *adv*

blister *n* **1** small bubble on the skin. **2** swelling, as on a painted surface. ◆ *v* **3** (cause to) have blisters. **blistering** *adj* **1** (of weather) very hot. **2** (of criticism) extremely harsh.

blithe *adj* casual and indifferent. **blithely** *adv*

blitz *n* **1** violent and sustained attack by aircraft. **2** intensive attack or concerted effort. ◆ *v* **3** attack suddenly and intensively.

blizzard *n* blinding storm of wind and snow.

bloat *v* cause to swell, as with liquid or air.

bloater *n Brit* salted smoked herring.

blob *n* **1** soft mass or drop. **2** indistinct or shapeless form.

bloc *n* people or countries combined by a common interest.

block *n* **1** large solid piece of wood, stone, etc. **2** large building of offices, flats, etc. **3** group of buildings enclosed by intersecting streets. **4** obstruction or hindrance. **5** *Slang* person's head. ◆ *v* **6** obstruct or impede by introducing an obstacle. **blockage** *n* **blockhead** *n* stupid person. **block letter** plain capital letter.

blockade *n* **1** sealing off of a place to prevent the passage of goods. ◆ *v* **2** impose a blockade on.

blockie *n Aust* owner of a small property, esp. a farm.

blog *n* short for WEBLOG.

bloke *n Informal* man.

blonde, (*masc*) **blond** *adj, n* fair-haired (person).

blood *n* **1** red fluid that flows around the body. **2** race or kinship. **in cold blood** done deliberately. **bloodless** *adj* **blood bath** massacre. **bloodhound** *n* large dog formerly used for tracking. **bloodshed** *n* slaughter or killing. **bloodshot** *adj* (of an eye) inflamed. **blood sport** sport involving the killing of animals. **bloodstream** *n* flow of blood round the body. **bloodsucker** *n* **1** animal that sucks blood. **2** *Informal* person who extorts money from other people. **bloodthirsty** *adj* taking pleasure in violence.

bloody *adj* **1** covered with blood. **2** marked by much killing. ◆ *adj, adv* *Slang* extreme or extremely. ◆ *v* **4** stain with blood. **bloody-minded** adj deliberately unhelpful.

bloom n 1 blossom on a flowering plant. 2 youthful or healthy glow. 3 v 4 bear flowers. 5 be in a healthy, glowing condition.

bloomer n Brit informal stupid mistake.

bloomers pl n woman's baggy knickers.

blooper n Chiefly US informal stupid mistake.

blossom n 1 flowers of a plant. ♦ v 2 (of plants) flower. 3 come to a promising stage.

blot n 1 spot or stain. 2 something that spoils. ♦ v **blotting, blotted** 3 cause a blemish in or on. 4 soak up (ink) by using blotting paper. **blotter** n **blot out** v darken or hide completely. **blotting paper** soft absorbent paper for soaking up ink.

blotch n discoloured area or stain. **blotchy** adj

blotto adj Brit, Aust & NZ slang extremely drunk.

blouse n woman's shirtlike garment.

blow[1] v **blowing, blew, blown** 1 (of air, the wind, etc.) move. 2 move or be carried as if by the wind. 3 expel (air etc.) through the mouth or nose. 4 cause (a musical instrument) to sound by forcing air into it. 5 burn out (a fuse etc.). 6 Slang spend (money) freely. **blower** n **blowy** adj windy. **blow-dry** v style (the hair) with a hand-held dryer. **blowout** n 1 sudden loss of air in a tyre. 2 escape of oil or gas from a well. 3 Slang filling meal. **blow up** v 1 explode. 2 fill with air. 3 Informal lose one's temper. 4 Informal enlarge (a photograph).

blow[2] n 1 hard hit. 2 sudden setback. 3 attacking action.

blowie n Aust informal bluebottle.

blown v past participle of BLOW[1].

blowsy adj fat, untidy, and red-faced.

blubber n 1 fat of whales, seals, etc. ♦ v 2 sob without restraint.

bludge Informal ♦ v 1 Aust & NZ evade work. 2 Aust & NZ scrounge. ♦ n 3 Aust easy task. **bludger** n person who scrounges.

bludgeon n 1 short thick club. ♦ v 2 hit with a bludgeon. 3 force or bully.

blue n 1 colour of a clear unclouded sky. 2 pl 3 feeling of depression. 4 type of folk music of Black American origin. ♦ adj **bluer, bluest** 5 of the colour blue. 6 depressed. 7 pornographic. **out of the blue** unexpectedly. **bluish** adj **bluebell** n flower with blue bell-shaped flowers. **bluebottle** n large fly with a dark-blue body. **blue-collar** adj denoting manual industrial workers. **blue heeler** Aust & NZ informal dog that controls cattle by biting their heels. **blueprint** n 1 photographic print of a plan. 2 description of how a plan is expected to work. **bluetongue** n Australian lizard with a blue tongue.

bluff[1] v 1 pretend to be confident in order to influence (someone). ♦ n 2 act of bluffing.

bluff[2] n 1 steep cliff or bank. ♦ adj 2 good-naturedly frank and hearty.

blunder n 1 clumsy mistake. ♦ v 2 make a blunder. 3 act clumsily.

blunderbuss n obsolete gun with a wide flared muzzle.

blunt adj 1 not having a sharp edge or point. 2 (of people, speech, etc.) straightforward or uncomplicated. ♦ v 3 make less sharp. **bluntly** adv

blur v **blurring, blurred** 1 make or become vague or less distinct. 2 n 3 something vague, hazy, or indistinct. **blurry** adj

blurb n promotional description, as on the jacket of a book.

blurt v (foll. by out) utter suddenly and involuntarily.

blush v **1** become red in the face, esp. from embarrassment or shame. ♦ n **2** reddening of the face.

bluster v **1** speak loudly or in a bullying way. ♦ n **2** empty threats or protests. **blustery** adj (of weather) rough and windy.

BMA British Medical Association.

BO Informal body odour.

boa n **1** large nonvenomous snake. **2** long scarf of fur or feathers. **boa constrictor** large snake that kills its prey by crushing.

boab [**boh**-ab] n Aust informal **short for** BAOBAB.

boar n **1** uncastrated male pig. **2** wild pig.

board n **1** long flat piece of sawn timber. **2** smaller flat piece of rigid material for a specific purpose, e.g. ironing board; chess board. **3** group of people who administer a company, trust, etc. **4** meals provided for money. **5** v **6** go aboard (a train, aeroplane, etc.). **7** cover with boards. **8** receive meals and lodgings in return for money. **on board** on or in a ship, aeroplane, etc. **boarder** n **1** person who pays rent in return for accommodation in someone else's home. **2** Brit pupil who lives at school during the school term. **boarding house** private house that provides meals and accommodation for paying guests. **boardroom** n room where the board of a company meets.

boast v **1** speak too proudly about one's talents etc. **2** possess (something to be proud of). ♦ n **3** bragging statement. **boastful** adj

boat n small vehicle for travelling across water. **boater** n flat straw hat. **boating** n

boatswain n same as BOSUN.

bob[1] v **bobbing, bobbed 1** move up and down repeatedly. ♦ n **2** short

abrupt movement.

bob[2] n **1** hairstyle in which the hair is cut short evenly all round the head. **2** v **bobbing, bobbed 3** cut (the hair) in a bob.

bobbin n reel on which thread is wound.

bobble n small ball of material, usu. for decoration.

bobby n, pl **-bies** Brit informal policeman.

bobotie [ba-**boot**-ee] n S Afr dish of curried mince.

bobsleigh n **1** sledge for racing down an icy track. ♦ v **2** ride on a bobsleigh.

bode v be an omen of (good or ill).

bodice n upper part of a dress.

bodkin n blunt large-eyed needle.

body n, pl **bodies 1** entire physical structure of an animal or human. **2** trunk or torso. **3** corpse. **4** group regarded as a single entity. **5** main part of anything. **6** woman's one-piece undergarment. **bodily** adj **1** relating to the body. ♦ adv **2** by taking hold of the body. **body-board** n small polystyrene surfboard. **body-boarder** n **bodyguard** n person or group of people employed to protect someone. **bodywork** n outer shell of a motor vehicle.

Boer n descendant of the Dutch settlers in S Africa. **boerewors** n S Afr spiced sausage.

boffin n Brit, Austral, NZ & S Afr informal scientist or expert.

bog n **1** wet spongy ground. **2** Slang toilet. **boggy** adj **bog down** v **bogging, bogged** impede physically or mentally.

bogan n Aust dated & NZ slang youth who dresses and behaves rebelliously.

bogey, bogy n **1** something that worries or annoys. **2** Golf score of one stroke over par on a hole.

boggle v be surprised, confused, or alarmed.

bogong, bugong n large nocturnal Australian moth.

bogus adj not genuine.

bogy n, pl **-gies** same as BOGEY.

bohemian n, adj (person) leading an unconventional life.

boil[1] v **1** (cause to) change from a liquid to a vapour so quickly that bubbles are formed. **2** cook by the process of boiling. **3** n **4** state or action of boiling. **boiler** n piece of equipment which provides hot water.

boil[2] n red pus-filled swelling on the skin.

boisterous adj noisy and lively. **boisterously** adv

bold adj **1** confident and fearless. **2** immodest or impudent. **boldly** adv **boldness** n

bole n tree trunk.

bolero n, pl **-ros 1** (music for) traditional Spanish dance. **2** short open jacket.

bollard n short thick post used to prevent the passage of motor vehicles.

boloney n same as BALONEY.

Bolshevik n (formerly) Russian Communist. **bolshie, bolshy** adj Informal difficult or rebellious.

bolster v **1** support or strengthen. ♦ n **2** Slang long narrow pillow.

bolt n **1** sliding metal bar for fastening a door etc. **2** metal pin which screws into a nut. **3** flash (of lightning). **4** v **5** run away suddenly. **6** fasten with a bolt. **7** eat hurriedly. **bolt upright** stiff and rigid. **bolt hole** place of escape.

bomb n **1** container fitted with explosive material. **2** Slang large amount of money. ♦ v **3** attack with bombs. **4** move very quickly. **the bomb** nuclear bomb. **bomber** n **1** aircraft that drops bombs. **2** person

who throws or puts a bomb in a particular place. **bomb out** v Aust, NZ & S Afr informal fail disastrously. **bombshell** n shocking or unwelcome surprise.

bombard v **1** attack with heavy gunfire or bombs. **2** attack verbally, esp. with questions. **bombardment** n

bombast n pompous language. **bombastic** adj

bona fide [**bone**-a **fide**-ee] adj genuine.

bonanza n sudden good luck or wealth.

bond n **1** something that binds, fastens or holds together. **2** something that unites people. **3** written or spoken agreement. **4** Finance certificate of debt issued to raise funds. **5** S Afr conditional pledging of property, esp. a house, as security for the repayment of a loan. ♦ pl **6** something that restrains or imprisons. ♦ v **7** bind. **bonded** adj

bondage n slavery.

bone n **1** any of the hard parts in the body that form the skeleton. **2** v **3** remove the bones from (meat for cooking etc.). **boneless** adj **bony** adj **1** having many bones. **2** thin or emaciated. **bone-dry** adj completely dry. **bone-idle** adj extremely lazy.

bonfire n large outdoor fire.

bongo n, pl **-gos, -goes** small drum played with the fingers.

bonhomie [**bon**-om-ee] n cheerful friendliness.

bonito [ba-**nee**-toh] n, pl **-os** small tunny-like marine food fish related fish, whose flesh is dried and flaked and used in Japanese cookery.

bonk v Informal **1** have sex with. **2** hit.

bonnet n **1** metal cover over a vehicle's engine. **2** hat which ties under the chin.

bonny adj **-nier, -niest** Scot beautiful.

bonsai *n, pl* **-sai** ornamental miniature tree or shrub.

bonus *n* something given, paid, or received above what is due or expected.

boo *interj* **1** shout of disapproval. **2** *v* **booing, booed 3** shout 'boo' to show disapproval.

boob *Slang* ♦ *n* **1** foolish mistake. **2** female breast. **3** *Aust slang* prison.

boobook [**boo**-book] *n* small spotted Australian brown owl.

booby *n, pl* **-bies** foolish person. **booby prize** prize given for the lowest score in a competition. **booby trap 1** hidden bomb primed to be set off by an unsuspecting victim. **2** trap for an unsuspecting person, intended as a joke.

boogie *v Informal* dance to fast pop music.

book *n* **1** number of pages bound together between covers. **2** long written work. **3** number of tickets, stamps, etc. fastened together. **4** *pl* **5** record of transactions of a business or society. ♦ *v* **6** reserve (a place, passage, etc.) in advance. **7** record the name of (a person) who has committed an offence. **booklet** *n* thin book with paper covers.

book-keeping *n* systematic recording of business transactions.

bookmaker *n* person whose occupation is taking bets.

bookmark *n* **1** person whose occupation is taking bets. **2** *Computers* marker on a website that enables the user to return to it quickly and easily. ♦ *v* **3** *Computers* identify and store (a website) so that one can return to it quickly and easily.

bookworm *n* person devoted to reading.

boom¹ *v* **1** make a loud deep echoing sound. **2** prosper vigorously and rapidly. ♦ *n* **3** loud deep echoing sound. **4** period of high economic growth. **boomer** *n Aust* large male kangaroo.

boom² *n* **1** pole to which the foot of a sail is attached. **2** pole carrying an overhead microphone. **3** barrier across a waterway.

boomerang *n* **1** curved wooden missile which can be made to return to the thrower. ♦ *v* **2** (of a plan) recoil unexpectedly.

boon *n* something helpful or beneficial.

boongary [**boong**-gar-ree] *n, pl* **-garies** tree kangaroo of NE Queensland, Australia.

boor *n* rude or insensitive person. **boorish** *adj*

boost *n* **1** encouragement or help. **2** increase. ♦ *v* **3** improve. **4** increase. **booster** *n* small additional injection of a vaccine.

boot¹ *n* **1** outer covering for the foot that extends above the ankle. **2** space in a car for luggage. **3** *Informal* kick. **4** *v* **5** *Informal* kick. **6** start up (a computer). **bootee** *n* baby's soft shoe. **boot camp** centre for young offenders, with strict discipline and hard physical exercise. **boot-cut** *adj* (of trousers) slightly flared at the bottom of the legs.

boot² *n* **to boot** in addition.

booth *n* **1** small partly enclosed cubicle. **2** stall at a fair or market.

bootleg *adj* **1** produced, distributed, or sold illicitly. ♦ *v* **-legging, -legged 2** make, carry, or sell (illicit goods). **bootlegger** *n*

booty *n, pl* **-ties** valuable articles obtained as plunder.

booze *v, n Informal* (consume) alcoholic drink. **boozy** *adj* **boozer** *n* *Informal* **1** person who is fond of drinking. **2** *Brit, Aust & NZ* pub. **booze-up** *n Informal* drinking spree.

bop v **bopping, bopped** Informal dance to pop music.

bora n Aust Aboriginal ceremony.

borax n white mineral used in making glass.

border n **1** dividing line between political or geographical regions. **2** band around or along the edge of something. ♦ v **3** provide with a border. **4** be nearly the same as, e.g. resentment that borders on hatred.

bore[1] v **1** make (a hole) with a drill etc. ♦ n **2** (diameter of) the hollow of a gun barrel or other tube.

bore[2] v **1** make weary by being dull or repetitious. ♦ n **2** dull or repetitious person or thing. **bored** adj **boredom** n

bore[3] n high wave in a narrow estuary, caused by the tide.

bore[4] v past tense of BEAR[1].

boree [baw-ree] n Aust same as MYALL

born v **1** a past participle of BEAR[1]. ♦ adj **2** possessing certain qualities from birth, e.g. a born musician.

borne v a past participle of BEAR[1].

boron n Chem element used in hardening steel.

boronia n Australian aromatic flowering shrub.

borough n Chiefly Brit town or district with its own council.

borrow v **1** obtain (something) temporarily. **2** adopt (ideas etc.) from another source. **borrower** n

borstal n (formerly in Britain) prison for young criminals.

borzoi n tall dog with a long silky coat.

bosh n Brit, Aust & NZ informal empty talk, nonsense.

bosom n **1** chest of a person, esp. the female breasts. ♦ adj **2** very dear, e.g. a bosom friend.

boss[1] n **1** person in charge of or employing others. ♦ v **2** boss around, **about** be domineering towards. **bossy** adj

boss[2] n raised knob or stud.

bosun n officer responsible for the maintenance of a ship.

botany n study of plants. **botanical, botanic** adj **botanist** n

botch v **1** spoil through clumsiness. **2** n **3** (also **botch-up**) badly done piece of work or repair.

both adj, pron two considered together.

bother v **1** take the time or trouble. **2** give annoyance or trouble to. **3** pester. ♦ n **4** trouble, fuss, or difficulty **bothersome** adj

bottle n **1** container for holding liquids. **2** Brit informal courage. ♦ v **3** put in a bottle. **bottleneck** n narrow stretch of road where traffic is held up. **bottle shop** Aust & NZ shop licensed to sell alcohol for drinking elsewhere. **bottle store** S Afr shop licensed to sell alcohol for drinking elsewhere. **bottle tree** Australian tree with a bottle-shaped swollen trunk. **bottle up** v restrain (powerful emotion).

bottom n **1** lowest, deepest, or farthest removed part of a thing. **2** buttocks. ♦ adj **3** lowest or last. **bottomless** adj

botulism n severe food poisoning.

boudoir [boo-dwahr] n woman's bedroom or private sitting room.

bougainvillea n climbing plant with red or purple flowers.

bough n large branch of a tree.

bought v past of BUY.

boulder n large rounded rock.

boulevard n wide, usu. tree-lined, street.

bounce v **1** (of a ball etc.) rebound from an impact. **2** Slang (of a cheque) be returned uncashed owing to a lack of funds in the account. ♦ n **3** act of rebounding. **4** springiness. **5** Informal vitality or vigour. **bouncer** n person employed at a disco etc. to remove unwanted people. **bouncing** *adj* vigorous and robust.

bound¹ *v* **1** past of BIND. ♦ *adj* **2** destined or certain. **3** compelled or obliged.

bound² *v* **1** move forwards by jumps. ♦ *n* **2** jump upwards or forwards.

bound³ *v* **1** form a boundary of. ♦ *pl n* **2** limit. **boundary** *n* dividing line that indicates the farthest limit.

bound⁴ *adj* going or intending to go towards, e.g. *homeward bound*.

bounty *n, pl* -**ties** **1** generosity. **2** generous gift or reward. **bountiful, bounteous** *adj*

bouquet *n* **1** bunch of flowers. **2** aroma of wine.

bourbon [**bur**-bn] *n* whiskey made from maize.

bourgeois [**boor**-zhwah] *adj, n Offens* middle-class (person).

bout *n* **1** period of activity or illness. **2** boxing or wrestling match.

boutique *n* small clothes shop.

bovine *adj* **1** relating to cattle. **2** rather slow and stupid.

bow¹ [rhymes with **now**] *v* **1** lower (one's head) or bend (one's knee or body) as a sign of respect or shame. **2** comply or accept. ♦ *n* **3** movement made when bowing.

bow² [rhymes with **go**] *n* **1** knot with two loops and loose ends. **2** weapon for shooting arrows. **3** long stick stretched with horsehair for playing stringed instruments. **bow-legged** *adj* having legs that curve outwards at the knees.

bow³ [rhymes with **now**] *n* front end of a ship.

bowdlerize *v* remove words regarded as indecent from (a play, novel, etc.).

bowel *n* **1** intestine, esp. the large intestine. ♦ *pl* **2** innermost part.

bower *n* shady leafy shelter. **bowerbird** *n* songbird of Australia and New Guinea, the males of which build bower-like display grounds to attract females.

bowl¹ *n* **1** round container with an open top. **2** the rounded or hollow part of an object, especially of a spoon or tobacco pipe.

bowl² *n* **1** large heavy ball. ♦ *pl* **2** game played on smooth grass with wooden bowls. ♦ *v* **3** *Cricket* send (a ball) towards the batsman. **bowling** *n* game in which bowls are rolled at a group of pins.

bowler¹ *n* **1** *Cricket* player who sends (a ball) towards the batsman. **2** person who plays bowls or bowling.

bowler² *n* stiff felt hat with a rounded crown.

box¹ *n* **1** container with a firm flat base and sides. **2** separate compartment in a theatre, stable, etc. **3** *v* **4** put into a box. **the box** *Informal* television. **box jellyfish** highly venomous jellyfish with a cuboidal body that lives in Australian tropical waters. **box office** place where theatre or cinema tickets are sold.

box² *v* fight (an opponent) in a boxing match. **boxer** *n* **1** person who participates in the sport of boxing. **2** medium-sized dog with smooth hair and a short nose. **boxer shorts, boxers** *pl n* men's underpants shaped like shorts but with a front opening. **boxing** *n* sport of fighting with the fists.

box³ *n* **1** evergreen tree with shiny leaves. **2** eucalyptus with similar timber and foliage, and with rough bark.

boy *n* male child. **boyish** *adj* **boyhood** *n* **boyfriend** *n* male friend with whom a person is romantically or sexually involved.

boycott *v* **1** refuse to deal with (an

organization or country). ♦ *n* **2** instance of boycotting.

☑ SPELLING TIP

The word **boycott** has two *ts*, whether or not it has an ending such as in **boycotting**.

---

bra *n* woman's undergarment for supporting the breasts.

braaivlies [**brye**-flayss], **braai** *S Afr* ♦ *n* grill on which food is cooked over hot charcoal, usu. outdoors. **1** outdoor party at which food like this is served. ♦ *v* **2** cook (food) on in this way.

brace *n* **1** object fastened to something to straighten or support it. **2** pair, esp. of game birds. ♦ *pl* **3** straps worn over the shoulders to hold up trousers. ♦ *v* **4** steady or prepare (oneself) for something unpleasant. **5** strengthen or fit with a brace. **bracing** *adj* refreshing and invigorating.

bracelet *n* ornamental chain or band for the wrist.

bracken *n* large fern.

bracket *n* **1** pair of characters used to enclose a section of writing. **2** group falling within certain defined limits. **3** support fixed to a wall. ♦ *v* **-eting, -eted 4** put in brackets. **5** class together.

brackish *adj* (of water) slightly salty.

bract *n* leaf at the base of a flower.

brag *v* **bragging, bragged** speak arrogantly and boastfully. **braggart** *n*

braid *v* **1** interweave (hair, thread, etc.). ♦ *n* **2** length of hair etc. that has been braided. **3** narrow ornamental tape of woven silk etc.

Braille *n* system of writing for the blind, consisting of raised dots interpreted by touch.

brain *n* **1** soft mass of nervous tissue in the head. **2** intellectual ability. ♦ *v* **3** hit (someone) hard on the head.

brainless *adj* stupid. **brainy** *adj Informal* clever. **brainchild** *n* idea produced by creative thought. **brain up** *v Brit* make (something) more intellectually demanding or sophisticated. **brainwash** *v* cause (a person) to alter his or her beliefs, esp. by methods based on isolation, sleeplessness, etc. **brainwave** *n* sudden idea.

braise *v* cook slowly in a covered pan with a little liquid.

brake *n* **1** device for slowing or stopping a vehicle. ♦ *v* **2** slow down or stop by using a brake.

bramble *n* prickly shrub that produces blackberries.

bran *n* husks of cereal grain.

branch *n* **1** secondary stem of a tree. **2** offshoot or subsidiary part of something larger or more complex. ♦ *v* **3** (of stems, roots, etc.) divide, then develop in different directions. **branch out** *v* expand one's interests.

brand *n* **1** particular product. **2** particular kind or variety. **3** identifying mark burnt onto the skin of an animal. **4** *v* **5** mark with a brand. **6** denounce as being. **brand-new** *adj* absolutely new.

brandish *v* wave (a weapon etc.) in a threatening way.

brandy *n, pl* **-dies** alcoholic spirit distilled from wine.

brash *adj* offensively loud, showy, or self-confident. **brashness** *n*

brass *n* **1** alloy of copper and zinc. **2** family of wind instruments made of brass. **3** *N English dialect* money. **brassy** *adj* **1** brazen or flashy. **2** like brass, esp. in colour.

brassiere *n* bra.

brat *n* unruly child.

bravado *n* showy display of self-confidence.

brave *adj* **1** having or showing

courage, resolution, and daring. **2** n **3** Native American warrior. ♦ v **4** confront with resolution or courage. **bravery** n

bravo interj well done!

brawl n **1** noisy fight. ♦ v **2** fight noisily.

brawn n **1** physical strength. **2** pressed meat from the head of a pig or calf. **brawny** adj

bray v **1** (of a donkey) utter its loud harsh sound. ♦ n **2** donkey's loud harsh sound.

brazen adj shameless and bold. ♦ v **brazenly** adv

brazier [**bray**-zee-er] n portable container for burning charcoal or coal.

breach n **1** breaking of a promise, obligation, etc. **2** gap or break. ♦ v **3** break (a promise, law, etc.). **4** make a gap in.

bread n **1** food made by baking a mixture of flour and water or milk. **2** Slang money. **breadwinner** n person whose earnings support a family.

breadth n extent of something from side to side.

break v **breaking, broke, broken 1** separate or become separated into two or more pieces. **2** damage or become damaged so as to be inoperative. **3** fail to observe (an agreement etc.). **4** disclose or be disclosed, e.g. he broke the news. **5** bring or come to an end, e.g. the good weather broke at last. **6** weaken or be weakened, as in spirit. **7** improve on or surpass, e.g. break a record. **8** (of the male voice) become permanently deeper at puberty. ♦ n **9** act or result of breaking. **10** gap or interruption in continuity. **11** Informal fortunate opportunity. **break even** make neither a profit nor a loss. **breakable** adj **breakage** n **breaker** n large wave. **break down** v **1** cease to function. **2** yield to strong emotion.

breakdown n **1** act or instance of breaking down. **2** nervous breakdown. **break-in** n illegal entering of a building, esp. by thieves. **breakneck** adj fast and dangerous. **break off** v **1** sever or detach. **2** end (a relationship etc.). **break out** v begin or arise suddenly. **breakthrough** n important development or discovery. **break up** v **1** (cause to) separate. **2** come to an end. **3** (of a school) close for the holidays. **breakwater** n wall that extends into the sea to protect a harbour or beach from the force of waves.

breakfast v, n (eat) the first meal of the day.

bream n **1** freshwater fish with silvery scales. **2** food fish of European seas.

breast n **1** either of the two soft fleshy milk-secreting glands on a woman's chest. **2** chest. **breastbone** n long flat bone in the front of the body, to which most of the ribs are attached. **breaststroke** n swimming stroke in which the arms are extended in front of the head and swept back on either side.

breath n **1** taking in and letting out of air during breathing. **2** air taken in and let out during breathing. **breathless** adj **breathtaking** adj causing awe or excitement. **breathe** v **1** take in oxygen and give out carbon dioxide. **2** whisper. **breather** n Informal short rest. **breathing** n

Breathalyser n ® device for estimating the amount of alcohol in the breath. **breathalyse** v

bred v past of BREED.

breech n **1** buttocks. **2** back part of gun where bullet or shell is loaded. **breech birth** birth of a baby with the feet or buttocks appearing first.

breeches pl n trousers extending to just below the knee.

breed v **breeding, bred 1** produce new or improved strains of (domestic animals or plants). **2** bear (offspring). **3** produce or be produced, e.g. *breed trouble.* ♦ n **4** group of animals etc. within a species that have certain clearly defined characteristics. **5** kind or sort. **breeder** n **breeding** n result of good upbringing or training.

breeze n **1** gentle wind. ♦ v **2** move quickly or casually. **breezy** adj **1** windy. **2** casual or carefree.

brethren pl n Old-fashioned (used in religious contexts) brothers.

brevity n shortness.

brew v **1** make (beer etc.) by steeping, boiling, and fermentation. **2** prepare (a drink) by infusing. **3** be about to happen or forming. ♦ n **4** beverage produced by brewing.

brewer n person or company that brews beer. **brewery** n, pl -**eries** place where beer etc. is brewed.

briar[1], **brier** n **1** European shrub with a hard woody root. **2** tobacco pipe made from this root.

briar[2] n same as BRIER[1].

bribe v **1** offer or give something to someone to gain favour, influence, etc. ♦ n **2** something given or offered as a bribe. **bribery** n

bric-a-brac n miscellaneous small ornamental objects.

brick n **1** (rectangular block of) baked clay used in building. ♦ v **2** (foll. by up or over) build, enclose, or fill with bricks. **bricklayer** n person who builds with bricks.

bride n woman who has just been or is about to be married. **bridal** adj **bridegroom** n man who has just been or is about to be married. **bridesmaid** n girl or woman who attends a bride at her wedding.

bridge[1] n **1** structure for crossing a river etc. **2** platform from which a ship

is steered or controlled. **3** upper part of the nose. **4** piece of wood supporting the strings of a violin etc. ♦ v **5** build a bridge over (something). **bridgehead** n fortified position at the end of a bridge nearest the enemy.

bridge[2] n card game based on whist, played between two pairs.

bridle n **1** headgear for controlling a horse. **2** v **3** show anger or indignation. **bridle path** path suitable for riding horses.

brief adj **1** short in duration. **2** n **3** condensed statement or written synopsis. **4** (also **briefing**) set of instructions. ♦ pl **5** men's or women's underpants. ♦ v **6** give information and instructions to (a person). **briefly** adv **briefcase** n small flat case for carrying papers, books, etc.

brier[1], **briar** n wild rose with long thorny stems.

brier[2] n same as BRIER[1].

brig n two-masted square-rigged ship.

brigade n **1** army unit smaller than a division. **2** group of people organized for a certain task.

brigadier n high-ranking army officer.

brigalow n Aust type of acacia tree.

brigand n Lit bandit.

brigantine n two-masted sailing ship.

bright adj **1** emitting or reflecting much light. **2** (of colours) intense. **3** clever. **brightly** adv **brightness** n **brighten** v

brilliant adj **1** shining with light. **2** splendid. **3** extremely clever. **brilliance, brilliancy** n

brim n **1** upper rim of a cup etc. **2** projecting edge of a hat. ♦ v **brimming, brimmed 3** be full to the brim.

brimstone n Obs sulphur.

brine n salt water. **briny** adj very salty. **the briny** Informal the sea.

bring v **bringing, brought** **1** carry, convey, or take to a designated place or person. **2** cause to happen. **3** *Law* put forward (charges) officially. **bring about** v cause to happen. **bring off** v succeed in achieving. **bring out** v **1** publish or have (a book) published. **2** reveal or cause to be seen. **bring up** v **1** rear (a child). **2** mention. **3** vomit (food).

brinjal n S Afr dark purple tropical fruit, cooked and eaten as a vegetable.

brink n edge of a steep place.

brisk adj lively and quick. **briskly** adv

brisket n beef from the breast of a cow.

bristle n **1** short stiff hair. ♦ v **2** (cause to) stand up like bristles. **3** show anger. **bristly** adj

Brit n Informal British person.

British adj **1** of Great Britain or the British Commonwealth. ♦ pl n **2** people of Great Britain.

brittle adj hard but easily broken. **brittleness** n

broach v **1** introduce (a topic) for discussion. **2** open (a bottle or barrel).

broad adj **1** having great breadth or width. **2** not detailed. **3** extensive, e.g. *broad support*. **4** strongly marked, e.g. *a broad American accent*. **broadly** adv **broaden** v **broadband** n telecommunication transmission technique using a wide range of frequencies. **broad bean** thick flat edible bean. **broad-minded** adj tolerant. **broadside** n **1** strong verbal or written attack. **2** Naval firing of all the guns on one side of a ship at once.

broadcast n **1** programme or announcement on radio or television. ♦ v **2** transmit (a programme or announcement) on radio or television. **3** make widely known. **broadcaster** n **broadcasting** n

brocade n rich fabric woven with a raised design.

broccoli n type of cabbage with greenish flower heads.

☑ **SPELLING TIP**
You might expect a word that sounds like **broccoli** to have two *l*s at the end, but it has only one because it comes from Italian and ends with an *i*.

brochure n booklet that contains information about a product or service.

broekies [**brook**-eez] pl n S Afr informal underpants.

brogue[1] n sturdy walking shoe.

brogue[2] n strong accent, esp. Irish.

broil v Aust, NZ, US & Canadian cook by direct heat under a grill.

broke v **1** past tense of BREAK. ♦ adj **2** Informal having no money.

broken v **1** past participle of BREAK. ♦ adj **2** fractured or smashed. **3** (of the speech of a foreigner) noticeably imperfect, e.g. *broken English*. **brokenhearted** adj overwhelmed by grief.

broker n agent who buys or sells goods, securities, etc.

brolga n large grey Australian crane with a trumpeting call (also **native companion**).

brolly n, pl **-lies** Informal umbrella.

bromide n chemical compound used in medicine and photography.

bromine n Chem dark red liquid element that gives off a pungent vapour.

bronchial [**bronk**-ee-al] adj of the bronchi.

bronchitis [bronk-**eye**-tiss] n inflammation of the bronchi.

bronchus [**bronk**-uss] n, pl **bronchi** [**bronk**-eye] either of the two branches of the windpipe.

bronco n, pl **-cos** (in the US) wild or partially tamed pony.

brontosaurus n very large plant-eating four-footed dinosaur.

bronze n 1 alloy of copper and tin. 2 statue, medal, etc. made of bronze. ♦ adj 3 made of, or coloured like, bronze. ♦ v 4 (esp. of the skin) make or become brown. **Bronze Age** era when bronze tools and weapons were used.

brooch n ornament with a pin, worn fastened to clothes.

brood n 1 number of birds produced at one hatching. 2 all the children of a family. ♦ v 3 think long and unhappily. **broody** adj 1 moody and sullen. 2 Informal (of a woman) wishing to have a baby.

brook¹ n small stream.

brook² v bear or tolerate.

broom n 1 long-handled sweeping brush. 2 yellow-flowered shrub. **broomstick** n handle of a broom.

broth n soup, usu. containing vegetables.

brothel n house where men pay to have sex with prostitutes.

brother n 1 boy or man with the same parents as another person. 2 member of a male religious order. **brotherly** adj **brotherhood** n 1 fellowship. 2 association, such as a trade union. **brother-in-law** n, pl **brothers-in-law** 1 brother of one's husband or wife. 2 husband of one's sister.

brought v past of BRING.

brow n 1 part of the face from the eyes to the hairline. 2 eyebrow. 3 top of a hill.

browbeat v frighten (someone) with threats.

brown n 1 colour of earth or wood. ♦ adj 2 of the colour brown. ♦ v 3 make or become brown. **brownish** adj **browned-off** adj Informal bored and depressed.

Brownie Guide, Brownie n junior Guide.

browse v 1 look through (a book or articles for sale) in a casual manner. 2 nibble on young shoots or leaves. ♦ n 3 instance of browsing. **browser** n Computers software package that enables a user to read hypertext, esp. on the Internet.

bruise n 1 discoloured area on the skin caused by an injury. ♦ v 2 cause a bruise on. **bruiser** n strong tough person.

brumby n, pl **-bies** Aust 1 wild horse. 2 unruly person.

brunch n Informal breakfast and lunch combined.

brunette n girl or woman with dark brown hair.

brunt n main force or shock of a blow, attack, etc.

brush¹ n 1 device made of bristles, wires, etc. used for cleaning, painting, etc. 2 brief unpleasant encounter. 3 fox's tail. ♦ v 4 clean, scrub, or paint with a brush. 5 touch lightly and briefly. **brush off** v Slang dismiss or ignore (someone). **brush up** v refresh one's knowledge of (a subject).

brush² n thick growth of shrubs.

brush turkey n bird of New Guinea and Australia resembling the domestic fowl, with black plumage.

brusque adj blunt or curt in manner or speech. **brusquely** adv **brusqueness** n

Brussels sprout n vegetable like a tiny cabbage.

brute n 1 brutal person. 2 animal other than man. ♦ adj 3 wholly instinctive or physical, like an animal. 4 without reason. **brutish** adj of or like an animal. **brutal** adj 1 cruel and vicious. 2 extremely honest in speech or manner. **brutally** adv **brutality** n **brutalize** v

BSc Bachelor of Science.

BSE bovine spongiform encephalopathy: fatal virus disease of cattle.

BST British Summer Time.

bubble n **1** ball of air in a liquid or solid. **2** v **3** form bubbles. **4** move or flow with a gurgling sound. **bubbly** adj **1** excited and lively. **2** full of bubbles. **bubble over** v express an emotion freely.

bubonic plague [bew-**bonn**-ik] n acute infectious disease characterized by swellings.

buccaneer n Hist pirate.

buck¹ n **1** male of the goat, hare, kangaroo, rabbit, and reindeer. ♦ v **2** (of a horse etc.) jump with legs stiff and back arched. **buck up** v make or become more cheerful.

buck² n **1** US, Canadian, Aust & NZ slang dollar. **2** S Afr rand.

buck³ n **pass the buck** Informal shift blame or responsibility onto someone else.

bucket n **1** open-topped round container with a handle. ♦ v **-eting, -eted 2** rain heavily. **bucketful** n

buckle n **1** clasp for fastening a belt or strap. ♦ v **2** fasten or be fastened with a buckle. **3** (cause to) bend out of shape through pressure or heat. **buckle down** v Informal apply oneself with determination.

buckshee adj Slang free.

buckteeth pl n projecting upper front teeth. **buck-toothed** adj

buckwheat n small black grain used for making flour.

bucolic [bew-**koll**-ik] adj of the countryside or country life.

bud n **1** swelling on a tree or plant that develops into a leaf or flower. **2** v **budding, budded 3** produce buds. **budding** adj beginning to develop or grow.

Buddhism n eastern religion founded by Buddha. **Buddhist** n, adj

buddleia n shrub with long spikes of purple flowers.

buddy n, pl **-dies** Informal friend.

budge v move slightly.

budgerigar n small cage bird bred in many different-coloured varieties.

budget n **1** financial plan for a period of time. **2** money allocated for a specific purpose. ♦ v **-eting, -eted 3** plan the expenditure of (money or time). ♦ adj **4** cheap. **budgetary** adj

---

☑ SPELLING TIP

A lot of verbs ending in et, have two ts when you add an ending like -ing, but **budget** is not one of them: **budgeting** and **budgeted** have a single t.

---

budgie n Informal short for BUDGERIGAR.

buff¹ **1** adj **2** dull yellowish-brown. ♦ v **3** clean or polish with soft material.

buff² n Informal expert on or devotee of a given subject.

buffalo n **1** type of cattle. **2** US bison.

buffer n something that lessens shock or protects from damaging impact, circumstances, etc.

buffet¹ [**boof**-ay, **buff**-ay] n counter where drinks and snacks are served.

buffet² [**buff**-it] v **-feting, -feted** knock against or about.

buffoon n clown or fool. **buffoonery** n

bug n **1** small insect. **2** Informal minor illness. **3** small mistake in a computer program. **4** concealed microphone. **5** Aust flattish edible shellfish. ♦ v **bugging, bugged 6** Informal irritate (someone). **7** conceal a microphone in (a room or phone).

bugbear n thing that causes obsessive anxiety.

bugger Slang ♦ n **1** unpleasant or

difficult person or thing. **2** person who practises buggery. ♦ v **3** tire. **4** practise buggery with. **buggery** n anal intercourse.

bugle n instrument like a small trumpet. **bugler** n

build v **building, built 1** make, construct, or form by joining parts or materials. **2** n **3** shape of the body. **builder** n **building** n structure with walls and a roof. **building society** organization where money can be borrowed or invested. **build-up** n gradual increase.

built v past of BUILD. **built-up** adj having many buildings.

bulb n **1** same as LIGHT BULB. **2** onion-shaped root which grows into a flower or plant. **bulbous** adj round and fat.

bulge n **1** swelling on a normally flat surface. **2** sudden increase in number. ♦ v **3** swell outwards. **bulging** adj

bulimia n disorder characterized by compulsive overeating followed by vomiting. **bulimic** adj, n

bulk n **1** size or volume, esp. when great. **2** main part. **in bulk** in large quantities. **bulky** adj

bulkhead n partition in a ship or aeroplane.

bull¹ n male of some animals, such as cattle, elephants, and whales. **bullock** n castrated bull. **bulldog** n thickset dog with a broad head and a muscular body. **bulldozer** n powerful tractor for moving earth. **bulldoze** v **bullfight** n public show in which a matador kills a bull. **bull's-eye** n central disc of a target. **bullswool** n Aust dated & NZ slang nonsense.

bull² n Informal complete nonsense.

bull³ n papal decree.

bullet n small piece of metal fired from a gun.

bulletin n short official report or announcement.

bullion n gold or silver in the form of bars.

bully n, pl **-lies 1** person who hurts, persecutes, or intimidates a weaker person. ♦ v **-lying, -lied 2** hurt, intimidate, or persecute (a weaker person).

bulrush n tall stiff reed.

bulwark n **1** wall used as a fortification. **2** person or thing acting as a defence.

bum¹ n Slang buttocks or anus.

bum² Informal ♦ n **1** disreputable idler **2** adj **3** of poor quality.

bumble v speak, do, or move in a clumsy way. **bumbling** adj, n

bumblebee n large hairy bee.

bumf, bumph n Informal official documents or forms.

bump v **1** knock or strike with a jolt. **2** travel in jerks and jolts. ♦ n **3** dull thud from an impact or collision. **4** raised uneven part. **bumpy** adj **bump off** v Informal murder.

bumper¹ n bar on the front and back of a vehicle to protect against damage.

bumper² **1** adj **2** unusually large or abundant.

bumph n same as BUMF.

bumpkin n awkward simple country person.

bumptious adj offensively self-assertive.

bun n **1** small sweet bread roll or cake. **2** hair gathered into a bun shape at the back of the head.

bunch n **1** number of things growing, fastened, or grouped together. **2** v **3** group or be grouped together in a bunch.

bundle n **1** number of things gathered loosely together. ♦ v **2** cause to go roughly or unceremoniously. **bundle up** v make into a bundle.

bung n **1** stopper for a cask etc. ♦ v **2**

(foll. by *up*) *Informal* close with a bung. **3** *Brit slang* throw (something) somewhere in a careless manner.

bungalow *n* one-storey house.

bungee jumping, bungy jumping *n* sport of leaping from a high bridge, tower, etc., to which one is connected by a rubber rope.

bungle *v* spoil through incompetence. **bungler** *n* **bungling** *adj, n*

bunion *n* inflamed swelling on the big toe.

bunk[1] *n* narrow shelflike bed. **bunk bed** one of a pair of beds constructed one above the other.

bunk[2] *n* same as BUNKUM.

bunk[3] *Slang* ♦ *n* **1** *Brit* **do a bunk** make a hurried and secret departure. ♦ *v* **2** *Brit, NZ & S Afr* be absent without permission.

bunker *n* **1** sand-filled hollow forming an obstacle on a golf course. **2** underground shelter. **3** large storage container for coal etc.

bunkum *n* nonsense.

bunny *n, pl* **-nies** child's word for a rabbit.

Bunsen burner *n* gas burner used in laboratories.

bunting *n* decorative flags.

bunya *n* tall dome-shaped Australian coniferous tree (also **bunya-bunya**).

bunyip *n Aust* legendary monster said to live in swamps and lakes.

buoy *n* **1** floating marker anchored in the sea. ♦ *v* **2** prevent from sinking. **3** encourage or hearten. **buoyant** *adj* **1** able to float. **2** cheerful or resilient. **buoyancy** *n*

bur *n* same as BURR[1].

burble *v* **1** make a bubbling sound. **2** talk quickly and excitedly.

burden[1] *n* **1** heavy load. **2** something difficult to cope with. ♦ *v* **3** put a burden on. **4** oppress.

burdensome *adj*

burden[2] *n* theme of a speech etc.

bureau *n, pl* **-reaus, -reaux** **1** office that provides a service. **2** writing desk with shelves and drawers.

bureaucracy *n, pl* **-cies** **1** administrative system based on complex rules and procedures. **2** excessive adherence to complex procedures. **bureaucrat** *n* **bureaucratic** *adj*

burgeon *v* develop or grow rapidly.

burgh *n* Scottish borough.

burglar *n* person who enters a building to commit a crime, esp. theft. **burglary** *n* **burgle** *v*

Burgundy *n* type of French wine. **burgundy** *adj* dark-purplish red.

burial *n* burying of a dead body.

burlesque *n* artistic work which satirizes a subject by caricature.

burly *adj* **-lier, -liest** (of a person) broad and strong.

burn[1] *v* **burning, burnt** *or* **burned** **1** be or set on fire. **2** destroy or be destroyed by fire. **3** damage, injure, or mark by heat. **4** feel strong emotion. **5** record data on (a compact disc). ♦ *n* **6** injury or mark caused by fire or exposure to heat. **burning** *adj* **1** intense. **2** urgent or crucial.

burn[2] *n Scot* small stream.

burnish *v* make smooth and shiny by rubbing.

burp *v, n Informal* belch.

burr[1] *n* head of a plant with prickles or hooks.

burr[2] *n* **1** soft trilling sound given to the letter *r* in some dialects. **2** whirring sound.

burrawang *n* Australian plant with fernlike leaves and an edible nut.

burrow *n* **1** hole dug in the ground by a rabbit etc. ♦ *v* **2** dig holes in the ground.

bursar n treasurer of a school, college, or university. **bursary** n scholarship.

burst v **bursting, burst** 1 (cause to) break open or apart noisily and suddenly. 2 come or go suddenly and forcibly. 3 be full to the point of breaking open. ♦ n 4 instance of breaking open suddenly. 5 sudden outbreak or occurrence. **burst into** v give vent to (an emotion) suddenly.

bury v **burying, buried** 1 place in a grave. 2 place in the earth and cover with soil. 3 conceal or hide.

bus n 1 large motor vehicle for carrying passengers. ♦ v **bussing, bussed** 2 travel or transport by bus.

busby n, pl **-bies** tall fur hat worn by some soldiers.

bush n 1 dense woody plant, smaller than a tree. 2 wild uncultivated part of a country. **bushy** adj (of hair) thick and shaggy. **bushbaby** n small African tree-living mammal with large eyes.

bushel n obsolete unit of measure equal to 8 gallons (36.4 litres).

business n 1 purchase and sale of goods and services. 2 commercial establishment. 3 trade or profession. 4 proper concern or responsibility. 5 affair, e.g. *it's a dreadful business.* **businesslike** adj efficient and methodical. **businessman, businesswoman** n

busker n street entertainer. **busk** v act as a busker.

bust¹ n 1 woman's bosom. 2 sculpture of the head and shoulders.

bust² Informal ♦ v **busting, bust** or **busted** 1 burst or break. 2 (of the police) raid (a place) or arrest (someone). ♦ adj 3 broken. **go bust** become bankrupt.

bustard n bird with long strong legs, a heavy body, a long neck, and speckled plumage.

bustle¹ v 1 hurry with a show of activity or energy. ♦ n 2 energetic and noisy activity. **bustling** adj

bustle² n cushion or framework formerly worn under the back of a woman's skirt to hold it out.

busy adj **busier, busiest** 1 actively employed. 2 crowded or full of activity. ♦ v **busying, busied** 3 keep (someone, esp. oneself) busy. **busily** adv **busybody** n meddlesome or nosy person.

but conj 1 contrary to expectation. 2 in contrast. 3 other than. 4 without it happening. ♦ prep 5 except. ♦ adv 6 only. **but for** were it not for.

butane n gas used for fuel.

butch adj Slang markedly or aggressively masculine.

butcher n 1 person who slaughters animals or sells their meat. 2 brutal murderer. ♦ v 3 kill and prepare (animals) for meat. 4 kill (people) brutally or indiscriminately. **butchery** n **butcherbird** n Australian magpie that impales its prey on thorns.

butler n chief male servant.

butt¹ n 1 thicker end of something. 2 unused end of a cigar or cigarette. 3 slang buttocks.

butt² n person or thing that is the target of ridicule.

butt³ v strike with the head or horns. **butt in** v interrupt a conversation.

butt⁴ n large cask.

butter n 1 edible fatty solid made by churning cream. ♦ v 2 put butter on. **buttery** adj **butter up** v flatter.

butter bean n large pale flat edible bean.

buttercup n small yellow flower.

butterfingers n Informal person who drops things by mistake.

butterfly n 1 insect with brightly coloured wings. 2 swimming stroke in which both arms move together in a forward circular action.

buttermilk n sourish milk that remains after the butter has been separated from milk.

butterscotch n kind of hard brittle toffee.

buttock n either of the two fleshy masses that form the human rump.

button n 1 small disc or knob sewn to clothing, which can be passed through a slit in another piece of fabric to fasten them. 2 knob that operates a piece of equipment when pressed. ♦ v 3 fasten with buttons. **buttonhole** n 1 slit in a garment through which a button is passed. 2 flower worn on a lapel. ♦ v 3 detain (someone) in conversation.

buttress n 1 structure to support a wall. ♦ v 2 support with, or as if with, a buttress.

buxom adj (of a woman) healthily plump and full-bosomed.

buy v **buying, bought** 1 acquire by paying money for. 2 Slang accept as true. 3 n 4 thing acquired through payment. **buyer** n 1 customer. 2 person employed to buy merchandise.

buzz n 1 rapidly vibrating humming sound. 2 Informal sense of excitement. ♦ v 3 make a humming sound. 4 be filled with an air of excitement. **buzzer** n **buzz around** v move around quickly and busily. **buzz word** jargon word which becomes

fashionably popular.

buzzard n bird of prey of the hawk family.

by prep 1 indicating the doer of an action, nearness, movement past, time before or during which, etc., e.g. bitten by a dog; down by the river; driving by the school; in bed by midnight. ♦ adv 2 near. 3 past. **by and by** eventually. **by and large** in general.

bye, bye-bye interj Informal goodbye.

by-election n election held during parliament to fill a vacant seat.

bygone adj past or former.

bylaw, bye-law n rule made by a local authority.

BYO, BYOG n Aust & NZ unlicensed restaurant at which diners may bring their own alcoholic drink.

bypass n 1 main road built to avoid a city. 2 operation to divert blood flow away from a damaged part of the heart. ♦ v 3 go round or avoid.

by-product n secondary or incidental product of a process.

byre n Brit shelter for cows.

bystander n person present but not involved.

byte n Computers group of bits processed as one unit of data.

byway n minor road.

byword n person or thing regarded as a perfect example of something.

C c

C 1 *Chem* carbon. **2** Celsius. **3** centigrade. **4** century.

c. circa.

cab *n* **1** taxi. **2** enclosed driver's compartment on a train, truck, etc. **cabbie, cabby** *n, pl* **-bies** *Informal* taxi driver.

cabal [kab-**bal**] *n* **1** small group of political plotters. **2** secret plot.

cabaret [**kab**-a-ray] *n* dancing and singing show in a nightclub.

cabbage *n* vegetable with a large head of green leaves. **cabbage tree** *NZ* palm-like tree with a bare trunk and spiky leaves.

caber *n* tree trunk tossed in competition at Highland games.

cabin *n* **1** compartment in a ship or aircraft. **2** small hut. **cabin cruiser** motorboat with a cabin.

cabinet *n* **1** piece of furniture with drawers or shelves. **2** (C-) committee of senior government ministers. **cabinet-maker** *n* person who makes fine furniture.

cable *n* **1** strong thick rope. **2** bundle of wires that carries electricity or electronic signals. **3** telegram sent abroad. ♦ *v* **4** send (someone) a message by cable. **cable car** vehicle pulled up a steep slope by a moving cable. **cable television** television service conveyed by cable to subscribers.

caboodle *n* **the whole caboodle** *Informal* the whole lot.

cabriolet [kab-ree-oh-**lay**] *n* small horse-drawn carriage with a folding hood.

cacao [kak-**kah**-oh] *n* tropical tree with seed pods from which chocolate and cocoa are made.

cache [**kash**] *n* hidden store of weapons or treasure.

cachet [**kash**-shay] *n* prestige, distinction.

cack-handed *adj Informal* clumsy.

cackle *v* **1** laugh shrilly. **2** (of a hen) squawk with shrill broken notes. ♦ *n* **3** cackling noise.

cacophony [kak-**koff**-on-ee] *n* harsh discordant sound. **cacophonous** *adj*

cactus *n, pl* **-tuses, -ti** fleshy desert plant with spines but no leaves.

cad *n Old-fashioned* dishonourable man. **caddish** *adj*

cadaver [kad-**dav**-ver] *n* corpse. **cadaverous** *adj* pale, thin, and haggard.

caddie, caddy *n, pl* **-dies 1** person who carries a golfer's clubs. ♦ *v* **-dying, -died 2** act as a caddie.

caddis fly *n* insect whose larva (**caddis worm**) lives underwater in a protective case of sand and stones.

caddy *n, pl* **-dies** small container for tea.

cadence [**kade**-enss] *n* **1** rise and fall in the pitch of the voice. **2** close of a musical phrase.

cadenza *n* complex solo passage in a piece of music.

cadet *n* young person training for the armed forces or police.

cadge *v Informal* get (something) by taking advantage of someone's generosity. **cadger** *n*

cadmium *n Chem* bluish-white metallic element used in alloys.

cadre [**kah**-der] *n* small group of people selected and trained to form the core of a political organization or military unit.

caecum [**seek**-um] *n, pl* -**ca** [-ka] pouch at the beginning of the large intestine.

Caesarean section [see-**zair**-ee-an] *n* surgical incision into the womb to deliver a baby.

caesium *n Chem* silvery-white metallic element used in photocells.

café *n* **1** small or inexpensive restaurant serving light refreshments. **2** *S Afr* corner shop or grocer. **cafeteria** *n* self-service restaurant.

caffeine *n* stimulant found in tea and coffee.

caftan *n* **same as** KAFTAN.

cage *n* **1** enclosure of bars or wires, for keeping animals or birds. **2** enclosed platform of a lift in a mine. **caged** *adj* kept in a cage.

cagey *adj* **cagier, cagiest** *Informal* reluctant to go into details.

cagoule *n Brit* lightweight hooded waterproof jacket.

cahoots *pl n* **in cahoots** *Informal* conspiring together.

cairn *n* mound of stones erected as a memorial or marker.

cajole *v* persuade by flattery. **cajolery** *n*

cake *n* **1** sweet food baked from a mixture of flour, eggs, etc. **2** flat compact mass of something, such as soap. ♦ *v* **3** form into a hardened mass or crust.

calamine *n* pink powder consisting chiefly of zinc oxide, used in skin lotions and ointments.

calamity *n, pl* -**ties** disaster. **calamitous** *adj*

calcify *v* -**fying, -fied** harden by the depositing of calcium salts. **calcification** *n*

calcium *n Chem* silvery-white metallic element found in bones, teeth, limestone, and chalk.

calculate *v* **1** solve or find out by a mathematical procedure or by reasoning. **2** aim to have a particular effect. **calculable** *adj* **calculating** *adj* selfishly scheming. **calculation** *n* **calculator** *n* small electronic device for making calculations.

calculus *n, pl* -**luses 1** branch of mathematics dealing with infinitesimal changes to a variable number or quantity. **2** *Pathology* hard deposit in kidney or bladder.

Caledonian *adj* Scottish.

calendar *n* **1** chart showing a year divided up into months, weeks, and days. **2** system for determining the beginning, length, and division of years. **3** schedule of events or appointments.

calendula *n* marigold.

calf[1] *n, pl* **calves 1** young cow, bull, elephant, whale, or seal. **2** leather made from calf skin. **calve** *v* give birth to a calf.

calf[2] *n, pl* **calves** back of the leg between the ankle and knee.

calibre *n* **1** person's ability or worth. **2** diameter of the bore of a gun or of a shell or bullet. **calibrate** *v* mark the scale or check the accuracy of (a measuring instrument). **calibration** *n*

calico *n, pl* -**coes** white cotton fabric.

caliph *n Hist* Muslim ruler.

call *v* **1** name. **2** shout to attract attention. **3** telephone. **4** summon. **5** (often foll. by *on*) visit. **6** arrange (a meeting, strike, etc.). ♦ *n* **7** cry, shout. **8** animal's or bird's cry. **9** telephone communication. **10** short visit. **11** summons, invitation. **12** need, demand. **caller** *n* **calling** *n* vocation, profession. **call box** kiosk for a public telephone. **call centre** office where staff carry out an organization's telephone transactions. **call for** *v* require. **call off** *v* cancel. **call up** *v* **1** summon to serve in the armed forces.

2 cause one to remember.

calligraphy n (art of) beautiful handwriting. **calligrapher** n

calliper n **1** metal splint for supporting the leg. **2** instrument for measuring diameters.

callisthenics pl n light keep-fit exercises.

callous adj showing no concern for other people's feelings. **calloused** adj (of skin) thickened and hardened. **callously** adv **callousness** n

callow adj young and inexperienced.

callus n, pl **-luses** area of thick hardened skin.

calm adj **1** not agitated or excited. **2** not ruffled by the wind. **3** windless. ♦ n **4** peaceful state. ♦ v **5** (often foll. by *down*) make or become calm. **calmly** adv **calmness** n

calorie n **1** unit of measurement for the energy value of food. **2** unit of heat. **calorific** adj of calories or heat.

calumny n, pl **-nies** false or malicious statement.

calypso n, pl **-sos** West Indian song with improvised topical lyrics.

calyx n, pl **calyxes, calyces** outer leaves that protect a flower bud.

cam n device that converts a circular motion to a to-and-fro motion. **camshaft** n part of an engine consisting of a rod to which cams are fixed.

camaraderie n comradeship.

camber n slight upward curve to the centre of a surface.

cambric n fine white linen fabric.

camcorder n combined portable video camera and recorder.

came v past tense of COME.

camel n humped mammal that can survive long periods without food or water in desert regions.

camellia [kam-**meal**-ya] n evergreen ornamental shrub with white, pink, or red flowers.

Camembert [**kam**-mem-bare] n soft creamy French cheese.

cameo n, pl **cameos 1** brooch or ring with a profile head carved in relief. **2** small part in a film or play performed by a well-known actor or actress.

camera n apparatus used for taking photographs or pictures for television or cinema. **in camera** in private session. **cameraman** n man who operates a camera for television or cinema.

camiknickers pl n Brit woman's undergarment consisting of knickers attached to a camisole.

camisole n woman's bodice-like garment.

camomile n aromatic plant, used to make herbal tea.

camouflage [**kam**-moo-flahzh] n **1** use of natural surroundings or artificial aids to conceal or disguise something. ♦ v **2** conceal by camouflage.

camp[1] n **1** (place for) temporary lodgings consisting of tents, huts, or cabins. **2** group supporting a particular doctrine. ♦ v **3** stay in a camp. **camper** n

camp[2] adj Informal **1** effeminate or homosexual. **2** consciously artificial or affected. **camp it up** Informal behave in a camp way.

campaign n **1** series of coordinated activities designed to achieve a goal. **2** v **3** take part in a campaign.

campanology n art of ringing bells.

campanula n plant with blue or white bell-shaped flowers.

camphor n aromatic crystalline substance used medicinally and in mothballs.

campion n red, pink, or white wild flower.

campus n, pl **-puses** grounds of a university or college.

can[1] v, past **could 1** be able to. **2** be allowed to.

can[2] n **1** metal container for food or liquids. ♦ v **canning, canned 2** put (something) into a can. **canned** adj **1** preserved in a can. **2** (of music) prerecorded. **cannery** n, pl factory where food is canned.

canal n **1** artificial waterway. **2** passage in the body.

canapé [kan-nap-pay] n small piece of bread or toast with a savoury topping.

canary n, pl **-ries** small yellow songbird often kept as a pet.

canasta n card game like rummy, played with two packs.

cancan n lively high-kicking dance performed by a female group.

cancel v **-celling, -celled 1** stop (something that has been arranged) from taking place. **2** mark (a cheque or stamp) with an official stamp to prevent further use. **cancellation** n **cancel out** v counterbalance, neutralize.

cancer n **1** serious disease resulting from a malignant growth or tumour. **2** malignant growth or tumour. **cancerous** adj

candela [kan-**dee**-la] n unit of luminous intensity.

candelabrum n, pl **-bra** large branched candle holder.

candid adj honest and straightforward. **candidly** adv

candidate n **1** person seeking a job or position. **2** person taking an examination. **candidacy, candidature** n

candle n stick of wax enclosing a wick, which is burned to produce light. **candlestick** n holder for a candle. **candlewick** n cotton fabric with a tufted surface.

candour n honesty and straightforwardness.

candy n, pl **-dies** US sweet or sweets. **candied** adj coated with sugar. **candyfloss** n light fluffy mass of spun sugar on a stick. **candy-striped** adj having coloured stripes on a white background.

cane n **1** stem of the bamboo or similar plant. **2** flexible rod used to beat someone. **3** slender walking stick. ♦ v **4** beat with a cane. **cane toad** large toad used to control insects and other pests of sugar-cane plantations.

canine adj **1** of or like a dog. ♦ n **2** sharp pointed tooth between the incisors and the molars.

canister n metal container.

canker n **1** ulceration, ulcerous disease. **2** something evil that spreads and corrupts.

cannabis n **1** Asian plant with tough fibres. **2** drug obtained from the dried leaves and flowers of this plant, which can be smoked or chewed.

cannelloni pl n tubular pieces of pasta filled with meat etc.

cannibal n **1** person who eats human flesh. **2** animal that eats others of its own kind. **cannibalism** n **cannibalize** v use parts from (one machine) to repair another.

cannon n **1** large gun on wheels. **2** billiard stroke in which the cue ball hits two balls successively. **cannonade** n continuous heavy gunfire. **cannonball** n heavy metal ball fired from a cannon. **cannon into** v collide with.

cannot can not.

canny adj **-nier, -niest** shrewd, cautious. **cannily** adv

canoe n light narrow open boat propelled by a paddle or paddles. **canoeing** n sport of rowing in a canoe. **canoeist** n

canon[1] n priest serving in a cathedral.

canon[2] n 1 Church decree regulating morals or religious practices. 2 general rule or standard. 3 list of the works of an author that are accepted as authentic. **canonical** adj **canonize** v declare (a person) officially to be a saint. **canonization** n

canoodle v Slang kiss and cuddle.

canopy n, pl -pies 1 covering above a bed, door, etc. 2 any large or wide covering. **canopied** adj covered with a canopy.

cant[1] n 1 insincere talk. 2 specialized vocabulary of a particular group.

cant[2] n 1 tilted position. ♦ v 2 tilt, overturn.

can't can not.

cantaloupe, cantaloup n kind of melon with sweet orange flesh.

cantankerous adj quarrelsome, bad-tempered.

cantata n musical work consisting of arias, duets, and choruses.

canteen n 1 restaurant attached to a workplace or school. 2 box containing a set of cutlery.

canter n 1 horse's gait between a trot and a gallop. ♦ v 2 move at a canter.

canticle n short hymn with words from the Bible.

cantilever n beam or girder fixed at one end only.

canto n, pl -tos main division of a long poem.

canton n political division of a country, esp. Switzerland.

cantor n man employed to lead services in a synagogue.

canvas n 1 heavy coarse cloth used for sails and tents, and for oil painting. 2 oil painting on canvas.

canvass v 1 try to get votes or support (from). 2 find out the opinions of (people) by conducting a survey. ♦ n 3 canvassing.

canyon n deep narrow valley.

cap n 1 soft close-fitting covering for the head. 2 small lid. 3 small explosive device used in a toy gun. 4 v **capping, capped** 5 cover or top with something. 6 select (a player) for a national team. 7 impose an upper limit on (a tax). 8 outdo, excel.

capable adj 1 (foll. by of) having the ability (for). 2 competent and efficient. **capably** adv **capability** n, pl -ties

capacity n, pl -ties 1 ability to contain, absorb, or hold. 2 maximum amount that can be contained or produced. 3 physical or mental ability. 4 position, function. **capacious** adj roomy. **capacitance** n (measure of) the ability of a system to store electrical charge. **capacitor** n device for storing electrical charge.

caparisoned adj magnificently decorated.

cape[1] n short cloak.

cape[2] n large piece of land that juts out into the sea.

caper n 1 high-spirited prank. ♦ v 2 skip about.

capercaillie, capercailzie [kap-per-**kale**-yee] n large black European grouse.

capers pl n pickled flower buds of a Mediterranean shrub used in sauces.

capillary n, pl -laries very fine blood vessel.

capital[1] n 1 chief city of a country. 2 accumulated wealth. 3 wealth used to produce more wealth. 4 large letter, as used at the beginning of a name or sentence. ♦ adj 5 involving or punishable by death. 6 Old-fashioned excellent. **capitalize** v 1 write or print (words) in capitals. 2 convert into or provide with capital. **capitalize on** v take advantage of (a situation).

capital[2] n top part of a pillar.

capitalism n economic system based on the private ownership of industry. **capitalist** adj 1 of capitalists or capitalism. 2 supporting capitalism. ♦ n 3 supporter of capitalism. 4 person who owns a business.

capitation n tax of a fixed amount per person.

capitulate v surrender on agreed terms. **capitulation** n

capon n castrated cock fowl fattened for eating.

cappuccino [kap-poo-**cheen**-oh] n, pl -nos coffee with steamed milk, sprinkled with powdered chocolate.

caprice [kap-**reess**] n sudden change of attitude. **capricious** adj tending to have sudden changes of attitude. **capriciously** adv

capsicum n kind of pepper used as a vegetable or as a spice.

capsize v (of a boat) overturn accidentally.

capstan n rotating cylinder round which a ship's rope is wound.

capsule n 1 soluble gelatine case containing a dose of medicine. 2 plant's seed case. 3 detachable crew compartment of a spacecraft.

captain n 1 commander of a ship or civil aircraft. 2 middle-ranking naval officer. 3 junior officer in the army. 4 leader of a team or group. ♦ v 5 be captain of. **captaincy** n

caption n 1 title or explanation accompanying an illustration. ♦ v 2 provide with a caption.

captious adj tending to make trivial criticisms.

captivate v attract and hold the attention of. **captivating** adj

captive n 1 person kept in confinement. ♦ adj 2 kept in confinement. 3 (of an audience) unable to leave. **captivity** n

captor n person who captures a person or animal.

capture v 1 take by force. 2 succeed in representing (something elusive) artistically. ♦ n 3 capturing.

car n 1 motor vehicle designed to carry a small number of people. 2 passenger compartment of a cable car, lift, etc. 3 US railway carriage. **car park** area or building reserved for parking cars.

carafe [kar-**raff**] n glass bottle for serving water or wine.

caramel n 1 chewy sweet made from sugar and milk. 2 burnt sugar, used for colouring and flavouring food. **caramelize** v turn into caramel.

carapace n hard upper shell of tortoises and crustaceans.

carat n 1 unit of weight of precious stones. 2 measure of the purity of gold in an alloy.

caravan n 1 large enclosed vehicle for living in, designed to be towed by a car or horse. 2 group travelling together in Eastern countries.

caraway n plant whose seeds are used as a spice.

carbide n compound of carbon with a metal.

carbine n light automatic rifle.

carbohydrate n any of a large group of energy-producing compounds in food, such as sugars and starches.

carbolic acid n disinfectant derived from coal tar.

carbon n nonmetallic element occurring as charcoal, graphite, and diamond, found in all organic matter. **carbonate** n salt or ester of carbonic acid. **carbonated** adj (of a drink) containing carbon dioxide. **carbonize** v 1 turn into carbon as a result of heating. 2 coat with carbon. **carbon copy 1** copy made with carbon paper. 2 very similar person or thing. **carbon dioxide** colourless gas exhaled by people and animals. **carbonic acid** weak acid formed from carbon dioxide and water. **carbon paper** paper coated on one side with a dark waxy pigment, used to make a copy of something as it is typed or written.

Carborundum n ® compound of silicon and carbon, used for grinding and polishing.

carbuncle n inflamed boil.

carburettor n device which mixes petrol and air in an internal-combustion engine.

carcass, carcase n dead body of an animal.

carcinogen n substance that produces cancer. **carcinogenic** adj **carcinoma** n malignant tumour.

card n 1 piece of thick stiff paper or cardboard used for identification, reference, or sending greetings or messages. 2 one of a set of cards with a printed pattern, used for playing games. 3 small rectangle of stiff plastic with identifying numbers for use as a credit card, cheque card, or charge card. 4 Old-fashioned witty or eccentric person. ♦ pl 5 any card game, or card games in general. **cardboard** n thin stiff board made from paper pulp. **cardsharp** n professional card player who cheats.

cardiac adj of the heart. **cardiogram** n electrocardiogram. **cardiograph** n electrocardiograph. **cardiology** n study of the heart and its diseases. **cardiologist** n **cardiovascular** adj of the heart and the blood vessels.

cardigan n knitted jacket.

cardinal n 1 any of the high-ranking clergymen of the RC Church who elect the Pope and act as his counsellors. ♦ adj 2 fundamentally important. **cardinal number** number denoting quantity but not order in a group, for example four as distinct from fourth.

cardinal points the four main points of the compass.

care v 1 be concerned. 2 like (to do something). 3 (foll. by for) like, be fond of. 4 (foll. by for) look after. ♦ n 5 careful attention, caution. 6 protection, charge. 7 trouble, worry. **careful** adj **carefully** adv **carefulness** n **careless** adj **carelessly** adv **carelessness** n

careen v tilt over to one side.

career n 1 series of jobs in a profession or occupation that a person has through their life. 2 part of a person's life spent in a particular occupation. ♦ v 3 rush in an uncontrolled way. **careerist** n person who seeks advancement by any possible means.

carefree adj without worry or responsibility.

caress n 1 gentle affectionate touch or embrace. ♦ v 2 touch gently and affectionately.

caret [**kar**-rett] n symbol (ʌ) indicating a place in written or printed matter where something is to be inserted.

caretaker n person employed to look after a place.

careworn adj showing signs of worry.

cargo n, pl **-goes** goods carried by a ship, aircraft, etc. **cargo pants, trousers** loose trousers with a large pocket on the outside of each leg.

caribou n, pl **-bou** or **-bous** large N American reindeer.

caricature n 1 drawing or description of a person that exaggerates features for comic effect. ♦ v 2 make a caricature of.

caries [**care**-reez] n tooth decay.

carillon [kar-**rill**-yon] n 1 set of bells played by keyboard or mechanically. 2 tune played on such bells.

cark v **cark it** Aust & NZ slang die.

carmine adj vivid red.

carnage n extensive slaughter of people.

carnal adj of a sexual or sensual nature. **carnal knowledge** sexual intercourse.

carnation n cultivated plant with fragrant white, pink, or red flowers.

carnival n festive period with processions, music, and dancing in the street.

carnivore n meat-eating animal. **carnivorous** adj

carob n pod of a Mediterranean tree, used as a chocolate substitute.

carol n 1 joyful Christmas hymn. ♦ v -olling, -olled 2 sing carols. 3 sing joyfully.

carotid adj, n (of) either of the two arteries supplying blood to the head.

carouse v have a merry drinking party.

carousel [kar-roo-**sell**] n 1 revolving conveyor belt for luggage or photographic slides. 2 US merry-go-round.

carp[1] n large freshwater fish.

carp[2] v complain, find fault.

carpel n female reproductive organ of a flowering plant.

carpenter n person who makes or repairs wooden structures. **carpentry** n

carpet n 1 heavy fabric for covering floors. 2 v **carpeting, carpeted** 3 cover with a carpet. **on the carpet** Informal being reprimanded. **carpet snake** or **python** large nonvenomous Australian snake with a carpet-like pattern on its back

carpus n, pl -pi set of eight bones of the wrist.

carriage n 1 one of the sections of a train for passengers. 2 way a person holds his or her head and body. 3 four-wheeled horse-drawn vehicle. 4 moving part of a machine that supports and shifts another part. 5 charge made for conveying goods. **carriageway** n Brit part of a road along which traffic passes in one direction.

carrier n 1 person or thing that carries something. 2 person or animal that does not suffer from a disease but can transmit it to others. **carrier pigeon** homing pigeon used for carrying messages.

carrion n dead and rotting flesh.

carrot n 1 long tapering orange root vegetable. 2 something offered as an incentive. **carroty** adj (of hair) reddish-orange.

carry v -rying, -ried 1 take from one place to another. 2 have with one habitually, in one's pocket etc. 3 transmit (a disease). 4 have as a factor or result. 5 hold (one's head or body) in a specified manner. 6 secure the adoption of (a bill or motion). 7 (of sound) travel a certain distance. **carry on** v 1 continue. 2 Informal cause a fuss. **carry out** v follow, accomplish.

cart n 1 open two-wheeled horse-drawn vehicle for carrying goods or passengers. 2 v 3 carry, usu. with some effort. **carthorse** n large heavily built horse. **cartwheel** n 1 sideways somersault supported by the hands with legs outstretched. 2 large spoked wheel of a cart.

carte blanche [kaht **blahntsh**] n French complete authority.

cartel n association of competing firms formed to fix prices.

cartilage n strong flexible tissue forming part of the skeleton. **cartilaginous** adj

cartography n map making. **cartographer** n **cartographic** adj

carton n container made of cardboard or waxed paper.

cartoon n 1 humorous or satirical drawing. 2 sequence of these telling a story. **3** film made by photographing a series of drawings which give the illusion of movement when projected. **cartoonist** n

cartridge n **1** casing containing an explosive charge and bullet for a gun. **2** part of the pick-up of a record player that converts the movements of the stylus into electrical signals. **3** sealed container of film, tape, etc. **cartridge paper** strong thick drawing paper.

carve v **1** cut to form an object. **2** form (an object or design) by cutting. **3** slice (cooked meat). **carving** n

caryatid [kar-ree-**at**-id] n supporting column in the shape of a female figure.

Casanova n promiscuous man.

casbah n citadel of a N African city.

cascade n **1** waterfall. **2** something flowing or falling like a waterfall. ♦ v **3** flow or fall in a cascade.

case[1] n **1** instance, example. **2** condition, state of affairs. **3** set of arguments supporting an action or cause. **4** person or problem dealt with by a doctor, social worker, or solicitor. **5** action, lawsuit. **6** Grammar form of a noun, pronoun, or adjective showing its relation to other words in the sentence. **in case** so as to allow for the possibility that.

case[2] n **1** container, protective covering. **2** v **3** Slang inspect (a building) with the intention of burgling it. **case-hardened** adj having been made callous by experience.

casement n window that is hinged on one side.

cash n **1** banknotes and coins. **2** v **3** obtain cash for. **cash in on** v Informal gain profit or advantage from. **cash register** till that displays and adds the prices of the goods sold.

cashew n edible kidney-shaped nut.

cashier[1] n person responsible for handling cash in a bank, shop, etc.

cashier[2] v dismiss with dishonour from the armed forces.

cashmere n fine soft wool obtained from goats.

casing n protective case, covering.

casino n, pl **-nos** public building or room where gambling games are played.

cask n **1** barrel used to hold alcoholic drink. **2** Aust cubic carton containing wine, with a tap for dispensing.

casket n **1** small box for valuables. **2** US coffin.

cassava n starch obtained from the roots of a tropical American plant, used to make tapioca.

casserole n **1** covered dish in which food is cooked slowly, usu. in an oven. **2** dish cooked in this way. ♦ v **3** cook in a casserole.

cassette n plastic case containing a reel of film or magnetic tape.

cassock n long tunic, usu. black, worn by priests.

cassowary n, pl **-waries** large flightless bird of Australia and New Guinea.

cast n **1** actors in a play or film collectively. **2** object shaped by a mould while molten. **3** mould used to shape such an object. **4** rigid plaster-of-Paris casing for immobilizing broken bones while they heal. **5** sort, kind. **6** slight squint in the eye. ♦ v **casting, cast 7** select (an actor) to play a part in a play or film. **8** give (a vote). **9** let fall, shed. **10** shape (molten material) in a mould. **11** throw with force. **12** direct (a glance). **castaway** n shipwrecked person. **casting vote** deciding vote used by the chairperson of a meeting when the votes on each side are equal. **cast-iron** adj **1** made of a hard but brittle type of iron. **2** definite, unchallengeable. **cast-off**

adj, n discarded (person or thing).

castanets *pl n* musical instrument, used by Spanish dancers, consisting of curved pieces of hollow wood clicked together in the hand.

caste *n* **1** any of the hereditary classes into which Hindu society is divided. **2** social rank.

castellated *adj* having battlements.

caster sugar finely ground white sugar.

castigate *v* reprimand severely. **castigation** *n*

castle *n* **1** large fortified building, often built as a ruler's residence. **2** rook in chess.

castor *n* small swivelling wheel fixed to the bottom of a piece of furniture for easy moving.

castor oil *n* oil obtained from an Indian plant, used as a lubricant and purgative.

castrate *v* **1** remove the testicles of. **2** deprive of vigour or masculinity. **castration** *n*

casual *adj* **1** careless, nonchalant. **2** (of work or workers) occasional or not permanent. **3** for informal wear. **4** happening by chance. **casually** *adv*

casualty *n, pl* **-ties 1** person killed or injured in an accident or war. **2** person or thing that has suffered as the result of something.

casuarina [kass-yew-a-**reen**-a] *n* Australian tree with jointed green branches.

casuistry *n* reasoning that is misleading or oversubtle.

cat *n* **1** small domesticated furry mammal. **2** related wild mammal, such as the lion or tiger. **catty** *adj Informal* spiteful. **catkin** *n* drooping flower spike of certain trees. **catcall** *n* derisive whistle or cry. **catfish** *n* fish with whisker-like barbels round the mouth. **catgut** *n* strong cord used to

string musical instruments and sports rackets. **catnap** *n, v* doze. **Catseyes** *pl n* ® glass reflectors set in the road to indicate traffic lanes. **cat's paw** person used by another to do unpleasant things for him or her. **catwalk** *n* narrow pathway or platform.

cataclysm [**kat**-a-kliz-zum] *n* **1** violent upheaval. **2** disaster, such as an earthquake. **cataclysmic** *adj*

catacombs [**kat**-a-koomz] *pl n* underground burial place consisting of tunnels with recesses for tombs.

catafalque [**kat**-a-falk] *n* raised platform on which a body lies in state before or during a funeral.

catalepsy *n* trancelike state in which the body is rigid. **cataleptic** *adj*

catalogue *n* **1** book containing details of items for sale. **2** systematic list of items. ◆ *v* **3** make a systematic list of.

catalyst *n* substance that speeds up a chemical reaction without itself changing. **catalyse** *v* speed up (a chemical reaction) by a catalyst. **catalysis** *n* **catalytic** *adj*

catamaran *n* boat with twin parallel hulls.

catapult *n* **1** Y-shaped device with a loop of elastic, used by children for firing stones. ◆ *v* **2** shoot forwards or upwards violently.

cataract *n* **1** eye disease in which the lens becomes opaque. **2** opaque area of an eye. **3** large waterfall.

catarrh [kat-**tar**] *n* excessive mucus in the nose and throat, during or following a cold. **catarrhal** *adj*

catastrophe [kat-**ass**-trof-fee] *n* great and sudden disaster. **catastrophic** *adj*

catch *v* **catching, caught 1** seize, capture. **2** surprise in an act, e.g. *two boys were caught stealing*. **3** hit unexpectedly. **4** be in time for (a bus, train, etc.). **5** see or hear. **6** be infected with (an illness). **7** entangle. **8** understand, make out. **9** *n* **10** device for fastening a door, window, etc. **11** *Informal* concealed or unforeseen drawback. **catch it** *Informal* be punished. **catching** *adj* infectious. **catchy** *adj* (of a tune) pleasant and easily remembered. **catchment area 1** area served by a particular school or hospital. **2** area of land draining into a river, basin, or reservoir. **catch on** *v Informal* **1** become popular. **2** understand. **catch out** *v Informal* trap (someone) in an error or lie. **catch phrase** well-known phrase associated with a particular entertainer. **catch 22** inescapable dilemma. **catchword** *n* well-known and frequently used phrase.

catechism [**kat**-ti-kiz-zum] *n* instruction on the doctrine of a Christian Church in a series of questions and answers.

category *n, pl* **-ries** class, group. **categorical** *adj* absolutely clear and certain. **categorically** *adv* **categorize** *v* put in a category. **categorization** *n*

cater *v* provide what is needed or wanted, esp. food or services. **caterer** *n*

caterpillar *n* **1** wormlike larva of a moth or butterfly. **2** ® endless track, driven by cogged wheels, used to propel a heavy vehicle.

caterwaul *v* wail, yowl.

catharsis [kath-**thar**-siss] *n, pl* **-ses** relief of strong suppressed emotions. **cathartic** *adj*

cathedral *n* principal church of a diocese.

Catherine wheel *n* rotating firework.

catheter [**kath**-it-er] *n* tube inserted into a body cavity to drain fluid.

cathode *n* negative electrode, by which electrons leave a circuit.

cathode rays stream of electrons from a cathode in a vacuum tube.

catholic *adj* **1** (of tastes or interests) covering a wide range. ♦ *n, adj* **2** (C-) (member) of the Roman Catholic Church. **Catholicism** *n*

cation [**kat**-eye-on] *n* positively charged ion.

cattle *pl n* domesticated cows and bulls.

Caucasian *n, adj* (member) of the light-skinned racial group of humankind.

caucus *n, pl* **-cuses 1** local committee or faction of a political party. **2** political meeting to decide future plans.

caught *v* past of CATCH.

cauldron *n* large pot used for boiling.

cauliflower *n* vegetable with a large head of white flower buds surrounded by green leaves.

caulk *v* fill in (cracks) with paste etc.

causal *adj* of or being a cause. **causally** *adv* **causation, causality** *n* relationship of cause and effect.

cause *n* **1** something that produces a particular effect. **2** (foll. by *for*) reason, motive. **3** aim or principle supported by a person or group. ♦ *v* **4** be the cause of.

cause célèbre [kawz sill-**leb**-ra] *n, pl* **causes célèbres** [kawz sill-**leb**-ra] controversial legal case or issue.

causeway *n* raised path or road across water or marshland.

caustic *adj* **1** capable of burning by chemical action. **2** bitter and sarcastic. **caustically** *adv*

cauterize *v* burn (a wound) with heat or a caustic agent to prevent infection.

caution *n* **1** care, esp. in the face of danger. **2** warning. ♦ *v* **3** warn, advise. **cautionary** *adj* warning. **cautious** *adj* showing caution. **cautiously** *adv*

cavalcade *n* procession of people on

horseback or in cars.

cavalier adj **1** showing haughty disregard. ♦ n **2** (C-) supporter of Charles I in the English Civil War.

cavalry n, pl **-ries** part of the army orig. on horseback, but now often using fast armoured vehicles.

cave n hollow in the side of a hill or cliff. **caving** n sport of exploring caves. **cave in** v **1** collapse inwards. **2** Informal yield under pressure. **caveman** n prehistoric cave dweller.

caveat [**kav**-vee-at] n warning.

cavern n large cave. **cavernous** adj

caviar, caviare n salted sturgeon roe, regarded as a delicacy.

cavil v **-illing, -illed** **1** make petty objections. ♦ n **2** petty objection.

cavity n, pl **-ties** **1** hollow space. **2** decayed area on a tooth.

cavort v skip about.

caw n **1** cry of a crow, rook, or raven. ♦ v **2** make this cry.

cayenne pepper, cayenne n hot red spice made from capsicum seeds.

cayman n, pl **-mans** S American reptile similar to an alligator.

CB Citizens' Band.

CBE (in Britain) Commander of the Order of the British Empire.

CBI Confederation of British Industry.

cc 1 cubic centimetre. **2** carbon copy.

CD compact disc.

CD-ROM compact disc read-only memory.

cease v bring or come to an end. **ceaseless** adj **ceaselessly** adv **ceasefire** n temporary truce.

cedar n **1** evergreen coniferous tree. **2** its wood.

cede v surrender (territory or legal rights).

cedilla n character (¸) placed under a c in some languages, to show that it is pronounced s, not k.

ceilidh [**kay**-lee] n informal social gathering for singing and dancing, esp. in Scotland.

ceiling n **1** inner upper surface of a room. **2** upper limit set on something.

celandine n wild plant with yellow flowers.

celebrate v **1** hold festivities to mark (a happy event, anniversary, etc.). **2** perform (a religious ceremony). **celebrated** adj well known. **celebration** n **celebrant** n person who performs a religious ceremony. **celebrity** n, pl **-rities** **1** famous person. **2** state of being famous.

celeriac [sill-**ler**-ee-ak] n variety of celery with a large turnip-like root.

celerity [sill-**ler**-rit-tee] n swiftness.

celery n vegetable with long green crisp edible stalks.

celestial adj **1** heavenly, divine. **2** of the sky.

celibate adj **1** unmarried or abstaining from sex, esp. because of a religious vow of chastity. ♦ n **2** celibate person. **celibacy** n

cell n **1** smallest unit of an organism that is able to function independently. **2** small room for a prisoner, monk, or nun. **3** small compartment of a honeycomb etc. **4** small group operating as the core of a larger organization. **5** device that produces electrical energy by chemical reaction. **cellular** adj of or consisting of cells.

cellar n **1** underground room for storage. **2** stock of wine.

cello [**chell**-oh] n, pl **-los** large low-pitched instrument of the violin family. **cellist** n

Cellophane n ® thin transparent cellulose sheeting used as wrapping.

celluloid n kind of plastic used to make toys and, formerly, photographic film.

cellulose n main constituent of plant

cell walls, used in making paper, plastics, etc.

Celsius adj of the temperature scale in which water freezes at 0° and boils at 100°.

Celt [**kelt**] n person from Scotland, Ireland, Wales, Cornwall, or Brittany.

Celtic [**kel**-tik, **sel**-tik] n 1 group of languages including Gaelic and Welsh. ♦ adj 2 of the Celts or the Celtic languages.

cement n 1 fine grey powder mixed with water and sand to make mortar or concrete. 2 something that unites, binds, or joins. 3 material used to fill teeth. ♦ v 4 join, bind, or cover with cement. 5 make (a relationship) stronger.

cemetery n, pl **-teries** place where dead people are buried.

cenotaph n monument honouring soldiers who died in a war.

censer n container for burning incense.

censor n 1 person authorized to examine films, books, etc., to ban or cut anything considered obscene or objectionable. ♦ v 2 ban or cut parts of (a film, book, etc.). **censorship** n **censorious** adj harshly critical.

censure n 1 severe disapproval. ♦ v 2 criticize severely.

census n, pl **-suses** official count of a population.

cent n hundredth part of a monetary unit such as the dollar or euro.

centaur n mythical creature with the head, arms, and torso of a man, and the lower body and legs of a horse.

centenary [sen-**teen**-a-ree] n Chiefly Brit pl **-naries** 100th anniversary or its celebration. **centenarian** n person at least 100 years old.

centennial n 100th anniversary or its celebration.

centi- prefix one hundredth.

centigrade adj same as CELSIUS.

centigram, centigramme n one hundredth of a gram.

centilitre n one hundredth of a litre.

centimetre n one hundredth of a metre.

centipede n small wormlike creature with many legs.

central adj 1 of, at, or forming the centre. 2 main, principal. **centrally** adv **centrality** n **centralism** n principle of central control of a country or organization. **centralize** v bring under central control. **centralization** n **central heating** system for heating a building from one central source of heat.

centre n 1 middle point or part. 2 place for a specified activity. 3 political party or group favouring moderation. 4 Sport player who plays in the middle of the field. ♦ v 5 put in the centre of something. **centrist** n person favouring political moderation. **centre on** v have as a centre or main theme.

centrifugal adj moving away from a centre. **centrifuge** n machine that separates substances by centrifugal force.

centripetal adj moving towards a centre.

centurion n (in ancient Rome) officer commanding 100 men.

century n, pl **-ries** 1 period of 100 years. 2 cricket score of 100 runs.

CEO chief executive officer.

cephalopod [**seff**-a-loh-pod] n sea mollusc with a head and tentacles, such as the octopus.

ceramic n 1 hard brittle material made by heating clay to a very high temperature. 2 object made of this. ♦ pl 3 art of producing ceramic objects. ♦ adj 4 made of ceramic.

cereal n 1 grass plant with edible grain, such as oat or wheat. 2 this grain. 3

breakfast food made from this grain, eaten mixed with milk.

cerebral [**ser**-rib-ral, ser-**reeb**-ral] *adj* **1** of the brain. **2** intellectual.

cerebrum [**serr**-rib-rum] *n, pl* **-brums, -bra** [-bra] main part of the brain.

ceremony *n, pl* **-nies 1** formal act or ritual. **2** formally polite behaviour. **ceremonial** *adj, n* **ceremonially** *adv* **ceremonious** *adj* excessively polite or formal. **ceremoniously** *adv*

cerise [ser-**reess**] *adj* cherry-red.

certain *adj* **1** positive and confident. **2** definite. **3** some but not much. **certainly** *adv* **certainty** *n* **1** state of being sure. **2** *pl* -**ties**) something that is inevitable.

certificate *n* official document stating the details of a birth, academic course, etc.

certify *v* **-fying, -fied 1** confirm, attest to. **2** guarantee. **3** declare legally insane. **certifiable** *adj* considered legally insane. **certification** *n*

certitude *n* confidence, certainty.

cervix *n, pl* **cervixes, cervices 1** narrow entrance of the womb. **2** neck. **cervical** *adj*

cessation *n* ceasing.

cesspit, cesspool *n* covered tank or pit for sewage.

cetacean [sit-**tay**-shun] *n* fish-shaped sea mammal such as a whale or dolphin.

cf compare.

CFC chlorofluorocarbon.

CGI computer-generated image(s).

ch. 1 chapter. **2** church.

chafe *v* **1** make sore or worn by rubbing. **2** be annoyed or impatient.

chaff[1] *n* grain husks.

chaff[2] *v* *Old-fashioned* tease good-naturedly.

chaffinch *n* small European songbird.

chagrin [**shag**-grin] *n* annoyance and disappointment. **chagrined** *adj* annoyed and disappointed.

chain *n* **1** flexible length of connected metal links. **2** series of connected facts or events. **3** group of shops, hotels, etc. owned by one firm. ♦ *v* **4** restrict or fasten with or as if with a chain. **chain reaction** series of events, each of which causes the next. **chain-smoke** *v* smoke (cigarettes) continuously. **chain smoker**

chair *n* **1** seat with a back, for one person. **2** official position of authority. **3** person holding this. **4** professorship. ♦ *v* **5** preside over (a meeting). **chairlift** series of chairs suspended from a moving cable for carrying people up a slope. **chairman, chairwoman** *n* person in charge of a company's board of directors or a meeting (also **chairperson**).

chaise [**shaze**] *n* *Hist* light horse-drawn carriage.

chaise longue [**long**] *n* couch with a back and a single armrest.

chalcedony [kal-**sed**-don-ee] *n, pl* -**nies** variety of quartz.

chalet *n* **1** kind of Swiss wooden house with a steeply sloping roof. **2** similar house, used as a holiday home.

chalice *n* large goblet.

chalk *n* **1** soft white rock consisting of calcium carbonate. **2** piece of chalk, often coloured, used for drawing and writing on blackboards. ♦ *v* **3** draw or mark with chalk. **chalky** *adj*

challenge *n* **1** demanding or stimulating situation. **2** call to take part in a contest or fight. **3** questioning of a statement of fact. **4** demand by a sentry for identification or a password. ♦ *v* **5** issue a challenge to. **challenged** *adj* disabled as specified, e.g. *physically challenged.* **challenger** *n*

chamber *n* **1** hall used for formal meetings. **2** legislative or judicial assembly. **3** *Old-fashioned* bedroom. **4** compartment, cavity. **5** *pl* **6** set of rooms used as offices by a barrister. **chambermaid** *n* woman employed to clean bedrooms in a hotel. **chamber music** classical music to be performed by a small group of musicians. **chamber pot** bowl for urine, formerly used in bedrooms.

chamberlain *n Hist* officer who managed the household of a king or nobleman.

chameleon [kam-**meal**-yon] *n* small lizard that changes colour to blend in with its surroundings.

chamfer [**cham**-fer] *v* bevel the edge of.

chamois [**sham**-wah] *n, pl* -**ois 1** small mountain antelope. **2** [**sham**-ee] soft suede leather. **3** piece of this, used for cleaning or polishing.

chamomile [**kam**-mo-mile] *n* same as CAMOMILE.

champ[1] *v* chew noisily. **champ at the bit** *Informal* be impatient to do something.

champ[2] *n* short for CHAMPION.

champagne *n* sparkling white French wine.

champion *n* **1** overall winner of a competition. **2** (foll. by *of*) someone who defends a person or cause. ♦ *v* **3** support. ♦ *adj* **4** *Dialect* excellent. **championship** *n*

chance *n* **1** likelihood, probability. **2** opportunity to do something. **3** risk, gamble. **4** unpredictable element that causes things to happen one way rather than another. ♦ *v* **5** risk, hazard. **chancy** *adj* uncertain, risky.

chancel *n* part of a church containing the altar and choir.

chancellor *n* **1** head of government in some European countries. **2** honorary head of a university. **chancellorship** *n*

Chancery *n* division of the British High Court of Justice.

chandelier [shan-dill-**eer**] *n* ornamental light with branches and holders for several candles or bulbs.

chandler *n* dealer, esp. in ships' supplies.

change *n* **1** becoming different. **2** variety or novelty. **3** different set, esp. of clothes. **4** balance received when the amount paid is more than the cost of a purchase. **5** coins of low value. ♦ *v* **6** make or become different. **7** give and receive (something) in return. **8** exchange (money) for its equivalent in a smaller denomination or different currency. **9** put on other clothes. **10** leave one vehicle and board another. **changeable** *adj* changing often. **changeling** *n* child believed to have been exchanged by fairies for another.

channel *n* **1** band of broadcasting frequencies. **2** means of access or communication. **3** broad strait connecting two areas of sea. **4** bed or course of a river, stream, or canal. **5** groove. ♦ *v* -**nelling**, -**nelled 6** direct or convey through a channel.

chant *v* **1** utter or sing (a slogan or psalm). ♦ *n* **2** rhythmic or repetitious slogan. **3** psalm that has a short simple melody with several words sung on one note.

chanter *n* (on bagpipes) pipe on which the melody is played.

chaos *n* complete disorder or confusion. **chaotic** *adj* **chaotically** *adv*

chap *n Informal* man or boy.

chapati, chapatti *n* (in Indian cookery) flat thin unleavened bread.

chapel *n* **1** place of worship with its own altar, within a church. **2** similar place of worship in a large house or institution. **3** Nonconformist place of worship.

chaperone [**shap**-per-rone] *n* **1** older

person who accompanies and supervises a young person or young people on a social occasion. ♦ v **2** act as a chaperone to.

chaplain n clergyman attached to a chapel, military body, or institution. **chaplaincy** n, pl **-cies**

chaplet n garland for the head.

chapped adj (of the skin) raw and cracked, through exposure to cold.

chapter n **1** division of a book. **2** period in a life or history. **3** branch of a society or club.

char[1] v **charring, charred** blacken by partial burning.

char[2] Brit informal ♦ n **1** charwoman. ♦ v **charring, charred 2** clean other people's houses as a job.

char[3] n Brit old-fashioned slang tea.

charabanc [**shar**-rab-bang] n Old-fashioned coach for sightseeing.

character n **1** combination of qualities distinguishing a person, group, or place. **2** reputation, esp. good reputation. **3** person represented in a play, film, or story. **4** unusual or amusing person. **5** letter, numeral, or symbol used in writing or printing. **characteristic** n **1** distinguishing feature or quality. ♦ adj **2** typical. **characteristically** adv **characterize** v **1** be a characteristic of. **2** (foll. by as) describe. **characterization** n

charade [shar-**rahd**] n **1** absurd pretence. ♦ pl **2** game in which one team acts out a word or phrase, which the other team has to guess.

charcoal n black substance formed by partially burning wood.

charge v **1** ask as a price. **2** enter a debit against a person's account for (a purchase). **3** accuse formally. **4** make a rush at or sudden attack upon. **5** fill (a glass). **6** fill (a battery) with electricity. **7** command, assign. ♦ n **8** price charged. **9** formal accusation. **10**

attack. **11** command, exhortation. **12** custody, guardianship. **13** person or thing entrusted to someone's care. **14** amount of electricity stored in a battery. **in charge of** in control of. **chargeable** adj **charger** n **1** device for charging an accumulator. **2** (in the Middle Ages) warhorse.

chargé d'affaires [**shar**-zhay daf-**fair**] n, pl **chargés d'affaires** head of a diplomatic mission in the absence of an ambassador or in a small mission.

chariot n two-wheeled horse-drawn vehicle used in ancient times in wars and races. **charioteer** n chariot driver.

charisma [kar-**rizz**-ma] n person's power to attract or influence people. **charismatic** [kar-rizz-**mat**-ik] adj

charity n, pl **-ties 1** organization that gives help, such as money or food, to those in need. **2** giving of help to those in need. **3** help given to those in need. **4** kindly attitude towards people. **charitable** adj **charitably** adv

charlady n Brit informal **same as** CHARWOMAN.

charlatan [**shar**-lat-tan] n person who claims expertise that he or she does not have.

charleston n lively dance of the 1920s.

charm n **1** attractive quality. **2** trinket worn on a bracelet. **3** magic spell. ♦ v **4** attract, delight. **5** influence by personal charm. **6** protect or influence as if by magic. **charmer** n **charming** adj attractive.

charnel house n Hist building or vault for the bones of the dead.

chart n **1** graph, table, or diagram showing information. **2** map of the sea or stars. ♦ v **3** plot the course of. **4** make a chart of. **the charts** Informal weekly lists of the bestselling pop records.

charter n **1** document granting or demanding certain rights. **2**

fundamental principles of an organization. **3** hire of transport for private use. ♦ v **4** hire by charter. **5** grant a charter to. **chartered** adj officially qualified to practise a profession.

chartreuse [shar-**trerz**] n sweet-smelling green or yellow liqueur.

charwoman n woman whose job is to clean other people's homes.

chary [**chair**-ee] adj -rier, -riest wary, careful.

chase¹ v **1** run after quickly in order to catch or drive away. **2** Informal rush, run. **3** Informal try energetically to obtain. ♦ n **4** chasing, pursuit. **chaser** n milder drink drunk after another stronger one.

chase² v engrave or emboss (metal).

chasm [**kaz**-zum] n deep crack in the earth.

chassis [**shass**-ee] n, pl -sis frame, wheels, and mechanical parts of a vehicle.

chaste adj **1** abstaining from sex outside marriage or altogether. **2** (of style) simple. **chastely** adv **chastity** n

chasten [**chase**-en] v subdue by criticism.

chastise v **1** scold severely. **2** punish by beating. **chastisement** n

chat n **1** informal conversation. ♦ v **chatting, chatted 2** have an informal conversation. **chatty** adj **chatroom** n site on the Internet where users have group discussions by e-mail.

chateau [**shat**-toe] n, pl -teaux, -teaus French castle.

chatelaine [**shat**-tell-lane] n (formerly) mistress of a large house or castle.

chattels pl n possessions.

chatter v **1** speak quickly and continuously about unimportant things. **2** (of the teeth) rattle with cold or fear. ♦ n **3** idle talk. **chatterbox** n person who chatters a lot.

chauffeur n person employed to drive a car for someone.

chauvinism [**show**-vin-iz-zum] n irrational belief that one's own country, race, group, or sex is superior. **chauvinist** n, adj **chauvinistic** adj

cheap adj **1** costing relatively little. **2** of poor quality. **3** not valued highly. **4** mean, despicable. **cheaply** adv **cheapen** v **1** lower the reputation of. **2** reduce the price of. **cheapskate** n Informal miserly person.

cheat v **1** act dishonestly to gain profit or advantage. **2** n **3** person who cheats. **4** fraud, deception.

check v **1** examine, investigate. **2** slow the growth or progress of. **3** correspond, agree. ♦ n **4** test to ensure accuracy or progress. **5** break in progress. **6** US cheque. **7** pattern of squares or crossed lines. **8** Chess position of a king under attack. **check in** v register one's arrival. **checkmate** n **1** Chess winning position in which an opponent's king is under attack and unable to escape. **2** utter defeat. ♦ v **3** Chess place the king of (one's opponent) in checkmate. **4** thwart, defeat. **check out** v **1** pay the bill and leave a hotel. **2** examine, investigate. **3** Informal have a look at. **checkout** n counter in a supermarket, where customers pay. **checkup** n thorough medical examination.

Cheddar n firm orange or yellowy-white cheese.

cheek n **1** either side of the face below the eye. **2** Informal impudence, boldness. ♦ v **3** Brit, Aust & NZ informal speak impudently to. **cheeky** adj impudent, disrespectful. **cheekily** adv **cheekiness** n

cheep n **1** young bird's high-pitched cry. ♦ v **2** utter a cheep.

cheer v **1** applaud or encourage with shouts. **2** make or become happy. ♦ n **3** shout of applause or encouragement. **cheerful** adj **cheerfully** adv **cheerfulness** n **cheerless** adj dreary, gloomy. **cheery** adj **cheerily** adv

cheerio interj **1** Informal goodbye. ♦ n **2** Aust & NZ small red cocktail sausage.

cheese n **1** food made from coagulated milk curd. **2** block of this. **cheesy** adj **cheeseburger** n hamburger topped with melted cheese. **cheesecake** n **1** dessert with a biscuit-crumb base covered with a sweet cream-cheese mixture. **2** Slang photographs of naked or near-naked women. **cheesecloth** n light cotton cloth. **cheesed off** bored, annoyed.

cheetah n large fast-running spotted African wild cat.

chef n cook in a restaurant.

chef-d'oeuvre [shay-**durv**] n, pl **chefs-d'oeuvre** masterpiece.

chemical n **1** substance used in or resulting from a reaction involving changes to atoms or molecules. ♦ adj **2** of chemistry or chemicals. **chemically** adv

chemise [shem-**meez**] n Old-fashioned woman's loose-fitting slip.

chemistry n science of the composition, properties, and reactions of substances. **chemist** n **1** shop selling medicines and cosmetics. **2** qualified dispenser of prescribed medicines. **3** specialist in chemistry.

chemotherapy n treatment of disease, often cancer, using chemicals.

chenille [shen-**neel**] n (fabric of) thick tufty yarn.

cheque n written order to one's bank to pay money from one's account. **cheque card** Brit plastic card issued by a bank guaranteeing payment of a customer's cheques.

chequer n **1** piece used in Chinese chequers. ♦ pl **2** game of draughts.

chequered adj **1** marked by varied fortunes. **2** having a pattern of squares.

cherish v **1** cling to (an idea or feeling). **2** care for.

cheroot [sher-**root**] n cigar with both ends cut flat.

cherry n, pl **-ries 1** small red or black fruit with a stone. **2** tree on which it grows. ♦ adj **3** deep red.

cherub n, pl **-ubs, -ubim 1** angel, often represented as a winged child. **2** sweet child. **cherubic** [cher-**rew**-bik] adj

chervil n aniseed-flavoured herb.

chess n game for two players with 16 pieces each, played on a chequered board of 64 squares. **chessman** n piece used in chess.

chest n **1** front of the body, from neck to waist. **2** large strong box. **chest of drawers** piece of furniture consisting of drawers in a frame.

chesterfield n couch with high padded sides and back.

chestnut n **1** reddish-brown edible nut. **2** tree on which it grows. **3** reddish-brown horse. **4** Informal old joke. ♦ adj **5** (of hair or a horse) reddish-brown.

chevron [**shev**-ron] n V-shaped pattern, esp. on the sleeve of a military uniform to indicate rank.

chew v grind (food) between the teeth. **chewy** adj requiring a lot of chewing. **chewing gum** flavoured gum to be chewed but not swallowed.

chianti [kee-**ant**-ee] n dry red Italian wine.

chiaroscuro [kee-ah-roh-**skew**-roh] n, pl **-ros** distribution of light and shade in a picture.

chic [**sheek**] adj **1** stylish, elegant. ♦ n **2** stylishness, elegance.

chicane [shik-**kane**] n obstacle in a motor-racing circuit.

chicanery n trickery, deception.

chick n baby bird. **chickpea** n edible yellow pealike seed. **chickweed** n weed with small white flowers.

chicken n 1 domestic fowl. 2 its flesh, used as food. 3 Slang coward. ♦ adj 4 Slang cowardly. **chicken feed** Slang trifling amount of money. **chicken out** v Informal fail to do something through cowardice. **chickenpox** n infectious disease with an itchy rash.

chicory n, pl **-ries** 1 plant whose leaves are used in salads. 2 root of this plant, used as a coffee substitute.

chide v chiding, chided or chid, chid or chidden rebuke, scold.

chief n 1 head of a group of people. ♦ adj 2 most important. **chiefly** adv 1 especially. 2 mainly. **chieftain** n leader of a tribe.

chiffon [**shif**-fon] n fine see-through fabric.

chignon [**sheen**-yon] n knot of hair pinned up at the back of the head.

chihuahua [chee-**wah**-wah] n tiny short-haired dog.

chilblain n inflammation of the fingers or toes, caused by exposure to cold.

child n, pl children 1 young human being, boy or girl. 2 son or daughter. **childhood** n **childish** adj 1 immature, silly. 2 of or like a child. **childishly** adv **childless** adj **childlike** adj innocent, trustful. **childbirth** n giving birth to a child. **child's play** very easy task.

chill n 1 feverish cold. 2 moderate coldness. ♦ v 3 make (something) cool or cold. 4 cause (someone) to feel cold or frightened. ♦ adj 5 unpleasantly cold. **chilly** adj 1 moderately cold. 2 unfriendly. **chilly-bin** n NZ informal insulated container for carrying food and drink. **chilliness** n **chill (out)** v

Informal relax. **chill-out** adj Informal suitable for relaxation, esp. after energetic activity, e.g. a chill-out area.

chilli, chili n 1 small red or green hot-tasting capsicum pod, used in cooking. 2 (also **chilli con carne**) hot-tasting Mexican dish of meat, onions, beans, and chilli powder.

chime n 1 musical ringing sound of a bell or clock. ♦ v 2 make a musical ringing sound. 3 indicate (the time) by chiming. 4 (foll. by with) be consistent with.

chimera [kime-**meer**-a] n 1 unrealistic hope or idea. 2 fabled monster with a lion's head, goat's body, and serpent's tail.

chimney n hollow vertical structure for carrying away smoke from a fire. **chimney pot** short pipe on the top of a chimney. **chimney sweep** person who cleans soot from chimneys.

chimp n Informal short for CHIMPANZEE.

chimpanzee n intelligent black African ape.

chin n part of the face below the mouth. **chinwag** n Brit, Aust & NZ informal chat.

china n 1 fine earthenware or porcelain. 2 dishes or ornaments made of this. 3 Brit, Aust, NZ & S Afr informal friend.

chinchilla n 1 S American rodent bred for its soft grey fur. 2 its fur.

chine n cut of meat including part of the backbone.

Chinese adj 1 of China. ♦ n 2 pl **-nese** person from China. 3 any of the languages of China.

chink[1] n small narrow opening.

chink[2] v, n (make) a light ringing sound.

chintz n printed cotton fabric with a glazed finish.

chip n 1 strip of potato, fried in deep fat. 2 tiny wafer of semiconductor material forming an integrated circuit. **3** counter used to represent money in gambling games. **4** small piece removed by chopping, breaking, etc. **5** mark left where a small piece has been broken off something. ♦ v **chipping, chipped 6** break small pieces from. **have a chip on one's shoulder** Informal bear a grudge. **chip in** v Informal **1** contribute (money). **2** interrupt with a remark. **chippie** n Brit, Aust & NZ informal carpenter.

chipboard n thin board made of compressed wood particles.

chipmunk n small squirrel-like N American rodent with a striped back.

chiropodist [kir-**rop**-pod-ist] n person who treats minor foot complaints. **chiropody** n

chiropractic [kire-oh-**prak**-tik] n system of treating bodily disorders by manipulation of the spine. **chiropractor** n

chirp v **1** (of a bird or insect) make a short high-pitched sound. **2** n **3** chirping sound. **chirpy** adj Informal lively and cheerful.

chisel n **1** metal tool with a sharp end for shaping wood or stone. ♦ v **-elling, -elled 2** carve or form with a chisel.

chit[1] n short official note, such as a receipt.

chit[2] n Brit, Aust & NZ old-fashioned pert or impudent girl.

chitchat n chat, gossip.

chitterlings pl n pig's intestines cooked as food.

chivalry n **1** courteous behaviour, esp. by men towards women. **2** medieval system and principles of knighthood. **chivalrous** adj

chives pl n herb with a mild onion flavour.

chivvy v **-vying, -vied** Informal harass, nag.

chlorine n strong-smelling

greenish-yellow gaseous element, used to disinfect water. **chlorinate** v disinfect (water) with chlorine. **chlorination** n **chloride** n compound of chlorine and another substance.

chlorofluorocarbon n any of various gaseous compounds of carbon, hydrogen, chlorine, and fluorine, used in refrigerators and aerosol propellants, some of which break down the ozone in the atmosphere.

chloroform n strong-smelling liquid formerly used as an anaesthetic.

chlorophyll n green colouring matter of plants, which enables them to convert sunlight into energy.

chock n block or wedge used to prevent a heavy object from moving. **chock-full, chock-a-block** adj completely full.

chocolate n **1** sweet food made from cacao seeds. **2** sweet or drink made from this. ♦ adj **3** dark brown.

choice n **1** choosing. **2** opportunity or power of choosing. **3** person or thing chosen or that may be chosen. **4** alternative action or possibility. ♦ adj **5** of high quality.

choir n **1** organized group of singers, esp. in church. **2** part of a church occupied by the choir.

choke v **1** hinder or stop the breathing of (a person) by strangling or smothering. **2** have trouble in breathing. **3** block, clog up. ♦ n **4** device controlling the amount of air that is mixed with the fuel in a petrol engine. **choker** n tight-fitting necklace. **choke back** v suppress (tears or anger).

cholera [**kol**-ler-a] n serious infectious disease causing severe vomiting and diarrhoea.

choleric [**kol**-ler-ik] adj bad-tempered.

cholesterol [kol-**lest**-er-oll] n fatty substance found in animal tissue, an excess of which can cause heart disease.

chomp v chew noisily.

chook n Aust & NZ hen or chicken.

choose v **choosing, chose, chosen 1** select from a number of alternatives. **2** decide (to do something) because one wants to. **choosy** adj Informal fussy, hard to please.

chop[1] v **chopping, chopped 1** cut with a blow from an axe or knife. **2** cut into pieces. **3** dispense with. **4** Boxing, karate hit (an opponent) with a short sharp blow. ♦ n **5** cutting or sharp blow. **6** slice of lamb or pork, usu. with a rib. **chopper** n **1** Informal helicopter. **2** small axe. **choppy** adj (of the sea) fairly rough.

chop[2] v **chopping, chopped. chop and change** change one's mind repeatedly.

chops pl n Brit, Aust & NZ informal jaws, cheeks.

chopsticks pl n pair of thin sticks used to eat Chinese food.

chop suey n Chinese dish of chopped meat and vegetables in a sauce.

choral adj of a choir.

chorale [kor-**rahl**] n slow stately hymn tune.

chord[1] n Maths straight line joining two points on a curve.

chord[2] n simultaneous sounding of three or more musical notes.

chore n routine task.

choreography n composition of steps and movements for dancing. **choreographer** n **choreographic** adj

chorister n singer in a choir.

chortle v **1** chuckle in amusement. ♦ n **2** amused chuckle.

chorus n, pl **-ruses 1** large choir. **2** part of a song repeated after each verse. **3** something expressed by many people at once. **4** group of singers or dancers

who perform together in a show. ♦ v **chorusing, chorused 5** sing or say together. **in chorus** in unison.

chose v past tense of CHOOSE. **chosen** v past participle of CHOOSE.

choux pastry [**shoo**] n very light pastry made with eggs.

chow n thick-coated dog with a curled tail, orig. from China.

chowder n thick soup containing clams or fish.

chow mein n Chinese-American dish of chopped meat or vegetables fried with noodles.

Christ n Jesus of Nazareth, regarded by Christians as the Messiah.

christen v **1** baptize. **2** give a name to. **3** Informal use for the first time. **christening** n

Christendom n all Christian people or countries.

Christian n **1** person who believes in and follows Christ. ♦ adj **2** of Christ or Christianity. **3** kind, good. **Christianity** n religion based on the life and teachings of Christ. **Christian name** personal name given to Christians at baptism: loosely used to mean a person's first name. **Christian Science** religious system which emphasizes spiritual healing.

Christmas n **1** annual festival on Dec. 25 commemorating the birth of Christ. **2** period around this time. **Christmassy** adj **Christmas Day** Dec. 25. **Christmas Eve** Dec. 24. **Christmas tree** evergreen tree or imitation of one, decorated as part of Christmas celebrations.

chromatic adj **1** of colour or colours. **2** Music (of a scale) proceeding by semitones.

chromatography n separation and analysis of the components of a substance by slowly passing it through an adsorbing material.

chromium, chrome *n Chem* grey metallic element used in steel alloys and for electroplating.

chromosome *n* microscopic gene-carrying body in the nucleus of a cell.

chronic *adj* **1** (of an illness) lasting a long time. **2** habitual, e.g. *chronic drinking*. **3** *Brit, Aust & NZ informal* of poor quality. **chronically** *adv*

chronicle *n* **1** record of events in order of occurrence. ♦ *v* **2** record in or as if in a chronicle. **chronicler** *n*

chronology *n, pl* **-gies** arrangement or list of events in order of occurrence. **chronological** *adj* **chronologically** *adv*

chronometer *n* timepiece designed to be accurate in all conditions.

chrysalis [**kriss**-a-liss] *n* insect in the stage between larva and adult, when it is in a cocoon.

chrysanthemum *n* garden flower with a large head made up of thin petals.

chub *n* European freshwater fish of the carp family.

chubby *adj* **-bier, -biest** plump and round.

chuck[1] *v* **1** *Informal* throw. **2** *Informal* give up, reject. **3** touch (someone) affectionately under the chin. **4** *Aust & NZ informal* vomit.

chuck[2] *n* **1** cut of beef from the neck to the shoulder. **2** device that holds a workpiece in a lathe or a tool in a drill.

chuckle *v* **1** laugh softly. ♦ *n* **2** soft laugh.

chuffed *adj Informal* very pleased.

chug *n* **1** short dull sound like the noise of an engine. ♦ *v* **chugging, chugged** **2** operate or move with this sound.

chukka *n* period of play in polo.

chum *Informal* ♦ *n* **1** close friend. ♦ *v* **chumming, chummed** **2** **chum up**

with form a close friendship with. **chummy** *adj*

chump *n* **1** *Informal* stupid person. **2** thick piece of meat.

chunk *n* **1** thick solid piece. **2** considerable amount. **chunky** *adj* **1** (of a person) broad and heavy. **2** (of an object) large and thick.

church *n* **1** building for public Christian worship. **2** particular Christian denomination. **3** (**C-**) Christians collectively. **4** clergy. **churchgoer** *n* person who attends church regularly. **churchwarden** *n* member of a congregation who assists the vicar. **churchyard** *n* grounds round a church, used as a graveyard.

churlish *adj* surly and rude.

churn *n* **1** machine in which cream is shaken to make butter. **2** large container for milk. ♦ *v* **3** stir (cream) vigorously to make butter. **4** move about violently. **churn out** *v Informal* produce (things) rapidly in large numbers.

chute[1] [**shoot**] *n* steep slope down which things may be slid.

chute[2] *n Informal* **short for** PARACHUTE.

chutney *n* pickle made from fruit, vinegar, spices, and sugar.

CIA (in the US) Central Intelligence Agency.

cicada [sik-**kah**-da] *n* large insect that makes a high-pitched drone.

cicatrix [**sik**-a-trix] *n, pl* **-trices** scar.

CID (in Britain) Criminal Investigation Department.

cider *n* alcoholic drink made from fermented apple juice.

cigar *n* roll of cured tobacco leaves for smoking.

cigarette *n* thin roll of shredded tobacco in thin paper, for smoking.

cinch [**sinch**] *n Informal* easy task.

cinder *n* piece of material that will not

burn, left after burning coal.

cine camera n camera for taking moving pictures.

cinema n **1** place for showing films. **2** films collectively. **cinematic** adj **cinematography** n technique of making films. **cinematographer** n

cineraria n garden plant with daisy-like flowers.

cinnamon n spice obtained from the bark of an Asian tree.

☑ **SPELLING TIP**

Cinnamon is a tricky word to spell. The Bank of English shows at least 3 different ways of getting it wrong. The correct spelling has two *n*s in the middle and only one *m*.

---

cipher [**sife**-er] n **1** system of secret writing. **2** unimportant person.

circa [**sir**-ka] prep Latin approximately, about.

circle n **1** perfectly round geometric figure, line, or shape. **2** group of people sharing an interest or activity. **3** Theatre section of seats above the main level of the auditorium. ♦ v **4** move in a circle (round). **5** enclose in a circle.

circlet n circular ornament worn on the head.

circuit n **1** complete route or course, esp. a circular one. **2** complete path through which an electric current can flow. **3** periodical journey round a district, as made by judges. **4** motor-racing track. **circuitous** [sir-**kew**-it-uss] adj indirect and lengthy. **circuitry** [**sir**-kit-tree] n electrical circuit(s).

circular adj **1** in the shape of a circle. **2** moving in a circle. ♦ n **3** letter for general distribution. **circularity** n

circulate v send, go, or pass from place to place or person to person.

circulation n **1** flow of blood around the body. **2** number of copies of a newspaper or magazine sold. **3** sending or moving round. **circulatory** adj

circumcise v remove the foreskin of. **circumcision** n

circumference n **1** boundary of a specified area or shape, esp. of a circle. **2** distance round this.

circumflex n mark (ˆ) over a vowel to show that it is pronounced in a particular way.

circumlocution n indirect way of saying something.

circumnavigate v sail right round. **circumnavigation** n

circumscribe v **1** limit, restrict. **2** draw a line round. **circumscription** n

circumspect adj cautious and careful not to take risks. **circumspectly** adv **circumspection** n

circumstance n (usu. pl) occurrence or condition that accompanies or influences a person or event. **circumstantial** adj **1** (of evidence) strongly suggesting something but not proving it. **2** very detailed.

circumvent v avoid or get round (a rule etc.). **circumvention** n

circus n, pl **-cuses** (performance given by) a travelling company of acrobats, clowns, performing animals, etc.

cirrhosis [sir-**roh**-siss] n serious liver disease, often caused by drinking too much alcohol.

cirrus n, pl **-ri** high wispy cloud.

cistern n water tank, esp. one that holds water for flushing a toilet.

citadel n fortress in a city.

cite v **1** quote, refer to. **2** bring forward as proof. **citation** n

citizen n **1** native or naturalized member of a state or nation. **2** inhabitant of a city or town.

citizenship n **Citizens' Band** range of radio frequencies for private communication by the public.

citric acid n weak acid found in citrus fruits.

citrus fruit n juicy sharp-tasting fruit such as an orange or lemon.

city n, pl **-ties** large or important town. **the City** Brit area of London as a financial centre.

civet [**siv**-vit] n **1** spotted catlike African mammal. **2** musky fluid from its glands used in perfume.

civic adj of a city or citizens. **civics** n study of the rights and responsibilities of citizenship.

civil adj **1** relating to the citizens of a state as opposed to the armed forces or the Church. **2** polite, courteous. **civilly** adv **civility** n polite or courteous behaviour. **civilian** n, adj (person) not belonging to the armed forces. **civil service** service responsible for the administration of the government. **civil servant** member of the civil service. **civil war** war between people of the same country.

civilize v **1** refine or educate (a person). **2** make (a place) more pleasant or more acceptable. **civilization** n **1** high level of human cultural and social development. **2** particular society which has reached this level.

civvies pl n Brit, Aust & NZ slang ordinary clothes that are not part of a uniform.

clack n **1** sound made by two hard objects striking each other. ♦ v **2** make this sound.

clad v a past of CLOTHE.

cladding n material used to cover the outside of a building.

claim v **1** assert as a fact. **2** demand as a right. **3** need, require. ♦ n **4** assertion

that something is true. **5** assertion of a right. **6** something claimed as a right. **claimant** n

clairvoyance n power of perceiving things beyond the natural range of the senses. **clairvoyant** n, adj

clam n **1** edible shellfish with a hinged shell. ♦ v **clamming, clammed** **2** **clam up** Informal stop talking, esp. through nervousness.

clamber v climb awkwardly.

clammy adj **-mier, -miest** unpleasantly moist and sticky.

clamour n **1** loud protest. **2** loud persistent noise or outcry. ♦ v **3** make a loud noise or outcry. **clamorous** adj **clamour for** v demand noisily.

clamp n **1** tool with movable jaws for holding things together tightly. **2** ♦ v **3** fasten with a clamp. **clamp down on** v **1** become stricter about. **2** suppress.

clan n **1** group of families with a common ancestor, esp. among Scottish Highlanders. **2** close group. **clannish** adj (of a group) tending to exclude outsiders.

clandestine adj secret and concealed.

clang v **1** make a loud ringing metallic sound. ♦ n **2** ringing metallic sound.

clanger n Informal obvious mistake.

clangour n loud continuous clanging sound.

clank n **1** harsh metallic sound. ♦ v **2** make such a sound.

clap[1] v **clapping, clapped** **1** applaud by hitting the palms of one's hands sharply together. **2** put quickly or forcibly. **3** ♦ n **4** act or sound of clapping. **5** sudden loud noise, e.g. a clap of thunder. **clapped out** Slang worn out, dilapidated.

clap[2] n Slang gonorrhoea.

clapper n piece of metal inside a bell, which causes it to sound when struck against the side. **clapperboard** n pair of hinged boards clapped together during filming to help in synchronizing sound and picture.

claptrap n Informal foolish or pretentious talk.

claret [**klar**-rit] n dry red wine from Bordeaux.

clarify v -fying, -fied make (a matter) clear and unambiguous. **clarification** n

clarinet n keyed woodwind instrument with a single reed. **clarinettist** n

clarion n 1 obsolete high-pitched trumpet. 2 its sound. **clarion call** strong encouragement to do something.

clarity n clearness.

clash v 1 come into conflict. 2 (of events) happen at the same time. 3 (of colours) look unattractive together. 4 (of objects) make a loud harsh sound by being hit together. ♦ n 5 fight, argument. 6 fact of two events happening at the same time.

clasp n 1 device for fastening things. 2 firm grasp or embrace. ♦ v 3 grasp or embrace firmly. 4 fasten with a clasp.

class n 1 group of people sharing a similar social position. 2 system of dividing society into such groups. 3 group of people or things sharing a common characteristic. 4 group of pupils or students taught together. 5 standard of quality. 6 Informal elegance or excellence, e.g. a touch of class. ♦ v 7 place in a class.

classic adj 1 being a typical example of something. 2 of lasting interest because of excellence. 3 attractive because of simplicity of form. ♦ n 4 author, artist, or work of art of recognized excellence. ♦ pl 5 study of ancient Greek and Roman literature and culture. **classical** adj 1 of or in a restrained conservative style. 2 denoting serious art music. 3 of or

influenced by ancient Greek and Roman culture. **classically** adv **classicism** n artistic style showing emotional restraint and regularity of form. **classicist** n

classify v -fying, -fied 1 divide into groups with similar characteristics. 2 declare (information) to be officially secret. **classifiable** adj **classification** n

classy adj **classier, classiest** Informal stylish and elegant.

clatter v, n (make) a rattling noise.

clause n 1 section of a legal document. 2 part of a sentence, containing a verb.

claustrophobia n abnormal fear of confined spaces. **claustrophobic** adj

clavichord n early keyboard instrument.

clavicle n same as COLLARBONE.

claw n 1 sharp hooked nail of a bird or beast. 2 similar part, such as a crab's pincer. ♦ v 3 tear with claws or nails.

clay n fine-grained earth, soft when moist and hardening when baked, used to make bricks and pottery. **clayey** adj **clay pigeon** baked clay disc hurled into the air as a target for shooting.

claymore n large two-edged sword formerly used by Scottish Highlanders.

clean adj 1 free from dirt or impurities. 2 not yet used. 3 morally acceptable, inoffensive. 4 (of a reputation or record) free from dishonesty or corruption. 5 complete, e.g. a clean break. 6 smooth and regular. ♦ v 7 make (something) free from dirt. ♦ adv 8 Not standard completely, e.g. I clean forgot. **come clean** Informal reveal or admit something. **cleaner** n **cleanly** adv **cleanliness** n

cleanse v make clean. **cleanser** n

clear adj 1 free from doubt or confusion. 2 easy to see or hear. 3 able to be seen through. 4 free of obstruction. **5** (of weather) free from clouds. **6** (of skin) without blemish. **7** *adv* **8** out of the way. ♦ *v* **9** make or become clear. **10** pass by or over (something) without contact. **11** prove (someone) innocent of a crime or mistake. **12** make as profit. **clearly** *adv* **clearance** *n* **1** clearing. **2** official permission. **clearing** *n* treeless area in a wood. **clear off** *v Brit, Aust & NZ informal* go away. **clear out** *v* **1** remove and sort the contents of. **2** *Brit, Aust & NZ informal* go away. **clear-sighted** *adj* having good judgment. **clearway** *n* stretch of road on which motorists may stop in an emergency.

cleat *n* **1** wedge. **2** piece of wood, metal, or plastic with two projecting ends round which ropes are fastened.

cleave[1] *v* **cleaving, cleft, cleaved** *or* **clove, cleft, cleaved** *or* **cloven** split apart. **cleavage** *n* **1** space between a woman's breasts, as revealed by a low-cut dress. **2** division, split.

cleave[2] *v* cling or stick.

cleaver *n* butcher's heavy knife with a square blade.

clef *n Music* symbol at the beginning of a stave to show the pitch.

cleft *n* **1** narrow opening or crack. ♦ *v* **2** **a** past of CLEAVE[1]. **in a cleft stick** in a very difficult position.

clematis *n* climbing plant with large colourful flowers.

clement *adj* (of weather) mild. **clemency** *n* kind or lenient treatment.

clementine *n* small orange citrus fruit.

clench *v* **1** close or squeeze (one's teeth or fist) tightly. **2** grasp firmly.

clerestory [**clear**-store-ee] *n, pl* -**ries** row of windows at the top of a wall above an adjoining roof.

clergy *n* priests and ministers as a group. **clergyman** *n*

cleric *n* member of the clergy.

clerical *adj* **1** of clerks or office work. **2** of the clergy.

clerk *n* employee in an office, bank, or court who keeps records, files, and accounts.

clever *adj* **1** intelligent, quick at learning. **2** showing skill. **cleverly** *adv* **cleverness** *n*

clianthus [klee-**anth**-us] *n* Australian or NZ plant with slender scarlet flowers.

cliché [klee-shay] *n* expression or idea that is no longer effective because of overuse. **clichéd** *adj*

click *n* **1** short sharp sound. ♦ *v* **2** make this sound. **3** *Informal* (of two people) get on well together. **4** *Informal* become suddenly clear. **5** *Computers* press and release (a button on a mouse). **6** *Slang* be a success.

client *n* **1** person who uses the services of a professional person or company. **2** *Computers* program or work station that requests data from a server. **clientele** [klee-on-**tell**] *n* clients collectively.

cliff *n* steep rock face, esp. along the sea shore. **cliffhanger** *n* film, game, etc., that is tense and exciting because its outcome is uncertain.

climate *n* typical weather conditions of an area. **climatic** *adj*

climax *n* **1** most intense point of an experience, series of events, or story. **2** same as ORGASM. **climactic** *adj*

climb *v* **1** go up, ascend. **2** rise to a higher point or intensity. ♦ *n* **3** climbing. **4** place to be climbed. **climber** *n* **climb down** *v* retreat from an opinion or position.

clime *n Poetic* place or its climate.

clinch *v* settle (an argument or agreement) decisively. **clincher** *n Informal* something decisive.

cling *v* **clinging, clung** hold tightly or stick closely. **clingfilm** *n* thin polythene material for wrapping food.

clinic n 1 building where outpatients receive medical treatment or advice. 2 private or specialized hospital. **clinical** adj 1 of a clinic. 2 logical and unemotional. **clinically** adv

clink[1] v, n (make) a light sharp metallic sound.

clink[2] n Brit, Aust & NZ slang prison.

clinker n fused coal left over in a fire or furnace.

clinker-built adj (of a boat) made of overlapping planks.

clip[1] v **clipping, clipped** 1 cut with shears or scissors. 2 Informal hit sharply. ♦ n 3 short extract of a film. 4 Informal sharp blow. **clippers** pl n tool for clipping. **clipping** n something cut out, esp. an article from a newspaper.

clip[2] n 1 device for attaching or holding things together. ♦ v **clipping, clipped** 2 attach or hold together with a clip.

clipper n fast commercial sailing ship.

clique [kleek] n small exclusive group.

clitoris [klit-or-iss] n small sexually sensitive organ at the front of the vulva. **clitoral** adj

cloak n 1 loose sleeveless outer garment. 2 v 3 cover or conceal. **cloakroom** n room where coats may be left temporarily.

clobber[1] v Informal 1 hit. 2 defeat utterly.

clobber[2] n Brit, Aust & NZ informal belongings, esp. clothes.

cloche [klosh] n 1 cover to protect young plants. 2 woman's close-fitting hat.

clock n 1 instrument for showing the time. 2 device with a dial for recording or measuring. **clockwise** adv, adj in the direction in which the hands of a clock rotate. **clock in** or **on, out** or **off** v register arrival at or departure from work on an automatic time recorder. **clock up** v reach (a total).

clockwork n mechanism similar to the kind in a clock, used in wind-up toys.

clod n 1 lump of earth. 2 Brit, Aust & NZ stupid person.

clog v **clogging, clogged** 1 obstruct. ♦ n 2 wooden or wooden-soled shoe.

cloister n covered pillared arcade, usu. in a monastery. **cloistered** adj sheltered.

clone n 1 animal or plant produced artificially from the cells of another animal or plant, and identical to the original. 2 Informal person who closely resembles another. ♦ v 3 produce as a clone.

close[1] v [rhymes with **nose**] 1 shut. 2 prevent access to. 3 end, terminate. 4 bring or come nearer together. ♦ n 5 end, conclusion. 6 [rhymes with **dose**] street closed at one end. 7 [rhymes with **dose**] Brit courtyard, quadrangle. **closed shop** place of work in which all workers must belong to a particular trade union.

close[2] adj [rhymes with **dose**] 1 near. 2 intimate. 3 careful, thorough. 4 compact, dense. 5 oppressive, stifling. 6 secretive. ♦ adv 7 closely, tightly. **closely** adv **closeness** n **close season** period when it is illegal to kill certain game or fish. **close shave** Informal narrow escape. **close-up** n photograph or film taken at close range.

closet n 1 US cupboard. 2 small private room. ♦ adj 3 private, secret. ♦ v **closeting, closeted** 4 shut (oneself) away in private.

closure n closing.

clot n 1 soft thick lump formed from liquid. 2 Brit, Aust & NZ informal stupid person. ♦ v **clotting, clotted** 3 form soft thick lumps.

cloth n (piece of) woven fabric.

clothe v **clothing, clothed** or **clad** 1 put clothes on. 2 provide with clothes.

clothes pl n **1** articles of dress. **2** bed coverings. **clothing** n clothes collectively.

cloud n **1** mass of condensed water vapour floating in the sky. **2** floating mass of smoke, dust, etc. **3** ♦ v **4** (foll. by over) become cloudy. **5** confuse. **6** make gloomy or depressed. **cloudless** adj **cloudy** adj **1** having a lot of clouds. **2** (of liquid) not clear. **cloudburst** n heavy fall of rain.

clout Informal ♦ n **1** hard blow. **2** power, influence. ♦ v **3** hit hard.

clove[1] n dried flower bud of a tropical tree, used as a spice.

clove[2] n segment of a bulb of garlic.

clove[3] v a past tense of CLEAVE[1]. **clove hitch** knot used to fasten a rope to a spar.

cloven v a past participle of CLEAVE[1]. **cloven hoof** divided hoof of a cow, goat, etc.

clover n plant with three-lobed leaves. **in clover** in luxury.

clown n **1** comic entertainer in a circus. **2** amusing person. **3** stupid person. ♦ v **4** behave foolishly. **5** perform as a clown. **clownish** adj

club n **1** association of people with common interests. **2** building used by such a group. **3** thick stick used as a weapon. **4** stick with a curved end used to hit the ball in golf. **5** playing card with black three-leaved symbols. ♦ v **clubbing, clubbed 6** hit with a club. **club together** v combine resources for a common purpose.

club foot n deformity of the foot causing inability to put the foot flat on the ground.

cluck n **1** low clicking noise made by a hen. ♦ v **2** make this noise.

clue n something that helps to solve a mystery or puzzle. **not have a clue** be completely baffled. **clueless** adj stupid.

clump n **1** small group of things or people. **2** dull heavy tread. ♦ v **3** walk heavily. **4** form into clumps.

clumsy adj **-sier, -siest 1** lacking skill or physical coordination. **2** badly made or done. **clumsily** adv **clumsiness** n

clung v past of CLING.

clunk n **1** dull metallic sound. ♦ v **2** make such a sound.

cluster n **1** small close group. ♦ v **2** gather in clusters.

clutch[1] v **1** grasp tightly. **2** (foll. by at) try to get hold of. ♦ n **3** device enabling two revolving shafts to be connected and disconnected, esp. in a motor vehicle. **4** tight grasp.

clutch[2] n set of eggs laid at the same time.

clutter v **1** scatter objects about a (place) untidily. ♦ n **2** untidy mess.

cm centimetre.

CND Campaign for Nuclear Disarmament.

CO Commanding Officer.

Co. 1 Company. **2** County.

co- prefix together, joint, or jointly, e.g. coproduction.

c/o 1 care of. **2** Book-keeping carried over.

coach n **1** long-distance bus. **2** railway carriage. **3** large four-wheeled horse-drawn carriage. **4** trainer, instructor. ♦ v **5** train, teach.

coagulate [koh-**ag**-yew-late] v change from a liquid to a semisolid mass. **coagulation** n **coagulant** n substance causing coagulation.

coal n black rock consisting mainly of carbon, used as fuel. **coalfield** n area with coal under the ground.

coalesce [koh-a-**less**] v come together, merge. **coalescence** n

coalition [koh-a-**lish**-un] n temporary alliance, esp. between political parties.

coarse adj **1** rough in texture. **2**

unrefined, indecent. **coarsely** adv
coarseness n **coarsen** v **coarse fish**
any freshwater fish not of the salmon
family.

coast n **1** place where the land meets
the sea. ♦ v **2** move by momentum,
without the use of power. **coastal** adj
coaster n small mat placed under a
glass. **coastguard** n **1** organization
that aids ships and swimmers in
trouble and prevents smuggling. **2**
member of this. **coastline** n outline of
a coast.

coat n **1** outer garment with long
sleeves. **2** animal's fur or hair. **3**
covering layer, e.g. a coat of paint. ♦ v
4 cover with a layer. **coating** n
covering layer. **coat of arms** heraldic
emblem of a family or institution.

coax v **1** persuade gently. **2** obtain by
persistent coaxing.

coaxial [koh-**ax**-ee-al] adj (of a cable)
transmitting by means of two
concentric conductors separated by an
insulator.

cob n **1** stalk of an ear of maize. **2**
thickset type of horse. **3** round loaf of
bread. **4** male swan.

cobalt n Chem brittle silvery-white
metallic element.

cobber n Aust & old-fashioned NZ
informal friend.

cobble n cobblestone. **cobblestone** n
rounded stone used for paving.
cobble together v put together
clumsily.

cobbler n shoe mender.

cobia [**koh**-bee-a] n large dark-striped
game fish of tropical and subtropical
seas.

cobra n venomous hooded snake of
Asia and Africa.

cobweb n spider's web.

cocaine n addictive drug used as a
narcotic and as an anaesthetic.

coccyx [**kok**-six] n, pl **coccyges**

[kok-**sije**-eez] bone at the base of the
spinal column.

cochineal n red dye obtained from a
Mexican insect, used for food
colouring.

cock n **1** male bird, esp. of domestic
fowl. **2** stopcock. ♦ v **3** draw back (the
hammer of a gun) to firing position. **4**
lift and turn (part of the body).
cockerel n young domestic cock.
cock-a-hoop adj Brit, Aust & NZ in
high spirits. **cock-and-bull story**
highly improbable story.

cockade n feather or rosette worn on a
hat as a badge.

cockatiel, cockateel n crested
Australian parrot with a greyish-brown
and yellow plumage.

cockatoo n crested parrot of Australia
or the East Indies.

cocker spaniel n small spaniel.

cockeyed adj **1** Informal crooked,
askew. **2** foolish, absurd.

cockie, cocky n, pl **-kies** Aust & NZ
informal farmer.

cockle n edible shellfish.

Cockney n **1** native of the East End of
London. **2** London dialect.

cockpit n **1** pilot's compartment in an
aircraft. **2** driver's compartment in a
racing car.

cockroach n beetle-like insect which is
a household pest.

cocksure adj overconfident, arrogant.

cocktail n **1** mixed alcoholic drink. **2**
appetizer of seafood or mixed fruits.

cocky adj **cockier, cockiest** conceited
and overconfident. **cockily** adv
cockiness n

cocoa n **1** powder made from the seed
of the cacao tree. **2** drink made from
this powder.

coconut n **1** large hard fruit of a type
of palm tree. **2** edible flesh of this fruit.

cocoon n **1** silky protective covering of

a silkworm. **2** protective covering. ♦ *v* **3** wrap up tightly for protection.

cod *n* **1** large food fish of the North Atlantic **2** any other Australian fish of the same family.

COD cash on delivery.

coda *n* final part of a musical composition.

coddle *v* pamper, overprotect.

code *n* **1** system of letters, symbols, or prearranged signals by which messages can be communicated secretly or briefly. **2** set of principles or rules. ♦ *v* **3** put into code. **codify** *v* **-fying, -fied** organize (rules or procedures) systematically. **codification** *n*

codeine [**kode**-een] *n* drug used as a painkiller.

codex *n, pl* **codices** volume of manuscripts of an ancient text.

codger *n Brit, Aust & NZ informal* old man.

codicil [**kode**-iss-ill] *n* addition to a will.

coeducation *n* education of boys and girls together. **coeducational** *adj*

coefficient *n Maths* number or constant placed before and multiplying a quantity.

coelacanth [**seel**-a-kanth] *n* primitive marine fish.

coeliac disease [**seel**-ee-ak] *n* disease which hampers digestion of food.

coerce [koh-**urss**] *v* compel, force. **coercion** *n* **coercive** *adj*

coeval [koh-**eev**-al] *adj, n* contemporary.

coexist *v* exist together, esp. peacefully despite differences. **coexistence** *n*

C of E Church of England.

coffee *n* **1** drink made from the roasted and ground seeds of a tropical shrub. **2** beanlike seeds of this shrub. ♦ *adj* **3** medium-brown. **coffee bar** café, snack bar. **coffee table** small low table.

coffer *n* **1** chest for valuables. ♦ *pl* **2** store of money.

coffin *n* box in which a corpse is buried or cremated.

cog *n* **1** one of the teeth on the rim of a gearwheel. **2** unimportant person in a big organization.

cogent [**koh**-jent] *adj* forcefully convincing. **cogency** *n*

cogitate [**koj**-it-tate] *v* think deeply about. **cogitation** *n*

cognac [**kon**-yak] *n* French brandy.

cognate *adj* derived from a common original form.

cognition *n* act or experience of knowing or acquiring knowledge. **cognitive** *adj*

cognizance *n* knowledge, understanding. **cognizant** *adj*

cognoscenti [kon-yo-**shen**-tee] *pl n* connoisseurs.

cohabit *v* live together as husband and wife without being married. **cohabitation** *n*

cohere *v* **1** hold or stick together. **2** be logically connected or consistent.

coherent *adj* **1** logical and consistent. **2** capable of intelligible speech. **coherence** *n* **coherently** *adv*

cohesion *n* sticking together.

cohesive *adj* sticking together to form a whole.

cohort *n* **1** band of associates. **2** tenth part of an ancient Roman legion.

coiffure *n* hairstyle. **coiffeur, coiffeuse** *n* hairdresser.

coil *v* **1** wind in loops. **2** move in a winding course. ♦ *n* **3** something coiled. **4** single loop of this. **5** coil-shaped contraceptive device inserted in the womb.

coin *n* **1** piece of metal money. **2** metal currency collectively. ♦ *v* **3** invent (a word or phrase). **coin it in** *Informal* earn money quickly. **coinage** n **1** coins collectively. **2** word or phrase coined. **3** coining.

coincide v **1** happen at the same time. **2** agree or correspond exactly. **coincidence** n **1** occurrence of simultaneous or apparently connected events. **2** coinciding. **coincident** adj in agreement. **coincidental** adj resulting from coincidence. **coincidentally** adv

coir n coconut fibre, used for matting.

coitus [**koh**-it-uss], **coition** [koh-**ish**-un] n sexual intercourse. **coital** adj

coke[1] n solid fuel left after gas has been distilled from coal.

coke[2] n Slang cocaine.

col n high mountain pass.

cola n dark brown fizzy soft drink.

colander n perforated bowl for straining or rinsing foods.

cold adj **1** lacking heat. **2** lacking affection or enthusiasm. **3** (of a colour) giving an impression of coldness. **4** Slang unconscious, e.g. out cold. ♦ n **5** lack of heat. **6** mild illness causing a runny nose, sneezing, and coughing. **coldly** adv **coldness** n **cold-blooded** adj **1** cruel, unfeeling. **2** having a body temperature that varies according to the surrounding temperature. **cold cream** creamy preparation for softening and cleansing the skin. **cold feet** Slang nervousness, fear. **cold-shoulder** v treat with indifference. **cold war** political hostility between countries without actual warfare.

coleslaw n salad dish of shredded raw cabbage in a dressing.

coley n codlike food fish of the N Atlantic.

colic n severe pains in the stomach and bowels. **colicky** adj

colitis [koh-**lie**-tiss] n inflammation of the colon.

collaborate v **1** work with another on a project. **2** cooperate with an enemy invader. **collaboration** n **collaborative** adj **collaborator** n

collage [kol-**lahzh**] n **1** art form in which various materials or objects are glued onto a surface. **2** picture made in this way.

collapse v **1** fall down suddenly. **2** fail completely. **3** fold compactly. ♦ n **4** collapsing. **5** sudden failure or breakdown. **collapsible** adj

collar n **1** part of a garment round the neck. **2** band put round an animal's neck. **3** cut of meat from an animal's neck. ♦ v **4** Brit, Aust & NZ informal seize, arrest. **5** catch in order to speak to. **collarbone** n bone joining the shoulder blade to the breastbone.

collate v gather together, examine, and put in order. **collation** n **1** collating. **2** light meal.

collateral n security pledged for the repayment of a loan.

colleague n fellow worker, esp. in a profession.

collect[1] v **1** gather together. **2** accumulate (stamps etc.) as a hobby. **3** fetch. **collected** adj calm and controlled. **collection** n **1** things collected. **2** collecting. **3** sum of money collected. **collector** n

collect[2] n short prayer.

collective adj **1** of or done by a group. ♦ n **2** group of people working together on an enterprise and sharing the benefits from it. **collectively** adv

colleen n Irish girl.

college n **1** place of higher education. **2** group of people of the same profession or with special duties. **collegiate** adj

collide v **1** crash together violently. **2** have an argument. **collision** n

collie n silky-haired sheepdog.

collier n 1 coal miner. 2 coal ship.

colliery n, pl **-lieries** coal mine.

collocate v (of words) occur together regularly. **collocation** n

colloid n suspension of particles in a solution.

colloquial adj suitable for informal speech or writing. **colloquialism** n colloquial word or phrase.

collusion n secret or illegal cooperation. **collude** v act in collusion.

collywobbles pl n Slang nervousness.

cologne n mild perfume.

colon[1] n punctuation mark (:).

colon[2] n part of the large intestine connected to the rectum.

colonel n senior commissioned army or air-force officer.

colonnade n row of columns.

colony n, pl **-nies** 1 group of people who settle in a new country but remain under the rule of their homeland. 2 territory occupied by a colony. 3 group of people or animals of the same kind living together. **colonial** adj, n (inhabitant) of a colony. **colonialism** n policy of acquiring and maintaining colonies. **colonist** n settler in a colony. **colonize** v make into a colony. **colonization** n

Colorado beetle n black-and-yellow beetle that is a serious pest of potatoes.

coloration n arrangement of colours.

colossal adj very large.

colossus n, pl **-si, -suses** 1 huge statue. 2 huge or important person or thing.

colostomy n, pl **-mies** operation to form an opening from the colon onto the surface of the body, for emptying the bowel.

colour n 1 appearance of things as a result of reflecting light. 2 substance that gives colour. 3 complexion. 4 pl 5 flag of a country or regiment. 6 Sport badge or symbol denoting membership of a team. ♦ v 7 apply colour to. 8 influence (someone's judgment). 9 blush. **coloured** adj 1 having colour. 2 (C-) (in S Africa) of mixed White and non-White parentage. **colourful** adj 1 with bright or varied colours. 2 vivid, distinctive. **colourfully** adv **colourless** adj **colour-blind** adj unable to distinguish between certain colours.

colt n young male horse.

columbine n garden flower with five petals.

column n 1 pillar. 2 vertical division of a newspaper page. 3 regular feature in a newspaper. 4 vertical arrangement of numbers. 5 narrow formation of troops. **columnist** n journalist who writes a regular feature in a newspaper.

coma n state of deep unconsciousness. **comatose** adj 1 in a coma. 2 sound asleep.

comb n 1 toothed implement for arranging the hair. 2 cock's crest. 3 honeycomb. ♦ v 4 use a comb on. 5 search with great care.

combat n, v **-bating, -bated** fight, struggle. **combatant** n **combative** adj **combat trousers, combats** loose casual trousers with large pockets on the legs.

combine v 1 join together. 2 n 3 association of people or firms for a common purpose. **combination** n 1 combining. 2 people or things combined. 3 set of numbers that opens a special lock. ♦ pl 4 Brit old-fashioned undergarment with long sleeves and long legs. **combine harvester** machine that reaps and threshes grain in one process.

combustion n process of burning.

combustible *adj* burning easily.

come *v* **coming, came, come 1** move towards a place, arrive. **2** occur. **3** reach a specified point or condition. **4** be produced. **5** (foll. by *from*) be born in. **6** become, e.g. *a dream come true*. **come across** *v* **1** meet or find by accident. **2** (often foll. by *as*) give an impression of (being). **comeback** *n Informal* **1** return to a former position. **2** retort. **comedown** *n* **1** decline in status. **2** disappointment. **comeuppance** *n Informal* deserved punishment.

comedy *n, pl* **-dies** humorous play, film, or programme. **comedian, comedienne** *n* **1** entertainer who tells jokes. **2** person who performs in comedy.

comely *adj* **-lier, -liest** *Old-fashioned* nice-looking.

comestibles *pl n Formal* food.

comet *n* heavenly body with a long luminous tail.

comfit *n Old-fashioned* sugar-coated sweet.

comfort *n* **1** physical ease or wellbeing. **2** consolation. **3** means of consolation. ♦ *v* **4** soothe, console. **comfortable** *adj* **1** giving comfort. **2** free from pain. **3** *Informal* well-off financially. **comfortably** *adv* **comforter** *n*

comfrey *n* tall plant with bell-shaped flowers.

comfy *adj* **-fier, -fiest** *Informal* comfortable.

comic *adj* **1** humorous, funny. **2** of comedy. ♦ *n* **3** comedian. **4** magazine containing strip cartoons. **comical** *adj* amusing. **comically** *adv*

comma *n* punctuation mark (,).

command *v* **1** order. **2** have authority over. **3** deserve and get. **4** look down over. ♦ *n* **5** authoritative instruction that something must be done. **6** authority to command. **7** knowledge.

8 military or naval unit with a specific function. **commandant** *n* officer commanding a military group. **commandeer** *v* seize for military use. **commandment** *n* command from God.

commander *n* **1** military officer in command of a group or operation. **2** middle-ranking naval officer. **commander-in-chief** *n, pl* **commanders-in-chief** supreme commander of a nation's armed forces.

commando *n, pl* **-dos, -does** (member of) a military unit trained for swift raids in enemy territory.

commemorate *v* honour the memory of. **commemoration** *n* **commemorative** *adj*

☑ **SPELLING TIP**

The problem in deciding how to spell **commemorate** seems to be how many *m*s it should have. The Bank of English shows that people often decide on four. In fact, it should have three, as in **commemoration**.

---

commence *v* begin. **commencement** *n US and Canadian* a ceremony for the presentation of awards at secondary schools.

commend *v* **1** praise. **2** recommend. **commendable** *adj* **commendably** *adv* **commendation** *n*

commensurable *adj* measurable by the same standards.

commensurate *adj* corresponding in degree, size, or value.

comment *n* **1** remark. **2** talk, gossip. **3** explanatory note. ♦ *v* **4** make a comment. **commentary** *n, pl* **-taries** **1** spoken accompaniment to a broadcast or film. **2** explanatory notes. **commentate** *v* provide a commentary. **commentator** *n* person who provides a spoken commentary, especially of a sporting event.

commerce n buying and selling, trade.
commercial adj **1** of commerce. **2** (of television or radio) paid for by advertisers. **3** having profit as the main aim. ♦ n **4** television or radio advertisement. **commercialize** v make commercial or exploit for profit. **commercialization** n

commiserate v (foll. by with) express sympathy (for). **commiseration** n

> ☑ **SPELLING TIP**
> The most popular way to misspell **commiserate** and **commiseration** is to double the s as well as the m. There should indeed be two ms, but only one s.

commissar n (formerly) official responsible for political education in Communist countries.

commissariat n Brit, Aust & NZ military department in charge of food supplies.

commission n **1** piece of work that an artist is asked to do. **2** duty, task. **3** percentage paid to a salesperson for each sale made. **4** group of people appointed to perform certain duties. **5** committing of a crime. **6** Mil rank or authority officially given to an officer. ♦ v **7** place an order for. **8** Mil give a commission to. **9** grant authority to. **out of commission** not in working order. **commissioner** n **1** appointed official in a government department. **2** member of a commission.

commissionaire n uniformed doorman at a hotel, theatre, etc.

commit v **-mitting, -mitted 1** perform (a crime or error). **2** pledge (oneself) to a course of action. **3** send (someone) to prison or hospital. **committal** n sending someone to prison or hospital. **commitment** n **1**

dedication to a cause. **2** responsibility that restricts freedom of action.

> ☑ **SPELLING TIP**
> The correct spelling of **commitment** has three ms altogether, but only two ts (which are not next to each other). Although the Bank of English has 176 examples of committment, with three ms and three ts, this spelling is wrong.

committee n group of people appointed to perform a specified service or function.

> ☑ **SPELLING TIP**
> The commonest misspelling of **committee** is commitee, with 81 occurrences in the Bank of English, which also has examples of comittee. The correct spelling is with two ms and two ts.

commode n **1** seat with a hinged flap concealing a chamber pot. **2** chest of drawers.

commodious adj roomy.

commodity n, pl **-ities** something that can be bought or sold.

commodore n senior commissioned officer in the navy.

common adj **1** occurring often. **2** belonging to two or more people. **3** public, general. **4** lacking in taste or manners. ♦ n **5** area of grassy land belonging to a community. **House of Commons, the Commons** lower chamber of the British parliament. **commonly** adv **commoner** n person who does not belong to the nobility. **common-law** adj (of a relationship) regarded as a marriage through being long-standing. **Common Market** former name for EUROPEAN UNION. **commonplace** adj **1** ordinary, everyday. ♦ n **2** trite remark. **common**

sense good practical understanding.

commonwealth n **1** state or nation viewed politically. **2** (C-) association of independent states that used to be ruled by Britain.

commotion n noisy disturbance.

commune¹ n group of people who live together and share everything. **communal** adj shared. **communally** adv

commune² v (foll. by with) feel very close (to), e.g. communing with nature.

communion n **1** sharing of thoughts or feelings. **2** (C-) Christian ritual of sharing consecrated bread and wine. **3** religious group with shared beliefs and practices.

communicate v make known or share (information, thoughts, or feelings). **communicable** adj (of a disease) able to be passed on. **communicant** n person who receives Communion. **communicating** adj (of a door) joining two rooms. **communication** n **1** communicating. **2** thing communicated. ♦ pl **3** means of travelling or sending messages. **communicative** adj talking freely.

communiqué [kom-**mune**-ik-kay] n official announcement.

communism n **1** belief that all property and means of production should be shared by the community. **2** (C-) system of state control of the economy and society in some countries. **communist** n, adj

community n, pl **-ties 1** all the people living in one district. **2** group with shared origins or interests. **3** the public, society. **community centre** building used by a community for activities.

commute v **1** travel daily to and from work. **2** reduce (a sentence) to a less severe one. **commutator** n device used to change alternating electric current into direct current.

commuter n person who commutes to and from work.

compact¹ adj **1** closely packed. **2** neatly arranged. **3** concise, brief. ♦ n **4** small flat case containing a mirror and face powder. ♦ v **5** pack closely together. **compactly** adv **compactness** n **compact disc** small digital audio disc on which the sound is read by an optical laser system.

compact² n contract, agreement.

companion n person who associates with or accompanies someone. **companionable** adj friendly. **companionship** n

companionway n ladder linking the decks of a ship.

company n, pl **-nies 1** business organization. **2** group of actors. **3** fact of being with someone. **4** guest or guests.

compare v **1** examine (things) and point out the resemblances or differences. **2** (foll. by to) declare to be (like). **3** (foll. by with) be worthy of comparison. **comparable** adj **comparability** n **comparative** adj **1** relative. **2** involving comparison. **3** Grammar denoting the form of an adjective or adverb indicating more. ♦ n **4** Grammar comparative form of a word. **comparatively** adv **comparison** n **1** comparing. **2** similarity or equivalence.

compartment n **1** section of a railway carriage. **2** separate section.

compass n **1** instrument for showing direction, with a needle that points north. **2** limits, range. ♦ pl **3** hinged instrument for drawing circles.

compassion n pity, sympathy. **compassionate** adj

compatible adj able to exist, work, or be used together. **compatibility** n

compatriot n fellow countryman or

countrywoman.

compel v **-pelling, -pelled** force (to be or do).

compendium n, pl **-diums, -dia** selection of board games in one box. **compendious** adj brief but comprehensive.

compensate v **1** make amends to (someone), esp. for injury or loss. **2** (foll. by for) cancel out (a bad effect). **compensation** n payment to make up for loss or injury. **compensatory** adj

compere n **1** person who presents a stage, radio, or television show. ♦ v **2** be the compere of.

compete v try to win or achieve (a prize, profit, etc.). **competition** n **1** competing. **2** event in which people compete. **3** people against whom one competes. **competitive** adj **competitor** n

competent adj having the skill or knowledge to do something well. **competently** adv **competence** n

compile v collect and arrange (information), esp. to make a book. **compilation** n **compiler** n

complacent adj self-satisfied. **complacently** adv **complacency** n

complain v **1** express resentment or displeasure. **2** (foll. by of) say that one is suffering from (an illness). **complaint** n **1** complaining. **2** mild illness. **complainant** n Law plaintiff.

complaisant [kom-**play**-zant] adj willing to please. **complaisance** n

complement n **1** thing that completes something. **2** complete amount or number. **3** Grammar word or words added to a verb to complete the meaning. ♦ v **5** make complete. **complementary** adj

complete adj **1** thorough, absolute. **2** finished. **3** having all the necessary parts. ♦ v **4** finish. **5** make whole or perfect. **completely** adv

completeness n **completion** n finishing.

complex adj **1** made up of parts. **2** complicated. ♦ n **3** whole made up of parts. **4** group of unconscious feelings that influences behaviour. **complexity** n

complexion n **1** skin of the face. **2** character, nature.

compliance n **1** complying. **2** tendency to do what others want. **compliant** adj

complicate v make or become complex or difficult to deal with. **complication** n

complicity n fact of being an accomplice in a crime.

compliment n **1** expression of praise. ♦ pl **2** formal greetings. ♦ v **3** praise. **complimentary** adj **1** expressing praise. **2** free of charge.

compline n last service of the day in the Roman Catholic Church.

comply v **-plying, -plied** (foll. by with) act in accordance (with).

component n, adj (being) part of a whole.

comport v Formal behave (oneself) in a specified way.

compose v **1** put together. **2** be the component parts of. **3** create (a piece of music or writing). **4** calm (oneself). **5** arrange artistically.

composer n person who writes music.

composite n, adj (something) made up of separate parts.

composition n **1** way that something is put together or arranged. **2** work of art, esp. a musical one. **3** essay. **4** composing.

compositor n person who arranges type for printing.

compos mentis adj Latin sane.

compost n decayed plants used as a fertilizer.

composure n calmness.

compote n fruit stewed with sugar.

compound[1] n, adj **1** (thing, esp. chemical) made up of two or more combined parts or elements. ♦ v **2** combine or make by combining. **3** intensify, make worse.

compound[2] n fenced enclosure containing buildings.

comprehend v understand. **comprehensible** adj **comprehension** n **comprehensive** adj **1** of broad scope, fully inclusive. ♦ n **2** Brit comprehensive school. **comprehensive school** Brit secondary school for children of all abilities.

compress v [kum-**press**] **1** squeeze together. **2** make shorter. ♦ n [**kom**-press] **3** pad applied to stop bleeding or cool inflammation. **compression** n **compressor** n machine that compresses gas or air.

comprise v be made up of or make up.

compromise [**kom**-prom-mize] n **1** settlement reached by concessions on each side. ♦ v **2** settle a dispute by making concessions. **3** put in a dishonourable position.

comptroller n (in titles) financial controller.

compulsion n **1** irresistible urge. **2** forcing by threats or violence. **compulsive** adj **compulsively** adv **compulsory** adj required by rules or laws.

compunction n feeling of guilt or shame.

compute v calculate, esp. using a computer. **computation** n

computer n electronic machine that stores and processes data. **computerize** v **1** adapt (a system) to be handled by computer. **2** store or process in a computer. **computerization** n

comrade n **1** fellow member of a union or socialist political party. **2** companion. **comradeship** n

con[1] Informal ♦ n **1** short for CONFIDENCE TRICK. ♦ v conning, conned **2** deceive, swindle.

con[2] n pros and cons see PRO[1].

concatenation n series of linked events.

concave adj curving inwards.

conceal v **1** cover and hide. **2** keep secret. **concealment** n

concede v **1** admit to be true. **2** acknowledge defeat in (a contest or argument). **3** grant as a right.

conceit n **1** too high an opinion of oneself. **2** far-fetched or clever comparison. **conceited** adj

conceive v **1** imagine, think. **2** form in the mind. **3** become pregnant. **conceivable** adj imaginable, possible. **conceivably** adv

concentrate v **1** fix one's attention or efforts on something. **2** bring or come together in large numbers in one place. **3** make (a liquid) stronger by removing water from it. ♦ n **4** concentrated liquid. **concentration** n **1** concentrating. **2** proportion of a substance in a mixture or solution. **concentration camp** prison camp for civilian prisoners, esp. in Nazi Germany.

concentric adj having the same centre.

concept n abstract or general idea. **conceptual** adj of or based on concepts. **conceptualize** v form a concept of.

conception n **1** general idea. **2** becoming pregnant.

concern n **1** anxiety, worry. **2** something that is of importance to someone. **3** business, firm. ♦ v **4** worry (someone). **5** involve (oneself). **6** be relevant or important to. **concerned** adj **1** interested, involved. **2** anxious, worried. **concerning** prep about, regarding.

concert n musical entertainment. **in concert 1** working together. **2** (of musicians) performing live. **concerted** adj done together.

concertina n **1** small musical instrument similar to an accordion. ♦ v **-naing, -naed 2** collapse or fold up like a concertina.

concerto [kon-**chair**-toe] n, pl **-tos**, **-ti** large-scale composition for a solo instrument and orchestra.

concession n **1** grant of rights, land, or property. **2** reduction in price for a specified category of people. **3** conceding. **4** thing conceded. **concessionary** adj

conch n **1** shellfish with a large spiral shell. **2** its shell.

concierge [kon-see-**airzh**] n (in France) caretaker in a block of flats.

conciliate v try to end a disagreement (with). **conciliation** n **conciliator** n

conciliatory adj intended to end a disagreement.

concise adj brief and to the point. **concisely** adv **concision, conciseness** n

conclave n **1** secret meeting. **2** private meeting of cardinals to elect a new pope.

conclude v **1** decide by reasoning. **2** end, finish. **3** arrange or settle finally. **conclusion** n **1** decision based on reasoning. **2** ending. **3** final arrangement or settlement. **conclusive** adj ending doubt, convincing. **conclusively** adv

concoct v **1** make up (a story or plan). **2** make by combining ingredients. **concoction** n

concomitant adj existing along with something else.

concord n state of peaceful agreement, harmony. **concordance** n **1** similarity or consistency. **2** index of words in a book. **concordant** adj agreeing.

concourse n **1** large open public place where people can gather. **2** large crowd.

concrete n **1** mixture of cement, sand, stone, and water, used in building. **2** adj **3** made of concrete. **4** particular, specific. **5** real or solid, not abstract.

concubine [**kon**-kew-bine] n Hist woman living in a man's house but not married to him and kept for his sexual pleasure.

concupiscence [kon-**kew**-piss-enss] n Formal lust.

concur v **-curring, -curred** agree. **concurrence** n **concurrent** adj happening at the same time or place. **concurrently** adv at the same time.

concussion n period of unconsciousness caused by a blow to the head. **concussed** adj having concussion.

condemn v **1** express disapproval of. **2** sentence, e.g. he was condemned to death. **3** force into an unpleasant situation. **4** declare unfit for use. **condemnation** n **condemnatory** adj

condense v **1** make shorter. **2** turn from gas into liquid. **condensation** n **condenser** n Electricity capacitor.

condescend v **1** behave patronizingly towards someone. **2** agree to do something, but as if doing someone a favour. **condescension** n

condiment n seasoning for food, such as salt or pepper.

condition n **1** particular state of being. **2** necessary requirement for something else to happen. **3** restriction, qualification. **4** state of health, physical fitness. **5** medical problem. ♦ pl **6** circumstances. ♦ v **7** train or influence to behave in a particular way. **8** treat with conditioner. **9** control. **on condition that** only if. **conditional** adj depending on circumstances.

conditioner n thick liquid used when washing to make hair or clothes feel softer.

condolence n 1 sympathy. ♦ pl 2 expression of sympathy.

condom n rubber sheath worn on the penis or in the vagina during sexual intercourse to prevent conception or infection.

condominium n Aust, US & Canadian block of flats in which each flat is owned by the occupant.

condone v overlook or forgive (wrongdoing).

condor n large vulture of S America.

conducive adj (foll. by to) likely to lead (to).

conduct n 1 management of an activity. 2 behaviour. ♦ v 3 carry out (a task). 4 behave (oneself). 5 direct (musicians) by moving the hands or a baton. 6 lead, guide. 7 transmit (heat or electricity). **conduction** n transmission of heat or electricity. **conductivity** n ability to transmit heat or electricity. **conductive** adj **conductor** n 1 person who conducts musicians. 2 (fem **conductress**) official on a bus who collects fares. 3 something that conducts heat or electricity.

conduit [kon-dew-it] n channel or tube for fluid or cables.

cone n 1 object with a circular base, tapering to a point. 2 cone-shaped ice-cream wafer. 3 Brit, Aust & NZ plastic cone used as a traffic marker on the roads. 4 scaly fruit of a conifer tree.

coney n same as CONY.

confab n Informal conversation (also **confabulation**).

confection n 1 any sweet food. 2 Old-fashioned elaborate article of clothing.

confectioner n maker or seller of confectionery. **confectionery** n

sweets.

confederate n 1 member of a confederacy. 2 accomplice. ♦ adj 3 united, allied. ♦ v 4 unite in a confederacy. **confederacy** n, pl -cies union of states or people for a common purpose. **confederation** n alliance of political units.

confer v -ferring, -ferred 1 discuss together. 2 grant, give. **conferment** n granting, giving.

conference n meeting for discussion.

confess v 1 admit (a fault or crime). 2 admit to be true. 3 declare (one's sins) to God or a priest, in hope of forgiveness. **confession** n 1 something confessed. 2 confessing. **confessional** n small stall in which a priest hears confessions. **confessor** n priest who hears confessions.

confetti n small pieces of coloured paper thrown at weddings.

confidant n person confided in. **confidante** n fem

confide v 1 tell someone (a secret). 2 entrust.

confidence n 1 trust. 2 self-assurance. 3 something confided. **confidence trick** swindle involving gaining a person's trust in order to cheat him or her. **in confidence** as a secret.

confident adj sure, esp. of oneself. **confidently** adv **confidential** adj 1 private, secret. 2 entrusted with someone's secret affairs. **confidentially** adv **confidentiality** n

configuration n arrangement of parts.

confine v 1 keep within bounds. 2 restrict the free movement of. **confines** pl n boundaries, limits. **confinement** n 1 being confined. 2 period of childbirth.

confirm v 1 prove to be true. 2 reaffirm, strengthen. 3 administer the rite of confirmation to. **confirmation** n 1 confirming. 2 something that confirms. **3** *Christianity* rite that admits a baptized person to full church membership. **confirmed** *adj* firmly established in a habit or condition.

confiscate *v* seize (property) by authority. **confiscation** *n*

conflagration *n* large destructive fire.

conflate *v* combine or blend into a whole. **conflation** *n*

conflict *n* **1** disagreement. **2** struggle or fight. ♦ *v* **3** be incompatible.

confluence *n* place where two rivers join.

conform *v* **1** comply with accepted standards or customs. **2** (foll. by *to* or *with*) be like or in accordance with. **conformist** *n*, *adj* person who adopts the attitudes and behaviour of the group to which he belongs. **conformity** *n* compliance with accepted standards or customs.

confound *v* **1** astound, bewilder. **2** confuse. **confounded** *adj* *Old-fashioned* damned.

confront *v* come face to face with. **confrontation** *n* serious argument.

confuse *v* **1** mix up. **2** perplex, disconcert. **3** make unclear. **confusion** *n*

confute *v* prove wrong.

conga *n* **1** dance performed by a number of people in single file. **2** large single-headed drum played with the hands.

congeal *v* (of a liquid) become thick and sticky.

congenial *adj* **1** pleasant, agreeable. **2** having similar interests and attitudes. **congeniality** *n*

congenital *adj* (of a condition) existing from birth. **congenitally** *adv*

conger *n* large sea eel.

congested *adj* crowded to excess. **congestion** *n*

conglomerate *n* **1** large corporation made up of many companies. **2** thing made up of several different elements. ♦ *v* **3** form into a mass. ♦ *adj* **4** made up of several different elements. **conglomeration** *n*

congratulate *v* express one's pleasure to (someone) at his or her good fortune or success. **congratulations** *pl n*, *interj* **congratulatory** *adj*

congregate *v* gather together in a crowd. **congregation** *n* people who attend a church. **congregational** *adj* **Congregationalism** *n* Protestant denomination in which each church is self-governing. **Congregationalist** *adj*, *n*

congress *n* **1** formal meeting for discussion. **2** (C-) federal parliament of the US. **congressional** *adj* **Congressman**, **Congresswoman** *n* member of Congress.

congruent *adj* **1** similar, corresponding. **2** *Geom* identical in shape and size. **congruence** *n*

conical *adj* cone-shaped.

conifer *n* cone-bearing tree, such as the fir or pine. **coniferous** *adj*

conjecture *n*, *v* guess. **conjectural** *adj*

conjugal *adj* of marriage.

conjugate *v* give the inflections of (a verb). **conjugation** *n* complete set of inflections of a verb.

conjunction *n* **1** combination. **2** simultaneous occurrence of events. **3** part of speech joining words, phrases, or clauses.

conjunctivitis *n* inflammation of the membrane covering the eyeball and inner eyelid. **conjunctiva** *n* this membrane.

conjure *v* perform tricks that appear to be magic. **conjuror** *n* person who practises conjuring, especially for people's entertainment. **conjure up** *v* produce as if by magic.

conk *n* *Brit, Aust & NZ slang* nose.

conker n Informal nut of the horse chestnut.

conk out v Informal (of a machine) break down.

connect v 1 join together. 2 associate in the mind. **connection, connexion** n 1 relationship, association. 2 link or bond. 3 opportunity to transfer from one public vehicle to another. 4 influential acquaintance. **connective** adj

conning tower n raised observation tower containing the periscope on a submarine.

connive v 1 (foll. by at) allow (wrongdoing) by ignoring it. 2 conspire. **connivance** n

connoisseur [kon-noss-**sir**] n person with special knowledge of the arts, food, or drink.

connotation n associated idea conveyed by a word. **connote** v

connubial adj Formal of marriage.

conquer v 1 defeat. 2 overcome (a difficulty). 3 take (a place) by force. **conqueror** n **conquest** n 1 conquering. 2 person or thing conquered.

conscience n sense of right or wrong as regards thoughts and actions.

conscientious adj painstaking, diligent. **conscientiously** adv **conscientious objector** person who refuses to serve in the armed forces on moral or religious grounds.

conscious adj 1 alert and awake. 2 aware. 3 deliberate, intentional. **consciously** adv **consciousness** n

conscript n 1 person enrolled for compulsory military service. ♦ v 2 enrol (someone) for compulsory military service. **conscription** n

consecrate v 1 make sacred. 2 dedicate to a specific purpose. **consecration** n

consecutive adj in unbroken

succession. **consecutively** adv

consensus n general agreement.

☑ SPELLING TIP

The Bank of English has 6694 examples of the word **consensus** and another 112 of *concensus* with a *c* in the middle. The correct spelling is **consensus** and it has only one *c*.

---

consent n 1 agreement, permission. ♦ v 2 (foll. by to) permit, agree to.

consequence n 1 result, effect. 2 importance. **consequent** adj resulting. **consequently** adv as a result, therefore. **consequential** adj important.

conservative adj 1 opposing change. 2 moderate, cautious. 3 conventional in style. 4 (C-) of the Conservative Party, the British right-wing political party which believes in private enterprise and capitalism. ♦ n 5 conservative person. 6 (C-) supporter or member of the Conservative Party. **conservatism** n

conservatoire [kon-**serv**-a-twahr] n school of music.

conservatory n, pl -ries 1 room with glass walls and a glass roof, attached to a house. 2 Chiefly US conservatoire.

conserve v 1 protect from harm, decay, or loss. 2 preserve (fruit) with sugar. ♦ n 3 jam containing large pieces of fruit. **conservancy** n environmental conservation. **conservation** n 1 protection of natural resources and the environment. 2 conserving. **conservationist** n

consider v 1 regard as. 2 think about. 3 be considerate of. 4 discuss. 5 look at. **considerable** adj large in amount or degree. **considerably** adv **considerate** adj thoughtful towards others. **considerately** adv **consideration** n 1 careful thought. 2

fact that should be considered. **3** thoughtfulness. **4** payment for a service. **considering** *prep* taking (a specified fact) into account.

consign *v* **1** put somewhere. **2** send (goods). **consignment** *n* shipment of goods.

consist *v* **1** consist of be made up of. **2 consist in** have as its main or only feature.

consistent *adj* **1** unchanging, constant. **2** (foll. by *with*) in agreement. **consistently** *adv* **consistency** *n, pl* **-cies 1** being consistent. **2** degree of thickness or smoothness.

console[1] *v* comfort in distress. **consolation** *n* **1** consoling. **2** person or thing that consoles.

console[2] *n* **1** panel of controls for electronic equipment. **2** cabinet for a television or audio equipment. **3** ornamental wall bracket. **4** part of an organ containing the pedals, stops, and keys.

consolidate *v* **1** make or become stronger or more stable. **2** combine into a whole. **consolidation** *n*

consommé [kon-**som**-may] *n* thin clear meat soup.

consonant *n* **1** speech sound made by partially or completely blocking the breath stream, such as *b* or *f*. **2** letter representing this. ♦ *adj* **3** (foll. by *with*) agreeing (with). **consonance** *n* agreement, harmony.

consort *v* **1** (foll. by *with*) keep company (with). ♦ *n* **2** husband or wife of a monarch.

consortium *n, pl* **-tia** association of business firms.

conspectus *n* Formal survey or summary.

conspicuous *adj* **1** clearly visible. **2** noteworthy, attracting attention. **conspicuously** *adv*

conspire *v* **1** plan a crime together in secret. **2** act together as if by design. **conspiracy** *n* **1** conspiring. **2** *pl* **-cies** plan made by conspiring. **conspirator** *n* **conspiratorial** *adj*

constable *n* police officer of the lowest rank. **constabulary** *n, pl* **-laries** police force of an area.

constant *adj* **1** continuous. **2** unchanging. **3** faithful. ♦ *n* **4** unvarying quantity. **5** something that stays the same. **constantly** *adv* **constancy** *n*

constellation *n* group of stars.

consternation *n* anxiety or dismay.

constipation *n* difficulty in defecating. **constipated** *adj* having constipation.

constituent *n* **1** member of a constituency. **2** component part. ♦ *adj* **3** forming part of a whole. **constituency** *n, pl* **-cies 1** area represented by a Member of Parliament. **2** voters in such an area.

constitute *v* form, make up. **constitution** *n* **1** principles on which a state is governed. **2** physical condition. **3** structure. **constitutional** *adj* **1** of a constitution. **2** in accordance with a political constitution. **3** *n* **4** walk taken for exercise. **constitutionally** *adv*

constrain *v* **1** compel, force. **2** limit, restrict. **constraint** *n*

constrict *v* make narrower by squeezing. **constriction** *n* **constrictive** *adj* **constrictor** *n* **1** large snake that squeezes its prey to death. **2** muscle that compresses an organ.

construct *v* build or put together. **construction** *n* **1** constructing. **2** thing constructed. **3** interpretation. **4** *Grammar* way in which words are arranged in a sentence, clause, or phrase. **constructive** *adj* (of advice, criticism, etc.) useful and helpful. **constructively** *adv*

construe *v* **-struing, -strued** interpret.

consul *n* **1** official representing a state

in a foreign country. **2** one of the two chief magistrates in ancient Rome. **consular** *adj* **consulate** *n* workplace or position of a consul. **consulship** *n*

consult *v* go to for advice or information. **consultant** *n* **1** specialist doctor with a senior position in a hospital. **2** specialist who gives professional advice. **consultancy** *n, pl* **-cies** work or position of a consultant. **consultation** *n* (meeting for) consulting. **consultative** *adj* giving advice.

consume *v* **1** eat or drink. **2** use up. **3** destroy. **4** obsess. **consumption** *n* **1** amount consumed. **2** consuming. **3** *Old-fashioned* tuberculosis. **consumptive** *n, adj Old-fashioned* (person) having tuberculosis.

consumer *n* person who buys goods or uses services.

consummate [**kon**-sum-mate] *v* **1** make (a marriage) legal by sexual intercourse. **2** complete or fulfil. ♦ *adj* [kon-**sum**-mit] **3** supremely skilled. **4** complete, extreme. **consummation** *n*

cont. continued.

contact *n* **1** communicating. **2** touching. **3** useful acquaintance. **4** connection between two electrical conductors in a circuit. ♦ *v* **5** get in touch with. **contact lens** lens placed on the eyeball to correct defective vision.

contagion *n* **1** passing on of disease by contact. **2** disease spread by contact. **3** spreading of a harmful influence. **contagious** *adj* spreading by contact, catching.

contain *v* **1** hold or be capable of holding. **2** consist of. **3** control, restrain. **container** *n* **1** object used to hold or store things in. **2** large standard-sized box for transporting cargo by truck or ship. **containment** *n* prevention of the spread of

something harmful.

contaminate *v* **1** make impure, pollute. **2** make radioactive. **contaminant** *n* contaminating substance. **contamination** *n*

contemplate *v* **1** think deeply. **2** consider as a possibility. **3** gaze at. **contemplation** *n* **contemplative** *adj*

contemporary *adj* **1** present-day, modern. **2** living or occurring at the same time. **3** *n, pl* **-raries 4** person or thing living or occurring at the same time as another. **contemporaneous** *adj* happening at the same time.

☑ SPELLING TIP

It's easy to miss a syllable out when you say **contemporary**. The Bank of English shows that syllables get lost from spellings too - for example, *contempory* is a common mistake. But remember that the correct spelling ends in *orary*.

---

contempt *n* **1** dislike and disregard. **2** open disrespect for the authority of a court. **contemptible** *adj* deserving contempt. **contemptuous** *adj* showing contempt. **contemptuously** *adv*

contend *v* **1** (foll. by *with*) deal with. **2** state, assert. **3** compete.

contender *n* competitor, esp. a strong one.

content[1] *n* **1** meaning or substance of a piece of writing. **2** amount of a substance in a mixture. ♦ *pl* **3** what something contains. **4** list of chapters at the front of a book.

content[2] *adj* **1** satisfied with things as they are. **2** *v* **3** make (someone) content. ♦ *n* **4** happiness and satisfaction. **contented** *adj* **contentment** *n*

contention *n* **1** disagreement or dispute. **2** point asserted in argument.

contentious *adj* **1** causing disagreement. **2** quarrelsome.

contest *n* **1** competition or struggle. ♦ *v* **2** dispute, object to. **3** fight or compete for. **contestant** *n*

context *n* **1** circumstances of an event or fact. **2** words before and after a word or sentence that help make its meaning clear. **contextual** *adj*

contiguous *adj* very near or touching.

continent[1] *n* one of the earth's large masses of land. **the Continent** mainland of Europe. **continental** *adj* **continental breakfast** light breakfast of coffee and rolls.

continent[2] *adj* **1** able to control one's bladder and bowels. **2** sexually restrained. **continence** *n*

contingent *n* **1** group of people that represents or is part of a larger group. ♦ *adj* **2** (foll. by *on*) dependent on (something uncertain). **contingency** *n, pl* **-cies** something that may happen.

continue *v* **-tinuing, -tinued 1** (cause to) remain in a condition or place. **2** carry on (doing something). **3** resume. **continual** *adj* **1** constant. **2** recurring frequently. **continually** *adv* **continuance** *n* continuing. **continuation** *n* **1** continuing. **2** part added. **continuity** *n, pl* smooth development or sequence. **continuous** *adj* continuing uninterrupted. **continuously** *adv*

continuo *n, pl* **-tinuos** *Music* continuous bass part, usu. played on a keyboard instrument.

continuum *n, pl* **-tinua, -tinuums** continuous series.

contort *v* twist out of shape. **contortion** *n* **contortionist** *n* performer who contorts his or her body to entertain.

contour *n* **1** outline. **2** (also **contour line**) line on a map joining places of the same height.

contra- *prefix* against or contrasting, e.g. *contraflow*.

contraband *n, adj* smuggled (goods).

contraception *n* prevention of pregnancy by artificial means. **contraceptive** *n* **1** device used or pill taken to prevent pregnancy. ♦ *adj* **2** preventing pregnancy.

contract *n* **1** (document setting out) a formal agreement. ♦ *v* **2** make a formal agreement (to do something). **3** make or become smaller or shorter. **4** catch (an illness). **contraction** *n* **contractor** *n* firm that supplies materials or labour. **contractual** *adj*

contradict *v* **1** declare the opposite of (a statement) to be true. **2** be at variance with. **contradiction** *n* **contradictory** *adj*

contraflow *n* flow of traffic going alongside but in an opposite direction to the usual flow.

contralto *n, pl* **-tos** (singer with) the lowest female voice.

contraption *n* strange-looking device.

contrapuntal *adj Music* of or in counterpoint.

contrary *n* **1** complete opposite. ♦ *adj* **2** opposed, completely different. **3** perverse, obstinate. ♦ *adv* **4** in opposition. **contrarily** *adv* **contrariness** *n* **contrariwise** *adv*

contrast *n* **1** obvious difference. **2** person or thing very different from another. **3** *v* **4** compare in order to show differences. **5** (foll. by *with*) be very different (from).

contravene *v* break (a rule or law). **contravention** *n*

contretemps [**kon**-tra-tahn] *n, pl* **-temps** embarrassing minor disagreement.

contribute *v* **1** give for a common purpose or fund. **2** (foll. by *to*) be partly responsible (for). **contribution** *n* **contributor** *n* **contributory** *adj*

contrite *adj* sorry and apologetic.
contritely *adv* **contrition** *n*
contrive *v* **1** make happen. **2** devise or
construct. **contrivance** *n* **1** device. **2**
plan. **3** contriving. **contrived** *adj*
planned or artificial.
control *n* **1** power to direct something.
2 curb or check. **3** *pl* **4** instruments
used to operate a machine. ◆ *v*
-trolling, -trolled 5 have power over.
6 limit, restrain. **7** regulate, operate.
controllable *adj* **controller** *n*
controversy *n, pl* **-sies** fierce
argument or debate. **controversial**
adj causing controversy.
contumely [**kon**-tume-mill-ee] *n Lit*
scornful or insulting treatment.
contusion *n Formal* bruise.
conundrum *n* riddle.
conurbation *n* large urban area
formed by the growth and merging of
towns.
convalesce *v* recover after an illness or
operation. **convalescence** *n*
convalescent *n, adj*
convection *n* transmission of heat in
liquids or gases by the circulation of
currents. **convector** *n* heater that
gives out hot air.
convene *v* gather or summon for a
formal meeting. **convener, convenor**
n person who calls a meeting.
convenient *adj* **1** suitable or
opportune. **2** easy to use. **3** nearby.
conveniently *adv* **convenience** *n* **1**
quality of being convenient. **2** useful
object. **3** *Euphemistic* public toilet.
convent *n* **1** building where nuns live.
2 school run by nuns.
convention *n* **1** widely accepted view
of proper behaviour. **2** assembly or
meeting. **3** formal agreement.
conventional *adj* **1** (unthinkingly)
following the accepted customs. **2**
customary. **3** (of weapons or warfare)
not nuclear. **conventionally** *adv*

conventionality *n*
converge *v* meet or join.
convergence *n*
conversant *adj* **conversant with**
having knowledge or experience of.
conversation *n* informal talk.
conversational *adj*
conversationalist *n* person with a
specified ability at conversation.
converse¹ *v* have a conversation.
converse² *adj, n* opposite or contrary.
conversely *adv*
convert *v* **1** change in form, character,
or function. **2** cause to change in
opinion or belief. **3** *n* **4** person who
has converted to a different belief or
religion. **conversion** *n* **1** (thing
resulting from) converting. **2** *Rugby*
score made after a try by kicking the
ball over the crossbar. **convertible**
adj **1** capable of being converted. ◆ *n*
2 car with a folding or removable roof.
convex *adj* curving outwards.
convey *v* **1** communicate
(information). **2** carry, transport.
conveyance *n* **1** *Old-fashioned* vehicle.
2 transfer of the legal title to property.
conveyancing *n* branch of law
dealing with the transfer of ownership
of property. **conveyor belt**
continuous moving belt for
transporting things, esp. in a factory.
convict *v* **1** declare guilty. ◆ *n* **2** person
serving a prison sentence. **conviction**
n **1** firm belief. **2** instance of being
convicted.
convince *v* persuade by argument or
evidence. **convincing** *adj*
convincingly *adv*
convivial *adj* sociable, lively.
conviviality *n*
convocation *n* **1** calling together. **2**
large formal meeting. **convoke** *v* call
together.
convoluted *adj* **1** coiled, twisted. **2** (of
an argument or sentence) complex

and hard to understand. **convolution** n

convolvulus n twining plant with funnel-shaped flowers.

convoy n group of vehicles or ships travelling together.

convulse v **1** (of part of the body) undergo violent spasms. **2** Informal (be) overcome with laughter. **convulsion** n **1** violent muscular spasm. ♦ pl **2** uncontrollable laughter. **convulsive** adj

cony n, pl **conies** Brit **1** rabbit. **2** rabbit fur.

coo v **cooing, cooed** (of a dove or pigeon) make a soft murmuring sound.

cooee interj Brit, Aust & NZ call to attract attention.

cook v **1** prepare (food) by heating. **2** (of food) be cooked. ♦ n **3** person who cooks food. **cook the books** falsify accounts. **cooker** n **1** Chiefly Brit apparatus for cooking heated by gas or electricity. **2** Chiefly Brit apple suitable for cooking. **cookery** n art of cooking. **cookie** n US biscuit. **cook up** v Informal devise (a story or scheme).

Cooktown orchid n purple Australian orchid.

cool adj **1** moderately cold. **2** calm and unemotional. **3** indifferent or unfriendly. **4** Informal sophisticated or excellent. **5** Informal (of a large sum of money) without exaggeration, e.g. a cool million. ♦ v **6** make or become cool. ♦ n **7** coolness. **8** Slang calmness, composure. **coolly** adv **coolness** n **coolant** n fluid used to cool machinery while it is working. **cool drink** S Afr nonalcoholic drink. **cooler** n container for making or keeping things cool.

coolibah n Australian eucalypt that grows beside rivers.

coolie n Old-fashioned offens unskilled Oriental labourer.

coomb, coombe n S English short valley or deep hollow.

coon n S Afr offens person of mixed race.

coop[1] n cage or pen for poultry. **coop up** v confine in a restricted place.

coop[2] [koh-op] n Brit, US & Aust (shop run by) a cooperative society.

cooper n person who makes or repairs barrels.

cooperate v work or act together. **cooperation** n **cooperative** adj **1** willing to cooperate. **2** (of an enterprise) owned and managed collectively. ♦ n **3** cooperative organization.

coopt [koh-**opt**] v add (someone) to a group by the agreement of the existing members.

coordinate v **1** bring together and cause to work together efficiently. ♦ n **2** Maths any of a set of numbers defining the location of a point. ♦ pl **3** clothes designed to be worn together. **coordination** n **coordinator** n

coot n small black water bird

cop Slang ♦ n **1** policeman. ♦ v **copping, copped 2** take or seize. **cop it** get into trouble or be punished. **cop out** v avoid taking responsibility or committing oneself.

cope[1] v (often foll. by with) deal successfully (with).

cope[2] n large ceremonial cloak worn by some Christian priests.

coping n sloping top row of a wall.

copious [kope-ee-uss] adj abundant, plentiful. **copiously** adv

copper[1] n **1** soft reddish-brown metal. **2** copper or bronze coin. **copper-bottomed** adj financially reliable. **copperplate** n fine handwriting style.

copper[2] n Brit slang policeman.

coppice, copse n small group of trees growing close together.

copra n dried oil-yielding kernel of the coconut.

copulate v have sexual intercourse. **copulation** n

copy n, pl **copies** 1 thing made to look exactly like another. 2 single specimen of a book etc. 3 material for printing. 4 v **copying, copied** 5 make a copy of. 6 act or try to be like. **copyright** n 1 exclusive legal right to reproduce and control a book, work of art, etc. ♦ v 2 take out a copyright on. ♦ adj 3 protected by copyright. **copywriter** n person who writes advertising copy.

coquette n woman who flirts. **coquettish** adj

coracle n small round boat of wicker covered with skins.

coral n 1 hard substance formed from the skeletons of very small sea animals. ♦ adj 2 orange-pink.

cor anglais n, pl **cors anglais** woodwind instrument similar to the oboe.

cord n 1 thin rope or thick string. 2 cordlike structure in the body. 3 corduroy. 4 pl 5 corduroy trousers.

cordial adj 1 warm and friendly. ♦ n 2 drink with a fruit base. **cordially** adv **cordiality** n

cordite n explosive used in guns and bombs.

cordon n chain of police, soldiers, etc., guarding an area. **cordon off** v form a cordon round.

cordon bleu [**bluh**] adj (of cookery or cooks) of the highest standard.

corduroy n cotton fabric with a velvety ribbed surface.

core n 1 central part of certain fruits, containing the seeds. 2 central or essential part. 3 v 4 remove the core from.

corella n white Australian cockatoo.

co-respondent n Brit, Aust & NZ person with whom someone being sued for divorce is claimed to have committed adultery.

corgi n short-legged sturdy dog.

coriander n plant grown for its aromatic seeds and leaves.

cork n 1 thick light bark of a Mediterranean oak. 2 piece of this used as a stopper. ♦ v 3 seal with a cork. **corkage** n restaurant's charge for serving wine bought elsewhere. **corkscrew** n spiral metal tool for pulling corks from bottles.

corm n bulblike underground stem of certain plants.

cormorant n large dark-coloured long-necked sea bird.

corn¹ n 1 cereal plant such as wheat or oats. 2 grain of such plants. 3 US, Canadian, Aust & NZ maize. 4 Slang something unoriginal or oversentimental. **corny** adj Slang unoriginal or oversentimental. **cornflakes** pl n breakfast cereal made from toasted maize. **cornflour** n 1 Chiefly Brit fine maize flour. 2 NZ fine wheat flour. **cornflower** n plant with blue flowers.

corn² n painful hard skin on the toe.

cornea [**korn**-ee-a] n, pl **-neas, -neae** transparent membrane covering the eyeball. **corneal** adj

corned beef n beef preserved in salt.

corner n 1 area or angle where two converging lines or surfaces meet. 2 place where two streets meet. 3 remote place. 4 Sport free kick or shot from the corner of the field. ♦ v 5 force into a difficult or inescapable position. 6 (of a vehicle) turn a corner. 7 obtain a monopoly of. **cornerstone** n indispensable part or basis.

cornet n 1 brass instrument similar to the trumpet. 2 cone-shaped ice-cream wafer.

cornice *n* decorative moulding round the top of a wall.

corn on the cob *n* corn cooked and eaten on the cob.

cornucopia [korn-yew-**kope**-ee-a] *n* 1 great abundance. 2 symbol of plenty, consisting of a horn overflowing with fruit and flowers.

corolla *n* petals of a flower collectively.

corollary *n, pl* **-laries** idea, fact, or proposition which is the natural result of something else.

corona *n, pl* **-nas, -nae** ring of light round the moon or sun.

coronary [**kor**-ron-a-ree] *adj* 1 of the arteries surrounding the heart. ♦ *n, pl* **-naries** 2 coronary thrombosis. **coronary thrombosis** condition in which the flow of blood to the heart is blocked by a blood clot.

coronation *n* ceremony of crowning a monarch.

coroner *n Brit, Aust & NZ* official responsible for the investigation of violent, sudden, or suspicious deaths.

coronet *n* small crown.

corpora *n* plural of CORPUS.

corporal[1] *n* noncommissioned officer in an army.

corporal[2] *adj* of the body. **corporal punishment** physical punishment, such as caning.

corporation *n* 1 large business or company. 2 city or town council. **corporate** *adj* 1 of business corporations. 2 shared by a group.

corporeal [kore-**pore**-ee-al] *adj* physical or tangible.

corps [kore] *n, pl* **corps** 1 military unit with a specific function. 2 organized body of people.

corpse *n* dead body.

corpulent *adj* fat or plump. **corpulence** *n*

corpus *n, pl* **corpora** collection of writings, esp. by a single author.

corpuscle *n* red or white blood cell.

corral *US* ♦ *n* 1 enclosure for cattle or horses. ♦ *v* **-ralling, -ralled** 2 put in a corral.

correct *adj* 1 free from error, true. 2 in accordance with accepted standards. ♦ *v* 3 put right. 4 indicate the errors in. 5 rebuke or punish. **correctly** *adv* **correctness** *n* **correction** *n* 1 correcting. 2 alteration correcting something. **corrective** *adj* intended to put right something wrong.

correlate *v* place or be placed in a mutual relationship. **correlation** *n*

correspond *v* 1 be consistent or compatible (with). 2 be the same or similar. 3 communicate by letter. **corresponding** *adj* **correspondingly** *adv* **correspondence** *n* 1 communication by letters. 2 letters so exchanged. 3 relationship or similarity. **correspondent** *n* 1 person employed by a newspaper etc. to report on a special subject or from a foreign country. 2 letter writer.

corridor *n* 1 passage in a building or train. 2 strip of land or airspace providing access through foreign territory.

corrigendum [kor-rij-**end**-um] *n, pl* **-da** error to be corrected.

corroborate *v* support (a fact or opinion) by giving proof. **corroboration** *n* **corroborative** *adj*

corroboree *n Aust* Aboriginal gathering or dance.

corrode *v* eat or be eaten away by chemical action or rust. **corrosion** *n* **corrosive** *adj*

corrugated *adj* folded into alternate grooves and ridges.

corrupt *adj* 1 open to or involving bribery. 2 morally depraved. 3 (of a text or data) unreliable through errors

or alterations. ♦ *v* **4** make corrupt.
corruptly *adv* **corruption** *n*
corruptible *adj*

corsage [kor-**sahzh**] *n* small bouquet worn on the bodice of a dress.

corsair *n* **1** pirate. **2** pirate ship.

corset *n* women's close-fitting undergarment worn to shape the torso.

cortege [kor-**tayzh**] *n* funeral procession.

cortex *n, pl* **-tices** *Anat* outer layer of the brain or other internal organ. **cortical** *adj*

cortisone *n* steroid hormone used to treat various diseases.

corundum *n* hard mineral used as an abrasive.

coruscate *v Formal* sparkle.

corvette *n* lightly armed escort warship.

cos *Maths* cosine.

cosh *n Brit* **1** heavy blunt weapon. ♦ *v* **2** hit with a cosh.

cosine [**koh**-sine] *n* (in trigonometry) ratio of the length of the adjacent side to that of the hypotenuse in a right-angled triangle.

cosmetic *n* **1** preparation used to improve the appearance of a person's skin. ♦ *adj* **2** improving the appearance only.

cosmic *adj* of the whole universe. **cosmic rays** electromagnetic radiation from outer space.

cosmonaut *n* Russian name for an astronaut.

cosmopolitan *adj* **1** composed of people or elements from many countries. **2** having lived and travelled in many countries. ♦ *n* **3** cosmopolitan person. **cosmopolitanism** *n*

cosmos *n* the universe. **cosmology** *n* study of the origin and nature of the universe. **cosmological** *adj*

Cossack *n* member of a S Russian

people famous as horsemen and dancers.

cosset *v* **cosseting, cosseted** pamper.

cost *n* **1** amount of money, time, labour, etc., required for something. ♦ *pl* **2** expenses of a lawsuit. ♦ *v* **costing, cost 3** have as its cost. **4** involve the loss or sacrifice of. **5** *past* **costed**) estimate the cost of. **costly** *adj* **1** expensive. **2** involving great loss or sacrifice. **costliness** *n*

costermonger *n Brit* person who sells fruit and vegetables from a street barrow.

costume *n* **1** style of dress of a particular place or time, or for a particular activity. **2** clothes worn by an actor or performer. **costumier** *n* maker or seller of costumes. **costume jewellery** inexpensive artificial jewellery.

cosy *adj* **-sier, -siest 1** warm and snug. **2** intimate, friendly. ♦ *n* **3** cover for keeping things warm, e.g. *a tea cosy*. **cosily** *adv* **cosiness** *n*

cot *n* **1** baby's bed with high sides. **2** small portable bed. **cot death** unexplained death of a baby while asleep.

cote *n* shelter for birds or animals.

coterie [**kote**-er-ee] *n* exclusive group, clique.

cotoneaster [kot-tone-ee-**ass**-ter] *n* garden shrub with red berries.

cottage *n* small house in the country. **cottage cheese** soft mild white cheese. **cottage industry** craft industry in which employees work at home. **cottage pie** dish of minced meat topped with mashed potato.

cotter *n* pin or wedge used to secure machine parts.

cotton *n* **1** white downy fibre covering the seeds of a tropical plant. **2** cloth or thread made from this. **cottony** *adj* **cotton on (to)** *v Informal* understand.

cotton wool fluffy cotton used for surgical dressings etc.

cotyledon [kot-ill-**ee**-don] *n* first leaf of a plant embryo.

couch *n* **1** piece of upholstered furniture for seating more than one person. ♦ *v* **2** express in a particular way. **couch potato** *Slang* lazy person whose only hobby is watching television.

couchette [koo-**shett**] *n* bed converted from seats on a train or ship.

couch grass *n* quickly spreading grassy weed.

cougan *n Aust slang* drunk and rowdy person.

cougar *n* puma.

cough *v* **1** expel air from the lungs abruptly and noisily. ♦ *n* **2** act or sound of coughing. **3** illness which causes coughing.

could *v* past tense of CAN¹.

couldn't could not.

coulomb [**koo**-lom] *n* SI unit of electric charge.

coulter *n* blade at the front of a ploughshare.

council *n* **1** group meeting for discussion or consultation. **2** local governing body of a town or region. ♦ *adj* **3** of or by a council. **councillor** *n* member of a council. **council tax** (in Britain) tax based on the value of property, to fund local services.

counsel *n* **1** advice or guidance. **2** barrister or barristers. ♦ *v* **-selling, -selled** **3** give guidance to. **4** urge, recommend. **counsellor** *n*

count¹ *v* **1** say numbers in order. **2** find the total of. **3** be important. **4** regard as. **5** take into account. ♦ *n* **6** counting. **7** number reached by counting. **8** *Law* one of a number of charges. **countless** *adj* too many to count. **count on** *v* rely or depend on.

count² *n* European nobleman.

countdown *n* counting backwards to zero of the seconds before an event.

countenance *n* **1** (expression of) the face. ♦ *v* **2** allow or tolerate.

counter¹ *n* **1** long flat surface in a bank or shop, on which business is transacted. **2** small flat disc used in board games.

counter² *v* **1** oppose, retaliate against. ♦ *adv* **2** in the opposite direction. **3** in direct contrast. ♦ *n* **4** opposing or retaliatory action.

counter- *prefix* **1** opposite, against, e.g. *counterattack*. **2** complementary, corresponding, e.g. *counterpart*.

counteract *v* act against or neutralize. **counteraction** *n*

counterattack *n*, *v* attack in response to an attack.

counterbalance *n* **1** weight or force balancing or neutralizing another. ♦ *v* **2** act as a counterbalance to.

counterblast *n* aggressive response to a verbal attack.

counterfeit *adj* **1** fake, forged. ♦ *n* **2** fake, forgery. ♦ *v* **3** fake, forge.

counterfoil *n* part of a cheque or receipt kept as a record.

countermand *v* cancel (a previous order).

counterpane *n* bed covering.

counterpart *n* person or thing complementary to or corresponding to another.

counterpoint *n Music* technique of combining melodies.

counterpoise *n*, *v* counterbalance.

counterproductive *adj* having an effect opposite to the one intended.

countersign *v* sign (a document already signed by someone) as confirmation.

countersink *v* drive (a screw) into a shaped hole so that its head is below the surface.

countertenor n male alto.

countess n 1 woman holding the rank of count or earl. 2 wife or widow of a count or earl.

country n, pl **-tries** 1 nation. 2 nation's territory. 3 nation's people. 4 part of the land away from cities. **countrified** adj rustic in manner or appearance. **country and western, country music** popular music based on American White folk music. **countryman, countrywoman** n 1 person from one's native land. 2 Brit, Aust & NZ person who lives in the country. **countryside** n land away from cities.

county n, pl **-ties** (in some countries) division of a country

coup [koo] n 1 successful action. 2 coup d'état.

coup de grâce [koo de **grahss**] n final or decisive action.

coup d'état [koo day-**tah**] n sudden violent overthrow of a government.

coupé [koo-**pay**] n sports car with two doors and a sloping fixed roof.

couple n 1 two people who are married or romantically involved. 2 two partners in a dance or game. ♦ v 3 connect, associate. **a couple** 1 pair. 2 Informal small number. **couplet** n two consecutive lines of verse, usu. rhyming and of the same metre. **coupling** n device for connecting things, such as railway carriages.

coupon n 1 piece of paper entitling the holder to a discount or gift. 2 detachable order form. 3 football pools entry form.

courage n ability to face danger or pain without fear. **courageous** adj **courageously** adv

courgette n type of small vegetable marrow.

courier n 1 person employed to look

after holiday-makers. 2 person employed to deliver urgent messages.

course n 1 series of lessons or medical treatment. 2 route or direction taken. 3 area where golf is played or a race is run. 4 any of the successive parts of a meal. 5 mode of conduct or action. 6 natural development of events. ♦ v 7 (of liquid) run swiftly. **of course** as expected, naturally.

court n 1 body which decides legal cases. 2 place where it meets. 3 marked area for playing a racket game. 4 courtyard. 5 residence, household, or retinue of a sovereign. ♦ v 6 Old-fashioned try to gain the love of. 7 try to win the favour of. 8 invite, e.g. to court disaster. **courtier** n attendant at a royal court. **courtly** adj ceremoniously polite. **courtliness** n **courtship** n courting of an intended spouse or mate. **court martial** n, pl **courts martial** court for trying naval or military offences. **court shoe** woman's low-cut shoe without straps or laces. **courtyard** n paved space enclosed by buildings or walls.

courtesan [kor-tiz-**zan**] n Hist mistress or high-class prostitute.

courtesy n 1 politeness, good manners. 2 pl **-sies** courteous act. **(by) courtesy of** by permission of. **courteous** adj polite. **courteously** adv

cousin n child of one's uncle or aunt.

couture [koo-**toor**] n high-fashion designing and dressmaking. **couturier** n person who designs women's fashion clothes.

cove n small bay or inlet.

coven [kuv-ven] n meeting of witches.

covenant [kuv-ven-ant] n 1 contract. 2 Chiefly Brit formal agreement to make an annual (charitable) payment. ♦ v 3 agree by a covenant.

Coventry n **send someone to Coventry** punish someone by refusing to speak to them.

cover v **1** place something over, to protect or conceal. **2** extend over or lie on the surface of. **3** travel over. **4** insure against loss or risk. **5** include. **6** report (an event) for a newspaper. **7** be enough to pay for. ♦ n **8** anything that covers. **9** outside of a book or magazine. **10** insurance. **11** shelter or protection. **coverage** n amount or extent covered. **coverlet** n bed cover.

covert adj **1** concealed, secret. ♦ n **2** thicket giving shelter to game birds or animals. **covertly** adv

covet v **coveting, coveted** long to possess (what belongs to someone else). **covetous** adj **covetousness** n

covey [**kuv**-vee] n small flock of grouse or partridge.

cow[1] n **1** mature female of cattle and of certain other mammals, such as the elephant or seal. **2** Informal, offens disagreeable woman. **cowboy** n **1** (in the US) ranch worker who herds and tends cattle, usu. on horseback. **2** Informal irresponsible or unscrupulous worker.

cow[2] v intimidate, subdue.

coward n person who lacks courage. **cowardly** adj **cowardice** n lack of courage.

cower v cringe in fear.

cowl n **1** loose hood. **2** monk's hooded robe. **3** cover on a chimney to increase ventilation.

cowling n cover on an engine.

cowrie n brightly-marked sea shell.

cowslip n small yellow wild European flower.

cox n **1** coxswain. ♦ v **2** act as cox of (a boat).

coxswain [**kok**-sn] n person who steers a rowing boat.

coy adj affectedly shy or modest. **coyly** adv **coyness** n

coyote [koy-**ote**-ee] n prairie wolf of N America.

coypu n beaver-like aquatic rodent native to S America, bred for its fur.

cozen v Lit cheat, trick.

CPU Computers central processing unit.

crab n edible shellfish with ten legs, the first pair modified into pincers.

crab apple n small sour apple.

crabbed adj **1** (of handwriting) hard to read. **2** (also **crabby**) bad-tempered.

crack v **1** break or split partially. **2** (cause to) make a sharp noise. **3** break down or yield under strain. **4** hit suddenly. **5** solve (a code or problem). **6** tell (a joke). ♦ n **7** sudden sharp noise. **8** narrow gap. **9** sharp blow. **10** Informal gibe, joke. **11** Slang highly addictive form of cocaine. ♦ adj **12** Informal first-rate, excellent, e.g. a crack shot. **cracking** adj very good. **crackdown** n severe disciplinary measures. **crack down on** v take severe measures against.

cracker n **1** thin dry biscuit. **2** decorated cardboard tube, pulled apart with a bang, containing a paper hat and a joke or toy. **3** small explosive firework. **4** Slang outstanding thing or person.

crackers adj Slang insane.

crackle v **1** make small sharp popping noises. ♦ n **2** crackling sound. **crackling** n **1** crackle. **2** crisp skin of roast pork.

crackpot n, adj Informal eccentric (person).

cradle n **1** baby's bed on rockers. **2** place where something originates. **3** supporting structure. ♦ v **4** hold gently as if in a cradle.

craft n **1** occupation requiring skill with the hands. **2** skill or ability. **3** pl **craft**) boat, ship, aircraft, or spaceship. **crafty** adj skilled in deception. **craftily** adv **craftiness** n **craftsman,**

craftswoman n skilled worker. **craftsmanship** n

crag n steep rugged rock. **craggy** adj

cram v **cramming, crammed 1** force into too small a space. **2** fill too full. **3** study hard just before an examination.

cramp[1] n **1** painful muscular contraction. **2** clamp for holding masonry or timber together.

cramp[2] v confine, restrict.

crampon n spiked plate strapped to a boot for climbing on ice.

cranberry n sour edible red berry.

crane n **1** machine for lifting and moving heavy weights. **2** large wading bird with a long neck and legs. ♦ v **3** stretch (one's neck) to see something.

crane fly n long-legged insect with slender wings.

cranium n, pl **-niums, -nia** Anat skull. **cranial** adj

crank n **1** arm projecting at right angles from a shaft, for transmitting or converting motion. **2** Informal eccentric person. ♦ v **3** start (an engine) with a crank. **cranky** adj Informal **1** eccentric. **2** bad-tempered. **crankshaft** n shaft driven by a crank.

cranny n, pl **-nies** narrow opening.

crape n same as CREPE.

craps n gambling game played with two dice.

crash n **1** collision involving a vehicle or vehicles. **2** sudden loud smashing noise. **3** financial collapse. ♦ v **4** (cause to) collide violently with a vehicle, a stationary object, or the ground. **5** (cause to) make a loud smashing noise. **6** (cause to) fall with a crash. **7** collapse or fail financially. **crash course** short, very intensive course in a particular subject. **crash helmet** protective helmet worn by a motorcyclist. **crash-land** v (of an aircraft) land in an emergency, causing damage. **crash-landing** n

crass adj stupid and insensitive. **crassly** adv **crassness** n

crate n large wooden container for packing goods.

crater n very large hole in the ground or in the surface of the moon.

cravat n man's scarf worn like a tie.

crave v **1** desire intensely. **2** beg or plead for. **craving** n

craven adj cowardly.

crawfish n same as CRAYFISH.

crawl v **1** move on one's hands and knees. **2** move very slowly. **3** (foll. by to) flatter in order to gain some advantage. **4** feel as if covered with crawling creatures. ♦ n **5** crawling motion or pace. **6** overarm swimming stroke. **crawler** n

crayfish n **1** edible shellfish like a lobster **2** Australian freshwater crustacean.

crayon v, n (draw or colour with) a stick or pencil of coloured wax or clay.

craze n short-lived fashion or enthusiasm. **crazed** adj **1** wild and uncontrolled. **2** (of porcelain) having fine cracks.

crazy adj **1** ridiculous. **2** (foll. by about) very fond (of). **3** insane. **craziness** n **crazy paving** paving made of irregularly shaped slabs of stone.

creak v, n (make) a harsh squeaking sound. **creaky** adj

cream n **1** fatty part of milk. **2** food or cosmetic resembling cream in consistency. **3** best part (of something). ♦ adj **4** yellowish-white. ♦ v **5** beat to a creamy consistency. **creamy** adj **cream cheese** rich soft white cheese. **cream off** v take the best part from.

crease n **1** line made by folding or pressing. **2** Cricket line marking the bowler's and batsman's positions. ♦ v **3** crush or line.

create v 1 make, cause to exist. 2 appoint to a new rank or position. 3 *Slang* make an angry fuss. **creation** n **creative** adj imaginative or inventive. **creativity** n **creator** n

creature n animal, person, or other being.

crèche n place where small children are looked after while their parents are working, shopping, etc.

credence n belief in the truth or accuracy of a statement.

credentials pl n document giving evidence of a person's identity or qualifications.

credible adj 1 believable. 2 trustworthy. **credibly** adv **credibility** n

credit n 1 system of allowing customers to receive goods and pay later. 2 reputation for trustworthiness in paying debts. 3 money at one's disposal in a bank account. 4 side of an account book on which such sums are entered. 5 (source or cause of) praise or approval. 6 influence or reputation based on the good opinion of others. 7 belief or trust. ♦ pl 8 list of people responsible for the production of a film, programme, or record. ♦ v **crediting, credited** 9 enter as a credit in an account. 10 (foll. by *with*) attribute (to). 11 believe. **creditable** adj praiseworthy. **creditably** adv **creditor** n person to whom money is owed. **credit card** card allowing a person to buy on credit.

credulous adj too willing to believe. **credulity** n

creed n statement or system of (Christian) beliefs or principles.

creek n 1 narrow inlet or bay. 2 *Aust, NZ, US & Canadian* small stream.

creel n wicker basket used by anglers.

creep v **creeping, crept** 1 move quietly and cautiously. 2 crawl with the body near to the ground. 3 (of a plant) grow along the ground or over rocks. ♦ n 4 *Slang* obnoxious or servile person. **give one the creeps** *Informal* make one feel fear or disgust. **creeper** n creeping plant. **creepy** adj *Informal* causing a feeling of fear or disgust.

cremate v burn (a corpse) to ash. **cremation** n **crematorium** n building where corpses are cremated.

crenellated adj having battlements.

creole n 1 language developed from a mixture of languages. 2 (C-) native-born W Indian or Latin American of mixed European and African descent.

creosote n 1 dark oily liquid made from coal tar and used for preserving wood. ♦ v 2 treat with creosote.

crepe [**krayp**] n 1 fabric or rubber with a crinkled texture. 2 very thin pancake. **crepe paper** paper with a crinkled texture.

crept v past of CREEP.

crepuscular adj *Lit* of or like twilight.

crescendo [krish-**end**-oh] n, pl **-dos** gradual increase in loudness, esp. in music.

crescent n 1 (curved shape of) the moon as seen in its first or last quarter. 2 crescent-shaped street.

cress n plant with strong-tasting leaves, used in salads.

crest n 1 top of a mountain, hill, or wave. 2 tuft or growth on a bird's or animal's head. 3 heraldic design used on a coat of arms and elsewhere. **crested** adj **crestfallen** adj disheartened.

cretin n 1 *Informal* stupid person. 2 *Obs* person afflicted with physical and mental retardation caused by a thyroid deficiency. **cretinous** adj

crevasse n deep open crack in a glacier.

crevice n narrow crack or gap in rock.

crew n 1 people who work on a ship or aircraft. 2 group of people working together. 3 Informal any group of people. ◆ v 4 serve as a crew member (on). **crew cut** man's closely cropped haircut.

crewel n fine worsted yarn used in embroidery.

crib n 1 piece of writing stolen from elsewhere. 2 translation or list of answers used by students, often illicitly. 3 baby's cradle. 4 rack for fodder. 5 short for CRIBBAGE. ◆ v **cribbing, cribbed 6** copy (someone's work) dishonestly. **crib-wall** n NZ retaining wall built against an earth bank.

cribbage n card game for two to four players.

crick n 1 muscle spasm or cramp in the back or neck. ◆ v 2 cause a crick in.

cricket[1] n outdoor game played with bats, a ball, and wickets by two teams of eleven. **cricketer** n

cricket[2] n chirping insect like a grasshopper.

crime n 1 unlawful act. 2 unlawful acts collectively. **criminal** n 1 person guilty of a crime. ◆ adj 2 of crime. 3 Informal deplorable. **criminally** adv **criminality** n **criminology** n study of crime. **criminologist** n

crimp v fold or press into ridges.

crimson adj deep purplish-red.

cringe v 1 flinch in fear. 2 behave in a submissive or timid way.

crinkle v, n wrinkle, crease, or fold.

crinoline n hooped petticoat.

cripple n 1 person who is lame or disabled. 2 v 3 make lame or disabled. 4 damage (something).

crisis n, pl **-ses 1** crucial stage, turning point. 2 time of extreme trouble.

crisp adj 1 fresh and firm. 2 dry and brittle. 3 clean and neat. 4 (of

weather) cold but invigorating. 5 lively or brisk. ◆ n 6 Brit very thin slice of potato fried till crunchy. **crisply** adv **crispness** n **crispy** adj hard and crunchy. **crispbread** n thin dry biscuit.

crisscross v 1 move in or mark with a crosswise pattern. ◆ adj 2 (of lines) crossing in different directions.

criterion n, pl **-ria** standard of judgment.

critic n 1 professional judge of any of the arts. 2 person who finds fault. **critical** adj 1 very important or dangerous. 2 fault-finding. 3 able to examine and judge carefully. 4 of a critic or criticism. **critically** adv **criticism** n 1 fault-finding. 2 analysis of a book, work of art, etc. **criticize** v find fault with. **critique** n critical essay.

croak v 1 (of a frog or crow) give a low hoarse cry. 2 utter or speak with a croak. 3 n 4 low hoarse sound. **croaky** adj hoarse.

crochet [**kroh**-shay] v **-cheting, -cheted 1** make by looping and intertwining yarn with a hooked needle. ◆ n 2 work made in this way.

crock[1] n earthenware pot or jar. **crockery** n dishes.

crock[2] n Brit, Aust & NZ informal old or decrepit person or thing.

crocodile n 1 large amphibious tropical reptile. 2 Brit, Aust & NZ line of people, esp. schoolchildren, walking two by two. **crocodile tears** insincere show of grief.

crocus n, pl **-cuses** small plant with yellow, white, or purple flowers in spring.

croft n small farm worked by one family in Scotland. **crofter** n

croissant [**krwah**-son] n rich flaky crescent-shaped roll.

cromlech n Brit circle of prehistoric standing stones.

crone n witchlike old woman.

crony n, pl **-nies** close friend.

crook n 1 Informal criminal. 2 bent or curved part. 3 hooked pole. 4 adj 5 Aust & NZ slang unwell, injured. 6 **go crook** Aust & NZ slang become angry. **crooked** adj 1 bent or twisted. 2 set at an angle. 3 Informal dishonest.

croon v sing, hum, or speak in a soft low tone.

crooner n male singer of sentimental ballads.

crop n 1 cultivated plant. 2 season's total yield of produce. 3 group of things appearing at one time. 4 (handle of) a whip. 5 pouch in a bird's gullet. 6 very short haircut. ♦ v **cropping, cropped** 7 cut very short. 8 produce or harvest as a crop. 9 (of animals) feed on (grass). **cropper** n **come a cropper** Informal have a disastrous failure or heavy fall. **crop-top** n short T-shirt or vest that reveals the wearer's midriff. **crop up** v Informal happen unexpectedly.

croquet [**kroh**-kay] n game played on a lawn in which balls are hit through hoops.

croquette [kroh-**kett**] n fried cake of potato, meat, or fish.

crosier n same as CROZIER.

cross v 1 move or go across (something). 2 meet and pass. 3 (with out) delete with a cross or lines. 4 place (one's arms or legs) crosswise. 5 n 6 structure, symbol, or mark of two intersecting lines. 7 such a structure of wood as a means of execution. 8 representation of the Cross as an emblem of Christianity. 9 mixture of two things. 10 adj 11 angry, annoyed. **the Cross** Christianity the cross on which Christ was crucified. **crossing** n 1 place where a street may be crossed safely. 2 place where one thing crosses another. 3 journey across water.

crossly adv **crossbar** n horizontal bar across goalposts or on a bicycle.

crossbow n weapon consisting of a bow fixed across a wooden stock.

crossbred adj bred from two different types of animal or plant. **crossbreed** n crossbred animal or plant.

cross-check v check using a different method. **cross-country** adj, adv by way of open country or fields.

cross-examine v Law question (a witness for the opposing side) to check his or her testimony.

cross-examination n **cross-eyed** adj with eyes looking towards each other. **cross-fertilize** v fertilize (an animal or plant) from one of a different kind.

cross-fertilization n **crossfire** n gunfire crossing another line of fire.

cross-purposes pl n **at cross-purposes** misunderstanding each other. **cross-reference** n reference within a text to another part.

crossroads n place where roads intersect. **cross section** 1 (diagram of) a surface made by cutting across something. 2 representative sample.

crosswise adj, adv 1 across. 2 in the shape of a cross. **crossword puzzle, crossword** n puzzle in which words suggested by clues are written into a grid of squares.

crotch n part of the body between the tops of the legs.

crotchet n musical note half the length of a minim.

crotchety adj Informal bad-tempered.

crouch v 1 bend low with the legs and body close. ♦ n 2 this position.

croup¹ [**kroop**] n throat disease of children, with a cough.

croup² [**kroop**] n hind quarters of a horse.

croupier [**kroop**-ee-ay] n person who collects bets and pays out winnings at a gambling table in a casino.

crouton n small piece of fried or toasted bread served in soup.

crow[1] n large black bird with a harsh call. **as the crow flies** in a straight line. **crow's feet** wrinkles at the corners of the eyes. **crow's nest** lookout platform at the top of a ship's mast. **stone the crows!** Brit & Aust slang expression of surprise, dismay, etc.

crow[2] v 1 (of a cock) make a shrill squawking sound. 2 boast or gloat.

crowbar n iron bar used as a lever.

crowd n 1 large group of people or things. 2 particular group of people. ♦ v 3 gather together in large numbers. 4 press together in a confined space. 5 fill or occupy fully.

crown n 1 monarch's headdress of gold and jewels. 2 wreath for the head, given as an honour. 3 top of the head or of a hill. 4 artificial cover for a broken or decayed tooth. 5 former British coin worth 25 pence. ♦ v 6 put a crown on the head of (someone) to proclaim him or her monarch. 7 put on or form the top of. 8 put the finishing touch to (a series of events). 9 Informal hit on the head. **the Crown** power of the monarchy. **crown court** local criminal court in England and Wales. **crown-of-thorns** n starfish with a spiny outer covering that feeds on living coral. **crown prince, crown princess** heir to a throne.

crozier n bishop's hooked staff.

crucial adj very important. **crucially** adv

crucible n pot in which metals are melted.

crucify v -fying, -fied put to death by fastening to a cross. **crucifix** n model of Christ on the Cross. **crucifixion** n crucifying. **the Crucifixion** Christianity crucifying of Christ.

cruciform adj cross-shaped.

crude adj 1 rough and simple. 2 tasteless, vulgar. 3 in a natural or unrefined state. **crudely** adv **crudity** n

cruel adj 1 delighting in others' pain. 2 causing pain or suffering. **cruelly** adv **cruelty** n

cruet n small container for salt, pepper, etc., at table.

cruise n 1 sail for pleasure. ♦ v 2 sail from place to place for pleasure. 3 (of a vehicle) travel at a moderate and economical speed. **cruiser** n 1 fast warship. 2 motorboat with a cabin. **cruise missile** low-flying guided missile.

crumb n 1 small fragment of bread or other dry food. 2 small amount.

crumble v 1 break into fragments. 2 fall apart or decay. ♦ n 3 pudding of stewed fruit with a crumbly topping. **crumbly** adj

crummy adj -mier, -miest Slang of poor quality.

crumpet n 1 round soft yeast cake, eaten buttered. 2 Brit, Aust & NZ slang sexually attractive women collectively.

crumple v 1 crush, crease. 2 collapse, esp. from shock. **crumpled** adj

crunch v 1 bite or chew with a noisy crushing sound. 2 make a crisp or brittle sound. ♦ n 3 crunching sound. 4 Informal critical moment. **crunchy** adj

crupper n strap that passes from the back of a saddle under a horse's tail.

crusade n 1 medieval Christian war to recover the Holy Land from the Muslims. 2 vigorous campaign in favour of a cause. ♦ v 3 take part in a crusade.

crusader n 1 person who took part in the medieval Christian war to recover the Holy Land from the Muslims. 2 person who campaigns vigorously in favour of a cause.

crush v 1 compress so as to injure, break, or crumple. 2 break into small pieces. 3 defeat or humiliate utterly. ♦ n 4 dense crowd. 5 *Informal* infatuation. 6 drink made by crushing fruit.

crust n 1 hard outer part of something, esp. bread. 2 v 3 cover with or form a crust. **crusty** adj 1 having a crust. 2 irritable.

crustacean n hard-shelled, usu. aquatic animal with several pairs of legs, such as the crab or lobster.

crutch n 1 long sticklike support with a rest for the armpit, used by a lame person. 2 person or thing that gives support. 3 crotch.

crux n, pl **cruxes** crucial or decisive point.

cry v **crying, cried** 1 shed tears. 2 call or utter loudly. ♦ n, pl **cries** 3 fit of weeping. 4 loud utterance. 5 urgent appeal, e.g. *a cry for help.* **crybaby** n person, esp. a child, who cries too readily. **cry off** v *Informal* withdraw from an arrangement. **cry out for** v need urgently.

cryogenics n branch of physics concerned with very low temperatures. **cryogenic** adj

crypt n vault under a church, esp. one used as a burial place.

cryptic adj obscure in meaning, secret. **cryptically** adv **cryptography** n art of writing in and deciphering codes.

crystal n 1 (single grain of) a symmetrically shaped solid formed naturally by some substances. 2 very clear and brilliant glass, usu. with the surface cut in many planes. 3 tumblers, vases, etc., made of crystal. ♦ adj 4 bright and clear. **crystalline** adj 1 of or like crystal or crystals. 2 clear. **crystallize** v 1 make or become definite. 2 form into crystals. **crystallization** n

cu. cubic.

cub n 1 young wild animal such as a bear or fox. 2 (C-) Cub Scout. 3 v **cubbing, cubbed** 4 give birth to cubs. **Cub Scout** member of a junior branch of the Scout Association.

cubbyhole n small enclosed space or room.

cube n 1 object with six equal square sides. 2 number resulting from multiplying a number by itself twice. ♦ v 3 cut into cubes. 4 find the cube of (a number). **cubic** adj 1 having three dimensions. 2 cube-shaped. **cubism** n style of art in which objects are represented by geometrical shapes. **cubist** adj, n **cube root** number whose cube is a given number.

cubicle n enclosed part of a large room, screened for privacy.

cuckold n 1 man whose wife has been unfaithful. ♦ v 2 be unfaithful to (one's husband).

cuckoo n 1 migratory bird with a characteristic two-note call, which lays its eggs in the nests of other birds. ♦ adj 2 *Informal* insane or foolish.

cucumber n long green-skinned fleshy fruit used in salads.

cud n partially digested food which a ruminant brings back into its mouth to chew again. **chew the cud** think deeply.

cuddle v, n hug. **cuddly** adj

cudgel n short thick stick used as a weapon.

cue¹ n 1 signal to an actor or musician to begin speaking or playing. 2 signal or reminder. ♦ v **cueing, cued** 3 give a cue to.

cue² n 1 long tapering stick used in billiards, snooker, or pool. ♦ v **cueing, cued** 2 hit (a ball) with a cue.

cuff¹ n end of a sleeve. **off the cuff** *Informal* without preparation. **cuff link** one of a pair of decorative fastenings for shirt cuffs.

cuff² *Brit, Aust & NZ* ♦ *v* **1** hit with an open hand. ♦ *n* **2** blow with an open hand.

cuisine [quiz-**zeen**] *n* style of cooking.

cul-de-sac *n* road with one end blocked off.

culinary *adj* of kitchens or cookery.

cull *v* **1** choose, gather. **2** remove or kill (inferior or surplus animals) from a herd. ♦ *n* **3** culling.

culminate *v* reach the highest point or climax. **culmination** *n*

culottes *pl n* women's knee-length trousers cut to look like a skirt.

culpable *adj* deserving blame. **culpability** *n*

culprit *n* person guilty of an offence or misdeed.

cult *n* **1** specific system of worship. **2** devotion to a person, idea, or activity. **3** popular fashion.

cultivate *v* **1** prepare (land) to grow crops. **2** grow (plants). **3** develop or improve (something). **4** try to develop a friendship with (someone). **cultivated** *adj* well-educated. **cultivation** *n*

culture *n* **1** ideas, customs, and art of a particular society. **2** particular society. **3** developed understanding of the arts. **4** cultivation of plants or rearing of animals. **5** growth of bacteria for study. **cultural** *adj* **cultured** *adj* showing good taste or manners. **cultured pearl** pearl artificially grown in an oyster shell.

culvert *n* drain under a road or railway.

cumbersome *adj* awkward because of size or shape.

cumin, cummin *n* sweet-smelling seeds of a Mediterranean plant, used in cooking.

cummerbund *n* wide sash worn round the waist.

cumulative *adj* increasing steadily.

cumulus [**kew**-myew-luss] *n, pl* **-li** thick white or dark grey cloud.

cuneiform [**kew**-nif-form] *n, adj* (written in) an ancient system of writing using wedge-shaped characters.

cunjevoi *n Aust* **1** plant of tropical Asia and Australia with small flowers, cultivated for its edible rhizome. **2** sea squirt.

cunning *adj* **1** clever at deceiving. **2** ingenious. ♦ *n* **3** cleverness at deceiving. **4** ingenuity. **cunningly** *adv*

cup *n* **1** small bowl-shaped drinking container with a handle. **2** contents of a cup. **3** (competition with) a cup-shaped trophy given as a prize. **4** hollow rounded shape. ♦ *v* **cupping, cupped 5** form (one's hands) into the shape of a cup. **6** hold in cupped hands. **cupful** *n*

cupboard *n* piece of furniture or alcove with a door, for storage.

cupidity [kew-**pid**-it-ee] *n* greed for money or possessions.

cupola [**kew**-pol-la] *n* domed roof or ceiling.

cur *n Lit* **1** mongrel dog. **2** contemptible person.

curaçao [**kew**-rah-so] *n* orange-flavoured liqueur.

curare [kew-**rah**-ree] *n* poisonous resin of a S American tree, used as a muscle relaxant in medicine.

curate *n* clergyman who assists a parish priest. **curacy** [**kew**-rah-see] *n, pl* **-cies** work or position of a curate.

curative *adj, n* (something) able to cure.

curator *n* person in charge of a museum or art gallery. **curatorship** *n*

curb *n* **1** something that restrains. **2** *v* **3** control, restrain.

curd *n* coagulated milk, used to make

cheese. **curdle** v turn into curd, coagulate.

cure v **1** get rid of (an illness or problem). **2** make (someone) well again. **3** preserve by salting, smoking, or drying. ♦ n **4** (treatment causing) curing of an illness or person. **5** remedy or solution. **curable** adj

curette n **1** surgical instrument for scraping tissue from body cavities. ♦ v **2** scrape with a curette. **curettage** n

curfew n **1** law ordering people to stay inside their homes after a specific time at night. **2** time set as a deadline by such a law.

curie n standard unit of radioactivity.

curio n, pl **-rios** rare or unusual object valued as a collector's item.

curious adj **1** eager to learn or know. **2** eager to find out private details. **3** unusual or peculiar. **curiously** adv **curiosity** n **1** eagerness to know or find out. **2** pl **-ties** rare or unusual object.

curl n **1** curved piece of hair. **2** curved spiral shape. ♦ v **3** make (hair) into curls or (of hair) grow in curls. **4** make into a curved spiral shape. **curly** adj **curling** n game like bowls, played with heavy stones on ice.

curlew n long-billed wading bird.

curmudgeon n bad-tempered person.

currant n **1** small dried grape. **2** small round berry, such as a redcurrant.

currajong n same as KURRAJONG.

currawong n Australian songbird.

current adj **1** of the immediate present. **2** most recent, up-to-date. **3** commonly accepted. ♦ n **4** flow of water or air in one direction. **5** flow of electricity. **6** general trend. **currently** adv **currency** n, pl **-cies** **1** money in use in a particular country. **2** general acceptance or use.

curriculum n, pl **-la**, **-lums** all the courses of study offered by a school or college. **curriculum vitae** [**vee**-tie] outline of someone's educational and professional history, prepared for job applications.

☑ **SPELLING TIP**
You possibly read the word **curriculum** more often than you have to write it. It's easy not to notice that the only letter that is doubled is the r in the middle.

curry¹ n, pl **-ries** **1** Indian dish of meat or vegetables in a hot spicy sauce. ♦ v **-rying**, **-ried** **2** prepare (food) with curry powder. **curry powder** mixture of spices for making curry.

curry² v **-rying**, **-ried** groom (a horse). **curry favour** ingratiate oneself with an important person. **curry comb** ridged comb for grooming a horse.

curse v **1** swear (at). **2** ask a supernatural power to cause harm to. ♦ n **3** swearword. **4** (result of) a call to a supernatural power to cause harm to someone. **5** something causing trouble or harm. **cursed** adj

cursive adj, n (handwriting) done with joined letters.

cursor n movable point of light that shows a specific position on a visual display unit.

cursory adj quick and superficial. **cursorily** adv

curt adj brief and rather rude. **curtly** adv **curtness** n

curtail v **1** cut short. **2** restrict. **curtailment** n

curtain n **1** piece of cloth hung at a window or opening as a screen. **2** hanging cloth separating the audience and the stage in a theatre. **3** fall or closing of the curtain at the end, or the rise or opening of the curtain at the start of a theatrical performance. **4** something forming a barrier or screen.

5 *v* **6** provide with curtains. **7** (foll. by *off*) separate by a curtain.

curtsy, curtsey *n, pl* **-sies, -seys 1** woman's gesture of respect made by bending the knees and bowing the head. ♦ *v* **-sying, -sied** *or* **-seying, -seyed 2** make a curtsy.

curve *n* **1** continuously bending line with no straight parts. **2** *v* **3** form or move in a curve. **curvy** *adj* **curvaceous** *adj Informal* (of a woman) having a shapely body. **curvature** *n* curved shape. **curvilinear** *adj* consisting of or bounded by a curve.

cuscus *n, pl* **-cuses** large Australian nocturnal possum.

cushion *n* **1** bag filled with soft material, to make a seat more comfortable. **2** something that provides comfort or absorbs shock. **3** *v* **4** lessen the effects of. **5** protect from injury or shock.

cushy *adj* **cushier, cushiest** *Informal* easy.

cusp *n* **1** pointed end, esp. on a tooth. **2** *Astrol* division between houses or signs of the zodiac.

cuss *Informal* ♦ *n* **1** curse, oath. **2** annoying person. ♦ *v* **3** swear (at). **cussed [kuss-**id] *adj Informal* obstinate.

custard *n* sweet yellow sauce made from milk and eggs.

custody *n* **1** protective care. **2** imprisonment prior to being tried. **custodial** *adj* **custodian** *n* person in charge of a public building.

custom *n* **1** long-established activity or action. **2** usual habit. **3** regular use of a shop or business. ♦ *pl* **4** duty charged on imports or exports. **5** government department which collects these. **6** area at a port, airport, or border where baggage and freight are examined for dutiable goods. **customary** *adj* **1** usual. **2** established by custom. **customarily** *adv* **custom-built,**

custom-made *adj* made to the specifications of an individual customer.

customer *n* person who buys goods or services.

cut *v* **cutting, cut 1** open up, penetrate, wound, or divide with a sharp instrument. **2** divide. **3** trim or shape by cutting. **4** abridge, shorten. **5** reduce, restrict. **6** *Informal* hurt the feelings of. **7** pretend not to recognize. **8** *n* **9** stroke or incision made by cutting. **10** piece cut off. **11** reduction. **12** deletion in a text, film, or play. **13** *Informal* share, esp. of profits. **14** style in which hair or a garment is cut. **cut in** *v* **1** interrupt. **2** obstruct another vehicle in overtaking it.

cutaneous [kew-**tane**-ee-uss] *adj* of the skin.

cute *adj* **1** appealing or attractive. **2** *Informal* clever or shrewd. **cutely** *adv* **cuteness** *n*

cuticle *n* skin at the base of a fingernail or toenail.

cutlass *n* curved one-edged sword formerly used by sailors.

cutlery *n* knives, forks, and spoons. **cutler** *n* maker of cutlery.

cutlet *n* **1** small piece of meat like a chop. **2** flat croquette of chopped meat or fish.

cutter *n* **1** person or tool that cuts. **2** any of various small fast boats.

cut-throat *adj* **1** fierce or relentless. ♦ *n* **2** murderer.

cutting *n* **1** article cut from a newspaper or magazine. **2** piece cut from a plant from which to grow a new plant. **3** passage cut through high ground for a road or railway. ♦ *adj* **4** (of a remark) hurtful.

cuttlefish *n* squidlike sea mollusc.

CV curriculum vitae.

cwt hundredweight.

cyanide n extremely poisonous chemical compound.

cyber- combining form computers, e.g. cyberspace.

cybernetics n branch of science in which electronic and mechanical systems are studied and compared to biological systems.

cyberspace n place said to contain all the data stored in computers.

cyclamen [**sik**-la-men] n plant with red, pink, or white flowers.

cycle v 1 ride a bicycle. ♦ n 2 Brit, Aust & NZ bicycle. 3 US motorcycle. 4 complete series of recurring events. 5 time taken for one such series. **cyclical, cyclic** adj occurring in cycles. **cyclist** n person who rides a bicycle.

cyclone n violent wind moving round a central area.

cyclotron n apparatus that accelerates charged particles by means of a strong vertical magnetic field.

cygnet n young swan.

cylinder n 1 solid or hollow body with straight sides and circular ends. 2 chamber within which the piston moves in an internal-combustion engine. **cylindrical** adj

cymbal n percussion instrument consisting of a brass plate which is struck against another or hit with a stick.

cynic [**sin**-ik] n person who believes that people always act selfishly. **cynical** adj **cynically** adv **cynicism** n

cynosure [**sin**-oh-zyure] n centre of attention.

cypher n same as CIPHER.

cypress n evergreen tree with dark green leaves.

cyst [**sist**] n (abnormal) sac in the body containing fluid or soft matter. **cystic** adj **cystitis** [siss-**tite**-iss] n inflammation of the bladder.

cytology [site-**ol**-a-jee] n study of plant and animal cells. **cytological** adj **cytologist** n

czar [**zahr**] n same as TSAR.

D d

d *Physics* density.

D *Chem* deuterium.

d. 1 *Brit* (before decimalization) penny.
2 died.

dab[1] *v* **dabbing, dabbed 1** pat lightly.
2 apply with short tapping strokes. ♦ *n*
3 small amount of something soft or
moist. **4** light stroke or tap. **dab hand**
Informal person who is particularly
good at something.

dab[2] *n* small European flatfish with
rough scales.

dabble *v* **1** be involved in something
superficially. **2** splash about. **dabbler** *n*

dace *n* small European freshwater fish.

dachshund *n* dog with a long body
and short legs.

dad *n Informal* father.

daddy *n, pl* **-dies** *Informal* father.

daddy-longlegs *n* **1** *Brit* crane fly. **2**
US & Canadian small web-spinning
spider with long legs.

dado [**day**-doe] *n, pl* **-does, -dos** lower
part of an interior wall, below a rail,
decorated differently from the upper
part.

daffodil *n* yellow trumpet-shaped
flower that blooms in spring.

daft *adj Informal* foolish or crazy.

dag *NZ* ♦ *n* **1** dried dung on a sheep's
rear. **2** *Informal* amusing person. ♦ *pl n*
3 rattle one's dags *Informal* hurry up.
♦ *v* **4** remove the dags from a sheep.
daggy *adj Informal* amusing.

dagga *n S Afr informal* cannabis.

dagger *n* short knifelike weapon with a
pointed blade.

daguerreotype [dag-**gair**-oh-type] *n*
type of early photograph produced on
chemically treated silver.

dahlia [**day**-lya] *n* brightly coloured
garden flower.

daily *adj* **1** occurring every day or every
weekday. ♦ *adv* **2** every day. ♦ *n, pl*
-lies 3 daily newspaper. **4** *Brit informal*
person who cleans other people's
houses.

dainty *adj* **-tier, -tiest** delicate or
elegant **daintily** *adv*

daiquiri [**dak**-eer-ee] *n* iced drink
containing rum, lime juice, and sugar.

dairy *n, pl* **dairies 1** place for the
processing or sale of milk and its
products. **2** *NZ* small shop selling
groceries and milk often outside
normal trading hours. ♦ *adj* **3** of milk
or its products.

dais [**day**-iss, **dayss**] *n* raised platform
in a hall, used by a speaker.

daisy *n, pl* **-sies** small wild flower with
a yellow centre and white petals.
daisy wheel flat disc in a word
processor with radiating spokes for
printing letters.

Dalai Lama *n* chief lama and (until
1959) ruler of Tibet.

dale *n* (esp. in N England) valley.

dally *v* **-lying, -lied 1** waste time. **2**
(foll. by *with*) deal frivolously (with).
dalliance *n* flirtation.

Dalmatian *n* large dog with a white
coat and black spots.

dam[1] *n* **1** barrier built across a river to
create a lake. **2** lake created by this.
♦ *v* **damming, dammed 3** build a
dam across (a river).

dam[2] *n* mother of an animal such as a
sheep or horse.

damage *v* **1** harm, spoil. ♦ *n* **2** harm to
a person or thing. **3** *Informal* cost, e.g.
what's the damage? ♦ *pl* **4** money
awarded as compensation for injury or
loss.

damask n fabric with a pattern woven into it, used for tablecloths etc.

dame n 1 *Chiefly US & Canadian slang* woman. 2 (D-) title of a woman who has been awarded the OBE or another order of chivalry.

damn interj 1 *Slang* exclamation of annoyance. ♦ adv, adj 2 (also **damned**) *Slang* extreme(ly). ♦ v 3 condemn as bad or worthless. 4 (of God) condemn to hell. **damnable** adj annoying. **damnably** adv **damnation** interj, n **damning** adj proving or suggesting guilt, e.g. *a damning report*.

damp adj 1 slightly wet. ♦ n 2 slight wetness, moisture. ♦ v (also **dampen**) 3 make damp. 4 (foll. by *down*) reduce the intensity of (feelings or actions). **damply** adv **dampness** n **damper** n 1 movable plate to regulate the draught in a fire. 2 pad in a piano that deadens the vibration of each string. **put a damper on** have a depressing or inhibiting effect on.

damsel n *Old-fashioned* young woman.

damson n small blue-black plumlike fruit.

dance v 1 move the feet and body rhythmically in time to music. 2 perform (a particular dance). 3 skip or leap. 4 move rhythmically. ♦ n 5 series of steps and movements in time to music. 6 social meeting arranged for dancing. **dancer** n

D and C n *Med* dilatation and curettage: a minor operation in which the neck of the womb is stretched and the lining of the womb scraped, to clear the womb or remove tissue for diagnosis.

dandelion n yellow-flowered wild plant.

dander n **get one's dander up** *Slang* become angry.

dandle v move (a child) up and down on one's knee.

dandruff n loose scales of dry dead skin shed from the scalp.

dandy n, pl **-dies** 1 man who is overconcerned with the elegance of his appearance. ♦ adj **-dier, -diest** 2 *Informal* very good. **dandified** adj

danger n 1 possibility of being injured or killed. 2 person or thing that may cause injury or harm. 3 likelihood that something unpleasant will happen. **dangerous** adj **dangerously** adv

dangle v 1 hang loosely. 2 display as an enticement.

dank adj unpleasantly damp and chilly.

dapper adj (of a man) neat in appearance.

dappled adj marked with spots of a different colour. **dapple-grey** n horse with a grey coat and darker coloured spots.

dare v 1 be courageous enough to try (to do something). 2 challenge to do something risky. ♦ n 3 challenge to do something risky. **daring** adj 1 willing to take risks. ♦ n 2 courage to do dangerous things. **daringly** adv **daredevil** adj, n recklessly bold (person).

☑ **WORD TIP**
When *dare* is used in a question or as a negative, it does not take an -s: *He dare not come*.

dark adj 1 having little or no light. 2 (of a colour) reflecting little light. 3 (of hair or skin) brown or black. 4 gloomy, sad. 5 sinister, evil. 6 secret, e.g. *keep it dark*. ♦ n 7 absence of light. 8 night. **darkly** adv **darkness** n **darken** v **dark horse** person about whom little is known. **darkroom** n darkened room for processing photographic film.

darling n 1 much-loved person. 2 favourite. ♦ adj 3 much-loved.

darn[1] v **1** mend (a garment) with a series of interwoven stitches. ♦ n **2** patch of darned work.

darn[2] interj, adv, adj, v Euphemistic damn.

dart n **1** small narrow pointed missile that is thrown or shot, esp. in the game of darts. **2** sudden quick movement. **3** tapered tuck made in dressmaking. ♦ pl **4** game in which darts are thrown at a circular numbered board. ♦ v **5** move or direct quickly and suddenly.

Darwinism n theory of the origin of animal and plant species by evolution. **Darwinian, Darwinist** adj, n

dash v **1** move quickly. **2** hurl or crash. **3** frustrate (someone's hopes). ♦ n **4** sudden quick movement. **5** small amount. **6** mixture of style and courage. **7** punctuation mark (–) indicating a change of subject. **8** longer symbol used in Morse code. **dashing** adj stylish and attractive. **dashboard** n instrument panel in a vehicle.

dassie n S Afr type of hoofed rodent-like animal (also **hyrax**).

dastardly adj wicked and cowardly.

dasyure [**dass**-ee-your] n small marsupial of Australia, New Guinea, and adjacent islands.

data n **1** information consisting of observations, measurements, or facts. **2** numbers, digits, etc., stored by a computer. **data base** store of information that can be easily handled by a computer. **data capture** process for converting information into a form that can be handled by a computer. **data processing** series of operations performed on data, esp. by a computer, to extract or interpret information.

date[1] n **1** specified day of the month. **2** particular day or year when an event

happened. **3** Informal appointment, esp. with a person to whom one is sexually attracted. **4** Informal person with whom one has a date. ♦ v **5** mark with the date. **6** assign a date of occurrence to. **7** become old-fashioned. **8** (foll. by from) originate from. **dated** adj old-fashioned.

date[2] n dark-brown sweet-tasting fruit of the date palm. **date palm** tall palm grown in tropical regions for its fruit.

dative n (in certain languages) the form of the noun that expresses the indirect object.

datum n, pl **data** single piece of information in the form of a fact or statistic.

daub v smear or spread quickly or clumsily.

daughter n **1** female child. **2** woman who comes from a certain place or is connected with a certain thing. **daughterly** adj **daughter-in-law** n, pl **daughters-in-law** son's wife.

daunting adj intimidating or worrying. **dauntless** adj fearless.

dauphin [**doe**-fan] n (formerly) eldest son of the king of France.

davenport n **1** Chiefly Brit small writing table with drawers. **2** Aust, US & Canadian large couch.

davit [**dav**-vit] n crane, usu. one of a pair, at a ship's side, for lowering and hoisting a lifeboat.

Davy lamp n miner's lamp designed to prevent it from igniting gas.

dawdle v walk slowly, lag behind.

dawn n **1** daybreak. **2** beginning (of something). ♦ v **3** begin to grow light. **4** begin to develop or appear. **5** (foll. by on) become apparent (to).

day n **1** period of 24 hours. **2** period of light between sunrise and sunset. **3** part of a day occupied with regular activity, esp. work. **4** period or point in time. **5** time of success. **daybreak** n time in the morning when light first appears. **daydream** n **1** pleasant fantasy indulged in while awake. ♦ v **2** indulge in idle fantasy. **daydreamer** n **daylight** n light from the sun. **day release** Brit system in which workers go to college one day a week. **day-to-day** adj routine.

daze v **1** stun, by a blow or shock. ♦ n **2** state of confusion or shock.

dazzle v **1** impress greatly. **2** blind temporarily by sudden excessive light. ♦ n **3** bright light that dazzles. **dazzling** adj **dazzlingly** adv

dB, db decibel(s).

DC direct current.

DD Doctor of Divinity.

D-day n day selected for the start of some operation, orig. the Allied invasion of Europe in 1944.

DDT n kind of insecticide.

de- prefix indicating: **1** removal, e.g. dethrone. **2** reversal, e.g. declassify. **3** departure, e.g. decamp.

deacon n Christianity **1** ordained minister ranking immediately below a priest. **2** (in some Protestant churches) lay official who assists the minister.

dead adj **1** no longer alive. **2** no longer in use. **3** numb, e.g. my leg has gone dead. **4** complete, absolute, e.g. dead silence. **5** Informal very tired. **6** (of a place) lacking activity. ♦ n **7** period during which coldness or darkness is most intense, e.g. in the dead of night. ♦ adv **8** extremely. **9** suddenly, e.g. I stopped dead. **the dead** dead people. **dead set** firmly decided. **deadbeat** n Informal lazy useless person. **dead beat** Informal exhausted. **dead end 1** road with one end blocked off. **2** situation in which further progress is impossible. **dead heat** tie for first place between two participants in a contest. **deadline** n time limit.

deadlock n point in a dispute at which no agreement can be reached. **deadlocked** adj **deadpan** adj, adv showing no emotion or expression. **dead reckoning** method of establishing one's position using the distance and direction travelled. **dead weight** heavy weight.

deaden v make less intense.

deadly adj -lier, -liest **1** likely to cause death. **2** Informal extremely boring. ♦ adv **3** extremely. **deadly nightshade** plant with poisonous black berries.

deaf adj unable to hear. **deaf to** refusing to listen to or take notice of. **deafen** v make deaf, esp. temporarily. **deafness** n

deal¹ n **1** agreement or transaction. **2** kind of treatment, e.g. a fair deal. **3** large amount. ♦ v **dealing, dealt** [**delt**] **4** inflict (a blow) on. **5** Cards give out (cards) to the players. **dealer** n **dealings** pl n transactions or business relations. **deal in** v buy or sell (goods). **deal out** v distribute. **deal with** v **1** take action on. **2** be concerned with.

deal² n plank of fir or pine wood.

dean n **1** chief administrative official of a college or university faculty. **2** chief administrator of a cathedral. **deanery** n, pl -eries **1** office or residence of a dean. **2** parishes of a dean.

dear n **1** someone regarded with affection. ♦ adj **2** much-loved. **3** costly. **dearly** adv **dearness** n

dearth [**dirth**] n inadequate amount, scarcity.

death n **1** permanent end of life in a person or animal. **2** instance of this. **3** ending, destruction. **deathly** adj, adv like death, e.g. a deathly silence; deathly pale. **death duty (in Britain)** former name for INHERITANCE TAX. **death's-head** n human skull or a representation of one. **death trap** place or vehicle considered very unsafe. **deathwatch beetle** beetle that bores into wood and makes a tapping sound.

deb n Informal debutante.

debacle [day-**bah**-kl] n disastrous failure.

debar v prevent, bar.

debase v lower in value, quality, or character. **debasement** n

debate n 1 discussion. 2 v 3 discuss formally. 4 consider (a course of action). **debatable** adj not absolutely certain.

debauch [dib-**bawch**] v make (someone) bad or corrupt, esp. sexually. **debauched** adj immoral, sexually corrupt. **debauchery** n

debenture n long-term bond bearing fixed interest, issued by a company or a government agency.

debilitate v weaken, make feeble. **debilitation** n **debility** n weakness, infirmity.

debit n 1 acknowledgment of a sum owing by entry on the left side of an account. ♦ v debiting, debited 2 charge (an account) with a debt.

debonair adj (of a man) charming and refined.

debouch v move out from a narrow place to a wider one.

debrief v receive a report from (a soldier, diplomat, etc.) after an event. **debriefing** n

debris [**deb**-ree] n fragments of something destroyed.

debt n something owed, esp. money. **in debt** owing money. **debtor** n

debunk v Informal expose the falseness of.

debut [**day**-byoo] n first public appearance of a performer. **debutante** [**day**-byoo-tont] n young

upper-class woman being formally presented to society.

Dec. December.

decade n period of ten years.

decadence n deterioration in morality or culture. **decadent** adj

decaffeinated [dee-**kaf**-fin-ate-id] adj (of coffee, tea, or cola) with caffeine removed.

decagon n geometric figure with ten faces.

decahedron [deck-a-**heed**-ron] n solid figure with ten sides.

Decalogue n the Ten Commandments.

decamp v depart secretly or suddenly.

decant v 1 pour (a liquid) from one container to another. 2 Chiefly Brit rehouse (people) while their homes are being renovated.

decanter n stoppered bottle for wine or spirits.

decapitate v behead. **decapitation** n

decathlon n athletic contest with ten events.

decay v 1 become weaker or more corrupt. 2 rot. ♦ n 3 process of decaying. 4 state brought about by this process.

decease n Formal death.

deceased adj Formal dead. **the deceased** dead person.

deceive v 1 mislead by lying. 2 be unfaithful to (one's sexual partner). **deceiver** n **deceit** n behaviour intended to deceive. **deceitful** adj

decelerate v slow down. **deceleration** n

December n twelfth month of the year.

decent adj 1 (of a person) polite and morally acceptable. 2 fitting or proper. 3 conforming to conventions of sexual behaviour. 4 Informal kind. **decently** adv **decency** n

decentralize v reorganize into smaller local units. **decentralization** n

deception n **1** deceiving. **2** something that deceives, trick. **deceptive** adj likely to or designed to deceive. **deceptively** adv **deceptiveness** n

deci- combining form one tenth.

decibel n unit for measuring the intensity of sound.

decide v **1** (cause to) reach a decision. **2** settle (a contest or question). **decided** adj **1** unmistakable. **2** determined. **decidedly** adv

deciduous adj (of a tree) shedding its leaves annually.

decimal n **1** fraction written in the form of a dot followed by one or more numbers. ♦ adj **2** relating to or using powers of ten. **3** expressed as a decimal. **decimalization** n **decimal currency** system of currency in which the units are parts or powers of ten. **decimal point** dot between the unit and the fraction of a number in the decimal system. **decimal system** number system with a base of ten, in which numbers are expressed by combinations of the digits 0 to 9.

decimate v destroy or kill a large proportion of. **decimation** n

decipher v work out the meaning of (something illegible or in code). **decipherable** adj

decision n **1** judgment, conclusion, or resolution. **2** act of making up one's mind. **3** firmness of purpose. **decisive** adj **1** having a definite influence. **2** having the ability to make quick decisions. **decisively** adv **decisiveness** n

deck n **1** area of a ship that forms a floor. **2** similar area in a bus. **3** platform that supports the turntable and pick-up of a record player. **deck chair** folding chair made of canvas over a wooden frame. **decking** n wooden platform in a garden. **deck out** v decorate.

declaim v **1** speak loudly and dramatically. **2** protest loudly. **declamation** n **declamatory** adj

declare v **1** state firmly and forcefully. **2** announce officially. **3** acknowledge for tax purposes. **declaration** n **declaratory** adj

declension n Grammar changes in the form of nouns, pronouns, or adjectives to show case, number, and gender.

decline v **1** become smaller, weaker, or less important. **2** refuse politely to accept or do. **3** Grammar list the inflections of (a noun, pronoun, or adjective). ♦ n **4** gradual weakening or loss.

declivity n, pl **-ties** downward slope.

declutch v disengage the clutch of a motor vehicle.

decoct v extract the essence from (a substance) by boiling. **decoction** n

decode v convert from code into ordinary language. **decoder** n

décolleté [day-**kol**-tay] adj (of a woman's garment) low-cut.

decommission v dismantle (a nuclear reactor, weapon, etc.) which is no longer needed.

decompose v be broken down through chemical or bacterial action. **decomposition** n

decompress v **1** free from pressure. **2** return (a diver) to normal atmospheric pressure. **decompression** n **decompression sickness** severe pain and difficulty in breathing, caused by a sudden change in atmospheric pressure.

decongestant n medicine that relieves nasal congestion.

decontaminate v make safe by removing poisons, radioactivity, etc. **decontamination** n

decor [**day**-core] n style in which a room or house is decorated.

decorate v 1 make more attractive by adding something ornamental. 2 paint or wallpaper. 3 award a (military) medal to. **decoration** n **decorative** adj **decorator** n

decorous [**dek**-a-russ] adj polite, calm, and sensible in behaviour. **decorously** adv

decorum [dik-**core**-um] n polite and socially correct behaviour.

decoy n 1 person or thing used to lure someone into danger. 2 dummy bird or animal, used to lure game within shooting range. ♦ v 3 lure away by means of a trick.

decrease v 1 make or become less. ♦ n 2 lessening, reduction. 3 amount by which something has decreased.

decree n 1 law made by someone in authority. 2 court judgment. ♦ v 3 order by decree.

decrepit adj weakened or worn out by age or long use. **decrepitude** n

decry v -crying, -cried express disapproval of.

dedicate v 1 commit (oneself or one's time) wholly to a special purpose or cause. 2 inscribe or address (a book etc.) to someone as a tribute. **dedicated** adj devoted to a particular purpose or cause. **dedication** n

deduce v reach (a conclusion) by reasoning from evidence. **deducible** adj

deduct v subtract.

deduction n 1 deducting. 2 something that is deducted. 3 deducing. 4 conclusion reached by deducing. **deductive** adj

deed n 1 something that is done. 2 legal document.

deem v consider, judge.

deep adj 1 extending or situated far down, inwards, backwards, or sideways. 2 of a specified dimension downwards, inwards, or backwards. 3 difficult to understand. 4 of great intensity. 5 (foll. by in) absorbed in (an activity). 6 (of a colour) strong or dark. 7 low in pitch. **the deep** Poetic the sea. **deeply** adv profoundly or intensely (also **deep down**). **deepen** v **deep-freeze** n same as FREEZER.

deer n, pl **deer** large wild animal, the male of which has antlers. **deerstalker** n cloth hat with peaks at the back and front and earflaps.

deface v deliberately spoil the appearance of. **defacement** n

de facto adv 1 in fact. ♦ adj 2 existing in fact, whether legally recognized or not.

defame v attack the good reputation of. **defamation** n **defamatory** [dif-**fam**-a-tree] adj

default n 1 failure to do something. 2 Computers instruction to a computer to select a particular option unless the user specifies otherwise. ♦ v 3 fail to fulfil an obligation. **in default of** in the absence of. **defaulter** n

defeat v 1 win a victory over. 2 thwart, frustrate. ♦ n 3 defeating. **defeatism** n ready acceptance or expectation of defeat. **defeatist** adj, n

defecate v discharge waste from the body through the anus. **defecation** n

defect n 1 imperfection, blemish. ♦ v 2 desert one's cause or country to join the opposing forces. **defective** adj imperfect, faulty. **defection** n **defector** n

defence n 1 resistance against attack. 2 argument in support of something. 3 country's military resources. 4 defendant's case in a court of law. **defenceless** adj

defend v 1 protect from harm or danger. 2 support in the face of criticism. 3 represent (a defendant) in court. **defendant** n person accused of a crime. **defensible** adj capable of being defended because believed to be right. **defensibility** n **defensive** adj **1** intended for defence. **2** overanxious to protect oneself against (threatened) criticism. **defensively** adv

defender n **1** person who supports someone or something in the face of criticism. **2** player whose chief task is to stop the opposition scoring.

defer¹ v **-ferring, -ferred** delay (something) until a future time. **deferment, deferral** n

defer² v **-ferring, -ferred** (foll. by to) comply with the wishes (of). **deference** n polite and respectful behaviour. **deferential** adj **deferentially** adv

defiance n see DEFY.

deficient adj **1** lacking some essential thing or quality. **2** inadequate in quality or quantity. **deficiency** n **1** state of being deficient. **2** lack, shortage.

deficit n amount by which a sum of money is too small.

defile¹ v treat (something sacred or important) without respect. **defilement** n

defile² n narrow valley or pass.

define v **1** state precisely the meaning of. **2** show clearly the outline of. **definable** adj **definite** adj **1** firm, clear, and precise. **2** having precise limits. **3** known for certain. **definitely** adv **definition** n **1** statement of the meaning of a word or phrase. **2** quality of being clear and distinct. **definitive** adj **1** providing an unquestionable conclusion. **2** being the best example of something.

deflate v **1** (cause to) collapse through the release of air. **2** take away the self-esteem or conceit from. **3** Economics cause deflation of (an economy). **deflation** n **1** Economics

reduction in economic activity resulting in lower output and investment. **2** feeling of sadness following excitement. **deflationary** adj

deflect v (cause to) turn aside from a course. **deflection** n **deflector** n

deflower v Lit deprive (a woman) of her virginity.

defoliate v deprive (a plant) of its leaves. **defoliant** n **defoliation** n

deforestation n destruction of all the trees in an area.

deform v put out of shape or spoil the appearance of. **deformation** n **deformity** n

defraud v cheat out of money, property, etc.

defray v provide money for (costs or expenses).

defrock v deprive (a priest) of priestly status.

defrost v **1** make or become free of ice. **2** thaw (frozen food) by removing it from a freezer.

deft adj quick and skilful in movement. **deftly** adv **deftness** n

defunct adj no longer existing or operative.

defuse v **1** remove the fuse of (an explosive device). **2** remove the tension from (a situation).

defy v **-fying, -fied** resist openly and boldly. **2** make impossible, e.g. the condition of the refugees defied description. **defiance** n **defiant** adj

degenerate adj **1** having deteriorated to a lower mental, moral, or physical level. ♦ n **2** degenerate person. ♦ v **3** become degenerate. **degeneracy** n degenerate behaviour. **degeneration** n

degrade v **1** reduce to dishonour or disgrace. **2** reduce in status or quality. **3** Chem decompose into smaller molecules. **degradation** n

degree n 1 stage in a scale of relative amount or intensity. 2 academic award given by a university or college on successful completion of a course. 3 unit of measurement for temperature, angles, or latitude and longitude.

dehumanize v 1 deprive of human qualities. 2 make (an activity) mechanical or routine. **dehumanization** n

dehydrate v remove water from (food) to preserve it. **be dehydrated** become weak through losing too much water from the body. **dehydration** n

de-ice v free of ice. **de-icer** n

deify [**day**-if-fie] v -**fying, -fied** treat or worship as a god. **deification** n

deign [**dane**] v agree (to do something), but as if doing someone a favour.

deity [**dee**-it-ee, **day**-it-ee] n, pl -**ties** 1 god or goddess. 2 state of being divine.

déjà vu [**day**-zhah **voo**] n feeling of having experienced before something that is actually happening now.

dejected adj unhappy. **dejectedly** adv **dejection** n

de jure adv, adj according to law.

dekko n Brit, Aust & NZ slang **have a dekko** have a look.

delay v 1 put off to a later time. 2 slow up or cause to be late. ♦ n 3 act of delaying. 4 interval of time between events.

delectable adj delightful, very attractive. **delectation** n Formal great pleasure.

delegate n 1 person chosen to represent others, esp. at a meeting. ♦ v 2 entrust (duties or powers) to someone. 3 appoint as a delegate. **delegation** n 1 group chosen to represent others. 2 delegating.

delete v remove (something written or printed). **deletion** n

deleterious [del-lit-**eer**-ee-uss] adj harmful, injurious.

deliberate adj 1 planned in advance, intentional. 2 careful and unhurried. ♦ v 3 think something over. **deliberately** adv **deliberation** n **deliberative** adj

delicate adj 1 fine or subtle in quality or workmanship. 2 having a fragile beauty. 3 (of a taste etc.) pleasantly subtle. 4 easily damaged. 5 requiring tact. **delicately** adv **delicacy** n 1 being delicate. 2 pl -**cies**) something particularly good to eat.

delicatessen n shop selling imported or unusual foods, often already cooked or prepared.

delicious adj very appealing to taste or smell. **deliciously** adv

delight n 1 (source of) great pleasure. ♦ v 2 please greatly. 3 (foll. by in) take great pleasure (in). **delightful** adj **delightfully** adv

delimit v mark or lay down the limits of. **delimitation** n

delineate [dill-**lin**-ee-ate] v 1 show by drawing. 2 describe in words. **delineation** n

delinquent n 1 someone, esp. a young person, who repeatedly breaks the law. ♦ adj 2 repeatedly breaking the law. **delinquency** n

delirium n 1 state of excitement and mental confusion, often with hallucinations. 2 great excitement. **delirious** adj **deliriously** adv

deliver v 1 carry (goods etc.) to a destination. 2 hand over. 3 aid in the birth of. 4 present (a lecture or speech). 5 release or rescue. 6 strike (a blow). **deliverance** n rescue from captivity or evil. **delivery** n, pl -**eries** 1 delivering. 2 something that is delivered. 3 act of giving birth to a baby. **4** style in public speaking.

dell n Chiefly Brit small wooded hollow.

Delphic adj ambiguous, like the ancient Greek oracle at Delphi.

delphinium n large garden plant with blue flowers.

delta n **1** fourth letter in the Greek alphabet. **2** flat area at the mouth of some rivers where the main stream splits up into several branches.

delude v deceive.

deluge [del-lyooj] n **1** great flood. **2** torrential rain. **3** overwhelming number. ♦ v **4** flood. **5** overwhelm.

delusion n **1** mistaken idea or belief. **2** state of being deluded. **delusive** adj

de luxe adj rich or sumptuous, superior in quality.

delve v research deeply (for information).

demagogue n political agitator who appeals to the prejudice and passions of the mob. **demagogic** adj **demagogy** n

demand v **1** request forcefully. **2** require as just, urgent, etc. **3** claim as a right. ♦ n **4** forceful request. **5** Economics willingness and ability to purchase goods and services. **6** something that requires special effort or sacrifice. **demanding** adj requiring a lot of time or effort.

demarcation n Formal establishing limits or boundaries, esp. between the work performed by different trade unions.

demean v **demean oneself** do something unworthy of one's status or character.

demeanour n way a person behaves.

demented adj mad. **dementedly** adv **dementia** [dim-men-sha] n state of serious mental deterioration.

demerara sugar n brown crystallized cane sugar.

demerit n fault, disadvantage.

demesne [dim-mane] n **1** land surrounding a house. **2** Law possession of one's own property or land.

demi- combining form half.

demijohn n large bottle with a short neck, often encased in wicker.

demilitarize v remove the military forces from. **demilitarization** n

demimonde n **1** (esp. in the 19th century) class of women considered to be outside respectable society because of promiscuity. **2** group considered not wholly respectable.

demise n **1** eventual failure (of something successful). **2** Formal death.

demo n, pl **demos** Informal demonstration, organized expression of public opinion.

demob v Brit, Aust & NZ informal demobilize.

demobilize v release from the armed forces. **demobilization** n

democracy n, pl -cies **1** government by the people or their elected representatives. **2** state governed in this way. **democrat** n **1** advocate of democracy. **2** (D-) member or supporter of the Democratic Party in the US. **democratic** adj **1** of democracy. **2** upholding democracy. **3** (D-) of the Democratic Party, the more liberal of the two main political parties in the US. **democratically** adv

demography n study of population statistics, such as births and deaths. **demographer** n **demographic** adj

demolish v **1** knock down or destroy (a building). **2** disprove (an argument). **demolition** n

demon n **1** evil spirit. **2** person who does something with great energy or skill. **demonic** adj evil. **demoniac**, **demoniacal** adj **1** appearing to be possessed by a devil. **2** frenzied. **demonology** n study of demons.

demonstrate v 1 show or prove by reasoning or evidence. 2 display and explain the workings of. 3 reveal the existence of. 4 show support or opposition by public parades or rallies. **demonstrable** adj able to be proved. **demonstrably** adv **demonstration** n 1 organized expression of public opinion. 2 explanation or display of how something works. 3 proof. **demonstrative** adj tending to show one's feelings unreservedly. **demonstratively** adv **demonstrator** n 1 person who demonstrates how a device or machine works. 2 person who takes part in a public demonstration.

demoralize v undermine the morale of. **demoralization** n

demote v reduce in status or rank. **demotion** n

demur v -murring, -murred 1 show reluctance. ♦ n 2 without demur without objecting.

demure adj quiet, reserved, and rather shy. **demurely** adv

den n 1 home of a wild animal. 2 small secluded room in a home. 3 place where people indulge in criminal or immoral activities.

denationalize v transfer (an industry) from public to private ownership. **denationalization** n

denature v 1 change the nature of. 2 make (alcohol) unfit to drink.

denier [**den**-yer] n unit of weight used to measure the fineness of nylon or silk.

denigrate v criticize unfairly. **denigration** n

denim n 1 hard-wearing cotton fabric, usu. blue. ♦ pl 2 jeans made of denim.

denizen n inhabitant.

denominate v give a specific name to.

denomination n 1 group having a distinctive interpretation of a religious faith. 2 unit in a system of weights,

values, or measures. **denominational** adj

denominator n number below the line in a fraction.

denote v 1 be a sign of. 2 have as a literal meaning. **denotation** n

denouement [day-**noo**-mon] n final outcome or solution in a play or book.

denounce v 1 speak vehemently against. 2 give information against. **denunciation** n open condemnation.

dense adj 1 closely packed. 2 difficult to see through. 3 stupid. **densely** adv **density** n, pl -ties 1 degree to which something is filled or occupied. 2 measure of the compactness of a substance, expressed as its mass per unit volume.

dent n 1 hollow in the surface of something, made by hitting it. ♦ v 2 make a dent in.

dental adj of teeth or dentistry. **dental floss** waxed thread used to remove food particles from between the teeth. **dentine** [**den**-teen] n hard dense tissue forming the bulk of a tooth. **denture** n false tooth.

dentist n person qualified to practise dentistry. **dentistry** n branch of medicine concerned with the teeth and gums.

denude v remove the covering or protection from.

deny v -nying, -nied 1 declare to be untrue. 2 refuse to give or allow. 3 refuse to acknowledge. **deniable** adj **denial** n 1 statement that something is not true. 2 rejection of a request.

deodorant n substance applied to the body to mask the smell of perspiration.

deodorize v remove or disguise the smell of.

depart v 1 leave. 2 differ, deviate. **departed** adj Euphemistic dead. **the departed** Euphemistic dead person. **departure** n

department *n* **1** specialized division of a large organization. **2** major subdivision of the administration of a government. **departmental** *adj* **department store** large shop selling many kinds of goods.

depend *v* (foll. by *on*) **1** put trust (in). **2** be influenced or determined (by). **3** rely (on) for income or support. **dependable** *adj* **dependably** *adv* **dependability** *n* **dependant** *n* person who depends on another for financial support. **dependence** *n* state of being dependent. **dependency** *n, pl* **-cies 1** country controlled by another country. **2** overreliance on another person or on a drug. **dependent** *adj* depending on someone or something.

> ☑ **SPELLING TIP**
> The words **dependant** and **dependent** are easy to confuse. The first, ending in *-ant*, is a noun meaning a person who is dependent (adjective ending in *-ent*) on someone else.

depict *v* **1** produce a picture of. **2** describe in words. **depiction** *n*

depilatory [dip-**pill**-a-tree] *n, pl* **-tories**, *adj* (substance) designed to remove unwanted hair.

deplete *v* **1** use up. **2** reduce in number. **depletion** *n*

deplore *v* condemn strongly. **deplorable** *adj* very bad or unpleasant.

deploy *v* organize (troops or resources) into a position ready for immediate action. **deployment** *n*

depopulate *v* reduce the population of. **depopulation** *n*

deport *v* remove forcibly from a country. **deport oneself** behave in a specified way. **deportation** *n* **deportee** *n*

deportment *n* way in which a person moves or stands.

depose *v* **1** remove from an office or position of power. **2** *Law* testify on oath.

deposit *v* **1** put down. **2** entrust for safekeeping, esp. to a bank. **3** lay down naturally. ♦ *n* **4** sum of money paid into a bank account. **5** money given in part payment for goods or services. **6** accumulation of sediments, minerals, etc. **depositary** *n* person to whom something is entrusted for safety. **depositor** *n* **depository** *n* store for furniture etc.

deposition *n* **1** *Law* sworn statement of a witness used in court in his or her absence. **2** deposing. **3** depositing. **4** something deposited.

depot [**dep**-oh] *n* **1** building where goods or vehicles are kept when not in use. **2** *NZ & US* bus or railway station.

depraved *adj* morally bad. **depravity** *n*

deprecate *v* express disapproval of. **deprecation** *n* **deprecatory** *adj*

depreciate *v* **1** decline in value or price. **2** criticize. **depreciation** *n*

depredation *n* plundering.

depress *v* **1** make sad. **2** lower (prices or wages). **3** push down. **depressing** *adj* **depressingly** *adv* **depressant** *n, adj* (drug) able to reduce nervous activity. **depression** *n* **1** mental state in which a person has feelings of gloom and inadequacy. **2** economic condition in which there is high unemployment and low output and investment. **3** area of low air pressure. **4** sunken place. **depressive** *adj* **1** tending to cause depression. ♦ *n* **2** person who suffers from depression.

deprive *v* (foll. by *of*) prevent from (having or enjoying). **deprivation** *n* **deprived** *adj* lacking adequate living conditions, education, etc.

depth n **1** distance downwards, backwards, or inwards. **2** intensity of emotion. **3** profundity of character or thought. **depth charge** bomb used to attack submarines by exploding at a preset depth of water.

depute v appoint (someone) to act on one's behalf. **deputation** n body of people appointed to represent others.

deputy n, pl **-ties** person appointed to act on behalf of another. **deputize** v act as deputy.

derail v cause (a train) to go off the rails. **derailment** n

deranged adj **1** insane or uncontrolled. **2** in a state of disorder. **derangement** n

derby [**dah**-bee] n, pl **-bies 1** sporting event between teams from the same area. ♦ n **2** any of various horse races.

deregulate v remove regulations or controls from. **deregulation** n

derelict adj **1** unused and falling into ruins. ♦ n **2** social outcast, vagrant. **dereliction** n state of being abandoned. **dereliction of duty** failure to do one's duty.

deride v treat with contempt or ridicule. **derision** n **derisive** adj mocking, scornful. **derisory** adj too small or inadequate to be considered seriously.

de rigueur [de rig-**gur**] adj required by fashion.

derive v (foll. by from) take or develop (from). **derivation** n **derivative** adj word, idea, etc., derived from another.

dermatitis n inflammation of the skin.

dermatology n branch of medicine concerned with the skin. **dermatologist** n

derogatory [dir-**rog**-a-tree] adj intentionally offensive.

derrick n **1** simple crane. **2** framework erected over an oil well.

derv n Brit diesel oil, when used for road transport.

dervish n member of a Muslim religious order noted for a frenzied whirling dance.

descant n Music tune played or sung above a basic melody.

descend v **1** move down (a slope etc.). **2** move to a lower level, pitch, etc. **3** (foll. by to) stoop to (unworthy behaviour). **4** (foll. by on) visit unexpectedly. **be descended from** be connected by a blood relationship to. **descendant** n person or animal descended from an individual, race, or species. **descendent** adj descending. **descent** n **1** descending. **2** downward slope. **3** derivation from an ancestor.

describe v **1** give an account of (something or someone) in words. **2** trace the outline of (a circle etc.). **description** n **1** statement that describes something or someone. **2** sort, e.g. flowers of every description. **descriptive** adj **descriptively** adv

descry v **-scrying, -scried 1** catch sight of. **2** discover by looking carefully.

desecrate v damage or insult (something sacred). **desecration** n

desegregate v end racial segregation in. **desegregation** n

deselect v Brit politics refuse to select (an MP) for re-election. **deselection** n

desert[1] n region with little or no vegetation because of low rainfall.

desert[2] v **1** abandon (a person or place) without intending to return. **2** Mil leave (a post or duty) with no intention of returning. **deserter** n **desertion** n

deserts pl n **get one's just deserts** get the punishment one deserves.

deserve v be entitled to or worthy of. **deserved** adj rightfully earned. **deservedly** adv **deserving** adj worthy of help, praise, or reward.

deshabille [day-zab-**beel**] *n* state of being partly dressed.

desiccate *v* remove most of the water from. **desiccation** *n*

☑ SPELLING TIP

The word **desiccate** has two *c*s because it comes from the Latin word *siccus*, which means 'dry'.

---

design *v* **1** work out the structure or form of (something), by making a sketch or plans. **2** plan and make artistically. **3** intend for a specific purpose. ♦ *n* **4** preliminary drawing. **5** arrangement or features of an artistic or decorative work. **6** art of designing. **7** intention, e.g. *by design*. **designedly** [dee-**zine**-id-lee] *adv* intentionally. **designer** *n* **1** person who draws up original sketches or plans from which things are made. ♦ *adj* **2** designed by a well-known designer. **designing** *adj* cunning and scheming.

designate [**dez**-zig-nate] *v* **1** give a name to. **2** select (someone) for an office or duty. ♦ *adj* **3** appointed but not yet in office. **designation** *n* name.

desire *v* **1** want very much. ♦ *n* **2** wish, longing. **3** sexual appetite. **4** person or thing desired. **desirable** *adj* **1** worth having. **2** arousing sexual desire. **desirability** *n* **desirous of** having a desire for.

desist *v* (foll. by *from*) stop (doing something).

desk *n* **1** piece of furniture with a writing surface and drawers. **2** service counter in a public building. **3** section of a newspaper covering a specific subject, e.g. *the sports desk*. **desktop** *adj* (of a computer) small enough to use at a desk.

desolate *adj* **1** uninhabited and bleak. **2** very sad. ♦ *v* **3** deprive of

inhabitants. **4** make (someone) very sad. **desolation** *n*

despair *n* **1** total loss of hope. ♦ *v* **2** lose hope.

despatch *v, n* same as DISPATCH.

desperado *n, pl* **-does, -dos** reckless person ready to commit any violent illegal act.

desperate *adj* **1** in despair and reckless. **2** (of an action) undertaken as a last resort. **3** having a strong need or desire. **desperately** *adv* **desperation** *n*

☑ SPELLING TIP

It's often difficult to decide whether to write an *a* or an *e* when it wouldn't seem to make much difference to a word's pronunciation. An example in the Bank of English is *desparate*, which should, of course, be spelt **desperate**.

---

despise *v* regard with contempt. **despicable** *adj* deserving contempt. **despicably** *adv*

despite *prep* in spite of.

despoil *v Formal* plunder. **despoliation** *n*

despondent *adj* unhappy. **despondently** *adv* **despondency** *n*

despot *n* person in power who acts unfairly or cruelly. **despotic** *adj* **despotism** *n* unfair or cruel government or behaviour.

dessert *n* sweet course served at the end of a meal. **dessertspoon** *n* spoon between a tablespoon and a teaspoon in size.

destination *n* place to which someone or something is going.

destined *adj* certain to be or to do something.

destiny *n, pl* **-nies 1** future marked out for a person or thing. **2** the power that predetermines the course of events.

destitute *adj* having no money or possessions. **destitution** *n*

destroy *v* 1 ruin, demolish. 2 put an end to. 3 kill (an animal). **destroyer** *n* 1 small heavily armed warship. 2 person or thing that destroys.

destruction *n* 1 destroying. 2 cause of ruin. **destructive** *adj* (capable of) causing destruction. **destructively** *adv*

desuetude [diss-**syoo**-it-tude] *n* condition of not being in use.

desultory [**dez**-zl-tree] *adj* 1 jumping from one thing to another, disconnected. 2 random. **desultorily** *adv*

detach *v* disengage and separate. **detachable** *adj* **detached** *adj* 1 *Brit, Aust & S Afr* (of a house) not joined to another house. 2 showing no emotional involvement. **detachment** *n* 1 lack of emotional involvement. 2 small group of soldiers.

detail *n* 1 individual piece of information. 2 unimportant item. 3 small individual features of something, considered collectively. 4 *Chiefly mil* (personnel assigned) a specific duty. ♦ *v* 5 list fully.

detain *v* 1 delay (someone). 2 hold (someone) in custody. **detainee** *n*

detect *v* 1 notice. 2 discover, find. **detectable** *adj* **detection** *n* **detective** *n* policeman or private agent who investigates crime. **detector** *n* instrument used to find something.

detente [day-**tont**] *n* easing of tension between nations.

detention *n* 1 imprisonment. 2 form of punishment in which a pupil is detained after school.

deter *v* -terring, -terred discourage (someone) from doing something by instilling fear or doubt. **deterrent** *n* 1 something that deters. 2 weapon, esp. nuclear, intended to deter attack. ♦ *adj*

3 tending to deter.

detergent *n* chemical substance for washing clothes or dishes.

deteriorate *v* become worse. **deterioration** *n*

determine *v* 1 settle (an argument or a question) conclusively. 2 find out the facts about. 3 make a firm decision (to do something). **determinant** *n* factor that determines. **determinate** *adj* definitely limited or fixed. **determination** *n* being determined or resolute. **determined** *adj* firmly decided, unable to be dissuaded. **determinedly** *adv* **determiner** *n* *Grammar* word that determines the object to which a noun phrase refers, e.g. *all*. **determinism** *n* theory that human choice is not free, but decided by past events. **determinist** *n, adj*

detest *v* dislike intensely. **detestable** *adj* **detestation** *n*

dethrone *v* remove from a throne or position of power.

detonate *v* explode. **detonation** *n* **detonator** *n* small amount of explosive, or a device, used to set off an explosion.

detour *n* route that is not the most direct one.

detract *v* (foll. by *from*) make (something) seem less good. **detractor** *n*

detriment *n* disadvantage or damage. **detrimental** *adj* **detrimentally** *adv*

detritus [dit-**trite**-uss] *n* 1 loose mass of stones and silt worn away from rocks. 2 debris.

de trop [de **troh**] *adj French* unwanted, unwelcome.

deuce [**dyewss**] *n* 1 *Tennis* score of forty all. 2 playing card with two symbols or dice with two spots.

deuterium *n* isotope of hydrogen twice as heavy as the normal atom.

Deutschmark [**doytch**-mark],

Deutsche Mark [**doytch**-a] *n* former monetary unit of Germany.

devalue *v* **-valuing, -valued** **1** reduce the exchange value of (a currency). **2** reduce the value of (something or someone). **devaluation** *n*

devastate *v* destroy. **devastated** *adj* shocked and extremely upset. **devastation** *n*

develop *v* **1** grow or bring to a later, more elaborate, or more advanced stage. **2** come or bring into existence. **3** build houses or factories on (an area of land). **4** produce (photographs) by making negatives or prints from a film. **developer** *n* **1** person who develops property. **2** chemical used to develop photographs or films. **development** *n* **developing country** poor or nonindustrial country that is trying to develop its resources by industrialization.

deviate *v* **1** differ from others in belief or thought. **2** depart from one's previous behaviour. **deviation** *n* **deviant** *n, adj* (person) deviating from what is considered acceptable behaviour. **deviance** *n*

device *n* **1** machine or tool used for a specific task. **2** scheme or plan.

devil *n* **1** evil spirit. **2** evil person. **3** person, e.g. *poor devil.* **4** daring person, e.g. *be a devil!* **5** *Informal* something difficult or annoying, e.g. *a devil of a long time.* ♦ *v* **-illing, -illed** **6** prepare (food) with a highly flavoured spiced mixture. **the Devil** *Theology* chief spirit of evil and enemy of God. **devilish** *adj* **1** cruel or unpleasant. ♦ *adv* **2** (also **devilishly**) *Informal* extremely. **devilment** *n* mischievous conduct. **devilry** *n* mischievousness. **devil-may-care** *adj* carefree and cheerful. **devil's advocate** person who takes an opposing or unpopular point of view for the sake of argument.

devious *adj* **1** insincere and dishonest. **2** indirect. **deviously** *adv* **deviousness** *n*

devise *v* work out (something) in one's mind.

devoid *adj* (foll. by *of*) completely lacking (in).

devolve *v* (foll. by *on* or *to*) pass (power or duties) or (of power or duties) be passed to a successor or substitute. **devolution** *n* transfer of authority from a central government to regional governments.

devote *v* apply or dedicate to a particular purpose. **devoted** *adj* showing loyalty or devotion. **devotedly** *adv* **devotee** *n* **1** person who is very enthusiastic about something. **2** zealous follower of a religion. **devotion** *n* **1** strong affection for or loyalty to someone or something. **2** religious zeal. ♦ *pl* **3** prayers. **devotional** *adj*

devour *v* **1** eat greedily. **2** (of an emotion) engulf and destroy. **3** read eagerly.

devout *adj* deeply religious. **devoutly** *adv*

dew *n* drops of water that form on the ground at night from vapour in the air. **dewy** *adj*

dewlap *n* loose fold of skin hanging under the throat in dogs, cattle, etc.

dexterity *n* **1** skill in using one's hands. **2** mental quickness. **dexterous** *adj* **dexterously** *adv*

dextrose *n* glucose occurring in fruit, honey, and the blood of animals.

DH (in Britain) Department of Health.

DI donor insemination: method of making a woman pregnant by transferring sperm from a man other than her regular partner using artificial means.

diabetes [die-a-**beet**-eez] *n* disorder in which an abnormal amount of urine containing an excess of sugar is excreted. **diabetic** n, adj

diabolic adj of the Devil. **diabolism** n witchcraft, devil worship.

diabolical adj Informal extremely bad. **diabolically** adv

diaconate n position or period of office of a deacon.

diacritic n sign above or below a character to indicate phonetic value or stress.

diadem n Old-fashioned crown.

diaeresis n, pl **-ses** mark (¨) placed over a vowel to show that it is pronounced separately from the preceding one, for example in Noël.

diagnosis [die-ag-**no**-siss] n, pl **-ses** [-seez] discovery and identification of diseases from the examination of symptoms. **diagnose** v **diagnostic** adj

diagonal adj 1 from corner to corner. 2 slanting. ♦ n 3 diagonal line. **diagonally** adv

diagram n sketch showing the form or workings of something. **diagrammatic** adj

dial n 1 face of a clock or watch. 2 graduated disc on a measuring instrument. 3 control on a radio or television set used to change the station. 4 numbered disc on the front of some telephones. ♦ v **dialling, dialled** 5 operate the dial or buttons on a telephone in order to contact (a number).

dialect n form of a language spoken in a particular area. **dialectal** adj

dialectic n logical debate by question and answer to resolve differences between two views. **dialectical** adj

dialogue n 1 conversation between two people, esp. in a book, film, or play. 2 discussion between representatives of two nations or groups. **dialogue box** n small

window that may open on a computer screen to prompt the user to enter information or select an option.

dialysis [die-**al**-iss-iss] n Med filtering of blood through a membrane to remove waste products.

diamanté [die-a-**man**-tee] adj decorated with artificial jewels or sequins.

diameter n (length of) a straight line through the centre of a circle or sphere. **diametric, diametrical** adj 1 of a diameter. 2 completely opposed, e.g. the diametric opposite. **diametrically** adv

diamond n 1 exceptionally hard, usu. colourless, precious stone. 2 Geom figure with four sides of equal length forming two acute and two obtuse angles. 3 playing card marked with red diamond-shaped symbols. **diamond wedding** sixtieth anniversary of a wedding.

diaper n US nappy.

diaphanous [die-**af**-fan-ous] adj fine and almost transparent.

diaphragm [**die**-a-fram] n 1 muscular partition that separates the abdominal cavity and chest cavity. 2 contraceptive device placed over the neck of the womb.

diarrhoea [die-a-**ree**-a] n frequent discharge of abnormally liquid faeces.

☑ **SPELLING TIP**
It's possibly because people don't write the word **diarrhoea** very often that there's only one example of diarhoea, with only one r, in the Bank of English. Or is it because it's such a difficult word to spell, we always look it up to get it right?

diary n, pl **-ries** (book for) a record of daily events, appointments, or observations. **diarist** n

diatribe *n* bitter critical attack.

dibble *n* small hand tool used to make holes in the ground for seeds or plants.

dice *n, pl* **dice 1** small cube each of whose sides has a different number of spots (1 to 6), used in games of chance. **2** *v* **3** cut (food) into small cubes. **dice with death** take a risk. **dicey** *adj Informal* dangerous or risky.

dichotomy [die-**kot**-a-mee] *n, pl* **-mies** division into two opposed groups or parts.

dicky[1] *n, pl* **dickies** false shirt front. **dicky-bird** *n* child's word for a bird.

dicky[2] *adj* **dickier, dickiest** *Informal* shaky or weak.

Dictaphone *n* ® tape recorder for recording dictation for subsequent typing.

dictate *v* **1** say aloud for someone else to write down. **2** (foll. by *to*) seek to impose one's will on (other people). ♦ *n* **3** authoritative command. **4** guiding principle. **dictation** *n* **dictator** *n* **1** ruler who has complete power. **2** person in power who acts unfairly or cruelly. **dictatorship** *n* **dictatorial** *adj* like a dictator.

diction *n* manner of pronouncing words and sounds.

dictionary *n, pl* **-aries 1** book consisting of an alphabetical list of words with their meanings. **2** alphabetically ordered reference book of terms relating to a particular subject.

dictum *n, pl* **-tums, -ta 1** formal statement. **2** popular saying.

did *v* past tense of DO.

didactic *adj* intended to instruct. **didactically** *adv*

diddle *v Informal* swindle.

didgeridoo *n* Australian musical instrument made from a long hollow piece of wood.

didn't did not.

die[1] *v* **dying, died 1** (of a person, animal, or plant) cease all biological activity permanently. **2** (of something inanimate) cease to exist or function. **be dying for, to do something** *Informal* be eager for *or* to do something. **die-hard** *n* person who resists change.

die[2] *n* shaped block used to cut or form metal.

dieresis [die-**air**-iss-iss] *n, pl* **-ses** [-seez] **same as** DIAERESIS.

diesel *n* **1** diesel engine. **2** vehicle driven by a diesel engine. **3** diesel oil. **diesel engine** internal-combustion engine in which oil is ignited by compression. **diesel oil** fuel obtained from petroleum distillation.

diet[1] *n* **1** food that a person or animal regularly eats. **2** specific range of foods, to control weight or for health reasons. ♦ *v* **3** follow a special diet so as to lose weight. ♦ *adj* **4** (of food) suitable for a weight-reduction diet. **dietary** *adj* **dietary fibre** fibrous substances in fruit and vegetables that aid digestion. **dieter** *n* **dietetic** *adj* prepared for special dietary requirements. **dietetics** *n* study of diet and nutrition. **dietician** *n* person who specializes in dietetics.

diet[2] *n* parliament of some countries.

differ *v* **1** be unlike. **2** disagree.

different *adj* **1** unlike. **2** unusual. **difference** *n* **1** state of being unlike. **2** disagreement. **3** remainder left after subtraction. **differently** *adv*

differential *adj* **1** of or using a difference. **2** *Maths* involving differentials. ♦ *n* **3** factor that differentiates between two comparable things. **4** *Maths* tiny difference between values in a scale. **5** difference between rates of pay for different types of work. **differential calculus** branch of calculus concerned with derivatives and differentials.

differentiate v **1** perceive or show the difference (between). **2** make (one thing) distinct from other such things. **differentiation** n

difficult adj **1** requiring effort or skill to do or understand. **2** not easily pleased. **difficulty** n

diffident adj lacking self-confidence. **diffidence** n **diffidently** adv

diffraction n Physics **1** deviation in the direction of a wave at the edge of an obstacle in its path. **2** formation of light and dark fringes by the passage of light through a small aperture.

diffuse v **1** spread over a wide area. ♦ adj **2** widely spread. **3** lacking concision. **diffusion** n

dig v **digging**, **dug** **1** cut into, break up, and turn over or remove (earth), esp. with a spade. **2** (foll. by out or up) find by effort or searching. **3** (foll. by in or into) thrust or jab. ♦ n **4** digging. **5** archaeological excavation. **6** thrust or poke. **7** spiteful remark. ♦ pl **8** Brit, Aust & S Afr informal lodgings. **digger** n machine used for digging.

digest v **1** subject to a process of digestion. **2** absorb mentally. ♦ n **3** shortened version of a book, report, or article. **digestible** adj **digestion** n (body's system for) breaking down food into easily absorbed substances. **digestive** adj **digestive biscuit** biscuit made from wholemeal flour.

digit [**dij**-it] n **1** finger or toe. **2** numeral from 0 to 9. **digital** adj displaying information as numbers rather than with hands and a dial, e.g. a digital clock. **digital recording** sound-recording process that converts audio or analogue signals into a series of pulses. **digital television** television in which the picture is transmitted in digital form and then decoded. **digitally** adv

digitalis n drug made from foxglove leaves, used as a heart stimulant.

dignity n, pl **-ties** **1** serious, calm, and controlled behaviour or manner. **2** quality of being worthy of respect. **3** sense of self-importance. **dignify** v add distinction to. **dignitary** n person of high official position.

digress v depart from the main subject in speech or writing. **digression** n

dike n same as DYKE.

dilapidated adj (of a building) having fallen into ruin. **dilapidation** n

dilate v make or become wider or larger. **dilation, dilatation** n

dilatory [**dill**-a-tree] adj tending or intended to waste time.

dildo n, pl **-dos** object used as a substitute for an erect penis.

dilemma n situation offering a choice between two equally undesirable alternatives.

dilettante [dill-it-**tan**-tee] n, pl **-tantes**, **-tanti** person whose interest in a subject is superficial rather than serious. **dilettantism** n

diligent adj **1** careful and persevering in carrying out duties. **2** carried out with care and perseverance. **diligently** adv **diligence** n

dill n sweet-smelling herb.

dilly-dally v **-lying**, **-lied** Brit, Aust & NZ informal dawdle, waste time.

dilute v **1** make (a liquid) less concentrated, esp. by adding water. **2** make (a quality etc.) weaker in force. **dilution** n

diluvial, diluvian adj of a flood, esp. the great Flood described in the Old Testament.

dim adj **dimmer**, **dimmest** **1** badly lit. **2** not clearly seen. **3** unintelligent. ♦ v **dimming**, **dimmed** **4** make or become dim. **take a dim view of** disapprove of. **dimly** adv **dimness** n

dimmer n device for dimming an electric light.

dime n coin of the US and Canada, worth ten cents.

dimension n 1 measurement of the size of something in a particular direction. 2 aspect, factor.

diminish v make or become smaller, fewer, or less. **diminution** n **diminutive** adj 1 very small. ♦ n 2 word or affix which implies smallness or unimportance.

diminuendo n Music gradual decrease in loudness.

dimple n 1 small natural dent, esp. in the cheeks or chin. ♦ v 2 produce dimples by smiling.

din n 1 loud unpleasant confused noise. ♦ v **dinning, dinned** 2 (foll. by into) instil (something) into someone by constant repetition.

dinar [**dee**-nahr] n monetary unit of various Balkan, Middle Eastern, and North African countries.

dine v eat dinner. **diner** n 1 person eating a meal. 2 Chiefly US small cheap restaurant. **dining car** railway coach where meals are served. **dining room** room where meals are eaten.

ding n Aust dated & NZ informal small dent in a vehicle.

ding-dong n 1 sound of a bell. 2 Informal lively quarrel or fight.

dinghy [**ding**-ee] n, pl **-ghies** small boat, powered by sails, oars, or a motor.

dingo n, pl **-goes** Australian wild dog.

dingy [**din**-jee] adj **-gier, -giest** Brit, Aust & NZ dull and drab. **dinginess** n

dinkum adj Aust & NZ informal genuine or right.

dinky adj **-kier, -kiest** Brit, Aust & NZ informal small and neat.

dinky-di adj Aust informal typical.

dinner n main meal of the day, eaten either in the evening or at midday. **dinner jacket** man's semiformal black evening jacket.

dinosaur n type of extinct prehistoric reptile, many of which were of gigantic size.

dint n **by dint of** by means of.

diocese [**die**-a-siss] n district over which a bishop has control. **diocesan** adj

diode n semiconductor device for converting alternating current to direct current.

dioptre [die-**op**-ter] n unit for measuring the refractive power of a lens.

dioxide n oxide containing two oxygen atoms per molecule.

dip v **dipping, dipped** 1 plunge quickly or briefly into a liquid. 2 slope downwards. 3 switch (car headlights) from the main to the lower beam. 4 lower briefly. ♦ n 5 dipping. 6 brief swim. 7 liquid chemical in which farm animals are dipped to rid them of insects. 8 depression in a landscape. 9 creamy mixture into which pieces of food are dipped before being eaten. **dip into** v read passages at random from (a book or journal).

diphtheria [dif-**theer**-ya] n contagious disease producing fever and difficulty in breathing and swallowing.

diphthong n union of two vowel sounds in a single compound sound.

diploma n qualification awarded by a college on successful completion of a course.

diplomacy n 1 conduct of the relations between nations by peaceful means. 2 tact or skill in dealing with people. **diplomat** n official engaged in diplomacy. **diplomatic** adj 1 of diplomacy. 2 tactful in dealing with people. **diplomatically** adv

dipper n 1 ladle used for dipping. 2

(also **ousel, ouzel**) European songbird that lives by a river.

diprotodont [die-**pro**-toe-dont] *n* marsupial with fewer than three upper incisor teeth on each side of the jaw.

dipsomania *n* compulsive craving for alcohol. **dipsomaniac** *n, adj*

diptych [**dip**-tik] *n* painting on two hinged panels.

dire *adj* disastrous, urgent, or terrible.

direct *adj* **1** (of a route) shortest, straight. **2** without anyone or anything intervening. **3** likely to have an immediate effect. **4** honest, frank. ◆ *adv* **5** in a direct manner. ◆ *v* **6** lead and organize. **7** tell (someone) to do something. **8** tell (someone) the way to a place. **9** address (a letter, package, remark, etc.). **10** provide guidance to (actors, cameramen, etc.) in (a play or film). **directly** *adv* **1** in a direct manner. **2** at once. ◆ *conj* **3** as soon as. **directness** *n* **direct current** electric current that flows in one direction only.

direction *n* **1** course or line along which a person or thing moves, points, or lies. **2** management or guidance. ◆ *pl* **3** instructions for doing something or for reaching a place. **directional** *adj*

directive *n* instruction, order.

director *n* **1** person or thing that directs or controls. **2** member of the governing board of a business etc. **3** person responsible for the artistic and technical aspects of the making of a film etc. **directorial** *adj* **directorship** *n* **directorate** *n* **1** board of directors. **2** position of director.

directory *n, pl* **-tories 1** book listing names, addresses, and telephone numbers. **2** *Computers* area of a disk containing the names and locations of the files it currently holds.

dirge *n* slow sad song of mourning.

dirigible [**dir**-rij-jib-bl] *adj* **1** able to be

steered. ◆ *n* **2** airship.

dirk *n* dagger, formerly worn by Scottish Highlanders.

dirndl *n* full gathered skirt originating from Tyrolean peasant wear.

dirt *n* **1** unclean substance, filth. **2** earth, soil. **3** obscene speech or writing. **4** *Informal* harmful gossip. **dirt track** racetrack made of packed earth or cinders.

dirty *adj* **dirtier, dirtiest 1** covered or marked with dirt. **2** unfair or dishonest. **3** obscene. **4** displaying dislike or anger, e.g. *a dirty look.* ◆ *v* **dirtying, dirtied 5** make dirty. **dirtiness** *n*

dis- *prefix* indicating: **1** reversal, e.g. *disconnect.* **2** negation or lack, e.g. *dissimilar; disgrace.* **3** removal or release, e.g. *disembowel.*

disable *v* make ineffective, unfit, or incapable. **disabled** *adj* lacking a physical power, such as the ability to walk. **disablement** *n* **disability** *n, pl* **-ties 1** condition of being disabled. **2** something that disables someone.

disabuse *v* (foll. by *of*) rid (someone) of a mistaken idea.

disadvantage *n* unfavourable or harmful circumstance. **disadvantageous** *adj* **disadvantaged** *adj* socially or economically deprived.

disaffected *adj* having lost loyalty to or affection for someone or something. **disaffection** *n*

disagree *v* **-greeing, -greed 1** argue or have different opinions. **2** be different, conflict. **3** (foll. by *with*) cause physical discomfort (to), e.g. *curry disagrees with me.* **disagreement** *n* **disagreeable** *adj* **1** unpleasant. **2** (of a person) unfriendly or unhelpful. **disagreeably** *adv*

disallow *v* reject as untrue or invalid.

disappear *v* **1** cease to be visible. **2** cease to exist. **disappearance** *n*

disappoint v fail to meet the expectations or hopes of. **disappointment** n 1 feeling of being disappointed. 2 person or thing that disappoints.

☑ SPELLING TIP

It is a more common mistake to spell **disappointment** with no double letters at all, than to spell it with two ss, although *dissappointment* does occur in the Bank of English.

---

disapprobation n disapproval.

disapprove v (foll. by *of*) consider wrong or bad. **disapproval** n

disarm v 1 deprive of weapons. 2 win the confidence or affection of. 3 (of a country) decrease the size of one's armed forces. **disarmament** n **disarming** adj removing hostility or suspicion. **disarmingly** adv

disarrange v throw into disorder.

disarray n 1 confusion and lack of discipline. 2 extreme untidiness.

disaster n 1 occurrence that causes great distress or destruction. 2 project etc. that fails. **disastrous** adj **disastrously** adv

disavow v deny connection with or responsibility for. **disavowal** n

disband v (cause to) cease to function as a group.

disbelieve v 1 reject as false. 2 (foll. by *in*) have no faith (in). **disbelief** n

disburse v pay out. **disbursement** n

disc n 1 flat circular object. 2 gramophone record. 3 *Anat* circular flat structure in the body, esp. between the vertebrae. 4 *Computers* same as DISK. **disc jockey** person who introduces and plays pop records on a radio programme or at a disco.

discard v get rid of (something or someone) as useless or undesirable.

discern v see or be aware of (something) clearly. **discernible** adj **discerning** adj having good judgment. **discernment** n

discharge v 1 release, allow to go. 2 dismiss (someone) from duty or employment. 3 fire (a gun). 4 pour forth, send out. 5 meet the demands of (a duty or responsibility). 6 relieve oneself of (a debt). ♦ n 7 substance that comes out from a place. 8 discharging.

disciple [diss-**sipe**-pl] n follower of the doctrines of a teacher, esp. Jesus Christ.

discipline n 1 practice of imposing strict rules of behaviour. 2 area of academic study. ♦ v 3 attempt to improve the behaviour of (oneself or another) by training or rules. 4 punish. **disciplined** adj able to behave and work in a controlled way. **disciplinarian** n person who practises strict discipline. **disciplinary** adj

disclaimer n statement denying responsibility. **disclaim** v

disclose v 1 make known. 2 allow to be seen. **disclosure** n

disco n, pl **-cos** 1 nightclub where people dance to amplified pop records. 2 occasion at which people dance to amplified pop records. 3 mobile equipment for providing music for a disco.

discolour v change in colour, fade. **discoloration** n

discomfit v make uneasy or confused. **discomfiture** n

discomfort n inconvenience, distress, or mild pain.

discommode v cause inconvenience to.

disconcert v embarrass or upset.

disconnect v 1 undo or break the connection between (two things). 2 stop the supply of electricity or gas of. **disconnected** adj (of speech or ideas) not logically connected.

disconnection n

disconsolate adj sad beyond comfort. **disconsolately** adv

discontent n lack of contentment. **discontented** adj

discontinue v come or bring to an end. **discontinuous** adj characterized by interruptions. **discontinuity** n

discord n 1 lack of agreement or harmony between people. 2 harsh confused sounds. **discordant** adj **discordance** n

discotheque n same as DISCO.

discount v 1 take no account of (something) because it is considered to be unreliable, prejudiced, or irrelevant. 2 deduct (an amount) from the price of something. ♦ n 3 deduction from the full price of something.

discourage v 1 deprive of the will to persist in something. 2 oppose by expressing disapproval. **discouragement** n

discourse n 1 conversation. 2 formal treatment of a subject in speech or writing. ♦ v 3 (foll. by on) speak or write (about) at length.

discourteous adj showing bad manners. **discourtesy** n

discover v 1 be the first to find or to find out about. 2 learn about for the first time. 3 find after study or search. **discoverer** n **discovery** n, pl **-eries** 1 discovering. 2 person, place, or thing that has been discovered.

discredit v 1 damage the reputation of. 2 cause (an idea) to be disbelieved or distrusted. ♦ n 3 damage to someone's reputation. **discreditable** adj bringing shame.

discreet adj 1 careful to avoid embarrassment, esp. by keeping confidences secret. 2 unobtrusive. **discreetly** adv

discrepancy n, pl **-cies** conflict or variation between facts, figures, or claims.

discrete adj separate, distinct.

discretion n 1 quality of behaving in a discreet way. 2 freedom or authority to make judgments and decide what to do. **discretionary** adj

discriminate v 1 (foll. by against or in favour of) single out (a particular person or group) for worse or better treatment than others. 2 (foll. by between) recognize or understand the difference (between). **discriminating** adj showing good taste and judgment. **discrimination** n **discriminatory** adj based on prejudice.

discursive adj passing from one topic to another.

discus n heavy disc-shaped object thrown in sports competitions.

discuss v 1 consider (something) by talking it over. 2 treat (a subject) in speech or writing. **discussion** n

disdain n 1 feeling of superiority and dislike. ♦ v 2 refuse with disdain. **disdainful** adj **disdainfully** adv

disease n illness, sickness. **diseased** adj

disembark v get off a ship, aircraft, or bus. **disembarkation** n

disembodied adj 1 lacking a body. 2 seeming not to be attached to or coming from anyone.

disembowel v **-elling, -elled** remove the entrails of.

disenchanted adj disappointed and disillusioned. **disenchantment** n

disenfranchise v deprive (someone) of the right to vote or of other rights of citizenship.

disengage v release from a connection. **disengagement** n

disentangle v release from entanglement or confusion.

disfavour n disapproval or dislike.

disfigure v spoil the appearance of.
disfigurement n

disfranchise v same as DISENFRANCHISE.

disgorge v empty out, discharge.

disgrace n 1 condition of shame, loss of reputation, or dishonour. 2 shameful person or thing. ♦ v 3 bring shame upon (oneself or others). **disgraceful** adj **disgracefully** adv

disgruntled adj sulky or discontented. **disgruntlement** n

disguise v 1 change the appearance or manner in order to conceal the identity of (someone or something). 2 misrepresent (something) in order to obscure its actual nature or meaning. ♦ n 3 mask, costume, or manner that disguises. 4 state of being disguised.

disgust n 1 great loathing or distaste. ♦ v 2 sicken, fill with loathing.

dish n 1 shallow container used for holding or serving food. 2 particular kind of food. 3 short for DISH AERIAL. 4 Informal attractive person. **dish aerial** aerial consisting of a concave disc-shaped reflector, used esp. for satellite television. **dishcloth** n cloth for washing dishes. **dish out** v Informal distribute. **dish up** v Informal serve (food).

dishabille [diss-a-**beel**] n same as DESHABILLE.

dishearten v weaken or destroy the hope, courage, or enthusiasm of.

dishevelled adj (of a person's hair, clothes, or general appearance) disordered and untidy.

dishonest adj not honest or fair. **dishonestly** adv **dishonesty** n

dishonour v 1 treat with disrespect. 2 n 3 lack of respect. 4 state of shame or disgrace. 5 something that causes a loss of honour. **dishonourable** adj **dishonourably** adv

disillusion v 1 destroy the illusions or false ideas of. ♦ n 2 (also

disillusionment) state of being disillusioned.

disincentive n something that acts as a deterrent.

disinclined adj unwilling, reluctant. **disinclination** n

disinfect v rid of harmful germs, chemically. **disinfectant** n substance that destroys harmful germs. **disinfection** n

disinformation n false information intended to mislead.

disingenuous adj not sincere. **disingenuously** adv

disinherit v Law deprive (an heir) of inheritance. **disinheritance** n

disintegrate v break up. **disintegration** n

disinter v **-terring, -terred** 1 dig up. 2 reveal, make known.

disinterested adj free from bias or involvement. **disinterest** n

☑ **WORD TIP**
Distinguish *disinterested* from *uninterested,* meaning 'apathetic, not caring': *We asked him to decide because he was a disinterested observer.*

disjointed adj having no coherence, disconnected.

disk n Computers storage device, consisting of a stack of plates coated with a magnetic layer, which rotates rapidly as a single unit.

dislike v 1 consider unpleasant or disagreeable. ♦ n 2 feeling of not liking something or someone.

dislocate v 1 displace (a bone or joint) from its normal position. 2 disrupt or shift out of place. **dislocation** n

dislodge v remove (something) from a previously fixed position.

disloyal adj not loyal, deserting one's allegiance. **disloyalty** n

dismal adj 1 gloomy and depressing. 2

Informal of poor quality. **dismally** *adv*

dismantle *v* take apart piece by piece.

dismay *v* **1** fill with alarm or depression. ♦ *n* **2** alarm mixed with sadness.

dismember *v* **1** remove the limbs of. **2** cut to pieces. **dismemberment** *n*

dismiss *v* **1** remove (an employee) from a job. **2** allow (someone) to leave. **3** put out of one's mind. **4** (of a judge) state that (a case) will not be brought to trial. **dismissal** *n* **dismissive** *adj* scornful, contemptuous.

dismount *v* get off a horse or bicycle.

disobey *v* neglect or refuse to obey. **disobedient** *adj* **disobedience** *n*

disobliging *adj* unwilling to help.

disorder *n* **1** state of untidiness and disorganization. **2** public violence or rioting. **3** illness. **disordered** *adj* untidy. **disorderly** *adj* **1** untidy and disorganized. **2** uncontrolled, unruly.

disorganize *v* disrupt the arrangement or system of. **disorganization** *n*

disorientate, disorient *v* cause (someone) to lose his or her bearings. **disorientation** *n*

disown *v* deny any connection with (someone).

disparage *v* speak contemptuously of. **disparagement** *n*

disparate *adj* completely different. **disparity** *n*

dispassionate *adj* not influenced by emotion. **dispassionately** *adv*

dispatch *v* **1** send off to a destination or to perform a task. **2** carry out (a duty or a task) with speed. **3** *Old-fashioned* kill. ♦ *n* **4** official communication or report, sent in haste. **5** report sent to a newspaper by a correspondent. **dispatch rider** *Brit, Aust & NZ* motorcyclist who carries dispatches.

dispel *v* **-pelling, -pelled** destroy or remove.

dispense *v* **1** distribute in portions. **2** prepare and distribute (medicine). **3** administer (the law etc.). **dispensable** *adj* not essential. **dispensation** *n* **1** dispensing. **2** exemption from an obligation. **dispenser** *n* **dispensary** *n, pl* **-saries** place where medicine is dispensed. **dispense with** *v* do away with, manage without.

disperse *v* **1** scatter over a wide area. **2** (cause to) leave a gathering. **dispersal, dispersion** *n*

dispirit *v* make downhearted.

displace *v* **1** move from the usual location. **2** remove from office. **displacement** *n* **displaced person** person forced from his or her home or country, esp. by war.

display *v* **1** make visible or noticeable. ♦ *n* **2** displaying. **3** something displayed. **4** exhibition.

displease *v* annoy or upset. **displeasure** *n*

disport *v* **disport oneself** indulge oneself in pleasure.

dispose *v* place in a certain order. **disposed** *adj* **1** willing or eager. **2** having an attitude as specified, e.g. *he felt well disposed towards her.* **disposable** *adj* **1** designed to be thrown away after use. **2** available for use, e.g. *disposable income.* **disposal** *n* getting rid of something. **at one's disposal** available for use. **disposition** *n* **1** person's usual temperament. **2** desire or tendency to do something. **3** arrangement. **dispose of** *v* **1** throw away, get rid of. **2** deal with (a problem etc.). **3** kill.

dispossess *v* (foll. by *of*) deprive (someone) of (a possession). **dispossession** *n*

disproportion *n* lack of proportion or equality.

disproportionate *adj* out of proportion. **disproportionately** *adv*

disprove *v* show (an assertion or claim) to be incorrect.

dispute *n* 1 disagreement, argument. ♦ *v* 2 argue about (something). 3 doubt the validity of. 4 fight over possession of.

disqualify *v* stop (someone) officially from taking part in something for wrongdoing. **disqualification** *n*

disquiet *n* 1 feeling of anxiety. ♦ *v* 2 make (someone) anxious. **disquietude** *n*

disregard *v* 1 give little or no attention to. ♦ *n* 2 lack of attention or respect.

disrepair *n* condition of being worn out or in poor working order.

disrepute *n* loss or lack of good reputation. **disreputable** *adj* having or causing a bad reputation.

disrespect *n* lack of respect. **disrespectful** *adj* **disrespectfully** *adv*

disrobe *v* undress.

disrupt *v* interrupt the progress of. **disruption** *n* **disruptive** *adj*

dissatisfied *adj* not pleased or contented. **dissatisfaction** *n*

dissect *v* 1 cut open (a corpse) to examine it. 2 examine critically and minutely. **dissection** *n*

dissemble *v* conceal one's real motives or emotions by pretence.

disseminate *v* spread (information). **dissemination** *n*

dissent *v* 1 disagree. 2 *Christianity* reject the doctrines of an established church. ♦ *n* 3 disagreement. 4 *Christianity* separation from an established church. **dissension** *n* **dissenter** *n*

dissertation *n* 1 written thesis, usu. required for a higher university degree.

2 long formal speech.

disservice *n* harmful action.

dissident *n* 1 person who disagrees with and criticizes the government. ♦ *adj* 2 disagreeing with the government. **dissidence** *n*

dissimilar *adj* not alike, different. **dissimilarity** *n*

dissimulate *v* conceal one's real feelings by pretence. **dissimulation** *n*

dissipate *v* 1 waste or squander. 2 scatter, disappear. **dissipated** *adj* showing signs of overindulgence in alcohol and other physical pleasures. **dissipation** *n*

dissociate *v* regard or treat as separate. **dissociate oneself from** deny or break an association with. **dissociation** *n*

dissolute *adj* leading an immoral life.

dissolution *n* 1 official breaking up of an organization or institution, such as Parliament. 2 official ending of a formal agreement, such as a marriage.

dissolve *v* 1 (cause to) become liquid. 2 break up or end officially. 3 break down emotionally, e.g. *she dissolved into tears.*

dissonance *n* lack of agreement or harmony. **dissonant** *adj*

dissuade *v* deter (someone) by persuasion from doing something. **dissuasion** *n*

distaff *n* rod on which wool etc. is wound for spinning. **distaff side** female side of a family.

distance *n* 1 space between two points. 2 state of being apart. 3 remoteness in manner. **the distance** most distant part of the visible scene. **distance oneself from** separate oneself mentally from. **distant** *adj* 1 far apart. 2 separated by a specified distance. 3 remote in manner. **distantly** *adv*

distaste *n* dislike, disgust. **distasteful**

adj unpleasant, offensive.

distemper[1] *n* highly contagious viral disease of dogs.

distemper[2] *n* paint mixed with water, glue, etc., used for painting walls.

distend *v* (of part of the body) swell. **distension** *n*

distil *v* **-tilling, -tilled 1** subject to or obtain by distillation. **2** give off (a substance) in drops. **3** extract the essence of. **distillation** *n* **1** process of evaporating a liquid and condensing its vapour. **2** (also **distillate**) concentrated essence.

distiller *n* person or company that makes strong alcoholic drink, esp. whisky. **distillery** *n, pl* **-leries** place where a strong alcoholic drink, esp. whisky, is made.

distinct *adj* **1** not the same. **2** easily sensed or understood. **3** clear and definite. **distinctly** *adv* **distinction** *n* **1** act of distinguishing. **2** distinguishing feature. **3** state of being different. **4** special honour, recognition, or fame. **distinctive** *adj* easily recognizable. **distinctively** *adv* **distinctiveness** *n*

distinguish *v* **1** (usu. foll. by *between*) make, show, or recognize a difference (between). **2** be a distinctive feature of. **3** make out by hearing, seeing, etc. **distinguishable** *adj* **distinguished** *adj* **1** dignified in appearance. **2** highly respected.

distort *v* **1** misrepresent (the truth or facts). **2** twist out of shape. **distortion** *n*

distract *v* **1** draw the attention of (a person) away from something. **2** entertain. **distracted** *adj* unable to concentrate, preoccupied. **distraction** *n*

distrait [diss-**tray**] *adj* absent-minded or preoccupied.

distraught [diss-**trawt**] *adj* extremely anxious or agitated.

distress *n* **1** extreme unhappiness. **2** great physical pain. **3** poverty. ♦ *v* **4** upset badly. **distressed** *adj* **1** extremely upset. **2** in financial difficulties. **distressing** *adj* **distressingly** *adv*

distribute *v* **1** hand out or deliver. **2** share out. **distribution** *n* **1** distributing. **2** arrangement or spread. **distributor** *n* **1** wholesaler who distributes goods to retailers in a specific area. **2** device in a petrol engine that sends the electric current to the spark plugs. **distributive** *adj*

district *n* area of land regarded as an administrative or geographical unit. **district court judge** *Aust & NZ* judge presiding over a lower court.

distrust *v* **1** regard as untrustworthy. ♦ *n* **2** feeling of suspicion or doubt. **distrustful** *adj*

disturb *v* **1** intrude on. **2** worry, make anxious. **3** change the position or shape of. **disturbance** *n* **disturbing** *adj* **disturbingly** *adv* **disturbed** *adj* *Psychiatry* emotionally upset or maladjusted.

disunite *v* cause disagreement among. **disunity** *n*

disuse *n* state of being no longer used. **disused** *adj*

ditch *n* **1** narrow channel dug in the earth for drainage or irrigation. ♦ *v* **2** *Slang* abandon.

dither *v* **1** be uncertain or indecisive. ♦ *n* **2** state of indecision or agitation. **ditherer** *n* **dithery** *adj*

ditto *n, pl* **-tos 1** the same. ♦ *adv* **2** in the same way.

ditty *n, pl* **-ties** short simple poem or song.

diuretic [die-yoor-**et**-ik] *n* drug that increases the flow of urine.

diurnal [die-**urn**-al] *adj* happening during the day or daily.

diva *n* distinguished female singer.

divan *n* **1** low backless bed. **2** backless sofa or couch.

dive *v* **diving, dived 1** plunge headfirst into water. **2** (of a submarine or diver) submerge under water. **3** fly in a steep nose-down descending path. **4** move quickly in a specified direction. **5** (foll. by *in* or *into*) start doing (something) enthusiastically. ♦ *n* **6** diving. **7** steep nose-down descent. **8** *Slang* disreputable bar or club. **diver** *n* **1** person who works or explores underwater. **2** person who dives for sport. **dive bomber** military aircraft designed to release bombs during a dive.

diverge *v* **1** separate and go in different directions. **2** deviate (from a prescribed course). **divergence** *n* **divergent** *adj*

divers *adj Old-fashioned* various.

diverse *adj* **1** having variety, assorted. **2** different in kind. **diversity** *n, pl* **-ties 1** quality of being different or varied. **2** range of difference. **diversify** *v* **-fying, -fied** **diversification** *n*

divert *v* **1** change the direction of. **2** entertain, distract the attention of. **diversion** *n* **1** official detour used by traffic when a main route is closed. **2** something that distracts someone's attention. **3** diverting. **4** amusing pastime. **diversionary** *adj*

divest *v* **1** strip (of clothes). **2** deprive (of a role or function).

divide *v* **1** separate into parts. **2** share or be shared out in parts. **3** (cause to) disagree. **4** keep apart, be a boundary between. **5** calculate how many times (one number) can be contained in (another). ♦ *n* **6** division, split. **dividend** *n* **1** sum of money representing part of the profit made, paid by a company to its shareholders.

2 extra benefit. **divider** *n* **1** screen used to divide a room into separate areas. ♦ *pl* **2** compasses with two pointed arms, used for measuring or dividing lines.

divine *adj* **1** of God or a god. **2** godlike. **3** *Informal* splendid. ♦ *v* **4** discover (something) by intuition or guessing. **divinely** *adv* **divination** *n* art of discovering future events, as though by supernatural powers. **divinity** *n* **1** study of religion. **2** *pl* **-ties**) god. **3** state of being divine. **divining rod** forked twig said to move when held over ground in which water or metal is to be found.

division *n* **1** dividing, sharing out. **2** one of the parts into which something is divided. **3** mathematical operation of dividing. **4** difference of opinion. **divisional** *adj* of a division in an organization. **divisible** *adj* **divisibility** *n* **divisive** *adj* tending to cause disagreement. **divisor** *n* number to be divided into another number.

divorce *n* **1** legal ending of a marriage. **2** any separation, esp. a permanent one. ♦ *v* **3** legally end one's marriage (to). **4** separate, consider separately. **divorcée,** (*masc*) **divorcé** *n* person who is divorced.

divulge *v* make known, disclose. *n*

Dixie *n* southern states of the US (also **Dixieland**).

DIY *Brit, Aust & NZ* do-it-yourself.

dizzy *adj* **-zier, -ziest 1** having or causing a whirling sensation. **2** mentally confused. ♦ *v* **-zying, -zied 3** make dizzy. **dizzily** *adv* **dizziness** *n*

DJ 1 disc jockey. **2** *Brit* dinner jacket.

DNA *n* deoxyribonucleic acid, the main constituent of the chromosomes of all living things.

do *v* **does, doing, did, done 1** perform or complete (a deed or action). **2** be adequate, e.g. *that one will do.* **3** suit or improve, e.g. *that style does nothing for you.* **4** find the answer to (a problem or puzzle). **5** cause, produce, e.g. *it does no harm to think ahead.* **6** give, grant, e.g. *do me a favour.* **7** work at, as a course of study or a job. **8** used to form questions, e.g. *how do you know?* **9** used to intensify positive statements and commands, e.g. *I like port; do go on.* **10** used to form negative statements and commands, e.g. *I do not know her well; do not get up.* **11** used to replace an earlier verb, e.g. *he gets paid more than I do.* ♦ *n, pl* **dos, do's 12** *Informal* party, celebration. **do away with** *v* get rid of. **do-it-yourself** *n* constructing and repairing things oneself. **do up** *v* **1** fasten. **2** decorate and repair. **do with** *v* find useful or benefit from, e.g. *I could do with a rest.* **do without** *v* manage without.

Doberman pinscher, Doberman *n* large dog with a black-and-tan coat.

dob in *v* **dobbing, dobbed** *Aust & NZ informal* **1** inform against. **2** contribute to a fund.

DOC (in New Zealand) Department of Conservation.

docile *adj* (of a person or animal) easily controlled. **docilely** *adv* **docility** *n*

dock[1] *n* **1** enclosed area of water where ships are loaded, unloaded, or repaired. ♦ *v* **2** bring or be brought into dock. **3** link (two spacecraft) or (of two spacecraft) be linked together in space. **docker** *n Brit* person employed to load and unload ships. **dockyard** *n* place where ships are built or repaired.

dock[2] *v* **1** deduct money from (a person's wages). **2** remove part of (an animal's tail) by cutting through the bone.

dock[3] *n* enclosed space in a court of law where the accused person sits or stands.

dock[4] *n* weed with broad leaves.

docket *n* label on a package or other delivery, stating contents, delivery instructions, etc.

doctor *n* **1** person licensed to practise medicine. **2** person who has been awarded a doctorate. ♦ *v* **3** alter in order to deceive. **4** poison or drug (food or drink). **5** *Informal* castrate (an animal). **doctoral** *adj* **doctorate** *n* highest academic degree in any field of knowledge.

doctrine *n* **1** body of teachings of a religious, political, or philosophical group. **2** principle or body of principles that is taught or advocated. **doctrinal** *adj* of doctrines. **doctrinaire** *adj* stubbornly insistent on the application of a theory without regard to practicality.

document *n* **1** piece of paper providing an official record of something. ♦ *v* **2** record or report (something) in detail. **3** support (a claim) with evidence. **documentation** *n*

documentary *n, pl* **-ries 1** film or television programme presenting the facts about a particular subject. ♦ *adj* **2** (of evidence) based on documents.

docu-soap *n* television documentary series presenting the lives of the people filmed as entertainment.

dodder *v* move unsteadily. **doddery** *adj*

dodecagon [doe-**deck**-a-gon] *n* geometric figure with twelve sides.

dodge *v* **1** avoid (a blow, being seen, etc.) by moving suddenly. **2** evade by cleverness or trickery. ♦ *n* **3** cunning or deceitful trick. **dodgy** *adj* **dodgier, dodgiest** *Informal* **1** dangerous, risky. **2** untrustworthy.

Dodgem *n* ® small electric car driven and bumped against similar cars in a rink at a funfair.

dodger n person who evades by a responsibility or duty.

dodo n, pl **dodos, dodoes** large flightless extinct bird.

doe n female deer, hare, or rabbit.

does v **third person singular of the present tense of** DO.

doesn't does not.

doff v take off or lift (one's hat) in polite greeting.

dog n **1** domesticated four-legged mammal of many different breeds. **2** related wild mammal, such as the dingo or coyote. **3** male animal of the dog family. **4** Informal person, e.g. you lucky dog! ♦ v **dogging, dogged 5** follow (someone) closely. **6** trouble, plague. **go to the dogs** Informal go to ruin physically or morally. **let sleeping dogs lie** leave things undisturbed. **doggy, doggie** n, pl **-gies** child's word for a dog. **dogcart** n light horse-drawn two-wheeled cart. **dog collar 1** collar for a dog. **2** Informal white collar fastened at the back, worn by members of the clergy. **dog-eared** adj **1** (of a book) having pages folded down at the corner. **2** shabby, worn. **dogfight** n close-quarters combat between fighter aircraft. **dogfish** n small shark. **doghouse** n US kennel. **in the doghouse** Informal in disgrace. **dogleg** n sharp bend. **dog-roll** n NZ sausage-shaped roll of meat processed as dog food. **dog rose** wild rose with pink or white flowers. **dog-tired** adj Informal exhausted.

doge [**doje**] n (formerly) chief magistrate of Venice or Genoa.

dogged [**dog**-gid] adj obstinately determined. **doggedly** adv **doggedness** n

doggerel n poorly written poetry, usu. comic.

doggo adv **lie doggo** Informal hide and keep quiet.

dogma n doctrine or system of doctrines proclaimed by authority as true. **dogmatic** adj habitually stating one's opinions forcefully or arrogantly. **dogmatically** adv **dogmatism** n

dogsbody n, pl **-bodies** Informal person who carries out boring tasks for others.

doily n, pl **-lies** decorative lacy paper mat, laid on a plate.

doldrums pl n **1** depressed state of mind. **2** state of inactivity.

dole n **1** Brit, Aust & NZ informal money received from the state while unemployed. ♦ v **2** (foll. by out) distribute in small quantities.

doleful adj dreary, unhappy. **dolefully** adv

doll n **1** small model of a human being, used as a toy. **2** Slang pretty girl or young woman.

dollar n standard monetary unit of many countries.

dollop n Informal lump (of food).

dolly n, pl **-lies 1** child's word for a doll. **2** wheeled support on which a camera may be moved.

dolman sleeve n sleeve that is very wide at the armhole, tapering to a tight wrist.

dolmen n prehistoric monument consisting of a horizontal stone supported by vertical stones.

dolomite n mineral consisting of calcium magnesium carbonate.

dolorous adj sad, mournful.

dolphin n sea mammal of the whale family, with a beaklike snout. **dolphinarium** n aquarium for dolphins.

dolt n stupid person. **doltish** adj

domain n **1** field of knowledge or activity. **2** land under one ruler or government. **3** *Computers* group of computers with the same name on the Internet. **4** *NZ* public park.

dome *n* **1** rounded roof built on a circular base. **2** something shaped like this. **domed** *adj*

domestic *adj* **1** of one's own country or a specific country. **2** of the home or family. **3** enjoying running a home. **4** (of an animal) kept as a pet or to produce food. ♦ *n* **5** person whose job is to do housework in someone else's house. **domestically** *adv* **domesticity** *n* **domesticate** *v* **1** bring or keep (a wild animal or plant) under control or cultivation. **2** accustom (someone) to home life. **domestication** *n* **domestic science** study of household skills.

domicile [**dom**-miss-ile] *n* place where one lives.

dominant *adj* **1** having authority or influence. **2** main, chief. **dominance** *n*

dominate *v* **1** control or govern. **2** tower above (surroundings). **3** be very significant in. **domination** *n*

domineering *adj* forceful and arrogant.

Dominican *n, adj* (friar or nun) of an order founded by Saint Dominic.

dominion *n* **1** control or authority. **2** land governed by one ruler or government. **3** (formerly) self-governing division of the British Empire.

domino *n, pl* **-noes 1** small rectangular block marked with dots, used in dominoes. ♦ *pl* **2** game in which dominoes with matching halves are laid together.

don[1] *v* **donning, donned** put on (clothing).

don[2] *n* **1** *Brit* member of the teaching staff at a university or college. **2** Spanish gentleman or nobleman. **donnish** *adj* serious and academic.

donate *v* give, esp. to a charity or organization. **donation** *n* **1** donating. **2** thing donated. **donor** *n* **1** *Med* person who gives blood or organs for use in the treatment of another person. **2** person who makes a donation.

done *v* **past participle of** DO

doner kebab *n* see KEBAB.

donga [**dong**-ga] *n* *S Afr, Aust & NZ* steep-sided gully created by soil erosion.

donkey *n* long-eared member of the horse family. **donkey jacket** *Brit, Aust & NZ* man's long thick jacket with a waterproof panel across the shoulders. **donkey's years** *Informal* long time. **donkey-work** *n* tedious hard work.

don't do not.

doodle *v* **1** scribble or draw aimlessly. ♦ *n* **2** shape or picture drawn aimlessly.

doom *n* **1** death or a terrible fate. ♦ *v* **2** destine or condemn to death or a terrible fate. **doomsday** *n* **1** *Christianity* day on which the Last Judgment will occur. **2** any dreaded day.

door *n* **1** hinged or sliding panel for closing the entrance to a building, room, etc. **2** entrance. **doormat** *n* **1** mat for wiping dirt from shoes before going indoors. **2** *Informal* person who offers little resistance to ill-treatment. **doorway** *n* opening into a building or room.

dope *n* **1** *Slang* illegal drug, usu. cannabis. **2** medicine, drug. **3** *Informal* stupid person. ♦ *v* **4** give a drug to, esp. in order to improve performance in a race. **dopey, dopy** *adj* **1** half-asleep, drowsy. **2** *Slang* silly.

dorba *n* *Aust slang* stupid, inept, or clumsy person (also **dorb**).

dork *n* *Slang* stupid person.

dormant *adj* temporarily quiet, inactive, or not being used.

dormancy n

dormer, dormer window n window that sticks out from a sloping roof.

dormitory n, pl **-ries** large room, esp. at a school, containing several beds

dormouse n, pl **-mice** small mouselike rodent with a furry tail.

dorp n S Afr small town.

dorsal adj of or on the back.

dory, John Dory n, pl **-ries** spiny-finned edible sea fish.

dose n **1** specific quantity of a medicine taken at one time. **2** Informal something unpleasant to experience. ♦ v **3** give a dose to. **dosage** n size of a dose.

doss v **doss down** slang sleep in an uncomfortable place. **dosshouse** n Brit & S Afr slang cheap lodging house for homeless people.

dossier [**doss**-ee-ay] n collection of documents about a subject or person.

dot n **1** small round mark. **2** shorter symbol used in Morse code. ♦ v **dotting, dotted 3** mark with a dot. **4** scatter, spread around. **on the dot** at exactly the arranged time. **dotty** adj Slang rather eccentric. **dotcom, dot.com** n company that does most of its business on the Internet.

dote v **dote on** love to an excessive degree. **dotage** n weakness as a result of old age.

double adj **1** as much again in number, amount, size, etc. **2** composed of two equal or similar parts. **3** designed for two users, e.g. double room. **4** folded in two. ♦ adv **5** twice over. ♦ n **6** twice the number, amount, size, etc. **7** person who looks almost exactly like another. ♦ pl **8** game between two pairs of players. ♦ v **9** make or become twice as much or as many. **10** bend or fold (material etc.). **11** play two parts. **12** turn sharply. **at, on the double** quickly or

immediately. **doubly** adv **double agent** spy employed by two enemy countries at the same time. **double bass** stringed instrument, largest and lowest member of the violin family. **double chin** fold of fat under the chin. **double cream** Brit thick cream with a high fat content. **double-cross** v **1** cheat or betray. ♦ n **2** double-crossing. **double-dealing** n treacherous or deceitful behaviour. **double-decker** n bus with two passenger decks one on top of the other. **double Dutch** Informal incomprehensible talk, gibberish. **double glazing** two panes of glass in a window, fitted to reduce heat loss. **double talk** deceptive or ambiguous talk. **double whammy** Informal devastating setback made up of two elements.

double entendre [**doob**-bl on-**tond**-ra] n word or phrase that can be interpreted in two ways, one of which is rude.

doublet [**dub**-lit] n Hist man's close-fitting jacket, with or without sleeves.

doubloon n former Spanish gold coin.

doubt n **1** uncertainty about the truth, facts, or existence of something. **2** unresolved difficulty or point. ♦ v **3** question the truth of. **4** distrust or be suspicious of (someone). **doubter** n **doubtful** adj **1** unlikely. **2** feeling doubt. **doubtfully** adv **doubtless** adv probably or certainly.

> ☑ **WORD TIP**
> If doubt is followed by a clause it is connected by whether: I doubt whether she means it. If it is used with a negative it is followed by that: I don't doubt that he is sincere.

douche [**doosh**] n **1** (instrument for

applying) a stream of water directed onto or into the body for cleansing or medical purposes. ♦ *v* **2** cleanse or treat by means of a douche.

dough *n* **1** thick mixture of flour and water or milk, used for making bread etc. **2** *Slang* money. **doughnut** *n* small cake of sweetened dough fried in deep fat.

doughty [**dowt**-ee] *adj* **-tier, -tiest** *Old-fashioned* brave and determined.

dour [**doo**-er] *adj* sullen and unfriendly. **dourness** *n*

douse [rhymes with **mouse**] *v* **1** drench with water or other liquid. **2** put out (a light).

dove *n* **1** bird with a heavy body, small head, and short legs. **2** *Politics* person opposed to war. **dovecote, dovecot** *n* structure for housing pigeons.

dovetail *n* **1** joint containing wedge-shaped tenons. ♦ *v* **2** fit together neatly.

dowager *n* widow possessing property or a title obtained from her husband.

dowdy *adj* **-dier, -diest** dull and old-fashioned. **dowdiness** *n*

dowel *n* wooden or metal peg that fits into two corresponding holes to join two adjacent parts.

dower *n* life interest in a part of her husband's estate allotted to a widow by law.

down[1] *prep, adv* **1** indicating movement to or position in a lower place. ♦ *adv* **2** indicating completion of an action, lessening of intensity, etc., e.g. *drink down.* ♦ *adj* **3** depressed, unhappy. ♦ *v* **4** *Informal* drink quickly. **have a down on** *Informal* feel hostile towards. **down under** *Informal* (in or to) Australia or New Zealand. **downward** *adj, adv* (descending) from a higher to a lower level, condition, or position. **downwards** *adv* from a higher to a lower level, condition, or

position. **down-and-out** *n* **1** person who is homeless and destitute. ♦ *adj* **2** without any means of support. **down-to-earth** *adj* sensible or practical.

down[2] *n* soft fine feathers. **downy** *adj*

downbeat *adj* **1** *Informal* gloomy. **2** *Brit, Aust & NZ* relaxed.

downcast *adj* **1** sad, dejected. **2** (of the eyes) directed downwards.

downfall *n* (cause of) a sudden loss of position or reputation.

downgrade *v* reduce in importance or value.

downhearted *adj* sad and discouraged.

downhill *adj* **1** going or sloping down. ♦ *adv* **2** towards the bottom of a hill.

download *v* transfer (data) from the memory of one computer to that of another.

downpour *n* heavy fall of rain.

downright *adj, adv* extreme(ly).

downs *pl n* low grassy hills, esp. in S England.

Down's syndrome *n* genetic disorder characterized by a flat face, slanting eyes, and mental retardation.

downstairs *adv* **1** to or on a lower floor. ♦ *n* **2** lower or ground floor.

downtrodden *adj* oppressed and lacking the will to resist.

dowry *n, pl* **-ries** property brought by a woman to her husband at marriage.

dowse [rhymes with **cows**] *v* search for underground water or minerals using a divining rod.

doxology *n, pl* **-gies** short hymn of praise to God.

doyen [**doy**-en] *n* senior member of a group, profession, or society. **doyenne** [doy-**en**] *n fem*

doze *v* **1** sleep lightly or briefly. ♦ *n* **2** short sleep. **dozy** *adj* **dozier, doziest 1** feeling sleepy. **2** *Informal* stupid.

doze off v fall into a light sleep.

dozen adj, n twelve. **dozenth** adj

DPB (in New Zealand) Domestic Purposes Benefit.

DPP (in Britain) Director of Public Prosecutions.

Dr 1 Doctor. **2** Drive.

drab adj **drabber, drabbest** dull and dreary. **drabness** n

drachm [**dram**] n Brit one eighth of a fluid ounce.

drachma n, pl **-mas, -mae** former monetary unit of Greece.

draconian adj severe, harsh.

draft n **1** plan, sketch, or drawing of something. **2** preliminary outline of a book, speech, etc. **3** written order for payment of money by a bank. **4** US & Aust selection for compulsory military service. ♦ v **5** draw up an outline or plan of. **6** send (people) from one place to another to do a specific job. **7** US & Aust select for compulsory military service.

drag v **dragging, dragged 1** pull with force, esp. along the ground. **2** trail on the ground. **3** persuade or force (oneself or someone else) to go somewhere. **4** (foll. by on or out) last or be prolonged tediously. **5** search (a river) with a dragnet or hook. **6** Computers move (an image) on the screen by use of the mouse. ♦ n **7** person or thing that slows up progress. **8** Informal tedious thing or person. **9** Slang women's clothes worn by a man. **dragnet** n net used to scour the bottom of a pond or river to search for something. **drag race** race in which specially built cars or motorcycles are timed over a measured course.

dragon n **1** mythical fire-breathing monster like a huge lizard. **2** Informal fierce woman. **dragonfly** n brightly coloured insect with a long slender body and two pairs of wings.

dragoon n **1** heavily armed cavalryman. ♦ v **2** coerce, force.

drain n **1** pipe or channel that carries off water or sewage. **2** cause of a continuous reduction in energy or resources. ♦ v **3** draw off or remove liquid from. **4** flow away or filter off. **5** drink the entire contents of a (glass or cup). **6** make constant demands on (energy or resources), exhaust. **drainage** n **1** system of drains. **2** process or method of draining.

drake n male duck.

dram n **1** small amount of a strong alcoholic drink, esp. whisky. **2** one sixteenth of an ounce.

drama n **1** serious play for theatre, television, or radio. **2** writing, producing, or acting in plays. **3** situation that is exciting or highly emotional. **dramatic** adj **1** of or like drama. **2** behaving flamboyantly. **dramatically** adv **dramatist** n person who writes plays. **dramatize** v **1** rewrite (a book) in the form of a play. **2** express (something) in a dramatic or exaggerated way. **dramatization** n

drank v past tense of DRINK.

drape v **1** cover with material, usu. in folds. **2** place casually. ♦ n **3** Aust, US & Canadian piece of cloth hung at a window or opening as a screen. **drapery** n, pl **-peries 1** fabric or clothing arranged and draped. **2** fabrics and cloth collectively.

draper n Brit person who sells fabrics and sewing materials.

drastic adj strong and severe.

draught n **1** current of cold air, esp. in an enclosed space. **2** portion of liquid to be drunk, esp. medicine. **3** gulp or swallow. **4** one of the flat discs used in the game of draughts. ♦ pl **5** game for two players using a chessboard and twelve draughts each. ♦ adj **6** (of an

animal) used for pulling heavy loads.
draughty adj exposed to draughts of
air. **draughtsman** n person employed
to prepare detailed scale drawings of
machinery, buildings, etc.
draughtsmanship n **draught beer**
beer stored in a cask.

draw v **drawing, drew, drawn 1**
sketch (a figure, picture, etc.) with a
pencil or pen. **2** pull (a person or
thing) closer to or further away from a
place. **3** move in a specified direction,
e.g. *the car drew near*. **4** take from a
source, e.g. *draw money from bank
accounts*. **5** attract, interest. **6**
formulate or decide, e.g. *to draw
conclusions*. **7** (of two teams or
contestants) finish a game with an
equal number of points. ♦ n **8** raffle or
lottery. **9** contest or game ending in a
tie. **10** event, act, etc., that attracts a
large audience. **drawing** n **1** picture
or plan made by means of lines on a
surface. **2** art of making drawings.
drawing pin short tack with a broad
smooth head. **drawing room**
Old-fashioned room where visitors are
received and entertained. **drawback**
n disadvantage. **drawbridge** n bridge
that may be raised to prevent access
or to enable vessels to pass. **draw out**
v **1** encourage (someone) to talk freely.
2 make longer. **drawstring** n cord
run through a hem around an
opening, so that when it is pulled
tighter, the opening closes. **draw up**
v **1** prepare and write out (a contract).
2 (of a vehicle) come to a stop.

drawer n **1** sliding box-shaped part of
a piece of furniture, used for storage.
♦ pl **2** *Old-fashioned* undergarment
worn on the lower part of the body.

drawl v **1** speak slowly, with long vowel
sounds. ♦ n **2** drawling manner of
speech.

drawn v **1** past participle of DRAW. ♦ adj

2 haggard, tired, or tense in
appearance.

dray n low cart used for carrying heavy
loads.

dread v **1** anticipate with apprehension
or fear. ♦ n **2** great fear. **dreadful** adj
1 very disagreeable or shocking. **2**
extreme. **dreadfully** adv

dreadlocks pl n hair worn in the
Rastafarian style of tightly twisted
strands.

dream n **1** imagined series of events
experienced in the mind while asleep.
2 cherished hope. **3** *Informal*
wonderful person or thing. ♦ v
dreaming, dreamed or **dreamt 4** see
imaginary pictures in the mind while
asleep. **5** (often foll. by *of* or *about*)
have an image (of) or fantasy (about).
6 (foll. by *of*) consider the possibility
(of). ♦ adj **7** ideal, e.g. *a dream house*.
dreamer n **dreamy** adj **1** vague or
impractical. **2** *Informal* wonderful.
dreamily adv

dreary adj **drearier, dreariest** dull,
boring. **drearily** adv **dreariness** n

dredge¹ v clear or search (a river bed
or harbour) by removing silt or mud.
dredger n boat fitted with machinery
for dredging.

dredge² v sprinkle (food) with flour etc.

dregs pl n **1** solid particles that settle at
the bottom of some liquids. **2** most
despised elements.

drench v make completely wet.

dress n **1** one-piece garment for a
woman or girl, consisting of a skirt and
bodice and sometimes sleeves. **2**
complete style of clothing. ♦ v **3** put
clothes on. **4** put on formal clothes. **5**
apply a protective covering to (a
wound). **6** arrange or prepare.
dressing n **1** sauce for salad. **2**
covering for a wound.
dressing-down n *Informal* severe
scolding. **dressing gown**

coat-shaped garment worn over pyjamas or nightdress. **dressing room** room used for changing clothes, esp. backstage in a theatre. **dressy** *adj* (of clothes) elegant. **dress circle** first gallery in a theatre. **dressmaker** *n* person who makes women's clothes. **dressmaking** *n* **dress rehearsal** last rehearsal of a play or show, using costumes, lighting, etc.

dressage [**dress**-ahzh] *n* training of a horse to perform manoeuvres in response to the rider's body signals.

dresser[1] *n* piece of furniture with shelves and with cupboards, for storing or displaying dishes.

dresser[2] *n* *Theatre* person employed to assist actors with their costumes.

drew *v* past tense of DRAW.

drey *n* squirrel's nest.

dribble *v* 1 (allow to) flow in drops. 2 allow saliva to trickle from the mouth. 3 *Sport* propel (a ball) by repeatedly tapping it with the foot, hand, or a stick. ♦ *n* 4 small quantity of liquid falling in drops. **dribbler** *n*

dried *v* past of DRY.

drier[1] *adj* a comparative of DRY.

drier[2] *n* same as DRYER.

driest *adj* a superlative of DRY.

drift *v* 1 be carried along by currents of air or water. 2 move aimlessly from one place or activity to another. 3 *n* 4 something piled up by the wind or current, such as a snowdrift. 5 general movement or development. 6 point, meaning, e.g. *catch my drift?* **drifter** *n* person who moves aimlessly from place to place or job to job. **driftwood** *n* wood floating on or washed ashore by the sea.

drill[1] *n* 1 tool or machine for boring holes. 2 strict and often repetitive training. 3 *Informal* correct procedure. ♦ *v* 4 bore a hole in (something) with or as if with a drill. 5 teach by rigorous

exercises or training.

drill[2] *n* 1 machine for sowing seed in rows. 2 small furrow for seed.

drill[3] *n* hard-wearing cotton cloth.

drily *adv* see DRY.

drink *v* **drinking, drank, drunk** 1 swallow (a liquid). 2 consume alcohol, esp. to excess. ♦ *n* 3 (portion of) a liquid suitable for drinking. 4 alcohol, or its habitual or excessive consumption. **drinkable** *adj* **drinker** *n* **drink in** *v* pay close attention to. **drink to** *v* drink a toast to.

drip *v* **dripping, dripped** 1 (let) fall in drops. ♦ *n* 2 falling of drops of liquid. 3 sound made by falling drops. 4 *Informal* weak dull person. 5 *Med* device by which a solution is passed in small drops through a tube into a vein. **drip-dry** *adj* denoting clothing that will dry free of creases if hung up when wet.

dripping *n* fat that comes from meat while it is being roasted or fried.

drive *v* **driving, drove, driven** 1 guide the movement of (a vehicle). 2 transport in a vehicle. 3 goad into a specified state. 4 push or propel. 5 *Sport* hit (a ball) very hard and straight. 6 *n* 7 journey by car, van, etc. 8 (also **driveway**) path for vehicles connecting a building to a public road. 9 united effort towards a common goal. 10 energy and ambition. 11 *Psychol* motive or interest, e.g. *sex drive.* 12 means by which power is transmitted in a mechanism. **drive at** *v* *Informal* intend or mean, e.g. *what was he driving at?* **drive-in** *adj, n* (denoting) a cinema, restaurant, etc., used by people in their cars.

drivel *n* 1 foolish talk. ♦ *v* **-elling, -elled** 2 speak foolishly.

driver *n* person who drives a vehicle.

drizzle *n* 1 very light rain. ♦ *v* 2 rain

lightly. **drizzly** adj

droll adj quaintly amusing. **drolly** adv **drollery** n

dromedary [**drom**-mid-er-ee] n, pl **-daries** camel with a single hump.

drone[1] n male bee.

drone[2] v, n (make) a monotonous low dull sound. **drone on** v talk for a long time in a monotonous tone.

drongo n, pl **-gos** tropical songbird with a glossy black plumage, a forked tail, and a stout bill.

drool v 1 (foll. by over) show excessive enthusiasm (for). 2 allow saliva to flow from the mouth.

droop v hang downwards loosely. **droopy** adj

drop v **dropping, dropped** 1 (allow to) fall vertically. 2 decrease in amount, strength, or value. 3 mention (a hint or name) casually. 4 discontinue. ♦ n 5 small quantity of liquid forming a round shape. 6 any small quantity of liquid. 7 decrease in amount, strength, or value. 8 vertical distance that something may fall. ♦ pl 9 liquid medication applied in small drops. **droplet** n **droppings** pl n faeces of certain animals, such as rabbits or birds. **drop in, by** v pay someone a casual visit. **drop off** v 1 Informal fall asleep. 2 grow smaller or less. **dropout** n 1 person who rejects conventional society. 2 person who does not complete a course of study. **drop out (of)** v abandon or withdraw from (a school, job, etc.).

dropsy n illness in which watery fluid collects in the body.

dross n 1 scum formed on the surfaces of molten metals. 2 anything worthless.

drought n prolonged shortage of rainfall.

drove[1] v past tense of DRIVE.

drove[2] n very large group, esp. of people. **drover** n person who drives

sheep or cattle.

drown v 1 die or kill by immersion in liquid. 2 forget (one's sorrows) temporarily by drinking alcohol. 3 drench thoroughly. 4 make (a sound) inaudible by being louder.

drowse v be sleepy, dull, or sluggish. **drowsy** adj **drowsily** adv **drowsiness** n

drubbing n utter defeat in a contest etc.

drudge n person who works hard at uninteresting tasks. **drudgery** n

drug n 1 substance used in the treatment or prevention of disease. 2 chemical substance, esp. a narcotic, taken for the effects it produces. ♦ v **drugging, drugged** 3 give a drug to (a person or animal) to cause sleepiness or unconsciousness. 4 mix a drug with (food or drink). **drugstore** n US pharmacy where a wide range of goods are available.

Druid n member of an ancient order of Celtic priests. **Druidic, Druidical** adj

drum n 1 percussion instrument sounded by striking a membrane stretched across the opening of a hollow cylinder. 2 cylindrical object or container. ♦ v **drumming, drummed** 3 play (music) on a drum. 4 tap rhythmically or regularly. **drum into** v instil into (someone) by constant repetition. **drumstick** n 1 stick used for playing a drum. 2 lower joint of the leg of a cooked chicken etc. **drum up** v obtain (support or business) by making requests or canvassing.

drummer n person who plays a drum or drums.

drunk v 1 past participle of DRINK. ♦ adj 2 intoxicated with alcohol to the extent of losing control over normal functions. 3 overwhelmed by a strong influence or emotion. ♦ n 4 person who is drunk or who frequently gets drunk. **drunkard** *n* person who frequently gets drunk. **drunken** *adj* **1** drunk or frequently drunk. **2** caused by or relating to alcoholic intoxication. **drunkenly** *adv* **drunkenness** *n*

dry *adj* **drier, driest** *or* **dryer, dryest 1** lacking moisture. **2** having little or no rainfall. **3** *Informal* thirsty. **4** (of wine) not sweet. **5** uninteresting. **6** (of humour) subtle and sarcastic. **7** prohibiting the sale of alcohol, e.g. *a dry town.* ♦ *v* **drying, dried 8** make or become dry. **9** preserve (food) by removing the moisture. **drily, dryly** *adv* **dryness** *n* **dryer** *n* apparatus for removing moisture. **dry-clean** *v* clean (clothes etc.) with chemicals rather than water. **dry-cleaner** *n* **dry-cleaning** *n* **dry out** *v* **1** make or become dry. **2** (cause to) undergo treatment for alcoholism. **dry rot** crumbling and drying of timber, caused by certain fungi. **dry run** *Informal* rehearsal. **dry stock** *NZ* cattle raised for meat.

dryad *n* wood nymph.

DSS (in Britain) Department of Social Security.

dual *adj* having two parts, functions, or aspects. **duality** *n* **dual carriageway** *Brit, Aust & NZ* road on which traffic travelling in opposite directions is separated by a central strip of grass or concrete.

dub¹ *v* **dubbing, dubbed** give (a person or place) a name or nickname.

dub² *v* **dubbing, dubbed 1** provide (a film) with a new soundtrack, esp. in a different language. **2** provide (a film or tape) with a soundtrack.

dubbin *n Brit* thick grease applied to leather to soften and waterproof it.

dubious [**dew**-bee-uss] *adj* feeling or causing doubt. **dubiously** *adv* **dubiety** [dew-**by**-it-ee] *n*

ducal [**duke**-al] *adj* of a duke.

ducat [**duck**-it] *n* former European gold or silver coin.

duchess *n* **1** woman who holds the rank of duke. **2** wife or widow of a duke.

duchesse *n NZ* dressing table with a mirror.

duchy *n, pl* **duchies** territory of a duke or duchess.

duck¹ *n* **1** water bird with short legs, webbed feet, and a broad blunt bill. **2** its flesh, used as food. **3** female of this bird. **4** *Cricket* score of nothing. **duckling** *n* baby duck.

duck² *v* **1** move (the head or body) quickly downwards, to avoid being seen or to dodge a blow. **2** plunge suddenly under water. **3** *Informal* dodge (a duty or responsibility).

duct *n* **1** tube, pipe, or channel through which liquid or gas is conveyed. **2** bodily passage conveying secretions or excretions.

ductile *adj* (of a metal) able to be shaped into sheets or wires.

dud *Informal* ♦ *n* **1** ineffectual person or thing. ♦ *adj* **2** bad or useless.

dude *n US informal* **1** man. **2** *Old-fashioned* dandy. **3** any person.

dudgeon *n* **in high dudgeon** angry, resentful.

due *adj* **1** expected or scheduled to be present or arrive. **2** owed as a debt. **3** fitting, proper. ♦ *n* **4** something that is owed or required. ♦ *pl* **5** charges for membership of a club or organization. ♦ *adv* **6** directly or exactly, e.g. *due south.* **due to** attributable to or caused by.

☑ **WORD TIP**
The use of *due to* as a compound preposition as in *the performance has been cancelled due to bad weather* was formerly considered incorrect, but is now acceptable.

duel n 1 formal fight with deadly weapons between two people, to settle a quarrel. ♦ v **duelling, duelled** 2 fight in a duel. **duellist** n

duet n piece of music for two performers.

duff adj Chiefly Brit broken or useless. **duff up** v Brit informal beat (someone) severely.

duffel, duffle n short for DUFFEL COAT. **duffel bag** cylindrical canvas bag fastened with a drawstring. **duffel coat** wool coat with toggle fastenings, usu. with a hood.

duffer n Informal dull or incompetent person.

dug[1] v past of DIG.

dug[2] n teat or udder.

dugite [**doo**-gyte] n medium-sized Australian venomous snake.

dugong n whalelike mammal of tropical waters.

dugout n 1 Brit (at a sports ground) covered bench where managers and substitutes sit. 2 canoe made by hollowing out a log. 3 Mil covered excavation to provide shelter.

duke n 1 nobleman of the highest rank. 2 prince or ruler of a small principality or duchy. **dukedom** n

dulcet [**dull**-sit] adj (of a sound) soothing or pleasant.

dulcimer n tuned percussion instrument consisting of a set of strings stretched over a sounding board and struck with hammers.

dull adj 1 not interesting. 2 (of an ache) not acute. 3 (of weather) not bright or clear. 4 lacking in spirit. 5 not very intelligent. 6 (of a blade) not sharp. ♦ v 7 make or become dull. **dullness** n **dully** adv **dullard** n dull or stupid person.

duly adv 1 in a proper manner. 2 at the proper time.

dumb adj 1 lacking the power to speak. 2 silent. 3 Informal stupid. **dumbly** adv **dumbness** n **dumbbell** n short bar with a heavy ball or disc at each end, used for physical exercise. **dumbfounded** adj speechless with astonishment. **dumb down** make less intellectually demanding or sophisticated. **dumb show** meaningful gestures without speech.

dumdum n soft-nosed bullet that expands on impact and causes serious wounds.

dummy n, pl -mies 1 figure representing the human form, used for displaying clothes etc. 2 copy of an object, often lacking some essential feature of the original. 3 rubber teat for a baby to suck. 4 Slang stupid person. ♦ adj 5 imitation, substitute. **dummy run** rehearsal.

dump v 1 drop or let fall in a careless manner. 2 Informal get rid of (someone or something no longer wanted). 3 n 4 place where waste materials are left. 5 Informal dirty unattractive place. 6 Mil place where weapons or supplies are stored. **down in the dumps** Informal depressed and miserable.

dumpling n 1 small ball of dough cooked and served with stew. 2 round pastry case filled with fruit.

dumpy adj **dumpier, dumpiest** short and plump.

dun adj brownish-grey.

dunce n person who is stupid or slow to learn.

dunderhead n slow-witted person.

dune n mound or ridge of drifted sand.

dung n faeces from animals such as cattle.

dungarees pl n trousers with a bib attached.

dungeon n underground prison cell.

dunk v 1 dip (a biscuit or bread) in a

drink or soup before eating it. **2** put (something) in liquid.

dunny n, pl **-nies** Aust & old-fashioned NZ informal toilet.

duo n, pl **duos 1** pair of performers. **2** Informal pair of closely connected people.

duodenum [dew-oh-**deen**-um] n, pl **-na, -nums** first part of the small intestine, just below the stomach. **duodenal** adj

dupe v **1** deceive or cheat. ♦ n **2** person who is easily deceived.

duple adj Music having two beats in a bar.

duplex n Chiefly US apartment on two floors

duplicate adj **1** copied exactly from an original. ♦ n **2** exact copy. ♦ v **3** make an exact copy of. **4** do again (something that has already been done). **duplication** n **duplicator** n

duplicity n deceitful behaviour.

durable adj long-lasting. **durability** n **durable goods, durables** pl n goods that require infrequent replacement.

duration n length of time that something lasts.

duress n compulsion by use of force or threats.

during prep throughout or within the limit of (a period of time).

dusk n time just before nightfall, when it is almost dark. **dusky** adj **1** dark in colour. **2** shadowy.

dust n **1** small dry particles of earth, sand, or dirt. ♦ v **2** remove dust from (furniture) by wiping. **3** sprinkle (something) with a powdery substance. **duster** n cloth used for dusting. **dusty** adj covered with dust. **dustbin** n large container for household rubbish. **dust bowl** dry area in which the surface soil is exposed to wind erosion. **dust jacket** removable paper cover used to protect

a book. **dustman** n Brit man whose job is to collect household rubbish. **dustpan** n short-handled shovel into which dust is swept from floors.

Dutch adj of the Netherlands. **go Dutch** Informal share the expenses on an outing. **Dutch courage** false courage gained from drinking alcohol.

duty n, pl **-ties 1** work or a task performed as part of one's job. **2** task that a person feels morally bound to do. **3** government tax on imports. **on duty** at work. **dutiable** adj (of goods) requiring payment of duty. **dutiful** adj doing what is expected. **dutifully** adv

duvet [**doo**-vay] n kind of quilt used in bed instead of a top sheet and blankets.

DVD Digital Versatile (or Video) Disk.

DVT deep-vein thrombosis.

dwang n NZ & S Afr short piece of wood inserted in a timber-framed wall.

dwarf n, pl **dwarfs, dwarves 1** person who is smaller than average. **2** (in folklore) small ugly manlike creature, often possessing magical powers. ♦ adj **3** (of an animal or plant) much smaller than the usual size for the species. ♦ v **4** cause (someone or something) to seem small by being much larger.

dwell v **dwelling, dwelt** or **dwelled** live, reside. **dwelling** n place of residence. **dwell on, upon** v think, speak, or write at length about.

dweller n person who lives in a specified place, e.g. city dweller.

dwindle v grow less in size, strength, or number.

dye n **1** colouring substance. **2** colour produced by dyeing. ♦ v **dyeing, dyed 3** colour (hair or fabric) by applying a dye. **dyer** n **dyed-in-the-wool** adj uncompromising or unchanging in opinion.

dying *v* present participle of DIE¹.

dyke¹ *n* wall built to prevent flooding.

dyke² *n Slang* lesbian.

dynamic *adj* **1** full of energy, ambition, and new ideas. **2** *Physics* of energy or forces that produce motion. **dynamically** *adv* **dynamism** *n* great energy and enthusiasm.

dynamics *n* **1** branch of mechanics concerned with the forces that change or produce the motions of bodies. ◆ *pl* **2** forces that produce change in a system.

dynamite *n* **1** explosive made of nitroglycerine. **2** *Informal* dangerous or exciting person or thing. ◆ *v* **3** blow (something) up with dynamite.

dynamo *n, pl* **-mos** device for converting mechanical energy into electrical energy.

dynasty *n, pl* **-ties** sequence of hereditary rulers. **dynastic** *adj*

dysentery *n* infection of the intestine causing severe diarrhoea.

dysfunction *n Med* disturbance or abnormality in the function of an organ or part. **dysfunctional** *adj*

dyslexia *n* disorder causing impaired ability to read. **dyslexic** *adj*

dysmenorrhoea *n* painful menstruation.

dyspepsia *n* indigestion. **dyspeptic** *adj*

dystrophy [**diss**-trof-fee] *n* see MUSCULAR DYSTROPHY.

E e

E 1 East(ern). ♦ *n, pl* **Es** *or* **E's 2** *Slang* ecstasy (the drug).

e- *prefix* electronic, e.g. *e-mail.*

each *adj, pron* every (one) taken separately.

eager *adj* showing or feeling great desire, keen. **eagerly** *adv* **eagerness** *n*

eagle *n* **1** large bird of prey with keen eyesight. **2** *Golf* score of two strokes under par for a hole. **eaglet** *n* young eagle.

ear¹ *n* **1** organ of hearing, esp. the external part of it. **2** sensitivity to musical or other sounds. **earache** *n* pain in the ear. **earbash** *v Aust & NZ informal* talk incessantly. **earbashing** *n* **eardrum** *n* thin piece of skin inside the ear which enables one to hear sounds. **earmark** *v* set (something) aside for a specific purpose. **earphone** *n* receiver for a radio etc., held to or put in the ear. **earring** *n* ornament for the lobe of the ear. **earshot** *n* hearing range.

ear² *n* head of corn.

earl *n* British nobleman ranking next below a marquess. **earldom** *n*

early *adj, adv* **-lier, -liest 1** before the expected or usual time. **2** in the first part of a period. **3** in a period far back in time.

earn *v* **1** obtain by work or merit. **2** (of investments etc.) gain (interest). **earnings** *pl n* money earned.

earnest¹ *adj* serious and sincere. **in earnest** seriously. **earnestly** *adv*

earnest² *n* part payment given in advance, esp. to confirm a contract.

earth *n* **1** planet that we live on. **2** land, the ground. **3** soil. **4** fox's hole. **5** wire connecting an electrical apparatus with the earth. ♦ *v* **6** connect (a circuit) to earth. **earthen** *adj* made of baked clay or earth. **earthenware** *n* pottery made of baked clay. **earthly** *adj* conceivable or possible. **earthy** *adj* **1** coarse or crude. **2** of or like earth. **earthquake** *n* violent vibration of the earth's surface. **earthwork** *n* fortification made of earth. **earthworm** *n* worm which burrows in the soil.

earwig *n* small insect with a pincer-like tail.

ease *n* **1** freedom from difficulty, discomfort, or worry. **2** rest or leisure. ♦ *v* **3** give bodily or mental ease to. **4** lessen (severity, tension, pain, etc.). **5** move carefully or gradually.

easel *n* frame to support an artist's canvas or a blackboard.

east *n* **1** (direction towards) the part of the horizon where the sun rises. **2** region lying in this direction. ♦ *adj* **3** to or in the east. **4** (of a wind) from the east. ♦ *adv* **5** in, to, or towards the east. **easterly** *adj* **eastern** *adj* **eastward** *adj, adv* **eastwards** *adv*

Easter *n* Christian spring festival commemorating the Resurrection of Jesus Christ. **Easter egg** chocolate egg given at Easter.

easy *adj* **easier, easiest 1** not needing much work or effort. **2** free from pain, care, or anxiety. **3** easy-going. **easily** *adv* **easiness** *n* **easy chair** comfortable armchair. **easy-going** *adj* relaxed in attitude, tolerant.

eat *v* **eating, ate, eaten 1** take (food) into the mouth and swallow it. **2** have a meal. **3** (foll. by *away* or *up*) destroy. **eatable** *adj* fit or suitable for eating.

eau de Cologne [**oh** de kol-**lone**] *n*

French light perfume.

eaves *pl n* overhanging edges of a roof.

eavesdrop *v* **-dropping, -dropped** listen secretly to a private conversation. **eavesdropper** *n* **eavesdropping** *n*

ebb *v* **1** (of tide water) flow back. **2** fall away or decline. ♦ *n* **3** flowing back of the tide. **at a low ebb** in a state of weakness.

ebony *n, pl* **-onies 1** hard black wood. ♦ *adj* **2** deep black.

ebullient *adj* full of enthusiasm or excitement. **ebullience** *n*

EC 1 European Commission. **2** European Community: a former name for the European Union.

eccentric *adj* **1** odd or unconventional. **2** (of circles) not having the same centre. ♦ *n* **3** eccentric person. **eccentrically** *adv* **eccentricity** *n*

ecclesiastic *n* **1** member of the clergy. ♦ *adj* **2** (also **ecclesiastical**) of the Christian Church or clergy.

ECG electrocardiogram.

echelon [**esh**-a-lon] *n* **1** level of power or responsibility. **2** *Mil* formation in which units follow one another but are spaced out sideways to allow each a line of fire ahead.

echidna [ik-**kid**-na] *n, pl* **-nas, -nae** [-nee] Australian spiny egg-laying mammal (also **spiny anteater**).

echo *n, pl* **-oes 1** repetition of sounds by reflection of sound waves off a surface. **2** close imitation. ♦ *v* **-oing, -oed 3** repeat or be repeated as an echo. **4** imitate (what someone else has said). **echo sounder** sonar.

éclair *n* finger-shaped pastry filled with cream and covered with chocolate.

éclat [ake-**lah**] *n* **1** brilliant success. **2** splendour.

eclectic *adj* selecting from various styles, ideas, or sources. **eclecticism** *n*

eclipse *n* **1** temporary obscuring of one star or planet by another. ♦ *v* **2** surpass or outclass. **ecliptic** *n* apparent path of the sun.

ecological *adj* **1** of ecology. **2** intended to protect the environment. **ecologically** *adv* **ecology** *n* study of the relationships between living things and their environment. **ecologist** *n*

e-commerce, ecommerce *n* business transactions done on the Internet.

economy *n, pl* **-mies 1** system of interrelationship of money, industry, and employment in a country. **2** careful use of money or resources to avoid waste. **economic** *adj* **1** of economics. **2** profitable. **3** *Informal* inexpensive or cheap. **economics** *n* **1** social science concerned with the production and consumption of goods and services. ♦ *pl* **2** financial aspects. **economical** *adj* not wasteful, thrifty. **economically** *adv* **economist** *n* specialist in economics. **economize** *v* reduce expense or waste.

ecosystem *n* system involving interactions between a community and its environment.

ecru *adj* pale creamy-brown.

ecstasy *n* **1** state of intense delight. **2** *Slang* powerful drug that can produce hallucinations. **ecstatic** *adj* **ecstatically** *adv*

> ☑ **SPELLING TIP**
> People get confused about how many *c*s there are in **ecstasy**. The Bank of English has 119 occurrences of *ecstacy*, but 3379 of the correct spelling **ecstasy**.

ectoplasm *n* *Spiritualism* substance that supposedly is emitted from the body of a medium during a trance.

ecumenical *adj* of the Christian

Church throughout the world, esp. with regard to its unity.

eczema [ek-sim-a] *n* skin disease causing intense itching.

Edam *n* round Dutch cheese with a red waxy cover.

eddy *n, pl* **eddies 1** circular movement of air, water, etc. ♦ *v* **eddying, eddied 2** move with a circular motion.

edelweiss [ade-el-vice] *n* alpine plant with white flowers.

Eden *n Bible* garden in which Adam and Eve were placed at the Creation.

edge *n* **1** border or line where something ends or begins. **2** cutting side of a blade. **3** sharpness of tone. ♦ *v* **4** provide an edge or border for. **5** push (one's way) gradually. **have the edge on** have an advantage over. **on edge** nervous or irritable. **edgeways** *adv* with the edge forwards or uppermost. **edging** *n* anything placed along an edge to finish it. **edgy** *adj* nervous or irritable.

edible *adj* fit to be eaten. **edibility** *n*

edict [ee-dikt] *n* order issued by an authority.

edifice [ed-if-iss] *n* large building.

edify [ed-if-fie] *v* **-fying, -fied** improve morally by instruction. **edification** *n*

edit *v* prepare (a book, film, etc.) for publication or broadcast. **edition** *n* number of copies of a new publication printed at one time. **editor** *n* **1** person who edits. **2** person in charge of one section of a newspaper or magazine. **editorial** *n* **1** newspaper article stating the opinion of the editor. ♦ *adj* **2** of editing or editors.

educate *v* **1** teach. **2** provide schooling for. **education** *n* **educational** *adj* **educationally** *adv* **educationalist** *n* expert in the theory of education. **educative** *adj* educating.

Edwardian *adj* of the reign of King Edward VII of Great Britain and Ireland

(1901–10).

EEG electroencephalogram.

eel *n* snakelike fish.

eerie *adj* **eerier, eeriest** uncannily frightening or disturbing. **eerily** *adv*

efface *v* **1** remove by rubbing. **2** make (oneself) inconspicuous. **effacement** *n*

effect *n* **1** change or result caused by someone or something. **2** condition of being operative, e.g. *the law comes into effect next month.* **3** overall impression. ♦ *pl* **4** personal belongings. **5** lighting, sounds, etc. to accompany a film or a broadcast. ♦ *v* **6** cause to happen, accomplish. **effective** *adj* **1** producing a desired result. **2** operative. **3** impressive. **effectively** *adv* **effectual** *adj* producing the intended result. **effectually** *adv*

effeminate *adj* (of a man) displaying characteristics thought to be typical of a woman. **effeminacy** *n*

effervescent *adj* **1** (of a liquid) giving off bubbles of gas. **2** (of a person) lively and enthusiastic. **effervescence** *n*

effete [if-**feet**] *adj* powerless, feeble.

efficacious *adj* producing the intended result. **efficacy** *n*

efficient *adj* functioning effectively with little waste of effort. **efficiently** *adv* **efficiency** *n*

effigy [ef-fij-ee] *n, pl* **-gies** image or likeness of a person.

efflorescence *n* flowering.

effluent *n* liquid discharged as waste.

effluvium *n, pl* **-via** unpleasant smell, as of decaying matter or gaseous waste.

effort *n* **1** physical or mental exertion. **2** attempt. **effortless** *adj*

effrontery *n* brazen impudence.

effusion *n* unrestrained outburst. **effusive** *adj* openly emotional, demonstrative. **effusively** *adv*

EFTA European Free Trade Association.

e.g. for example.

egalitarian adj 1 upholding the equality of all people. ♦ n 2 person who holds egalitarian beliefs. **egalitarianism** n

egg[1] n 1 oval or round object laid by the females of birds and other creatures, containing a developing embryo. 2 hen's egg used as food. 3 (also **egg cell**) ovum. **egghead** n Informal intellectual person. **eggplant** n US, Canadian, Aust & NZ dark purple tropical fruit, cooked and eaten as a vegetable.

egg[2] v **egg on** encourage or incite, esp. to do wrong.

ego n, pl **egos** 1 the conscious mind of an individual. 2 self-esteem. **egoism, egotism** n 1 excessive concern for one's own interests. 2 excessively high opinion of oneself. **egotist, egoist** n **egotistic, egoistic** adj **egocentric** adj self-centred.

egregious [ig-**greej**-uss] adj outstandingly bad.

egress [**ee**-gress] n 1 departure. 2 way out.

egret [**ee**-grit] n lesser white heron.

Egyptology n study of the culture of ancient Egypt.

eider n Arctic duck. **eiderdown** n quilt (orig. stuffed with eider feathers).

eight adj, n 1 one more than seven. ♦ n 2 eight-oared boat. 3 its crew. **eighth** adj, n (of) number eight in a series. **eighteen** adj, n eight and ten. **eighteenth** adj, n **eighty** adj, n eight times ten. **eightieth** adj, n

eisteddfod [ice-**sted**-fod] n Welsh festival with competitions in music and other performing arts.

either adj, pron 1 one or the other (of two). 2 each of two. ♦ conj 3 used preceding two or more possibilities joined by or. ♦ adv 4 likewise, e.g. I

don't eat meat and he doesn't either.

ejaculate v 1 eject (semen). 2 utter abruptly. **ejaculation** n

eject v force out, expel. **ejection** n **ejector** n

eke out v 1 make (a supply) last by frugal use. 2 make (a living) with difficulty.

elaborate adj 1 with a lot of fine detail. ♦ v 2 expand upon. **elaboration** n

élan [ale-**an**] n style and vigour.

eland [**eel**-and] n large antelope of southern Africa.

elapse v (of time) pass by.

elastic adj 1 resuming normal shape after distortion. 2 adapting easily to change. ♦ n 3 tape or fabric containing interwoven strands of flexible rubber. **elasticity** n

elated v extremely happy and excited. **elation** n

elbow n 1 joint between the upper arm and the forearm. 2 v 3 shove or strike with the elbow. **elbow grease** vigorous physical labour. **elbow room** sufficient room to move freely.

elder[1] adj 1 older. ♦ n 2 older person. 3 (in certain Protestant Churches) lay officer. **elderly** adj (fairly) old. **eldest** adj oldest.

elder[2] n small tree with white flowers and black berries.

El Dorado [el dor-**rah**-doe] n fictitious country rich in gold.

eldritch adj Scot weird, uncanny.

elect v 1 choose by voting. 2 decide (to do something). ♦ adj 3 appointed but not yet in office, e.g. president elect. **election** n 1 choosing of representatives by voting. 2 act of choosing. **electioneering** n active participation in a political campaign. **elective** adj 1 chosen by election. 2 optional. **elector** n someone who has the right to vote in an election. **electoral** adj **electorate** n people who have the right to vote.

electricity n 1 form of energy associated with stationary or moving electrons or other charged particles. 2 electric current or charge. **electric** adj 1 produced by, transmitting, or powered by electricity. 2 exciting or tense. **electrical** adj using or concerning electricity. **electrician** n person trained to install and repair electrical equipment. **electrics** pl n Brit electric appliances. **electric chair** US chair in which criminals who have been sentenced to death are electrocuted.

electrify v -**fying**, -**fied** 1 adapt for operation by electric power. 2 charge with electricity. 3 startle or excite intensely. **electrification** n

electro- combining form operated by or caused by electricity.

electrocardiograph n instrument for recording the electrical activity of the heart. **electrocardiogram** n tracing produced by this.

electrocute v kill or injure by electricity. **electrocution** n

electrode n conductor through which an electric current enters or leaves a battery, vacuum tube, etc.

electrodynamics n branch of physics concerned with the interactions between electrical and mechanical forces.

electroencephalograph [ill-lek-tro-en-**sef**-a-loh-graf] n instrument for recording the electrical activity of the brain. **electroencephalogram** n tracing produced by this.

electrolysis [ill-lek-**troll**-iss-iss] n 1 conduction of electricity by an electrolyte, esp. to induce chemical change. 2 destruction of living tissue

such as hair roots by an electric current.

electrolyte n solution or molten substance that conducts electricity. **electrolytic** adj

electromagnet n magnet containing a coil of wire through which an electric current is passed. **electromagnetic** adj of or operated by an electomagnet. **electromagnetism** n

electron n elementary particle in all atoms that has a negative electrical charge. **electron microscope** microscope that uses electrons, rather than light, to produce a magnified image. **electronvolt** n unit of energy used in nuclear physics.

electronic adj 1 (of a device) dependent on the action of electrons. 2 (of a process) using electronic devices. **electronic mail** see E-MAIL. **electronics** n technology concerned with the development of electronic devices and circuits.

electroplate v coat with silver etc. by electrolysis.

elegant adj pleasing or graceful in dress, style, or design. **elegance** n

elegy [**el**-lij-ee] n, pl -**egies** mournful poem, esp. a lament for the dead. **elegiac** adj mournful or plaintive.

element n 1 component part. 2 substance which cannot be separated into other substances by ordinary chemical techniques. 3 section of people within a larger group, e.g. the rowdy element. 4 heating wire in an electric kettle, stove, etc. ♦ pl 5 basic principles of something. 6 weather conditions, esp. wind, rain, and cold. **in one's element** in a situation where one is happiest. **elemental** adj of primitive natural forces or passions. **elementary** adj simple and straightforward.

elephant n huge four-footed thick-skinned animal with ivory tusks and a long trunk. **elephantine** adj unwieldy, clumsy. **elephantiasis** [el-lee-fan-**tie**-a-siss] n disease with hardening of the skin and enlargement of the legs etc.

elevate v 1 raise in rank or status. 2 lift up. **elevation** n 1 raising. 2 height above sea level. 3 scale drawing of one side of a building. **elevator** n Aust, US & Canadian lift for carrying people.

eleven adj, n 1 one more than ten. ♦ n 2 Sport team of eleven people. **eleventh** adj, n (of) number eleven in a series. **elevenses** n Brit & S Afr informal mid-morning snack.

elf n, pl **elves** (in folklore) small mischievous fairy. **elfin** adj small and delicate.

elicit v 1 bring about (a response or reaction). 2 find out (information) by careful questioning.

elide v omit (a vowel or syllable) from a spoken word. **elision** n

eligible adj 1 meeting the requirements or qualifications needed. 2 desirable as a spouse. **eligibility** n

eliminate v get rid of. **elimination** n

elite [ill-**eet**] n most powerful, rich, or gifted members of a group. **elitism** n belief that society should be governed by a small group of superior people. **elitist** n, adj

elixir [ill-**ix**-er] n imaginary liquid that can prolong life or turn base metals into gold.

Elizabethan adj of the reign of Elizabeth I of England (1558–1603).

elk n large deer of N Europe and Asia.

ellipse n oval shape. **elliptical** adj 1 oval-shaped. 2 (of speech or writing) obscure or ambiguous.

ellipsis n, pl **-ses** omission of letters or words in a sentence.

elm n tree with serrated leaves.

elocution n art of speaking clearly in public.

elongate [**eel**-long-gate] v make or become longer. **elongation** n

elope v (of two people) run away secretly to get married. **elopement** n

eloquence n fluent powerful use of language. **eloquent** adj **eloquently** adv

else adv 1 in addition or more, e.g. what else can I do? 2 other or different, e.g. it was unlike anything else that had happened. **elsewhere** adv in or to another place.

elucidate v make (something difficult) clear. **elucidation** n

elude v 1 escape from by cleverness or quickness. 2 baffle. **elusive** adj difficult to catch or remember.

elver n young eel.

elves n plural of ELF.

emaciated [im-**mace**-ee-ate-id] adj abnormally thin. **emaciation** n

e-mail, email n 1 (also **electronic mail**) sending of messages between computer terminals. ♦ v 2 communicate in this way.

emanate [**em**-a-nate] v issue, proceed from a source. **emanation** n

emancipate v free from social, political, or legal restraints. **emancipation** n

emasculate v deprive of power. **emasculation** n

embalm v preserve (a corpse) from decay by the use of chemicals etc.

embankment n man-made ridge that carries a road or railway or holds back water.

embargo n, pl **-goes** 1 order by a government prohibiting trade with a country. ♦ v **-going, -goed** 2 put an embargo on.

embark v 1 board a ship or aircraft. 2 (foll. by on) begin (a new project).

embarkation n

embarrass v cause to feel self-conscious or ashamed. **embarrassed** adj **embarrassing** adj **embarrassment** n

✓ **SPELLING TIP**
There are 32 examples of the misspelling *embarras* in the Bank of English and another mistake, *embarassment*, occurs 64 times. Both these words should have two *rs* and two *ss*.

embassy n, pl **-sies 1** offices or official residence of an ambassador. **2** ambassador and his staff.

embattled adj having a lot of difficulties.

embed v **-bedding, -bedded** fix firmly in something solid.

embellish v **1** decorate. **2** embroider (a story). **embellishment** n

ember n glowing piece of wood or coal in a dying fire.

embezzle v steal money that has been entrusted to one. **embezzlement** n **embezzler** n

embittered adj feeling anger as a result of misfortune.

emblazon v **1** decorate with bright colours. **2** proclaim or publicize.

emblem n object or design that symbolizes a quality, type, or group. **emblematic** adj

embody v **-bodying, -bodied 1** be an example or expression of. **2** comprise, include. **embodiment** n

embolden v encourage (someone).

embolism n blocking of a blood vessel by a blood clot or air bubble.

embossed adj (of a design or pattern) standing out from a surface.

embrace v **1** clasp in the arms, hug. **2** accept (an idea) eagerly. **3** comprise. ♦ n **4** act of embracing.

embrasure n **1** door or window having splayed sides so that the opening is larger on the inside. **2** opening like this in a fortified wall, for shooting through.

embrocation n lotion for rubbing into the skin to relieve pain.

embroider v **1** decorate with needlework. **2** make (a story) more interesting with fictitious detail. **embroidery** n

embroil v involve (a person) in problems.

embryo [**em**-bree-oh] n, pl **-bryos 1** unborn creature in the early stages of development. **2** something at an undeveloped stage. **embryonic** adj at an early stage. **embryology** n

emend v remove errors from. **emendation** n

emerald n **1** bright green precious stone. ♦ adj **2** bright green.

emerge v **1** come into view. **2** (foll. by *from*) come out of. **3** become known. **emergence** n **emergent** adj

emergency n, pl **-cies** sudden unforeseen occurrence needing immediate action.

emeritus [im-**mer**-rit-uss] adj retired, but retaining an honorary title, e.g. *emeritus professor.*

emery n hard mineral used for smoothing and polishing. **emery board** cardboard strip coated with crushed emery, for filing the nails.

emetic [im-**met**-ik] n **1** substance that causes vomiting. ♦ adj **2** causing vomiting.

emigrate v go and settle in another country. **emigrant** n **emigration** n

émigré [**em**-mig-gray] n someone who has left his native country for political reasons.

eminent adj distinguished, well-known. **eminently** adv **eminence** n **1** position of superiority or fame. **2** (E-) title of a cardinal.

emir [em-**meer**] *n* Muslim ruler.
emirate *n* his country.

emissary *n, pl* -saries agent sent on a mission by a government.

emit *v* **emitting, emitted 1** give out (heat, light, or a smell). **2** utter.
emission *n*

emollient *adj* **1** softening, soothing. ♦ *n* **2** substance which softens or soothes the skin.

emolument *n formal* fees or wages from employment.

emoticon [i-**mote**-i-kon] *n Computers* same as SMILEY.

emotion *n* strong feeling. **emotional** *adj* readily affected by or appealing to the emotions. **emotionally** *adv* **emotive** *adj* tending to arouse emotion.

empathy *n* ability to understand someone else's feelings as if they were one's own.

emperor *n* ruler of an empire.
empress *n fem*

emphasis *n, pl* -ses **1** special importance or significance. **2** stress on a word or phrase in speech.
emphasize *v* **emphatic** *adj* showing emphasis. **emphatically** *adv*

emphysema [em-fiss-**see**-ma] *n* condition in which the air sacs of the lungs are grossly enlarged, causing breathlessness.

empire *n* **1** group of territories under the rule of one state or person. **2** large organization that is directed by one person or group.

empirical *adj* relying on experiment or experience, not on theory.
empirically *adv* **empiricism** *n* doctrine that all knowledge derives from experience. **empiricist** *n*

emplacement *n* prepared position for a gun.

employ *v* **1** hire (a person). **2** provide work or occupation for. **3** use. ♦ *n* **4 in the employ of** doing regular paid work for. **employee** *n* **employment** *n* **1** state of being employed. **2** work done by a person to earn money.

employer *n* person or organization that employs someone.

emporium *n, pl* -riums, -ria *Old-fashioned* large general shop.

empower *v* enable, authorize.

empress *n see* EMPEROR.

empty *adj* -tier, -tiest **1** containing nothing. **2** unoccupied. **3** without purpose or value. **4** (of words) insincere. ♦ *v* -tying, -tied **5** make or become empty. **empties** *pl n* empty boxes, bottles, etc. **emptiness** *n*

emu *n* large Australian flightless bird with long legs.

emulate *v* attempt to equal or surpass by imitating. **emulation** *n*

emulsion *n* **1** light-sensitive coating on photographic film. **2** type of water-based paint. ♦ *v* **3** paint with emulsion paint. **emulsify** *v* (of two liquids) join together or join (two liquids) together. **emulsifier** *n*

enable *v* provide (a person) with the means, opportunity, or authority (to do something).

enact *v* **1** establish by law. **2** perform (a story or play) by acting. **enactment** *n*

enamel *n* **1** glasslike coating applied to metal etc. to preserve the surface. **2** hard white coating on a tooth. ♦ *v* -elling, -elled **3** cover with enamel.

enamoured *adj* inspired with love.

en bloc *adv French* as a whole, all together.

encamp *v* set up in a camp.
encampment *n*

encapsulate *v* **1** summarize. **2** enclose as in a capsule.

encephalitis [en-sef-a-**lite**-iss] *n*

inflammation of the brain.

encephalogram n short for ELECTROENCEPHALOGRAM.

enchant v delight and fascinate. **enchantment** n **enchanter** n **enchantress** n fem

encircle v form a circle around. **encirclement** n

enclave n part of a country entirely surrounded by foreign territory.

enclose v 1 surround completely. 2 include along with something else. **enclosure** n

encomium n, pl -miums, -mia formal expression of praise.

encompass v 1 surround. 2 include comprehensively.

encore interj 1 again, once more. ♦ n 2 extra performance due to enthusiastic demand.

encounter v 1 meet unexpectedly. 2 be faced with. ♦ n 3 unexpected meeting. 4 game or battle.

encourage v 1 inspire with confidence. 2 spur on. **encouragement** n

encroach v intrude gradually on a person's rights or land. **encroachment** n

encrust v cover with a layer of something.

encumber v hinder or impede. **encumbrance** n something that impedes or is burdensome.

encyclical [en-**sik**-lik-kl] n letter sent by the Pope to all bishops.

encyclopedia, encyclopaedia n book or set of books containing facts about many subjects, usu. in alphabetical order. **encyclopedic, encyclopaedic** adj

end n 1 furthest point or part. 2 limit. 3 last part of something. 4 fragment. 5 death or destruction. 6 purpose. 7 Sport either of the two defended areas of a playing field. ♦ v 8 bring or come to a finish. **make ends meet** have just enough money for one's needs. **ending** n **endless** adj **endways** adv having the end forwards or upwards.

endanger v put in danger.

endear v cause to be liked. **endearing** adj **endearment** n affectionate word or phrase.

endeavour v 1 try. ♦ n 2 effort.

endemic adj present within a localized area or peculiar to a particular group of people.

endive n curly-leaved plant used in salads.

endocrine adj relating to the glands which secrete hormones directly into the bloodstream.

endogenous [en-**dodge**-in-uss] adj originating from within.

endorse v 1 give approval to. 2 sign the back of (a cheque). 3 record a conviction on (a driving licence). **endorsement** n

endow v provide permanent income for. **endowed with** provided with. **endowment** n

endure v 1 bear (hardship) patiently. 2 last for a long time. **endurable** adj **endurance** n act or power of enduring.

enema [**en**-im-a] n medicine injected into the rectum to empty the bowels.

enemy n, pl -mies hostile person or nation, opponent.

energy n, pl -gies 1 capacity for intense activity. 2 capacity to do work and overcome resistance. 3 source of power, such as electricity. **energetic** adj **energetically** adv **energize** v give vigour to. **energy drink** soft drink supposed to boost the drinker's energy levels.

enervate v deprive of strength or vitality. **enervation** n

enfant terrible [**on**-fon ter-**reeb**-la] *n*, *pl* **enfants terribles** *French* clever but unconventional or indiscreet person.

enfeeble *v* weaken.

enfold *v* **1** cover by wrapping something around. **2** embrace.

enforce *v* **1** impose obedience (to a law etc.). **2** impose (a condition). **enforceable** *adj* **enforcement** *n*

enfranchise *v* grant (a person) the right to vote. **enfranchisement** *n*

engage *v* **1** take part, participate. **2** involve (a person or his or her attention) intensely. **3** employ (a person). **4** begin a battle with. **5** bring (a mechanism) into operation. **engaged** *adj* **1** pledged to be married. **2** in use. **engagement** *n* **engaging** *adj* charming.

engender *v* produce, cause to occur.

engine *n* **1** any machine which converts energy into mechanical work. **2** railway locomotive.

engineer *n* **1** person trained in any branch of engineering. ♦ *v* **2** plan in a clever manner. **3** design or construct as an engineer.

engineering *n* profession of applying scientific principles to the design and construction of engines, cars, buildings, or machines.

English *n* **1** official language of Britain, Ireland, Australia, New Zealand, South Africa, Canada, the US, and several other countries. ♦ *adj* **2** relating to England. **the English** the people of England.

engrave *v* **1** carve (a design) onto a hard surface. **2** fix deeply in the mind. **engraver** *n* **engraving** *n* print made from an engraved plate.

engross [en-**groce**] *v* occupy the attention of (a person) completely.

engulf *v* cover or surround completely.

enhance *v* increase in quality, value, or attractiveness. **enhancement** *n*

enigma *n* puzzling thing or person. **enigmatic** *adj* **enigmatically** *adv*

enjoin *v* order (someone) to do something.

enjoy *v* **1** take joy in. **2** have the benefit of. **3** experience. **enjoyable** *adj* **enjoyment** *n*

enlarge *v* **1** make or grow larger. **2** (foll. by *on*) speak or write about in greater detail. **enlargement** *n*

enlighten *v* give information to. **enlightenment** *n*

enlist *v* **1** enter the armed forces. **2** obtain the support of. **enlistment** *n*

enliven *v* make lively or cheerful.

en masse [on **mass**] *adv French* in a group, all together.

enmeshed *adj* deeply involved.

enmity *n*, *pl* **-ties** ill will, hatred.

ennoble *v* make noble, elevate.

ennui [on-**nwee**] *n* boredom, dissatisfaction.

enormous *adj* very big, vast. **enormity** *n*, *pl* **-ties 1** great wickedness. **2** gross offence. **3** *Informal* great size.

enough *adj* **1** as much or as many as necessary. ♦ *n* **2** sufficient quantity. ♦ *adv* **3** sufficiently. **4** fairly or quite, e.g. *that's a common enough experience.*

en passant [on **pass**-on] *adv French* in passing, by the way.

enquire *v* same as INQUIRE. **enquiry** *n*

enraptured *adj* filled with delight and fascination.

enrich *v* **1** improve in quality. **2** make wealthy or wealthier.

enrol *v* **-rolling, -rolled** (cause to) become a member. **enrolment** *n*

en route *adv French* on the way.

ensconce *v* settle firmly or comfortably.

ensemble [on-**som**-bl] *n* **1** all the parts of something taken together. **2** complete outfit of clothes. **3** company of actors or musicians. **4** *Music* group of musicians playing together.

enshrine v cherish or treasure.

ensign n **1** naval flag. **2** banner. **3** US naval officer.

enslave v make a slave of (someone). **enslavement** n

ensnare v catch in or as if in a snare.

ensue v come next, result.

en suite adv French connected to a bedroom and entered directly from it.

ensure v **1** make certain or sure. **2** make safe or protect.

entail v bring about or impose inevitably.

entangle v catch or involve in or as if in a tangle. **entanglement** n

entente [on-**tont**] n friendly understanding between nations.

enter v **1** come or go in. **2** join. **3** become involved in, take part in. **4** record (an item) in a journal etc. **5** begin. **entrance** n **1** way into a place. **2** act of entering. **3** right of entering. **entrant** n person who enters a university, contest, etc. **entry** n, pl -tries **1** entrance. **2** entering. **3** item entered in a journal etc.

enteric [en-**ter**-ik] adj intestinal. **enteritis** [en-ter-**rite**-iss] n inflammation of the intestine, causing diarrhoea.

enterprise n **1** company or firm. **2** bold or difficult undertaking. **3** boldness and energy. **enterprising** adj full of boldness and initiative.

entertain v **1** amuse. **2** receive as a guest. **3** consider (an idea). **entertainer** n **entertainment** n

enthral [en-**thrawl**] v -thralling, -thralled hold the attention of. **enthralling** adj

enthusiasm n ardent interest, eagerness. **enthuse** v (cause to) show enthusiasm. **enthusiast** n ardent supporter of something. **enthusiastic**

adj **enthusiastically** adv

entice v attract by exciting hope or desire, tempt. **enticement** n

entire adj including every detail, part, or aspect of something. **entirely** adv **entirety** n

entitle v **1** give a right to. **2** give a title to. **entitlement** n

entity n, pl -ties separate distinct thing.

entomology n study of insects. **entomological** adj **entomologist** n

entourage [on-toor-ahzh] n group of people who assist an important person.

entrails pl n **1** intestines. **2** innermost parts of something.

entrance[1] n see ENTER.

entrance[2] v **1** delight. **2** put into a trance.

entreat v ask earnestly. **entreaty** n, pl -ties earnest request.

entrée [on-tray] n **1** dish served before a main course. **2** main course. **3** right of admission.

entrench v **1** establish firmly. **2** establish in a fortified position with trenches. **entrenchment** n

entrepreneur n business person who attempts to make a profit by risk and initiative.

entropy [en-trop-ee] n lack of organization.

entrust v put into the care or protection of.

entwine v twist together or around.

E number n any of a series of numbers with the prefix E indicating a specific food additive recognized by the EU.

enumerate v name one by one. **enumeration** n

enunciate v **1** pronounce clearly. **2** state precisely or formally. **enunciation** n

envelop v enveloping, enveloped wrap up, enclose. **envelopment** n

envelope n folded gummed paper

cover for a letter.

environment [en-**vire**-on-ment] *n* external conditions and surroundings in which people, animals, or plants live. **environmental** *adj* **environmentalist** *n* person concerned with the protection of the natural environment.

☑ **SPELLING TIP**

For every thousand correct appearances of the word **environment** in the Bank of English, there is one *enviroment*, without the middle *n*.

---

environs *pl n* surrounding area, esp. of a town.

envisage *v* conceive of as a possibility.

envoy *n* **1** messenger. **2** diplomat ranking below an ambassador.

envy *n* **1** feeling of discontent aroused by another's good fortune. ♦ *v* **-vying, -vied 2** grudge (another's good fortune, success, or qualities). **enviable** *adj* arousing envy, fortunate. **envious** *adj* full of envy.

enzyme *n* any of a group of complex proteins that act as catalysts in specific biochemical reactions.

Eolithic *adj* of the early part of the Stone Age.

epaulette *n* shoulder ornament on a uniform.

ephemeral *adj* short-lived.

epic *n* **1** long poem, book, or film about heroic events or actions. ♦ *adj* **2** very impressive or ambitious.

epicentre *n* point on the earth's surface immediately above the origin of an earthquake.

epicure *n* person who enjoys good food and drink. **epicurean** *adj* **1** devoted to sensual pleasures, esp. food and drink. ♦ *n* **2** epicure.

epidemic *n* **1** widespread occurrence

of a disease. **2** rapid spread of something.

epidermis *n* outer layer of the skin.

epidural [ep-pid-**dure**-al] *adj, n* (of) spinal anaesthetic injected to relieve pain during childbirth.

epiglottis *n* thin flap that covers the opening of the larynx during swallowing.

epigram *n* short witty remark or poem. **epigrammatic** *adj*

epigraph *n* **1** quotation at the start of a book. **2** inscription.

epilepsy *n* disorder of the nervous system causing loss of consciousness and sometimes convulsions. **epileptic** *adj* **1** of or having epilepsy. ♦ *n* **2** person who has epilepsy.

epilogue *n* short speech or poem at the end of a literary work, esp. a play.

Epiphany *n* Christian festival held on January 6 commemorating the manifestation of Christ to the Magi.

episcopal [ip-**piss**-kop-al] *adj* of or governed by bishops. **episcopalian** *adj* **1** advocating Church government by bishops. ♦ *n* **2** advocate of such Church government.

episode *n* **1** incident in a series of incidents. **2** section of a serialized book, television programme, etc. **episodic** *adj* occurring at irregular intervals.

epistemology [ip-iss-stem-**ol**-a-jee] *n* study of the source, nature, and limitations of knowledge. **epistemological** *adj*

epistle *n* letter, esp. of an apostle. **epistolary** *adj*

epitaph *n* **1** commemorative inscription on a tomb. **2** commemorative speech or passage.

epithet *n* descriptive word or name.

epitome [ip-**pit**-a-mee] *n* typical example, embodiment. **epitomize** *v* be the epitome of.

epoch [**ee**-pok] n period of notable events. **epoch-making** adj extremely important.

eponymous [ip-**pon**-im-uss] adj after whom a book, play, etc. is named.

equable [**ek**-wab-bl] adj even-tempered. **equably** adv

equal adj 1 identical in size, quantity, degree, etc. 2 having identical rights or status. 3 evenly balanced. 4 (foll. by to) having the necessary ability (for). ♦ n 5 person or thing equal to another. ♦ v **equalling, equalled** 6 be equal to. **equally** adv **equality** n state of being equal. **equalize** v 1 make or become equal. 2 reach the same score as one's opponent. **equalization** n **equal opportunity** nondiscrimination as to sex, race, etc. in employment.

equanimity n calmness of mind.

equate v make or regard as equivalent. **equation** n 1 mathematical statement that two expressions are equal. 2 act of equating.

equator n imaginary circle round the earth, equidistant from the poles. **equatorial** adj

equerry [**ek**-kwer-ee] n, pl **-ries** Brit officer who acts as an attendant to a member of a royal family.

equestrian adj of horses and riding.

equidistant adj equally distant.

equilateral adj having equal sides.

equilibrium n, pl **-ria** steadiness or stability.

equine adj of or like a horse.

equinox n time of year when day and night are of equal length. **equinoctial** adj

equip v **equipping, equipped** provide with supplies, components, etc. **equipment** n 1 set of tools or devices used for a particular purpose. 2 act of equipping.

equipoise n perfect balance.

equity n, pl **-ties** 1 fairness. 2 legal system, founded on the principles of natural justice, that supplements common law. ♦ pl 3 interest of ordinary shareholders in a company. **equitable** adj fair and reasonable. **equitably** adv

equivalent adj 1 equal in value. 2 having the same meaning or result. ♦ n 3 something that is equivalent. **equivalence** n

equivocal adj 1 ambiguous. 2 deliberately misleading. 3 of doubtful character or sincerity. **equivocally** adv **equivocate** v use vague or ambiguous language to mislead people. **equivocation** n

ER Queen Elizabeth.

era n period of time considered as distinctive.

eradicate v destroy completely. **eradication** n

erase v 1 rub out. 2 remove sound or information from (a magnetic tape or disk). **eraser** n object for erasing something written. **erasure** n 1 erasing. 2 place or mark where something has been erased.

ere prep, conj Poetic before.

erect v 1 build. 2 found or form. ♦ adj 3 upright. 4 (of the penis, clitoris, or nipples) rigid as a result of sexual excitement. **erectile** adj capable of becoming erect from sexual excitement. **erection** n

erg n unit of work or energy.

ergonomics n study of the relationship between workers and their environment. **ergonomic** adj

ergot n 1 fungal disease of cereal. 2 dried fungus used in medicine.

ermine n 1 stoat in northern regions. 2 its white winter fur.

erode v wear away. **erosion** n

erogenous [ir-**roj**-in-uss] *adj* sensitive to sexual stimulation.

erotic *adj* relating to sexual pleasure or desire. **eroticism** *n* **erotica** *n* sexual literature or art.

err *v* make a mistake. **erratum** *n, pl* **-ta** error in writing or printing. **erroneous** *adj* incorrect, mistaken.

errand *n* short trip to do something for someone.

errant *adj* behaving in a manner considered to be unacceptable.

erratic *adj* irregular or unpredictable. **erratically** *adv*

error *n* mistake, inaccuracy, or misjudgment.

ersatz [**air**-zats] *adj* made in imitation, e.g. *ersatz coffee.*

erstwhile *adj* former.

erudite *adj* having great academic knowledge. **erudition** *n*

erupt *v* **1** eject (steam, water, or volcanic material) violently. **2** burst forth suddenly and violently. **3** (of a blemish) appear on the skin. **eruption** *n*

erysipelas [err-riss-**sip**-pel-ass] *n* acute skin infection causing purplish patches.

escalate *v* increase in extent or intensity. **escalation** *n*

escalator *n* moving staircase.

escalope [**ess**-kal-lop] *n* thin slice of meat, esp. veal.

escapade *n* mischievous adventure.

escape *v* **1** get free (of). **2** avoid, e.g. *escape attention.* **3** (of a gas, liquid, etc.) leak gradually. **4** *n* **5** act of escaping. **6** means of relaxation. **escapee** *n* person who has escaped. **escapism** *n* taking refuge in fantasy to avoid unpleasant reality. **escapologist** *n* entertainer who specializes in freeing himself from confinement. **escapology** *n*

escarpment *n* steep face of a ridge or mountain.

eschew [iss-**chew**] *v* abstain from, avoid.

escort *n* **1** people or vehicles accompanying another person for protection or as an honour. **2** person who accompanies a person of the opposite sex to a social event. ♦ *v* **3** act as an escort to.

escudo [ess-**kyoo**-doe] *n, pl* **-dos** former monetary unit of Portugal.

escutcheon *n* shield with a coat of arms. **blot on one's escutcheon** stain on one's honour.

Eskimo *n* **1** member of the aboriginal race inhabiting N Canada, Greenland, Alaska, and E Siberia. **2** their language.

esoteric [ee-so-**ter**-rik] *adj* understood by only a small number of people with special knowledge.

ESP extrasensory perception.

esp. especially.

espadrille [**ess**-pad-drill] *n* light canvas shoe with a braided cord sole.

espalier [ess-**pal**-yer] *n* **1** shrub or fruit tree trained to grow flat. **2** trellis for this.

esparto *n, pl* **-tos** grass of S Europe and N Africa used for making rope etc.

especial *adj Formal* special.

especially *adv* particularly.

Esperanto *n* universal artificial language.

espionage [**ess**-pyon-ahzh] *n* spying.

esplanade *n* wide open road used as a public promenade.

espouse *v* adopt or give support to (a cause etc.). **espousal** *n*

espresso *n, pl* **-sos** strong coffee made by forcing steam or boiling water through ground coffee beans.

esprit [ess-**pree**] *n* spirit, liveliness, or wit. **esprit de corps** [de **core**] pride in and loyalty to a group.

espy *v* **espying, espied** catch sight of.

Esq. esquire.

esquire *n* courtesy title placed after a man's name.

essay *n* **1** short literary composition. **2** short piece of writing on a subject done as an exercise by a student. ♦ *v* **3** attempt. **essayist** *n*

essence *n* **1** most important feature of a thing which determines its identity. **2** concentrated liquid used to flavour food. **essential** *adj* **1** vitally important. **2** basic or fundamental. ♦ *n* **3** something fundamental or indispensable. **essentially** *adv*

establish *v* **1** set up on a permanent basis. **2** make secure or permanent in a certain place, job, etc. **3** prove. **4** cause to be accepted. **establishment** *n* **1** act of establishing. **2** commercial or other institution. **the Establishment** group of people having authority within a society.

estate *n* **1** landed property. **2** large area of property development, esp. of new houses or factories. **3** property of a deceased person. **estate agent** agent concerned with the valuation, lease, and sale of property. **estate car** car with a rear door and luggage space behind the rear seats.

esteem *n* **1** high regard. ♦ *v* **2** think highly of. **3** judge or consider.

ester *n Chem* compound produced by the reaction between an acid and an alcohol.

estimate *v* **1** calculate roughly. **2** form an opinion about. ♦ *n* **3** approximate calculation. **4** statement from a workman etc. of the likely charge for a job. **5** opinion. **estimable** *adj* worthy of respect. **estimation** *n* considered opinion.

estranged *adj* no longer living with one's spouse. **estrangement** *n*

estuary *n, pl* **-aries** mouth of a river.

ETA estimated time of arrival.

et al. and elsewhere.

etc. et cetera.

et cetera [et set-ra] *Latin* **1** and the rest, and others. **2** or the like. **etceteras** *pl n* miscellaneous extra things or people.

etch *v* **1** wear away or cut the surface of (metal, glass, etc.) with acid. **2** imprint vividly (on someone's mind). **etching** *n*

eternal *adj* **1** without beginning or end. **2** unchanging. **eternally** *adv* **eternity** *n* **1** infinite time. **2** timeless existence after death. **eternity ring** ring given as a token of lasting affection.

ether *n* **1** colourless sweet-smelling liquid used as an anaesthetic. **2** region above the clouds. **ethereal** [eth-**eer**-ee-al] *adj* extremely delicate.

ethic *n* moral principle. **ethical** *adj* **ethically** *adv* **ethics** *n* **1** code of behaviour. **2** study of morals.

ethnic *adj* **1** relating to a people or group that shares a culture, religion, or language. **2** belonging or relating to such a group, esp. one that is a minority group in a particular place. **ethnic cleansing** practice, by the dominant ethnic group in an area, of removing other ethnic groups by expulsion or extermination. **ethnology** *n* study of human races. **ethnological** *adj* **ethnologist** *n*

ethos [**eeth**-oss] *n* distinctive spirit and attitudes of a people, culture, etc.

ethyl [**eeth**-ile] *adj* of, consisting of, or containing the hydrocarbon group C_2H_5. **ethylene** *n* poisonous gas used as an anaesthetic and as fuel.

etiolate [**ee**-tee-oh-late] *v* **1** become pale and weak. **2** *Botany* whiten through lack of sunlight.

etiology *n* study of the causes of diseases.

etiquette *n* conventional code of

conduct.

étude [**ay**-tewd] n short musical composition for a solo instrument, esp. intended as a technical exercise.

etymology n, pl **-gies** study of the sources and development of words. **etymological** adj

EU European Union.

eucalyptus, eucalypt n tree, mainly grown in Australia, that provides timber, gum, and medicinal oil from the leaves.

Eucharist [**yew**-kar-ist] n 1 Christian sacrament commemorating Christ's Last Supper. 2 consecrated elements of bread and wine. **Eucharistic** adj

eugenics [yew-**jen**-iks] n study of methods of improving the human race.

eulogy n, pl **-gies** speech or writing in praise of a person. **eulogize** v praise (a person or thing) highly in speech or writing. **eulogistic** adj

eunuch n castrated man, esp. (formerly) a guard in a harem.

euphemism n inoffensive word or phrase substituted for one considered offensive or upsetting. **euphemistic** adj **euphemistically** adv

euphony n, pl **-nies** pleasing sound. **euphonious** adj pleasing to the ear. **euphonium** n brass musical instrument, tenor tuba.

euphoria n sense of elation. **euphoric** adj

Eurasian adj 1 of Europe and Asia. 2 of mixed European and Asian parentage. ♦ n 3 person of Eurasian parentage.

eureka [yew-**reek**-a] interj exclamation of triumph at finding something.

euro n, pl **euros** unit of the single currency of the European Union.

European n, adj (person) from Europe. **European Union** economic and political association of a number of European nations.

Eustachian tube n passage leading from the ear to the throat.

euthanasia n act of killing someone painlessly, esp. to relieve his or her suffering.

evacuate v 1 send (someone) away from a place of danger. 2 empty. **evacuation** n **evacuee** n

evade v 1 get away from or avoid. 2 elude. **evasion** n **evasive** adj not straightforward. **evasively** adv

evaluate v find or judge the value of. **evaluation** n

evanescent adj quickly fading away. **evanescence** n

evangelical adj 1 of or according to gospel teaching. 2 of certain Protestant sects which maintain the doctrine of salvation by faith. ♦ n 3 member of an evangelical sect. **evangelicalism** n

evangelist n 1 writer of one of the four gospels. 2 travelling preacher. **evangelism** n teaching and spreading of the Christian gospel. **evangelize** v preach the gospel. **evangelization** n

evaporate v 1 change from a liquid or solid to a vapour. 2 disappear. **evaporation** n **evaporated milk** thick unsweetened tinned milk.

eve n 1 evening or day before some special event. 2 period immediately before an event. **evensong** n evening prayer.

even adj 1 flat or smooth. 2 (foll. by with) on the same level (as). 3 constant. 4 calm. 5 equally balanced. 6 divisible by two. ♦ adv 7 equally. 8 simply. 9 nevertheless. ♦ v 10 make even.

evening n 1 end of the day or early part of the night. ♦ adj 2 of or in the evening.

event n 1 anything that takes place. 2 planned and organized occasion. 3 contest in a sporting programme.

eventful *adj* full of exciting incidents.

eventing *n Brit, Aust & NZ* riding competitions. usu. involving cross-country, jumping, and dressage.

eventual *adj* ultimate. **eventuality** *n* possible event.

eventually *adv* at the end of a situation or process.

ever *adv* 1 at any time. 2 always.

evergreen *n, adj* (tree or shrub) having leaves throughout the year.

everlasting *adj* **evermore** *adv* for all time to come.

every *adj* 1 each without exception. 2 all possible. **everybody** *pron* every person. **everyday** *adj* usual or ordinary. **everyone** *pron* every person. **everything** *pron* **everywhere** *adv* in all places.

evict *v* legally expel (someone) from his or her home. **eviction** *n*

evidence *n* 1 ground for belief. 2 matter produced before a law court to prove or disprove a point. 3 sign, indication. ♦ *v* 4 demonstrate, prove. **in evidence** conspicuous. **evident** *adj* easily seen or understood. **evidently** *adv* **evidential** *adj* of, serving as, or based on evidence.

evil *n* 1 wickedness. 2 wicked deed. ♦ *adj* 3 harmful. 4 morally bad. 5 very unpleasant. **evilly** *adv* **evildoer** *n* wicked person.

evince *v* make evident.

eviscerate *v* disembowel. **evisceration** *n*

evoke *v* call or summon up (a memory, feeling, etc.). **evocation** *n* **evocative** *adj*

evolve *v* 1 develop gradually. 2 (of an animal or plant species) undergo evolution. **evolution** *n* gradual change in the characteristics of living things over successive generations, esp. to a more complex form. **evolutionary** *adj*

ewe *n* female sheep.

ewer *n* large jug with a wide mouth.

ex *n Informal* former wife or husband.

ex- *prefix* 1 out of, outside, from, e.g. *exodus*. 2 former, e.g. *ex-wife*.

exacerbate [ig-**zass**-er-bate] *v* make (pain, emotion, or a situation) worse. **exacerbation** *n*

exact *adj* 1 correct and complete in every detail. 2 precise, as opposed to approximate. ♦ *v* 3 demand (payment or obedience). **exactly** *adv* precisely, in every respect. **exactness, exactitude** *n* **exacting** *adj* making rigorous or excessive demands.

exaggerate *v* 1 regard or represent as greater than is true. 2 make greater or more noticeable. **exaggeratedly** *adv* **exaggeration** *n*

☑ **SPELLING TIP**

Some apparently tricky words, like **exaggerate** for example, appear wrongly spelt relatively rarely in the Bank of English. Similarly, there is only one occurrence of *exagerration*, instead of the correct **exaggeration**.

---

exalt *v* 1 praise highly. 2 raise to a higher rank. **exalted** *adj* **exaltation** *n*

exam *n* short for EXAMINATION.

examine *v* 1 look at closely. 2 test the knowledge of. 3 ask questions of. **examination** *n* 1 examining. 2 test of a candidate's knowledge or skill. **examinee** *n* **examiner** *n*

example *n* 1 specimen typical of its group. 2 person or thing worthy of imitation. 3 punishment regarded as a warning to others.

exasperate *v* cause great irritation to. **exasperation** *n*

excavate *v* 1 unearth buried objects from (a piece of land) methodically to learn about the past. 2 make (a hole) in solid matter by digging.

excavation n **excavator** n large machine used for digging.

exceed v 1 be greater than. 2 go beyond (a limit). **exceedingly** adv very.

excel v -celling, -celled 1 be superior to. 2 be outstandingly good at something.

Excellency n title used to address a high-ranking official, such as an ambassador.

excellent adj exceptionally good. **excellence** n

except prep 1 (sometimes foll. by for) other than, not including. ♦ v 2 not include. **except that** but for the fact that. **excepting** prep except. **exception** n 1 excepting. 2 thing that is excluded from or does not conform to the general rule. **exceptional** adj 1 not ordinary. 2 much above the average.

excerpt n passage taken from a book, speech, etc.

excess n 1 state or act of exceeding the permitted limits. 2 immoderate amount. 3 amount by which a thing exceeds the permitted limits. **excessive** adj **excessively** adv

exchange v 1 give or receive (something) in return for something else. ♦ n 2 act of exchanging. 3 thing given or received in place of another. 4 centre in which telephone lines are interconnected. 5 Finance place where securities or commodities are traded. 6 transfer of sums of money of equal value between different currencies. **exchangeable** adj

Exchequer n Brit government department in charge of state money.

excise¹ n tax on goods produced for the home market.

excise² v cut out or away. **excision** n

excite v 1 arouse to strong emotion. 2 arouse or evoke (an emotion). 3 arouse

sexually. **excitement** n **excitable** adj easily excited. **excitability** n

exclaim v speak suddenly, cry out. **exclamation** n **exclamation mark** punctuation mark (!) used after exclamations. **exclamatory** adj

exclude v 1 keep out, leave out. 2 leave out of consideration. **exclusion** n **exclusive** adj 1 excluding everything else. 2 not shared. 3 catering for a privileged minority. ♦ n 4 story reported in only one newspaper. **exclusively** adv **exclusivity, exclusiveness** n

excommunicate v exclude from membership and the sacraments of the Church. **excommunication** n

excoriate v 1 censure severely. 2 strip skin from. **excoriation** n

excrement n waste matter discharged from the body.

excrete v discharge (waste matter) from the body. **excretion** n **excreta** [ik-**skree**-ta] n excrement. **excretory** adj

excruciating adj 1 agonizing. 2 hard to bear. **excruciatingly** adv

exculpate v free from blame or guilt.

excursion n short journey, esp. for pleasure.

excuse n 1 explanation offered to justify (a fault etc.). ♦ v 2 put forward a reason or justification for (a fault etc.). 3 forgive (a person) or overlook (a fault etc.). 4 make allowances for. 5 allow to leave. **excusable** adj

ex-directory adj not listed in a telephone directory by request.

execrable [**eks**-sik-rab-bl] adj of very poor quality.

execute v 1 put (a condemned person) to death. 2 carry out or accomplish. 3 produce (a work of art). 4 render (a legal document) effective, as by signing. **execution** n **executioner** n

executive n 1 person or group in an

administrative position. **2** branch of government responsible for carrying out laws etc. ♦ *adj* **3** having the function of carrying out plans, orders, laws, etc.

executor, executrix *n* person appointed to perform the instructions of a will.

exegesis [eks-sij-**jee**-siss] *n, pl* **-ses** [-seez] explanation of a text, esp. of the Bible.

exemplar *n* **1** person or thing to be copied, model. **2** example. **exemplary** *adj* **1** being a good example. **2** serving as a warning.

exemplify *v* **-fying, -fied 1** show an example of. **2** be an example of. **exemplification** *n*

exempt *adj* **1** not subject to an obligation etc. ♦ *v* **2** release from an obligation etc. **exemption** *n*

exequies [**eks**-sik-wiz] *pl n* funeral rites.

exercise *n* **1** activity to train the body or mind. **2** set of movements or tasks designed to improve or test a person's ability. **3** performance of a function. ♦ *v* **4** make use of, e.g. *to exercise one's rights*. **5** take exercise.

exert *v* use (influence, authority, etc.) forcefully or effectively. **exert oneself** make a special effort. **exertion** *n*

exeunt [**eks**-see-unt] *Latin* they go out: used as a stage direction.

ex gratia [eks **gray**-sha] *adj* given as a favour where no legal obligation exists.

exhale *v* breathe out. **exhalation** *n*

exhaust *v* **1** tire out. **2** use up. **3** discuss (a subject) thoroughly. ♦ *n* **4** gases ejected from an engine as waste products. **5** pipe through which an engine's exhaust fumes pass. **exhaustion** *n* **1** extreme tiredness. **2** exhausting. **exhaustive** *adj* comprehensive. **exhaustively** *adv*

exhibit *v* **1** display to the public. **2** show (a quality or feeling). ♦ *n* **3** object exhibited to the public. **4** *Law* document or object produced in court as evidence. **exhibitor** *n* **exhibition** *n* **1** public display of art, skills, etc. **2** exhibiting. **exhibitionism** *n* **1** compulsive desire to draw attention to oneself. **2** compulsive desire to display one's genitals publicly. **exhibitionist** *n*

exhilarate *v* make lively and cheerful. **exhilaration** *n*

☑ **SPELLING TIP**
It may surprise you that it's the vowels, not the consonants that are a problem when people try to spell **exhilarate** or **exhilaration**. They often make the mistake of writing an *e* instead of an *a* in the middle.

exhort *v* urge earnestly. **exhortation** *n*

exhume [ig-**zyume**] *v* dig up (something buried, esp. a corpse). **exhumation** *n*

exigency *n, pl* **-cies** urgent demand or need. **exigent** *adj*

exiguous *adj* scanty or meagre.

exile *n* **1** prolonged, usu. enforced, absence from one's country. **2** person banished or living away from his or her country. ♦ *v* **3** expel from one's country.

exist *v* **1** have being or reality. **2** eke out a living. **3** live. **existence** *n* **existent** *adj*

☑ **SPELLING TIP**
People often write *-ance* at the end of a word when it should be *-ence*. The Bank of English shows this is the case for *existance* which occurs 43 times. However, the correct spelling **existence** is over 350 times commoner.

existential *adj* of or relating to existence, esp. human existence.

existentialism *n* philosophical movement stressing the personal experience and responsibility of the individual, who is seen as a free agent. **existentialist** *adj, n*

exit *n* **1** way out. **2** going out. **3** actor's going off stage. ♦ *v* **4** go out. **5** go offstage: used as a stage direction.

exocrine *adj* relating to a gland, such as the sweat gland, that secretes externally through a duct.

exodus [**eks**-so-duss] *n* departure of a large number of people.

ex officio [eks off-**fish**-ee-oh] *adv, adj Latin* by right of position or office.

exonerate *v* free from blame or a criminal charge. **exoneration** *n*

exorbitant *adj* (of prices, demands, etc.) excessive, immoderate. **exorbitantly** *adv*

exorcize *v* expel (evil spirits) by prayers and religious rites. **exorcism** *n* **exorcist** *n*

exotic *adj* **1** having a strange allure or beauty. **2** originating in a foreign country. ♦ *n* **3** non-native plant. **exotically** *adv* **exotica** *pl n* (collection of) exotic objects.

expand *v* **1** make or become larger. **2** spread out. **3** (foll. by *on*) enlarge (on). **4** become more relaxed, friendly, and talkative. **expansion** *n* **expanse** *n* uninterrupted wide area. **expansive** *adj* **1** wide or extensive. **2** friendly and talkative.

expat *adj, n* short for EXPATRIATE.

expatiate [iks-**pay**-shee-ate] *v* (foll. by *on*) speak or write at great length (on).

expatriate [eks-**pat**-ree-it] *adj* **1** living outside one's native country. ♦ *n* **2** person living outside his or her native country. **expatriation** *n*

expect *v* **1** regard as probable. **2** look forward to, await. **3** require as an obligation. **expectancy** *n* **1** something expected on the basis of an average, e.g. *life expectancy*. **2** feeling of anticipation. **expectant** *adj* **1** expecting or hopeful. **2** pregnant. **expectantly** *adv* **expectation** *n* **1** act or state of expecting. **2** something looked forward to. **3** attitude of anticipation or hope.

expectorant *n* medicine that helps to bring up phlegm from the respiratory passages.

expectorate *v* spit out (phlegm etc.). **expectoration** *n*

expedient *n* **1** something that achieves a particular purpose. ♦ *adj* **2** suitable to the circumstances, appropriate. **expediency** *n*

expedite *v* hasten the progress of. **expedition** *n* **1** organized journey, esp. for exploration. **2** people and equipment comprising an expedition. **3** pleasure trip or excursion. **expeditionary** *adj* relating to an expedition, esp. a military one. **expeditious** *adj* done quickly and efficiently.

expel *v* -**pelling, -pelled 1** drive out with force. **2** dismiss from a school etc. permanently. **expulsion** *n*

expend *v* spend, use up. **expendable** *adj* able to be sacrificed to achieve an objective. **expenditure** *n* **1** something expended, esp. money. **2** amount expended.

expense *n* **1** cost. **2** (cause of) spending. ♦ *pl* **3** charges, outlay incurred.

expensive *adj* high-priced.

experience *n* **1** direct personal participation. **2** particular incident, feeling, etc. that a person has undergone. **3** accumulated knowledge. ♦ *v* **4** participate in. **5** be affected by (an emotion). **experienced** *adj* skilful from extensive participation.

experiment *n* **1** test to provide

evidence to prove or disprove a theory. **2** attempt at something new. ◆ *v* **3** carry out an experiment. **experimental** *adj* **experimentally** *adv* **experimentation** *n*

expert *n* **1** person with extensive skill or knowledge in a particular field. ◆ *adj* **2** skilful or knowledgeable. **expertise** [eks-per-**teez**] *n* special skill or knowledge.

expiate *v* make amends for. **expiation** *n*

expire *v* **1** finish or run out. **2** breathe out. **3** *Lit* die. **expiration** *n* **expiry** *n* end, esp. of a contract period.

explain *v* **1** make clear and intelligible. **2** account for. **explanation** *n* **explanatory** *adj*

expletive *n* swearword.

explicable *adj* able to be explained. **explicate** *v Formal* explain. **explication** *n*

explicit *adj* **1** precisely and clearly expressed. **2** shown in realistic detail. **explicitly** *adv*

explode *v* **1** burst with great violence, blow up. **2** react suddenly with emotion. **3** increase rapidly. **4** show (a theory etc.) to be baseless. **explosion** *n* **explosive** *adj* **1** tending to explode. ◆ *n* **2** substance that causes explosions.

exploit *v* **1** take advantage of for one's own purposes. **2** make the best use of. ◆ *n* **3** notable feat or deed. **exploitation** *n* **exploiter** *n*

explore *v* **1** investigate. **2** travel into (unfamiliar regions), esp. for scientific purposes. **exploration** *n* **exploratory** *adj* **explorer** *n*

expo *n, pl* **expos** *Informal* exposition, large public exhibition.

exponent *n* **1** person who advocates an idea, cause, etc. **2** skilful performer, esp. a musician.

exponential *adj Informal* very rapid. **exponentially** *adv*

export *n* **1** selling or shipping of goods to a foreign country. **2** product shipped or sold to a foreign country. ◆ *v* **3** sell or ship (goods) to a foreign country. **exporter** *n*

expose *v* **1** uncover or reveal. **2** make vulnerable, leave unprotected. **3** subject (a photographic film) to light. **expose oneself** display one's sexual organs in public. **exposure** *n* **1** exposing. **2** lack of shelter from the weather, esp. the cold. **3** appearance before the public, as on television.

exposé [iks-**pose**-ay] *n* bringing of a crime, scandal, etc. to public notice.

exposition *n* see EXPOUND.

expostulate *v* (foll. by *with*) reason (with), esp. to dissuade.

expound *v* explain in detail. **exposition** *n* **1** explanation. **2** large public exhibition.

express *v* **1** put into words. **2** show (an emotion). **3** indicate by a symbol or formula. **4** squeeze out (juice etc.). ◆ *adj* **5** explicitly stated. **6** (of a purpose) particular. **7** of or for rapid transportation of people, mail, etc. ◆ *n* **8** fast train or bus stopping at only a few stations. ◆ *adv* **9** by express delivery. **expression** *n* **1** expressing. **2** word or phrase. **3** showing or communication of emotion. **4** look on the face that indicates mood. **5** *Maths* variable, function, or some combination of these. **expressionless** *adj* **expressive** *adj*

expressionism *n* early 20th-century artistic movement which sought to express emotions rather than represent the physical world. **expressionist** *n, adj*

expropriate *v* deprive an owner of (property). **expropriation** *n*

expunge *v* delete, erase, blot out.

expurgate *v* remove objectionable parts from (a book etc.).

exquisite adj 1 of extreme beauty or delicacy. 2 intense in feeling. **exquisitely** adv

extant adj still existing.

extemporize v speak, perform, or compose without preparation.

extend v 1 draw out or be drawn out, stretch. 2 last for a certain time. 3 (foll. by to) include. 4 increase in size or scope. 5 offer, e.g. *extend one's sympathy*. **extendable** adj **extension** n 1 room or rooms added to an existing building. 2 additional telephone connected to the same line as another. 3 extending. **extensive** adj having a large extent, widespread. **extensor** n muscle that extends a part of the body. **extent** n range over which something extends, area.

☑ **SPELLING TIP**
Lots of nouns in English end with *-tion*, but **extension** is not one of them.

---

extenuate v make (an offence or fault) less blameworthy. **extenuation** n

exterior n 1 part or surface on the outside. 2 outward appearance or behaviour of a person. ♦ adj 3 of, on, or coming from the outside.

exterminate v destroy (animals or people) completely. **extermination** n **exterminator** n

external adj of, situated on, or coming from the outside. **externally** adv

extinct adj 1 having died out. 2 (of a volcano) no longer liable to erupt. **extinction** n

extinguish v 1 put out (a fire or light). 2 remove or destroy entirely.

extinguisher n device for extinguishing a fire or light.

extirpate v destroy utterly.

extol v **-tolling, -tolled** praise highly.

extort v get (something) by force or threats. **extortion** n **extortionate** adj (of prices) excessive.

extra adj 1 more than is usual, expected or needed. ♦ n 2 additional person or thing. 3 something for which an additional charge is made. 4 *Films* actor hired for crowd scenes. 5 adv 6 unusually or exceptionally.

extra- prefix outside or beyond an area or scope, e.g. *extrasensory; extraterritorial*.

extract v 1 pull out by force. 2 remove. 3 derive. 4 copy out (an article, passage, etc.) from a publication. ♦ n 5 something extracted, such as a passage from a book etc. 6 preparation containing the concentrated essence of a substance, e.g. *beef extract*. **extraction** n **extractor** n

extradite v send (an accused person) back to his or her own country for trial. **extradition** n

extramural adj connected with but outside the normal courses of a university or college.

extraneous [iks-**train**-ee-uss] adj irrelevant.

extraordinary adj 1 very unusual. 2 (of a meeting) specially arranged to deal with a particular subject. **extraordinarily** adv

extrapolate v 1 infer (something not known) from the known facts. 2 *Maths* estimate (a value of a function or measurement) beyond the known values by the extension of a curve. **extrapolation** n

extrasensory adj **extrasensory perception** supposed ability to obtain information other than through the normal senses.

extravagant adj 1 spending money excessively. 2 going beyond reasonable limits. **extravagance** n excessive or wasteful spending.

extravaganza *n* elaborate and lavish entertainment, display, etc.

✓ **SPELLING TIP**

Make sure that **extravagant** ends in *-ant*, even though *-ent* sounds like a possibility.

extreme *adj* **1** of a high or the highest degree or intensity. **2** severe. **3** immoderate. **4** farthest or outermost. ♦ *n* **5** either of the two limits of a scale or range. **extremely** *adv* **extreme sport** sport with a high risk of injury or death. **extremist** *n* **1** person who favours immoderate methods. ♦ *adj* **2** holding extreme opinions. **extremity** *n, pl* **-ties 1** farthest point. **2** extreme condition, as of misfortune. ♦ *pl* **3** hands and feet.

extricate *v* free from complication or difficulty. **extrication** *n*

extrovert *adj* **1** lively and outgoing. **2** concerned more with external reality than inner feelings. ♦ *n* **3** extrovert person.

extrude *v* squeeze or force out. **extrusion** *n*

exuberant *adj* **1** high-spirited. **2** growing luxuriantly. **exuberance** *n*

exude *v* **1** (of a liquid or smell) seep or flow out slowly and steadily. **2** make apparent by mood or behaviour, e.g. *exude confidence.*

exult *v* be joyful or jubilant. **exultation** *n* **exultant** *adj*

eye *n* **1** organ of sight. **2** ability to judge or appreciate, e.g. *a good eye for detail.* **3** one end of a sewing needle. **4** dark spot on a potato from which a stem grows. ♦ *v* **eyeing** *or* **eying, eyed 5** look at carefully or warily. **eyeless** *adj* **eyelet** *n* **1** small hole for a lace or cord to be passed through. **2** ring that strengthens this. **eyeball** *n* ball-shaped part of the eye. **eyebrow** *n* line of hair on the bony ridge above the eye. **eyeglass** *n* lens for aiding defective vision. **eyelash** *n* short hair that grows out from the eyelid. **eyelid** *n* fold of skin that covers the eye when it is closed. **eyeliner** *n* cosmetic used to outline the eyes. **eye-opener** *n Informal* something startling or revealing. **eye shadow** coloured cosmetic worn on the upper eyelids. **eyesight** *n* ability to see. **eyesore** *n* ugly object. **eye tooth** canine tooth. **eyewitness** *n* person who was present at an event and can describe what happened.

eyrie *n* **1** nest of an eagle. **2** high isolated place.

F f

f *Music* forte.

F 1 Fahrenheit. **2** farad.

FA Football Association (of England).

fable *n* **1** story with a moral. **2** false or fictitious account. **3** legend. **fabled** *adj* made famous in legend.

fabric *n* **1** knitted or woven cloth. **2** framework or structure.

fabricate *v* **1** make up (a story or lie). **2** make or build. **fabrication** *n*

fabulous *adj* **1** *Informal* excellent. **2** astounding. **3** told of in fables. **fabulously** *adv*

facade [fas-**sahd**] *n* **1** front of a building. **2** (false) outward appearance.

face *n* **1** front of the head. **2** facial expression. **3** distorted expression. **4** outward appearance. **5** front or main side. **6** dial of a clock. **7** dignity, self-respect. ◆ *v* **8** look or turn towards. **9** be opposite. **10** be confronted by. **11** provide with a surface. **faceless** *adj* impersonal, anonymous. **face-lift** *n* operation to tighten facial skin, to remove wrinkles. **face-saving** *adj* maintaining dignity or self-respect. **face up to** *v* accept (an unpleasant fact or reality). **face value** apparent worth or meaning.

facet *n* **1** aspect. **2** surface of a cut gem.

facetious [fas-**see**-shuss] *adj* funny or trying to be funny, esp. at inappropriate times.

facia *n, pl* **-ciae** same as **FASCIA**.

facial *adj* **1** of the face. ◆ *n* **2** beauty treatment for the face.

facile [**fas**-sile] *adj* (of a remark, argument, etc.) superficial and showing lack of real thought.

facilitate *v* make easy. **facilitation** *n*

facility *n, pl* **-ties 1** skill. **2** easiness. ◆ *pl*
3 means or equipment for an activity.

facing *n* **1** lining or covering for decoration or reinforcement. ◆ *pl* **2** contrasting collar and cuffs on a jacket.

facsimile [fak-**sim**-ill-ee] *n* exact copy.

fact *n* **1** event or thing known to have happened or existed. **2** provable truth. **facts of life** details of sex and reproduction. **factual** *adj*

faction *n* **1** (dissenting) minority group within a larger body. **2** dissension. **factious** *adj* of or producing factions.

factitious *adj* artificial.

factor *n* **1** element contributing to a result. **2** *Maths* one of the integers multiplied together to give a given number. **3** *Scot* property manager. **factorial** *n* product of all the integers from one to a given number. **factorize** *v* calculate the factors of (a number).

factory *n, pl* **-ries** building where goods are manufactured.

factotum *n* person employed to do all sorts of work.

faculty *n, pl* **-ties 1** physical or mental ability. **2** department in a university or college.

fad *n* **1** short-lived fashion. **2** whim. **faddy, faddish** *adj*

fade *v* **1** (cause to) lose brightness, colour, or strength. **2** vanish slowly.

faeces [**fee**-seez] *pl n* waste matter discharged from the anus. **faecal** [**fee**-kl] *adj*

fag[1] *n* **1** *Informal* boring task. **2** *Brit* young public schoolboy who does menial chores for a senior boy. ◆ *v* **3** *Brit* do menial chores in a public school.

fag[2] *n Brit slang* cigarette. **fag end 1** last and worst part. **2** *Slang* cigarette stub.

faggot[1] n **1** Brit, Aust & NZ ball of chopped liver, herbs, and bread. **2** bundle of sticks for fuel.

faggot[2] n Offens male homosexual.

Fahrenheit [**far**-ren-hite] adj of a temperature scale with the freezing point of water at 32° and the boiling point at 212°.

faïence [**fie**-ence] n tin-glazed earthenware.

fail v **1** be unsuccessful. **2** stop operating. **3** be or judge to be below the required standard in a test. **4** disappoint or be useless to (someone). **5** neglect or be unable to do (something). **6** go bankrupt. ♦ n **7** instance of not passing an exam or test. **without fail 1** regularly. **2** definitely. **failing** n **1** weak point. ♦ prep **2** in the absence of. **failure** n **1** act or instance of failing. **2** unsuccessful person or thing.

fain adv Obs gladly.

faint adj **1** lacking clarity, brightness, or volume. **2** feeling dizzy or weak. **3** lacking conviction or force. ♦ v **4** lose consciousness temporarily. ♦ n **5** temporary loss of consciousness.

fair[1] adj **1** unbiased and reasonable. **2** light in colour. **3** beautiful. **4** quite good, e.g. a fair attempt. **5** quite large, e.g. a fair amount of money. **6** (of weather) fine. ♦ adv **7** fairly. **fairly** adv **1** moderately. **2** to a great degree or extent. **3** as deserved, reasonably. **fairness** n **fairway** n Golf smooth area between the tee and the green.

fair[2] n **1** travelling entertainment with sideshows, rides, and amusements. **2** exhibition of commercial or industrial products. **fairground** n open space used for a fair.

Fair Isle n intricate multicoloured knitted pattern.

fairy n, pl **fairies 1** imaginary small creature with magic powers. **2** Offens male homosexual. **fairy godmother** person who helps in time of trouble. **fairyland** n **fairy lights** small coloured electric bulbs used as decoration. **fairy penguin** small penguin with a bluish head and back, found on the Australian coast. **fairy tale, story 1** story about fairies or magic. **2** unbelievable story or explanation.

fait accompli [**fate** ak-**kom**-plee] n French something already done that cannot be altered.

faith n **1** strong belief, esp. without proof. **2** religion. **3** complete confidence or trust. **4** allegiance to a person or cause. **faithful** adj **1** loyal. **2** consistently reliable. **3** accurate in detail. **faithfully** adv **faithless** adj disloyal or dishonest. **faith school** Brit school that provides a general education within a framework of a specific religious belief.

fake v **1** cause something not genuine to appear real or more valuable by fraud. **2** pretend to have (an illness, emotion, etc.). ♦ n **3** person, thing, or act that is not genuine. ♦ adj **4** not genuine.

fakir [**fay**-keer] n **1** Muslim who spurns worldly possessions. **2** Hindu holy man.

falcon n small bird of prey. **falconry** n **1** art of training falcons. **2** sport of hunting with falcons. **falconer** n

fall v **falling, fell, fallen 1** drop from a higher to a lower place through the force of gravity. **2** collapse to the ground. **3** decrease in number or quality. **4** pass into a specified condition. **5** occur. **6** n **7** falling. **8** thing or amount that falls. **9** decrease in value or number. **10** decline in power or influence. **11** US autumn. ♦ pl **12** waterfall. **fall for** v **1** Informal fall in love with. **2** be deceived by (a lie or trick). **fall guy 1** *Informal* victim of a confidence trick. **2** scapegoat.

fallout *n* radioactive particles spread as a result of a nuclear explosion.

fallacy *n, pl* **-cies 1** false belief. **2** unsound reasoning. **fallacious** *adj*

fallible *adj* (of a person) liable to make mistakes. **fallibility** *n*

Fallopian tube *n* either of a pair of tubes through which egg cells pass from the ovary to the womb.

fallow *adj* (of land) ploughed but left unseeded to regain fertility.

false *adj* **1** not true or correct. **2** artificial, fake. **3** deceptive, e.g. *false promises.* **falsely** *adv* **falseness** *n* **falsity** *n* **falsehood** *n* **1** quality of being untrue. **2** lie.

falsetto *n, pl* **-tos** voice pitched higher than one's natural range.

falsify *v* **-fying, -fied** alter fraudulently. **falsification** *n*

falter *v* **1** be hesitant, weak, or unsure. **2** lose power momentarily. **3** utter hesitantly. **4** move unsteadily.

fame *n* state of being widely known or recognized. **famed** *adj* famous.

familiar *adj* **1** well-known. **2** intimate, friendly. **3** too friendly. ♦ *n* **4** demon supposed to attend a witch. **5** friend. **familiarly** *adv* **familiarity** *n* **familiarize** *v* acquaint fully with a particular subject. **familiarization** *n*

family *n, pl* **-lies 1** group of parents and their children. **2** one's spouse and children. **3** group descended from a common ancestor. **4** group of related objects or beings. ♦ *adj* **5** suitable for parents and children together. **familial** *adj* **family planning** control of the number of children in a family by the use of contraception.

famine *n* severe shortage of food.

famished *adj* very hungry.

famous *adj* very well-known. **famously** *adv* *Informal* excellently.

fan[1] *n* **1** hand-held or mechanical object used to create a current of air for ventilation or cooling. ♦ *v* **fanning, fanned 2** blow or cool with a fan. **3** spread out like a fan. **fanbase** *n* body of admirers of a particular pop singer, sports team, etc. **fan belt** belt that drives a cooling fan in a car engine. **fantail** *n* small New Zealand bird with a tail like a fan.

fan[2] *n* *Informal* devotee of a pop star, sport, or hobby.

fanatic *n* person who is excessively enthusiastic about something. **fanatical** *adj* **fanatically** *adv* **fanaticism** *n*

fancy *adj* **-cier, -ciest 1** elaborate, not plain. **2** (of prices) higher than usual. ♦ *n, pl* **-cies 3** sudden irrational liking or desire. **4** uncontrolled imagination. ♦ *v* **-cying, -cied 5** *Informal* be sexually attracted to. **6** *Informal* have a wish for. **7** picture in the imagination. **8** suppose. **fancy oneself** *Informal* have a high opinion of oneself. **fanciful** *adj* **1** not based on fact. **2** excessively elaborate. **fancifully** *adv* **fancy dress** party costume representing a historical figure, animal, etc. **fancy-free** *adj* not in love.

fandango *n, pl* **-gos** lively Spanish dance.

fanfare *n* short loud tune played on brass instruments.

fang *n* **1** snake's tooth which injects poison. **2** long pointed tooth.

fantasia *n* musical composition of an improvised nature.

fantastic *adj* **1** *Informal* very good. **2** unrealistic or absurd. **3** strange or difficult to believe. **fantastically** *adv*

fantasy *n, pl* **-sies 1** far-fetched notion. **2** imagination unrestricted by reality. **3** daydream. **4** fiction with a large fantasy content. **fantasize** *v* indulge in daydreams.

FAQ *Computers* frequently asked question *or* questions.

far *adv* **farther** *or* **further, farthest** *or* **furthest 1** at, to, or from a great distance. **2** at or to a remote time. **3** very much. ♦ *adj* **4** remote in space or time. **Far East** East Asia. **far-fetched** *adj* hard to believe.

farad *n* unit of electrical capacitance.

farce *n* **1** boisterous comedy. **2** ludicrous situation. **farcical** *adj* ludicrous. **farcically** *adv*

fare *n* **1** charge for a passenger's journey. **2** passenger. **3** food provided. ♦ *v* **4** get on (as specified), e.g. *we fared badly*.

farewell *interj* **1** goodbye. ♦ *n* **2** act of saying goodbye and leaving. ♦ *v* **3** *NZ* say goodbye.

farinaceous *adj* containing starch or having a starchy texture.

farm *n* **1** area of land for growing crops or rearing livestock. **2** area of land or water for growing or rearing a specified animal or plant, e.g. *fish farm*. ♦ *v* **3** cultivate (land). **4** rear (stock). **farmhouse** *n* **farm out** *v* send (work) to be done by others. **farmstead** *n* farm and its buildings. **farmyard** *n*

farmer *n* person who owns or runs a farm.

farrago [far-**rah**-go] *n, pl* **-gos, -goes** jumbled mixture of things.

farrier *n* person who shoes horses.

farrow *n* **1** litter of piglets. ♦ *v* **2** (of a sow) give birth.

fart *Vulgar slang* ♦ *n* **1** emission of gas from the anus. ♦ *v* **2** emit gas from the anus.

farther, farthest *adv, adj see* FAR.

farthing *n* former British coin equivalent to a quarter of a penny.

fascia [**fay**-shya] *n, pl* **-ciae, -cias 1** outer surface of a dashboard. **2** flat

surface above a shop window.

fascinate *v* **1** attract and interest strongly. **2** make motionless from fear or awe. **fascinating** *adj* **fascination** *n*

> ☑ **SPELLING TIP**
> Remember that there is a silent *c* after the *s* in **fascinate**, **fascinated**, and **fascinating**.

fascism [**fash**-iz-zum] *n* right-wing totalitarian political system characterized by state control and extreme nationalism. **fascist** *adj, n*

fashion *n* **1** style in clothes, hairstyle, etc., popular at a particular time. **2** way something happens or is done. ♦ *v* **3** form or make into a particular shape. **fashionable** *adj* currently popular. **fashionably** *adv*

fast[1] *adj* **1** (capable of) acting or moving quickly. **2** done in or lasting a short time. **3** adapted to or allowing rapid movement. **4** (of a clock or watch) showing a time later than the correct time. **5** dissipated. **6** firmly fixed, fastened, or shut. ♦ *adv* **7** quickly. **8** soundly, deeply, e.g. *fast asleep*. **10** tightly and firmly. **fast food** food, such as hamburgers, prepared and served very quickly. **fast-track** *adj* **1** taking the quickest but most competitive route to success, e.g. *fast-track executives*. ♦ *v* **2** speed up the progress of (a project or person).

fast[2] *v* **1** go without food, esp. for religious reasons. ♦ *n* **2** period of fasting.

fasten *v* **1** make or become firmly fixed or joined. **2** close by fixing in place or locking. **3** (foll. by *on*) direct (one's attention) towards. **fastener, fastening** *n* device that fastens.

fastidious *adj* **1** very fussy about

details. **2** excessively concerned with cleanliness. **fastidiously** adv **fastidiousness** n

fastness n fortress, safe place.

fat adj **fatter, fattest 1** having excess flesh on the body. **2** (of meat) containing a lot of fat. **3** thick. **4** profitable. ♦ n **5** extra flesh on the body. **6** oily substance obtained from animals or plants. **fatness** n **fatten** v (cause to) become fat. **fatty** adj containing fat. **fathead** n Informal stupid person. **fat-headed** adj

fatal adj causing death or ruin. **fatally** adv **fatality** n, pl **-ties** death caused by an accident or disaster.

fatalism n belief that all events are predetermined and people are powerless to change their destinies. **fatalist** n **fatalistic** adj

fate n **1** power supposed to predetermine events. **2** inevitable fortune that befalls a person or thing. **fated** adj **1** destined. **2** doomed to death or destruction. **fateful** adj having important, usu. disastrous, consequences.

father n **1** male parent. **2** person who founds a line or family. **3** man who starts, creates, or invents something. **4** (F-) God. **5** (F-) title of some priests. ♦ v **6** be the father of (offspring). **fatherhood** n **fatherless** adj **fatherly** adj **father-in-law** n, pl **fathers-in-law** father of one's husband or wife. **fatherland** n one's native country.

fathom n **1** unit of length, used in navigation, equal to six feet (1.83 metres). ♦ v **2** understand. **fathomable** adj **fathomless** adj too deep or difficult to fathom.

fatigue [fat-**eeg**] n **1** extreme physical or mental tiredness. **2** weakening of a material due to stress. **3** soldier's nonmilitary duty. **4** v **5** tire out.

fatuous adj foolish. **fatuously** adv **fatuity** n

faucet [**faw**-set] n US tap.

fault n **1** responsibility for something wrong. **2** defect or flaw. **3** mistake or error. **4** Geology break in layers of rock. **5** Tennis, squash, etc. invalid serve. ♦ v **6** criticize or blame. **at fault** guilty of error. **find fault with** seek out minor imperfections in. **to a fault** excessively. **faulty** adj **faultless** adj **faultlessly** adv

faun n (in Roman legend) creature with a human face and torso and a goat's horns and legs.

fauna n, pl **-nas, -nae** animals of a given place or time.

faux pas [foe **pah**] n, pl **faux pas** social blunder.

favour n **1** approving attitude. **2** act of goodwill or generosity. **3** partiality. ♦ v **4** prefer. **5** regard or treat with especial kindness. **6** support or advocate.

favourable adj **1** encouraging or advantageous. **2** giving consent. **3** useful or beneficial. **favourably** adv

favourite adj **1** most liked. ♦ n **2** preferred person or thing. **3** Sport competitor expected to win. **favouritism** n practice of giving special treatment to a person or group.

fawn[1] n **1** young deer. ♦ adj **2** light yellowish-brown.

fawn[2] v **1** (foll. by on) seek attention from (someone) by insincere flattery. **2** (of a dog) try to please by a show of extreme affection.

fax n **1** electronic system for sending facsimiles of documents by telephone. **2** document sent by this system. ♦ v **3** send (a document) by this system.

FBI US Federal Bureau of Investigation.

FC (in Britain) Football Club.

Fe Chem iron.

fealty n (in feudal society)

subordinate's loyalty to his ruler or lord.

fear *n* **1** distress or alarm caused by impending danger or pain. **2** something that causes distress. ♦ *v* **3** be afraid of (something or someone). **fear for** feel anxiety about something. **fearful** *adj* **1** feeling fear. **2** causing fear. **3** *Informal* very unpleasant. **fearfully** *adv* **fearless** *adj* **fearlessly** *adv* **fearsome** *adj* terrifying.

feasible *adj* able to be done, possible. **feasibly** *adv* **feasibility** *n*

feast *n* **1** lavish meal. **2** something extremely pleasing. **3** annual religious celebration. ♦ *v* **4** eat a feast. **5** give a feast to. **6** (foll. by *on*) eat a large amount of.

feat *n* remarkable, skilful, or daring action.

feather *n* **1** one of the barbed shafts forming the plumage of birds. ♦ *v* **2** fit or cover with feathers. **3** turn (an oar) edgeways. **feather in one's cap** achievement one can be pleased with. **feather one's nest** make one's life comfortable. **feathered** *adj* **feathery** *adj* **featherweight** *n* **1** boxer weighing up to 126lb (professional) or 57kg (amateur). **2** insignificant person or thing.

feature *n* **1** part of the face, such as the eyes. **2** prominent or distinctive part. **3** special article in a newspaper or magazine. **4** main film in a cinema programme. ♦ *v* **5** have as a feature or be a feature in. **6** give prominence to. **featureless** *adj*

Feb. February.

febrile [**fee**-brile] *adj* feverish.

February *n* second month of the year.

feckless *adj* ineffectual or irresponsible.

fecund *adj* fertile. **fecundity** *n*

fed *v* past of FEED. **fed up** *Informal* bored, dissatisfied.

federal *adj* **1** of a system in which power is divided between one central government and several regional governments. **2** of the central government of a federation. **federalism** *n* **federalist** *n* **federate** *v* unite in a federation. **federation** *n* **1** union of several states, provinces, etc. **2** association.

fedora [fid-**or**-a] *n* man's soft hat with a brim.

fee *n* **1** charge paid to be allowed to do something. **2** payment for professional services.

feeble *adj* **1** lacking physical or mental power. **2** unconvincing. **feebleness** *n* **feebly** *adv* **feeble-minded** *adj* unable to think or understand effectively.

feed *v* **feeding, fed 1** give food to. **2** give (something) as food. **3** eat. **4** supply or prepare food for. **5** supply (what is needed). ♦ *n* **6** act of feeding. **7** food, esp. for babies or animals. **8** *Informal* meal. **feeder** *n* road or railway line linking outlying areas to the main traffic network. **feedback** *n* **1** information received in response to something done. **2** return of part of the output of an electrical circuit or loudspeaker to its source.

feel *v* **feeling, felt 1** have a physical or emotional sensation of. **2** become aware of or examine by touch. **3** believe. ♦ *n* **4** act of feeling. **5** impression. **6** way something feels. **7** sense of touch. **8** instinctive aptitude. **feeler** *n* **1** organ of touch in some animals. **2** remark made to test others' opinion. **feeling** *n* **1** emotional reaction. **2** intuitive understanding. **3** opinion. **4** sympathy, understanding. **5** ability to experience physical sensations. **6** sensation experienced. ♦ *pl* **7** emotional sensitivities. **feel like** wish for, want.

feet *n* plural of FOOT.

feign [fane] v pretend.

feint[1] [faint] n 1 sham attack or blow meant to distract an opponent. ♦ v 2 make a feint.

feint[2] [faint] n narrow lines on ruled paper.

feldspar n hard mineral that is the main constituent of igneous rocks.

felicity n 1 happiness. 2 pl -ties) appropriate expression or style. **felicitations** pl n congratulations. **felicitous** adj

feline adj 1 of cats. 2 catlike. ♦ n 3 member of the cat family.

fell[1] v past tense of FALL.

fell[2] v 1 cut down (a tree). 2 knock down.

fell[3] adj in one fell swoop in a single action or occurrence.

fell[4] n Scot & N English mountain, hill, or moor.

felloe n (segment of) the rim of a wheel.

fellow n 1 man or boy. 2 comrade or associate. 3 person in the same group or condition. 4 member of a learned society or the governing body of a college. ♦ adj 5 in the same group or condition. **fellowship** n 1 sharing of aims or interests. 2 group with shared aims or interests. 3 feeling of friendliness. 4 paid research post in a college or university.

felon n Criminal law (formerly) person guilty of a felony. **felony** n, pl -nies serious crime. **felonious** adj

felspar n same as FELDSPAR.

felt[1] v past of FEEL.

felt[2] n matted fabric made by bonding fibres by pressure. **felt-tip pen** pen with a writing point made from pressed fibres.

fem. feminine.

female adj 1 of the sex which bears offspring. 2 (of plants) producing fruits. ♦ n 3 female person or animal.

feminine adj 1 having qualities traditionally regarded as suitable for, or typical of, women. 2 of women. 3 belonging to a particular class of grammatical inflection in some languages. **femininity** n **feminism** n advocacy of equal rights for women. **feminist** n, adj

femme fatale [fam fat-**tahl**] n, pl **femmes fatales** alluring woman who leads men into dangerous situations by her charm.

femur [**fee**-mer] n thighbone. **femoral** adj of the thigh.

fen n Brit low-lying flat marshy land.

fence n 1 barrier of posts linked by wire or wood, enclosing an area. 2 Slang dealer in stolen property. ♦ v 3 enclose with or as if with a fence. 4 fight with swords as a sport. 5 avoid a question. **fencing** n 1 sport of fighting with swords. 2 material for making fences. **fencer** n

fend v fend for oneself provide for oneself. **fend off** v defend oneself against (verbal or physical attack).

fender n 1 low metal frame in front of a fireplace. 2 soft but solid object hung over a ship's side to prevent damage when docking. 3 Chiefly US wing of a car.

feng shui [fung **shway**] n Chinese art of deciding the best design of a building, etc., in order to bring good luck.

fennel n fragrant plant whose seeds, leaves, and root are used in cookery.

fenugreek n Mediterranean plant grown for its heavily scented seeds.

feral adj wild.

ferment n 1 commotion, unrest. ♦ v 2 undergo or cause to undergo fermentation. **fermentation** n reaction in which an organic molecule splits into simpler substances, esp. the conversion of sugar to alcohol.

fern *n* flowerless plant with fine fronds.

ferocious *adj* savagely fierce or cruel. **ferocity** *n*

ferret *n* **1** tamed polecat used to catch rabbits or rats. ♦ *v* **ferreting, ferreted 2** hunt with ferrets. **3** search around. **ferret out** *v* find by searching.

ferric, ferrous *adj* of or containing iron.

Ferris wheel *n* large vertical fairground wheel with hanging seats for riding in.

ferry *n, pl* **-ries 1** boat for transporting people and vehicles. **2** *v* **-rying, -ried 3** carry by ferry. **4** convey (goods or people). **ferryman** *n*

fertile *adj* **1** capable of producing young, crops, or vegetation. **2** highly productive, e.g. *a fertile mind*. **fertility** *n* **fertilize** *v* **1** provide (an animal or plant) with sperm or pollen to bring about fertilization. **2** supply (soil) with nutrients. **fertilization** *n*

fertilizer *n* substance added to the soil to increase its productivity.

fervent, fervid *adj* intensely passionate and sincere. **fervently** *adv* **fervour** *n* intensity of feeling.

fescue *n* pasture and lawn grass with stiff narrow leaves.

fester *v* **1** grow worse and increasingly hostile. **2** (of a wound) form pus. **3** rot and decay.

festival *n* **1** organized series of special events or performances. **2** day or period of celebration. **festive** *adj* of or like a celebration. **festivity** *n, pl* **-ties 1** happy celebration. ♦ *pl* **2** celebrations.

festoon *v* hang decorations in loops.

feta *n* white salty Greek cheese.

fetch *v* **1** go after and bring back. **2** be sold for. **3** *Informal* deal (a blow). **fetching** *adj* attractive. **fetch up** *v*

Informal arrive or end up.

fete [**fate**] *n* **1** gala, bazaar, etc., usu. held outdoors. ♦ *v* **2** honour or entertain regally.

fetid *adj* stinking.

fetish *n* **1** form of behaviour in which sexual pleasure is derived from looking at or handling an inanimate object. **2** thing with which one is excessively concerned. **3** object believed to have magical powers. **fetishism** *n* **fetishist** *n*

fetlock *n* projection behind and above a horse's hoof.

fetter *n* **1** chain or shackle for the foot. ♦ *pl* **2** restrictions. ♦ *v* **3** restrict. **4** bind in fetters.

fettle *n* state of health or spirits.

fetus [**fee**-tuss] *n, pl* **-tuses** embryo of a mammal in the later stages of development. **fetal** *adj*

feu *n* (in Scotland) right of use of land in return for a fixed annual payment.

feud *n* **1** long bitter hostility between two people or groups. ♦ *v* **2** carry on a feud.

feudalism *n* medieval system in which people held land from a lord, and in return worked and fought for him. **feudal** *adj* of or like feudalism.

fever *n* **1** (illness causing) high body temperature. **2** nervous excitement. **fevered** *adj* **feverish** *adj* **1** suffering from fever. **2** in a state of nervous excitement. **feverishly** *adv*

few *adj* not many. **a few** small number. **quite a few, a good few** several.

☑ **WORD TIP**
Few(er) is used of things that can be counted: *Fewer than five visits.* Compare *less*, which is used for quantity: *It uses less sugar.*

---

fey *adj* **1** whimsically strange. **2** having

the ability to look into the future.

fez n, pl **fezzes** brimless tasselled cap, orig. from Turkey.

ff Music fortissimo.

fiancé [fee-**on**-say] n man engaged to be married. **fiancée** n fem

fiasco n, pl **-cos, -coes** ridiculous or humiliating failure.

fiat [fee-at] n 1 arbitrary order. 2 official permission.

fib n 1 trivial lie. ♦ v **fibbing, fibbed** 2 tell a lie. **fibber** n

fibre n 1 thread that can be spun into yarn. 2 threadlike animal or plant tissue. 3 fibrous material in food. 4 strength of character. 5 essential substance or nature. **fibrous** adj **fibreglass** n material made of fine glass fibres. **fibre optics** transmission of information by light along very thin flexible fibres of glass.

fibro n Aust mixture of cement and asbestos fibre, used in sheets for building (also **fibrocement**).

fibroid [fibe-royd] 1 n 2 benign tumour composed of fibrous connective tissue. **fibrositis** [fibe-roh-**site**-iss] n inflammation of the tissues of muscle sheaths.

fibula n, pl **-lae, -las** slender outer bone of the lower leg.

fiche [feesh] n sheet of film for storing publications in miniaturized form.

fickle adj changeable, inconstant. **fickleness** n

fiction n 1 literary works of the imagination, such as novels. 2 invented story. **fictional** adj **fictionalize** v turn into fiction. **fictitious** adj 1 not genuine. 2 of or in fiction.

fiddle n 1 violin. 2 Informal dishonest action or scheme. ♦ v 3 play the violin. 4 falsify (accounts). 5 move or touch something restlessly. **fiddling** adj trivial. **fiddly** adj awkward to do or

use. **fiddlesticks** interj expression of annoyance or disagreement.

fidelity n 1 faithfulness. 2 accuracy in detail. 3 quality of sound reproduction.

fidget v 1 move about restlessly. ♦ n 2 person who fidgets. ♦ pl 3 restlessness. **fidgety** adj

fiduciary [fid-**yew**-she-er-ee] Law ♦ n, pl **-aries** 1 person bound to act for someone else's benefit, as a trustee. ♦ adj 2 of a trust or trustee.

fief [feef] n Hist land granted by a lord in return for war service.

field n 1 enclosed piece of agricultural land. 2 marked off area for sports. 3 area rich in a specified natural resource. 4 sphere of knowledge or activity. 5 place away from the laboratory or classroom where practical work is done. 6 v 7 Sport catch and return (a ball). 8 deal with (a question) successfully. **fielder** n Sport player whose task is to field the ball. **field day** day or time of exciting activity. **field events** throwing and jumping events in athletics. **fieldfare** n type of large Old World thrush. **field glasses** binoculars. **field marshal** army officer of the highest rank. **field sports** hunting, shooting, and fishing. **fieldwork** n investigation made in the field as opposed to the classroom or the laboratory.

fiend [feend] n 1 evil spirit. 2 cruel or wicked person. 3 Informal person devoted to something, e.g. fitness fiend. **fiendish** adj **fiendishly** adv

fierce adj 1 wild or aggressive. 2 intense or strong. **fiercely** adv **fierceness** n

fiery adj **fierier, fieriest** 1 consisting of or like fire. 2 easily angered. 3 (of food) very spicy.

fiesta n religious festival, carnival.

fife n small high-pitched flute.

fifteen adj, n five and ten. **fifteenth**

adj, n

fifth *adj, n* (of) number five in a series. **fifth column** group secretly helping the enemy.

fifty *adj, n, pl* **-ties** five times ten. **fiftieth** *adj, n*

fig *n* **1** soft pear-shaped fruit. **2** tree bearing it.

fight *v* **fighting, fought 1** struggle (against) in battle or physical combat. **2** struggle to overcome someone or obtain something. **3** carry on (a battle or contest). **4** make (one's way) somewhere with difficulty. ♦ *n* **5** aggressive conflict between two (groups of) people. **6** quarrel or contest. **7** resistance. **8** boxing match. **fighter** *n* **1** boxer. **2** determined person. **3** aircraft designed to destroy other aircraft. **fight off** *v* drive away (an attacker). **2** struggle to avoid.

figment *n* **figment of one's imagination** imaginary thing.

figure *n* **1** numerical symbol. **2** amount expressed in numbers. **3** bodily shape. **4** well-known person. **5** representation in painting or sculpture of a human form. **6** *Maths* any combination of lines, planes, points, or curves. **7** *v* **8** consider, conclude. **9** (usu. foll. by *in*) be included (in). **figure of speech** expression in which words do not have their literal meaning. **figurative** *adj* (of language) abstract, imaginative, or symbolic. **figuratively** *adv* **figurine** *n* statuette. **figurehead** *n* **1** nominal leader. **2** carved bust at the bow of a ship. **figure out** *v* solve or understand.

filament *n* **1** fine wire in a light bulb that gives out light. **2** fine thread.

filbert *n* hazelnut.

filch *v* steal (small amounts).

file¹ *n* **1** box or folder used to keep documents in order. **2** documents in a file. **3** information about a person or subject. **4** line of people one behind the other. **5** *Computers* organized collection of related material. ♦ *v* **6** place (a document) in a file. **7** place (a legal document) on official record. **8** bring a lawsuit, esp. for divorce. **9** walk or march in a line.

file² *n* **1** tool with a roughened blade for smoothing or shaping. ♦ *v* **2** shape or smooth with a file. **filings** *pl n* shavings removed by a file.

filial *adj* of or befitting a son or daughter.

filibuster *n* **1** obstruction of legislation by making long speeches. **2** person who filibusters. ♦ *v* **3** obstruct (legislation) with such delaying tactics.

filigree *n* **1** delicate ornamental work of gold or silver wire. ♦ *adj* **2** made of filigree.

fill *v* **1** make or become full. **2** occupy completely. **3** plug (a gap). **4** satisfy (a need). **5** hold and perform the duties of (a position). **6** appoint to (a job or position). **one's fill** sufficient for one's needs or wants. **filler** *n* substance that fills a gap or increases bulk. **filling** *n* **1** substance that fills a gap or cavity, esp. in a tooth. ♦ *adj* **2** (of food) substantial and satisfying. **filling station** *Chiefly Brit* garage selling petrol, oil, etc.

fillet *n* **1** boneless piece of meat or fish. ♦ *v* **filleting, filleted 2** remove the bones from.

fillip *n* something that adds stimulation or enjoyment.

filly *n, pl* **-lies** young female horse.

film *n* **1** sequence of images projected on a screen, creating the illusion of movement. **2** story told in such a sequence of images. **3** thin strip of light-sensitive cellulose used to make photographic negatives and transparencies. **4** thin sheet or layer. ♦ *v* **5** photograph with a movie or video camera. **6** make a film of (a scene, story, etc.). **7** cover or become covered with a thin layer. ♦ *adj* **8** connected with films or the cinema. **filmy** *adj* very thin, delicate. **film strip** set of pictures on a strip of film, projected separately as slides.

filter *n* **1** material or device permitting fluid to pass but retaining solid particles. **2** device that blocks certain frequencies of sound or light. **3** *Brit* traffic signal that allows vehicles to turn left or right while the main signals are at red. ♦ *v* **4** remove impurities from (a substance) with a filter. **5** pass slowly or faintly.

filth *n* **1** disgusting dirt. **2** offensive material or language. **filthy** *adj* **filthiness** *n*

filtrate *n* **1** filtered gas or liquid. ♦ *v* **2** remove impurities with a filter. **filtration** *n*

fin *n* **1** projection from a fish's body enabling it to balance and swim. **2** vertical tailplane of an aircraft.

finagle [fin-**nay**-gl] *v* get or achieve by craftiness or trickery.

final *adj* **1** at the end. **2** having no possibility of further change, action, or discussion. ♦ *n* **3** deciding contest between winners of previous rounds in a competition. ♦ *pl* **4** *Brit & S Afr* last examinations in an educational course. **finally** *adv* **finality** *n* **finalist** *n* competitor in a final. **finalize** *v* put into final form. **finale** [fin-**nah**-lee] *n* concluding part of a dramatic performance or musical work.

finance *v* **1** provide or obtain funds for. ♦ *n* **2** management of money, loans, or credits. **3** (provision of) funds. ♦ *pl* **4** money resources. **financial** *adj* **financially** *adv* **financier** *n* person involved in large-scale financial business. **financial year** twelve-month period used for financial

calculations.

finch *n, pl* **finches** small songbird with a short strong beak.

find *v* **finding, found** **1** discover by chance. **2** discover by search or effort. **3** become aware of. **4** consider to have a particular quality. **5** experience (a particular feeling). **6** *Law* pronounce (the defendant) guilty or not guilty. **7** provide, esp. with difficulty. ♦ *n* **8** person or thing found, esp. when valuable. **finder** *n* **finding** *n* conclusion from an investigation. **find out** *v* **1** gain knowledge of. **2** detect (a crime, deception, etc.).

fine¹ *adj* **1** very good. **2** (of weather) clear and dry. **3** in good health. **4** satisfactory. **5** of delicate workmanship. **6** thin or slender. **7** subtle or abstruse, e.g. *a fine distinction.* **finely** *adv* **fineness** *n* **finery** *n* showy clothing. **fine art** art produced to appeal to the sense of beauty. **fine-tune** *v* make small adjustments to (something) so that it works really well.

fine² *n* **1** payment imposed as a penalty. ♦ *v* **2** impose a fine on.

finesse [fin-**ness**] *n* **1** delicate skill. **2** subtlety and tact.

finger *n* **1** one of the four long jointed parts of the hand. **2** part of a glove that covers a finger. **3** quantity of liquid in a glass as deep as a finger is wide. ♦ *v* **4** touch or handle with the fingers. **fingering** *n* technique of using the fingers in playing a musical instrument. **fingerboard** *n* part of a stringed instrument against which the strings are pressed. **fingerprint** *n* **1** impression of the ridges on the tip of the finger. ♦ *v* **2** take the fingerprints of (someone). **finger stall** cover to protect an injured finger.

finicky *adj* **1** excessively particular, fussy. **2** overelaborate.

finish v **1** bring to an end, stop. **2** use up. **3** bring to a desired or completed condition. **4** put a surface texture on (wood, cloth, or metal). **5** defeat or destroy. ♦ n **6** end, last part. **7** death or defeat. **8** surface texture.

finite adj having limits in space, time, or size.

fiord n same as FJORD.

fir n pyramid-shaped tree with needle-like leaves and erect cones.

fire n **1** state of combustion producing heat, flames, and smoke. **2** Brit burning coal or wood, or a gas or electric device, used to heat a room. **3** uncontrolled destructive burning. **4** shooting of guns. **5** intense passion, ardour. ♦ v **6** operate (a weapon) so that a bullet or missile is released. **7** Informal dismiss from employment. **8** bake (ceramics etc.) in a kiln. **9** excite. **firearm** n rifle, pistol, or shotgun. **firebrand** n person who causes unrest. **firebreak** n strip of cleared land to stop the advance of a fire. **fire brigade** organized body of people whose job is to put out fires. **firedamp** n explosive gas, composed mainly of methane, formed in mines. **fire drill** rehearsal of procedures for escape from a fire. **fire engine** vehicle with apparatus for extinguishing fires. **fire escape** metal staircase or ladder down the outside of a building for escape in the event of fire. **firefighter** n member of a fire brigade. **firefly** n, pl **-flies** beetle that glows in the dark. **fireguard** n protective grating in front of a fire. **fire irons** tongs, poker, and shovel for tending a domestic fire. **fireplace** n recess in a room for a fire. **fire power** Mil amount a weapon or unit can fire. **fire station** building where firefighters are stationed. **firewall** n Computers computer that prevents unauthorized access to a computer network from the Internet. **firework** n **1** device containing chemicals that is ignited to produce spectacular explosions and coloured sparks. ♦ pl **2** show of fireworks. **3** Informal outburst of temper. **firing squad** group of soldiers ordered to execute an offender by shooting.

firm¹ adj **1** not soft or yielding. **2** securely in position. **3** definite. **4** having determination or strength. ♦ adv **5** in an unyielding manner, e.g. hold firm. ♦ v **6** make or become firm. **firmly** adv **firmness** n

firm² n business company.

firmament n Lit sky or the heavens.

first adj **1** earliest in time or order. **2** graded or ranked above all others. ♦ n **3** person or thing coming before all others. **4** outset or beginning. **5** first-class honours degree at university. **6** lowest forward gear in a motor vehicle. ♦ adv **7** before anything else. **8** for the first time. **firstly** adv **first aid** immediate medical assistance given in an emergency. **first-class** adj **1** of the highest class or grade. **2** excellent. **first-hand** adj, adv (obtained) directly from the original source. **first mate** officer of a merchant ship second in command to the captain. **first person** Grammar category of verbs and pronouns used by a speaker to refer to himself or herself. **first-rate** adj excellent. **first-strike** adj (of a nuclear missile) for use in an opening attack to destroy enemy weapons.

firth n narrow inlet of the sea, esp. in Scotland.

fiscal adj of government finances, esp. taxes.

fish n, pl **fish, fishes** **1** cold-blooded vertebrate with gills, that lives in water. **2** its flesh as food. ♦ v **3** try to catch fish. **4** fish in (a particular area of water). **5** (foll. by for) grope for and find with difficulty. **6** (foll. by *for*) seek indirectly. **fisherman** *n* person who catches fish for a living or for pleasure. **fishery** *n, pl* **-eries** area of the sea used for fishing. **fishy** *adj* **1** of or like fish. **2** *Informal* suspicious or questionable. **fishfinger** *n* oblong piece of fish covered in breadcrumbs. **fishmeal** dried ground fish used as animal feed or fertilizer. **fishmonger** *n* seller of fish. **fishnet** *n* open mesh fabric resembling netting. **fishwife** *n, pl* **-wives** coarse scolding woman.

fishplate *n* metal plate holding rails together.

fission *n* **1** splitting. **2** *Biol* asexual reproduction involving a division into two or more equal parts. **3** splitting of an atomic nucleus with the release of a large amount of energy. **fissionable** *adj* **fissile** *adj* **1** capable of undergoing nuclear fission. **2** tending to split.

fissure [**fish**-er] *n* long narrow cleft or crack.

fist *n* clenched hand. **fisticuffs** *pl n* fighting with the fists.

fit[1] *v* **fitting, fitted 1** be appropriate or suitable for. **2** be of the correct size or shape (for). **3** adjust so as to make appropriate. **4** try (clothes) on and note any adjustments needed. **5** make competent or ready. **6** correspond with the facts or circumstances. ♦ *adj* **7** appropriate. **8** in good health. **9** worthy or deserving. ♦ *n* **10** way in which something fits. **fitness** *n* **fitter** *n* **1** person skilled in the installation and adjustment of machinery. **2** person who fits garments. **fitting** *adj* **1** appropriate, suitable. ♦ *n* **2** accessory or part. **3** trying on of clothes for size. ♦ *pl* **4** furnishings and accessories in a building. **fitment** *n* detachable part of the furnishings of a room. **fit in** *v* **1** give a place or time to. **2** belong or

conform. **fit out** *v* provide with the necessary equipment.

fit[2] *n* **1** sudden attack or convulsion, such as an epileptic seizure. **2** sudden short burst or spell.

fitful *adj* occurring in irregular spells. **fitfully** *adv*

five *adj, n* one more than four. **fiver** *n* *Informal* five-pound note. **fives** *n* ball game resembling squash but played with bats or the hands.

fix *v* **1** make or become firm, stable, or secure. **2** repair. **3** place permanently. **4** settle definitely. **5** direct (the eyes etc.) steadily. **6** *Informal* unfairly influence the outcome of. ♦ *n* **7** *Informal* difficult situation. **8** ascertaining of the position of a ship by radar etc. **9** *Slang* injection of a narcotic drug. **fixed** *adj* **fixedly** *adv* steadily. **fixer** *n* **1** solution used to make a photographic image permanent. **2** *Slang* person who arranges things. **fix up** *v* **1** arrange. **2** provide (with).

fixation *n* obsessive interest in something. **fixated** *adj* obsessed.

fixative *n* liquid used to preserve or hold things in place.

fixture *n* **1** permanently fitted piece of household equipment. **2** person whose presence seems permanent. **3** sports match or the date fixed for it.

fizz *v* **1** make a hissing or bubbling noise. **2** give off small bubbles. ♦ *n* **3** hissing or bubbling noise. **4** releasing of small bubbles of gas by a liquid. **5** effervescent drink. **fizzy** *adj*

fizzle *v* make a weak hissing or bubbling sound. **fizzle out** *v* *Informal* come to nothing, fail.

fjord [fee-**ord**] *n* long narrow inlet of the sea between cliffs, esp. in Norway.

flab *n* *Informal* unsightly body fat.

flabbergasted *adj* completely astonished.

flabby *adj* **-bier, -biest 1** having flabby flesh. **2** loose or limp.

flaccid [**flas**-sid] *adj* soft and limp. **flaccidity** *n*

flag¹ *n* **1** piece of cloth attached to a pole as an emblem or signal. ♦ *v* **flagging, flagged 2** mark with a flag or sticker. **3** (often foll. by *down*) signal (a vehicle) to stop by waving the arm. **flag day** *Brit* day on which small stickers are sold in the streets for charity. **flagpole, flagstaff** *n* pole for a flag. **flagship** *n* **1** admiral's ship. **2** most important product of an organization.

flag² *v* **flagging, flagged** lose enthusiasm or vigour.

flag³, flagstone *n* flat paving-stone. **flagged** *adj* paved with flagstones.

flagellate [**flaj**-a-late] *v* whip, esp. in religious penance or for sexual pleasure. **flagellation** *n* **flagellant** *n* person who whips himself or herself.

flageolet [flaj-a-**let**] *n* small instrument like a recorder.

flagon *n* **1** wide bottle for wine or cider. **2** narrow-necked jug for liquid.

flagrant [**flayg**-rant] *adj* openly outrageous. **flagrantly** *adv*

flail *v* **1** wave about wildly. **2** beat or thrash. ♦ *n* **3** tool formerly used for threshing grain by hand.

flair *n* **1** natural ability. **2** stylishness.

flak *n* **1** anti-aircraft fire. **2** *Informal* severe criticism.

flake¹ *n* **1** small thin piece, esp. chipped off something. **2** *Aust & NZ informal* unreliable person. ♦ *v* **3** peel off in flakes. **flaky** *adj* **flake out** *v Informal* collapse or fall asleep from exhaustion.

flake² *n* (in Australia) the commercial name for the meat of the gummy shark.

flambé [**flahm**-bay] *v* **flambéing, flambéed** cook or serve (food) in flaming brandy.

flamboyant *adj* **1** behaving in a very noticeable, extravagant way. **2** very bright and showy. **flamboyance** *n*

flame *n* **1** luminous burning gas coming from burning material. ♦ *v* **2** burn brightly. **3** become bright red. **old flame** *Informal* former sweetheart.

flamenco *n, pl* **-cos 1** rhythmical Spanish dance accompanied by a guitar and vocalist. **2** music for this dance.

flamingo *n, pl* **-gos, -goes** large pink wading bird with a long neck and legs.

flammable *adj* easily set on fire. **flammability** *n*

> ☑ **WORD TIP**
> This now replaces *inflammable* in labelling and packaging because *inflammable* was often mistaken to mean 'not flammable'.

flan *n* open sweet or savoury tart.

flange *n* projecting rim or collar.

flank *n* **1** part of the side between the hips and ribs. **2** side of a body of troops. ♦ *v* **3** be at or move along the side of.

flannel *n* **1** *Brit* small piece of cloth for washing the face. **2** soft woollen fabric for clothing. **3** *Informal* evasive talk. ♦ *pl* **4** trousers made of flannel. ♦ *v* **-nelling, -nelled 5** *Informal* talk evasively. **flannelette** *n* cotton imitation of flannel.

flap *v* **flapping, flapped 1** move back and forwards or up and down. ♦ *n* **2** action or sound of flapping. **3** piece of something attached by one edge only. **4** *Informal* state of excitement or panic.

flapjack *n* chewy biscuit made with oats.

flare *v* **1** blaze with a sudden unsteady flame. **2** *Informal* (of temper, violence, or trouble) break out suddenly. **3** (of a skirt or trousers) become wider towards the hem. ♦ *n* **4** sudden unsteady flame. **5** signal light. ♦ *pl* **6** flared trousers. **flared** *adj* (of a skirt or trousers) becoming wider towards the hem.

flash *n* **1** sudden burst of light or flame. **2** sudden occurrence (of intuition or emotion). **3** very short time. **4** brief unscheduled news announcement. **5** *Photog* small bulb that produces an intense flash of light. ♦ *adj* **6** (also **flashy**) vulgarly showy. ♦ *v* **7** (cause to) burst into flame. **8** (cause to) emit light suddenly or intermittently. **9** move very fast. **10** come rapidly (to mind or view). **11** *Informal* display ostentatiously. **12** *Slang* expose oneself indecently. **flasher** *n Slang* man who exposes himself indecently. **flashback** *n* scene in a book, play, or film, that shows earlier events. **flash flood** sudden short-lived flood. **flashlight** *n US* torch. **flash point 1** critical point beyond which a situation will inevitably erupt into violence. **2** lowest temperature at which vapour given off by a liquid can ignite.

flashing *n* watertight material used to cover joins in a roof.

flask *n* **1** same as VACUUM FLASK. **2** flat bottle for carrying alcoholic drink in the pocket. **3** narrow-necked bottle.

flat¹ *adj* **flatter, flattest 1** level and horizontal. **2** even and smooth. **3** (of a tyre) deflated. **4** outright. **5** fixed. **6** without variation or emotion. **7** (of a drink) no longer fizzy. **8** (of a battery) with no electrical charge. **9** *Music* below the true pitch. ♦ *adv* **10** in or into a flat position. **11** completely or absolutely. **12** exactly. **13** *Music* too low in pitch. ♦ *n* **14** *Music* symbol lowering the pitch of a note by a semitone. **15** mud bank exposed at low tide. **flat out** with maximum

speed or effort. **flatly** *adv* **flatness** *n* **flatten** *v* **flatfish** *n* sea fish, such as the sole, which has a flat body.

flat-pack *adj* (of furniture, etc.) supplied in pieces in a flat box for assembly by the buyer. **flat racing** horse racing over level ground with no jumps.

flat² *n* **1** set of rooms for living in which are part of a larger building. ♦ *v* **flatting, flatted 2** *Aust & NZ* live in a flat. **flatlet** *n Brit, Aust & S Afr* small flat. **flatmate** *n* person with whom one shares a flat.

flatter *v* **1** praise insincerely. **2** show to advantage. **3** make (a person) appear more attractive in a picture than in reality. **flatterer** *n* **flattery** *n*

flattie *n NZ & S Afr informal* flat tyre.

flatulent *adj* suffering from or caused by too much gas in the intestines. **flatulence** *n*

flaunt *v* display (oneself or one's possessions) arrogantly.

> ☑ **WORD TIP**
> Be careful not to confuse this with *flout* meaning 'disobey'.

flautist *n* flute player.

flavour *n* **1** distinctive taste. **2** distinctive characteristic or quality. ♦ *v* **3** give flavour to. **flavouring** *n* substance used to flavour food. **flavourless** *adj*

flaw *n* **1** imperfection or blemish. **2** mistake that makes a plan or argument invalid. **flawed** *adj* **flawless** *adj*

flax *n* **1** plant grown for its stem fibres and seeds. **2** its fibres, spun into linen thread. **flaxen** *adj* (of hair) pale yellow.

flay *v* **1** strip the skin off. **2** criticize severely.

flea *n* small wingless jumping

bloodsucking insect. **flea market** market for cheap goods. **fleapit** n Informal shabby cinema or theatre.

fleck n 1 small mark, streak, or speck. ♦ v 2 speckle.

fled v past of FLEE.

fledged adj 1 (of young birds) able to fly. 2 (of people) fully trained. **fledgling, fledgeling** n 1 young bird. ♦ adj 2 new or inexperienced.

flee v **fleeing, fled** run away (from).

fleece n 1 sheep's coat of wool. 2 sheepskin used as a lining for coats etc. 3 warm polyester fabric. 4 Brit jacket or top made of this fabric. ♦ v 5 defraud or overcharge. **fleecy** adj made of or like fleece.

fleet[1] n 1 number of warships organized as a unit. 2 number of vehicles under the same ownership.

fleet[2] adj swift in movement. **fleeting** adj rapid and soon passing. **fleetingly** adv

flesh n 1 soft part of a human or animal body. 2 Informal excess fat. 3 meat of animals as opposed to fish or fowl. 4 thick soft part of a fruit or vegetable. 5 human body as opposed to the soul. **in the flesh** in person, actually present. **one's own flesh and blood** one's family. **flesh-coloured** adj yellowish-pink. **fleshly** adj 1 carnal. 2 worldly. **fleshy** adj 1 plump. 2 like flesh. **flesh wound** wound affecting only superficial tissue.

fleur-de-lys, fleur-de-lis [flur-de-**lee**] n, pl **fleurs-de-lys, fleurs-de-lis** heraldic lily with three petals.

flew v past tense of FLY[1].

flex n 1 flexible insulated electric cable. ♦ v 2 bend. **flexible** adj 1 easily bent. 2 adaptable. **flexibly** adv **flexibility** n **flexitime, flextime** n system permitting variation in starting and finishing times of work.

flick v 1 touch or move with the finger

or hand in a quick movement. 2 move with a short sudden movement, often repeatedly. ♦ v 3 tap or quick stroke. ♦ pl 4 Slang the cinema. **flick knife** knife with a spring-loaded blade which shoots out when a button is pressed. **flick through** v look at (a book or magazine) quickly or idly.

flicker v 1 shine unsteadily or intermittently. 2 move quickly to and fro. ♦ n 3 unsteady brief light. 4 brief faint indication.

flier n see FLY[1].

flight[1] n 1 journey by air. 2 act or manner of flying through the air. 3 group of birds or aircraft flying together. 4 aircraft flying on a scheduled journey. 5 set of stairs between two landings. 6 stabilizing feathers or plastic fins on an arrow or dart. **flightless** adj (of certain birds or insects) unable to fly. **flight attendant** person who looks after passengers on an aircraft. **flight deck** 1 crew compartment in an airliner. 2 runway deck on an aircraft carrier. **flight recorder** electronic device in an aircraft storing information about its flight.

flight[2] n act of running away.

flighty adj **flightier, flightiest** frivolous and fickle.

flimsy adj **-sier, -siest** 1 not strong or substantial. 2 thin. 3 not very convincing. **flimsily** adv **flimsiness** n

flinch v draw back or wince, as from pain. **flinch from** v shrink from or avoid.

fling v **flinging, flung** 1 throw, send, or move forcefully or hurriedly. ♦ n 2 spell of self-indulgent enjoyment. 3 brief romantic or sexual relationship. **fling oneself into** (start to) do with great vigour.

flint n 1 hard grey stone. 2 piece of this. 3 small piece of an iron alloy, used in cigarette lighters. **flinty** adj 1 cruel. 2 of or like flint.

flip v **flipping, flipped** 1 throw (something small or light) carelessly. 2 turn (something) over. 3 (also **flip one's lid**) Slang fly into an emotional state. ♦ n 4 snap or tap. ♦ adj 5 Informal flippant. **flipper** n 1 limb of a sea animal adapted for swimming. 2 one of a pair of paddle-like rubber devices worn on the feet to help in swimming. **flip-flop** n Brit & S Afr rubber-soled sandal held on by a thong between the big toe and the next toe. **flip through** v look at (a book or magazine) quickly or idly.

flippant adj treating serious things lightly. **flippancy** n

flirt v 1 behave as if sexually attracted to someone. 2 consider lightly, toy (with). ♦ n 3 person who flirts. **flirtation** n **flirtatious** adj

flit v **flitting, flitted** 1 move lightly and rapidly. 2 Scot move house. 3 Informal depart hurriedly and secretly. ♦ n 4 act of flitting.

float v 1 rest on the surface of a liquid. 2 move lightly and freely. 3 move about aimlessly. 4 launch (a company). 5 offer for sale on the stock market. 6 allow (a currency) to fluctuate against other currencies. ♦ n 7 light object used to help someone or something float. 8 indicator on a fishing line that moves when a fish bites. 9 decorated truck in a procession. 10 Brit small delivery vehicle. 11 sum of money used for minor expenses or to provide change. **floating** adj 1 moving about, changing, e.g. floating population. 2 (of a voter) not committed to one party.

flock[1] n 1 number of animals of one kind together. 2 large group of people. 3 Christianity congregation. ♦ v 4 gather in a crowd.

flock[2] n 1 wool or cotton waste used as stuffing. ♦ adj 2 (of wallpaper) with a velvety raised pattern.

floe n sheet of floating ice.

flog v **flogging, flogged** 1 beat with a whip or stick. 2 (sometimes foll. by off) Brit, NZ & S Afr informal sell. 3 NZ informal steal. **flogging** n

flood n 1 overflow of water onto a normally dry area. 2 large amount of water. 3 rising of the tide. ♦ v 4 cover or become covered with water. 5 fill to overflowing. 6 come in large numbers or quantities. **floodgate** n gate used to control the flow of water. **floodlight** n 1 lamp that casts a broad intense beam of light. ♦ v **-lighting, -lit** 2 illuminate by floodlight.

floor n 1 lower surface of a room. 2 level of a building. 3 flat bottom surface. 4 (right to speak in) a legislative hall. ♦ v 5 knock down. 6 Informal disconcert or defeat. **floored** adj covered with a floor. **flooring** n material for floors. **floor show** entertainment in a nightclub.

floozy n, pl **-zies** Old-fashioned slang disreputable woman.

flop v **flopping, flopped** 1 bend, fall, or collapse loosely or carelessly. 2 Informal fail. ♦ n 3 Informal failure. 4 flopping movement. **floppy** adj hanging downwards, loose. **floppy disk** Computers flexible magnetic disk that stores information.

flora n plants of a given place or time.

floral adj consisting of or decorated with flowers.

floret n small flower forming part of a composite flower head.

floribunda n type of rose whose flowers grow in large clusters.

florid adj 1 with a red or flushed complexion. 2 ornate.

florin n former British and Australian coin.

florist *n* seller of flowers.

floss *n* fine silky fibres.

flotation *n* launching or financing of a business enterprise.

flotilla *n* small fleet or fleet of small ships.

flotsam *n* floating wreckage. **flotsam and jetsam 1** odds and ends. **2** *Brit* homeless or vagrant people.

flounce¹ *v* **1** go with emphatic movements. ♦ *n* **2** flouncing movement.

flounce² *n* ornamental frill on a garment.

flounder¹ *v* **1** move with difficulty, as in mud. **2** behave or speak in a bungling or hesitating manner.

flounder² *n* edible flatfish.

flour *n* **1** powder made by grinding grain, esp. wheat. ♦ *v* **2** sprinkle with flour. **floury** *adj*

flourish *v* **1** be active, successful, or widespread. **2** be at the peak of development. **3** wave (something) dramatically. ♦ *n* **4** dramatic waving motion. **5** ornamental curly line in writing. **flourishing** *adj*

flout *v* deliberately disobey (a rule, law, etc.).

☑ WORD TIP

Be careful not to confuse this with *flaunt* meaning 'display'.

---

flow *v* **1** (of liquid) move in a stream. **2** (of blood or electricity) circulate. **3** proceed smoothly. **4** hang loosely. **5** be abundant. ♦ *n* **6** act, rate, or manner of flowing. **7** continuous stream or discharge. **flow chart** diagram showing a sequence of operations in a process.

flower *n* **1** part of a plant that produces seeds. **2** plant grown for its colourful flowers. **3** best or finest part. ♦ *v* **4** produce flowers, bloom. **5** reach full growth or maturity. **in flower** with flowers open. **flowered** *adj* decorated with a floral design. **flowery** *adj* **1** decorated with a floral design. **2** (of language or style) elaborate.

flowerbed *n* piece of ground for growing flowers.

flown *v* past participle of FLY¹.

fl. oz. fluid ounce(s).

flu *n* short for INFLUENZA.

fluctuate *v* change frequently and erratically. **fluctuation** *n*

flue *n* passage or pipe for smoke or hot air.

fluent *adj* **1** able to speak or write with ease. **2** spoken or written with ease. **fluently** *adv* **fluency** *n*

fluff *n* **1** soft fibres. **2** *Brit, Aust & NZ informal* mistake. ♦ *v* **3** make or become soft and puffy. **4** *Informal* make a mistake. **fluffy** *adj*

fluid *n* **1** substance able to flow and change its shape; a liquid or a gas. ♦ *adj* **2** able to flow or change shape easily. **fluidity** *n* **fluid ounce** *Brit* one twentieth of a pint (28.4 ml).

fluke¹ *n* accidental stroke of luck.

fluke² *n* **1** flat triangular point of an anchor. **2** lobe of a whale's tail.

fluke³ *n* parasitic worm.

flume *n* **1** narrow sloping channel for water. **2** enclosed water slide at a swimming pool.

flummox *v* puzzle or confuse.

flung *v* past of FLING.

flunk *v* *US, Aust, NZ & S Afr informal* fail.

flunky, flunkey *n, pl* **flunkies, flunkeys 1** servile person. **2** manservant who wears a livery.

fluorescence *n* emission of light from a substance bombarded by particles, such as electrons, or by radiation. **fluoresce** *v* exhibit fluorescence.

fluorescent *adj* of or resembling fluorescence.

fluoride n compound containing fluorine. **fluoridate** v add fluoride to (water) as protection against tooth decay. **fluoridation** n

fluorine n Chem toxic yellow gas, most reactive of all the elements.

flurry n, pl -ries 1 sudden commotion. 2 gust of rain or wind or fall of snow. ♦ v -rying, -ried 3 confuse.

flush¹ v 1 blush or cause to blush. 2 send water through (a toilet or pipe) so as to clean it. 3 elate. ♦ n 4 blush. 5 rush of water. 6 excitement or elation.

flush² adj 1 level with the surrounding surface. 2 Informal having plenty of money.

flush³ v drive out of a hiding place.

flush⁴ n (in card games) hand all of one suit.

fluster v 1 make nervous or upset. ♦ n 2 nervous or upset state.

flute n 1 wind instrument consisting of a tube with sound holes and a mouth hole in the side. 2 tall narrow wineglass. **fluted** adj having decorative grooves.

flutter v 1 wave rapidly. 2 flap the wings. 3 move quickly and irregularly. 4 (of the heart) beat abnormally quickly. ♦ n 5 flapping movement. 6 nervous agitation. 7 Informal small bet. 8 abnormally fast heartbeat.

fluvial adj of rivers.

flux n 1 constant change or instability. 2 flow or discharge. 3 substance mixed with metal to assist in fusion.

fly¹ v flying, flew, flown 1 move through the air on wings or in an aircraft. 2 control the flight of. 3 float, flutter, display, or be displayed in the air. 4 transport or be transported by air. 5 move quickly or suddenly. 6 (of time) pass rapidly. 7 flee. ♦ n, pl flies 8 (often pl) Brit fastening at the front of trousers. 9 flap forming the entrance to a tent. ♦ pl 10 space above a stage,

used for storage. **flyer, flier** n 1 small advertising leaflet. 2 aviator. **flying fox** Aust & NZ platform suspended from an overhead cable, used for transporting people or materials. **flying phalanger** phalanger with black-striped greyish fur, which moves with gliding leaps. **flyleaf** n blank leaf at the beginning or end of a book. **flyover** n road passing over another by a bridge. **flywheel** n heavy wheel regulating the speed of a machine.

fly² n, pl flies two-winged insect. **flycatcher** n small insect-eating songbird. **fly-fishing** n fishing with an artificial fly as a lure. **flypaper** n paper with a sticky poisonous coating, used to kill flies. **flyweight** n boxer weighing up to 112lb (professional) or 51kg (amateur).

fly³ adj Slang sharp and cunning.

flying adj hurried and brief. **flying boat** aircraft fitted with floats instead of landing wheels. **flying colours** conspicuous success. **flying fish** fish with winglike fins used for gliding above the water. **flying fox** large fruit-eating bat. **flying saucer** unidentified disc-shaped flying object, supposedly from outer space. **flying squad** small group of police, soldiers, etc., ready to act quickly. **flying start** very good start.

FM frequency modulation.

foal n 1 young of a horse or related animal. ♦ v 2 give birth to a foal.

foam n 1 mass of small bubbles on a liquid. 2 frothy saliva. 3 light spongelike solid used for insulation, packing, etc. ♦ v 4 produce foam. **foamy** adj

fob n 1 short watch chain. 2 small pocket in a waistcoat.

fob off v fobbing, fobbed 1 pretend to satisfy (a person) with lies or excuses. 2 sell or pass off (inferior goods) as valuable.

fo'c's'le *n* same as FORECASTLE.

focus *n, pl* **-cuses, -ci** [-sye] **1** point at which light or sound waves converge. **2** state of an optical image when it is clearly defined. **3** state of an instrument producing such an image. **4** centre of interest or activity. ♦ *v* **-cusing, -cused** *or* **-cussing, -cussed** **5** bring or come into focus. **6** concentrate (on). **focal** *adj* of or at a focus. **focus group** group of people gathered by a market-research company to discuss and assess a product or service.

fodder *n* feed for livestock.

foe *n* enemy, opponent.

foetid *adj* same as FETID.

foetus *n, pl* **-tuses** same as FETUS.

fog *n* **1** mass of condensed water vapour in the lower air, often greatly reducing visibility. **2** *v* **fogging, fogged 3** cover with steam. **foggy** *adj* **foghorn** *n* large horn sounded to warn ships in fog.

fogey, fogy *n, pl* **-geys, -gies** old-fashioned person.

foible *n* minor weakness or slight peculiarity.

foil[1] *v* ruin (someone's plan).

foil[2] *n* **1** metal in a thin sheet, esp. for wrapping food. **2** anything which sets off another thing to advantage.

foil[3] *n* light slender flexible sword tipped with a button.

foist *v* (foll. by *on* or *upon*) force or impose on.

fold[1] *v* **1** bend so that one part covers another. **2** interlace (the arms). **3** clasp (in the arms). **4** *Cooking* mix gently. **5** *Informal* fail or go bankrupt. ♦ *n* **6** folded piece or part. **7** mark, crease, or hollow made by folding. **folder** *n* piece of folded cardboard for holding loose papers.

fold[2] *n* **1** *Brit, Aust & S Afr* enclosure for sheep. **2** church or its members.

foliage *n* leaves. **foliation** *n* process of producing leaves.

folio *n, pl* **-lios 1** sheet of paper folded in half to make two leaves of a book. **2** book made up of such sheets. **3** page number.

folk *n* **1** people in general. **2** race of people. **3** *pl* **4** relatives. **folksy** *adj* simple and unpretentious. **folk dance** traditional country dance. **folklore** *n* traditional beliefs and stories of a people. **folk song 1** song handed down among the common people. **2** modern song like this. **folk singer**

follicle *n* small cavity in the body, esp. one from which a hair grows.

follow *v* **1** go or come after. **2** be a logical or natural consequence of. **3** keep to the course or track of. **4** act in accordance with. **5** accept the ideas or beliefs of. **6** understand. **7** have a keen interest in. **follower** *n* disciple or supporter. **following** *adj* **1** about to be mentioned. **2** next in time. ♦ *n* **3** group of supporters. ♦ *prep* **4** as a result of. **follow up** *v* **1** investigate. **2** do a second, often similar, thing after (a first). **follow-up** *n* something done to reinforce an initial action.

folly *n, pl* **-lies 1** foolishness. **2** foolish action or idea. **3** useless extravagant building.

foment [foam-**ent**] *v* encourage or stir up (trouble).

fond *adj* **1** tender, loving. **2** unlikely to be realized, e.g. *a fond hope*. **fond of** having a liking for. **fondly** *adv* **fondness** *n*

fondant *n* (sweet made from) flavoured paste of sugar and water.

fondle *v* caress.

fondue *n* Swiss dish of a hot melted cheese sauce into which pieces of bread are dipped.

font¹ *n* bowl in a church for baptismal water.

font² *n* set of printing type of one style and size.

fontanelle *n* soft membranous gap between the bones of a baby's skull.

food *n* what one eats, solid nourishment. **foodie** *n Informal* gourmet. **foodstuff** *n* substance used as food.

fool¹ *n* **1** person lacking sense or judgment. **2** person made to appear ridiculous. **3** *Hist* jester, clown. ♦ *v* **4** deceive (someone). **foolish** *adj* unwise, silly, or absurd. **foolishly** *adv* **foolishness** *n* **foolery** *n* foolish behaviour. **fool around** *v* act or play irresponsibly or aimlessly. **foolproof** *adj* unable to fail.

fool² *n* dessert of puréed fruit mixed with cream.

foolhardy *adj* recklessly adventurous. **foolhardiness** *n*

foolscap *n* size of paper, 34.3 × 43.2 centimetres.

foot *n, pl* **feet** **1** part of the leg below the ankle. **2** unit of length of twelve inches (0.3048 metre). **3** lowest part of anything. **4** unit of poetic rhythm. **foot it** *Informal* walk. **foot the bill** pay the entire cost. **footage** *n* amount of film used.

foot-and-mouth disease infectious viral disease of sheep, cattle, etc.

footbridge *n* bridge for pedestrians. **footfall** *n* sound of a footstep. **foothills** *pl n* hills at the foot of a mountain. **foothold** *n* **1** secure position from which progress may be made. **2** small place giving a secure grip for the foot. **footlights** *pl n* lights across the front of a stage. **footloose** *adj* free from ties. **footman** *n* male servant in uniform. **footnote** *n* note printed at the foot of a page. **footpath** *n* **1** narrow path for walkers

only. **2** *Aust* raised space alongside a road, for pedestrians. **footplate** *n* platform in the cab of a locomotive for the driver. **footprint** *n* mark left by a foot. **footstep** *n* **1** step in walking. **2** sound made by walking. **footstool** *n* low stool used to rest the feet on while sitting. **footwear** *n* anything worn to cover the feet. **footwork** *n* skilful use of the feet, as in sport or dancing.

football *n* **1** game played by two teams of eleven players kicking a ball in an attempt to score goals. **2** any of various similar games, such as rugby. **3** ball used for this. **footballer** *n* **football pools** form of gambling on the results of soccer matches.

footing *n* **1** basis or foundation. **2** relationship between people. **3** secure grip by or for the feet.

footling *adj Chiefly Brit informal* trivial.

footsie *n Informal* flirtation involving the touching together of feet.

fop *n* man excessively concerned with fashion. **foppery** *n* **foppish** *adj*

for *prep* **1** indicating a person intended to benefit from or receive something, span of time or distance, person or thing represented by someone, etc., e.g. *a gift for you; for five miles; playing for his country.* ♦ *conj* **2** because. **for it** *Informal* liable for punishment or blame.

forage *v* **1** search about (for). ♦ *n* **2** food for cattle or horses.

foray *n* **1** brief raid or attack. **2** first attempt or new undertaking.

forbear *v* cease or refrain (from doing something). **forbearance** *n* tolerance, patience.

forbid *v* prohibit, refuse to allow. **forbidden** *adj* **forbidding** *adj* severe, threatening.

force *n* **1** strength or power. **2** compulsion. **3** *Physics* influence tending to produce a change in a physical system. **4** mental or moral strength. **5** person or thing with strength or influence. **6** vehemence or intensity. **7** group of people organized for a particular task or duty. ♦ v **8** compel, make (someone) do something. **9** acquire or produce through effort, strength, etc. **10** propel or drive. **11** break open. **12** impose or inflict. **13** cause to grow at an increased rate. **in force 1** having legal validity. **2** in great numbers. **forced** adj **1** compulsory. **2** false or unnatural. **3** due to an emergency. **forceful** adj **1** emphatic and confident. **2** effective. **forcefully** adv **forcible** adj **1** involving physical force or violence. **2** strong and emphatic. **forcibly** adv

forceps pl n surgical pincers.

ford n **1** shallow place where a river may be crossed. ♦ v **2** cross (a river) at a ford.

fore adj **1** in, at, or towards the front. ♦ n **2** front part. **to the fore** in a conspicuous position.

fore- prefix **1** before in time or rank, e.g. forefather. **2** at the front, e.g. forecourt.

fore-and-aft adj located at both ends of a ship.

forearm[1] n arm from the wrist to the elbow.

forearm[2] v prepare beforehand.

forebear n ancestor.

foreboding n feeling that something bad is about to happen.

forecast v -casting, -cast or -casted **1** predict (weather, events, etc.). ♦ n **2** prediction.

forecastle [**foke**-sl] n raised front part of a ship.

foreclose v take possession of (property bought with borrowed money which has not been repaid). **foreclosure** n

forecourt n courtyard or open space in front of a building.

forefather n ancestor.

forefinger n finger next to the thumb.

forefront n **1** most active or prominent position. **2** very front.

foregather v meet together or assemble.

forego v same as FORGO.

foregoing adj going before, preceding. **foregone conclusion** inevitable result.

foreground n part of a view, esp. in a picture, nearest the observer.

forehand n Tennis etc. stroke played with the palm of the hand facing forward.

forehead n part of the face above the eyebrows.

foreign adj **1** not of, or in, one's own country. **2** relating to or connected with other countries. **3** unfamiliar, strange. **4** in an abnormal place or position, e.g. foreign matter. **foreigner** n

foreleg n either of the front legs of an animal.

forelock n lock of hair over the forehead.

foreman n **1** person in charge of a group of workers. **2** leader of a jury.

foremast n mast nearest the bow of a ship.

foremost adj, adv first in time, place, or importance.

forename n first name.

forenoon n Chiefly US & Canadian morning.

forensic adj used in or connected with courts of law. **forensic medicine** use of medical knowledge for the purposes of the law.

foreplay n sexual stimulation before intercourse.

forerunner n person or thing that goes before, precursor.

foresail *n* main sail on the foremast of a ship.

foresee *v* see or know beforehand. **foreseeable** *adj*

☑ **SPELLING TIP**

There are 665 occurrences of the word **unforeseen** in the Bank of English. The misspelling *unforseen* occurs 50 times.

foreshadow *v* show or indicate beforehand.

foreshore *n* part of the shore between high- and low-tide marks.

foreshorten *v* represent (an object) in a picture as shorter than it really is, in accordance with perspective.

foresight *n* ability to anticipate and provide for future needs.

foreskin *n* fold of skin covering the tip of the penis.

forest *n* large area with a thick growth of trees. **forested** *adj* **forestry** *n* **1** science of planting and caring for trees. **2** management of forests. **forester** *n* person skilled in forestry.

forestall *v* prevent or guard against in advance.

foretaste *n* early limited experience of something to come.

foretell *v* tell or indicate beforehand.

forethought *n* thoughtful planning for future events.

forever, for ever *adv* **1** without end. **2** at all times. **3** *Informal* for a long time.

forewarn *v* warn beforehand.

foreword *n* introduction to a book.

forfeit [**for**-fit] *n* **1** thing lost or given up as a penalty for a fault or mistake. ♦ *v* **2** lose as a forfeit. ♦ *adj* **3** lost as a forfeit. **forfeiture** *n*

forge[1] *n* **1** place where metal is worked, smithy. **2** furnace for melting metal. ♦ *v* **3** make a fraudulent imitation of

(something). **4** shape (metal) by heating and hammering it. **5** create (an alliance etc.).

forge[2] *v* advance steadily. **forge ahead** increase speed or take the lead.

forger *n* person who makes an illegal copy of something.

forgery *n*, *pl* **-ries 1** illegal copy of something. **2** crime of making an illegal copy.

forget *v* **-getting, -got, -gotten 1** fail to remember. **2** neglect. **3** leave behind by mistake. **forgetful** *adj* tending to forget. **forgetfulness** *n* **forget-me-not** *n* plant with clusters of small blue flowers.

forgive *v* **-giving, -gave, -given** cease to blame or hold resentment against, pardon. **forgiveness** *n*

forgo *v* do without or give up.

forgot *v* past tense of FORGET.

forgotten *v* past participle of FORGET.

fork *n* **1** tool for eating food, with prongs and a handle. **2** large similarly-shaped tool for digging or lifting. **3** point where a road, river, etc. divides into branches. **4** one of the branches. ♦ *v* **5** pick up, dig, etc. with a fork. **6** branch. **7** take one or other branch at a fork in the road. **forked** *adj* **fork-lift truck** vehicle with a forklike device at the front which can be raised or lowered to move loads. **fork out** *v Informal* pay.

forlorn *adj* lonely and unhappy. **forlorn hope** hopeless enterprise. **forlornly** *adv*

form *n* **1** shape or appearance. **2** mode in which something appears. **3** type or kind. **4** printed document with spaces for details. **5** physical or mental condition. **6** previous record of an athlete, racehorse, etc. **7** class in school. **8** *v* **9** give a (particular) shape to or take a (particular) shape. **10** come or bring into existence. **11** make or be made. **12** train. **13** acquire or develop. **formless** *adj*

formal *adj* **1** of or characterized by established conventions of ceremony and behaviour. **2** of or for formal occasions. **3** stiff in manner. **4** organized. **5** symmetrical. **formally** *adv* **formality** *n, pl* **-ties 1** requirement of custom or etiquette. **2** necessary procedure without real importance. **formalize** *v* make official or formal.

formaldehyde [for-**mal**-de-hide] *n* colourless pungent gas used to make formalin. **formalin** *n* solution of formaldehyde in water, used as a disinfectant or a preservative for biological specimens.

format *n* **1** style in which something is arranged. ♦ *v* **-matting, -matted 2** arrange in a format.

formation *n* **1** forming. **2** thing formed. **3** structure or shape. **4** arrangement of people or things acting as a unit.

formative *adj* **1** of or relating to development. **2** shaping.

former *adj* of an earlier time, previous. **the former** first mentioned of two. **formerly** *adv*

Formica *n* ® kind of laminated sheet used to make heat-resistant surfaces.

formic acid *n* acid derived from ants.

formidable *adj* **1** frightening because difficult to overcome or manage. **2** extremely impressive. **formidably** *adv*

formula *n, pl* **-las, -lae 1** group of numbers, letters, or symbols expressing a scientific or mathematical rule. **2** method or rule for doing or producing something. **3** set form of words used in religion, law, etc. **4** specific category of car in motor racing. **formulaic** *adj* **formulate** *v* plan or describe precisely and clearly. **formulation** *n*

fornicate *v* have sexual intercourse without being married. **fornication** *n* **fornicator** *n*

forsake *v* **-saking, -sook, -saken 1** withdraw support or friendship from. **2** give up, renounce.

forsooth *adv Obs* indeed.

forswear *v* **-swearing, -swore, -sworn** renounce or reject.

forsythia [for-**syth**-ee-a] *n* shrub with yellow flowers in spring.

fort *n* fortified building or place. **hold the fort** *Informal* keep things going during someone's absence.

forte[1] [**for**-tay] *n* thing at which a person excels.

forte[2] [**for**-tay] *adv Music* loudly.

forth *adv* forwards, out, or away.

forthcoming *adj* **1** about to appear or happen. **2** available. **3** (of a person) communicative.

forthright *adj* direct and outspoken.

forthwith *adv* at once.

fortieth *adj, n see* FORTY.

fortify *v* **-fying, -fied 1** make (a place) defensible, as by building walls. **2** strengthen. **3** add vitamins etc. to (food). **4** add alcohol to (wine) to make sherry or port. **fortification** *n*

fortissimo *adv Music* very loudly.

fortitude *n* courage in adversity or pain.

fortnight *n* two weeks. **fortnightly** *adv, adj*

FORTRAN *n Computers* programming language for mathematical and scientific purposes.

fortress *n* large fort or fortified town.

fortuitous [for-**tyew**-it-uss] *adj* happening by (lucky) chance. **fortuitously** *adv*

fortunate *adj* **1** having good luck. **2** occurring by good luck. **fortunately** *adv*

fortune *n* **1** luck, esp. when favourable.

2 power regarded as influencing human destiny. **3** wealth, large sum of money. ♦ *pl* **4** person's destiny. **fortune-teller** *n* person who claims to predict the future of others.

forty *adj, n, pl* **-ties** four times ten. **fortieth** *adj, n*

forum *n* meeting or medium for open discussion or debate.

forward *adj* **1** directed or moving ahead. **2** in, at, or near the front. **3** presumptuous. **4** well developed or advanced. **5** relating to the future. ♦ *n* **6** attacking player in various team games, such as soccer or hockey. ♦ *adv* **7** forwards. ♦ *v* **8** send (a letter etc.) on to an ultimate destination. **9** advance or promote. **forwards** *adv* **1** towards or at a place further ahead in space or time. **2** towards the front.

fossick *v Aust & NZ* search, esp. for gold or precious stones.

fossil *n* hardened remains of a prehistoric animal or plant preserved in rock. **fossilize** *v* **1** turn into a fossil. **2** become out-of-date or inflexible.

foster *v* **1** promote the growth or development of. **2** bring up (a child not one's own). ♦ *adj* **3** of or involved in fostering a child, e.g. *foster parents*.

fought *v* past of FIGHT.

foul *adj* **1** loathsome or offensive. **2** stinking or dirty. **3** (of language) obscene or vulgar. **4** unfair. **5** *n* **6** *Sport* violation of the rules. ♦ *v* **7** make dirty or polluted. **8** make or become entangled or clogged. **9** *Sport* commit a foul against (an opponent). **fall foul of** come into conflict with. **foul-mouthed** *adj* habitually using foul language. **foul play** unfair conduct, esp. involving violence.

found[1] *v* past of FIND.

found[2] *v* **1** establish or bring into being. **2** lay the foundation of. **3** (foll. by *on* or *upon*) have a basis (in).

founder *n*

found[3] *v* **1** cast (metal or glass) by melting and setting in a mould. **2** make (articles) by this method.

foundation *n* **1** basis or base. **2** part of a building or wall below the ground. **3** act of founding. **4** institution supported by an endowment. **5** cosmetic used as a base for make-up.

founder *v* **1** break down or fail. **2** (of a ship) sink. **3** stumble or fall.

foundling *n Chiefly Brit* abandoned baby.

foundry *n, pl* **-ries** place where metal is melted and cast.

fount[1] *n* **1** *Lit* fountain. **2** source.

fount[2] *n* set of printing type of one style and size.

fountain *n* **1** jet of water. **2** structure from which such a jet spurts. **3** source. **fountainhead** *n* original source. **fountain pen** pen supplied with ink from a container inside it.

four *adj, n* **1** one more than three. ♦ *n* **2** (crew of) four-oared rowing boat. **on all fours** on hands and knees. **four-letter word** short obscene word referring to sex or excrement. **four-poster** *n* bed with four posts supporting a canopy. **foursome** *n* group of four people.

fourteen *adj, n* four and ten. **fourteenth** *adj, n*

fourth *adj, n* **1** (of) number four in a series. ♦ *n* **2** quarter. **fourth dimension** time. **fourth estate** the press.

fowl *n* **1** domestic cock or hen. **2** any bird used for food or hunted as game.

fox *n* **1** reddish-brown bushy-tailed animal of the dog family. **2** its fur. **3** cunning person. ♦ *v* **4** *Informal* perplex or deceive. **foxy** *adj* of or like a fox, esp. in craftiness. **foxglove** *n* tall plant with purple or white flowers. **foxhole** *n Mil* small pit dug for protection.

foxhound n dog bred for hunting foxes. **fox terrier** small short-haired terrier. **foxtrot** n **1** ballroom dance with slow and quick steps. **2** music for this.

foyer [**foy**-ay] n entrance hall in a theatre, cinema, or hotel.

fracas [**frak**-ah] n, pl -cas noisy quarrel.

fraction n **1** numerical quantity that is not a whole number. **2** fragment, piece. **3** Chem substance separated by distillation. **fractional** adj **fractionally** adv

fractious adj easily upset and angered.

fracture n **1** breaking, esp. of a bone. ♦ v **2** break.

fragile adj **1** easily broken or damaged. **2** in a weakened physical state. **fragility** n

fragment n **1** piece broken off. **2** incomplete piece. ♦ v **3** break into pieces. **fragmentary** adj **fragmentation** n

fragrant adj sweet-smelling. **fragrance** n **1** pleasant smell. **2** perfume, scent.

frail adj **1** physically weak. **2** easily damaged. **frailty** n, pl -ties physical or moral weakness.

frame n **1** structure giving shape or support. **2** enclosing case or border, as round a picture. **3** person's build. **4** individual exposure on a strip of film. **5** individual game of snooker in a match. ♦ v **6** put together, construct. **7** put into words. **8** put into a frame. **9** Slang incriminate (a person) on a false charge. **frame of mind** mood or attitude. **frame-up** n Slang false incrimination. **framework** n supporting structure.

franc n monetary unit of Switzerland, various African countries, and formerly of France and Belgium.

franchise n **1** right to vote. **2** authorization to sell a company's goods.

Franciscan n, adj (friar or nun) of the order founded by St. Francis of Assisi.

francium n Chem radioactive metallic element.

Franco- combining form of France or the French.

frangipani [fran-jee-**pah**-nee] n **1** Australian evergreen tree with large yellow fragrant flowers. **2** tropical shrub with fragrant white or pink flowers.

frank adj **1** honest and straightforward in speech or attitude. ♦ n **2** official mark on a letter permitting delivery. ♦ v **3** put such a mark on (a letter). **frankly** adv **frankness** n

frankfurter n smoked sausage.

frankincense n aromatic gum resin burned as incense.

frantic adj **1** distracted with rage, grief, joy, etc. **2** hurried and disorganized. **frantically** adv

fraternal adj of a brother, brotherly. **fraternally** adv **fraternity** n **1** group of people with shared interests, aims, etc. **2** brotherhood. **3** US male social club at college. **fraternize** v associate on friendly terms. **fraternization** n **fratricide** n **1** crime of killing one's brother. **2** person who does this.

Frau [rhymes with **how**] n, pl **Fraus**, **Frauen** German title, equivalent to Mrs. **Fräulein** [**froy**-line] n, pl -leins, -lein German title, equivalent to Miss.

fraud n **1** (criminal) deception, swindle. **2** person who acts in a deceitful way. **fraudulent** adj **fraudulence** n

fraught [**frawt**] adj tense or anxious. **fraught with** involving, filled with.

fray[1] n Brit, Aust & NZ noisy quarrel or conflict.

fray[2] v **1** make or become ragged at the edge. **2** become strained.

frazzle n Informal exhausted state.

freak n 1 abnormal person or thing. 2 person who is excessively enthusiastic about something. ♦ adj 3 abnormal. **freakish** adj **freak out** v Informal (cause to) be in a heightened emotional state.

freckle n small brown spot on the skin. **freckled** adj marked with freckles.

free adj **freer, freest** 1 able to act at will, not compelled or restrained. 2 not subject (to). 3 provided without charge. 4 not in use. 5 (of a person) not busy. 6 not fixed or joined. 7 v **freeing, freed** 8 release, liberate. 9 remove (obstacles, pain, etc.) from. 10 make available or usable. **a free hand** unrestricted freedom to act. **freely** adv **free fall** part of a parachute descent before the parachute opens. **free-for-all** n Informal brawl. **freehand** adj drawn without guiding instruments. **freehold** n tenure of land for life without restrictions. **freeholder** n **free house** Brit public house not bound to sell only one brewer's products. **freelance** adj, n (of) a self-employed person doing specific pieces of work for various employers. **freeloader** n Slang habitual scrounger. **free-range** adj kept or produced in natural conditions. **freeway** n US & Aust motorway. **freewheel** v travel downhill on a bicycle without pedalling.

-free combining form without, e.g. a trouble-free journey.

freedom n 1 being free. 2 right or privilege of unlimited access, e.g. the freedom of the city.

Freemason n member of a secret fraternity pledged to help each other.

freesia n plant with fragrant tubular flowers.

freeze v **freezing, froze, frozen** 1 change from a liquid to a solid by the reduction of temperature, as water to ice. 2 preserve (food etc.) by extreme cold. 3 (cause to) be very cold. 4 become motionless with fear, shock, etc. 5 fix (prices or wages) at a particular level. 6 ban the exchange or collection of (loans, assets, etc.). ♦ n 7 period of very cold weather. 8 freezing of prices or wages. **freezer** n insulated cabinet for cold-storage of perishable foods. **freeze-dry** v preserve (food) by rapid freezing and drying in a vacuum. **freezing** adj Informal very cold.

freight [**frate**] n 1 commercial transport of goods. 2 cargo transported. 3 cost of this. ♦ v 4 send by freight. **freighter** n ship or aircraft for transporting goods.

French n 1 language of France, also spoken in parts of Belgium, Canada, and Switzerland. ♦ adj 2 of France, its people, or their language. **French bread** white bread in a long thin crusty loaf. **French dressing** salad dressing of oil and vinegar. **French fries** potato chips. **French horn** brass wind instrument with a coiled tube. **French letter** Slang condom. **French polish** shellac varnish for wood. **French window** window extending to floor level, used as a door.

frenetic [frin-**net**-ik] adj uncontrolled, excited. **frenetically** adv

frenzy n, pl **-zies** 1 violent mental derangement. 2 wild excitement. **frenzied** adj **frenziedly** adv

frequent adj 1 happening often. 2 habitual. ♦ v 3 visit habitually. **frequently** adv **frequency** n, pl **-cies** 1 rate of occurrence. 2 Physics number of times a wave repeats itself in a given time.

fresco n, pl **-coes, -cos** watercolour painting done on wet plaster on a wall.

fresh adj 1 newly made, acquired, etc.

2 novel, original. **3** further, additional. **4** (of food) not preserved. **5** (of water) not salty. **6** (of weather) brisk or invigorating. **7** not tired. **freshly** *adv* **freshness** *n* **freshen** *v* make or become fresh or fresher. **fresher,** (US) **freshman** *n Brit & US* first-year student.

fret¹ *v* **fretting, fretted** be worried. **fretful** *adj* irritable.

fret² *n* small bar on the fingerboard of a guitar etc.

fretwork *n* decorative carving in wood. **fretsaw** *n* fine saw with a narrow blade, used for fretwork.

Freudian [**froy**-dee-an] *adj* of or relating to the psychoanalyst Sigmund Freud or his theories.

friable *adj* easily crumbled.

friar *n* member of a male Roman Catholic religious order. **friary** *n, pl* **-ries** house of friars.

fricassee *n* stewed meat served in a thick white sauce.

friction *n* **1** resistance met with by a body moving over another. **2** rubbing. **3** clash of wills or personalities. **frictional** *adj*

Friday *n* sixth day of the week. **Good Friday** Friday before Easter.

fridge *n* apparatus in which food and drinks are kept cool.

fried *v* past of FRY¹.

friend *n* **1** person whom one knows well and likes. **2** supporter or ally. **3** (F-) Quaker. **friendly** *adj* **1** showing or expressing liking. **2** not hostile, on the same side. ♦ *n, pl* **-lies 3** *Sport* match played for its own sake and not as part of a competition. **-friendly** *combining form* good or easy for the person or thing specified, e.g. *user-friendly*. **friendly society** (in Britain) association of people who pay regular dues in return for pensions, sickness benefits, etc. **friendliness** *n* **friendless** *adj* **friendship** *n*

Friesian [**free**-zhan] *n* breed of black-and-white dairy cattle.

frieze [**freeze**] *n* ornamental band on a wall.

frigate [**frig**-it] *n* medium-sized fast warship.

fright *n* **1** sudden fear or alarm. **2** sudden alarming shock. **frightful** *adj* **1** horrifying. **2** *Informal* very great. **frightfully** *adv*

frighten *v* **1** scare or terrify. **2** force (someone) to do something from fear. **frightening** *adj*

frigid [**frij**-id] *adj* **1** (of a woman) sexually unresponsive. **2** very cold. **3** excessively formal. **frigidity** *n*

frill *n* **1** gathered strip of fabric attached at one edge. ♦ *pl* **2** superfluous decorations or details. **frilled** *adj* **frilled lizard** large tree-living Australian lizard with an erectile fold of skin round the neck. **frilly** *adj*

fringe *n* **1** hair cut short and hanging over the forehead. **2** ornamental edge of hanging threads, tassels, etc. **3** outer edge. **4** less important parts of an activity or group. ♦ *v* **5** decorate with a fringe. ♦ *adj* **6** (of theatre) unofficial or unconventional. **fringed** *adj* **fringe benefit** benefit given in addition to a regular salary.

frippery *n, pl* **-peries 1** useless ornamentation. **2** trivia.

frisk *v* **1** move or leap playfully. **2** *Informal* search (a person) for concealed weapons etc. **frisky** *adj* lively or high-spirited.

frisson [**frees**-sonn] *n* shiver of fear or excitement.

fritter *n* piece of food fried in batter.

fritter away *v* waste.

frivolous *adj* **1** not serious or sensible. **2** enjoyable but trivial. **frivolity** *n*

frizz *v* form (hair) into stiff wiry curls. **frizzy** *adj*

frizzle v cook or heat until crisp and shrivelled.

frock n dress. **frock coat** man's skirted coat as worn in the 19th century.

frog n smooth-skinned tailless amphibian with long back legs used for jumping. **frog in one's throat** phlegm on the vocal cords, hindering speech. **frogman** n swimmer with a rubber suit and breathing equipment for working underwater. **frogspawn** n jelly-like substance containing frog's eggs.

frolic v **-icking, -icked 1** run and play in a lively way. ♦ n **2** lively and merry behaviour. **frolicsome** adj playful.

from prep indicating the point of departure, source, distance, cause, change of state, etc.

☑ **WORD TIP**
The use of *off* to mean *from* is very informal: *They bought milk from* (rather than *off*) *a farmer.*

frond n long leaf or leaflike part of a fern, palm, or seaweed.

front n **1** fore part. **2** position directly before or ahead **3** battle line or area. **4** *Meteorol* dividing line between two different air masses. **5** outward appearance. **6** *Informal* cover for another, usu. criminal, activity. **7** particular field of activity, e.g. *on the economic front.* ♦ adj **8** of or at the front. ♦ v **9** face (onto). **10** be the presenter of (a television show). **frontal** adj **frontage** n facade of a building. **front bench** (in Britain) parliamentary leaders of the government or opposition. **front-bencher** n **frontrunner** n *Informal* person regarded as most likely to win a race, election, etc.

frontier n area of a country bordering on another.

frontispiece n illustration facing the title page of a book.

frost n **1** white frozen dew or mist. **2** atmospheric temperature below freezing point. ♦ v **3** become covered with frost. **frosted** adj (of glass) having a rough surface to make it opaque. **frosting** n *Chiefly US* sugar icing. **frosty** adj **1** characterized or covered by frost. **2** unfriendly. **frostily** adv **frostiness** n **frostbite** n destruction of tissue, esp. of the fingers or ears, by cold. **frostbitten** adj

froth n **1** mass of small bubbles. **2** v **3** foam. **frothy** adj

frown v **1** wrinkle one's brows in worry, anger, or thought. **2** look disapprovingly (on). ♦ n **3** frowning expression.

frowsty adj *Brit* stale or musty.

frowzy, frowsy adj **-zier, -ziest** or **-sier, -siest** dirty or unkempt.

froze v past tense of FREEZE. **frozen** v past participle of FREEZE.

frugal adj **1** thrifty, sparing. **2** meagre and inexpensive. **frugally** adv **frugality** n

fruit n **1** part of a plant containing seeds, esp. if edible. **2** any plant product useful to humans. **3** (often pl) result of an action or effort. ♦ v **4** bear fruit. **fruiterer** n person who sells fruit. **fruit fly 1** small fly that feeds on and lays its eggs in plant tissues. **2** similar fly that feeds on plant sap, decaying fruit, etc., and is widely used in genetics experiments. **fruitful** adj useful or productive. **fruitfully** adv **fruitless** adj useless or unproductive. **fruitlessly** adv **fruity** adj **1** of or like fruit. **2** (of a voice) mellow. **3** *Brit informal* mildly bawdy. **fruit machine** coin-operated gambling machine.

fruition [froo-**ish**-on] n fulfilment of something worked for or desired.

frump n dowdy woman. **frumpy** adj

frustrate v **1** upset or anger. **2** hinder or prevent. **frustrated** adj **frustrating** adj **frustration** n

fry¹ v **frying, fried 1** cook or be cooked in fat or oil. ♦ n, pl **fries 2** (also **fry-up**) dish of fried food. ♦ pl **3** potato chips.

fry² pl n young fishes. **small fry** young or insignificant people.

ft. 1 foot. **2** feet.

fuchsia [**fyew**¹-sha] n ornamental shrub with hanging flowers.

fuddle v cause to be intoxicated or confused **fuddled** adj

fuddy-duddy adj, n, pl **-dies** Informal old-fashioned (person).

fudge¹ n soft caramel-like sweet.

fudge² v avoid making a firm statement or decision.

fuel n **1** substance burned or treated to produce heat or power. **2** something that intensifies (a feeling etc.). ♦ v **fuelling, fuelled 3** provide with fuel.

fug n hot stale atmosphere. **fuggy** adj

fugitive [**fyew**-jit-iv] n **1** person who flees, esp. from arrest or pursuit. ♦ adj **2** fleeing. **3** transient.

fugue [**fyewg**] n musical composition in which a theme is repeated in different parts.

fulcrum n, pl **-crums, -cra** pivot about which a lever turns.

fulfil v **-filling, -filled 1** bring about the achievement of (a desire or promise). **2** carry out (a request or order). **3** do what is required. **fulfilment** n **fulfil oneself** v achieve one's potential.

full adj **1** containing as much or as many as possible. **2** abundant in supply. **3** having had enough to eat. **4** plump. **5** complete, whole. **6** (of a garment) of ample cut. **7** (of a sound or flavour) rich and strong. ♦ adv **8** completely. **9** directly. **10** very. **fully**

adv **fullness** n **in full** without shortening. **full-blooded** adj vigorous or enthusiastic. **full-blown** adj fully developed. **full moon** phase of the moon when it is visible as a fully illuminated disc. **full-scale** adj **1** (of a plan) of actual size. **2** using all resources. **full stop** punctuation mark (.) at the end of a sentence and after abbreviations.

fulmar n Arctic sea bird.

fulminate v (foll. by against) criticize or denounce angrily.

fulsome adj distastefully excessive or insincere.

fumble v **1** handle awkwardly. **2** say awkwardly. ♦ n **3** act of fumbling.

fume v **1** be very angry. **2** give out smoke or vapour. **3** pl n **4** pungent smoke or vapour.

fumigate [**fyew**-mig-gate] v disinfect with fumes. **fumigation** n

fun n enjoyment or amusement. **make fun of** mock or tease. **funny** adj **1** comical, humorous. **2** odd. **funny bone** part of the elbow where the nerve is near the surface. **funnily** adv

function n **1** purpose something exists for. **2** way something works. **3** large or formal social event. **4** Maths quantity whose value depends on the varying value of another. **5** sequence of operations performed by a computer at a key stroke. ♦ v **6** operate or work. **7** (foll. by as) fill the role of. **functional** adj **1** of or as a function. **2** practical rather than decorative. **3** in working order. **functionally** adv **functionary** n, pl **-aries** official.

fund n **1** stock of money for a special purpose. **2** supply or store. ♦ pl **3** money resources. ♦ v **4** provide money to. **funding** n

fundamental adj **1** essential or primary. **2** basic. ♦ n **3** basic rule or fact. **fundamentally** adv

fundamentalism n literal or strict interpretation of a religion. **fundamentalist** n, adj

fundi n S Afr expert or boffin.

funeral n ceremony of burying or cremating a dead person.

funerary adj of or for a funeral.

funereal [fyew-**neer**-ee-al] adj gloomy or sombre.

funfair n entertainment with machines to ride on and stalls.

fungus n, pl **-gi**, **-guses** plant without leaves, flowers, or roots, such as a mushroom or mould. **fungal**, **fungous** adj **fungicide** n substance that destroys fungi.

funicular n cable railway on a mountainside or cliff.

funk[1] n style of dance music with a strong beat. **funky** adj (of music) having a strong beat.

funk[2] Informal ♦ n 1 nervous or fearful state. ♦ v 2 avoid (doing something) through fear.

funnel n 1 cone-shaped tube for pouring liquids into a narrow opening. 2 chimney of a ship or locomotive. ♦ v **-nelling**, **-nelled** 3 (cause to) move through or as if through a funnel. **funnel-web** n large poisonous black spider that builds funnel-shaped webs.

fur n 1 soft hair of a mammal. 2 animal skin with the fur left on. 3 garment made of this. 4 whitish coating on the tongue or inside a kettle. ♦ v 5 cover or become covered with fur. **furry** adj **furrier** n dealer in furs.

furbish v smarten up.

furious adj 1 very angry. 2 violent or unrestrained. **furiously** adv

furl v roll up and fasten (a sail, umbrella, or flag).

furlong n unit of length equal to 220 yards (201.168 metres).

furlough [**fur**-loh] n leave of absence.

furnace n enclosed chamber containing a very hot fire.

furnish v 1 provide (a house or room) with furniture. 2 supply, provide. **furnishings** pl n furniture, carpets, and fittings. **furniture** n large movable articles such as chairs and wardrobes.

furore [fyew-**ror**-ee] n very excited or angry reaction.

furrow n 1 trench made by a plough. 2 groove, esp. a wrinkle on the forehead. ♦ v 3 make or become wrinkled. 4 make furrows in.

further adv 1 in addition. 2 to a greater distance or extent. ♦ adj 3 additional. 4 more distant. ♦ v 5 assist the progress of. **further education** Brit education beyond school other than at a university. **furthest** adv 1 to the greatest distance or extent. ♦ adj 2 most distant. **furtherance** n **furthermore** adv besides. **furthermost** adj most distant.

furtive adj sly and secretive. **furtively** adv

fury n, pl **-ries** 1 wild anger. 2 uncontrolled violence.

furze n gorse.

fuse[1] n cord containing an explosive for detonating a bomb.

fuse[2] n 1 safety device for electric circuits, containing a wire that melts and breaks the connection when the circuit is overloaded. ♦ v 2 (cause to) fail as a result of a blown fuse. 3 join or combine. 4 unite by melting. 5 melt with heat.

fuselage [**fyew**-zill-lahzh] n body of an aircraft.

fusilier [fyew-zill-**leer**] n soldier of certain regiments.

fusillade [fyew-zill-**lade**] n 1 continuous discharge of firearms. 2 outburst of criticism, questions, etc.

fusion n 1 melting. 2 product of fusing.

3 combination of the nucleus of two atoms with the release of energy. **4** something new created by a mixture of qualities, ideas, or things. **5** popular music blending styles, esp. jazz and funk. ♦ *adj* **6** of a style of cooking that combines traditional Western techniques and ingredients with those used in Eastern cuisine.

fuss *n* **1** needless activity or worry. **2** complaint or objection. **3** great display of attention. ♦ *v* **4** make a fuss. **fussy** *adj* **1** inclined to fuss. **2** overparticular. **3** overelaborate. **fussily** *adv* **fussiness** *n*

fusty *adj* **-tier, -tiest 1** stale-smelling. **2** behind the times. **fustiness** *n*

futile *adj* unsuccessful or useless.

futility *n*

futon [**foo**-tonn] *n* Japanese-style bed.

future *n* **1** time to come. **2** what will happen. **3** prospects. ♦ *adj* **4** yet to come or be. **5** of or relating to time to come. **6** (of a verb tense) indicating that the action specified has not yet taken place. **futuristic** *adj* of a design appearing to belong to some future time.

fuzz¹ *n* mass of fine or curly hairs or fibres. **fuzzy** *adj* **1** of, like, or covered with fuzz. **2** blurred or indistinct. **3** (of hair) tightly curled. **fuzzily** *adv* **fuzziness** *n*

fuzz² *n Slang* police.

G g

g 1 gram(s). **2** (acceleration due to) gravity.

gab *n, v* **gabbing, gabbed** *Informal* talk or chatter. **gift of the gab** eloquence. **gabby** *adj* **-bier, -biest** *Informal* talkative.

gabardine, gaberdine *n* strong twill cloth used esp. for raincoats.

gabble *v* **1** speak rapidly and indistinctly. ♦ *n* **2** rapid indistinct speech.

gable *n* triangular upper part of a wall between sloping roofs. **gabled** *adj*

gad *v* **gadding, gadded. gad about, around** go around in search of pleasure. **gadabout** *n* pleasure-seeker.

gadfly *n* **1** fly that bites cattle. **2** constantly annoying person.

gadget *n* small mechanical device or appliance. **gadgetry** *n* gadgets.

Gael [gayl] *n* speaker of Gaelic. **Gaelic** [**gal**-lik, **gay**-lik] *n* **1** any of the Celtic languages of Ireland and the Scottish Highlands. ♦ *adj* **2** of the Gaels or their language.

gaff[1] *n* stick with an iron hook for landing large fish.

gaff[2] *n* **blow the gaff** *Slang* divulge a secret.

gaffe *n* social blunder.

gaffer *n* **1** *Brit informal* foreman or boss. **2** *Informal* old man. **3** senior electrician on a TV or film set.

gag[1] *v* **gagging, gagged 1** choke or retch. **2** stop up the mouth of (a person) with cloth etc. **3** deprive of free speech. ♦ *n* **4** cloth etc. put into or tied across the mouth.

gag[2] *n* *Informal* joke.

gaga [**gah**-gah] *adj Slang* senile.

gaggle *n* **1** *Informal* disorderly crowd. **2** flock of geese.

gaiety *n* **1** cheerfulness. **2** merrymaking. **gaily** *adv* **1** merrily. **2** colourfully.

gain *v* **1** acquire or obtain. **2** increase or improve. **3** reach. **4** (of a watch or clock) be or become too fast. ♦ *n* **5** profit or advantage. **6** increase or improvement. **gainful** *adj* useful or profitable. **gainfully** *adv* **gain on, upon** *v* get nearer to or catch up with.

gainsay *v* **-saying, -said** deny or contradict.

gait *n* manner of walking.

gaiter *n* cloth or leather covering for the lower leg.

gala [**gah**-la] *n* **1** festival. **2** competitive sporting event.

galaxy *n, pl* **-axies 1** system of stars. **2** gathering of famous people. **galactic** *adj*

gale *n* **1** strong wind. **2** *Informal* loud outburst.

gall[1] [**gawl**] *n* **1** *Informal* impudence. **2** bitter feeling. **gall bladder** sac attached to the liver, storing bile. **gallstone** *n* hard mass formed in the gall bladder or its ducts.

gall[2] [**gawl**] *v* **1** annoy. **2** make sore by rubbing.

gall[3] [**gawl**] *n* abnormal outgrowth on a tree or plant.

gallant *adj* **1** brave and noble. **2** (of a man) attentive to women. **gallantly** *adv* **gallantry** *n* **1** showy, attentive treatment of women. **2** bravery.

galleon *n* large three-masted sailing ship of the 15th–17th centuries.

gallery *n, pl* **-ries 1** room or building for displaying works of art. **2** balcony in a church, theatre, etc. **3** passage in a mine. **4** long narrow room for a specific purpose, e.g. *shooting gallery.*

galley *n* **1** kitchen of a ship or aircraft. **2** *Hist* ship propelled by oars, usu. rowed by slaves. **galley slave 1** *Hist* slave forced to row in a galley. **2** *Informal* drudge.

Gallic *adj* **1** French. **2** of ancient Gaul.

gallium *n Chem* soft grey metallic element used in semiconductors.

gallivant *v* go about in search of pleasure.

gallon *n* liquid measure of eight pints, equal to 4.55 litres.

gallop *n* **1** horse's fastest pace. **2** galloping. ♦ *v* **galloping, galloped 3** go or ride at a gallop. **4** move or progress rapidly.

☑ **SPELLING TIP**
Although **gallop** has two *l*s, remember that **galloping** and **galloped** have only one *p*.

gallows *n* wooden structure used for hanging criminals.

Gallup poll *n* public opinion poll carried out by questioning a cross section of the population.

galore *adv* in abundance.

galoshes *pl n Brit, Aust & NZ* waterproof overshoes.

galumph *v Brit, Aust & NZ informal* leap or move about clumsily.

galvanic *adj* **1** of or producing an electric current generated by chemical means. **2** *Informal* stimulating or startling. **galvanize** *v* **1** stimulate into action. **2** coat (metal) with zinc.

gambit *n* **1** opening line or move intended to secure an advantage. **2** *Chess* opening move involving the sacrifice of a pawn.

gamble *v* **1** play games of chance to win money. **2** act on the expectation of something. ♦ *n* **3** risky undertaking. **4** bet or wager. **gambler** *n*

gambling *n*

gamboge [gam-**boje**] *n* gum resin used as a yellow pigment and purgative.

gambol *v* **-bolling, -bolled 1** jump about playfully, frolic. ♦ *n* **2** frolic.

☑ **SPELLING TIP**
Although the pronunciation is the same as 'gamble', both the verb and the noun **gambol** must always contain an o.

game[1] *n* **1** amusement or pastime. **2** contest for amusement. **3** single period of play in a contest. **4** animals or birds hunted for sport or food. **5** their flesh. **6** scheme or trick. **7** *v* **8** gamble. ♦ *adj* **9** brave. **10** willing. **gamely** *adv* **gaming** *n* gambling. **gamekeeper** *n Brit, Aust & S Afr* person employed to breed game and prevent poaching. **gamer** *n* person who plays computer games. **gamesmanship** *n* art of winning by cunning practices without actually cheating.

game[2] *adj Brit, Aust & NZ* lame, crippled.

gamete *n Biol* reproductive cell.

gamine [**gam**-een] *n* slim boyish young woman.

gamma *n* third letter of the Greek alphabet. **gamma ray** electromagnetic ray of shorter wavelength and higher energy than an x-ray.

gammon *n* cured or smoked ham.

gammy *adj* **-mier, -miest** same as GAME[2].

gamut *n* whole range or scale (of music, emotions, etc.).

gander *n* **1** male goose. **2** *Informal* quick look.

gang *n* **1** (criminal) group. **2** organized group of workmen. **gangland** *n* criminal underworld. **gang up** *v* form an alliance (against).

gangling *adj* lanky and awkward.

ganglion *n* **1** group of nerve cells. **2** small harmless tumour.

gangplank *n* portable bridge for boarding or leaving a ship.

gangrene *n* decay of body tissue as a result of disease or injury. **gangrenous** *adj*

gangsta rap *n* style of music portraying life in Black ghettos in the US.

gangster *n* member of a criminal gang.

gangway *n* **1** passage between rows of seats. **2** gangplank.

gannet *n* **1** large sea bird. **2** *Brit slang* greedy person.

gantry *n, pl* -tries structure supporting something such as a crane or rocket.

gaol [**jayl**] *n* same as JAIL.

gap *n* **1** break or opening. **2** interruption or interval. **3** divergence or difference. **gappy** *adj*

gape *v* **1** stare in wonder. **2** open the mouth wide. **3** be or become wide open. **gaping** *adj*

garage *n* **1** building used to house cars. **2** place for the refuelling, sale, and repair of cars. ♦ *v* **3** put or keep a car in a garage.

garb *n* **1** clothes. ♦ *v* **2** clothe.

garbage *n* rubbish.

garbled *adj* (of a story etc.) jumbled and confused.

garden *n* **1** piece of land for growing flowers, fruit, or vegetables. ♦ *pl* **2** ornamental park. ♦ *v* **3** cultivate a garden. **gardener** *n* **gardening** *n* **garden centre** place selling plants and gardening equipment.

gardenia [gar-**deen**-ya] *n* **1** large fragrant white waxy flower. **2** shrub bearing this.

garfish *n* freshwater fish with a long body and very long toothed jaws sea

fish with similar characteristics.

gargantuan *adj* huge.

gargle *v* **1** wash the throat with (a liquid) by breathing out slowly through the liquid. ♦ *n* **2** liquid used for gargling.

gargoyle *n* waterspout carved in the form of a grotesque face, esp. on a church.

garish *adj* crudely bright or colourful. **garishly** *adv* **garishness** *n*

garland *n* **1** wreath of flowers worn or hung as a decoration. ♦ *v* **2** decorate with garlands.

garlic *n* pungent bulb of a plant of the onion family, used in cooking.

garment *n* **1** article of clothing. ♦ *pl* **2** clothes.

garner *v* collect or store.

garnet *n* red semiprecious stone.

garnish *v* **1** decorate (food). ♦ *n* **2** decoration for food.

garret *n* attic in a house.

garrison *n* **1** troops stationed in a town or fort. **2** fortified place. ♦ *v* **3** station troops in.

garrotte, garotte *n* **1** Spanish method of execution by strangling. **2** cord or wire used for this. ♦ *v* **3** kill by this method.

garrulous *adj* talkative.

garter *n* band worn round the leg to hold up a sock or stocking.

gas *n, pl* **gases, gasses** **1** airlike substance that is not liquid or solid. **2** fossil fuel in the form of a gas, used for heating. **3** gaseous anaesthetic. **4** *Chiefly US* petrol. **5** *v* **gassing, gassed** **6** poison or render unconscious with gas. **7** *Informal* talk idly or boastfully. **gassy** *adj* filled with gas. **gaseous** *adj* of or like gas. **gasbag** *n* *Informal* person who talks too much. **gas chamber** airtight room which is filled with poison gas to kill people or animals. **gasholder, gasometer** [gas-**som**-it-er] *n* large tank for storing gas. **gas mask** mask with a chemical filter to protect the wearer against poison gas.

gash *v* **1** make a long deep cut in. ♦ *n* **2** long deep cut.

gasket *n* piece of rubber etc. placed between the faces of a metal joint to act as a seal.

gasoline *n US* petrol.

gasp *v* **1** draw in breath sharply or with difficulty. **2** utter breathlessly. **3** *n* **4** convulsive intake of breath.

gastric *adj* of the stomach. **gastritis** *n* inflammation of the stomach lining.

gastroenteritis *n* inflammation of the stomach and intestines.

gastronomy *n* art of good eating. **gastronomic** *adj*

gastropod *n* mollusc, such as a snail, with a single flattened muscular foot.

gate *n* **1** movable barrier, usu. hinged, in a wall or fence. **2** opening with a gate. **3** any entrance or way in. **4** (entrance money paid by) those attending a sporting event. **gate-crash** *v* enter (a party) uninvited. **gatehouse** *n* building at or above a gateway. **gateway** *n* **1** entrance with a gate. **2** means of access, e.g. *London's gateway to Scotland.*

gâteau [**gat**-toe] *n, pl* **-teaux** [-toes] rich elaborate cake.

gather *v* **1** assemble. **2** collect gradually. **3** increase gradually. **4** learn from information given. **5** pick or harvest. **6** draw (material) into small tucks or folds. **gathers** *pl n* gathered folds in material. **gathering** *n* assembly.

gauche [**gohsh**] *adj* socially awkward. **gaucheness** *n*

gaucho [**gow**-choh] *n, pl* **-chos** S American cowboy.

gaudy *adj* **gaudier, gaudiest** vulgarly bright or colourful. **gaudily** *adv* **gaudiness** *n*

gauge [**gayj**] *v* **1** estimate or judge. **2** measure the amount or condition of. ♦ *n* **3** measuring instrument. **4** scale or standard of measurement. **5** distance between the rails of a railway track. **6**

☑ **SPELLING TIP**
The vowels in **gauge** are often confused so that the misspelling *guage* is common in the Bank of English.

gaunt *adj* lean and haggard. **gauntness** *n*

gauntlet[1] *n* heavy glove with a long cuff. **throw down the gauntlet** offer a challenge.

gauntlet[2] *n* **run the gauntlet** be exposed to criticism or unpleasant treatment.

gauze *n* transparent loosely-woven fabric, often used for surgical dressings. **gauzy** *adj*

gave *v* past tense of GIVE.

gavel [**gav**-el] *n* small hammer banged on a table by a judge, auctioneer, or chairman to call for attention.

gavotte *n* **1** old formal dance. **2** music for this.

gawk *v* stare stupidly. **gawky** *adj* clumsy or awkward. **gawkiness** *n*

gawp *v Slang* stare stupidly.

gay *adj* **1** homosexual. **2** carefree and merry. **3** colourful. ♦ *n* **4** homosexual. **gayness** *n* homosexuality.

gaze *v* **1** look fixedly. ♦ *n* **2** fixed look.

gazebo [gaz-**zee**-boh] *n, pl* **-bos, -boes** summerhouse with a good view.

gazelle *n* small graceful antelope.

gazette *n* official publication containing announcements. **gazetteer** *n* (part of) a book that lists and describes places.

gazump *v Brit & Aust* raise the price of

a property after verbally agreeing it with (a prospective buyer).

GB Great Britain.

GBH (in Britain) grievous bodily harm.

GCE (in Britain) General Certificate of Education.

GCSE (in Britain) General Certificate of Secondary Education.

gear n **1** set of toothed wheels connecting with another or with a rack to change the direction or speed of transmitted motion. **2** mechanism for transmitting motion by gears. **3** setting of a gear to suit engine speed, e.g. *first gear*. **4** clothing or belongings. **5** equipment. ♦ v **6** prepare or organize for something. **in, out of gear** with the gear mechanism engaged *or* disengaged. **gearbox** n case enclosing a set of gears in a motor vehicle. **gear up** v prepare for an activity.

gecko n, pl **geckos, geckoes** small tropical lizard.

geebung [**gee**-bung] n Australian tree or shrub with an edible but tasteless fruit fruit of this tree.

geek n Informal boring, unattractive person. **geeky** adj

geelbek n S Afr edible marine fish.

geese n plural of GOOSE.

geezer n Brit, Aust & NZ informal man.

Geiger counter [**guy**-ger] n instrument for detecting and measuring radiation.

geisha [**gay**-sha] n, pl **-sha, -shas** (in Japan) professional female companion for men.

gel [**jell**] n **1** jelly-like substance, esp. one used to secure a hairstyle. ♦ v **gelling, gelled 2** form a gel. **3** Informal take on a definite form.

gelatine [**jel**-at-teen], **gelatin** n **1** substance made by boiling animal bones. **2** edible jelly made of this.

gelatinous [jel-**at**-in-uss] adj of or like jelly.

geld v castrate.

gelding n castrated horse.

gelignite n type of dynamite used for blasting.

gem n **1** precious stone or jewel. **2** highly valued person or thing.

gemfish n Australian food fish with a delicate flavour.

gen n Informal information. **gen up on** v **genning, genned** Brit informal make or become fully informed about.

gendarme [**zhohn**-darm] n member of the French police force.

gender n **1** state of being male or female. **2** Grammar classification of nouns in certain languages as masculine, feminine, or neuter.

gene [**jean**] n part of a cell which determines inherited characteristics.

genealogy [jean-ee-**al**-a-gee] n, pl **-gies** (study of) the history and descent of a family or families. **genealogical** adj **genealogist** n

genera [**jen**-er-a] n plural of GENUS.

general adj **1** common or widespread. **2** of or affecting all or most. **3** not specific. **4** including or dealing with various or miscellaneous items. **5** highest in authority or rank, e.g. *general manager*. ♦ n **6** very senior army officer. **in general** mostly or usually. **generally** adv **generality** n, pl **-ties 1** general principle. **2** state of being general. **generalize** v **1** draw general conclusions. **2** speak in generalities. **3** make widely known or used. **generalization** n **general election** election in which representatives are chosen for every constituency. **general practitioner** nonspecialist doctor serving a local area.

generate v produce or bring into being. **generative** adj capable of producing. **generator** n machine for converting mechanical energy into electrical energy.

generation n **1** all the people born about the same time. **2** average time between two generations (about 30 years). **3** generating.

generic [jin-**ner**-ik] adj of a class, group, or genus. **generically** adv

generous adj **1** free in giving. **2** free from pettiness. **3** plentiful. **generously** adv **generosity** n

genesis [**jen**-iss-iss] n, pl -eses [-iss-eez] beginning or origin.

genetic [jin-**net**-tik] adj of genes or genetics. **genetics** n study of heredity and variation in organisms. **geneticist** n **genetic engineering** alteration of the genetic structure of an organism for a particular purpose. **genetic fingerprinting** use of a person's unique DNA pattern as a means of identification.

genial [**jean**-ee-al] adj cheerful and friendly. **genially** adv **geniality** n

genie [**jean**-ee] n (in fairy tales) servant who appears by magic and grants wishes.

genital adj of the sexual organs or reproduction. **genitals, genitalia** [jen-it-**ail**-ya] pl n external sexual organs.

genitive n grammatical case indicating possession or association.

genius [**jean**-yuss] n (person with) exceptional ability in a particular field.

genocide [**jen**-no-side] n murder of a race of people.

genre [**zhohn**-ra] n style of literary, musical, or artistic work.

gent n Brit, Aust & NZ informal gentleman. **gents** n men's public toilet.

genteel adj affectedly proper and polite. **genteelly** adv

gentian [**jen**-shun] n mountain plant with deep blue flowers.

gentile adj, n non-Jewish (person).

gentle adj **1** mild or kindly. **2** not rough or severe. **3** gradual. **4** easily controlled, tame. **gentleness** n **gently** adv **gentleman** n **1** polite well-bred man. **2** man of high social position. **3** polite name for a man. **gentlemanly** adj **gentlewoman** n fem

gentry n people just below the nobility in social rank. **gentrification** n taking-over of a traditionally working-class area by middle-class incomers. **gentrify** v

genuflect v bend the knee as a sign of reverence or deference. **genuflection, genuflexion** n

genuine adj **1** not fake, authentic. **2** sincere. **genuinely** adv **genuineness** n

genus [**jean**-uss] n, pl genera **1** group into which a family of animals or plants is divided. **2** kind, type.

geocentric adj **1** having the earth as a centre. **2** measured as from the earth's centre.

geography n study of the earth's physical features, climate, population, etc. **geographer** n **geographical, geographic** adj **geographically** adv

geology n study of the earth's origin, structure, and composition. **geological** adj **geologically** adv **geologist** n

geometry n branch of mathematics dealing with points, lines, curves, and surfaces. **geometric, geometrical** adj **geometrically** adv

Geordie n person from, or dialect of, Tyneside, an area of NE England.

Georgian adj of the time of any of the four kings of Britain called George, esp. 1714–1830.

geostationary adj (of a satellite) orbiting so as to remain over the same point of the earth's surface.

geothermal adj of or using the heat in the earth's interior.

geranium n cultivated plant with red, pink, or white flowers.

gerbil [**jer**-bill] n burrowing desert rodent of Asia and Africa.

geriatrics n branch of medicine dealing with old age and its diseases. **geriatric** adj, n old (person).

germ n 1 microbe, esp. one causing disease. 2 beginning from which something may develop. 3 simple structure that can develop into a complete organism.

German n 1 language of Germany, Austria, and part of Switzerland. 2 person from Germany. ♦ adj 3 of Germany or its language. **Germanic** adj **German measles** contagious disease accompanied by a cough, sore throat, and red spots. **German shepherd dog** Alsatian.

germane adj **germane to** relevant to.

germanium n Chem brittle grey element that is a semiconductor.

germinate v (cause to) sprout or begin to grow. **germination** n **germinal** adj of or in the earliest stage of development.

gerrymandering n alteration of voting constituencies in order to give an unfair advantage to one party.

gerund [**jer**-rund] n noun formed from a verb, such as *living*.

Gestapo n secret state police of Nazi Germany.

gestation n 1 (period of) carrying of young in the womb between conception and birth. 2 developing of a plan or idea in the mind.

gesticulate v make expressive movements with the hands and arms. **gesticulation** n

gesture n 1 movement to convey meaning. 2 thing said or done to show one's feelings. ♦ v 3 gesticulate.

get v getting, got 1 obtain or receive. 2 bring or fetch. 3 contract (an illness). 4 (cause to) become as specified, e.g. get wet. 5 understand. 6 (often foll. by to) come (to) or arrive (at). 7 go on board (a plane, bus, etc.). 8 persuade. 9 Informal annoy. **get across** v (cause to) be understood. **get at** v 1 gain access to. 2 imply or mean. 3 criticize. **getaway** adj, n (used in) escape. **get by** v manage in spite of difficulties. **get off** v (cause to) avoid the consequences of, or punishment for, an action. **get off with** v Informal start a romantic or sexual relationship with. **get over** v recover from. **get through** v 1 (cause to) succeed. 2 use up (money or supplies). **get through to** v 1 make (a person) understand. 2 contact by telephone. **get-up** n Informal costume. **get up to** v be involved in.

geyser [**geez**-er] n 1 spring that discharges steam and hot water. 2 Brit & S Afr domestic gas water heater.

ghastly adj -lier, -liest 1 Informal unpleasant. 2 deathly pale. 3 Informal unwell. 4 Informal horrible. **ghastliness** n

ghat n 1 (in India) steps leading down to a river. 2 mountain pass.

ghee [**gee**] n (in Indian cookery) clarified butter.

gherkin n small pickled cucumber.

ghetto n, pl -tos, -toes slum area inhabited by a deprived minority. **ghetto-blaster** n Informal large portable cassette recorder or CD player.

ghillie n same as GILLIE.

ghost n 1 disembodied spirit of a dead person. 2 faint trace. 3 ♦ v 4 ghostwrite. **ghost gum** Aust eucalyptus with white trunk and branches. **ghostly** adj

ghost town deserted town.

ghostwriter *n* writer of a book or article on behalf of another person who is credited as the author.

ghoul [**gool**] *n* **1** person with morbid interests. **2** demon that eats corpses. **ghoulish** *adj*

GI *n Informal* US soldier.

giant *n* **1** mythical being of superhuman size. **2** very large person or thing. **3** *adj* **4** huge.

gibber[1] [**jib**-ber] *v* speak or utter rapidly and unintelligibly. **gibberish** *n* rapid unintelligible talk.

gibber[2] [**gib**-ber] *n Aust* **1** boulder. **2** barren land covered with stones.

gibbet [**jib**-bit] *n* gallows for displaying executed criminals.

gibbon [**gib**-bon] *n* agile tree-dwelling ape of S Asia.

gibbous *adj* (of the moon) more than half but less than fully illuminated.

gibe [**jibe**] *v*, *n* **same as** JIBE[1].

giblets [**jib**-lets] *pl n* gizzard, liver, heart, and neck of a fowl.

gidday, g'day *interj Aust & NZ* expression of greeting.

giddy *adj* **-dier, -diest** having or causing a feeling of dizziness. **giddily** *adv* **giddiness** *n*

gift *n* **1** present. **2** natural talent. ♦ *v* **3** make a present of. **gifted** *adj* talented.

gig[1] *n* **1** single performance by pop or jazz musicians. ♦ *v* **gigging, gigged** **2** play a gig or gigs.

gig[2] *n* light two-wheeled horse-drawn carriage.

gigantic *adj* enormous.

giggle *v* **1** laugh nervously or foolishly. ♦ *n* **2** such a laugh. **giggly** *adj*

gigolo [**jig**-a-lo] *n, pl* **-los** man paid by an older woman to be her escort or lover.

gigot *n Chiefly Brit* leg of lamb or mutton.

gild *v* **gilding, gilded** *or* **gilt** **1** put a thin layer of gold on. **2** make falsely attractive.

gill [**jill**] *n* liquid measure of quarter of a pint, equal to 0.142 litres.

gillie *n* (in Scotland) attendant for hunting or fishing.

gills [**gillz**] *pl n* breathing organs in fish and other water creatures.

gilt **1** *adj* **2** covered with a thin layer of gold. ♦ *n* **3** thin layer of gold used as decoration. **gilt-edged** *adj* denoting government stocks on which interest payments and final repayments are guaranteed.

gimbals *pl n* set of pivoted rings which allow nautical instruments to remain horizontal at sea.

gimcrack [**jim**-krak] *adj* **1** showy but cheap. **2** shoddy.

gimlet [**gim**-let] *n* small tool with a screwlike tip for boring holes in wood. **gimlet-eyed** *adj* having a piercing glance.

gimmick *n* something designed to attract attention or publicity. **gimmickry** *n* **gimmicky** *adj*

gin[1] *n* spirit flavoured with juniper berries.

gin[2] *n* **1** wire noose used to trap small animals. **2** machine for separating seeds from raw cotton.

gin[3] *n Aust offens* Aboriginal woman.

ginger *n* **1** root of a tropical plant, used as a spice. **2** light orange-brown colour. **gingery** *adj* **ginger ale, beer** fizzy ginger-flavoured soft drink. **gingerbread** *n* moist cake flavoured with ginger. **ginger group** *Brit, Aust & NZ* group within a larger group that agitates for a more active policy. **ginger nut, snap** crisp ginger-flavoured biscuit.

gingerly *adv* cautiously.

gingham *n* cotton cloth, usu. checked or striped.

gingivitis [jin-jiv-**vite**-iss] *n* inflammation of the gums.

ginkgo [**gink**-go] *n, pl* -**goes** ornamental Chinese tree.

ginseng [**jin**-seng] *n* (root of) a plant believed to have tonic and energy-giving properties.

Gipsy *n, pl* -**sies** same as GYPSY.

giraffe *n* African ruminant mammal with a spotted yellow skin and long neck and legs.

gird *v* **girding, girded** *or* **girt** **1** put a belt round. **2** secure with or as if with a belt. **3** surround. **gird (up) one's loins** prepare for action.

girder *n* large metal beam.

girdle¹ *n* **1** woman's elastic corset. **2** belt. **3** *Anat* encircling structure or part. ♦ *v* **4** surround or encircle.

girdle² *n Scot* griddle.

girl *n* **1** female child. **2** young woman. **3** girlfriend. **4** *Informal* any woman. **girlhood** *n* **girlish** *adj* **girlie, girly** *adj Informal* featuring photographs of naked or scantily clad women.

girlfriend *n* **1** girl or woman with whom a person is romantically or sexually involved. **2** female friend.

giro [**jire**-oh] *n, pl* -**ros** **1** (in some countries) system of transferring money within a post office or bank directly from one account to another. **2** *Brit informal* social security payment by giro cheque.

girt *v* a past of GIRD.

girth *n* **1** measurement round something. **2** band round a horse to hold the saddle in position.

gist [**jist**] *n* substance or main point of a matter.

give *v* **giving, gave, given** **1** present (something) to another person. **2** impart. **3** administer. **4** utter or emit. **5** sacrifice or devote. **6** organize or host. **7** yield or break under pressure. ♦ *n* **8** resilience or elasticity. **give away** *v* **1**

donate as a gift. **2** reveal. **giveaway** *n* **1** something that reveals hidden feelings or intentions. ♦ *adj* **2** very cheap or free. **give in** *v* admit defeat. **give off** *v* emit. **give out** *v* **1** distribute. **2** emit. **3** come to an end or fail. **give over** *v* **1** set aside for a specific purpose. **2** *Informal* cease. **give up** *v* **1** abandon. **2** acknowledge defeat.

gizzard *n* part of a bird's stomach.

glacé [**glass**-say] *adj* preserved in a thick sugary syrup.

glacier *n* slow-moving mass of ice formed by accumulated snow. **glacial** *adj* **1** of ice or glaciers. **2** very cold. **3** unfriendly. **glaciated** *adj* covered with or affected by glaciers. **glaciation** *n*

glad *adj* **gladder, gladdest** **1** pleased and happy. **2** causing happiness. **glad to** very willing to (do something). **the glad eye** *Chiefly Brit informal* inviting or seductive glance. **gladly** *adv* **gladness** *n* **gladden** *v* make glad. **glad rags** *Informal* best clothes.

glade *n* open space in a forest.

gladiator *n* (in ancient Rome) man trained to fight in arenas to provide entertainment.

gladiolus *n, pl* -**lus, -li, -luses** garden plant with sword-shaped leaves.

glamour *n* alluring charm or fascination. **glamorous** *adj* alluring. **glamorize** *v*

☑ **SPELLING TIP**

People often forget to drop the *u* in **glamour** when they add *ous*. That's why there are 124 occurrences of *glamourous* in the Bank of English. But the correct spelling is **glamorous**.

---

glance *v* **1** look rapidly or briefly. **2** glint or gleam. ♦ *n* **3** brief look. **glancing** *adj* hitting at an oblique angle. **glance off** *v* strike and be deflected off (an object) at an oblique angle.

gland *n* organ that produces and secretes substances in the body. **glandular** *adj*

glare *v* 1 stare angrily. 2 be unpleasantly bright. ♦ *n* 3 angry stare. 4 unpleasant brightness. **glaring** *adj* 1 conspicuous. 2 unpleasantly bright. **glaringly** *adv*

glass *n* 1 hard brittle, usu. transparent substance consisting of metal silicates or similar compounds. 2 tumbler. 3 its contents. 4 objects made of glass. 5 mirror. 6 barometer. ♦ *pl* 7 spectacles. **glassy** *adj* 1 like glass. 2 expressionless. **glasshouse** *n* 1 greenhouse. 2 *Brit informal* army prison.

glaucoma *n* eye disease.

glaze *v* 1 fit or cover with glass. 2 cover with a protective shiny coating. 3 *n* 4 transparent coating. 5 substance used for this. **glazier** *n* person who fits windows with glass.

gleam *n* 1 small beam or glow of light. 2 brief or faint indication. ♦ *v* 3 emit a gleam. **gleaming** *adj*

glean *v* 1 gather (facts etc.) bit by bit. 2 gather (the useful remnants of a crop) after harvesting. **gleaner** *n*

glee *n* triumph and delight. **gleeful** *adj* **gleefully** *adv*

glen *n* deep narrow valley, esp. in Scotland.

glib *adj* **glibber, glibbest** fluent but insincere or superficial. **glibly** *adv* **glibness** *n*

glide *v* 1 move easily and smoothly. 2 (of an aircraft) move without the use of engines. 3 *n* 4 smooth easy movement. **glider** *n* *Aust* flying phalanger. **gliding** *n* sport of flying gliders.

glimmer *v* 1 shine faintly, flicker. ♦ *n* 2 faint gleam. 3 faint indication.

glimpse *n* 1 brief or incomplete view. 2 *v* 3 catch a glimpse of.

glint *v* 1 gleam brightly. ♦ *n* 2 bright gleam.

glissando *n* *Music* slide between two notes in which all intermediate notes are played.

glisten *v* gleam by reflecting light.

glitch *n* small problem that stops something from working properly.

glitter *v* 1 shine with bright flashes. 2 be showy. ♦ *n* 3 sparkle or brilliance. 4 tiny pieces of shiny decorative material.

gloaming *n* *Scot poetic* twilight.

gloat *v* (often foll. by *over*) regard one's own good fortune or the misfortune of others with smug or malicious pleasure.

glob *n* rounded mass of thick fluid.

globe *n* 1 sphere with a map of the earth on it. 2 spherical object. 3 *S Afr* light bulb. **the globe** the earth. **global** *adj* 1 worldwide. 2 total or comprehensive. **globalization** *n* process by which a company, etc., expands to operate internationally. **global warming** increase in the overall temperature worldwide believed to be caused by the greenhouse effect. **globally** *adv* **globetrotter** *n* habitual worldwide traveller. **globetrotting** *n, adj*

globule *n* small round drop. **globular** *adj*

glockenspiel *n* percussion instrument consisting of small metal bars played with hammers.

gloom *n* 1 melancholy or depression. 2 darkness. **gloomy** *adj* **gloomier, gloomiest** **gloomily** *adv*

glory *n, pl* **-ries** 1 praise or honour. 2 splendour. 3 praiseworthy thing. 4 *v* **-rying, -ried** 5 (foll. by *in*) triumph or exalt. **glorify** *v* 1 make (something) seem more worthy than it is. 2 praise. **glorification** *n* **glorious** *adj* 1 brilliantly beautiful. 2 delightful. 3 full

of or conferring glory. **gloriously** adv
glory hole Informal untidy cupboard
or storeroom.

gloss[1] n **1** surface shine or lustre. **2**
paint or cosmetic giving a shiny finish.
glossy adj **-sier, -siest 1** smooth and
shiny. **2** (of a magazine) printed on
shiny paper. **glossily** adv **glossiness**
n **gloss over** v (try to) cover up or
pass over (a fault or error).

gloss[2] n **1** explanatory comment added
to the text of a book. ♦ v **2** add glosses
to.

glossary n, pl **-ries** list of special or
technical words with definitions.

glottal adj of the glottis.

glottis n, pl **-tises, -tides** vocal cords
and the space between them.

glove n covering for the hand with
individual sheaths for each finger and
the thumb. **gloved** adj covered by a
glove or gloves. **glove compartment**
or **box** small storage area in the
dashboard of a car.

glow v **1** emit light and heat without
flames. **2** shine. **3** have a feeling of
wellbeing or satisfaction. **4** (of a
colour) look warm. **5** be hot. ♦ n **6**
glowing light. **7** warmth of colour. **8**
feeling of wellbeing. **glow-worm** n
insect giving out a green light.

glower [rhymes with **power**] v, n scowl.

gloxinia n tropical plant with large
bell-shaped flowers.

glucose n kind of sugar found in fruit.

glue n **1** natural or synthetic sticky
substance used as an adhesive. ♦ v
gluing or **glueing, glued 2** fasten
with glue. **3** (foll. by to) pay full
attention to, e.g. her eyes were glued to
the TV. **gluey** adj **glue-sniffing** n
inhaling of glue fumes for intoxicating
or hallucinatory effects.

glum adj **glummer, glummest** sullen
or gloomy. **glumly** adv

glut n **1** excessive supply. ♦ v **glutting,**

glutted **2** oversupply.

gluten [**gloo**-ten] n protein found in
cereal grain.

glutinous [**gloo**-tin-uss] adj sticky or
gluey.

glutton n **1** greedy person. **2** person
with a great capacity for something.
gluttonous adj **gluttony** n

glycerine, glycerin n colourless
sweet liquid used widely in chemistry
and industry.

glycerol [**gliss**-ser-ol] n technical name
for GLYCERINE.

gm gram.

GM genetically modified

GMO genetically modified organism.

GMT Greenwich Mean Time.

gnarled adj rough, twisted, and
knobbly.

gnash v grind (the teeth) together in
anger or pain.

gnat n small biting two-winged fly.

gnaw v **gnawing, gnawed** or
gnawn 1 bite or chew steadily. **2** (foll.
by at) cause constant distress (to).

gneiss n coarse-grained metamorphic
rock.

gnome n imaginary creature like a little
old man.

gnomic [**no**-mik] adj of pithy sayings.

Gnosticism n religious movement
believing in intuitive spiritual
knowledge. **Gnostic** n, adj

gnu [**noo**] n oxlike S African antelope.

go v **going, went, gone 1** move to or
from a place. **2** be in regular
attendance at. **3** depart. **4** be, do, or
become as specified. **5** be allotted to a
specific purpose or recipient. **6** blend
or harmonize. **7** fail or break down. **8**
elapse. **9** be got rid of. **10** attend. **11**
be acceptable. **12** n **13** attempt. **14**
verbal attack. **15** turn. **make a go of**
be successful at. **go back on** v break
(a promise etc.). **go-between** n

intermediary. **go for** v 1 *Informal* choose. **2** attack. **3** apply to equally. **go-getter** n energetically ambitious person. **go-go dancer** scantily dressed erotic dancer. **go off** v 1 explode. **2** ring or sound. **3** *Informal* become stale or rotten. **4** *Informal* stop liking. **go out** v 1 go to entertainments or social functions. **2** be romantically involved (with). **3** be extinguished. **go over** v examine or check. **go-slow** n deliberate slowing of work-rate as an industrial protest. **go through** v 1 suffer or undergo. **2** examine or search.

goad v 1 provoke (someone) to take some kind of action, usu. in anger. ♦ n **2** spur or provocation. **3** spiked stick for driving cattle.

goal n 1 *Sport* posts through which the ball or puck has to be propelled to score. **2** score made in this way. **3** aim or purpose. **goalie** n *Informal* goalkeeper. **goalkeeper** n player whose task is to stop shots entering the goal. **goalpost** n one of the two posts marking the limit of a goal. **move the goalposts** change the aims of an activity to ensure the desired result.

goanna n large Australian lizard.

goat n sure-footed ruminant animal with horns. **get someone's goat** *Slang* annoy someone. **goatee** n pointed tuftlike beard.

gob n 1 lump of a soft substance. **2** *Brit, Aust & NZ slang* mouth.

gobbet n lump, esp. of food.

gobble[1] v eat hastily and greedily.

gobble[2] n 1 rapid gurgling cry of the male turkey. ♦ v 2 make this noise.

gobbledegook, gobbledygook n unintelligible (official) language or jargon.

goblet n drinking cup without handles.

goblin n (in folklore) small malevolent creature.

goby n, pl **-by, -bies** small spiny-finned fish.

god n 1 spirit or being worshipped as having supernatural power. **2** object of worship, idol. **3** (G-) (in monotheistic religions) the Supreme Being, creator and ruler of the universe. **the gods** top balcony in a theatre. **goddess** n *fem* **godlike** adj **godly** adj devout or pious. **godliness** n **god-fearing** adj pious and devout. **godforsaken** adj desolate or dismal. **godsend** n something unexpected but welcome.

godetia n plant with showy flowers.

godparent n person who promises at a child's baptism to bring the child up as a Christian. **godchild** n child for whom a person stands as godparent. **goddaughter** n **godfather** n 1 male godparent. **2** head of a criminal, esp. Mafia, organization. **godmother** n **godson** n

gogga n *S Afr informal* any small insect.

goggle v 1 (of the eyes) bulge. **2** stare. **goggles** pl n protective spectacles.

going n 1 condition of the ground for walking or riding over. **2** speed or progress. **3** departure. ♦ adj **4** thriving. **5** current or accepted. **going-over** n, pl **goings-over** 1 *Informal* investigation or examination. **2** scolding or thrashing. **goings-on** pl n mysterious or unacceptable events.

goitre [**goy**-ter] n swelling of the thyroid gland in the neck.

go-kart n small low-powered racing car.

gold n 1 yellow precious metal. **2** coins or articles made of this. **3** colour of gold. **4** adj **5** made of gold. **6** gold-coloured. **goldcrest** n small bird with a yellow crown. **gold-digger** n *Informal* woman who uses her sexual attractions to get money from a man. **goldfinch** n kind of finch, the male of

which has yellow-and-black wings.
goldfish n orange fish kept in ponds or aquariums. **gold leaf** thin gold sheet used for gilding. **gold medal** medal given to the winner of a competition or race.

golden adj 1 made of gold. 2 gold-coloured. 3 very successful or promising. **golden eagle** large mountain eagle of the N hemisphere. **golden handshake** Informal payment to a departing employee. **golden rule** important principle. **golden wattle** Australian plant with yellow flowers that yields a useful gum and bark. **golden wedding** fiftieth wedding anniversary.

golf n 1 outdoor game in which a ball is struck with clubs into a series of holes. ♦ v 2 play golf. **golfer** n

golliwog n soft black-faced doll.

gonad n organ producing reproductive cells, such as a testicle or ovary.

gondola n 1 long narrow boat used in Venice. 2 suspended cabin of a cable car, airship, etc. **gondolier** n person who propels a gondola.

gone v past participle of GO. **goner** n Informal person or thing beyond help or recovery.

gong n 1 rimmed metal disc that produces a note when struck. 2 Slang medal.

gonorrhoea [gon-or-**ree**-a] n venereal disease with a discharge from the genitals.

good adj **better, best** 1 giving pleasure. 2 morally excellent. 3 beneficial. 4 kindly. 5 talented. 6 well-behaved. 7 valid. 8 reliable. 9 complete or full. ♦ n 10 benefit. 11 positive moral qualities. ♦ pl 12 merchandise. 13 property. **as good as** virtually. **for good** permanently. **goodness** n **goodly** adj considerable. **goody** n 1 Informal hero in a book or

film. 2 enjoyable thing. **goody-goody** adj, n smugly virtuous (person).

good-for-nothing adj, n irresponsible or worthless (person). **Good Samaritan** person who helps another in distress. **goodwill** n 1 kindly feeling. 2 value of a business in reputation etc. over and above its tangible assets.

goodbye interj, n expression used on parting.

gooey adj **gooier, gooiest** Informal sticky and soft.

goof Informal ♦ n 1 mistake. ♦ v 2 make a mistake.

googly n, pl -lies Cricket ball that spins unexpectedly from off to leg on the bounce.

goon n 1 Informal stupid person. 2 Chiefly US hired thug.

goose n, pl geese 1 web-footed bird like a large duck. 2 female of this bird. **goose flesh, pimples** bumpy condition of the skin and bristling of the hair due to cold or fright. **goose step** march step in which the leg is raised rigidly.

gooseberry n 1 edible yellowy-green berry. 2 Brit informal unwanted third person accompanying a couple.

gopher [**go**-fer] n American burrowing rodent.

gore¹ n blood from a wound.

gore² v pierce with horns.

gorge n 1 deep narrow valley. ♦ v 2 eat greedily. **make one's gorge rise** cause feelings of disgust or nausea.

gorgeous adj 1 strikingly beautiful or attractive. 2 Informal very pleasant. **gorgeously** adv

gorgon n terrifying or repulsive woman.

Gorgonzola n sharp-flavoured blue-veined Italian cheese.

gorilla n largest of the apes, found in Africa.

gormless *adj Informal* stupid.

gorse *n* prickly yellow-flowered shrub.

gory *adj* **gorier, goriest 1** horrific or bloodthirsty. **2** involving bloodshed.

goshawk *n* large hawk.

gosling *n* young goose.

gospel *n* **1** (G-) any of the first four books of the New Testament. **2** unquestionable truth. **3** Black religious music originating in the churches of the Southern US.

gossamer *n* **1** very fine fabric. **2** filmy cobweb.

gossip *n* **1** idle talk, esp. about other people. **2** person who engages in gossip. ♦ *v* **gossiping, gossiped 3** engage in gossip. **gossipy** *adj*

got *v* past of GET. **have got** possess. **have got to** need or be required to.

Gothic *adj* **1** (of architecture) of or in the style common in Europe from the 12th–16th centuries, with pointed arches. **2** of or in an 18th-century literary style characterized by gloom and the supernatural. **3** (of print) using a heavy ornate typeface.

gouache *n* (painting using) watercolours mixed with glue.

Gouda *n* mild-flavoured Dutch cheese.

gouge [**gowj**] *v* **1** scoop or force out. **2** cut (a hole or groove) in (something). ♦ *n* **3** hole or groove. **4** chisel with a curved cutting edge.

goulash [**goo**-lash] *n* rich stew seasoned with paprika.

gourd [**goord**] *n* **1** fleshy fruit of a climbing plant. **2** its dried shell, used as a container.

gourmand [**goor**-mand] *n* person who is very keen on food and drink.

gourmet [**goor**-may] *n* connoisseur of food and drink.

gout [**gowt**] *n* disease causing inflammation of the joints.

govern *v* **1** rule, direct, or control. **2** exercise restraint over (temper etc.). **governable** *adj* **governance** *n* governing. **governess** *n* woman teacher in a private household. **governor** *n* **1** official governing a province or state. **2** senior administrator of a society, institution, or prison **governor general** representative of the Crown in a Commonwealth country.

government *n* **1** executive policy-making body of a state. **2** exercise of political authority over a country or state. **3** system by which a country or state is ruled. **governmental** *adj*

☑ **SPELLING TIP**

In the Bank of English, there are hundreds of examples of *goverment* without its middle *n*. Remember it has two *n*s: **government**.

---

gown *n* **1** woman's long formal dress. **2** surgeon's overall. **3** official robe worn by judges, clergymen, etc.

goy *n, pl* **goyim, goys** *Slang* Jewish word for a non-Jew.

GP general practitioner.

GPS Global Positioning System: a satellite-based navigation system.

grab *v* **grabbing, grabbed 1** grasp suddenly, snatch. **2** *n* **3** sudden snatch. **4** mechanical device for gripping.

grace *n* **1** beauty and elegance. **2** polite, kind behaviour. **3** goodwill or favour. **4** delay granted. **5** short prayer of thanks for a meal. **6** (G-) title of a duke, duchess, or archbishop. **7** *v* **8** add grace to. **graceful** *adj* **gracefully** *adv* **graceless** *adj* **gracious** *adj* **1** kind and courteous. **2** condescendingly polite. **3** elegant. **graciously** *adv* **grace note** *Music* note ornamenting a melody.

grade *n* **1** place on a scale of quality,

rank, or size. **2** mark or rating. **3** *US, Aust & S Afr* class in school. ♦ *v* **4** arrange in grades. **5** assign a grade to. **make the grade** succeed. **gradation** *n* **1** (stage in) a series of degrees or steps. **2** arrangement in stages.

gradient *n* (degree of) slope.

gradual *adj* occurring, developing, or moving in small stages. **gradually** *adv*

graduate *v* **1** receive a degree or diploma. **2** group by type or quality. **3** mark (a container etc.) with units of measurement. ♦ *n* **4** holder of a degree. **graduation** *n*

graffiti [graf-**fee**-tee] *pl n* words or drawings scribbled or sprayed on walls etc.

☑ SPELLING TIP

People get confused about the number of *f*s and *t*s in **graffiti**. The favourite misspelling in the Bank of English is *grafitti*. The correct spelling has two *f*s and only one *t*.

---

graft¹ *n* **1** surgical transplant of skin or tissue. **2** shoot of a plant set in the stalk of another. ♦ *v* **3** transplant (living tissue) surgically. **4** insert (a plant shoot) in another stalk.

graft² *Brit informal* ♦ *n* **1** hard work. **2** obtaining of money by misusing one's position. ♦ *v* **3** work hard. **grafter** *n*

grail *n* same as HOLY GRAIL.

grain *n* **1** seedlike fruit of a cereal plant. **2** cereal plants in general. **3** small hard particle. **4** very small amount. **5** arrangement of fibres, as in wood. **6** texture or pattern resulting from this. **go against the grain** be contrary to one's natural inclination. **grainy** *adj*

gram, gramme *n* metric unit of mass equal to one thousandth of a kilogram.

grammar *n* **1** branch of linguistics dealing with the form, function, and order of words. **2** use of words. **3** book

on the rules of grammar. **grammarian** *n* **grammatical** *adj* according to the rules of grammar. **grammatically** *adv* **grammar school** *Brit* esp. formerly, a secondary school providing an education with a strong academic bias.

gramophone *n* old-fashioned type of record player.

grampus *n, pl* -**puses** dolphin-like mammal.

gran *n Brit, Aust & NZ informal* grandmother.

granary *n, pl* -**ries** storehouse for grain.

grand *adj* **1** large or impressive, imposing. **2** dignified or haughty. **3** *Informal* excellent. **4** (of a total) final. ♦ *n* **5** *Slang* thousand pounds or dollars. **6** grand piano. **grandchild** *n* child of one's child. **granddaughter** *n* female grandchild. **grandfather** *n* male grandparent. **grandfather clock** tall standing clock with a pendulum and wooden case. **grandmother** *n* female grandparent. **grandparent** *n* parent of one's parent. **grand piano** large harp-shaped piano with the strings set horizontally. **grand slam** winning of all the games or major tournaments in a sport in one season. **grandson** *n* male grandchild. **grandstand** *n* terraced block of seats giving the best view at a sports ground.

grandee *n* person of high station.

grandeur *n* **1** magnificence. **2** nobility or dignity.

grandiloquent *adj* using pompous language. **grandiloquence** *n*

grandiose *adj* **1** imposing. **2** pretentiously grand. **grandiosity** *n*

grange *n Brit* country house with farm buildings.

granite [**gran**-nit] *n* very hard igneous rock often used in building.

granny, grannie *n, pl* -**nies** *Informal*

grandmother. **granny flat** flat in or added to a house, suitable for an elderly parent.

grant v 1 consent to fulfil (a request). 2 give formally. 3 admit. ♦ n 4 sum of money provided by a government for a specific purpose, such as education. **take for granted** 1 accept as true without proof. 2 take advantage of without due appreciation.

granule n small grain. **granular** adj of or like grains. **granulated** adj (of sugar) in the form of coarse grains.

grape n small juicy green or purple berry, eaten raw or used to produce wine, raisins, currants, or sultanas. **grapevine** n 1 grape-bearing vine. 2 Informal unofficial way of spreading news.

grapefruit n large round yellow citrus fruit.

graph n drawing showing the relation of different numbers or quantities plotted against a set of axes.

graphic adj 1 vividly descriptive. 2 of or using drawing, painting, etc. **graphics** pl n diagrams, graphs, etc., esp. as used on a television programme or computer screen. **graphically** adv

graphite n soft black form of carbon, used in pencil leads.

graphology n study of handwriting. **graphologist** n

grapnel n device with several hooks, used to grasp or secure things.

grapple v 1 try to cope with (something difficult). 2 come to grips with (a person). **grappling iron** grapnel.

grasp v 1 grip something firmly. 2 understand. 3 try to seize. ♦ n 4 grip or clasp. 5 understanding. 6 total rule or possession. **grasping** adj greedy or avaricious.

grass n 1 common type of plant with

jointed stems and long narrow leaves, including cereals and bamboo. 2 lawn. 3 pasture land. 4 Slang marijuana. 5 Brit slang person who informs, esp. on criminals. ♦ v 6 cover with grass. 7 (often foll. by on) Brit slang inform on. **grassy** adj **-sier, -siest grasshopper** n jumping insect with long hind legs. **grass roots** 1 ordinary members of a group, as distinct from its leaders. 2 essentials. **grassroots** adj **grass tree** Australian plant with stiff grasslike leaves and small white flowers.

grate[1] v 1 rub into small bits on a rough surface. 2 scrape with a harsh rasping noise. 3 annoy. **grater** n **grating** adj 1 harsh or rasping. 2 annoying.

grate[2] n framework of metal bars for holding fuel in a fireplace. **grating** n framework of metal bars covering an opening.

grateful adj feeling or showing gratitude. **gratefully** adv

gratify v **-fying, -fied** 1 satisfy or please. 2 indulge (a desire or whim). **gratification** n

gratis adv, adj free, for nothing.

gratitude n feeling of being thankful for a favour or gift.

gratuitous adj 1 unjustified, e.g. gratuitous violence. 2 given free. **gratuitously** adv

gratuity n, pl **-ties** money given for services rendered, tip.

grave[1] n hole for burying a corpse. **gravestone** n stone marking a grave. **graveyard** n cemetery.

grave[2] adj 1 causing concern. 2 serious and solemn. **gravely** adv

grave[3] [rhymes with **halve**] n accent (`) over a vowel to indicate a special pronunciation.

gravel n mixture of small stones and coarse sand. **gravelled** adj covered with gravel. **gravelly** adj 1 covered with gravel. **2** rough-sounding.

graven adj carved or engraved.

gravid [**grav**-id] adj Med pregnant.

gravitate v **1** be influenced or drawn towards. **2** Physics move by gravity. **gravitation** n **gravitational** adj

gravity n, pl **-ties 1** force of attraction of one object for another, esp. of objects to the earth. **2** seriousness or importance. **3** solemnity.

gravy n, pl **-vies 1** juices from meat in cooking. **2** sauce made from these.

gray adj Chiefly US grey.

grayling n fish of the salmon family.

graze[1] v feed on grass.

graze[2] v **1** scratch or scrape the skin. **2** touch lightly in passing. ♦ n **3** slight scratch or scrape.

grease n **1** soft melted animal fat. **2** any thick oily substance. ♦ v **3** apply grease to. **greasy** adj **greasier, greasiest** covered with or containing grease. **greasiness** n **greasepaint** n theatrical make-up.

great adj **1** large in size or number. **2** important. **3** pre-eminent. **4** Informal excellent. **great-** prefix one generation older or younger than, e.g. great-grandfather. **greatly** adv **greatness** n **greatcoat** n heavy overcoat. **Great Dane** very large dog with short smooth hair.

greave n piece of armour for the shin.

grebe n diving water bird.

Grecian [**gree**-shan] adj of ancient Greece.

greed n excessive desire for food, wealth, etc. **greedy** adj **greedily** adv **greediness** n

Greek n **1** language of Greece. **2** person from Greece. ♦ adj **3** of Greece, the Greeks, or the Greek language.

green adj **1** of a colour between blue and yellow. **2** characterized by green plants or foliage. **3** (**G-**) of or

concerned with environmental issues. **4** unripe. **5** envious or jealous. **6** immature or gullible. ♦ n **7** colour between blue and yellow. **8** area of grass kept for a special purpose. **9** (**G-**) person concerned with environmental issues. ♦ pl **10** green vegetables. ♦ v **11** make or become green. **greenness** n **greenish, greeny** adj **greenery** n vegetation. **green belt** protected area of open country around a town. **greenfinch** n European finch with dull green plumage in the male. **green fingers** skill in gardening. **greenfly** n green aphid, a common garden pest. **greengage** n sweet green plum. **greengrocer** n Brit shopkeeper selling vegetables and fruit. **greenhorn** n Chiefly US novice. **greenhouse** n glass building for rearing plants. **greenhouse effect** rise in the temperature of the earth caused by heat absorbed from the sun being unable to leave the atmosphere. **green light 1** signal to go. **2** permission to proceed with something. **greenshank** n large European sandpiper. **greenstone** n NZ type of green jade used for Maori ornaments.

greet v **1** meet with expressions of welcome. **2** receive in a specified manner. **3** be immediately noticeable to. **greeting** n

gregarious adj **1** fond of company. **2** (of animals) living in flocks or herds.

gremlin n imaginary being blamed for mechanical malfunctions.

grenade n small bomb thrown by hand or fired from a rifle. **grenadier** n soldier of a regiment formerly trained to throw grenades.

grenadine [gren-a-**deen**] n syrup made from pomegranates.

grevillea n any of various Australian evergreen trees and shrubs.

grew v past tense of GROW.

grey adj **1** of a colour between black and white. **2** (of hair) partly turned white. **3** dismal or dark. **4** dull or boring. ♦ n **5** grey colour. **6** grey or white horse. **greying** adj (of hair) turning grey. **greyish** adj **greyness** n **grey matter** Informal brains.

greyhound n swift slender dog used in racing.

grid n **1** network of horizontal and vertical lines, bars, etc. **2** national network of electricity supply cables.

griddle n flat iron plate for cooking.

gridiron n **1** frame of metal bars for grilling food. **2** American football pitch.

gridlock n **1** situation where traffic is not moving. **2** point in a dispute at which no agreement can be reached. **gridlocked** adj

grief n deep sadness. **grieve** v (cause to) feel grief. **grievance** n real or imaginary cause for complaint. **grievous** adj **1** very severe or painful. **2** very serious.

griffin n mythical monster with an eagle's head and wings and a lion's body.

grill n **1** device on a cooker that radiates heat downwards. **2** grilled food. **3** gridiron. ♦ v **5** cook under a grill. **6** question relentlessly. **grilling** n relentless questioning.

grille, grill n grating over an opening.

grilse [**grillss**] n salmon on its first return from the sea to fresh water.

grim adj **grimmer, grimmest 1** stern. **2** harsh or forbidding. **3** very unpleasant. **grimly** adv **grimness** n

grimace n **1** ugly or distorted facial expression of pain, disgust, etc. ♦ v **2** make a grimace.

grime n **1** ingrained dirt. ♦ v **2** make very dirty. **grimy** adj

grin v **grinning, grinned 1** smile broadly, showing the teeth. ♦ n **2** broad smile.

grind v **grinding, ground 1** crush or rub to a powder. **2** smooth or sharpen by friction. **3** scrape together with a harsh noise. **4** oppress. **5** n **6** Informal hard work. **7** act or sound of grinding. **grind out** v produce in a routine or uninspired manner. **grindstone** n stone used for grinding.

grip n **1** firm hold or grasp. **2** way in which something is grasped. **3** mastery or understanding. **4** US travelling bag. **5** handle. ♦ v **gripping, gripped 6** grasp or hold tightly. **7** hold the interest or attention of. **gripping** adj

gripe v **1** Informal complain persistently. ♦ n **2** Informal complaint. **3** sudden intense bowel pain.

grisly adj **-lier, -liest** horrifying or ghastly.

grist n grain for grinding. **grist to one's mill** something which can be turned to advantage.

gristle n tough stringy animal tissue found in meat. **gristly** adj

grit n **1** rough particles of sand. **2** courage. ♦ pl **4** coarsely ground grain. ♦ v **gritting, gritted 5** spread grit on (an icy road etc.). **6** clench or grind (the teeth). **gritty** adj **-tier, -tiest** **grittiness** n

grizzle v Brit, Aust & NZ informal whine or complain.

grizzled adj grey-haired.

grizzly n, pl **-zlies** large American bear (also **grizzly bear**).

groan n **1** deep sound of grief or pain. **2** Informal complaint. ♦ v **3** utter a groan. **4** Informal complain.

groat n Hist fourpenny piece.

grocer n shopkeeper selling foodstuffs. **grocery** n, pl **-ceries 1** business or premises of a grocer. ♦ pl **2** goods sold by a grocer.

grog n Brit, Aust & NZ spirit, usu. rum,

and water.

groggy adj **-gier**, **-giest** Informal faint, shaky, or dizzy.

groin n place where the legs join the abdomen.

grommet n **1** ring or eyelet. **2** Med tube inserted in the ear to drain fluid from the middle ear.

groom n **1** person who looks after horses. **2** bridegroom. **3** officer in a royal household. ♦ v **4** make or keep one's clothes and appearance neat and tidy. **5** brush or clean a horse. **6** train (someone) for a future role.

groove n long narrow channel in a surface.

grope v **1** feel about or search uncertainly. **2** Slang fondle (someone) in a rough sexual way. **groping** n

gross adj **1** flagrant. **2** vulgar. **3** Slang disgusting or repulsive. **4** repulsively fat. **5** total, without deductions. ♦ n **6** twelve dozen. ♦ v **7** make as total revenue before deductions. **grossly** adv **grossness** n

grotesque [grow-**tesk**] adj **1** strangely distorted. **2** absurd. ♦ n **3** grotesque person or thing. **4** artistic style mixing distorted human, animal, and plant forms. **grotesquely** adv

grotto n, pl **-toes**, **-tos** small picturesque cave.

grotty adj **-tier**, **-tiest** Informal nasty or in bad condition.

grouch Informal ♦ v **1** grumble or complain. ♦ n **2** person who is always complaining. **3** persistent complaint. **grouchy** adj

ground¹ n **1** surface of the earth. **2** soil. **3** area used for a specific purpose, e.g. rugby ground. **4** position in an argument or controversy. **5** pl **6** enclosed land round a house. **7** reason or motive. **8** coffee dregs. **9** v **10** base or establish. **11** instruct in the basics. **12** ban an aircraft or pilot from flying.

13 run (a ship) aground. **groundless** adj without reason. **grounding** n basic knowledge of a subject. **ground-breaking** adj innovative. **ground floor** floor of a building level with the ground. **groundnut** n peanut. **groundsheet** n waterproof sheet put on the ground under a tent. **groundsman** n person employed to maintain a sports ground or park. **groundswell** n rapidly developing general feeling or opinion. **groundwork** n preliminary work.

ground² v past of GRIND.

group n **1** number of people or things regarded as a unit. **2** small band of musicians or singers. ♦ v **3** place or form into a group.

grouse¹ n **1** stocky game bird. **2** its flesh.

grouse² v **1** grumble or complain. ♦ n **2** complaint.

grout n **1** thin mortar. ♦ v **2** fill up with grout.

grove n small group of trees.

grovel [**grov**-el] v **-elling**, **-elled 1** behave humbly in order to win a superior's favour. **2** crawl on the floor.

grow v **growing**, **grew**, **grown 1** develop physically. **2** (of a plant) exist. **3** cultivate (plants). **4** increase in size or degree. **5** originate. **6** become gradually, e.g. it was growing dark. **growth** n **1** growing. **2** increase. **3** something grown or growing. **4** tumour. **grown-up** adj, n adult. **grow up** v mature.

growl v **1** make a low rumbling sound. **2** utter with a growl. ♦ n **3** growling sound.

groyne n wall built out from the shore to control erosion.

grub n **1** legless insect larva. **2** Slang food. ♦ v **grubbing**, **grubbed 3** search carefully for something by digging or by moving things about. **4**

dig up the surface of (soil).

grubby adj -bier, -biest dirty. **grubbiness** n

grudge v 1 be unwilling to give or allow. ♦ n 2 resentment.

gruel n thin porridge.

gruelling adj exhausting or severe.

gruesome adj causing horror and disgust.

gruff adj rough or surly in manner or voice. **gruffly** adv **gruffness** n

grumble v 1 complain. 2 rumble. ♦ n 3 complaint. 4 rumble. **grumbler** n **grumbling** adj, n

grumpy adj grumpier, grumpiest bad-tempered. **grumpily** adv **grumpiness** n

grunge n 1 style of rock music with a fuzzy guitar sound. 2 deliberately untidy and uncoordinated fashion style.

grunt v 1 make a low short gruff sound, like a pig. ♦ n 2 pig's sound. 3 gruff noise.

Gruyère [**grew**-yair] n hard yellow Swiss cheese with holes.

gryphon n same as GRIFFIN.

GST (in Australia, New Zealand, and Canada) Goods and Services Tax.

G-string n small strip of cloth covering the genitals and attached to a waistband.

GT gran turismo, used of a sports car.

guano [**gwah**-no] n dried sea-bird manure, used as fertilizer.

guarantee n 1 formal assurance, esp. in writing, that a product will meet certain standards. 2 something that makes a specified condition or outcome certain. 3 v -teeing, -teed 4 give a guarantee. 5 secure against risk etc. 6 ensure. **guarantor** n person who gives or is bound by a guarantee.

guard v 1 watch over to protect or to prevent escape. 2 n 3 person or group that guards. 4 official in charge of a

train. 5 protection. 6 screen for enclosing anything dangerous. 7 posture of defence in sports such as boxing or fencing. ♦ pl 8 (G-) regiment with ceremonial duties. **guarded** adj cautious or noncommittal. **guardedly** adv **guard against** v take precautions against. **guardsman** n member of the Guards.

guardian n 1 keeper or protector. 2 person legally responsible for a child, mentally ill person, etc. **guardianship** n

guava [**gwah**-va] n yellow-skinned tropical American fruit.

gudgeon n small freshwater fish.

Guernsey [**gurn**-zee] n breed of dairy cattle.

guerrilla, guerilla n member of an unofficial armed force fighting regular forces.

guess v 1 estimate or draw a conclusion without proper knowledge. 2 estimate correctly by guessing. 3 suppose. ♦ n 4 estimate or conclusion reached by guessing. **guesswork** n process or results of guessing.

guest n 1 person entertained at another's house or at another's expense. 2 invited performer or speaker. 3 customer at a hotel or restaurant. ♦ v 4 appear as a visiting player or performer. **guesthouse** n boarding house.

guff n Brit, Aust & NZ slang nonsense.

guffaw n 1 crude noisy laugh. ♦ v 2 laugh in this way.

guide n 1 person who conducts tour expeditions. 2 person who shows the way. 3 book of instruction or information. 4 model for behaviour. 5 something to gauge something or to help in planning one's actions. 6 (G-) member of an organization for girls equivalent to the Scouts. ♦ v 7 act as a guide for. 8 control, supervise, or influence. **guidance** n leadership, instruction, or advice. **guided missile** missile whose flight is controlled electronically. **guide dog** dog trained to lead a blind person. **guideline** n set principle for doing something.

guild n 1 organization or club. 2 Hist society of men in the same trade or craft.

guilder n former monetary unit of the Netherlands.

guile [gile] n cunning or deceit. **guileful** adj **guileless** adj

guillemot [gil-lee-mot] n black-and-white diving sea bird of N hemisphere.

guillotine n 1 machine for beheading people. 2 device for cutting paper or sheet metal. 3 method of preventing lengthy debate in parliament by fixing a time for taking the vote. ♦ v 4 behead by guillotine. 5 limit debate by the guillotine.

guilt n 1 fact or state of having done wrong. 2 remorse for wrongdoing. **guiltless** adj innocent. **guilty** adj 1 responsible for an offence or misdeed. 2 feeling or showing guilt. **guiltily** adv

guinea n 1 former British monetary unit worth 21 shillings (1.05 pounds). 2 former gold coin of this value. **guinea fowl** wild bird related to the pheasant. **guinea pig** 1 tailless S American rodent, commonly kept as a pet. 2 Informal person used for experimentation.

guise [rhymes with **size**] n 1 false appearance. 2 external appearance.

guitar n stringed instrument with a flat back and a long neck, played by plucking or strumming. **guitarist** n

gulch n US deep narrow valley.

gulf n 1 large deep bay. 2 chasm. 3 large difference in opinion or understanding.

gull n long-winged sea bird.

gullet n muscular tube through which food passes from the mouth to the stomach.

gullible adj easily tricked. **gullibility** n

gully n, pl **-lies** channel cut by running water.

gulp v 1 swallow hastily. 2 gasp. ♦ n 3 gulping. 4 thing gulped.

gum[1] n firm flesh in which the teeth are set. **gummy** adj **-mier, -miest** toothless.

gum[2] n 1 sticky substance obtained from certain trees. 2 adhesive. 3 chewing gum. 4 gumdrop. 5 gum tree. ♦ v **gumming, gummed** 6 stick with gum. **gummy** adj **-mier, -miest** **gumboots** pl n Chiefly Brit Wellington boots. **gumdrop** n hard jelly-like sweet. **gum tree** eucalyptus tree.

gumption n Informal 1 resourcefulness. 2 courage.

gun n 1 weapon with a metal tube from which missiles are fired by explosion. 2 device from which a substance is ejected under pressure. 3 v **gunning, gunned** 4 cause (an engine) to run at high speed. **jump the gun** act prematurely. **gunner** n artillery soldier. **gunnery** n use or science of large guns. **gunboat** n small warship. **gun dog** dog used to retrieve game. **gun down** v shoot (a person). **gun for** v seek or pursue vigorously. **gunman** n armed criminal. **gunmetal** n 1 alloy of copper, tin, and zinc. ♦ adj 2 dark grey. **gunpowder** n explosive mixture of potassium nitrate, sulphur, and charcoal. **gunrunning** n smuggling of guns and ammunition. **gunrunner** n **gunshot** n shot or range of a gun.

gunge n Informal sticky unpleasant substance. **gungy** adj **-gier, -giest**

gunny n strong coarse fabric used for sacks.

gunwale, gunnel [gun-nel] n top of

a ship's side.

gunyah *n Aust* hut or shelter in the bush.

guppy *n, pl* **-pies** small colourful aquarium fish.

gurgle *v, n* (make) a bubbling noise.

Gurkha *n* person, esp. a soldier, belonging to a Hindu people of Nepal.

guru *n* **1** Hindu or Sikh religious teacher or leader. **2** leader, adviser, or expert.

gush *v* **1** flow out suddenly and profusely. **2** express admiration effusively. ♦ *n* **3** sudden copious flow. **4** sudden surge of strong feeling. **gusher** *n* spurting oil well.

gusset *n* piece of material sewn into a garment to strengthen it.

gust *n* **1** sudden blast of wind. **2** *v* **3** blow in gusts. **gusty** *adj*

gusto *n* enjoyment or zest.

gut *n* **1** intestine. **2** *Informal* fat stomach. **3** short for CATGUT. ♦ *pl* **4** internal organs. **5** *Informal* courage. **6** *v* **gutting, gutted 7** remove the guts from. **8** (of a fire) destroy the inside of (a building). ♦ *adj* **9** basic or instinctive, e.g. *a gut reaction.* **gutsy** *adj* **-sier, -siest** *Informal* **1** courageous. **2** vigorous or robust, e.g. *a gutsy performance.* **gutted** *adj Brit, Aust & NZ informal* disappointed and upset.

gutta-percha *n* whitish rubbery substance obtained from an Asian tree.

gutter *n* **1** shallow channel for carrying away water from a roof or roadside. ♦ *v* **2** (of a candle) burn unsteadily, with wax running down the sides. **the gutter** degraded or criminal environment. **guttering** *n* material for gutters. **gutter press** newspapers that rely on sensationalism. **guttersnipe** *n Brit* neglected slum child.

guttural *adj* **1** (of a sound) produced at the back of the throat. **2** (of a voice)

harsh-sounding.

guy[1] *n* **1** *Informal* man or boy. **2** effigy of Guy Fawkes burnt on Nov. 5th **(Guy Fawkes Day).**

guy[2] *n* rope or chain to steady or secure something. **guy rope**

guzzle *v* eat or drink greedily.

gybe [**jibe**] *v* **1** (of a fore-and-aft sail) swing suddenly from one side to the other. **2** (of a boat) change course by letting the sail gybe.

gym *n* **1** gymnasium. **2** gymnastics.

gymkhana [jim-**kah**-na] *n* horse-riding competition.

gymnasium *n* large room with equipment for physical training. **gymnast** *n* expert in gymnastics. **gymnastic** *adj* **gymnastics** *pl n* exercises to develop strength and agility.

gynaecology [guy-nee-**kol**-la-jee] *n* branch of medicine dealing with diseases and conditions specific to women. **gynaecological** *adj* **gynaecologist** *n*

gypsophila *n* garden plant with small white flowers.

gypsum *n* chalklike mineral used to make plaster of Paris.

Gypsy *n, pl* **-sies** member of a travelling people found throughout Europe.

gyrate [jire-**rate**] *v* rotate or spiral about a point or axis. **gyration** *n* **gyratory** *adj* gyrating.

gyrocompass *n* compass using a gyroscope.

gyroscope [**jire**-oh-skohp] *n* disc rotating on an axis that can turn in any direction, so the disc maintains the same position regardless of the movement of the surrounding structure. **gyroscopic** *adj*

H h

H *Chem* hydrogen.

habeas corpus [hay-bee-ass **kor**-puss] *n* writ ordering a prisoner to be brought before a court.

haberdasher *n Brit, Aust & NZ* dealer in small articles used for sewing. **haberdashery** *n*

habit *n* **1** established way of behaving. **2** addiction to a drug. **3** costume of a monk or nun.

habitable *adj* fit to be lived in. **habitation** *n* (occupation of) a dwelling place.

habitat *n* natural home of an animal or plant.

habitual *adj* done regularly and repeatedly. **habitually** *adv*

habituate *v* accustom. **habituation** *n* **habitué** [hab-**it**-yew-ay] *n* frequent visitor to a place.

hacienda [hass-ee-**end**-a] *n* ranch or large estate in Latin America.

hack¹ *v* **1** cut or chop violently. **2** *Brit & NZ informal* tolerate.

hack² *n* **1** (inferior) writer or journalist. **2** horse kept for riding.

hacker *n Slang* computer enthusiast, esp. one who breaks into the computer system of a company or government.

hackles *pl n* **make one's hackles rise** make one feel angry or hostile.

hackney *n Brit* taxi.

hackneyed *adj* (of a word or phrase) unoriginal and overused.

hacksaw *n* small saw for cutting metal.

had *v* past of HAVE.

haddock *n* edible sea fish of N Atlantic.

Hades [**hay**-deez] *n Greek myth* underworld home of the dead.

hadj *n* same as HAJJ.

haematology *n* study of blood and its diseases.

haemoglobin [hee-moh-**globe**-in] *n* protein found in red blood cells which carries oxygen.

haemophilia [hee-moh-**fill**-lee-a] *n* hereditary illness in which the blood does not clot. **haemophiliac** *n*

haemorrhage [**hem**-or-ij] *n* **1** heavy bleeding. ♦ *v* **2** bleed heavily.

> ☑ **SPELLING TIP**
> The Bank of English shows that the most usual mistake in spelling **haemorrhage** is to miss out the second h, which is silent.

---

haemorrhoids [**hem**-or-oydz] *pl n* swollen veins in the anus (also **piles**).

hafnium *n Chem* metallic element found in zirconium ores.

haft *n* handle of an axe, knife, or dagger.

hag *n* ugly old woman. **hag-ridden** *adj* distressed or worried.

haggard *adj* looking tired and ill.

haggis *n* Scottish dish made from sheep's offal, oatmeal, suet, and seasonings, boiled in a bag made from the sheep's stomach.

haggle *v* bargain or wrangle over a price.

hagiography *n, pl* -**phies** writing about the lives of the saints.

hail¹ *n* **1** (shower of) small pellets of ice. **2** large number of insults, missiles, blows, etc. ♦ *v* **3** fall as or like hail. **hailstone** *n*

hail² *v* **1** call out to, greet. **2** stop (a taxi) by waving. **3** acknowledge publicly. **hail from** *v* come originally from.

hair n **1** threadlike growth on the skin. **2** such growths collectively, esp. on the head. **hairy** adj **1** covered with hair. **2** Slang dangerous or exciting. **hairiness** n **hairclip** n small bent metal hairpin. **hairdo** n Informal hairstyle. **hairdresser** n person who cuts and styles hair. **hairgrip** n Brit **same as** HAIRCLIP. **hairline** n **1** edge of hair at the top of the forehead. ♦ adj **2** very fine or narrow. **hairpin** n U-shaped wire used to hold the hair in place. **hairpin bend** very sharp bend in a road. **hair-raising** adj frightening or exciting. **hair-splitting** n, adj making petty distinctions. **hairstyle** n cut and arrangement of a person's hair.

hajj n pilgrimage a Muslim makes to Mecca.

haka n NZ **1** ceremonial Maori dance with chanting. **2** similar dance performed by a sports team before a match.

hake n edible sea fish of N hemisphere. Aust **same as** BARRACOUTA.

hakea [**hah**-kee-a] n Australian tree or shrub with hard woody fruit.

halal n meat from animals slaughtered according to Muslim law.

halberd n Hist spear with an axe blade.

halcyon [**hal**-see-on] adj peaceful and happy. **halcyon days** time of peace and happiness.

hale adj healthy, robust.

half n, pl **halves 1** either of two equal parts. **2** Informal half-pint of beer etc. **3** half-price ticket. ♦ adj **4** denoting one of two equal parts. ♦ adv **5** to the extent of half. **6** partially. **half-baked** adj Informal not properly thought out. **half-brother, half-sister** n brother or sister related through one parent only. **half-caste** n Offens person with parents of different races. **half-cocked** adj **go off half-cocked, (at) half-cock** fail because of inadequate preparation. **half-hearted** adj unenthusiastic. **half-life** n time taken for half the atoms in radioactive material to decay. **half-nelson** n wrestling hold in which one wrestler's arm is pinned behind his back by his opponent. **half-pie** adj NZ informal incomplete. **half-pipe** large U-shaped ramp used for skateboarding, snowboarding, etc. **half-timbered** adj (of a house) having an exposed wooden frame filled in with plaster. **half-time** n Sport short rest period between two halves of a game. **halftone** n illustration showing lights and shadows by means of very small dots. **halfway** adv, adj at or to half the distance. **halfwit** n foolish or stupid person.

halfpenny [**hayp**-nee] n former British coin worth half an old penny.

halibut n large edible flatfish of N Atlantic.

halitosis n unpleasant-smelling breath.

hall n **1** (also **hallway**) entrance passage. **2** large room or building for public meetings, dances, etc. **3** Brit large country house.

hallelujah [hal-ee-**loo**-ya] interj exclamation of praise to God.

hallmark n **1** typical feature. **2** mark indicating the standard of tested gold and silver. ♦ v **3** stamp with a hallmark.

hallo interj **same as** HELLO.

hallowed adj regarded as holy.

Halloween, Hallowe'en n October 31, celebrated by children by dressing up as ghosts, witches, etc.

hallucinate v seem to see something that is not really there. **hallucination** n **hallucinatory** adj **hallucinogen** n drug that causes hallucinations. **hallucinogenic** adj

halo [**hay**-loh] n, pl **-loes, -los 1** ring of light round the head of a sacred figure. **2** circle of refracted light round the sun or moon.

halogen [**hal**-oh-jen] *n Chem* any of a group of nonmetallic elements including chlorine and iodine.

halt *v* **1** come or bring to a stop. ♦ *n* **2** temporary stop. **3** minor railway station without a building. **halting** *adj* hesitant, uncertain.

halter *n* strap round a horse's head with a rope to lead it with. **halterneck** *n* woman's top or dress with a strap fastened at the back of the neck.

halve *v* **1** divide in half. **2** reduce by half.

halves *n* plural of HALF.

halyard *n* rope for raising a ship's sail or flag.

ham¹ *n* smoked or salted meat from a pig's thigh. **ham-fisted** *adj* clumsy.

ham² *Informal* ♦ *n* **1** amateur radio operator. **2** actor who overacts. ♦ *v* **hamming, hammed 3 ham it up** overact.

hamburger *n* minced beef shaped into a flat disc, cooked and usu. served in a bread roll.

hamlet *n* small village.

hammer *n* **1** tool with a heavy metal head and a wooden handle, used to drive in nails etc. **2** part of a gun which causes the bullet to be fired. **3** heavy metal ball on a wire, thrown as a sport. **4** auctioneer's mallet. **5** striking mechanism in a piano. ♦ *v* **6** hit (as if) with a hammer. **7** *Informal* punish or defeat utterly. **go at it hammer and tongs** do something, esp. argue, very vigorously. **hammerhead** *n* shark with a wide flattened head. **hammer toe** condition in which a toe is permanently bent at the joint.

hammock *n* hanging bed made of canvas or net.

hamper¹ *v* make it difficult for (someone or something) to move or progress.

hamper² *n* **1** large basket with a lid. **2** selection of food and drink packed as a gift.

hamster *n* small rodent with a short tail and cheek pouches.

☑ **SPELLING TIP**

The word **hamster** appears 750 times in the Bank of English. The misspelling *hampster*, with a *p*, appears 13 times.

hamstring *n* **1** tendon at the back of the knee. ♦ *v* **2** make it difficult for (someone) to take any action.

hand *n* **1** part of the body at the end of the arm, consisting of a palm, four fingers, and a thumb. **2** style of handwriting. **3** round of applause. **4** manual worker. **5** pointer on a dial, esp. on a clock. **6** cards dealt to a player in a card game. **7** unit of length of four inches (10.16 centimetres) used to measure horses. ♦ *v* **8** pass, give. **have a hand in** be involved in. **lend a hand** help. **out of hand 1** beyond control. **2** definitely and finally. **to hand, at hand, on hand** nearby. **win hands down** win easily. **handbag** *n* woman's small bag for carrying personal articles in. **handbill** *n* small printed notice. **handbook** *n* small reference or instruction book. **handcuff** *n* **1** one of a linked pair of metal rings designed to be locked round a prisoner's wrists by the police. ♦ *v* **2** put handcuffs on. **hand-held** *adj* **1** (of a film camera) held rather than mounted, as in close-up action shots. **2** (of a computer) able to be held in the hand. ♦ *n* computer that can be held in the hand. **hand-out** *n* **1** clothing, food, or money given to a needy person. **2** written information given out at a talk etc. **hands-on** *adj* involving practical experience of equipment. **handstand** n act of supporting the body on the hands in an upside-down position. **handwriting** n (style of) writing by hand.

handful n 1 amount that can be held in the hand. 2 small number. 3 Informal person or animal that is difficult to control.

handicap n 1 physical or mental disability. 2 something that makes progress difficult. 3 contest in which the competitors are given advantages or disadvantages in an attempt to equalize their chances. 4 advantage or disadvantage given. ♦ v 5 make it difficult for (someone) to do something.

handicraft n objects made by hand.

handiwork n result of someone's work or activity.

handkerchief n small square of fabric used to wipe the nose.

☑ **SPELLING TIP**

People often forget to write a d in **handkerchief**, probably because they don't say it or hear it either.

---

handle n 1 part of an object that is held so that it can be used. ♦ v 2 hold, feel, or move with the hands. 3 control or deal with. **handler** n person who controls an animal. **handlebars** pl n curved metal bar used to steer a cycle.

handsome adj 1 (esp. of a man) good-looking. 2 large or generous, e.g. a handsome profit.

handy adj handier, handiest 1 convenient, useful. 2 good at manual work. **handily** adv **handyman** n man who is good at making or repairing things.

hang v hanging, hung 1 attach or be attached at the top with the lower

part free. 2 past **hanged**) suspend or be suspended by the neck until dead. 3 fasten to a wall. **get the hang of** Informal begin to understand. **hanger** n curved piece of wood, wire, or plastic, with a hook, for hanging up clothes (also **coat hanger**). **hang back** v hesitate, be reluctant. **hangman** n man who executes people by hanging. **hangover** n headache and nausea as a result of drinking too much alcohol. **hang-up** n Informal emotional or psychological problem.

hangar n large shed for storing aircraft.

hangdog adj guilty, ashamed, e.g. a hangdog look.

hang-glider n glider with a light framework from which the pilot hangs in a harness. **hang-gliding** n

hangi n, pl -gi, -gis NZ Maori oven consisting of a hole in the ground filled with hot stones.

hank n coil, esp. of yarn.

hanker v (foll. by after or for) desire intensely.

hanky, hankie n, pl hankies Informal handkerchief.

hanky-panky n Informal illicit sexual relations.

hansom cab n (formerly) two-wheeled horse-drawn carriage for hire.

haphazard adj not organized or planned. **haphazardly** adv

hapless adj unlucky.

happen v 1 take place, occur. 2 chance (to be or do something). **happening** n event, occurrence.

happy adj -pier, -piest 1 feeling or causing joy. 2 lucky, fortunate. **happily** adv **happiness** n **happy-go-lucky** adj carefree and cheerful.

hara-kiri n (formerly, in Japan) ritual suicide by disembowelling.

harangue v **1** address angrily or forcefully. ♦ n **2** angry or forceful speech.

harass v annoy or trouble constantly. **harassed** adj **harassment** n

> ☑ **SPELLING TIP**
>
> The commonest misspelling of **harass** is *harrass*. There should be only one r, but it's obviously difficult to remember: there are 232 instances of *harrassment* in the Bank of English and 10 of *harrasment*. The correct spelling is **harassment**.

harbinger [**har**-binj-a] n someone or something that announces the approach of something.

harbour n **1** sheltered port. ♦ v **2** maintain secretly in the mind. **3** give shelter or protection to.

hard adj **1** firm, solid, or rigid. **2** difficult. **3** requiring a lot of effort. **4** unkind, unfeeling. **5** causing pain, sorrow, or hardship. **6** (of water) containing calcium salts which stop soap lathering freely. **7** (of a drug) strong and addictive. ♦ adv **8** with great energy or effort. **9** with great intensity. **hard of hearing** unable to hear properly. **hard up** *Informal* short of money. **harden** v **hardness** n **hardship** n **1** suffering. **2** difficult circumstances. **hard-bitten** adj tough and determined. **hard-boiled** adj **1** (of an egg) boiled until solid. **2** *Informal* tough, unemotional. **hard copy** computer output printed on paper. **hardfill** n NZ & S Afr stone waste material used for landscaping. **hard-headed** adj shrewd, practical. **hardhearted** adj unsympathetic, uncaring. **hard sell** aggressive sales technique. **hard shoulder** surfaced verge at the edge of a motorway for emergency stops.

hardboard n thin stiff board made of compressed sawdust and wood chips.

hardly adv **1** scarcely or not at all. **2** with difficulty.

hardware n **1** metal tools or implements. **2** machinery used in a computer system. **3** heavy military equipment, such as tanks and missiles.

hardwood n wood of a broadleaved tree such as oak or ash.

hardy adj **hardier, hardiest** able to stand difficult conditions. **hardiness** n

hare n **1** animal like a large rabbit, with longer ears and legs. ♦ v **2** (usu. foll. by *off*) run (away) quickly. **harebell** n blue bell-shaped flower. **harebrained** adj foolish or impractical. **harelip** n slight split in the upper lip.

harem n (apartments of) a Muslim man's wives and concubines.

haricot bean [**har**-rik-oh] n small pale edible bean, usu. sold dried.

hark v *Old-fashioned* listen. **hark back** v return (to an earlier subject).

harlequin n **1** stock comic character with a diamond-patterned costume and mask. ♦ adj **2** in many colours.

harlot n *Lit* prostitute.

harm v **1** injure physically, mentally, or morally. ♦ n **2** physical, mental, or moral injury. **harmful** adj **harmless** adj

harmonica n small wind instrument played by sucking and blowing.

harmonium n keyboard instrument like a small organ.

harmony n, pl **-nies 1** peaceful agreement and cooperation. **2** pleasant combination of notes sounded at the same time. **harmonious** adj **harmoniously** adv **harmonic** adj of harmony. **harmonics** n science of musical sounds. **harmonize** v blend well together. **harmonization** n

harness n **1** arrangement of straps for attaching a horse to a cart or plough. **2** set of straps fastened round someone's body to attach something, e.g. *a safety harness.* ♦ v **3** put a harness on. **4** control (something) in order to make use of it.

harp n large triangular stringed instrument played with the fingers. **harpist** n **harp on about** v talk about continuously.

harpoon n **1** barbed spear attached to a rope used for hunting whales. ♦ v **2** spear with a harpoon.

harpsichord n stringed keyboard instrument.

harpy n, pl **-pies** nasty or bad-tempered woman.

harridan n nagging or vicious woman.

harrier n cross-country runner.

harrow n **1** implement used to break up lumps of soil. ♦ v **2** draw a harrow over.

harrowing adj very distressing.

harry v **-rying, -ried** keep asking (someone) to do something, pester.

harsh adj **1** severe and difficult to cope with. **2** unkind, unsympathetic. **3** extremely hard, bright, or rough. **harshly** adv **harshness** n

hart n adult male deer.

harum-scarum adj reckless.

harvest n **1** (season for) the gathering of crops. **2** crops gathered. ♦ v **3** gather (a ripened crop). **harvester** n

has v third person singular of the present tense of HAVE. **has-been** n *Informal* person who is no longer popular or successful.

hash[1] n dish of diced cooked meat and vegetables reheated. **make a hash of** *Informal* spoil, do badly.

hash[2] n *Informal* hashish.

hashish [**hash**-eesh] n drug made from the cannabis plant, smoked for its

intoxicating effects.

hasp n clasp that fits over a staple and is secured by a bolt or padlock, used as a fastening.

hassle *Informal* ♦ n **1** trouble, bother. **2** v **3** bother or annoy.

hassock n cushion for kneeling on in church.

haste n (excessive) quickness. **make haste** hurry, rush. **hasten** v (cause to) hurry. **hasty** adj (too) quick. **hastily** adv

hat n covering for the head, often with a brim, usu. worn to give protection from the weather. **keep something under one's hat** keep something secret. **hat trick** any three successive achievements, esp. in sport.

hatch[1] v **1** (cause to) emerge from an egg. **2** devise (a plot).

hatch[2] n **1** hinged door covering an opening in a floor or wall. **2** opening in the wall between a kitchen and a dining area. **3** door in an aircraft or spacecraft. **hatchback** n car with a lifting door at the back. **hatchway** n opening in the deck of a ship.

hatchet n small axe. **bury the hatchet** become reconciled. **hatchet job** malicious verbal or written attack. **hatchet man** *Informal* person carrying out unpleasant tasks for an employer.

hate v **1** dislike intensely. **2** be unwilling (to do something). ♦ n **3** intense dislike. **4** person or thing hated. **hateful** adj causing or deserving hate. **hater** n **hatred** n intense dislike.

haughty adj **-tier, -tiest** proud, arrogant. **haughtily** adv **haughtiness** n

haul v **1** pull or drag with effort. ♦ n **2** amount gained by effort or theft. **long haul** something that takes a lot of time and effort. **haulage** n (charge for) transporting goods. **haulier** n firm or person that transports goods by road.

haunch n human hip or fleshy hindquarter of an animal.

haunt v 1 visit in the form of a ghost. 2 remain in the memory or thoughts of. ♦ n 3 place visited frequently. **haunted** adj 1 frequented by ghosts. 2 worried. **haunting** adj memorably beautiful or sad.

haute couture [oat koo-**ture**] n French high fashion.

hauteur [oat-**ur**] n haughtiness.

have v has, having, had 1 possess, hold. 2 receive, take, or obtain. 3 experience or be affected by. 4 (foll. by to) be obliged, must, e.g. I had to go. 5 cause to be done. 6 give birth to. 7 used to form past tenses (with a past participle), e.g. we have looked; she had done enough. **have it out** Informal settle a matter by argument. **have on** v 1 wear. 2 Informal tease or trick. **have up** v bring to trial.

haven n place of safety.

haversack n canvas bag carried on the back or shoulder.

havoc n disorder and confusion.

haw n hawthorn berry.

hawk¹ n 1 bird of prey with a short hooked bill and very good eyesight. 2 Politics supporter or advocate of warlike policies. **hawkish, hawklike** adj **hawk-eyed** adj having very good eyesight.

hawk² v offer (goods) for sale in the street or door-to-door. **hawker** n

hawk³ v cough noisily.

hawser n large rope used on a ship.

hawthorn n thorny shrub or tree.

hay n grass cut and dried as fodder. **hay fever** allergy to pollen, causing sneezing and watery eyes. **haystack** n large pile of stored hay. **haywire** adj **go haywire** Informal not function properly.

hazard n 1 something that could be dangerous. ♦ v 2 put in danger. 3 make (a guess). **hazardous** adj

haze n mist, often caused by heat. **hazy** adj 1 not clear, misty. 2 confused or vague.

hazel n 1 small tree producing edible nuts. ♦ adj 2 (of eyes) greenish-brown. **hazelnut** n

H-bomb n hydrogen bomb.

he pron refers to: 1 male person or animal. n 2 male person or animal a he-goat.

head n 1 upper or front part of the body, containing the sense organs and the brain. 2 mind and mental abilities. 3 upper or most forward part of anything. 4 person in charge of a group, organization, or school. 5 pus-filled tip of a spot or boil. 6 white froth on beer. 7 pl **head**) person or animal considered as a unit. 8 adj 9 chief, principal. ♦ v 10 be at the top or front of. 11 be in charge of. 12 move (in a particular direction). 13 hit (a ball) with the head. 14 provide with a heading. **go to one's head** make one drunk or conceited. **head over heels (in love)** very much in love. **not make head nor tail of** not understand. **off one's head** Slang foolish or insane. **heads** adv Informal with the side of a coin which has a portrait of a head on it uppermost. **header** n 1 striking a ball with the head. 2 headlong fall. **heading** n title written or printed at the top of a page. **heady** adj intoxicating or exciting. **headache** n 1 continuous pain in the head. 2 cause of worry or annoyance. **headboard** n vertical board at the top end of a bed. **headdress** n decorative head covering. **head-hunt** v (of a company) approach and offer a job to (a person working for a rival company). **head-hunter** n **headland**

n area of land jutting out into the sea.
headlight *n* powerful light on the front of a vehicle. **headline** *n* **1** title at the top of a newspaper article, esp. on the front page. ♦ *pl* **2** main points of a news broadcast. **headlong** *adv, adj* **1** with the head first. **2** hastily.
headphones *pl n* two small loudspeakers held against the ears.
headquarters *pl n* centre from which operations are directed. **head start** advantage in a competition.
headstone *n* memorial stone on a grave. **headstrong** *adj* self-willed, obstinate. **headway** *n* progress.
headwind *n* wind blowing against the course of an aircraft or ship.
heal *v* make or become well. **healer** *n*
health *n* normal (good) condition of someone's body. **health food** natural food, organically grown and free from additives. **healthy** *adj* **1** having good health. **2** of or producing good health. **3** functioning well, sound. **healthily** *adv*
heap *n* **1** pile of things one on top of another. **2** (also **heaps**) large number or quantity. ♦ *v* **3** gather into a pile. **4** (foll. by *on*) give liberally (to).
hear *v* **hearing, heard 1** perceive (a sound) by ear. **2** listen to. **3** learn or be informed. **4** *Law* try (a case). **hear! hear!** exclamation of approval or agreement. **hearer** *n* **hearing** *n* **1** ability to hear. **2** trial of a case. **within hearing** close enough to be heard.
hearsay *n* gossip, rumour.
hearse *n* funeral car used to carry a coffin.
heart *n* **1** organ that pumps blood round the body. **2** centre of emotions, esp. love. **3** courage, spirit. **4** central or most important part. **5** figure representing a heart. **6** playing card with red heart heart-shaped symbols. **break someone's heart** cause

someone great grief. **by heart** from memory. **set one's heart on something** greatly desire something. **take something to heart** be upset about something. **hearten** *v* encourage, make cheerful. **heartless** *adj* cruel, unkind. **hearty** *adj* **1** substantial, nourishing. **2** friendly, enthusiastic. **heartily** *adv* **heart attack** sudden severe malfunction of the heart. **heart failure** sudden stopping of the heartbeat.
heart-rending *adj* causing great sorrow. **heart-throb** *n Slang* very attractive man, esp. a film or pop star.
heartache *n* intense anguish.
heartbeat *n* one complete pulsation of the heart.
heartbreak *n* intense grief.
heartburn *n* burning sensation in the chest caused by indigestion.
heartfelt *adj* felt sincerely or strongly.
hearth *n* floor of a fireplace.
heat *v* **1** make or become hot. ♦ *n* **2** state of being hot. **3** energy transferred as a result of a difference in temperature. **4** hot weather. **5** intensity of feeling. **6** preliminary eliminating contest in a competition. **on, in heat** (of some female animals) ready for mating. **heated** *adj* angry and excited. **heatedly** *adv* **heater** *n*
heath *n Brit* area of open uncultivated land.
heathen *adj, n* (of) a person who does not believe in an established religion.
heather *n* low-growing plant with small purple, pinkish, or white flowers, growing on heaths and mountains.
heave *v* **1** lift with effort. **2** throw (something heavy). **3** utter (a sigh). **4** rise and fall. **5** vomit. **6** *n* **7** heaving.
heaven *n* **1** place believed to be the home of God, where good people go when they die. **2** place or state of bliss. **the heavens** sky. **heavenly** *adj* **1** of

or like heaven. **2** of or occurring in space. **3** wonderful or beautiful.

heavy adj **heavier, heaviest 1** of great weight. **2** having a high density. **3** great in degree or amount. **4** Informal (of a situation) serious. **heavily** adv **heaviness** n **heavy industry** large-scale production of raw material or machinery. **heavy metal** very loud rock music featuring guitar riffs. **heavyweight** n boxer weighing over 175lb (professional) or 81kg (amateur).

Hebrew n **1** member of an ancient Semitic people. **2** ancient language of the Hebrews. **3** its modern form, used in Israel. ♦ adj **4** of the Hebrews.

heckle v interrupt (a public speaker) with comments, questions, or taunts. **heckler** n

hectare n one hundred ares or 10 000 square metres (2.471 acres).

hectic adj rushed or busy.

hector v bully.

hedge n **1** row of bushes forming a barrier or boundary. ♦ v **2** be evasive or noncommittal. **3** (foll. by against) protect oneself (from). **hedgerow** n bushes forming a hedge.

hedgehog n small mammal with a protective covering of spines.

hedonism n doctrine that pleasure is the most important thing in life. **hedonist** n **hedonistic** adj

heed n **1** careful attention. ♦ v **2** pay careful attention to. **heedless** adj **heedless of** taking no notice of.

heel¹ n **1** back part of the foot. **2** part of a shoe supporting the heel. **3** Old-fashioned contemptible person. ♦ v **4** repair the heel of (a shoe). **heeler** n Aust & NZ dog that herds cattle by biting at their heels.

heel² v (foll. by over) lean to one side.

hefty adj **heftier, heftiest** large, heavy, or strong.

hegemony [hig-**em**-on-ee] n political

domination.

Hegira n Mohammed's flight from Mecca to Medina in 622 AD.

heifer [**hef**-fer] n young cow.

height n **1** distance from base to top. **2** distance above sea level. **3** highest degree or topmost point. **heighten** v make or become higher or more intense.

heinous adj evil and shocking.

heir n person entitled to inherit property or rank. **heiress** n fem **heirloom** n object that has belonged to a family for generations.

held v past of HOLD¹.

helical adj spiral.

helicopter n aircraft lifted and propelled by rotating overhead blades. **heliport** n airport for helicopters.

heliotrope n **1** plant with purple flowers. ♦ adj **2** light purple.

helium [**heel**-ee-um] n Chem very light colourless odourless gas.

helix [**heel**-iks] n, pl **helices, helixes** spiral.

hell n **1** place believed to be where wicked people go when they die. **2** place or state of wickedness, suffering, or punishment. **hell for leather** at great speed. **hellish** adj **hellbent** adj (foll. by on) intent.

Hellenic adj of the (ancient) Greeks or their language.

hello interj expression of greeting or surprise.

helm n tiller or wheel for steering a ship.

helmet n hard hat worn for protection.

help v **1** make something easier, better, or quicker for (someone). **2** improve (a situation). **3** refrain from, e.g. I can't help smiling. ♦ n **4** assistance or support. **help oneself 1** take something, esp. food or drink, without being served. **2** Informal steal something. **helper** n **helpful** adj

helping n single portion of food.
helpless adj weak or incapable.
helplessly adv **helpline** n telephone line set aside for callers to contact an organization for help with a problem.
helpmate n companion and helper, esp. a husband or wife.

helter-skelter adj 1 haphazard and careless. ♦ adv 2 in a haphazard and careless manner. ♦ n 3 high spiral slide at a fairground.

hem n 1 bottom edge of a garment, folded under and stitched down. ♦ v **hemming, hemmed** 2 provide with a hem. **hem in** v surround and prevent from moving. **hemline** n level to which the hem of a skirt hangs.

hemisphere n half of a sphere, esp. the earth. **hemispherical** adj

hemlock n poison made from a plant with spotted stems and small white flowers.

hemp n 1 (also **cannabis**) Asian plant with tough fibres. 2 its fibre, used to make canvas and rope. 3 narcotic drug obtained from hemp.

hen n 1 female domestic fowl. 2 female of any bird. **hen night, party** party for women only. **henpecked** adj (of a man) dominated by his wife.

hence conj 1 for this reason. ♦ adv 2 from this time. **henceforth** adv from now on.

henchman n person employed by someone powerful to carry out orders.

henna n 1 reddish dye made from a shrub or tree. ♦ v 2 dye (the hair) with henna.

henry n, pl **-ry, -ries, -rys** unit of electrical inductance.

hepatitis n inflammation of the liver.

heptagon n geometric figure with seven sides.

heptathlon n athletic contest for women, involving seven events.

her pron 1 refers to a female person or animal or anything personified as feminine when the object of a sentence or clause. ♦ adj 2 belonging to her.

herald n 1 person who announces important news. 2 forerunner. ♦ v 3 signal the approach of. **heraldry** n study of coats of arms and family trees. **heraldic** adj

herb n plant used for flavouring in cookery, and in medicine. **herbal** adj **herbalist** n person who grows or specializes in the use of medicinal herbs. **herbaceous** adj (of a plant) soft-stemmed. **herbicide** n chemical used to destroy plants, esp. weeds. **herbivore** n animal that eats only plants. **herbivorous** [her-**biv**-or-uss] adj

herculean [her-kew-**lee**-an] adj requiring great strength or effort.

herd n 1 group of animals feeding and living together. 2 large crowd of people. ♦ v 3 collect into a herd. **herdsman** n man who looks after a herd of animals.

here adv in, at, or to this place or point. **hereabouts** adv near here. **hereafter** adv after this point or time. **the hereafter** life after death. **hereby** adv by means of or as a result of this. **herein** adv in this place, matter, or document. **herewith** adv with this.

heredity [hir-**red**-it-ee] n passing on of characteristics from one generation to another. **hereditary** adj 1 passed on genetically from one generation to another. 2 passed on by inheritance.

☑ **SPELLING TIP**
There are several ways to misspell **hereditary**. The problems always come after the t, where there should be three more letters: -ary.

heresy [**herr**-iss-ee] n, pl **-sies** opinion

contrary to accepted opinion or belief. **heretic** [**herr**-it-ik] n person who holds unorthodox opinions. **heretical** [hir-**ret**-ik-al] adj

heritage n 1 something inherited. 2 anything from the past, considered as the inheritance of present-day society.

hermaphrodite [her-**maf**-roe-dite] n animal, plant, or person with both male and female reproductive organs.

hermetic adj sealed so as to be airtight. **hermetically** adv

hermit n person living in solitude, esp. for religious reasons. **hermitage** n home of a hermit.

hernia n protrusion of an organ or part through the lining of the surrounding body cavity.

hero n, pl **heroes** 1 principal character in a film, book, etc. 2 man greatly admired for his exceptional qualities or achievements. **heroine** n fem **heroic** adj 1 courageous. 2 of or like a hero. **heroics** pl n extravagant behaviour. **heroically** adv **heroism** [**herr**-oh-izz-um] n

heroin n highly addictive drug derived from morphine.

heron n long-legged wading bird.

herpes [**her**-peez] n any of several inflammatory skin diseases, including shingles and cold sores.

Herr [**hair**] n, pl **Herren** German term of address equivalent to Mr.

herring n important food fish of northern seas. **herringbone** n pattern of zigzag lines.

hertz n, pl **hertz** Physics unit of frequency.

hesitate v 1 be slow or uncertain in doing something. 2 be reluctant (to do something). **hesitation** n **hesitant** adj undecided or wavering. **hesitantly** adv **hesitancy** n

hessian n coarse jute fabric.

heterodox adj differing from accepted doctrines or beliefs. **heterodoxy** n

heterogeneous [het-er-oh-**jean**-ee-uss] adj composed of diverse elements. **heterogeneity** n

heterosexual n, adj (person) sexually attracted to members of the opposite sex. **heterosexuality** n

heuristic [hew-**rist**-ik] adj involving learning by investigation.

hew v **hewing, hewed, hewed** or **hewn** 1 cut with an axe. 2 carve from a substance.

hexagon n geometrical figure with six sides. **hexagonal** adj

hey interj expression of surprise or for catching attention.

heyday n time of greatest success, prime.

hiatus [hie-**ay**-tuss] n, pl **-tuses, -tus** pause or interruption in continuity.

hibernate v (of an animal) pass the winter as if in a deep sleep. **hibernation** n

Hibernian adj Poetic Irish.

hibiscus n, pl **-cuses** tropical plant with large brightly coloured flowers.

hiccup, hiccough n 1 spasm of the breathing organs with a sharp coughlike sound. 2 Informal small problem, hitch. ♦ v 3 make a hiccup.

hick n US, Aust & NZ informal unsophisticated country person.

hickory n, pl **-ries** 1 N American nut-bearing tree. 2 its wood.

hide[1] v **hiding, hid, hidden** 1 put (oneself or an object) somewhere difficult to see or find. 2 keep secret. ♦ n 3 place of concealment, esp. for a bird-watcher. **hiding** n state of concealment, e.g. in hiding. **hide-out** n place to hide in.

hide[2] n skin of an animal. **hiding** n Slang severe beating. **hidebound** adj unwilling to accept new ideas.

hideous [**hid**-ee-uss] *adj* ugly, revolting. **hideously** *adv*

hierarchy [**hire**-ark-ee] *n, pl* -chies system of people or things arranged in a graded order. **hierarchical** *adj*

hieroglyphic [hire-oh-**gliff**-ik] *adj* 1 of a form of writing using picture symbols, as used in ancient Egypt. ♦ *n* 2 symbol that is difficult to decipher. 3 (also **hieroglyph**) symbol representing an object, idea, or sound.

hi-fi *n* 1 set of high-quality sound-reproducing equipment. ♦ *adj* 2 high-fidelity.

higgledy-piggledy *adv, adj* in a muddle.

high *adj* 1 of a great height. 2 far above ground or sea level. 3 being at its peak. 4 greater than usual in intensity or amount. 5 (of a sound) acute in pitch. 6 of great importance, quality, or rank. 7 *Informal* under the influence of alcohol or drugs. ♦ *adv* 8 at or to a high level. **highly** *adv* **highly strung** nervous and easily upset. **Highness** *n* title used to address or refer to a royal person. **High-Church** *adj* belonging to a section within the Church of England stressing the importance of ceremony and ritual. **higher education** education at colleges and universities. **high-fidelity** *adj* able to reproduce sound with little or no distortion. **high-flown** *adj* (of language) extravagant or pretentious. **high-handed** *adj* excessively forceful. **high-rise** *adj* (of a building) having many storeys. **high tea** early evening meal consisting of a cooked dish, bread, cakes, and tea. **high time** latest possible time.

highbrow *adj, n* intellectual and serious (person).

highlands *pl n* area of high ground.

highlight *n* 1 outstanding part or feature. 2 light-toned area in a painting or photograph. 3 lightened streak in the hair. ♦ *v* 4 give emphasis to.

highway *n US, Aust & NZ* main road. **Highway Code** regulations and recommendations applying to all road users. **highwayman** *n* (formerly) robber, usu. on horseback, who robbed travellers at gunpoint.

hijack *v* seize control of (an aircraft or other vehicle) while travelling. **hijacker** *n*

hike *n* 1 long walk in the country, esp. for pleasure. 2 *v* 3 go for a long walk. 4 (foll. by *up*) pull (up) or raise. **hiker** *n*

hilarious *adj* very funny. **hilariously** *adv* **hilarity** *n*

hill *n* raised part of the earth's surface, less high than a mountain. **hilly** *adj* **hillock** *n* small hill. **hillbilly** *n US* unsophisticated country person.

hilt *n* handle of a sword or knife.

him *pron* refers to a male person or animal when the object of a sentence or clause.

hind¹ *adj* **hinder, hindmost** situated at the back.

hind² *n* female deer.

hinder *v* get in the way of. **hindrance** *n*

Hindu *n* 1 person who practises Hinduism. ♦ *adj* 2 of Hinduism. **Hindi** *n* language of N central India. **Hinduism** *n* dominant religion of India, which involves the worship of many gods and a belief in reincarnation.

hinge *n* 1 device for holding together two parts so that one can swing freely. ♦ *v* 2 (foll. by *on*) depend (on). 3 fit a hinge to.

hint *n* 1 indirect suggestion. 2 piece of advice. 3 small amount. ♦ *v* 4 suggest indirectly.

hinterland *n* land lying behind a coast or near a city, esp. a port.

hip[1] *n* either side of the body between the pelvis and the thigh.

hip[2] *n* rosehip.

hip-hop *n* pop-culture movement originating in the 1980s, comprising rap music, graffiti, and break dancing.

hippie *adj, n* same as HIPPY.

hippo *n, pl* **-pos** *Informal* hippopotamus.

hippodrome *n* music hall, variety theatre, or circus.

hippopotamus *n, pl* **-muses, -mi** large African mammal with thick wrinkled skin, living near rivers.

hippy *adj, n, pl* **-pies** (esp. in the 1960s) (of) a person whose behaviour and dress imply a rejection of conventional values.

hire *v* **1** pay to have temporary use of. **2** employ for wages. ◆ *n* **3** hiring. **for hire** available to be hired. **hireling** *n* person who works only for wages. **hire-purchase** *n* system of purchase by which the buyer pays for goods by instalments.

hirsute [**her**-suit] *adj* hairy.

his *pron, adj* (something) belonging to him.

Hispanic *adj* Spanish or Latin-American.

hiss *n* **1** sound like that of a long *s* (as an expression of contempt). ◆ *v* **2** utter a hiss. **3** show derision or anger towards.

histamine [**hiss**-ta-meen] *n* substance released by the body tissues in allergic reactions.

histogram *n* statistical graph in which the frequency of values is represented by vertical bars of varying heights and widths.

histology *n* study of the tissues of an animal or plant.

history *n, pl* **-ries 1** (record or account of) past events and developments. **2** study of these. **3** record of someone's past. **historian** *n* writer of history. **historic** *adj* famous or significant in history. **historical** *adj* **1** occurring in the past. **2** based on history. **historically** *adv*

histrionic *adj* excessively dramatic. **histrionics** *pl n* excessively dramatic behaviour.

hit *v* **hitting, hit 1** strike, touch forcefully. **2** come into violent contact with. **3** affect badly. **4** reach (a point or place). ◆ *n* **5** hitting. **6** successful record, film, etc. **7** *Computers* single visit to a website. **hit it off** *Informal* get on well together. **hit the road** *Informal* start a journey. **hit-and-miss** *adj* sometimes successful and sometimes not. **hit man** hired assassin. **hit on** *v* think of (an idea).

hitch *n* **1** minor problem. ◆ *v* **2** *Informal* obtain (a lift) by hitchhiking. **3** fasten with a knot or tie. **4** (foll. by *up*) pull up with a jerk. **hitchhike** *v* travel by obtaining free lifts. **hitchhiker** *n*

hi-tech *adj* using sophisticated technology.

hither *adv* Old-fashioned to or towards this place.

hitherto *adv* until this time.

HIV human immunodeficiency virus, the cause of AIDS.

hive *n* same as BEEHIVE. **hive of activity** place where people are very busy. **hive off** *v* separate from a larger group.

hives *n* allergic reaction in which itchy red or whitish patches appear on the skin.

HM (in Britain) Her (or His) Majesty.

HMS (in Britain) Her (or His) Majesty's Ship.

HNC (in Britain) Higher National Certificate.

HND (in Britain) Higher National Diploma.

hoard *n* **1** store hidden away for future

use. ♦ v **2** save or store. **hoarder** n

hoarding n large board for displaying advertisements.

hoarfrost n white ground frost.

hoarse adj **1** (of a voice) rough and unclear. **2** having a rough and unclear voice. **hoarsely** adv **hoarseness** n

hoary adj **hoarier, hoariest 1** grey or white(-haired). **2** very old.

hoax n **1** deception or trick. ♦ v **2** deceive or play a trick upon. **hoaxer** n

hob n Brit flat top part of a cooker, or a separate flat surface, containing gas or electric rings for cooking on.

hobble v **1** walk lamely. **2** tie the legs of (a horse) together.

hobby n, pl **-bies** activity pursued in one's spare time. **hobbyhorse** n **1** favourite topic. **2** toy horse.

hobgoblin n mischievous goblin.

hobnail boots pl n heavy boots with short nails in the soles.

hobnob v **-nobbing, -nobbed** (foll. by with) be on friendly terms (with).

hobo n, pl **-bos** US, Aust & NZ tramp or vagrant.

hock[1] n joint in the back leg of an animal such as a horse that corresponds to the human ankle.

hock[2] n white German wine.

hock[3] v Informal pawn. **in hock** Informal in debt.

hockey n **1** team game played on a field with sticks and a curved ball. **2** US ice hockey.

hocus-pocus n trickery.

hod n open wooden box attached to a pole, for carrying bricks or mortar.

hoe n **1** long-handled tool used for loosening soil or weeding. ♦ v **2** scrape or weed with a hoe.

hog n **1** castrated male pig. **2** Informal greedy person. ♦ v **hogging, hogged 3** Informal take more than one's share of. **hogshead** n large cask. **hogwash**

n Informal nonsense.

Hogmanay n (in Scotland) New Year's Eve.

hoick v raise abruptly and sharply.

hoi polloi n the ordinary people.

hoist v **1** raise or lift up. ♦ n **2** device for lifting things.

hoity-toity adj Informal arrogant or haughty.

hokey-pokey n NZ brittle toffee sold in lumps.

hold[1] v **holding, held 1** keep or support in or with the hands or arms. **2** arrange for (a meeting, party, etc.) to take place. **3** consider to be as specified, e.g. who are you holding responsible? **4** maintain in a specified position or state. **5** have the capacity for. **6** Informal wait, esp. on the telephone. **7** restrain or keep back. **8** own, possess. **9** n **10** act or way of holding. **11** controlling influence. **holder** n **holding** n property, such as land or stocks and shares. **holdall** n large strong travelling bag. **hold-up** n **1** armed robbery. **2** delay.

hold[2] n cargo compartment in a ship or aircraft.

hole n **1** area hollowed out in a solid. **2** opening or hollow. **3** animal's burrow. **4** Informal unattractive place. **5** Informal difficult situation. ♦ v **6** make holes in. **7** hit (a golf ball) into the target hole.

holiday n **1** time spent away from home for rest or recreation. **2** day or other period of rest from work or studies.

holiness n **1** state of being holy. **2** (H-) title used to address or refer to the Pope.

holistic adj considering the complete person, physically and mentally, in the treatment of an illness. **holism** n

hollow adj **1** having a hole or space inside. **2** (of a sound) as if echoing in a hollow place. **3** without any real value or worth. ♦ *n* **4** cavity or space. **5** dip in the land. ♦ *v* **6** form a hollow in.

holly *n* evergreen tree with prickly leaves and red berries.

hollyhock *n* tall garden plant with spikes of colourful flowers.

holocaust *n* destruction or loss of life on a massive scale.

hologram *n* three-dimensional photographic image.

holograph *n* document handwritten by the author.

holster *n* leather case for a pistol, hung from a belt.

holy *adj* **-lier, -liest 1** of God or a god. **2** devout or virtuous.

holier-than-thou *adj* self-righteous. **Holy Communion** *Christianity* service in which people take bread and wine in remembrance of the death and resurrection of Jesus Christ. **Holy Grail** (in medieval legend) the bowl used by Jesus Christ at the Last Supper. **Holy Spirit, Ghost** *Christianity* one of the three aspects of God. **Holy Week** *Christianity* week before Easter.

homage *n* show of respect or honour towards someone or something.

home *n* **1** place where one lives. **2** institution for the care of the elderly, orphans, etc. ♦ *adj* **3** of one's home, birthplace, or native country. **4** *Sport* played on one's own ground. ♦ *adv* **5** to or at home. ♦ *v* **6** (foll. by *in* or *in on*) direct towards (a point or target). **at home** at ease. **bring home to** make clear to. **home and dry** *Informal* safe or successful. **homeless** *adj* **1** having nowhere to live. ♦ *pl n* **2** people who have nowhere to live. **homelessness** *n* **homely** *adj* **1** simple, ordinary, and comfortable. **2** *US* unattractive. **homeward** *adj, adv* **homewards** *adv* **home-brew** *n* beer

made at home. **home-made** *adj* made at home or on the premises. **home page** *Computers* introductory information about a website with links to the information or services provided. **home truths** unpleasant facts told to a person about himself or herself.

homeland *n* country from which a person's ancestors came.

homeopathy [home-ee-**op**-ath-ee] *n* treatment of disease by small doses of a drug that produces symptoms of the disease in healthy people. **homeopath** *n* person who practises homeopathy. **homeopathic** *adj*

homesick *adj* sad because missing one's home and family. **homesickness** *n*

homework *n* school work done at home.

homicide *n* **1** killing of a human being. **2** person who kills someone. **homicidal** *adj*

homily *n, pl* **-lies** speech telling people how they should behave.

hominid *n* man or any extinct forerunner of man.

homo- *combining form* same, like, e.g. *homosexual.*

homogeneous [home-oh-**jean**-ee-uss] *adj* formed of similar parts. **homogeneity** *n* **homogenize** *v* **1** break up fat globules in (milk or cream) to distribute them evenly. **2** make homogeneous.

homograph *n* word spelt the same as another, but with a different meaning.

homologous [hom-**ol**-log-uss] *adj* having a related or similar position or structure.

homonym *n* word spelt or pronounced the same as another, but with a different meaning.

homophobia *n* hatred or fear of homosexuals. **homophobic** *adj*

homophone n word pronounced the same as another, but with a different meaning or spelling.

Homo sapiens [**hoe**-moh **sap**-ee-enz] n human beings as a species.

homosexual n, adj (person) sexually attracted to members of the same sex. **homosexuality** n

hone v sharpen.

honest adj **1** truthful and moral. **2** open and sincere. **honestly** adv **honesty** n **1** quality of being honest. **2** plant with silvery seed pods.

honey n **1** sweet edible sticky substance made by bees from nectar. **2** term of endearment. **honeycomb** n waxy structure of six-sided cells in which honey is stored by bees in a beehive. **honeydew melon** melon with a yellow skin and sweet pale flesh. **honeymoon** n holiday taken by a newly married couple. **honeysuckle** n **1** climbing shrub with sweet-smelling flowers **2** Australian tree or shrub with nectar–rich flowers.

hongi [**hong**-jee] n NZ Maori greeting in which people touch noses.

honk n **1** sound made by a car horn. **2** sound made by a goose. ♦ v **3** (cause to) make this sound.

honour n **1** sense of honesty and fairness. **2** (award given out of) respect. **3** pleasure or privilege. ♦ pl **4** university degree of a higher standard than an ordinary degree. ♦ v **5** give praise and attention to. **6** give an award to (someone) out of respect. **7** accept or pay (a cheque or bill). **8** keep (a promise). **do the honours** act as host or hostess by pouring drinks or giving out food.
honourable adj worthy of respect or esteem. **honourably** adv **honorary** adj **1** held or given only as an honour. **2** unpaid. **honorific** adj showing respect.

hood¹ n **1** head covering, often attached to a coat or jacket. **2** folding roof of a convertible car or a pram. **3** US & Aust car bonnet. **hooded** adj **1** (of a garment) having a hood. **2** (of eyes) having heavy eyelids that appear to be half-closed.

hood² n Chiefly US slang hoodlum.

hoodlum n Slang violent criminal, gangster.

hoodoo n, pl -**doos** (cause of) bad luck.

hoodwink v trick, deceive.

hoof n, pl **hooves, hoofs** horny covering of the foot of a horse, deer, etc. **hoof it** Slang walk.

hoo-ha n fuss or commotion.

hook n **1** curved piece of metal, plastic, etc., used to hang, hold, or pull something. **2** short swinging punch. ♦ v **3** fasten or catch (as if) with a hook. **hooked** adj **1** bent like a hook. **2** (foll. by on) Slang addicted (to) or obsessed (with). **hooker** n **1** Chiefly US slang prostitute. **2** Rugby player who uses his feet to get the ball in a scrum. **hook-up** n linking of radio or television stations. **hookworm** n blood-sucking worm with hooked mouthparts.

hookah n oriental pipe in which smoke is drawn through water and a long tube.

hooligan n rowdy young person. **hooliganism** n

hoon n Aust & NZ slang loutish youth who drives irresponsibly.

hoop n rigid circular band, used esp. as a child's toy or for animals to jump through in the circus. **jump, be put through the hoops** go through an ordeal or test. **hoop pine** Australian tree or shrub with flowers in dense spikes.

hoopla n fairground game in which hoops are thrown over objects in an attempt to win them.

hooray *interj* same as HURRAH.

hoot *n* **1** sound of a car horn. **2** cry of an owl. **3** cry of derision. **4** *Informal* amusing person or thing. ♦ *v* **5** sound (a car horn). **6** jeer or yell contemptuously (at someone). **hooter** *n* **1** device that hoots. **2** *Chiefly Brit slang* nose.

Hoover *n* **1** ® vacuum cleaner. ♦ *v* **2** (h-) clean with a vacuum cleaner.

hooves *n* a plural of HOOF.

hop¹ *v* **hopping, hopped 1** jump on one foot. **2** move in short jumps. **3** *Informal* move quickly. ♦ *n* **4** instance of hopping. **5** *Informal* dance. **6** short journey, esp. by air. **catch someone on the hop** *Informal* catch someone unprepared.

hop² *n* (often pl) climbing plant, the dried flowers of which are used to make beer.

hope *v* **1** want (something) to happen or be true. ♦ *n* **2** expectation of something desired. **3** thing that gives cause for hope or is desired. **hopeful** *adj* **1** having, expressing, or inspiring hope. ♦ *n* **2** person considered to be on the brink of success. **hopefully** *adv* **1** in a hopeful manner. **2** it is hoped. **hopeless** *adj*

hopper *n* container for storing substances such as grain or sand.

hopscotch *n* children's game of hopping in a pattern drawn on the ground.

horde *n* large crowd.

horizon *n* **1** apparent line that divides the earth and the sky. ♦ *pl* **2** limits of scope, interest, or knowledge.

horizontal *adj* parallel to the horizon, level, flat. **horizontally** *adv*

hormone *n* **1** substance secreted by certain glands which stimulates certain organs of the body. **2** synthetic substance with the same effect. **hormonal** *adj*

horn *n* **1** one of a pair of bony growths sticking out of the heads of cattle, sheep, etc. **2** substance of which horns are made. **3** musical instrument with a tube or pipe of brass fitted with a mouthpiece. **4** device on a vehicle sounded as a warning. **horned** *adj* **horny** *adj* **1** of or like horn. **2** *Slang* (easily) sexually aroused. **hornbeam** *n* tree with smooth grey bark. **hornbill** *n* bird with a bony growth on its large beak. **hornpipe** *n* (music for) a solo dance, traditionally performed by sailors.

hornblende *n* mineral containing aluminium, calcium, sodium, magnesium, and iron.

hornet *n* large wasp with a severe sting.

horoscope *n* prediction of a person's future based on the positions of the planets, sun, and moon at his or her birth.

horrendous *adj* very unpleasant and shocking.

horrible *adj* **1** disagreeable, unpleasant. **2** causing horror. **horribly** *adv*

horrid *adj* **1** disagreeable, unpleasant. **2** *Informal* nasty.

horrify *v* **-fying, -fied** cause to feel horror or shock. **horrific** *adj* causing horror.

horror *n* (thing or person causing) terror or hatred.

hors d'oeuvre [or durv] *n* appetizer served before a main meal.

horse *n* **1** large animal with hooves, a mane, and a tail, used for riding and pulling carts etc. **2** piece of gymnastic equipment used for vaulting over. **(straight) from the horse's mouth** from the original source. **horsey, horsy** *adj* **1** very keen on horses. **2** of or like a horse. **horse around** *v* *Informal* play roughly or boisterously. **horse chestnut** tree with broad leaves and inedible large brown shiny nuts in spiky cases. **horsefly** n large bloodsucking fly. **horsehair** n hair from the tail or mane of a horse. **horse laugh** loud coarse laugh. **horseman, horsewoman** n person riding a horse. **horseplay** n rough or rowdy play. **horsepower** n unit of power (equivalent to 745.7 watts), used to measure the power of an engine. **horseradish** n strong-tasting root of a plant, usu. made into a sauce. **horseshoe** n protective U-shaped piece of iron nailed to a horse's hoof, regarded as a symbol of good luck.

horticulture n art or science of cultivating gardens. **horticultural** adj **horticulturalist, horticulturist** n

hosanna interj exclamation of praise to God.

hose¹ n 1 flexible pipe for conveying liquid. ♦ v 2 water with a hose.

hose² n stockings, socks, and tights. **hosiery** n stockings, socks, and tights collectively.

hospice [**hoss**-piss] n nursing home for the terminally ill.

hospital n place where people who are ill are looked after and treated. **hospitalize** v send or admit to hospital. **hospitalization** n

hospitality n kindness in welcoming strangers or guests. **hospitable** adj welcoming to strangers or guests.

host¹ n 1 (fem **hostess**) person who entertains guests, esp. in his own home. 2 place or country providing the facilities for an event. 3 compere of a show. 4 animal or plant on which a parasite lives. 5 v 6 be the host of.

host² n large number.

Host n Christianity bread used in Holy Communion.

hostage n person who is illegally held prisoner until certain demands are met

by other people.

hostel n building providing accommodation at a low cost for a specific group of people such as students, travellers, homeless people, etc.

hostelry n, pl **-ries** Old-fashioned or facetious inn, pub.

hostile adj 1 unfriendly. 2 (foll. by to) opposed (to). 3 of an enemy. **hostility** n, pl **-ties** 1 unfriendly and aggressive feelings or behaviour. ♦ pl 2 acts of warfare.

hot adj **hotter, hottest** 1 having a high temperature. 2 strong, spicy. 3 (of news) very recent. 4 (of a contest) fiercely fought. 5 (of a temper) quick to rouse. 6 liked very much, e.g. a hot favourite. 7 Slang stolen. **in hot water** Informal in trouble. **hotly** adv **hot air** Informal empty talk. **hot-blooded** adj passionate or excitable. **hot dog** long roll split lengthways with a hot frankfurter inside. **hot-headed** adj rash, having a hot temper. **hotline** n direct telephone link for emergency use. **hot pool** NZ geothermally heated pool.

hotbed n any place encouraging a particular activity, e.g. hotbeds of unrest.

hotchpotch n jumbled mixture.

hotel n commercial establishment providing lodging and meals. **hotelier** n owner or manager of a hotel.

hotfoot adv Informal quickly and eagerly. **hotfoot it** Informal go quickly and eagerly.

hothouse n greenhouse.

hotplate n 1 heated metal surface on an electric cooker. 2 portable device for keeping food warm.

hound n 1 hunting dog. ♦ v 2 pursue relentlessly.

hour n 1 twenty-fourth part of a day,

sixty minutes. **2** time of day. ♦ *pl* **3** period regularly appointed for work or business. **hourly** *adj, adv* **1** (happening) every hour. **2** frequent(ly). **hourglass** *n* device with two glass compartments, containing a quantity of sand that takes an hour to trickle from the top section to the bottom one.

houri *n Islam* any of the nymphs of paradise.

house *n* **1** building used as a home. **2** building used for some specific purpose, e.g. *the opera house.* **3** business firm. **4** law-making body or the hall where it meets. **5** family or dynasty. **6** theatre or cinema audience. ♦ *v* **7** give accommodation to. **8** contain or cover. **get on like a house on fire** *Informal* get on very well together. **on the house** *Informal* provided free by the management. **housing** *n* **1** (providing of) houses. **2** protective case or covering of a machine. **house arrest** confinement to one's home rather than in prison. **houseboat** *n* stationary boat used as a home. **housebreaker** *n* burglar. **housecoat** *n* woman's long loose coat-shaped garment for wearing at home. **household** *n* all the people living in a house. **householder** *n* person who owns or rents a house. **housekeeper** *n* person employed to run someone else's household. **housekeeping** *n* (money for) running a household. **housemaid** *n* female servant employed to do housework. **house-train** *v* train (a pet) to urinate and defecate outside. **house-warming** *n* party to celebrate moving into a new home. **housewife** *n* woman who runs her own household and does not have a job. **housework** *n* work of running a home, such as cleaning and cooking.

House music, House *n* electronic funk-based disco music with samples of other recordings edited in.

hovea *n* Australian plant with purple flowers.

hovel *n* small dirty house or hut.

hover *v* **1** (of a bird etc.) remain suspended in one place in the air. **2** loiter. **3** be in a state of indecision. **hovercraft** *n* vehicle which can travel over land or sea on a cushion of air.

how *adv* **1** in what way, by what means. **2** to what degree, e.g. *I know how hard it is.* **however** *adv* **1** nevertheless. **2** by whatever means. **3** no matter how, e.g. *however much it hurt, he could do it.*

howdah *n* canopied seat on an elephant's back.

howitzer *n* large gun firing shells at a steep angle.

howl *n* **1** loud wailing cry. **2** loud burst of laughter. ♦ *v* **3** utter a howl. **howler** *n Informal* stupid mistake.

hoyden *n Old-fashioned* wild or boisterous girl.

HP, h.p. 1 hire-purchase. **2** horsepower.

HQ headquarters.

HRH Her (or His) Royal Highness.

HRT hormone replacement therapy.

HTML hypertext markup language: text description language used on the Internet.

hub *n* **1** centre of a wheel, through which the axle passes. **2** central point of activity.

hubbub *n* confused noise of many voices.

hubby *n, pl* **-bies** *Informal* husband.

hubris [**hew**-briss] *n Formal* pride, arrogance.

huckster *n* person using aggressive methods of selling.

huddle *v* **1** hunch (oneself) through cold or fear. **2** crowd closely together.

♦ n **3** small group. **4** Informal impromptu conference.

hue n colour, shade.

hue and cry n public outcry.

huff n **1** passing mood of anger or resentment. ♦ v **2** blow or puff heavily. **huffy** adj **huffily** adv

hug v **hugging, hugged 1** clasp tightly in the arms, usu. with affection. **2** keep close to (the ground, kerb, etc.). ♦ n **3** tight or fond embrace.

huge adj very big. **hugely** adv

huh interj exclamation of derision, bewilderment, or inquiry.

hui [**hoo**-ee] n NZ **1** meeting of Maori people. **2** meeting to discuss Maori matters.

hula n swaying Hawaiian dance. **Hula Hoop** ® plastic hoop twirled round the body by gyrating the hips.

hulk n **1** body of an abandoned ship. **2** Offens large heavy person or thing. **hulking** adj bulky, unwieldy.

hull n **1** main body of a boat. **2** leaves round the stem of a strawberry, raspberry, etc. ♦ v **3** remove the hulls from.

hullabaloo n, pl **-loos** loud confused noise or clamour.

hum v **humming, hummed 1** make a low continuous vibrating sound. **2** sing with the lips closed. **3** Slang (of a place) be very busy. ♦ n **4** humming sound. **hummingbird** n very small American bird whose powerful wings make a humming noise as they vibrate.

human adj **1** of or typical of people. ♦ n **2** human being. **humanly** adv by human powers or means. **human being** man, woman, or child.

humane adj kind or merciful. **humanely** adv

humanism n belief in human effort rather than religion. **humanist** n

humanitarian n, adj (person) having the interests of humankind at heart.

humanity n, pl **-ties 1** human race. **2** the quality of being human. **3** kindness or mercy. ♦ pl **4** study of literature, philosophy, and the arts.

humanize v make human or humane.

humankind n human race.

humble adj **1** conscious of one's failings. **2** modest, unpretentious. **3** unimportant. ♦ v **4** cause to feel humble, humiliate. **humbly** adv

humbug n **1** Brit hard striped peppermint sweet. **2** nonsense. **3** dishonest person.

humdinger n Slang excellent person or thing.

humdrum adj ordinary, dull.

humerus [**hew**-mer-uss] n, pl **-meri** [-mer-rye] bone from the shoulder to the elbow.

humid adj damp and hot. **humidity** n **humidify** v **-fying, -fied humidifier** n device for increasing the amount of water vapour in the air in a room.

humiliate v lower the dignity or hurt the pride of. **humiliating** adj **humiliation** n

humility n quality of being humble.

hummock n very small hill.

humour n **1** ability to say or perceive things that are amusing. **2** amusing quality in a situation, film, etc. **3** state of mind, mood. **4** Old-fashioned fluid in the body. ♦ v **5** be kind and indulgent to. **humorous** adj **humorously** adv **humorist** n writer or entertainer who uses humour.

☑ **SPELLING TIP**
A lot of people simply add -ous to the noun **humour** to make humourous, but this is a mistake; you have to drop the second u when you write **humorous** or **humorist**.

hump n **1** raised piece of ground. **2**

large lump on the back of an animal or person. ♦ v **3** Slang carry or heave. **get, take the hump** Informal be annoyed, sulk. **hump-back, humpbacked bridge** road bridge with a sharp slope on each side.

humus [**hew**-muss] n decomposing vegetable and animal mould in the soil.

hunch n **1** feeling or suspicion not based on facts. ♦ v **2** draw (one's shoulders) up or together. **hunchback** n Offens person with an abnormal curvature of the spine.

hundred adj, n **1** ten times ten. ♦ n **2** (often pl) large but unspecified number. **hundredth** adj, n **hundredweight** n Brit unit of weight of 112 pounds (50.8 kilograms).

hung v **1** past of HANG. ♦ adj **2** (of a parliament or jury) with no side having a clear majority. **hung over** Informal suffering the effects of a hangover.

hunger n **1** discomfort or weakness from lack of food. **2** desire or craving. ♦ v **3** (foll. by for) want very much. **hunger strike** refusal of all food, as a means of protest.

hungry adj **hungrier, hungriest 1** desiring food. **2** (foll. by for) having a desire or craving (for). **hungrily** adv

hunk n **1** large piece. **2** Slang sexually attractive man.

hunt v **1** seek out and kill (wild animals) for food or sport. **2** (foll. by for) search (for). ♦ n **3** hunting. **4** (party organized for) hunting wild animals for sport. **huntaway** n NZ sheepdog trained to drive sheep by barking. **huntsman** n man who hunts wild animals, esp. foxes.

hunter n person or animal that hunts wild animals for food or sport.

hurdle n **1** Sport light barrier for jumping over in some races. **2** problem or difficulty. ♦ pl **3** race involving hurdles. ♦ v **4** jump over

(something). **hurdler** n

hurdy-gurdy n, pl **-dies** mechanical musical instrument, such as a barrel organ.

hurl v throw or utter forcefully.

hurling, hurley n Irish game like hockey.

hurly-burly n loud confusion.

hurrah, hurray interj exclamation of joy or applause.

hurricane n very strong, often destructive, wind or storm. **hurricane lamp** paraffin lamp with a glass covering.

hurry v **-rying, -ried 1** (cause to) move or act very quickly. ♦ n **2** doing something quickly or the need to do something quickly. **hurriedly** adv

hurt v **hurting, hurt 1** cause physical or mental pain to. **2** be painful. **3** Informal feel pain. ♦ n **4** physical or mental pain. **hurtful** adj unkind.

hurtle v move quickly or violently.

husband n **1** woman's partner in marriage. ♦ v **2** use economically. **husbandry** n **1** farming. **2** management of resources.

hush v **1** make or be silent. ♦ n **2** stillness or silence. **hush-hush** adj Informal secret. **hush up** v suppress information about.

husk n **1** outer covering of certain seeds and fruits. ♦ v **2** remove the husk from.

husky[1] adj **huskier, huskiest 1** slightly hoarse. **2** Informal big and strong. **huskily** adv

husky[2] n, pl **huskies** Arctic sledge dog with thick hair and a curled tail.

hussar [hoo-**zar**] n Hist lightly armed cavalry soldier.

hussy n, pl **-sies** immodest or promiscuous woman.

hustings pl n political campaigns and speeches before an election.

hustle v **1** push about, jostle. ♦ n **2** lively activity or bustle.

hut n small house, shelter, or shed.

hutch n cage for pet rabbits etc.

hyacinth n sweet-smelling spring flower that grows from a bulb.

hyaena n same as HYENA.

hybrid n **1** offspring of two plants or animals of different species. **2** anything of mixed origin. ♦ adj **3** of mixed origin.

hydra n mythical many-headed water serpent.

hydrangea n ornamental shrub with clusters of pink, blue, or white flowers.

hydrant n outlet from a water main with a nozzle for a hose.

hydrate n chemical compound of water with another substance.

hydraulic adj operated by pressure forced through a pipe by a liquid such as water or oil. **hydraulics** n study of the mechanical properties of fluids as they apply to practical engineering. **hydraulically** adv

hydro[1] n, pl **hydros** hotel offering facilities for hydropathy.

hydro[2] adj short for HYDROELECTRIC.

hydro- combining form **1** water, e.g. hydroelectric. **2** hydrogen, e.g. hydrochloric acid.

hydrocarbon n compound of hydrogen and carbon.

hydrochloric acid n strong colourless acid used in many industrial and laboratory processes.

hydroelectric adj of the generation of electricity by water pressure.

hydrofoil n fast light boat with its hull raised out of the water on one or more pairs of fins.

hydrogen n Chem light flammable colourless gas that combines with oxygen to form water. **hydrogen bomb** extremely powerful bomb in which energy is released by fusion of hydrogen nuclei to give helium nuclei

hydrogen peroxide colourless liquid used as a hair bleach and as an antiseptic.

hydrolysis [hie-**drol**-iss-iss] n decomposition of a chemical compound reacting with water.

hydrometer [hie-**drom**-it-er] n instrument for measuring the density of a liquid.

hydropathy n method of treating disease by the use of large quantities of water both internally and externally.

hydrophobia n **1** rabies. **2** fear of water.

hydroplane n light motorboat that skims the water.

hydroponics n method of growing plants in water rather than soil.

hydrotherapy n Med treatment of certain diseases by exercise in water.

hyena n scavenging doglike mammal of Africa and S Asia.

hygiene n principles and practice of health and cleanliness. **hygienic** adj **hygienically** adv

hymen n membrane partly covering the opening of a girl's vagina, which breaks before puberty or at the first occurrence of sexual intercourse.

hymn n Christian song of praise sung to God or a saint. **hymnal** n book of hymns (also **hymn book**).

hype n **1** intensive or exaggerated publicity or sales promotion. ♦ v **2** promote (a product) using intensive or exaggerated publicity.

hyper adj Informal overactive or overexcited.

hyper- prefix over, above, excessively, e.g. hyperactive.

hyperbola [hie-**per**-bol-a] n Geom curve produced when a cone is cut by a plane at a steeper angle to its base than its side.

hyperbole [hie-**per**-bol-ee] n deliberate exaggeration for effect. **hyperbolic** adj

hyperlink Computers ♦ n link from a hypertext file that gives users instant access to related material in another file. ♦ v link (files) in this way.

hypermarket n huge self-service store.

hypersensitive adj **1** extremely sensitive to certain drugs, extremes of temperature, etc. **2** very easily upset.

hypersonic adj having a speed of at least five times the speed of sound.

hypertension n very high blood pressure.

hypertext n computer software and hardware that allows users to store and view text and move between related items easily.

hyphen n punctuation mark (-) indicating that two words or syllables are connected. **hyphenated** adj (of two words or syllables) having a hyphen between them. **hyphenation** n

hypnosis n artificially induced state of relaxation in which the mind is more than usually receptive to suggestion. **hypnotic** adj of or (as if) producing hypnosis. **hypnotism** n inducing hypnosis in someone. **hypnotist** n **hypnotize** v

hypo- prefix beneath, less than, e.g. hypothermia.

hypoallergenic adj (of cosmetics) not likely to cause an allergic reaction.

hypochondria n undue preoccupation with one's health. **hypochondriac** n

hypocrisy [hip-**ok**-rass-ee] n, pl -**sies** (instance of) pretence of having standards or beliefs that are contrary to one's real character or actual behaviour. **hypocrite** [**hip**-oh-krit] n person who pretends to be what he or she is not. **hypocritical** adj **hypocritically** adv

hypodermic adj, n (denoting) a syringe or needle used to inject a drug beneath the skin.

hypotension n very low blood pressure.

hypotenuse [hie-**pot**-a-news] n side of a right-angled triangle opposite the right angle.

hypothermia n condition in which a person's body temperature is dangerously low as a result of prolonged exposure to severe cold.

hypothesis [hie-**poth**-iss-iss] n, pl -**ses** [-seez] suggested but unproved explanation of something. **hypothetical** adj based on assumption rather than fact or reality. **hypothetically** adv

hyrax n, pl -**raxes** or -**races** type of hoofed rodent-like animal of Africa and Asia.

hysterectomy n, pl -**mies** surgical removal of the womb.

hysteria n state of uncontrolled excitement, anger, or panic. **hysterical** adj **hysterically** adv **hysterics** pl n **1** attack of hysteria. **2** Informal uncontrollable laughter.

Hz hertz.

I i

I *pron* used by a speaker or writer to refer to himself or herself as the subject of a verb.

Iberian *adj* of Iberia, the peninsula comprising Spain and Portugal.

ibex [**ibe**-eks] *n* wild goat of N with large backward-curving horns.

ibid. (referring to a book, page, or passage already mentioned) in the same place.

ibis [**ibe**-iss] *n* large wading bird with long legs.

ice *n* **1** frozen water. **2** *Chiefly Brit* portion of ice cream. **3 the Ice** *NZ informal* Antarctica. ♦ *v* **4** (foll. by *up* or *over*) become covered with ice. **5** cover with icing. **break the ice** create a relaxed atmosphere, esp. between people meeting for the first time. **iced** *adj* **1** covered with icing. **2** (of a drink) containing ice. **icy** *adj* **icier, iciest 1** very cold. **2** covered with ice. **3** aloof and unfriendly. **icily** *adv* **iciness** *n* **Ice Age** period when much of the earth's surface was covered in glaciers. **iceberg** *n* large floating mass of ice. **icebox** *n* *US* refrigerator. **icecap** *n* mass of ice permanently covering an area. **ice cream** sweet creamy frozen food. **ice cube** small square block of ice added to a drink to cool it. **ice floe** sheet of ice floating in the sea. **ice hockey** team game like hockey played on ice with a puck. **ice lolly** flavoured ice on a stick. **ice pick** pointed tool for breaking ice. **ice skate** boot with a steel blade fixed to the sole, to enable the wearer to glide over ice. **ice-skate** *v* **ice-skater** *n*

icicle *n* tapering spike of ice hanging where water has dripped.

icing *n* mixture of sugar and water etc., used to cover and decorate cakes. **icing sugar** finely ground sugar for making icing.

icon *n* **1** picture of Christ or another religious figure, regarded as holy in the Orthodox Church. **2** picture on a computer screen representing a function that can be activated by moving the cursor over it.

iconoclast *n* person who attacks established ideas or principles. **iconoclastic** *adj*

id *n* *Psychoanalysis* the mind's instinctive unconscious energies.

idea *n* **1** plan or thought formed in the mind. **2** thought of something. **3** belief or opinion.

ideal *adj* **1** most suitable. **2** perfect. ♦ *n* **3** conception of something that is perfect. **4** perfect person or thing. **ideally** *adv* **idealism** *n* tendency to seek perfection in everything. **idealist** *n* **idealistic** *adj* **idealize** *v* regard or portray as perfect or nearly perfect. **idealization** *n*

idem *pron, adj Latin* the same: used to refer to an article, chapter, or book already quoted.

identical *adj* exactly the same. **identically** *adv*

identify *v* **-fying, -fied 1** prove or recognize as being a certain person or thing. **2** (foll. by *with*) understand and sympathize with (a person or group that one regards as being similar or similarly situated). **3** treat as being the same. **identifiable** *adj* **identification** *n*

Identikit *n* ® composite picture, assembled from descriptions given, of a person wanted by the police.

identity *n, pl* **-ties 1** state of being a

specified person or thing. **2** individuality or personality. **3** state of being the same.

ideology *n, pl* **-gies** body of ideas and beliefs of a group, nation, etc. **ideological** *adj* **ideologist** *n*

idiocy *n* utter stupidity.

idiom *n* **1** group of words which when used together have a different meaning from the words individually, e.g. *raining cats and dogs*. **2** way of expression natural or peculiar to a language or group. **idiomatic** *adj* **idiomatically** *adv*

idiosyncrasy *n, pl* **-sies** personal peculiarity of mind, habit, or behaviour.

idiot *n* **1** foolish or stupid person. **2** *Offens* mentally retarded person. **idiotic** *adj* **idiotically** *adv*

idle *adj* **1** not doing anything. **2** not willing to work, lazy. **3** not being used. **4** useless or meaningless, e.g. *an idle threat*. ♦ *v* **5** (usu. foll. by *away*) spend (time) doing very little. **6** (of an engine) run slowly with the gears disengaged. **idleness** *n* **idler** *n* **idly** *adv*

idol *n* **1** object of excessive devotion. **2** image of a god as an object of worship. **idolatry** *n* worship of idols. **idolatrous** *adj* **idolize** *v* love or admire excessively.

idyll [**id**-ill] *n* scene or time of great peace and happiness. **idyllic** *adj* **idyllically** *adv*

i.e. that is to say.

if *conj* **1** on the condition or supposition that. **2** whether. **3** even though. ♦ *n* **4** uncertainty or doubt, e.g. *no ifs, ands, or buts*. **iffy** *adj Informal* doubtful, uncertain.

igloo *n, pl* **-loos** dome-shaped Inuit house made of snow and ice.

igneous [**ig**-nee-uss] *adj* (of rock) formed as molten rock cools and hardens.

ignite *v* catch fire or set fire to.

ignition *n* **1** system that ignites the fuel-and-air mixture to start an engine. **2** igniting.

ignoble *adj* dishonourable.

ignominy [**ig**-nom-in-ee] *n* humiliating disgrace. **ignominious** *adj* **ignominiously** *adv*

ignoramus *n, pl* **-muses** ignorant person.

ignorant *adj* **1** lacking knowledge. **2** rude through lack of knowledge of good manners. **ignorance** *n*

ignore *v* refuse to notice, disregard deliberately.

iguana *n* large tropical American lizard.

ileum *n* lowest part of the small intestine.

ilk *n* type, e.g. *others of his ilk*.

ill *adj* **1** not in good health. **2** harmful or unpleasant, e.g. *ill effects*. ♦ *n* **3** evil, harm. ♦ *adv* **4** badly. **5** hardly, with difficulty, e.g. *I can ill afford to lose him*. **ill at ease** uncomfortable, unable to relax. **illness** *n* **ill-advised** *adj* **1** badly thought out. **2** unwise. **ill-disposed** *adj* (often foll. by *towards*) unfriendly, unsympathetic. **ill-fated** *adj* doomed to end unhappily. **ill-gotten** *adj* obtained dishonestly. **ill-health** *n* condition of being unwell. **ill-mannered** *adj* having bad manners. **ill-treat** *v* treat cruelly. **ill will** unkind feeling, hostility.

illegal *adj* against the law. **illegally** *adv* **illegality** *n, pl* **-ties**

illegible *adj* unable to be read or deciphered.

illegitimate *adj* **1** born of parents not married to each other. **2** not lawful. **illegitimacy** *n*

illicit *adj* **1** illegal. **2** forbidden or disapproved of by society.

illiterate *n, adj* (person) unable to read

or write. **illiteracy** n

illogical adj **1** unreasonable. **2** not logical. **illogicality** n

illuminate v **1** light up. **2** make clear, explain. **3** decorate with lights. **4** Hist decorate (a manuscript) with designs of gold and bright colours. **illumination** n **illuminating** adj

illusion n deceptive appearance or belief. **illusory** adj seeming to be true, but actually false.

illustrate v **1** explain by use of examples. **2** provide (a book or text) with pictures. **3** be an example of. **illustration** n **1** picture or diagram. **2** example. **illustrative** adj **illustrator** n

illustrious adj famous and distinguished.

image n **1** mental picture of someone or something. **2** impression people have of a person, organization, etc. **3** representation of a person or thing in a work of art. **4** optical reproduction of someone or something, for example in a mirror. **5** person or thing that looks almost exactly like another. **imagery** n images collectively, esp. in the arts.

imagine v **1** form a mental image of. **2** think, believe, or guess. **imaginable** adj **imaginary** adj existing only in the imagination. **imagination** n **1** ability to make mental images of things that may not exist in real life. **2** creative mental ability. **imaginative** adj having or showing a lot of creative mental ability. **imaginatively** adv

---

☑ **SPELLING TIP**

Remembering that an e changes to an a to form **imagination** is a good way of getting **imaginary** right, because it has an a instead of an e too.

---

imago [im-**may**-go] n, pl **imagoes**, **imagines** [im-**maj**-in-ees] sexually

mature adult insect.

imam n **1** leader of prayers in a mosque. **2** title of some Islamic leaders.

IMAX [**eye**-max] n ® film projection process which produces an image ten times larger than standard.

imbalance n lack of balance or proportion.

imbecile [**imb**-ess-eel] n **1** stupid person. **2** adj **3** (also **imbecilic**) stupid or senseless. **imbecility** n

imbibe v **1** drink (alcoholic drinks). **2** Lit absorb (ideas etc.).

imbroglio [imb-**role**-ee-oh] n, pl **-ios** confusing and complicated situation.

imbue v **-buing, -bued** (usu. foll. by with) fill or inspire with (ideals or principles).

IMF International Monetary Fund.

imitate v **1** take as a model. **2** copy the voice and mannerisms of, esp. for entertainment. **imitation** n **1** copy of an original. **2** imitating. **imitative** adj **imitator** n

immaculate adj **1** completely clean or tidy. **2** completely flawless. **immaculately** adv

immanent adj present within and throughout something. **immanence** n

immaterial adj not important, not relevant.

immature adj **1** not fully developed. **2** lacking wisdom or stability because of youth. **immaturity** n

immediate adj **1** occurring at once. **2** next or nearest in time, space, or relationship. **immediately** adv **immediacy** n

immemorial adj **since, from time immemorial** longer than anyone can remember.

immense adj extremely large. **immensely** adv to a very great degree. **immensity** n

immerse v **1** involve deeply, engross. **2**

plunge (something or someone) into liquid. **immersion** n **immersion heater** electrical device in a domestic hot-water tank for heating water.

immigration n coming to a foreign country in order to settle there. **immigrant** n

imminent adj about to happen. **imminently** adv **imminence** n

immobile adj 1 not moving. 2 unable to move. **immobility** n **immobilize** v make unable to move or work.

immoderate adj excessive or unreasonable.

immolate v kill as a sacrifice. **immolation** n

immoral adj 1 morally wrong, corrupt. 2 sexually depraved or promiscuous. **immorality** n

---

✓ **WORD TIP**
Do not confuse *immoral* with *amoral*, which means 'having no moral standards'.

---

immortal adj 1 living forever. 2 famous for all time. ◆ n 3 person whose fame will last for all time. 4 immortal being. **immortality** n **immortalize** v

immune adj 1 protected against a specific disease. 2 (foll. by to) secure (against). 3 (foll. by from) exempt (from). **immunity** n, pl **-ties** 1 ability to resist disease. 2 freedom from prosecution, tax, etc. **immunize** v make immune to a disease. **immunization** n

immunodeficiency n deficiency in or breakdown of a person's ability to fight diseases.

immunology n branch of medicine concerned with the study of immunity. **immunological** adj **immunologist** n

immutable [im-**mute**-a-bl] adj unchangeable. **immutability** n

imp n 1 (in folklore) mischievous small creature with magical powers. 2 mischievous child.

impact n 1 strong effect. 2 (force of) a collision. ◆ v 3 press firmly into something.

impair v weaken or damage. **impairment** n

impala [imp-**ah**-la] n southern African antelope.

impale v pierce with a sharp object.

impalpable adj difficult to define or understand.

impart v 1 communicate (information). 2 give.

impartial adj not favouring one side or the other. **impartially** adv **impartiality** n

impassable adj (of a road etc.) impossible to travel through or over.

impasse [**am**-pass] n situation in which progress is impossible.

impassioned adj full of emotion.

impassive adj showing no emotion, calm.

impatient adj 1 irritable at any delay or difficulty. 2 restless (to have or do something). **impatiently** adv **impatience** n

impeach v charge with a serious crime against the state. **impeachment** n

impeccable adj without fault, excellent. **impeccably** adv

impecunious adj penniless, poor.

impedance [imp-**eed**-anss] n Electricity measure of the opposition to the flow of an alternating current.

impede v hinder in action or progress. **impediment** n something that makes action, speech, or progress difficult. **impedimenta** pl n objects impeding progress, esp. baggage or equipment.

impel v **-pelling, -pelled** push or force (someone) to do something.

impending adj (esp. of something bad) about to happen.

impenetrable *adj* **1** impossible to get through. **2** impossible to understand.

imperative *adj* **1** extremely urgent, vital. **2** *Grammar* denoting a mood of verbs used in commands. ♦ *n* **3** *Grammar* imperative mood.

imperceptible *adj* too slight or gradual to be noticed. **imperceptibly** *adv*

imperfect *adj* **1** having faults or mistakes. **2** not complete. **3** *Grammar* denoting a tense of verbs describing continuous, incomplete, or repeated past actions. ♦ *n* **4** *Grammar* imperfect tense. **imperfection** *n*

imperial *adj* **1** of or like an empire or emperor. **2** denoting a system of weights and measures formerly used in Britain. **imperialism** *n* rule by one country over many others. **imperialist** *adj, n*

imperil *v* **-illing, -illed** put in danger.

imperious *adj* proud and domineering.

impersonal *adj* **1** not relating to any particular person, objective. **2** lacking human warmth or sympathy. **3** *Grammar* (of a verb) without a personal subject, e.g. *it is snowing*. **impersonality** *n*

impersonate *v* **1** pretend to be (another person). **2** copy the voice and mannerisms of, esp. for entertainment. **impersonation** *n* **impersonator** *n*

impertinent *adj* disrespectful or rude. **impertinently** *adv* **impertinence** *n*

imperturbable *adj* calm, not excitable.

impervious *adj* (foll. by *to*) **1** not letting (water etc.) through. **2** not influenced by (a feeling, argument, etc.).

impetigo [imp-it-**tie**-go] *n* contagious skin disease.

impetuous *adj* done or acting without thought, rash. **impetuously** *adv* **impetuosity** *n*

impetus [**imp**-it-uss] *n, pl* **-tuses 1** incentive, impulse. **2** force that starts a body moving.

impinge *v* (foll. by *on*) affect or restrict.

impious [**imp**-ee-uss] *adj* showing a lack of respect or reverence.

impish *adj* mischievous.

implacable *adj* not prepared to be appeased, unyielding. **implacably** *adv* **implacability** *n*

implant *n* **1** *Med* something put into someone's body, usu. by surgical operation. ♦ *v* **2** put (something) into someone's body, usu. by surgical operation. **3** fix firmly in someone's mind. **implantation** *n*

implement *v* **1** carry out (instructions etc.). ♦ *n* **2** tool, instrument. **implementation** *n*

implicate *v* show to be involved, esp. in a crime. **implication** *n* something implied.

implicit *adj* **1** expressed indirectly. **2** absolute and unquestioning, e.g. *implicit support*. **implicitly** *adv*

implore *v* beg earnestly.

imply *v* **-plying, -plied 1** indicate by hinting, suggest. **2** involve as a necessary consequence.

impolitic *adj* unwise or inadvisable.

imponderable *n, adj* (something) impossible to assess.

import *v* **1** bring in (goods) from another country. ♦ *n* **2** something imported. **3** importance. **4** meaning. **importation** *n* **importer** *n*

important *adj* **1** of great significance or value. **2** having influence or power. **importance** *n*

importunate *adj* persistent or demanding. **importune** *v* harass with persistent requests. **importunity** *n, pl* **-ties**

impose *v* **1** force the acceptance of. **2** (foll. by *on*) take unfair advantage (of).

imposing *adj* grand, impressive.
imposition *n* unreasonable demand.
impossible *adj* **1** not able to be done or to happen. **2** absurd or unreasonable. **impossibly** *adv* **impossibility** *n*, *pl* **-ties**
imposter, impostor *n* person who cheats or swindles by pretending to be someone else.
impotent [**imp**-a-tent] *adj* **1** powerless. **2** (of a man) incapable of sexual intercourse. **impotence** *n* **impotently** *adv*
impound *v* take legal possession of, confiscate.
impoverish *v* make poor or weak. **impoverishment** *n*
impracticable *adj* incapable of being put into practice.
impractical *adj* not sensible.
imprecation *n* curse.
impregnable *adj* impossible to break into. **impregnability** *n*
impregnate *v* **1** saturate, spread all through. **2** make pregnant. **impregnation** *n*
impresario *n*, *pl* **-ios** person who runs theatre performances, concerts, etc.

☑ SPELLING TIP
Don't be fooled into spelling impresario as *impressario*, which occurs 33 times in the Bank of English. The correct spelling has only one *s*.

---

impress *v* **1** affect strongly, usu. favourably. **2** stress, emphasize. **3** imprint, stamp. **impression** *n* **1** effect, esp. a strong or favourable one. **2** vague idea. **3** impersonation for entertainment. **4** mark made by pressing. **impressionable** *adj* easily impressed or influenced.
Impressionism *n* art style that gives a general effect or mood rather than

form or structure. **Impressionist** *n* **Impressionistic** *adj*
impressive *adj* making a strong impression, esp. through size, importance, or quality.
imprimatur [imp-rim-**ah**-ter] *n* official approval to print a book.
imprint *n* **1** mark made by printing or stamping. **2** publisher's name and address on a book. ♦ *v* **3** produce (a mark) by printing or stamping.
imprison *v* put in prison. **imprisonment** *n*
improbable *adj* not likely to be true or to happen. **improbability** *n*, *pl* **-ties**
impromptu *adj* without planning or preparation.
improper *adj* **1** indecent. **2** incorrect or irregular. **improper fraction** fraction in which the numerator is larger than the denominator, as in ⅗.
impropriety [imp-roe-**pry**-a-tee] *n*, *pl* **-ties** unsuitable or slightly improper behaviour.
improve *v* make or become better. **improvement** *n*
improvident *adj* not planning for future needs. **improvidence** *n*
improvise *v* **1** make use of whatever materials are available. **2** make up (a piece of music, speech, etc.) as one goes along. **improvisation** *n*
impudent *adj* cheeky, disrespectful. **impudently** *adv* **impudence** *n*
impugn [imp-**yoon**] *v* challenge the truth or validity of.
impulse *n* **1** sudden urge to do something. **2** short electrical signal passing along a wire or nerve or through the air. **on impulse** suddenly and without planning. **impulsive** *adj* acting or done without careful consideration. **impulsively** *adv*
impunity [imp-**yoon**-it-ee] *n* **with impunity** without punishment.

impure *adj* **1** having dirty or unwanted substances mixed in. **2** immoral, obscene. **impurity** *n*

impute *v* attribute responsibility to. **imputation** *n*

in *prep* **1** indicating position inside, state or situation, etc., e.g. *in the net; in tears.* ♦ *adv* **2** indicating position inside, entry into, etc., e.g. *she stayed in; come in.* ♦ *adj* **3** fashionable.

inward *adj* **1** directed towards the middle. **2** situated within. **3** spiritual or mental. ♦ *adv* **4** (also **inwards**) towards the inside or middle. **inwardly** *adv*

inability *n* lack of means or skill to do something.

inaccurate *adj* not correct. **inaccuracy** *n, pl* **-cies**

inadequate *adj* **1** not enough. **2** not good enough. **inadequacy** *n*

inadvertent *adj* unintentional. **inadvertently** *adv*

inalienable *adj* not able to be taken away, e.g. *an inalienable right.*

inane *adj* senseless, silly. **inanity** *n*

inanimate *adj* not living.

inappropriate *adj* not suitable.

inarticulate *adj* unable to express oneself clearly or well.

inasmuch as *conj* because or in so far as.

inaugurate *v* **1** open or begin the use of, esp. with ceremony. **2** formally establish (a new leader) in office. **inaugural** *adj* **inauguration** *n*

inauspicious *adj* unlucky, likely to have an unfavourable outcome.

inboard *adj* (of a boat's engine) inside the hull.

inborn *adj* existing from birth, natural.

inbred *adj* **1** produced as a result of inbreeding. **2** inborn or ingrained.

inbreeding *n* breeding of animals or people that are closely related.

inbuilt *adj* present from the start.

Inc. *US & Aust* (of a company) incorporated.

incalculable *adj* too great to be estimated.

in camera *adv see* CAMERA.

incandescent *adj* glowing with heat. **incandescence** *n*

incantation *n* ritual chanting of magic words or sounds.

incapable *adj* **1** (foll. by *of*) unable (to do something). **2** incompetent.

incapacitate *v* deprive of strength or ability. **incapacity** *n*

incarcerate *v* imprison. **incarceration** *n*

incarnate *adj* in human form. **incarnation** *n* **Incarnation** *n* *Christianity* God's coming to earth in human form as Jesus Christ.

incendiary [in-**send**-ya-ree] *adj* **1** (of a bomb, attack, etc.) designed to cause fires. ♦ *n, pl* **-aries** **2** bomb designed to cause fires.

incense¹ *v* make very angry.

incense² *n* substance that gives off a sweet perfume when burned.

incentive *n* something that encourages effort or action.

inception *n* beginning.

incessant *adj* never stopping. **incessantly** *adv*

incest *n* sexual intercourse between two people too closely related to marry. **incestuous** *adj*

inch *n* **1** unit of length equal to one twelfth of a foot or 2.54 centimetres. ♦ *v* **2** move slowly and gradually.

inchoate [in-**koe**-ate] *adj* just begun and not yet properly developed.

incidence *n* extent or frequency of occurrence.

incident *n* **1** something that happens. **2** event involving violence.

incidental *adj* occurring in connection

with or resulting from something more important. **incidentally** adv
incidental music background music for a film or play.

incinerate v burn to ashes.
incineration n **incinerator** n furnace for burning rubbish.

incipient adj just starting to appear or happen.

incise v cut into with a sharp tool.
incision n **incisor** n front tooth, used for biting into food.

incisive adj direct and forceful.

incite v stir up, provoke. **incitement** n

incivility n, pl **-ties** rudeness or a rude remark.

inclement adj (of weather) stormy or severe.

incline v 1 lean, slope. 2 (cause to) have a certain disposition or tendency.
♦ n 3 slope. **inclination** n 1 liking, tendency, or preference. 2 slope.

include v 1 have as part of the whole.
2 put in as part of a set or group.
inclusion n **inclusive** adj including everything (specified). **inclusively** adv

incognito [in-kog-**nee**-toe] adj, adv 1 having adopted a false identity. ♦ n, pl **-tos** 2 false identity.

incoherent adj unclear and impossible to understand. **incoherence** n
incoherently adv

income n amount of money earned from work, investments, etc. **income support** (in New Zealand) allowance paid by the government to people with a very low income. **income tax** personal tax levied on annual income.

incoming adj 1 coming in. 2 about to come into office.

incommode v cause inconvenience to.

incommunicado adj, adv deprived of communication with other people.

incomparable adj beyond comparison, unequalled.

incomparably adv

incompatible adj inconsistent or conflicting. **incompatibility** n

incompetent adj not having the necessary ability or skill to do something. **incompetence** n

inconceivable adj extremely unlikely, unimaginable.

inconclusive adj not giving a final decision or result.

incongruous adj inappropriate or out of place. **incongruously** adv
incongruity n, pl **-ties**

inconsequential adj unimportant, insignificant.

inconsiderable adj **not inconsiderable** fairly large.

inconstant adj liable to change one's loyalties or opinions.

incontinent adj unable to control one's bladder or bowels.
incontinence n

incontrovertible adj impossible to deny or disprove.

inconvenience n 1 trouble or difficulty. ♦ v 2 cause trouble or difficulty to. **inconvenient** adj

incorporate v include or be included as part of a larger unit.

incorporeal adj without material form.

incorrigible adj beyond correction or reform.

incorruptible adj 1 too honest to be bribed or corrupted. 2 not subject to decay.

increase v 1 make or become greater in size, number, etc. ♦ n 2 rise in number, size, etc. 3 amount by which something increases. **increasingly** adv

incredible adj 1 hard to believe or imagine. 2 Informal marvellous, amazing. **incredibly** adv

incredulous adj not willing to believe something. **incredulity** n

increment n increase in money or

value, esp. a regular salary increase. **incremental** *adj*

incriminate *v* make (someone) seem guilty of a crime. **incriminating** *adj*

incubate [**in**-cube-ate] *v* **1** (of a bird) hatch (eggs) by sitting on them. **2** grow (bacteria). **3** (of bacteria) remain inactive in an animal or person before causing disease. **incubation** *n* **incubator** *n* **1** heated enclosed apparatus for rearing premature babies. **2** apparatus for artificially hatching birds' eggs.

incubus [**in**-cube-uss] *n, pl* **-bi, -buses 1** (in folklore) demon believed to have sex with sleeping women. **2** nightmarish burden or worry.

inculcate *v* fix in someone's mind by constant repetition. **inculcation** *n*

incumbent *n* **1** person holding a particular office or position. ♦ *adj* **2 it is incumbent on** it is the duty of. **incumbency** *n, pl* **-cies**

incur *v* **-curring, -curred** cause (something unpleasant) to happen.

incurable *adj* not able to be cured. **incurably** *adv*

incurious *adj* showing no curiosity or interest.

incursion *n* sudden brief invasion.

indebted *adj* **1** owing gratitude for help or favours. **2** owing money. **indebtedness** *n*

indecent *adj* **1** morally or sexually offensive. **2** unsuitable or unseemly, e.g. *indecent haste*. **indecently** *adv* **indecency** *n* **indecent assault** sexual attack which does not include rape. **indecent exposure** showing of one's genitals in public.

indecipherable *adj* impossible to read.

indeed *adv* **1** really, certainly. ♦ *interj* **2** expression of indignation or surprise.

indefatigable *adj* never getting tired. **indefatigably** *adv*

indefensible *adj* **1** unable to be justified. **2** impossible to defend.

indefinite *adj* **1** without exact limits, e.g. *for an indefinite period.* **2** vague, unclear. **indefinite article** *Grammar* the word *a* or *an*. **indefinitely** *adv*

indelible *adj* **1** impossible to erase or remove. **2** making indelible marks. **indelibly** *adv*

indelicate *adj* offensive or embarrassing.

indemnify *v* **-ifying, -ified 1** secure against loss, damage, or liability. **2** compensate for loss or damage.

indemnity *n, pl* **-ties 1** insurance against loss or damage. **2** compensation for loss or damage.

indent *v* **1** start (a line of writing) further from the margin than the other lines. **2** order (goods) using a special order form. **indentation** *n* dent in a surface or edge.

indenture *n* contract, esp. one binding an apprentice to his or her employer.

independent *adj* **1** free from the control or influence of others. **2** separate. **3** financially self-reliant. **4** capable of acting for oneself or on one's own. ♦ *n* **5** politician who does not represent any political party. **independently** *adv* **independence** *n*

☑ SPELLING TIP

People often get confused about how to spell **independent**. It is spelt *independant* 44 times in the Bank of English. It should be spelt with an *e* at the end in the same way as the noun it is related to: **independent** and **independence**.

---

in-depth *adj* detailed, thorough.

indescribable *adj* too intense or extreme for words. **indescribably** *adv*

indeterminate *adj* uncertain in

extent, amount, or nature.
indeterminacy n

index n, pl **indices** [**in**-diss-eez] **1** alphabetical list of names or subjects dealt with in a book. **2** file or catalogue used to find things. **3** v **4** provide (a book) with an index. **5** enter in an index. **6** make index-linked. **index finger** finger next to the thumb. **index-linked** adj (of pensions, wages, etc.) rising or falling in line with the cost of living.

Indian n, adj **1** (person) from India. **2** Native American. **Indian summer** period of warm sunny weather in autumn.

indicate v **1** be a sign or symptom of. **2** point out. **3** state briefly. **4** (of a measuring instrument) show a reading of. **indication** n **indicative** adj **1** (foll. by of) suggesting. **2** Grammar denoting a mood of verbs used to make a statement. ♦ n **3** Grammar indicative mood. **indicator** n **1** something acting as a sign or indication. **2** flashing light on a vehicle showing the driver's intention to turn. **3** dial or gauge.

indict [in-**dite**] v formally charge with a crime. **indictable** adj **indictment** n

indie adj Informal (of rock music) released by an independent record company.

indifferent adj **1** showing no interest or concern. **2** of poor quality. **indifference** n **indifferently** adv

indigenous [in-**dij**-in-uss] adj born in or natural to a country.

indigent adj extremely poor. **indigence** n

indigestion n (discomfort or pain caused by) difficulty in digesting food. **indigestible** adj

indignation n anger at something unfair or wrong. **indignant** adj feeling or showing indignation.

indignantly adv

indignity n, pl -**ties** embarrassing or humiliating treatment.

indigo adj **1** deep violet-blue. ♦ n **2** dye of this colour.

indirect adj **1** done or caused by someone or something else. **2** not by a straight route. **indirect object** Grammar person or thing indirectly affected by the action of a verb, e.g. Amy in I bought Amy a bag. **indirect tax** tax added to the price of something.

indiscreet adj incautious or tactless in revealing secrets. **indiscreetly** adv **indiscretion** n

indiscriminate adj showing lack of careful thought.

indispensable adj absolutely essential.

☑ **SPELLING TIP**
For every twenty examples of the word **indispensable** in the Bank of English, there is one example of the misspelling indispensible. So remember that it ends in -able.

indisposed adj unwell, ill. **indisposition** n

indisputable adj beyond doubt. **indisputably** adv

indissoluble adj permanent.

indium n Chem soft silvery-white metallic element.

individual adj **1** characteristic of or meant for a single person or thing. **2** separate, distinct. **3** distinctive, unusual. ♦ n **4** single person or thing. **individually** adv **individuality** n **individualism** n principle of living one's life in one's own way. **individualist** n **individualistic** adj

indoctrinate v teach (someone) to accept a doctrine or belief uncritically. **indoctrination** n

Indo-European *adj, n* (of) a family of languages spoken in most of Europe and much of Asia, including English, Russian, and Hindi.

indolent *adj* lazy. **indolence** *n*

indomitable *adj* too strong to be defeated or discouraged. **indomitably** *adv*

indoor *adj* inside a building. **indoors** *adv*

indubitable *adj* beyond doubt, certain. **indubitably** *adv*

induce *v* **1** persuade or influence. **2** cause. **3** *Med* cause (a woman) to go into labour or bring on (labour) by the use of drugs etc. **inducement** *n* something used to persuade someone to do something.

induct *v* formally install (someone, esp. a clergyman) in office.

inductance *n* property of an electric circuit creating voltage by a change of current.

induction *n* **1** reasoning process by which general conclusions are drawn from particular instances. **2** process by which electrical or magnetic properties are produced by the proximity of an electrified or magnetic object. **3** formal introduction into an office or position. **inductive** *adj* **induction coil** transformer for producing a high voltage from a low voltage. **induction course** training course to help familiarize someone with a new job.

indulge *v* **1** allow oneself pleasure. **2** allow (someone) to have or do everything he or she wants. **indulgence** *n* **1** something allowed because it gives pleasure. **2** act of indulging oneself or someone else. **3** liberal or tolerant treatment. **indulgent** *adj* **indulgently** *adv*

industrial *adj* of, used in, or employed in industry. **industrialize** *v* develop large-scale industry in (a country or region). **industrialization** *n*

industrial action ways in which workers can protest about their conditions, e.g. by striking or working to rule. **industrial estate** area of land set aside for factories and warehouses. **industrial relations** relations between management and workers.

industry *n, pl* **-tries 1** manufacture of goods. **2** branch of this, e.g. *the music industry*. **3** quality of working hard. **industrious** *adj* hard-working.

inebriate *n, adj* (person who is) habitually drunk. **inebriated** *adj* drunk. **inebriation** *n*

inedible *adj* not fit to be eaten.

ineffable *adj* too great for words. **ineffably** *adv*

ineffectual *adj* having very little effect.

ineligible *adj* not qualified for or entitled to something.

ineluctable *adj* impossible to avoid.

inept *adj* clumsy, lacking skill. **ineptitude** *n*

inequitable *adj* unfair.

ineradicable *adj* impossible to remove.

inert *adj* **1** without the power of motion or resistance. **2** chemically unreactive. **inertness** *n*

inertia *n* **1** feeling of unwillingness to do anything. **2** *Physics* tendency of a body to remain still or continue moving unless a force is applied to it.

inescapable *adj* unavoidable.

inestimable *adj* too great to be estimated. **inestimably** *adv*

inevitable *adj* unavoidable, sure to happen. **the inevitable** something that cannot be prevented. **inevitably** *adv* **inevitability** *n*

inexorable *adj* unable to be prevented from continuing or progressing. **inexorably** *adv*

inexpert *adj* lacking skill.

inexplicable *adj* impossible to explain.
 inexplicably *adv*
in extremis *adv Latin* **1** in great
 difficulty. **2** on the point of death.
inextricable *adj* **1** impossible to
 escape from. **2** impossible to
 disentangle or separate.
infallible *adj* never wrong. **infallibly**
 adv **infallibility** *n*
infamous [**in**-fam-uss] *adj* well-known
 for something bad. **infamously** *adv*
 infamy *n*
infant *n* very young child. **infancy** *n* **1**
 early childhood. **2** early stage of
 development. **infantile** *adj* childish.
infanticide *n* **1** murder of an infant. **2**
 person guilty of this.
infantry *n* soldiers who fight on foot.
infatuated *adj* feeling intense
 unreasoning passion.
infatuation *n* intense unreasoning
 passion.
infect *v* **1** affect with a disease. **2** affect
 with a feeling. **infection** *n*
 infectious *adj* **1** (of a disease)
 spreading without actual contact. **2**
 spreading from person to person, e.g.
 infectious enthusiasm.
infer *v* **-ferring, -ferred** work out from
 evidence. **inference** *n*

> ☑ **WORD TIP**
> Someone *infers* something by
> 'reading between the lines' of a
> remark. Do not confuse with *imply*,
> which means 'to hint'.

inferior *adj* **1** lower in quality, position,
 or status. ♦ *n* **2** person of lower
 position or status. **inferiority** *n*
infernal *adj* **1** of hell. **2** *Informal*
 irritating. **infernally** *adv*
inferno *n, pl* **-nos** intense raging fire.
infertile *adj* **1** unable to produce
 offspring. **2** (of soil) barren, not
 productive. **infertility** *n*

infest *v* inhabit or overrun in
 unpleasantly large numbers.
 infestation *n*
infidel *n* **1** person with no religion. **2**
 person who rejects a particular
 religion, esp. Christianity or Islam.
infidelity *n, pl* **-ties** (act of) sexual
 unfaithfulness to one's husband, wife,
 or lover.
infighting *n* quarrelling within a
 group.
infiltrate *v* enter gradually and
 secretly. **infiltration** *n* **infiltrator** *n*
infinite [**in**-fin-it] *adj* without any limit
 or end. **infinitely** *adv*
infinitesimal *adj* extremely small.
infinitive *n Grammar* form of a verb
 not showing tense, person, or
 number, e.g. *to sleep*.
infinity *n* endless space, time, or
 number.
infirm *adj* physically or mentally weak.
 infirmity *n, pl* **-ties**
infirmary *n, pl* **-ries** hospital.
inflame *v* make angry or excited.
 inflamed *adj* (of part of the body) red,
 swollen, and painful because of
 infection. **inflammation** *n*
inflammable *adj* easily set on fire.

> ☑ **WORD TIP**
> *Inflammable* means the same as
> *flammable* but is falling out of general
> use as it was often mistaken to mean
> 'not flammable'.

inflammatory *adj* likely to provoke
 anger.
inflate *v* **1** expand by filling with air or
 gas. **2** cause economic inflation in.
 inflatable *adj* **1** able to be inflated.
 ♦ *n* **2** plastic or rubber object which
 can be inflated.
inflation *n* **1** inflating. **2** increase in
 prices and fall in the value of money.
 inflationary *adj*

inflection, inflexion *n* **1** change in the pitch of the voice. **2** *Grammar* change in the form of a word to show grammatical use.

inflexible *adj* **1** unwilling to be persuaded, obstinate. **2** (of a policy etc.) firmly fixed, unalterable. **inflexibly** *adv* **inflexibility** *n*

inflict *v* impose (something unpleasant) on. **infliction** *n*

inflorescence *n Botany* arrangement of flowers on a stem.

influence *n* **1** effect of one person or thing on another. **2** (person with) the power to have such an effect. ♦ *v* **3** have an effect on. **influential** *adj*

influenza *n* contagious viral disease causing headaches, muscle pains, and fever.

influx *n* arrival or entry of many people or things.

info *n Informal* information.

inform *v* **1** tell. **2** give incriminating information to the police. **informant** *n* person who gives information. **information** *n* knowledge or facts. **informative** *adj* giving useful information. **information superhighway** worldwide network of computers transferring information at high speed. **information technology** use of computers and electronic technology to store and communicate information. **informer** *n* person who informs to the police.

informal *adj* **1** relaxed and friendly. **2** appropriate for everyday life or use. **informally** *adv* **informality** *n*

infra dig *adj Informal* beneath one's dignity.

infrared *adj* of or using rays below the red end of the visible spectrum.

infrastructure *n* basic facilities, services, and equipment needed for a country or organization to function properly.

infringe *v* break (a law or agreement). **infringement** *n*

infuriate *v* make very angry.

infuse *v* **1** fill (with an emotion or quality). **2** soak to extract flavour. **infusion** *n* **1** infusing. **2** liquid obtained by infusing.

ingenious [in-**jean**-ee-uss] *adj* showing cleverness and originality. **ingeniously** *adv* **ingenuity** [in-jen-**new**-it-ee] *n*

ingénue [**an**-jay-new] *n* naive young woman, esp. as a role played by an actress.

ingenuous [in-**jen**-new-uss] *adj* unsophisticated and trusting. **ingenuously** *adv*

ingest *v* take (food or liquid) into the body. **ingestion** *n*

inglorious *adj* dishonourable, shameful.

ingot *n* oblong block of cast metal.

ingrained *adj* firmly fixed.

ingratiate *v* try to make (oneself) popular with someone. **ingratiating** *adj* **ingratiatingly** *adv*

ingredient *n* component of a mixture or compound.

ingress *n* act or right of entering.

ingrowing *adj* (of a toenail) growing abnormally into the flesh.

inhabit *v* **-habiting, -habited** live in. **inhabitable** *adj* **inhabitant** *n*

inhale *v* breathe in (air, smoke, etc.). **inhalation** *n* **inhalant** *n* medical preparation inhaled to help breathing problems. **inhaler** *n* container for an inhalant.

inherent *adj* existing as an inseparable part. **inherently** *adv*

inherit *v* **-heriting, -herited** **1** receive (money etc.) from someone who has died. **2** receive (a characteristic) from an earlier generation. **3** receive from a predecessor. **inheritance** *n* inheritance tax tax paid on property left at death. **inheritor** n

inhibit v -hibiting, -hibited **1** restrain (an impulse or desire). **2** hinder or prevent (action). **inhibited** adj **inhibition** n feeling of fear or embarrassment that stops one from behaving naturally.

inhospitable adj **1** not welcoming, unfriendly. **2** difficult to live in, harsh.

inhuman adj **1** cruel or brutal. **2** not human.

inhumane adj cruel or brutal. **inhumanity** n

inimical adj unfavourable or hostile.

inimitable adj impossible to imitate, unique.

iniquity n, pl -ties **1** injustice or wickedness. **2** wicked act. **iniquitous** adj

initial adj **1** first, at the beginning. ◆ n **2** first letter, esp. of a person's name. ◆ v -tialling, -tialled **3** sign with one's initials. **initially** adv

initiate v **1** begin or set going. **2** admit (someone) into a closed group. **3** instruct in the basics of something. ◆ n **4** recently initiated person. **initiation** n **initiator** n

initiative n **1** first step, commencing move. **2** ability to act independently.

inject v **1** put (a fluid) into the body with a syringe. **2** introduce (a new element), e.g. try to inject a bit of humour. **injection** n

injudicious adj showing poor judgment, unwise.

injunction n court order not to do something.

injure v hurt physically or mentally. **injury** n, pl -ries **injury time** Sport playing time added at the end of a match to compensate for time spent treating injured players. **injurious** adj

injustice n **1** unfairness. **2** unfair action.

ink n **1** coloured liquid used for writing or printing. ◆ v **2** (foll. by in) mark in ink (something already marked in pencil). **inky** adj **1** dark or black. **2** covered in ink.

inkling n slight idea or suspicion.

inlaid adj **1** set in another material so that the surface is smooth. **2** made like this, e.g. an inlaid table.

inland adj, adv in or towards the interior of a country, away from the sea. **Inland Revenue** (in Britain) government department that collects taxes.

in-laws pl n one's husband's or wife's family.

inlay n inlaid substance or pattern.

inlet n **1** narrow strip of water extending from the sea into the land. **2** valve etc. through which liquid or gas enters.

in loco parentis Latin in place of a parent.

inmate n person living in an institution such as a prison.

inmost adj innermost.

inn n pub or small hotel, esp. in the country. **innkeeper** n

innards pl n Informal **1** internal organs. **2** working parts of a machine.

innate adj being part of someone's nature, inborn.

inner adj **1** happening or located inside. **2** relating to private feelings, e.g. the inner self. **innermost** adj furthest inside. **inner city** parts of a city near the centre, esp. having severe social and economic problems.

innings n **1** Sport player's or side's turn of batting. **2** period of opportunity.

innocent adj **1** not guilty of a crime. **2** without experience of evil. **3** without malicious intent. ◆ n **4** innocent person, esp. a child. **innocently** adv **innocence** n

innocuous adj not harmful.
innocuously adv

☑ **SPELLING TIP**

Always make sure there are two ns in **innocuous**. It is more common to miss out an n than to double the c by mistake.

innovation n 1 new idea or method. 2 introduction of new ideas or methods. **innovate** v **innovative** adj **innovator** n

innuendo n, pl -does (remark making) an indirect reference to something rude or unpleasant.

innumerable adj too many to be counted.

innumerate adj having no understanding of mathematics or science. **innumeracy** n

inoculate v protect against disease by injecting with a vaccine. **inoculation** n

☑ **SPELLING TIP**

The verb **inoculate** has only one n and one c. There are 235 occurrences of the correct spelling of the noun **inoculation** in the Bank of English, with lots of different misspellings. The most popular one, *innoculation*, occurs 31 times.

inoperable adj (of a tumour or cancer) unable to be surgically removed.

inopportune adj badly timed, unsuitable.

inordinate adj excessive.

inorganic adj 1 not having the characteristics of living organisms. 2 of chemical substances that do not contain carbon.

inpatient n patient who stays in a hospital for treatment.

input n 1 resources put into a project etc. 2 data fed into a computer. ♦ v -putting, -put 3 enter (data) in a computer.

inquest n official inquiry into a sudden death.

inquire v seek information or ask (about). **inquirer** n

inquiry n, pl -ries 1 question. 2 investigation.

inquisition n 1 thorough investigation. 2 (I-) *Hist* organization within the Catholic Church for suppressing heresy. **inquisitor** n **inquisitorial** adj

inquisitive adj excessively curious about other people's affairs. **inquisitively** adv

inquorate adj without enough people present to make a quorum.

inroads pl n **make inroads into** start affecting or reducing.

insalubrious adj unpleasant, unhealthy, or sordid.

insane adj 1 mentally ill. 2 stupidly irresponsible. **insanely** adv **insanity** n

insanitary adj dirty or unhealthy.

insatiable [in-**saysh**-a-bl] adj unable to be satisfied.

inscribe v write or carve words on. **inscription** n words inscribed.

inscrutable adj mysterious, enigmatic. **inscrutably** adv

insect n small animal with six legs and usu. wings, such as an ant or fly. **insecticide** n substance for killing insects. **insectivorous** adj insect-eating.

insecure adj 1 anxious, not confident. 2 not safe or well-protected.

insemination n putting semen into a woman's or female animal's body to try to make her pregnant. **inseminate** v

insensate adj 1 without sensation,

unconscious. **2** unfeeling.

insensible adj **1** unconscious, without feeling. **2** (foll. by to or of) not aware (of) or affected (by).

insensitive adj unaware of or ignoring other people's feelings. **insensitivity** n

inseparable adj **1** (of two people) spending most of the time together. **2** (of two things) impossible to separate.

☑ **SPELLING TIP**

The word **inseparable** occurs in the Bank of English 914 times. The misspelling inseperable, with an e instead of an a in the middle, appears 6 times.

---

insert v **1** put inside or include. ♦ n **2** something inserted. **insertion** n

inset n small picture inserted within a larger one.

inshore adj **1** close to the shore. ♦ adj, adv **2** towards the shore.

inside prep **1** in or to the interior of. ♦ adj **2** on or of the inside. **3** by or from someone within an organization, e.g. inside information. ♦ adv **4** on, in, or to the inside, indoors. **5** Brit, Aust & NZ slang in(to) prison. ♦ n **6** inner side, surface, or part. ♦ pl **7** Informal stomach and bowels. **inside out** with the inside facing outwards. **know inside out** know thoroughly. **insider** n member of a group who has privileged knowledge about it.

☑ **WORD TIP**

Avoid using the expression inside of, as the second preposition of is superfluous.

---

insidious adj subtle or unseen but dangerous. **insidiously** adv

insight n deep understanding.

insignia n, pl -nias, -nia badge or emblem of honour or office.

insignificant adj not important. **insignificance** n

insincere adj showing false feelings, not genuine. **insincerely** adv **insincerity** n, pl -ties

insinuate v **1** suggest indirectly. **2** work (oneself) into a position by gradual manoeuvres. **insinuation** n

insipid adj lacking interest, spirit, or flavour.

insist v demand or state firmly. **insistent** adj **1** making persistent demands. **2** demanding attention. **insistently** adv **insistence** n

in situ adv, adj Latin in its original position.

in so far as, insofar as prep to the extent that.

insole n inner sole of a shoe or boot.

insolent adj rude and disrespectful. **insolence** n **insolently** adv

insoluble adj **1** incapable of being solved. **2** incapable of being dissolved.

insolvent adj unable to pay one's debts. **insolvency** n

insomnia n inability to sleep. **insomniac** n

insouciant adj carefree and unconcerned. **insouciance** n

inspect v check closely or officially. **inspection** n **inspector** n **1** person who inspects. **2** high-ranking police officer.

inspire v **1** fill with enthusiasm, stimulate. **2** arouse (an emotion). **inspiration** n **1** creative influence or stimulus. **2** brilliant idea. **inspirational** adj

instability n lack of steadiness or reliability.

install v **1** put in and prepare (equipment) for use. **2** place (a person) formally in a position or rank. **installation** n **1** installing. **2** equipment installed. **3** place containing equipment for a particular purpose, e.g. *oil installations*.

instalment *n* any of the portions of a thing presented or a debt paid in successive parts.

instance *n* **1** particular example. ♦ *v* **2** mention as an example. **for instance** as an example.

instant *n* **1** very brief time. **2** particular moment. ♦ *adj* **3** happening at once. **4** (of foods) requiring little preparation. **instantly** *adv*

instantaneous *adj* happening at once. **instantaneously** *adv*

instead *adv* as a replacement or substitute.

instep *n* **1** part of the foot forming the arch between the ankle and toes. **2** part of a shoe or boot covering this.

instigate *v* cause to happen. **instigation** *n* **instigator** *n*

instil *v* **-stilling, -stilled** introduce (an idea etc.) gradually into someone's mind.

instinct *n* inborn tendency to behave in a certain way. **instinctive** *adj* **instinctively** *adv*

institute *n* **1** organization set up for a specific purpose, esp. research or teaching. ♦ *v* **2** start or establish.

institution *n* **1** large important organization such as a university or bank. **2** hospital etc. for people with special needs. **3** long-established custom. **institutional** *adj* **institutionalize** *v*

instruct *v* **1** order to do something. **2** teach (someone) how to do something. **instruction** *n* **1** order to do something. **2** teaching. ♦ *pl* **3** information on how to do or use something. **instructive** *adj* informative or helpful. **instructor** *n*

instrument *n* **1** tool used for particular work. **2** object played to produce a musical sound. **3** measuring device to show height, speed, etc. **4** *Informal* someone or something used to achieve an aim. **instrumental** *adj* **1** (foll. by *in*) having an important function (in). **2** played by or composed for musical instruments.

instrumentalist *n* player of a musical instrument. **instrumentation** *n* **1** set of instruments in a car etc. **2** arrangement of music for instruments.

insubordinate *adj* not submissive to authority. **insubordination** *n*

insufferable *adj* unbearable.

insular *adj* not open to new ideas, narrow-minded. **insularity** *n*

insulate *v* **1** prevent or reduce the transfer of electricity, heat, or sound by surrounding or lining with a nonconducting material. **2** isolate or set apart. **insulation** *n* **insulator** *n*

insulin *n* hormone produced in the pancreas that controls the amount of sugar in the blood.

insult *v* **1** behave rudely to, offend. ♦ *n* **2** insulting remark or action. **insulting** *adj*

insuperable *adj* impossible to overcome.

insupportable *adj* **1** impossible to tolerate. **2** impossible to justify.

insurance *n* **1** agreement by which one makes regular payments to a company who pay an agreed sum if damage, loss, or death occurs. **2** money paid to or by an insurance company. **3** means of protection. **insure** *v* protect by insurance. **insurance policy** contract of insurance.

insurgent *n, adj* (person) in revolt against an established authority.

insurrection *n* rebellion.

intact *adj* not changed or damaged in any way.

intaglio [in-**tah**-lee-oh] *n, pl* **-lios** (gem carved with) an engraved design.

intake n amount or number taken in.

integer n positive or negative whole number or zero.

integral adj 1 being an essential part of a whole. ♦ n 2 Maths sum of a large number of very small quantities.

integrate v 1 combine into a whole. 2 amalgamate (a religious or racial group) into a community. **integration** n **integrated circuit** tiny electronic circuit on a chip of semiconducting material.

integrity n 1 quality of having high moral principles. 2 quality of being united.

intellect n power of thinking and reasoning.

intellectual adj 1 of or appealing to the intellect. 2 clever, intelligent. ♦ n 3 intellectual person. **intellectually** adv

intelligent adj 1 able to understand, learn, and think things out quickly. 2 (of a computerized device) able to initiate or modify action in the light of ongoing events. **intelligence** n 1 quality of being intelligent. 2 secret government or military information. 3 people or department collecting such information. **intelligently** adv

intelligentsia n intellectual or cultured people in a society.

intelligible adj able to be understood. **intelligibility** n

intemperate adj 1 unrestrained, uncontrolled. 2 drinking alcohol to excess. **intemperance** n

intend v 1 propose or plan (to do something). 2 have as one's purpose.

intense adj 1 of great strength or degree. 2 deeply emotional. **intensity** n **intensify** v -fying, -fied make or become more intense. **intensification** n

intensive adj using or needing concentrated effort or resources. **intensively** adv

intent n 1 intention. 2 adj 3 paying close attention. **intently** adv **intentness** n intent on doing something determined to do something.

intention n something intended. **intentional** adj planned in advance, deliberate. **intentionally** adv

inter [in-**ter**] v -terring, -terred bury (a corpse). **interment** n

inter- prefix between or among, e.g. international.

interact v act on or in close relation with each other. **interaction** n **interactive** adj

interbreed v breed within a related group.

intercede v try to end a dispute between two people or groups. **intercession** n

intercept v seize or stop in transit. **interception** n

interchange v 1 (cause to) exchange places. ♦ n 2 motorway junction. **interchangeable** adj

Intercity adj ® (in Britain) denoting a fast train (service) travelling between cities.

intercom n internal communication system with loudspeakers.

intercontinental adj travelling between or linking continents.

intercourse n 1 sexual intercourse. 2 communication or dealings between people or groups.

interdiction, interdict n formal order forbidding something.

interdisciplinary adj involving more than one branch of learning.

interest n 1 desire to know or hear more about something. 2 something in which one is interested. 3 (often pl) advantage, benefit. 4 sum paid for the use of borrowed money. 5 (often pl) right or share. ♦ v 6 arouse the interest of. **interested** *adj* **1** feeling or showing interest. **2** involved in or affected by something. **interesting** *adj* **interestingly** *adv*

interface *n* **1** area where two things interact or link. **2** circuit linking a computer and another device.

interfere *v* **1** try to influence other people's affairs where one is not involved or wanted. **2** (foll. by *with*) clash (with). **3** (foll. by *with*) *Brit, Aust & NZ euphemistic* abuse (a child) sexually. **interfering** *adj* **interference** *n* **1** interfering. **2** *Radio* interruption of reception by atmospherics or unwanted signals.

interferon *n* protein that stops the development of an invading virus.

interim *adj* temporary or provisional.

interior *n* **1** inside. **2** inland region. ♦ *adj* **3** inside, inner. **4** mental or spiritual.

interject *v* make (a remark) suddenly or as an interruption. **interjection** *n*

interlace *v* join together as if by weaving.

interlink *v* connect together.

interlock *v* join firmly together.

interlocutor [in-ter-**lok**-yew-ter] *n* person who takes part in a conversation.

interloper [**in**-ter-lope-er] *n* person in a place or situation where he or she has no right to be.

interlude *n* short rest or break in an activity or event.

intermarry *v* (of families, races, or religions) become linked by marriage. **intermarriage** *n*

intermediary *n, pl* -ries person trying to create agreement between others.

intermediate *adj* coming between two points or extremes.

intermezzo [in-ter-**met**-so] *n, pl* -zos short piece of music, esp. one

performed between the acts of an opera.

interminable *adj* seemingly endless because boring. **interminably** *adv*

intermingle *v* mix together.

intermission *n* interval between parts of a play, film, etc.

intermittent *adj* occurring at intervals. **intermittently** *adv*

intern *v* **1** imprison, esp. during a war. ♦ *n* **2** trainee doctor in a hospital. **internment** *n* **internee** *n* person who is interned.

internal *adj* **1** of or on the inside. **2** within a country or organization. **3** spiritual or mental. **internally** *adv* **internal-combustion engine** engine powered by the explosion of a fuel-and-air mixture within the cylinders.

international *adj* **1** of or involving two or more countries. ♦ *n* **2** game or match between teams of different countries. **3** player in such a match. **internationally** *adv*

internecine *adj* mutually destructive.

Internet, internet *n* large international computer network.

interplanetary *adj* of or linking planets.

interplay *n* action and reaction of two things upon each other.

interpolate [in-**ter**-pole-ate] *v* insert (a comment or passage) into (a conversation or text). **interpolation** *n*

interpose *v* **1** insert between or among things. **2** say as an interruption.

interpret *v* **1** explain the meaning of. **2** translate orally from one language into another. **3** convey the meaning of (a poem, song, etc.) in performance. **interpretation** *n*

interpreter *n* person who translates orally from one language into another.

interregnum *n, pl* -nums, -na interval

between reigns.

interrogate v question closely. **interrogation** n **interrogative** adj 1 questioning. ♦ n 2 word used in asking a question, such as *how* or *why*. **interrogator** n

interrupt v 1 break into (a conversation etc.). 2 stop (a process or activity) temporarily. **interruption** n

intersect v 1 (of roads) meet and cross. 2 divide by passing across or through. **intersection** n

interspersed adj scattered (among, between, or on).

interstellar adj between or among stars.

interstice [in-**ter**-stiss] n small crack or gap between things.

intertwine v twist together.

interval n 1 time between two particular moments or events. 2 break between parts of a play, concert, etc. 3 difference in pitch between musical notes. **at intervals** 1 repeatedly. 2 with spaces left between.

intervene v 1 involve oneself in a situation, esp. to prevent conflict. 2 happen so as to stop something. **intervention** n

interview n 1 formal discussion, esp. between a job-seeker and an employer. 2 questioning of a well-known person about his or her career, views, etc., by a reporter. ♦ v 3 conduct an interview with. **interviewee** n **interviewer** n

interweave v weave together.

intestate adj not having made a will. **intestacy** n

intestine n (often pl) lower part of the alimentary canal between the stomach and the anus. **intestinal** adj **intestinally** adv

intimate¹ adj 1 having a close personal relationship. 2 personal or private. 3 (of knowledge) extensive and detailed.

4 (foll. by *with*) Euphemistic having a sexual relationship (with). 5 having a friendly quiet atmosphere. ♦ n 6 close friend. **intimately** adv **intimacy** n

intimate² v 1 hint at or suggest. 2 announce. **intimation** n

intimidate v subdue or influence by fear. **intimidating** adj **intimidation** n

into prep 1 indicating motion towards the centre, result of a change, division, etc., e.g. *into the valley; turned into a madman; cut into pieces.* 2 Informal interested in.

intolerable adj more than can be endured. **intolerably** adv

intolerant adj refusing to accept practices and beliefs different from one's own. **intolerance** n

intonation n sound pattern produced by variations in the voice.

intone v speak or recite in an unvarying tone of voice.

intoxicate v 1 make drunk. 2 excite to excess. **intoxicant** n intoxicating drink.

intoxication n 1 state of being drunk. 2 overexcited state.

intractable adj 1 (of a person) difficult to control. 2 (of a problem or issue) difficult to deal with.

intranet n Computers internal network that makes use of Internet technology.

intransigent adj refusing to change one's attitude. **intransigence** n

intransitive adj (of a verb) not taking a direct object.

intrauterine adj within the womb.

intravenous [in-tra-**vee**-nuss] adj into a vein. **intravenously** adv

intrepid adj fearless, bold. **intrepidity** n

intricate adj 1 involved or complicated. 2 full of fine detail. **intricately** adv **intricacy** n, pl **-cies**

intrigue v 1 make interested or

curious. **2** plot secretly. ♦ *n* **3** secret plotting. **4** secret love affair. **intriguing** *adj*

intrinsic *adj* essential to the basic nature of something. **intrinsically** *adv*

introduce *v* **1** present (someone) by name (to another person). **2** present (a radio or television programme). **3** bring forward for discussion. **4** bring into use. **5** insert. **introduction** *n* **1** presentation of one person to another. **2** preliminary part or treatment. **introductory** *adj*

introspection *n* examination of one's own thoughts and feelings. **introspective** *adj*

introvert *n* person concerned more with his or her thoughts and feelings than with the outside world. **introverted** *adj* **introversion** *n*

intrude *v* come in or join in without being invited. **intrusion** *n* **intrusive** *adj*

intruder *n* person who enters a place without permission.

intuition *n* instinctive knowledge or insight without conscious reasoning. **intuitive** *adj* **intuitively** *adv*

Inuit *n* indigenous inhabitant of North America or Greenland.

inundate *v* **1** flood. **2** overwhelm. **inundation** *n*

inured *adj* accustomed, esp. to hardship or danger.

invade *v* **1** enter (a country) by military force. **2** enter in large numbers. **3** disturb (someone's privacy). **invader** *n*

invalid[1] *adj, n* **1** disabled or chronically ill (person). ♦ *v* **2** (often foll. by *out*) dismiss from active service because of illness or injury. **invalidity** *n*

invalid[2] *adj* **1** having no legal force. **2** (of an argument etc.) not valid because based on a mistake. **invalidate** *v* make or show to be invalid.

invaluable *adj* of very great value or worth.

invasion *n* **1** invading. **2** intrusion, e.g. *an invasion of privacy*.

invective *n* abusive speech or writing.

inveigh [in-**vay**] *v* (foll. by *against*) criticize strongly.

inveigle *v* coax by cunning or trickery.

invent *v* **1** think up or create (something new). **2** make up (a story, excuse, etc.). **invention** *n* **1** something invented. **2** ability to invent. **inventive** *adj* creative and resourceful. **inventiveness** *n* **inventor** *n*

inventory *n, pl* -**tories** detailed list of goods or furnishings.

inverse *adj* **1** reversed in effect, sequence, direction, etc. **2** *Maths* linking two variables in such a way that one increases as the other decreases. **inversely** *adv*

invert *v* turn upside down or inside out. **inversion** *n* **inverted commas** quotation marks.

invertebrate *n* animal with no backbone.

invest *v* **1** spend (money, time, etc.) on something with the expectation of profit. **2** (foll. by *with*) give (power or rights) to. **investment** *n* **1** money invested. **2** something invested in. **investor** *n* **invest in** *v* buy.

investigate *v* inquire into, examine. **investigation** *n* **investigative** *adj* **investigator** *n*

investiture *n* formal installation of a person in an office or rank.

inveterate *adj* firmly established in a habit or condition.

invidious *adj* likely to cause resentment.

invigilate *v* supervise people sitting an examination. **invigilator** *n*

invigorate *v* give energy to, refresh.

invincible *adj* impossible to defeat. **invincibility** *n*

inviolable *adj* unable to be broken or violated.

inviolate *adj* unharmed, unaffected.

invisible *adj* not able to be seen. **invisibly** *adv* **invisibility** *n*

invite *v* **1** request the company of. **2** ask politely for. **3** encourage or provoke, e.g. *the two works inevitably invite comparison.* ♦ *n* **4** *Informal* invitation. **inviting** *adj* tempting, attractive. **invitation** *n*

in-vitro *adj* happening outside the body in an artificial environment.

invoice *v, n* (present with) a bill for goods or services supplied.

invoke *v* **1** put (a law or penalty) into operation. **2** prompt or cause (a certain feeling). **3** call on (a god or spirit) for help, inspiration, etc. **invocation** *n*

involuntary *adj* not done consciously, unintentional. **involuntarily** *adv*

involve *v* **1** include as a necessary part. **2** affect, concern. **3** implicate (a person). **involved** *adj* **1** complicated. **2** concerned, taking part. **involvement** *n*

invulnerable *adj* not able to be wounded or harmed.

inward *adj, adv* see IN.

iodine *n Chem* bluish-black element used in medicine and photography. **iodize** *v* treat with iodine.

ion *n* electrically charged atom. **ionic** *adj* **ionize** *v* change into ions. **ionization** *n* **ionosphere** *n* region of ionized air in the upper atmosphere that reflects radio waves.

iota *n* very small amount.

IOU *n* signed paper acknowledging debt.

IPA International Phonetic Alphabet.

ipso facto *adv Latin* by that very fact.

IQ intelligence quotient.

IRA Irish Republican Army.

irascible *adj* easily angered. **irascibility** *n*

irate *adj* very angry.

ire *n Lit* anger.

iridescent *adj* having shimmering changing colours like a rainbow. **iridescence** *n*

iridium *n Chem* very hard corrosion-resistant metal.

iris *n* **1** coloured circular membrane of the eye containing the pupil. **2** tall plant with purple, yellow, or white flowers.

Irish *adj* of Ireland.

irk *v* irritate, annoy. **irksome** *adj* irritating, annoying.

iron *n* **1** strong silvery-white metallic element, widely used for structural and engineering purposes. **2** appliance used, when heated, to press clothes. **3** metal-headed golf club. ♦ *pl* **4** chains, restraints. ♦ *adj* **5** made of iron. **6** strong, inflexible, e.g. *iron will.* ♦ *v* **7** smooth (clothes or fabric) with an iron. **ironbark** *n* Australian eucalyptus with hard rough bark. **ironing** *n* clothes to be ironed. **ironing board** long cloth-covered board with folding legs, for ironing clothes on. **Iron Age** era when iron tools were used. **iron out** *v* settle (a problem) through discussion.

ironic, ironical *adj* **1** using irony. **2** odd or amusing because the opposite of what one would expect. **ironically** *adv*

ironmonger *n* shopkeeper or shop dealing in hardware. **ironmongery** *n*

ironstone *n* rock consisting mainly of iron ore.

irony *n, pl* **-nies 1** mildly sarcastic use of words to imply the opposite of what is said. **2** aspect of a situation that is odd or amusing because the opposite of what one would expect.

irradiate v subject to or treat with radiation. **irradiation** n

irrational adj not based on or not using logical reasoning.

irredeemable adj not able to be reformed or corrected.

irreducible adj impossible to put in a simpler form.

irrefutable adj impossible to deny or disprove.

irregular adj 1 not regular or even. 2 not conforming to accepted practice. 3 (of a word) not following the typical pattern of formation in a language. **irregularly** adv **irregularity** n, pl -ties

irrelevant adj not connected with the matter in hand. **irrelevantly** adv **irrelevance** n

irreparable adj not able to be repaired or put right. **irreparably** adv

irreplaceable adj impossible to replace.

irreproachable adj blameless, faultless.

irresistible adj too attractive or strong to resist. **irresistibly** adv

irrespective of prep without taking account of.

irresponsible adj 1 not showing or not done with due care for the consequences of one's actions or attitudes. 2 not capable of accepting responsibility. **irresponsibility** n

irreverent adj not showing due respect. **irreverence** n

irreversible adj not able to be reversed or put right again, e.g. irreversible change. **irreversibly** adv

irrevocable adj not possible to change or undo. **irrevocably** adv

irrigate v supply (land) with water by artificial channels or pipes. **irrigation** n

irritate v 1 annoy, anger. 2 cause (a

body part) to itch or become inflamed. **irritable** adj easily annoyed. **irritably** adv **irritant** n, adj (person or thing) causing irritation. **irritation** n

is v third person singular present tense of BE.

ISA (in Britain) Individual Savings Account.

isinglass [**ize**-ing-glass] n kind of gelatine obtained from some freshwater fish.

Islam n 1 Muslim religion teaching that there is one God and that Mohammed is his prophet. 2 Muslim countries and civilization. **Islamic** adj

island n piece of land surrounded by water. **islander** n 1 person who lives on an island. 2 (I-) NZ Pacific Islander.

isle n Poetic island. **islet** n small island.

isobar [**ice**-oh-bar] n line on a map connecting places of equal atmospheric pressure.

isolate v 1 place apart or alone. 2 Chem obtain (a substance) in uncombined form. **isolation** n **isolationism** n policy of not participating in international affairs. **isolationist** n, adj

isomer [**ice**-oh-mer] n substance whose molecules contain the same atoms as another but in a different arrangement.

isometric adj relating to muscular contraction without shortening of the muscle. **isometrics** pl n isometric exercises.

isosceles triangle [ice-**soss**-ill-eez] n triangle with two sides of equal length.

isotherm [**ice**-oh-therm] n line on a map connecting points of equal temperature.

isotope [**ice**-oh-tope] n one of two or more atoms with the same number of protons in the nucleus but a different number of neutrons.

ISP Internet service provider.

issue n 1 topic of interest or discussion.

2 reason for quarrelling. **3** particular edition of a magazine or newspaper. **4** outcome or result. ♦ v **6** make (a statement etc.) publicly. **7** supply officially (with). **8** produce and make available. **take issue with** disagree with.

isthmus [**iss**-muss] n, pl **-muses** narrow strip of land connecting two areas of land.

it pron **1** refers to a nonhuman, animal, plant, or inanimate object. **2** refers to a thing mentioned or being discussed. **3** used as the subject of impersonal verbs, e.g. it's windy. **4** Informal crucial or ultimate point. **its** adj, pron belonging to it. **it's 1** it is. **2** it has. **itself** pron **emphatic form of** IT.

☑ SPELLING TIP

Many people find **its** and **it's** confusing. But it's quite simple really. **It's** only needs an apostrophe when it is used as the informal short form of 'it is' or 'it has'.

IT information technology.

italic adj (of printing type) sloping to the right. **italics** pl n this type, used for emphasis. **italicize** v put in italics.

itch n **1** skin irritation causing a desire to scratch. **2** restless desire. ♦ v **3** have an itch. **itchy** adj

item n **1** single thing in a list or collection. **2** piece of information. **itemize** v make a list of.

iterate v repeat. **iteration** n

itinerant adj travelling from place to place.

itinerary n, pl **-aries** detailed plan of a journey.

ITV (in Britain) Independent Television.

IUD intrauterine device: a coil-shaped contraceptive fitted into the womb.

IVF in-vitro fertilization.

ivory n **1** hard white bony substance forming the tusks of elephants. ♦ adj **2** yellowish-white. **ivory tower** remoteness from the realities of everyday life.

ivy n, pl **ivies** evergreen climbing plant.

iwi [**ee**-wee] n NZ Maori tribe.

J j

jab *v* jabbing, jabbed **1** poke sharply.
♦ *n* **2** quick punch or poke. **3** *Informal*
injection.

jabber *v* talk rapidly or incoherently.

jabiru *n* large white-and-black
Australian stork.

jacaranda *n* tropical tree with
sweet-smelling wood.

jack *n* **1** device for raising a motor
vehicle or other heavy object. **2**
playing card with a picture of a
pageboy. **3** *Bowls* small white bowl
aimed at by the players. **4** socket in
electrical equipment into which a plug
fits. **5** flag flown at the bow of a ship,
showing nationality. **jack-up** *n NZ
informal* something achieved
dishonestly. **jack up** *v* **1** raise with a
jack. **2** *NZ informal* organize by
dishonest means.

jackal *n* doglike wild animal of Africa
and Asia.

jackaroo, jackeroo *n, pl* -roos *Aust*
trainee on a sheep station.

jackass *n* **1** fool. **2** male of the ass.
laughing jackass same as KOOKABURRA.

jackboot *n* high military boot.

jackdaw *n* black-and-grey Eurasian
bird of the crow family.

jacket *n* **1** short coat. **2** skin of a baked
potato. **3** outer paper cover on a
hardback book.

jackknife *v* **1** (of an articulated truck)
go out of control so that the trailer
swings round at a sharp angle to the
cab. ♦ *n* **2** large clasp knife.

jackpot *n* largest prize that may be
won in a game. **hit the jackpot** be
very successful through luck.

Jacobean [jak-a-**bee**-an] *adj* of the
reign of James I of England.

Jacobite *n* supporter of James II of
England and his descendants.

Jacquard [**jak**-ard] *n* fabric in which
the design is incorporated into the
weave.

Jacuzzi [jak-**oo**-zee] *n* ® circular bath
with a device that swirls the water.

jade *n* **1** ornamental semiprecious
stone, usu. dark green. ♦ *adj* **2**
bluish-green.

jaded *adj* tired and unenthusiastic.

jagged [**jag**-gid] *adj* having an uneven
edge with sharp points.

jaguar *n* large S American spotted cat.

jail *n* **1** prison. ♦ *v* **2** send to prison.
jailer *n* **jailbird** *n Informal* person
who has often been in prison.

jalopy [jal-**lop**-ee] *n, pl* -lopies *Informal*
old car.

jam¹ *v* jamming, jammed **1** pack
tightly into a place. **2** crowd or
congest. **3** make or become stuck. **4**
Radio block (another station) with
impulses of equal wavelength. **5** *n* **6**
hold-up of traffic. **7** *Informal* awkward
situation. **jam on the brakes** apply
brakes fiercely. **jam-packed** *adj* filled
to capacity. **jam session** informal
rock or jazz performance.

jam² *n* food made from fruit boiled with
sugar.

jamb *n* side post of a door or window
frame.

jamboree *n* large gathering or
celebration.

Jan. January.

jandal *n NZ* sandal with a strap
between the toes.

jangle *v* **1** (cause to) make a harsh
ringing noise. **2** (of nerves) be upset or
irritated.

janitor *n* caretaker of a school or other

building.

January *n* first month of the year.

japan *n* **1** very hard varnish, usu. black. ♦ *v* **-panning, -panned 2** cover with this varnish.

jape *n Old-fashioned* joke or prank.

japonica *n* shrub with red flowers.

jar[1] *n* wide-mouthed container, usu. round and made of glass.

jar[2] *v* **jarring, jarred 1** have a disturbing or unpleasant effect. **2** jolt or bump. ♦ *n* **3** jolt or shock.

jargon *n* specialized technical language of a particular subject.

jarrah *n* Australian eucalypt yielding valuable timber.

jasmine *n* shrub with sweet-smelling yellow or white flowers.

jasper *n* red, yellow, dark green, or brown variety of quartz.

jaundice *n* disease marked by yellowness of the skin. **jaundiced** *adj* **1** (of an attitude or opinion) bitter or cynical. **2** having jaundice.

jaunt *n* short journey for pleasure.

jaunty *adj* **-tier, -tiest 1** sprightly and cheerful. **2** smart. **jauntily** *adv*

javelin *n* light spear thrown in sports competitions.

jaw *n* **1** one of the bones in which the teeth are set. **2** *pl* **3** mouth. **4** gripping part of a tool. **5** narrow opening of a gorge or valley. ♦ *v* **6** *Slang* talk lengthily.

jay *n* bird with a pinkish body and blue-and-black wings.

jaywalker *n* person who crosses the road in a careless or dangerous manner. **jaywalking** *n*

jazz *n* kind of music with an exciting rhythm, usu. involving improvisation. **jazzy** *adj* flashy or showy. **jazz up** *v* make more lively.

JCB *n* ® *Brit* construction machine with a shovel at the front and an excavator

at the rear.

jealous *adj* **1** fearful of losing a partner or possession to a rival. **2** envious. **3** suspiciously watchful. **jealously** *adv* **jealousy** *n, pl* **-sies**

jeans *pl n* casual denim trousers.

Jeep *n* ® four-wheel-drive motor vehicle.

jeer *v* **1** scoff or deride. ♦ *n* **2** cry of derision.

Jehovah *n* God.

jejune *adj* **1** simple or naive. **2** dull or boring.

jell *v* **1** form into a jelly-like substance. **2** take on a definite form.

jelly *n, pl* **-lies 1** soft food made of liquid set with gelatine. **2** jam made from fruit juice and sugar. **jellied** *adj* prepared in a jelly.

jellyfish *n* small jelly-like sea animal.

jemmy *n, pl* **-mies** short steel crowbar used by burglars.

jenny *n, pl* **-nies** female ass or wren.

jeopardy *n* danger. **jeopardize** *v* place in danger.

jerboa *n* small mouselike rodent with long hind legs.

jerk *v* **1** move or throw abruptly. ♦ *n* **2** sharp or abruptly stopped movement. **3** *Slang* contemptible person. **jerky** *adj* sudden or abrupt. **jerkily** *adv* **jerkiness** *n*

jerkin *n* sleeveless jacket.

jerry-built *adj* built badly using flimsy materials.

jerry can *n* flat-sided can for carrying petrol etc.

jersey *n* **1** knitted jumper. **2** machine-knitted fabric. **3** (J-) breed of cow.

Jerusalem artichoke *n* small yellowish-white root vegetable.

jest *n, v* joke.

jester *n Hist* professional clown at court.

Jesuit [**jezz**-yoo-it] *n* member of the

Society of Jesus, a Roman Catholic order.

jet¹ n **1** aircraft driven by jet propulsion. **2** stream of liquid or gas, esp. one forced from a small hole. **3** nozzle from which gas or liquid is forced. ♦ v **jetting, jetted 4** fly by jet aircraft. **jetboat** n motorboat propelled by a jet of water. **jet lag** fatigue caused by crossing time zones in an aircraft. **jet propulsion** propulsion by thrust provided by a jet of gas or liquid. **jet-propelled** adj **jet set** rich and fashionable people who travel the world for pleasure.

jet² n hard black mineral. **jet-black** adj glossy black.

jetsam n goods thrown overboard to lighten a ship.

jettison v -**soning**, -**soned 1** abandon. **2** throw overboard.

jetty n, pl -**ties** small pier.

Jew n **1** person whose religion is Judaism. **2** descendant of the ancient Hebrews. **Jewish** adj **Jewry** n Jews collectively. **jew's-harp** n musical instrument held between the teeth and played by plucking a metal strip with one's finger.

jewel n **1** precious stone. **2** special person or thing. **jeweller** n dealer in jewels. **jewellery** n objects decorated with precious stones.

jewfish n Aust freshwater catfish.

jib¹ n triangular sail set in front of a mast.

jib² v **jibbing, jibbed** (of a horse, person, etc.) stop and refuse to go on. **jib at** v object to (a proposal etc.).

jib³ n projecting arm of a crane or derrick.

jibe¹ n, v taunt or jeer.

jibe² v same as GYBE.

jiffy n, pl -**fies** Informal very short period of time.

jig n **1** type of lively dance. **2** music for it. **3** device that holds a component in place for cutting etc. ♦ v **jigging, jigged 4** make jerky up-and-down movements.

jiggery-pokery n Informal trickery or mischief.

jiggle v move up and down with short jerky movements.

jigsaw n **1** (also **jigsaw puzzle**) picture cut into interlocking pieces, which the user tries to fit together again. **2** mechanical saw for cutting along curved lines.

jihad n Islamic holy war against unbelievers.

jilt v leave or reject (one's lover).

jingle n **1** catchy verse or song used in a radio or television advert. **2** gentle ringing noise. ♦ v **3** (cause to) make a gentle ringing sound.

jingoism n aggressive nationalism. **jingoistic** adj

jinks pl n **high jinks** boisterous merrymaking.

jinni n, pl **jinn** spirit in Muslim mythology.

jinx n **1** person or thing bringing bad luck. ♦ v **2** be or put a jinx on.

jitters pl n worried nervousness. **jittery** adj nervous.

jive n **1** lively dance of the 1940s and '50s. ♦ v **2** dance the jive.

job n **1** occupation or paid employment. **2** task to be done. **3** Informal difficult task. **4** Brit, Aust & NZ informal crime, esp. robbery. **jobbing** adj doing individual jobs for payment. **jobless** adj, pl n unemployed (people). **job lot** assortment sold together. **job sharing** splitting of one post between two people working part-time.

jockey n **1** (professional) rider of racehorses. ♦ v **2** **jockey for position** manoeuvre to obtain an advantage.

jockstrap n belt with a pouch to support the genitals, worn by male athletes.

jocose [joke-**kohss**] adj playful or humorous.

jocular adj 1 fond of joking. 2 meant as a joke. **jocularity** n **jocularly** adv

jocund [**jok**-kund] adj Lit merry or cheerful.

jodhpurs pl n riding trousers, loose-fitting above the knee but tight below.

joey n Aust young kangaroo.

jog v jogging, jogged 1 run at a gentle pace, esp. for exercise. 2 nudge slightly. ♦ n 3 slow run. **jogger** n **jogging** n

joggle v shake or move jerkily.

joie de vivre [jwah de **veev**-ra] n French enjoyment of life.

join v 1 become a member (of). 2 come into someone's company. 3 take part (in). 4 come or bring together. 5 n 6 place where two things are joined. **join up** v enlist in the armed services. **joined-up** adj integrated by an overall strategy joined-up government.

joiner n maker of finished woodwork. **joinery** n joiner's work.

joint adj 1 shared by two or more. ♦ n 2 place where bones meet but can move. 3 junction of two or more parts or objects. 4 piece of meat for roasting. 5 Slang house or place, esp. a disreputable bar or nightclub. 6 Slang marijuana cigarette. ♦ v 7 divide meat into joints. **out of joint 1** disorganized. 2 dislocated. **jointed** adj **jointly** adv

joist n horizontal beam that helps support a floor or ceiling.

jojoba [hoe-**hoe**-ba] n shrub of SW North America whose seeds yield oil used in cosmetics.

joke n 1 thing said or done to cause laughter. 2 amusing or ridiculous person or thing. ♦ v 3 make jokes. **jokey** adj **jokingly** adv **joker** n 1 person who jokes. 2 Slang fellow. 3 extra card in a pack, counted as any other in certain games.

jolly adj -lier, -liest 1 (of a person) happy and cheerful. 2 (of an occasion) merry and festive. 3 v -lying, -lied 4 **jolly along** try to keep (someone) cheerful by flattery or coaxing. **jollity** n **jollification** n merrymaking.

jolt n 1 unpleasant surprise or shock. 2 sudden jerk or bump. ♦ v 3 surprise or shock. 4 move or shake with a jerk.

jonquil n fragrant narcissus.

josh v Chiefly US slang tease.

joss stick n stick of incense giving off a sweet smell when burnt.

jostle v knock or push against.

jot v jotting, jotted 1 write briefly. ♦ n 2 very small amount. **jotter** n notebook. **jottings** pl n notes jotted down.

joule [jool] n Physics unit of work or energy.

journal n 1 daily newspaper or magazine. 2 daily record of events. **journalese** n superficial style of writing, found in some newspapers. **journalism** n writing in or editing of newspapers and magazines. **journalist** n **journalistic** adj

journey n 1 act or process of travelling from one place to another. 2 v 3 travel.

journeyman n qualified craftsman employed by another.

joust Hist ♦ n 1 combat with lances between two mounted knights. ♦ v 2 fight on horseback using lances.

jovial adj happy and cheerful. **jovially** adv **joviality** n

jowl[1] n 1 lower jaw. ♦ pl 2 cheeks.

jowl[2] n fatty flesh hanging from the lower jaw.

joy n 1 feeling of great delight or

pleasure. **2** cause of this feeling.
joyful *adj* **joyless** *adj* **joyous** *adj*
extremely happy and enthusiastic.
joyriding *n* driving for pleasure, esp.
in a stolen car. **joyride** *n* **joyrider** *n*
joystick *n* control device for an aircraft
or computer.

JP (in Britain) Justice of the Peace.

JPEG [**jay**-peg] *Computing* **1** standard
compressed file format used for
pictures. **2** picture held in this file
format.

Jr Junior.

JSA jobseeker's allowance: in Britain, a
payment made to unemployed people.

jubilant *adj* feeling or expressing great
joy. **jubilantly** *adv* **jubilation** *n*

jubilee *n* special anniversary, esp. 25th
(**silver jubilee**) or 50th (**golden
jubilee**).

Judaism *n* religion of the Jews, based
on the Old Testament and the Talmud.
Judaic *adj*

judder *v* **1** vibrate violently. ♦ *n* **2**
violent vibration. **judder bar** *NZ*
raised strip across a road designed to
slow down vehicles.

judge *n* **1** public official who tries cases
and passes sentence in a court of law.
2 person who decides the outcome of
a contest. **3** *v* **4** act as a judge. **5**
appraise critically. **6** consider
something to be the case. **judgment,
judgement** *n* **1** opinion reached after
careful thought. **2** verdict of a judge. **3**
ability to appraise critically.
judgmental, judgemental *adj*

judicial *adj* **1** of or by a court or judge.
2 showing or using judgment.
judicially *adv*

judiciary *n* system of courts and
judges.

judicious *adj* well-judged and sensible.
judiciously *adv*

judo *n* sport in which two opponents
try to throw each other to the ground.

jug *n* container for liquids, with a
handle and small spout. **jugged hare**
hare stewed in an earthenware pot.

juggernaut *n* **1** *Brit* large heavy truck.
2 any irresistible destructive force.

juggle *v* **1** throw and catch (several
objects) so that most are in the air at
the same time. **2** manipulate (figures,
situations, etc.) to suit one's purposes.
juggler *n*

jugular, jugular vein *n* one of three
large veins of the neck that return
blood from the head to the heart.

juice *n* **1** liquid part of vegetables, fruit,
or meat. **2** *Brit, Aust & NZ informal*
petrol. ♦ *pl* **3** fluids secreted by an
organ of the body. **juicy** *adj* **1** full of
juice. **2** interesting.

jujitsu *n* Japanese art of wrestling and
self-defence.

juju *n* W African magic charm or fetish.

jukebox *n* coin-operated machine on
which records, CDs, or videos can be
played.

Jul. July.

julep *n* sweet alcoholic drink.

July *n* seventh month of the year.

jumble *n* **1** confused heap or state. **2**
articles for a jumble sale. ♦ *v* **3** mix in a
disordered way. **jumble sale** sale of
miscellaneous second-hand items.

jumbo *adj* **1** *Informal* very large. ♦ *n* **2**
(also **jumbo jet**) large jet airliner.

jumbuck *n* *Aust* old-fashioned slang
sheep.

jump *v* **1** leap or spring into the air
using the leg muscles. **2** move quickly
and suddenly. **3** jerk with surprise. **4**
increase suddenly. **5** change the
subject abruptly. **6** *Informal* attack
without warning. **7** pass over or miss
out (intervening material). ♦ *n* **8** act of
jumping. **9** sudden rise. **10** break in
continuity. **jump the gun** act
prematurely. **jump the queue** not
wait one's turn. **jumpy** *adj* nervous.

jump at v accept (a chance etc.) gladly. **jumped-up** adj arrogant because of recent promotion. **jump jet** fixed-wing jet that can take off and land vertically. **jump leads** electric cables to connect a flat car battery to an external battery to aid starting an engine. **jump on** v attack suddenly and forcefully. **jump suit** one-piece garment of trousers and top.

jumper n sweater or pullover.

Jun. 1 June. **2** Junior.

junction n place where routes, railway lines, or roads meet.

juncture n point in time, esp. a critical one.

June n sixth month of the year.

jungle n **1** tropical forest of dense tangled vegetation. **2** confusion or mess. **3** place of intense struggle for survival.

junior adj **1** of lower standing. **2** younger. ♦ n **3** junior person.

juniper n evergreen shrub with purple berries.

junk[1] n **1** discarded or useless objects. **2** Informal rubbish. **3** Slang narcotic drug, esp. heroin. **junkie, junky** n, pl **junkies** Slang drug addict. **junk food** snack food of low nutritional value. **junk mail** unwanted mail advertising goods or services.

junk[2] n flat-bottomed Chinese sailing boat.

junket n **1** excursion by public officials paid for from public funds. **2** sweetened milk set with rennet.

junta n group of military officers holding power in a country, esp. after a coup.

Jupiter n **1** king of the Roman gods. **2** largest of the planets.

juridical adj of law or the administration of justice.

jurisdiction n **1** right or power to administer justice and apply laws. **2** extent of this right or power.

jurisprudence n science or philosophy of law.

jurist n expert in law.

jury n, pl **-ries** group of people sworn to deliver a verdict in a court of law. **juror** n member of a jury.

just adv **1** very recently. **2** at this instant. **3** merely, only. **4** exactly. **5** barely. **6** really. ♦ adj **7** fair or impartial in action or judgment. **8** proper or right. **justly** adv **justness** n

justice n **1** quality of being just. **2** judicial proceedings. **3** judge or magistrate. **justice of the peace** (in Britain) person who is authorized to act as a judge in a local court of law.

justify v **-fying, -fied 1** prove right or reasonable. **2** explain the reasons for an action. **3** align (text) so the margins are straight. **justifiable** adj **justifiably** adv **justification** n

jut v **jutting, jutted** project or stick out.

jute n plant fibre, used for rope, canvas, etc.

juvenile adj **1** young. **2** of or suitable for young people. **3** immature and rather silly. ♦ n **4** young person or child. **juvenilia** pl n works produced in an author's youth. **juvenile delinquent** young person guilty of a crime.

juxtapose v put side by side. **juxtaposition** n

K k

K *Informal* thousand(s).

Kaffir [**kaf**-fer] *n S Afr taboo* Black African.

kaftan *n* **1** long loose Eastern garment. **2** woman's dress resembling this.

kaiser [**kize**-er] *n Hist* German or Austro-Hungarian emperor.

kak *n S Afr slang* **1** faeces. **2** rubbish.

Kalashnikov *n* Russian-made automatic rifle.

kale *n* cabbage with crinkled leaves.

kaleidoscope *n* tube-shaped toy containing loose coloured pieces reflected by mirrors so that intricate patterns form when the tube is twisted. **kaleidoscopic** *adj*

kamikaze [kam-mee-**kah**-zee] *n* **1** (in World War II) Japanese pilot who performed a suicide mission. ♦ *adj* **2** (of an action) undertaken in the knowledge that it will kill or injure the person performing it.

kangaroo *n, pl* **-roos** Australian marsupial which moves by jumping with its powerful hind legs. **kangaroo court** unofficial court set up by a group to discipline its members. **kangaroo paw** Australian plant with green-and-red flowers.

kaolin *n* fine white clay used to make porcelain and in some medicines.

kapok *n* fluffy fibre from a tropical tree, used to stuff cushions etc.

kaput [kap-**poot**] *adj Informal* ruined or broken.

karaoke *n* form of entertainment in which people sing over a prerecorded backing tape.

karate *n* Japanese system of unarmed combat using blows with the feet, hands, elbows, and legs.

karma *n Buddhism, Hinduism* person's actions affecting his or her fate in the next reincarnation.

karri *n, pl* **-ris** **1** Australian eucalypt. **2** its wood, used for building.

katipo *n* small poisonous New Zealand spider.

kayak *n* **1** Inuit canoe made of sealskins stretched over a frame. **2** fibreglass or canvas-covered canoe of this design.

kbyte *Computers* kilobyte.

kebab *n* **1** dish of small pieces of meat grilled on skewers. **2** (also **doner kebab**) grilled minced lamb served in a split slice of unleavened bread.

kedgeree *n* dish of fish with rice and eggs.

keel *n* main lengthways timber or steel support along the base of a ship. **keel over** *v* **1** turn upside down. **2** *Informal* collapse suddenly.

keen[1] *adj* **1** eager or enthusiastic. **2** intense or strong. **3** intellectually acute. **4** (of the senses) capable of recognizing small distinctions. **5** sharp. **6** cold and penetrating. **7** competitive. **keenly** *adv* **keenness** *n*

keen[2] *v* wail over the dead.

keep *v* **keeping, kept** **1** have or retain possession of. **2** store. **3** stay or cause to stay (in, on, or at a place or position). **4** continue or persist. **5** detain (someone). **6** look after or maintain. **7** *n* **8** cost of food and everyday expenses. **keeper** *n* **1** person who looks after animals in a zoo. **2** person in charge of a museum or collection. **3** short for GOALKEEPER. **keeping** *n* care or charge. **in, out of keeping with** appropriate *or* inappropriate for. **keep fit** exercises designed to promote physical fitness.

keepsake n gift treasured for the sake of the giver. **keep up** v maintain at the current level. **keep up with** v maintain a pace set by (someone).

keg n small metal beer barrel.

kelp n large brown seaweed.

kelpie n Australian sheepdog with a smooth coat and upright ears.

kelvin n SI unit of temperature. **Kelvin scale** temperature scale starting at absolute zero (-273.15° Celsius).

ken v **kenning**, **kenned** or **kent** Scot know. **beyond one's ken** beyond one's range of knowledge.

kendo n Japanese sport of fencing using wooden staves.

kennel n 1 hutlike shelter for a dog. ♦ pl 2 place for breeding, boarding, or training dogs.

kept v past of KEEP.

keratin n fibrous protein found in the hair and nails.

kerb n edging to a footpath. **kerb crawling** Brit act of driving slowly beside a pavement to pick up a prostitute.

kerchief n piece of cloth worn over the head or round the neck.

kerfuffle n Informal commotion or disorder.

kernel n 1 seed of a nut, cereal, or fruit stone. 2 central and essential part of something.

kerosene n US, Canadian, Aust & NZ liquid mixture distilled from petroleum and used as a fuel or solvent.

kestrel n type of small falcon.

ketch n two-masted sailing ship.

ketchup n thick cold sauce, usu. made of tomatoes.

kettle n container with a spout and handle used for boiling water. **kettledrum** n large bowl-shaped metal drum.

key n 1 device for operating a lock by moving a bolt. 2 device turned to wind a clock, operate a machine, etc. 3 any of a set of levers or buttons pressed to operate a typewriter, computer, or musical keyboard instrument. 4 Music set of related notes. 5 something crucial in providing an explanation or interpretation. 6 means of achieving a desired end. 7 list of explanations of codes, symbols, etc. ♦ adj 8 of great importance. ♦ v 9 (also **key in**) enter (text) using a keyboard. **keyed up** very excited or nervous.

keyboard n 1 set of keys on a piano, computer, etc. 2 musical instrument played using a keyboard. ♦ v 3 enter (text) using a keyboard.

keyhole n opening for inserting a key into a lock.

keynote 1 n 2 dominant idea of a speech etc. 3 basic note of a musical key.

keystone n 1 most important part of a process, organization, etc. 2 central stone of an arch which locks the others in position.

kg kilogram(s).

KGB n (formerly) Soviet secret police.

khaki adj 1 dull yellowish-brown. ♦ n 2 hard-wearing fabric of this colour used for military uniforms.

kHz kilohertz.

kia ora [kee-a **aw**-ra] interj NZ Maori greeting.

kibbutz n, pl **kibbutzim** communal farm or factory in Israel.

kibosh n **put the kibosh on** Slang put a stop to.

kick v 1 drive, push, or strike with the foot. 2 (of a gun) recoil when fired. 3 Informal object or resist. 4 Informal free oneself of (an addiction). 5 Rugby score with a kick. ♦ n 6 thrust or blow with the foot. 7 recoil of a gun. 8 Informal excitement or thrill.

kickback n money paid illegally for favours done. **kick off** v 1 start a game of soccer. 2 Informal begin. **kick out** v dismiss or expel forcibly. **kick-start** v start (a motorcycle) by kicking a pedal. **kick up** v Informal create (a fuss).

kid[1] n 1 Informal child. 2 young goat. 3 leather made from the skin of a young goat.

kid[2] v kidding, kidded Informal tease or deceive (someone).

kidnap v -napping, -napped seize and hold (a person) to ransom. **kidnapper** n

kidney n 1 either of the pair of organs that filter waste products from the blood to produce urine. 2 animal kidney used as food. **kidney bean** reddish-brown kidney-shaped bean, edible when cooked.

kill v 1 cause the death of. 2 Informal cause (someone) pain or discomfort. 3 put an end to. 4 pass (time). 5 act of killing. 6 animals or birds killed in a hunt. **killer** n **killing** Informal ♦ adj 1 very tiring. 2 very funny. ♦ n 3 sudden financial success. **killjoy** n person who spoils others' pleasure.

kiln n oven for baking, drying, or processing pottery, bricks, etc.

kilo n short for KILOGRAM.

kilo- combining form one thousand, e.g. kilometre.

kilobyte n Computers 1024 units of information.

kilogram, kilogramme n one thousand grams.

kilohertz n one thousand hertz.

kilometre n one thousand metres.

kilowatt n Electricity one thousand watts.

kilt n knee-length pleated tartan skirt worn orig. by Scottish Highlanders. **kilted** adj

kimono n, pl -nos 1 loose wide-sleeved Japanese robe, fastened with a sash. 2 European dressing gown resembling this.

kin, kinsfolk n person's relatives collectively. **kinship** n

kind[1] adj considerate, friendly, and helpful. **kindness** n **kindly** adj 1 having a warm-hearted nature. 2 pleasant or agreeable. ♦ adv 3 in a considerate way. 4 please, e.g. will you kindly be quiet! **kindliness** n **kind-hearted** adj

kind[2] n 1 class or group with common characteristics. 2 essential nature or character. **in kind** 1 (of payment) in goods rather than money. 2 with something similar. **kind of** to a certain extent.

kindergarten n class or school for children under six years old.

kindle v 1 set (a fire) alight. 2 (of a fire) start to burn. 3 arouse or be aroused. **kindling** n dry wood or straw for starting fires.

kindred adj 1 having similar qualities. 2 related by blood or marriage. ♦ n 3 same as KIN.

kindy, kindie n, pl -dies Aust & NZ informal kindergarten.

kinetic [kin-net-ik] adj relating to or caused by motion.

king n 1 male ruler of a monarchy. 2 ruler or chief. 3 best or most important of its kind. 4 piece in chess that must be defended. 5 playing card with a picture of a king on it. **kingdom** n 1 state ruled by a king or queen. 2 division of the natural world. **king prawn** large prawn, fished commercially in Australian waters. **kingship** n **king-size, king-sized** adj larger than standard size.

kingfisher n small bird, often with a bright-coloured plumage, that dives for fish.

kingpin n most important person in an organization.

kink n **1** twist or bend in rope, wire, hair, etc. **2** Informal quirk in someone's personality. **kinky** adj **1** Slang given to unusual sexual practices. **2** full of kinks.

kiosk n **1** small booth selling drinks, cigarettes, newspapers, etc. **2** public telephone box.

kip n, v **kipping**, **kipped** Informal sleep.

kipper n cleaned, salted, and smoked herring.

kirk n Scot church.

Kirsch n brandy made from cherries.

kismet n fate or destiny.

kiss v **1** touch with the lips in affection or greeting. **2** join lips with a person in love or desire. ♦ n **3** touch with the lips. **kisser** n Slang mouth or face. **kissagram** n greetings service in which a messenger kisses the person celebrating. **kissing crust** NZ & S Afr soft end of a loaf of bread where two loaves have been separated. **kiss of life** mouth-to-mouth resuscitation.

kist n S Afr large wooden chest.

kit n **1** outfit or equipment for a specific purpose. **2** set of pieces of equipment sold ready to be assembled. **3** NZ flax basket. **kitbag** n bag for a soldier's or traveller's belongings. **kit out** v **kitting**, **kitted** provide with clothes or equipment needed for a particular activity. **kitset** n NZ unassembled pieces for constructing a piece of furniture.

kitchen n room used for cooking. **kitchenette** n small kitchen. **kitchen garden** garden for growing vegetables, herbs, etc.

kite n **1** light frame covered with a thin material flown on a string in the wind. **2** large hawk with a forked tail. **Kite mark** Brit official mark on articles approved by the British Standards Institution.

kith n **kith and kin** friends and relatives.

kitsch n art or literature with popular sentimental appeal.

kitten n young cat. **kittenish** adj lively and flirtatious.

kittiwake n type of seagull.

kitty n, pl **-ties 1** communal fund. **2** total amount wagered in certain gambling games.

kiwi n **1** New Zealand flightless bird with a long beak and no tail. **2** Informal New Zealander. **kiwi fruit** edible fruit with a fuzzy brownish skin and green flesh.

klaxon n loud horn used on emergency vehicles as a warning signal.

kleptomania n compulsive tendency to steal. **kleptomaniac** n

kloof n S Afr mountain pass or gorge.

km kilometre(s).

knack n **1** skilful way of doing something. **2** innate ability.

knacker n Brit buyer of old horses for killing.

knackered adj Slang **1** extremely tired. **2** no longer functioning.

knapsack n soldier's or traveller's bag worn strapped on the back.

knave n **1** jack at cards. **2** Obs dishonest man.

knead v **1** work (dough) into a smooth mixture with the hands. **2** squeeze or press with the hands.

knee n **1** joint between thigh and lower leg. **2** lap. **3** part of a garment covering the knee. ♦ v **kneeing**, **kneed 4** strike or push with the knee. **kneecap** n **1** bone in front of the knee. ♦ v **2** shoot in the kneecap. **kneejerk** adj (of a reply or reaction) automatic and predictable. **knees-up** n Brit informal party.

kneel *v* **kneeling, kneeled** *or* **knelt** fall or rest on one's knees.

knell *n* **1** sound of a bell, esp. at a funeral or death. **2** portent of doom.

knew *v* past tense of KNOW.

knickerbockers *pl n* loose-fitting short trousers gathered in at the knee.

knickers *pl n* woman's or girl's undergarment covering the lower trunk and having legs or legholes.

knick-knack *n* trifle or trinket.

knife *n, pl* **knives 1** cutting tool or weapon consisting of a sharp-edged blade with a handle. ♦ *v* **2** cut or stab with a knife.

knight *n* **1** man who has been given a knighthood. **2** *Hist* man who served his lord as a mounted armoured soldier. **3** chess piece shaped like a horse's head. ♦ *v* **4** award a knighthood to. **knighthood** *n* honorary title given to a man by the British sovereign. **knightly** *adj*

knit *v* **knitting, knitted** *or* **knit 1** make (a garment) by interlocking a series of loops in wool or other yarn. **2** join closely together. **3** draw (one's eyebrows) together. **knitting** *n* **knitwear** *n* knitted clothes, such as sweaters.

knob *n* **1** rounded projection, such as a switch on a radio. **2** rounded handle on a door or drawer. **3** small amount of butter. **knobbly** *adj* covered with small bumps.

knobkerrie *n* S Afr club with a rounded end.

knock *v* **1** give a blow or push to. **2** rap audibly with the knuckles. **3** make or drive by striking. **4** *Informal* criticize adversely. **5** (of an engine) make a regular banging noise as a result of a fault. ♦ *n* **6** blow or rap. **7** knocking sound. **knocker** *n* metal fitting for knocking on a door. **knock about, around** *v* **1** wander or spend time aimlessly. **2** hit or kick brutally.

knockabout *adj* (of comedy) boisterous. **knock back** *v* *Informal* **1** drink quickly. **2** cost. **3** reject or refuse.

knock down *v* **1** demolish. **2** reduce the price of. **knockdown** *adj* (of a price) very low. **knock-knees** *pl n* legs that curve in at the knees. **knock off** *v* **1** *Informal* cease work. **2** *Informal* make or do (something) hurriedly or easily. **3** take (a specified amount) off a price. **4** *Brit, Aust & NZ informal* steal.

knock out *v* **1** render (someone) unconscious. **2** *Informal* overwhelm or amaze. **3** defeat in a knockout competition. **knockout** *n* **1** blow that renders an opponent unconscious. **2** competition from which competitors are progressively eliminated. **3** *Informal* overwhelmingly attractive person or thing. **knock up** *v* **1** *Informal* assemble (something) quickly. **2** *Informal* waken. **knock-up** *n* practice session at tennis, squash, or badminton.

knoll *n* small rounded hill.

knot *n* **1** fastening made by looping and pulling tight strands of string, cord, or rope. **2** tangle (of hair). **3** small cluster or huddled group. **4** round lump or spot in timber. **5** feeling of tightness, caused by tension or nervousness. **6** unit of speed used by ships, equal to one nautical mile (1.85 kilometres) per hour. ♦ *v* **knotting, knotted 7** tie with or into a knot. **knotty** *adj* **1** full of knots. **2** puzzling or difficult.

know *v* **knowing, knew, known 1** be or feel certain of the truth of (information etc.). **2** be acquainted with. **3** have a grasp of or understand (a skill or language). **4** be aware of. **in the know** *Informal* informed or aware. **knowable** *adj* **knowing** *adj* suggesting secret knowledge.

knowingly adv 1 deliberately. 2 in a way that suggests secret knowledge.

know-all n Offens person who acts as if knowing more than other people.

know-how n Informal ingenuity, aptitude, or skill.

knowledge n 1 facts or experiences known by a person. 2 state of knowing. 3 specific information on a subject. **knowledgeable, knowledgable** adj intelligent or well-informed.

knuckle n 1 bone at the finger joint. 2 knee joint of a calf or pig. **near the knuckle** Informal rather rude or offensive. **knuckle-duster** n metal appliance worn on the knuckles to add force to a blow. **knuckle under** v yield or submit.

KO knockout.

koala n tree-dwelling Australian marsupial with dense grey fur.

kohanga reo, kohanga n NZ infant class where children are taught in Maori.

kohl n cosmetic powder used to darken the edges of the eyelids.

kookaburra n large Australian kingfisher with a cackling cry.

koori n, pl **-ris** Australian Aborigine.

kopje, koppie n S Afr small hill.

Koran n sacred book of Islam.

kosher [**koh**-sher] adj 1 conforming to Jewish religious law, esp. (of food) to Jewish dietary law. 2 Informal legitimate or authentic. ♦ n 3 kosher food.

kowhai n New Zealand tree with clusters of yellow flowers.

kowtow v be servile (towards).

kph kilometres per hour.

kraal n S African village surrounded by a strong fence.

Kremlin n central government of Russia and, formerly, the Soviet Union.

krill n, pl **krill** small shrimplike sea creature.

krypton n Chem colourless gas present in the atmosphere and used in fluorescent lights.

kudos n fame or credit.

kugel [**koog**-el] n S Afr rich, fashion-conscious, materialistic young woman.

kumara n NZ tropical root vegetable with yellow flesh.

kumquat [**kumm**-kwott] n citrus fruit resembling a tiny orange.

kung fu n Chinese martial art combining hand, foot, and weapon techniques.

kura kaupapa Maori n NZ primary school where the teaching is done in Maori.

kurrajong n Australian tree or shrub with tough fibrous bark.

kW kilowatt.

kWh kilowatt-hour.

L l

l litre.

L 1 large. **2** learner (driver).

lab *n Informal short for* LABORATORY.

label *n* **1** piece of card or other material fixed to an object to show its ownership, destination, etc. **2** *v* **-elling, -elled 3** give a label to.

labia *pl n, sing* **labium** four liplike folds of skin forming part of the female genitals. **labial** [**lay**-bee-al] *adj* of the lips.

labor *n US & Aust same as* LABOUR. **Labor Day 1** (in the US and Canada) public holiday in honour of labour, held on the first Monday in September. **2** (in Australia) public holiday observed on different days in different states.

laboratory *n, pl* **-ries** building or room designed for scientific research or for the teaching of practical science.

laborious *adj* involving great prolonged effort. **laboriously** *adv*

Labor Party *n* main left-wing political party in Australia.

labour, (*US & Aust*) **labor** *n* **1** physical work or exertion. **2** workers in industry. **3** final stage of pregnancy, leading to childbirth. ♦ *v* **4** work hard. **5** stress to excess or too persistently. **6** be at a disadvantage because of a mistake or false belief. **laboured** *adj* uttered or done with difficulty. **labourer** *n* person who labours, esp. someone doing manual work for wages. **Labour Day 1** (in Britain) a public holiday in honour of work, held on May 1. **2** (in New Zealand) a public holiday commemorating the introduction of the eight-hour day, held on the 4th Monday in October. **Labour Party** main left-wing political party in a number of countries including Britain and New Zealand.

labrador *n* large retriever dog with a usu. gold or black coat.

laburnum *n* ornamental tree with yellow hanging flowers.

labyrinth [**lab**-er-inth] *n* **1** complicated network of passages. **2** interconnecting cavities in the internal ear. **labyrinthine** *adj*

lace *n* **1** delicate decorative fabric made from threads woven into an open weblike pattern. **2** cord drawn through eyelets and tied. ♦ *v* **3** fasten with laces. **4** thread a cord or string through holes in something. **5** add a small amount of alcohol, a drug, etc. to (food or drink). **lacy** *adj* fine, like lace. **lace-ups** *pl n* shoes which fasten with laces.

lacerate [**lass**-er-rate] *v* tear (flesh). **laceration** *n*

lachrymose *adj* **1** tearful. **2** sad.

lack *n* **1** shortage or absence of something needed or wanted. ♦ *v* **2** need or be short of (something).

lackadaisical *adj* lazy and careless in a dreamy way.

lackey *n* **1** servile follower. **2** uniformed male servant.

lacklustre *adj* lacking brilliance or vitality.

laconic *adj* using only a few words, terse. **laconically** *adv*

lacquer *n* **1** hard varnish for wood or metal. **2** clear sticky substance sprayed onto the hair to hold it in place.

lacrimal *adj* of tears or the glands which produce them.

lacrosse *n* sport in which teams catch and throw a ball using long sticks with a pouched net at the end, in an attempt to score goals.

lactation *n* secretion of milk by female mammals to feed young. **lactic** *adj* of or derived from milk. **lactose** *n* white crystalline sugar found in milk.

lacuna [lak-**kew**-na] *n, pl* **-nae** gap or missing part, esp. in a document or series.

lad *n* boy or young man.

ladder *n* **1** frame of two poles connected by horizontal steps used for climbing. **2** line of stitches that have come undone in tights or stockings. ♦ *v* **3** have or cause to have such a line of undone stitches.

laden *adj* **1** loaded. **2** burdened.

la-di-da, lah-di-dah *adj Informal* affected or pretentious.

ladle *n* **1** spoon with a long handle and a large bowl, used for serving soup etc. ♦ *v* **2** serve out.

lady *n, pl* **-dies** **1** woman regarded as having characteristics of good breeding or high rank. **2** polite term of address for a woman. **3** (L-) title of some female members of the British nobility. **Our Lady** the Virgin Mary. **lady-in-waiting** *n, pl* **ladies-in-waiting** female servant of a queen or princess. **ladykiller** *n Informal* man who is or thinks he is irresistible to women. **ladylike** *adj* polite and dignified.

ladybird *n* small red beetle with black spots.

lag[1] *v* **lagging, lagged** **1** go too slowly, fall behind. ♦ *n* **2** delay between events. **laggard** *n* person who lags behind.

lag[2] *v* **lagging, lagged** wrap (a boiler, pipes, etc.) with insulating material. **lagging** *n* insulating material.

lag[3] *n* **old lag** *Brit, Aust & NZ slang* convict.

lager *n* light-bodied beer.

lagoon *n* body of water cut off from the open sea by coral reefs or sand bars.

laid *v* past of LAY[1]. **laid-back** *adj Informal* relaxed.

lain *v* past participle of LIE[2].

lair *n* resting place of an animal.

laird *n* Scottish landowner.

laissez-faire [less-ay-**fair**] *n* principle of nonintervention, esp. by a government in commercial affairs.

laity [**lay**-it-ee] *n* people who are not members of the clergy.

lake[1] *n* expanse of water entirely surrounded by land. **lakeside** *n*

lake[2] *n* red pigment.

lama *n* Buddhist priest in Tibet or Mongolia.

lamb *n* **1** young sheep. **2** its meat. ♦ *v* **3** (of sheep) give birth to a lamb or lambs. **lamb's fry** *Aust & NZ* lamb's liver for cooking. **lambskin** *n* **lambswool** *n*

lambast, lambaste *v* **1** beat or thrash. **2** reprimand severely.

lambent *adj Lit* (of a flame) flickering softly.

lame *adj* **1** having an injured or disabled leg or foot. **2** (of an excuse) unconvincing. ♦ *v* **3** make lame. **lamely** *adv* **lameness** *n* **lame duck** person or thing unable to cope without help.

lamé [**lah**-may] *n, adj* (fabric) interwoven with gold or silver thread.

lament *v* **1** feel or express sorrow (for). ♦ *n* **2** passionate expression of grief. **lamentable** *adj* very disappointing. **lamentation** *n* **lamented** *adj* grieved for.

laminate *v* **1** make (a sheet of material) by sticking together thin sheets. **2** cover with a thin sheet of material. **3** *n* **4** laminated sheet. **laminated** *adj*

lamington *n Aust & NZ* sponge cake

coated with a sweet coating.

Lammas n August 1, formerly a harvest festival.

lamp n device which produces light from electricity, oil, or gas. **lamppost** n post supporting a lamp in the street. **lampshade** n

lampoon n 1 humorous satire ridiculing someone. ♦ v 2 satirize or ridicule.

lamprey n eel-like fish with a round sucking mouth.

lance n 1 long spear used by a mounted soldier. ♦ v 2 pierce (a boil or abscess) with a lancet. **lancer** n formerly, cavalry soldier armed with a lance. **lance corporal** noncommissioned army officer of the lowest rank.

lancet n 1 pointed two-edged surgical knife. 2 narrow window in the shape of a pointed arch.

land n 1 solid part of the earth's surface. 2 ground, esp. with reference to its type or use. 3 rural or agricultural area. 4 property consisting of land. 5 country or region. ♦ v 6 come or bring to earth after a flight, jump, or fall. 7 go or take from a ship at the end of a voyage. 8 come to or touch shore. 9 come or bring to some point or condition. 10 Informal obtain. 11 take (a hooked fish) from the water. 12 Informal deliver (a punch). **landed** adj possessing or consisting of lands. **landless** adj **landward** adj 1 nearest to or facing the land. ♦ adv 2 (also **landwards**) towards land. **landfall** n ship's first landing after a voyage. **landlocked** adj completely surrounded by land. **land up** v arrive at a final point or condition.

landau [**lan**-daw] n four-wheeled carriage with two folding hoods.

landing n 1 floor area at the top of a flight of stairs. 2 bringing or coming to

land. 3 (also **landing stage**) place where people or goods go onto or come off a boat.

landlord, landlady n 1 person who rents out land, houses, etc. 2 owner or manager of a pub or boarding house.

landlubber n person who is not experienced at sea.

landmark n 1 prominent object in or feature of a landscape. 2 event, decision, etc. considered as an important development.

landscape n 1 extensive piece of inland scenery seen from one place. 2 picture of it. ♦ v 3 improve natural features of (a piece of land).

landslide n 1 (also **landslip**) falling of soil, rock, etc. down the side of a mountain. 2 overwhelming electoral victory.

lane n 1 narrow road. 2 area of road for one stream of traffic. 3 specified route followed by ships or aircraft. 4 strip of a running track or swimming pool for use by one competitor.

language n 1 system of sounds, symbols, etc. for communicating thought. 2 particular system used by a nation or people. 3 system of words and symbols for computer programming.

languid adj lacking energy or enthusiasm. **languidly** adv

languish v 1 suffer neglect or hardship. 2 lose or diminish in strength or vigour. 3 pine (for).

languor [**lang**-ger] n 1 state of dreamy relaxation. 2 laziness or weariness. **languorous** adj

lank adj 1 (of hair) straight and limp. 2 thin or gaunt. **lanky** adj ungracefully tall and thin.

lanolin n grease from sheep's wool used in ointments etc.

lantana [lan-**tay**-na] n shrub with orange or yellow flowers, considered a weed in Australia.

lantern n light in a transparent protective case. **lantern jaw** long thin jaw. **lantern-jawed** adj

lanthanum n Chem silvery-white metallic element. **lanthanide series** class of 15 elements chemically related to lanthanum.

lanyard n 1 cord worn round the neck to hold a knife or whistle. 2 Naut short rope.

lap¹ n part between the waist and knees of a person when sitting. **laptop** adj 1 (of a computer) small enough to fit on a user's lap. ♦ n 2 computer small enough to fit on a user's lap.

lap² n 1 single circuit of a racecourse or track. 2 stage of a journey. ♦ v **lapping, lapped** 3 overtake an opponent so as to be one or more circuits ahead.

lap³ v **lapping, lapped** (of waves) beat softly against (a shore etc.). **lap up** v 1 drink by scooping up with the tongue. 2 accept (information or attention) eagerly.

lapel [lap-**pel**] n part of the front of a coat or jacket folded back towards the shoulders.

lapidary adj of or relating to stones.

lapis lazuli [**lap**-iss **lazz**-yoo-lie] n bright blue gemstone.

lapse n 1 temporary drop in a standard, esp. through forgetfulness or carelessness. 2 instance of bad behaviour by someone usually well-behaved. 3 break in occurrence or usage. ♦ v 4 drop in standard. 5 end or become invalid, esp. through disuse. 6 abandon religious faith. 7 (of time) slip away. **lapsed** adj

lapwing n plover with a tuft of feathers on the head.

larboard adj, n Old-fashioned port (side of a ship).

larceny n, pl **-nies** Law theft.

larch n deciduous coniferous tree.

lard n 1 soft white fat obtained from a pig. ♦ v 2 insert strips of bacon in (meat) before cooking. 3 decorate (speech or writing) with strange words unnecessarily.

larder n storeroom for food.

large adj great in size, number, or extent. **at large** 1 in general. 2 free, not confined. 3 fully. **largely** adv **largish** adj **large-scale** adj wide-ranging or extensive.

largesse, largess [lar-**jess**] n generous giving, esp. of money.

largo n, pl **-gos**, adv Music (piece to be played) in a slow and dignified manner.

lariat n lasso.

lark¹ n small brown songbird, skylark.

lark² n Informal 1 harmless piece of mischief or fun. 2 unnecessary activity or job. **lark about** v play pranks.

larkspur n plant with spikes of blue, pink, or white flowers with spurs.

larrikin n Aust & NZ old-fashioned slang mischievous or unruly person.

larva n, pl **-vae** insect in an immature stage, often resembling a worm. **larval** adj

larynx n, pl **larynges** part of the throat containing the vocal cords. **laryngeal** adj **laryngitis** n inflammation of the larynx.

lasagne, lasagna [laz-**zan**-ya] n 1 pasta in wide flat sheets. 2 dish made from layers of lasagne, meat, and cheese.

lascivious [lass-**iv**-ee-uss] adj showing or producing sexual desire. **lasciviously** adv

laser [**lay**-zer] n device that produces a very narrow intense beam of light, used for cutting very hard materials and in surgery etc.

lash¹ n 1 eyelash. 2 sharp blow with a whip. 3 v 4 hit with a whip. 5 (of rain or waves) beat forcefully against. **6** attack verbally, scold. **7** flick or wave sharply to and fro. **lash out** *v* **1** make a sudden physical or verbal attack. **2** *Informal* spend (money) extravagantly.

lash² *v* fasten or bind tightly with cord etc.

lashings *pl n Old-fashioned* large amounts.

lass, lassie *n Scot & N English* girl.

lassitude *n* physical or mental weariness.

lasso [lass-**oo**] *n, pl* -**sos, -soes 1** rope with a noose for catching cattle and horses. ♦ *v* -**soing, -soed 2** catch with a lasso.

last¹ *adj, adv* **1** coming at the end or after all others. **2** most recent(ly). ♦ *adj* **3** only remaining. ♦ *n* **4** last person or thing. **lastly** *adv* **last-ditch** *adj* done as a final resort. **last post** army bugle-call played at sunset or funerals. **last straw** small irritation or setback that, coming after others, is too much to bear. **last word 1** final comment in an argument. **2** most recent or best example of something.

last² *v* **1** continue. **2** be sufficient for (a specified amount of time). **3** remain fresh, uninjured, or unaltered. **lasting** *adj*

last³ *n* model of a foot on which shoes and boots are made or repaired.

latch *n* **1** fastening for a door with a bar and lever. **2** lock which can only be opened from the outside with a key. ♦ *v* **3** fasten with a latch. **latch onto** *v* become attached to (a person or idea).

late *adj* **1** after the normal or expected time. **2** towards the end of a period. **3** being at an advanced time. **4** recently dead. **5** recent. **6** former. ♦ *adv* **7** after the normal or expected time. **8** at a relatively advanced age. **9** recently. **lately** *adv* in recent times. **lateness** *n*

latent *adj* hidden and not yet

developed. **latency** *n*

lateral [**lat**-ter-al] *adj* of or relating to the side or sides. **laterally** *adv*

latex *n* milky fluid found in some plants, esp. the rubber tree, used in making rubber.

lath *n* thin strip of wood used to support plaster, tiles, etc.

lathe *n* machine for turning wood or metal while it is being shaped.

lather *n* **1** froth of soap and water. **2** frothy sweat. **3** *Informal* state of agitation. ♦ *v* **4** make frothy. **5** rub with soap until lather appears.

Latin *n* **1** language of the ancient Romans. ♦ *adj* **2** of or in Latin. **3** of a people whose language derives from Latin. **Latin America** parts of South and Central America whose official language is Spanish or Portuguese. **Latin American** *n, adj*

latitude *n* **1** angular distance measured in degrees N or S of the equator. **2** scope for freedom of action or thought. ♦ *pl* **3** regions considered in relation to their distance from the equator.

latrine *n* toilet in a barracks or camp.

latter *adj* **1** second of two. **2** later. **3** recent. **latterly** *adv* **latter-day** *adj* modern.

lattice [**lat**-iss] *n* **1** framework of intersecting strips of wood, metal, etc. **2** gate, screen, etc. formed of such a framework. **latticed** *adj*

laud *v* praise or glorify. **laudable** *adj* praiseworthy. **laudably** *adv* **laudatory** *adj* praising or glorifying.

laudanum [**lawd**-a-num] *n* opium-based sedative.

laugh *v* **1** make inarticulate sounds with the voice expressing amusement, merriment, or scorn. **2** utter or express with laughter. ♦ *n* **3** act or instance of laughing. **4** *Informal* person or thing causing amusement. **laughable** *adj*

ridiculously inadequate. **laughter** n sound or action of laughing.
laughing gas nitrous oxide as an anaesthetic. **laughing stock** object of general derision. **laugh off** v treat (something serious or difficult) lightly.

launch¹ v **1** put (a ship or boat) into the water, esp. for the first time. **2** begin (a campaign, project, etc.). **3** put a new product on the market. **4** send (a missile or spacecraft) into space or the air. ♦ n **5** launching. **launcher** n **launch into** v start doing something enthusiastically. **launch out** v start doing something new.

launch² n open motorboat.

launder v **1** wash and iron (clothes and linen). **2** make (illegally obtained money) seem legal by passing it through foreign banks or legitimate businesses. **laundry** n, pl **-dries 1** clothes etc. for washing or which have recently been washed. **2** place for washing clothes and linen.
Launderette n ® shop with coin-operated washing and drying machines.

laureate [**lor**-ee-at] adj see POET LAUREATE.

laurel n **1** glossy-leaved shrub, bay tree. ♦ pl **2** wreath of laurel, an emblem of victory or merit.

lava n molten rock thrown out by volcanoes, which hardens as it cools.

lavatory n, pl **-ries** toilet.

lavender n **1** shrub with fragrant flowers. ♦ adj **2** bluish-purple. **lavender water** light perfume made from lavender.

lavish adj **1** great in quantity or richness. **2** giving or spending generously. **3** extravagant. ♦ v **4** give or spend generously. **lavishly** adv

law n **1** rule binding on a community. **2** system of such rules. **3** Informal police. **4** invariable sequence of events in nature. **5** general principle deduced from facts. **lawful** adj allowed by law. **lawfully** adv **lawless** adj breaking the law, esp. in a violent way. **lawlessness** n **law-abiding** adj obeying the laws. **law-breaker** n **lawsuit** n court case brought by one person or group against another.

lawn¹ n area of tended and mown grass. **lawn mower** machine for cutting grass. **lawn tennis** tennis, esp. when played on a grass court.

lawn² n fine linen or cotton fabric.

lawyer n professionally qualified legal expert.

lax adj not strict. **laxity** n

laxative n, adj (medicine) inducing the emptying of the bowels.

lay¹ v **laying, laid 1** cause to lie. **2** devise or prepare. **3** set in a particular place or position. **4** attribute (blame). **5** put forward (a plan, argument, etc.). **6** (of a bird or reptile) produce eggs. **7** arrange (a table) for a meal. **lay waste** devastate. **lay-by** n stopping place for traffic beside a road. **lay off** v dismiss staff during a slack period. **lay-off** n **lay on** v provide or supply. **lay out** v **1** arrange or spread out. **2** prepare (a corpse) for burial. **3** Informal spend money, esp. lavishly. **4** Informal knock unconscious. **layout** n arrangement, esp. of matter for printing or of a building.

lay² v past tense of LIE². **layabout** n lazy person.

lay³ adj **1** of or involving people who are not clergymen. **2** nonspecialist. **layman** n **1** person who is not a member of the clergy. **2** person without specialist knowledge.

lay⁴ n short narrative poem designed to be sung.

layer n **1** single thickness of some substance, as a cover or coating on a surface. **2** laying hen. **3** shoot of a plant pegged down or partly covered with earth to encourage root growth. ♦ *v* **4** form a layer. **5** propagate plants by layers. **layered** *adj*

layette *n* clothes for a newborn baby.

laze *v* **1** be idle or lazy. ♦ *n* **2** time spent lazing.

lazy *adj* **lazier, laziest 1** not inclined to work or exert oneself. **2** done in a relaxed manner without much effort. **3** (of movement) slow and gentle. **lazily** *adv* **laziness** *n*

lb pound (weight).

lbw *Cricket* leg before wicket.

lea *n Poetic* meadow.

leach *v* remove or be removed from a substance by a liquid passing through it.

lead¹ *v* **leading, led 1** guide or conduct. **2** cause to feel, think, or behave in a certain way. **3** be, go, or play first. **4** (of a road, path, etc.) go towards. **5** control or direct. **6** (foll. by *to*) result in. **7** pass or spend (one's life). ♦ *n* **8** first or most prominent place. **9** amount by which a person or group is ahead of another. **10** clue. **11** length of leather or chain attached to a dog's collar to control it. **12** principal role or actor in a film, play, etc. **13** cable bringing current to an electrical device. ♦ *adj* **14** acting as a leader or lead. **leading** *adj* **1** principal. **2** in the first position. **leading question** question worded to prompt the answer desired. **lead-in** *n* introduction to a subject.

lead² *n* **1** soft heavy grey metal. **2** (in a pencil) graphite. **3** lead weight on a line, used for sounding depths of water. **leaded** *adj* (of windows) made from many small panes of glass held together by lead strips. **leaden** *adj* **1** heavy or sluggish. **2** dull grey. **3** made from lead.

leader *n* **1** person who leads. **2** article

in a newspaper expressing editorial views. **leadership** *n*

leaf *n, pl* **leaves 1** flat usu. green blade attached to the stem of a plant. **2** single sheet of paper in a book. **3** very thin sheet of metal. **4** extending flap on a table. **leafy** *adj* **leafless** *adj* **leaf mould** rich soil composed of decayed leaves. **leaf through** *v* turn pages without reading them.

leaflet *n* **1** sheet of printed matter for distribution. **2** small leaf.

league¹ *n* **1** association promoting the interests of its members. **2** association of sports clubs organizing competitions between its members. **3** *Informal* class or level.

league² *n Obs* measure of distance, about three miles.

leak *n* **1** hole or defect that allows the escape or entrance of liquid, gas, radiation, etc. **2** liquid etc. that escapes or enters. **3** disclosure of secrets. ♦ *v* **4** let liquid etc. in or out. **5** (of liquid etc.) find its way through a leak. **6** disclose secret information. **leakage** *n* act or instance of leaking. **leaky** *adj*

lean¹ *v* **leaning, leaned** *or* **leant 1** rest against. **2** bend or slope from an upright position. **3** tend (towards). **leaning** *n* tendency. **lean on** *v* **1** *Informal* threaten or intimidate. **2** depend on for help or advice. **lean-to** *n* shed built against an existing wall.

lean² *adj* **1** thin but healthy-looking. **2** (of meat) lacking fat. **3** unproductive. ♦ *n* **4** lean part of meat. **leanness** *n*

leap *v* **leaping, leapt** *or* **leaped 1** make a sudden powerful jump. ♦ *n* **2** sudden powerful jump. **3** abrupt increase, as in costs or prices. **leapfrog** *n* game in which a player vaults over another bending down. **leap year** year with February 29th as an extra day.

learn v learning, learned or learnt 1 gain skill or knowledge by study, practice, or teaching. 2 memorize (something). 3 find out or discover. **learned** adj 1 erudite, deeply read. 2 showing much learning. **learner** n **learning** n knowledge got by study.

lease n 1 contract by which land or property is rented for a stated time by the owner to a tenant. ♦ v 2 let or rent by lease. **leasehold** n, adj (land or property) held on lease. **leaseholder** n

leash n lead for a dog.

least adj 1 superlative of LITTLE. 2 smallest. ♦ n 3 smallest one. ♦ adv 4 in the smallest degree.

leather n 1 material made from specially treated animal skins. ♦ adj 2 made of leather. ♦ v 3 beat or thrash. **leathery** adj like leather, tough.

leave¹ v leaving, left 1 go away from. 2 allow to remain, accidentally or deliberately. 3 cause to be or remain in a specified state. 4 discontinue membership of. 5 permit. 6 entrust. 7 bequeath. **leave out** v exclude or omit.

leave² n 1 permission to be absent from work or duty. 2 period of such absence. 3 permission to do something. 4 formal parting.

leaven [lev-ven] n 1 substance that causes dough to rise. 2 influence that produces a gradual change. ♦ v 3 raise with leaven. 4 spread through and influence (something).

lecher n man who has or shows excessive sexual desire. **lechery** n

lecherous [letch-er-uss] adj (of a man) having or showing excessive sexual desire.

lectern n sloping reading desk, esp. in a church.

lecture n 1 informative talk to an audience on a subject. 2 lengthy rebuke or scolding. ♦ v 3 give a talk. 4 scold.

lecturer n person who lectures, esp. in a university or college. **lectureship** n appointment as a lecturer.

ledge n 1 narrow shelf sticking out from a wall. 2 shelflike projection from a cliff etc.

ledger n book of debit and credit accounts of a firm.

lee n sheltered part or side. **leeward** adj, n 1 (on) the lee side. ♦ adv 2 towards this side. **leeway** n room for free movement within limits.

leech n 1 species of bloodsucking worm. 2 person who lives off others.

leek n vegetable of the onion family with a long bulb and thick stem.

leer v 1 look or grin at in a sneering or suggestive manner. ♦ n 2 sneering or suggestive look or grin.

leery adj Informal suspicious or wary (of).

lees pl n sediment of wine.

left¹ adj 1 of the side that faces west when the front faces north. ♦ adv 2 on or towards the left. ♦ n 3 left hand or part. 4 Politics people supporting socialism rather than capitalism. **leftist** n, adj (person) of the political left. **left-handed** adj more adept with the left hand than with the right. **left-wing** adj 1 socialist. 2 belonging to the more radical part of a political party.

left² v past of LEAVE¹.

leftover n unused portion of food or material.

leg n 1 one of the limbs on which a person or animal walks, runs, or stands. 2 part of a garment covering the leg. 3 structure that supports, such as one of the legs of a table. 4 stage of a journey. 5 Sport (part of) one game or race in a series. **pull someone's leg** tease someone. **leggy** adj having long legs. **legless** adj 1 without legs.

2 *Slang* very drunk. **leggings** *pl n* **1** covering of leather or other material for the legs. **2** close-fitting trousers for women or children.

legacy *n, pl* **-cies 1** thing left in a will. **2** thing handed down to a successor.

legal *adj* **1** established or permitted by law. **2** relating to law or lawyers. **legally** *adv* **legality** *n* **legalize** *v* make legal. **legalization** *n*

legate *n* messenger or representative, esp. from the Pope. **legation** *n* **1** diplomatic minister and his staff. **2** official residence of a diplomatic minister.

legatee *n* recipient of a legacy.

legato [leg-**ah**-toe] *n, pl* **-tos,** *adv Music* (piece to be played) smoothly.

legend *n* **1** traditional story or myth. **2** traditional literature. **3** famous person or event. **4** stories about such a person or event. **5** inscription. **legendary** *adj* **1** famous. **2** of or in legend.

legerdemain [lej-er-de-**main**] *n* **1** sleight of hand. **2** cunning deception.

legible *adj* easily read. **legibility** *n* **legibly** *adv*

legion *n* **1** large military force. **2** large number. **3** association of veterans. **4** infantry unit in the Roman army. **legionary** *adj, n* **legionnaire** *n* member of a legion. **legionnaire's disease** serious bacterial disease similar to pneumonia.

legislate *v* make laws. **legislative** *adj* **legislator** *n* maker of laws. **legislature** *n* body of people that makes, amends, or repeals laws.

legislation *n* **1** legislating. **2** laws made.

legitimate *adj* **1** authorized by or in accordance with law. **2** fairly deduced. **3** born to parents married to each other. ♦ *v* **4** make legitimate. **legitimacy** *n* **legitimately** *adv* **legitimize** *v* make legitimate, legalize.

legitimization *n*

Lego *n* ® construction toy of plastic bricks fitted together by studs.

leguaan [**leg**-oo-ahn] *n* large S African lizard.

legume *n* **1** pod of a plant of the pea or bean family. ♦ *pl* **2** peas or beans. **leguminous** *adj* (of plants) pod-bearing.

lei *n* (in Hawaii) garland of flowers.

leisure *n* time for relaxation or hobbies. **at one's leisure** when one has time. **leisurely** *adj* **1** deliberate, unhurried. ♦ *adv* **2** slowly. **leisured** *adj* with plenty of spare time. **leisure centre** building with facilities such as a swimming pool, gymnasium, and café.

leitmotif [**lite**-mote-eef] *n Music* recurring theme associated with a person, situation, or thought.

lekker *adj S Afr slang* **1** attractive or nice. **2** tasty.

lemming *n* rodent of arctic regions, reputed to run into the sea and drown during mass migrations.

lemon *n* **1** yellow oval fruit that grows on trees. **2** *Slang* useless or defective person or thing. ♦ *adj* **3** pale-yellow. **lemonade** *n* lemon-flavoured soft drink, often fizzy. **lemon curd** creamy spread made of lemons, butter, etc. **lemon sole** edible flatfish.

lemur *n* nocturnal animal like a small monkey, found in Madagascar.

lend *v* **lending, lent 1** give the temporary use of. **2** provide (money) temporarily, often for interest. **3** add (a quality or effect), e.g. *her presence lent beauty to the scene.* **lend itself to** be suitable for. **lender** *n*

length *n* **1** extent or measurement from end to end. **2** period of time for which something happens. **3** quality of being long. **4** piece of something narrow and long. **at length 1** at last. **2** in full detail. **lengthy** *adj* very long or tiresome. **lengthily** adv **lengthen** v make or become longer. **lengthways, lengthwise** adj, adv

lenient [**lee**-nee-ent] adj tolerant, not strict or severe. **leniency** n **leniently** adv

lens n, pl **lenses** 1 piece of glass or similar material with one or both sides curved, used to bring together or spread light rays in cameras, spectacles, telescopes, etc. 2 transparent structure in the eye that focuses light.

lent v past of LEND.

Lent n period from Ash Wednesday to Easter Saturday. **Lenten** adj of, in, or suitable to Lent.

lentil n edible seed of a leguminous Asian plant.

lento n, pl **-tos,** adv Music (piece to be played) slowly.

leonine adj like a lion.

leopard n large spotted carnivorous animal of the cat family.

leotard n tight-fitting garment covering the upper body, worn for dancing or exercise.

leper n 1 person suffering from leprosy. 2 ignored or despised person.

lepidoptera pl n order of insects with four wings covered with fine gossamer scales, as moths and butterflies. **lepidopterist** n person who studies or collects butterflies or moths.

leprechaun n mischievous elf of Irish folklore.

leprosy n disease attacking the nerves and skin, resulting in loss of feeling in the affected parts. **leprous** adj

lesbian n 1 homosexual woman. ♦ adj 2 of homosexual women. **lesbianism** n

lese-majesty [lezz-**maj**-est-ee] n 1 treason. 2 taking of liberties against people in authority.

lesion n 1 structural change in an organ of the body caused by illness or injury. 2 injury or wound.

less adj 1 smaller in extent, degree, or duration. 2 not so much. 3 **comparative of** LITTLE. ♦ pron 4 smaller part or quantity. ♦ adv 5 to a smaller extent or degree. ♦ prep 6 after deducting, minus. **lessen** v make or become smaller or not as much. **lesser** adj not as great in quantity, size, or worth.

lessee n person to whom a lease is granted.

lesson n 1 single period of instruction in a subject. 2 content of this. 3 experience that teaches. 4 portion of Scripture read in church.

lest conj 1 so as to prevent any possibility that. 2 for fear that.

let[1] v **letting, let** 1 allow, enable, or cause. 2 used as an auxiliary to express a proposal, command, threat, or assumption. 3 grant use of for rent, lease. 4 allow to escape. **let alone** not to mention. **let down** v 1 disappoint. 2 lower. 3 deflate. **letdown** n disappointment. **let off** v 1 excuse from (a duty or punishment). 2 fire or explode (a weapon). 3 emit (gas, steam, etc.). **let on** v Informal reveal (a secret). **let out** v 1 emit. 2 release. **let up** v diminish or stop. **let-up** n lessening.

let[2] n 1 Tennis minor infringement or obstruction of the ball requiring a replay of the point. 2 hindrance.

lethal adj deadly.

lethargy n 1 sluggishness or dullness. 2 abnormal lack of energy. **lethargic** adj **lethargically** adv

letter n 1 written message, usu. sent by post. 2 alphabetical symbol. 3 strict meaning (of a law etc.). ♦ pl 4 literary knowledge or ability. **lettered** adj learned. **lettering** n **letter bomb**

explosive device in a parcel or letter that explodes on opening. **letter box 1** slot in a door through which letters are delivered. **2** box in a street or post office where letters are posted. **letterhead** n printed heading on stationery giving the sender's name and address.

lettuce n plant with large green leaves used in salads.

leucocyte [**loo**-koh-site] n white blood cell.

leukaemia [loo-**kee**-mee-a] n disease caused by uncontrolled overproduction of white blood cells.

levee n US natural or artificial river embankment.

level adj **1** horizontal. **2** having an even surface. **3** of the same height as something else. **4** equal to or even with (someone or something else). **5** not going above the top edge of (a spoon etc.). **6** v **-elling, -elled 7** make even or horizontal. **8** make equal in position or status. **9** direct (a gun, accusation, etc.) at. **10** raze to the ground. ♦ n **11** horizontal line or surface. **12** device for showing or testing if something is horizontal. **13** position on a scale. **14** standard or grade. **15** flat area of land. **on the level** Informal honest or trustworthy. **level crossing** point where a railway line and road cross. **level-headed** adj not apt to be carried away by emotion.

lever n **1** handle used to operate machinery. **2** bar used to move a heavy object or to open something. **3** rigid bar pivoted about a fulcrum to transfer a force to a load. **4** means of exerting pressure to achieve an aim. ♦ v **5** prise or move with a lever. **leverage** n **1** action or power of a lever. **2** influence or strategic advantage.

leveret [**lev**-ver-it] n young hare.

leviathan [lev-**vie**-ath-an] n **1** sea monster. **2** anything huge or formidable.

Levis pl n ® denim jeans.

levitation n raising of a solid body into the air supernaturally. **levitate** v rise or cause to rise into the air.

levity n, pl **-ties** inclination to make a joke of serious matters.

levy [**lev**-vee] v **levying, levied 1** impose and collect (a tax). **2** raise (troops). ♦ n, pl **levies 3** imposition or collection of taxes. **4** money levied.

lewd adj lustful or indecent. **lewdly** adv **lewdness** n

lexicon n **1** dictionary. **2** vocabulary of a language. **lexical** adj relating to the vocabulary of a language. **lexicographer** n writer of dictionaries. **lexicography** n

liable adj **1** legally obliged or responsible. **2** given to or at risk from a condition. **liability** n **1** hindrance or disadvantage. **2** state of being liable. **3** financial obligation.

liaise v establish and maintain communication (with). **liaison** n **1** communication and contact between groups. **2** secret or adulterous relationship.

☑ **SPELLING TIP**

A lot of people forget to include a second i in **liaise**. They make the same mistake when they write *liason*, which occurs 58 times in the Bank of English and which should, of course, be **liaison**.

---

liana n climbing plant in tropical forests.

liar n person who tells lies.

lib n Informal short for LIBERATION.

libation [lie-**bay**-shun] n drink poured as an offering to the gods.

libel n **1** published statement falsely damaging a person's reputation. ♦ v

-belling, -belled **2** falsely damage the reputation of (someone). **libellous** adj

liberal adj **1** having social and political views that favour progress and reform. **2** generous in behaviour or temperament. **3** tolerant. **4** abundant. **5** (of education) designed to develop general cultural interests. ♦ n **6** person who has liberal ideas or opinions. **liberally** adv **liberalism** n belief in democratic reforms and individual freedom. **liberality** n generosity. **liberalize** v make (laws, a country, etc.) less restrictive. **liberalization** n **Liberal Democrat, Lib Dem** member of the Liberal Democrats, a British political party favouring a mixed economy and individual freedom. **Liberal Party** main right-wing political party in Australia.

liberate v set free. **liberation** n **liberator** n

libertarian n **1** believer in freedom of thought and action. ♦ adj **2** having such a belief.

libertine [**lib**-er-teen] n morally dissolute person.

liberty n, pl **-ties 1** freedom. **2** act or comment regarded as forward or socially unacceptable. **at liberty 1** free. **2** having the right. **take liberties** be presumptuous.

libido [lib-**ee**-doe] n, pl **-dos 1** psychic energy. **2** emotional drive, esp. of sexual origin. **libidinous** adj lustful.

library n, pl **-braries 1** room or building where books are kept. **2** collection of books, records, etc. for consultation or borrowing. **librarian** n keeper of or worker in a library. **librarianship** n

libretto n, pl **-tos, -ti** words of an opera. **librettist** n

lice n a plural of LOUSE.

licence n **1** document giving official permission to do something. **2** formal permission. **3** disregard of conventions for effect, e.g. *poetic licence*. **4** excessive liberty. **license** v grant a licence to. **licensed** adj **licensee** n holder of a licence, esp. to sell alcohol.

licentiate n person licensed as competent to practise a profession.

licentious adj sexually unrestrained or promiscuous.

lichen n small flowerless plant forming a crust on rocks, trees, etc.

licit adj lawful, permitted.

lick v **1** pass the tongue over. **2** touch lightly or flicker round. **3** Slang defeat. **4** n **5** licking. **6** small amount (of paint etc.). **7** Informal fast pace.

licorice n same as LIQUORICE.

lid n **1** movable cover. **2** short for EYELID.

lido [**lee**-doe] n, pl **-dos** open-air centre for swimming and water sports.

lie¹ v **lying, lied 1** make a deliberately false statement. **2** n **3** deliberate falsehood. **white lie** see WHITE.

lie² v **lying, lay, lain 1** place oneself or be in a horizontal position. **2** be situated. **3** be or remain in a certain state or position. **4** exist or be found. ♦ n **5** way something lies. **lie-down** n rest. **lie in** v remain in bed late into the morning. **lie-in** n long stay in bed in the morning.

lied [**leed**] n, pl **lieder** Music setting for voice and piano of a romantic poem.

liege [**leej**] adj **1** bound to give or receive feudal service. ♦ n **2** lord.

lien n Law right to hold another's property until a debt is paid.

lieu [**lyew**] n in lieu of instead of.

lieutenant [lef-**ten**-ant] n **1** junior officer in the army or navy. **2** main assistant.

life n, pl **lives 1** state of living beings, characterized by growth, reproduction, and response to stimuli. **2** period between birth and death or between birth and the present time. **3** way of living. **4** amount of time something is active or functions. **5** biography. **6** liveliness or high spirits. **7** living beings collectively. **lifeless** adj **1** dead. **2** not lively or exciting. **3** unconscious. **lifelike** adj **lifelong** adj lasting all of a person's life. **life belt, jacket** buoyant device to keep afloat a person in danger of drowning. **lifeboat** n boat used for rescuing people at sea. **life cycle** series of changes undergone by each generation of an animal or plant. **lifeline** n **1** means of contact or support. **2** rope used in rescuing a person in danger. **life science** any science concerned with living organisms, such as biology, botany, or zoology. **lifestyle** n particular attitudes, habits, etc. **life-support** adj (of equipment or treatment) necessary to keep a person alive. **lifetime** n length of time a person is alive.

lift v **1** move upwards in position, status, volume, etc. **2** revoke or cancel. **3** take (plants) out of the ground for harvesting. **4** (of fog, etc.) disappear. **5** make or become more cheerful. **6** n **7** cage raised and lowered in a vertical shaft to transport people or goods. **8** ride in a car etc. as a passenger. **9** Informal feeling of cheerfulness. **10** lifting. **liftoff** n moment a rocket leaves the ground.

ligament n band of tissue joining bones.

ligature n link, bond, or tie.

light[1] n **1** electromagnetic radiation by which things are visible. **2** source of this, lamp. **3** anything that lets in light, such as a window. **4** aspect or view. **5** mental vision. **6** means of setting fire to. ♦ pl **7** traffic lights. ♦ adj **8** bright. **9** (of a colour) pale. ♦ v **lighting, lighted** or **lit 10** ignite. **11** illuminate

or cause to illuminate. **lighten** v make less dark. **lighting** n apparatus for and use of artificial light in theatres, films, etc. **light bulb** glass part of an electric lamp. **lighthouse** n tower with a light to guide ships. **light year** Astronomy distance light travels in one year, about six million million miles.

light[2] adj **1** not heavy, weighing relatively little. **2** relatively low in strength, amount, density, etc. **3** not clumsy. **4** not serious or profound. **5** easily digested. **6** adv **7** with little equipment or luggage. ♦ v **lighting, lighted, lit 8** (esp. of birds) settle after flight. **9** come (upon) by chance. **lightly** adv **lightness** n **lighten** v **1** make less heavy or burdensome. **2** make more cheerful or lively. **light-fingered** adj skilful at stealing. **light-headed** adj feeling faint, dizzy. **light-hearted** adj carefree. **lightweight** n, adj **1** (person) of little importance. ♦ n **2** boxer weighing up to 135lb (professional) or 60kg (amateur).

lighter[1] n device for lighting cigarettes etc.

lighter[2] n flat-bottomed boat for unloading ships.

lightning n **1** visible discharge of electricity in the atmosphere. ♦ adj **2** fast and sudden.

> ☑ **SPELLING TIP**
> Do not confuse this noun with the verb 'lighten', which has the form 'lightening'. The Bank of English shows that people often make the mistake of writing *lightening*, when they mean the noun **lightning**, which doesn't have an *e* in the middle.

lights pl n lungs of animals as animal food.

ligneous *adj* of or like wood.

lignite [**lig**-nite] *n* woody textured rock used as fuel.

like¹ *prep, conj, adj, pron* indicating similarity, comparison, etc. **liken** *v* compare. **likeness** *n* **1** resemblance. **2** portrait. **likewise** *adv* similarly.

like² *v* **1** find enjoyable. **2** be fond of. **3** prefer, choose, or wish. **likeable, likable** *adj* **liking** *n* **1** fondness. **2** preference.

likely *adj* **1** tending or inclined. **2** probable. **3** hopeful, promising. ♦ *adv* **4** probably. **not likely** *Informal* definitely not. **likelihood** *n* probability.

lilac *n* **1** shrub with pale mauve or white flowers. ♦ *adj* **2** light-purple.

Lilliputian [lil-lip-**pew**-shun] *adj* tiny.

Lilo *n, pl* **-los** ® inflatable rubber mattress.

lilt *n* **1** pleasing musical quality in speaking. **2** jaunty rhythm. **3** graceful rhythmic motion. **lilting** *adj*

lily *n, pl* **lilies** plant which grows from a bulb and has large, often white, flowers.

limb *n* **1** arm, leg, or wing. **2** main branch of a tree.

limber *v* (foll. by *up*) **1** loosen stiff muscles by exercising. ♦ *adj* **2** pliant or supple.

limbo¹ *n* **in limbo** not knowing the result or next stage of something and powerless to influence it.

limbo² *n, pl* **-bos** West Indian dance in which dancers lean backwards to pass under a bar.

lime¹ *n* calcium compound used as a fertilizer or in making cement. **limelight** *n* glare of publicity. **limestone** *n* sedimentary rock used in building.

lime² *n* small green citrus fruit. **lime-green** *adj* greenish-yellow.

lime³ *n* deciduous tree with heart-shaped leaves and fragrant flowers.

limerick [**lim**-mer-ik] *n* humorous verse of five lines.

limey *n US slang* British person.

limit *n* **1** ultimate extent, degree, or amount of something. **2** boundary or edge. ♦ *v* **-iting, -ited 3** restrict or confine. **limitation** *n* **limitless** *adj* **limited company** company whose shareholders' liability for debts is restricted.

limousine *n* large luxurious car.

limp¹ *v* **1** walk with an uneven step. **2** *n* **3** limping walk.

limp² *adj* without firmness or stiffness. **limply** *adv*

limpet *n* shellfish which sticks tightly to rocks.

limpid *adj* **1** clear or transparent. **2** easy to understand. **limpidity** *n*

linchpin, lynchpin *n* **1** pin to hold a wheel on its axle. **2** essential person or thing.

linctus *n, pl* **-tuses** syrupy cough medicine.

linden *n* same as LIME³.

line¹ *n* **1** long narrow mark. **2** indented mark or wrinkle. **3** boundary or limit. **4** edge or contour of a shape. **5** string or wire for a particular use. **6** telephone connection. **7** wire or cable for transmitting electricity. **8** shipping company. **9** railway track. **10** course or direction of movement. **11** prescribed way of thinking. **12** field of interest or activity. **13** row or queue of people. **14** class of goods. **15** row of words. **16** *pl* **17** words of a theatrical part. **18** school punishment of writing out a sentence a specified number of times. ♦ *v* **19** mark with lines. **20** be or form a border or edge. **in line for** likely to receive. **in line with** in accordance with. **line dancing** form of dancing performed by rows of people to country and western music. **line-up** n people or things assembled for a particular purpose.

line² v **1** give a lining to. **2** cover the inside of.

lineage [**lin**-ee-ij] n descent from an ancestor.

lineament n facial feature.

linear [**lin**-ee-er] adj of or in lines.

linen n **1** cloth or thread made from flax. **2** sheets, tablecloths, etc.

liner¹ n large passenger ship or aircraft.

liner² n something used as a lining.

linesman n **1** (in some sports) an official who helps the referee or umpire. **2** person who maintains railway, electricity, or telephone lines.

ling¹ n slender food fish.

ling² n heather.

linger v **1** delay or prolong departure. **2** continue in a weakened state for a long time before dying or disappearing. **3** spend a long time doing something.

lingerie [**lan**-zher-ee] n women's underwear or nightwear.

lingo n, pl **-goes** Informal foreign or unfamiliar language or jargon.

lingua franca n language used for communication between people of different mother tongues.

lingual adj of the tongue.

linguist n **1** person skilled in foreign languages. **2** person who studies linguistics. **linguistic** adj of languages. **linguistics** n scientific study of language.

liniment n medicated liquid rubbed on the skin to relieve pain or stiffness.

lining n **1** layer of cloth attached to the inside of a garment etc. **2** inner covering of anything.

link n **1** any of the rings forming a chain. **2** person or thing forming a connection. **3** type of communications connection, e.g. *a radio link*. ♦ v **4** connect with or as if with links. **5** connect by association. **linkage** n **link-up** n joining together of two systems or groups.

links pl n golf course, esp. one by the sea.

linnet n songbird of the finch family.

lino n short for LINOLEUM.

linoleum n floor covering of hessian or jute with a smooth decorative coating of powdered cork.

Linotype n ® typesetting machine which casts lines of words in one piece.

linseed n seed of the flax plant.

lint n soft material for dressing a wound.

lintel n horizontal beam at the top of a door or window.

lion n large animal of the cat family, the male of which has a shaggy mane. **lioness** n fem **the lion's share** the biggest part. **lion-hearted** adj brave.

lip n **1** either of the fleshy edges of the mouth. **2** rim of a jug etc. **3** Slang impudence. **lip-reading** n method of understanding speech by interpreting lip movements. **lip service** insincere tribute or respect. **lipstick** n cosmetic in stick form, for colouring the lips.

liquefy v **-fying, -fied** make or become liquid. **liquefaction** n

liqueur [lik-**cure**] n flavoured and sweetened alcoholic spirit.

liquid n **1** substance in a physical state which can change shape but not size. ♦ adj **2** of or being a liquid. **3** flowing smoothly. **4** (of assets) in the form of money or easily converted into money. **liquidize** v make or become liquid. **liquidizer** n kitchen appliance that liquidizes food. **liquidity** n state of being able to meet financial obligations.

liquidate v **1** pay (a debt). **2** dissolve a company and share its assets among

creditors. **3** wipe out or kill.
liquidation n **liquidator** n official
appointed to liquidate a business.
liquor n **1** alcoholic drink, esp. spirits. **2**
liquid in which food has been cooked.
liquorice [**lik**-ker-iss] n black substance
used in medicine and as a sweet.
lira n, pl **-re, -ras** monetary unit of
Turkey and formerly of Italy.
lisle [rhymes with **mile**] n strong fine
cotton thread or fabric.
lisp n **1** speech defect in which s and z
are pronounced th. ♦ v **2** speak or
utter with a lisp.
lissom, lissome adj supple, agile.
list[1] n **1** item-by-item record of names
or things, usu. written one below
another. ♦ v **2** make a list of. **3** include
in a list.
list[2] v **1** (of a ship) lean to one side. ♦ n
2 leaning to one side.
listen v **1** concentrate on hearing
something. **2** heed or pay attention to.
listener n **listen in** v listen secretly,
eavesdrop.
listeriosis n dangerous form of food
poisoning.
listless adj lacking interest or energy.
listlessly adv
lit v past of LIGHT[1] or LIGHT[2].
litany n, pl **-nies 1** prayer with
responses from the congregation. **2**
any tedious recital.
literacy n ability to read and write.
literal adj **1** according to the explicit
meaning of a word or text, not
figurative. **2** (of a translation) word for
word. **3** actual, true. **literally** adv
literary adj **1** of or knowledgeable
about literature. **2** (of a word) formal,
not colloquial.
literate adj **1** able to read and write. **2**
educated. **literati** pl n literary people.
literature n **1** written works such as
novels, plays, and poetry. **2** books and

writings of a country, period, or
subject.
lithe adj flexible or supple, pliant.
lithium n Chem chemical element, the
lightest known metal.
litho n, pl **-thos 1** short for LITHOGRAPH.
♦ adj **2** short for LITHOGRAPHIC.
lithography [lith-**og**-ra-fee] n method
of printing from a metal or stone
surface in which the printing areas are
made receptive to ink. **lithograph** n **1**
print made by lithography. ♦ v **2**
reproduce by lithography.
lithographer n **lithographic** adj
litigant n person involved in a lawsuit.
litigation n legal action. **litigate** v **1**
bring or contest a law suit. **2** engage
in legal action. **litigious** [lit-**ij**-uss] adj
frequently going to law.
litmus n blue dye turned red by acids
and restored to blue by alkalis. **litmus
test** something which is regarded as a
simple and accurate test of a particular
thing.
litotes [lie-**toe**-teez] n ironical
understatement used for effect.
litre n unit of liquid measure equal to
1000 cubic centimetres or 1.76 pints.
litter n **1** untidy rubbish dropped in
public places. **2** group of young
animals produced at one birth. **3** straw
etc. as bedding for an animal. **4** dry
material to absorb a cat's excrement. **5**
bed or seat on parallel sticks for
carrying people. ♦ v **6** strew with litter.
7 scatter or be scattered about
untidily. **8** give birth to young.
little adj **1** small or smaller than
average. **2** young. ♦ adv **3** not a lot. **4**
hardly. **5** not much or often. ♦ n **6**
small amount, extent, or duration.
littoral adj **1** of or by the seashore. ♦ n
2 coastal district.
liturgy n, pl **-gies** prescribed form of
public worship. **liturgical** adj
live[1] v **1** be alive. **2** remain in life or

existence. **3** exist in a specified way, e.g. *we live well.* **4** reside. **5** continue or last. **6** subsist. **7** enjoy life to the full. **liver** *n* person who lives in a specified way. **live down** *v* wait till people forget a past mistake or misdeed. **live-in** *adj* resident. **live together** *v* (of an unmarried couple) share a house and have a sexual relationship. **live up to** *v* meet (expectations). **live with** *v* tolerate.

live² *adj* **1** living, alive. **2** (of a broadcast) transmitted during the actual performance. **3** (of a performance) done in front of an audience. **4** (of a wire, circuit, etc.) carrying an electric current. **5** causing interest or controversy. **6** capable of exploding. **7** glowing or burning. ♦ *adv* **8** in the form of a live performance. **lively** *adj* **1** full of life or vigour. **2** animated. **3** vivid. **liveliness** *n* **liven up** *v* make (more) lively.

livelihood *n* occupation or employment.

liver *n* **1** organ secreting bile. **2** animal liver as food. **liverish** *adj* **1** having a disorder of the liver. **2** touchy or irritable.

livery *n, pl* **-eries 1** distinctive dress, esp. of a servant or servants. **2** distinctive design or colours of a company. **liveried** *adj* **livery stable** stable where horses are kept at a charge or hired out.

livestock *n* farm animals.

livid *adj* **1** *Informal* angry or furious. **2** bluish-grey.

living *adj* **1** possessing life, not dead or inanimate. **2** currently in use or existing. **3** of everyday life, e.g. *living conditions.* ♦ *n* **4** condition of being alive. **5** manner of life. **6** financial means. **living room** room in a house used for relaxation and entertainment.

lizard *n* four-footed reptile with a long body and tail.

llama *n* woolly animal of the camel family used as a beast of burden in S America.

LLB Bachelor of Laws.

loach *n* carplike freshwater fish.

load *n* **1** burden or weight. **2** amount carried. **3** source of worry. **4** amount of electrical energy drawn from a source. ♦ *pl* **5** *Informal* lots. ♦ *v* **6** put a load on or into. **7** burden or oppress. **8** cause to be biased. **9** put ammunition into (a weapon). **10** put film into (a camera). **11** transfer (a program) into computer memory. **loaded** *adj* **1** (of a question) containing a hidden trap or implication. **2** (of dice) dishonestly weighted. **3** *Slang* wealthy.

loaf¹ *n, pl* **loaves 1** shaped mass of baked bread. **2** shaped mass of food. **3** *Slang* head, esp. as the source of common sense, e.g. *use your loaf.*

loaf² *v* idle, loiter. **loafer** *n*

loam *n* fertile soil.

loan *n* **1** money lent at interest. **2** lending. **3** thing lent. ♦ *v* **4** lend. **loan shark** person who lends money at an extremely high interest rate.

loath, loth [rhymes with **both**] *adj* unwilling or reluctant (to).

✓ **WORD TIP**
Distinguish between *loath* 'reluctant' and *loathe* 'be disgusted by'.

loathe *v* hate, be disgusted by. **loathing** *n* **loathsome** *adj*

lob *Sport* ♦ *n* **1** ball struck or thrown in a high arc. ♦ *v* **lobbing, lobbed 2** strike or throw (a ball) in a high arc.

lobby *n, pl* **-bies 1** corridor into which rooms open. **2** group which tries to influence legislators. **3** hall in a legislative building to which the public has access. ♦ *v* **4** try to influence (legislators) in the formulation of policy. **lobbyist** n

lobe n 1 rounded projection. 2 soft hanging part of the ear. 3 subdivision of a body organ. **lobed** adj

lobelia n garden plant with blue, red, or white flowers.

lobola [law-**bawl**-a] n S Afr (in African custom) price paid by a bridegroom's family to his bride's family.

lobotomy n, pl -**mies** surgical incision into a lobe of the brain to treat mental disorders.

lobster n 1 shellfish with a long tail and claws, which turns red when boiled. 2 Austral informal $20 note.

local adj 1 of or existing in a particular place. 2 confined to a particular place. ♦ n 3 person belonging to a particular district. 4 Informal pub close to one's home. **locally** adv **locality** n neighbourhood or area. **localize** v restrict to a particular place. **locale** [loh-**kahl**] n scene of an event. **local anaesthetic** anaesthetic which produces loss of feeling in one part of the body. **local authority** governing body of a county, district, or region. **local government** government of towns, counties, and districts by locally elected political bodies.

locate v 1 discover the whereabouts of. 2 situate or place. **location** n 1 site or position. 2 act of discovering where something is. 3 site of a film production away from the studio. 4 S Afr Black African or coloured township.

loch n Scot 1 lake. 2 long narrow bay.

lock[1] n 1 appliance for fastening a door, case, etc. 2 section of a canal shut off by gates between which the water level can be altered to aid boats moving from one level to another. 3 extent to which a vehicle's front wheels will turn. 4 interlocking of parts. 5 mechanism for firing a gun. 6 wrestling hold. ♦ v 7 fasten or become

fastened securely. 8 become or cause to become fixed or united. 9 become or cause to become immovable. 10 embrace closely. **lockout** n closing of a workplace by an employer to force workers to accept terms. **locksmith** n person who makes and mends locks. **lockup** n 1 prison. 2 garage or storage place away from the main premises.

lock[2] n strand of hair.

locker n small cupboard with a lock.

locket n small hinged pendant for a portrait etc.

lockjaw n tetanus.

locomotive n 1 self-propelled engine for pulling trains. ♦ adj 2 of locomotion. **locomotion** n action or power of moving.

locum n temporary stand-in for a doctor or clergyman.

locus [**loh**-kuss] n, pl **loci** [**loh**-sigh] 1 area or place where something happens. 2 Maths set of points or lines satisfying one or more specified conditions.

locust n destructive African insect that flies in swarms and eats crops.

lode n vein of ore. **lodestar** n star used in navigation or astronomy as a point of reference. **lodestone** n magnetic iron ore.

lodge n 1 Chiefly Brit gatekeeper's house. 2 house or cabin used occasionally by hunters, skiers, etc. 3 porters' room in a university or college. 4 local branch of some societies. 5 v 6 live in another's house at a fixed charge. 7 stick or become stuck (in a place). 8 make (a complaint etc.) formally. **lodger** n **lodging** n 1 temporary residence. ♦ pl 2 rented room or rooms in another person's house.

loft n 1 space between the top storey and roof of a building. 2 gallery in a church etc. 3 v 4 Sport strike, throw, or kick (a ball) high into the air.

lofty adj **loftier, loftiest 1** of great height. **2** exalted or noble. **3** haughty. **loftily** adv haughtily.

log[1] n **1** portion of a felled tree stripped of branches. **2** detailed record of a journey of a ship, aircraft, etc. ◆ v **logging, logged 3** saw logs from a tree. **4** record in a log. **logging** n work of cutting and transporting logs. **logbook** n book recording the details about a car or a ship's journeys. **log in, out** v gain entrance to or leave a computer system by keying in a special command.

log[2] n short for LOGARITHM.

loganberry n purplish-red fruit, similar to a raspberry.

logarithm n one of a series of arithmetical functions used to make certain calculations easier.

loggerheads pl n **at loggerheads** quarrelling, disputing.

loggia [**loj**-ya] n covered gallery at the side of a building.

logic n **1** philosophy of reasoning. **2** reasoned thought or argument. **logical** adj **1** of logic. **2** capable of or using clear valid reasoning. **3** reasonable. **logically** adv **logician** n

logistics n detailed planning and organization of a large, esp. military, operation. **logistical, logistic** adj

logo [**loh**-go] n, pl **-os** emblem used by a company or other organization.

loin n **1** part of the body between the ribs and the hips. **2** cut of meat from this part of an animal. ◆ pl **3** hips and inner thighs. **loincloth** n piece of cloth covering the loins only.

loiter v stand or wait aimlessly or idly.

loll v **1** lounge lazily. **2** hang loosely.

lollipop n boiled sweet on a small wooden stick. **lollipop man, lady** Brit informal person holding a circular sign on a pole, who controls traffic so that children may cross the road safely.

lolly n, pl **-ies 1** Informal lollipop or ice lolly. **2** Aust & NZ informal sweet. **3** Slang money. **lolly scramble** NZ sweets scattered on the ground for children to collect.

lone adj solitary. **lonely** adj **1** sad because alone. **2** resulting from being alone. **3** unfrequented. **loneliness** n **loner** n Informal person who prefers to be alone. **lonesome** adj lonely.

long[1] adj **1** having length, esp. great length, in space or time. ◆ adv **2** for an extensive period. **long-distance** adj going between places far apart. **long face** glum expression. **longhand** n ordinary writing, not shorthand or typing. **long johns** Informal long underpants. **long-life** adj (of milk, batteries, etc.) lasting longer than the regular kind. **long-lived** adj living or lasting for a long time. **long-range** adj **1** extending into the future. **2** (of vehicles, weapons, etc.) designed to cover great distances. **long shot** competitor, undertaking, or bet with little chance of success. **long-sighted** adj able to see distant objects in focus but not nearby ones. **long-standing** adj existing for a long time. **long-suffering** adj enduring trouble or unhappiness without complaint. **long-term** adj lasting or effective for a long time. **long wave** radio wave with a wavelength of over 1000 metres. **long-winded** adj speaking or writing at tedious length.

long[2] v have a strong desire (for). **longing** n yearning. **longingly** adv

longevity [lon-**jev**-it-ee] n long life.

longitude n distance east or west from a standard meridian. **longitudinal** adj **1** of length or longitude. **2** lengthways.

longshoreman n US docker.

loo n Informal toilet.

loofah n sponge made from the dried

pod of a gourd.

look v 1 direct the eyes or attention (towards). 2 have the appearance of being. 3 face in a particular direction. 4 search (for). 5 hope (for). ♦ n 6 instance of looking. 7 (often pl) appearance. **look after** v take care of. **lookalike** n person who is the double of another. **look down on** v treat as inferior or unimportant. **look forward to** v anticipate with pleasure. **look on** v 1 be a spectator. 2 consider or regard. **lookout** n 1 guard. 2 place for watching. 3 Informal worry or concern. 4 chances or prospect. **look out** v be careful. **look up** v 1 discover or confirm by checking in a book. 2 improve. 3 visit. **look up to** v respect.

loom¹ n machine for weaving cloth.

loom² v 1 appear dimly. 2 seem ominously close.

loony Slang ♦ adj **loonier, looniest** 1 foolish or insane. ♦ n, pl **loonies** 2 foolish or insane person.

loop n 1 rounded shape made by a curved line or rope crossing itself. 2 v 3 form or fasten with a loop. **loop the loop** fly or be flown in a complete vertical circle. **loophole** n means of evading a rule without breaking it.

loose adj 1 not tight, fastened, fixed, or tense. 2 vague. 3 dissolute or promiscuous. ♦ adv 4 in a loose manner. ♦ v 5 free. 6 unfasten. 7 slacken. 8 let fly (an arrow, bullet, etc.). **at a loose end** bored, with nothing to do. **loosely** adv **looseness** n **loosen** v make loose. **loosen up** v relax, stop worrying. **loose-leaf** adj allowing the addition or removal of pages.

loot n, v 1 plunder. ♦ n 2 Informal money. **looter** n **looting** n

lop v **lopping, lopped** 1 cut away twigs and branches. 2 chop off.

lope v run with long easy strides.

lop-eared adj having drooping ears.

lopsided adj greater in height, weight, or size on one side.

loquacious adj talkative. **loquacity** n

lord n 1 person with power over others, such as a monarch or master. 2 male member of the British nobility. 3 Hist feudal superior. 4 (L-) God or Jesus. 5 (L-) (in Britain) title given to certain male officials and peers. **House of Lords** unelected upper chamber of the British parliament. **lord it over** act in a superior manner towards. **the Lord's Prayer** prayer taught by Christ to his disciples. **lordly** adj imperious, proud. **Lordship** n (in Britain) title of some male officials and peers.

lore n body of traditions on a subject.

lorgnette [lor-**nyet**] n pair of spectacles mounted on a long handle.

lorikeet n small brightly coloured Australian parrot.

lorry n, pl **-ries** Brit & S Afr large vehicle for transporting loads by road.

lose v **losing, lost** 1 come to be without, esp. by accident or carelessness. 2 fail to keep or maintain. 3 be deprived of. 4 fail to get or make use of. 5 be defeated in a competition etc. 6 be or become engrossed, e.g. lost in thought. **loser** n 1 person or thing that loses. 2 Informal person who seems destined to fail.

☑ **SPELLING TIP**

The verb **lose** (I don't want to lose my hair) should not be confused with **loose**, which, although existing as a verb, is more often used as an adjective (a loose tooth) or adverb (to work loose).

---

loss n 1 losing. 2 that which is lost. 3 damage resulting from losing. **at a loss** 1 confused or bewildered. 2 not earning enough to cover costs. **loss**

leader item sold at a loss to attract customers.

lost v **1** past of LOSE. ♦ adj **2** unable to find one's way. **3** unable to be found.

lot pron **1** great number. ♦ n **2** collection of people or things. **3** fate or destiny. **4** one of a set of objects drawn at random to make a selection or choice. **5** item at auction. **6** pl **7** Informal great numbers or quantities. **a lot** Informal great deal.

loth adj same as LOATH.

lotion n medical or cosmetic liquid for use on the skin.

lottery n, pl **-teries 1** method of raising money by selling tickets that win prizes by chance. **2** gamble.

lotto n **1** game of chance like bingo. **2** (L-) national lottery.

lotus n **1** legendary plant whose fruit induces forgetfulness. **2** Egyptian water lily.

loud adj **1** relatively great in volume. **2** capable of making much noise. **3** insistent and emphatic. **4** unpleasantly patterned or colourful. **loudly** adv **loudness** n **loudspeaker** n instrument for converting electrical signals into sound.

lough n Irish loch.

lounge n **1** living room in a private house. **2** more expensive bar in a pub. **3** area for waiting in an airport. ♦ v **4** sit, lie, or stand in a relaxed manner. **lounge suit** man's suit for daytime wear.

lour v same as LOWER².

louse n **1** pl **lice** wingless parasitic insect. **2** pl **louses**) unpleasant person. **lousy** adj **1** Slang mean or unpleasant. **2** bad, inferior. **3** unwell.

lout n crude, oafish, or aggressive person. **loutish** adj

louvre [**loo**-ver] n one of a set of parallel slats slanted to admit air but not rain. **louvred** adj

love v **1** have a great affection for. **2** feel sexual passion for. **3** enjoy (something) very much. ♦ n **4** great affection. **5** sexual passion. **6** wholehearted liking for something. **7** beloved person. **8** Tennis, squash, etc. score of nothing. **fall in love** become in love. **in love (with)** feeling a strong emotional (and sexual) attraction (for). **make love (to)** have sexual intercourse (with). **lovable, loveable** adj **loveless** adj **lovely** adj **-lier, -liest 1** very attractive. **2** highly enjoyable. **lover** n **1** person having a sexual relationship outside marriage. **2** person in love. **3** someone who loves a specified person or thing. **loving** adj affectionate, tender. **lovingly** adv **love affair** romantic or sexual relationship between two people who are not married to each other. **lovebird** n small parrot. **love child** Euphemistic child of an unmarried couple. **love life** person's romantic or sexual relationships. **lovelorn** adj miserable because of unhappiness in love. **lovemaking** n

low¹ adj **1** not tall, high, or elevated. **2** of little or less than the usual amount, degree, quality, or cost. **3** coarse or vulgar. **4** dejected. **5** not loud. **6** deep in pitch. **7** adv **8** in or to a low position, level, or degree. ♦ n **9** low position, level, or degree. **10** area of low atmospheric pressure, depression. **lowly** adj modest, humble. **lowliness** n **lowbrow** n, adj (person) with nonintellectual tastes and interests. **Low Church** section of the Anglican Church stressing evangelical beliefs and practices. **lowdown** n Informal inside information. **low-down** adj Informal mean, underhand, or dishonest. **low-key** adj subdued, restrained, not intense. **lowland** n **1** low-lying country. ♦ pl **2** (L-) less mountainous parts of Scotland. **low profile** position or attitude avoiding prominence or publicity. **low-spirited** adj depressed.

low² n 1 cry of cattle, moo. ♦ v 2 moo.

lower¹ adj 1 below one or more other things. 2 smaller or reduced in amount or value. ♦ v 3 cause or allow to move down. 4 lessen. **lower case** small, as distinct from capital, letters.

lower², lour v (of the sky or weather) look gloomy or threatening. **lowering** adj

loyal adj faithful to one's friends, country, or government. **loyally** adv **loyalty** n **loyalty card** swipe card issued by a supermarket or chain store to a customer, used to record credit points awarded for money spent in the store. **loyalist** n

lozenge n 1 medicated tablet held in the mouth until it dissolves. 2 four-sided diamond-shaped figure.

LP n record playing approximately 20–25 minutes each side.

L-plate n Brit & Aust sign on a car being driven by a learner driver.

LSD lysergic acid diethylamide, a hallucinogenic drug.

Lt Lieutenant.

Ltd Brit Limited (Liability).

lubricate [loo-brik-ate] v oil or grease to lessen friction. **lubricant** n lubricating substance, such as oil. **lubrication** n

lubricious adj Lit lewd.

lucerne n fodder plant like clover, alfalfa.

lucid adj 1 clear and easily understood. 2 able to think clearly. 3 bright and clear. **lucidly** adv **lucidity** n

Lucifer n Satan.

luck n 1 fortune, good or bad. 2 good fortune. **lucky** adj having or bringing good luck. **lucky dip** game in which

prizes are picked from a tub at random. **luckily** adv fortunately. **luckless** adj having bad luck.

lucrative adj very profitable.

lucre [loo-ker] n filthy lucre Facetious money.

Luddite n person opposed to change in industrial methods.

luderick n Australian fish, usu. black or dark brown in colour.

ludicrous adj absurd or ridiculous. **ludicrously** adv

ludo n game played with dice and counters on a board.

lug¹ v lugging, lugged carry or drag with great effort.

lug² n 1 projection serving as a handle. 2 Brit informal ear.

luggage n traveller's cases, bags, etc.

lugubrious adj mournful, gloomy. **lugubriously** adv

lugworm n large worm used as bait.

lukewarm adj 1 moderately warm, tepid. 2 indifferent or half-hearted.

lull v 1 soothe (someone) by soft sounds or motions. 2 calm (fears or suspicions) by deception. ♦ n 3 brief time of quiet in a storm etc.

lullaby n, pl -bies quiet song to send a child to sleep.

lumbago [lum-bay-go] n pain in the lower back. **lumbar** adj relating to the lower back.

lumber¹ n 1 Brit unwanted disused household articles. 2 Chiefly US sawn timber. ♦ v 3 Informal burden with something unpleasant. **lumberjack** n US man who fells trees and prepares logs for transport.

lumber² v move heavily and awkwardly. **lumbering** adj

luminous adj reflecting or giving off light. **luminosity** n **luminary** n 1 famous person. 2 Lit heavenly body giving off light. **luminescence** n emission of light at low temperatures by any process other than burning. **luminescent** *adj*

lump[1] *n* **1** shapeless piece or mass. **2** swelling. **3** *Informal* awkward or stupid person. ♦ *v* **4** consider as a single group. **lump in one's throat** tight dry feeling in one's throat, usu. caused by great emotion. **lumpy** *adj* **lump sum** relatively large sum of money paid at one time.

lump[2] *v* **lump it** *Informal* tolerate or put up with it.

lunar *adj* relating to the moon.

lunatic *adj* **1** foolish and irresponsible. ♦ *n* **2** foolish or annoying person. **3** *Old-fashioned* insane person. **lunacy** *n*

lunch *n* **1** meal taken in the middle of the day. ♦ *v* **2** eat lunch. **luncheon** *n* formal lunch. **luncheon meat** tinned ground mixture of meat and cereal. **luncheon voucher** *Brit* voucher for a certain amount, given to an employee and accepted by some restaurants as payment for a meal.

lung *n* organ that allows an animal or bird to breathe air: humans have two lungs in the chest. **lungfish** *n* freshwater bony fish with an air-breathing lung of South America and Australia.

lunge *n* **1** sudden forward motion. **2** thrust with a sword. ♦ *v* **3** move with or make a lunge.

lupin *n* garden plant with tall spikes of flowers.

lupine *adj* like a wolf.

lurch[1] *v* **1** tilt or lean suddenly to one side. **2** stagger. ♦ *n* **3** lurching movement.

lurch[2] *n* **leave someone in the lurch** abandon someone in difficulties.

lurcher *n* crossbred dog trained to hunt silently.

lure *v* **1** tempt or attract by the promise of reward. ♦ *n* **2** person or thing that

lures. **3** brightly-coloured artificial angling bait.

lurid *adj* **1** vivid in shocking detail, sensational. **2** glaring in colour. **luridly** *adv*

lurk *v* **1** lie hidden or move stealthily, esp. for sinister purposes. **2** be latent.

luscious [**lush**-uss] *adj* **1** extremely pleasurable to taste or smell. **2** very attractive.

lush[1] *adj* **1** (of grass etc.) growing thickly and healthily. **2** opulent.

lush[2] *n* *Slang* alcoholic.

lust *n* **1** strong sexual desire. **2** any strong desire. ♦ *v* **3** have passionate desire (for). **lustful** *adj* **lusty** *adj* vigorous, healthy. **lustily** *adv*

lustre *n* **1** gloss, sheen. **2** splendour or glory. **3** metallic pottery glaze. **lustrous** *adj* shining, luminous.

lute *n* ancient guitar-like musical instrument with a body shaped like a half pear.

Lutheran *adj* of Martin Luther (1483–1546), German Reformation leader, his doctrines, or a Church following these doctrines.

luxuriant *adj* **1** rich and abundant. **2** very elaborate. **luxuriance** *n* **luxuriantly** *adv*

luxuriate *v* **1** take self-indulgent pleasure (in). **2** flourish.

luxury *n, pl* -**ries 1** enjoyment of rich, very comfortable living. **2** enjoyable but not essential thing. ♦ *adj* **3** of or providing luxury, sumptuous. **luxurious** *adj* full of luxury, sumptuous. **luxuriously** *adv*

lychee [lie-**chee**] *n* Chinese fruit with a whitish juicy pulp.

lych gate *n* roofed gate to a churchyard.

Lycra *n* ® elastic fabric used for tight-fitting garments, such as swimsuits.

lye *n* caustic solution obtained by

leaching wood ash.

lying *v* **present participle of** LIE¹ *or* LIE².

lymph *n* colourless bodily fluid consisting mainly of white blood cells. **lymphatic** *adj*

lymphocyte *n* type of white blood cell.

lynch *v* put to death without a trial.

lynx *n* animal of the cat family with tufted ears and a short tail.

lyre *n* ancient musical instrument like a U-shaped harp.

lyric *adj* **1** (of poetry) expressing personal emotion in songlike style. **2** like a song. ♦ *n* **3** short poem in a songlike style. ♦ *pl* **4** words of a popular song. **lyrical** *adj* **1** lyric. **2** enthusiastic. **lyricist** *n* person who writes the words of songs or musicals.

M m

m 1 metre(s). **2** mile(s). **3** minute(s).

M 1 Motorway. **2** Monsieur.

m. 1 male. **2** married. **3** masculine. **4** meridian. **5** month.

ma *n Informal* mother.

MA Master of Arts.

ma'am *n* madam.

mac *n Brit informal* mackintosh.

macabre [mak-**kahb**-ra] *adj* strange and horrible, gruesome.

macadam *n* road surface of pressed layers of small broken stones.

macadamia *n* Australian tree with edible nuts.

macaroni *n* pasta in short tube shapes.

macaroon *n* small biscuit or cake made with ground almonds.

macaw *n* large tropical American parrot.

mace[1] *n* **1** ceremonial staff of office. **2** medieval weapon with a spiked metal head.

mace[2] *n* spice made from the dried husk of the nutmeg.

macerate [**mass**-er-ate] *v* soften by soaking. **maceration** *n*

machete [mash-**ett**-ee] *n* broad heavy knife used for cutting or as a weapon.

Machiavellian [mak-ee-a-**vel**-yan] *adj* unprincipled, crafty, and opportunist.

machinations [mak-in-**nay**-shunz] *pl n* cunning plots and ploys.

machine *n* **1** apparatus, usu. powered by electricity, designed to perform a particular task. **2** vehicle, such as a car or aircraft. **3** controlling system of an organization. ♦ *v* **4** make or produce by machine. **machinery** *n* machines or machine parts collectively.

machinist *n* person who operates a machine. **machine gun** automatic gun that fires rapidly and continuously. **machine-gun** *v* fire at with such a gun. **machine-readable** *adj* (of data) in a form suitable for processing by a computer.

machismo [mak-**izz**-moh] *n* exaggerated or strong masculinity.

Mach number [**mak**] *n* ratio of the speed of a body in a particular medium to the speed of sound in that medium.

macho [**match**-oh] *adj* strongly or exaggeratedly masculine.

mackerel *n* edible sea fish.

mackintosh *n* waterproof raincoat of rubberized cloth.

macramé [mak-**rah**-mee] *n* ornamental work of knotted cord.

macrobiotics *n* dietary system advocating whole grains and vegetables grown without chemical additives. **macrobiotic** *adj*

macrocosm *n* **1** the universe. **2** any large complete system.

mad *adj* **madder, maddest 1** mentally deranged, insane. **2** very foolish. **3** *Informal* angry. **4** frantic. **5** (foll. by *about* or *on*) very enthusiastic (about). **like mad** *Informal* with great energy, enthusiasm, or haste. **madly** *adv* **madness** *n* **madden** *v* infuriate or irritate. **maddening** *adj* **madman, madwoman** *n*

madam *n* **1** polite form of address to a woman. **2** *Informal* precocious or conceited girl.

madame [mad-**dam**] *n, pl* **mesdames** [may-**dam**] French title equivalent to *Mrs.*

madcap *adj* foolish or reckless.

madder *n* **1** climbing plant. **2** red dye made from its root.

made v past of MAKE.

Madeira [mad-**deer**-a] n fortified white wine. **Madeira cake** rich sponge cake.

mademoiselle [mad-mwah-**zel**] n, pl **mesdemoiselles** [maid-mwah-**zel**] French title equivalent to *Miss*.

Madonna n 1 the Virgin Mary. 2 picture or statue of her.

madrigal n 16th–17th-century part song for unaccompanied voices.

maelstrom [**male**-strom] n 1 great whirlpool. 2 turmoil.

maestro [**my**-stroh] n, pl **-tri, -tros** 1 outstanding musician or conductor. 2 any master of an art.

Mafia n international secret criminal organization founded in Sicily. **mafioso** n, pl **-sos, -si** member of the Mafia.

magazine n 1 periodical publication with articles by different writers. 2 television or radio programme made up of short nonfictional items. 3 appliance for automatically supplying cartridges to a gun or slides to a projector. 4 storehouse for explosives or arms.

magenta [maj-**jen**-ta] adj deep purplish-red.

maggot n larva of an insect. **maggoty** adj

Magi [**maje**-eye] pl n wise men from the East who came to worship the infant Jesus.

magic n 1 supposed art of invoking supernatural powers to influence events. 2 mysterious quality or power. ♦ adj 3 (also **magical**) of, using, or like magic. 4 *Informal* wonderful, marvellous. **magically** adv **magician** n 1 conjuror. 2 person with magic powers.

magistrate n 1 public officer administering the law. 2 *Brit* justice of the peace. 3 *Aust & NZ* former name for DISTRICT COURT JUDGE. **magisterial** adj 1 commanding or authoritative. 2 of a magistrate.

magma n molten rock inside the earth's crust.

magnanimous adj noble and generous. **magnanimously** adv **magnanimity** n

magnate n influential or wealthy person, esp. in industry.

magnesia n white tasteless substance used as an antacid and a laxative; magnesium oxide.

magnesium n *Chem* silvery-white metallic element.

magnet n piece of iron or steel capable of attracting iron and pointing north when suspended. **magnetic** adj 1 having the properties of a magnet. 2 powerfully attractive. **magnetically** adv **magnetism** n 1 magnetic property. 2 powerful personal charm. 3 science of magnetic properties. **magnetize** v 1 make into a magnet. 2 attract strongly. **magnetic tape** plastic strip coated with a magnetic substance for recording sound or video signals.

magneto [mag-**nee**-toe] n, pl **-tos** apparatus for ignition in an internal-combustion engine.

magnificent adj 1 splendid or impressive. 2 excellent. **magnificently** adv **magnificence** n

magnify v **-fying, -fied** 1 increase in apparent size, as with a lens. 2 exaggerate. **magnification** n

magnitude n relative importance or size.

magnolia n shrub or tree with showy white or pink flowers.

magnum n large wine bottle holding about 1.5 litres.

magpie n 1 black-and-white bird 2 any of various similar Australian birds, e.g. the butcherbird.

maharajah n former title of some

Indian princes. **maharani** *n fem*

mah jong, mah-jongg *n* Chinese table game for four, played with tiles bearing different designs.

mahogany *n* hard reddish-brown wood of several tropical trees.

mahout [ma-**howt**] *n* (in India and the East Indies) elephant driver or keeper.

maid *n* 1 (also **maidservant**) female servant. 2 *Lit* young unmarried woman.

maiden *n* 1 *Lit* young unmarried woman. ♦ *adj* 2 unmarried. 3 first, e.g. *maiden voyage*. **maidenly** *adj* modest. **maidenhair** *n* fern with delicate fronds. **maidenhead** *n* virginity. **maiden name** woman's surname before marriage. **maiden over** *Cricket* over in which no runs are scored.

mail[1] *n* 1 letters and packages transported and delivered by the post office. 2 postal system. 3 single collection or delivery of mail. 4 train, ship, or aircraft carrying mail. 5 same as E-MAIL. ♦ *v* 6 send by mail. **mailbox** *n US, Canadian & Aust* box into which letters and parcels are delivered. **mail order** system of buying goods by post. **mailshot** *n Brit* posting of advertising material to many selected people at once.

mail[2] *n* flexible armour of interlaced rings or links.

maim *v* cripple or mutilate.

main *adj* 1 chief or principal. ♦ *n* 2 principal pipe or line carrying water, gas, or electricity. ♦ *pl* 3 main distribution network for water, gas, or electricity. **in the main** on the whole. **mainly** *adv* for the most part, chiefly. **mainframe** *n, adj Computers* (denoting) a high-speed general-purpose computer. **mainland** *n* stretch of land which forms the main part of a country. **mainmast** *n* chief mast of a ship. **mainsail** *n* largest sail on a mainmast. **mainspring** *n* 1 chief

cause or motive. 2 chief spring of a watch or clock. **mainstay** *n* 1 chief support. 2 rope securing a mainmast. **mainstream** *adj* (of) a prevailing cultural trend.

maintain *v* 1 continue or keep in existence. 2 keep up or preserve. 3 support financially. 4 assert. **maintenance** *n* 1 maintaining. 2 upkeep of a building, car, etc. 3 provision of money for a separated or divorced spouse.

maisonette *n Brit* flat with more than one floor.

maître d'hôtel [**met**-ra dote-**tell**] *n French* head waiter.

maize *n* type of corn with spikes of yellow grains.

majesty *n, pl* **-ties** 1 stateliness or grandeur. 2 supreme power. **majestic** *adj* **majestically** *adv*

major *adj* 1 greater in number, quality, or extent. 2 significant or serious. ♦ *n* 3 middle-ranking army officer. 4 scale in music. 5 *US, Canadian, S Afr, Aust & NZ* principal field of study at a university etc. ♦ *v* 6 (foll. by *in*) *US, Canadian, S Afr, Aust & NZ* do one's principal study in (a particular subject). **major-domo** *n, pl* **-domos** chief steward of a great household.

majority *n, pl* **-ties** 1 greater number. 2 number by which the votes on one side exceed those on the other. 3 largest party voting together. 4 state of being legally an adult.

make *v* **making, made** 1 create, construct, or establish. 2 cause to do or be. 3 bring about or produce. 4 perform (an action). 5 serve as or become. 6 amount to. 7 earn. ♦ *n* 8 brand, type, or style. **make do** manage with an inferior alternative. **make it** *Informal* be successful. **on the make** *Informal* out for profit or conquest. **maker** *n* **making** *n* 1 creation or production. ♦ *pl* **2** necessary requirements or qualities.

make-believe *n* fantasy or pretence.

make for *v* head towards. **make off with** *v* steal or abduct. **makeshift** *adj* serving as a temporary substitute.

make up *v* **1** form or constitute. **2** prepare. **3** invent. **4** supply what is lacking, complete. **5** (foll. by *for*) compensate (for). **6** settle a quarrel. **7** apply cosmetics. **make-up** *n* **1** cosmetics. **2** way something is made. **3** mental or physical constitution.

makeweight *n* something unimportant added to make up a lack.

mal- *combining form* bad or badly, e.g. *malformation*.

malachite [**mal**-a-kite] *n* green mineral.

maladjusted *adj Psychol* unable to meet the demands of society. **maladjustment** *n*

maladministration *n* inefficient or dishonest administration.

maladroit *adj* clumsy or awkward.

malady *n, pl* **-dies** disease or illness.

malaise [mal-**laze**] *n* vague feeling of unease, illness, or depression.

malapropism *n* comical misuse of a word by confusion with one which sounds similar, e.g. *I am not under the affluence of alcohol.*

malaria *n* infectious disease caused by the bite of some mosquitoes. **malarial** *adj*

Malay *n* **1** member of a people of Malaysia or Indonesia. **2** language of this people. **Malayan** *adj, n*

malcontent *n* discontented person.

male *adj* **1** of the sex which can fertilize female reproductive cells. ♦ *n* **2** male person or animal.

malediction [mal-lid-**dik**-shun] *n* curse.

malefactor [**mal**-if-act-or] *n* criminal or wrongdoer.

malevolent [mal-**lev**-a-lent] *adj*

wishing evil to others. **malevolently** *adv* **malevolence** *n*

malfeasance [mal-**fee**-zanss] *n* misconduct, esp. by a public official.

malformed *adj* misshapen or deformed. **malformation** *n*

malfunction *v* **1** function imperfectly or fail to function. ♦ *n* **2** defective functioning or failure to function.

malice [**mal**-iss] *n* desire to cause harm to others. **malicious** *adj* **maliciously** *adv*

malign [mal-**line**] *v* **1** slander or defame. ♦ *adj* **2** evil in influence or effect. **malignity** *n* evil disposition.

malignant [mal-**lig**-nant] *adj* **1** seeking to harm others. **2** (of a tumour) harmful and uncontrollable. **malignancy** *n*

malinger *v* feign illness to avoid work. **malingerer** *n*

mall [**mawl**] *n* street or shopping area closed to vehicles.

mallard *n* wild duck.

malleable [**mal**-lee-a-bl] *adj* **1** capable of being hammered or pressed into shape. **2** easily influenced. **malleability** *n*

mallee *n Aust* low-growing eucalypt in dry regions.

mallet *n* **1** (wooden) hammer. **2** stick with a head like a hammer, used in croquet or polo.

mallow *n* plant with pink or purple flowers.

malnutrition *n* inadequate nutrition.

malodorous [mal-**lode**-or-uss] *adj* bad-smelling.

malpractice *n* immoral, illegal, or unethical professional conduct.

malt *n* grain, such as barley, prepared for use in making beer or whisky.

maltreat *v* treat badly. **maltreatment** *n*

mama *n Old-fashioned* mother.

mamba n deadly S African snake.

mamma n same as MAMA.

mammal n animal of the type that suckles its young. **mammalian** adj

mammary adj of the breasts or milk-producing glands.

mammon n wealth regarded as a source of evil.

mammoth n 1 extinct elephant-like mammal. ♦ adj 2 colossal.

man n, pl **men** 1 adult male. 2 human being or person. 3 mankind. 4 manservant. 5 piece used in chess etc. ♦ v **manning, manned** 6 supply with sufficient people for operation or defence. **manhood** n **mankind** n human beings collectively. **manly** adj (possessing qualities) appropriate to a man. **manliness** n **mannish** adj (of a woman) like a man. **man-hour** n work done by one person in one hour. **man-made** adj made artificially.

mana n NZ authority, influence.

manacle [**man**-a-kl] n, v handcuff or fetter.

manage v 1 succeed in doing. 2 be in charge of, administer. 3 handle or control. 4 cope with (financial) difficulties. **manageable** adj **management** n 1 managers collectively. 2 administration or organization.

manager, manageress n person in charge of a business, institution, actor, sports team, etc. **managerial** adj

manatee n large tropical plant-eating aquatic mammal.

mandarin n 1 high-ranking government official. 2 kind of small orange.

mandate n 1 official or authoritative command. 2 authorization or instruction from an electorate to its representative or government. ♦ v 3 give authority to. **mandatory** adj compulsory.

mandible n lower jawbone or jawlike part.

mandolin n musical instrument with four pairs of strings.

mandrake n plant with a forked root, formerly used as a narcotic.

mandrel n shaft on which work is held in a lathe.

mandrill n large blue-faced baboon.

mane n long hair on the neck of a horse, lion, etc.

manful adj determined and brave. **manfully** adv

manganese n Chem brittle greyish-white metallic element.

mange n skin disease of domestic animals.

mangelwurzel n variety of beet used as cattle food.

manger n eating trough in a stable or barn.

mangetout [**mawnzh**-too] n variety of pea with an edible pod.

mangle¹ v 1 destroy by crushing and twisting. 2 spoil.

mangle² n 1 machine with rollers for squeezing water from washed clothes. ♦ v 2 put through a mangle.

mango n, pl **-goes, -gos** tropical fruit with sweet juicy yellow flesh.

mangrove n tropical tree with exposed roots, which grows beside water.

mangy adj **mangier, mangiest** 1 having mange. 2 scruffy or shabby.

manhandle v treat roughly.

manhole n hole with a cover, through which a person can enter a drain or sewer.

mania n 1 extreme enthusiasm. 2 madness. **maniac** n 1 mad person. 2 Informal person who has an extreme enthusiasm for something. **maniacal** [man-**eye**-a-kl] adj

manic adj affected by mania.

manicure n **1** cosmetic care of the fingernails and hands. ♦ v **2** care for (the fingernails and hands) in this way. **manicurist** n

manifest adj **1** easily noticed, obvious. ♦ v **2** show plainly. **3** be evidence of. ♦ n **4** list of cargo or passengers for customs. **manifestation** n

manifesto n, pl -tos, -toes declaration of policy as issued by a political party.

manifold adj **1** numerous and varied. ♦ n **2** pipe with several outlets, esp. in an internal-combustion engine.

manikin n **1** little man or dwarf. **2** model of the human body.

manila, manilla n strong brown paper used for envelopes.

manipulate v **1** handle skilfully. **2** control cleverly or deviously. **manipulation** n **manipulative** adj **manipulator** n

manna n **1** Bible miraculous food which sustained the Israelites in the wilderness. **2** windfall.

mannequin n **1** woman who models clothes at a fashion show. **2** life-size dummy of the human body used to fit or display clothes.

manner n **1** way a thing happens or is done. **2** person's bearing or behaviour. **3** type or kind. **4** custom or style. ♦ pl **5** (polite) social behaviour. **mannered** adj affected. **mannerism** n person's distinctive habit or trait.

mannikin n same as MANIKIN.

manoeuvre [man-**noo**-ver] n **1** skilful movement. **2** contrived, complicated, and possibly deceptive plan or action. ♦ pl **3** military or naval exercises. ♦ v **4** manipulate or contrive skilfully or cunningly. **5** perform manoeuvres. **manoeuvrable** adj

manor n Brit large country house and its lands. **manorial** adj

manpower n available number of workers.

manqué [**mong**-kay] adj would-be, e.g. an actor manqué.

mansard roof n roof with a break in its slope, the lower part being steeper than the upper.

manse n house provided for a minister in some religious denominations.

manservant n, pl **menservants** male servant, esp. a valet.

mansion n large house.

manslaughter n unlawful but unintentional killing of a person.

mantel n structure round a fireplace. **mantelpiece, mantel shelf** n shelf above a fireplace.

mantilla n (in Spain) a lace scarf covering a woman's head and shoulders.

mantis n, pl -tises, -tes carnivorous insect like a grasshopper.

mantle n **1** loose cloak. **2** covering. **3** responsibilities and duties which go with a particular job or position.

mantra n Hinduism, Buddhism any sacred word or syllable used as an object of concentration.

manual adj **1** of or done with the hands. **2** by human labour rather than automatic means. ♦ n **3** handbook. **4** organ keyboard. **manually** adv

manufacture v **1** process or make (goods) on a large scale using machinery. **2** invent or concoct (an excuse etc.). ♦ n **3** process of manufacturing goods.

manufacturer n company that manufactures goods.

manure n animal excrement used as a fertilizer.

manuscript n **1** book or document, orig. one written by hand. **2** copy for printing.

Manx adj **1** of the Isle of Man or its inhabitants. ♦ n **2** almost extinct language of the Isle of Man. **Manx**

cat tailless breed of cat.

many *adj* **more, most 1** numerous. ♦ *n* **2** large number.

Maoism *n* form of Marxism advanced by Mao Tse-tung in China. **Maoist** *n, adj*

Maori *n, pl* **-ri, -ris 1** member of the indigenous race of New Zealand. **2** language of the Maoris. ♦ *adj* **3** of the Maoris or their language.

map *n* **1** representation of the earth's surface or some part of it, showing geographical features. **2** *v* **mapping, mapped 3** make a map of. **map out** *v* plan.

maple *n* tree with broad leaves, a variety of which (**sugar maple**) yields sugar.

mar *v* **marring, marred** spoil or impair.

Mar. March.

marabou *n* **1** large black-and-white African stork. **2** its soft white down, used to trim hats etc.

maraca [mar-**rak**-a] *n* shaken percussion instrument made from a gourd containing dried seeds etc.

marae *n NZ* **1** enclosed space in front of a Maori meeting house. **2** Maori meeting house and its buildings.

maraschino cherry [mar-rass-**kee**-no] *n* cherry preserved in a cherry liqueur with a taste like bitter almonds.

marathon *n* **1** long-distance race of 26 miles 385 yards (42.195 kilometres). **2** long or arduous task.

marauding *adj* wandering or raiding in search of plunder. **marauder** *n*

marble *n* **1** kind of limestone with a mottled appearance, which can be highly polished. **2** slab or sculpture in this. **3** small glass ball used in playing marbles. ♦ *pl* **4** game of rolling these at one another. **marbled** *adj* having a mottled appearance like marble.

march[1] *v* **1** walk with a military step. **2** make (a person or group) proceed. **3** progress steadily. ♦ *n* **4** action of marching. **5** steady progress. **6** distance covered by marching. **7** piece of music, as for a march. **marcher** *n*

marching girl *Aust & NZ* girl who does team formation marching as a sport.

march[2] *n* border or frontier.

March *n* third month of the year.

marchioness [marsh-on-**ness**] *n* **1** woman holding the rank of marquis. **2** wife or widow of a marquis.

mare *n* female horse or zebra. **mare's nest** discovery which proves worthless.

margarine *n* butter substitute made from animal or vegetable fats.

marge *n Informal* margarine.

margin *n* **1** edge or border. **2** blank space round a printed page. **3** additional amount or one greater than necessary. **4** limit. **marginal** *adj* **1** insignificant, unimportant. **2** near a limit. **3** *Politics* (of a constituency) won by only a small margin. ♦ *n* **4** *Politics* marginal constituency. **marginalize** *v* make or treat as insignificant. **marginally** *adv*

marguerite *n* large daisy.

marigold *n* plant with yellow or orange flowers.

marijuana [mar-ree-**wah**-na] *n* dried flowers and leaves of the cannabis plant, used as a drug, esp. in cigarettes.

marina *n* harbour for yachts and other pleasure boats.

marinade *n* **1** seasoned liquid in which fish or meat is soaked before cooking. ♦ *v* **2** same as MARINATE. **marinate** *v* soak in marinade.

marine *adj* **1** of the sea or shipping. **2** *n* **3** (esp. in Britain and the US) soldier trained for land and sea combat. **4** country's shipping or fleet. **mariner** *n* sailor.

marionette *n* puppet worked with strings.

marital *adj* relating to marriage.

maritime *adj* **1** relating to shipping. **2** of, near, or living in the sea.

marjoram *n* aromatic herb used for seasoning food and in salads.

mark¹ *n* **1** line, dot, scar, etc. visible on a surface. **2** distinguishing sign or symbol. **3** written or printed symbol. **4** letter or number used to grade academic work. **5** indication of position. **6** indication of some quality. **7** target or goal. ♦ *v* **8** make a mark on. **9** characterize or distinguish. **10** indicate. **11** pay attention to. **12** notice or watch. **13** grade (academic work). **14** stay close to (a sporting opponent) to hamper his or her play. **marked** *adj* noticeable. **markedly** *adv* **marker** *n*

mark² *n* same as DEUTSCHMARK.

market *n* **1** assembly or place for buying and selling. **2** demand for goods. ♦ *v* **-keting, -keted 3** offer or produce for sale. **on the market** for sale. **marketable** *adj* **marketing** *n* part of a business that controls the way that goods or services are sold. **market garden** place where fruit and vegetables are grown for sale. **market maker** (in London Stock Exchange) person who uses a firm's money to create a market for a stock. **marketplace** *n* **1** market. **2** commercial world. **market research** research into consumers' needs and purchases.

marksman *n* person skilled at shooting. **marksmanship** *n*

marl *n* soil formed of clay and lime, used as fertilizer.

marlin *n* large food and game fish of warm and tropical seas, with a very long upper jaw.

marlinespike, marlinspike *n*

pointed hook used to separate strands of rope.

marmalade *n* jam made from citrus fruits.

marmoreal *adj* of or like marble.

marmoset *n* small bushy-tailed monkey.

marmot *n* burrowing rodent.

maroon¹ *adj* reddish-purple.

maroon² *v* **1** abandon ashore, esp. on an island. **2** isolate without resources.

marquee *n* large tent used for a party or exhibition.

marquess [**mar**-kwiss] *n Brit* nobleman of the rank below a duke.

marquetry *n* ornamental inlaid work of wood.

marquis *n* (in some European countries) nobleman of the rank above a count.

marram grass *n* grass that grows on sandy shores.

marrow *n* **1** fatty substance inside bones. **2** long thick striped green vegetable with whitish flesh.

marry *v* **-rying, -ried 1** take as a husband or wife. **2** join or give in marriage. **3** unite closely. **marriage** *n* **1** state of being married. **2** wedding. **marriageable** *adj*

Mars *n* **1** Roman god of war. **2** fourth planet from the sun.

Marsala [mar-**sah**-la] *n* dark sweet wine.

marsh *n* low-lying wet land. **marshy** *adj*

marshal *n* **1** officer of the highest rank. **2** official who organizes ceremonies or events. **3** *US* law officer. ♦ *v* **-shalling, -shalled 4** arrange in order. **5** assemble. **6** conduct with ceremony. **marshalling yard** railway depot for goods trains.

marshmallow *n* spongy pink or white sweet.

marsupial [mar-**soop**-ee-al] *n* animal

that carries its young in a pouch, such as a kangaroo.

mart *n* market.

Martello tower *n* round tower for coastal defence, formerly used in Europe.

marten *n* weasel-like animal.

martial *adj* of war, warlike. **martial art** any of various philosophies and techniques of self-defence, orig. Eastern, such as karate. **martial law** law enforced by military authorities in times of danger or emergency.

Martian [**marsh**-an] *adj* **1** of Mars. ◆ *n* **2** supposed inhabitant of Mars.

martin *n* bird with a slightly forked tail.

martinet *n* person who maintains strict discipline.

martini *n* cocktail of vermouth and gin.

martyr *n* **1** person who dies or suffers for his or her beliefs. ◆ *v* **2** make a martyr of. **be a martyr to** be constantly suffering from. **martyrdom** *n*

marvel *v* -velling, -velled **1** be filled with wonder. ◆ *n* **2** wonderful thing. **marvellous** *adj* **1** amazing. **2** wonderful.

Marxism *n* political philosophy of Karl Marx. **Marxist** *n*, *adj*

marzipan *n* paste of ground almonds, sugar, and egg whites.

masc. masculine.

mascara *n* cosmetic for darkening the eyelashes.

mascot *n* person, animal, or thing supposed to bring good luck.

masculine *adj* **1** relating to males. **2** manly. **3** *Grammar* of the gender of nouns that includes some male animate things. **masculinity** *n*

mash *n* **1** *Informal* mashed potatoes. **2** bran or meal mixed with warm water as food for horses etc. ◆ *v* **3** crush into a soft mass.

mask *n* **1** covering for the face, as a disguise or protection. **2** behaviour that hides one's true feelings. ◆ *v* **3** cover with a mask. **4** hide or disguise.

masochism [**mass**-oh-kiz-zum] *n* condition in which (sexual) pleasure is obtained from feeling pain or from being humiliated. **masochist** *n* **masochistic** *adj*

mason *n* **1** person who works with stone. **2** (M-) Freemason. **Masonic** *adj* of Freemasonry. **masonry** *n* **1** stonework. **2** (M-) Freemasonry.

masque [**mask**] *n Hist* 16th–17th-century form of dramatic entertainment.

masquerade [mask-er-**aid**] *n* **1** deceptive show or pretence. **2** party at which masks and costumes are worn. ◆ *v* **3** pretend to be someone or something else.

mass *n* **1** coherent body of matter. **2** large quantity or number. **3** *Physics* amount of matter in a body. ◆ *adj* **4** large-scale. **5** involving many people. ◆ *v* **6** form into a mass. **the masses** ordinary people. **massive** *adj* large and heavy. **mass-market** *adj* for or appealing to a large number of people. **mass media** means of communication to many people, such as television and newspapers. **mass-produce** *v* manufacture (standardized goods) in large quantities.

Mass *n* service of the Eucharist, esp. in the RC Church.

massacre [**mass**-a-ker] *n* **1** indiscriminate killing of large numbers of people. ◆ *v* **2** kill in large numbers.

massage [**mass**-ahzh] *n* **1** rubbing and kneading of parts of the body to reduce pain or stiffness. ◆ *v* **2** give a massage to. **masseur,** (*fem*) **masseuse** *n* person who gives massages.

massif [**mass**-seef] *n* connected group of mountains.

mast[1] *n* tall pole for supporting something, esp. a ship's sails.

mast[2] *n* fruit of the beech, oak, etc., used as pig fodder.

mastectomy [mass-**tek**-tom-ee] *n, pl* **-mies** surgical removal of a breast.

master *n* **1** person in control, such as an employer or an owner of slaves or animals. **2** expert. **3** great artist. **4** original thing from which copies are made. **5** male teacher. **6** *adj* **7** overall or controlling. **8** main or principal. ♦ *v* **9** acquire knowledge of or skill in. **10** overcome. **masterful** *adj* **1** domineering. **2** showing great skill. **masterly** *adj* showing great skill. **mastery** *n* **1** expertise. **2** control or command. **master key** key that opens all the locks of a set. **mastermind** *v* **1** plan and direct (a complex task). ♦ *n* **2** person who plans and directs a complex task. **masterpiece** *n* outstanding work of art.

mastic *n* **1** gum obtained from certain trees. **2** putty-like substance used as a filler, adhesive, or seal.

masticate *v* chew. **mastication** *n*

mastiff *n* large dog.

mastitis *n* inflammation of a breast or udder.

mastodon *n* extinct elephant-like mammal.

mastoid *n* projection of the bone behind the ear.

masturbate *v* fondle the genitals (of). **masturbation** *n*

mat *n* **1** piece of fabric used as a floor covering or to protect a surface. **2** thick tangled mass. ♦ *v* **matting**, **matted 3** tangle or become tangled into a dense mass.

matador *n* man who kills the bull in bullfights.

match[1] *n* **1** contest in a game or sport. **2** person or thing exactly like, equal to, or in harmony with another. **3** marriage. ♦ *v* **4** be exactly like, equal to, or in harmony with. **5** put in competition (with). **6** find a match for. **7** join (in marriage). **matchless** *adj* unequalled. **matchmaker** *n* person who schemes to bring about a marriage. **matchmaking** *n, adj*

match[2] *n* small stick with a tip which ignites when scraped on a rough surface. **matchbox** *n* **matchstick** *n* **1** wooden part of a match. ♦ *adj* **2** (of drawn figures) thin and straight. **matchwood** *n* small splinters.

mate[1] *n* **1** *Informal* friend **2** associate or colleague, e.g. *team-mate*. **3** sexual partner of an animal. **4** officer in a merchant ship. **5** tradesman's assistant. ♦ *v* **6** pair (animals) or (of animals) be paired for reproduction.

mate[2] *n, v Chess* checkmate.

material *n* **1** substance of which a thing is made. **2** cloth. **3** information on which a piece of work may be based. ♦ *pl* **4** things needed for an activity. ♦ *adj* **5** of matter or substance. **6** not spiritual. **7** affecting physical wellbeing. **8** relevant. **materially** *adv* considerably. **materialism** *n* **1** excessive interest in or desire for money and possessions. **2** belief that only the material world exists. **materialist** *adj, n* **materialistic** *adj* **materialize** *v* **1** actually happen. **2** come into existence or view. **materialization** *n*

maternal *adj* **1** of a mother. **2** related through one's mother. **maternity** *n* **1** motherhood. ♦ *adj* **2** of or for pregnant women.

matey *adj Brit informal* friendly or intimate.

mathematics *n* science of number, quantity, shape, and space.

mathematical *adj* **mathematically** *adv* **mathematician** *n*

maths *n Informal* mathematics.

Matilda *n Aust hist* swagman's bundle of belongings. **waltz Matilda** *Aust* travel about carrying one's bundle of belongings.

matinée [**mat**-in-nay] *n* afternoon performance in a theatre or cinema.

matins *pl n* early morning service in various Christian Churches.

matriarch [**mate**-ree-ark] *n* female head of a tribe or family. **matriarchal** *adj* **matriarchy** *n* society governed by a female, in which descent is traced through the female line.

matricide *n* **1** crime of killing one's mother. **2** person who does this.

matriculate *v* enrol or be enrolled in a college or university. **matriculation** *n*

matrimony *n* marriage. **matrimonial** *adj*

matrix [**may**-trix] *n, pl* **matrices** **1** substance or situation in which something originates, takes form, or is enclosed. **2** mould for casting. **3** *Maths* rectangular array of numbers or elements.

matron *n* **1** staid or dignified married woman. **2** woman who supervises the domestic or medical arrangements of an institution. **3** former name for NURSING OFFICER. **matronly** *adj*

matt *adj* dull, not shiny.

matter *n* **1** substance of which something is made. **2** physical substance. **3** event, situation, or subject. **4** written material in general. **5** pus. ◆ *v* **6** be of importance. **what's the matter?** what is wrong?

mattock *n* large pick with one of its blade ends flattened for loosening soil.

mattress *n* large stuffed flat case, often with springs, used on or as a bed.

mature *adj* **1** fully developed or grown-up. **2** ripe. ◆ *v* **3** make or become mature. **4** (of a bill or bond) become due for payment. **maturity** *n* state of being mature. **maturation** *n*

maudlin *adj* foolishly or tearfully sentimental.

maul *v* **1** handle roughly. **2** beat or tear.

maunder *v* talk or act aimlessly or idly.

mausoleum [maw-so-**lee**-um] *n* stately tomb.

mauve *adj* pale purple.

maverick *n, adj* independent and unorthodox (person).

maw *n* animal's mouth, throat, or stomach.

mawkish *adj* foolishly sentimental.

maxim *n* general truth or principle.

maximum *adj, n, pl* **-mums, -ma** greatest possible (amount or number). **maximal** *adj* **maximize** *v* increase to a maximum.

may *v, past tense* **might** used as an auxiliary to express possibility, permission, opportunity, etc.

May *n* **1** fifth month of the year. **2** (m-) same as HAWTHORN. **mayfly** *n* short-lived aquatic insect. **maypole** *n* pole set up for dancing round on the first day of May to celebrate spring.

maybe *adv* perhaps, possibly.

Mayday *n* international radio distress signal.

mayhem *n* violent destruction or confusion.

mayonnaise *n* creamy sauce of egg yolks, oil, and vinegar.

☑ SPELLING TIP

There are two *n*s to remember in the middle of **mayonnaise** - possibly a good reason for the increasing use of the abbreviation 'mayo'.

---

mayor *n* head of a municipality. **mayoress** *n* **1** mayor's wife. **2** female mayor. **mayoralty** n (term of) office of a mayor.

maze n **1** complex network of paths or lines designed to puzzle. **2** any confusing network or system.

mazurka n **1** lively Polish dance. **2** music for this.

MB Bachelor of Medicine.

MBE (in Britain) Member of the Order of the British Empire.

MC Master of Ceremonies.

MD Doctor of Medicine.

me pron **objective form of** I.

ME myalgic encephalomyelitis: painful muscles and general weakness sometimes persisting long after a viral illness.

mead n alcoholic drink made from honey.

meadow n piece of grassland. **meadowsweet** n plant with dense heads of small fragrant flowers.

meagre adj scanty or insufficient.

meal[1] n **1** occasion when food is served and eaten. **2** the food itself.

meal[2] n grain ground to powder. **mealy** adj **mealy-mouthed** adj not outspoken enough.

mealie n S Afr maize.

mean[1] v **meaning, meant 1** intend to convey or express. **2** signify, denote, or portend. **3** intend. **4** have importance as specified. **meaning** n sense, significance. **meaningful** adj **meaningless** adj

mean[2] adj **1** miserly, ungenerous, or petty. **2** despicable or callous. **3** Chiefly US informal bad-tempered. **meanly** adv **meanness** n

mean[3] n **1** middle point between two extremes. **2** average. ◆ pl **3** method by which something is done. **4** money. ◆ adj **5** intermediate in size or quantity. **6** average. **by all means** certainly. **by no means** in no way.

means test inquiry into a person's means to decide on eligibility for financial aid.

meander [mee-**and**-er] v **1** follow a winding course. **2** wander aimlessly. ◆ n **3** winding course.

meantime n **1** intervening period. ◆ adv **2** meanwhile.

meanwhile adv **1** during the intervening period. **2** at the same time.

measles n infectious disease producing red spots. **measly** adj Informal meagre.

measure n **1** size or quantity. **2** graduated scale etc. for measuring size or quantity. **3** unit of size or quantity. **4** extent. **5** action taken. **6** law. **7** poetical rhythm. ◆ v **8** determine the size or quantity of. **9** be (a specified amount) in size or quantity. **measurable** adj **measured** adj **1** slow and steady. **2** carefully considered. **measurement** n **1** measuring. **2** size. **measure up to** v fulfil (expectations or requirements).

meat n animal flesh as food. **meaty** adj **1** (tasting) of or like meat. **2** brawny. **3** full of significance or interest.

Mecca n **1** holy city of Islam. **2** place that attracts visitors.

mechanic n person skilled in repairing or operating machinery. **mechanics** n scientific study of motion and force. **mechanical** adj **1** of or done by machines. **2** (of an action) without thought or feeling. **mechanically** adv

mechanism n **1** way a machine works. **2** piece of machinery. **3** process or technique, e.g. defence mechanism. **mechanize** v **1** equip with machinery. **2** make mechanical or automatic. **3** Mil equip (an army) with armoured vehicles. **mechanization** n

med. **1** medical. **2** medicine. **3** medieval. **4** medium.

medal *n* piece of metal with an inscription etc., given as a reward or memento. **medallion** *n* **1** disc-shaped ornament worn on a chain round the neck. **2** large medal. **3** circular decorative device in architecture. **medallist** *n* winner of a medal.

meddle *v* interfere annoyingly. **meddler** *n* **meddlesome** *adj*

media *n* **1** a plural of MEDIUM. **2** the mass media collectively.

mediaeval *adj* same as MEDIEVAL.

medial *adj* of or in the middle.

median *adj, n* middle (point or line).

mediate *v* intervene in a dispute to bring about agreement. **mediation** *n* **mediator** *n*

medic *n* Informal doctor or medical student.

medical *adj* **1** of the science of medicine. ♦ *n* **2** Informal medical examination. **medically** *adv* **medicate** *v* treat with a medicinal substance. **medication** *n* (treatment with) a medicinal substance.

medicine *n* **1** substance used to treat disease. **2** science of preventing, diagnosing, or curing disease. **medicinal** [med-**diss**-in-al] *adj* having therapeutic properties. **medicine man** witch doctor.

medieval [med-ee-**eve**-al] *adj* of the Middle Ages.

mediocre [mee-dee-**oak**-er] *adj* **1** average in quality. **2** second-rate. **mediocrity** [mee-dee-**ok**-rit-ee] *n*

meditate *v* **1** reflect deeply, esp. on spiritual matters. **2** think about or plan. **meditation** *n* **meditative** *adj* **meditatively** *adv* **meditator** *n*

medium *adj* **1** midway between extremes, average. ♦ *n, pl* **-dia, -diums 2** middle state, degree, or condition. **3** intervening substance producing an effect. **4** means of communicating news or information to the public, such as radio or newspapers. **5** person who can supposedly communicate with the dead. **6** surroundings or environment. **7** category of art according to the material used. **medium wave** radio wave with a wavelength between 100 and 1000 metres.

medlar *n* apple-like fruit of a small tree, eaten when it begins to decay.

medley *n* **1** miscellaneous mixture. **2** musical sequence of different tunes.

medulla [mid-**dull**-la] *n, pl* **-las, -lae** marrow, pith, or inner tissue.

meek *adj* submissive or humble. **meekly** *adv* **meekness** *n*

meerkat *n* S African mongoose.

meerschaum [**meer**-shum] *n* **1** white substance like clay. **2** tobacco pipe with a bowl made of this.

meet[1] *v* **meeting, met 1** come together (with). **2** come into contact (with). **3** be at the place of arrival of. **4** make the acquaintance of. **5** satisfy (a need etc.). **6** experience. ♦ *n* **7** meeting, esp. a sports meeting. **8** assembly of a hunt. **meeting** *n* **1** coming together. **2** assembly.

meet[2] *adj* Obs fit or suitable.

mega- *combining form* **1** denoting one million, e.g. megawatt. **2** very great, e.g. megastar.

megabyte *n* Computers 2^{20} or 1 048 576 bytes.

megahertz *n, pl* **-hertz** one million hertz.

megalith *n* great stone, esp. as part of a prehistoric monument. **megalithic** *adj*

megalomania *n* craving for or mental delusions of power. **megalomaniac** *adj, n*

megaphone *n* cone-shaped instrument used to amplify the voice.

megapode *n* bird of Australia, New

Guinea, and adjacent islands.

megaton *n* explosive power equal to that of one million tons of TNT.

melaleuca [mel-a-**loo**-ka] *n* Australian shrub or tree with a white trunk and black branches.

melancholy [**mel**-an-kol-lee] *n* **1** sadness or gloom. ♦ *adj* **2** sad or gloomy. **melancholia** [mel-an-**kole**-lee-a] *n* state of depression. **melancholic** *adj, n*

melange [may-**lahnzh**] *n* mixture.

melanin *n* dark pigment found in the hair, skin, and eyes of humans and animals.

mêlée [**mel**-lay] *n* noisy confused fight or crowd.

mellifluous [mel-**lif**-flew-uss] *adj* (of sound) smooth and sweet.

mellow *adj* **1** soft, not harsh. **2** kind-hearted, esp. through maturity. **3** (of fruit) ripe. ♦ *v* **4** make or become mellow.

melodrama *n* **1** play full of extravagant action and emotion. **2** overdramatic behaviour or emotion. **melodramatic** *adj*

melody *n, pl* **-dies 1** series of musical notes which make a tune. **2** sweet sound. **melodic** [mel-**lod**-ik] *adj* **1** of melody. **2** melodious. **melodious** [mel-**lode**-ee-uss] *adj* **1** pleasing to the ear. **2** tuneful.

melon *n* large round juicy fruit with a hard rind.

melt *v* **1** (cause to) become liquid by heat. **2** dissolve. **3** disappear. **4** blend (into). **5** soften through emotion. **meltdown** *n* (in a nuclear reactor) melting of the fuel rods, with the possible release of radiation.

member *n* **1** individual making up a body or society. **2** limb. **membership** *n* **Member of Parliament** person elected to parliament.

membrane *n* thin flexible tissue in a plant or animal body. **membranous** *adj*

memento *n, pl* **-tos, -toes** thing serving to remind, souvenir.

memo *n, pl* **memos** short for MEMORANDUM.

memoir [**mem**-wahr] *n* **1** biography or historical account based on personal knowledge. ♦ *pl* **2** collection of these. **3** autobiography.

memorable *adj* worth remembering, noteworthy. **memorably** *adv*

memorandum *n, pl* **-dums, -da 1** written record or communication within a business. **2** note of things to be remembered.

memory *n, pl* **-ries 1** ability to remember. **2** sum of things remembered. **3** particular recollection. **4** length of time one can remember. **5** commemoration. **6** part of a computer which stores information. **memorize** *v* commit to memory. **memorial** *n* **1** something serving to commemorate a person or thing. ♦ *adj* **2** serving as a memorial.

men *n* plural of MAN.

menace *n* **1** threat. **2** *Informal* nuisance. ♦ *v* **3** threaten, endanger. **menacing** *adj*

ménage [may-**nahzh**] *n* household.

menagerie [min-**naj**-er-ee] *n* collection of wild animals for exhibition.

mend *v* **1** repair or patch. **2** recover or heal. **3** make or become better. ♦ *n* **4** mended area. **on the mend** regaining health.

mendacity *n* (tendency to) untruthfulness. **mendacious** *adj*

mendicant *adj* **1** begging. ♦ *n* **2** beggar.

menhir [**men**-hear] *n* single upright prehistoric stone.

menial [**mean**-nee-al] *adj* **1** involving boring work of low status. ♦ *n* **2**

person with a menial job.

meningitis [men-in-**jite**-iss] n inflammation of the membranes of the brain.

meniscus n 1 curved surface of a liquid. 2 crescent-shaped lens.

menopause n time when a woman's menstrual cycle ceases. **menopausal** adj

menstruation n approximately monthly discharge of blood and cellular debris from the womb of a nonpregnant woman. **menstruate** v **menstrual** adj

mensuration n measuring, esp. in geometry.

mental adj 1 of, in, or done by the mind. 2 of or for mental illness. 3 Informal insane. **mentally** adv **mentality** n way of thinking.

menthol n organic compound found in peppermint, used medicinally.

mention v 1 refer to briefly. 2 acknowledge. ♦ n 3 brief reference to a person or thing. 4 acknowledgment.

mentor n adviser or guide.

menu n 1 list of dishes to be served, or from which to order. 2 Computers list of options displayed on a screen.

MEP Member of the European Parliament.

mercantile adj of trade or traders.

mercenary adj 1 influenced by greed. 2 working merely for reward. ♦ n, pl -aries 3 hired soldier.

merchandise n commodities.

merchant n person engaged in trade, wholesale trader. **merchant bank** bank dealing mainly with businesses and investment. **merchantman** n trading ship. **merchant navy** ships or crew engaged in a nation's commercial shipping.

mercury n 1 Chem silvery liquid metal. 2 (M-) Roman myth messenger of the gods. 3 (M-) planet nearest the sun. **mercurial** adj lively, changeable.

mercy n, pl -cies 1 compassionate treatment of an offender or enemy who is in one's power. 2 merciful act. **merciful** adj 1 compassionate. 2 giving relief. **merciless** adj

mere¹ adj nothing more than, e.g. mere chance. **merely** adv

mere² n Brit obs lake.

meretricious adj superficially or garishly attractive but of no real value.

merganser [mer-**gan**-ser] n large crested diving duck.

merge v combine or blend.

merger n combination of business firms into one.

meridian n imaginary circle of the earth passing through both poles.

meringue [mer-**rang**] n 1 baked mixture of egg whites and sugar. 2 small cake of this.

merino n, pl -nos 1 breed of sheep with fine soft wool. 2 this wool.

merit n 1 excellence or worth. ♦ pl 2 admirable qualities. ♦ v -iting, -ited 3 deserve. **meritorious** adj deserving praise. **meritocracy** [mer-it-**tok**-rass-ee] n rule by people of superior talent or intellect.

merlin n small falcon.

mermaid n imaginary sea creature with the upper part of a woman and the lower part of a fish.

merry adj -rier, -riest 1 cheerful or jolly. 2 Informal slightly drunk. **merrily** adv **merriment** n **merry-go-round** n roundabout. **merrymaking** n noisy, cheerful celebrations or fun.

mesdames n plural of MADAME.

mesdemoiselles n plural of MADEMOISELLE.

mesh n 1 network or net. 2 (open space between) strands forming a network. ♦ v 3 (of gear teeth) engage.

mesmerize v 1 hold spellbound. 2 Obs hypnotize.

meson [**mee**-zon] n elementary atomic particle.

mess n 1 untidy or dirty confusion. 2 trouble or difficulty. 3 place where servicemen eat. 4 group of servicemen who regularly eat together. ♦ v 5 muddle or dirty. 6 (foll. by about) potter about. 7 (foll. by with) interfere with. 8 Brit, Aust & NZ (of servicemen) eat in a group.

message n 1 communication sent. 2 meaning or moral. **messaging** n sending and receiving of textual communications by mobile phone. **messenger** n bearer of a message.

Messiah n 1 Jews' promised deliverer. 2 Christ. **Messianic** adj

messieurs n plural of MONSIEUR.

Messrs [**mess**-erz] n plural of MR.

messy adj **messier**, **messiest** dirty, confused, or untidy. **messily** adv

met v past of MEET[1].

metabolism [met-**tab**-oh-liz-zum] n chemical processes of a living body. **metabolic** adj **metabolize** v produce or be produced by metabolism.

metal n chemical element, such as iron or copper, that is malleable and capable of conducting heat and electricity. **metallic** adj **metallurgy** n scientific study of the structure, properties, extraction, and refining of metals. **metallurgical** adj **metallurgist** n **metal road** NZ unsealed road covered in gravel.

metamorphosis [met-a-**more**-foss-is] n, pl -**phoses** [-foss-eez] change of form or character. **metamorphic** adj (of rocks) changed in texture or structure by heat and pressure. **metamorphose** v transform.

metaphor n figure of speech in which a term is applied to something it does not literally denote in order to imply a resemblance, e.g. he is a lion in battle. **metaphorical** adj **metaphorically** adv

metaphysics n branch of philosophy concerned with being and knowing. **metaphysical** adj

mete v (usu. with out) deal out as punishment.

meteor n small fast-moving heavenly body, visible as a streak of incandescence if it enters the earth's atmosphere. **meteoric** [meet-ee-**or**-rik] adj 1 of a meteor. 2 brilliant and very rapid. **meteorite** n meteor that has fallen to earth.

meteorology n study of the earth's atmosphere, esp. for weather forecasting. **meteorological** adj **meteorologist** n

meter n 1 instrument for measuring and recording something, such as the consumption of gas or electricity. ♦ v 2 measure by meter.

methane n colourless inflammable gas.

methanol n colourless poisonous liquid used as a solvent and fuel (also **methyl alcohol**).

methinks v, past tense **methought** Obs it seems to me.

method n 1 way or manner. 2 technique. 3 orderliness. **methodical** adj orderly. **methodically** adv **methodology** n particular method or procedure.

Methodist n 1 member of any of the Protestant churches originated by John Wesley and his followers. ♦ adj 2 of Methodists or their Church. **Methodism** n

meths n Informal methylated spirits.

methyl n (compound containing) a saturated hydrocarbon group of atoms. **methylated spirits** alcohol with methanol added, used as a solvent and for heating.

meticulous *adj* very careful about details. **meticulously** *adv*

métier [**met**-ee-ay] *n* **1** profession or trade. **2** one's strong point.

metonymy [mit-**on**-im-ee] *n* figure of speech in which one thing is replaced by another associated with it, such as 'the Crown' for 'the queen'.

metre *n* **1** basic unit of length equal to about 1.094 yards (100 centimetres). **2** rhythm of poetry. **metric** *adj* of the decimal system of weights and measures based on the metre. **metrical** *adj* **1** of measurement. **2** of poetic metre. **metrication** *n* conversion to the metric system.

metronome *n* instrument which marks musical time by means of a ticking pendulum.

metropolis [mit-**trop**-oh-liss] *n* chief city of a country or region.

metropolitan *adj* of a metropolis.

mettle *n* courage or spirit.

mew *n* **1** cry of a cat. ♦ *v* **2** utter this cry.

mews *n* yard or street orig. of stables, now often converted into houses.

mezzanine [**mez**-zan-een] *n* intermediate storey, esp. between the ground and first floor.

mezzo-soprano [**met**-so-] *n* voice or singer between a soprano and contralto (also **mezzo**).

mezzotint [**met**-so-tint] *n* **1** method of engraving by scraping the roughened surface of a metal plate. **2** print so made.

mg milligram(s).

MHz megahertz.

miaow [mee-**ow**] *n*, *v* same as MEW.

miasma [mee-**azz**-ma] *n* unwholesome or foreboding atmosphere.

mica [**my**-ka] *n* glasslike mineral used as an electrical insulator.

mice *n* plural of MOUSE.

Michaelmas [**mik**-kl-mass] *n* Sept.

29th, feast of St Michael the archangel.

mickey *n* take the mickey (out of) *Informal* tease.

micro *n*, *pl* **-cros** short for MICROCOMPUTER *or* MICROPROCESSOR.

microbe *n* minute organism, esp. one causing disease. **microbial** *adj*

microchip *n* small wafer of silicon containing electronic circuits.

microcomputer *n* computer with a central processing unit contained in one or more silicon chips.

microcosm *n* miniature representation of something.

microfiche [**my**-kroh-feesh] *n* microfilm in sheet form.

microfilm *n* miniaturized recording of books or documents on a roll of film.

microlight *n* very small light private aircraft with large wings.

micrometer [my-**krom**-it-er] *n* instrument for measuring very small distances or angles.

micron [**my**-kron] *n* one millionth of a metre.

microorganism *n* organism of microscopic size.

microphone *n* instrument for amplifying or transmitting sounds.

microprocessor *n* integrated circuit acting as the central processing unit in a small computer.

microscope *n* instrument with lens(es) which produces a magnified image of a very small object. **microscopic** *adj* **1** too small to be seen except with a microscope. **2** very small. **3** of a microscope. **microscopically** *adv* **microscopy** *n* use of a microscope.

microsurgery *n* intricate surgery using a special microscope and miniature precision instruments.

microwave *n* **1** electromagnetic wave with a wavelength of a few centimetres, used in radar and cooking. **2** microwave oven. ♦ v **3** cook in a microwave oven. **microwave oven** oven using microwaves to cook food quickly.

mid adj intermediate, middle.

midday n noon.

midden n Brit & Aust dunghill or rubbish heap.

middle adj **1** equidistant from two extremes. **2** medium, intermediate. ♦ n **3** middle point or part. **middle age** period of life between youth and old age. **middle-aged** adj **Middle Ages** period from about 1000 AD to the 15th century. **middle class** social class of business and professional people. **middle-class** adj **Middle East** area around the eastern Mediterranean up to and including Iran. **middleman** n trader who buys from the producer and sells to the consumer. **middle-of-the-road** adj **1** politically moderate. **2** (of music) generally popular. **middleweight** n boxer weighing up to 160lb (professional) or 75kg (amateur).

middling adj **1** mediocre. **2** moderate.

midge n small mosquito-like insect.

midget n very small person or thing.

midland n **1** Brit, Aust & US middle part of a country. ♦ pl **2** (M-) central England.

midnight n twelve o'clock at night.

midriff n middle part of the body.

midst n **in the midst of 1** surrounded by. **2** at a point during.

midsummer n **1** middle of summer. **2** summer solstice. **Midsummer's Day, Midsummer Day** (in Britain and Ireland) June 24th.

midway adj, adv halfway.

midwife n trained person who assists at childbirth. **midwifery** n

midwinter n **1** middle or depth of winter. **2** winter solstice.

mien [**mean**] n Lit person's bearing, demeanour, or appearance.

miffed adj Informal offended or upset.

might¹ v past tense of MAY.

might² n power or strength. **with might and main** energetically or forcefully. **mighty** adj **1** powerful. **2** important. ♦ adv **3** US & Aust informal very. **mightily** adv

migraine [**mee**-grain] n severe headache, often with nausea and visual disturbances.

migrate v **1** move from one place to settle in another. **2** (of animals) journey between different habitats at specific seasons. **migration** n **migrant** n **1** person or animal that moves from one place to another. ♦ adj **2** moving from one place to another. **migratory** adj (of an animal) migrating every year.

mike n Informal microphone.

milch adj Chiefly Brit (of a cow) giving milk.

mild adj **1** not strongly flavoured. **2** gentle. **3** calm or temperate. **mildly** adv **mildness** n

mildew n destructive fungus on damp plants or fabric. **mildewed** adj

mile n unit of length equal to 1760 yards or 1.609 kilometres. **mileage** n **1** distance travelled in miles. **2** miles travelled by a motor vehicle per gallon of petrol. **3** Informal usefulness of something. **mileometer** n Brit device that records the number of miles a vehicle has travelled. **milestone** n **1** significant event. **2** stone marker showing the distance to a certain place.

milieu [meal-**yer**] n, pl **milieux**, **milieus** [meal-**yerz**] environment or surroundings.

militant adj aggressive or vigorous in support of a cause. **militancy** n

military adj **1** of or for soldiers, armies, or war. ♦ n **2** armed services.

militarism *n* belief in the use of military force and methods. **militarist** *n* **militarized** *adj*

militate *v* (usu. with *against* or *for*) have a strong influence or effect.

militia [mill-**ish**-a] *n* military force of trained citizens for use in emergency.

milk *n* **1** white fluid produced by female mammals to feed their young. **2** milk of cows, goats, etc., used by humans as food. **3** fluid in some plants. ♦ *v* **4** draw milk from. **5** exploit (a person or situation). **milky** *adj* **Milky Way** luminous band of stars stretching across the night sky. **milk float** *Brit* small electrically powered vehicle used to deliver milk to houses. **milkmaid** *n* (esp. in former times) woman who milks cows. **milkman** *n* *Brit, Aust & NZ* man who delivers milk to people's houses. **milkshake** *n* frothy flavoured cold milk drink. **milksop** *n* feeble man. **milk teeth** first set of teeth in young children.

mill *n* **1** factory. **2** machine for grinding, processing, or rolling. ♦ *v* **3** grind, press, or process in or as if in a mill. **4** cut fine grooves across the edges of (coins). **5** (of a crowd) move in a confused manner.

millennium *n, pl* **-nia, -niums 1** period of a thousand years. **2** future period of peace and happiness. **millennium bug** computer problem caused by the date change at the beginning of the 21st century.

✔ SPELLING TIP

If you spell **millennium** with only one *n*, you are not alone: there are 338 occurrences of this in the Bank of English. The correct spelling has two *l*s and two *n*s.

---

miller *n* person who works in a mill.

millet *n* type of cereal grass.

milli- *combining form* denoting a thousandth part, e.g. *millisecond*.

millibar *n* unit of atmospheric pressure.

millimetre *n* thousandth part of a metre.

milliner *n* maker or seller of women's hats. **millinery** *n*

million *n* one thousand thousands. **millionth** *adj, n* **millionaire** *n* person who owns at least a million pounds, dollars, etc.

✔ SPELLING TIP

Lots of people find it difficult to decide how many *l*s and *n*s to put in **millionaire**. They usually get the double *l* right, but remembering the single *n* is trickier.

---

millipede *n* small animal with a jointed body and many pairs of legs.

millstone *n* flat circular stone for grinding corn.

millwheel *n* waterwheel that drives a mill.

milometer *n Brit same as* MILEOMETER.

milt *n* sperm of fish.

mime *n* **1** acting without the use of words. **2** performer who does this. ♦ *v* **3** act in mime.

mimic *v* **-icking, -icked 1** imitate (a person or manner), esp. for satirical effect. ♦ *n* **2** person or animal that is good at mimicking. **mimicry** *n*

min. 1 minimum. **2** minute(s).

minaret *n* tall slender tower of a mosque.

mince *v* **1** cut or grind into very small pieces. **2** walk or speak in an affected manner. **3** soften or moderate (one's words). ♦ *n* **4** minced meat. **mincer** *n* machine for mincing meat. **mincing** *adj* affected in manner. **mincemeat** *n* sweet mixture of dried fruit and spices. **mince pie** pie containing mincemeat.

mind *n* **1** thinking faculties. **2** memory

or attention. **3** intention. **4** sanity. ◆ *v* **5** take offence at. **6** pay attention to. **7** take care of. **8** be cautious or careful about (something). **minded** *adj* having an inclination as specified, e.g. *politically minded*. **minder** *n Informal* aide or bodyguard. **mindful** *adj* **1** heedful. **2** keeping aware. **mindless** *adj* **1** stupid. **2** requiring no thought. **3** careless.

mine¹ *pron* belonging to me.

mine² *n* **1** deep hole for digging out coal, ores, etc. **2** bomb placed under the ground or in water. **3** profitable source. ◆ *v* **4** dig for minerals. **5** dig (minerals) from a mine. **6** place explosive mines in or on. **miner** *n* person who works in a mine. **minefield** *n* area of land or water containing mines. **minesweeper** *n* ship for clearing away mines.

mineral *n* **1** naturally occurring inorganic substance, such as metal. ◆ *adj* **2** of, containing, or like minerals. **mineralogy** [min-er-**al**-a-jee] *n* study of minerals. **mineral water** water containing dissolved mineral salts or gases.

minestrone [min-ness-**strone**-ee] *n* soup containing vegetables and pasta.

minger *n Brit informal* unattractive person. **minging** *adj Brit informal* unattractive or unpleasant.

mingle *v* **1** mix or blend. **2** come into association (with).

mingy *adj* -**gier**, -**giest** *Informal* miserly.

mini *n, adj* **1** (something) small or miniature. **2** short (skirt).

miniature *n* **1** small portrait, model, or copy. ◆ *adj* **2** small-scale. **miniaturist** *n* **miniaturize** *v* make to a very small scale.

minibar *n* selection of drinks and confectionery provided in a hotel room.

minibus *n* small bus.

minicab *n Brit* ordinary car used as a taxi.

minicomputer *n* computer smaller than a mainframe but more powerful than a microcomputer.

minidisc *n* small recordable compact disc.

minim *n Music* note half the length of a semibreve.

minimum *adj, n, pl* -**mums**, -**ma** least possible (amount or number). **minimal** *adj* minimum. **minimize** *v* **1** reduce to a minimum. **2** belittle.

minion *n* servile assistant.

miniseries *n* TV programme shown in several parts, often on consecutive days.

minister *n* **1** head of a government department. **2** diplomatic representative. **3** (in nonconformist churches) member of the clergy. ◆ *v* **4** (foll. by *to*) attend to the needs of. **ministerial** *adj* **ministration** *n* giving of help. **ministry** *n, pl* -**tries** **1** profession or duties of a clergyman. **2** ministers collectively. **3** government department.

mink *n* **1** stoatlike animal. **2** its highly valued fur.

minnow *n* small freshwater fish.

minor *adj* **1** lesser. **2** *Music* (of a scale) having a semitone between the second and third notes. ◆ *n* **3** person regarded legally as a child. **4** *Music* minor scale. **minority** *n* **1** lesser number. **2** smaller party voting together. **3** group in a minority in any state.

minster *n Brit* cathedral or large church.

minstrel *n* medieval singer or musician.

mint¹ *n* **1** plant with aromatic leaves used for seasoning and flavouring. **2** sweet flavoured with this.

mint² *n* **1** place where money is coined. ◆ *v* **2** make (coins).

minuet [min-new-**wet**] n 1 stately dance. 2 music for this.

minus prep, adj 1 indicating subtraction. ♦ adj 2 less than zero. ♦ n 3 sign (-) denoting subtraction or a number less than zero.

minuscule [**min**-niss-skyool] adj very small.

☑ **SPELLING TIP**

The pronunciation of **minuscule** often influences the way people spell it. It's spelt *miniscule* 121 times in the Bank of English, but it should only one i and two us.

---

minute¹ [**min**-it] n 1 60th part of an hour or degree. 2 moment. ♦ pl 3 record of the proceedings of a meeting. ♦ v 4 record in the minutes.

minute² [my-**newt**] adj 1 very small. 2 precise. **minutely** adv **minutiae** [my-**new**-shee-eye] pl n trifling or precise details.

minx n bold or flirtatious girl.

miracle n 1 wonderful supernatural event. 2 marvel. **miraculous** adj **miraculously** adv **miracle play** medieval play based on a sacred subject.

mirage [mir-**rahzh**] n optical illusion, esp. one caused by hot air.

mire n 1 swampy ground. 2 mud.

mirror n 1 coated glass surface for reflecting images. ♦ v 2 reflect in or as if in a mirror.

mirth n laughter, merriment, or gaiety. **mirthful** adj **mirthless** adj

mis- prefix wrong(ly), bad(ly).

misadventure n unlucky chance.

misanthrope [**miz**-zan-thrope] n person who dislikes people in general. **misanthropic** [miz-zan-**throp**-ik] adj **misanthropy** [miz-**zan**-throp-ee] n

misapprehend v misunderstand. **misapprehension** n

misappropriate v take and use (money) dishonestly. **misappropriation** n

miscarriage n 1 spontaneous premature expulsion of a fetus from the womb. 2 failure, e.g. *a miscarriage of justice.* **miscarry** v 1 have a miscarriage. 2 fail.

miscast v -casting, -cast cast (a role or actor) in (a play or film) inappropriately.

miscegenation [miss-ij-in-**nay**-shun] n interbreeding of races.

miscellaneous [miss-sell-**lane**-ee-uss] adj mixed or assorted. **miscellany** [miss-**sell**-a-nee] n mixed assortment.

mischance n unlucky event.

mischief n 1 annoying but not malicious behaviour. 2 inclination to tease. 3 harm. **mischievous** adj 1 full of mischief. 2 intended to cause harm. **mischievously** adv

miscible [**miss**-sib-bl] adj able to be mixed.

misconception n wrong idea or belief.

misconduct n immoral or unethical behaviour.

miscreant [**miss**-kree-ant] n wrongdoer.

misdeed n wrongful act.

misdemeanour n minor wrongdoing.

miser n person who hoards money and hates spending it. **miserly** adj

miserable adj 1 very unhappy, wretched. 2 causing misery. 3 squalid. 4 mean. **misery** n, pl -eries 1 great unhappiness. 2 *Informal* complaining person.

misfire v 1 (of a firearm or engine) fail to fire correctly. 2 (of a plan) fail to turn out as intended.

misfit n person not suited to his or her social environment.

misfortune n (piece of) bad luck.

misgiving n feeling of fear or doubt.

misguided adj mistaken or unwise.

mishandle v handle badly or inefficiently.

mishap n minor accident.

misinform v give incorrect information to. **misinformation** n

misjudge v judge wrongly or unfairly. **misjudgment, misjudgement** n

mislay v lose (something) temporarily.

mislead v give false or confusing information to. **misleading** adj

mismanage v organize or run (something) badly. **mismanagement** n

misnomer [miss-**no**-mer] n 1 incorrect or unsuitable name. 2 use of this.

misogyny [miss-**oj**-in-ee] n hatred of women. **misogynist** n

misplace v 1 mislay. 2 put in the wrong place. 3 give (trust or affection) inappropriately.

misprint n printing error.

misrepresent v represent wrongly or inaccurately.

miss v 1 fail to notice, hear, hit, reach, find, or catch. 2 not be in time for. 3 notice or regret the absence of. 4 avoid. 5 (of an engine) misfire. ♦ n 6 fact or instance of missing. **missing** adj lost or absent.

Miss n title of a girl or unmarried woman.

missal n book containing the prayers and rites of the Mass.

misshapen adj badly shaped, deformed.

missile n object or weapon thrown, shot, or launched at a target.

mission n 1 specific task or duty. 2 group of people sent on a mission. 3 building in which missionaries work. 4 S Afr long and difficult process. **missionary** n, pl **-aries** person sent abroad to do religious and social work.

missive n letter.

misspent adj wasted or misused.

mist n 1 thin fog. 2 fine spray of liquid. **misty** adj 1 full of mist. 2 dim or obscure.

mistake n 1 error or blunder. ♦ v -taking, -took, -taken 2 misunderstand. 3 confuse (a person or thing) with another.

Mister n polite form of address to a man.

mistletoe n evergreen plant with white berries growing as a parasite on trees.

mistral n strong dry northerly wind of S France.

mistress n 1 woman who has a continuing sexual relationship with a married man. 2 woman in control of people or animals. 3 female teacher.

mistrial n Law trial made void because of some error.

mistrust v 1 have doubts or suspicions about. ♦ n 2 lack of trust. **mistrustful** adj

misunderstand v fail to understand properly. **misunderstanding** n

misuse n 1 incorrect, improper, or careless use. ♦ v 2 use wrongly. 3 treat badly.

mite n 1 very small spider-like animal. 2 very small thing or amount.

mitigate v make less severe. **mitigation** n

mitre [**my**-ter] n 1 bishop's pointed headdress. 2 joint between two pieces of wood bevelled to meet at right angles. ♦ v 3 join with a mitre joint.

mitt n 1 short for MITTEN. 2 baseball catcher's glove.

mitten n glove with one section for the thumb and one for the four fingers together.

mix v 1 combine or blend into one mass. 2 form (something) by mixing. 3 be sociable. ♦ n 4 mixture. **mixed** adj **mix up** v 1 confuse. 2 make into a

mixture. **mixed up** adj **mix-up** n
mixer n **mixture** n **1** something
mixed. **2** combination.

mizzenmast n (on a vessel with three
or more masts) third mast from the
bow.

mm millimetre(s).

mnemonic [nim-**on**-ik] n, adj
(something, such as a rhyme)
intended to help the memory.

mo n, pl **mos** Informal **short for** MOMENT.

MO Medical Officer.

moa n large extinct flightless New
Zealand bird.

moan n **1** low cry of pain. **2** Informal
grumble. ♦ v **3** make or utter with a
moan. **4** Informal grumble.

moat n deep wide ditch, esp. round a
castle.

mob n **1** disorderly crowd. **2** Slang
gang. ♦ v **mobbing, mobbed 3**
surround in a mob to acclaim or attack.

mobile adj **1** able to move. ♦ n **2** same
as MOBILE PHONE. **3** hanging structure
designed to move in air currents.
mobile phone cordless phone
powered by batteries. **mobility** n

mobilize v **1** (of the armed services)
prepare for active service. **2** organize
for a purpose. **mobilization** n

moccasin n soft leather shoe.

☑ SPELLING TIP

One **moccasin** has a double c, but
only one s. The plural, **moccasins**,
has two ss, but they are not together.

---

mocha [**mock**-a] n **1** kind of strong
dark coffee. **2** flavouring made from
coffee and chocolate.

mock v **1** make fun of. **2** mimic. ♦ adj **3**
sham or imitation. **mocks** pl n
Informal (in England and Wales)
practice exams taken before public
exams. **put the mockers on** Brit, Aust
& NZ informal ruin the chances of

success of. **mockery** n **1** derision. **2**
inadequate or worthless attempt.
mockingbird n N American bird
which imitates other birds' songs.
mock orange shrub with white
fragrant flowers. **mock-up** n full-scale
model for test or study.

mod. **1** moderate. **2** modern.

mode n **1** method or manner. **2** current
fashion.

model n **1** (miniature) representation. **2**
pattern. **3** person or thing worthy of
imitation. **4** person who poses for an
artist or photographer. **5** person who
wears clothes to display them to
prospective buyers. **6** v **-elling, -elled**
7 make a model of. **8** mould. **9** display
(clothing) as a model.

modem [**mode**-em] n device for
connecting two computers by a
telephone line.

moderate adj **1** not extreme. **2**
self-restrained. **3** average. ♦ n **4** person
of moderate views. ♦ v **5** make or
become less violent or extreme.
moderately adv **moderation** n
moderator n **1** (Presbyterian Church)
minister appointed to preside over a
Church court, general assembly, etc. **2**
person who presides over a public or
legislative assembly.

modern adj **1** of present or recent
times. **2** up-to-date. **modernity** n
modernism n (support of) modern
tendencies, thoughts, or styles.
modernist adj, n **modernize** v bring
up to date. **modernization** n

modest adj **1** not vain or boastful. **2**
not excessive. **3** not showy. **4** shy.
modestly adv **modesty** n

modicum n small quantity.

modify v **-fying, -fied 1** change
slightly. **2** tone down. **3** (of a word)
qualify (another word). **modifier** n
word that qualifies the sense of
another. **modification** n

modish [**mode**-ish] *adj* in fashion.

modulate *v* **1** vary in tone. **2** adjust. **3** change the key of (music). **modulation** *n* **modulator** *n*

module *n* self-contained unit, section, or component with a specific function.

modus operandi [**mode**-uss op-er-**an**-die] *n Latin* method of operating.

mogul [**moh**-gl] *n* important or powerful person.

mohair *n* **1** fine hair of the Angora goat. **2** yarn or fabric made from this.

mohican *n* punk hairstyle with shaved sides and a stiff central strip of hair, often brightly coloured.

moiety [**moy**-it-ee] *n, pl* **-ties** half.

moist *adj* slightly wet. **moisten** *v* make or become moist. **moisture** *n* liquid diffused as vapour or condensed in drops. **moisturize** *v* add moisture to (the skin etc.).

molar *n* large back tooth used for grinding.

molasses *n* dark syrup, a by-product of sugar refining.

mole[1] *n* small dark raised spot on the skin.

mole[2] *n* **1** small burrowing mammal. **2** *Informal* spy who has infiltrated and become a trusted member of an organization.

mole[3] *n* unit of amount of substance.

mole[4] *n* **1** breakwater. **2** harbour protected by this.

molecule [**mol**-lik-kyool] *n* **1** simplest freely existing chemical unit, composed of two or more atoms. **2** very small particle. **molecular** [**mol**-**lek**-yew-lar] *adj*

molest *v* **1** interfere with sexually. **2** annoy or injure. **molester** *n* **molestation** *n*

moll *n Slang* gangster's female accomplice.

mollify *v* **-fying, -fied** pacify or soothe.

mollusc *n* soft-bodied, usu. hard-shelled, animal, such as a snail or oyster.

mollycoddle *v* pamper.

Molotov cocktail *n* petrol bomb.

molten *adj* liquefied or melted.

molybdenum [mol-**lib**-din-um] *n Chem* hard silvery-white metallic element.

moment *n* **1** short space of time. **2** (present) point in time. **momentary** *adj* lasting only a moment. **momentarily** *adv*

momentous [moh-**men**-tuss] *adj* of great significance.

momentum *n* **1** impetus of a moving body. **2** product of a body's mass and velocity.

monarch *n* sovereign ruler of a state. **monarchical** *adj* **monarchist** *n* supporter of monarchy. **monarchy** *n* government by or a state ruled by a sovereign.

monastery *n, pl* **-teries** residence of a community of monks. **monastic** *adj* **1** of monks, nuns, or monasteries. **2** simple and austere. **monasticism** *n*

Monday *n* second day of the week.

monetary *adj* of money or currency. **monetarism** *n* theory that inflation is caused by an increase in the money supply. **monetarist** *n, adj*

money *n* medium of exchange, coins or banknotes. **moneyed, monied** *adj* rich.

mongol *n, adj Offens* (person) affected by Down's syndrome. **mongolism** *n*

mongoose *n, pl* **-gooses** stoatlike mammal of Asia and Africa that kills snakes.

mongrel *n* **1** animal, esp. a dog, of mixed breed. **2** something arising from a variety of sources. ♦ *adj* **3** of mixed breed or origin.

monitor n 1 person or device that checks, controls, warns, or keeps a record of something. 2 *Brit, Aust & NZ* pupil assisting a teacher with duties. 3 television set used in a studio to check what is being transmitted. 4 large lizard of Africa, Asia, and Australia. ♦ v 5 watch and check on.

monk n member of an all-male religious community bound by vows. **monkish** *adj*

monkey n 1 long-tailed primate. 2 mischievous child. ♦ v 3 (usu. foll. by *about* or *around*) meddle or fool. **monkey nut** *Brit* peanut. **monkey puzzle** coniferous tree with sharp stiff leaves. **monkey wrench** wrench with adjustable jaws.

mono- *combining form* single, e.g. *monosyllable.*

monochrome *adj* 1 *Photog* black-and-white. 2 in only one colour.

monocle n eyeglass for one eye only.

monogamy n custom of being married to one person at a time.

monogram n design of combined letters, esp. a person's initials.

monograph n book or paper on a single subject.

monolith n large upright block of stone. **monolithic** *adj*

monologue n 1 long speech by one person. 2 dramatic piece for one performer.

monomania n obsession with one thing. **monomaniac** *n, adj*

monoplane n aeroplane with one pair of wings.

monopoly n 1 pl **-lies** exclusive possession of or right to do something. 2 (M-) ® board game for four to six players who deal in 'property' as they move around the board. **monopolize** v have or take exclusive possession of.

monorail n single-rail railway.

monotheism n belief in only one God. **monotheistic** *adj*

monotone n unvaried pitch in speech or sound. **monotonous** *adj* tedious due to lack of variety. **monotonously** *adv* **monotony** n

Monseigneur [mon-sen-**nyur**] *n, pl* **Messeigneurs** [may-sen-**nyur**] title of French prelates.

monsieur [muss-**syur**] *n, pl* **messieurs** [may-**syur**] French title of address equivalent to *sir* or *Mr.*

Monsignor n *RC Church* title attached to certain offices.

monsoon n 1 seasonal wind of SE Asia. 2 rainy season accompanying this.

monster n 1 imaginary, usu. frightening, beast. 2 huge person, animal, or thing. 3 very wicked person. ♦ *adj* 4 huge. **monstrosity** n large ugly thing. **monstrous** *adj* 1 unnatural or ugly. 2 outrageous or shocking. 3 huge. **monstrously** *adv*

monstrance n *RC Church* container in which the consecrated Host is exposed for adoration.

montage [mon-**tahzh**] *n* 1 (making of) a picture composed from pieces of others. 2 method of film editing incorporating several shots to form a single image.

month n 1 one of the twelve divisions of the calendar year. 2 period of four weeks. **monthly** *adj* 1 happening or payable once a month. ♦ *adv* 2 once a month. ♦ *n* 3 monthly magazine.

monument n something, esp. a building or statue, that commemorates something. **monumental** *adj* 1 large, impressive, or lasting. 2 of or being a monument. 3 *Informal* extreme. **monumentally** *adv*

moo n 1 long deep cry of a cow. ♦ v 2 make this noise.

mooch v *Slang* loiter about aimlessly.

mood[1] n temporary (gloomy) state of mind. **moody** adj 1 sullen or gloomy. 2 changeable in mood. **moodily** adv

mood[2] n Grammar form of a verb indicating whether it expresses a fact, wish, supposition, or command.

moon n 1 natural satellite of the earth. 2 natural satellite of any planet. ♦ v 3 (foll. by about or around) be idle in a listless or dreamy way. **moonlight** n 1 light from the moon. 2 v 3 Informal work at a secondary job, esp. illegally. **moonshine** n 1 US & Canadian illicitly distilled whisky. 2 nonsense. **moonstone** n translucent semiprecious stone. **moonstruck** adj slightly mad or odd.

moor[1] n Brit tract of open uncultivated ground covered with grass and heather. **moorhen** n small black water bird.

moor[2] v secure (a ship) with ropes etc. **mooring** n 1 place for mooring a ship. ♦ pl 2 ropes etc. used in mooring a ship.

Moor n member of a Muslim people of NW Africa who ruled Spain between the 8th and 15th centuries. **Moorish** adj

moose n large N American deer.

moot adj 1 debatable, e.g. a moot point. ♦ v 2 bring up for discussion.

mop n 1 long stick with twists of cotton or a sponge on the end, used for cleaning. 2 thick mass of hair. ♦ v **mopping, mopped** 3 clean or soak up with or as if with a mop.

mope v be gloomy and apathetic.

moped n light motorized cycle.

mopoke n small spotted owl of Australia and New Zealand.

moraine n accumulated mass of debris deposited by a glacier.

moral adj 1 concerned with right and wrong conduct. 2 based on a sense of right and wrong. 3 (of support or a

victory) psychological rather than practical. ♦ n 4 lesson to be obtained from a story or event. ♦ pl 5 principles of behaviour with respect to right and wrong. **morally** adv **moralist** n person with a strong sense of right and wrong. **morality** n 1 good moral conduct. 2 moral goodness or badness. **morality play** medieval play with a moral lesson. **moralize** v make moral pronouncements.

morale [mor-**rahl**] n degree of confidence or hope of a person or group.

morass n 1 marsh. 2 mess.

moratorium n, pl -ria, -riums legally authorized ban or delay.

moray n large voracious eel.

morbid adj 1 unduly interested in death or unpleasant events. 2 gruesome.

mordant adj 1 sarcastic or scathing. ♦ n 2 substance used to fix dyes.

more adj 1 greater in amount or degree. 2 comparative of MUCH or MANY. 3 additional or further. ♦ adv 4 to a greater extent. 5 in addition. ♦ pron 6 greater or additional amount or number. **moreover** adv in addition to what has already been said.

mores [**more**-rayz] pl n customs and conventions embodying the fundamental values of a community.

Moreton Bay bug n Australian flattish edible shellfish.

morganatic marriage n marriage of a person of high rank to a lower-ranking person whose status remains unchanged.

morgue n mortuary.

moribund adj without force or vitality.

Mormon n member of a religious sect founded in the USA.

morn n Poetic morning.

morning n part of the day before

noon. **morning-glory** n plant with trumpet-shaped flowers which close in the late afternoon.

morocco n goatskin leather.

moron n 1 Informal foolish or stupid person. 2 (formerly) person with a low intelligence quotient. **moronic** adj

morose [mor-**rohss**] adj sullen or moody.

morphine, morphia n drug extracted from opium, used as an anaesthetic and sedative.

morphology n science of forms and structures of organisms or words. **morphological** adj

morris dance n traditional English folk dance.

morrow n Poetic next day.

Morse n former system of signalling in which letters of the alphabet are represented by combinations of short and long signals.

morsel n small piece, esp. of food.

mortal adj 1 subject to death. 2 causing death. ♦ n 3 human being. **mortally** adv **mortality** n 1 state of being mortal. 2 great loss of life. 3 death rate. **mortal sin** RC Church sin meriting damnation.

mortar n 1 small cannon with a short range. 2 mixture of lime, sand, and water for holding bricks and stones together. 3 bowl in which substances are pounded. **mortarboard** n black square academic cap.

mortgage n 1 conditional pledging of property, esp. a house, as security for the repayment of a loan. 2 the loan itself. ♦ v 3 pledge (property) as security thus. **mortgagee** n creditor in a mortgage. **mortgagor** n debtor in a mortgage.

mortice, mortise [**more**-tiss] n hole in a piece of wood or stone shaped to receive a matching projection on another piece. **mortice lock** lock set

into a door.

mortify v -fying, -fied 1 humiliate. 2 subdue by self-denial. 3 (of flesh) become gangrenous. **mortification** n

mortuary n, pl -aries building where corpses are kept before burial or cremation.

mosaic [mow-**zay**-ik] n design or decoration using small pieces of coloured stone or glass.

Mosaic adj of Moses.

Moselle n light white German wine.

Moslem n, adj same as MUSLIM.

mosque n Muslim temple.

mosquito n, pl -toes, -tos blood-sucking flying insect.

moss n small flowerless plant growing in masses on moist surfaces. **mossy** adj

most n 1 greatest number or degree. ♦ adj 2 greatest in number or degree. 3 superlative of MUCH or MANY. ♦ adv 4 in the greatest degree. **mostly** adv for the most part, generally.

MOT, MOT test n (in Britain) compulsory annual test of the roadworthiness of vehicles over a certain age.

motel n roadside hotel for motorists.

motet n short sacred choral song.

moth n nocturnal insect like a butterfly. **mothball** n 1 small ball of camphor or naphthalene used to repel moths from stored clothes. ♦ v 2 store (something operational) for future use. 3 postpone (a project etc.). **moth-eaten** adj 1 decayed or scruffy. 2 eaten or damaged by moth larvae.

mother n 1 female parent. 2 head of a female religious community. ♦ adj 3 native or inborn, e.g. mother wit. ♦ v 4 look after as a mother. **motherhood** n **motherly** adj **motherless** adj **mother-in-law** n mother of one's husband or wife. **mother of pearl**

iridescent lining of certain shells.
mother tongue one's native language.
motif [moh-**teef**] n (recurring) theme or design.
motion n **1** process, action, or way of moving. **2** proposal in a meeting. **3** evacuation of the bowels. ♦ v **4** direct (someone) by gesture. **motionless** adj not moving. **motion picture** cinema film.
motive n **1** reason for a course of action. ♦ adj **2** causing motion. **motivate** v give incentive to. **motivation** n
motley adj **1** miscellaneous. **2** multicoloured.
motocross n motorcycle race over a rough course.
motor n **1** engine, esp. of a vehicle. **2** machine that converts electrical energy into mechanical energy. **3** Chiefly Brit car. ♦ v **4** travel by car. **motorist** n driver of a car. **motorized** adj equipped with a motor or motor transport. **motorbike** n **motorboat** n **motorcar** n **motorcycle** n **motorcyclist** n **motor scooter** light motorcycle with small wheels and an enclosed engine. **motorway** n main road for fast-moving traffic.
mottled adj marked with blotches.
motto n, pl **-toes, -tos 1** saying expressing an ideal or rule of conduct. **2** verse or maxim in a paper cracker.
mould¹ n **1** hollow container in which metal etc. is cast. **2** shape, form, or pattern. **3** nature or character. ♦ v **4** shape. **5** influence or direct. **moulding** n moulded ornamental edging.
mould² n fungal growth caused by dampness. **mouldy** adj **1** stale or musty. **2** dull or boring.
mould³ n loose soil. **moulder** v decay into dust.
moult v **1** shed feathers, hair, or skin to make way for new growth. ♦ n **2** process of moulting.
mound n **1** heap, esp. of earth or stones. **2** small hill.
mount v **1** climb or ascend. **2** get up on (a horse etc.). **3** increase or accumulate. **4** fix on a support or backing. **5** organize, e.g. mount a campaign. ♦ n **6** backing or support on which something is fixed. **7** horse for riding. **8** hill.
mountain n **1** hill of great size. **2** large heap. **mountainous** adj **1** full of mountains. **2** huge. **mountaineer** n person who climbs mountains. **mountaineering** n **mountain bike** bicycle with straight handlebars and heavy-duty tyres, for cycling over rough terrain. **mountain oyster** NZ informal sheep's testicle eaten as food.
mountebank n charlatan or fake.
Mountie n Informal member of the Royal Canadian Mounted Police.
mourn v feel or express sorrow for (a dead person or lost thing). **mournful** adj sad or dismal. **mournfully** adv **mourning** n **1** grieving. **2** conventional symbols of grief for death, such as the wearing of black.
mourner n person attending a funeral.
mouse n, pl **mice 1** small long-tailed rodent. **2** timid person. **3** Computers hand-held device for moving the cursor without keying. **mouser** n cat used to catch mice. **mousy** adj **1** like a mouse, esp. in hair colour. **2** meek and shy.
mousse n dish of flavoured cream whipped and set.
moustache n hair on the upper lip.
mouth n **1** opening in the head for eating and issuing sounds. **2** entrance. **3** point where a river enters the sea. **4** opening. ♦ v **5** form (words) with the lips without speaking. **6** speak or utter insincerely, esp. in public. **mouthful** n

amount of food or drink put into the mouth at any one time when eating or drinking. **mouth organ same as** HARMONICA. **mouthpiece** *n* **1** part of a telephone into which a person speaks. **2** part of a wind instrument into which the player blows. **3** spokesperson.

move *v* **1** change in place or position. **2** change (one's house etc.). **3** take action. **4** stir the emotions of. **5** incite. **6** suggest (a proposal) formally. ◆ *n* **7** moving. **8** action towards some goal. **movable, moveable** *adj* **movement** *n* **1** action or process of moving. **2** group with a common aim. **3** division of a piece of music. **4** moving parts of a machine.

movie *n Informal* cinema film.

mow *v* **mowing, mowed, mowed** *or* **mown** cut (grass or crops). **mow down** *v* kill in large numbers.

mower *n* machine for cutting grass.

mozzarella [mot-sa-**rel**-la] *n* moist white cheese originally made in Italy from buffalo milk.

MP 1 Member of Parliament. **2** Military Police(man).

MP3 *Computing* Motion Picture Expert Group-1, Audio Layer-3: a digital compression format used to compress audio files to a fraction of their original size without loss of sound quality.

MPEG [**em**-peg] *Computing* **1** Motion Picture Expert Group: standard compressed file format used for audio and video files. **2** file in this format.

mpg miles per gallon.

mph miles per hour.

Mr Mister.

Mrs *n* title of a married woman.

Ms [**mizz**] *n* title used instead of Miss or Mrs.

MS 1 manuscript. **2** multiple sclerosis.

MSc Master of Science.

MSP (in Britain) Member of the Scottish Parliament.

MSS manuscripts.

Mt Mount.

much *adj* **more, most 1** large amount or degree of. ◆ *n* **2** large amount or degree. ◆ *adv* **more, most 3** to a great degree. **4** nearly.

mucilage [**mew**-sill-ij] *n* gum or glue.

muck *n* **1** dirt, filth. **2** manure. **mucky** *adj*

mucus [**mew**-kuss] *n* slimy secretion of the mucous membranes. **mucous membrane** tissue lining body cavities or passages.

mud *n* wet soft earth. **muddy** *adj* **mudguard** *n* cover over a wheel to prevent mud or water from being thrown up by it. **mud pack** cosmetic paste to improve the complexion.

muddle *v* **1** (often foll. by *up*) confuse. **2** mix up. ◆ *n* **3** state of confusion.

muesli [**mewz**-lee] *n* mixture of grain, nuts, and dried fruit, eaten with milk.

muezzin [moo-**ezz**-in] *n* official who summons Muslims to prayer.

muff[1] *n* tube-shaped covering to keep the hands warm.

muff[2] *v* bungle (an action).

muffin *n* light round flat yeast cake.

muffle *v* wrap up for warmth or to deaden sound. **muffler** *n* **1** *Brit* scarf. **2** device to reduce the noise of an engine exhaust.

mufti *n* civilian clothes worn by a person who usually wears a uniform.

mug[1] *n* large drinking cup.

mug[2] *n* **1** *Slang* face. **2** *Slang* gullible person. ◆ *v* **mugging, mugged 3** *Informal* attack in order to rob. **mugger** *n*

mug[3] *v* **mugging, mugged** (foll. by *up*) *Informal* study hard.

muggins *n Informal* stupid or gullible person.

muggy *adj* **-gier, -giest** (of weather)

damp and stifling.

mulatto [mew-**lat**-toe] *n, pl* -**tos**, -**toes** child of one Black and one White parent.

mulberry *n* **1** tree whose leaves are used to feed silkworms. **2** purple fruit of this tree.

mulch *n* **1** mixture of wet straw, leaves, etc., used to protect the roots of plants. ♦ *v* **2** cover (land) with mulch.

mule[1] *n* offspring of a horse and a donkey. **mulish** *adj* obstinate.

mule[2] *n* backless shoe or slipper.

mulga *n* **1** Australian acacia shrub growing in desert regions. **2** *Aust* the outback.

mull *v* think (over) or ponder. **mulled** *adj* (of wine or ale) flavoured with sugar and spices and served hot.

mullah *n* Muslim scholar, teacher, or religious leader.

mullet[1] *n* edible sea fish.

mullet[2] *n* haircut in which the hair is short at the top and sides and long at the back.

mulligatawny *n* soup made with curry powder.

mullion *n* vertical dividing bar in a window. **mullioned** *adj*

mulloway *n* large Australian sea fish, valued for sport and food.

multi- *combining form* many, e.g. *multicultural; multistorey.*

multifarious [mull-tee-**fare**-ee-uss] *adj* having many various parts.

multiple *adj* **1** having many parts. ♦ *n* **2** quantity which contains another an exact number of times.

multiplex *n* **1** purpose-built complex containing several cinemas and usu. restaurants and bars. ♦ *adj* **2** having many elements, complex.

multiplicity *n, pl* -**ties** large number or great variety.

multiply *v* -**plying**, -**plied** **1** (cause to) increase in number, quantity, or degree. **2** add (a number or quantity) to itself a given number of times. **3** increase in number by reproduction. **multiplication** *n* **multiplicand** *n* *Maths* number to be multiplied.

multipurpose *adj* having many uses, e.g. *a multipurpose tool.* **multipurpose vehicle** large vanlike car designed to carry up to eight passengers.

multitude *n* **1** great number. **2** great crowd. **multitudinous** *adj* very numerous.

mum[1] *n Informal* mother.

mum[2] *adj* keep mum remain silent.

mumble *v* speak indistinctly, mutter.

mumbo jumbo *n* **1** meaningless language. **2** foolish religious ritual or incantation.

mummer *n* actor in a traditional English folk play or mime.

mummy[1] *n, pl* -**mies** body embalmed and wrapped for burial in ancient Egypt. **mummified** *adj* (of a body) preserved as a mummy.

mummy[2] *n, pl* -**mies** child's word for MOTHER.

mumps *n* infectious disease with swelling in the glands of the neck.

munch *v* chew noisily and steadily.

mundane *adj* **1** everyday, banal. **2** earthly.

municipal *adj* relating to a city or town. **municipality** *n* **1** city or town with local self-government. **2** governing body of this.

munificent [mew-**niff**-fiss-sent] *adj* very generous. **munificence** *n*

muniments *pl n* title deeds or similar documents.

munitions *pl n* military stores.

munted *adj NZ slang* **1** destroyed or ruined. **2** abnormal or peculiar.

mural *n* painting on a wall.

murder n **1** unlawful intentional killing of a human being. ♦ v **2** kill in this way. **murderer, murderess** n **murderous** adj

murky adj dark or gloomy. **murk** n thick darkness.

murmur v **-muring, -mured 1** speak or say in a quiet indistinct way. **2** complain. ♦ n **3** continuous low indistinct sound.

muscle n **1** tissue in the body which produces movement by contracting. **2** strength or power. **muscular** adj **1** with well-developed muscles. **2** of muscles. **muscular dystrophy** disease with wasting of the muscles. **muscle in** v Informal force one's way in.

muse v ponder quietly.

Muse n **1** Greek myth one of nine goddesses, each of whom inspired an art or science. **2** (m-) force that inspires a creative artist.

museum n building where natural, artistic, historical, or scientific objects are exhibited and preserved.

mush n **1** soft pulpy mass. **2** Informal cloying sentimentality. **mushy** adj

mushroom n **1** edible fungus with a stem and cap. ♦ v **2** grow rapidly.

music n **1** art form using a melodious and harmonious combination of notes. **2** written or printed form of this. **musical** adj **1** of or like music. **2** talented in or fond of music. **3** pleasant-sounding. ♦ n **4** play or film with songs and dancing. **musically** adv **musician** n **musicology** n scientific study of music. **musicologist** n **music centre** Brit combined record or CD player, radio, and cassette player. **music hall** variety theatre.

musk n scent obtained from a gland of the musk deer or produced synthetically. **musky** adj **muskrat** n **1** N American beaver-like rodent. **2** its fur.

musket n Hist long-barrelled gun. **musketeer** n **musketry** n (use of) muskets.

Muslim n **1** follower of the religion of Islam. ♦ adj **2** of or relating to Islam.

muslin n fine cotton fabric.

mussel n edible shellfish with a dark hinged shell.

must[1] v **1** used as an auxiliary to express obligation, certainty, or resolution. ♦ n **2** essential or necessary thing.

must[2] n newly pressed grape juice.

mustang n wild horse of SW USA.

mustard n **1** paste made from the powdered seeds of a plant, used as a condiment. **2** the plant. **mustard gas** poisonous gas causing blistering burns and blindness.

muster v **1** assemble. ♦ n **2** assembly of military personnel.

musty adj **mustier, mustiest** smelling mouldy and stale. **mustiness** n

mutable [mew-tab-bl] adj liable to change. **mutability** n

mutation n (genetic) change. **mutate** v (cause to) undergo mutation. **mutant** n mutated animal, plant, etc.

mute adj **1** silent. **2** unable to speak. ♦ n **3** person who is unable to speak. **4** Music device to soften the tone of an instrument. **muted** adj **1** (of sound or colour) softened. **2** (of a reaction) subdued. **mutely** adv

muti [moo-ti] n S Afr informal medicine, esp. herbal medicine.

mutilate [mew-till-ate] v **1** deprive of a limb or other part. **2** damage (a book or text). **mutilation** n

mutiny [mew-tin-ee] n, pl **-nies 1** rebellion against authority, esp. by soldiers or sailors. ♦ v **-nying, -nied 2** commit mutiny. **mutineer** n

mutinous *adj*

mutt *n Slang* **1** mongrel dog. **2** stupid person.

mutter *v* **1** utter or speak indistinctly. **2** grumble. ♦ *n* **3** muttered sound or grumble.

mutton *n* flesh of sheep, used as food. **mutton bird 1** *Aust* sea bird with dark plumage. **2** *NZ* any of a number of migratory sea birds, the young of which are a Maori delicacy.

mutual [**mew**-chew-al] *adj* **1** felt or expressed by each of two people about the other. **2** common to both or all. **mutually** *adv*

Muzak *n* ® recorded light music played in shops etc.

muzzle *n* **1** animal's mouth and nose. **2** cover for these to prevent biting. **3** open end of a gun. ♦ *v* **4** prevent from being heard or noticed. **5** put a muzzle on.

muzzy *adj* **-zier**, **-ziest 1** confused or muddled. **2** blurred or hazy.

mW milliwatt(s).

MW megawatt(s).

my *adj* belonging to me.

myall *n* Australian acacia with hard scented wood.

mycology *n* study of fungi.

myna, mynah, mina *n* Asian bird which can mimic human speech.

myopia [my-**oh**-pee-a] *n* short-sightedness. **myopic** [my-**op**-ik] *adj*

myriad [**mir**-ree-ad] *adj* **1** innumerable. ♦ *n* **2** large indefinite number.

myrrh [**mur**] *n* aromatic gum used in perfume, incense, and medicine.

myrtle [**mur**-tl] *n* flowering evergreen shrub.

myself *pron* emphatic or reflexive form of I or ME.

mystery *n, pl* **-teries 1** strange or inexplicable event or phenomenon. **2** obscure or secret thing. **3** story or film that arouses suspense. **mysterious** *adj* **mysteriously** *adv*

mystic *n* **1** person who seeks spiritual knowledge. ♦ *adj* **2** mystical. **mystical** *adj* having a spiritual or religious significance beyond human understanding. **mysticism** *n*

mystify *v* **-fying**, **-fied** bewilder or puzzle. **mystification** *n*

mystique [miss-**steek**] *n* aura of mystery or power.

myth *n* **1** tale with supernatural characters, usu. of how the world and mankind began. **2** untrue idea or explanation. **3** imaginary person or object. **mythical, mythic** *adj* **mythology** *n* **1** myths collectively. **2** study of myths. **mythological** *adj*

myxomatosis [mix-a-mat-**oh**-siss] *n* contagious fatal viral disease of rabbits.

N n

N 1 *Chem* nitrogen. **2** *Physics* newton(s). **3** North(ern).

n. 1 neuter. **2** noun. **3** number.

Na *Chem* sodium.

Naafi *n Brit* canteen or shop for military personnel.

naan *n same as* NAN BREAD.

naartjie [**nahr**-chee] *n S Afr* tangerine.

nab *v* **nabbing, nabbed** *Informal* **1** arrest (someone). **2** catch (someone) in wrongdoing.

nadir *n* **1** point in the sky opposite the zenith. **2** lowest point.

naevus [**nee**-vuss] *n, pl* **-vi** birthmark or mole.

naff *adj Brit slang* lacking quality or taste.

nag[1] *v* **nagging, nagged 1** scold or find fault constantly. **2** be a constant source of discomfort or worry to. ♦ *n* **3** person who nags. **nagging** *adj, n*

nag[2] *n Informal* old horse.

naiad [**nye**-ad] *n Greek myth* nymph living in a lake or river.

nail *n* **1** pointed piece of metal with a head, hit with a hammer to join two objects together. **2** hard covering of the upper tips of the fingers and toes. ♦ *v* **3** attach (something) with nails. **4** *Informal* catch or arrest. **hit the nail on the head** say something exactly correct. **nail file** small metal file used to smooth or shape the finger or toe nails. **nail varnish, polish** cosmetic lacquer applied to the finger or toe nails.

naive [nye-**eev**] *adj* **1** innocent and gullible. **2** simple and lacking sophistication. **naively** *adv* **naivety, naïveté** [nye-**eev**-tee] *n*

naked *adj* **1** without clothes. **2** without any covering. **the naked eye** the eye unassisted by any optical instrument. **nakedness** *n*

namby-pamby *adj Brit, Aust & NZ* sentimental or insipid.

name *n* **1** word by which a person or thing is known. **2** reputation, esp. a good one. **3** *v* **4** give a name to. **5** refer to by name. **6** fix or specify. **call someone names, a name** insult someone by using rude words to describe him or her. **nameless** *adj* **1** without a name. **2** unspecified. **3** too horrible to be mentioned. **namely** *adv* that is to say. **namesake** *n* person with the same name as another.

nan bread *n* slightly leavened Indian bread in a large flat leaf shape.

nanny *n, pl* **-nies** woman whose job is looking after young children. **nanny goat** female goat.

nap[1] *n* **1** short sleep. ♦ *v* **napping, napped 2** have a short sleep.

nap[2] *n* raised fibres of velvet or similar cloth.

nap[3] *n* card game similar to whist.

napalm *n* highly inflammable jellied petrol, used in bombs.

nape *n* back of the neck.

naphtha *n* liquid mixture distilled from coal tar or petroleum, used as a solvent and in petrol. **naphthalene** *n* white crystalline product distilled from coal tar or petroleum, used in disinfectants, mothballs, and explosives.

napkin *n* piece of cloth or paper for wiping the mouth or protecting the clothes while eating.

nappy *n, pl* **-pies** piece of absorbent material fastened round a baby's lower torso to absorb urine and faeces.

narcissism *n* exceptional interest in or admiration for oneself. **narcissistic** *adj*

narcissus *n, pl* **-cissi** yellow, orange, or white flower related to the daffodil.

narcotic *n, adj* (of) a drug, such as morphine or opium, which produces numbness and drowsiness, used medicinally but addictive. **narcosis** *n* effect of a narcotic.

nark *Slang* ♦ *v* **1** annoy. ♦ *n* **2** informer or spy. **3** *Brit* someone who complains in an irritating manner. **narky** *adj Slang* irritable or complaining.

narrate *v* **1** tell (a story). **2** speak the words accompanying and telling what is happening in a film or TV programme. **narration** *n* **narrator** *n*

narrative *n* account, story.

narrow *adj* **1** small in breadth in comparison to length. **2** limited in range, extent, or outlook. **3** with little margin, e.g. *a narrow escape.* ♦ *v* **4** make or become narrow. **5** (often foll. by *down*) limit or restrict. **narrows** *pl n* narrow part of a strait, river, or current. **narrowly** *adv* **narrowness** *n* **narrow boat** *Brit* long bargelike canal boat. **narrow-minded** *adj* intolerant or bigoted.

narwhal *n* arctic whale with a long spiral tusk.

NASA *US* National Aeronautics and Space Administration.

nasal *adj* **1** of the nose. **2** (of a sound) pronounced with air passing through the nose. **nasally** *adv*

nascent *adj* starting to grow or develop.

nasturtium *n* plant with yellow, red, or orange trumpet-shaped flowers.

nasty *adj* **-tier, -tiest** **1** unpleasant. **2** (of an injury) dangerous or painful. **3** spiteful or unkind. **nastily** *adv* **nastiness** *n*

natal *adj* of or relating to birth.

nation *n* people of one or more cultures or races organized as a single state.

national *adj* **1** characteristic of a particular nation. ♦ *n* **2** citizen of a nation. **nationally** *adv* **National Curriculum** curriculum of subjects taught in state schools in England and Wales since 1989. **National Health Service** (in Britain) system of national medical services financed mainly by taxation. **national insurance** (in Britain) state insurance scheme providing payments to the unemployed, sick, and retired. **national park** area of countryside protected by a government for its natural or environmental importance. **national service** compulsory military service.

nationalism *n* **1** policy of national independence. **2** patriotism, sometimes to an excessive degree. **nationalist** *n, adj*

nationality *n, pl* **-ities** **1** fact of being a citizen of a particular nation. **2** group of people of the same race.

nationalize *v* put (an industry or a company) under state control. **nationalization** *n*

native *adj* **1** relating to a place where a person was born. **2** born in a specified place. **3** (foll. by *to*) originating (in). **4** inborn. ♦ *n* **5** person born in a specified place. **6** indigenous animal or plant. **7** member of the original race of a country. **Native American** (person) descended from the original inhabitants of the American continent. **native bear** *Aust* same as KOALA. **native companion** *Aust* same as BROLGA. **native dog** *Aust* dingo.

Nativity *n Christianity* birth of Jesus Christ.

NATO North Atlantic Treaty Organization.

natter *Informal* ♦ *v* **1** talk idly or

chatter. ♦ *n* **2** long idle chat.

natty *adj* **-tier, -tiest** *Informal* smart and spruce.

natural *adj* **1** normal or to be expected. **2** genuine or spontaneous. **3** of, according to, existing in, or produced by nature. **4** not created by human beings. **5** not synthetic. **6** *n* **7** person with an inborn talent or skill. **naturally** *adv* **1** of course. **2** in a natural or normal way. **3** instinctively. **natural gas** gas found below the ground, used mainly as a fuel. **natural history** study of animals and plants in the wild. **natural selection** process by which only creatures and plants well adapted to their environment survive.

naturalism *n* movement in art and literature advocating detailed realism. **naturalistic** *adj*

naturalist *n* student of natural history.

naturalize *v* give citizenship to (a person born in another country). **naturalization** *n*

nature *n* **1** whole system of the existence, forces, and events of the physical world that are not controlled by human beings. **2** fundamental or essential qualities. **3** kind or sort.

naturism *n* nudism. **naturist** *n*

naught *n Lit* nothing.

naughty *adj* **-tier, -tiest 1** disobedient or mischievous. **2** mildly indecent. **naughtily** *adv* **naughtiness** *n*

nausea [**naw**-zee-a] *n* feeling of being about to vomit. **nauseate** *v* **1** make (someone) feel sick. **2** disgust. **nauseous** *adj* **1** as if about to vomit. **2** sickening.

nautical *adj* of the sea or ships. **nautical mile** 1852 metres (6076.12 feet).

nautilus *n, pl* **-luses, -li** shellfish with many tentacles.

naval *adj see* NAVY.

nave *n* long central part of a church.

navel *n* hollow in the middle of the abdomen where the umbilical cord was attached.

navigate *v* **1** direct or plot the path or position of a ship, aircraft, or car. **2** travel over or through. **navigation** *n* **navigator** *n* **navigable** *adj* **1** wide, deep, or safe enough to be sailed through. **2** able to be steered.

navvy *n, pl* **-vies** *Brit* labourer employed on a road or a building site.

navy *n, pl* **-vies 1** branch of a country's armed services comprising warships with their crews and organization. **2** warships of a nation. ♦ *adj* **3** navy-blue. **naval** *adj* of or relating to a navy or ships. **navy-blue** *adj* very dark blue.

nay *interj Obs* no.

Nazi *n* **1** member of the fascist National Socialist Party, which came to power in Germany in 1933 under Adolf Hitler. ♦ *adj* **2** of or relating to the Nazis. **Nazism** *n*

NB note well.

NCO *Mil* noncommissioned officer.

NE northeast(ern).

Neanderthal [nee-**ann**-der-tahl] *adj* of a type of primitive man that lived in Europe before 12 000 BC.

neap tide *n* tide at the first and last quarters of the moon when there is the smallest rise and fall in tidal level.

near *prep, adv, adj* **1** indicating a place or time not far away. ♦ *adj* **2** almost being the thing specified, e.g. *a near disaster.* ♦ *v* **3** draw close (to). **nearly** *adv* almost. **nearness** *n* **nearby** *adj* not far away. **nearside** *n* side of a vehicle that is nearer the kerb.

neat *adj* **1** tidy and clean. **2** smoothly or competently done. **3** undiluted. **neatly** *adv* **neatness** *n*

nebula *n, pl* **-lae** *Astronomy* hazy cloud of particles and gases. **nebulous** *adj* vague and unclear, e.g. *a nebulous concept.*

necessary *adj* 1 needed to obtain the desired result, e.g. *the necessary skills.* 2 certain or unavoidable, e.g. *the necessary consequences.* **necessarily** *adv* **necessitate** *v* compel or require. **necessity** *n* 1 circumstances that inevitably require a certain result. 2 something needed. 3

> ☑ **SPELLING TIP**
> There are 41 examples of the misspelling *neccessary* in the Bank of English; single letters throughout (*necesary*) are also popular. The correct spelling, **necessary**, has one *c* and two *s*s. When you add *un-* at the beginning, you end up with a double *n* too: **unnecessary.**

neck *n* 1 part of the body joining the head to the shoulders. 2 part of a garment round the neck. 3 long narrow part of a bottle or violin. ♦ *v* 4 *Slang* kiss and cuddle. **neck and neck** absolutely level in a race or competition. **neckerchief** *n* piece of cloth worn tied round the neck. **necklace** *n* 1 decorative piece of jewellery worn around the neck. 2 *S Afr* burning petrol-filled tyre placed round someone's neck to kill him or her.

necromancy *n* 1 communication with the dead. 2 sorcery.

necropolis [neck-**rop**-pol-liss] *n* cemetery.

nectar *n* 1 sweet liquid collected from flowers by bees. 2 drink of the gods.

nectarine *n* smooth-skinned peach.

née [**nay**] *prep* indicating the maiden name of a married woman.

need *v* 1 require or be in want of. 2 be obliged (to do something). ♦ *n* 3 condition of lacking something. 4

requirement or necessity. 5 poverty. **needs** *adv* (preceded or foll. by *must*) necessarily. **needy** *adj* poor, in need of financial support. **needful** *adj* necessary or required. **needless** *adj* unnecessary.

needle *n* 1 thin pointed piece of metal with an eye through which thread is passed for sewing. 2 long pointed rod used in knitting. 3 pointed part of a hypodermic syringe. 4 small pointed part in a record player that touches the record and picks up the sound signals, stylus. 5 pointer on a measuring instrument or compass. 6 long narrow stiff leaf. 7 *v* 8 *Informal* goad or provoke. **needlework** *n* sewing and embroidery.

ne'er *adv Lit* never. **ne'er-do-well** *n* useless or lazy person.

nefarious [nif-**fair**-ee-uss] *adj* wicked.

negate *v* 1 invalidate. 2 deny the existence of. **negation** *n*

negative *adj* 1 expressing a denial or refusal. 2 lacking positive qualities. 3 (of an electrical charge) having the same electrical charge as an electron. 4 *n* 5 negative word or statement. 6 *Photog* image with a reversal of tones or colours from which positive prints are made.

neglect *v* 1 take no care of. 2 fail (to do something) through carelessness. 3 disregard. ♦ *n* 4 neglecting or being neglected. **neglectful** *adj*

negligee [**neg**-lee-zhay] *n* woman's lightweight usu. lace-trimmed dressing gown.

negligence *n* neglect or carelessness. **negligent** *adj* **negligently** *adv*

negligible *adj* so small or unimportant as to be not worth considering.

negotiate *v* 1 discuss in order to reach (an agreement). 2 succeed in passing round or over (a place or problem). **negotiation** *n* **negotiator** *n*

negotiable *adj*

Negro *n, pl* **-groes** *Old-fashioned* member of any of the Black peoples originating in Africa. **Negroid** *adj* of or relating to the Negro race.

neigh *n* **1** loud high-pitched sound made by a horse. ♦ *v* **2** make this sound.

neighbour *n* person who lives or is situated near another. **neighbouring** *adj* situated nearby. **neighbourhood** *n* **1** district. **2** surroundings. **3** people of a district. **neighbourly** *adj* kind, friendly, and helpful.

neither *adj, pron* **1** not one nor the other. ♦ *conj* **2** not.

nemesis [**nem**-miss-iss] *n, pl* **-ses** retribution or vengeance.

neo- *combining form* new, recent, or a modern form of, e.g. *neoclassicism*.

Neolithic *adj* of the later Stone Age.

neologism [nee-**ol**-a-jiz-zum] *n* newly-coined word or an established word used in a new sense.

neon *n Chem* colourless odourless gaseous element used in illuminated signs and lights.

neophyte *n* **1** beginner or novice. **2** new convert.

nephew *n* son of one's sister or brother.

nephritis [nif-**frite**-tiss] *n* inflammation of a kidney.

nepotism [**nep**-a-tiz-zum] *n* favouritism in business shown to relatives and friends.

Neptune *n* **1** Roman god of the sea. **2** eighth planet from the sun.

nerd *n Slang* **1** boring person obsessed with a particular subject. **2** stupid and feeble person.

nerve *n* **1** cordlike bundle of fibres that conducts impulses between the brain and other parts of the body. **2** bravery and determination. **3** impudence. ♦ *pl* **4** anxiety or tension. **5** ability or inability to remain calm in a difficult situation. **get on someone's nerves** irritate someone. **nerve oneself** prepare oneself (to do something difficult or unpleasant). **nerveless** *adj* **1** numb, without feeling. **2** fearless.

nervy *adj* excitable or nervous. **nerve centre** place from which a system or organization is controlled. **nerve-racking** *adj* very distressing or harrowing.

nervous *adj* **1** apprehensive or worried. **2** of or relating to the nerves. **nervously** *adv* **nervousness** *n* **nervous breakdown** mental illness in which the sufferer ceases to function properly.

nest *n* **1** place or structure in which birds or certain animals lay eggs or give birth to young. **2** secluded place. **3** set of things of graduated sizes designed to fit together. ♦ *v* **4** make or inhabit a nest. **nest egg** fund of money kept in reserve.

nestle *v* **1** snuggle. **2** be in a sheltered position.

nestling *n* bird too young to leave the nest.

net[1] *n* **1** fabric of meshes of string, thread, or wire with many openings. **2** piece of net used to protect or hold things or to trap animals. **3** *v* **netting, netted 4** catch (a fish or animal) in a net. **netting** *n* material made of net. **netball** *n* team game in which a ball has to be thrown through a net hanging from a ring at the top of a pole.

net[2], **nett** *adj* **1** left after all deductions. **2** (of weight) excluding the wrapping or container. **3** *v* **netting, netted 4** yield or earn as a clear profit.

nether *adj* lower.

nettle *n* plant with stinging hairs on the leaves. **nettled** *adj* irritated or annoyed.

network n 1 system of intersecting lines, roads, etc. 2 interconnecting group or system. 3 (in broadcasting) group of stations that all transmit the same programmes simultaneously.

neural adj of a nerve or the nervous system.

neuralgia n severe pain along a nerve.

neuritis [nyoor-**rite**-tiss] n inflammation of a nerve or nerves.

neurology n scientific study of the nervous system. **neurologist** n

neurosis n, pl -ses mental disorder producing hysteria, anxiety, depression, or obsessive behaviour. **neurotic** adj 1 emotionally unstable. 2 suffering from neurosis. ♦ n 3 neurotic person.

neuter adj 1 belonging to a particular class of grammatical inflections in some languages. 2 v 3 castrate (an animal).

neutral adj 1 taking neither side in a war or dispute. 2 of or belonging to a neutral party or country. 3 (of a colour) not definite or striking. ♦ n 4 neutral person or nation. 5 neutral gear. **neutrality** n **neutralize** v make ineffective or neutral. **neutral gear** position of the controls of a gearbox that leaves the gears unconnected to the engine.

neutrino [new-**tree**-no] n, pl -nos elementary particle with no mass or electrical charge.

neutron n electrically neutral elementary particle of about the same mass as a proton. **neutron bomb** nuclear bomb designed to kill people and animals while leaving buildings virtually undamaged.

never adv at no time. **nevertheless** adv in spite of that.

never-never n Informal hire-purchase.

new adj 1 not existing before. 2 recently acquired. 3 having lately come into some state. 4 additional. 5 (foll. by to) unfamiliar. ♦ adv 6 recently. **newness** n **New Age** philosophy, originating in the late 1980s, characterized by a belief in alternative medicine and spiritualism. **newbie** Informal ♦ n person new to a job, club, etc. **newborn** adj recently or just born. **newcomer** n recent arrival or participant. **newfangled** adj objectionably or unnecessarily modern. **newlyweds** pl n recently married couple. **new moon** moon when it appears as a narrow crescent at the beginning of its cycle.

newel n post at the top or bottom of a flight of stairs that supports the handrail.

news n 1 important or interesting new happenings. 2 information about such events reported in the mass media. **newsy** adj full of news. **newsagent** n Brit shopkeeper who sells newspapers and magazines. **newsflash** n brief important news item, which interrupts a radio or television programme. **newsletter** n bulletin issued periodically to members of a group. **newspaper** n weekly or daily publication containing news. **newsprint** n inexpensive paper used for newspapers. **newsreader, newscaster** n person who reads the news on the television or radio. **newsreel** n short film giving news. **newsroom** n room where news is received and prepared for publication or broadcasting. **newsworthy** adj sufficiently interesting to be reported as news.

newt n small amphibious creature with a long slender body and tail.

newton n unit of force.

next adj, adv 1 immediately following. 2 nearest. **next-of-kin** n closest relative.

nexus n, pl **nexus** connection or link.

NHS (in Britain) National Health Service.

nib n writing point of a pen.

nibble v 1 take little bites (of). ♦ n 2 little bite.

nibs n **his, her nibs** Slang mock title of respect.

nice adj 1 pleasant. 2 kind. 3 good or satisfactory. 4 subtle, e.g. a nice distinction. **nicely** adv **niceness** n

nicety n, pl **-ties** 1 subtle point. 2 refinement or delicacy.

niche [**neesh**] n 1 hollow area in a wall. 2 suitable position for a particular person.

nick v 1 make a small cut in. 2 Chiefly Brit slang steal. 3 Chiefly Brit slang arrest. ♦ n 4 small cut. 5 Slang prison or police station. **in good nick** Informal in good condition. **in the nick of time** just in time.

nickel n 1 Chem silvery-white metal often used in alloys. 2 US coin worth five cents.

nickelodeon n US early type of jukebox.

nickname n 1 familiar name given to a person or place. ♦ v 2 call by a nickname.

nicotine n poisonous substance found in tobacco.

niece n daughter of one's sister or brother.

nifty adj **-tier, -tiest** Informal neat or smart.

niggardly adj stingy. **niggard** n stingy person.

nigger n Offens Black person.

niggle v 1 worry slightly. 2 continually find fault (with). ♦ n 3 small worry or doubt.

nigh adv, prep Lit near.

night n time of darkness between sunset and sunrise. **nightly** adj, adv (happening) each night. **nightcap** n 1 drink taken just before bedtime. 2 soft cap formerly worn in bed. **nightclub** n establishment for dancing, music, etc., open late at night. **nightdress** n woman's loose dress worn in bed. **nightfall** n approach of darkness. **nightie** n Informal nightdress. **nightingale** n small bird with a musical song usu. heard at night. **nightjar** n nocturnal bird with a harsh cry. **nightlife** n entertainment and social activities available at night in a town or city. **nightmare** n 1 very bad dream. 2 very unpleasant experience. **night school** place where adults can attend educational courses in the evenings. **nightshade** n plant with bell-shaped flowers which are often poisonous. **nightshirt** n long loose shirt worn in bed. **night-time** n time from sunset to sunrise.

nihilism [**nye**-ill-liz-zum] n rejection of all established authority and institutions. **nihilist** n **nihilistic** adj

nil n nothing, zero.

nimble adj 1 agile and quick. 2 mentally alert or acute. **nimbly** adv

nimbus n, pl **-bi, -buses** dark grey rain cloud.

nincompoop n Informal stupid person.

nine adj, n one more than eight. **ninth** adj, n (of) number nine in a series. **ninepins** n game of skittles.

nineteen adj, n ten and nine. **nineteenth** adj, n

ninety adj, n ten times nine. **ninetieth** adj, n

niobium n Chem white superconductive metallic element.

nip[1] v **nipping, nipped** 1 Informal hurry. 2 pinch or squeeze. 3 bite lightly. 4 ♦ n 5 pinch or light bite. 6 sharp coldness. **nipper** n Brit, Aust & NZ informal small child. **nippy** adj 1 frosty or chilly. 2 Informal quick or nimble.

nip² n small alcoholic drink.

nipple n projection in the centre of a breast.

nirvana [near-**vah**-na] n Buddhism, Hinduism absolute spiritual enlightenment and bliss.

nit n 1 egg or larva of a louse. 2 Informal short for NITWIT. **nit-picking** adj Informal overconcerned with insignificant detail, esp. to find fault. **nitwit** n Informal stupid person.

nitrogen [**nite**-roj-jen] n Chem colourless odourless gas that forms four fifths of the air. **nitric, nitrous, nitrogenous** adj of or containing nitrogen. **nitrate** n compound of nitric acid, used as a fertilizer. **nitroglycerine, nitroglycerin** n explosive liquid.

nitty-gritty n Informal basic facts.

no interj 1 expresses denial, disagreement, or refusal. ♦ adj 2 not any, not a. ♦ adv 3 not at all. ♦ n, pl **noes, nos** 4 answer or vote of 'no'. 5 person who answers or votes 'no'. **no-go area** district barricaded off so that the police or army can enter only by force. **no-man's-land** n land between boundaries, esp. contested land between two opposing forces. **no-one, no one** pron nobody.

no. number.

nob n Chiefly Brit slang person of wealth or social distinction.

nobble v Brit slang 1 attract the attention of (someone) in order to talk to him or her. 2 bribe or threaten.

nobelium n Chem artificially-produced radioactive element.

Nobel Prize n prize awarded annually for outstanding achievement in various fields.

noble adj 1 showing or having high moral qualities. 2 of the nobility. 3 impressive and magnificent. ♦ n 4 member of the nobility. **nobility** n 1 quality of being noble. 2 class of people holding titles and high social rank. **nobly** adv **nobleman, noblewoman** n

nobody pron 1 no person. ♦ n, pl **-bodies** 2 person of no importance.

nocturnal adj 1 of the night. 2 active at night.

nocturne n short dreamy piece of music.

nod v **nodding, nodded** 1 lower and raise (one's head) briefly in agreement or greeting. 2 let one's head fall forward with sleep. ♦ n 3 act of nodding. **nod off** v Informal fall asleep.

noddle n Chiefly Brit informal the head.

node n 1 point on a plant stem from which leaves grow. 2 point at which a curve crosses itself.

nodule n 1 small knot or lump. 2 rounded mineral growth on the root of a plant.

Noel n Christmas.

noggin n 1 Informal head. 2 small quantity of an alcoholic drink.

noise n sound, usu. a loud or disturbing one. **noisy** adj 1 making a lot of noise. 2 full of noise. **noisily** adv **noiseless** adj

noisome adj 1 (of smells) offensive. 2 harmful or poisonous.

nomad n member of a tribe with no fixed dwelling place, wanderer. **nomadic** adj

nom de plume n, pl **noms de plume** pen name.

nomenclature n system of names used in a particular subject.

nominal adj 1 in name only. 2 very small in comparison with real worth. **nominally** adv

nominate v 1 suggest as a candidate. 2 appoint to an office or position. **nomination** n **nominee** n candidate.

nominative n form of a noun indicating the subject of a verb.

non- prefix indicating: **1** negation, e.g. nonexistent. **2** refusal or failure, e.g. noncooperation. **3** exclusion from a specified class, e.g. nonfiction. **4** lack or absence, e.g. nonevent.

nonagenarian n person aged between ninety and ninety-nine.

nonaggression n policy of not attacking other countries.

nonagon n geometric figure with nine sides.

nonalcoholic adj containing no alcohol.

nonaligned adj (of a country) not part of a major alliance or power bloc.

nonce n **for the nonce** for the present.

nonchalant adj casually unconcerned or indifferent. **nonchalantly** adv **nonchalance** n

noncombatant n member of the armed forces whose duties do not include fighting.

noncommissioned officer n (in the armed forces) a subordinate officer, risen from the ranks.

noncommittal adj not committing oneself to any particular opinion.

non compos mentis adj of unsound mind.

nonconductor n substance that is a poor conductor of heat, electricity, or sound.

nonconformist n **1** person who does not conform to generally accepted patterns of behaviour or thought. **2** (N-) member of a Protestant group separated from the Church of England. ♦ adj **3** (of behaviour or ideas) not conforming to accepted patterns. **nonconformity** n

noncontributory adj Brit denoting a pension scheme for employees, the premiums of which are paid entirely by the employer.

nondescript adj lacking outstanding features.

none pron **1** not any. **2** no-one. **nonetheless** adv despite that, however.

nonentity [non-**enn**-tit-tee] n, pl -**ties** insignificant person or thing.

nonevent n disappointing or insignificant occurrence.

nonflammable adj not easily set on fire.

nonintervention n refusal to intervene in the affairs of others.

nonpareil [non-par-**rail**] n person or thing that is unsurpassed.

nonpayment n failure to pay money owed.

nonplussed adj perplexed.

nonsense n **1** something that has or makes no sense. **2** absurd language. **3** foolish behaviour. **nonsensical** adj

non sequitur [**sek**-wit-tur] n statement with little or no relation to what preceded it.

nonstandard adj denoting language that is not regarded as correct by educated native speakers.

nonstarter n person or idea that has little chance of success.

nonstick adj coated with a substance that food will not stick to when cooked.

nonstop adj, adv without a stop.

nontoxic adj not poisonous.

noodles pl n long thin strips of pasta.

nook n sheltered place.

noon n twelve o'clock midday. **noonday** adj happening at noon.

noose n loop in the end of a rope, tied with a slipknot.

nor conj and not.

Nordic adj of Scandinavia or its typically tall blond and blue-eyed people.

norm *n* standard that is regarded as normal.

normal *adj* 1 usual, regular, or typical. 2 free from mental or physical disorder. **normally** *adv* **normality** *n* **normalize** *v*

Norse *n, adj* (language) of ancient and medieval Norway.

north *n* 1 direction towards the North Pole, opposite south. 2 area lying in or towards the north. ♦ *adj* 3 to or in the north. 4 (of a wind) from the north. ♦ *adv* 5 in, to, or towards the north. **northerly** *adj* **northern** *adj* **northerner** *n* person from the north of a country or area. **northward** *adj, adv* **northwards** *adv* **North Pole** northernmost point on the earth's axis.

nos. numbers.

nose *n* 1 organ of smell, used also in breathing. 2 front part of a vehicle. 3 *v* 4 move forward slowly and carefully. 5 pry or snoop. **nose dive** sudden drop. **nosegay** *n* small bunch of flowers. **nosey, nosy** *adj Informal* prying or inquisitive. **nosiness** *n*

nosh *Brit, Aust & NZ slang* ♦ *n* 1 food. ♦ *v* 2 eat.

nostalgia *n* sentimental longing for the past. **nostalgic** *adj*

nostril *n* one of the two openings at the end of the nose.

nostrum *n* 1 quack medicine. 2 favourite remedy.

not *adv* expressing negation, refusal, or denial.

notable *adj* 1 worthy of being noted, remarkable. ♦ *n* 2 person of distinction. **notably** *adv* **notability** *n*

notary *n, pl* -ries person authorized to witness the signing of legal documents.

notation *n* 1 representation of numbers or quantities in a system by a series of symbols. 2 set of such symbols.

notch *n* 1 V-shaped cut. 2 *Informal* step or level. ♦ *v* 3 make a notch in. 4 (foll. by *up*) score or achieve.

note *n* 1 short letter. 2 brief comment or record. 3 banknote. 4 (symbol for) a musical sound. 5 hint or mood. ♦ *v* 6 notice, pay attention to. 7 record in writing. 8 remark upon. **noted** *adj* well-known. **notebook** *n* book for writing in. **noteworthy** *adj* worth noting, remarkable.

nothing *pron* 1 not anything. 2 matter of no importance. 3 figure 0. ♦ *adv* 4 not at all. **nothingness** *n* 1 nonexistence. 2 insignificance.

☑ **WORD TIP**

Nothing is usually followed by a singular verb but, if it comes before a plural noun, this can sound odd: *Nothing but books was/were on the shelf.* A solution is to rephrase the sentence: *Only books were....*

---

notice *n* 1 observation or attention. 2 sign giving warning or an announcement. 3 advance notification of intention to end a contract of employment. 4 *v* 5 observe, become aware of. 6 point out or remark upon. **noticeable** *adj* easily seen or detected, appreciable.

notify *v* -fying, -fied inform. **notification** *n* **notifiable** *adj* having to be reported to the authorities.

notion *n* 1 idea or opinion. 2 whim. **notional** *adj* speculative, imaginary, or unreal.

notorious *adj* well known for something bad. **notoriously** *adv* **notoriety** *n*

notwithstanding *prep* in spite of.

nougat *n* chewy sweet containing nuts and fruit.

nought *n* 1 figure 0. 2 nothing. **noughties** *Informal* ♦ *pl n* decade from 2000 to 2009.

noun *n* word that refers to a person, place, or thing.

nourish *v* 1 feed. 2 encourage or foster (an idea or feeling). **nourishment** *n* **nourishing** *adj* providing the food necessary for life and growth.

nouvelle cuisine [noo-vell kwee-zeen] *n* style of preparing and presenting food with light sauces and unusual combinations of flavours.

Nov. November.

nova *n*, *pl* -vae, -vas star that suddenly becomes brighter and then gradually decreases to its original brightness.

novel¹ *n* long fictitious story in book form. **novelist** *n* writer of novels. **novella** *n*, *pl* -las, -lae short novel.

novel² *adj* fresh, new, or original. **novelty** *n* 1 newness. 2 something new or unusual

November *n* eleventh month of the year.

novena [no-vee-na] *n*, *pl* -nas RC Church set of prayers or services on nine consecutive days.

novice *n* 1 beginner. 2 person who has entered a religious order but has not yet taken vows.

now *adv* 1 at or for the present time. 2 immediately. ♦ *conj* 3 seeing that, since. **just now** very recently. **now and again, then** occasionally. **nowadays** *adv* in these times.

nowhere *adv* not anywhere.

noxious *adj* 1 poisonous or harmful. 2 extremely unpleasant.

nozzle *n* projecting spout through which fluid is discharged.

NSPCC (in Britain) National Society for the Prevention of Cruelty to Children.

NSW New South Wales.

NT 1 (in Britain) National Trust. 2 New Testament. 3 Northern Territory.

nuance [new-ahnss] *n* subtle difference in colour, meaning, or tone.

nub *n* point or gist (of a story etc.).

nubile [new-bile] *adj* (of a young woman) 1 sexually attractive. 2 old enough to get married.

nuclear *adj* 1 of nuclear weapons or energy. 2 of a nucleus, esp. the nucleus of an atom. **nuclear energy** energy released as a result of nuclear fission or fusion. **nuclear fission** splitting of an atomic nucleus. **nuclear fusion** combination of two nuclei to form a heavier nucleus with the release of energy. **nuclear power** power produced by a nuclear reactor. **nuclear reaction** change in structure and energy content of an atomic nucleus by interaction with another nucleus or particle. **nuclear reactor** device in which a nuclear reaction is maintained and controlled to produce nuclear energy. **nuclear weapon** weapon whose force is due to uncontrolled nuclear fusion or fission. **nuclear winter** theoretical period of low temperatures and little light after a nuclear war.

nucleic acid *n* complex compound, such as DNA or RNA, found in all living cells.

nucleus *n*, *pl* -clei 1 centre, esp. of an atom or cell. 2 central thing around which others are grouped.

nude *adj* 1 naked. ♦ *n* 2 naked figure in painting, sculpture, or photography. **nudity** *n* **nudism** *n* practice of not wearing clothes. **nudist** *n*

nudge *v* 1 push gently, esp. with the elbow. ♦ *n* 2 gentle push or touch.

nugatory [new-gat-tree] *adj* 1 of little value. 2 not valid.

nugget *n* 1 small lump of gold in its natural state. 2 something small but valuable. ♦ *v* 3 NZ & S Afr polish footwear.

nuisance *n* something or someone that causes annoyance or bother.

nuke *Slang* ♦ *v* **1** attack with nuclear weapons. ♦ *n* **2** nuclear weapon.

null *adj* **null and void** not legally valid. **nullity** *n* **nullify** *v* **1** make ineffective. **2** cancel.

nulla-nulla *n* wooden club used by Australian Aborigines.

numb *adj* **1** without feeling, as through cold, shock, or fear. ♦ *v* **2** make numb. **numbly** *adv* **numbness** *n* **numbskull** *n* stupid person.

numbat *n* small Australian marsupial with a long snout and tongue.

number *n* **1** sum or quantity. **2** word or symbol used to express a sum or quantity, numeral. **3** numeral or string of numerals used to identify a person or thing. **4** one of a series, such as a copy of a magazine. **5** song or piece of music. **6** group of people. **7** *Grammar* classification of words depending on how many persons or things are referred to. ♦ *v* **8** count. **9** give a number to. **10** amount to. **11** include in a group. **numberless** *adj* too many to be counted. **number crunching** *Computers* large-scale processing of numerical data. **number one** *n* *Informal* **1** oneself. **2** bestselling pop record in any one week. ♦ *adj* **3** first in importance or quality. **numberplate** *n* plate on a car showing the registration number.

numeral *n* word or symbol used to express a sum or quantity.

numerate *adj* able to do basic arithmetic. **numeracy** *n*

numeration *n* act or process of numbering or counting.

numerator *n* *Maths* number above the line in a fraction.

numerical *adj* measured or expressed in numbers. **numerically** *adv*

numerous *adj* existing or happening in large numbers.

numismatist *n* coin collector.

numskull *n* same as NUMBSKULL.

nun *n* female member of a religious order. **nunnery** *n* convent.

nuncio *n* *RC Church* pope's ambassador.

nuptial *adj* relating to marriage. **nuptials** *pl n* wedding.

nurse *n* **1** person employed to look after sick people, usu. in a hospital. **2** woman employed to look after children. ♦ *v* **3** look after (a sick person). **4** breast-feed (a baby). **5** try to cure (an ailment). **6** harbour or foster (a feeling). **nursing home** private hospital or home for old people. **nursing officer** (in Britain) administrative head of the nursing staff of a hospital.

nursery *n, pl* **-ries** **1** room where children sleep or play. **2** place where children are taken care of while their parents are at work. **3** place where plants are grown for sale. **nurseryman** *n* person who raises plants for sale. **nursery school** school for children from 3 to 5 years old. **nursery slopes** gentle ski slopes for beginners.

nurture *n* **1** act or process of promoting the development of a child or young plant. ♦ *v* **2** promote or encourage the development of.

nut *n* **1** fruit consisting of a hard shell and a kernel. **2** small piece of metal that screws onto a bolt. **3** (also **nutcase**) *Slang* insane or eccentric person. **4** *Slang* head. **nutter** *n* *Brit slang* insane person. **nutty** *adj* **1** containing or resembling nuts. **2** *Slang* insane or eccentric. **nutcracker** *n* device for cracking the shells of nuts. **nuthatch** *n* small songbird. **nutmeg** *n* spice made from the seed of a tropical tree.

nutria *n* fur of the coypu.

nutrient *n* substance that provides nourishment.

nutriment *n* food or nourishment required by all living things to grow and stay healthy.

nutrition *n* **1** process of taking in and absorbing nutrients. **2** process of being nourished. **nutritional** *adj* **nutritious, nutritive** *adj* nourishing.

nuzzle *v* push or rub gently with the nose or snout.

NW northwest(ern).

nylon *n* **1** synthetic material used for clothing etc. ♦ *pl* **2** stockings made of nylon.

nymph *n* **1** mythical spirit of nature, represented as a beautiful young woman. **2** larva of certain insects, resembling the adult form.

nymphet *n* sexually precocious young girl.

nymphomaniac *n* woman with an abnormally intense sexual desire.

NZ New Zealand.

NZE New Zealand English.

NZRFU New Zealand Rugby Football Union.

NZSE40 Index New Zealand Share Price 40 Index.

O o

O *Chem* oxygen.

oaf *n* stupid or clumsy person. **oafish** *adj*

oak *n* 1 deciduous forest tree. 2 its wood, used for furniture. **oaken** *adj* **oak apple** brownish lump found on oak trees.

oakum *n* fibre obtained by unravelling old rope.

OAP (in Britain) old-age pensioner.

oar *n* pole with a broad blade, used for rowing a boat.

oasis *n, pl* **-ses** fertile area in a desert.

oast *n Chiefly Brit* oven for drying hops.

oat *n* 1 hard cereal grown as food. ♦ *pl* 2 grain of this cereal. **sow one's wild oats** have many sexual relationships when young. **oatmeal** 1 *adj* 2 pale brownish-cream.

oath *n* 1 solemn promise, esp. to be truthful in court. 2 swearword.

obbligato [ob-lig-**gah**-toe] *n, pl* **-tos** *Music* essential part or accompaniment.

obdurate *adj* hardhearted or stubborn. **obduracy** *n*

OBE (in Britain) Officer of the Order of the British Empire.

obedient *adj* obeying or willing to obey. **obedience** *n* **obediently** *adv*

obeisance [oh-**bay**-sanss] *n* 1 attitude of respect. 2 bow or curtsy.

obelisk [**ob**-bill-isk] *n* four-sided stone column tapering to a pyramid at the top.

obese [oh-**beess**] *adj* very fat. **obesity** *n*

obey *v* carry out instructions or orders.

obfuscate *v* make (something) confusing.

obituary *n, pl* **-aries** announcement of someone's death, esp. in a newspaper. **obituarist** *n*

object[1] *n* 1 physical thing. 2 focus of thoughts or action. 3 aim or purpose. 4 *Grammar* word that a verb or preposition affects. **no object** not a hindrance.

object[2] *v* express disapproval. **objection** *n* **objectionable** *adj* unpleasant. **objector** *n*

objective *n* 1 aim or purpose. ♦ *adj* 2 not biased. 3 existing in the real world outside the human mind. **objectively** *adv* **objectivity** *n*

objet d'art [ob-zhay **dahr**] *n, pl* **objets d'art** small object of artistic value.

oblation *n* religious offering.

oblige *v* 1 compel (someone) morally or by law to do something. 2 do a favour for (someone). **obliging** *adj* ready to help other people. **obligingly** *adv* **obligated** *adj* obliged to do something. **obligation** *n* duty. **obligatory** *adj* required by a rule or law.

oblique [oh-**bleak**] *adj* 1 slanting. 2 indirect. ♦ *n* 3 the symbol (/). **obliquely** *adv* **oblique angle** angle that is not a right angle.

obliterate *v* wipe out, destroy. **obliteration** *n*

oblivious *adj* unaware. **oblivion** *n* 1 state of being forgotten. 2 state of being unaware or unconscious.

oblong *adj* 1 having two long sides, two short sides, and four right angles. ♦ *n* 2 oblong figure.

obloquy [**ob**-lock-wee] *n, pl* **-quies** 1 verbal abuse. 2 discredit.

obnoxious *adj* offensive.

oboe *n* double-reeded woodwind instrument. **oboist** *n*

obscene *adj* **1** portraying sex offensively. **2** disgusting. **obscenity** *n*

obscure *adj* **1** not well known. **2** hard to understand. **3** indistinct. ♦ *v* **4** make (something) obscure. **obscurity** *n*

obsequies [ob-sick-weez] *pl n* funeral rites.

obsequious [ob-**seek**-wee-uss] *adj* overattentive in order to gain favour. **obsequiousness** *n*

observe *v* **1** see or notice. **2** watch (someone or something) carefully. **3** remark. **4** act according to (a law or custom). **observation** *n* **1** action or habit of observing. **2** remark. **observable** *adj* **observance** *n* observing of a custom. **observant** *adj* quick to notice things. **observatory** *n* building equipped for studying the weather and the stars.

observer *n* person who observes, esp. one who watches someone or something carefully.

obsess *v* preoccupy (someone) compulsively. **obsessed** *adj* **obsessive** *adj* **obsession** *n*

> ☑ **SPELLING TIP**
> Some people get carried away with doubling *ss* and write *obssession* instead of **obsession**.

obsidian *n* dark glassy volcanic rock.

obsolete *adj* no longer in use. **obsolescent** *adj* becoming obsolete. **obsolescence** *n*

obstacle *n* something that makes progress difficult.

obstetrics *n* branch of medicine concerned with pregnancy and childbirth. **obstetric** *adj* **obstetrician** *n*

obstinate *adj* **1** stubborn. **2** difficult to remove or change. **obstinately** *adv* **obstinacy** *n*

obstreperous *adj* unruly, noisy.

obstruct *v* block with an obstacle. **obstruction** *n* **obstructive** *adj*

obtain *v* **1** acquire intentionally. **2** be customary. **obtainable** *adj*

obtrude *v* push oneself or one's ideas on others. **obtrusive** *adj* unpleasantly noticeable. **obtrusively** *adv*

obtuse *adj* **1** mentally slow. **2** *Maths* (of an angle) between 90° and 180°. **3** not pointed. **obtuseness** *n*

obverse *n* **1** opposite way of looking at an idea. **2** main side of a coin or medal.

obviate *v* make unnecessary.

obvious *adj* easy to see or understand, evident. **obviously** *adv*

ocarina *n* small oval wind instrument.

occasion *n* **1** time at which a particular thing happens. **2** reason, e.g. *no occasion for complaint*. **3** special event. ♦ *v* **4** cause. **occasional** *adj* happening sometimes. **occasionally** *adv*

> ☑ **SPELLING TIP**
> The commonest misspelling of **occasion** is *occassion*, with 44 occurrences in the Bank of English. As you might expect, there are also examples of *ocasion* and *ocassion*. The correct spelling has two *cs* and one *s*.

Occident *n Lit* the West. **Occidental** *adj*

occiput [**ox**-sip-put] *n* back of the head.

occlude *v* **1** obstruct. **2** close off. **occlusion** *n* **occluded front** *Meteorol* front formed when a cold front overtakes a warm front and warm air rises.

occult *adj* relating to the supernatural. **the occult** knowledge or study of the supernatural.

occupant *n* person occupying a specified place. **occupancy** *n* (length of) a person's stay in a specified place.

occupation n 1 profession. 2 activity that occupies one's time. 3 control of a country by a foreign military power. 4 being occupied. **occupational** adj **occupational therapy** purposeful activities, designed to aid recovery from illness etc.

occupy v -pying, -pied 1 live or work in (a building). 2 take up the attention of (someone). 3 take up (space or time). 4 take possession of (a place) by force. **occupier** n

occur v -curring, -curred 1 happen. 2 exist. **occur to** come to the mind of. **occurrence** n 1 something that occurs. 2 fact of occurring.

> ☑ **SPELLING TIP**
> Rather surprisingly, there are no examples in the Bank of English where **occurrence** has been spelt with only one c. However, there are 85 examples of *occurence*, with only one r, as opposed to 2013 instances where the word is spelt correctly: **occurrence**.

ocean n vast area of sea between continents. **oceanic** adj **oceanography** n scientific study of the oceans. **ocean-going** adj able to sail on the open sea.

ocelot [oss-ill-lot] n American wild cat with a spotted coat.

oche [ok-kee] n Darts mark on the floor behind which a player must stand.

ochre [oak-er] adj, n brownish-yellow (earth).

o'clock adv used after a number to specify an hour.

Oct. October.

octagon n geometric figure with eight sides. **octagonal** adj

octahedron [ok-ta-heed-ron] n, pl -drons, -dra three-dimensional geometric figure with eight faces.

octane n hydrocarbon found in petrol. **octane rating** measure of petrol quality.

octave n Music (interval between the first and) eighth note of a scale.

octet n 1 group of eight performers. 2 music for such a group.

October n tenth month of the year.

octogenarian n person aged between eighty and eighty-nine.

octopus n, pl -puses sea creature with a soft body and eight tentacles.

ocular adj relating to the eyes or sight.

OD Informal ♦ n 1 overdose. ♦ v OD'ing, OD'd 2 take an overdose.

odd adj 1 unusual. 2 occasional. 3 not divisible by two. 4 not part of a set. **odds** pl n (ratio showing) the probability of something happening. **at odds** in conflict. **odds and ends** small miscellaneous items. **oddity** n odd person or thing. **oddness** n quality of being odd. **oddments** pl n things left over.

ode n lyric poem, usu. addressed to a particular subject.

odium [oh-dee-um] n widespread dislike. **odious** adj offensive.

odour n particular smell. **odorous** adj **odourless** adj

odyssey [odd-iss-ee] n long eventful journey.

OE NZ informal overseas experience, e.g. he's away on his OE..

OECD Organization for Economic Cooperation and Development.

oedema [id-deem-a] n, pl -mata Med abnormal swelling.

oesophagus [ee-soff-a-guss] n, pl -gi passage between the mouth and stomach.

oestrogen [ee-stra-jen] n female hormone that controls the reproductive cycle.

of prep 1 belonging to. 2 consisting of.

3 connected with. **4** characteristic of.

off *prep* **1** away from. ♦ *adv* **2** away. **3** *adj* **4** not operating. **5** cancelled. **6** (of food) gone bad. ♦ *n* **7** *Cricket* side of the field to which the batsman's feet point. **off colour** slightly ill. **off-line** *adj* (of a computer) not directly controlled by a central processor. **off-message** *adj* (esp. of a politician) not following the official Party line. **off-road** *adj* (of a motor vehicle) designed for use away from public roads.

offal *n* edible organs of an animal, such as liver or kidneys. **offal pit, offal hole** *NZ* place on a farm for the disposal of animal offal.

offcut *n* piece remaining after the required parts have been cut out.

offend *v* **1** hurt the feelings of, insult. **2** commit a crime. **offence** *n* **1** (cause of) hurt feelings or annoyance. **2** illegal act. **offensive** *adj* **1** disagreeable. **2** insulting. **3** aggressive. ♦ *n* **4** position or action of attack.

offender *n* person who commits a crime.

offer *v* **1** present (something) for acceptance or rejection. **2** provide. **3** be willing (to do something). **4** propose as payment. ♦ *n* **5** instance of offering something. **offering** *n* thing offered. **offertory** *n* *Christianity* offering of the bread and wine for Communion.

offhand *adj* **1** casual, curt. ♦ *adv* **2** without preparation.

office *n* **1** room or building where people work at desks. **2** department of a commercial organization. **3** formal position of responsibility. **4** place where tickets or information can be obtained.

officer *n* **1** person in authority in the armed services. **2** member of the police force. **3** person with special responsibility in an organization.

official *adj* **1** of a position of authority. **2** approved or arranged by someone in authority. **3** *n* **4** person who holds a position of authority. **officially** *adv* **officialdom** *n* officials collectively. **Official Receiver** *Brit* person who deals with the affairs of a bankrupt company.

officiate *v* act in an official role.

officious *adj* interfering unnecessarily.

offing *n* area of the sea visible from the shore. **in the offing** *Brit, Aust & NZ* likely to happen soon.

off-licence *n* *Brit* shop licensed to sell alcohol for drinking elsewhere.

offset *v* cancel out, compensate for.

offshoot *n* something developed from something else.

offside *adj*, *adv* *Sport* (positioned) illegally ahead of the ball.

offspring *n*, *pl* **offspring** child.

often *adv* frequently, much of the time. **oft** *adv* *Poetic* often.

ogle *v* stare at (someone) lustfully.

ogre *n* **1** giant that eats human flesh. **2** monstrous or cruel person.

oh *interj* exclamation of surprise, pain, etc.

ohm *n* unit of electrical resistance.

OHMS *Brit* On Her *or* His Majesty's Service.

oil *n* **1** viscous liquid, insoluble in water and usu. flammable. **2** same as PETROLEUM. **3** petroleum derivative, used as a fuel or lubricant. ♦ *pl* **4** oil-based paints used in art. ♦ *v* **5** lubricate (a machine) with oil. **oily** *adj* **oilfield** *n* area containing oil reserves. **oil rig** platform constructed for drilling oil wells. **oilskin** *n* (garment made from) waterproof material.

ointment *n* greasy substance used for healing skin or as a cosmetic.

O.K., okay *Informal* ♦ *interj* **1**

expression of approval. **2** v **3** approve (something). ♦ n **4** approval.

okapi [ok-**kah**-pee] n African animal related to the giraffe but with a shorter neck.

okra n tropical plant with edible green pods.

old adj **1** having lived or existed for a long time. **2** of a specified age, e.g. *two years old*. **3** former. **olden** adj old, e.g. *in the olden days*. **oldie** n Informal old but popular song or film. **old-fashioned** adj no longer commonly used or valued. **old guard** group of people in an organization who have traditional values. **old hat** boring because so familiar. **old maid** elderly unmarried woman. **old master** European painter or painting from the period 1500–1800. **Old Nick** Brit, Aust & NZ informal the Devil. **old school tie** system of mutual help between former pupils of public schools. **Old Testament** part of the Bible recording Hebrew history. **Old World** world as it was known before the discovery of the Americas.

oleaginous [ol-lee-**aj**-in-uss] adj oily, producing oil.

oleander [ol-lee-**ann**-der] n Mediterranean flowering evergreen shrub.

olfactory adj relating to the sense of smell.

oligarchy [**ol**-lee-gark-ee] n, pl -chies **1** government by a small group of people. **2** state governed this way. **oligarchic, oligarchical** adj

olive n **1** small green or black fruit used as food or pressed for its oil. **2** tree on which this fruit grows. ♦ adj **3** greyish-green. **olive branch** peace offering.

Olympic Games pl n four-yearly international sports competition.

ombudsman n official who investigates complaints against government organizations.

omelette n dish of eggs beaten and fried.

> ☑ **SPELLING TIP**
> You don't hear it in the pronunciation, but there is an *e* after the *m* in **omelette**.

omen n happening or object thought to foretell success or misfortune. **ominous** adj worrying, seeming to foretell misfortune.

omit v **omitting, omitted 1** leave out. **2** neglect (to do something). **omission** n

omnibus n **1** several books or TV or radio programmes made into one. **2** Old-fashioned bus.

omnipotent adj having unlimited power. **omnipotence** n

omnipresent adj present everywhere. **omnipresence** n

omniscient [om-**niss**-ee-ent] adj knowing everything. **omniscience** n

omnivorous [om-**niv**-vor-uss] adj eating food obtained from both animals and plants. **omnivore** n omnivorous animal.

on prep **1** indicating position above, attachment, closeness, etc., e.g. *lying on the ground; a puppet on a string; on the coast*. ♦ adv **2** in operation. **3** continuing. **4** forwards. ♦ adj **5** operating. **6** taking place. ♦ n **7** Cricket side of the field on which the batsman stands. **on line, online** adj **1** (of a computer) directly controlled by a central processor. **2** relating to the Internet, e.g. *online shopping*. **on-message** adj (esp. of a politician) following the official Party line.

once adv **1** on one occasion. **2** formerly. ♦ conj **3** as soon as. **at once 1** immediately. **2** simultaneously.

once-over n Informal quick examination.

oncogene [**on**-koh-jean] n gene that can cause cancer when abnormally activated.

oncoming adj approaching from the front.

one adj **1** single, lone. **2** n **3** number or figure 1. **4** single unit. ♦ pron **5** any person. **oneness** n unity. **oneself** pron **reflexive form of** ONE.

one-armed bandit fruit machine operated by a lever on one side.

one-liner n witty remark. **one-night stand** sexual encounter lasting one night. **one-sided** adj considering only one point of view. **one-way** adj allowing movement in one direction only.

onerous [**own**-er-uss] adj (of a task) difficult to carry out.

ongoing adj in progress, continuing.

onion n strongly flavoured edible bulb.

onlooker n person who watches without taking part.

only adj **1** alone of its kind. ♦ adv **2** exclusively. **3** merely. **4** no more than. ♦ conj **5** but.

onomatopoeia [on-a-mat-a-**pee**-a] n use of a word which imitates the sound it represents, such as hiss. **onomatopoeic** adj

onset n beginning.

onslaught n violent attack.

onto prep **1** to a position on. **2** aware of, e.g. she's onto us.

ontology n branch of philosophy concerned with existence. **ontological** adj

onus [**own**-uss] n, pl **onuses** responsibility or burden.

onward adj **1** directed or moving forward. ♦ adv **2** (also **onwards**) ahead, forward.

onyx n type of quartz with coloured layers.

oodles pl n Informal great quantities.

ooze[1] v **1** flow slowly. **2** n **3** sluggish flow. **oozy** adj

ooze[2] n soft mud at the bottom of a lake or river.

opal n iridescent precious stone. **opalescent** adj iridescent like an opal.

opaque adj not able to be seen through, not transparent. **opacity** n

op. cit. [**op** sit] in the work cited.

OPEC Organization of Petroleum-Exporting Countries.

open adj **1** not closed. **2** not covered. **3** unfolded. **4** ready for business. **5** free from obstruction, accessible. **6** frank. ♦ v **7** (cause to) become open. **8** begin. ♦ n **9** Sport competition which all may enter. **in the open** outdoors. **openly** adv without concealment. **opening** n **1** opportunity. **2** hole. ♦ adj **3** first. **opencast mining** mining at the surface and not underground. **open day** day on which a school or college is open to the public. **open-handed** adj generous. **open-hearted** adj **1** generous. **2** frank. **open-heart surgery** surgery on the heart during which the blood circulation is maintained by machine. **open house** hospitality to visitors at any time. **open letter** letter to an individual that the writer makes public in a newspaper or magazine. **open-minded** adj receptive to new ideas. **open-plan** adj (of a house or office) having few interior walls. **open prison** prison with minimal security. **open verdict** coroner's verdict not stating the cause of death.

opera[1] n drama in which the text is sung to an orchestral accompaniment. **operatic** adj **operetta** n light-hearted comic opera.

opera[2] n a plural of OPUS.

operate v **1** (cause to) work. **2** direct. **3**

perform an operation. **operator** n
operation n **1** method or procedure
of working. **2** medical procedure in
which the body is worked on to repair
a damaged part. **operational** adj **1** in
working order. **2** relating to an
operation. **operative** adj **1** working. **2**
n **3** worker with a special skill.

ophthalmic adj relating to the eye.
ophthalmology n study of the eye
and its diseases. **ophthalmologist** n

opiate n narcotic drug containing
opium.

opinion n personal belief or judgment.
opinionated adj having strong
opinions. **opine** v Old-fashioned
express an opinion. **opinion poll** see
POLL.

opium n addictive narcotic drug made
from poppy seeds.

opossum n small marsupial of America
or Australasia.

opponent n person one is working
against in a contest, battle, or
argument.

opportunity n, pl **-ties 1** favourable
time or condition. **2** good chance.
opportunity shop Aust & NZ shop
selling second-hand clothes,
sometimes for charity (also **op-shop**).
opportune adj happening at a
suitable time. **opportunist** n, adj
(person) doing whatever is
advantageous without regard for
principles. **opportunism** n

☑ **SPELLING TIP**

Lots of people forget that
opportunity, which is a very
common word, has two *p*s.

---

oppose v work against. **be opposed
to** disagree with or disapprove of.
opposition n **1** obstruction or
hostility. **2** group opposing another. **3**
political party not in power.

opposite adj **1** situated on the other
side. **2** facing. **3** completely different.
♦ n **4** person or thing that is opposite.
♦ prep **5** facing. ♦ adv **6** on the other
side.

oppress v **1** control by cruelty or force.
2 depress. **oppression** n **oppressor**
n **oppressive** adj **1** tyrannical. **2** (of
weather) hot and humid.
oppressively adv

opprobrium [op-**probe**-ree-um] n state
of being criticized severely for wrong
one has done.

opt v show a preference, choose. **opt
out** v choose not to be part (of).

optic adj relating to the eyes or sight.
optics n science of sight and light.
optical adj **optical character reader**
device that electronically reads and
stores text. **optical fibre** fine
glass-fibre tube used to transmit
information.

optician n **1** (also **ophthalmic
optician**) person qualified to prescribe
glasses. **2** (also **dispensing optician**)
person who supplies and fits glasses.

optimism n tendency to take the most
hopeful view. **optimist** n **optimistic**
adj **optimistically** adv

optimum n, pl **-ma, -mums 1** best
possible conditions. ♦ adj **2** most
favourable. **optimal** adj **optimize** v
make the most of.

option n **1** choice. **2** thing chosen. **3**
right to buy or sell something at a
specified price within a given time.
optional adj possible but not
compulsory.

optometrist n person qualified to
prescribe glasses. **optometry** n

opulent [**op**-pew-lent] adj having or
indicating wealth. **opulence** n

opus n, pl **opuses, opera** artistic
creation, esp. a musical work.

or conj used to join alternatives, e.g. *tea
or coffee.*

oracle n 1 shrine of an ancient god. 2 prophecy, often obscure, revealed at a shrine. 3 person believed to make infallible predictions. **oracular** adj

oral adj 1 spoken. 2 (of a drug) to be taken by mouth. ♦ n 3 spoken examination. **orally** adv

orange n 1 reddish-yellow citrus fruit. ♦ adj 2 reddish-yellow. **orangeade** n Brit orange-flavoured, usu. fizzy drink. **orangery** n greenhouse for growing orange trees.

orang-utan, orang-utang n large reddish-brown ape with long arms.

orator [**or**-rat-tor] n skilful public speaker. **oration** n formal speech.

oratorio [or-rat-**tor**-ee-oh] n, pl -rios musical composition for choir and orchestra, usu. with a religious theme.

oratory[1] [**or**-rat-tree] n art of making speeches. **oratorical** adj

oratory[2] n, pl -ries small private chapel.

orb n ceremonial decorated sphere with a cross on top, carried by a monarch.

orbit n 1 curved path of a planet, satellite, or spacecraft around another body. 2 sphere of influence. ♦ v **orbiting, orbited** 3 move in an orbit around. 4 put (a satellite or spacecraft) into orbit. **orbital** adj

orchard n area where fruit trees are grown.

orchestra n 1 large group of musicians, esp. playing a variety of instruments. 2 (also **orchestra pit**) area of a theatre in front of the stage, reserved for the musicians. **orchestral** adj **orchestrate** v 1 arrange (music) for orchestra. 2 organize (something) to produce a particular result. **orchestration** n

orchid n plant with flowers that have unusual lip-shaped petals.

ordain v 1 make (someone) a member of the clergy. 2 order or establish with authority.

ordeal n painful or difficult experience.

order n 1 instruction to be carried out. 2 methodical arrangement or sequence. 3 established social system. 4 condition of a law-abiding society. 5 request for goods to be supplied. 6 kind, sort. 7 religious society of monks or nuns. 8 v 9 give an instruction to. 10 request (something) to be supplied. **in order** so that it is possible. **orderly** adj 1 well-organized. 2 well-behaved. ♦ n, pl -lies 3 male hospital attendant. **orderliness** n

ordinal number n number showing a position in a series, e.g. first; second.

ordinance n official rule or order.

ordinary adj 1 usual or normal. 2 dull or commonplace. **ordinarily** adv

ordination n act of making someone a member of the clergy.

ordnance n weapons and military supplies. **Ordnance Survey** official organization making maps of Britain.

ordure n excrement.

ore n (rock containing) a mineral which yields metal.

oregano [or-rig-**gah**-no] n sweet-smelling herb used in cooking.

organ n 1 part of an animal or plant that has a particular function, such as the heart or lungs. 2 musical keyboard instrument in which notes are produced by forcing air through pipes. 3 means of conveying information, esp. a newspaper. **organist** n organ player.

organdie n fine cotton fabric.

organic adj 1 of or produced from animals or plants. 2 grown without artificial fertilizers or pesticides. 3 Chem relating to compounds of carbon. 4 organized systematically. **organically** adv **organism** n any living animal or plant.

organize v 1 make arrangements for. 2 arrange systematically. **organization**

n **1** group of people working together. **2** act of organizing. **organizational** *adj* **organizer** *n*

orgasm *n* most intense point of sexual pleasure. **orgasmic** *adj*

orgy *n, pl* **-gies 1** party involving promiscuous sexual activity. **2** unrestrained indulgence, e.g. *an orgy of destruction.* **orgiastic** *adj*

oriel window *n* upper window built out from a wall.

orient, orientate *v* **1** position (oneself) according to one's surroundings. **2** position (a map) in relation to the points of the compass. **orientation** *n* **orienteering** *n* sport in which competitors hike over a course using a compass and map.

Orient *n* the Orient *Lit* East Asia. **Oriental** *adj* **Orientalist** *n* specialist in the languages and history of the Far East.

orifice [**or**-rif-fiss] *n* opening or hole.

origami [or-rig-**gah**-mee] *n* Japanese decorative art of paper folding.

origin *n* **1** point from which something develops. **2** ancestry. **original** *adj* **1** first or earliest. **2** new, not copied or based on something else. **3** able to think up new ideas. ♦ *n* **4** first version, from which others are copied. **original sin** human imperfection and mortality as a result of Adam's disobedience. **originality** *n* **originally** *adv* **originate** *v* come or bring into existence. **origination** *n* **originator** *n*

oriole *n* tropical or American songbird.

ormolu *n* gold-coloured alloy used for decoration.

ornament *n* **1** decorative object. **2** *v* **3** decorate. **ornamental** *adj* **ornamentation** *n*

ornate *adj* highly decorated, elaborate.

ornithology *n* study of birds. **ornithological** *adj* **ornithologist** *n*

orphan *n* child whose parents are dead. **orphanage** *n* children's home for orphans. **orphaned** *adj* having no living parents.

orrery *n, pl* **-ries** mechanical model of the solar system.

orris *n* **1** kind of iris. **2** (also **orris root**) fragrant root used for perfume.

orthodontics *n* branch of dentistry concerned with correcting irregular teeth. **orthodontist** *n*

orthodox *adj* conforming to established views. **orthodoxy** *n* **Orthodox Church** dominant Christian Church in Eastern Europe.

orthography *n* correct spelling.

orthopaedics *n* branch of medicine concerned with disorders of the bones or joints. **orthopaedic** *adj*

oryx *n* large African antelope.

Oscar *n* award in the form of a statuette given for achievements in films.

oscillate [**oss**-ill-late] *v* swing back and forth. **oscillation** *n* **oscillator** *n* **oscilloscope** [oss-**sill**-oh-scope] *n* instrument that shows the shape of a wave on a cathode-ray tube.

osier [**oh**-zee-er] *n* willow tree.

osmium *n* *Chem* heaviest known metallic element.

osmosis *n* **1** movement of a liquid through a membrane from a lower to a higher concentration. **2** process of subtle influence. **osmotic** *adj*

osprey *n* large fish-eating bird of prey.

ossify *v* **-fying, -fied 1** (cause to) become bone, harden. **2** become inflexible. **ossification** *n*

ostensible *adj* apparent, seeming. **ostensibly** *adv*

ostentation *n* pretentious display. **ostentatious** *adj* **ostentatiously** *adv*

osteopathy *n* medical treatment involving manipulation of the joints.

osteopath n

osteoporosis n brittleness of the bones, caused by lack of calcium.

ostracize v exclude (a person) from a group. **ostracism** n

ostrich n large African bird that runs fast but cannot fly.

OT Old Testament.

other adj **1** remaining in a group of which one or some have been specified. **2** different from the ones specified or understood. **3** additional. ♦ n **4** other person or thing. **otherwise** conj **1** or else, if not. ♦ adv **2** differently, in another way. **otherworldly** adj concerned with spiritual rather than practical matters.

otiose [oh-tee-oze] adj not useful, e.g. otiose language.

otter n small brown freshwater mammal that eats fish.

ottoman n, pl **-mans** storage chest with a padded lid for use as a seat. **Ottoman** n, adj Hist (member) of the former Turkish empire.

oubliette [oo-blee-**ett**] n dungeon entered only by a trapdoor.

ouch interj exclamation of sudden pain.

ought v used to express: **1** obligation, e.g. you ought to pay. **2** advisability, e.g. you ought to diet. **3** probability, e.g. you ought to know by then.

Ouija board n ® lettered board on which supposed messages from the dead are spelt out.

ounce n unit of weight equal to one sixteenth of a pound (28.4 grams).

our adj belonging to us. **ours** pron thing(s) belonging to us. **ourselves** pron emphatic and reflexive form of WE or US.

ousel n see DIPPER.

oust v force (someone) out, expel.

out adv, adj **1** denoting movement or distance away from, a state of being used up or extinguished, public availability, etc., e.g. oil was pouring out; turn the light out; her new book is out. ♦ v **2** Informal name (a public figure) as being homosexual. **out of** at or to a point outside. **out-of-date** adj old-fashioned. **outer** adj on the outside. **outermost** adj furthest out. **outer space** space beyond the earth's atmosphere. **outing** n leisure trip. **outward** adj **1** apparent. **2** adv **3** (also **outwards**) away from somewhere. **outwardly** adv

out- prefix surpassing, e.g. outlive; outdistance.

outback n remote bush country of Australia.

outbid v offer a higher price than.

outboard motor n engine externally attached to the stern of a boat.

outbreak n sudden occurrence (of something unpleasant).

outburst n sudden expression of emotion.

outcast n person rejected by a particular group.

outclass v surpass in quality.

outcome n result.

outcrop n part of a rock formation that sticks out of the earth.

outcry n, pl **-cries** vehement or widespread protest.

outdo v surpass in performance.

outdoors adv **1** in(to) the open air. ♦ n **2** the open air. **outdoor** adj

outface v subdue or disconcert (someone) by staring.

outfield n Cricket area far from the pitch.

outfit n **1** matching set of clothes. **2** Informal group of people working together. **outfitter** n supplier of men's clothes.

outflank v **1** get round the side of (an enemy army). **2** outdo (someone).

outgoing *adj* 1 leaving. 2 sociable. **outgoings** *pl n* expenses.

outgrow *v* become too large or too old for. **outgrowth** *n* natural development.

outhouse *n* building near a main building.

outlandish *adj* extremely unconventional.

outlaw *n* 1 *Hist* criminal deprived of legal protection, bandit. ♦ *v* 2 make illegal. 3 *Hist* make (someone) an outlaw.

outlay *n* expenditure.

outlet *n* 1 means of expressing emotion. 2 market for a product. 3 place where a product is sold. 4 opening or way out.

outline *n* 1 short general explanation. 2 line defining the shape of something. ♦ *v* 3 summarize. 4 show the general shape of.

outlook *n* 1 attitude. 2 probable outcome.

outlying *adj* distant from the main area.

outmanoeuvre *v* get an advantage over.

outmoded *adj* no longer fashionable or accepted.

outnumber *v* exceed in number.

outpatient *n* patient who does not stay in hospital overnight.

outpost *n* outlying settlement.

outpouring *n* passionate outburst.

output *n* 1 amount produced. 2 power, voltage, or current delivered by an electrical circuit. 3 *Computers* data produced. ♦ *v* 4 *Computers* produce (data) at the end of a process.

outrage *n* 1 great moral indignation. 2 gross violation of morality. ♦ *v* 3 offend morally. **outrageous** *adj* 1 shocking. 2 offensive. **outrageously** *adv*

outré [**oo**-tray] *adj* shockingly eccentric.

outrider *n* motorcyclist acting as an escort.

outrigger *n* stabilizing frame projecting from a boat.

outright *adj, adv* 1 absolute(ly). 2 open(ly) and direct(ly).

outrun *v* 1 run faster than. 2 exceed.

outset *n* beginning.

outshine *v* surpass (someone) in excellence.

outside *prep, adj, adv* 1 indicating movement to or position on the exterior. ♦ *adj* 2 unlikely, e.g. *an outside chance.* 3 coming from outside. ♦ *n* 4 external area or surface. **outsider** *n* 1 person outside a specific group. 2 contestant thought unlikely to win.

outsize, outsized *adj* larger than normal.

outskirts *pl n* outer areas, esp. of a town.

outsmart *v* *Informal* outwit.

outspan *v* *S Afr* relax.

outspoken *adj* 1 tending to say what one thinks. 2 said openly.

outstanding *adj* 1 excellent. 2 still to be dealt with or paid.

outstrip *v* 1 surpass. 2 go faster than.

outtake *n* unreleased take from a recording session, film, or TV programme.

outweigh *v* be more important, significant, or influential than.

outwit *v* **-witting, -witted** get the better of (someone) by cunning.

ouzel [**ooze**-el] *n see* DIPPER.

ova *n* plural of OVUM.

oval *adj* 1 egg-shaped. ♦ *n* 2 anything that is oval in shape.

ovary *n, pl* **-ries** female egg-producing organ. **ovarian** *adj*

ovation *n* enthusiastic round of applause.

oven *n* heated compartment or

container for cooking or for drying or firing ceramics.

over *prep, adv* **1** indicating position on the top of, movement to the other side of, amount greater than, etc., e.g. *a room over the garage; climbing over the fence; over fifty pounds.* ♦ *adj* **2** finished. ♦ *n* **3** *Cricket* series of six balls bowled from one end. **overly** *adv* excessively.

over- *prefix* **1** too much, e.g. *overeat.* **2** above, e.g. *overlord.* **3** on top, e.g. *overshoe.*

overall *adj, adv* **1** in total. ♦ *n* **2** coat-shaped protective garment. ♦ *pl* **3** protective garment consisting of trousers with a jacket or bib and braces attached.

overarm *adj, adv* (thrown) with the arm above the shoulder.

overawe *v* affect (someone) with an overpowering sense of awe.

overbalance *v* lose balance.

overbearing *adj* unpleasantly forceful.

overblown *adj* excessive.

overboard *adv* from a boat into the water. **go overboard** go to extremes, esp. in enthusiasm.

overcast *adj* (of the sky) covered by clouds.

overcoat *n* heavy coat.

overcome *v* **1** gain control over after an effort. **2** (of an emotion) affect strongly.

overcrowded *adj* containing more people or things than is desirable.

overdo *v* **1** do to excess. **2** exaggerate (something). **overdo it** do something to a greater degree than is advisable.

overdose *n* **1** excessive dose of a drug. ♦ *v* **2** take an overdose.

overdraft *n* **1** overdrawing. **2** amount overdrawn.

overdraw *v* withdraw more money than is in (one's bank account).

overdrawn *adj* **1** having overdrawn one's account. **2** (of an account) in debit.

overdrive *n* very high gear in a motor vehicle.

overdue *adj* still due after the time allowed.

overgrown *adj* thickly covered with plants and weeds.

overhaul *v* **1** examine and repair. **2** *n* **3** examination and repair.

overhead *adv, adj* above one's head. **overheads** *pl n* general cost of maintaining a business.

overhear *v* hear (a speaker or remark) unintentionally or without the speaker's knowledge.

overjoyed *adj* extremely pleased.

overkill *n* treatment that is greater than required.

overland *adj, adv* by land.

overlap *v* **1** share part of the same space or period of time (as). ♦ *n* **2** area overlapping.

overleaf *adv* on the back of the current page.

overlook *v* **1** fail to notice. **2** ignore. **3** look at from above.

overnight *adj, adv* **1** (taking place) during one night. **2** (happening) very quickly.

overpower *v* subdue or overcome (someone).

overreach *v* **overreach oneself** fail by trying to be too clever.

override *v* **1** overrule. **2** replace.

overrule *v* **1** reverse the decision of (a person with less power). **2** reverse (someone else's decision).

overrun *v* **1** spread over (a place) rapidly. **2** extend beyond a set limit.

overseas *adv, adj* to, of, or from a distant country.

oversee *v* watch over from a position of authority. **overseer** *n*

overshadow v **1** reduce the significance of (a person or thing) by comparison. **2** sadden the atmosphere of.

oversight n mistake caused by not noticing something.

overspill n Brit rehousing of people from crowded cities in smaller towns.

overstay v overstay one's welcome stay longer than one's host or hostess would like. **overstayer** n NZ person who remains in New Zealand after their permit has expired.

overt adj open, not hidden. **overtly** adv

overtake v move past (a vehicle or person) travelling in the same direction.

overthrow v **1** defeat and replace. ♦ n **2** downfall, destruction.

overtime n, adv (paid work done) in addition to one's normal working hours.

overtone n additional meaning.

overture n **1** Music orchestral introduction. ♦ pl **2** opening moves in a new relationship.

overturn v **1** turn upside down. **2** overrule (a legal decision). **3** overthrow (a government).

overweight adj weighing more than is healthy.

overwhelm v **1** overpower, esp. emotionally. **2** defeat by force. **overwhelming** adj **overwhelmingly** adv

overwrought adj nervous and agitated.

ovoid [**oh**-void] adj egg-shaped.

ovulate [**ov**-yew-late] v produce or release an egg cell from an ovary. **ovulation** n

ovum [**oh**-vum] n, pl ova unfertilized egg cell.

owe v be obliged to pay (a sum of money) to (a person). **owing to** as a result of.

owl n night bird of prey. **owlish** adj

own adj **1** used to emphasize possession, e.g. my own idea. **2** v **3** possess. **owner** n **ownership** n **own up** v confess.

ox n, pl oxen castrated bull.

Oxfam Oxford Committee for Famine Relief.

oxide n compound of oxygen and one other element. **oxidize** v combine chemically with oxygen, as in burning or rusting.

oxygen n Chem gaseous element essential to life and combustion. **oxygenate** v add oxygen to.

oxymoron [ox-see-**more**-on] n figure of speech that combines two apparently contradictory ideas, e.g. cruel kindness.

oyez interj Hist shouted three times by a public crier, listen.

oyster n edible shellfish. **oystercatcher** n wading bird with black-and-white feathers.

Oz n Slang Australia.

oz. ounce.

ozone n strong-smelling form of oxygen. **ozone layer** layer of ozone in the upper atmosphere that filters out ultraviolet radiation.

P p

p 1 *Brit, Aust & NZ* penny. **2** *Brit* pence.
P parking.

p. *pl* **pp** page.

pa *n NZ* (formerly) a fortified Maori settlement.

PA 1 personal assistant. **2** public-address system.

p.a. each year.

pace *n* **1** single step in walking. **2** length of a step. **3** rate of progress. ♦ *v* **4** walk up and down, esp. in anxiety. **5** (foll. by *out*) cross or measure with steps. **pacemaker** *n* **1** electronic device surgically implanted in a person with heart disease to regulate the heartbeat. **2** person who, by taking the lead early in a race, sets the pace for the rest of the competitors.

pachyderm [**pak**-ee-durm] *n* thick-skinned animal such as an elephant.

pacifist *n* person who refuses on principle to take part in war. **pacifism** *n*

pacify *v* **-fying, -fied** soothe, calm. **pacification** *n*

pack *v* **1** put (clothes etc.) together in a suitcase or bag. **2** put (goods) into containers or parcels. **3** fill with people or things. ♦ *n* **4** bag carried on a person's or animal's back. **5** *Chiefly US* **same as** PACKET. **6** set of playing cards. **7** group of dogs or wolves that hunt together. **pack ice** mass of floating ice in the sea. **pack in** *v Informal* stop doing. **pack off** *v* send away.

package *n* **1** small parcel. **2** (also **package deal**) deal in which separate items are presented together as a unit. ♦ *v* **3** put into a package. **packaging** *n* **package holiday** holiday in which everything is arranged by one company for a fixed price.

packet *n* **1** small container (and contents). **2** small parcel. **3** *Slang* large sum of money.

packhorse *n* horse used for carrying goods.

pact *n* formal agreement.

pad *n* **1** piece of soft material used for protection, support, absorption of liquid, etc. **2** number of sheets of paper fastened at the edge. **3** fleshy underpart of an animal's paw. **4** place for launching rockets. **5** *Slang* home. ♦ *v* **padding, padded 6** protect or fill with soft material. **7** walk with soft steps. **padding** *n* **1** soft material used to pad something. **2** unnecessary words put into a speech or written work to make it longer.

paddle¹ *n* **1** short oar with a broad blade at one or each end. ♦ *v* **2** move (a canoe etc.) with a paddle. **paddle steamer** ship propelled by paddle wheels. **paddle wheel** wheel with crosswise blades that strike the water successively to propel a ship.

paddle² *v* walk barefoot in shallow water.

paddock *n* small field or enclosure for horses.

paddy *n Brit informal* fit of temper.

paddy field *n* field where rice is grown (also **paddy**).

pademelon, paddymelon [**pad**-ee-mel-an] *n* small Australian wallaby.

padlock *n* detachable lock with a hinged hoop fastened over a ring on the object to be secured.

padre [**pah**-dray] *n* chaplain to the armed forces.

paean [**pee**-an] *n* song of triumph or

thanksgiving.

paediatrics n branch of medicine concerned with diseases of children. **paediatrician** n

paedophilia n condition of being sexually attracted to children. **paedophile** n person who is sexually attracted to children.

paella [pie-**ell**-a] n Spanish dish of rice, chicken, shellfish, and vegetables.

pagan n, adj (person) not belonging to one of the world's main religions.

page¹ n 1 (one side of) a sheet of paper forming a book etc. 2 screenful of information from a website or teletext service.

page² n 1 (also **pageboy**) small boy who attends a bride at her wedding. 2 Hist boy in training for knighthood. ♦ v 3 summon (someone) by bleeper or loudspeaker, in order to pass on a message.

pageant n parade or display of people in costume, usu. illustrating a scene from history. **pageantry** n

pagination n numbering of the pages of a book etc.

pagoda n pyramid-shaped Asian temple or tower.

paid v past of PAY. **put paid to** Informal end or destroy.

pail n (contents of) a bucket.

pain n 1 physical or mental suffering. ♦ pl 2 trouble, effort. **on pain of** subject to the penalty of. **painful** adj **painfully** adv **painless** adj **painlessly** adv **painkiller** n drug that relieves pain.

painstaking adj extremely thorough and careful.

paint n 1 coloured substance, spread on a surface with a brush or roller. ♦ v 2 colour or coat with paint. 3 use paint to make a picture of. **painter** n **painting** n

painter n rope at the front of a boat, for tying it up.

pair n 1 set of two things matched for use together. 2 v 3 group or be grouped in twos.

paisley pattern n pattern of small curving shapes, used in fabric.

Pakeha [**pah**-kee-ha] n NZ New Zealander who is not of Maori descent.

pal n Informal, old-fashioned in NZ friend.

palace n 1 residence of a king, bishop, etc. 2 large grand building.

palaeography [pal-ee-**og**-ra-fee] n study of ancient manuscripts.

Palaeolithic [pal-ee-oh-**lith**-ik] adj of the Old Stone Age.

palaeontology [pal-ee-on-**tol**-a-jee] n study of past geological periods and fossils.

Palagi [pa-**lang**-gee] n, pl **-gis** NZ Samoan name for a Pakeha.

palatable adj pleasant to taste.

palate n 1 roof of the mouth. 2 sense of taste.

palatial adj like a palace, magnificent.

palaver [pal-**lah**-ver] n time-wasting fuss.

pale¹ adj 1 light, whitish. 2 whitish in the face, esp. through illness or shock. ♦ v 3 become pale.

pale² n wooden or metal post used in fences. **beyond the pale** outside the limits of social convention.

palette n artist's flat board for mixing colours on.

palindrome n word or phrase that reads the same backwards as forwards.

paling n wooden or metal post used in fences.

palisade n fence made of wooden posts driven into the ground.

pall¹ n 1 cloth spread over a coffin. 2 dark cloud (of smoke). 3 depressing oppressive atmosphere. **pallbearer** n person who helps to carry the coffin at a funeral.

pall[2] v become boring.

palladium n Chem silvery-white element of the platinum metal group.

pallet[1] n portable platform for storing and moving goods.

pallet[2] n straw-filled mattress or bed.

palliate v lessen the severity of (something) without curing it.

palliative adj 1 giving temporary or partial relief. ♦ n 2 something, for example a drug, that palliates.

pallid adj pale, esp. because ill or weak. **pallor** n

pally adj -lier, -liest Informal on friendly terms.

palm[1] n inner surface of the hand. **palm off** v get rid of (an unwanted thing or person), esp. by deceit.

palm[2] n tropical tree with long pointed leaves growing out of the top of a straight trunk. **Palm Sunday** Sunday before Easter.

palmistry n fortune-telling from lines on the palm of the hand. **palmist** n

palmtop adj 1 (of a computer) small enough to be held in the hand. ♦ n 2 computer small enough to be held in the hand.

palomino n, pl -nos gold-coloured horse with a white mane and tail.

palpable adj 1 obvious, e.g. a palpable hit. 2 so intense as to seem capable of being touched, e.g. the tension is almost palpable. **palpably** adv

palpate v Med examine (an area of the body) by touching.

palpitate v 1 (of the heart) beat rapidly. 2 flutter or tremble. **palpitation** n

palsy [pawl-zee] n paralysis. **palsied** adj affected with palsy.

paltry adj -trier, -triest insignificant.

pampas pl n vast grassy plains in S

America. **pampas grass** tall grass with feathery ornamental flower branches.

pamper v treat (someone) with great indulgence, spoil.

pamphlet n thin paper-covered booklet. **pamphleteer** n writer of pamphlets.

pan[1] n 1 wide long-handled metal container used in cooking. 2 bowl of a toilet. ♦ v panning, panned 3 sift gravel from (a river) in a pan to search for gold. 4 Informal criticize harshly. **pan out** v result.

pan[2] v panning, panned (of a film camera) be moved slowly so as to cover a whole scene or follow a moving object.

pan- combining form all, e.g. pan-American.

panacea [pan-a-**see**-a] n remedy for all diseases or problems.

panache [pan-**ash**] n confident elegant style.

panama hat n straw hat.

panatella n long slender cigar.

pancake n thin flat circle of fried batter.

panchromatic adj Photog sensitive to light of all colours.

pancreas [**pang**-kree-ass] n large gland behind the stomach that produces insulin and helps digestion. **pancreatic** adj

panda n large black-and-white bearlike mammal from China. **panda car** Brit police patrol car.

pandemic adj (of a disease) occurring over a wide area.

pandemonium n wild confusion, uproar.

pander[1] v (foll. by to) indulge (a person his or her desires).

pander[2] n Old-fashioned person who procures a sexual partner for someone.

p & p postage and packing.

pane n sheet of glass in a window or door.

panegyric [pan-ee-**jire**-ik] n formal speech or piece of writing in praise of someone or something.

panel n 1 flat distinct section of a larger surface, for example in a door. 2 group of people as a team in a quiz etc. 3 list of jurors, doctors, etc. 4 board or surface containing switches and controls to operate equipment. ♦ v -elling, -elled 5 cover or decorate with panels. **panelling** n panels collectively, esp. on a wall. **panellist** n member of a panel. **panel beater** person who repairs damage to car bodies.

pang n sudden sharp feeling of pain or sadness.

pangolin n animal of tropical countries with a scaly body and a long snout for eating ants and termites (also **scaly anteater**).

panic n 1 sudden overwhelming fear, often affecting a whole group of people. ♦ v -icking, -icked 2 feel or cause to feel panic. **panicky** adj **panic-stricken** adj

pannier n 1 bag fixed on the back of a cycle. 2 basket carried by a beast of burden.

panoply n magnificent array.

panorama n wide unbroken view of a scene. **panoramic** adj

pansy n, pl -sies 1 small garden flower with velvety purple, yellow, or white petals. 2 Offens effeminate or homosexual man.

pant v breathe quickly and noisily during or after exertion.

pantaloons pl n baggy trousers gathered at the ankles.

pantechnicon n large van for furniture removals.

pantheism n belief that God is present in everything. **pantheist** n

pantheistic adj

pantheon n (in ancient Greece and Rome) temple built to honour all the gods.

panther n leopard, esp. a black one.

panties pl n women's underpants.

pantile n roofing tile with an S-shaped cross section.

pantomime n play based on a fairy tale, performed at Christmas time.

pantry n, pl -tries small room or cupboard for storing food.

pants pl n 1 undergarment for the lower part of the body. 2 US, Canadian, Aust & NZ trousers.

pap n 1 soft food for babies or invalids. 2 worthless entertainment or information.

papacy [**pay**-pa-see] n, pl -cies position or term of office of a pope. **papal** adj of the pope.

paparazzo [pap-a-**rat**-so] n, pl -razzi photographer specializing in candid photographs of famous people.

papaya [pa-**pie**-ya] n large sweet West Indian fruit.

paper n 1 material made in sheets from wood pulp or other fibres. 2 printed sheet of this. 3 newspaper. 4 set of examination questions. 5 article or essay. ♦ pl 6 personal documents. ♦ v 7 cover (walls) with wallpaper. **paperback** n book with covers made of flexible card. **paperweight** n heavy decorative object placed on top of loose papers. **paperwork** n clerical work, such as writing reports and letters.

papier-mâché [**pap**-yay **mash**-ay] n material made from paper mixed with paste and moulded when moist.

papist n, adj Offens Roman Catholic.

papoose n Native American child.

paprika n mild powdered seasoning made from red peppers.

papyrus [pap-**ire**-uss] n, pl **-ri**, **-ruses 1** tall water plant. **2** (manuscript written on) a kind of paper made from this plant.

par n **1** usual or average condition, e.g. *feeling under par.* **2** *Golf* expected standard score. **3** face value of stocks and shares. **on a par with** equal to.

parable n story that illustrates a religious teaching.

parabola [par-**ab**-bol-a] n regular curve resembling the course of an object thrown forward and up. **parabolic** adj

paracetamol n mild pain-relieving drug.

parachute n **1** large fabric canopy that slows the descent of a person or object from an aircraft. ♦ v **2** land or drop by parachute. **parachutist** n

parade n **1** procession or march. **2** street or promenade. ♦ v **3** display or flaunt. **4** march in procession.

paradigm [**par**-a-dime] n example or model.

paradise n **1** heaven. **2** place or situation that is near-perfect.

paradox n statement that seems self-contradictory but may be true. **paradoxical** adj **paradoxically** adv

paraffin n *Brit & S Afr* liquid mixture distilled from petroleum and used as a fuel or solvent.

☑ **SPELLING TIP**

People have trouble remembering whether the *r* or the *f* is doubled in **paraffin**, but according to the Bank of English, the most popular mistake is to decide on neither, as in *parafin*.

---

paragliding n cross-country gliding wearing a parachute shaped like wings.

paragon n model of perfection.

paragraph n section of a piece of writing starting on a new line.

parakeet n small long-tailed parrot.

parallax n apparent change in an object's position due to a change in the observer's position.

parallel adj **1** separated by an equal distance at every point. **2** exactly corresponding. ♦ n **3** line separated from another by an equal distance at every point. **4** thing with similar features to another. **5** line of latitude. ♦ v **6** correspond to.

parallelogram n four-sided geometric figure with opposite sides parallel.

paralysis n inability to move or feel, because of damage to the nervous system. **paralyse** v **1** affect with paralysis. **2** make temporarily unable to move or take action. **paralytic** n, adj (person) affected with paralysis.

paramedic n person working in support of the medical profession. **paramedical** adj

parameter [par-**am**-it-er] n limiting factor, boundary.

paramilitary adj organized on military lines.

paramount adj of the greatest importance.

paramour n *Old-fashioned* lover, esp. of a person married to someone else.

paranoia n **1** mental illness causing delusions of grandeur or persecution. **2** *Informal* intense fear or suspicion. **paranoid, paranoiac** adj, n

paranormal adj beyond scientific explanation.

parapet n low wall or railing along the edge of a balcony or roof.

paraphernalia n personal belongings or bits of equipment.

paraphrase v put (a statement or text) into other words.

paraplegia [par-a-**pleej**-ya] n paralysis of the lower half of the body. **paraplegic** adj, n

parapsychology n study of mental

phenomena such as telepathy.

Paraquat n ® extremely poisonous weedkiller.

parasite n **1** animal or plant living in or on another. **2** person who lives at the expense of others. **parasitic** adj

parasol n umbrella-like sunshade.

paratrooper n soldier trained to be dropped by parachute into a battle area. **paratroops** pl n

parboil v boil until partly cooked.

parcel n **1** something wrapped up, package. ◆ v **-celling, -celled 2** (often foll. by up) wrap up. **parcel out** v divide into parts.

parch v **1** make very hot and dry. **2** make thirsty.

parchment n thick smooth writing material made from animal skin.

pardon v **1** forgive, excuse. ◆ n **2** forgiveness. **3** official release from punishment for a crime. **pardonable** adj

pare v **1** cut off the skin or top layer of. **2** (often foll. by down) reduce in size or amount. **paring** n piece pared off.

parent n father or mother. **parental** adj **parenthood** n **parentage** n ancestry or family. **parenting** n activity of bringing up children.

parenthesis [par-**en**-thiss-iss] n, pl **-ses 1** word or sentence inserted into a passage, marked off by brackets or dashes. ◆ pl **2** round brackets, ( ). **parenthetical** adj

pariah [par-**rye**-a] n social outcast.

parietal [par-**rye**-it-al] adj of the walls of a body cavity such as the skull.

parish n area that has its own church and a priest or pastor. **parishioner** n inhabitant of a parish.

parity n equality or equivalence.

park n **1** area of open land for recreational use by the public. **2** area containing a number of related enterprises, e.g. a business park. **3** Brit area of private land around a large country house. ◆ v **4** stop and leave (a vehicle) temporarily.

parka n large waterproof jacket with a hood.

parky adj **parkier, parkiest** Brit informal (of the weather) chilly.

parlance n particular way of speaking, idiom.

parley n **1** meeting between leaders or representatives of opposing forces to discuss terms. ◆ v **2** have a parley.

parliament n law-making assembly of a country. **parliamentary** adj

parlour n Old-fashioned living room for receiving visitors.

parlous adj Old-fashioned **1** dire. **2** dangerously bad.

Parmesan n hard strong-flavoured Italian cheese, used grated on pasta dishes and soups.

parochial adj **1** narrow in outlook. **2** of a parish. **parochialism** n

parody n, pl **-dies 1** exaggerated and amusing imitation of someone else's style. ◆ v **-dying, -died 2** make a parody of.

parole n **1** early freeing of a prisoner on condition that he or she behaves well. ◆ v **2** put on parole. **on parole** (of a prisoner) released on condition that he or she behaves well.

paroxysm n **1** uncontrollable outburst of rage, delight, etc. **2** spasm or convulsion of coughing, pain, etc.

parquet [**par**-kay] n floor covering made of wooden blocks arranged in a geometric pattern. **parquetry** n

parricide n **1** crime of killing either of one's parents. **2** person who does this.

parrot n **1** tropical bird with a short hooked beak and an ability to imitate human speech. ◆ v **-roting, -roted 2** repeat (someone else's words) without thinking.

parry v -rying, -ried 1 ward off (an attack). 2 cleverly avoid (an awkward question).

parse [**parz**] v analyse (a sentence) in terms of grammar.

parsimony n extreme caution in spending money. **parsimonious** adj

parsley n herb used for seasoning and decorating food.

parsnip n long tapering cream-coloured root vegetable.

parson n 1 Anglican parish priest. 2 any member of the clergy. **parsonage** n parson's house.

part n 1 one of the pieces that make up a whole. 2 one of several equal divisions. 3 actor's role. 4 (often pl) region, area. 5 component of a vehicle or machine. ♦ v 6 divide or separate. 7 (of people) leave each other. **take someone's part** support someone in an argument etc. **take (something) in good part** respond to (teasing or criticism) with good humour. **parting** n 1 occasion when one person leaves another. 2 line of scalp between sections of hair combed in opposite directions. 3 dividing or separating. **partly** adv not completely. **part of speech** particular grammatical class of words, such as noun or verb. **part-time** adj occupying or working less than the full working week. **part with** v give away, hand over.

partake v -taking, -took, -taken 1 (foll. by of) take (food or drink). 2 (foll. by in) take part in.

partial adj 1 not complete. 2 prejudiced. **partial to** having a liking for. **partiality** n **partially** adv

participate v become actively involved. **participant** n **participation** n

participle n form of a verb used in compound tenses or as an adjective,

e.g. worried; worrying.

particle n 1 extremely small piece or amount. 2 Physics minute piece of matter, such as a proton or electron.

particular adj 1 relating to one person or thing, not general. 2 exceptional or special. 3 very exact. 4 difficult to please, fastidious. ♦ n 5 item of information, detail. **particularly** adv **particularize** v give details about.

partisan n 1 strong supporter of a party or group. 2 guerrilla, member of a resistance movement. ♦ adj 3 prejudiced or one-sided.

partition n 1 screen or thin wall that divides a room. 2 division of a country into independent parts. ♦ v 3 divide with a partition.

partner n 1 either member of a couple in a relationship or activity. 2 member of a business partnership. ♦ v 3 be the partner of. **partnership** n joint business venture between two or more people.

partridge n game bird of the grouse family.

parturition n act of giving birth.

party n, pl -ties 1 social gathering for pleasure. 2 group of people travelling or working together. 3 group of people with a common political aim. 4 person or people forming one side in a lawsuit or dispute. **party line** 1 official view of a political party. 2 telephone line shared by two or more subscribers. **party wall** common wall separating adjoining buildings.

parvenu [**par**-ven-new] n person newly risen to a position of power or wealth.

pascal n unit of pressure.

paspalum [pass-**pale**-um] n Aust & NZ type of grass with wide leaves.

pass v 1 go by, past, or through. 2 be successful in (a test or examination). 3 spend (time) or (of time) go by. 4 give, hand. 5 be inherited by. 6 Sport hit, kick, or throw (the ball) to another player. **7** (of a law-making body) agree to (a law). **8** exceed. **9** *n* **10** successful result in a test or examination. **11** permit or licence. **make a pass at** *Informal* make sexual advances to. **passable** *adj* **1** (just) acceptable. **2** (of a road) capable of being travelled along. **passing** *adj* **1** brief or transitory. **2** cursory or casual. **pass away** *v* die. **pass out** *v Informal* faint. **pass up** *v Informal* fail to take advantage of (something).

passage *n* **1** channel or opening providing a way through. **2** hall or corridor. **3** section of a book etc. **4** journey by sea. **5** right or freedom to pass. **passageway** *n* passage or corridor.

passbook *n* **1** book issued by a bank or building society for keeping a record of deposits and withdrawals. **2** *S Afr* formerly, an official identity document.

passé [**pas**-say] *adj* out-of-date.

passenger *n* **1** person travelling in a vehicle driven by someone else. **2** member of a team who does not pull his or her weight.

passer-by *n, pl* **passers-by** person who is walking past something or someone.

passim *adv Latin* everywhere, throughout.

passion *n* **1** intense sexual love. **2** any strong emotion. **3** great enthusiasm. **4** (P-) *Christianity* the suffering of Christ. **passionate** *adj* **passionflower** *n* tropical American plant. **passion fruit** edible fruit of the passionflower. **Passion play** play about Christ's suffering.

passive *adj* **1** not playing an active part. **2** submissive and receptive to outside forces. **3** *Grammar* (of a verb) in a form indicating that the subject receives the action, e.g. *was jeered* in *he was jeered by the crowd*. **passivity** *n* **passive resistance** resistance to a government, law, etc. by nonviolent acts. **passive smoking** inhalation of smoke from others' cigarettes by a nonsmoker.

Passover *n* Jewish festival commemorating the sparing of the Jews in Egypt.

passport *n* official document of nationality granting permission to travel abroad.

password *n* secret word or phrase that ensures admission.

past *adj* **1** of the time before the present. **2** ended, gone by. **3** *Grammar* (of a verb tense) indicating that the action specified took place earlier. ♦ *n* **4** period of time before the present. **5** person's earlier life, esp. a disreputable period. **6** *Grammar* past tense. ♦ *adv* **7** by, along. ♦ *prep* **8** beyond. **past it** *Informal* unable to do the things one could do when younger. **past master** person with great talent or experience in a particular subject.

pasta *n* type of food, such as spaghetti, that is made in different shapes from flour and water.

paste *n* **1** moist soft mixture, such as toothpaste. **2** adhesive, esp. for paper. **3** *Brit* pastry dough. **4** shiny glass used to make imitation jewellery. ♦ *v* **5** fasten with paste. **pasting** *n Informal* **1** heavy defeat. **2** strong criticism. **pasteboard** *n* stiff thick paper.

pastel *n* **1** coloured chalk crayon for drawing. **2** picture drawn in pastels. **3** pale delicate colour. ♦ *adj* **4** pale and delicate in colour.

pasteurize *v* sterilize by heating. **pasteurization** *n*

pastiche [pass-**teesh**] *n* work of art that mixes styles or copies the style of another artist.

pastille n small fruit-flavoured and sometimes medicated sweet.

pastime n activity that makes time pass pleasantly.

pastor n member of the clergy in charge of a congregation. **pastoral** adj 1 of or depicting country life. 2 of a clergyman or his duties.

pastrami n highly seasoned smoked beef.

pastry n, pl -**ries** 1 baking dough made of flour, fat, and water. 2 cake or pie.

pasture n grassy land for farm animals to graze on.

pasty[1] [**pay**-stee] adj **pastier, pastiest** (of a complexion) pale and unhealthy.

pasty[2] [**pass**-tee] n, pl **pasties** round of pastry folded over a savoury filling.

pat[1] v **patting, patted** 1 tap lightly. ◆ n 2 gentle tap or stroke. 3 small shaped mass of butter etc.

pat[2] adj quick, ready, or glib. **off pat** learned thoroughly.

patch n 1 piece of material sewn on a garment. 2 small contrasting section. 3 plot of ground. 4 protective pad for the eye. ◆ v 5 mend with a patch. **patchy** adj of uneven quality or intensity. **patch up** v 1 repair clumsily. 2 make up (a quarrel). **patchwork** n needlework made of pieces of different materials sewn together.

pate n Old-fashioned head.

pâté [**pat**-ay] n spread of finely minced liver etc.

patella n, pl -**lae** kneecap.

patent n 1 document giving the exclusive right to make or sell an invention. ◆ adj 2 open to public inspection, e.g. letters patent. 3 obvious. 4 protected by a patent. ◆ v 5 obtain a patent for. **patently** adv obviously. **patent leather** leather processed to give a hard glossy surface.

paternal adj 1 fatherly. 2 related through one's father. **paternity** n fact or state of being a father. **paternalism** n authority exercised in a way that limits individual responsibility. **paternalistic** adj

path n 1 surfaced walk or track. 2 course of action.

pathetic adj 1 causing feelings of pity or sadness. 2 distressingly inadequate. **pathetically** adv

pathogen n thing that causes disease. **pathogenic** adj

pathology n scientific study of diseases. **pathological** adj 1 of pathology. 2 Informal compulsively motivated. **pathologist** n

pathos n power of arousing pity or sadness.

patient adj 1 enduring difficulties or delays calmly. ◆ n 2 person receiving medical treatment. **patience** n 1 quality of being patient. 2 card game for one.

patina n 1 fine layer on a surface. 2 sheen of age on woodwork.

patio n, pl -**tios** paved area adjoining a house.

patois [**pat**-wah] n, pl **patois** [**pat**-wahz] regional dialect, esp. of French.

patriarch n 1 male head of a family or tribe. 2 highest-ranking bishop in Orthodox Churches. **patriarchal** adj **patriarchy** n, pl -**chies** society in which men have most of the power.

patrician n 1 member of the nobility. ◆ adj 2 of noble birth.

patricide n 1 crime of killing one's father. 2 person who does this.

patrimony n, pl -**nies** property inherited from ancestors.

patriot n person who loves his or her country and supports its interests. **patriotic** adj **patriotism** n

patrol n 1 regular circuit by a guard. 2 person or small group patrolling. 3 unit of Scouts or Guides. ♦ v **-trolling, -trolled** go round on guard, or reconnoitring.

patron n 1 person who gives financial support to charities, artists, etc. 2 regular customer of a shop, pub, etc. **patronage** n support given by a patron. **patronize** v 1 treat in a condescending way. 2 be a patron of. **patron saint** saint regarded as the guardian of a country or group.

patronymic n name derived from one's father or a male ancestor.

patter[1] v 1 make repeated soft tapping sounds. ♦ n 2 quick succession of taps.

patter[2] n glib rapid speech.

pattern n 1 arrangement of repeated parts or decorative designs. 2 regular way that something is done. 3 diagram or shape used as a guide to make something. **patterned** adj decorated with a pattern.

patty n, pl **-ties** small flattened cake of minced food.

paucity n 1 scarcity. 2 smallness of amount or number.

paunch n protruding belly.

pauper n very poor person.

pause v 1 stop for a time. 2 n 3 stop or rest in speech or action.

pave v form (a surface) with stone or brick. **pavement** n paved path for pedestrians.

pavilion n 1 building on a playing field etc. 2 building for housing an exhibition etc.

paw n 1 animal's foot with claws and pads. ♦ v 2 scrape with the paw or hoof. 3 Informal touch in a rough or overfamiliar way.

pawn[1] v deposit (an article) as security for money borrowed. **in pawn** deposited as security with a pawnbroker. **pawnbroker** n lender of money on goods deposited.

pawn[2] n 1 chessman of the lowest value. 2 person manipulated by someone else.

pay v **paying, paid** 1 give money etc. in return for goods or services. 2 settle a debt or obligation. 3 compensate (for). 4 give. 5 be profitable to. ♦ n 6 wages or salary. **payment** n 1 act of paying. 2 money paid. **payable** adj due to be paid. **payee** n person to whom money is paid or due. **paying guest** lodger or boarder. **pay off** v 1 pay (debt) in full. 2 turn out successfully. **pay out** v 1 spend. 2 release (a rope) bit by bit.

PAYE pay as you earn: system by which income tax is paid by an employer straight to the government.

payload n 1 passengers or cargo of an aircraft. 2 explosive power of a missile etc.

payola n Chiefly US informal bribe to get special treatment, esp. to promote a commercial product.

pc per cent.

PC 1 personal computer. 2 (in Britain) Police Constable. 3 politically correct. 4 (in Britain) Privy Councillor.

PDA personal digital assistant.

PE physical education.

pea n 1 climbing plant with seeds growing in pods. 2 its seed, eaten as a vegetable.

peace n 1 calm, quietness. 2 absence of anxiety. 3 freedom from war. 4 harmony between people. **peaceable** adj inclined towards peace. **peaceably** adv **peaceful** adj **peacefully** adv

peach n 1 soft juicy fruit with a stone and a downy skin. 2 Informal very pleasing person or thing. ♦ adj 3 pinkish-orange.

peacock n large male bird with a brilliantly coloured fanlike tail.

peahen *n fem*

peak *n* **1** pointed top, esp. of a mountain. **2** point of greatest development etc. **3** projecting piece on the front of a cap. ♦ *v* **4** form or reach a peak. ♦ *adj* **5** of or at the point of greatest demand. **peaked** *adj* **peaky** *adj* pale and sickly.

peal *n* **1** long loud echoing sound, esp. of bells or thunder. ♦ *v* **2** sound with a peal or peals.

peanut *n* **1** pea-shaped nut that ripens underground. ♦ *pl* **2** *Informal* trifling amount of money.

pear *n* sweet juicy fruit with a narrow top and rounded base.

pearl *n* hard round shiny object found inside some oyster shells and used as a jewel. **pearly** *adj*

peasant *n* person working on the land, esp. in poorer countries or in the past. **peasantry** *n* peasants collectively.

peat *n* decayed vegetable material found in bogs, used as fertilizer or fuel.

pebble *n* small roundish stone. **pebbly** *adj* **pebble dash** coating for exterior walls consisting of small stones set in plaster.

pecan [**pee**-kan] *n* edible nut of a N American tree.

peccadillo *n, pl* **-loes, -los** trivial misdeed.

peck *v* **1** strike or pick up with the beak. **2** *Informal* kiss quickly. ♦ *n* **3** pecking movement. **peckish** *adj Informal* slightly hungry. **peck at** *v* nibble, eat reluctantly.

pecs *pl n Informal* pectoral muscles.

pectin *n* substance in fruit that makes jam set.

pectoral *adj* **1** of the chest or thorax. ♦ *n* **2** pectoral muscle or fin.

peculiar *adj* **1** strange. **2** distinct, special. **3** belonging exclusively to. **peculiarity** *n, pl* **-ties 1** oddity,

eccentricity. **2** distinguishing trait.

pecuniary *adj* relating to, or consisting of, money.

pedagogue *n* schoolteacher, esp. a pedantic one.

pedal *n* **1** foot-operated lever used to control a vehicle or machine, or to modify the tone of a musical instrument. ♦ *v* **-alling, -alled 2** propel (a bicycle) by using its pedals.

pedant *n* person who is excessively concerned with details and rules, esp. in academic work. **pedantic** *adj* **pedantry** *n*

peddle *v* sell (goods) from door to door.

peddler *n* person who sells illegal drugs.

pederast *n* man who has homosexual relations with boys. **pederasty** *n*

pedestal *n* base supporting a column, statue, etc.

pedestrian *n* **1** person who walks. ♦ *adj* **2** dull, uninspiring. **pedestrian crossing** place marked where pedestrians may cross a road. **pedestrian precinct** *Brit* (shopping) area for pedestrians only.

pedicure *n* medical or cosmetic treatment of the feet.

pedigree *n* register of ancestors, esp. of a purebred animal.

pediment *n* triangular part over a door etc.

pedlar *n* person who sells goods from door to door.

pee *Informal* ♦ *v* **peeing, peed 1** urinate. ♦ *n* **2** act of urinating.

peek *v, n* peep or glance.

peel *v* **1** remove the skin or rind of (a vegetable or fruit). **2** (of skin or a surface) come off in flakes. ♦ *n* **3** rind or skin. **peelings** *pl n*

peep[1] *v* **1** look slyly or quickly. ♦ *n* **2** peeping look. **Peeping Tom** man who furtively watches women undressing.

peep[2] v **1** make a small shrill noise. ♦ n **2** small shrill noise.

peer[1] n **1** (fem **peeress**) (in Britain) member of the nobility. **2** person of the same status, age, etc. **peerage** n Brit **1** whole body of peers. **2** rank of a peer. **peerless** adj unequalled, unsurpassed. **peer group** group of people of similar age, status, etc.

peer[2] v look closely and intently.

peeved adj Informal annoyed.

peevish adj fretful or irritable. **peevishly** adv

peewee n black-and-white Australian bird.

peewit n same as LAPWING.

peg n **1** pin or clip for joining, fastening, marking, etc. **2** hook or knob for hanging things on. ♦ v **pegging, pegged 3** fasten with pegs. **4** stabilize (prices). **off the peg** (of clothes) ready-to-wear, not tailor-made.

peggy square n NZ small hand-knitted square.

peignoir [**pay**-nwahr] n woman's light dressing gown.

pejorative [pij-**jor**-a-tiv] adj (of words etc.) with an insulting or critical meaning.

Pekingese, Pekinese n, pl -ese small dog with a short wrinkled muzzle.

pelargonium n plant with red, white, purple, or pink flowers.

pelican n large water bird with a pouch beneath its bill for storing fish. **pelican crossing** (in Britain) road crossing with pedestrian-operated traffic lights.

pellagra n disease caused by lack of vitamin B.

pellet n small ball of something.

pell-mell adv in utter confusion, headlong.

pellucid adj very clear.

pelmet n ornamental drapery or board, concealing a curtain rail.

pelt[1] v **1** throw missiles at. **2** run fast, rush. **3** rain heavily. **at full pelt** at top speed.

pelt[2] n skin of a fur-bearing animal.

pelvis n framework of bones at the base of the spine, to which the hips are attached. **pelvic** adj

pen[1] n **1** instrument for writing in ink. ♦ v **penning, penned 2** write or compose. **pen friend** friend with whom a person corresponds without meeting. **penknife** n small knife with blade(s) that fold into the handle. **pen name** name used by a writer instead of his or her real name.

pen[2] n **1** small enclosure for domestic animals. ♦ v **penning, penned 2** put or keep in a pen.

pen[3] n female swan.

penal [**pee**-nal] adj of or used in punishment. **penalize** v **1** impose a penalty on. **2** handicap, hinder.

penalty n, pl -ties **1** punishment for a crime or offence. **2** Sport handicap or disadvantage imposed for breaking a rule.

penance n voluntary self-punishment to make amends for wrongdoing.

pence n Brit a plural of PENNY.

penchant [**pon**-shon] n inclination or liking.

pencil n **1** thin cylindrical instrument containing graphite, for writing or drawing. ♦ v -cilling, -cilled **2** draw, write, or mark with a pencil.

pendant n ornament worn on a chain round the neck.

pendent adj hanging.

pending prep **1** while waiting for. ♦ adj **2** not yet decided or settled.

pendulous adj hanging, swinging.

pendulum n suspended weight swinging to and fro, esp. as a regulator for a clock.

penetrate v **1** find or force a way into or through. **2** arrive at the meaning of. **penetrable** adj capable of being penetrated. **penetrating** adj **1** (of a sound) loud and unpleasant. **2** quick to understand. **penetration** n

penguin n flightless black-and-white sea bird of the southern hemisphere.

penicillin n antibiotic drug effective against a wide range of diseases and infections.

peninsula n strip of land nearly surrounded by water. **peninsular** adj

penis n organ of copulation and urination in male mammals.

penitent adj **1** feeling sorry for having done wrong. ♦ n **2** someone who is penitent. **penitence** n **penitentiary** n, pl **-ries 1** US prison. ♦ adj **2** (also **penitential**) relating to penance.

pennant n long narrow flag.

penny n, pl **pence, pennies 1** British bronze coin worth one hundredth of a pound. **2** former British and Australian coin worth one twelfth of a shilling. **penniless** adj very poor.

pension¹ n regular payment to people above a certain age, retired employees, widows, etc. **pensionable** adj **pensioner** n person receiving a pension. **pension off** v force (someone) to retire from a job and pay him or her a pension.

pension² [**pon**-syon] n boarding house in Europe.

pensive adj deeply thoughtful, often with a tinge of sadness.

pentagon n **1** geometric figure with five sides. **2** (P-) headquarters of the US military. **pentagonal** adj

pentameter [pen-**tam**-it-er] n line of poetry with five metrical feet.

Pentateuch [**pent**-a-tyuke] n first five books of the Old Testament.

Pentecost n Christian festival celebrating the descent of the Holy Spirit to the apostles, Whitsuntide.

penthouse n flat built on the roof or top floor of a building.

pent-up adj (of an emotion) not released, repressed.

penultimate adj second last.

penumbra n, pl **-brae, -bras 1** (in an eclipse) the partially shadowed region which surrounds the full shadow. **2** partial shadow.

penury n extreme poverty. **penurious** adj

peony n, pl **-nies** garden plant with showy red, pink, or white flowers.

people pl n **1** persons generally. **2** the community. **3** one's family. ♦ n **4** race or nation. ♦ v **5** provide with inhabitants. **people mover** Brit, Aust & NZ same as MULTIPURPOSE VEHICLE.

pep n Informal high spirits, energy, or enthusiasm. **pep talk** Informal talk designed to increase confidence and enthusiasm. **pep up** v **pepping, pepped** stimulate, invigorate.

pepper n **1** sharp hot condiment made from the fruit of an East Indian climbing plant. **2** colourful tropical fruit used as a vegetable, capsicum. ♦ v **3** season with pepper. **4** sprinkle, dot. **5** pelt with missiles. **peppery** adj **1** tasting of pepper. **2** irritable. **peppercorn** n dried berry of the pepper plant. **peppercorn rent** Chiefly Brit low or nominal rent.

peppermint n **1** plant that yields an oil with a strong sharp flavour. **2** sweet flavoured with this.

peptic adj relating to digestion or the digestive juices.

per prep for each. **as per** in accordance with.

perambulate v Old-fashioned walk through or about (a place).

perambulation *n* **perambulator** *n* pram.

per annum *adv Latin* in each year.

per capita *adj, adv Latin* of or for each person.

perceive *v* **1** become aware of (something) through the senses. **2** understand.

per cent in each hundred. **percentage** *n* proportion or rate per hundred.

perceptible *adj* discernible, recognizable.

perception *n* **1** act of perceiving. **2** intuitive judgment. **perceptive** *adj*

perch[1] *n* **1** resting place for a bird. ♦ *v* **2** alight, rest, or place on or as if on a perch.

perch[2] *n* any of various edible fishes.

perchance *adv Old-fashioned* perhaps.

percipient *adj* quick to notice things, observant.

percolate *v* **1** pass or filter through small holes. **2** spread gradually. **3** make (coffee) or (of coffee) be made in a percolator. **percolation** *n* **percolator** *n* coffeepot in which boiling water is forced through a tube and filters down through coffee.

percussion *n* striking of one thing against another. **percussion instrument** musical instrument played by being struck, such as drums or cymbals.

perdition *n Christianity* spiritual ruin.

peregrination *n Obs* travels, roaming.

peregrine falcon *n* falcon with dark upper parts and a light underside.

peremptory *adj* authoritative, imperious.

perennial *adj* **1** lasting through many years. ♦ *n* **2** plant lasting more than two years. **perennially** *adv*

perfect *adj* **1** having all the essential elements. **2** faultless. **3** correct, precise.

4 utter or absolute. **5** excellent. **6** *n* **7** *Grammar* perfect tense. ♦ *v* **8** improve. **9** make fully correct. **perfectly** *adv*

perfection *n* state of being perfect.

perfectionist *n* person who demands the highest standards of excellence. **perfectionism** *n*

perfidious *adj Lit* treacherous, disloyal. **perfidy** *n*

perforate *v* make holes in. **perforation** *n*

perforce *adv* of necessity.

perform *v* **1** carry out (an action). **2** act, sing, or present a play before an audience. **3** fulfil (a request etc.). **performance** *n* **performer** *n*

perfume *n* **1** liquid cosmetic worn for its pleasant smell. **2** fragrance. ♦ *v* **3** give a pleasant smell to. **perfumery** *n* perfumes in general.

perfunctory *adj* done only as a matter of routine, superficial. **perfunctorily** *adv*

pergola *n* arch or framework of trellis supporting climbing plants.

perhaps *adv* possibly, maybe.

pericardium *n, pl* **-dia** membrane enclosing the heart.

perihelion *n, pl* **-lia** point in the orbit of a planet or comet that is nearest to the sun.

peril *n* great danger. **perilous** *adj* **perilously** *adv*

perimeter [per-**rim**-it-er] *n* (length of) the outer edge of an area.

perinatal *adj* of or in the weeks shortly before or after birth.

period *n* **1** particular portion of time. **2** single occurrence of menstruation. **3** division of time at school etc. when a particular subject is taught. **4** *US* full stop. ♦ *adj* **5** (of furniture, dress, a play, etc.) dating from or in the style of an earlier time. **periodic** *adj* recurring at intervals. **periodic table** *Chem* chart of the elements, arranged to show their relationship to each other. **periodical** n **1** magazine issued at regular intervals. ♦ adj **2** periodic.

peripatetic [per-rip-a-**tet**-ik] adj travelling about from place to place.

periphery [per-**if**-er-ee] n, pl **-eries 1** boundary or edge. **2** fringes of a field of activity. **peripheral** [per-**if**-er-al] adj **1** unimportant, not central. **2** of or on the periphery.

periscope n instrument used, esp. in submarines, to give a view of objects on a different level.

perish v **1** be destroyed or die. **2** decay, rot. **perishable** adj liable to rot quickly. **perishing** adj Informal very cold.

peritoneum [per-rit-toe-**nee**-um] n, pl **-nea, -neums** membrane lining the internal surface of the abdomen. **peritonitis** [per-rit-tone-**ite**-iss] n inflammation of the peritoneum.

periwinkle[1] n small edible shellfish, the winkle.

periwinkle[2] n plant with trailing stems and blue flowers.

perjury n, pl **-juries** act or crime of lying while under oath in a court. **perjure oneself** commit perjury.

perk n Informal incidental benefit gained from a job, such as a company car.

perk up v cheer up. **perky** adj lively or cheerful.

perlemoen n S Afr edible sea creature with a shell lined with mother of pearl.

perm n **1** long-lasting curly hairstyle produced by treating the hair with chemicals. ♦ v **2** give (hair) a perm.

permafrost n permanently frozen ground.

permanent adj lasting forever. **permanence** n **permanently** adv

permeate v pervade or pass through the whole of (something).

permeable adj able to be permeated, esp. by liquid.

permit v **-mitting, -mitted 1** give permission, allow. ♦ n **2** document giving permission to do something. **permission** n authorization to do something. **permissible** adj **permissive** adj (excessively) tolerant, esp. in sexual matters.

permutation n any of the ways a number of things can be arranged or combined.

pernicious adj **1** wicked. **2** extremely harmful, deadly.

pernickety adj Informal (excessively) fussy about details.

peroration n concluding part of a speech, usu. summing up the main points.

peroxide n **1** hydrogen peroxide used as a hair bleach. **2** oxide containing a high proportion of oxygen.

perpendicular adj **1** at right angles to a line or surface. **2** upright or vertical. ♦ n **3** line or plane at right angles to another.

perpetrate v commit or be responsible for (a wrongdoing). **perpetration** n **perpetrator** n

perpetual adj **1** lasting forever. **2** continually repeated. **perpetually** adv **perpetuate** v cause to continue or be remembered. **perpetuation** n **in perpetuity** forever.

perplex v puzzle, bewilder. **perplexity** n, pl **-ties**

perquisite n Formal same as PERK.

perry n, pl **-ries** alcoholic drink made from fermented pears.

per se [per **say**] adv Latin in itself.

persecute v **1** treat cruelly because of race, religion, etc. **2** subject to persistent harassment. **persecution** n **persecutor** n

persevere v keep making an effort

despite difficulties. **perseverance** n

persimmon n sweet red tropical fruit.

persist v **1** continue to be or happen, last. **2** continue in spite of obstacles or objections. **persistent** adj **persistently** adv **persistence** n

person n **1** human being. **2** body of a human being. **3** Grammar form of pronouns and verbs that shows if a person is speaking, spoken to, or spoken of. **in person** actually present.

persona [per-**soh**-na] n, pl **-nae** [-nee] someone's personality as presented to others.

personable adj pleasant in appearance and personality.

personage n important person.

personal adj **1** individual or private. **2** of the body, e.g. personal hygiene. **3** (of a remark etc.) offensive. **personally** adv **1** directly, not by delegation to others. **2** in one's own opinion. **personal computer** small computer used for word processing or computer games. **personal pronoun** pronoun like I or she that stands for a definite person. **personal stereo** very small portable cassette player with headphones.

personality n, pl **-ties 1** person's distinctive characteristics. **2** celebrity. ♦ pl **3** personal remarks, e.g. the discussion degenerated into personalities.

personify v **-fying, -fied 1** give human characteristics to. **2** be an example of, typify. **personification** n

personnel n **1** people employed in an organization. **2** department in an organization that appoints or keeps records of employees.

perspective n **1** view of the relative importance of situations or facts. **2** method of drawing that gives the effect of solidity and relative distances and sizes.

Perspex n ® transparent acrylic substitute for glass.

perspicacious adj having quick mental insight. **perspicacity** n

perspire v sweat. **perspiration** n

persuade v **1** make (someone) do something by argument, charm, etc. **2** convince. **persuasion** n **1** act of persuading. **2** way of thinking or belief. **persuasive** adj

pert adj saucy and cheeky.

pertain v belong or be relevant (to).

pertinacious adj Formal very persistent and determined. **pertinacity** n

pertinent adj relevant. **pertinence** n

perturb v disturb greatly. **perturbation** n

peruse v read in a careful or leisurely manner. **perusal** n

pervade v spread right through (something). **pervasive** adj

perverse adj deliberately doing something different from what is thought normal or proper. **perversely** adv **perversity** n

pervert v **1** use or alter for a wrong purpose. **2** lead into abnormal (sexual) behaviour. ♦ n **3** person who practises sexual perversion. **perversion** n **1** sexual act or desire considered abnormal. **2** act of perverting.

pervious adj able to be penetrated, permeable.

peseta [pa-**say**-ta] n former monetary unit of Spain.

pessary n, pl **-ries 1** appliance worn in the vagina, either to prevent conception or to support the womb. **2** vaginal suppository.

pessimism n tendency to expect the worst in all things. **pessimist** n **pessimistic** adj **pessimistically** adv

pest n **1** annoying person. **2** insect or animal that damages crops. **pesticide** n chemical for killing insect pests.

pester v annoy or nag continually.

pestilence n deadly epidemic disease. **pestilent** adj 1 annoying, troublesome. 2 deadly. **pestilential** adj

pestle n club-shaped implement for grinding things to powder in a mortar.

pet n 1 animal kept for pleasure and companionship. 2 person favoured or indulged. ♦ adj 3 particularly cherished. ♦ v **petting, petted** 4 treat as a pet. 5 pat or stroke affectionately. 6 Old-fashioned kiss and caress erotically.

petal n one of the brightly coloured outer parts of a flower. **petalled** adj

petard n hoist with one's own petard being the victim of one's own schemes.

peter out v gradually come to an end.

petite adj (of a woman) small and dainty.

petition n 1 formal request, esp. one signed by many people and presented to parliament. ♦ v 2 present a petition to. **petitioner** n

petrel n sea bird with a hooked bill and tubular nostrils.

petrify v **-fying, -fied** 1 frighten severely. 2 turn to stone. **petrification** n

petrochemical n substance, such as acetone, obtained from petroleum.

petrol n flammable liquid obtained from petroleum, used as fuel in internal-combustion engines. **petrol bomb** home-made incendiary device consisting of a bottle filled with petrol.

petroleum n thick dark oil found underground.

petticoat n woman's skirt-shaped undergarment.

pettifogging adj excessively concerned with unimportant detail.

petty adj **-tier, -tiest** 1 unimportant, trivial. 2 small-minded. 3 on a small scale, e.g. *petty crime.* **pettiness** n **petty cash** cash kept by a firm to pay minor expenses. **petty officer** noncommissioned officer in the navy.

petulant adj childishly irritable or peevish. **petulance** n **petulantly** adv

petunia n garden plant with funnel-shaped flowers.

pew n 1 fixed benchlike seat in a church. 2 Informal chair, seat.

pewter n greyish metal made of tin and lead.

pH Chem measure of the acidity of a solution.

phalanger n long-tailed Australian tree-dwelling marsupial.

phalanx n, pl **phalanxes** closely grouped mass of people.

phallus n, pl **-luses, -li** penis, esp. as a symbol of reproductive power in primitive rites. **phallic** adj

phantasm n unreal vision, illusion. **phantasmal** adj

phantasmagoria n shifting medley of dreamlike figures.

phantom n 1 ghost. 2 unreal vision.

Pharaoh [**fare**-oh] n title of the ancient Egyptian kings.

pharmaceutical adj of pharmacy.

pharmacology n study of drugs. **pharmacological** adj **pharmacologist** n

pharmacopoeia [far-ma-koh-**pee**-a] n book with a list of and directions for the use of drugs.

pharmacy n, pl **-cies** 1 preparation and dispensing of drugs and medicines. 2 pharmacist's shop. **pharmacist** n person qualified to prepare and sell drugs and medicines.

pharynx [**far**-rinks] n, pl **pharynges, pharynxes** cavity forming the back part of the mouth. **pharyngitis** [far-rin-**jite**-iss] n inflammation of the pharynx.

phase n **1** any distinct or characteristic stage in a development or chain of events. ♦ v **2** arrange or carry out in stages or to coincide with something else. **phase in, out** v introduce or discontinue gradually.

PhD Doctor of Philosophy.

pheasant n game bird with bright plumage.

phenobarbitone n drug inducing sleep or relaxation.

phenol n chemical used in disinfectants and antiseptics.

phenomenon n, pl **-ena 1** anything appearing or observed. **2** remarkable person or thing. **phenomenal** adj extraordinary, outstanding. **phenomenally** adv

phial n small bottle for medicine etc.

philadelphus n shrub with sweet-scented flowers.

philanderer n man who flirts or has many casual love affairs. **philandering** adj, n

philanthropy n practice of helping people less well-off than oneself. **philanthropic** adj **philanthropist** n

philately [fill-**lat**-a-lee] n stamp collecting. **philatelist** n

philharmonic adj (in names of orchestras etc.) music-loving.

philistine adj, n boorishly uncultivated (person). **philistinism** n

philology n science of the structure and development of languages. **philological** adj **philologist** n

philosopher n person who studies philosophy.

philosophy n, pl **-phies 1** study of the meaning of life, knowledge, thought, etc. **2** theory or set of ideas held by a particular philosopher. **3** person's outlook on life. **philosophical, philosophic** adj **1** of philosophy. **2**

calm in the face of difficulties or disappointments. **philosophically** adv **philosophize** v discuss in a philosophical manner.

philtre n magic drink supposed to arouse love in the person who drinks it.

phlebitis [fleb-**bite**-iss] n inflammation of a vein.

phlegm [**flem**] n thick yellowish substance formed in the nose and throat during a cold.

phlegmatic [fleg-**mat**-ik] adj not easily excited, unemotional. **phlegmatically** adv

phlox n, pl **phlox, phloxes** flowering garden plant.

phobia n intense and unreasoning fear or dislike.

phoenix n legendary bird said to set fire to itself and rise anew from its ashes.

phone n, v Informal telephone. **phonecard** n card used to operate certain public telephones. **phone-in** n Brit, Aust & S Afr broadcast in which telephone comments or questions from the public are transmitted live.

phonetic adj **1** of speech sounds. **2** (of spelling) written as it is sounded. **phonetics** n science of speech sounds. **phonetically** adv

phoney, phony Informal ♦ adj **phonier, phoniest 1** not genuine. **2** insincere. ♦ n, pl **phoneys, phonies 3** phoney person or thing.

phonograph n US old-fashioned record player.

phosphorescence n faint glow in the dark. **phosphorescent** adj

phosphorus n Chem toxic flammable nonmetallic element which appears luminous in the dark. **phosphate** n **1** compound of phosphorus. **2** fertilizer containing phosphorus.

photo n, pl **photos** short for PHOTOGRAPH. **photo finish** finish of a race in which the contestants are so close that a photograph is needed to decide the result.

photocopy *n, pl* **-copies 1** photographic reproduction. ♦ *v* **-copying, -copied 2** make a photocopy of. **photocopier** *n*

photoelectric *adj* using or worked by electricity produced by the action of light.

photogenic *adj* always looking attractive in photographs.

photograph *n* **1** picture made by the chemical action of light on sensitive film. ♦ *v* **2** take a photograph of. **photographic** *adj* **photography** *n* art of taking photographs.

photographer *n* person who takes photographs, esp. professionally.

photostat *n* copy made by photocopying machine.

photosynthesis *n* process by which a green plant uses sunlight to build up carbohydrate reserves.

phrase *n* **1** group of words forming a unit of meaning, esp. within a sentence. **2** short effective expression. ♦ *v* **3** express in words. **phrasal verb** phrase consisting of a verb and an adverb or preposition, with a meaning different from the parts, such as *take in* meaning *deceive*.

phraseology *n, pl* **-gies** way in which words are used.

physical *adj* **1** of the body, as contrasted with the mind or spirit. **2** of material things or nature. **3** of physics. **physically** *adv* **physical education** training and practice in sports and gymnastics.

physician *n* doctor of medicine.

physics *n* science of the properties of matter and energy. **physicist** *n* person skilled in or studying physics.

physiognomy [fiz-ee-**on**-om-ee] *n* face.

physiology *n* science of the normal

function of living things. **physiological** *adj* **physiologist** *n*

physiotherapy *n* treatment of disease or injury by physical means such as massage, rather than by drugs. **physiotherapist** *n*

physique *n* person's bodily build and muscular development.

pi *n Maths* ratio of the circumference of a circle to its diameter.

pianissimo *adv Music* very quietly.

piano¹ *n, pl* **pianos** musical instrument with strings which are struck by hammers worked by a keyboard (also **pianoforte**). **pianist** *n* **Pianola** *n* ® mechanically played piano.

piano² *adv Music* quietly.

piazza *n* square or marketplace, esp. in Italy.

pic *n, pl* **pics, pix** *Informal* photograph or illustration.

picador *n* mounted bullfighter with a lance.

picaresque *adj* denoting a type of fiction in which the hero, a rogue, has a series of adventures.

piccalilli *n* pickle of vegetables in mustard sauce.

piccolo *n, pl* **-los** small flute.

pick¹ *v* **1** choose. **2** remove (flowers or fruit) from a plant. **3** take hold of and move with the fingers. **4** provoke (a fight etc.) deliberately. **5** open (a lock) by means other than a key. ♦ *n* **6** choice. **7** best part. **pick-me-up** *n Informal* stimulating drink, tonic. **pick on** *v* continually treat unfairly. **pick out** *v* recognize, distinguish. **pick up** *v* **1** raise, lift. **2** collect. **3** improve, get better. **4** become acquainted with for a sexual purpose. **pick-up** *n* **1** small truck. **2** casual acquaintance made for a sexual purpose. **3** device for conversion of vibrations into electrical signals, as in a record player.

pick² *n* tool with a curved iron crossbar

and wooden shaft, for breaking up hard ground or rocks.

pickaxe n large pick.

picket n 1 person or group standing outside a workplace to deter would-be workers during a strike. 2 sentry or sentries posted to give warning of an attack. 3 pointed stick used as part of a fence. ♦ v 4 form a picket outside (a workplace). **picket line** line of people acting as pickets.

pickings pl n money easily acquired.

pickle n 1 food preserved in vinegar or salt water. 2 Informal awkward situation. ♦ v 3 preserve in vinegar or salt water. **pickled** adj 1 (of food) preserved. 2 Informal drunk.

pickpocket n thief who steals from someone's pocket.

picnic n 1 informal meal out of doors. 2 v -nicking, -nicked 3 have a picnic.

Pict n member of an ancient race of N Britain. **Pictish** adj

pictorial adj of or in painting or pictures.

picture n 1 drawing or painting. 2 photograph. 3 mental image. 4 beautiful or picturesque object. 5 image on a TV screen. ♦ pl 6 cinema. ♦ v 7 visualize, imagine. 8 represent in a picture. **picturesque** adj 1 (of a place or view) pleasant to look at. 2 (of language) forceful, vivid. **picture window** large window made of a single sheet of glass.

piddle v Informal urinate.

pidgin n language, not a mother tongue, made up of elements of two or more other languages.

pie n dish of meat, fruit, etc. baked in pastry. **pie chart** circular diagram with sectors representing quantities.

piebald n, adj (horse) with irregular black-and-white markings.

piece n 1 separate bit or part. 2 instance, e.g. a piece of luck. 3

example, specimen. 4 literary or musical composition. 5 coin. 6 small object used in draughts, chess, etc. **piece together** v make or assemble bit by bit.

pièce de résistance [pyess de ray-**ziss**-tonss] n French most impressive item.

piecemeal adv bit by bit.

piecework n work paid for according to the quantity produced.

pied adj having markings of two or more colours.

pied-à-terre [pyay-à **tair**] n, pl **pieds-à-terre** [pyay da **tair**] small flat or house for occasional use.

pier n 1 platform on stilts sticking out into the sea. 2 pillar, esp. one supporting a bridge.

pierce v 1 make a hole in or through with a sharp instrument. 2 make a way through. **piercing** adj (of a sound) shrill and high-pitched.

Pierrot [**pier**-roe] n pantomime clown with a whitened face.

piety n, pl -ties deep devotion to God and religion.

piffle n Informal nonsense.

pig n 1 animal kept and killed for pork, ham, and bacon. 2 Informal greedy, dirty, or rude person. 3 Offens slang policeman. **piggish, piggy** adj 1 Informal dirty. 2 greedy. 3 stubborn. **piggery** n, pl -geries place for keeping and breeding pigs. **pig-headed** adj obstinate. **pig iron** crude iron produced in a blast furnace.

pigeon¹ n bird with a heavy body and short legs, sometimes trained to carry messages. **pigeonhole** n 1 compartment for papers in a desk etc. ♦ v 2 classify. 3 put aside and do nothing about. **pigeon-toed** adj with the feet or toes turned inwards.

pigeon² n Informal concern or responsibility.

piggyback *n* **1** ride on someone's shoulders. ♦ *adv* **2** carried on someone's shoulders.

pigment *n* colouring matter, paint or dye. **pigmentation** *n*

Pigmy *n, pl* **-mies** same as PYGMY.

pigtail *n* plait of hair hanging from the back or either side of the head.

pike¹ *n* large predatory freshwater fish.

pike² *n Hist* long-handled spear.

pikelet *n Aust & NZ* small thick pancake.

piker *n Aust & NZ slang* shirker.

pilaster *n* square column, usu. set in a wall.

pilau, pilaf, pilaff *n* Middle Eastern dish of meat, fish, or poultry boiled with rice, spices, etc.

pilchard *n* small edible sea fish of the herring family.

pile¹ *n* **1** number of things lying on top of each other. **2** *Informal* large amount. **3** large building. ♦ *v* **4** collect into a pile. **5** (foll. by *in* or *out*) move in a group. **pile-up** *n Informal* traffic accident involving several vehicles.

pile² *n* beam driven into the ground, esp. as a foundation for building.

pile³ *n* fibres of a carpet or a fabric, esp. velvet, that stand up from the weave.

piles *pl n* swollen veins in the rectum, haemorrhoids.

pilfer *v* steal in small quantities.

pilgrim *n* person who journeys to a holy place. **pilgrimage** *n*

pill *n* small ball of medicine swallowed whole. **the pill** pill taken by a woman to prevent pregnancy.

pillage *v* **1** steal property by violence in war. ♦ *n* **2** violent seizure of goods, esp. in war.

pillar *n* **1** upright post, usu. supporting a roof. **2** strong supporter. **pillar box** (in Britain) red pillar-shaped letter box in the street.

pillion *n* seat for a passenger behind the rider of a motorcycle.

pillory *n, pl* **-ries** **1** *Hist* frame with holes for the head and hands in which an offender was locked and exposed to public abuse. ♦ *v* **-rying, -ried** **2** ridicule publicly.

pillow *n* **1** stuffed cloth bag for supporting the head in bed. ♦ *v* **2** rest as if on a pillow. **pillowcase, pillowslip** *n* removable cover for a pillow.

pilot *n* **1** person qualified to fly an aircraft or spacecraft. **2** person employed to steer a ship entering or leaving a harbour. ♦ *adj* **3** experimental and preliminary. ♦ *v* **4** act as the pilot of. **5** guide, steer. **pilot light** small flame lighting the main one in a gas appliance.

pimento *n, pl* **-tos** mild-tasting red pepper.

pimp *n* **1** man who gets customers for a prostitute in return for a share of his or her earnings. ♦ *v* **2** act as a pimp.

pimpernel *n* wild plant with small star-shaped flowers.

pimple *n* small pus-filled spot on the skin. **pimply** *adj*

pin *n* **1** short thin piece of stiff wire with a point and head, for fastening things. **2** wooden or metal peg or stake. ♦ *v* **pinning, pinned** **3** fasten with a pin. **4** seize and hold fast. **pin down** *v* **1** force (someone) to make a decision, take action, etc. **2** define clearly. **pin money** small amount earned to buy small luxuries. **pin-up** *n* picture of a sexually attractive person, esp. (partly) naked.

pinafore *n* **1** apron. **2** dress with a bib top.

pinball *n* electrically operated table game in which a small ball is shot through various hazards.

pince-nez [panss-**nay**] *n, pl* **pince-nez**

glasses kept in place only by a clip on the bridge of the nose.

pincers pl n **1** tool consisting of two hinged arms, for gripping. **2** claws of a lobster etc.

pinch v **1** squeeze between finger and thumb. **2** cause pain by being too tight. **3** Informal steal. **4** n **5** act of pinching. **6** as much as can be taken up between the finger and thumb. **at a pinch** if absolutely necessary. **feel the pinch** have to economize.

pinchbeck n alloy of zinc and copper, used as imitation gold.

pine¹ n **1** evergreen coniferous tree. **2** its wood. **pine cone** woody seed case of the pine tree. **pine marten** wild mammal of the coniferous forests of Europe and Asia.

pine² v **1** (foll. by for) feel great longing (for). **2** become thin and ill through grief etc.

pineal gland n small cone-shaped gland at the base of the brain.

pineapple n large tropical fruit with juicy yellow flesh and a hard skin.

ping v, n (make) a short high-pitched sound.

Ping-Pong n ® table tennis.

pinion¹ n **1** bird's wing. ♦ v **2** immobilize (someone) by tying or holding his or her arms.

pinion² n small cogwheel.

pink n **1** pale reddish colour. **2** fragrant garden plant. ♦ adj **3** of the colour pink. ♦ v **4** (of an engine) make a metallic noise because not working properly, knock. **in the pink** in good health.

pinking shears pl n scissors with a serrated edge that give a wavy edge to material to prevent fraying.

pinnacle n **1** highest point of fame or success. **2** mountain peak. **3** small slender spire.

pinotage [**pin**-no-tajj] n blended red wine of S Africa.

pinpoint v locate or identify exactly.

pinstripe n **1** very narrow stripe in fabric. **2** the fabric itself.

pint n liquid measure, ⅛ gallon (.568 litre).

pioneer n **1** explorer or early settler of a new country. **2** originator or developer of something new. ♦ v **3** be the pioneer or leader of.

pious adj deeply religious, devout.

pip¹ n small seed in a fruit.

pip² n **1** high-pitched sound used as a time signal on radio. **2** Informal star on a junior army officer's shoulder showing rank.

pip³ n **give someone the pip** Brit, NZ & S Afr slang annoy.

pipe n **1** tube for conveying liquid or gas. **2** tube with a small bowl at the end for smoking tobacco. **3** tubular musical instrument. ♦ pl **4** bagpipes. ♦ v **5** play on a pipe. **6** utter in a shrill tone. **7** convey by pipe. **8** decorate with piping. **piper** n player on a pipe or bagpipes. **piping** n **1** system of pipes. **2** decoration of icing on a cake etc. **3** fancy edging on clothes etc. **piped music** recorded music played as background music in public places. **pipe down** v Informal stop talking. **pipe dream** fanciful impossible plan. **pipeline** n **1** long pipe for transporting oil, water, etc. **2** means of communication. **in the pipeline** in preparation. **pipe up** v speak suddenly or shrilly.

pipette n slender glass tube used to transfer or measure fluids.

pipi n **1** Aust mollusc often used as bait. **2** NZ edible shellfish.

pipit n small brownish songbird.

pippin n type of eating apple.

piquant [**pee**-kant] adj **1** having a pleasant spicy taste. **2** mentally stimulating. **piquancy** n

pique [**peek**] n **1** feeling of hurt pride, baffled curiosity, or resentment. ♦ v **2** hurt the pride of. **3** arouse (curiosity).

piqué [**pee**-kay] n stiff ribbed cotton fabric.

piquet [pik-**ket**] n card game for two.

piranha n small fierce freshwater fish of tropical America.

pirate n **1** sea robber. **2** person who illegally publishes or sells work owned by someone else. **3** person or company that broadcasts illegally. ♦ v **4** sell or reproduce (artistic work etc.) illegally. **piracy** n **piratical** adj

pirouette v, n (make) a spinning turn balanced on the toes of one foot.

piss Vulgar slang ♦ v **1** urinate. ♦ n **2** act of urinating. **3** urine.

pistachio n, pl **-chios** edible nut of a Mediterranean tree.

piste [**peest**] n ski slope.

pistil n seed-bearing part of a flower.

pistol n short-barrelled handgun.

piston n cylindrical part in an engine that slides to and fro in a cylinder.

pit n **1** deep hole in the ground. **2** coal mine. **3** dent or depression. **4** servicing and refuelling area on a motor-racing track. **5** same as ORCHESTRA PIT. ♦ v **pitting, pitted 6** mark with small dents or scars. **pit one's wits against** compete against in a test or contest. **pit bull terrier** strong muscular terrier with a short coat.

pitch¹ v **1** throw, hurl. **2** set up (a tent). **3** fall headlong. **4** (of a ship or plane) move with the front and back going up and down alternately. **5** set the level or tone of. ♦ n **6** area marked out for playing sport. **7** degree or angle of slope. **8** degree of highness or lowness of a (musical) sound. **9** place where a street or market trader regularly sells. **10** Informal persuasive sales talk. **pitch in** v join in enthusiastically. **pitch into**

v Informal attack.

pitch² n dark sticky substance obtained from tar. **pitch-black, pitch-dark** adj very dark.

pitchblende n mineral composed largely of uranium oxide, yielding radium.

pitcher n large jug with a narrow neck.

pitchfork n **1** large long-handled fork for lifting hay. ♦ v **2** thrust abruptly or violently.

pitfall n hidden difficulty or danger.

pith n **1** soft white lining of the rind of oranges etc. **2** essential part. **3** soft tissue in the stems of certain plants. **pithy** adj short and full of meaning.

piton [**peet**-on] n metal spike used in climbing to secure a rope.

pittance n very small amount of money.

pituitary n, pl **-taries** gland at the base of the brain, that helps to control growth (also **pituitary gland**).

pity n, pl **pities 1** sympathy or sorrow for others' suffering. **2** regrettable fact. ♦ v **pitying, pitied 3** feel pity for. **piteous, pitiable** adj arousing pity. **pitiful** adj **1** arousing pity. **2** woeful, contemptible. **pitifully** adv **pitiless** adj feeling no pity or mercy. **pitilessly** adv

pivot n **1** central shaft on which something turns. ♦ v **2** provide with or turn on a pivot. **pivotal** adj of crucial importance.

pix n Informal a plural of PIC.

pixie n (in folklore) fairy.

pizza n flat disc of dough covered with a wide variety of savoury toppings and baked.

pizzazz n Informal attractive combination of energy and style.

pizzicato [pit-see-**kah**-toe] adj Music played by plucking the string of a violin etc. with the finger.

placard *n* notice that is carried or displayed in public.

placate *v* make (someone) stop feeling angry or upset. **placatory** *adj*

place *n* 1 particular part of an area or space. 2 particular town, building, etc. 3 position or point reached. 4 seat or space. 5 duty or right. 6 position of employment. 7 usual position. ♦ *v* 8 put in a particular place. 9 identify, put in context. 10 make (an order, bet, etc.). **be placed** (of a competitor in a race) be among the first three. **take place** happen, occur.

placebo [plas-**see**-bo] *n, pl* -bos, -boes sugar pill etc. given to an unsuspecting patient instead of an active drug.

placenta [plass-**ent**-a] *n, pl* -tas, -tae organ formed in the womb during pregnancy, providing nutrients for the fetus. **placental** *adj*

placid *adj* not easily excited or upset, calm. **placidity** *n*

plagiarize [**play**-jer-ize] *v* steal ideas, passages, etc. from (someone else's work) and present them as one's own. **plagiarism** *n*

plague *n* 1 fast-spreading fatal disease. 2 *Hist* bubonic plague. 3 widespread infestation. ♦ *v* **plaguing, plagued** 4 trouble or annoy continually.

plaice *n* edible European flatfish.

plaid *n* 1 long piece of tartan cloth worn as part of Highland dress. 2 tartan cloth or pattern.

plain *adj* 1 easy to see or understand. 2 expressed honestly and clearly. 3 without decoration or pattern. 4 not beautiful. 5 simple, ordinary. ♦ *n* 6 large stretch of level country. **plainly** *adv* **plainness** *n* **plain clothes** ordinary clothes, as opposed to uniform. **plain sailing** easy progress. **plain speaking** saying exactly what one thinks.

plainsong *n* unaccompanied singing, esp. in a medieval church.

plaintiff *n* person who sues in a court of law.

plaintive *adj* sad, mournful. **plaintively** *adv*

plait [**platt**] *n* 1 intertwined length of hair. ♦ *v* 2 intertwine separate strands in a pattern.

plan *n* 1 way thought out to do or achieve something. 2 diagram showing the layout or design of something. ♦ *v* **planning, planned** 3 arrange beforehand. 4 make a diagram of. **planner** *n*

plane[1] *n* 1 aeroplane. 2 *Maths* flat surface. 3 level of attainment etc. ♦ *adj* 4 perfectly flat or level. ♦ *v* 5 glide or skim.

plane[2] *n* 1 tool for smoothing wood. ♦ *v* 2 smooth (wood) with a plane.

plane[3] *n* tree with broad leaves.

planet *n* large body in space that revolves round the sun or another star. **planetary** *adj*

planetarium *n, pl* -iums, -ia building where the movements of the stars, planets, etc. are shown by projecting lights on the inside of a dome.

plangent *adj* (of sounds) mournful and resounding.

plank *n* long flat piece of sawn timber.

plankton *n* minute animals and plants floating in the surface water of a sea or lake.

plant *n* 1 living organism that grows in the ground and has no power to move. 2 equipment or machinery used in industrial processes. 3 factory or other industrial premises. ♦ *v* 4 put in the ground to grow. 5 place firmly in position. 6 *Informal* put (a person) secretly in an organization to spy. 7 *Informal* hide (stolen goods etc.) on a person to make him or her seem guilty. **planter** *n* owner of a plantation.

plantain[1] n low-growing wild plant with broad leaves.

plantain[2] n tropical fruit like a green banana.

plantation n 1 estate for the cultivation of tea, tobacco, etc. 2 wood of cultivated trees.

plaque n 1 inscribed commemorative stone or metal plate. 2 filmy deposit on teeth that causes decay.

plasma n clear liquid part of blood.

plaster n 1 mixture of lime, sand, etc. for coating walls. 2 adhesive strip of material for dressing cuts etc. ♦ v 3 cover with plaster. 4 coat thickly. **plastered** adj Slang drunk. **plaster of Paris** white powder which dries to form a hard solid when mixed with water, used for sculptures and casts for broken limbs.

plastic n 1 synthetic material that can be moulded when soft but sets in a hard long-lasting shape. 2 credit cards etc. as opposed to cash. ♦ adj 3 made of plastic. 4 easily moulded, pliant. **plasticity** n ability to be moulded. **plastic bullet** solid PVC cylinder fired by police in riot control. **plastic surgery** repair or reconstruction of missing or malformed parts of the body.

Plasticine n ® soft coloured modelling material used esp. by children.

plate n 1 shallow dish for holding food. 2 flat thin sheet of metal, glass, etc. 3 thin coating of metal on another metal. 4 dishes or cutlery made of gold or silver. 5 illustration, usu. on fine quality paper, in a book. 6 Informal set of false teeth. ♦ v 7 cover with a thin coating of gold, silver, or other metal. **plateful** n **plate glass** glass in thin sheets, used for mirrors and windows. **plate tectonics** study of the structure of the earth's crust,

esp. the movement of layers of rocks.

plateau n, pl **-teaus, -teaux** 1 area of level high land. 2 stage when there is no change or development.

platen n roller of a typewriter, against which the paper is held.

platform n 1 raised floor. 2 raised area in a station from which passengers board trains. 3 structure in the sea which holds machinery, stores, etc. for drilling an oil well. 4 programme of a political party.

platinum n Chem valuable silvery-white metal. **platinum blonde** woman with silvery-blonde hair.

platitude n remark that is true but not interesting or original. **platitudinous** adj

platonic adj (of a relationship) friendly or affectionate but not sexual.

platoon n smaller unit within a company of soldiers.

platteland n S Afr rural district.

platter n large dish.

platypus n Australian egg-laying amphibious mammal, with dense fur, webbed feet, and a ducklike bill (also **duck-billed platypus**).

plaudits pl n expressions of approval.

plausible adj 1 apparently true or reasonable. 2 persuasive but insincere. **plausibly** adv **plausibility** n

play v 1 occupy oneself in (a game or recreation). 2 compete against in a game or sport. 3 behave carelessly. 4 act (a part) on the stage. 5 perform on (a musical instrument). 6 cause (a radio, record player, etc.) to give out sound. 7 move lightly or irregularly, flicker. ♦ n 8 story performed on stage or broadcast. 9 activities children take part in for amusement. 10 playing of a game. 11 conduct, e.g. fair play. 12 (scope for) freedom of movement. **playful** adj lively. **play back** v listen to or watch (something recorded).

playcentre n NZ & S Afr centre for preschool children run by parents. **play down** v minimize the importance of. **playgroup** n regular meeting of very young children for supervised play. **playhouse** n theatre. **playing card** one of a set of 52 cards used in card games. **playing field** extensive piece of ground for sport. **play-lunch** n Aust & NZ child's mid-morning snack at school. **play off** v set (two people) against each other for one's own ends. **play on** v exploit or encourage (someone's sympathy or weakness). **playschool** n nursery group for young children. **plaything** n 1 toy. 2 person regarded or treated as a toy. **play up** v 1 give prominence to. 2 cause trouble. **playwright** n author of plays.

playboy n rich man who lives only for pleasure.

player n 1 person who plays a game or sport. 2 actor or actress. 3 person who plays a musical instrument.

plaza n 1 open space or square. 2 modern shopping complex.

PLC, plc (in Britain) Public Limited Company.

plea n 1 serious or urgent request, entreaty. 2 statement of a prisoner or defendant. 3 excuse.

plead v 1 ask urgently or with deep feeling. 2 give as an excuse. 3 Law declare oneself to be guilty or innocent of a charge made against one.

pleasant adj pleasing, enjoyable. **pleasantly** adv **pleasantry** n, pl -tries polite or joking remark.

please v 1 give pleasure or satisfaction to. ♦ adv 2 polite word of request. **please oneself** do as one likes. **pleased** adj **pleasing** adj

pleasure n 1 feeling of happiness and satisfaction. 2 something that causes

this. **pleasurable** adj giving pleasure. **pleasurably** adv

pleat n 1 fold made by doubling material back on itself. ♦ v 2 arrange (material) in pleats.

plebeian [pleb-**ee**-an] adj 1 of the lower social classes. 2 vulgar or rough. ♦ n 3 (also **pleb**) member of the lower social classes.

plebiscite [pleb-**iss**-ite] n decision by direct voting of the people of a country.

plectrum n, pl -trums, -tra small implement for plucking the strings of a guitar etc.

pledge n 1 solemn promise. 2 something valuable given as a guarantee that a promise will be kept or a debt paid. ♦ v 3 promise solemnly. 4 bind by or as if by a pledge.

plenary adj (of a meeting) attended by all members.

plenipotentiary adj 1 having full powers. ♦ n, pl -aries 2 diplomat or representative having full powers.

plenitude n completeness, abundance.

plenteous adj plentiful.

plenty n 1 large amount or number. 2 quite enough. **plentiful** adj existing in large amounts or numbers. **plentifully** adv

pleonasm n use of more words than necessary.

plethora n excess.

pleurisy n inflammation of the membrane covering the lungs.

pliable adj 1 easily bent. 2 easily influenced. **pliability** n

pliant adj pliable. **pliancy** n

pliers pl n tool with hinged arms and jaws for gripping.

plight[1] n difficult or dangerous situation.

plight[2] v **plight one's troth**

Old-fashioned promise to marry.

Plimsoll line *n* mark on a ship showing the level water should reach when the ship is fully loaded.

plimsolls *pl n Brit* rubber-soled canvas shoes.

plinth *n* slab forming the base of a statue, column, etc.

PLO Palestine Liberation Organization.

plod *v* **plodding, plodded 1** walk with slow heavy steps. **2** work slowly but determinedly. **plodder** *n*

plonk[1] *v* put (something) down heavily and carelessly.

plonk[2] *n Informal* cheap inferior wine.

plop *n* **1** sound of an object falling into water without a splash. ♦ *v* **plopping, plopped 2** make this sound.

plot[1] *n* **1** secret plan to do something illegal or wrong. **2** story of a film, novel, etc. ♦ *v* **plotting, plotted 3** plan secretly, conspire. **4** mark the position or course of (a ship or aircraft) on a map. **5** mark and join up (points on a graph).

plot[2] *n* small piece of land.

plough *n* **1** agricultural tool for turning over soil. ♦ *v* **2** turn over (earth) with a plough. **3** move or work through slowly and laboriously. **ploughman** *n* **ploughshare** *n* blade of a plough.

plover *n* shore bird with a straight bill and long pointed wings.

ploy *n* manoeuvre designed to gain an advantage.

pluck *v* **1** pull or pick off. **2** pull out the feathers of (a bird for cooking). **3** sound the strings of (a guitar etc.) with the fingers or a plectrum. ♦ *n* **4** courage. **plucky** *adj* brave. **pluckily** *adv* **pluck up** *v* summon up (courage).

plug *n* **1** thing fitting into and filling a hole. **2** device connecting an appliance to an electricity supply. **3** *Informal* favourable mention of a product etc.,

to encourage people to buy it. ♦ *v* **plugging, plugged 4** block or seal (a hole or gap) with a plug. **5** *Informal* advertise (a product etc.) by constant repetition. **plug away** *v Informal* work steadily. **plug in** *v* connect (an electrical appliance) to a power source by pushing a plug into a socket.

plum *n* **1** oval usu. dark red fruit with a stone in the middle. ♦ *adj* **2** dark purplish-red. **3** very desirable.

plumage *n* bird's feathers.

plumb *v* **1** understand (something obscure). **2** test with a plumb line. ♦ *adv* **3** exactly. **plumb the depths of** experience the worst extremes of (an unpleasant quality or emotion). **plumbing** *n* pipes and fixtures used in water and drainage systems. **plumb in** *v* connect (an appliance such as a washing machine) to a water supply. **plumb line** string with a weight at the end, used to test the depth of water or to test whether something is vertical.

plumber *n* person who fits and repairs pipes and fixtures for water and drainage systems.

plume *n* feather, esp. one worn as an ornament.

plummet *v* **-meting, -meted** plunge downward.

plump[1] *adj* moderately or attractively fat. **plumpness** *n* **plump up** *v* make (a pillow) fuller or rounded.

plump[2] *v* sit or fall heavily and suddenly. **plump for** *v* choose, vote for.

plunder *v* **1** take by force, esp. in time of war. ♦ *n* **2** things plundered, spoils.

plunge *v* **1** put or throw forcibly or suddenly (into). **2** descend steeply. ♦ *n* **3** plunging, dive. **take the plunge** *Informal* embark on a risky enterprise. **plunger** *n* rubber suction cup used to clear blocked pipes. **plunge into** *v* become deeply involved in.

plunket baby n NZ baby brought up on the diet recommended by the Plunket Society. **plunket nurse** NZ nurse working for the Plunket Society.

pluperfect n, adj Grammar (tense) expressing an action completed before a past time, e.g. had gone in his wife had gone already.

plural adj 1 of or consisting of more than one. ♦ n 2 word indicating more than one.

pluralism n existence and toleration of a variety of peoples, opinions, etc. in a society. **pluralist** n **pluralistic** adj

plus prep, adj 1 indicating addition. ♦ adj 2 more than zero. 3 positive. 4 advantageous. ♦ n 5 sign (+) denoting addition. 6 advantage.

plus fours pl n trousers gathered in just below the knee.

plush n 1 fabric with long velvety pile. ♦ adj 2 (also **plushy**) luxurious.

Pluto n 1 Greek god of the underworld. 2 farthest planet from the sun.

plutocrat n person who is powerful because of being very rich. **plutocratic** adj

plutonium n Chem radioactive metallic element used esp. in nuclear reactors and weapons.

ply[1] v **plying, plied** 1 work at (a job or trade). 2 use (a tool). 3 (of a ship) travel regularly along or between. **ply with** v supply with or subject to persistently.

ply[2] n thickness of wool, fabric, etc.

plywood n board made of thin layers of wood glued together.

PM prime minister.

p.m. 1 after noon. 2 postmortem.

PMT premenstrual tension.

pneumatic adj worked by or inflated with wind or air.

pneumonia n inflammation of the lungs.

PO 1 Brit postal order. 2 Post Office.

poach[1] v 1 catch (animals) illegally on someone else's land. 2 encroach on or steal something belonging to someone else.

poach[2] v simmer (food) gently in liquid.

poacher n person who catches animals illegally on someone else's land.

pocket n 1 small bag sewn into clothing for carrying things. 2 pouchlike container, esp. for catching balls at the edge of a snooker table. 3 isolated or distinct group or area. ♦ v **pocketing, pocketed** 4 put into one's pocket. 5 take secretly or dishonestly. ♦ adj 6 small. **out of pocket** having made a loss. **pocket money** 1 small regular allowance given to children by parents. 2 money for small personal expenses.

pockmarked adj (of the skin) marked with hollow scars where diseased spots have been.

pod n long narrow seed case of peas, beans, etc.

podgy adj **podgier, podgiest** short and fat.

podium n, pl **-diums, -dia** small raised platform for a conductor or speaker.

poem n imaginative piece of writing in rhythmic lines.

poep n S Afr slang emission of gas from the anus.

poesy n Obs poetry.

poet n writer of poems. **poetry** n 1 poems. 2 art of writing poems. 3 beautiful or pleasing quality. **poetic, poetical** adj of or like poetry. **poetically** adv **poetic justice** suitable reward or punishment for someone's past actions. **poet laureate** poet appointed by the British sovereign to write poems on important occasions.

pogrom n organized persecution and massacre.

poignant adj sharply painful to the

feelings. **poignancy** n

poinsettia n Central American shrub widely grown for its clusters of scarlet leaves, which resemble petals.

point n **1** main idea in a discussion, argument, etc. **2** aim or purpose. **3** detail or item. **4** characteristic. **5** particular position, stage, or time. **6** dot indicating decimals. **7** sharp end. **8** unit for recording a value or score. **9** one of the direction marks of a compass. **10** electrical socket. **11** v **12** show the direction or position of something or draw attention to it by extending a finger or other pointed object towards it. **13** direct or face towards. **on the point of** very shortly going to. **pointed** adj **1** having a sharp end. **2** (of a remark) obviously directed at a particular person. **pointedly** adv **pointer** n **1** helpful hint. **2** indicator on a measuring instrument. **3** breed of gun dog. **pointless** adj meaningless, irrelevant. **point-blank** adj **1** fired at a very close target. **2** (of a remark or question) direct, blunt. ♦ adv **3** directly or bluntly. **point duty** control of traffic by a policeman at a road junction. **point of view** way of considering something. **point-to-point** n Brit horse race across open country.

poise n calm dignified manner. **poised** adj **1** absolutely ready. **2** behaving with or showing poise.

poison n **1** substance that kills or injures when swallowed or absorbed. ♦ v **2** give poison to. **3** have a harmful or evil effect on, spoil. **poisoner** n **poisonous** adj **poison-pen letter** malicious anonymous letter.

poke v **1** jab or prod with one's finger, a stick, etc. **2** thrust forward or out. ♦ n **3** poking. **poky** adj small and cramped.

poker[1] n metal rod for stirring a fire.

poker[2] n card game in which players bet on the hands dealt. **poker-faced** adj expressionless.

polar adj of or near either of the earth's poles. **polar bear** white bear that lives in the regions around the North Pole.

polarize v **1** form or cause to form into groups with directly opposite views. **2** Physics restrict (light waves) to certain directions of vibration. **polarization** n

Polaroid n ® **1** plastic which polarizes light and so reduces glare. **2** camera that develops a print very quickly inside itself.

polder n land reclaimed from the sea, esp. in the Netherlands.

pole[1] n long rounded piece of wood etc.

pole[2] n **1** point furthest north or south on the earth's axis of rotation. **2** either of the opposite ends of a magnet or electric cell. **Pole Star** star nearest to the North Pole in the northern hemisphere.

poleaxe v hit or stun with a heavy blow.

polecat n small animal of the weasel family.

polemic [pol-**em**-ik] n fierce attack on or defence of a particular opinion, belief, etc. **polemical** adj

police n **1** organized force in a state which keeps law and order. ♦ v **2** control or watch over with police or a similar body. **policeman, policewoman** n member of a police force.

policy[1] n, pl -cies plan of action adopted by a person, group, or state.

policy[2] n, pl -cies document containing an insurance contract.

polio n disease affecting the spinal cord, which often causes paralysis (also **poliomyelitis**).

polish v **1** make smooth and shiny by

rubbing. **2** make more nearly perfect.
♦ n **3** substance used for polishing. **4**
pleasing elegant style. **polished** adj **1**
accomplished. **2** done or performed
well or professionally. **polish off** v
finish completely, dispose of.

polite adj **1** showing consideration for
others in one's manners, speech, etc. **2**
socially correct or refined. **politely**
adv **politeness** n

politic adj wise and likely to prove
advantageous.

politics n **1** winning and using of
power to govern society. **2** (study of)
the art of government. **3** person's
beliefs about how a country should be
governed. **political** adj of the state,
government, or public administration.
politically adv **politically correct** (of
language) intended to avoid any
implied prejudice. **political prisoner**
person imprisoned because of his or
her political beliefs. **politician** n
person actively engaged in politics,
esp. a member of parliament.

polka n **1** lively 19th-century dance. **2**
music for this. **polka dots** pattern of
bold spots on fabric.

poll n **1** (also **opinion poll**) questioning
of a random sample of people to find
out general opinion. **2** voting. **3**
number of votes recorded. ♦ v **4**
receive (votes). **5** question in an
opinion poll. **pollster** n person who
conducts opinion polls. **polling
station** building where people vote in
an election.

pollarded adj (of a tree) growing very
bushy because its top branches have
been cut short.

pollen n fine dust produced by flowers
to fertilize other flowers. **pollinate** v
fertilize with pollen. **pollen count**
measure of the amount of pollen in
the air, esp. as a warning to people
with hay fever.

pollute v contaminate with something
poisonous or harmful. **pollution** n
pollutant n something that pollutes.

polo n game like hockey played by
teams of players on horseback. **polo
neck** sweater with tight turned-over
collar.

polonaise n **1** old stately dance. **2**
music for this.

polonium n Chem radioactive element
that occurs in trace amounts in
uranium ores.

poltergeist n spirit believed to move
furniture and throw objects around.

poltroon n Obs utter coward.

poly- combining form many, much.

polyandry n practice of having more
than one husband at the same time.

polyanthus n garden primrose.

polychromatic adj many-coloured.

polyester n synthetic material used to
make plastics and textile fibres.

polygamy [pol-**ig**-a-mee] n practice of
having more than one husband or wife
at the same time. **polygamous** adj
polygamist n

polyglot n, adj (person) able to speak
or write several languages.

polygon n geometrical figure with
three or more angles and sides.
polygonal adj

polyhedron n, pl **-drons, -dra** solid
figure with four or more sides.

polymer n chemical compound with
large molecules made of simple
molecules of the same kind.
polymerize v form into polymers.
polymerization n

polyp n **1** small simple sea creature
with a hollow cylindrical body. **2** small
growth on a mucous membrane.

polyphonic adj Music consisting of
several melodies played simultaneously.

polystyrene n synthetic material used
esp. as white rigid foam for packing

and insulation.

polytechnic n (in New Zealand and formerly in Britain) college offering courses in many subjects at and below degree level.

polytheism n belief in many gods. **polytheistic** adj

polythene n light plastic used for bags etc.

polyunsaturated adj of a group of fats that do not form cholesterol in the blood.

polyurethane n synthetic material used esp. in paints.

pom n Aust & NZ slang person from England (also **pommy**).

pomander n (container for) a mixture of sweet-smelling petals, herbs, etc.

pomegranate n round tropical fruit with a thick rind containing many seeds in a red pulp.

Pomeranian n small dog with long straight hair.

pommel n 1 raised part on the front of a saddle. 2 knob at the top of a sword hilt.

pomp n stately display or ceremony.

pompom n decorative ball of tufted wool, silk, etc.

pompous adj foolishly serious and grand; self-important. **pompously** adv **pomposity** n

ponce n Offens 1 effeminate man. 2 pimp. **ponce around** v Brit, Aust & NZ behave in a ridiculous or posturing way.

poncho n, pl **-chos** loose circular cloak with a hole for the head.

pond n small area of still water.

ponder v think thoroughly or deeply (about).

ponderous adj 1 serious and dull. 2 heavy and unwieldy. 3 (of movement) slow and clumsy. **ponderously** adv

pong v, n Informal (give off) a strong

unpleasant smell.

pontiff n the Pope. **pontificate** v 1 state one's opinions as if they were the only possible correct ones. ◆ n 2 period of office of a Pope.

pontoon[1] n floating platform supporting a temporary bridge.

pontoon[2] n gambling card game.

pony n, pl **ponies** small horse. **ponytail** n long hair tied in one bunch at the back of the head.

poodle n dog with curly hair often clipped fancifully.

poof, poofter n Brit, Aust & NZ offens homosexual man.

pool[1] n 1 small body of still water. 2 puddle of spilt liquid. 3 swimming pool.

pool[2] n 1 shared fund or group of workers or resources. 2 game like snooker. ◆ pl 3 Brit short for FOOTBALL POOLS. ◆ v 4 put in a common fund.

poop n raised part at the back of a sailing ship.

poor adj 1 having little money and few possessions. 2 less, smaller, or weaker than is needed or expected. 3 inferior. 4 unlucky, pitiable. **poorly** adv 1 in a poor manner. ◆ adj 2 not in good health.

pop[1] v **popping, popped** 1 make or cause to make a small explosive sound. 2 Informal go, put, or come unexpectedly or suddenly. ◆ n 3 small explosive sound. 4 Brit nonalcoholic fizzy drink. **popcorn** n grains of maize heated until they puff up and burst.

pop[2] n music of general appeal, esp. to young people.

pop[3] n Informal father.

Pope n head of the Roman Catholic Church. **popish** adj Offens Roman Catholic.

poplar n tall slender tree.

poplin n ribbed cotton material.

poppadom *n* thin round crisp Indian bread.

poppy *n, pl* **-pies** plant with a large red flower.

populace *n* the ordinary people.

popular *adj* **1** widely liked and admired. **2** of or for the public in general. **popularly** *adv* **popularity** *n* **popularize** *v* **1** make popular. **2** make (something technical or specialist) easily understood.

populate *v* **1** live in, inhabit. **2** fill with inhabitants. **populous** *adj* densely populated.

population *n* **1** all the people who live in a particular place. **2** the number of people living in a particular place.

porbeagle *n* kind of shark.

porcelain *n* **1** fine china. **2** objects made of it.

porch *n* covered approach to the entrance of a building.

porcine *adj* of or like a pig.

porcupine *n* animal covered with long pointed quills.

pore *n* tiny opening in the skin or in the surface of a plant.

pork *n* pig meat. **porker** *n* pig raised for food.

porn, porno *n, adj Informal* **short for** PORNOGRAPHY *or* PORNOGRAPHIC.

pornography *n* writing, films, or pictures designed to be sexually exciting. **pornographer** *n* producer of pornography. **pornographic** *adj*

porous *adj* allowing liquid to pass through gradually. **porosity** *n*

porpoise *n* fishlike sea mammal.

porridge *n* **1** breakfast food made of oatmeal cooked in water or milk. **2** *Chiefly Brit slang* term in prison.

port[1] *n* (town with) a harbour.

port[2] *n* left side of a ship or aircraft when facing the front of it.

port[3] *n* strong sweet wine, usu. red.

port[4] *n* **1** opening in the side of a ship. **2** porthole.

portable *adj* easily carried. **portability** *n*

portal *n* large imposing door or gate.

portcullis *n* grating suspended above a castle gateway, that can be lowered to block the entrance.

portend *v* be a sign of.

portent *n* sign of a future event. **portentous** *adj* **1** of great or ominous significance. **2** pompous, self-important.

porter[1] *n* **1** man who carries luggage. **2** hospital worker who transfers patients between rooms etc.

porter[2] *n* doorman or gatekeeper of a building.

portfolio *n, pl* **-os 1** (flat case for carrying) examples of an artist's work. **2** area of responsibility of a government minister. **3** list of investments held by an investor.

porthole *n* small round window in a ship or aircraft.

portico *n, pl* **-coes, -cos** porch or covered walkway with columns supporting the roof.

portion *n* **1** part or share. **2** helping of food for one person. **3** destiny or fate. **portion out** *v* divide into shares.

portly *adj* **-lier, -liest** rather fat.

portmanteau *n, pl* **-teaus, -teaux 1** *Old-fashioned* large suitcase that opens into two compartments. ♦ *adj* **2** combining aspects of different things.

portrait *n* **1** picture of a person. **2** lifelike description.

portray *v* describe or represent by artistic means, as in writing or film. **portrayal** *n*

Portuguese *adj* **1** of Portugal, its people, or their language. ♦ *n* **2** person from Portugal. **3** language of Portugal and Brazil. **Portuguese man-of-war**

sea creature resembling a jellyfish, with stinging tentacles.

pose *v* **1** place in or take up a particular position to be photographed or drawn. **2** raise (a problem). **3** ask (a question). ♦ *n* **4** position while posing. **5** behaviour adopted for effect. **pose as** pretend to be. **poser** *n* **1** puzzling question **2** poseur. **poseur** *n* person who behaves in an affected way to impress others.

posh *adj Informal* **1** smart, luxurious. **2** affectedly upper-class.

posit [**pozz**-it] *v* lay down as a basis for argument.

position *n* **1** place. **2** usual or expected place. **3** way in which something is placed or arranged. **4** attitude, point of view. **5** social standing. **6** job. ♦ *v* **7** place.

positive *adj* **1** feeling no doubts, certain. **2** confident, hopeful. **3** helpful, providing encouragement. **4** absolute, downright. **5** *Maths* greater than zero. **6** (of an electrical charge) having a deficiency of electrons. **positively** *adv* **positive discrimination** provision of special opportunities for a disadvantaged group.

positron *n Physics* particle with same mass as electron but positive charge.

posse [**poss**-ee] *n* **1** *US* group of men organized to maintain law and order. **2** *Brit & Aust informal* group of friends or associates.

possess *v* **1** have as one's property. **2** (of a feeling, belief, etc.) have complete control of, dominate. **possessor** *n* **possession** *n* **1** state of possessing, ownership. ♦ *pl* **2** things a person possesses. **possessive** *adj* **1** wanting all the attention or love of another person. **2** (of a word) indicating the person or thing that something belongs to. **possessiveness** *n*

possible *adj* **1** able to exist, happen, or be done. **2** worthy of consideration. ♦ *n* **3** person or thing that might be suitable or chosen. **possibility** *n, pl* **-ties** **possibly** *adv* perhaps, not necessarily.

possum *n* same as OPOSSUM; *Aust & NZ* same as PHALANGER. **play possum** pretend to be dead or asleep to deceive an opponent.

post[1] *n* **1** official system of delivering letters and parcels. **2** (single collection or delivery of) letters and parcels sent by this system. ♦ *v* **3** send by post. **keep someone posted** supply someone regularly with the latest information. **postage** *n* charge for sending a letter or parcel by post. **postal** *adj* **postal order** *Brit* written money order sent by post and cashed at a post office by the person who receives it. **postbag** *n* **1** postman's bag. **2** post received by a magazine, famous person, etc. **postcode** *n* system of letters and numbers used to aid the sorting of mail. **postie** *n Scot, Austral & NZ informal* postman. **postman, postwoman** *n* person who collects and delivers post. **postmark** *n* official mark stamped on letters showing place and date of posting. **postmaster, postmistress** *n* (in some countries) official in charge of a post office. **post office** place where postal business is conducted. **post shop** *NZ* shop providing postal services.

post[2] *n* **1** length of wood, concrete, etc. fixed upright to support or mark something. ♦ *v* **2** put up (a notice) in a public place.

post[3] *n* **1** job. **2** position to which someone, esp. a soldier, is assigned for duty. **3** military establishment. ♦ *v* **4** send (a person) to a new place to work. **5** put (a guard etc.) on duty.

post- *prefix* after, later than, e.g.

postwar.

postcard *n* card for sending a message by post without an envelope.

postdate *v* write a date on (a cheque) that is later than the actual date.

poster *n* large picture or notice stuck on a wall.

posterior *n* 1 buttocks. ♦ *adj* 2 behind, at the back of.

posterity *n* future generations, descendants.

postern *n* small back door or gate.

postgraduate *n* person with a degree who is studying for a more advanced qualification.

posthaste *adv* with great speed.

posthumous [**poss**-tume-uss] *adj* occurring after one's death. **posthumously** *adv*

postilion, postillion *n Hist* person riding one of a pair of horses drawing a carriage.

postmortem *n* medical examination of a body to establish the cause of death.

postnatal *adj* occurring after childbirth.

postpone *v* put off to a later time. **postponement** *n*

postscript *n* passage added at the end of a letter.

postulant *n* candidate for admission to a religious order.

postulate *v* assume to be true as the basis of an argument or theory.

posture *n* 1 position or way in which someone stands, walks, etc. ♦ *v* 2 behave in an exaggerated way to get attention.

posy *n, pl* **-sies** small bunch of flowers.

pot[1] *n* 1 round deep container. 2 teapot. ♦ *pl* 3 *Informal* large amount. ♦ *v* **potting, potted** 4 plant in a pot. 5 *Snooker* hit (a ball) into a pocket. **potted** *adj* 1 grown in a pot. 2 (of meat or fish) cooked or preserved in a pot. 3 *Informal* abridged. **pot shot** shot taken without aiming carefully. **potting shed** shed where plants are potted.

pot[2] *n Slang* cannabis.

potable [**pote**-a-bl] *adj* drinkable.

potash *n* white powdery substance obtained from ashes and used as fertilizer.

potassium *n Chem* silvery metallic element.

potato *n, pl* **-toes** roundish starchy vegetable that grows underground.

poteen *n* (in Ireland) illegally made alcoholic drink.

potent *adj* 1 having great power or influence. 2 (of a male) capable of having sexual intercourse. **potency** *n*

potentate *n* ruler or monarch.

potential *adj* 1 possible but not yet actual. ♦ *n* 2 ability or talent not yet fully used. 3 *Electricity* level of electric pressure. **potentially** *adv* **potentiality** *n, pl* **-ties**

pothole *n* 1 hole in the surface of a road. 2 deep hole in a limestone area. **potholing** *n* sport of exploring underground caves. **potholer** *n*

potion *n* dose of medicine or poison.

potluck *n* **take potluck** accept whatever happens to be available.

potoroo *n, pl* **-roos** Australian leaping rodent.

potpourri [po-**poor**-ee] *n* 1 fragrant mixture of dried flower petals. 2 assortment or medley.

pottage *n Old-fashioned* thick soup or stew.

potter[1] *n* person who makes pottery.

potter[2] *v* be busy in a pleasant but aimless way.

pottery *n, pl* **-ries** 1 articles made from baked clay. 2 place where they are made.

potty[1] *adj* **-tier, -tiest** *Informal* crazy or

silly.

potty² *n, pl* **-ties** bowl used by a small child as a toilet.

pouch *n* 1 small bag. 2 baglike pocket of skin on an animal.

pouf, pouffe [**poof**] *n* large solid cushion used as a seat.

poulterer *n Brit* person who sells poultry.

poultice [**pole**-tiss] *n* moist dressing, often heated, applied to inflamed skin.

poultry *n* domestic fowls.

pounce *v* 1 spring upon suddenly to attack or capture. ♦ *n* 2 pouncing.

pound¹ *n* 1 monetary unit of Britain and some other countries. 2 unit of weight equal to 0.454 kg.

pound² *v* 1 hit heavily and repeatedly. 2 crush to pieces or powder. 3 (of the heart) throb heavily. 4 run heavily.

pound³ *n* enclosure for stray animals or officially removed vehicles.

pour *v* 1 flow or cause to flow out in a stream. 2 rain heavily. 3 come or go in large numbers.

pout *v* 1 thrust out one's lips, look sulky. ♦ *n* 2 pouting look.

poverty *n* 1 state of being without enough food or money. 2 lack of, scarcity.

POW prisoner of war.

powder *n* 1 substance in the form of tiny loose particles. 2 medicine or cosmetic in this form. ♦ *v* 3 apply powder to. **powdered** *adj* in the form of a powder, e.g. *powdered milk*. **powdery** *adj* **powder room** ladies' toilet.

power *n* 1 ability to do or act. 2 strength. 3 position of authority or control. 4 *Maths* product from continuous multiplication of a number by itself. 5 *Physics* rate at which work is done. 6 electricity supply. 7 particular form of energy, e.g. *nuclear power*.

powered *adj* having or operated by mechanical or electrical power. **powerful** *adj* **powerless** *adj* **power cut** temporary interruption in the supply of electricity. **power point** socket on a wall for plugging in electrical appliances. **power station** installation for generating and distributing electric power.

powwow *n Informal* talk or conference.

pox *n* 1 disease in which skin pustules form. 2 *Informal* syphilis.

pp (in signing a document) for and on behalf of.

pp. pages.

PPTA (in New Zealand) Post Primary Teachers Association.

PR 1 proportional representation. 2 public relations.

practicable *adj* 1 capable of being done successfully. 2 usable. **practicability** *n*

practical *adj* 1 involving experience or actual use rather than theory. 2 sensible, useful, and effective. 3 good at making or doing things. 4 in effect though not in name. ♦ *n* 5 examination in which something has to be done or made. **practically** *adv* **practical joke** trick intended to make someone look foolish.

practice *n* 1 something done regularly or habitually. 2 repetition of something so as to gain skill. 3 doctor's or lawyer's place of work. **in practice** what actually happens as opposed to what is supposed to happen. **put into practice** carry out.

☑ **SPELLING TIP**
It is extremely common for people to confuse the noun, **practice**, which has a *c* at the end, and the verb **practise**, which has an *s*.

practise *v* 1 do repeatedly so as to

gain skill. **2** take part in, follow (a religion etc.). **3** work at, e.g. *practise medicine*. **4** do habitually.

practitioner *n* person who practises a profession.

pragmatic *adj* concerned with practical consequences rather than theory. **pragmatism** *n* **pragmatist** *n*

prairie *n* large treeless area of grassland, esp. in N America and Canada. **prairie dog** rodent that lives in burrows in the N American prairies.

praise *v* **1** express approval or admiration of (someone or something). **2** express honour and thanks to (one's God). ♦ *n* **3** something said or written to show approval or admiration. **sing someone's praises** praise someone highly. **praiseworthy** *adj*

praline [**prah**-leen] *n* sweet made of nuts and caramelized sugar.

pram *n* four-wheeled carriage for a baby, pushed by hand.

prance *v* walk with exaggerated bouncing steps.

prang *v, n Slang* (have) a crash in a car or aircraft.

prank *n* mischievous trick.

prat *n Brit, Aust & NZ informal* stupid person.

prattle *v* **1** chatter in a childish or foolish way. ♦ *n* **2** childish or foolish talk.

prawn *n* edible shellfish like a large shrimp.

praxis *n* practice as opposed to theory.

pray *v* **1** say prayers. **2** ask earnestly, entreat.

prayer *n* **1** thanks or appeal addressed to one's God. **2** set form of words used in praying. **3** earnest request.

pre- *prefix* before, beforehand, e.g. *prenatal; prerecorded; preshrunk.*

preach *v* **1** give a talk on a religious theme as part of a church service. **2** speak in support of (an idea, principle, etc.).

preacher *n* person who preaches, esp. in church.

preamble *n* introductory part to something said or written.

prearranged *adj* arranged beforehand.

prebendary *n, pl* **-daries** clergyman who is a member of the chapter of a cathedral.

precarious *adj* insecure, unsafe, likely to fall or collapse. **precariously** *adv*

precaution *n* action taken in advance to prevent something bad happening. **precautionary** *adj*

precede *v* go or be before. **precedence** [**press**-ee-denss] *n* formal order of rank or position. **take precedence over** be more important than. **precedent** *n* previous case or occurrence regarded as an example to be followed.

precentor *n* person who leads the singing in a church.

precept *n* rule of behaviour. **preceptive** *adj*

precinct *n* **1** *Brit, Aust & S Afr* area in a town closed to traffic. **2** *Brit, Aust & S Afr* enclosed area round a building. **3** *US* administrative area of a city. ♦ *pl* **4** surrounding region.

precious *adj* **1** of great value and importance. **2** loved and treasured. **3** (of behaviour) affected, unnatural. **precious metal** gold, silver, or platinum. **precious stone** rare mineral, such as a ruby, valued as a gem.

precipice *n* very steep face of cliff or rockface. **precipitous** *adj* sheer.

precipitate *v* **1** cause to happen suddenly. **2** *Chem* cause to be deposited in solid form from a solution. **3** throw headlong. ♦ *adj* **4** done rashly or hastily. ♦ *n* **5** *Chem*

substance precipitated from a solution.
precipitately adv **precipitation** n 1 precipitating. 2 rain, snow, etc.
précis [**pray**-see] n, pl **précis** 1 short written summary of a longer piece. ♦ v 2 make a précis of.
precise adj 1 exact, accurate in every detail. 2 strict in observing rules or standards. **precisely** adv **precision** n
preclude v make impossible to happen.
precocious adj having developed or matured early or too soon. **precocity** n
precognition n alleged ability to foretell the future.
preconceived adj (of an idea) formed without real experience or reliable information. **preconception** n
precondition n something that must happen or exist before something else can.
precursor n 1 something that precedes and is a signal of something else, forerunner. 2 predecessor.
predate v 1 occur at an earlier date than. 2 write a date on (a document) that is earlier than the actual date.
predatory [**pred**-a-tree] adj habitually hunting and killing other animals for food. **predator** n predatory animal.
predecease v die before (someone else).
predecessor n 1 person who precedes another in an office or position. 2 ancestor.
predestination n Theology belief that future events have already been decided by God or fate. **predestined** adj
predetermined adj decided in advance.
predicament n embarrassing or difficult situation.
predicate n 1 Grammar part of a sentence in which something is said

about the subject, e.g. went home in I went home. ♦ v 2 declare or assert.
predict v tell about in advance, prophesy. **predictable** adj **prediction** n **predictive** adj 1 relating to or able to make predictions. 2 (of a word processer) able to complete words after only part of a word has been keyed.
predilection n Formal preference or liking.
predispose v 1 influence (someone) in favour of something. 2 make (someone) susceptible to something. **predisposition** n
predominate v be the main or controlling element. **predominance** n **predominant** adj **predominantly** adv
pre-eminent adj excelling all others, outstanding. **pre-eminence** n
pre-empt v prevent an action by doing something which makes it pointless or impossible. **pre-emption** n **pre-emptive** adj
preen v (of a bird) clean or trim (feathers) with the beak. **preen oneself** 1 smarten oneself. 2 show self-satisfaction.
prefab n prefabricated house.
prefabricated adj (of a building) manufactured in shaped sections for rapid assembly on site.
preface [**pref**-iss] n 1 introduction to a book. ♦ v 2 serve as an introduction to (a book, speech, etc.). **prefatory** adj
prefect n 1 senior pupil in a school, with limited power over others. 2 senior administrative officer in some countries. **prefecture** n office or area of authority of a prefect.
prefer v -ferring, -ferred 1 like better. 2 Law bring (charges) before a court. **preferable** adj more desirable. **preferably** adv **preference** n **preferential** adj showing preference.

preferment *n* promotion or advancement.

prefigure *v* represent or suggest in advance.

prefix *n* **1** letter or group of letters put at the beginning of a word to make a new word, such as *un-* in *unhappy.* ♦ *v* **2** put as an introduction or prefix (to).

pregnant *adj* **1** carrying a fetus in the womb. **2** full of meaning or significance, e.g. *a pregnant pause.* **pregnancy** *n, pl* **-cies**

prehensile *adj* capable of grasping.

prehistoric *adj* of the period before written history begins. **prehistory** *n*

prejudice *n* **1** unreasonable or unfair dislike or preference. ♦ *v* **2** cause (someone) to have a prejudice. **3** harm, cause disadvantage to. **prejudicial** *adj* disadvantageous, harmful.

☑ SPELLING TIP

There are examples in the Bank of English of **prejudice** being misspelt as *predjudice*, with an extra *d*. Although *d* often combines with *g* in English, it is not necessary before *j*.

---

prelate [**prel**-it] *n* bishop or other churchman of high rank.

preliminary *adj* **1** happening before and in preparation, introductory. ♦ *n, pl* **-naries 2** preliminary remark, contest, etc.

prelude *n* **1** introductory movement in music. **2** event preceding and introducing something else.

premarital *adj* occurring before marriage.

premature *adj* **1** happening or done before the normal or expected time. **2** (of a baby) born before the end of the normal period of pregnancy. **prematurely** *adv*

premeditated *adj* planned in advance. **premeditation** *n*

premenstrual *adj* occurring or experienced before a menstrual period, e.g. *premenstrual tension.*

premier *n* **1** prime minister. ♦ *adj* **2** chief, leading. **premiership** *n*

première *n* first performance of a play, film, etc.

premise, premiss *n* statement assumed to be true and used as the basis of reasoning.

premises *pl n* house or other building and its land.

premium *n* **1** additional sum of money, as on a wage or charge. **2** (regular) sum paid for insurance. **at a premium** in great demand because scarce. **premium bonds** (in Britain) savings certificates issued by the government, on which no interest is paid but cash prizes can be won.

premonition *n* feeling that something unpleasant is going to happen; foreboding. **premonitory** *adj*

prenatal *adj* before birth, during pregnancy.

preoccupy *v* **-pying, -pied** fill the thoughts or attention of (someone) to the exclusion of other things. **preoccupation** *n*

preordained *adj* decreed or determined in advance.

prep. **1** preparatory. **2** preposition.

prepacked *adj* sold already wrapped.

prepaid *adj* paid for in advance.

prepare *v* make or get ready. **prepared** *adj* **1** willing. **2** ready. **preparation** *n* **1** preparing. **2** something done in readiness for something else. **3** mixture prepared for use as a cosmetic, medicine, etc. **preparatory** [prip-**par**-a-tree] *adj* preparing for. **preparatory school** *Brit & S Afr* private school for children between 7 and 13.

preponderance n greater force, amount, or influence. **preponderant** adj

preposition n word used before a noun or pronoun to show its relationship with other words, such as by in go by bus. **prepositional** adj

prepossessing adj making a favourable impression, attractive.

preposterous adj utterly absurd.

prep school n short for PREPARATORY SCHOOL.

prepuce [**pree**-pyewss] n retractable fold of skin covering the tip of the penis, foreskin.

prerecorded adj recorded in advance to be played or broadcast later.

prerequisite n, adj (something) required before something else is possible.

prerogative n special power or privilege.

☑ SPELLING TIP

The way **prerogative** is often pronounced is presumably the reason why *perogative* is a common way of misspelling it.

---

presage [**press**-ij] v be a sign or warning of.

Presbyterian n, adj (member) of a Protestant church governed by lay elders. **Presbyterianism** n

presbytery n, pl -**teries** 1 *Presbyterian Church* local church court. 2 *RC Church* priest's house.

prescience [**press**-ee-enss] n knowledge of events before they happen. **prescient** adj

prescribe v 1 recommend the use of (a medicine). 2 lay down as a rule. **prescription** n written instructions from a doctor for the making up and use of a medicine. **prescriptive** adj laying down rules.

presence n 1 fact of being in a specified place. 2 impressive dignified appearance. **presence of mind** ability to act sensibly in a crisis.

present[1] adj 1 being in a specified place. 2 existing or happening now. 3 *Grammar* (of a verb tense) indicating that the action specified is taking place now. ♦ n 4 present time or tense. **presently** adv 1 soon. 2 *US & Scot* now.

present[2] n 1 something given to bring pleasure to another person. ♦ v 2 introduce formally or publicly. 3 introduce and compere (a TV or radio show). 4 cause, e.g. *present a difficulty*. 5 give, award. **presentation** n **presentable** adj attractive, neat, fit for people to see. **presenter** n person introducing a TV or radio show.

presentiment [priz-**zen**-tim-ent] n sense of something unpleasant about to happen.

preserve v 1 keep from being damaged, changed, or ended. 2 treat (food) to prevent it decaying. ♦ n 3 area of interest restricted to a particular person or group. 4 fruit preserved by cooking in sugar. 5 area where game is kept for private hunting or fishing. **preservation** n **preservative** n chemical that prevents decay.

preshrunk adj (of fabric or a garment) having been shrunk during manufacture so that further shrinkage will not occur when washed.

preside v be in charge, esp. of a meeting.

president n 1 head of state in many countries. 2 head of a society, institution, etc. **presidential** adj **presidency** n, pl -**cies**

press[1] v 1 apply force or weight to. 2 squeeze. 3 smooth by applying pressure or heat. 4 urge insistently. 5

crowd, push. ♦ n **6** printing machine.
pressed for short of. **pressing** adj
urgent. **press box** room at a sports
ground reserved for reporters. **press
conference** interview for reporters
given by a celebrity.

press² v **press into service** force to be
involved or used. **press gang** Hist
group of men used to capture men
and boys and force them to join the
navy.

pressure n **1** force produced by
pressing. **2** urgent claims or demands.
3 Physics force applied to a surface per
unit of area. **pressure cooker** airtight
pot which cooks food quickly by steam
under pressure. **pressure group**
group that tries to influence policies,
public opinion, etc.

prestidigitation n skilful quickness
with the hands, conjuring.

prestige n high status or respect
resulting from success or
achievements. **prestigious** adj

presto adv Music very quickly.

prestressed adj (of concrete)
containing stretched steel wires to
strengthen it.

presume v **1** suppose to be the case. **2**
dare (to). **presumably** adv one
supposes (that). **presumption** n **1**
bold insolent behaviour. **2** strong
probability. **presumptive** adj
assumed to be true or valid until the
contrary is proved. **presumptuous**
adj doing things one has no right to
do.

presuppose v need as a previous
condition in order to be true.
presupposition n

pretend v claim or give the
appearance of (something untrue) to
deceive or in play. **pretender** n
person who makes a false or disputed
claim to a position of power.
pretence n behaviour intended to

deceive, pretending. **pretentious** adj
making (unjustified) claims to special
merit or importance. **pretension** n

preternatural adj beyond what is
natural, supernatural.

pretext n false reason given to hide the
real one.

pretty adj **-tier, -tiest 1** pleasing to
look at. ♦ adv **2** fairly, moderately, e.g.
I'm pretty certain. **prettily** adv
prettiness n

pretzel n brittle salted biscuit.

prevail v **1** gain mastery. **2** be generally
established. **prevailing** adj **1**
widespread. **2** predominant.
prevalence n **prevalent** adj
widespread, common.

prevaricate v avoid giving a direct or
truthful answer. **prevarication** n

prevent v keep from happening or
doing. **preventable** adj **prevention**
n **preventive** adj, n

preview n advance showing of a film
or exhibition before it is shown to the
public.

previous adj coming or happening
before. **previously** adv

prey n **1** animal hunted and killed for
food by another animal. **2** victim.
bird of prey bird that kills and eats
other birds or animals. **prey on** v **1**
hunt and kill for food. **2** worry, obsess.

price n **1** amount of money for which a
thing is bought or sold. **2** unpleasant
thing that must be endured to get
something desirable. ♦ v **3** fix or ask
the price of. **priceless** adj **1** very
valuable. **2** Informal very funny.
pricey adj **pricier, priciest** Informal
expensive.

prick v **1** pierce lightly with a sharp
point. **2** cause to feel mental pain. **3**
(of an animal) make (the ears) stand
erect. ♦ n **4** sudden sharp pain caused
by pricking. **5** mark made by pricking.
6 remorse. **prick up one's ears** listen

intently.

prickle n 1 thorn or spike on a plant. ♦ v 2 have a tingling or pricking sensation. **prickly** adj **prickly heat** itchy rash occurring in hot moist weather.

pride n 1 feeling of pleasure and satisfaction when one has done well. 2 too high an opinion of oneself. 3 sense of dignity and self-respect. 4 something that causes one to feel pride. 5 group of lions. **pride of place** most important position. **pride oneself on** feel pride about.

priest n 1 (in the Christian church) a person who can administer the sacraments and preach. 2 (in some other religions) an official who performs religious ceremonies. **priestess** n fem **priesthood** n **priestly** adj

prig n self-righteous person who acts as if superior to others. **priggish** adj

prim adj **primmer, primmest** formal, proper, and rather prudish. **primly** adv

prima ballerina n leading female ballet dancer.

primacy n, pl -cies 1 state of being first in rank, grade, etc. 2 office of an archbishop.

prima donna n 1 leading female opera singer. 2 Informal temperamental person.

primaeval adj same as PRIMEVAL.

prima facie [**prime**-a **fay**-shee] adv Latin as it seems at first.

primal adj of basic causes or origins.

primary adj 1 chief, most important. 2 being the first stage, elementary. **primarily** adv **primary colours** (in physics) red, green, and blue or (in art) red, yellow, and blue, from which all other colours can be produced by mixing. **primary school** school for children from five to eleven years or (in New Zealand) between five to thirteen years.

primate[1] n member of an order of mammals including monkeys and humans.

primate[2] n archbishop.

prime adj 1 main, most important. 2 of the highest quality. ♦ n 3 time when someone is at his or her best or most vigorous. ♦ v 4 give (someone) information in advance to prepare them for something. 5 prepare (a surface) for painting. 6 prepare (a gun, pump, etc.) for use. **primer** n special paint applied to bare wood etc. before the main paint. **Prime Minister** leader of a government. **prime number** number that can be divided exactly only by itself and one.

primer n beginners' school book or manual.

primeval [prime-**ee**-val] adj of the earliest age of the world.

primitive adj 1 of an early simple stage of development. 2 basic, crude.

primogeniture n system under which the eldest son inherits all his parents' property.

primordial adj existing at or from the beginning.

primrose n pale yellow spring flower.

primula n type of primrose with brightly coloured flowers.

Primus n ® portable cooking stove used esp. by campers.

prince n 1 male member of a royal family, esp. the son of the king or queen. 2 male ruler of a small country. **princely** adj 1 of or like a prince. 2 generous, lavish, or magnificent. **Prince of Wales** eldest son of the British sovereign. **princess** n female member of a royal family, esp. the daughter of the king or queen. **Princess Royal** title sometimes given to the eldest daughter of the British sovereign.

principal *adj* 1 main, most important.
♦ *n* 2 head of a school or college. 3 person taking a leading part in something. 4 sum of money lent on which interest is paid. **principally** *adv*

principality *n, pl* **-ties** territory ruled by a prince.

principle *n* 1 moral rule guiding behaviour. 2 general or basic truth. 3 scientific law concerning the working of something. **in principle** in theory but not always in practice. **on principle** because of one's beliefs.

print *v* 1 reproduce (a newspaper, book, etc.) in large quantities by mechanical or electronic means. 2 reproduce (text or pictures) by pressing ink onto paper etc. 3 write in letters that are not joined up. 4 stamp (fabric) with a design. 5 *Photog* produce (pictures) from negatives. ♦ *n* 6 printed words etc. 7 printed copy of a painting. 8 printed lettering. 9 photograph. 10 printed fabric. 11 mark left on a surface by something that has pressed against it. **out of print** no longer available from a publisher. **printer** *n* 1 person or company engaged in printing. 2 machine that prints. **printing** *n* **printed circuit** electronic circuit with wiring printed on an insulating base. **print-out** *n* printed information from a computer.

prior[1] *adj* earlier. **prior to** before.

prior[2] *n* head monk in a priory. **prioress** *n* deputy head nun in a convent. **priory** *n, pl* **-ries** home of certain orders of monks or nuns.

priority *n, pl* **-ties** 1 most important thing that must be dealt with first. 2 right to be or go before others.

prise *v* force open by levering.

prism *n* transparent block usu. with triangular ends and rectangular sides, used to disperse light into a spectrum or refract it in optical instruments.

prismatic *adj* 1 of or shaped like a prism. 2 (of colour) as if produced by refraction through a prism, rainbow-like.

prison *n* building where criminals and accused people are held.

prisoner *n* person held captive. **prisoner of war** serviceman captured by an enemy in wartime.

prissy *adj* **-sier, -siest** prim, correct, and easily shocked. **prissily** *adv*

pristine *adj* clean, new, and unused.

private *adj* 1 for the use of one person or group only. 2 secret. 3 personal, unconnected with one's work. 4 owned or paid for by individuals rather than by the government. 5 quiet, not likely to be disturbed. ♦ *n* 6 soldier of the lowest rank. **privately** *adv* **privacy** *n*

privateer *n* 1 *Hist* privately owned armed vessel authorized by the government to take part in a war. 2 captain of such a ship.

privation *n* loss or lack of the necessities of life.

privatize *v* sell (a publicly owned company) to individuals or a private company. **privatization** *n*

privet *n* bushy evergreen hedge shrub.

privilege *n* advantage or favour that only some people have. **privileged** *adj* enjoying a special right or immunity.

☑ **SPELLING TIP**

Although the Bank of English shows that people find it difficult to decide whether to use *is* or *es* when spelling **privilege**, the commonest mistake is to insert an extra *d* to make *prividilege*. The adjective, **privileged**, should not have a *d* in the middle either.

---

privy *adj* 1 sharing knowledge of something secret. ♦ *n, pl* **privies** 2 *Obs* toilet, esp. an outside one. **Privy Council** private council of the British monarch.

prize[1] n **1** reward given for success in a competition etc. ♦ adj **2** winning or likely to win a prize. **prizefighter** n boxer who fights for money.

prize[2] v value highly.

prize[3] v same as PRISE.

pro[1] adv, prep in favour of. **pros and cons** arguments for and against.

pro[2] n, pl **pros** Informal **1** professional. **2** prostitute.

pro- prefix **1** in favour of, e.g. pro-Russian. **2** instead of, e.g. pronoun.

probable adj likely to happen or be true. **probability** n, pl **-ties**

probably adv in all likelihood.

probate n **1** process of proving the validity of a will. **2** certificate stating that a will is genuine.

probation n **1** system of dealing with law-breakers, esp. juvenile ones, by placing them under supervision. **2** period when someone is assessed for suitability for a job etc. **probationer** n person on probation.

probe v **1** search into or examine closely. ♦ n **2** surgical instrument used to examine a wound, cavity, etc.

probiotic n **1** bacterium that protects the body from harmful bacteria. ♦ adj **2** relating to probiotics probiotic yogurts.

probity n honesty, integrity.

problem n **1** something difficult to deal with or solve. **2** question or puzzle set for solution. **problematic, problematical** adj

proboscis [pro-**boss**-iss] n **1** long trunk or snout. **2** elongated mouth of some insects.

procedure n way of doing something, esp. the correct or usual one. **procedural** adj

proceed v **1** start or continue doing. **2** Formal walk, go. **3** start a legal action. **4** arise from. **proceeds** pl n money obtained from an event or activity.

proceedings pl n **1** organized or related series of events. **2** minutes of a meeting. **3** legal action.

process n **1** series of actions or changes. **2** method of doing or producing something. ♦ v **3** handle or prepare by a special method of manufacture. **processed** adj (of food) treated to prevent it decaying. **processor** n

procession n line of people or vehicles moving forward together in order.

proclaim v declare publicly. **proclamation** n

proclivity n, pl **-ties** inclination, tendency.

procrastinate v put off taking action, delay. **procrastination** n

procreate v Formal produce offspring. **procreation** n

procurator fiscal n (in Scotland) law officer who acts as public prosecutor and coroner.

procure v **1** get, provide. **2** obtain (people) to act as prostitutes. **procurement** n **procurer, procuress** n person who obtains people to act as prostitutes.

prod v **prodding, prodded 1** poke with something pointed. **2** goad (someone) to take action. ♦ n **3** prodding.

prodigal adj recklessly extravagant, wasteful. **prodigality** n

prodigy n, pl **-gies 1** person with some marvellous talent. **2** wonderful thing. **prodigious** adj **1** very large, immense. **2** wonderful. **prodigiously** adv

produce v **1** bring into existence. **2** present to view, show. **3** make, manufacture. **4** present on stage, film, or television. ♦ n **5** food grown for sale. **producer** n 1 person with control over the making of a film, record, etc. 2 person or company that produces something.

product n 1 something produced. 2 number resulting from multiplication. **production** n 1 producing. 2 things produced. 3 presentation of a play, opera, etc. **productive** adj 1 producing large quantities. 2 useful, profitable. **productivity** n

profane adj 1 showing disrespect for religion or holy things. 2 (of language) coarse, blasphemous. ♦ v 3 treat (something sacred) irreverently, desecrate. **profanation** n act of profaning. **profanity** n, pl -ties profane conversation or behaviour, blasphemy.

profess v 1 state or claim (something as true), sometimes falsely. 2 have as one's belief or religion. **professed** adj supposed.

profession n 1 type of work, such as being a doctor, that needs special training. 2 all the people employed in a profession, e.g. *the legal profession*. 3 declaration of a belief or feeling. **professional** adj 1 working in a profession. 2 taking part in an activity, such as sport or music, for money. 3 very competent. ♦ n 4 person who works in a profession. 5 person paid to take part in sport, music, etc. **professionally** adv **professionalism** n

professor n teacher of the highest rank in a university. **professorial** adj **professorship** n

proffer v offer.

proficient adj skilled, expert. **proficiency** n

profile n 1 outline, esp. of the face, as seen from the side. 2 brief biographical sketch.

profit n 1 money gained. 2 benefit obtained. ♦ v 3 gain or benefit. **profitable** adj making profit. **profitably** adv **profitability** n **profiteer** n person who makes excessive profits at the expense of the public. **profiteering** n

profligate adj 1 recklessly extravagant. 2 shamelessly immoral. ♦ n 3 profligate person. **profligacy** n

pro forma adj Latin prescribing a set form.

profound adj 1 showing or needing great knowledge. 2 strongly felt, intense. **profundity** n, pl -ties

profuse adj plentiful. **profusion** n

progeny [**proj**-in-ee] n, pl -nies children. **progenitor** [pro-**jen**-it-er] n ancestor.

progesterone n hormone which prepares the womb for pregnancy and prevents further ovulation.

prognosis n, pl -noses 1 doctor's forecast about the progress of an illness. 2 any forecast.

prognostication n forecast or prediction.

program n 1 sequence of coded instructions for a computer. ♦ v -gramming, -grammed 2 arrange (data) so that it can be processed by a computer. 3 feed a program into (a computer). **programmer** n **programmable** adj

programme n 1 planned series of events. 2 broadcast on radio or television. 3 list of items or performers in an entertainment.

progress n 1 improvement, development. 2 movement forward. ♦ v 3 become more advanced or skilful. 4 move forward. **in progress** taking place. **progression** n **progressive** adj 1 favouring political or social reform. 2 happening gradually by steps or degrees. **progressively** adv

prohibit v forbid or prevent from happening. **prohibition** n 1 act of forbidding. 2 ban on the sale or drinking of alcohol. **prohibitive** adj (of prices) too high to be affordable. **prohibitively** adv

project n 1 planned scheme to do or examine something over a period. ◆ v 2 make a forecast based on known data. 3 make (a film or slide) appear on a screen. 4 communicate (an impression). 5 stick out beyond a surface or edge. **projector** n apparatus for projecting photographic images, films, or slides on a screen. **projection** n **projectionist** n person who operates a projector.

projectile n object thrown as a weapon or fired from a gun.

prolapse n slipping down of an internal organ of the body from its normal position.

prole adj, n Chiefly Brit slang proletarian.

proletariat [pro-lit-**air**-ee-at] n working class. **proletarian** adj, n

proliferate v grow or reproduce rapidly. **proliferation** n

prolific adj very productive. **prolifically** adv

prolix adj (of speech or a piece of writing) overlong and boring.

prologue n introduction to a play or book.

prolong v make (something) last longer. **prolongation** n

prom n short for PROMENADE or PROMENADE CONCERT.

promenade n 1 Chiefly Brit paved walkway along the seafront at a holiday resort. ◆ v, n 2 Old-fashioned (take) a leisurely walk. **promenade concert** Brit concert at which part of the audience stands rather than sits.

prominent adj 1 very noticeable. 2 famous, widely known. **prominently** adv **prominence** n

promiscuous adj having many casual sexual relationships. **promiscuity** n

promise v 1 say that one will definitely do or not do something. 2 show signs of, seem likely. ◆ n 3 undertaking to do or not to do something. 4 indication of future success. **promising** adj likely to succeed or turn out well.

promo n, pl -mos Informal short film to promote a product.

promontory n, pl -ries point of high land jutting out into the sea.

promote v 1 help to make (something) happen or increase. 2 raise to a higher rank or position. 3 encourage the sale of by advertising. **promoter** n person who organizes or finances an event et, esp. a sporting one. **promotion** n **promotional** adj

prompt v 1 cause (an action). 2 remind (an actor or speaker) of words that he or she has forgotten. ◆ adj 3 done without delay. ◆ adv 4 exactly, e.g. six o'clock prompt. **promptly** adv immediately, without delay. **promptness** n **prompter, prompt** n person offstage who prompts actors.

promulgate v 1 put (a law etc.) into effect by announcing it officially. 2 make widely known. **promulgation** n

prone adj 1 (foll. by to) likely to do or be affected by (something). 2 lying face downwards.

prong n one spike of a fork or similar instrument. **pronged** adj

pronoun n word, such as she or it, used to replace a noun.

pronounce v 1 form the sounds of (words or letters), esp. clearly or in a particular way. 2 declare formally or officially. **pronounceable** adj **pronounced** adj very noticeable. **pronouncement** n formal announcement. **pronunciation** n way in which a word or language is pronounced.

☑ **SPELLING TIP**
The noun **pronunciation**, which appears in the Bank of English 823 times, is spelt *pronounciation* 21 times, probably because of the way **pronounce** is spelt. Remember, there is no o between the n and the u.

pronto adv Informal at once.
proof n 1 evidence that shows that something is true or has happened. 2 copy of something printed, such as the pages of a book, for checking before final production. 3 adj 4 able to withstand, e.g. *proof against criticism.* 5 denoting the strength of an alcoholic drink, e.g. *seventy proof.* **proofread** v read and correct (printer's proofs). **proofreader** n
prop[1] v propping, propped 1 support (something) so that it stays upright or in place. ♦ n 2 pole, beam, etc. used as a support.
prop[2] n movable object used on the set of a film or play.
prop[3] n Informal propeller.
propaganda n (organized promotion of) information to assist or damage the cause of a government or movement. **propagandist** n
propagate v 1 spread (information and ideas). 2 reproduce, breed, or grow. **propagation** n
propane n flammable gas found in petroleum and used as a fuel.
propel v -pelling, -pelled cause to move forward. **propellant** n 1 something that provides or causes propulsion. 2 gas used in an aerosol spray. **propulsion** n 1 method by which something is propelled. 2 act of propelling or state of being propelled.
propeller n revolving shaft with blades for driving a ship or aircraft.

propensity n, pl -ties natural tendency.
proper adj 1 real or genuine. 2 suited to a particular purpose. 3 correct in behaviour. 4 excessively moral. 5 Brit, Aust & NZ informal complete. **properly** adv
property n, pl -ties 1 something owned. 2 possessions collectively. 3 land or buildings owned by somebody. 4 quality or attribute.
prophet n 1 person supposedly chosen by God to spread His word. 2 person who predicts the future. **prophetic** adj **prophetically** adv **prophecy** n, pl -cies 1 prediction. 2 message revealing God's will. **prophesy** v -sying, -sied foretell.
prophylactic n, adj (drug) used to prevent disease.
propitiate v appease, win the favour of. **propitiation** n **propitious** adj favourable or auspicious.
proponent n person who argues in favour of something.
proportion n 1 relative size or extent. 2 correct relation between connected parts. 3 part considered with respect to the whole. ♦ pl 4 dimensions or size. ♦ v 5 adjust in relative amount or size. **in proportion** 1 comparable in size, rate of increase, etc. 2 without exaggerating. **proportional, proportionate** adj being in proportion. **proportionally, proportionately** adv
propose v 1 put forward for consideration. 2 nominate. 3 intend or plan (to do). 4 make an offer of marriage. **proposal** n **proposition** n 1 offer. 2 statement or assertion. 3 Maths theorem. 4 Informal thing to be dealt with. ♦ v 5 Informal ask (someone) to have sexual intercourse.
propound v put forward for consideration.

proprietor n owner of a business establishment. **proprietress** n fem **proprietary** adj **1** made and distributed under a trade name. **2** denoting or suggesting ownership.

propriety n, pl **-ties** correct conduct.

propulsion n see PROPEL.

pro rata adv, adj Latin in proportion.

prorogue v suspend (parliament) without dissolving it. **prorogation** n

prosaic [pro-**zay**-ik] adj lacking imagination, dull. **prosaically** adv

proscenium n, pl **-nia**, **-niums** arch in a theatre separating the stage from the auditorium.

proscribe v prohibit, outlaw. **proscription** n **proscriptive** adj

prose n ordinary speech or writing in contrast to poetry.

prosecute v **1** bring a criminal charge against. **2** continue to do. **prosecution** n **prosecutor** n

proselyte [**pross**-ill-ite] n recent convert.

proselytize [**pross**-ill-it-ize] v attempt to convert.

prospect n **1** something anticipated. **2** Old-fashioned view from a place. ♦ pl **3** probability of future success. ♦ v **4** explore, esp. for gold. **prospective** adj **1** future. **2** expected. **prospector** n **prospectus** n booklet giving details of a university, company, etc.

prosper v be successful. **prosperity** n success and wealth. **prosperous** adj

prostate n gland in male mammals that surrounds the neck of the bladder.

prosthesis [pross-**theess**-iss] n, pl **-ses** [-seez] artificial body part, such as a limb or breast. **prosthetic** adj

prostitute n **1** person who offers sexual intercourse in return for payment. ♦ v **2** make a prostitute of. **3** offer (oneself or one's talents) for unworthy purposes. **prostitution** n

prostrate adj **1** lying face downwards. **2** physically or emotionally exhausted. ♦ v **3** lie face downwards. **4** exhaust physically or emotionally. **prostration** n

protagonist n **1** supporter of a cause. **2** leading character in a play or a story.

protea [**pro**-tee-a] n African shrub with showy flowers.

protean [pro-**tee**-an] adj constantly changing.

protect v defend from trouble, harm, or loss. **protection** n **protectionism** n policy of protecting industries by taxing competing imports. **protectionist** n, adj **protective** adj **1** giving protection, e.g. protective clothing. **2** tending or wishing to protect someone. **protector** n **1** person or thing that protects. **2** regent. **protectorate** n **1** territory largely controlled by a stronger state. **2** (period of) rule of a regent.

protégé, (fem) **protégée** [**pro**-ti-zhay] n person who is protected and helped by another.

protein n any of a group of complex organic compounds that are essential for life.

pro tempore adv, adj for the time being (also **pro tem**).

protest n **1** declaration or demonstration of objection. ♦ v **2** object, disagree. **3** assert formally. **protestation** n strong declaration.

Protestant n **1** follower of any of the Christian churches that split from the Roman Catholic Church in the sixteenth century. ♦ adj **2** of or relating to such a church. **Protestantism** n

proto- combining form first, e.g. protohuman.

protocol n rules of behaviour for formal occasions.

proton n positively charged particle in the nucleus of an atom.

protoplasm n substance forming the living contents of a cell.

prototype n original or model to be copied or developed.

protozoan [pro-toe-**zoe**-an] n, pl -**zoa** microscopic one-celled creature.

protracted adj lengthened or extended.

protractor n instrument for measuring angles.

protrude v stick out, project. **protrusion** n

protuberant adj swelling out, bulging. **protuberance** n

proud adj 1 feeling pleasure and satisfaction. 2 feeling honoured. 3 thinking oneself superior to other people. 4 dignified. **proudly** adv

prove v proving, proved, proved or proven 1 establish the validity of. 2 demonstrate, test. 3 be found to be. **proven** adj known from experience to work.

provenance [**prov**-in-anss] n place of origin.

provender n Old-fashioned fodder.

proverb n short saying that expresses a truth or gives a warning. **proverbial** adj

provide v make available. **provider** n **provided that, providing** on condition that. **provide for** v 1 take precautions (against). 2 support financially.

providence n God or nature seen as a protective force that arranges people's lives. **provident** adj 1 thrifty. 2 showing foresight. **providential** adj lucky.

province n 1 area governed as a unit of a country or empire. 2 area of learning, activity, etc. ♦ pl 3 parts of a country outside the capital. **provincial** adj 1 of a province or the provinces. 2 unsophisticated and narrow-minded. ♦ n 3 unsophisticated

person. 4 person from a province or the provinces. **provincialism** n narrow-mindedness and lack of sophistication.

provision n 1 act of supplying something. 2 something supplied. 3 Law condition incorporated in a document. ♦ pl 4 food. ♦ v 5 supply with food. **provisional** adj temporary or conditional. **provisionally** adv

proviso [pro-**vize**-oh] n, pl -sos, -soes condition, stipulation.

provoke v 1 deliberately anger. 2 cause (an adverse reaction). **provocation** n **provocative** adj

provost n 1 head of certain university colleges in Britain. 2 chief councillor of a Scottish town.

prow n bow of a vessel.

prowess n 1 superior skill or ability. 2 bravery, fearlessness.

prowl v 1 move stealthily around a place as if in search of prey or plunder. ♦ n 2 prowling.

prowler n person who moves stealthily around a place as if in search of prey or plunder.

proximity n 1 nearness in space or time. 2 nearness or closeness in a series. **proximate** adj

proxy n, pl proxies 1 person authorized to act on behalf of someone else. 2 authority to act on behalf of someone else.

prude n person who is excessively modest, prim, or proper. **prudish** adj **prudery** n

prudent adj cautious, discreet, and sensible. **prudence** n **prudential** adj Old-fashioned prudent.

prune¹ n dried plum.

prune² v 1 cut off dead parts or excessive branches from (a tree or plant). 2 shorten, reduce.

prurient adj excessively interested in

sexual matters. **prurience** n

pry v **prying, pried** make an impertinent or uninvited inquiry into a private matter.

PS postscript.

PSA (in New Zealand) Public Service Association.

psalm n sacred song. **psalmist** n writer of psalms.

Psalter n book containing (a version of) psalms from the Bible. **psaltery** n, pl -ries ancient instrument played by plucking strings.

PSBR (in Britain) public sector borrowing requirement.

psephology [sef-**fol**-a-jee] n statistical study of elections.

pseud n Informal pretentious person.

pseudo- combining form false, pretending, or unauthentic, e.g. pseudoclassical.

pseudonym n fictitious name adopted esp. by an author. **pseudonymous** adj

psittacosis n disease of parrots that can be transmitted to humans.

psyche [**sye**-kee] n human mind or soul.

psychedelic adj **1** denoting a drug that causes hallucinations. **2** having vivid colours and complex patterns similar to those experienced during hallucinations.

☑ **SPELLING TIP**

The main problem with **psychedelic** is which vowel follows the ch; it should be e of course.

---

psychiatry n branch of medicine concerned with mental disorders. **psychiatric** adj **psychiatrist** n

psychic adj (also **psychical**) **1** having mental powers which cannot be explained by natural laws. **2** relating to the mind. ♦ n **3** person with psychic powers.

psycho n, pl -chos Informal psychopath.

psychoanalysis n method of treating mental and emotional disorders by discussion and analysis of one's thoughts and feelings. **psychoanalyse** v **psychoanalyst** n

psychology n, pl -gies **1** study of human and animal behaviour. **2** Informal person's mental make-up. **psychologist** n **psychological** adj **1** of or affecting the mind. **2** of psychology. **psychologically** adv

psychopath n person afflicted with a personality disorder causing him or her to commit antisocial or violent acts. **psychopathic** adj

psychosis n, pl -ses severe mental disorder in which the sufferer's contact with reality becomes distorted. **psychotic** adj

psychosomatic adj (of a physical disorder) thought to have psychological causes.

psychotherapy n treatment of nervous disorders by psychological methods. **psychotherapeutic** adj **psychotherapist** n

psych up v prepare (oneself) mentally for a contest or task.

pt 1 part. **2** point.

PT Old-fashioned physical training.

pt. pint.

PTA Parent-Teacher Association.

ptarmigan [**tar**-mig-an] n bird of the grouse family which turns white in winter.

pterodactyl [terr-roe-**dak**-til] n extinct flying reptile with batlike wings.

PTO please turn over.

ptomaine [**toe**-main] n any of a group of poisonous alkaloids found in decaying matter.

Pty Aust, NZ & S Afr Proprietary.

pub n building with a bar licensed to sell alcoholic drinks.

puberty n beginning of sexual

maturity. **pubertal** adj

pubic adj of the lower abdomen, e.g. *pubic hair*.

public adj 1 of or concerning the people as a whole. 2 for use by everyone. 3 well-known. 4 performed or made openly. ♦ n 5 the community, people in general. **publicly** adv **public house** pub. **public relations** promotion of a favourable opinion towards an organization among the public. **public school** private fee-paying school in Britain. **public-spirited** adj having or showing an active interest in the good of the community.

publican n Brit, Aust & NZ person who owns or runs a pub.

publicity n 1 process or information used to arouse public attention. 2 public interest so aroused. **publicist** n person, esp. a press agent or journalist, who publicizes something. **publicize** v bring to public attention.

publish v 1 produce and issue (printed matter) for sale. 2 announce formally or in public. **publication** n **publisher** n

puce adj purplish-brown.

puck[1] n small rubber disc used in ice hockey.

puck[2] n mischievous or evil spirit. **puckish** adj

pucker v 1 gather into wrinkles. ♦ n 2 wrinkle or crease.

pudding n 1 dessert, esp. a cooked one served hot. 2 savoury dish with pastry or batter, e.g. *steak-and-kidney pudding*. 3 sausage-like mass of meat, e.g. *black pudding*.

puddle n small pool of water, esp. of rain.

puerile adj silly and childish.

puerperal [pew-**er**-per-al] adj concerning the period following childbirth.

puff n 1 (sound of) a short blast of breath, wind, etc. 2 act of inhaling cigarette smoke. ♦ v 3 blow or breathe in short quick draughts. 4 take draws at (a cigarette). 5 send out in small clouds. 6 swell. **out of puff** out of breath. **puffy** adj **puffball** n ball-shaped fungus. **puff pastry** light flaky pastry.

puffin n black-and-white sea bird with a brightly-coloured beak.

pug n small snub-nosed dog. **pug nose** short stubby upturned nose.

pugilist [pew-jil-ist] n boxer. **pugilism** n **pugilistic** adj

pugnacious adj ready and eager to fight. **pugnacity** n

puissance [pwee-sonce] n showjumping competition that tests a horse's ability to jump large obstacles.

puke Slang ♦ v 1 vomit. ♦ n 2 act of vomiting. 3 vomited matter.

pulchritude n Lit beauty.

pull v 1 exert force on (an object) to move it towards the source of the force. 2 strain or stretch. 3 remove or extract. 4 attract. ♦ n 5 act of pulling. 6 force used in pulling. 7 act of taking in drink or smoke. 8 Informal power, influence. **pull in** v 1 (of a vehicle or driver) draw in to the side of the road or stop. 2 reach a destination. 3 attract in large numbers. 4 Brit, Aust & NZ slang arrest. **pull off** v Informal succeed in performing. **pull out** v 1 (of a vehicle or driver) move away from the side of the road or move out to overtake. 2 (of a train) depart. 3 withdraw. 4 remove by pulling. **pull up** v 1 (of a vehicle or driver) stop. 2 remove by the roots. 3 reprimand.

pullet n young hen.

pulley n wheel with a grooved rim in which a belt, chain, or piece of rope runs in order to lift weights by a downward pull.

Pullman n, pl **-mans** luxurious railway coach.

pullover n sweater that is pulled on over the head.

pulmonary adj of the lungs.

pulp n **1** soft wet substance made from crushed or beaten matter. **2** flesh of a fruit. **3** poor-quality books and magazines. ♦ v **4** reduce to pulp.

pulpit n raised platform for a preacher.

pulsar n small dense star which emits regular bursts of radio waves.

pulse[1] n **1** regular beating of blood through the arteries at each heartbeat. **2** any regular beat or vibration. **pulsate** v throb, quiver. **pulsation** n

pulse[2] n edible seed of a pod-bearing plant such as a bean or pea.

pulverize v **1** reduce to fine pieces. **2** destroy completely.

puma n large American wild cat with a greyish-brown coat.

pumice [**pumm**-iss] n light porous stone used for scouring.

pummel v **-melling, -melled** strike repeatedly with or as if with the fists.

pump[1] n **1** machine used to force a liquid or gas to move in a particular direction. ♦ v **2** raise or drive with a pump. **3** supply in large amounts. **4** operate or work in the manner of a pump. **5** extract information from.

pump[2] n light flat-soled shoe.

pumpkin n large round fruit with an orange rind, soft flesh, and many seeds.

pun n **1** use of words to exploit double meanings for humorous effect. ♦ v **punning, punned 2** make puns.

punch[1] v **1** strike at with a clenched fist. ♦ n **2** blow with a clenched fist. **3** Informal effectiveness or vigour. **punchy** adj forceful. **punch-drunk** adj dazed by or as if by repeated blows to the head.

punch[2] n **1** tool or machine for shaping, piercing, or engraving. ♦ v **2** pierce, cut, stamp, shape, or drive with a punch.

punch[3] n drink made from a mixture of wine, spirits, fruit, sugar, and spices.

punctilious adj **1** paying great attention to correctness in etiquette. **2** careful about small details.

punctual adj arriving or taking place at the correct time. **punctuality** n **punctually** adv

punctuate v **1** put punctuation marks in. **2** interrupt at frequent intervals. **punctuation** n (use of) marks such as commas, colons, etc. in writing, to assist in making the sense clear.

puncture n **1** small hole made by a sharp object, esp. in a tyre. ♦ v **2** pierce a hole in.

pundit n expert who speaks publicly on a subject.

pungent adj having a strong sharp bitter flavour. **pungency** n

punish v cause (someone) to suffer or undergo a penalty for some wrongdoing. **punishing** adj harsh or difficult. **punishment** n **punitive** [**pew**-nit-tiv] adj relating to punishment.

punk n **1** anti-Establishment youth movement and style of rock music of the late 1970s. **2** follower of this music. **3** worthless person.

punnet n small basket for fruit.

punt[1] n **1** open flat-bottomed boat propelled by a pole. ♦ v **2** travel in a punt.

punt[2] Sport ♦ n **1** kick of a ball before it touches the ground when dropped from the hands. ♦ v **2** kick (a ball) in this way.

punt[3] n former monetary unit of the Irish Republic.

punter n **1** person who bets. **2** Brit, Aust & NZ any member of the public.

puny *adj* **-nier, -niest** small and feeble.

pup *n* young of certain animals, such as dogs and seals.

pupa *n, pl* **-pae, -pas** insect at the stage of development between a larva and an adult.

pupil[1] *n* person who is taught by a teacher.

pupil[2] *n* round dark opening in the centre of the eye.

puppet *n* **1** small doll or figure moved by strings or by the operator's hand. **2** person or country controlled by another. **puppeteer** *n*

puppy *n, pl* **-pies** young dog.

purchase *v* **1** obtain by payment. ♦ *n* **2** thing that is bought. **3** act of buying. **4** leverage, grip. **purchaser** *n*

purdah *n* Muslim and Hindu custom of keeping women in seclusion, with clothing that conceals them completely when they go out.

pure *adj* **1** unmixed, untainted. **2** innocent. **3** complete, e.g. *pure delight.* **4** concerned with theory only, e.g. *pure mathematics.* **purely** *adv* **purity** *n* **purify** *v* **-fying, -fied** make or become pure. **purification** *n* **purist** *n* person concerned with strict obedience to the traditions of a subject.

purée [**pure**-ray] *n* **1** pulp of cooked food. ♦ *v* **-réeing, -réed 2** make into a purée.

purgatory *n* **1** place or state of temporary suffering. **2** (P-) *RC Church* place where souls of the dead undergo punishment for their sins before being admitted to Heaven. **purgatorial** *adj*

purge *v* **1** rid (a thing or place) of (unwanted things or people). ♦ *n* **2** purging. **purgative** *n, adj* (medicine) designed to cause defecation.

Puritan *n* **1** *Hist* member of the English Protestant group who wanted simpler church ceremonies. **2** (p-) person with strict moral and religious principles. **puritanical** *adj* **puritanism** *n*

purl *n* **1** stitch made by knitting a plain stitch backwards. ♦ *v* **2** knit in purl.

purlieus [**per**-lyooz] *pl n Lit* outskirts.

purloin *v* steal.

purple *adj, n* (of) a colour between red and blue.

purport *v* **1** claim (to be or do something). ♦ *n* **2** apparent meaning, significance.

purpose *n* **1** reason for which something is done or exists. **2** determination. **3** practical advantage or use, e.g. *use the time to good purpose.* **purposely** *adv* intentionally (also **on purpose**).

purr *v* **1** (of cats) make low vibrant sound, usu. when pleased. ♦ *n* **2** this sound.

purse *n* **1** small bag for money. **2** *US & NZ* handbag. **3** financial resources. **4** prize money. ♦ *v* **5** draw (one's lips) together into a small round shape. **purser** *n* ship's officer who keeps the accounts.

pursue *v* **1** chase. **2** follow (a goal). **3** engage in. **4** continue to discuss or ask about (something). **pursuer** *n* **pursuit** *n* **1** pursuing. **2** occupation or pastime.

☑ SPELLING TIP

The misspelling *persue* is very common, occurring in the Bank of English 52 times. It should, of course, be spelt with a *u* in each half of the word, as in **pursuing** and **pursued**.

---

purulent [**pure**-yoo-lent] *adj* of or containing pus.

purvey *v* supply (provisions). **purveyor** *n*

purview *n* scope or range of activity or outlook.

pus *n* yellowish matter produced by

infected tissue.

push v 1 move or try to move by steady force. **2** drive or spur (oneself or another person) to do something. **3** Informal sell (drugs) illegally. ♦ n **4** act of pushing. **5** special effort. **the push** Slang dismissal from a job or relationship. **pusher** n person who sells illegal drugs. **pushy** adj too assertive or ambitious. **pushchair** n Brit folding chair on wheels for a baby.

pusillanimous adj timid and cowardly. **pusillanimity** n

puss, pussy n, pl **pusses, pussies** Informal cat.

pussyfoot v Informal behave too cautiously.

pustule n pimple containing pus.

put v **putting, put 1** cause to be (in a position, state, or place). **2** express. **3** throw (the shot) in the shot put. ♦ n **4** throw in putting the shot. **put across** v express successfully. **put off** v **1** postpone. **2** disconcert. **3** repel. **put up** v **1** erect. **2** accommodate. **3** nominate. **put-upon** adj taken advantage of.

putative adj reputed, supposed.

putrid adj rotten and foul-smelling. **putrefy** v **-fying, -fied** rot and produce an offensive smell. **putrefaction** n **putrescent** adj rotting.

putsch n sudden violent attempt to remove a government from power.

putt Golf ♦ n **1** stroke on the putting green to roll the ball into or near the hole. ♦ v **2** strike (the ball) in this way.

putter n golf club for putting.

putty n adhesive used to fix glass into frames and fill cracks in woodwork.

puzzle v **1** perplex and confuse or be perplexed or confused. ♦ n **2** problem that cannot be easily solved. **3** toy, game, or question that requires skill or ingenuity to solve. **puzzlement** n **puzzling** adj

PVC polyvinyl chloride: plastic material used in clothes etc.

Pygmy n, pl **-mies 1** member of one of the very short peoples of Equatorial Africa. **2** adj **3** (**p-**) very small.

pyjamas pl n loose-fitting trousers and top worn in bed.

pylon n steel tower-like structure supporting electrical cables.

pyramid n **1** solid figure with a flat base and triangular sides sloping upwards to a point. **2** building of this shape, esp. an ancient Egyptian one. **pyramidal** adj

pyre n pile of wood for burning a corpse on.

Pyrex n ® heat-resistant glassware.

pyromania n uncontrollable urge to set things on fire. **pyromaniac** n

pyrotechnics n **1** art of making fireworks. **2** firework display. **pyrotechnic** adj

Pyrrhic victory [**pir**-ik] n victory in which the victor's losses are as great as those of the defeated.

python n large nonpoisonous snake that crushes its prey.

Q q

QC Queen's Counsel.

QED which was to be shown or proved.

Qld Queensland.

QM Quartermaster.

qr. 1 quarter. **2** quire.

qt. quart.

qua [**kwah**] *prep* in the capacity of.

quack¹ *v* **1** (of a duck) utter a harsh guttural sound. **2** *n* **3** sound made by a duck.

quack² *n* unqualified person who claims medical knowledge.

quad *n* **1** see QUADRANGLE. **2** *Informal* quadruplet. ♦ *adj* **3** short for QUADRAPHONIC. **quad bike, quad** vehicle like a small motorcycle with four large wheels, designed for agricultural and sporting uses.

quadrangle *n* **1** (also **quad**) rectangular courtyard with buildings on all four sides. **2** geometric figure consisting of four points connected by four lines. **quadrangular** *adj*

quadrant *n* **1** quarter of a circle. **2** quarter of a circle's circumference. **3** instrument for measuring the altitude of the stars.

quadraphonic *adj* using four independent channels to reproduce or record sound.

quadratic *Maths* ♦ *n* **1** equation in which the variable is raised to the power of two, but nowhere raised to a higher power. ♦ *adj* **2** of the second power.

quadrennial *adj* **1** occurring every four years. **2** lasting four years.

quadri- *combining form* four, e.g. *quadrilateral.*

quadrilateral *adj* **1** having four sides. ♦ *n* **2** polygon with four sides.

quadrille *n* square dance for four couples.

quadriplegia *n* paralysis of all four limbs.

quadruped [**kwod**-roo-ped] *n* any animal with four legs.

quadruple *v* **1** multiply by four. ♦ *adj* **2** four times as much or as many. **3** consisting of four parts.

quadruplet *n* one of four offspring born at one birth.

quaff [**kwoff**] *v* drink heartily or in one draught.

quagmire [**kwog**-mire] *n* soft wet area of land.

quail¹ *n* small game bird of the partridge family.

quail² *v* shrink back with fear.

quaint *adj* attractively unusual, esp. in an old-fashioned style. **quaintly** *adv*

quake *v* **1** shake or tremble with or as if with fear. ♦ *n* **2** *Informal* earthquake.

Quaker *n* member of a Christian sect, the Society of Friends. **Quakerism** *n*

qualify *v* -**fying, -fied 1** provide or be provided with the abilities necessary for a task, office, or duty. **2** moderate or restrict (a statement). **qualified** *adj* **qualification** *n* **1** official record of achievement in a course or examination. **2** quality or skill needed for a particular activity. **3** condition that modifies or limits. **4** act of qualifying.

quality *n, pl* -**ties 1** degree or standard of excellence. **2** distinguishing characteristic or attribute. **3** basic character or nature of something. ♦ *adj* **4** excellent or superior. **qualitative** *adj* of or relating to quality.

qualm [**kwahm**] *n* **1** pang of conscience. **2** sudden sensation of misgiving.

quandary *n, pl* **-ries** difficult situation or dilemma.

quandong [**kwon**-dong] *n* small Australian tree with edible fruit and nuts used in preserves Australian tree with pale timber.

quango *n, pl* **-gos** *Chiefly Brit* quasi-autonomous nongovernmental organization: any partly independent official body set up by a government.

quanta *n* plural of QUANTUM.

quantify *v* **-fying, -fied** discover or express the quantity of. **quantifiable** *adj* **quantification** *n*

quantity *n, pl* **-ties 1** specified or definite amount or number. **2** aspect of anything that can be measured, weighed, or counted. **quantitative** *adj* of or relating to quantity. **quantity surveyor** person who estimates the cost of the materials and labour necessary for a construction job.

quantum *n, pl* **-ta** desired or required amount, esp. a very small one. **quantum leap, jump** *Informal* sudden large change, increase, or advance. **quantum theory** physics theory based on the idea that energy of electrons is discharged in discrete quanta.

quarantine *n* **1** period of isolation of people or animals to prevent the spread of disease. ◆ *v* **2** isolate in or as if in quarantine.

quark *n* *Physics* subatomic particle thought to be the fundamental unit of matter.

quarrel *n* **1** angry disagreement. **2** cause of dispute. ◆ *v* **-relling, -relled 3** have a disagreement or dispute. **quarrelsome** *adj*

quarry¹ *n, pl* **-ries 1** place where stone is dug from the surface of the earth. ◆ *v* **-rying, -ried 2** extract (stone) from a quarry.

quarry² *n, pl* **-ries** person or animal that is being hunted.

quart *n* unit of liquid measure equal to two pints (1.136 litres).

quarter *n* **1** one of four equal parts of something. **2** fourth part of a year. **3** *Informal* unit of weight equal to 4 ounces. **4** region or district of a town or city. **5** *US* 25-cent piece. **6** mercy or pity, as shown towards a defeated opponent. **7** *pl* **8** lodgings. ◆ *v* **9** divide into four equal parts. **10** billet or be billeted in lodgings. **quarterly** *adj* **1** occurring, due, or issued at intervals of three months. ◆ *n* **2** magazine issued every three months. ◆ *adv* **3** once every three months. **quarter day** *Brit* any of the four days in the year when certain payments become due. **quarterdeck** *n* *Naut* rear part of the upper deck of a ship. **quarterfinal** *n* round before the semifinal in a competition. **quartermaster** *n* military officer responsible for accommodation, food, and equipment.

quartet *n* **1** group of four performers. **2** music for such a group.

quarto *n, pl* **-tos** book size in which the sheets are folded into four leaves.

quartz *n* hard glossy mineral.

quasar [**kway**-zar] *n* extremely distant starlike object that emits powerful radio waves.

quash *v* **1** annul or make void. **2** subdue forcefully and completely.

quasi- [**kway**-zie] *combining form* almost but not really, e.g. *quasi-religious; a quasi-scholar.*

quatrain *n* stanza or poem of four lines.

quaver *v* **1** (of a voice) quiver or tremble. ◆ *n* **2** *Music* note half the length of a crotchet. **3** tremulous sound or note.

quay [**kee**] *n* wharf built parallel to the shore.

queasy *adj* **-sier, -siest 1** having the

feeling that one is about to vomit. **2** feeling or causing uneasiness. **queasiness** n

queen n **1** female sovereign who is the official ruler or head of state. **2** wife of a king. **3** woman, place, or thing considered to be the best of her or its kind. **4** Slang effeminate male homosexual. **5** only fertile female in a colony of bees, wasps, or ants. **6** the most powerful piece in chess. **queenly** adj **Queen's Counsel** barrister or advocate appointed Counsel to the Crown.

queer adj **1** not normal or usual. **2** Brit faint, giddy, or queasy. **3** Offens homosexual. ◆ n **4** Offens homosexual. **queer someone's pitch** Informal spoil someone's chances of something.

☑ WORD TIP
Although the term queer meaning homosexual is still considered derogatory when used by non-homosexuals, it is now being used by homosexuals of themselves as a positive term: queer politics, queer cinema.

quell v **1** suppress. **2** overcome.

quench v **1** satisfy (one's thirst). **2** put out or extinguish.

quern n stone hand mill for grinding corn.

querulous [**kwer**-yoo-luss] adj complaining or whining. **querulously** adv

query n, pl **-ries 1** question, esp. one raising doubt. **2** question mark. ◆ v **-rying, -ried 3** express uncertainty, doubt, or an objection concerning (something).

quest n **1** long and difficult search. ◆ v **2** (foll. by for or after) go in search of.

question n **1** form of words addressed to a person in order to obtain an answer. **2** point at issue. **3** difficulty or uncertainty. ◆ v **4** put a question or questions to (a person). **5** express uncertainty about. **in question** under discussion. **out of the question** impossible. **questionable** adj of disputable value or authority. **questionably** adv **questionnaire** n set of questions on a form, used to collect information from people. **question mark 1** punctuation mark (?) written at the end of questions. **2**

☑ SPELLING TIP
There are 28 occurrences of the misspelling questionaire (with only one n), in the Bank of English. The correct spelling, **questionnaire**, has two ns, and appears in the Bank of English over 3000 times.

queue n **1** line of people or vehicles waiting for something. ◆ v **queuing** or **queueing, queued 2** (often foll. by up) form or remain in a line while waiting.

quibble v **1** make trivial objections. ◆ n **2** trivial objection.

quiche [**keesh**] n savoury flan with an egg custard filling to which vegetables etc. are added.

quick adj **1** speedy, fast. **2** lasting or taking a short time. **3** alert and responsive. **4** easily excited or aroused. ◆ n **5** area of sensitive flesh under a nail. ◆ adv **6** Informal in a rapid manner. **cut someone to the quick** hurt someone's feelings deeply. **quickly** adv **quicken** v **1** make or become faster. **2** make or become more lively. **quicklime** n white solid used in the manufacture of glass and steel. **quicksand** n deep mass of loose wet sand that sucks anything on top of it into it. **quicksilver** n mercury. **quickstep** n fast modern ballroom dance.

quid *n, pl* **quid** *Brit slang* pound (sterling).

quid pro quo *n, pl* **quid pro quos** one thing, esp. an advantage or object, given in exchange for another.

quiescent [kwee-**ess**-ent] *adj* quiet, inactive, or dormant. **quiescence** *n*

quiet *adj* 1 with little noise. 2 calm or tranquil. 3 untroubled. 4 *n* 5 quietness. ♦ *v* 6 make or become quiet. **on the quiet** without other people knowing, secretly. **quietly** *adv* **quietness** *n* **quieten** *v* (often foll. by *down*) make or become quiet. **quietude** *n* quietness, peace, or tranquillity.

quietism *n* passivity and calmness of mind towards external events.

quiff *n* tuft of hair brushed up above the forehead.

quill *n* 1 pen made from the feather of a bird's wing or tail. 2 stiff hollow spine of a hedgehog or porcupine.

quilt *n* padded covering for a bed. **quilted** *adj* consisting of two layers of fabric with a layer of soft material between them.

quin *n* short for QUINTUPLET.

quince *n* acid-tasting pear-shaped fruit.

quinine *n* bitter drug used as a tonic and formerly to treat malaria.

quinquennial *adj* 1 occurring every five years. 2 lasting five years.

quinsy *n* inflammation of the throat or tonsils.

quintessence *n* most perfect representation of a quality or state. **quintessential** *adj*

quintet *n* 1 group of five performers. 2 music for such a group.

quintuplet *n* one of five offspring born at one birth.

quip *n* 1 witty saying. ♦ *v* **quipping, quipped** 2 make a quip.

quire *n* set of 24 or 25 sheets of paper.

quirk *n* 1 peculiarity of character. 2 unexpected twist or turn, e.g. *a quirk of fate.* **quirky** *adj*

quisling *n* traitor who aids an occupying enemy force.

quit *v* **quitting, quit** 1 stop (doing something). 2 give up (a job). 3 depart from. **quitter** *n* person who lacks perseverance. **quits** *adj Informal* on an equal footing.

quite *adv* 1 somewhat, e.g. *she's quite pretty.* 2 absolutely, e.g. *you're quite right.* 3 in actuality, truly. ♦ *interj* 4 expression of agreement.

> ☑ **WORD TIP**
> Note that because *quite* can mean 'extremely': *quite amazing;* or can express a reservation: *quite friendly,* it should be used carefully.

quiver[1] *v* 1 shake with a tremulous movement. ♦ *n* 2 shaking or trembling.

quiver[2] *n* case for arrows.

quixotic [kwik-**sot**-ik] *adj* romantic and unrealistic. **quixotically** *adv*

quiz *n, pl* **quizzes** 1 entertainment in which the knowledge of the players is tested by a series of questions. ♦ *v* **quizzing, quizzed** 2 investigate by close questioning. **quizzical** *adj* questioning and mocking, e.g. *a quizzical look.* **quizzically** *adv*

quod *n Brit slang* jail.

quoit *n* 1 large ring used in the game of quoits. ♦ *pl* 2 game in which quoits are tossed at a stake in the ground in attempts to encircle it.

quokka *n* small Australian wallaby.

quorum *n* minimum number of people required to be present at a meeting before any transactions can take place.

quota *n* 1 share that is due from, due to, or allocated to a group or person. 2 prescribed number or quantity allowed, required, or admitted.

quote *v* **1** repeat (words) exactly from (an earlier work, speech, or conversation). **2** state (a price) for goods or a job of work. ◆ *n* **3** *Informal* quotation. **quotable** *adj* **quotation** *n* **1** written or spoken passage repeated exactly in a later work, speech, or conversation. **2** act of quoting. **3** estimate of costs submitted by a contractor to a prospective client. **quotation marks** raised commas used in writing to mark the beginning and end of a quotation or passage of speech.

quoth *v Obs* said.

quotidian *adj* **1** daily. **2** commonplace.

quotient *n* result of the division of one number or quantity by another.

q.v. which see: used to refer a reader to another item in the same book.

R r

r 1 radius. **2** ratio. **3** right.

R 1 Queen. **2** King. **3** River.

RA 1 (in Britain) Royal Academy. **2** (in Britain) Royal Artillery.

RAAF Royal Australian Air Force.

rabbi [**rab**-bye] *n, pl* **-bis** Jewish spiritual leader. **rabbinical** *adj*

rabbit *n* small burrowing mammal with long ears. **rabbit on** *v* **rabbiting, rabbited** *Brit informal* talk too much.

rabble *n* disorderly crowd of noisy people.

rabid *adj* **1** fanatical. **2** having rabies. **rabidly** *adv*

rabies [**ray**-beez] *n* usu. fatal viral disease transmitted by dogs and certain other animals.

RAC (in Britain) Royal Automobile Club.

raccoon *n* small N American mammal with a long striped tail.

race¹ *n* **1** contest of speed. **2** *pl* **3** meeting for horse racing. ♦ *v* **4** compete with in a race. **5** run swiftly. **6** (of an engine) run faster than normal. **racer** *n* **racecourse** *n* **racehorse** *n* **racetrack** *n*

race² *n* group of people of common ancestry with distinguishing physical features, such as skin colour. **racial** *adj* **racism, racialism** *n* hostile attitude or behaviour to members of other races, based on a belief in the innate superiority of one's own race. **racist, racialist** *adj, n*

raceme [rass-**eem**] *n* cluster of flowers along a central stem, as in the foxglove.

rack¹ *n* **1** framework for holding particular articles, such as coats or luggage. **2** *Hist* instrument of torture that stretched the victim's body. ♦ *v* **3** cause great suffering to. **rack one's brains** try very hard to remember.

rack² *n* **go to rack and ruin** be destroyed.

racket¹ *n* **1** noisy disturbance. **2** occupation by which money is made illegally.

racket², racquet *n* bat with strings stretched in an oval frame, used in tennis etc. **rackets** *n* ball game played in a paved walled court.

racketeer *n* person making illegal profits.

raconteur [rak-on-**tur**] *n* skilled storyteller.

racy *adj* **racier, raciest 1** slightly shocking. **2** spirited or lively.

radar *n* device for tracking distant objects by bouncing high-frequency radio pulses off them.

radial *adj* **1** spreading out from a common central point. **2** of a radius. **3** (also **radial-ply**) (of a tyre) having flexible sides strengthened with radial cords.

radiant *adj* **1** looking happy. **2** shining. **3** emitting radiation. **radiance** *n*

radiate *v* **1** spread out from a centre. **2** emit or be emitted as radiation. **radiator** *n* **1** *Brit* arrangement of pipes containing hot water or steam to heat a room. **2** tubes containing water as cooling apparatus for a car engine. **3** *Aust & NZ* electric fire.

radiation *n* **1** transmission of energy from one body to another. **2** particles or waves emitted in nuclear decay. **3** process of radiating.

radical *adj* **1** fundamental. **2** thorough. **3** advocating fundamental change. ♦ *n* **4** person advocating fundamental (political) change. **5** number expressed as the root of another. **radically** *adv*

radicalism n

radicle n small or developing root.

radii n a plural of RADIUS.

radio n, pl **-dios 1** use of electromagnetic waves for broadcasting, communication, etc. **2** device for receiving and amplifying radio signals. **3** sound broadcasting. ♦ v **4** transmit (a message) by radio.

radio- combining form of radio, radiation, or radioactivity.

radioactive adj emitting radiation as a result of nuclear decay. **radioactivity** n

radiography [ray-dee-**og**-ra-fee] n production of an image on a film or plate by radiation. **radiographer** n

radiology [ray-dee-**ol**-a-jee] n science of using x-rays in medicine. **radiologist** n

radiotherapy n treatment of disease, esp. cancer, by radiation. **radiotherapist** n

radish n small hot-flavoured root vegetable eaten raw in salads.

radium n Chem radioactive metallic element.

radius n, pl **radii**, **radiuses 1** (length of) a straight line from the centre to the circumference of a circle. **2** outer of two bones in the forearm.

radon [**ray**-don] n Chem radioactive gaseous element.

RAF (in Britain) Royal Air Force.

raffia n prepared palm fibre for weaving mats etc.

raffish adj slightly disreputable.

raffle n **1** lottery with goods as prizes. ♦ v **2** offer as a prize in a raffle.

raft n floating platform of logs, planks, etc.

rafter n one of the main beams of a roof.

rag¹ n **1** fragment of cloth. **2** Brit, Aust & NZ informal newspaper. ♦ pl **3** tattered

clothing. **ragged** [**rag**-gid] adj **1** dressed in shabby or torn clothes. **2** torn. **3** lacking smoothness.

rag² Brit ♦ v **ragging, ragged 1** tease. **2** adj, n **3** (of) events organized by students to raise money for charities.

ragamuffin n ragged dirty child.

rage n **1** violent anger or passion. **2** v **3** speak or act with fury. **4** proceed violently and without check. **all the rage** very popular.

raglan adj (of a sleeve) joined to a garment by diagonal seams from the neck to the underarm.

ragout [rag-**goo**] n richly seasoned stew of meat and vegetables.

ragtime n style of jazz piano music.

raid n **1** sudden surprise attack or search. ♦ v **2** make a raid on. **raider** n

rail¹ n **1** horizontal bar, esp. as part of a fence or track. **2** railway. **railing** n fence made of rails supported by posts. **railway** n **1** track of iron rails on which trains run. **2** company operating a railway.

rail² v (foll. by at or against) complain bitterly or loudly. **raillery** n teasing or joking.

rail³ n small marsh bird.

raiment n Obs clothing.

rain n **1** water falling in drops from the clouds. **2** v **3** fall or pour down as rain. **4** fall rapidly and in large quantities. **rainy** adj **rainbow** n arch of colours in the sky. **rainbow nation** South African nation. **raincoat** n water-resistant overcoat. **rainfall** n amount of rain. **rainforest** n dense forest in tropical and temperate areas.

raise v **1** lift up. **2** set upright. **3** increase in amount or intensity. **4** collect or levy. **5** bring up (a family). **6** put forward for consideration

raisin n dried grape.

raison d'être [**ray**-zon **det**-ra] n, pl

raisons d'être *French* reason or justification for existence.

Raj *n* **the Raj** former British rule in India.

raja, rajah *n Hist* Indian prince or ruler.

rake[1] *n* **1** tool with a long handle and a crosspiece with teeth, used for smoothing earth or gathering leaves, hay, etc. ♦ *v* **2** gather or smooth with a rake. **3** search (through). **4** sweep (with gunfire). **rake it in** *Informal* make a large amount of money. **rake-off** *n Slang* share of profits, esp. illegal. **rake up** *v* revive memories of (a forgotten unpleasant event).

rake[2] *n* dissolute or immoral man. **rakish** *adj*

rakish *adj* dashing or jaunty.

rally *n, pl* **-lies 1** large gathering of people for a meeting. **2** marked recovery of strength. **3** *Tennis etc.* lively exchange of strokes. **4** car-driving competition on public roads. ♦ *v* **-lying, -lied 5** bring or come together after dispersal or for a common cause. **6** regain health or strength, revive.

ram *n* **1** male sheep. **2** hydraulic machine. ♦ *v* **ramming, rammed 3** strike against with force. **4** force or drive. **5** cram or stuff.

RAM *Computers* random access memory.

Ramadan *n* **1** 9th Muslim month. **2** strict fasting from dawn to dusk observed during this time.

ramble *v* **1** walk without a definite route. **2** talk incoherently. ♦ *n* **3** walk, esp. in the country.

rambler *n* **1** person who rambles. **2** climbing rose.

ramekin [**ram**-ik-in] *n* small ovenproof dish for a single serving of food.

ramifications *pl n* consequences resulting from an action.

ramp *n* slope joining two level surfaces.

rampage *v* dash about violently. **on the rampage** behaving violently or destructively.

rampant *adj* **1** growing or spreading uncontrollably. **2** (of a heraldic beast) on its hind legs.

rampart *n* mound or wall for defence.

ramshackle *adj* tumbledown, rickety, or makeshift.

ran *v* past tense of RUN.

ranch *n* large cattle farm in the American West. **rancher** *n*

rancid *adj* (of butter, bacon, etc.) stale and having an offensive smell. **rancidity** *n*

rancour *n* deep bitter hate. **rancorous** *adj*

rand *n* monetary unit of S Africa.

random *adj* made or done by chance or without plan. **at random** haphazard(ly).

randy *adj* **randier, randiest** *Informal* sexually aroused.

rang *v* past tense of RING[1].

range *n* **1** limits of effectiveness or variation. **2** distance that a missile or plane can travel. **3** distance of a mark shot at. **4** whole set of related things. **5** chain of mountains. **6** place for shooting practice or rocket testing. **7** kitchen stove. ♦ *v* **8** vary between one point and another. **9** cover or extend over. **10** roam. **ranger** *n* **1** official in charge of a nature reserve etc. **2** (R-) member of the senior branch of Guides. **rangefinder** *n* instrument for finding how far away an object is.

rangy [**rain**-jee] *adj* **rangier, rangiest** having long slender limbs.

rank[1] *n* **1** relative place or position. **2** status. **3** social class. **4** row or line. **5** *v* **6** have a specific rank or position. **7** arrange in rows or lines. **rank and file** ordinary people or members. **the ranks** common soldiers.

rank[2] *adj* **1** complete or absolute, e.g.

rank favouritism. **2** smelling offensively strong. **3** growing too thickly.

rankle v continue to cause resentment or bitterness.

ransack v **1** search thoroughly. **2** pillage, plunder.

ransom n money demanded in return for the release of someone who has been kidnapped.

rant v talk in a loud and excited way. **ranter** n

rap v **rapping, rapped 1** hit with a sharp quick blow. **2** utter (a command) abruptly. **3** perform a rhythmic monologue with musical backing. ♦ n **4** quick sharp blow. **5** rhythmic monologue performed to music. **take the rap** Slang suffer punishment for something whether guilty or not. **rapper** n

rapacious adj greedy or grasping. **rapacity** n

rape[1] v **1** force to submit to sexual intercourse. ♦ n **2** act of raping. **3** any violation or abuse. **rapist** n

rape[2] n plant with oil-yielding seeds, also used as fodder.

rapid adj quick, swift. **rapids** pl n part of a river with a fast turbulent current. **rapidly** adv **rapidity** n

rapier [**ray**-pyer] n fine-bladed sword.

rapport [rap-**pore**] n harmony or agreement.

rapprochement [rap-**prosh**-mong] n re-establishment of friendly relations, esp. between nations.

rapt adj engrossed or spellbound. **rapture** n ecstasy. **rapturous** adj

rare[1] adj **1** uncommon. **2** infrequent. **3** of uncommonly high quality. **4** (of air at high altitudes) having low density, thin. **rarely** adv seldom. **rarity** n

rare[2] adj (of meat) lightly cooked.

rarebit n see WELSH RAREBIT.

rarefied [**rare**-if-ide] adj **1** highly specialized, exalted. **2** (of air) thin.

raring adj **raring to** enthusiastic, willing, or ready to.

rascal n **1** rogue. **2** naughty (young) person. **rascally** adj

rash[1] adj hasty, reckless, or incautious. **rashly** adv

rash[2] n **1** eruption of spots or patches on the skin. **2** outbreak of (unpleasant) occurrences.

rasher n thin slice of bacon.

rasp n **1** harsh grating noise. **2** coarse file. ♦ v **3** speak in a grating voice. **4** make a scraping noise.

raspberry n **1** red juicy edible berry. **2** Informal spluttering noise made with the tongue and lips, to show contempt.

Rastafarian n, adj (member) of a religion originating in Jamaica and regarding Haile Selassie as God (also **Rasta**).

rat n **1** small rodent. **2** Informal contemptible person, esp. a deserter or informer. ♦ v **ratting, ratted 3** Informal inform (on). **4** hunt rats. **ratty** adj Brit & NZ informal bad-tempered, irritable. **rat race** continual hectic competitive activity.

ratafia [rat-a-**fee**-a] n liqueur made from fruit

ratatouille [rat-a-**twee**] n vegetable casserole of tomatoes, aubergines, etc.

ratchet n set of teeth on a bar or wheel allowing motion in one direction only.

rate n **1** degree of speed or progress. **2** proportion between two things. **3** charge. ♦ pl **4** local tax on business. **5** v **6** consider or value. **7** estimate the value of. **at any rate** in any case. **rateable** adj **1** able to be rated. **2** (of property) liable to payment of rates. **ratepayer** n

rather adv **1** to some extent. **2** more truly or appropriately. **3** more willingly.

ratify v **-fying, -fied** give formal approval to. **ratification** n

rating n **1** valuation or assessment. **2** classification. **3** noncommissioned sailor. ♦ pl **4** size of the audience for a TV programme.

ratio n, pl **-tios** relationship between two numbers or amounts expressed as a proportion.

ration n **1** fixed allowance of food etc. ♦ v **2** limit to a certain amount per person.

rational adj **1** reasonable, sensible. **2** capable of reasoning. **rationally** adv **rationality** n **rationale** [rash-a-**nahl**] n reason for an action or decision. **rationalism** n philosophy that regards reason as the only basis for beliefs or actions. **rationalist** n **rationalize** v **1** justify by plausible reasoning. **2** reorganize to improve efficiency or profitability. **rationalization** n

rattan n climbing palm with jointed stems used for canes.

rattle v **1** give out a succession of short sharp sounds. **2** shake briskly causing sharp sounds. **3** Informal confuse or fluster. **4** n **5** short sharp sound. **6** instrument for making such a sound. **rattlesnake** n poisonous snake with loose horny segments on the tail that make a rattling sound.

raucous adj hoarse or harsh.

raunchy adj **-chier, -chiest** Slang earthy, sexy.

ravage v cause extensive damage to. **ravages** pl n damaging effects.

rave v **1** talk wildly or with enthusiasm. ♦ n **2** Slang large-scale party with electronic dance music. **raving** adj **1** delirious. **2** Informal exceptional, e.g. a raving beauty.

ravel v **-elling, -elled** tangle or become entangled.

raven n **1** black bird like a large crow. ♦ adj **2** (of hair) shiny black.

ravenous adj very hungry.

ravine [rav-**veen**] n narrow steep-sided valley worn by a stream.

ravioli pl n small squares of pasta with a savoury filling.

ravish v **1** enrapture. **2** Lit rape. **ravishing** adj lovely or entrancing.

raw adj **1** uncooked. **2** not manufactured or refined. **3** inexperienced. **4** chilly. **raw deal** unfair or dishonest treatment. **rawhide** n untanned hide.

ray¹ n single line or narrow beam of light.

ray² n large sea fish with a flat body and a whiplike tail.

rayon n (fabric made of) a synthetic fibre.

raze v destroy (buildings or a town) completely.

razor n sharp instrument for shaving. **razorbill** n sea bird of the North Atlantic with a stout sideways flattened bill.

razzle-dazzle, razzmatazz n Slang showy activity.

RC 1 Roman Catholic. **2** Red Cross.

Rd Road.

re prep with reference to, concerning.

RE (in Britain) religious education.

re- prefix again, e.g. re-enter; retrial.

reach v **1** arrive at. **2** make a movement in order to grasp or touch. **3** succeed in touching. **4** make contact or communication with. **5** extend as far as. ♦ n **6** distance that one can reach. **7** range of influence. ♦ pl **8** stretch of a river. **reachable** adj

react v **1** act in response (to). **2** (foll. by against) act in an opposing or contrary manner. **reaction** n **1** physical or emotional response to a stimulus. **2** any action resisting another. **3** opposition to change. **4** chemical or nuclear change, combination, or decomposition. **reactionary** n, adj (person) opposed to change, esp. in politics. **reactance** n Electricity resistance to the flow of an alternating current caused by the inductance or capacitance of the circuit. **reactive** adj chemically active. **reactor** n apparatus in which a nuclear reaction is maintained and controlled to produce nuclear energy.

read v **reading, read 1** look at and understand or take in (written or printed matter). **2** look at and say aloud. **3** interpret the significance or meaning of. **4** (of an instrument) register. **5** study. ♦ n **6** matter suitable for reading, e.g. a good read. **readable** adj **1** enjoyable to read. **2** legible. **reading** n

reader n **1** person who reads. **2** textbook. **3** Chiefly Brit senior university lecturer. **readership** n readers of a publication collectively.

readjust v adapt to a new situation. **readjustment** n

ready adj **readier, readiest 1** prepared for use or action. **2** willing, prompt. **readily** adv **readiness** n **ready-made** adj for immediate use by any customer.

reagent [ree-**age**-ent] n chemical substance that reacts with another, used to detect the presence of the other.

real adj **1** existing in fact. **2** actual. **3** genuine. **really** adv **1** very. **2** truly. ♦ interj **3** exclamation of dismay, doubt, or surprise. **reality** n state of things as they are. **reality TV** television programmes focusing on members of the public living in conditions created especially by the programme makers. **real ale** Chiefly Brit beer allowed to ferment in the barrel. **real estate** property consisting of land and houses.

realistic adj seeing and accepting things as they really are, practical. **realistically** adv **realism** n **realist** n

realize v **1** become aware or grasp the significance of. **2** achieve (a plan, hopes, etc.). **3** convert into money. **realization** n

realm n **1** kingdom. **2** sphere of interest.

ream n **1** twenty quires of paper, generally 500 sheets. ♦ pl **2** Informal large quantity (of written matter).

reap v **1** cut and gather (a harvest). **2** receive as the result of a previous activity. **reaper** n

reappear v appear again. **reappearance** n

rear[1] n **1** back part. **2** part of an army, procession, etc. behind the others. **bring up the rear** come last. **rearmost** adj **rear admiral** high-ranking naval officer. **rearguard** n troops protecting the rear of an army.

rear[2] v **1** care for and educate (children). **2** breed (animals). **3** (of a horse) rise on its hind feet.

rearrange v organize differently, alter. **rearrangement** n

reason n **1** cause or motive. **2** faculty of rational thought. **3** sanity. ♦ v **4** think logically in forming conclusions. **reason with** persuade by logical argument into doing something. **reasonable** adj **1** sensible. **2** not excessive. **3** logical. **reasonably** adv

reassess v reconsider the value or importance of.

reassure v restore confidence to. **reassurance** n

rebate n discount or refund.

rebel v **-belling, -belled 1** revolt against the ruling power. **2** reject accepted conventions. ♦ n **3** person who rebels. **rebellion** n **1** organized open resistance to authority. **2** rejection of conventions.

rebellious *adj*

rebore, reboring *n* boring of a cylinder to restore its true shape.

rebound *v* **1** spring back. **2** misfire so as to hurt the perpetrator of a plan or deed. **on the rebound** *Informal* while recovering from rejection.

rebuff *v* **1** reject or snub. ♦ *n* **2** blunt refusal, snub.

rebuke *v* **1** scold sternly. ♦ *n* **2** stern scolding.

rebus *n, pl* **-buses** puzzle consisting of pictures and symbols representing words or syllables.

rebut *v* **-butting, -butted** prove that (a claim) is untrue. **rebuttal** *n*

recalcitrant *adj* wilfully disobedient. **recalcitrance** *n*

recall *v* **1** recollect or remember. **2** order to return. **3** annul or cancel. ♦ *n* **4** ability to remember. **5** order to return.

recant *v* withdraw (a statement or belief) publicly. **recantation** *n*

recap *Informal* ♦ *v* **-capping, -capped** **1** recapitulate. ♦ *n* **2** recapitulation.

recapitulate *v* state again briefly, repeat. **recapitulation** *n*

recapture *v* **1** experience again. **2** capture again.

recce *Chiefly Brit slang* ♦ *v* **-ceing, -ced** *or* **-ceed 1** reconnoitre. ♦ *n* **2** reconnaissance.

recede *v* **1** move to a more distant place. **2** (of the hair) stop growing at the front.

receipt *n* **1** written acknowledgment of money or goods received. **2** receiving or being received.

receive *v* **1** take, accept, or get. **2** experience. **3** greet (guests). **received** *adj* generally accepted. **receiver** *n* **1** part of telephone that is held to the ear. **2** equipment in a telephone, radio, or television that converts electrical signals into sound. **3** person appointed by a court to manage the property of a bankrupt. **receivership** *n* state of being administered by a receiver.

recent *adj* **1** having happened lately. **2** new. **recently** *adv*

receptacle *n* object used to contain something.

reception *n* **1** area for receiving guests, clients, etc. **2** formal party. **3** manner of receiving. **4** welcome. **5** (in broadcasting) quality of signals received. **receptionist** *n* person who receives guests, clients, etc.

receptive *adj* willing to accept new ideas, suggestions, etc. **receptivity** *n*

recess *n* **1** niche or alcove. **2** holiday between sessions of work. **3** secret hidden place. **recessed** *adj* hidden or placed in a recess.

recession *n* period of economic difficulty when little is being bought or sold. **recessive** *adj* receding.

recherché [rish-**air**-shay] *adj* **1** refined or elegant. **2** known only to experts.

recidivism *n* habitual relapse into crime. **recidivist** *n*

recipe *n* **1** directions for cooking a dish. **2** method for achieving something.

recipient *n* person who receives something.

reciprocal [ris-**sip**-pro-kl] *adj* **1** mutual. **2** given or done in return. **reciprocally** *adv* **reciprocate** *v* **1** give or feel in return. **2** (of a machine part) move backwards and forwards. **reciprocation** *n* **reciprocity** *n*

recite *v* repeat (a poem etc.) aloud to an audience. **recital** *n* **1** musical performance by a soloist or soloists. **2** act of reciting. **recitation** *n* recital, usu. from memory, of poetry or prose. **recitative** [ress-it-a-**teev**] *n* speechlike style of singing, used esp. for narrative passages in opera.

reckless *adj* heedless of danger.
recklessly *adv* **recklessness** *n*

reckon *v* **1** consider or think. **2** make
calculations, count. **3** expect.
reckoning *n*

reclaim *v* **1** regain possession of. **2**
make fit for cultivation. **reclamation** *n*

recline *v* rest in a leaning position.
reclining *adj*

recluse *n* person who avoids other
people. **reclusive** *adj*

recognize *v* **1** identify as (a person or
thing) already known. **2** accept as true
or existing. **3** treat as valid. **4** notice,
show appreciation of. **recognition** *n*
recognizable *adj* **recognizance**
[rik-**og**-nizz-anss] *n* undertaking before
a court to observe some condition.

recoil *v* **1** jerk or spring back. **2** draw
back in horror. **3** (of an action) go
wrong so as to hurt the doer. ♦ *n* **4**
backward jerk. **5** recoiling.

recollect *v* call back to mind,
remember. **recollection** *n*

recommend *v* **1** advise or counsel. **2**
praise or commend. **3** make
acceptable. **recommendation** *n*

✓ SPELLING TIP

If you wonder how many *c*s and *m*s
to put in **recommend**, you are not
alone. Most people who make the
wrong decision go for single letters
throughout (*recomend* and
recomendation); they should, of
course, double the *m*, as in
recommendation.

recompense *v* **1** pay or reward. **2**
compensate or make up for. ♦ *n* **3**
compensation. **4** reward or
remuneration.

reconcile *v* **1** harmonize (conflicting
beliefs etc.). **2** bring back into
friendship. **3** accept or cause to accept
(an unpleasant situation).

reconciliation *n*

recondite *adj* difficult to understand.

recondition *v* restore to good
condition or working order.

reconnaissance [rik-**kon**-iss-anss] *n*
survey for military or engineering
purposes.

✓ SPELLING TIP

The Bank of English shows that the
most common way to misspell
reconnaissance is to miss out an *s*,
although there are examples where
an *n* has been missed out instead.
Remember, there are two *n*s in the
middle and two *s*s.

reconnoitre [rek-a-**noy**-ter] *v* make a
reconnaissance of.

reconsider *v* think about again,
consider changing.

reconstitute *v* **1** reorganize. **2** restore
(dried food) to its former state by
adding water. **reconstitution** *n*

reconstruct *v* **1** rebuild. **2** use
evidence to re-create. **reconstruction**
n

record *n* [**rek**-ord] **1** document or
other thing that preserves information.
2 disc with indentations which a
record player transforms into sound. **3**
best recorded achievement. **4** known
facts about a person's past. ♦ *v*
[rik-**kord**] **5** put in writing. **6** preserve
(sound, TV programmes, etc.) on
plastic disc, magnetic tape, etc., for
reproduction on a playback device. **7**
show or register. **off the record** not
for publication. **recorder** *n* **1** person
or machine that records, esp. a video,
cassette, or tape recorder. **2** type of
flute, held vertically. **3** judge in certain
courts. **recording** *n* **record player**
instrument for reproducing sound on
records.

recount *v* tell in detail.

re-count v 1 count again. ◆ n 2 second or further count, esp. of votes.

recoup [rik-**koop**] v 1 regain or make good (a loss). 2 recompense or compensate.

recourse n source of help. **have recourse to** turn to a source of help or course of action.

recover v 1 become healthy again. 2 regain a former condition. 3 find again. 4 get back (a loss or expense). **recovery** n **recoverable** adj

re-create v make happen or exist again.

recreation n agreeable or refreshing occupation, relaxation, or amusement. **recreational** adj

recrimination n mutual blame. **recriminatory** adj

recruit v 1 enlist (new soldiers, members, etc.). ◆ n 2 newly enlisted soldier. 3 new member or supporter. **recruitment** n

rectangle n oblong four-sided figure with four right angles. **rectangular** adj

rectify v -fying, -fied 1 put right, correct. 2 Chem purify by distillation. 3 Electricity convert (alternating current) into direct current. **rectification** n **rectifier** n

rectilinear adj 1 in a straight line. 2 characterized by straight lines.

rectitude n moral correctness.

recto n, pl -tos right-hand page of a book.

rector n 1 clergyman in charge of a parish. 2 head of certain academic institutions. **rectory** n rector's house.

rectum n, pl -tums, -ta final section of the large intestine.

recumbent adj lying down.

recuperate v recover from illness. **recuperation** n **recuperative** adj

recur v -curring, -curred happen again. **recurrence** n repetition.

recurrent adj

recycle v reprocess (used materials) for further use. **recyclable** adj

red adj **redder, reddest** 1 of a colour varying from crimson to orange and seen in blood, fire, etc. 2 flushed in the face from anger, shame, etc. ◆ n 3 red colour. 4 (R-) Informal communist. **in the red** Informal in debt. **see red** Informal be angry. **redness** n **redden** v make or become red. **reddish** adj **redback spider** small venomous Australian spider with a red stripe on the back of the abdomen.

red-blooded adj Informal vigorous or virile. **redbrick** adj (of a university in Britain) founded in the late 19th or early 20th century. **red card** Soccer piece of red pasteboard shown by a referee to indicate that a player has been sent off. **red carpet** very special welcome for an important guest. **redcoat** n Hist British soldier. **Red Cross** international organization providing help for victims of war or natural disasters. **redcurrant** n small round edible red berry. **red-handed** adj Informal (caught) in the act of doing something wrong or illegal. **red herring** something which diverts attention from the main issue. **red-hot** adj 1 glowing red. 2 extremely hot. 3 very keen. **Red Indian** Offens Native American. **red light** 1 traffic signal to stop. 2 danger signal. **red meat** dark meat, esp. beef or lamb. **red tape** excessive adherence to official rules.

redeem v 1 make up for. 2 reinstate (oneself) in someone's good opinion. 3 free from sin. 4 buy back. 5 pay off (a loan or debt). **the Redeemer** Jesus Christ. **redeemable** adj **redemption** n **redemptive** adj

redeploy v assign to a new position or task. **redeployment** n

redevelop v rebuild or renovate (an area or building). **redevelopment** n

redolent adj 1 reminiscent (of). 2 smelling strongly (of).

redouble v increase, multiply, or intensify.

redoubt n small fort defending a hilltop or pass.

redoubtable adj formidable.

redound v cause advantage or disadvantage (to).

redox n chemical reaction in which one substance is reduced and the other is oxidized.

redress v 1 make amends for. ◆ n 2 compensation or amends.

reduce v 1 bring down, lower. 2 lessen, weaken. 3 bring by force or necessity to some state or action. 4 slim. 5 simplify. 6 make (a sauce) more concentrated. **reducible** adj **reduction** n

redundant adj 1 (of a worker) no longer needed. 2 superfluous. **redundancy** n

reed n 1 tall grass that grows in swamps and shallow water. 2 tall straight stem of this plant. 3 Music vibrating cane or metal strip in certain wind instruments. **reedy** adj harsh and thin in tone.

reef¹ n 1 ridge of rock or coral near the surface of the sea. 2 vein of ore.

reef² n 1 part of a sail which can be rolled up to reduce its area. ◆ v 2 take in a reef of. **reefer** n 1 short thick jacket worn esp. by sailors. 2 Old-fashioned slang hand-rolled cigarette containing cannabis. **reef knot** two simple knots turned opposite ways.

reek v 1 smell strongly. ◆ n 2 strong unpleasant smell. **reek of** give a strong suggestion of.

reel¹ n 1 cylindrical object on which film, tape, thread, or wire is wound. 2 winding apparatus, as of a fishing rod. **reel in** v draw in by means of a reel. **reel off** v recite or write fluently or quickly.

reel² v stagger, sway, or whirl.

reel³ n lively Scottish dance.

ref n Informal referee in sport.

refectory n, pl **-tories** room for meals in a college etc.

refer v **-ferring, -ferred** (foll. by to) 1 allude (to). 2 be relevant (to). 3 send (to) for information. 4 submit (to) for decision. **referral n reference** n 1 act of referring. 2 citation or direction in a book. 3 written testimonial regarding character or capabilities. **with reference to** concerning.

referee n 1 umpire in sports, esp. soccer or boxing. 2 person willing to testify to someone's character etc. 3 arbitrator. ◆ v **-eeing, -eed** 4 act as referee of.

referendum n, pl **-dums, -da** direct vote of the electorate on an important question.

refill v 1 fill again. ◆ n 2 second or subsequent filling. 3 replacement supply of something in a permanent container.

refine v 1 purify. 2 improve. **refined** adj 1 cultured or polite. 2 purified. **refinement** n 1 improvement or elaboration. 2 fineness of taste or manners. 3 subtlety. **refinery** n place where sugar, oil, etc. is refined.

reflation n increase in the supply of money and credit designed to encourage economic activity. **reflate** v **reflationary** adj

reflect v 1 throw back, esp. rays of light, heat, etc. 2 form an image of. 3 show. 4 consider at length. 5 bring credit or discredit upon. **reflection** n 1 act of reflecting. 2 return of rays of heat, light, etc. from a surface. 3 image of an object given back by a mirror etc. **4** conscious thought or meditation. **5** attribution of discredit or blame. **reflective** adj **1** quiet, contemplative. **2** capable of reflecting images. **reflector** n polished surface for reflecting light etc.

reflex n **1** involuntary response to a stimulus or situation. ♦ adj **2** (of a muscular action) involuntary. **3** reflected. **4** (of an angle) more than 180°. **reflexive** adj Grammar denoting a verb whose subject is the same as its object, e.g. dress oneself.

reflexology n foot massage as a therapy in alternative medicine.

reform n **1** improvement. ♦ v **2** improve. **3** abandon evil practices. **reformer** n **reformation** n **1** act or instance of something being reformed. **2** (R-) religious movement in 16th-century Europe that resulted in the establishment of the Protestant Churches. **reformatory** n (formerly) institution for reforming young offenders.

refract v change the course of (light etc.) passing from one medium to another. **refraction** n **refractive** adj **refractor** n

refractory adj **1** unmanageable or rebellious. **2** Med resistant to treatment. **3** resistant to heat.

refrain¹ v **refrain from** keep oneself from doing.

refrain² n frequently repeated part of a song.

refresh v **1** revive or reinvigorate, as through food, drink, or rest. **2** stimulate (the memory). **refresher** n **refreshing** adj **1** having a reviving effect. **2** pleasantly different or new. **refreshment** n something that refreshes, esp. food or drink.

refrigerate v cool or freeze in order to preserve. **refrigeration** n **refrigerator** n full name for FRIDGE.

refuge n (source of) shelter or protection. **refugee** n person who seeks refuge, esp. in a foreign country.

refulgent adj shining, radiant.

refund v **1** pay back. ♦ n **2** return of money. **3** amount returned.

refurbish v renovate and brighten up.

refuse¹ v decline, deny, or reject. **refusal** n denial of anything demanded or offered.

refuse² n rubbish or useless matter.

refute v disprove. **refutation** n

regain v **1** get back or recover. **2** reach again.

regal adj of or like a king or queen. **regally** adv **regalia** pl n ceremonial emblems of royalty or high office.

regale v entertain (someone) with stories etc.

regard v **1** consider. **2** look at. **3** heed. ♦ n **4** respect or esteem. **5** attention. **6** look. ♦ pl **7** expression of goodwill. **as regards, regarding** in respect of, concerning. **regardless** adj **1** heedless. ♦ adv **2** in spite of everything.

regatta n meeting for yacht or boat races.

regenerate v **1** (cause to) undergo spiritual, moral, or physical renewal. **2** reproduce or re-create. **regeneration** n **regenerative** adj

regent n **1** ruler of a kingdom during the absence, childhood, or illness of its monarch. ♦ adj **2** ruling as a regent, e.g. prince regent. **regency** n status or period of office of a regent.

reggae n style of Jamaican popular music with a strong beat.

regicide n **1** killing of a king. **2** person who kills a king.

regime [ray-**zheem**] n **1** system of government. **2** particular administration.

regimen n prescribed system of diet etc.

regiment n 1 organized body of troops as a unit of the army. **regimental** adj **regimentation** n **regimented** adj very strictly controlled.

region n 1 administrative division of a country. 2 area considered as a unit but with no definite boundaries. 3 part of the body. **regional** adj

register n 1 (book containing) an official list or record of things. 2 range of a voice or instrument. ♦ v 3 enter in a register or set down in writing. 4 show or be shown on a meter or the face. **registration** n **registration number** numbers and letters displayed on a vehicle to identify it. **registrar** n 1 keeper of official records. 2 senior hospital doctor, junior to a consultant. **register office, registry office** place where births, marriages, and deaths are recorded.

Regius professor [**reej**-yuss] n (in Britain) professor appointed by the Crown to a university chair founded by a royal patron.

regress v revert to a former worse condition. **regression** n 1 act of regressing. 2 Psychol use of an earlier (inappropriate) mode of behaviour. **regressive** adj

regret v -gretting, -gretted 1 feel sorry about. 2 express apology or distress. ♦ n 3 feeling of repentance, guilt, or sorrow. **regretful** adj **regrettable** adj

regular adj 1 normal, customary, or usual. 2 symmetrical or even. 3 done or occurring according to a rule. 4 periodical. 5 employed continuously in the armed forces. ♦ n 6 regular soldier. 7 Informal frequent customer. **regularity** n **regularize** v **regularly** adv

regulate v 1 control, esp. by rules. 2 adjust slightly. **regulation** n 1 rule. 2 regulating. **regulator** n device that

automatically controls pressure, temperature, etc.

regurgitate v 1 vomit. 2 (of some birds and animals) bring back (partly digested food) into the mouth. 3 reproduce (ideas, facts, etc.) without understanding them. **regurgitation** n

rehabilitate v 1 help (a person) to readjust to society after illness, imprisonment, etc. 2 restore to a former position or rank. 3 restore the good reputation of. **rehabilitation** n

rehash v 1 rework or reuse. ♦ n 2 old ideas presented in a new form.

rehearse v 1 practise (a play, concert, etc.). 2 repeat aloud. **rehearsal** n

rehouse v provide with a new (and better) home.

reign n 1 period of a sovereign's rule. 2 v 3 rule (a country). 4 be supreme.

reimburse v refund, pay back. **reimbursement** n

rein v 1 check or manage with reins. 2 control or limit. **reins** pl n 1 narrow straps attached to a bit to guide a horse. 2 means of control.

reincarnation n 1 rebirth of a soul in successive bodies. 2 one of a series of such transmigrations. **reincarnate** v

reindeer n, pl -deer, -deers deer of arctic regions with large branched antlers.

reinforce v 1 strengthen with new support, material, or force. 2 strengthen with additional troops, ships, etc. **reinforcement** n **reinforced concrete** concrete strengthened by having steel mesh or bars embedded in it.

reinstate v restore to a former position. **reinstatement** n

reiterate v repeat again and again. **reiteration** n

reject v 1 refuse to accept or believe. 2 rebuff (a person). 3 discard as useless. 4 n 5 person or thing rejected as not up to standard. **rejection** *n*

rejig *v* **-jigging, -jigged 1** re-equip (a factory or plant). **2** rearrange.

rejoice *v* feel or express great happiness.

rejoin[1] *v* join again.

rejoin[2] *v* reply. **rejoinder** *n* answer, retort.

rejuvenate *v* restore youth or vitality to. **rejuvenation** *n*

relapse *v* **1** fall back into bad habits, illness, etc. ♦ *n* **2** return of bad habits, illness, etc.

relate *v* **1** establish a relation between. **2** have reference or relation to. **3** have an understanding (of people or ideas). **4** tell (a story) or describe (an event). **related** *adj*

relation *n* **1** connection between things. **2** relative. **3** connection by blood or marriage. **4** act of relating (a story). ♦ *pl* **5** social or political dealings. **6** family. **relationship** *n* **1** dealings and feelings between people or countries. **2** emotional or sexual affair. **3** connection between two things. **4** association by blood or marriage, kinship.

relative *adj* **1** dependent on relation to something else, not absolute. **2** having reference or relation (to). **3** *Grammar* referring to a word or clause earlier in the sentence. ♦ *n* **4** person connected by blood or marriage. **relatively** *adv* **relativity** *n* **1** subject of two theories of Albert Einstein, dealing with relationships of space, time, and motion, and acceleration and gravity. **2** state of being relative.

relax *v* **1** make or become looser, less tense, or less rigid. **2** ease up from effort or attention, rest. **3** be less strict about. **4** become more friendly. **relaxing** *adj* **relaxation** *n*

relay *n* **1** fresh set of people or animals relieving others. **2** *Electricity* device for

making or breaking a local circuit. **3** broadcasting station receiving and retransmitting programmes. ♦ *v* **-laying, -layed 4** pass on (a message). **relay race** race between teams in which each runner races part of the distance.

release *v* **1** set free. **2** let go or fall. **3** issue (a record, film, etc.) for sale or public showing. **4** emit heat, energy, etc. ♦ *n* **5** setting free. **6** statement to the press. **7** act of issuing for sale or publication. **8** newly issued film, record, etc.

relegate *v* **1** put in a less important position. **2** demote (a sports team) to a lower league. **relegation** *n*

relent *v* give up a harsh intention, become less severe. **relentless** *adj* **1** unremitting. **2** merciless.

relevant *adj* to do with the matter in hand. **relevance** *n*

☑ **SPELLING TIP**

A common word in English, **relevant** is not always spelt correctly. The final syllable is the problem and sometimes appears incorrectly in the Bank of English as *-ent*.

---

reliable *adj* able to be trusted, dependable. **reliably** *adv* **reliability** *n*

reliance *n* dependence, confidence, or trust. **reliant** *adj*

relic *n* **1** something that has survived from the past. **2** body or possession of a saint, regarded as holy. ♦ *pl* **3** remains or traces. **relict** *n Obs* widow.

relief *n* **1** gladness at the end or removal of pain, distress, etc. **2** release from monotony or duty. **3** money or food given to victims of disaster, poverty, etc. **4** freeing of a besieged city etc. **5** person who replaces another. **6** projection of a carved design from the surface. **7** any vivid effect resulting from contrast, e.g. *comic relief*. **relieve** *v* bring relief to. **relieve oneself** urinate or defecate. **relief map** map showing the shape and height of land by shading.

religion *n* system of belief in and worship of a supernatural power or god. **religious** *adj* 1 of religion. 2 pious or devout. 3 scrupulous or conscientious. **religiously** *adv*

relinquish *v* give up or abandon.

reliquary *n, pl* **-quaries** case or shrine for holy relics.

relish *v* 1 enjoy, like very much. 2 *n* 3 liking or enjoyment. 4 appetizing savoury food, such as pickle. 5 zestful quality or flavour.

relocate *v* move to a new place to live or work. **relocation** *n*

reluctant *adj* unwilling or disinclined. **reluctantly** *adv* **reluctance** *n*

rely *v* **-lying, -lied** 1 depend (on). 2 trust.

remain *v* 1 continue. 2 stay, be left behind. 3 be left (over). 4 be left to be done, said, etc. **remains** *pl n* 1 relics, esp. of ancient buildings. 2 dead body. **remainder** *n* 1 part which is left. 2 amount left over after subtraction or division. 3 *v* 4 offer (copies of a poorly selling book) at reduced prices.

remand *v* send back into custody or put on bail before trial. **on remand** in custody or on bail before trial. **remand centre** (in Britain) place where accused people are detained awaiting trial.

remark *v* 1 make a casual comment (on). 2 say. 3 observe or notice. ♦ *n* 4 observation or comment. **remarkable** *adj* 1 worthy of note or attention. 2 striking or unusual. **remarkably** *adv*

remedy *n, pl* **-edies** 1 means of curing pain or disease. 2 means of solving a problem. ♦ *v* **-edying, -edied** 3 put

right. **remedial** *adj* intended to correct a specific disability, handicap, etc.

remember *v* 1 retain in or recall to one's memory. 2 keep in mind. **remembrance** *n* 1 memory. 2 token or souvenir. 3 honouring of the memory of a person or event.

remind *v* 1 cause to remember. 2 put in mind (of). **reminder** *n* 1 something that recalls the past. 2 note to remind a person of something not done.

reminisce *v* talk or write of past times, experiences, etc. **reminiscence** *n* 1 remembering. 2 thing recollected. ♦ *pl* 3 memoirs. **reminiscent** *adj* reminding or suggestive (of).

remiss *adj* negligent or careless.

remission *n* 1 reduction in the length of a prison term. 2 easing of intensity, as of an illness.

remit *v* [rim-**mitt**] **-mitting, -mitted** 1 send (money) for goods, services, etc., esp. by post. 2 cancel (a punishment or debt). 3 refer (a decision) to a higher authority or later date. ♦ *n* [**ree**-mitt] 4 area of competence or authority. **remittance** *n* money sent as payment.

remnant *n* 1 small piece, esp. of fabric, left over. 2 surviving trace.

remonstrate *v* argue in protest. **remonstrance** *n*

remorse *n* feeling of sorrow and regret for something one did. **remorseful** *adj* **remorseless** *adj* 1 pitiless. 2 persistent. **remorselessly** *adv*

remote *adj* 1 far away, distant. 2 aloof. 3 slight or faint. **remotely** *adv* **remote control** control of an apparatus from a distance by an electrical device.

remould *v* 1 *Brit* renovate (a worn tyre). ♦ *n* 2 *Brit* renovated tyre.

remove *v* 1 take away or off. 2 get rid of. 3 dismiss from office. ♦ *n* 4 degree

of difference. **removable** *adj*
removal *n* removing, esp. changing
residence.

remunerate *v* reward or pay.
remunerative *adj*

remuneration *n* reward or payment.

renaissance *n* 1 revival or rebirth. 2
(R-) revival of learning in the
14th–16th centuries.

renal [**ree**-nal] *adj* of the kidneys.

renascent *adj* becoming active or
vigorous again.

rend *v* **rending, rent** 1 tear or wrench
apart. 2 (of a sound) break (the
silence) violently.

render *v* 1 cause to become. 2 give or
provide (aid, a service, etc.). 3 submit
or present (a bill). 4 portray or
represent. 5 cover with plaster. 6 melt
down (fat).

rendezvous [**ron**-day-voo] *n, pl* **-vous**
1 appointment. 2 meeting place. ♦ *v* 3
meet as arranged.

rendition *n* 1 performance. 2
translation.

renegade *n* person who deserts a
cause.

renege [rin-**nayg**] *v* go back (on a
promise etc.).

renew *v* 1 begin again. 2 make valid
again. 3 grow again. 4 restore to a
former state. 5 replace (a worn part). 6
restate or reaffirm. **renewable** *adj*
renewal *n*

rennet *n* substance for curdling milk to
make cheese.

renounce *v* 1 give up (a belief, habit,
etc.) voluntarily. 2 give up (a title or
claim) formally. **renunciation** *n*

renovate *v* restore to good condition.
renovation *n*

renown *n* widespread good reputation.

renowned *adj* famous.

rent¹ *v* 1 give or have use of in return
for regular payments. ♦ *n* 2 regular

payment for use of land, a building,
machine, etc. **rental** *n* sum payable
as rent.

rent² *n* 1 tear or fissure. ♦ *v* 2 past of
REND.

renunciation *n* see RENOUNCE.

reorganize *v* organize in a new and
more efficient way. **reorganization** *n*

rep¹ *n* short for REPERTORY COMPANY.

rep² *n* short for REPRESENTATIVE.

repair¹ *v* 1 restore to good condition,
mend. ♦ *n* 2 act of repairing. 3
repaired part. 4 state or condition, e.g.
in good repair. **reparation** *n*
something done or given as
compensation.

repair² *v* go (to).

repartee *n* 1 interchange of witty
retorts. 2 witty retort.

repast *n* meal.

repatriate *v* send (someone) back to
his or her own country. **repatriation** *n*

repay *v* **repaying, repaid** 1 pay back,
refund. 2 do something in return for,
e.g. *repay hospitality.* **repayable** *adj*
repayment *n*

repeal *v* 1 cancel (a law) officially. ♦ *n* 2
act of repealing.

repeat *v* 1 say or do again. 2 happen
again, recur. ♦ *n* 3 act or instance of
repeating. 4 programme broadcast
again. **repeatedly** *adv* **repeater** *n*
firearm that may be discharged many
times without reloading.

repel *v* **-pelling, -pelled** 1 be
disgusting to. 2 drive back, ward off. 3
resist. **repellent** *adj* 1 distasteful. 2
resisting water etc. ♦ *n* 3 something
that repels, esp. a chemical to repel
insects.

repent *v* feel regret for (a deed or
omission). **repentance** *n* **repentant**
adj

repercussions *pl n* indirect effects,
often unpleasant.

repertoire n stock of plays, songs, etc. that a player or company can give.

repertory n, pl **-ries** repertoire. **repertory company** permanent theatre company producing a succession of plays.

repetition n 1 act of repeating. 2 thing repeated. **repetitive, repetitious** adj full of repetition.

rephrase v express in different words.

repine v fret or complain.

replace v 1 substitute for. 2 put back. **replacement** n

replay n 1 (also **action replay**) immediate reshowing on TV of an incident in sport, esp. in slow motion. 2 second sports match, esp. one following an earlier draw. ♦ v 3 play (a match, recording, etc.) again.

replenish v fill up again, resupply. **replenishment** n

replete adj filled or gorged.

replica n exact copy. **replicate** v make or be a copy of.

reply v **-plying, -plied** 1 answer or respond. ♦ n, pl **-plies** 2 answer or response.

report v 1 give an account of. 2 make a report (on). 3 make a formal complaint about. 4 present oneself (to). 5 be responsible (to). ♦ n 6 account or statement. 7 rumour. 8 written statement of a child's progress at school. 9 bang. **reportedly** adv according to rumour. **reporter** n person who gathers news for a newspaper, TV, etc.

repose n 1 peace. 2 composure. 3 sleep. ♦ v 4 lie or lay at rest.

repository n, pl **-ries** place where valuables are deposited for safekeeping, store.

repossess v (of a lender) take back property from a customer who is behind with payments. **repossession** n

reprehensible adj open to criticism, unworthy.

represent v 1 act as a delegate or substitute for. 2 stand for. 3 symbolize. 4 make out to be. 5 portray, as in art. **representation** n **representative** n 1 person chosen to stand for a group. 2 (travelling) salesperson. ♦ adj 3 typical.

repress v 1 keep (feelings) in check. 2 restrict the freedom of. **repression** n **repressive** adj

reprieve v 1 postpone the execution of (a condemned person). 2 give temporary relief to. ♦ n 3 (document granting) postponement or cancellation of a punishment. 4 temporary relief.

reprimand v 1 blame (someone) officially for a fault. ♦ n 2 official blame.

reprint v 1 print further copies of (a book). ♦ n 2 reprinted copy.

reprisal n retaliation.

reproach n, v blame, rebuke. **reproachful** adj **reproachfully** adv

reprobate adj, n depraved or disreputable (person).

reproduce v 1 produce a copy of. 2 bring new individuals into existence. 3 re-create. **reproducible** adj **reproduction** n 1 process of reproducing. 2 facsimile, as of a painting etc. 3 quality of sound from an audio system. **reproductive** adj

reprove v speak severely to (someone) about a fault. **reproof** n severe blaming of someone for a fault.

reptile n cold-blooded egg-laying vertebrate with horny scales or plates, such as a snake or tortoise. **reptilian** adj

republic n 1 form of government in which the people or their elected representatives possess the supreme power. 2 country in which a president is the head of state. **Republican** n, adj (member or supporter) of the

Republican Party, the more conservative of the two main political parties in the US. **Republicanism** n

repudiate [rip-**pew**-dee-ate] v 1 reject the authority or validity of. 2 disown. **repudiation** n

repugnant adj offensive or distasteful. **repugnance** n

repulse v 1 be disgusting to. 2 drive (an army) back. 3 rebuff or reject. ♦ n 4 driving back. 5 rejection or rebuff. **repulsion** n 1 distaste or aversion. 2 Physics force separating two objects. **repulsive** adj loathsome, disgusting.

reputation n estimation in which a person is held. **reputable** adj of good reputation, respectable. **repute** n reputation. **reputed** adj supposed. **reputedly** adv

request v 1 ask. ♦ n 2 asking. 3 thing asked for.

Requiem [**rek**-wee-em] n 1 Mass for the dead. 2 music for this.

require v 1 want or need. 2 demand. **requirement** n 1 essential condition. 2 specific need or want.

☑ WORD TIP

Require suggests a demand imposed by some regulation. *Need* is usually something that comes from a person.

---

requisite [**rek**-wizz-it] adj 1 necessary, essential. ♦ n 2 essential thing.

requisition v 1 demand (supplies). ♦ n 2 formal demand, such as for materials or supplies.

requite v return to someone (the same treatment or feeling as received).

reredos [**rear**-doss] n ornamental screen behind an altar.

rescind v annul or repeal.

rescue v -cuing, -cued 1 deliver from danger or trouble, save. ♦ n 2 rescuing. **rescuer** n

research n 1 systematic investigation to discover facts or collect information. ♦ v 2 carry out investigations. **researcher** n

resemble v be or look like. **resemblance** n

resent v feel bitter about. **resentful** adj **resentment** n

reservation n 1 doubt. 2 exception or limitation. 3 seat, room, etc. that has been reserved. 4 area of land reserved for use by a particular group. 5 (also **central reservation**) Brit strip of ground separating the two carriageways of a dual carriageway or motorway.

reserve v 1 set aside, keep for future use. 2 obtain by arranging beforehand, book. 3 retain. ♦ n 4 something, esp. money or troops, kept for emergencies. 5 area of land reserved for a particular purpose. 6 Sport substitute. 7 concealment of feelings or friendliness. **reserved** adj 1 not showing one's feelings, lacking friendliness. 2 set aside for use by a particular person. **reservist** n member of a military reserve.

reservoir n 1 natural or artificial lake storing water for community supplies. 2 store or supply of something.

reshuffle n 1 reorganization. ♦ v 2 reorganize.

reside v dwell permanently.

resident n 1 person who lives in a place. 2 adj 3 living in a place. **residence** n home or house. **residential** adj 1 (of part of a town) consisting mainly of houses. 2 providing living accommodation.

residue n what is left, remainder. **residual** adj

resign v 1 give up office, a job, etc. 2 reconcile (oneself) to. **resigned** adj content to endure. **resignation** n 1 resigning. 2 passive endurance of difficulties.

resilient adj 1 (of a person) recovering quickly from a shock etc. 2 able to return to normal shape after stretching etc. **resilience** n

resin [**rezz**-in] n 1 sticky substance from plants, esp. pines. 2 similar synthetic substance. **resinous** adj

resist v 1 withstand or oppose. 2 refrain from despite temptation. 3 be proof against. **resistance** n 1 act of resisting. 2 capacity to withstand something. 3 *Electricity* opposition offered by a circuit to the passage of a current through it. **resistant** adj **resistible** adj **resistor** n component of an electrical circuit producing resistance.

resit v 1 take (an exam) again. ♦ n 2 exam that has to be taken again.

resolute adj firm in purpose. **resolutely** adv

resolution n 1 firmness of conduct or character. 2 thing resolved upon. 3 decision of a court or vote of an assembly. 4 act of resolving.

resolve v 1 decide with an effort of will. 2 form (a resolution) by a vote. 3 separate the component parts of. 4 make clear, settle. **resolved** adj determined.

resonance n 1 echoing, esp. with a deep sound. 2 sound produced in one object by sound waves coming from another object. **resonant** adj **resonate** v

resort v 1 have recourse (to) for help etc. ♦ n 2 place for holidays. 3 recourse.

resound [riz-**zownd**] v echo or ring with sound. **resounding** adj 1 echoing. 2 clear and emphatic.

resource n 1 thing resorted to for support. 2 ingenuity. 3 means of achieving something. ♦ pl 4 sources of economic wealth. 5 stock that can be drawn on, funds. **resourceful** adj **resourcefulness** n

respect n 1 consideration. 2 deference or esteem. 3 point or aspect. 4 reference or relation, e.g. *with respect to.* 5 v 6 treat with esteem. 7 show consideration for. **respecter** n **respectful** adj **respecting** prep concerning.

respectable adj 1 worthy of respect. 2 fairly good. **respectably** adv **respectability** n

respective adj relating separately to each of those in question. **respectively** adv

respiration [ress-per-**ray**-shun] n breathing. **respirator** n apparatus worn over the mouth and breathed through as protection against dust, poison gas, etc., or to provide artificial respiration. **respiratory** adj **respire** v breathe.

respite n 1 pause, interval of rest. 2 delay.

resplendent adj 1 brilliant or splendid. 2 shining. **resplendence** n

respond v 1 answer. 2 act in answer to any stimulus. 3 react favourably. **respondent** n *Law* defendant. **response** n 1 answer. 2 reaction to a stimulus. **responsive** adj readily reacting to some influence. **responsiveness** n

responsible adj 1 having control and authority. 2 reporting or accountable (to). 3 sensible and dependable. 4 involving responsibility. **responsibly** adv **responsibility** n, pl -ties 1 state of being responsible. 2 person or thing for which one is responsible.

rest[1] n 1 freedom from exertion etc. 2 repose. 3 pause, esp. in music. 4 object used for support. ♦ v 5 take a rest. 6 give a rest (to). 7 be supported. 8 place on a support. **restful** adj **restless** adj

rest[2] n 1 what is left. 2 others. ♦ v 3 remain, continue to be.

restaurant n commercial establishment serving meals. **restaurateur** [rest-er-a-**tur**] n person who owns or runs a restaurant.

restitution n 1 giving back. 2 reparation or compensation.

restive adj restless or impatient.

restore v 1 return (a building, painting, etc.) to its original condition. 2 cause to recover health or spirits. 3 give back, return. 4 re-establish. **restoration** n **restorative** adj 1 restoring. ♦ n 2 food or medicine to strengthen etc. **restorer** n

restrain v 1 hold (someone) back from action. 2 control or restrict. **restrained** adj not displaying emotion. **restraint** n 1 control, esp. self-control. 2 restraining.

restrict v confine to certain limits. **restriction** n **restrictive** adj

restructure v organize in a different way.

result n 1 outcome or consequence. 2 score. 3 number obtained from a calculation. 4 exam mark or grade. ♦ v 5 (foll. by from) be the outcome or consequence (of). 6 (foll. by in) end (in). **resultant** adj

resume v 1 begin again. 2 occupy or take again. **resumption** n

résumé [**rezz**-yew-may] n summary.

resurgence n rising again to vigour. **resurgent** adj

resurrect v 1 restore to life. 2 use once more (something discarded etc.), revive. **resurrection** n 1 rising again (esp. from the dead). 2 revival.

resuscitate [ris-**suss**-it-tate] v restore to consciousness. **resuscitation** n

☑ **SPELLING TIP**
There is a silent c in **resuscitate**, but only one: it comes after the second s, not after the first one.

retail n 1 selling of goods individually or in small amounts to the public. 2 adv 3 by retail. ♦ v 4 sell or be sold retail. 5 recount in detail.

retailer n person or company that sells goods to the public.

retain v 1 keep in one's possession. 2 engage the services of. **retainer** n 1 fee to retain someone's services 2 old-established servant of a family.

retaliate v repay an injury or wrong in kind. **retaliation** n **retaliatory** adj

retard v delay or slow (progress or development). **retarded** adj underdeveloped, esp. mentally. **retardation** n

retch v try to vomit.

rethink v consider again, esp. with a view to changing one's tactics.

reticent adj uncommunicative, reserved. **reticence** n

retina n, pl **-nas, -nae** light-sensitive membrane at the back of the eye.

retinue n band of attendants.

retire v 1 (cause to) give up office or work, esp. through age. 2 go away or withdraw. 3 go to bed. **retired** adj having retired from work etc. **retirement** n **retiring** adj shy.

retort[1] v 1 reply quickly, wittily, or angrily. ♦ n 2 quick, witty, or angry reply.

retort[2] n glass container with a bent neck used for distilling.

retouch v restore or improve by new touches, esp. of paint.

retrace v go back over (a route etc.) again.

retract v 1 withdraw (a statement etc.). 2 draw in or back. **retractable, retractile** adj able to be retracted. **retraction** n

retread v, n same as REMOULD.

retreat v 1 move back from a position, withdraw. ♦ n 2 act of or military signal for retiring or withdrawal. **3** place to which anyone retires, refuge.

retrench v reduce expenditure, cut back. **retrenchment** n

retrial n second trial of a case or defendant in a court of law.

retribution n punishment or vengeance for evil deeds. **retributive** adj

retrieve v **1** fetch back again. **2** restore to a better state. **3** recover (information) from a computer. **retrievable** adj **retrieval** n **retriever** n dog trained to retrieve shot game.

retroactive adj effective from a date in the past.

retrograde adj tending towards an earlier worse condition.

retrogressive adj going back to an earlier worse condition. **retrogression** n

retrorocket n small rocket engine used to slow a spacecraft.

retrospect n **in retrospect** when looking back on the past. **retrospective** adj **1** looking back in time. **2** applying from a date in the past. ◆ n **3** exhibition of an artist's life's work.

retroussé [rit-**troo**-say] adj (of a nose) turned upwards.

retsina n Greek wine flavoured with resin.

return v **1** go or come back. **2** give, put, or send back. **3** reply. **4** elect. ◆ n **5** returning. **6** (thing) being returned. **7** profit. **8** official report, as of taxable income. **9** return ticket. **returnable** adj **returning officer** person in charge of an election. **return ticket** ticket allowing a passenger to travel to a place and back.

reunion n meeting of people who have been apart. **reunite** v bring or come together again after a separation.

reuse v use again. **reusable** adj

rev Informal ◆ n **1** revolution (of an engine). ◆ v **revving, revved 2** (foll. by up) increase the speed of revolution of (an engine).

Rev., Revd. Reverend.

revalue v adjust the exchange value of (a currency) upwards. **revaluation** n

revamp v renovate or restore.

reveal v **1** make known. **2** expose or show. **revelation** n

reveille [riv-**val**-ee] n morning bugle call to waken soldiers.

revel v **-elling, -elled 1** take pleasure (in). **2** make merry. **revels** pl n merrymaking. **reveller** n **revelry** n festivity.

revenge n **1** retaliation for wrong done. ◆ v **2** make retaliation for. **3** avenge (oneself or another). **revengeful** adj

revenue n income, esp. of a state.

reverberate v echo or resound. **reverberation** n

revere v be in awe of and respect greatly. **reverence** n awe mingled with respect and esteem. **Reverend** adj title of respect for a clergyman. **reverent** adj showing reverence. **reverently** adv **reverential** adj marked by reverence.

reverie n absent-minded daydream.

revers [riv-**veer**] n turned back part of a garment, such as the lapel.

reverse v **1** turn upside down or the other way round. **2** change completely. **3** move (a vehicle) backwards. ◆ n **4** opposite. **5** back side. **6** change for the worse. **7** reverse gear. ◆ adj **8** opposite or contrary. **reversal** n **reversible** adj **reverse gear** mechanism enabling a vehicle to move backwards.

revert v **1** return to a former state. **2** come back to a subject. **3** (of property) return to its former owner. **reversion** n

review n **1** critical assessment of a book, concert, etc. **2** publication with critical articles. **3** general survey. **4** formal inspection. ♦ v **5** hold or write a review of. **6** examine, reconsider, or look back on. **7** inspect formally. **reviewer** n writer of reviews.

revile v be abusively scornful of.

revise v **1** change or alter. **2** restudy (work) in preparation for an examination. **revision** n

revive v bring or come back to life, vigour, use, etc. **revival** n **1** reviving or renewal. **2** movement seeking to restore religious faith. **revivalism** n **revivalist** n

revoke v cancel (a will, agreement, etc.). **revocation** n

revolt n **1** uprising against authority. ♦ v **2** rise in rebellion. **3** cause to feel disgust. **revolting** adj disgusting, horrible.

revolution n **1** overthrow of a government by the governed. **2** great change. **3** spinning round. **4** complete rotation. **revolutionary** adj **1** advocating or engaged in revolution. **2** radically new or different. ♦ n, pl **-aries** **3** person advocating or engaged in revolution. **revolutionize** v change considerably.

revolve v turn round, rotate. **revolve around** be centred on.

revolver n repeating pistol.

revue n theatrical entertainment with topical sketches and songs.

revulsion n strong disgust.

reward n **1** something given in return for a service. **2** sum of money offered for finding a criminal or missing property. ♦ v **3** pay or give something to (someone) for a service, information, etc. **rewarding** adj giving personal satisfaction, worthwhile.

rewind v run (a tape or film) back to an earlier point in order to replay.

rewire v provide (a house, engine, etc.) with new wiring.

rewrite v **1** write again in a different way. ♦ n **2** something rewritten.

rhapsody n, pl **-dies** **1** freely structured emotional piece of music. **2** expression of ecstatic enthusiasm. **rhapsodic** adj **rhapsodize** v speak or write with extravagant enthusiasm.

rhea [**ree**-a] n S American three-toed ostrich.

rhenium n Chem silvery-white metallic element with a high melting point.

rheostat n instrument for varying the resistance of an electrical circuit.

rhesus [**ree**-suss] n small long-tailed monkey of S Asia. **rhesus factor, Rh factor** antigen commonly found in human blood.

rhetoric n **1** art of effective speaking or writing. **2** artificial or exaggerated language. **rhetorical** adj (of a question) not requiring an answer. **rhetorically** adv

rheumatism n painful inflammation of joints or muscles. **rheumatic** n, adj (person) affected by rheumatism. **rheumatoid** adj of or like rheumatism.

Rh factor n see RHESUS.

rhinestone n imitation diamond.

rhino n short for RHINOCEROS.

rhinoceros n, pl **-oses, -os** large thick-skinned animal with one or two horns on its nose.

☑ SPELLING TIP

The pronunciation of **rhinoceros** probably misleads some people into making the mistake of adding a u before the final s (rhinocerous).

---

rhizome n thick underground stem producing new plants.

rhodium n Chem hard metallic element.

rhododendron n evergreen flowering shrub.

rhombus n, pl -buses, -bi parallelogram with sides of equal length but no right angles, diamond-shaped figure. **rhomboid** n parallelogram with adjacent sides of unequal length.

rhubarb n garden plant of which the fleshy stalks are cooked as fruit.

rhyme n 1 sameness of the final sounds at the ends of lines of verse, or in words. 2 word identical in sound to another in its final sounds. 3 verse marked by rhyme. ♦ v 4 make a rhyme.

rhythm n 1 any regular movement or beat. 2 arrangement of the durations of and stress on the notes of a piece of music, usu. grouped into a regular pattern. 3 (in poetry) arrangement of words to form a regular pattern of stresses. **rhythmic, rhythmical** adj **rhythmically** adv **rhythm and blues** popular music, orig. Black American, influenced by the blues.

☑ **SPELLING TIP**

The second letter of **rhythm** is a silent h, which people often forget in writing.

---

rib¹ n 1 one of the curved bones forming the framework of the upper part of the body. 2 cut of meat including the rib(s). 3 curved supporting part, as in the hull of a boat. 4 raised series of rows in knitting. ♦ v **ribbing, ribbed** 5 provide or mark with ribs. 6 knit to form a rib pattern. **ribbed** adj **ribbing** n **ribcage** n bony structure of ribs enclosing the lungs.

rib² v **ribbing, ribbed** Informal tease or ridicule. **ribbing** n

ribald adj humorously or mockingly rude or obscene. **ribaldry** n

ribbon n 1 narrow band of fabric used for trimming, tying, etc. 2 any long strip, for example of inked tape in a typewriter.

riboflavin [rye-boe-**flay**-vin] n form of vitamin B.

rice n 1 cereal plant grown on wet ground in warm countries. 2 its seeds as food.

rich adj 1 owning a lot of money or property, wealthy. 2 abounding. 3 fertile. 4 (of food) containing much fat or sugar. 5 mellow. 6 amusing. **riches** pl n wealth. **richly** adv 1 elaborately. 2 fully. **richness** n

rick¹ n stack of hay etc.

rick² v, n sprain or wrench.

rickets n disease of children marked by softening of the bones, bow legs, etc., caused by vitamin D deficiency.

rickety adj shaky or unstable.

rickshaw n light two-wheeled man-drawn Asian vehicle.

ricochet [**rik**-osh-ay] v 1 (of a bullet) rebound from a solid surface. ♦ n 2 such a rebound.

rid v **ridding, rid** clear or relieve (of). **get rid of** free oneself of (something undesirable). **good riddance** relief at getting rid of something or someone.

ridden v 1 past participle of RIDE. ♦ adj 2 afflicted or affected by the thing specified, e.g. disease-ridden.

riddle¹ n 1 question made puzzling to test one's ingenuity. 2 puzzling person or thing.

riddle² v 1 pierce with many holes. ♦ n 2 coarse sieve for gravel etc. **riddled with** full of.

ride v **riding, rode, ridden** 1 sit on and control or propel (a horse, bicycle, etc.). 2 go on horseback or in a vehicle. 3 travel over. 4 be carried on or across. 5 lie at anchor. ♦ n 6 journey on a horse etc., or in a vehicle. 7 type of movement experienced in a vehicle.

ride up v (of a garment) move up from the proper position.

rider n **1** person who rides. **2** supplementary clause added to a document.

ridge n **1** long narrow hill. **2** long narrow raised part on a surface. **3** line where two sloping surfaces meet. **4** *Meteorol* elongated area of high pressure. **ridged** adj

ridiculous adj deserving to be laughed at, absurd. **ridicule** n **1** treatment of a person or thing as ridiculous. ♦ v **2** laugh at, make fun of.

Riding n former administrative district of Yorkshire.

riesling n type of white wine.

rife adj widespread or common. **rife with** full of.

riff n *Jazz, rock* short repeated melodic figure.

riffle v flick through (pages etc.) quickly.

riffraff n rabble, disreputable people.

rifle[1] n firearm with a long barrel.

rifle[2] v **1** search and rob. **2** steal.

rift n **1** break in friendly relations. **2** crack, split, or cleft. **rift valley** long narrow valley resulting from subsidence between faults.

rig v **rigging, rigged 1** arrange in a dishonest way. **2** equip, esp. a ship. ♦ n **3** apparatus for drilling for oil and gas. **4** way a ship's masts and sails are arranged. **5** *Informal* outfit of clothes. **rigging** n ship's spars and ropes. **rig up** v set up or build temporarily.

right adj **1** just. **2** true or correct. **3** proper. **4** in a satisfactory condition. **5** of the side that faces east when the front is turned to the north. **6** of the outer side of a fabric. ♦ adv **7** properly. **8** straight or directly. **9** on or to the right side. **10** n **11** claim, title, etc. allowed or due. **12** what is just or due. **13** (R-) conservative political party or

group. ♦ v **14** bring or come back to a normal or correct state. **15** bring or come back to a vertical position. **in the right** morally or legally correct. **right away** immediately. **rightly** adv **rightful** adj **rightfully** adv **rightist** n, adj (person) on the political right. **right angle** angle of 90°. **right-handed** adj using or for the right hand. **right-hand man** person's most valuable assistant. **right of way 1** right of one vehicle to go before another. **2** legal right to pass over someone's land. **right-wing** adj **1** conservative or reactionary. **2** belonging to the more conservative part of a political party.

righteous [rye-chuss] adj **1** upright, godly, or virtuous. **2** morally justified. **righteousness** n

rigid adj **1** inflexible or strict. **2** unyielding or stiff. **rigidly** adv **rigidity** n

rigmarole n long complicated procedure.

rigor mortis n stiffening of the body after death.

rigour n **1** harshness, severity, or strictness. **2** hardship. **rigorous** adj harsh, severe, or stern.

rile v anger or annoy.

rill n small stream.

rim n **1** edge or border. **2** outer ring of a wheel. **rimmed** adj

rime n *Lit* hoarfrost.

rimu n *NZ* New Zealand tree whose wood is used for building and furniture.

rind n tough outer coating of fruits, cheese, or bacon.

ring[1] v **ringing, rang, rung 1** give out a clear resonant sound, as a bell. **2** cause (a bell) to sound. **3** telephone. **4** resound. ♦ n **5** ringing. **6** telephone call. **ring off** v end a telephone call. **ringtone** n tune played by a mobile phone when it receives a call. **ring up**

v **1** telephone. **2** record on a cash register.

☑ **WORD TIP**
The simple past is *rang: He rang the bell.* Avoid the use of the past participle *rung* for the simple past.

---

ring² *n* **1** circle of gold etc., esp. for a finger. **2** any circular band, coil, or rim. **3** circle of people. **4** enclosed area, esp. a circle for a circus or a roped-in square for boxing. **5** group operating (illegal) control of a market. ♦ *v* **6** put a ring round. **7** mark (a bird) with a ring. **8** kill (a tree) by cutting the bark round the trunk. **ringer** *n Brit, Aust & NZ slang* person or thing apparently identical to another (also **dead ringer**). **ringlet** *n* curly lock of hair. **ringleader** *n* instigator of a mutiny, riot, etc. **ring road** *Brit, Aust & S Afr* main road that bypasses a town (centre). **ringside** *n* row of seats nearest a boxing or circus ring. **ringtail** *n Aust* possum with a curling tail used to grip branches while climbing. **ringworm** *n* fungal skin disease in circular patches.

rink *n* **1** sheet of ice for skating or curling. **2** floor for roller-skating.

rinse *v* **1** remove soap from (washed clothes, hair, etc.) by applying clean water. **2** wash lightly. ♦ *n* **3** rinsing. **4** liquid to tint hair.

riot *n* **1** disorderly unruly disturbance. **2** *Brit, Aust & NZ* loud revelry. **3** profusion. **4** *Slang* very amusing person or thing. ♦ *v* **5** take part in a riot. **read the riot act** reprimand severely. **run riot 1** behave without restraint. **2** grow profusely. **riotous** *adj* **1** unrestrained. **2** unruly or rebellious.

rip *v* **ripping, ripped** **1** tear violently. **2** tear away. **3** *Informal* rush. ♦ *n* **4** split or tear. **let rip** act or speak without restraint. **ripcord** *n* cord pulled to open a parachute. **rip-off** *v Slang* cheat by overcharging. **rip-off** *n Slang* cheat or swindle. **rip-roaring** *adj Informal* boisterous and exciting.

RIP rest in peace.

riparian [rip-**pair**-ee-an] *adj* of or on the banks of a river.

ripe *adj* **1** ready to be reaped, eaten, etc. **2** matured. **3** ready or suitable. **ripen** *v* **1** grow ripe. **2** mature.

riposte [rip-**posst**] *n* **1** verbal retort. **2** counterattack, esp. in fencing. ♦ *v* **3** make a riposte.

ripple *n* **1** slight wave or ruffling of a surface. **2** sound like ripples of water. ♦ *v* **3** flow or form into little waves (on). **4** (of sounds) rise and fall gently.

rise *v* **rising, rose, risen** **1** get up from a lying, sitting, or kneeling position. **2** move upwards. **3** (of the sun or moon) appear above the horizon. **4** reach a higher level. **5** (of an amount or price) increase. **6** rebel. **7** (of a court) adjourn. **8** *n* **9** rising. **10** upward slope. **11** increase, esp. of wages. **give rise to** cause. **riser** *n* **1** person who rises, esp. from bed. **2** vertical part of a step. **rising** *n* **1** revolt. ♦ *adj* **2** increasing in rank or maturity.

risible [**riz**-zib-bl] *adj* causing laughter, ridiculous.

risk *n* **1** chance of disaster or loss. **2** person or thing considered as a potential hazard. ♦ *v* **3** act in spite of the possibility of (injury or loss). **4** expose to danger or loss. **risky** *adj* full of risk, dangerous.

risotto *n, pl* **-tos** dish of rice cooked in stock with vegetables, meat, etc.

risqué [**risk**-ay] *adj* bordering on indecency.

rissole *n* cake of minced meat, coated with breadcrumbs and fried.

rite *n* formal practice or custom, esp.

religious.
ritual n 1 prescribed order of rites. 2 regular repeated action or behaviour. ♦ adj 3 concerning rites. **ritually** adv **ritualistic** adj like a ritual.

ritzy adj **ritzier, ritziest** Slang luxurious or elegant.

rival n 1 person or thing that competes with or equals another for favour, success, etc. ♦ adj 2 in the position of a rival. ♦ v **-valling, -valled** 3 (try to) equal. **rivalry** n keen competition.

riven adj split apart.

river n 1 large natural stream of water. 2 plentiful flow.

rivet [**riv-**vit] n 1 bolt for fastening metal plates, the end being put through holes and then beaten flat. ♦ v **riveting, riveted** 2 fasten with rivets. 3 cause to be fixed, as in fascination. **riveting** adj very interesting and exciting.

rivulet n small stream.

RN (in Britain) Royal Navy.

RNA ribonucleic acid: substance in living cells essential for the synthesis of protein.

RNZ Radio New Zealand.

RNZAF Royal New Zealand Air Force.

RNZN Royal New Zealand Navy.

roach n Eurasian freshwater fish.

road n 1 way prepared for passengers, vehicles, etc. 2 route in a town or city with houses along it. 3 way or course, e.g. the road to fame. **on the road** travelling. **roadie** n Brit, Aust & NZ informal person who transports and sets up equipment for a band. **roadblock** n barricade across a road to stop traffic for inspection etc. **road hog** Informal selfish aggressive driver. **roadhouse** n Brit, Aust & S Afr pub or restaurant on a country road. **roadside** n, adj **road test** test of a vehicle etc. in actual use. **roadway** n the part of a road used by vehicles.

roadworks pl n repairs to a road, esp. blocking part of the road. **roadworthy** adj (of a vehicle) mechanically sound.

roam v wander about.

roan adj 1 (of a horse) having a brown or black coat sprinkled with white hairs. ♦ n 2 roan horse.

roar v 1 make or utter a loud deep hoarse sound like that of a lion. 2 shout (something) as in anger. 3 laugh loudly. ♦ n 4 such a sound. **a roaring trade** Informal brisk and profitable business. **roaring drunk** noisily drunk.

roast v 1 cook by dry heat, as in an oven. 2 make or be very hot. ♦ n 3 roasted joint of meat. ♦ adj 4 roasted. **roasting** Informal ♦ adj 1 extremely hot. ♦ n 2 severe criticism or scolding.

rob v **robbing, robbed** 1 steal from. 2 deprive. **robber** n **robbery** n

robe n 1 long loose outer garment. ♦ v 2 put a robe on.

robin n small brown bird with a red breast.

robot n 1 automated machine, esp. one performing functions in a human manner. 2 person of machine-like efficiency. 3 S Afr set of coloured lights at a junction to control the traffic flow. **robotic** adj **robotics** n science of designing and using robots.

robust adj very strong and healthy. **robustly** adv **robustness** n

roc n monstrous bird of Arabian mythology.

rock[1] n 1 hard mineral substance that makes up part of the earth's crust, stone. 2 large rugged mass of stone 3 Brit hard sweet in sticks. **on the rocks** 1 (of a marriage) about to end. 2 (of an alcoholic drink) served with ice. **rocky** adj having many rocks. **rockery** n mound of stones in a garden for rock plants. **rock bottom** lowest possible level. **rock cake** small fruit cake with a rough surface.

rock² v **1** (cause to) sway to and fro. **2** NZ slang be very good. ♦ n **3** (also **rock music**) style of pop music with a heavy beat. **rocky** adj shaky or unstable. **rock and roll, rock'n'roll** style of pop music blending rhythm and blues and country music. **rocking chair** chair allowing the sitter to rock backwards and forwards.

rocker n **1** rocking chair. **2** curved piece of wood etc. on which something may rock. **off one's rocker** Informal insane.

rocket n **1** self-propelling device powered by the burning of explosive contents (used as a firework, weapon, etc.). **2** vehicle propelled by a rocket engine, as a weapon or carrying a spacecraft. **3** v **-eting, -eted 4** move fast, esp. upwards, like a rocket.

rock melon n US, Aust & NZ kind of melon with sweet orange flesh.

rococo [rok-**koe**-koe] adj (of furniture, architecture, etc.) having much elaborate decoration in an early 18th-century style.

rod n **1** slender straight bar, stick. **2** cane.

rode v past tense of RIDE.

rodent n animal with teeth specialized for gnawing, such as a rat, mouse, or squirrel.

rodeo n, pl **-deos** display of skill by cowboys, such as bareback riding.

roe¹ n mass of eggs in a fish, sometimes eaten as food.

roe² n small species of deer.

roentgen [**ront**-gan] n unit measuring a radiation dose.

rogue n **1** dishonest or unprincipled person. **2** mischief-loving person. **3** adj **4** (of a wild beast) having a savage temper and living apart from the herd. **roguish** adj

roister v make merry noisily or boisterously.

role, rôle n **1** task or function. **2** actor's part.

roll v **1** move by turning over and over. **2** move or sweep along. **3** wind round. **4** undulate. **5** smooth out with a roller. **6** (of a ship or aircraft) turn from side to side about a line from nose to tail. **7** n **8** act of rolling over or from side to side. **9** piece of paper etc. rolled up. **10** small round individually baked piece of bread. **11** list or register. **12** continuous sound, as of drums, thunder, etc. **13** swaying unsteady movement or gait. **roll call** calling out of a list of names, as in a school or the army, to check who is present. **rolled gold** metal coated with a thin layer of gold. **rolling pin** cylindrical roller for flattening pastry. **rolling stock** locomotives and coaches of a railway. **rolling stone** restless wandering person. **roll-on/roll-off** adj Brit, Aust & NZ denoting a ship allowing vehicles to be driven straight on and off. **roll-top** adj (of a desk) having a flexible lid sliding in grooves. **roll up** v Informal appear or arrive. **roll-up** n Brit informal cigarette made by the smoker from loose tobacco and cigarette paper.

roller n **1** rotating cylinder used for smoothing or supporting a thing to be moved, spreading paint, etc. **2** long wave of the sea. **Rollerblade** n ® roller skate with the wheels set in one straight line. **roller coaster** (at a funfair) narrow railway with steep slopes. **roller skate** skate with wheels.

rollicking adj boisterously carefree.

roly-poly adj round or plump.

ROM Computers read only memory.

Roman adj of Rome or the Roman Catholic Church. **Roman Catholic** (member) of that section of the Christian Church that acknowledges the supremacy of the Pope. **Roman numerals** the letters I, V, X, L, C, D, M, used to represent numbers. **roman type** plain upright letters in printing.

romance *n* **1** love affair. **2** mysterious or exciting quality. **3** novel or film dealing with love, esp. sentimentally. **4** story with scenes remote from ordinary life.

Romance *adj* (of a language) developed from Latin, such as French or Spanish.

romantic *adj* **1** of or dealing with love. **2** idealistic but impractical. **3** (of literature, music, etc.) displaying passion and imagination rather than order and form. ♦ *n* **4** romantic person or artist. **romantically** *adv* **romanticism** *n* **romanticize** *v* describe or regard in an idealized and unrealistic way.

Romany *n, pl* **-nies**, *adj* Gypsy.

romp *v* **1** play wildly and joyfully. ♦ *n* **2** boisterous activity. **romp home** win easily. **rompers** *pl n* child's overalls.

rondo *n, pl* **-dos** piece of music with a leading theme continually returned to.

roo *n Aust informal* kangaroo.

rood *n* **1** *Christianity* the Cross. **2** crucifix. **rood screen** (in a church) screen separating the nave from the choir.

roof *n, pl* **roofs 1** outside upper covering of a building, car, etc. ♦ *v* **2** put a roof on.

rooibos [**roy**-boss] *n S Afr* tea prepared from the dried leaves of an African plant.

rook[1] *n* Eurasian bird of the crow family. **rookery** *n, pl* **-eries** colony of rooks, penguins, or seals.

rook[2] *n* chess piece shaped like a castle.

rookie *n Informal* new recruit.

room *n* **1** enclosed area in a building. **2** unoccupied space. **3** scope or

opportunity. ♦ *pl* **4** lodgings. **roomy** *adj* spacious.

roost *n* **1** perch for fowls. ♦ *v* **2** perch.

rooster *n* domestic cock.

root[1] *n* **1** part of a plant that grows down into the earth obtaining nourishment. **2** plant with an edible root, such as a carrot. **3** part of a tooth, hair, etc. below the skin. **4** source or origin. **5** form of a word from which other words and forms are derived. **6** *Maths* factor of a quantity which, when multiplied by itself the number of times indicated, gives the quantity. ♦ *pl* **7** person's sense of belonging. ♦ *v* **8** establish a root and start to grow. **rootless** *adj* having no sense of belonging. **root for** *v Informal* cheer on. **root out** *v* get rid of completely.

root[2] *v* dig or burrow.

rope *n* thick cord. **know the ropes** be thoroughly familiar with an activity. **rope in** *v* persuade to join in.

ropey, ropy *adj* **ropier, ropiest** *Brit informal* **1** inferior or inadequate. **2** not well.

rorqual *n* toothless whale with a dorsal fin.

rort *Aust informal* ♦ *n* **1** dishonest scheme. ♦ *v* **2** take unfair advantage of something.

rosary *n, pl* **-saries 1** series of prayers. **2** string of beads for counting these prayers.

rose[1] *n* **1** shrub or climbing plant with prickly stems and fragrant flowers. **2** flower of this plant. **3** perforated flat nozzle for a hose. **4** pink colour. ♦ *adj* **5** pink. **roseate** [**roe**-zee-ate] *adj* rose-coloured. **rose window** circular window with spokes branching from the centre. **rosewood** *n* fragrant wood used to make furniture.

rose[2] *v* past tense of RISE.

rosé [**roe**-zay] *n* pink wine.

rosehip n berry-like fruit of a rose plant.

rosella n type of Australian parrot.

rosemary n 1 fragrant flowering shrub. 2 its leaves as a herb.

rosette n rose-shaped ornament, esp. a circular bunch of ribbons.

rosin [**rozz**-in] n resin used for treating the bows of violins etc.

roster n list of people and their turns of duty.

rostrum n, pl **-trums, -tra** platform or stage.

rosy adj **rosier, rosiest** 1 pink-coloured. 2 hopeful or promising.

rot v **rotting, rotted** 1 decompose or decay. 2 slowly deteriorate physically or mentally. ♦ n 3 decay. 4 Informal nonsense.

rota n list of people who take it in turn to do a particular task.

rotary adj 1 revolving. 2 operated by rotation.

rotate v 1 (cause to) move round a centre or on a pivot. 2 (cause to) follow a set sequence. **rotation** n

rote n mechanical repetition. **by rote** by memory.

rotisserie n rotating spit for cooking meat.

rotor n 1 revolving portion of a dynamo, motor, or turbine. 2 rotating device with long blades that provides thrust to lift a helicopter.

rotten adj 1 decaying. 2 Informal very bad. 3 corrupt.

rotter n Chiefly Brit slang despicable person.

Rottweiler [**rot**-vile-er] n large sturdy dog with a smooth black and tan coat and usu. a docked tail.

rotund [roe-**tund**] adj 1 round and plump. 2 sonorous. **rotundity** n

rotunda n circular building or room, esp. with a dome.

rouble [**roo**-bl] n monetary unit of Russia, Belarus, and Tajikistan.

roué [**roo**-ay] n man given to immoral living.

rouge n red cosmetic used to colour the cheeks.

rough adj 1 uneven or irregular. 2 not careful or gentle. 3 difficult or unpleasant. 4 approximate. 5 violent, stormy, or boisterous. 6 in preliminary form. 7 lacking refinement. ♦ v 8 make rough. ♦ n 9 rough state or area. **rough it** live without the usual comforts etc. **roughen** v **roughly** adv **roughness** n **roughage** n indigestible constituents of food which aid digestion. **rough-and-ready** adj hastily prepared but adequate. **rough-and-tumble** n playful fight. **rough-hewn** adj roughly shaped. **roughhouse** n Chiefly US slang fight. **rough out** v prepare (a sketch or report) in preliminary form.

roughcast n 1 mixture of plaster and small stones for outside walls. ♦ v 2 coat with this.

roughshod adv **ride roughshod over** act with total disregard for.

roulette n gambling game played with a revolving wheel and a ball.

round adj 1 spherical, cylindrical, circular, or curved. 2 adv, prep 3 indicating an encircling movement, presence on all sides, etc., e.g. tied round the waist; books scattered round the room. ♦ v 4 move round. ♦ n 5 customary course, as of a milkman. 6 game (of golf). 7 stage in a competition. 8 one of several periods in a boxing match etc. 9 number of drinks bought at one time. 10 bullet or shell for a gun. **roundly** adv thoroughly. **rounders** n bat-and-ball team game. **round robin 1** petition signed with names in a circle to conceal the order. 2 tournament in which each player plays against every other player. **round-the-clock** *adj* throughout the day and night. **round trip** journey out and back again. **round up** *v* gather (people or animals) together. **roundup** *n*

roundabout *n* **1** road junction at which traffic passes round a central island. **2** revolving circular platform on which people ride for amusement. ♦ *adj* **3** not straightforward.

roundel *n* small disc. **roundelay** *n* simple song with a refrain.

Roundhead *n Hist* supporter of Parliament against Charles I in the English Civil War.

rouse[1] [rhymes with **cows**] *v* **1** wake up. **2** provoke or excite. **rousing** *adj* lively, vigorous.

rouse[2] [rhymes with **mouse**] *v* (foll. by *on*) *Aust* scold or rebuke.

rouseabout *n Aust & NZ* labourer in a shearing shed.

roustabout *n* labourer on an oil rig.

rout *n* **1** overwhelming defeat. **2** disorderly retreat. ♦ *v* **3** defeat and put to flight.

route *n* **1** roads taken to reach a destination. **2** chosen way. **route march** long military training march.

routine *n* **1** usual or regular method of procedure. **2** set sequence. ♦ *adj* **3** ordinary or regular.

roux [**roo**] *n* fat and flour cooked together as a basis for sauces.

rove *v* wander.

rover *n* wanderer, traveller.

row[1] [rhymes with **go**] *n* straight line of people or things. **in a row** in succession.

row[2] [rhymes with **go**] *v* **1** propel (a boat) by oars. ♦ *n* **2** spell of rowing. **rowing boat** boat propelled by oars.

row[3] [rhymes with **now**] *Informal* ♦ *n* **1** dispute. **2** disturbance. **3** reprimand. ♦ *v* **4** quarrel noisily.

rowan *n* tree producing bright red berries, mountain ash.

rowdy *adj* **-dier, -diest 1** disorderly, noisy, and rough. ♦ *n, pl* **-dies 2** person like this.

rowel [rhymes with **towel**] *n* small spiked wheel on a spur.

rowlock [**rol**-luk] *n* device on a boat that holds an oar in place.

royal *adj* **1** of, befitting, or supported by a king or queen. **2** splendid. ♦ *n* **3** *Informal* member of a royal family. **royally** *adv* **royalist** *n* supporter of monarchy. **royalty** *n* **1** royal people. **2** rank or power of a monarch. **3** *pl* **-ties)** payment to an author, musician, inventor, etc. **royal blue** deep blue.

RPI (in Britain) retail price index: measure of change in the average level of prices

rpm revolutions per minute.

RSA 1 Republic of South Africa. **2** (in New Zealand) Returned Services Association.

RSI repetitive strain injury.

RSPCA (in Britain) Royal Society for the Prevention of Cruelty to Animals.

RSVP please reply.

rub *v* **rubbing, rubbed 1** apply pressure and friction to (something) with a circular or backwards-and-forwards movement. **2** clean, polish, or dry by rubbing. **3** chafe or fray through rubbing. ♦ *n* **4** act of rubbing. **rub it in** emphasize an unpleasant fact. **rub out** *v* remove with a rubber.

rubato *adv, n Music* (with) expressive flexibility of tempo.

rubber[1] *n* **1** strong waterproof elastic material, orig. made from the dried sap of a tropical tree, now usu. synthetic. **2** piece of rubber used for erasing writing. ♦ *adj* **3** made of or producing rubber. **rubbery** *adj* **rubberneck** *v* stare with unthinking curiosity. **rubber stamp 1** device for imprinting the date, a name, etc. **2** automatic authorization.

rubber[2] *n* **1** match consisting of three games of bridge, whist, etc. **2** series of matches.

rubbish *n* **1** waste matter. **2** anything worthless. **3** nonsense. **rubbishy** *adj*

rubble *n* fragments of broken stone, brick, etc.

rubella *n* same as GERMAN MEASLES.

rubicund *adj* ruddy.

rubidium *n* *Chem* soft highly reactive radioactive element.

rubric *n* heading or explanation inserted in a text.

ruby *n, pl* **-bies 1** red precious gemstone. ♦ *adj* **2** deep red.

ruck[1] *n* **1** rough crowd of common people. **2** *Rugby* loose scrummage.

ruck[2] *n, v* wrinkle or crease.

rucksack *n* *Brit, Aust & S Afr* large pack carried on the back.

ructions *pl n* *Informal* noisy uproar.

rudder *n* vertical hinged piece at the stern of a boat or at the rear of an aircraft, for steering.

ruddy *adj* **-dier, -diest** of a fresh healthy red colour.

rude *adj* **1** impolite or insulting. **2** coarse, vulgar, or obscene. **3** unexpected and unpleasant. **4** roughly made. **5** robust. **rudely** *adv* **rudeness** *n*

rudiments *pl n* simplest and most basic stages of a subject. **rudimentary** *adj* basic, elementary.

rue[1] *v* **ruing, rued** feel regret for. **rueful** *adj* regretful or sorry. **ruefully** *adv*

rue[2] *n* plant with evergreen bitter leaves.

ruff *n* **1** starched and frilled collar. **2** natural collar of feathers, fur, etc. on certain birds and animals.

ruffian *n* violent lawless person.

ruffle *v* **1** disturb the calm of. **2** annoy, irritate. ♦ *n* **3** frill or pleat.

rug *n* **1** small carpet. **2** thick woollen blanket.

rugby *n* form of football played with an oval ball which may be handled by the players.

rugged [**rug**-gid] *adj* **1** rocky or steep. **2** uneven and jagged. **3** strong-featured. **4** tough and sturdy.

rugger *n* *Chiefly Brit informal* rugby.

ruin *v* **1** destroy or spoil completely. **2** impoverish. ♦ *n* **3** destruction or decay. **4** loss of wealth, position, etc. **5** broken-down unused building. **ruination** *n* **1** act of ruining. **2** state of being ruined. **3** cause of ruin. **ruinous** *adj* **1** causing ruin. **2** more expensive than can be afforded. **ruinously** *adv*

rule *n* **1** statement of what is allowed, for example in a game or procedure. **2** what is usual. **3** government, authority, or control. **4** measuring device with a straight edge. ♦ *v* **5** govern. **6** be pre-eminent. **7** give a formal decision. **8** mark with straight line(s). **9** restrain. **as a rule** usually. **ruler** *n* **1** person who governs. **2** measuring device with a straight edge. **ruling** *n* formal decision. **rule of thumb** practical but imprecise approach. **rule out** *v* dismiss from consideration.

rum *n* alcoholic drink distilled from sugar cane.

rumba *n* lively ballroom dance of Cuban origin.

rumble *v* **1** make a low continuous noise. **2** *Brit informal* discover the (disreputable) truth about. ♦ *n* **3** deep resonant sound.

rumbustious *adj* boisterous or unruly.

ruminate *v* **1** chew the cud. **2** ponder or meditate. **ruminant** *adj, n* cud-chewing (animal, such as a cow, sheep, or deer). **rumination** *n* quiet meditation and reflection. **ruminative** *adj*

rummage *v* **1** search untidily and at length. ♦ *n* **2** untidy search through a collection of things.

rummy *n* card game in which players try to collect sets or sequences.

rumour *n* **1** unproved statement. **2** gossip or common talk. **rumoured** *adj* suggested by rumour.

rump *n* **1** buttocks. **2** rear of an animal.

rumple *v* make untidy, crumpled, or dishevelled.

rumpus *n, pl* **-puses** noisy commotion.

run *v* **running, ran, run** **1** move with a more rapid gait than walking. **2** compete in a race, election, etc. **3** travel according to schedule. **4** function. **5** manage. **6** continue in a particular direction or for a specified period. **7** expose oneself to (a risk). **8** flow. **9** spread. **10** (of stitches) unravel. **11** *n* **12** act or spell of running. **13** ride in a car. **14** continuous period. **15** series of unravelled stitches, ladder. **run away** *v* make one's escape, flee. **run down** *v* **1** be rude about. **2** reduce in number or size. **3** stop working. **rundown** *n* **run-down** *adj* exhausted. **run into** *v* meet. **run-of-the-mill** *adj* ordinary. **run out** *v* be completely used up. **run over** *v* knock down (a person) with a moving vehicle. **run up** *v* incur (a debt).

rune *n* any character of the earliest Germanic alphabet. **runic** *adj*

rung[1] *n* crossbar on a ladder.

rung[2] *v* past participle of RING[1].

runnel *n* small brook.

runner *n* **1** competitor in a race. **2** messenger. **3** part underneath an ice skate etc., on which it slides. **4** slender horizontal stem of a plant, such as a strawberry, running along the ground and forming new roots at intervals. **5** long strip of carpet or decorative

cloth. **runner-up** *n* person who comes second in a competition.

running *adj* **1** continuous. **2** consecutive. **3** (of water) flowing. ♦ *n* **4** act of moving or flowing quickly. **5** management of a business etc. **in, out of the running** having or not having a good chance in a competition.

runny *adj* **-nier, -niest** **1** tending to flow. **2** exuding moisture.

runt *n* **1** smallest animal in a litter. **2** undersized person.

runway *n* hard level roadway where aircraft take off and land.

rupee *n* monetary unit of India and Pakistan.

rupture *n* **1** breaking, breach. **2** hernia. ♦ *v* **3** break, burst, or sever.

rural *adj* in or of the countryside.

ruse [rooz] *n* stratagem or trick.

rush[1] *v* **1** move or do very quickly. **2** force (someone) to act hastily. **3** make a sudden attack upon (a person or place). ♦ *n* **4** sudden quick or violent movement. **5** *pl* **6** first unedited prints of a scene for a film. ♦ *adj* **7** done with speed, hasty. **rush hour** period at the beginning and end of the working day, when many people are travelling to or from work.

rush[2] *n* marsh plant with a slender pithy stem. **rushy** *adj* full of rushes.

rusk *n* hard brown crisp biscuit, used esp. for feeding babies.

russet *adj* **1** reddish-brown. ♦ *n* **2** apple with rough reddish-brown skin.

rust *n* **1** reddish-brown coating formed on iron etc. that has been exposed to moisture. **2** disease of plants which produces rust-coloured spots. ♦ *adj* **3** reddish-brown. ♦ *v* **4** become coated with rust. **rusty** *adj* **1** coated with rust. **2** of a rust colour. **3** out of practice.

rustic *adj* **1** of or resembling country

people. **2** rural. **3** crude, awkward, or uncouth. **4** (of furniture) made of untrimmed branches. ♦ *n* **5** person from the country.

rustle¹ *v, n* (make) a low whispering sound.

rustle² *v US* steal (cattle). **rustler** *n US* cattle thief. **rustle up** *v* prepare at short notice.

rut¹ *n* **1** furrow made by wheels. **2** dull settled habits or way of living.

rut² *n* **1** recurrent period of sexual excitability in male deer. ♦ *v* **rutting,** **rutted 2** be in a period of sexual excitability.

ruthenium *n Chem* rare hard brittle white element.

ruthless *adj* pitiless, merciless. **ruthlessly** *adv* **ruthlessness** *n*

rye *n* **1** kind of grain used for fodder and bread. **2** *US* whiskey made from rye.

rye-grass *n* any of several grasses cultivated for fodder.

S s

s second(s).

S South(ern).

SA 1 Salvation Army. **2** South Africa. **3** South Australia.

SAA South African Airways.

Sabbath *n* day of worship and rest: Saturday for Jews, Sunday for Christians. **sabbatical** *adj*, *n* (denoting) leave for study.

SABC South African Broadcasting Corporation.

sable *n* **1** dark fur from a small weasel-like Arctic animal. ♦ *adj* **2** black.

sabot [**sab**-oh] *n* wooden shoe traditionally worn by peasants in France.

sabotage *n* **1** intentional damage done to machinery, systems, etc. ♦ *v* **2** damage intentionally. **saboteur** *n* person who commits sabotage.

sabre *n* curved cavalry sword.

sac *n* pouchlike structure in an animal or plant.

saccharin *n* artificial sweetener. **saccharine** *adj* excessively sweet.

sacerdotal *adj* of priests.

sachet *n* small envelope or bag containing a single portion.

sack¹ *n* **1** large bag made of coarse material. **2** *Informal* dismissal. **3** *Slang* bed. ♦ *v* **4** *Informal* dismiss. **sackcloth** *n* coarse fabric used for sacks, formerly worn as a penance.

sack² *n* **1** plundering of a captured town. ♦ *v* **2** plunder (a captured town).

sacrament *n* ceremony of the Christian Church, esp. Communion. **sacramental** *adj*

sacred *adj* **1** holy. **2** connected with religion. **3** set apart, reserved.

sacrifice *n* **1** giving something up. **2** thing given up. **3** making of an offering to a god. **4** thing offered. ♦ *v* **5** offer as a sacrifice. **6** give (something) up. **sacrificial** *adj*

sacrilege *n* misuse or desecration of something sacred. **sacrilegious** *adj*

☑ **SPELLING TIP**

It may sound as if **sacrilegious** has something to do with the word 'religious', which might explain why the most common misspelling of the word in the Bank of English is *sacreligious*. But it should be spelt **sacrilegious**.

---

sacristan *n* person in charge of the contents of a church. **sacristy** *n*, *pl* **-ties** room in a church where sacred objects are kept.

sacrosanct *adj* regarded as sacred, inviolable.

sacrum [**say**-krum] *n*, *pl* **-cra** wedge-shaped bone at the base of the spine.

sad *adj* **sadder, saddest 1** sorrowful, unhappy. **2** deplorably bad. **sadden** *v* make sad.

saddo *n*, *pl* **-dos, -does** *Brit informal* socially inadequate or pathetic person. **sadly** *adv* **sadness** *n*

saddle *n* **1** rider's seat on a horse or bicycle. **2** joint of meat. ♦ *v* **3** put a saddle on (a horse). **4** burden (with a responsibility). **saddler** *n* maker or seller of saddles.

sadism [**say**-dizz-um] *n* gaining of (sexual) pleasure from inflicting pain. **sadist** *n* **sadistic** *adj* **sadistically** *adv*

sadomasochism *n* combination of sadism and masochism. **sadomasochist** *n*

s.a.e. *Brit, Aust & NZ* stamped addressed envelope.

safari *n, pl* **-ris** expedition to hunt or observe wild animals, esp. in Africa. **safari park** park where lions, elephants, etc. are kept uncaged so that people can see them from cars.

safe *adj* **1** secure, protected. **2** uninjured, out of danger. **3** not involving risk. **4** *n* **5** strong lockable container. **safely** *adv* **safe-conduct** *n* permit allowing travel through a dangerous area. **safekeeping** *n* protection.

safeguard *v* **1** protect. ♦ *n* **2** protection.

safety *n, pl* **-ties** state of being safe. **safety net** net to catch performers on a trapeze or high wire if they fall. **safety pin** pin with a spring fastening and a guard over the point when closed. **safety valve** valve that allows steam etc. to escape if pressure becomes excessive.

saffron *n* **1** orange-coloured flavouring obtained from a crocus. ♦ *adj* **2** orange.

sag *v* **sagging, sagged** **1** sink in the middle. **2** tire. **3** (of clothes) hang loosely. ♦ *n* **4** droop.

saga [**sah**-ga] *n* **1** legend of Norse heroes. **2** any long story or series of events.

sagacious *adj* wise. **sagacity** *n*

sage¹ *n* **1** very wise man. ♦ *adj* **2** *Lit* wise. **sagely** *adv*

sage² *n* aromatic herb with grey-green leaves.

sago *n* starchy cereal from the powdered pith of the sago palm tree.

said *v* past of SAY.

sail *n* **1** sheet of fabric stretched to catch the wind for propelling a sailing boat. **2** arm of a windmill. ♦ *v* **3** travel by water. **4** begin a voyage. **5** move smoothly. **sailor** *n* member of a ship's crew. **sailboard** *n* board with a mast

and single sail, used for windsurfing.

saint *n* **1** *Christianity* person venerated after death as specially holy. **2** exceptionally good person. **saintly** *adj* **saintliness** *n*

sake¹ *n* **1** benefit. **2** purpose. **for the sake of 1** for the purpose of. **2** to please or benefit (someone).

sake², saki [**sah**-kee] *n* Japanese alcoholic drink made from fermented rice.

salaam [sal-**ahm**] *n* low bow of greeting among Muslims.

salacious *adj* excessively concerned with sex.

salad *n* dish of raw vegetables, eaten as a meal or part of a meal.

salamander *n* amphibian which looks like a lizard.

salami *n* highly spiced sausage.

salary *n, pl* **-ries** fixed regular payment, usu. monthly, to an employee. **salaried** *adj*

sale *n* **1** exchange of goods for money. **2** selling of goods at unusually low prices. **3** auction. **saleable** *adj* fit or likely to be sold. **salesman, saleswoman, salesperson** *n* person who sells goods. **salesmanship** *n* skill in selling.

salient [**say**-lee-ent] *adj* **1** prominent, noticeable. ♦ *n* **2** *Mil* projecting part of a front line.

saline [**say**-line] *adj* containing salt. **salinity** *n*

saliva *n* liquid that forms in the mouth, spittle. **salivary** *adj* **salivate** *v* produce saliva.

sallee *n* *Aust* (also **snow gum**) SE Australian eucalyptus with a pale grey bark acacia tree.

sallow *adj* of an unhealthy pale or yellowish colour.

sally *n, pl* **-lies** **1** witty remark. **2** sudden brief attack by troops. ♦ *v*

-lying, -lied (foll. by *forth*) **3** rush out. **4** go out.

salmon *n* **1** large fish with orange-pink flesh valued as food. ♦ *adj* **2** orange-pink.

salmonella *n, pl* **-lae** bacterium causing food poisoning.

salon *n* **1** commercial premises of a hairdresser, beautician, etc. **2** elegant reception room for guests.

saloon *n* **1** two-door or four-door car with body closed off from rear luggage area. **2** large public room, as on a ship. **3** *US* bar serving alcoholic drinks. **saloon bar** more expensive bar in a pub.

salt *n* **1** white crystalline substance used to season food. **2** chemical compound of acid and metal. **3** *v* **4** season or preserve with salt. **old salt** experienced sailor. **with a pinch of salt** allowing for exaggeration. **worth one's salt** efficient. **salty** *adj* **saltbush** *n* shrub that grows in alkaline desert regions. **salt cellar** small container for salt at table.

saltire *n Heraldry* diagonal cross on a shield.

saltpetre *n* compound used in gunpowder and as a preservative.

salubrious *adj* favourable to health.

Saluki *n* tall hound with a silky coat.

salutary *adj* producing a beneficial result.

salute *n* **1** motion of the arm as a formal military sign of respect. **2** firing of guns as a military greeting of honour. ♦ *v* **3** greet with a salute. **4** make a salute. **5** acknowledge with praise. **salutation** *n* greeting by words or actions.

salvage *n* **1** saving of a ship or other property from destruction. **2** property so saved. ♦ *v* **3** save from destruction or waste.

salvation *n* fact or state of being saved from harm or the consequences of sin.

salve *n* **1** healing or soothing ointment. ♦ *v* **2** soothe or appease.

salver *n* (silver) tray on which something is presented.

salvia *n* plant with blue or red flowers.

salvo *n, pl* **-vos, -voes** **1** simultaneous discharge of guns etc. **2** burst of applause or questions.

sal volatile [sal vol-**at**-ill-ee] *n* preparation of ammonia, used to revive a person who feels faint.

SAM surface-to-air missile.

Samaritan *n* person who helps people in distress.

samba *n* lively Brazilian dance.

same *adj* **1** identical, not different, unchanged. **2** just mentioned. **sameness** *n*

samovar *n* Russian tea urn.

Samoyed *n* dog with a thick white coat and tightly curled tail.

sampan *n* small boat with oars used in China.

samphire *n* plant found on rocks by the seashore.

sample *n* **1** part taken as representative of a whole. **2** *Music* short extract from an existing recording mixed into a backing track to produce a new recording. ♦ *v* **3** take and test a sample of. **4** *Music* take a short extract from (one recording) and mix it into a backing track. **5** record (a sound) and feed it into a computerized synthesizer so that it can be reproduced at any pitch. **sampler** *n* **1** piece of embroidery showing the embroiderer's skill. **2** *Music* piece of electronic equipment used for sampling. **sampling** *n*

samurai *n, pl* **-rai** member of an ancient Japanese warrior caste.

sanatorium *n, pl* **-riums, -ria** **1** institution for invalids or convalescents. **2** room for sick pupils at a boarding school.

sanctify v **-fying, -fied** make holy.

sanctimonious adj pretending to be religious and virtuous.

sanction n **1** permission, authorization. **2** coercive measure or penalty. ♦ v **3** allow, authorize.

sanctity n sacredness, inviolability.

sanctuary n, pl **-aries 1** holy place. **2** part of a church nearest the altar. **3** place of safety for a fugitive. **4** place where animals or birds can live undisturbed.

sanctum n, pl **-tums, -ta 1** sacred place. **2** person's private room.

sand n **1** substance consisting of small grains of rock, esp. on a beach or in a desert. ♦ pl **2** stretches of sand forming a beach or desert. ♦ v **3** smooth with sandpaper. **sandy** adj **1** covered with sand. **2** (of hair) reddish-fair. **sandbag** n bag filled with sand, used as protection against gunfire or flood water. **sandblast** v, n (clean with) a jet of sand blown from a nozzle under pressure. **sandpaper** n paper coated with sand for smoothing a surface. **sandpiper** n shore bird with a long bill and slender legs. **sandstone** n rock composed of sand. **sandstorm** n desert wind that whips up clouds of sand.

sandal n light shoe consisting of a sole attached by straps.

sandalwood n sweet-scented wood.

sander n power tool for smoothing surfaces.

sandwich n **1** two slices of bread with a layer of food between. ♦ v **2** insert between two other things. **sandwich board** pair of boards hung over a person's shoulders to display advertisements in front and behind.

sane adj **1** of sound mind. **2** sensible, rational. **sanity** n

sang v past tense of SING.

sang-froid [sahng-**frwah**] n composure and calmness in a difficult situation.

sangoma n S Afr witch doctor or herbalist.

sanguinary adj **1** accompanied by bloodshed. **2** bloodthirsty.

sanguine adj cheerful, optimistic.

sanitary adj promoting health by getting rid of dirt and germs. **sanitation** n sanitary measures, esp. drainage or sewerage.

sank v past tense of SINK.

Sanskrit n ancient language of India.

sap[1] n **1** moisture that circulates in plants. **2** Informal gullible person.

sap[2] v **sapping, sapped 1** undermine. **2** weaken. **sapper** n soldier in an engineering unit.

sapient [**say**-pee-ent] adj Lit wise, shrewd.

sapling n young tree.

sapphire n **1** blue precious stone. ♦ adj **2** deep blue.

sarabande, saraband n slow stately Spanish dance.

Saracen n Hist Arab or Muslim who opposed the Crusades.

sarcasm n (use of) bitter or wounding ironic language. **sarcastic** adj **sarcastically** adv

sarcophagus n, pl **-gi, -guses** stone coffin.

sardine n small fish of the herring family, usu. preserved tightly packed in tins.

sardonic adj mocking or scornful. **sardonically** adv

sargassum, sargasso n type of floating seaweed.

sari, saree n long piece of cloth draped around the body and over one shoulder, worn by Hindu women.

sarmie n S Afr slang sandwich.

sarong n long piece of cloth tucked around the waist or under the armpits, worn esp. in Malaysia.

sarsaparilla n soft drink, orig. made from the root of a tropical American plant.

sartorial adj of men's clothes or tailoring.

SAS (in Britain) Special Air Service.

sash¹ n decorative strip of cloth worn round the waist or over one shoulder.

sash² n wooden frame containing the panes of a window. **sash window** window consisting of two sashes that can be opened by sliding one over the other.

sassafras n American tree with aromatic bark used medicinally.

Sassenach n Scot English person.

sat v past of SIT.

Satan n the Devil. **satanic** adj 1 of Satan. 2 supremely evil. **Satanism** n worship of Satan.

satay, saté [**sat**-ay] n Indonesian and Malaysian dish consisting of pieces of chicken, pork, etc., grilled on skewers and served with peanut sauce.

satchel n bag, usu. with a shoulder strap, for carrying books.

sate v satisfy (a desire or appetite) fully.

satellite n 1 man-made device orbiting in space. 2 heavenly body that orbits another. 3 country that is dependent on a more powerful one. ◆ adj 4 of or used in the transmission of television signals from a satellite to the home.

satiate [**say**-she-ate] v provide with more than enough, so as to disgust. **satiety** [sat-**tie**-a-tee] n feeling of having had too much.

satin n silky fabric with a glossy surface on one side. **satiny** adj of or like satin. **satinwood** n tropical tree yielding hard wood.

satire n 1 use of ridicule to expose vice or folly. 2 poem or other work that does this. **satirical** adj **satirist** n **satirize** v ridicule by means of satire.

satisfy v -**fying, -fied** 1 please, content. 2 provide amply for (a need or desire). 3 convince, persuade. **satisfaction** n **satisfactory** adj

satnav n Motoring Informal satellite navigation.

satsuma n kind of small orange.

saturate v 1 soak thoroughly. 2 cause to absorb the maximum amount of something. **saturation** n

Saturday n seventh day of the week.

Saturn n 1 Roman god of agriculture. 2 sixth planet from the sun. **saturnine** adj gloomy in temperament or appearance. **saturnalia** n wild party or orgy.

satyr n 1 woodland god, part man, part goat. 2 lustful man.

sauce n 1 liquid added to food to enhance flavour. 2 Chiefly Brit informal impudence. **saucy** adj 1 impudent. 2 pert, jaunty. **saucily** adv **saucepan** n cooking pot with a long handle.

saucer n small round dish put under a cup.

sauerkraut n shredded cabbage fermented in brine.

sauna n Finnish-style steam bath.

saunter v 1 walk in a leisurely manner, stroll. ◆ n 2 leisurely walk.

sausage n minced meat in an edible tube-shaped skin. **sausage roll** skinless sausage covered in pastry.

sauté [**so**-tay] v -**téing** or -**téeing,** -**téed** fry quickly in a little fat.

savage adj 1 wild, untamed. 2 cruel and violent. 3 uncivilized, primitive. ◆ n 4 uncivilized person. ◆ v 5 attack ferociously. **savagely** adv **savagery** n

savannah, savanna n extensive open grassy plain in Africa.

savant n learned person.

save v **1** rescue or preserve from harm, protect. **2** keep for the future. **3** set aside (money). **4** *Sport* prevent the scoring of (a goal). ♦ n **5** *Sport* act of preventing a goal. **saver** n **saving** n **1** economy. ♦ pl **2** money put by for future use.

saveloy n *Brit, Aust & NZ* spicy smoked sausage.

saviour n **1** person who rescues another. **2** (S-) Christ.

savoir-faire [sav-wahr-**fair**] n *French* ability to do and say the right thing in any situation.

savory n aromatic herb used in cooking.

savour v **1** enjoy, relish. **2** (foll. by *of*) have a flavour or suggestion of. ♦ n **3** characteristic taste or odour. **4** slight but distinctive quality. **savoury** adj **1** salty or spicy. **2** n, pl **-vouries 3** savoury dish served before or after a meal.

savoy n variety of cabbage.

savvy *Slang* ♦ v **-vying, -vied 1** understand. ♦ n **2** understanding, intelligence.

saw¹ n **1** cutting tool with a toothed metal blade. ♦ v **sawing, sawed, sawed** or **sawn 2** cut with a saw. **3** move (something) back and forth. **sawyer** n person who saws timber for a living. **sawdust** n fine wood fragments made in sawing. **sawfish** n fish with a long toothed snout. **sawmill** n mill where timber is sawn into planks.

saw² v past tense of SEE¹.

saw³ n wise saying, proverb.

sax n *Informal* short for SAXOPHONE.

saxifrage n alpine rock plant with small flowers.

Saxon n **1** member of the W Germanic people who settled widely in Europe in the early Middle Ages. ♦ adj **2** of the Saxons.

saxophone n brass wind instrument with keys and a curved body. **saxophonist** n

say v **saying, said 1** speak or utter. **2** express (an idea) in words. **3** give as one's opinion. **4** suppose as an example or possibility. ♦ n **5** right or chance to speak. **6** share in a decision. **saying** n maxim, proverb.

scab n **1** crust formed over a wound. **2** *Offens* blackleg. **scabby** adj **1** covered with scabs. **2** *Informal* despicable.

scabbard n sheath for a sword or dagger.

scabies [**skay**-beez] n itchy skin disease.

scabrous [**skay**-bruss] adj **1** rough and scaly. **2** indecent.

scaffold n **1** temporary platform for workmen. **2** gallows. **scaffolding** n (materials for building) scaffolds.

scalar n, adj (variable quantity) having magnitude but no direction.

scald v **1** burn with hot liquid or steam. **2** sterilize with boiling water. **3** heat (liquid) almost to boiling point. ♦ n **4** injury by scalding.

scale¹ n **1** one of the thin overlapping plates covering fishes and reptiles. **2** thin flake. **3** coating which forms in kettles etc. due to hard water. **4** tartar formed on the teeth. ♦ v **5** remove scales from. **6** come off in scales. **scaly** adj

scale² n (often pl) weighing instrument.

scale³ n **1** graduated table or sequence of marks at regular intervals, used as a reference in making measurements. **2** ratio of size between a thing and a representation of it. **3** relative degree or extent. **4** fixed series of notes in music. **5** v **6** climb. **scale up, down** v increase or decrease proportionately in size.

scalene adj (of a triangle) with three unequal sides.

scallop n **1** edible shellfish with two

fan-shaped shells. **2** one of a series of small curves along an edge.

scalloped *adj* decorated with small curves along the edge.

scallywag *n Informal* scamp, rascal.

scalp *n* **1** skin and hair on top of the head. **2** *v* **3** cut off the scalp of.

scalpel *n* small surgical knife.

scam *n Informal* dishonest scheme.

scamp *n* mischievous child.

scamper *v* **1** run about hurriedly or in play. ◆ *n* **2** scampering.

scampi *pl n* large prawns.

scan *v* **scanning, scanned 1** scrutinize carefully. **2** glance over quickly. **3** examine or search (an area) by passing a radar or sonar beam over it. **4** (of verse) conform to metrical rules. ◆ *n* **5** scanning. **scanner** *n* electronic device used for scanning. **scansion** *n* metrical scanning of verse.

scandal *n* **1** disgraceful action or event. **2** malicious gossip. **scandalize** *v* shock by scandal. **scandalous** *adj*

scandium *n Chem* rare silvery-white metallic element.

scant *adj* barely sufficient, meagre.

scanty *adj* **scantier, scantiest** barely sufficient or not sufficient. **scantily** *adv*

scapegoat *n* person made to bear the blame for others.

scapula *n, pl* **-lae, -las** shoulder blade. **scapular** *adj*

scar *n* **1** mark left by a healed wound. **2** permanent emotional damage left by an unpleasant experience. ◆ *v* **scarring, scarred 3** mark or become marked with a scar.

scarab *n* sacred beetle of ancient Egypt.

scarce *adj* **1** insufficient to meet demand. **2** not common, rarely found. **make oneself scarce** *Informal* go away. **scarcely** *adv* **1** hardly at all. **2** definitely or probably not. **scarcity** *n*

scare *v* **1** frighten or be frightened. **2** *n*

3 fright, sudden panic. **scary** *adj Informal* frightening. **scarecrow** *n* **1** figure dressed in old clothes, set up to scare birds away from crops. **2** raggedly dressed person.

scaremonger *n* person who spreads alarming rumours.

scarf¹ *n, pl* **scarves, scarfs** piece of material worn round the neck, head, or shoulders.

scarf² *n* **1** joint between two pieces of timber made by notching the ends and fastening them together. ◆ *v* **2** join in this way.

scarify *v* **-fying, -fied 1** scratch or cut slightly all over. **2** break up and loosen (topsoil). **3** criticize mercilessly. **scarification** *n*

scarlatina *n* scarlet fever.

scarlet *adj, n* brilliant red. **scarlet fever** infectious fever with a scarlet rash.

scarp *n* steep slope.

scarper *v Brit slang* run away.

scat¹ *v* **scatting, scatted** *Informal* go away.

scat² *n* jazz singing using improvised vocal sounds instead of words.

scathing *adj* harshly critical.

scatological *adj* preoccupied with obscenity, esp. with references to excrement. **scatology** *n*

scatter *v* **1** throw about in various directions. **2** disperse. **scatterbrain** *n* empty-headed person.

scatty *adj* **-tier, -tiest** *Informal* empty-headed.

scavenge *v* search for (anything usable) among discarded material.

scavenger *n* **1** person who scavenges. **2** animal that feeds on decaying matter.

scenario *n, pl* **-rios 1** summary of the plot of a play or film. **2** imagined sequence of future events.

scene n 1 place of action of a real or imaginary event. 2 subdivision of a play or film in which the action is continuous. 3 view of a place. 4 display of emotion. 5 *Informal* specific activity or interest, e.g. *the fashion scene.* **behind the scenes** 1 backstage. 2 in secret. **scenery** n 1 natural features of a landscape. 2 painted backcloths or screens used on stage to represent the scene of action. **scenic** adj picturesque.

scent n 1 pleasant smell. 2 smell left in passing, by which an animal can be traced. 3 series of clues. 4 perfume. ♦ v 5 detect by smell. 6 suspect. 7 fill with fragrance.

sceptic [**skep**-tik] n person who habitually doubts generally accepted beliefs. **sceptical** adj **sceptically** adv **scepticism** n

sceptre n ornamental rod symbolizing royal power.

schedule n 1 plan of procedure for a project. 2 list. 3 timetable. ♦ v 4 plan to occur at a certain time.

schema n, pl **-mata** overall plan or diagram. **schematic** adj presented as a plan or diagram.

scheme n 1 systematic plan. 2 secret plot. ♦ v 3 plan in an underhand manner. **scheming** adj, n

scherzo [**skairt**-so] n, pl **-zos, -zi** brisk lively piece of music.

schism [**skizz**-um] n (group resulting from) division in an organization. **schismatic** adj

schist [**skist**] n crystalline rock which splits into layers.

schizoid adj 1 abnormally introverted. 2 *Informal* contradictory. ♦ n 3 schizoid person.

schizophrenia n 1 mental disorder involving deterioration of or confusion about the personality. 2 *Informal* contradictory behaviour or attitudes.

schizophrenic adj, n

schmaltz n excessive sentimentality. **schmaltzy** adj

schnapps n strong alcoholic spirit.

schnitzel n thin slice of meat, esp. veal.

scholar n 1 learned person. 2 student receiving a scholarship. 3 pupil. **scholarly** adj learned. **scholarship** n 1 learning. 2 financial aid given to a student because of academic merit. **scholastic** adj of schools or scholars.

school[1] n 1 place where children are taught or instruction is given in a subject. 2 group of artists, thinkers, etc. with shared principles or methods. ♦ v 3 educate or train.

school[2] n shoal of fish, whales, etc.

schooner n 1 sailing ship rigged fore-and-aft. 2 large glass.

sciatica n severe pain in the large nerve in the back of the leg. **sciatic** adj 1 of the hip. 2 of or afflicted with sciatica.

science n systematic study and knowledge of natural or physical phenomena. **scientific** adj 1 of science. 2 systematic. **scientifically** adv **scientist** n person who studies or practises a science. **science fiction** stories making imaginative use of scientific knowledge. **science park** area where scientific research and commercial development are carried on in cooperation.

sci-fi n short for SCIENCE FICTION.

scimitar n curved oriental sword.

scintillate v give off sparks.

scintillating adj very lively and amusing.

scion [**sy**-on] n 1 descendant or heir. 2 shoot of a plant for grafting.

scissors pl n cutting instrument with two crossed pivoted blades.

sclerosis n, pl **-ses** abnormal hardening of body tissues.

scoff[1] v express derision.

scoff[2] v Informal eat rapidly.

scold v 1 find fault with, reprimand. ♦ n 2 person who scolds. **scolding** n

sconce n bracket on a wall for holding candles or lights.

scone n small plain cake baked in an oven or on a griddle.

scoop n 1 shovel-like tool for ladling or hollowing out. 2 news story reported in one newspaper before all its rivals. ♦ v 3 take up or hollow out with or as if with a scoop. 4 beat (rival newspapers) in reporting a news item.

scoot v Slang leave or move quickly.

scooter n 1 child's vehicle propelled by pushing on the ground with one foot. 2 light motorcycle.

scope n 1 opportunity for using abilities. 2 range of activity.

scorch v 1 burn on the surface. 2 parch or shrivel from heat. ♦ n 3 slight burn. **scorcher** n Informal very hot day.

score n 1 points gained in a game or competition. 2 twenty. 3 written version of a piece of music showing parts for each musician. 4 mark or cut. 5 grievance, e.g. settle old scores. ♦ pl 6 lots. ♦ v 7 gain (points) in a game. 8 keep a record of points. 9 mark or cut. 10 (foll. by out) cross out. 11 arrange music (for). 12 achieve a success.

scorn n 1 open contempt. ♦ v 2 despise. 3 reject with contempt. **scornful** adj **scornfully** adv

scorpion n small lobster-shaped animal with a sting at the end of a jointed tail.

Scot n person from Scotland. **Scottish** adj of Scotland, its people, or their languages. **Scotch** n whisky distilled in Scotland. **Scots** adj Scottish. **Scotsman, Scotswoman** n

scotch v put an end to.

scot-free adj without harm or punishment.

scoundrel n Old-fashioned cheat or deceiver.

scour[1] v 1 clean or polish by rubbing with something rough. 2 clear or flush out. **scourer** n small rough nylon pad used for cleaning pots and pans.

scour[2] v search thoroughly and energetically.

scourge n 1 person or thing causing severe suffering. 2 whip. ♦ v 3 cause severe suffering to. 4 whip.

scout n 1 person sent out to reconnoitre. 2 (S-) member of the Scout Association, an organization for young people which aims to develop character and promotes outdoor activities. ♦ v 3 act as a scout. 4 reconnoitre.

scowl v, n (have) an angry or sullen expression.

scrabble v scrape at with the hands, feet, or claws.

scrag n thin end of a neck of mutton. **scraggy** adj thin, bony.

scram v **scramming, scrammed** Informal go away quickly.

scramble v 1 climb or crawl hastily or awkwardly. 2 struggle with others (for). 3 mix up. 4 cook (eggs beaten up with milk). 5 (of an aircraft or aircrew) take off hurriedly in an emergency. 6 make (transmitted speech) unintelligible by the use of an electronic device. ♦ n 7 scrambling. 8 rough climb. 9 disorderly struggle. 10 motorcycle race over rough ground. **scrambler** n electronic device that makes transmitted speech unintelligible.

scrap[1] n 1 small piece. 2 waste metal collected for reprocessing. ♦ pl 3 leftover food. ♦ v **scrapping, scrapped** 4 discard as useless. **scrappy** adj fragmentary, disjointed. **scrapbook** n book with blank pages in which newspaper cuttings or pictures are stuck.

scrap² n, v **scrapping, scrapped** Informal fight or quarrel.

scrape v 1 rub with something rough or sharp. 2 clean or smooth thus. 3 rub with a harsh noise. 4 economize. ♦ n 5 act or sound of scraping. 6 mark or wound caused by scraping. 7 Informal awkward situation. **scraper** n **scrape through** v succeed in or obtain with difficulty.

scratch v 1 mark or cut with claws, nails, or anything rough or sharp. 2 scrape (skin) with nails or claws to relieve itching. 3 withdraw from a race or competition. ♦ n 4 wound, mark, or sound made by scratching. ♦ adj 5 put together at short notice. **from scratch** from the very beginning. **up to scratch** up to standard. **scratchy** adj **scratchcard** n ticket that reveals whether or not the holder has won a prize when the surface is removed by scratching.

scrawl v 1 write carelessly or hastily. ♦ n 2 scribbled writing.

scrawny adj **scrawnier, scrawniest** thin and bony.

scream v 1 utter a piercing cry, esp. of fear or pain. 2 utter with a scream. ♦ n 3 shrill piercing cry. 4 Informal very funny person or thing.

scree n slope of loose shifting stones.

screech v, n (utter) a shrill cry.

screed n long tedious piece of writing.

screen n 1 surface of a television set, VDU, etc., on which an image is formed. 2 white surface on which films or slides are projected. 3 movable structure used to shelter, divide, or conceal something. ♦ v 4 shelter or conceal with or as if with a screen. 5 examine (a person or group) to determine suitability for a task or to detect the presence of disease or weapons. 6 show (a film). **the screen**

cinema generally. **screen saver** Computers software that produces changing images on a monitor when the computer is operative but idle.

screw n 1 metal pin with a spiral ridge along its length, twisted into materials to fasten them together. 2 Slang prison guard. ♦ v 3 turn (a screw). 4 twist. 5 fasten with screw(s). 6 Informal extort. **screwy** adj Informal crazy or eccentric. **screwdriver** n tool for turning screws. **screw up** v 1 Informal bungle. 2 distort.

scribble v 1 write hastily or illegibly. 2 make meaningless or illegible marks. ♦ n 3 something scribbled.

scribe n 1 person who copied manuscripts before the invention of printing. 2 Bible scholar of the Jewish Law.

scrimmage n rough or disorderly struggle.

scrimp v be very economical.

scrip n certificate representing a claim to stocks or shares.

script n 1 text of a film, play, or TV programme. 2 particular system of writing, e.g. Arabic script. 3 handwriting.

scripture n sacred writings of a religion. **scriptural** adj

scrofula n tuberculosis of the lymphatic glands. **scrofulous** adj

scroggin n NZ mixture of nuts and dried fruits.

scroll n 1 roll of parchment or paper. 2 ornamental carving shaped like a scroll. ♦ v 3 move (text) up or down on a VDU screen.

scrotum n, pl **-ta, -tums** pouch of skin containing the testicles.

scrounge v Informal get by cadging or begging. **scrounger** n

scrub¹ v **scrubbing, scrubbed** 1 clean by rubbing, often with a hard brush and water. 2 Informal delete or cancel.

♦ *n* **3** scrubbing.

scrub[2] *n* **1** stunted trees. **2** area of land covered with scrub. **scrubby** *adj* **1** covered with scrub. **2** stunted. **3** *Informal* shabby.

scruff[1] *n* nape (of the neck).

scruff[2] *n Informal* untidy person. **scruffy** *adj* unkempt or shabby.

scrum, scrummage *n* **1** *Rugby* restarting of play in which opposing packs of forwards push against each other to gain possession of the ball. **2** disorderly struggle.

scrumptious *adj Informal* delicious.

scrunch *v* **1** crumple or crunch or be crumpled or crunched. ♦ *n* **2** act or sound of scrunching.

scruple *n* **1** doubt produced by one's conscience or morals. ♦ *v* **2** have doubts on moral grounds. **scrupulous** *adj* **1** very conscientious. **2** very careful or precise. **scrupulously** *adv*

scrutiny *n, pl* **-nies** close examination. **scrutinize** *v* examine closely.

scuba diving *n* sport of swimming under water using cylinders containing compressed air attached to breathing apparatus.

scud *v* **scudding, scudded** move along swiftly.

scuff *v* **1** drag (the feet) while walking. **2** scrape (one's shoes) by doing so. ♦ *n* **3** mark caused by scuffing.

scuffle *v* **1** fight in a disorderly manner. ♦ *n* **2** disorderly struggle. **3** scuffling sound.

scull *n* **1** small oar. ♦ *v* **2** row (a boat) using sculls.

scullery *n, pl* **-leries** small room where washing-up and other kitchen work is done.

sculpture *n* **1** art of making figures or designs in wood, stone, etc. **2** product of this art. ♦ *v* **3** (also **sculpt**) represent in sculpture. **sculptor, sculptress** *n* **sculptural** *adj*

scum *n* **1** impure or waste matter on the surface of a liquid. **2** worthless people. **scummy** *adj*

scungy *adj* **-ier, -iest** *Aust & NZ informal* sordid or dirty.

scupper *v Informal* defeat or ruin.

scurf *n* flaky skin on the scalp.

scurrilous *adj* untrue and defamatory.

scurry *v* **-rying, -ried** **1** move hastily. ♦ *n* **2** act or sound of scurrying.

scurvy *n* disease caused by lack of vitamin C.

scut *n* short tail of the hare, rabbit, or deer.

scuttle[1] *n* fireside container for coal.

scuttle[2] *v* **1** run with short quick steps. ♦ *n* **2** hurried run.

scuttle[3] *v* make a hole in (a ship) to sink it.

scythe *n* **1** long-handled tool with a curved blade for cutting grass. ♦ *v* **2** cut with a scythe.

SE southeast(ern).

sea *n* **1** mass of salt water covering three quarters of the earth's surface. **2** particular area of this. **3** vast expanse. **at sea 1** in a ship on the ocean. **2** confused or bewildered. **sea anemone** sea animal with suckers like petals. **seaboard** *n* coast. **sea dog** experienced sailor. **seafaring** *adj* working or travelling by sea. **seafood** *n* edible saltwater fish or shellfish. **seagull** *n* gull. **sea horse** small sea fish with a plated body and horselike head. **sea level** average level of the sea's surface in relation to the land. **sea lion** kind of large seal. **seaman** *n* sailor. **seaplane** *n* aircraft designed to take off from and land on water. **seasick** *adj* suffering from nausea caused by the motion of a ship. **seasickness** *n* **seaside** *n* area, esp. a holiday resort, on the coast. **sea**

urchin sea animal with a round spiky shell. **seaweed** n plant growing in the sea. **seaworthy** adj (of a ship) in fit condition for a sea voyage.

seal[1] n 1 piece of wax, lead, etc. with a special design impressed upon it, attached to a letter or document as a mark of authentication. 2 device or material used to close an opening tightly. ♦ v 3 close with or as if with a seal. 4 make airtight or watertight. 5 affix a seal to or stamp with a seal. 6 decide (one's fate) irrevocably. **sealant** n any substance used for sealing. **seal off** v enclose or isolate (a place) completely.

seal[2] n amphibious mammal with flippers as limbs. **sealskin** n

seam n 1 line where two edges are joined, as by stitching. 2 thin layer of coal or ore. ♦ v 3 mark with furrows or wrinkles. **seamless** adj **seamy** adj sordid.

seamstress n woman who sews, esp. professionally.

seance [say-anss] n meeting at which spiritualists attempt to communicate with the dead.

sear v scorch, burn the surface of. **searing** adj 1 (of pain) very sharp. 2 highly critical.

search v 1 examine closely in order to find something. 2 n 3 searching. **searching** adj keen or thorough. **search engine** Computers Internet service enabling users to search for items of interest. **searchlight** n powerful light with a beam that can be shone in any direction.

season n 1 one of four divisions of the year, each of which has characteristic weather conditions. 2 period during which a thing happens or is plentiful. 3 fitting or proper time. ♦ v 4 flavour with salt, herbs, etc. 5 dry (timber) till ready for use. **seasonable** adj 1

appropriate for the season. 2 timely or opportune. **seasonal** adj depending on or varying with the seasons. **seasoned** adj experienced. **seasoning** n salt, herbs, etc. added to food to enhance flavour. **season ticket** ticket for a series of journeys or events within a specified period.

seat n 1 thing designed or used for sitting on. 2 place to sit in a theatre, esp. one that requires a ticket. 3 buttocks. 4 Brit country house. 5 membership of a legislative or administrative body. ♦ v 6 cause to sit. 7 provide seating for. **seat belt** belt worn in a car or aircraft to prevent a person being thrown forward in a crash.

sebaceous adj of, like, or secreting fat or oil.

secateurs pl n small pruning shears.

secede v withdraw formally from a political alliance or federation. **secession** n

seclude v keep (a person) from contact with others. **secluded** adj private, sheltered. **seclusion** n

second[1] adj 1 coming directly after the first. 2 alternate, additional. 3 inferior. ♦ n 4 person or thing coming second. 5 attendant in a duel or boxing match. ♦ pl 6 inferior goods. ♦ v 7 express formal support for (a motion proposed in a meeting). **secondly** adv **second-class** adj 1 inferior. 2 cheaper, slower, or less comfortable than first-class. **second-hand** adj bought after use by another. **second nature** something so habitual that it seems part of one's character. **second sight** supposed ability to predict events. **second thoughts** revised opinion on a matter already considered. **second wind** renewed ability to continue effort.

second[2] n 1 sixtieth part of a minute of

an angle or time. **2** moment.

second³ [si-**kond**] *v* transfer (a person) temporarily to another job. **secondment** *n*

secondary *adj* **1** of less importance. **2** coming after or derived from what is primary or first. **3** relating to the education of people between the ages of 11 and 18 or, in New Zealand, between 13 and 18.

secret *adj* **1** kept from the knowledge of others. **2** *n* **3** something kept secret. **4** mystery. **5** underlying explanation, e.g. *the secret of my success.* **in secret** without other people knowing. **secretly** *adv* **secrecy** *n* **secretive** *adj* inclined to keep things secret. **secretiveness** *n*

secretariat *n* administrative office or staff of a legislative body.

secretary *n, pl* **-ries** **1** person who deals with correspondence and general clerical work. **2** (S-) head of a state department, e.g. *Home Secretary.* **secretarial** *adj* **Secretary of State** head of a major government department.

secrete¹ *v* (of an organ, gland, etc.) produce and release (a substance). **secretion** *n* **secretory** [sek-**reet**-or-ee] *adj*

secrete² *v* hide or conceal.

sect *n* subdivision of a religious or political group, esp. one with extreme beliefs. **sectarian** *adj* **1** of a sect. **2** narrow-minded.

section *n* **1** part cut off. **2** part or subdivision of something. **3** distinct part of a country or community. **4** cutting. **5** drawing of something as if cut through. ♦ *v* **6** cut or divide into sections. **sectional** *adj*

sector *n* **1** part or subdivision. **2** part of a circle enclosed by two radii and the arc which they cut off.

secular *adj* **1** worldly, as opposed to sacred. **2** not connected with religion or the church.

secure *adj* **1** free from danger. **2** free from anxiety. **3** firmly fixed. **4** reliable. ♦ *v* **5** obtain. **6** make safe. **7** make firm. **8** guarantee payment of (a loan) by giving something as security. **securely** *adv* **security** *n, pl* **-ties** **1** precautions against theft, espionage, or other danger. **2** state of being secure. **3** certificate of ownership of a share, stock, or bond. **4** something given or pledged to guarantee payment of a loan.

sedan *n US, Aust & NZ* two-door or four-door car with the body closed off from the rear luggage area. **sedan chair** *Hist* enclosed chair for one person, carried on poles by two bearers.

sedate¹ *adj* **1** calm and dignified. **2** slow or unhurried. **sedately** *adv*

sedate² *v* give a sedative drug to. **sedation** *n* **sedative** *adj* **1** having a soothing or calming effect. ♦ *n* **2** sedative drug.

sedentary *adj* done sitting down, involving little exercise.

sedge *n* coarse grasslike plant growing on wet ground.

sediment *n* **1** matter which settles to the bottom of a liquid. **2** material deposited by water, ice, or wind. **sedimentary** *adj*

sedition *n* speech or action encouraging rebellion against the government. **seditious** *adj*

seduce *v* **1** persuade into sexual intercourse. **2** tempt into wrongdoing. **seducer, seductress** *n* **seduction** *n* **seductive** *adj*

sedulous *adj* diligent or persevering. **sedulously** *adv*

see¹ *v* **seeing, saw, seen** **1** perceive with the eyes or mind. **2** understand. **3** watch. **4** find out. **5** make sure (of something). **6** consider or decide. **7** have experience of. **8** meet or visit. **9** accompany. **seeing 1** *conj* **2** in view of the fact that.

see² *n* diocese of a bishop.

seed *n* **1** mature fertilized grain of a plant. **2** such grains used for sowing. **3** origin. **4** *Obs* offspring. **5** *Sport* player ranked according to his or her ability. ♦ *v* **6** sow with seed. **7** remove seeds from. **8** arrange (the draw of a sports tournament) so that the outstanding competitors will not meet in the early rounds. **go, run to seed 1** (of plants) produce or shed seeds after flowering. **2** lose vigour or usefulness. **seedling** *n* young plant raised from a seed. **seedy** *adj* shabby.

seek *v* **seeking, sought 1** try to find or obtain. **2** try (to do something).

seem *v* appear to be. **seeming** *adj* apparent but not real. **seemingly** *adv*

seemly *adj* proper or fitting.

seen *v* past participle of SEE¹.

seep *v* trickle through slowly, ooze. **seepage** *n*

seer *n* prophet.

seersucker *n* light cotton fabric with a slightly crinkled surface.

seesaw *n* **1** plank balanced in the middle so that two people seated on either end ride up and down alternately. ♦ *v* **2** move up and down.

seethe *v* **seething, seethed 1** be very agitated. **2** (of a liquid) boil or foam.

segment *n* **1** one of several sections into which something may be divided. **2** *v* **3** divide into segments. **segmentation** *n*

segregate *v* set apart. **segregation** *n*

seine [**sane**] *n* large fishing net that hangs vertically from floats.

seismic *adj* relating to earthquakes. **seismology** *n* study of earthquakes. **seismological** *adj* **seismologist** *n*

seismograph, seismometer *n* instrument that records the strength of earthquakes.

seize *v* **1** take hold of forcibly or quickly. **2** take immediate advantage of. **3** (usu. foll. by *up*) (of mechanical parts) stick tightly through overheating. **seizure** *n* **1** sudden violent attack of an illness. **2** seizing or being seized.

seldom *adv* not often, rarely.

select *v* **1** pick out or choose. ♦ *adj* **2** chosen in preference to others. **3** restricted to a particular group, exclusive. **selection** *n* **1** selecting. **2** things that have been selected. **3** range from which something may be selected. **selective** *adj* chosen or choosing carefully. **selectively** *adv* **selectivity** *n* **selector** *n*

selenium *n* *Chem* nonmetallic element with photoelectric properties.

self *n, pl* **selves 1** distinct individuality or identity of a person or thing. **2** one's basic nature. **3** one's own welfare or interests. **selfish** *adj* caring too much about oneself and not enough about others. **selfishly** *adv* **selfishness** *n* **selfless** *adj* unselfish.

self- *prefix* used with many main words to mean: **1** of oneself or itself. **2** by, to, in, due to, for, or from the self. **3** automatic(ally). **self-assured** *adj* confident. **self-catering** *adj* (of accommodation) for people who provide their own food. **self-coloured** *adj* having only a single colour. **self-conscious** *adj* embarrassed at being the object of others' attention. **self-contained** *adj* **1** containing everything needed, complete. **2** (of a flat) having its own facilities. **self-determination** *n* the right of a nation to decide its own form of government. **self-evident** *adj* obvious without proof. **self-help** *n* **1**

use of one's own abilities to solve problems. **2** practice of solving one's problems within a group of people with similar problems. **self-interest** n one's own advantage. **self-made** adj having achieved wealth or status by one's own efforts. **self-possessed** adj having control of one's emotions, calm. **self-raising** adj (of flour) containing a raising agent. **self-righteous** adj thinking oneself more virtuous than others. **selfsame** adj the very same. **self-seeking** adj, n seeking to promote only one's own interests. **self-service** adj denoting a shop, café, or garage where customers serve themselves and then pay a cashier. **self-styled** adj using a title or name that one has taken without right. **self-sufficient** adj able to provide for oneself without help. **self-willed** adj stubbornly determined to get one's own way.

sell v **selling, sold 1** exchange (something) for money. **2** stock, deal in. **3** (of goods) be sold. **4** (foll. by for) have a specified price. **5** Informal persuade (someone) to accept (something). **6** n **7** manner of selling. **seller** n **sell-by date** Brit date on packaged food after which it should not be sold. **sell out** v **1** dispose of (something) completely by selling. **2** Informal betray. **sellout** n **1** performance of a show etc. for which all the tickets are sold. **2** Informal betrayal.

Sellotape n **1** ® type of adhesive tape. ♦ v **2** stick with Sellotape.

selvage, selvedge n edge of cloth, woven so as to prevent unravelling.

selves n plural of SELF.

semantic adj relating to the meaning of words. **semantics** n study of linguistic meaning.

semaphore n system of signalling by

holding two flags in different positions to represent letters of the alphabet.

semblance n outward or superficial appearance.

semen n sperm-carrying fluid produced by male animals.

semester n either of two divisions of the academic year.

semi n Brit & S Afr informal semidetached house.

semi- prefix used with many main words to mean: **1** half, e.g. semicircle. **2** partly or almost, e.g. semiprofessional.

semibreve n musical note four beats long.

semicolon n the punctuation mark (;).

semiconductor n substance with an electrical conductivity that increases with temperature.

semidetached adj (of a house) joined to another on one side.

semifinal n match or round before the final. **semifinalist** n

seminal adj **1** original and influential. **2** capable of developing. **3** of semen or seed.

seminar n meeting of a group of students for discussion.

seminary n, pl **-ries** college for priests.

semiprecious adj (of gemstones) having less value than precious stones.

semiquaver n musical note half the length of a quaver.

Semite n member of the group of peoples including Jews and Arabs.

Semitic adj of the group of peoples including Jews and Arabs.

semitone n smallest interval between two notes in Western music.

semitrailer n Aust large truck in two separate sections joined by a pivoted bar (also **semi**).

semolina n hard grains of wheat left after the milling of flour, used to make puddings and pasta.

Senate n 1 upper house of some parliaments. 2 governing body of some universities. **senator** n member of a Senate. **senatorial** adj

send v **sending, sent** 1 cause (a person or thing) to go to or be taken or transmitted to a place. 2 bring into a specified state or condition. **sendoff** n demonstration of good wishes at a person's departure. **send up** v Informal make fun of by imitating. **send-up** n Informal imitation.

senile adj mentally or physically weak because of old age. **senility** n

senior adj 1 superior in rank or standing. 2 older. 3 of or for older pupils. ♦ n 4 senior person. **seniority** n

senna n 1 tropical plant. 2 its dried leaves or pods used as a laxative.

señor [sen-**nyor**] n, pl **-ores** Spanish term of address equivalent to sir or Mr. **señora** [sen-**nyor**-a] n Spanish term of address equivalent to madam or Mrs. **señorita** [sen-nyor-**ee**-ta] n Spanish term of address equivalent to madam or Miss.

sensation n 1 ability to feel things physically. 2 physical feeling. 3 general feeling or awareness. 4 state of excitement. 5 exciting person or thing. **sensational** adj 1 causing intense shock, anger, or excitement. 2 Informal very good. **sensationalism** n deliberate use of sensational language or subject matter. **sensationalist** adj, n

sense n 1 any of the faculties of perception or feeling (sight, hearing, touch, taste, or smell). 2 ability to perceive. 3 feeling perceived through one of the senses. 4 awareness. 5 (sometimes pl) sound practical judgment or intelligence. 6 specific meaning. ♦ v 7 perceive. **senseless** adj

sensible adj 1 having or showing good

sense. 2 practical, e.g. sensible shoes. 3 (foll. by of) aware. **sensibly** adv **sensibility** n ability to experience deep feelings.

sensitive adj 1 easily hurt or offended. 2 responsive to external stimuli. 3 (of a subject) liable to arouse controversy or strong feelings. 4 (of an instrument) responsive to slight changes. **sensitively** adv **sensitivity** n **sensitize** v make sensitive.

sensor n device that detects or measures the presence of something, such as radiation.

sensory adj of the senses or sensation.

sensual adj 1 giving pleasure to the body and senses rather than the mind. 2 having a strong liking for physical pleasures. **sensually** adv **sensuality** n **sensualist** n

sensuous adj pleasing to the senses. **sensuously** adv

sent v past of SEND.

sentence n 1 sequence of words capable of standing alone as a statement, question, or command. 2 punishment passed on a criminal. ♦ v 3 pass sentence on (a convicted person).

sententious adj 1 trying to sound wise. 2 pompously moralizing.

sentient [sen-tee-ent] adj capable of feeling. **sentience** n

sentiment n 1 thought, opinion, or attitude. 2 feeling expressed in words. 3 exaggerated or mawkish emotion. **sentimental** adj excessively romantic or nostalgic. **sentimentalism** n **sentimentality** n **sentimentalize** v make sentimental.

sentinel n sentry.

sentry n, pl **-tries** soldier on watch.

sepal n leaflike division of the calyx of a flower.

separate v 1 act as a barrier between. 2 distinguish between. 3 divide up into parts. **4** (of a couple) stop living together. ♦ *adj* **5** not the same, different. **6** set apart. **7** not shared, individual. **separately** *adv* **separation** *n* **1** separating or being separated. **2** *Law* living apart of a married couple without divorce. **separable** *adj* **separatist** *n* person who advocates the separation of a group from an organization or country. **separatism** *n*

☑ SPELLING TIP

There are 101 examples of *seperate* in the Bank of English, which makes it the most popular misspelling of **separate**.

---

sepia *adj, n* reddish-brown (pigment).
sepsis *n* poisoning caused by pus-forming bacteria.
Sept. September.
September *n* ninth month of the year.
septet *n* **1** group of seven performers. **2** music for such a group.
septic *adj* **1** (of a wound) infected. **2** of or caused by harmful bacteria. **septic tank** tank in which sewage is decomposed by the action of bacteria.
septicaemia [sep-tis-**see**-mee-a] *n* infection of the blood.
septuagenarian *n* person aged between seventy and seventy-nine.
sepulchre [**sep**-pull-ker] *n* tomb or burial vault. **sepulchral** [sip-**pulk**-ral] *adj* gloomy.
sequel *n* **1** novel, play, or film that continues the story of an earlier one. **2** consequence.
sequence *n* **1** arrangement of two or more things in successive order. **2** the successive order of two or more things. **3** section of a film showing a single uninterrupted episode. **sequential** *adj*
sequester *v* **1** seclude. **2** sequestrate.

sequestrate *v* confiscate (property) until its owner's debts are paid or a court order is complied with. **sequestration** *n*
sequin *n* small ornamental metal disc on a garment. **sequined** *adj*
sequoia *n* giant Californian coniferous tree.
seraglio [sir-**ah**-lee-oh] *n, pl* -**raglios 1** harem of a Muslim palace. **2** Turkish sultan's palace.
seraph *n, pl* -**aphs, -aphim** member of the highest order of angels. **seraphic** *adj*
Serbian, Serb *adj* **1** of Serbia. ♦ *n* **2** person from Serbia. **Serbo-Croat, Serbo-Croatian** *adj, n* (of) the chief official language of Serbia and Croatia.
serenade *n* **1** music played or sung to a woman by a lover. **2** *v* **3** sing or play a serenade to (someone).
serendipity *n* gift of making fortunate discoveries by accident.
serene *adj* calm, peaceful. **serenely** *adv* **serenity** *n*
serf *n* medieval farm labourer who could not leave the land he worked on. **serfdom** *n*
serge *n* strong woollen fabric.
sergeant *n* **1** noncommissioned officer in the army. **2** police officer ranking between constable and inspector. **sergeant at arms** parliamentary or court officer with ceremonial duties. **sergeant major** highest rank of noncommissioned officer in the army.
serial *n* **1** story or play produced in successive instalments. ♦ *adj* **2** of or forming a series. **3** published or presented as a serial. **serialize** *v* publish or present as a serial. **serial killer** person who commits a series of murders.
series *n, pl* -**ries 1** group or succession of related things, usu. arranged in order. **2** set of radio or TV programmes

about the same subject or characters.

serious *adj* **1** giving cause for concern. **2** concerned with important matters. **3** not cheerful, grave. **4** sincere, not joking. **seriously** *adv* **seriousness** *n*

sermon *n* **1** speech on a religious or moral subject by a clergyman in a church service. **2** long moralizing speech. **sermonize** *v* make a long moralizing speech.

serpent *n Lit* snake. **serpentine** *adj* twisting like a snake.

serrated *adj* having a notched or sawlike edge.

serried *adj* in close formation.

serum [**seer**-um] *n* **1** watery fluid left after blood has clotted. **2** this fluid from the blood of immunized animals used for inoculation or vaccination.

servant *n* person employed to do household work for another.

serve *v* **1** work for (a person, community, or cause). **2** perform official duties. **3** attend to (customers). **4** provide (someone) with (food or drink). **5** provide with a service. **6** be a member of the armed forces. **7** spend (time) in prison. **8** be useful or suitable. **9** *Tennis etc.* put (the ball) into play. **10** *n* **11** *Tennis etc.* act of serving the ball.

server *n* **1** player who serves in racket games. **2** *Computers* computer or program that supplies data to other machines on a network.

service *n* **1** system that provides something needed by the public. **2** department of public employment and its employees. **3** availability for use. **4** overhaul of a machine or vehicle. **5** formal religious ceremony. **6** *Tennis etc.* act, manner, or right of serving the ball. ♦ *pl* **7** armed forces. **8** *v* **9** overhaul (a machine or vehicle). **serviceable** *adj* **1** useful or helpful. **2** able or ready to be used. **service**

area area beside a motorway with garage, restaurant, and toilet facilities. **serviceman, servicewoman** *n* member of the armed forces. **service road** narrow road giving access to houses and shops. **service station** garage selling fuel for motor vehicles.

serviette *n* table napkin.

servile *adj* **1** too eager to obey people, fawning. **2** suitable for a slave. **servility** *n*

servitude *n* bondage or slavery.

sesame [**sess**-am-ee] *n* plant cultivated for its seeds and oil, which are used in cooking.

session *n* **1** period spent in an activity. **2** meeting of a court, parliament, or council. **3** series or period of such meetings. **4** academic term or year.

set[1] *v* **setting, set 1** put in a specified position or state. **2** make ready. **3** make or become firm or rigid. **4** establish, arrange. **5** prescribe, assign. **6** (of the sun) go down. **7** *n* **8** scenery used in a play or film. ♦ *adj* **9** fixed or established beforehand. **10** rigid or inflexible. **11** determined (to do something). **setback** *n* anything that delays progress. **set square** flat right-angled triangular instrument used for drawing angles. **set-top box** *n* device which enables digital television broadcasts to be viewed on a standard television set. **set up** *v* arrange or establish. **setup** *n* way in which anything is organized or arranged.

set[2] *n* **1** number of things or people grouped or belonging together. **2** *Maths* group of numbers or objects that satisfy a given condition or share a property. **3** television or radio receiver. **4** *Sport* group of games in a match.

sett, set *n* badger's burrow.

settee *n* couch.

setter n long-haired gun dog.

setting n 1 background or surroundings. 2 time and place where a film, book, etc. is supposed to have taken place. 3 music written for the words of a text. 4 decorative metalwork in which a gem is set. 5 plates and cutlery for a single place at table. 6 position or level to which the controls of a machine can be adjusted.

settle¹ v 1 arrange or put in order. 2 come to rest. 3 establish or become established as a resident. 4 make quiet, calm, or stable. 5 pay (a bill). 6 bestow (property) legally. **settlement** n 1 act of settling. 2 place newly colonized. 3 subsidence (of a building). 4 property bestowed legally. **settler** n colonist.

settle² n long wooden bench with high back and arms.

seven adj, n one more than six. **seventh** adj, n (of) number seven in a series. **seventeen** adj, n ten and seven. **seventeenth** adj, n **seventy** adj, n ten times seven. **seventieth** adj, n

sever v 1 cut through or off. 2 break off (a relationship). **severance** n **severance pay** compensation paid by a firm to an employee who leaves because the job he or she was appointed to do no longer exists.

several adj 1 some, a few. 2 various, separate. **severally** adv separately.

severe adj 1 strict or harsh. 2 very intense or unpleasant. 3 strictly restrained in appearance. **severely** adv **severity** n

sew v sewing, sewed, sewn or sewed 1 join with thread repeatedly passed through with a needle. 2 make or fasten by sewing.

sewage n waste matter or excrement carried away in sewers.

sewer n drain to remove waste water and sewage. **sewerage** n system of sewers.

sewn v a past participle of SEW.

sex n 1 state of being male or female. 2 male or female category. 3 sexual intercourse. 4 sexual feelings or behaviour. ♦ v 5 find out the sex of. **sexy** adj 1 sexually exciting or attractive. 2 Informal exciting or trendy. **sexism** n discrimination on the basis of a person's sex. **sexist** adj, n **sexual** adj **sexually** adv **sexuality** n **sexual intercourse** sexual act in which the male's penis is inserted into the female's vagina. **sex up** vb Informal make (something) more exciting.

sexagenarian n person aged between sixty and sixty-nine.

sextant n navigator's instrument for measuring angles, as between the sun and horizon, to calculate one's position.

sextet n 1 group of six performers. 2 music for such a group.

sexton n official in charge of a church and churchyard.

SF science fiction.

shabby adj -bier, -biest 1 worn or dilapidated in appearance. 2 mean or unworthy, e.g. shabby treatment. **shabbily** adv **shabbiness** n

shack n rough hut. **shack up with** v Slang live with (one's lover).

shackle n 1 one of a pair of metal rings joined by a chain, for securing a person's wrists or ankles. 2 v 3 fasten with shackles.

shad n herring-like fish.

shade n 1 relative darkness. 2 place sheltered from sun. 3 screen or cover used to protect from a direct source of light. 4 depth of colour. 5 slight amount. 6 Lit ghost. ♦ pl 7 Slang sunglasses. ♦ v 8 screen from light. 9 darken. 10 represent (darker areas) in drawing. 11 change slightly or by degrees. **shady** adj **1** situated in or giving shade. **2** of doubtful honesty or legality.

shadow n **1** dark shape cast on a surface when something stands between a light and the surface. **2** patch of shade. **3** slight trace. **4** threatening influence. **5** inseparable companion. **6** v **7** cast a shadow over. **8** follow secretly. **shadowy** adj **shadow-boxing** n boxing against an imaginary opponent for practice. **Shadow Cabinet** members of the main opposition party in Parliament who would be ministers if their party were in power.

shaft n **1** long narrow straight handle of a tool or weapon. **2** ray of light. **3** revolving rod that transmits power in a machine. **4** vertical passageway, as for a lift or a mine. **5** one of the bars between which an animal is harnessed to a vehicle.

shag[1] n **1** coarse shredded tobacco. **2** adj **3** (of a carpet) having a long pile. **shaggy** adj **1** covered with rough hair or wool. **2** tousled, unkempt. **shaggy-dog story** long anecdote with a humorous twist at the end.

shag[2] n kind of cormorant.

shagreen n **1** sharkskin. **2** rough grainy untanned leather.

shah n formerly, ruler of Iran.

shake v **shaking, shook, shaken 1** move quickly up and down or back and forth. **2** make unsteady. **3** tremble. **4** grasp (someone's hand) in greeting or agreement. **5** shock or upset. **6** n **7** shaking. **8** vibration. **9** Informal short period of time. **shaky** adj **1** unsteady. **2** uncertain or questionable. **shakily** adv

shale n flaky sedimentary rock.

shall v, past tense **should** used as an auxiliary to make the future tense or to indicate intention, obligation, or inevitability.

shallot n kind of small onion.

shallow adj **1** not deep. **2** lacking depth of character or intellect. **shallows** pl n area of shallow water. **shallowness** n

sham n **1** thing or person that is not genuine. ♦ adj **2** not genuine. ♦ v **shamming, shammed 3** fake, feign.

shamble v walk in a shuffling awkward way.

shambles n disorderly event or place.

shame n **1** painful emotion caused by awareness of having done something dishonourable or foolish. **2** capacity to feel shame. **3** cause of shame. **4** cause for regret. ♦ v **5** cause to feel shame. **6** disgrace. **7** compel by shame. ♦ interj **8** S Afr informal exclamation of sympathy or endearment. **shameful** adj causing or deserving shame. **shamefully** adv **shameless** adj with no sense of shame. **shamefaced** adj looking ashamed.

shammy n, pl **-mies** Informal piece of chamois leather.

shampoo n **1** liquid soap for washing hair, carpets, or upholstery. **2** process of shampooing. ♦ v **3** wash with shampoo.

shamrock n clover leaf, esp. as the Irish emblem.

shandy n, pl **-dies** drink made of beer and lemonade.

shanghai v **-haiing, -haied 1** force or trick (someone) into doing something. ♦ n **2** Aust & NZ catapult.

shank n **1** lower leg. **2** shaft or stem.

shan't shall not.

shantung n soft Chinese silk with a knobbly surface.

shanty[1] n, pl **-ties** shack or crude dwelling. **shantytown** n slum consisting of shanties.

shanty[2] n, pl **-ties** sailor's traditional

song.

shape *n* **1** outward form of an object. **2** way in which something is organized. **3** pattern or mould. **4** condition or state. ♦ *v* **5** form or mould. **6** devise or develop. **shapeless** *adj* **shapely** *adj* having an attractive shape.

shard *n* broken piece of pottery or glass.

share¹ *n* **1** part of something that belongs to or is contributed by a person. **2** one of the equal parts into which the capital stock of a public company is divided. ♦ *v* **3** give or take a share of (something). **4** join with others in doing or using (something). **shareholder** *n* **sharemilker** *NZ* person who works on a dairy farm belonging to someone else.

share² *n* blade of a plough.

shark *n* **1** large usu. predatory sea fish. **2** person who cheats others.

sharkskin *n* stiff glossy fabric.

sharp *adj* **1** having a keen cutting edge or fine point. **2** not gradual. **3** clearly defined. **4** mentally acute. **5** shrill. **6** bitter or sour in taste. **7** *Music* above the true pitch. ♦ *adv* **8** promptly. **9** *Music* too high in pitch. ♦ *n* **10** *Music* symbol raising a note one semitone above natural pitch. **sharply** *adv* **sharpness** *n* **sharpen** *v* make or become sharp or sharper. **sharpener** *n* **sharpshooter** *n* marksman.

shatter *v* **1** break into pieces. **2** destroy completely. **shattered** *adj* *Informal* **1** completely exhausted. **2** badly upset.

shave *v* **shaving, shaved, shaved** *or* **shaven 1** remove (hair) from (the face, head, or body) with a razor or shaver. **2** pare away. **3** touch lightly in passing. ♦ *n* **4** shaving. **close shave** *Informal* narrow escape. **shaver** *n* electric razor. **shavings** *pl n* parings.

shawl *n* piece of cloth worn over a woman's head or shoulders or

wrapped around a baby.

she *pron* refers to: **1** female person or animal previously mentioned. **2** something regarded as female, such as a car, ship, or nation.

sheaf *n, pl* **sheaves 1** bundle of papers. **2** tied bundle of reaped corn.

shear *v* **shearing, sheared, sheared** *or* **shorn 1** clip hair or wool from. **2** cut through. **shears** *pl n* large scissors or a cutting tool shaped like these. **shearer** *n* **shearing shed** *Aust & NZ* farm building with equipment for shearing sheep.

shearwater *n* medium-sized sea bird.

sheath *n* **1** close-fitting cover, esp. for a knife or sword *Brit, Aust & NZ* condom. **sheathe** *v* put into a sheath.

shebeen *n* *Scot, Irish & S Afr* place where alcohol is sold illegally.

shed¹ *n* building used for storage or shelter or as a workshop.

shed² *v* **shedding, shed 1** pour forth (tears). **2** cast off (skin, hair, or leaves).

sheen *n* glistening brightness on the surface of something.

sheep *n, pl* **sheep** ruminant animal bred for wool and meat. **sheep-dip** *n* liquid disinfectant in which sheep are immersed. **sheepdog** *n* dog used for herding sheep. **sheepskin** *n* skin of a sheep with the fleece still on, used for clothing or rugs.

sheepish *adj* embarrassed because of feeling foolish. **sheepishly** *adv*

sheer¹ *adj* **1** absolute, complete, e.g. *sheer folly.* **2** perpendicular, steep. **3** (of material) so fine as to be transparent.

sheer² *v* change course suddenly.

sheet¹ *n* **1** large piece of cloth used as an inner bed cover. **2** broad thin piece of any material. **3** large expanse.

sheet² *n* rope for controlling the position of a sail. **sheet anchor 1** strong anchor for use in an emergency. **2** person or thing relied on.

sheikh, sheik [**shake**] n Arab chief. **sheikhdom, sheikdom** n

sheila n Aust & NZ slang girl or woman.

shekel n **1** monetary unit of Israel. ♦ pl **2** Informal money.

shelf n, pl **shelves 1** board fixed horizontally for holding things. **2** ledge. **shelf life** time a packaged product will remain fresh.

shell n **1** hard outer covering of an egg, nut, or certain animals. **2** external frame of something. **3** explosive projectile fired from a large gun. **4** v **5** take the shell from. **6** fire at with artillery shells. **shellfish** n sea-living animal, esp. one that can be eaten, with a shell. **shell out** v Informal pay out or hand over (money). **shell shock** nervous disorder caused by exposure to battle conditions. **shell suit** Brit lightweight tracksuit made of a waterproof nylon layer over a cotton layer.

shellac n **1** resin used in varnishes. ♦ v **-lacking, -lacked 2** coat with shellac.

shelter n **1** structure providing protection from danger or the weather. **2** protection. ♦ v **3** give shelter to. **4** take shelter.

shelve¹ v **1** put aside or postpone. **2** provide with shelves. **shelving** n (material for) shelves.

shelve² v slope.

shenanigans pl n Informal **1** mischief or nonsense. **2** trickery.

shepherd n **1** person who tends sheep. ♦ v **2** guide or watch over (people). **shepherdess** n fem **shepherd's pie** baked dish of mince covered with mashed potato.

sherbet n **1** Brit, Aust & NZ fruit-flavoured fizzy powder. **2** US, Canadian & S Afr flavoured water ice.

sheriff n **1** (in the US) chief law enforcement officer of a county. **2** (in England and Wales) chief executive officer of the Crown in a county. **3** (in Scotland) chief judge of a district. **4** (in Australia) officer of the Supreme Court.

Sherpa n member of a people of Tibet and Nepal.

sherry n, pl **-ries** pale or dark brown fortified wine.

shibboleth n slogan or principle, usu. considered outworn, characteristic of a particular group.

shield n **1** piece of armour carried on the arm to protect the body from blows or missiles. **2** anything that protects. **3** sports trophy in the shape of a shield. ♦ v **4** protect.

shift v **1** move. **2** transfer (blame or responsibility). **3** remove or be removed. ♦ n **4** shifting. **5** group of workers who work during a specified period. **6** period of time during which they work. **7** loose-fitting straight underskirt or dress. **shiftless** adj lacking in ambition or initiative. **shifty** adj evasive or untrustworthy. **shiftiness** n

shillelagh [shil-**lay**-lee] n (in Ireland) a cudgel.

shilling n **1** former British coin, replaced by the 5p piece. **2** former Australian coin, worth one twentieth of a pound.

shillyshally v **-lying, -lied** Informal be indecisive.

shimmer v, n (shine with) a faint unsteady light.

shin n **1** front of the lower leg. ♦ v **shinning, shinned 2** climb by using the hands or arms and legs. **shinbone** n tibia.

shindig n Informal **1** noisy party. **2** brawl.

shine v **shining, shone 1** give out or reflect light. **2** aim (a light). **3** polish. **4** excel. ♦ n **5** brightness or lustre. **shiny**

adj **take a shine to** *Informal* take a liking to (someone). **shiner** *n Informal* black eye.

shingle[1] *n* **1** wooden roof tile. ♦ *v* **2** cover (a roof) with shingles.

shingle[2] *n* coarse gravel found on beaches. **shingle slide** *NZ* loose stones on a steep slope.

shingles *n* disease causing a rash of small blisters along a nerve.

Shinto *n* Japanese religion in which ancestors and nature spirits are worshipped. **Shintoism** *n*

shinty *n* game like hockey.

ship *n* **1** large seagoing vessel. **2** *v* **shipping, shipped 3** send or transport by carrier, esp. a ship. **4** bring or go aboard a ship. **shipment** *n* **1** act of shipping cargo. **2** consignment of goods shipped. **shipping** *n* **1** freight transport business. **2** ships collectively. **shipshape** *adj* orderly or neat. **shipwreck** *n* **1** destruction of a ship through storm or collision. ♦ *v* **3** cause to undergo shipwreck. **shipyard** *n* place where ships are built.

shire *n* **1** *Brit* county. **2** *Aust* rural area with an elected council.

shire horse *n* large powerful breed of horse.

shirk *v* avoid (duty or work). **shirker** *n*

shirt *n* garment for the upper part of the body.

shirty *adj* **-tier, -tiest** *Chiefly Brit slang* bad-tempered or annoyed.

shish kebab *n* meat and vegetable dish cooked on a skewer.

shiver[1] *v* **1** tremble, as from cold or fear. ♦ *n* **2** shivering.

shiver[2] *v* splinter into pieces.

shoal[1] *n* large number of fish swimming together.

shoal[2] *n* **1** stretch of shallow water. **2** sandbank.

shock[1] *v* **1** horrify, disgust, or astonish. ♦ *n* **2** sudden violent emotional disturbance. **3** sudden violent blow or impact. **4** something causing this. **5** state of bodily collapse caused by physical or mental shock. **6** pain and muscular spasm caused by an electric current passing through the body. **shocker** *n* **shocking** *adj* **1** causing horror, disgust, or astonishment. **2** *Informal* very bad.

shock[2] *n* bushy mass (of hair).

shod *v* past of SHOE.

shoddy *adj* **-dier, -diest** made or done badly.

shoe *n* **1** outer covering for the foot, ending below the ankle. **2** horseshoe. ♦ *v* **shoeing, shod 3** fit with a shoe or shoes. **shoehorn** *n* smooth curved implement inserted at the heel of a shoe to ease the foot into it. **shoestring** *n* **on a shoestring** using a very small amount of money.

shone *v* past of SHINE.

shonky *adj* **-kier, -kiest** *Aust & NZ informal* unreliable or unsound.

shoo *interj* **1** go away! ♦ *v* **2** drive away as by saying 'shoo'.

shook *v* past tense of SHAKE.

shoot *v* **shooting, shot 1** hit, wound, or kill with a missile fired from a weapon. **2** fire (a missile from) a weapon. **3** hunt. **4** send out or move rapidly. **5** (of a plant) sprout. **6** photograph or film. **7** *Sport* take a shot at goal. ♦ *n* **8** new branch or sprout of a plant. **9** hunting expedition. **shooting star** meteor. **shooting stick** stick with a spike at one end and a folding seat at the other.

shop *n* **1** place for sale of goods and services. ♦ workshop. ♦ *v* **shopping, shopped 3** visit a shop or shops to buy goods. **4** *Brit, Aust & NZ slang* inform against (someone). **talk shop** discuss one's work, esp. on a social occasion. **shop around** v visit various shops to compare goods and prices. **shop floor** 1 production area of a factory. 2 workers in a factory. **shoplifter** n person who steals from a shop. **shop-soiled** adj soiled or faded from being displayed in a shop. **shop steward** (in some countries) trade-union official elected to represent his or her fellow workers.

shore¹ n edge of a sea or lake.

shore² v (foll. by up) prop or support.

shorn v a past participle of SHEAR.

short adj 1 not long. 2 not tall. 3 not lasting long, brief. 4 deficient, e.g. short of cash. 5 abrupt, rude. 6 (of a drink) consisting chiefly of a spirit. 7 (of pastry) crumbly. ♦ adv 8 abruptly. ♦ n 9 drink of spirits. 10 short film. 11 Informal short circuit. ♦ pl 12 short trousers. **shortage** n deficiency. **shorten** v make or become shorter. **shortly** adv 1 soon. 2 rudely. **shortbread, shortcake** n crumbly biscuit made with butter. **short-change** v 1 give (someone) less than the correct amount of change. 2 Slang swindle. **short circuit** faulty or accidental connection in a circuit, which deflects current through a path of low resistance. **shortcoming** n failing or defect. **short cut** quicker route or method. **shortfall** n deficit. **shorthand** n system of rapid writing using symbols to represent words. **short-handed** adj not having enough workers. **short list** selected list of candidates for a job or prize, from which the final choice will be made. **short-list** v put on a short list. **short shrift** brief and unsympathetic treatment. **short-sighted** adj 1 unable to see distant things clearly. 2 lacking in foresight. **short wave** radio wave with a wavelength of less than 60 metres.

shot¹ n 1 shooting. 2 small lead pellets used in a shotgun. 3 person with specified skill in shooting. 4 Slang attempt. 5 Sport act or instance of hitting, kicking, or throwing the ball. 6 photograph. 7 uninterrupted film sequence. 8 Informal injection. **shotgun** n gun for firing a charge of shot at short range.

shot² v 1 past of SHOOT. ♦ adj 2 woven to show changing colours.

shot put n athletic event in which contestants hurl a heavy metal ball as far as possible. **shot-putter** n

should v past tense of **shall** used as an auxiliary to make the subjunctive mood or to indicate obligation or possibility.

shoulder n 1 part of the body to which an arm, foreleg, or wing is attached. 2 cut of meat including the upper foreleg. 3 side of a road. ♦ v 4 bear (a burden or responsibility). 5 push with one's shoulder. 6 put on one's shoulder. **shoulder blade** large flat triangular bone at the shoulder.

shouldn't should not.

shout n 1 loud cry. 2 Informal person's turn to buy a round of drinks. ♦ v 3 cry out loudly. 4 Aust & NZ informal treat (someone) to (something, such as a drink). **shout down** v silence (someone) by shouting.

shove v 1 push roughly. 2 Informal put. ♦ n 3 rough push. **shove off** v Informal go away.

shovel n 1 tool for lifting or moving loose material. ♦ v -elling, -elled 2 lift or move as with a shovel.

show v showing, showed, shown or showed 1 make, be, or become noticeable or visible. 2 exhibit or display. 3 indicate. 4 instruct by demonstration. 5 prove. 6 guide. 7 reveal or display (an emotion). ♦ n 8 public exhibition. 9 theatrical or other entertainment. **10** mere display or pretence. **showy** *adj* **1** gaudy. **2** ostentatious. **showily** *adv* **show business** the entertainment industry. **showcase** *n* **1** situation in which something is displayed to best advantage. **2** glass case used to display objects. **showdown** *n* confrontation that settles a dispute. **showjumping** *n* competitive sport of riding horses to demonstrate skill in jumping. **showman** *n* man skilled at presenting anything spectacularly. **showmanship** *n* **show off** *v* **1** exhibit to invite admiration. **2** *Informal* behave flamboyantly in order to attract attention. **show-off** *n Informal* person who shows off. **showpiece** *n* excellent specimen shown for display or as an example. **showroom** *n* room in which goods for sale are on display. **show up** *v* **1** reveal or be revealed clearly. **2** expose the faults or defects of. **3** *Informal* embarrass. **4** *Informal* arrive.

shower *n* **1** kind of bath in which a person stands while being sprayed with water. **2** wash in this. **3** short period of rain, hail, or snow. **4** sudden abundant fall of objects. ♦ *v* **5** wash in a shower. **6** bestow (things) or present (someone) with things liberally. **showery** *adj*

shown *v* a past participle of SHOW.

shrank *v* a past tense of SHRINK.

shrapnel *n* **1** artillery shell filled with pellets which scatter on explosion. **2** fragments from this.

shred *n* **1** long narrow strip torn from something. **2** small amount. ♦ *v* **shredding, shredded** *or* **shred** **3** tear to shreds.

shrew *n* **1** small mouselike animal. **2** bad-tempered nagging woman. **shrewish** *adj*

shrewd *adj* clever and perceptive.

shrewdly *adv* **shrewdness** *n*

shriek *n* **1** shrill cry. ♦ *v* **2** utter (with) a shriek.

shrike *n* songbird with a heavy hooked bill.

shrill *adj* (of a sound) sharp and high-pitched. **shrillness** *n* **shrilly** *adv*

shrimp *n* **1** small edible shellfish. **2** *Informal* small person. **shrimping** *n* fishing for shrimps.

shrine *n* place of worship associated with a sacred person or object.

shrink *v* **shrinking, shrank** *or* **shrunk, shrunk** *or* **shrunken** **1** become or make smaller. **2** recoil or withdraw. ♦ *n* **3** *Slang* psychiatrist. **shrinkage** *n* decrease in size, value, or weight.

shrivel *v* **-elling, -elled** shrink and wither.

shroud *n* **1** piece of cloth used to wrap a dead body. **2** anything which conceals. ♦ *v* **3** conceal.

Shrove Tuesday *n* day before Ash Wednesday.

shrub *n* woody plant smaller than a tree. **shrubbery** *n, pl* **-beries** area planted with shrubs.

shrug *v* **shrugging, shrugged** **1** raise and then drop (the shoulders) as a sign of indifference, ignorance, or doubt. ♦ *n* **2** shrugging. **shrug off** *v* dismiss as unimportant.

shrunk *v* a past of SHRINK.

shrunken *v* a past participle of SHRINK.

shudder *v* **1** shake or tremble violently, esp. with horror. ♦ *n* **2** shaking or trembling.

shuffle *v* **1** walk without lifting the feet. **2** jumble together. **3** rearrange. ♦ *n* **4** shuffling. **5** rearrangement.

shun *v* **shunning, shunned** avoid.

shunt *v* **1** move (objects or people) to a different position. **2** move (a train) from one track to another.

shush *interj* be quiet!

shut v **shutting, shut 1** bring together or fold, close. **2** prevent access to. **3** (of a shop etc.) stop operating for the day. **shutter** n **1** hinged doorlike cover for closing off a window. **2** device in a camera letting in the light required to expose a film. **shut down** v close or stop (a factory, machine, or business). **shutdown** n

shuttle n **1** vehicle going to and fro over a short distance. **2** instrument which passes the weft thread between the warp threads in weaving. **3** v **4** travel by or as if by shuttle.

shuttlecock n small light cone with feathers stuck in one end, struck to and fro in badminton.

shy[1] adj **1** not at ease in company. **2** timid. **3** (foll. by of) cautious or wary. **4** v **shying, shied 5** start back in fear. **6** (foll. by away from) avoid (doing something) through fear or lack of confidence. **shyly** adv **shyness** n

shy[2] v **shying, shied 1** throw. ♦ n, pl **shies 2** throw.

SI French Système International (d'Unités), international metric system of units of measurement.

Siamese adj of Siam, former name of Thailand. **Siamese cat** breed of cat with cream fur, dark ears and face, and blue eyes. **Siamese twins** twins born joined to each other at some part of the body.

sibilant adj **1** hissing. ♦ n **2** consonant pronounced with a hissing sound.

sibling n brother or sister.

sibyl n (in ancient Greece and Rome) prophetess.

sic Latin thus: used to indicate that an odd spelling or reading is in fact accurate.

sick adj **1** vomiting or likely to vomit. **2** physically or mentally unwell. **3** Informal amused or fascinated by something sadistic or morbid. **4** (foll. by of) Informal disgusted (by) or weary (of). **sickness** n **sicken** v **1** make nauseated or disgusted. **2** become ill. **sickly** adj **1** unhealthy, weak. **2** causing revulsion or nausea. **sick bay** place for sick people, such as that on a ship.

sickle n tool with a curved blade for cutting grass or grain.

side n **1** line or surface that borders anything. **2** either of two halves into which something can be divided. **3** either surface of a flat object. **4** area immediately next to a person or thing. **5** aspect or part. **6** one of two opposing groups or teams. **7** adj **8** at or on the side. **9** subordinate. **on the side 1** as an extra. **2** unofficially. **siding** n short stretch of railway track on which trains or wagons are shunted from the main line. **sideboard** n piece of furniture for holding plates, cutlery, etc. in a dining room. **sideburns, sideboards** pl n man's side whiskers. **side effect** additional undesirable effect. **sidekick** n Informal close friend or associate. **sidelight** n either of two small lights on the front of a vehicle. **sideline** n **1** subsidiary interest or source of income. **2** Sport line marking the boundary of a playing area. **sidelong** adj **1** sideways. ♦ adv **2** obliquely. **side-saddle** n saddle designed to allow a woman rider to sit with both legs on the same side of the horse. **sidestep** v **1** dodge (an issue). **2** avoid by stepping sideways. **sidetrack** v divert from the main topic. **sidewalk** n US paved path for pedestrians, at the side of a road. **sideways** adv **1** to or from the side. **2** obliquely. **side with** v support (one side in a dispute).

sidereal [side-**eer**-ee-al] adj of or determined with reference to the stars.

sidle v walk in a furtive manner.

SIDS sudden infant death syndrome, cot death.

siege *n* surrounding and blockading of a place.

sienna *n* reddish- or yellowish-brown pigment made from natural earth.

sierra *n* range of mountains in Spain or America with jagged peaks.

siesta *n* afternoon nap, taken in hot countries.

sieve [siv] *n* **1** utensil with mesh through which a substance is sifted or strained. ◆ *v* **2** sift or strain through a sieve.

sift *v* **1** remove the coarser particles from a substance with a sieve. **2** examine (information or evidence) to select what is important.

sigh *n* **1** long audible breath expressing sadness, tiredness, relief, or longing. ◆ *v* **2** utter a sigh.

sight *n* **1** ability to see. **2** instance of seeing. **3** range of vision. **4** device for guiding the eye while using a gun or optical instrument. **5** thing worth seeing. **6** *Informal* a lot. ◆ *v* **7** catch sight of. **sightless** *adj* blind. **sight-read** *v* play or sing printed music without previous preparation. **sightseeing** *n* visiting places of interest. **sightseer** *n*

sign *n* **1** indication of something not immediately or outwardly observable. **2** gesture, mark, or symbol conveying a meaning. **3** notice displayed to advertise, inform, or warn. **4** omen. ◆ *v* **5** write (one's name) on (a document or letter) to show its authenticity or one's agreement. **6** communicate using sign language. **7** make a sign or gesture. **sign language** system of communication by gestures, as used by deaf people (also **signing**). **sign on** *v* **1** register as unemployed. **2** sign a document committing oneself to a job, course, etc. **signpost** *n* post

bearing a sign that shows the way.

signal *n* **1** sign or gesture to convey information. **2** sequence of electrical impulses or radio waves transmitted or received. ◆ *adj* **3** *Formal* very important. ◆ *v* **-nalling, -nalled** **4** convey (information) by signal. **signally** *adv* **signal box** building from which railway signals are operated. **signalman** *n* railwayman in charge of signals and points.

signatory *n, pl* **-ries** one of the parties who sign a document.

signature *n* **1** person's name written by himself or herself in signing something. **2** sign at the start of a piece of music to show the key or tempo. **signature tune** tune used to introduce a particular television or radio programme.

signet *n* small seal used to authenticate documents. **signet ring** finger ring bearing a signet.

significant *adj* **1** important. **2** having or expressing a meaning. **significantly** *adv* **significance** *n*

signify *v* **-fying, -fied** **1** indicate or suggest. **2** be a symbol or sign for. **3** be important. **signification** *n*

signor [see-**nyor**] *n* Italian term of address equivalent to *sir* or *Mr.* **signora** [see-**nyor**-a] *n* Italian term of address equivalent to *madam* or *Mrs.* **signorina** [see-nyor-**ee**-na] *n* Italian term of address equivalent to *madam* or *Miss.*

Sikh [**seek**] *n* member of an Indian religion having only one God.

silage [**sile**-ij] *n* fodder crop harvested while green and partially fermented in a silo or plastic bags.

silence *n* **1** absence of noise or speech. **2** *v* **3** make silent. **4** put a stop to. **silent** *adj* **silently** *adv* **silencer** *n* device to reduce the noise of an engine exhaust or gun.

silhouette n **1** outline of a dark shape seen against a light background. **2** v **3** show in silhouette.

silica n hard glossy mineral found as quartz and in sandstone. **silicosis** n lung disease caused by inhaling silica dust.

silicon n Chem brittle nonmetallic element widely used in chemistry and industry. **silicone** n tough synthetic substance made from silicon and used in lubricants, paints, and resins. **silicon chip** tiny wafer of silicon processed to form an integrated circuit.

silk n **1** fibre made by the larva (**silkworm**) of a certain moth. **2** thread or fabric made from this. **silky, silken** adj of or like silk.

sill n ledge at the bottom of a window or door.

silly adj -lier, -liest foolish. **silliness** n

silo n, pl -los **1** pit or airtight tower for storing silage or grains. **2** underground structure in which nuclear missiles are kept ready for launching.

silt n **1** mud deposited by moving water. ♦ v **2** (foll. by up) fill or be choked with silt.

silvan adj same as SYLVAN.

silver n **1** white precious metal. **2** coins or articles made of silver. ♦ adj **3** made of or of the colour of silver. **silverbeet** n Aust & NZ leafy green vegetable with white stalks. **silver birch** tree with silvery-white bark. **silver fern** NZ sporting symbol of New Zealand. **silverfish** n small wingless silver-coloured insect. **silverside** n cut of beef from below the rump and above the leg. **silver wedding** twenty-fifth wedding anniversary.

sim n computer game that simulates an activity such as flying or sport.

simian adj, n (of or like) a monkey or ape.

similar adj alike but not identical. **similarity** n **similarly** adv

simile [**sim**-ill-ee] n figure of speech comparing one thing to another, using 'as' or 'like', e.g. as blind as a bat.

similitude n similarity, likeness.

simmer v **1** cook gently at just below boiling point. **2** be in a state of suppressed rage. **simmer down** v Informal calm down.

simnel cake n Brit fruit cake covered with marzipan.

simper v **1** smile in a silly or affected way. **2** utter (something) with a simper. ♦ n **3** simpering smile.

simple adj **1** easy to understand or do. **2** plain or unpretentious. **3** not combined or complex. **4** sincere or frank. **5** feeble-minded. **simply** adv **simplicity** n **simplify** v make less complicated. **simplification** n **simplistic** adj too simple or naive. **simpleton** n foolish or half-witted person.

simulate v **1** make a pretence of. **2** imitate the conditions of (a particular situation). **3** have the appearance of. **simulation** n **simulator** n

simultaneous adj occurring at the same time. **simultaneously** adv

sin¹ n **1** breaking of a religious or moral law. **2** offence against a principle or standard. ♦ v sinning, sinned **3** commit a sin. **sinful** adj **1** guilty of sin. **2** being a sin. **sinfully** adv **sinner** n

sin² Maths sine.

since prep **1** during the period of time after. ♦ conj **2** from the time when. **3** for the reason that. ♦ adv **4** from that time.

sincere adj without pretence or deceit. **sincerely** adv **sincerity** n

sine n (in trigonometry) ratio of the length of the opposite side to that of the hypotenuse in a right-angled triangle.

sinecure [**sin**-ee-cure] *n* paid job with minimal duties.

sine die [**sin**-ay **dee**-ay] *adv Latin* with no date fixed for future action.

sine qua non [**sin**-ay kwah **non**] *n Latin* essential requirement.

sinew *n* **1** tough fibrous tissue joining muscle to bone. **2** muscles or strength. **sinewy** *adj*

sing *v* **singing, sang, sung 1** make musical sounds with the voice. **2** perform (a song). **3** make a humming or whistling sound. **singing telegram** service in which a messenger presents greetings to a person by singing. **singsong** *n* **1** informal singing session. ♦ *adj* **2** (of the voice) repeatedly rising and falling in pitch.

singe *v* **singeing, singed 1** burn the surface of. ♦ *n* **2** superficial burn.

singer *n* person who sings, esp. professionally.

single *adj* **1** one only. **2** distinct from others of the same kind. **3** unmarried. **4** designed for one user. **5** formed of only one part. **6** (of a ticket) valid for an outward journey only. ♦ *n* **7** single thing. **8** thing intended for one person. **9** record with one short song or tune on each side. **10** single ticket. ♦ *pl* **11** game between two players. ♦ *v* **12** (foll. by *out*) pick out from others. **singly** *adv* **single file** (of people or things) arranged in one line. **single-handed** *adj* without assistance. **single-minded** *adj* having one aim only.

singlet *n* sleeveless vest.

singular *adj* **1** (of a word or form) denoting one person or thing. **2** remarkable, unusual. ♦ *n* **3** singular form of a word. **singularity** *n* **singularly** *adv*

sinister *adj* threatening or suggesting evil or harm.

sink *v* **sinking, sank, sunk** *or* **sunken 1** submerge (in liquid). **2** descend or cause to descend. **3** decline in value or amount. **4** become weaker in health. **5** dig or drill (a hole or shaft). **6** invest (money). **7** *Golf, snooker* hit (a ball) into a hole or pocket. ♦ *n* **8** fixed basin with a water supply and drainage pipe. **sinker** *n* weight for a fishing line. **sink in** *v* penetrate the mind.

Sino- *combining form* Chinese.

sinuous *adj* **1** curving. **2** lithe. **sinuously** *adv*

sinus [**sine**-uss] *n* hollow space in a bone, esp. an air passage opening into the nose.

sip *v* **sipping, sipped 1** drink in small mouthfuls. ♦ *n* **2** amount sipped.

siphon *n* **1** bent tube which uses air pressure to draw liquid from a container. ♦ *v* **2** draw off thus. **3** redirect (resources).

sir *n* **1** polite term of address for a man. **2** (S-) title of a knight or baronet.

sire *n* **1** male parent of a horse or other domestic animal. **2** respectful term of address to a king. ♦ *v* **3** father.

siren *n* **1** device making a loud wailing noise as a warning. **2** dangerously alluring woman.

sirloin *n* prime cut of loin of beef.

sirocco *n, pl* **-cos** hot wind blowing from N Africa into S Europe.

sis *interj S Afr informal* exclamation of disgust.

sisal [**size**-al] *n* (fibre of) plant used in making ropes.

sissy *adj, n, pl* **-sies** weak or cowardly (person).

sister *n* **1** girl or woman with the same parents as another person. **2** female fellow-member of a group. **3** senior nurse. **4** nun. ♦ *adj* **5** closely related, similar. **sisterhood** *n* **1** state of being a sister. **2** group of women united by common aims or beliefs. **sisterly** *adj*

sister-in-law n, pl **sisters-in-law 1** sister of one's husband or wife. **2** one's brother's wife.

sit v **sitting, sat 1** rest one's body upright on the buttocks. **2** cause to sit. **3** perch. **4** occupy an official position. **5** (of an official body) hold a session. **6** take (an examination). **sitting room** room in a house where people sit and relax. **sit-in** n protest in which demonstrators occupy a place and refuse to move.

sitar n Indian stringed musical instrument.

sitcom n Informal situation comedy.

site n **1** place where something is, was, or is intended to be located. **2** same as WEBSITE. ♦ v **3** provide with a site.

situate v place.

situation n **1** state of affairs. **2** location and surroundings. **3** position of employment. **situation comedy** radio or television series involving the same characters in various situations.

six adj, n one more than five. **sixth** adj, n number six in a series. **sixteen** adj, n six and ten. **sixteenth** adj, n **sixty** adj, n six times ten. **sixtieth** adj, n

size[1] n **1** dimensions, bigness. **2** one of a series of standard measurements of goods. ♦ v **3** arrange according to size. **sizeable, sizable** adj quite large. **size up** v Informal assess.

size[2] n gluey substance used as a protective coating.

sizzle v make a hissing sound like frying fat.

skanky adj Slang **1** dirty or unattractive. **2** promiscuous.

skate[1] n **1** boot with a steel blade or sets of wheels attached to the sole for gliding over ice or a hard surface. ♦ v **2** glide on or as if on skates. **skateboard** n board mounted on small wheels for riding on while standing up. **skateboarding** n **skate**

over, round v avoid discussing or dealing with (a matter) fully.

skate[2] n large marine flatfish.

skedaddle v Informal run off.

skein n **1** yarn wound in a loose coil. **2** flock of geese in flight.

skeleton n **1** framework of bones inside a person's or animal's body. **2** essential framework of a structure. **3** adj **4** reduced to a minimum. **skeletal** adj **skeleton key** key which can open many different locks.

sketch n **1** rough drawing. **2** brief description. **3** short humorous play. ♦ v **4** make a sketch (of). **sketchy** adj incomplete or inadequate.

skew v **1** make slanting or crooked. ♦ adj **2** slanting or crooked. **skew-whiff** adj Brit informal slanting or crooked.

skewer n **1** pin to hold meat together during cooking. ♦ v **2** fasten with a skewer.

ski n **1** one of a pair of long runners fastened to boots for gliding over snow or water. ♦ v **skiing, skied** or **ski'd 2** travel on skis. **skier** n

skid v **skidding, skidded 1** (of a moving vehicle) slide sideways uncontrollably. ♦ n **2** skidding.

skiff n small boat.

skill n **1** special ability or expertise. **2** something requiring special expertise. **skilful** adj having or showing skill. **skilfully** adv **skilled** adj

☑ **SPELLING TIP**
When you make an adjective from **skill**, you should drop an l to make **skilful**. This is not the case in American English, and this is probably why there are over 100 examples of skillful in the Bank of English.

skillet n small frying pan or shallow

cooking pot.

skim *v* **skimming, skimmed 1** remove floating matter from the surface of (a liquid). **2** glide smoothly over. **3** read quickly. **skimmed, skim milk** milk from which the cream has been removed.

skimp *v* not invest enough time, money, material, etc. **skimpy** *adj* scanty or insufficient.

skin *n* **1** outer covering of the body. **2** complexion. **3** outer layer or covering. **4** film on a liquid. **5** animal skin used as a material or container. ♦ *v* **skinning, skinned 6** remove the skin of. **skinless** *adj* **skinny** *adj* thin. **skin-deep** *adj* superficial. **skin diving** underwater swimming using flippers and light breathing apparatus. **skin-diver** *n* **skinflint** *n* miser. **skinhead** *n* youth with very short hair.

skint *adj Brit slang* having no money.

skip¹ *v* **skipping, skipped 1** leap lightly from one toot to the other. **2** jump over a rope as it is swung under one. **3** *Informal* pass over, omit. **4** *n* **5** skipping.

skip² *n* large open container for builders' rubbish.

skipper *n, v* captain.

skirl *n* sound of bagpipes.

skirmish *n* **1** brief or minor fight or argument. ♦ *v* **2** take part in a skirmish.

skirt *n* **1** woman's garment hanging from the waist. **2** part of a dress or coat below the waist. **3** cut of beef from the flank. ♦ *v* **4** border. **5** go round. **6** avoid dealing with (an issue). **skirting board** narrow board round the bottom of an interior wall.

skit *n* brief satirical sketch.

skite *v, n Aust & NZ* boast.

skittish *adj* playful or lively.

skittle *n* **1** bottle-shaped object used as a target in some games. ♦ *pl* **2** game in which players try to knock over skittles

by rolling a ball at them.

skive *v Brit informal* evade work or responsibility.

skivvy *n, pl* **-vies** *Brit* female servant who does menial work.

skua *n* large predatory gull.

skulduggery *n Informal* trickery.

skulk *v* **1** move stealthily. **2** lurk.

skull *n* bony framework of the head. **skullcap** *n* close-fitting brimless cap.

skunk *n* **1** small black-and-white N American mammal which emits a foul-smelling fluid when attacked. **2** *Slang* despicable person.

sky *n, pl* **skies** upper atmosphere as seen from the earth. **skydiving** *n* sport of jumping from an aircraft and performing manoeuvres before opening one's parachute. **skylark** *n* lark that sings while soaring at a great height. **skylight** *n* window in a roof or ceiling. **skyscraper** *n* very tall building.

slab *n* broad flat piece.

slack *adj* **1** not tight. **2** negligent. **3** not busy. ♦ *n* **4** slack part. **5** *pl* **6** informal trousers. ♦ *v* **7** neglect one's work or duty. **slackness** *n* **slacken** *v* make or become slack. **slacker** *n*

slag *n* **1** waste left after metal is smelted. **2** *v* **slagging, slagged 3** (foll. by *off*) *Brit, Aust & NZ slang* criticize.

slain *v* past participle of SLAY.

slake *v* **1** satisfy (thirst or desire). **2** combine (quicklime) with water.

slalom *n* skiing or canoeing race over a winding course.

slam *v* **slamming, slammed 1** shut, put down, or hit violently and noisily. **2** *Informal* criticize harshly. ♦ *n* **3** act or sound of slamming. **grand slam see** GRAND.

slander *n* **1** false and malicious statement about a person. **2** crime of making such a statement. ♦ *v* **3** utter slander about. **slanderous** adj

slang n very informal language.
slangy adj **slanging match** abusive
argument.

slant v 1 lean at an angle, slope. 2
present (information) in a biased way.
♦ n 3 slope. 4 point of view, esp. a
biased one. **slanting** adj

slap n 1 blow with the open hand or a
flat object. ♦ v **slapping, slapped** 2
strike with the open hand or a flat
object. 3 Informal place forcefully or
carelessly. **slapdash** adj careless and
hasty. **slap-happy** adj Informal
cheerfully careless. **slapstick** n
boisterous knockabout comedy.
slap-up adj (of a meal) large and
luxurious.

slash v 1 cut with a sweeping stroke. 2
gash. 3 reduce drastically. 4 n 5
sweeping stroke. 6 gash.

slat n narrow strip of wood or metal.

slate[1] n 1 rock which splits easily into
thin layers. 2 piece of this for covering
a roof or, formerly, for writing on.

slate[2] v Informal criticize harshly.

slattern n Old-fashioned slovenly
woman. **slatternly** adj

slaughter v 1 kill (animals) for food. 2
kill (people) savagely or
indiscriminately. ♦ n 3 slaughtering.
slaughterhouse n place where
animals are killed for food.

Slav n member of any of the peoples of
E Europe or the former Soviet Union
who speak a Slavonic language.
Slavonic n 1 language group
including Russian, Polish, and Czech.
♦ adj 2 of this language group.

slave n 1 person owned by another for
whom he or she has to work. 2 person
dominated by another or by a habit. 3
drudge. ♦ v 4 work like a slave. **slaver**
n person or ship engaged in the slave
trade. **slavery** n 1 state or condition
of being a slave. 2 practice of owning

slaves. **slavish** adj 1 of or like a slave.
2 imitative. **slave-driver** n person
who makes others work very hard.

slaver [slav-ver] v dribble saliva from
the mouth.

slay v **slaying, slew, slain** kill.

sleazy adj -zier, -ziest run-down or
sordid. **sleaze** n

sledge[1], **sled** n 1 carriage on runners
for sliding on snow. 2 light wooden
frame for sliding over snow. ♦ v 3
travel by sledge.

sledge[2], **sledgehammer** n heavy
hammer with a long handle.

sleek adj glossy, smooth, and shiny.

sleep n 1 state of rest characterized by
unconsciousness. 2 period of this. ♦ v
sleeping, slept 3 be in or as if in a
state of sleep. 4 have sleeping
accommodation for (a specified
number). **sleeper** n 1 railway car
fitted for sleeping in. 2 beam
supporting the rails of a railway. 3 ring
worn in a pierced ear to stop the hole
from closing up. 4 person who sleeps.
sleepy adj **sleepily** adv **sleepiness** n
sleepless adj **sleeping bag** padded
bag for sleeping in. **sleeping
sickness** African disease spread by the
tsetse fly. **sleepout** n NZ small
building for sleeping in. **sleepover** n
occasion when a person stays over
night at a friend's house. **sleep with,
together** v have sexual intercourse
(with).

sleet n rain and snow or hail falling
together.

sleeve n 1 part of a garment which
covers the arm. 2 tubelike cover. 3
gramophone record cover. **up one's
sleeve** secretly ready. **sleeveless** adj

sleigh n, v sledge.

sleight of hand [slite] n skilful use of
the hands when performing conjuring
tricks.

slender adj 1 slim. 2 small in amount.

slept v past of SLEEP.

sleuth [**slooth**] n detective.

slew[1] v past tense of SLAY.

slew[2] v twist or swing round.

slice n 1 thin flat piece cut from something. 2 share. 3 kitchen tool with a broad flat blade. 4 *Sport* hitting of a ball so that it travels obliquely. ♦ v 5 cut into slices. 6 *Sport* hit (a ball) with a slice.

slick adj 1 persuasive and glib. 2 skilfully devised or carried out. 3 well-made and attractive, but superficial. ♦ n 4 patch of oil on water. ♦ v 5 make smooth or sleek.

slide v **sliding, slid** 1 slip smoothly along (a surface). 2 pass unobtrusively. 3 n 4 sliding. 5 piece of glass holding an object to be viewed under a microscope. 6 photographic transparency. 7 surface or structure for sliding on or down. 8 ornamental hair clip. **slide rule** mathematical instrument formerly used for rapid calculations. **sliding scale** variable scale according to which things such as wages alter in response to changes in other factors.

slight adj 1 small in quantity or extent. 2 not important. 3 slim and delicate. ♦ v, n 4 snub. **slightly** adv

slim adj **slimmer, slimmest** 1 not heavy or stout, thin. 2 slight. ♦ v **slimming, slimmed** 3 make or become slim by diet and exercise. **slimmer** n

slime n unpleasant thick slippery substance. **slimy** adj 1 of, like, or covered with slime. 2 ingratiating.

sling[1] n 1 bandage hung from the neck to support an injured hand or arm. 2 rope or strap for lifting something. 3 strap with a string at each end for throwing a stone. ♦ v **slinging, slung** 4 throw. 5 carry, hang, or throw with or as if with a sling.

sling[2] n sweetened drink with a spirit base, e.g. *gin sling*.

slink v **slinking, slunk** move furtively or guiltily. **slinky** adj (of clothes) figure-hugging.

slip[1] v **slipping, slipped** 1 lose balance by sliding. 2 move smoothly, easily, or quietly. 3 (foll. by *on* or *off*) put on or take off easily or quickly. 4 pass out of (the mind). 5 n 6 slipping. 7 mistake. 8 petticoat. **give someone the slip** escape from someone. **slippy** adj *Informal* slippery. **slipknot** n knot tied so that it will slip along the rope round which it is made. **slipped disc** painful condition in which one of the discs connecting the bones of the spine becomes displaced. **slip road** narrow road giving access to a motorway. **slipshod** adj (of an action) careless. **slipstream** n stream of air forced backwards by a fast-moving object. **slip up** v make a mistake. **slipway** n launching slope on which ships are built or repaired.

slip[2] n small piece (of paper).

slip[3] n clay mixed with water used for decorating pottery.

slipper n light shoe for indoor wear.

slippery adj 1 so smooth or wet as to cause slipping or be difficult to hold. 2 (of a person) untrustworthy.

slit n 1 long narrow cut or opening. ♦ v **slitting, slit** 2 make a long straight cut in.

slither v slide unsteadily.

sliver [**sliv**-ver] n small thin piece.

slob n *Informal* lazy and untidy person. **slobbish** adj

slobber v dribble or drool. **slobbery** adj

sloe n sour blue-black fruit.

slog v **slogging, slogged** 1 work hard and steadily. 2 make one's way with difficulty. 3 hit hard. ♦ n 4 long and exhausting work or walk.

slogan n catchword or phrase used in politics or advertising.

sloop n small single-masted ship.

slop v **slopping, slopped 1** splash or spill. ♦ n **2** spilt liquid. **3** liquid food. ♦ pl **4** liquid refuse and waste food used to feed animals. **sloppy** adj **1** careless or untidy. **2** gushingly sentimental.

slope v **1** slant. ♦ n **2** sloping surface. **3** degree of inclination. ♦ pl **4** hills. **slope off** v Informal go furtively.

slosh v **1** splash carelessly. **2** Slang hit hard. ♦ n **3** splashing sound. **sloshed** adj Slang drunk.

slot n **1** narrow opening for inserting something. **2** Informal place in a series or scheme. ♦ v **slotting, slotted 3** make a slot or slots in. **4** fit into a slot. **slot machine** automatic machine worked by placing a coin in a slot.

sloth [rhymes with **both**] n **1** slow-moving animal of tropical America. **2** laziness. **slothful** adj lazy or idle.

slouch v **1** sit, stand, or move with a drooping posture. ♦ n **2** drooping posture. **be no slouch** Informal be very good or talented.

slough[1] [rhymes with **now**] n bog.

slough[2] [**sluff**] v (of a snake) shed (its skin) or (of a skin) be shed. **slough off** v get rid of (something unwanted or unnecessary).

sloven n habitually dirty or untidy person. **slovenly** adj **1** dirty or untidy. **2** careless.

slow adj **1** taking a longer time than is usual or expected. **2** not fast. **3** (of a clock or watch) showing a time earlier than the correct one. **4** stupid. **5** v **6** reduce the speed (of). **slowly** adv **slowness** n **slowcoach** n Informal person who moves or works slowly.

slowworm n small legless lizard.

sludge n **1** thick mud. **2** sewage.

slug[1] n land snail with no shell. **sluggish** adj slow-moving, lacking energy. **sluggishly** adv **sluggishness** n **sluggard** n lazy person.

slug[2] n **1** bullet. **2** Informal mouthful of an alcoholic drink.

slug[3] v **slugging, slugged 1** hit hard. ♦ n **2** heavy blow.

sluice n **1** channel carrying off water. **2** sliding gate used to control the flow of water in this. **3** water controlled by a sluice. ♦ v **4** pour a stream of water over or through.

slum n **1** squalid overcrowded house or area. ♦ v **slumming, slummed 2** temporarily and deliberately experience poorer places or conditions than usual.

slumber v, n Lit sleep.

slump v **1** (of prices or demand) decline suddenly. **2** sink or fall heavily. ♦ n **3** sudden decline in prices or demand. **4** time of substantial unemployment.

slung v past of SLING[1].

slunk v past of SLINK.

slur v **slurring, slurred 1** pronounce or utter (words) indistinctly. **2** Music sing or play (notes) smoothly without a break. **3** n **4** slurring of words. **5** remark intended to discredit someone. **6** Music slurring of notes. **7** curved line indicating notes to be slurred.

slurp Informal ♦ v **1** eat or drink noisily. ♦ n **2** slurping sound.

slurry n, pl **-ries** muddy liquid mixture.

slush n **1** watery muddy substance. **2** sloppy sentimental talk or writing. **slushy** adj **slush fund** fund for financing bribery or corruption.

slut n Offens dirty or immoral woman. **sluttish** adj

sly adj **slyer, slyest** or **slier, sliest 1** crafty. **2** secretive and cunning. **3** roguish. **on the sly** secretly. **slyly**

adv **slyness** *n*

smack¹ *v* **1** slap sharply. **2** open and close (the lips) loudly in enjoyment or anticipation. ♦ *n* **3** sharp slap. **4** loud kiss. **5** slapping sound. ♦ *adv* **6** *Informal* squarely or directly, e.g. *smack in the middle*. **smacker** *n Slang* loud kiss.

smack² *n* **1** slight flavour or trace. **2** *Slang* heroin. ♦ *v* **3** have a slight flavour or trace (of).

smack³ *n* small single-masted fishing boat.

small *adj* **1** not large in size, number, or amount. **2** unimportant. **3** mean or petty. ♦ *n* **4** narrow part of the lower back. ♦ *pl* **5** *Informal* underwear. **smallness** *n* **smallholding** *n* small area of farming land. **small hours** hours just after midnight. **small-minded** *adj* intolerant, petty. **smallpox** *n* contagious disease with blisters that leave scars. **small talk** light social conversation. **small-time** *adj* insignificant or minor.

smarmy *adj* **smarmier, smarmiest** *Informal* unpleasantly suave or flattering.

smart *adj* **1** well-kept and neat. **2** astute. **3** witty. **4** fashionable. **5** brisk. **6** *v* **7** feel or cause stinging pain. ♦ *n* **8** stinging pain. **smartly** *adv* **smartness** *n* **smart aleck** *Informal* irritatingly clever person. **smart card** plastic card used for storing and processing computer data. **smarten** *v* make or become smart.

smash *v* **1** break violently and noisily. **2** throw (against) violently. **3** collide forcefully. **4** destroy. ♦ *n* **5** act or sound of smashing. **6** violent collision of vehicles. **7** *Informal* popular success. **8** *Sport* powerful overhead shot. **smasher** *n Informal* attractive person or thing. **smashing** *adj Informal* excellent.

smattering *n* slight knowledge.

smear *v* **1** spread with a greasy or sticky substance. **2** rub so as to produce a dirty mark or smudge. **3** slander. ♦ *n* **4** dirty mark or smudge. **5** slander. **6** *Med* sample of a secretion smeared on to a slide for examination under a microscope.

smell *v* **smelling, smelt** *or* **smelled 1** perceive (a scent or odour) by means of the nose. **2** have or give off a smell. **3** have an unpleasant smell. **4** detect by instinct. **5** *n* **6** ability to perceive odours by the nose. **7** odour or scent. **8** smelling. **smelly** *adj* having a nasty smell. **smelling salts** preparation of ammonia used to revive a person who feels faint.

smelt¹ *v* extract (a metal) from (an ore) by heating.

smelt² *n* small fish of the salmon family.

smelt³ *v* a past of SMELL.

smelter *n* industrial plant where smelting is carried out.

smile *n* **1** turning up of the corners of the mouth to show pleasure, amusement, or friendliness. ♦ *v* **2** give a smile. **smiley** *n* symbol depicting a smile or other facial expression, used in e-mail. **smile on, upon** *v* regard favourably.

smirch *v, n* stain.

smirk *n* **1** smug smile. ♦ *v* **2** give a smirk.

smite *v* **smiting, smote, smitten 1** *Old-fashioned* strike hard. **2** affect severely.

smith *n* worker in metal. **smithy** *n* blacksmith's workshop.

smithereens *pl n* shattered fragments.

smitten *v* past participle of SMITE.

smock *n* **1** loose overall. **2** woman's loose blouselike garment. ♦ *v* **3** gather (material) by sewing in a honeycomb pattern. **smocking** *n*

smog *n* mixture of smoke and fog.

smoke n **1** cloudy mass that rises from something burning. **2** act of smoking tobacco. **3** v **4** give off smoke. **5** inhale and expel smoke of (a cigar, cigarette, or pipe). **6** do this habitually. **7** cure (meat, fish, or cheese) by treating with smoke. **smokeless** adj **smoker** n **smoky** adj **smoke screen** something said or done to hide the truth.

smooch Informal ♦ v **1** kiss and cuddle. ♦ n **2** smooching.

smooth adj **1** even in surface, texture, or consistency. **2** without obstructions or difficulties. **3** charming and polite but possibly insincere. **4** free from jolts. **5** not harsh in taste. ♦ v **6** make smooth. **7** calm. **smoothie** n **1** Informal charming but possibly insincere man. **2** thick drink made from puréed fresh fruit. **smoothly** adv

smorgasbord n buffet meal of assorted dishes.

smote v past tense of SMITE.

smother v **1** suffocate or stifle. **2** suppress thickly. **3** cover thickly.

smoulder v **1** burn slowly with smoke but no flame. **2** (of feelings) exist in a suppressed state.

SMS short message system: used for sending data to mobile phones.

smudge v **1** make or become smeared or soiled. ♦ n **2** dirty mark. **3** blurred form. **smudgy** adj

smug adj **smugger**, **smuggest** self-satisfied. **smugly** adv **smugness** n

smuggle v **1** import or export (goods) secretly and illegally. **2** take somewhere secretly. **smuggler** n

smut n **1** obscene jokes, pictures, etc. **2** speck of soot or dark mark left by soot. **smutty** adj

snack n light quick meal. **snack bar** place where snacks are sold.

snaffle n **1** jointed bit for a horse. ♦ v **2** Brit, Aust & NZ slang steal.

snag n **1** difficulty or disadvantage. **2** sharp projecting point. **3** hole in fabric caused by a sharp object. ♦ v **snagging, snagged 4** catch or tear on a point.

snail n slow-moving mollusc with a spiral shell. **snail mail** Informal conventional post, as opposed to e-mail. **snail's pace** very slow speed.

snake n **1** long thin scaly limbless reptile. ♦ v **2** move in a winding course like a snake. **snake in the grass** treacherous person. **snaky** adj twisted or winding.

snap v **snapping, snapped 1** break suddenly. **2** (cause to) make a sharp cracking sound. **3** move suddenly. **4** bite (at) suddenly. **5** speak sharply and angrily. **6** take a snapshot of. ♦ n **7** act or sound of snapping. **8** Informal snapshot. **9** sudden brief spell of cold weather. **10** card game in which the word 'snap' is called when two similar cards are put down. ♦ adj **11** made on the spur of the moment. **snappy** adj **1** (also **snappish**) irritable. **2** Slang quick. **3** Slang smart and fashionable. **snapdragon** n plant with flowers that can open and shut like a mouth. **snapper** n food fish of Australia and New Zealand with a pinkish body covered with blue spots. **snapshot** n informal photograph. **snap up** v take eagerly and quickly.

snare n **1** trap with a noose. ♦ v **2** catch in or as if in a snare.

snarl¹ v **1** (of an animal) growl with bared teeth. **2** speak or utter fiercely. ♦ n **3** act or sound of snarling.

snarl² n **1** tangled mess. ♦ v **2** make tangled. **snarl-up** n Informal confused situation such as a traffic jam.

snatch v **1** seize or try to seize suddenly. **2** take (food, rest, etc.) hurriedly. **3** n **4** snatching. **5** fragment.

snazzy adj **-zier, -ziest** Informal stylish

and flashy.

sneak *v* **1** move furtively. **2** bring, take, or put furtively. **3** *Informal* tell tales. ♦ *n* **4** cowardly or underhand person. **sneaking** *adj* **1** slight but persistent. **2** secret. **sneaky** *adj*

sneakers *pl n* canvas shoes with rubber soles.

sneer *n* **1** contemptuous expression or remark. ♦ *v* **2** show contempt by a sneer.

sneeze *v* **1** expel air from the nose suddenly, involuntarily, and noisily. ♦ *n* **2** act or sound of sneezing.

snicker *n, v* same as SNIGGER.

snide *adj* critical in an unfair and nasty way.

sniff *v* **1** inhale through the nose in short audible breaths. **2** smell by sniffing. ♦ *n* **3** act or sound of sniffing. **sniffle** *v* **1** sniff repeatedly, as when suffering from a cold. ♦ *n* **2** slight cold. **sniff at** *v* express contempt for. **sniffer dog** police dog trained to detect drugs or explosives by smell.

snifter *n Informal* small quantity of alcoholic drink.

snigger *n* **1** sly disrespectful laugh, esp. one partly stifled. ♦ *v* **2** utter a snigger.

snip *v* **snipping, snipped** **1** cut in small quick strokes with scissors or shears. ♦ *n* **2** *Informal* bargain. **3** act or sound of snipping. **snippet** *n* small piece.

snipe *n* **1** wading bird with a long straight bill. ♦ *v* **2** (foll. by *at*) shoot at (a person) from cover. **3** make critical remarks about.

sniper *n* person who shoots at someone from cover.

snitch *Informal* ♦ *v* **1** act as an informer. **2** steal. ♦ *n* **3** informer.

snivel *v* **-elling, -elled** cry in a whining way.

snob *n* **1** person who judges others by social rank. **2** person who feels smugly superior in his or her tastes or interests. **snobbery** *n* **snobbish** *adj*

snoek *n S Afr* edible marine fish.

snood *n* pouch, often of net, loosely holding a woman's hair at the back.

snook *n* **cock a snook at** show contempt for.

snooker *n* **1** game played on a billiard table. ♦ *v* **2** leave (a snooker opponent) in a position such that another ball blocks the target ball. **3** *Informal* put (someone) in a position where he or she can do nothing.

snoop *Informal* ♦ *v* **1** pry. ♦ *n* **2** snooping. **snooper** *n*

snooty *adj* **snootier, snootiest** *Informal* haughty.

snooze *Informal* ♦ *v* **1** take a brief light sleep. ♦ *n* **2** brief light sleep.

snore *v* **1** make snorting sounds while sleeping. ♦ *n* **2** sound of snoring.

snorkel *n* **1** tube allowing a swimmer to breathe while face down on the surface of the water. **2** *v* **-kelling, -kelled 3** swim using a snorkel.

snort *v* **1** exhale noisily through the nostrils. **2** express contempt or anger by snorting. **3** *n* **4** act or sound of snorting.

snot *n Slang* mucus from the nose.

snout *n* animal's projecting nose and jaws.

snow *n* **1** frozen vapour falling from the sky in flakes. **2** *Slang* cocaine. ♦ *v* **3** fall as or like snow. **be snowed under** be overwhelmed, esp. with paperwork. **snowy** *adj* **snowball** *n* **1** snow pressed into a ball for throwing. ♦ *v* **2** increase rapidly. **snowboard** *n* board on which a person stands to slide across the snow. **snowboarding** *n* **snowdrift** *n* bank of deep snow. **snowdrop** *n* small white bell-shaped spring flower. **snowflake** *n* single crystal of snow. **snow gum** same as

SALLEE. **snow line** (on a mountain) height above which there is permanent snow. **snowman** n figure shaped out of snow. **snowplough** n vehicle for clearing away snow. **snowshoes** pl n racket-shaped shoes for travelling on snow.

snub v snubbing, snubbed 1 insult deliberately. ♦ n 2 deliberate insult. ♦ adj 3 (of a nose) short and blunt. **snub-nosed** adj

snuff[1] n powdered tobacco for sniffing up the nostrils.

snuff[2] v extinguish (a candle). **snuff it** Informal die.

snuffle v breathe noisily or with difficulty.

snug adj snugger, snuggest 1 warm and comfortable. 2 comfortably close-fitting. ♦ n 3 (in Britain and Ireland) small room in a pub. **snugly** adv

snuggle v nestle into a person or thing for warmth or from affection.

so adv 1 to such an extent. 2 in such a manner. 3 very. 4 also. 5 thereupon. ♦ conj 6 in order that. 7 with the result that. 8 therefore. ♦ interj 9 exclamation of surprise, triumph, or realization. **so-and-so** n 1 Informal person whose name is not specified. 2 unpleasant person or thing. **so-called** adj called (in the speaker's opinion, wrongly) by that name. **so long** goodbye. **so that** in order that.

soak v 1 make wet. 2 put or lie in liquid so as to become thoroughly wet. 3 (of liquid) penetrate. ♦ n 4 soaking. 5 Slang drunkard. **soaking** n, adj **soak up** v absorb.

soap n 1 compound of alkali and fat, used with water as a cleaning agent. 2 Informal soap opera. ♦ v 3 apply soap to. **soapy** adj **soap opera** radio or television serial dealing with domestic themes.

soar v 1 rise or fly upwards. 2 increase suddenly.

sob v sobbing, sobbed 1 weep with convulsive gasps. 2 utter with sobs. ♦ n 3 act or sound of sobbing. **sob story** tale of personal distress told to arouse sympathy.

sober adj 1 not drunk. 2 serious. 3 (of colours) plain and dull. ♦ v 4 make or become sober. **soberly** adv **sobriety** n state of being sober.

sobriquet [so-brik-ay] n nickname.

soccer n football played by two teams of eleven kicking a spherical ball.

sociable adj 1 friendly or companionable. 2 (of an occasion) providing companionship. **sociability** n **sociably** adv

social adj 1 living in a community. 2 of society or its organization. 3 sociable. ♦ n 4 informal gathering. **socially** adv **socialite** n member of fashionable society. **socialize** v meet others socially. **social security** state provision for the unemployed, elderly, or sick. **social services** welfare services provided by local authorities or the state. **social work** work which involves helping or advising people with serious financial or family problems.

socialism n political system which advocates public ownership of industries, resources, and transport. **socialist** n, adj

society n, pl -ties 1 human beings considered as a group. 2 organized community. 3 structure and institutions of such a community. 4 organized group with common aims and interests. 5 upper-class or fashionable people collectively. 6 companionship.

sociology n study of human societies. **sociological** adj **sociologist** n

sock[1] n knitted covering for the foot.

sock² _Slang_ ♦ _v_ **1** hit hard. ♦ _n_ **2** hard blow.

socket _n_ hole or recess into which something fits.

sod¹ _n_ (piece of) turf.

sod² _n Slang_ obnoxious person.

soda _n_ **1** compound of sodium. **2** soda water. **soda water** fizzy drink made from water charged with carbon dioxide.

sodden _adj_ soaked.

sodium _n Chem_ silvery-white metallic element. **sodium bicarbonate** white soluble compound used in baking powder.

sodomy _n_ anal intercourse. **sodomite** _n_ person who practises sodomy.

sofa _n_ couch.

soft _adj_ **1** easy to shape or cut. **2** not hard, rough, or harsh. **3** (of a breeze or climate) mild. **4** (too) lenient. **5** easily influenced or imposed upon. **6** (of drugs) not liable to cause addiction. **softly** _adv_ **soften** _v_ make or become soft or softer. **soft drink** nonalcoholic drink. **soft furnishings** curtains, rugs, lampshades, and furniture covers. **soft option** easiest alternative. **soft-pedal** _v_ deliberately avoid emphasizing something. **soft-soap** _v Informal_ flatter. **software** _n_ computer programs. **softwood** _n_ wood of a coniferous tree.

soggy _adj_ -gier, -giest **1** soaked. **2** moist and heavy. **sogginess** _n_

soigné, _(fem)_ **soignée** [**swah**-nyay] _adj_ well-groomed, elegant.

soil¹ _n_ **1** top layer of earth. **2** country or territory.

soil² _v_ **1** make or become dirty. **2** disgrace.

soiree [**swah**-ray] _n_ evening party or gathering.

sojourn [**soj**-urn] _n_ **1** temporary stay. ♦ _v_ **2** stay temporarily.

solace [**sol**-iss] _n, v_ comfort in distress.

solar _adj_ **1** of the sun. **2** using the energy of the sun. **solar plexus 1** network of nerves at the pit of the stomach. **2** this part of the stomach. **solar system** the sun and the heavenly bodies that go round it.

solarium _n, pl_ -lariums, -laria place with beds and ultraviolet lights used for acquiring an artificial suntan.

sold _v_ past of SELL.

solder _n_ **1** soft alloy used to join two metal surfaces. ♦ _v_ **2** join with solder. **soldering iron** tool for melting and applying solder.

soldier _n_ **1** member of an army. ♦ _v_ **2** serve in an army. **soldierly** _adj_ **soldier on** _v_ persist doggedly.

sole¹ _adj_ **1** one and only. **2** not shared, exclusive. **solely** _adv_ **1** only, completely. **2** alone. **sole charge school** _NZ_ country school with only one teacher.

sole² _n_ **1** underside of the foot. **2** underside of a shoe. **3** _v_ **4** provide (a shoe) with a sole.

sole³ _n_ small edible flatfish.

solecism [**sol**-iss-izz-um] _n_ **1** minor grammatical mistake. **2** breach of etiquette.

solemn _adj_ **1** serious, deeply sincere. **2** formal. **solemnly** _adv_ **solemnity** _n_

solenoid [**sole**-in-oid] _n_ coil of wire magnetized by passing a current through it.

sol-fa _n_ system of syllables used as names for the notes of a scale.

solicit _v_ -iting, -ited **1** request. **2** (of a prostitute) offer (a person) sex for money. **solicitation** _n_

solicitor _n Brit, Aust & NZ_ lawyer who advises clients and prepares documents and cases.

solicitous _adj_ anxious about someone's welfare. **solicitude** _n_

solid *adj* **1** (of a substance) keeping its shape. **2** not liquid or gas. **3** not hollow. **4** of the same substance throughout. **5** strong or substantial. **6** sound or reliable. **7** having three dimensions. ♦ *n* **8** three-dimensional shape. **9** solid substance. **solidly** *adv* **solidify** *v* make or become solid or firm. **solidity** *n*

solidarity *n* agreement in aims or interests, total unity.

soliloquy *n*, *pl* **-quies** speech made by a person while alone, esp. in a play.

solipsism *n* doctrine that the self is the only thing known to exist. **solipsist** *n*

solitaire *n* **1** game for one person played with pegs set in a board. **2** gem set by itself.

solitary *adj* **1** alone, single. **2** (of a place) lonely. **solitude** *n* state of being alone.

solo *n*, *pl* **-los** **1** music for one performer. **2** any act done without assistance. ♦ *adj* **3** done alone. ♦ *adv* **4** by oneself, alone. **soloist** *n* **solo parent** *NZ* parent bringing up a child or children alone.

solstice *n* either the shortest (in winter) or longest (in summer) day of the year.

soluble *adj* **1** able to be dissolved. **2** able to be solved. **solubility** *n*

solution *n* **1** answer to a problem. **2** act of solving a problem. **3** liquid with something dissolved in it. **4** process of dissolving.

solve *v* find the answer to (a problem). **solvable** *adj*

solvent *adj* **1** having enough money to pay one's debts. ♦ *n* **2** liquid capable of dissolving other substances. **solvency** *n* **solvent abuse** deliberate inhaling of intoxicating fumes from certain solvents.

sombre *adj* dark, gloomy.

sombrero *n*, *pl* **-ros** wide-brimmed Mexican hat.

some *adj* **1** unknown or unspecified. **2** unknown or unspecified quantity or number of. **3** considerable number or amount of. **4** *Informal* remarkable. ♦ *pron* **5** certain unknown or unspecified people or things. **6** unknown or unspecified number or quantity. **somebody** *pron* **1** some person. ♦ *n* **2** important person. **somehow** *adv* in some unspecified way. **someone** *pron* somebody. **something** *pron* **1** unknown or unspecified thing or amount. **2** impressive or important thing. **sometime** *adv* **1** at some unspecified time. ♦ *adj* **2** former. **sometimes** *adv* from time to time, now and then. **somewhat** *adv* to some extent, rather. **somewhere** *adv* in, to, or at some unspecified or unknown place.

somersault *n* **1** leap or roll in which the trunk and legs are turned over the head. ♦ *v* **2** perform a somersault.

somnambulist *n* person who walks in his or her sleep. **somnambulism** *n*

somnolent *adj* drowsy.

son *n* male offspring. **son-in-law** *n*, *pl* **sons-in-law** daughter's husband.

sonar *n* device for detecting underwater objects by the reflection of sound waves.

sonata *n* piece of music in several movements for one instrument with or without piano.

son et lumière [sawn eh **loo**-mee-er] *n French* night-time entertainment with lighting and sound effects, telling the story of the place where it is staged.

song *n* **1** music for the voice. **2** tuneful sound made by certain birds. **3** singing. **for a song** very cheaply. **songster, songstress** *n* singer. **songbird** *n* any bird with a musical call.

sonic *adj* of or producing sound. **sonic**

boom loud bang caused by an aircraft flying faster than sound.

sonnet *n* fourteen-line poem with a fixed rhyme scheme.

sonorous *adj* (of sound) deep or resonant. **sonorously** *adv* **sonority** *n*

soon *adv* in a short time.

sooner *adv* rather, e.g. *I'd sooner go alone.* **sooner or later** eventually.

soot *n* black powder formed by the incomplete burning of an organic substance. **sooty** *adj*

soothe *v* 1 make calm. 2 relieve (pain etc.).

soothsayer *n* seer or prophet.

sop *n* 1 concession to pacify someone. 2 *v* **sopping, sopped** 3 mop up or absorb (liquid). **sopping** *adj* completely soaked. **soppy** *adj* *Informal* oversentimental.

sophist *n* person who uses clever but invalid arguments.

sophisticate *v* 1 make less natural or innocent. 2 make more complex or refined. ◆ *n* 3 sophisticated person.

sophisticated *adj* 1 having or appealing to refined or cultured tastes and habits. 2 complex and refined. **sophistication** *n*

sophistry, sophism *n* clever but invalid argument.

sophomore *n* *US* student in second year at college.

soporific *adj* 1 causing sleep. ◆ *n* 2 drug that causes sleep.

soprano *n, pl* **-pranos** 1 (singer with) the highest female or boy's voice. 2 highest pitched of a family of instruments.

sorbet *n* flavoured water ice.

sorcerer *n* magician. **sorceress** *n fem* **sorcery** *n* witchcraft or magic.

sordid *adj* 1 dirty, squalid. 2 base, vile. 3 selfish and grasping. **sordidly** *adv* **sordidness** *n*

sore *adj* 1 painful. 2 causing annoyance. 3 resentful. 4 (of need) urgent. ◆ *n* 5 painful area on the body. ◆ *adv* 6 *Obs* greatly. **sorely** *adv* greatly. **soreness** *n*

sorghum *n* kind of grass cultivated for grain.

sorrel *n* bitter-tasting plant.

sorrow *n* 1 grief or sadness. 2 cause of sorrow. ◆ *v* 3 grieve. **sorrowful** *adj* **sorrowfully** *adv*

sorry *adj* **-rier, -riest** 1 feeling pity or regret. 2 pitiful or wretched.

sort *n* 1 group all sharing certain qualities or characteristics. 2 *Informal* type of character. ◆ *v* 3 arrange according to kind. 4 mend or fix. **out of sorts** slightly unwell or bad-tempered.

sortie *n* 1 relatively short return trip. 2 operational flight made by military aircraft.

SOS *n* 1 international code signal of distress. 2 call for help.

so-so *adj* *Informal* mediocre.

sot *n* habitual drunkard.

sotto voce [**sot**-toe **voe**-chay] *adv* in an undertone.

soubriquet [so-brik-ay] *n* same as **SOBRIQUET**.

soufflé [**soo**-flay] *n* light fluffy dish made with beaten egg whites and other ingredients.

sough [rhymes with **now**] *v* (of the wind) make a sighing sound.

sought [sawt] *v* past of **SEEK**.

souk [sook] *n* marketplace in Muslim countries, often open-air.

soul *n* 1 spiritual and immortal part of a human being. 2 essential part or fundamental nature. 3 deep and sincere feelings. 4 person regarded as typifying some quality. 5 person. 6 type of Black music combining blues, pop, and gospel. **soulful** *adj* full of emotion. **soulless** adj **1** lacking human qualities, mechanical. **2** (of a person) lacking sensitivity.

sound[1] n **1** something heard, noise. **2** v **3** make or cause to make a sound. **4** seem to be as specified. **5** pronounce. **sound barrier** Informal sudden increase in air resistance against an object as it approaches the speed of sound. **sound bite** short pithy sentence or phrase extracted from a longer speech, esp. by a politician, for use on television or radio. **soundproof** adj **1** not penetrable by sound. ♦ v **2** make soundproof. **soundtrack** n recorded sound accompaniment to a film.

sound[2] adj **1** in good condition. **2** firm, substantial. **3** financially reliable. **4** showing good judgment. **5** ethically correct. **6** (of sleep) deep. **7** thorough. **soundly** adv

sound[3] v **1** find the depth of (water etc.). **2** examine (the body) by tapping or with a stethoscope. **3** ascertain the views of. **soundings** pl n measurements of depth taken by sounding. **sounding board** person or group used to test a new idea.

sound[4] n channel or strait.

soup n liquid food made from meat, vegetables, etc. **soupy** adj **soup kitchen** place where food and drink is served to needy people. **souped-up** adj (of an engine) adjusted so as to be more powerful than normal.

soupçon [soop-sonn] n small amount.

sour adj **1** sharp-tasting. **2** (of milk) gone bad. **3** (of a person's temperament) sullen. ♦ v **4** make or become sour. **sourly** adv **sourness** n

source n **1** origin or starting point. **2** person, book, etc. providing information. **3** spring where a river or stream begins.

souse v **1** plunge (something) into

liquid. **2** drench. **3** pickle.

soutane [soo-**tan**] n Roman Catholic priest's cassock.

south n **1** direction towards the South Pole, opposite north. **2** area lying in or towards the south. ♦ adj **3** to or in the south. **4** (of a wind) from the south. ♦ adv **5** in, to, or towards the south. **southerly** adj **southern** adj **southerner** n person from the south of a country or area. **southward** adj, adv **southwards** adv **southpaw** n Informal left-handed person, esp. a boxer. **South Pole** southernmost point on the earth's axis.

souvenir n keepsake, memento.

sou'wester n seaman's waterproof hat covering the head and back of the neck.

sovereign n **1** king or queen. **2** former British gold coin worth one pound. ♦ adj **3** (of a state) independent. **4** supreme in rank or authority. **5** excellent. **sovereignty** n

soviet n **1** formerly, elected council at various levels of government in the USSR. ♦ adj **2** (S-) of the former USSR.

sow[1] [rhymes with **know**] v sowing, **sowed, sown** or **sowed 1** scatter or plant (seed) in or on (the ground). **2** implant or introduce.

sow[2] [rhymes with **cow**] n female adult pig.

soya n plant whose edible bean (**soya bean**) is used for food and as a source of oil. **soy sauce** sauce made from fermented soya beans, used in Chinese and Japanese cookery.

sozzled adj Brit, Aust & NZ slang drunk.

spa n resort with a mineral-water spring.

space n **1** unlimited expanse in which all objects exist and move. **2** interval. **3** blank portion. **4** unoccupied area. **5** the universe beyond the earth's atmosphere. ♦ v **6** place at intervals. **spacious** adj having a large capacity or area. **spacecraft, spaceship** n vehicle for travel beyond the earth's atmosphere. **space shuttle** manned reusable vehicle for repeated space flights. **spacesuit** n sealed pressurized suit worn by an astronaut.

spade¹ n tool for digging. **spadework** n hard preparatory work.

spade² n playing card of the suit marked with black leaf-shaped symbols.

spaghetti n pasta in the form of long strings.

span n 1 space between two points. 2 complete extent. 3 distance from thumb to little finger of the expanded hand. ♦ v **spanning, spanned** 4 stretch or extend across.

spangle n 1 small shiny metallic ornament. ♦ v 2 decorate with spangles.

spaniel n dog with long ears and silky hair.

spank v 1 slap with the open hand, on the buttocks or legs. ♦ n 2 such a slap. **spanking** n

spanking adj 1 Informal outstandingly fine or smart. 2 quick.

spanner n tool for gripping and turning a nut or bolt.

spar¹ n pole used as a ship's mast, boom, or yard.

spar² v **sparring, sparred** 1 box or fight using light blows for practice. 2 argue (with someone).

spare adj 1 extra. 2 in reserve. 3 (of a person) thin. 4 n 5 duplicate kept in case of damage or loss. ♦ v 6 refrain from punishing or harming. 7 protect (someone) from (something unpleasant). 8 afford to give. **to spare** in addition to what is needed. **sparing** adj economical. **spare ribs** pork ribs with most of the meat trimmed off.

spark n 1 fiery particle thrown out from a fire or caused by friction. 2 flash of light produced by an electrical discharge. 3 trace or hint (of a particular quality). 4 v 5 give off sparks. 6 initiate. **sparkie** n NZ informal electrician. **spark plug** device in an engine that ignites the fuel by producing an electric spark.

sparkle v 1 glitter with many points of light. 2 be vivacious or witty. ♦ n 3 sparkling points of light. 4 vivacity or wit. **sparkler** n hand-held firework that emits sparks. **sparkling** adj (of wine or mineral water) slightly fizzy.

sparrow n small brownish bird. **sparrowhawk** n small hawk.

sparse adj thinly scattered. **sparsely** adv **sparseness** n

spartan adj strict and austere.

spasm n 1 involuntary muscular contraction. 2 sudden burst of activity or feeling. **spasmodic** adj occurring in spasms. **spasmodically** adv

spastic n 1 person with cerebral palsy. ♦ adj 2 suffering from cerebral palsy. 3 affected by spasms.

spat¹ n slight quarrel.

spat² v past of SPIT¹.

spate n 1 large number of things happening within a period of time. 2 sudden outpouring or flood.

spatial adj of or in space.

spats pl n coverings formerly worn over the ankle and instep.

spatter v 1 scatter or be scattered in drops over (something). ♦ n 2 spattering sound. 3 something spattered.

spatula n utensil with a broad flat blade for spreading or stirring.

spawn n 1 jelly-like mass of eggs of fish, frogs, or molluscs. ♦ v 2 (of fish, frogs, or molluscs) lay eggs. 3 generate.

spay v remove the ovaries from (a female animal).

speak v speaking, spoke, spoken 1 say words, talk. 2 communicate or express in words. 3 give a speech or lecture. 4 know how to talk in (a specified language). **speaker** n 1 person who speaks, esp. at a formal occasion. 2 loudspeaker. 3 (S-) official chairman of a body.

spear¹ n 1 weapon consisting of a long shaft with a sharp point. ◆ v 2 pierce with or as if with a spear. **spearhead** v 1 lead (an attack or campaign). ◆ n 2 leading force in an attack or campaign.

spear² n slender shoot.

spearmint n type of mint.

spec n **on spec** Informal as a risk or gamble.

special adj 1 distinguished from others of its kind. 2 for a specific purpose. 3 exceptional. 4 particular. **specially** adv **specialist** n expert in a particular activity or subject. **speciality** n 1 special interest or skill. 2 product specialized in. **specialize** v be a specialist. **specialization** n

specie n coins as distinct from paper money.

species n, pl -cies group of plants or animals that are related closely enough to interbreed naturally.

specific adj 1 particular, definite. 2 n 3 drug used to treat a particular disease. ◆ pl 4 particular details. **specifically** adv **specification** n detailed description of something to be made or done. **specify** v refer to or state specifically. **specific gravity** ratio of the density of a substance to that of water.

specimen n 1 individual or part typifying a whole. 2 sample of blood etc. taken for analysis.

specious [spee-shuss] adj apparently true, but actually false.

speck n small spot or particle. **speckle** n 1 small spot. ◆ v 2 mark with speckles.

specs pl n Informal short for SPECTACLES.

spectacle n 1 strange, interesting, or ridiculous sight. 2 impressive public show. ◆ pl 3 pair of glasses for correcting faulty vision. **spectacular** adj 1 impressive. ◆ n 2 spectacular public show. **spectacularly** adv

spectator n person viewing anything, onlooker. **spectate** v watch.

spectre n 1 ghost. 2 menacing mental image. **spectral** adj

spectrum n, pl -tra 1 range of different colours, radio waves, etc. in order of their wavelengths. 2 entire range of anything. **spectroscope** n instrument for producing or examining spectra.

speculate v 1 guess, conjecture. 2 buy property, shares, etc. in the hope of selling them at a profit. **speculation** n **speculative** adj **speculator** n

sped v a past of SPEED.

speech n 1 act, power, or manner of speaking. 2 talk given to an audience. 3 language or dialect. **speechless** adj unable to speak because of great emotion.

speed n 1 swiftness. 2 rate at which something moves or acts. 3 Slang amphetamine. ◆ v speeding, sped or speeded 4 go quickly. 5 drive faster than the legal limit. **speedy** adj 1 prompt. 2 rapid. **speedily** adv **speedboat** n light fast motorboat. **speed camera** Brit, Aust & NZ camera for photographing vehicles breaking the speed limit. **speedometer** n instrument to show the speed of a vehicle. **speed up** v accelerate. **speedway** n 1 track for motorcycle racing. 2 US, Canadian & NZ track for motor racing. **speedwell** n plant with small blue flowers.

speleology n study and exploration of caves.

spell¹ v spelling, spelt or spelled 1

give in correct order the letters that form (a word). **2** (of letters) make up (a word). **3** indicate. **spelling** n **1** way a word is spelt. **2** person's ability to spell. **spellchecker** n Computing program that highlights wrongly spelled words in a word-processed document. **spell out** v make explicit.

spell² n **1** formula of words supposed to have magic power. **2** effect of a spell. **3** fascination. **spellbound** adj entranced.

spell³ n **1** period of time of weather or activity. **2** Scot, Aust & NZ period of rest.

spelt v a past of SPELL¹.

spend v **spending, spent 1** pay out (money). **2** use or pass (time). **3** use up completely. **spendthrift** n person who spends money wastefully.

sperm n, pl **sperms** or **sperm 1** male reproductive cell. **2** semen. **spermicide** n substance that kills sperm. **sperm whale** large toothed whale.

spermaceti [sper-ma-**set**-ee] n waxy solid obtained from the sperm whale.

spermatozoon [sper-ma-toe-**zoe**-on] n, pl **-zoa** sperm.

spew v **1** vomit. **2** send out in a stream.

sphagnum n moss found in bogs.

sphere n **1** perfectly round solid object. **2** field of activity. **spherical** adj

sphincter n ring of muscle which controls the opening and closing of a hollow organ.

Sphinx n **1** statue in Egypt with a lion's body and human head. **2** (s-) enigmatic person.

spice n **1** aromatic substance used as flavouring. **2** something that adds zest or interest. ♦ v **3** flavour with spices. **spicy** adj **1** flavoured with spices. **2** Informal slightly scandalous.

spick-and-span adj neat and clean.

spider n small eight-legged creature which spins a web to catch insects for food. **spidery** adj

spiel n speech made to persuade someone to do something.

spigot n stopper for, or tap fitted to, a cask.

spike n **1** sharp point. **2** sharp pointed metal object. ♦ pl **3** sports shoes with spikes for greater grip. ♦ v **4** put spikes on. **5** pierce or fasten with a spike. **6** add alcohol to (a drink). **spike someone's guns** thwart someone. **spiky** adj

spill¹ v **spilling, spilt** or **spilled 1** pour from or as if from a container. **2** n **3** fall. **4** amount spilt. **spill the beans** Informal give away a secret. **spillage** n

spill² n thin strip of wood or paper for lighting pipes or fires.

spin v **spinning, spun 1** revolve or cause to revolve rapidly. **2** draw out and twist (fibres) into thread. **3** Informal present information in a way that creates a favourable impression. ♦ n **4** revolving motion. **5** continuous spiral descent of an aircraft. **6** Informal short drive for pleasure. **7** Informal presenting of information in a way that creates a favourable impression. **spin a yarn** tell an improbable story. **spinner** n **spin doctor** Informal person who provides a favourable slant to a news item or policy on behalf of a politician or a political party. **spin-dry** v dry (clothes) in a spin-dryer. **spin-dryer** n machine in which washed clothes are spun in a perforated drum to remove excess water. **spin-off** n incidental benefit. **spin out** v prolong.

spina bifida n condition in which part of the spinal cord protrudes through a gap in the backbone, often causing paralysis.

spinach n dark green leafy vegetable.

spindle n 1 rotating rod that acts as an axle. 2 weighted rod rotated for spinning thread by hand. **spindly** adj long, slender, and frail.

spindrift n spray blown up from the sea.

spine n 1 backbone. 2 edge of a book on which the title is printed. 3 sharp point on an animal or plant. **spinal** adj of the spine. **spineless** adj lacking courage. **spiny** adj covered with spines.

spinet n small harpsichord.

spinifex n coarse spiny Australian grass.

spinnaker n large sail on a racing yacht.

spinney n Chiefly Brit small wood.

spinster n unmarried woman.

spiral n 1 continuous curve formed by a point winding about a central axis at an ever-increasing distance from it. 2 steadily accelerating increase or decrease. ♦ v -ralling, -ralled 3 move in a spiral. 4 increase or decrease with steady acceleration. ♦ adj 5 having the form of a spiral.

spire n pointed part of a steeple.

spirit[1] n 1 nonphysical aspect of a person concerned with profound thoughts. 2 nonphysical part of a person believed to live on after death. 3 courage and liveliness. 4 essential meaning as opposed to literal interpretation. 5 ghost. ♦ pl 6 emotional state. ♦ v -iting, -ited 7 carry away mysteriously. **spirited** adj lively.

spirit[2] n liquid obtained by distillation. **spirit level** glass tube containing a bubble in liquid, used to check whether a surface is level.

spiritual adj 1 relating to the spirit. 2 relating to sacred things. ♦ n 3 type of religious folk song originating among Black slaves in America. **spiritually** adv **spirituality** n

spiritualism n belief that the spirits of the dead can communicate with the living. **spiritualist** n

spit[1] v **spitting, spat** 1 eject (saliva or food) from the mouth. 2 throw out particles explosively. 3 rain slightly. 4 utter (words) in a violent manner. ♦ n 5 saliva. **spitting image** Informal person who looks very like another. **spittle** n fluid produced in the mouth, saliva. **spittoon** n bowl to spit into.

spit[2] n 1 sharp rod on which meat is skewered for roasting. 2 long narrow strip of land jutting out into the sea.

spite n 1 deliberate nastiness. ♦ v 2 annoy or hurt from spite. **in spite of** in defiance of. **spiteful** adj **spitefully** adv

spitfire n person with a fiery temper.

spiv n Brit, Aust & NZ slang smartly dressed man who makes a living by shady dealings.

splash v 1 scatter liquid on (something). 2 scatter (liquid) or (of liquid) be scattered in drops. 3 print (a story or photograph) prominently in a newspaper. ♦ n 4 splashing sound. 5 patch (of colour or light). 6 extravagant display. 7 small amount of liquid added to a drink. **splash out** v Informal spend extravagantly.

splatter v, n splash.

splay v spread out, with ends spreading in different directions.

spleen n 1 abdominal organ which filters bacteria from the blood. 2 bad temper. **splenetic** adj spiteful or irritable.

splendid adj 1 excellent. 2 brilliant in appearance. **splendidly** adv **splendour** n

splice v join by interweaving or overlapping ends. **get spliced** Slang get married.

splint n rigid support for a broken bone.

splinter *n* **1** thin sharp piece broken off, esp. from wood. ♦ *v* **2** break into fragments. **splinter group** group that has broken away from an organization.

split *v* **splitting, split** **1** break into separate pieces. **2** separate. **3** share. **4** *n* **5** crack or division caused by splitting. **6** *pl* **7** act of sitting with the legs outstretched in opposite directions. **split second** very short period of time.

splotch, splodge *n, v* splash, daub.

splurge *v* **1** spend money extravagantly. ♦ *n* **2** bout of extravagance.

splutter *v* **1** utter with spitting or choking sounds. **2** make hissing spitting sounds. ♦ *n* **3** spluttering.

spoil *v* **spoiling, spoilt** *or* **spoiled** **1** damage. **2** harm the character of (a child) by giving it all it wants. **3** rot, go bad. **spoils** *pl n* booty. **spoiling for** eager for. **spoilsport** *n* person who spoils the enjoyment of others.

spoke¹ *v* past tense of SPEAK.

spoke² *n* bar joining the hub of a wheel to the rim.

spoken *v* past participle of SPEAK.

spokesman, spokeswoman, spokesperson *n* person chosen to speak on behalf of a group.

spoliation *n* plundering.

sponge *n* **1** sea animal with a porous absorbent skeleton. **2** skeleton of a sponge, or a substance like it, used for cleaning. **3** type of light cake. **4** *v* **5** wipe with a sponge. **6** live at the expense of others. **sponger** *n Slang* person who sponges on others. **spongy** *adj*

sponsor *n* **1** person who promotes something. **2** person who agrees to give money to a charity on completion of a specified activity by another. **3** godparent. **4** *v* **5** act as a sponsor for. **sponsorship** *n*

spontaneous *adj* **1** not planned or arranged. **2** occurring through natural processes without outside influence. **spontaneously** *adv* **spontaneity** *n*

spoof *n* mildly satirical parody.

spook *n Informal* ghost. **spooky** *adj*

spool *n* cylinder round which something can be wound.

spoon *n* **1** shallow bowl attached to a handle for eating, stirring, or serving food. ♦ *v* **2** lift with a spoon. **spoonful** *n* **spoonbill** *n* wading bird of warm regions with a long flat bill. **spoon-feed** *v* **1** feed with a spoon. **2** give (someone) too much help.

spoonerism *n* accidental changing over of the initial sounds of a pair of words, such as *half-warmed fish* for *half-formed wish*.

spoor *n* trail of an animal.

sporadic *adj* intermittent, scattered. **sporadically** *adv*

spore *n* minute reproductive body of some plants.

sporran *n* pouch worn in front of a kilt.

sport *n* **1** activity for pleasure, competition, or exercise. **2** such activities collectively. **3** enjoyment. **4** playful joking. **5** person who reacts cheerfully. ♦ *v* **6** wear proudly. **sporting** *adj* **1** of sport. **2** behaving in a fair and decent way. **sporting chance** reasonable chance of success. **sporty** *adj* **sportive** *adj* playful. **sports car** fast low-built car, usu. open-topped. **sports jacket** man's casual jacket. **sportsman, sportswoman** *n* **1** person who plays sports. **2** person who plays fair and is good-humoured when losing. **sportsmanlike** *adj* **sportsmanship** *n*

spot *n* **1** small mark on a surface. **2** pimple. **3** location. **4** *Informal* small quantity. **5** *Informal* awkward situation. **6** *v* **spotting, spotted** **7** notice. **8** mark with spots. **9** watch for and take note of **on the spot 1** at the place in question. **2** immediately. **3** in an awkward predicament. **spotless** adj absolutely clean. **spotlessly** adv **spotty** adj with spots. **spot check** random examination. **spotlight** n **1** powerful light illuminating a small area. **2** centre of attention. **spot-on** adj Informal absolutely accurate.

spouse n husband or wife.

spout v **1** pour out in a stream or jet. **2** Slang utter (a stream of words) lengthily. ♦ n **3** projecting tube or lip for pouring liquids. **4** stream or jet of liquid.

sprain v **1** injure (a joint) by a sudden twist. ♦ n **2** such an injury.

sprang v a past tense of SPRING.

sprat n small sea fish.

sprawl v **1** lie or sit with the limbs spread out. **2** spread out in a straggling manner. ♦ n **3** part of a city that has spread untidily over a large area.

spray[1] n **1** (device for producing) fine drops of liquid. **2** v **3** scatter in fine drops. **4** cover with a spray. **spray gun** device for spraying paint etc.

spray[2] n **1** branch with buds, leaves, flowers, or berries. **2** ornament like this.

spread v **spreading, spread 1** open out or be displayed to the fullest extent. **2** extend over a larger expanse. **3** apply as a coating. **4** send or be sent in all directions. ♦ n **5** spreading. **6** extent. **7** Informal large meal. **8** soft food which can be spread. **spread-eagled** adj with arms and legs outstretched. **spreadsheet** n computer program for manipulating figures.

spree n session of overindulgence, usu. in drinking or spending money.

sprig n **1** twig or shoot. **2** NZ stud on the sole of a soccer or rugby boot.

sprightly adj **-lier, -liest** lively and

brisk. **sprightliness** n

spring v **springing, sprang** or **sprung, sprung 1** move suddenly upwards or forwards in a single motion, jump. **2** develop unexpectedly. **3** originate (from). **4** Informal arrange the escape of (someone) from prison. ♦ n **5** season between winter and summer. **6** jump. **7** coil which can be compressed, stretched, or bent and returns to its original shape when released. **8** natural pool forming the source of a stream. **9** elasticity. **springy** adj elastic.

springboard n flexible board used to gain height or momentum in diving or gymnastics. **spring-clean** v clean (a house) thoroughly. **spring tide** high tide at new or full moon.

springbok n S African antelope.

springer n small spaniel.

sprinkle v scatter (liquid or powder) in tiny drops or particles over (something). **sprinkler** n **sprinkling** n small quantity or number.

sprint n **1** short race run at top speed. **2** fast run. ♦ v **3** run a short distance at top speed. **sprinter** n

sprite n elf.

sprocket n wheel with teeth on the rim, that drives or is driven by a chain.

sprout v **1** put forth shoots. **2** begin to grow or develop. ♦ n **3** shoot. **4** short for BRUSSELS SPROUT.

spruce[1] n kind of fir.

spruce[2] adj neat and smart. **spruce up** v make neat and smart.

sprung v a past of SPRING.

spry adj **spryer, spryest** or **sprier, spriest** active or nimble.

spud n Informal potato.

spume n, v froth.

spun v past of SPIN.

spunk n Informal courage, spirit. **spunky** adj

spur n **1** stimulus or incentive. **2** spiked

wheel on the heel of a rider's boot used to urge on a horse. **3** projection. ♦ *v* **spurring, spurred 4** urge on, incite (someone). **on the spur of the moment** on impulse.

spurge *n* plant with milky sap.

spurious *adj* not genuine.

spurn *v* reject with scorn.

spurt *v* **1** gush or cause to gush out in a jet. ♦ *n* **2** short sudden burst of activity or speed. **3** sudden gush.

sputnik *n* early Soviet artificial satellite.

sputter *v, n* splutter.

sputum *n, pl* **-ta** spittle, usu. mixed with mucus.

spy *n, pl* **spies 1** person employed to obtain secret information. **2** person who secretly watches others. ♦ *v* **spying, spied 3** act as a spy. **4** catch sight of.

Sq. Square.

squabble *v, n* (engage in) a petty or noisy quarrel.

squad *n* small group of people working or training together.

squadron *n* division of an air force, fleet, or cavalry regiment.

squalid *adj* **1** dirty and unpleasant. **2** morally sordid. **squalor** *n* disgusting dirt and filth.

squall[1] *n* sudden strong wind.

squall[2] *v* **1** cry noisily, yell. ♦ *n* **2** harsh cry.

squander *v* waste (money or resources).

square *n* **1** geometric figure with four equal sides and four right angles. **2** open area in a town in this shape. **3** product of a number multiplied by itself. ♦ *adj* **4** square in shape. **5** denoting a measure of area. **6** straight or level. **7** fair and honest. **8** with all accounts or debts settled. **9** *v* **10** multiply (a number) by itself. **11** make square. **12** be or cause to be

consistent. ♦ *adv* **13** squarely, directly.

squarely *adv* **1** in a direct way. **2** in an honest and frank manner. **square dance** formation dance in which the couples form squares. **square meal** substantial meal. **square root** number of which a given number is the square. **square up to** *v* prepare to confront (a person or problem).

squash[1] *v* **1** crush flat. **2** suppress. **3** push into a confined space. **4** humiliate with a crushing retort. ♦ *n* **5** sweet fruit drink diluted with water. **6** crowd of people in a confined space. **7** game played in an enclosed court with a rubber ball and long-handled rackets. **squashy** *adj*

squash[2] *n* marrow-like vegetable.

squat *v* **squatting, squatted 1** crouch with the knees bent and the weight on the feet. **2** occupy unused premises to which one has no legal right. ♦ *n* **3** place where squatters live. ♦ *adj* **4** short and broad.

squatter *n* illegal occupier of unused premises.

squaw *n Offens* Native American woman.

squawk *n* **1** loud harsh cry. **2** *v* **3** utter a squawk.

squeak *n* **1** short shrill cry or sound. ♦ *v* **2** make or utter a squeak. **squeaky** *adj*

squeal *n* **1** long shrill cry or sound. ♦ *v* **2** make or utter a squeal. **3** *Slang* inform on someone to the police.

squeamish *adj* easily sickened or shocked.

squeegee *n* tool with a rubber blade for clearing water from a surface.

squeeze *v* **1** grip or press firmly. **2** crush or press to extract liquid. **3** push into a confined space. **4** hug. **5** obtain (something) by force or great effort. ♦ *n* **6** squeezing. **7** amount extracted by squeezing. **8** hug. **9** crush of people in a confined space. **10** restriction on borrowing.

squelch v **1** make a wet sucking sound, as by walking through mud. ♦ n **2** squelching sound.

squib n small firework that hisses before exploding.

squid n sea creature with a long soft body and ten tentacles.

squiggle n wavy line. **squiggly** adj

squint v **1** have eyes which face in different directions. **2** glance sideways. ♦ n **3** squinting condition of the eye. **4** Informal glance. ♦ adj **5** crooked.

squire n **1** country gentleman, usu. the main landowner in a community. **2** Hist knight's apprentice.

squirm v **1** wriggle, writhe. **2** feel embarrassed. ♦ n **3** wriggling movement.

squirrel n small bushy-tailed tree-living animal.

squirt v **1** force (a liquid) or (of a liquid) be forced out of a narrow opening. **2** squirt liquid at. ♦ n **3** jet of liquid. **4** Informal small or insignificant person.

squish v, n (make) a soft squelching sound. **squishy** adj

Sr 1 Senior. **2** Señor.

SS 1 Schutzstaffel: Nazi paramilitary security force. **2** steamship.

St 1 Saint. **2** Street.

st. stone (weight).

stab v **stabbing, stabbed 1** pierce with something pointed. **2** jab (at). ♦ n **3** stabbing. **4** sudden unpleasant sensation. **5** Informal attempt.

stabilize v make or become stable. **stabilization** n **stabilizer** n device for stabilizing a child's bicycle, an aircraft, or a ship.

stable¹ n **1** building in which horses are kept. **2** establishment that breeds and trains racehorses. **3** establishment that manages or trains several entertainers or athletes. ♦ v **4** put or keep (a horse) in a stable.

stable² adj **1** firmly fixed or established. **2** firm in character. **3** Science not subject to decay or decomposition. **stability** n

staccato [stak-**ah**-toe] adj, adv **1** Music with the notes sharply separated. ♦ adj **2** consisting of short abrupt sounds.

stack n **1** ordered pile. **2** large amount. **3** chimney. ♦ v **4** pile in a stack. **5** control (aircraft waiting to land) so that they fly at different altitudes.

stadium n, pl **-diums, -dia** sports arena with tiered seats for spectators.

staff¹ n **1** people employed in an organization. **2** stick used as a weapon, support, etc. ♦ v **3** supply with personnel.

staff² n, pl **staves** set of five horizontal lines on which music is written.

stag n adult male deer. **stag beetle** beetle with large branched jaws. **stag night, party** party for men only.

stage n **1** step or period of development. **2** platform in a theatre where actors perform. **3** portion of a journey. ♦ v **4** put (a play) on stage. **5** organize and carry out (an event). **the stage** theatre as a profession. **stagey** adj overtheatrical. **stagecoach** n large horse-drawn vehicle formerly used to carry passengers and mail. **stage fright** nervousness felt by a person about to face an audience. **stage whisper** loud whisper intended to be heard by an audience.

stagger v **1** walk unsteadily. **2** astound. **3** set apart to avoid congestion. ♦ n **4** staggering.

stagnant adj **1** (of water or air) stale from not moving. **2** not growing or developing. **stagnate** v be stagnant. **stagnation** n

staid adj sedate, serious, and rather dull.

stain v **1** discolour, mark. **2** colour with a penetrating pigment. ♦ n **3** discoloration or mark. **4** moral blemish or slur. **5** penetrating liquid used to colour things. **stainless** adj **stainless steel** steel alloy that does not rust.

stairs pl n flight of steps between floors, usu. indoors. **staircase, stairway** n flight of stairs with a handrail or banisters.

stake[1] n **1** pointed stick or post driven into the ground as a support or marker. ♦ v **2** support or mark out with stakes. **stake a claim to** claim a right to. **stake out** v Slang (of police) keep (a place) under surveillance.

stake[2] n **1** money wagered. **2** interest, usu. financial, held in something. **3** v **4** wager, risk. **5** support financially. **at stake** being risked. **stakeholder** n person who has a concern or interest in something, esp. a business.

stalactite n lime deposit hanging from the roof of a cave.

stalagmite n lime deposit sticking up from the floor of a cave.

stale adj **1** not fresh. **2** lacking energy or ideas through overwork or monotony. **3** uninteresting from overuse. **staleness** n

stalemate n **1** Chess position in which any of a player's moves would put his king in check, resulting in a draw. **2** deadlock, impasse.

stalk[1] n plant's stem.

stalk[2] v **1** follow or approach stealthily. **2** pursue persistently and, sometimes, attack (a person with whom one is obsessed). **3** walk in a stiff or haughty manner. **stalker** n **1** person who follows or stealthily approaches a person or an animal. **2** person who persistently pursues and, sometimes, attacks someone with whom he or she is obsessed. **stalking-horse** n pretext.

stall[1] n **1** small stand for the display and sale of goods. **2** compartment in a stable. **3** small room or compartment. ♦ pl **4** ground-floor seats in a theatre or cinema. **5** row of seats in a church for the choir or clergy. ♦ v **6** stop (a motor vehicle or engine) or (of a motor vehicle or engine) stop accidentally.

stall[2] v employ delaying tactics.

stallion n uncastrated male horse.

stalwart [**stawl**-wart] adj **1** strong and sturdy. **2** dependable. ♦ n **3** stalwart person.

stamen n pollen-producing part of a flower.

stamina n enduring energy and strength.

stammer v **1** speak or say with involuntary pauses or repetition of syllables. ♦ n **2** tendency to stammer.

stamp n **1** (also **postage stamp**) piece of gummed paper stuck to an envelope or parcel to show that the postage has been paid. **2** act of stamping. **3** instrument for stamping a pattern or mark. **4** pattern or mark stamped. **5** characteristic feature. ♦ v **6** bring (one's foot) down forcefully. **7** walk with heavy footsteps. **8** characterize. **9** impress (a pattern or mark) on. **10** stick a postage stamp on. **stamping ground** favourite meeting place. **stamp out** v suppress by force.

stampede n **1** sudden rush of frightened animals or of a crowd. ♦ v **2** (cause to) take part in a stampede.

stance n **1** attitude. **2** manner of standing.

stanch [**stahnch**] v same as STAUNCH[2].

stanchion n upright bar used as a support.

stand v **standing, stood 1** be in, rise to, or place in an upright position. **2** be situated. **3** be in a specified state or position. **4** remain unchanged or valid. **5** tolerate. **6** offer oneself as a candidate. **7** *Informal* treat to. ♦ *n* **8** stall for the sale of goods. **9** structure for spectators at a sports ground. **10** firmly held opinion. **11** *US & Aust* witness box. **12** rack or piece of furniture on which things may be placed. **standing** *adj* **1** permanent, lasting. **2** *n* **3** reputation or status. **4** duration. **stand for** *v* **1** represent or mean. **2** *Informal* tolerate. **stand in** *v* act as a substitute. **stand-in** *n* substitute. **standoffish** *adj* reserved or haughty. **stand up for** *v* support or defend.

standard *n* **1** level of quality. **2** example against which others are judged or measured. **3** moral principle. **4** distinctive flag. **5** upright pole. ♦ *adj* **6** usual, regular, or average. **7** of recognized authority. **8** accepted as correct. **standardize** *v* cause to conform to a standard. **standardization** *n* **standard lamp** lamp attached to an upright pole on a base.

standpipe *n* tap attached to a water main to provide a public water supply.

standpoint *n* point of view.

standstill *n* complete halt.

stank *v* a past tense of STINK.

stanza *n* verse of a poem.

staple¹ *n* **1** U-shaped piece of metal used to fasten papers or secure things. ♦ *v* **2** fasten with staples. **stapler** *n* small device for fastening papers together.

staple² *adj* **1** of prime importance, principal. ♦ *n* **2** main constituent of anything.

star *n* **1** hot gaseous mass in space, visible in the night sky as a point of light. **2** star-shaped mark used to indicate excellence. **3** asterisk. **4** celebrity in the entertainment or sports world. ♦ *pl* **5** astrological forecast, horoscope. ♦ *v* **starring,**

starred 6 feature or be featured as a star. **7** mark with a star or stars. ♦ *adj* **8** leading, famous. **stardom** *n* status of a star in the entertainment or sports world. **starry** *adj* full of or like stars. **starry-eyed** *adj* full of naive optimism. **starfish** *n* star-shaped sea creature.

starboard *n* **1** right-hand side of a ship, when facing forward. ♦ *adj* **2** of or on this side.

starch *n* **1** carbohydrate forming the main food element in bread, potatoes, etc., and used mixed with water for stiffening fabric. ♦ *v* **2** stiffen (fabric) with starch. **starchy** *adj* **1** containing starch. **2** stiff and formal.

stare *v* **1** look or gaze fixedly (at). ♦ *n* **2** fixed gaze.

stark *adj* **1** harsh, unpleasant, and plain. **2** desolate, bare. **3** absolute. ♦ *adv* **4** completely.

starling *n* songbird with glossy black speckled feathers.

start *v* **1** take the first step, begin. **2** set or be set in motion. **3** make a sudden involuntary movement from fright. **4** establish or set up. ♦ *n* **5** first part of something. **6** place or time of starting. **7** advantage or lead in a competitive activity. **8** sudden movement made from fright. **starter** *n* **1** first course of a meal. **2** device for starting a car's engine. **3** person who signals the start of a race. **start-up** *n* **1** recently launched project or business enterprise. ♦ *adj* **2** recently launched, e.g. *start-up grants*.

startle *v* slightly surprise or frighten.

starve *v* **1** die or suffer or cause to die or suffer from hunger. **2** deprive of something needed. **starvation** *n*

stash *Informal* ♦ *v* **1** store in a secret place. ♦ *n* **2** secret store.

state *n* **1** condition of a person or thing. **2** sovereign political power or its territory. **3** (S-) the government. **4**

Informal excited or agitated condition. **5** pomp. ♦ *adj* **6** of or concerning the State. **7** involving ceremony. ♦ *v* **8** express in words. **stately** *adj* dignified or grand. **statehouse** *n NZ* publicly-owned house rented to a low-income tenant. **statement** *n* **1** something stated. **2** printed financial account. **stateroom** *n* **1** private cabin on a ship. **2** large room in a palace, used for ceremonial occasions. **statesman, stateswoman** *n* experienced and respected political leader. **statesmanship** *n*

static *adj* **1** stationary or inactive. **2** (of a force) acting but producing no movement. ♦ *n* **3** crackling sound or speckled picture caused by interference in radio or television reception. **4** (also **static electricity**) electric sparks produced by friction.

station *n* **1** place where trains stop for passengers. **2** headquarters or local offices of the police or a fire brigade. **3** building with special equipment for a particular purpose, e.g. *power station*. **4** television or radio channel. **5** position in society. **6** large Australian sheep or cattle property. ♦ *v* **7** assign (someone) to a particular place. **station wagon** *US & Aust* car with a rear door and luggage space behind the rear seats.

stationary *adj* not moving.

☑ **SPELLING TIP**

The words **stationary** and **stationery** are completely different in meaning and should not be confused.

---

stationery *n* writing materials such as paper and pens. **stationer** *n* dealer in stationery.

statistic *n* numerical fact collected and classified systematically. **statistics** *n*

science of classifying and interpreting numerical information. **statistical** *adj* **statistically** *adv* **statistician** *n* person who compiles and studies statistics.

statue *n* large sculpture of a human or animal figure. **statuary** *n* statues collectively. **statuesque** *adj* (of a woman) tall and well-proportioned. **statuette** *n* small statue.

stature *n* **1** person's height. **2** reputation of a person or their achievements.

status *n* **1** social position. **2** prestige. **3** person's legal standing. **status quo** existing state of affairs.

statute *n* written law. **statutory** *adj* required or authorized by law.

staunch[1] *adj* loyal, firm.

staunch[2], **stanch** *v* stop (a flow of blood).

stave *n* **1** one of the strips of wood forming a barrel. **2** *Music* same as STAFF[2]. **stave in** *v* **staving, stove** burst a hole in. **stave off** *v* **staving, staved** ward off.

stay[1] *v* **1** remain in a place or condition. **2** reside temporarily. **3** endure. **4** *Scot & S Afr* live permanently, e.g. *where do you stay?* ♦ *n* **5** period of staying in a place. **6** postponement. **staying power** stamina.

stay[2] *n* **1** prop or buttress. ♦ *pl* **2** corset.

stay[3] *n* rope or wire supporting a ship's mast.

STD 1 sexually transmitted disease. **2** *Brit, Aust & S Afr* subscriber trunk dialling. **3** *NZ* subscriber toll dialling.

stead *n* **in someone's stead** in someone's place. **stand someone in good stead** be useful to someone.

steadfast *adj* firm, determined. **steadfastly** *adv*

steady *adj* **steadier, steadiest** **1** not shaky or wavering. **2** regular or continuous. **3** sensible and dependable. ♦ *v* **steadying, steadied**

4 make steady. ♦ *adv* **5** in a steady manner. **steadily** *adv* **steadiness** *n*

steak *n* **1** thick slice of meat, esp. beef. **2** slice of fish.

steal *v* **stealing, stole, stolen 1** take unlawfully or without permission. **2** move stealthily.

stealth *n* **1** secret or underhand behaviour. ♦ *adj* **2** (of technology) able to render an aircraft almost invisible to radar. **3** disguised or hidden , e.g. *stealth taxes.* **stealthy** *adj* **stealthily** *adv*

steam *n* **1** vapour into which water changes when boiled. **2** power, energy, or speed. ♦ *v* **3** give off steam. **4** (of a vehicle) move by steam power. **5** cook or treat with steam. **steamer** *n* **1** steam-propelled ship. **2** container used to cook food in steam. **steam engine** engine worked by steam. **steamroller** *n* **1** steam-powered vehicle with heavy rollers, used to level road surfaces. ♦ *v* **2** use overpowering force to make (someone) do what one wants.

steed *n Lit* horse.

steel *n* **1** hard malleable alloy of iron and carbon. **2** steel rod used for sharpening knives. **3** hardness of character or attitude. ♦ *v* **4** prepare (oneself) for something unpleasant. **steely** *adj*

steep¹ *adj* **1** sloping sharply. **2** *Informal* (of a price) unreasonably high. **steeply** *adv* **steepness** *n*

steep² *v* soak or be soaked in liquid. **steeped in** filled with.

steeple *n* church tower with a spire. **steeplejack** *n* person who repairs steeples and chimneys.

steeplechase *n* **1** horse race with obstacles to jump. **2** track race with hurdles and a water jump.

steer¹ *v* **1** direct the course of (a vehicle or ship). **2** direct (one's course).

steerage *n* cheapest accommodation on a passenger ship. **steering wheel** wheel turned by the driver of a vehicle in order to steer it.

steer² *n* castrated male ox.

stein [**stine**] *n* earthenware beer mug.

stellar *adj* of stars.

stem¹ *n* **1** long thin central part of a plant. **2** long slender part, as of a wineglass. **3** part of a word to which inflections are added. ♦ *v* **stemming, stemmed 4 stem from** originate from.

stem² *v* **stemming, stemmed** stop (the flow of something).

stench *n* foul smell.

stencil *n* **1** thin sheet with cut-out pattern through which ink or paint passes to form the pattern on the surface below. **2** pattern made thus. ♦ *v* **-cilling, -cilled 3** make (a pattern) with a stencil.

stenographer *n* shorthand typist.

stent *n* surgical implant used to keep an artery open.

stentorian *adj* (of a voice) very loud.

step *v* **stepping, stepped 1** move and set down the foot, as when walking. **2** walk a short distance. ♦ *n* **3** stepping. **4** distance covered by a step. **5** sound made by stepping. **6** foot movement in a dance. **7** one of a sequence of actions taken in order to achieve a goal. **8** degree in a series or scale. **9** flat surface for placing the foot on when going up or down. ♦ *pl* **10** stepladder. **step in** *v* intervene. **stepladder** *n* folding portable ladder with supporting frame. **stepping stone 1** one of a series of stones for stepping on in crossing a stream. **2** means of progress towards a goal. **step up** *v* increase (something) by stages.

step- *prefix* denoting a relationship created by the remarriage of a parent, e.g. *stepmother.*

steppes *pl n* wide grassy treeless plains in Russia and Ukraine.

stereo *adj* **1** short for STEREOPHONIC. ◆ *n* **2** stereophonic record player. **3** stereophonic sound.

stereophonic *adj* using two separate loudspeakers to give the effect of naturally distributed sound.

stereotype *n* **1** standardized idea of a type of person or thing. **2** *v* **3** form a stereotype of.

sterile *adj* **1** free from germs. **2** unable to produce offspring or seeds. **3** lacking inspiration or vitality. **sterility** *n* **sterilize** *v* make sterile. **sterilization** *n*

sterling *n* **1** British money system. ◆ *adj* **2** genuine and reliable.

stern[1] *adj* severe, strict. **sternly** *adv* **sternness** *n*

stern[2] *n* rear part of a ship.

sternum *n, pl* **-na, -nums** same as BREASTBONE.

steroid *n* organic compound containing a carbon ring system, such as many hormones.

stethoscope *n* medical instrument for listening to sounds made inside the body.

Stetson *n* ® tall broad-brimmed hat, worn mainly by cowboys.

stevedore *n* person who loads and unloads ships.

stew *n* **1** food cooked slowly in a closed pot. **2** *Informal* troubled or worried state. ◆ *v* **3** cook slowly in a closed pot.

steward *n* **1** person who looks after passengers on a ship or aircraft. **2** official who helps at a public event such as a race. **3** person who administers another's property. **stewardess** *n fem*

stick[1] *n* **1** long thin piece of wood. **2** such a piece of wood shaped for a special purpose, e.g. *hockey stick*. **3**

something like a stick, e.g. *stick of celery*. **4** *Slang* verbal abuse, criticism.

stick[2] *v* **sticking, stuck** **1** push (a pointed object) into (something). **2** fasten or be fastened by or as if by pins or glue. **3** (foll. by *out*) extend beyond something else, protrude. **4** *Informal* put. **5** remain for a long time. **sticker** *n* adhesive label or sign. **sticky** *adj* **1** covered with an adhesive substance. **2** *Informal* difficult, unpleasant. **3** (of weather) warm and humid. **stick-in-the-mud** *n* person who does not like anything new. **stick-up** *n Slang* robbery at gunpoint. **stick up for** *v Informal* support or defend.

stickleback *n* small fish with sharp spines on its back.

stickler *n* person who insists on something, e.g. *stickler for detail*.

stiff *adj* **1** not easily bent or moved. **2** severe, e.g. *stiff punishment*. **3** unrelaxed or awkward. **4** firm in consistency. **5** strong, e.g. *a stiff drink*. ◆ *n* **6** *Slang* corpse. **stiffly** *adv* **stiffness** *n* **stiffen** *v* make or become stiff. **stiff-necked** *adj* haughtily stubborn.

stifle *v* **1** suppress. **2** suffocate.

stigma *n, pl* **-mas, -mata** **1** mark of social disgrace. **2** part of a plant that receives pollen. **stigmata** *pl n* marks resembling the wounds of the crucified Christ. **stigmatize** *v* mark as being shameful.

stile *n* set of steps allowing people to climb a fence.

stiletto *n, pl* **-tos** **1** high narrow heel on a woman's shoe. **2** small slender dagger.

still[1] *adv* **1** now or in the future as before. **2** up to this or that time. **3** even or yet, e.g. *still more insults*. **4** quietly or without movement. ◆ *adj* **5** motionless. **6** silent and calm,

undisturbed. **7** (of a drink) not fizzy.
♦ *n* **8** photograph from a film scene.
♦ *v* **9** make still. **stillness** *n* **stillborn**
adj born dead. **still life** painting of
inanimate objects.

still² *n* apparatus for distilling alcoholic
drinks.

stilted *adj* stiff and formal in manner.

stilts *pl n* **1** pair of poles with footrests
for walking raised from the ground. **2**
long posts supporting a building
above ground level.

stimulus *n, pl* **-li** something that
rouses a person or thing to activity.
stimulant *n* something, such as a
drug, that acts as a stimulus.
stimulate *v* act as a stimulus (on).
stimulation *n*

sting *v* **stinging, stung 1** (of certain
animals or plants) wound by injecting
with poison. **2** feel or cause to feel
sharp physical or mental pain. **3** *Slang*
cheat (someone) by overcharging. ♦ *n*
4 wound or pain caused by or as if by
stinging. **5** mental pain. **6** sharp
pointed organ of certain animals or
plants by which poison can be injected.

stingy *adj* **-gier, -giest** mean or
miserly. **stinginess** *n*

stink *n* **1** strong unpleasant smell. **2**
Slang unpleasant fuss. ♦ *v* **stinking,
stank** or **stunk, stunk 3** give off a
strong unpleasant smell. **4** *Slang* be
very unpleasant.

stint *v* **1** (foll. by *on*) be miserly with
(something). ♦ *n* **2** allotted amount of
work.

stipend [**sty**-pend] *n* regular allowance
or salary, esp. that paid to a
clergyman. **stipendiary** *adj* receiving
a stipend.

stipple *v* paint, draw, or engrave using
dots.

stipulate *v* specify as a condition of an
agreement. **stipulation** *n*

stir *v* **stirring, stirred 1** mix up (a

liquid) by moving a spoon etc. around
in it. **2** move. **3** excite or stimulate (a
person) emotionally. ♦ *n* **4** a stirring. **5**
strong reaction, usu. of excitement.
stir-fry *v* **-fries, -frying, -fried 1** cook
(food) quickly by stirring it in a pan
over a high heat. ♦ *n, pl* **-fries 2** dish
cooked in this way.

stirrup *n* metal loop attached to a
saddle for supporting a rider's foot.

stitch *n* **1** link made by drawing thread
through material with a needle. **2** loop
of yarn formed round a needle or hook
in knitting or crochet. **3** sharp pain in
the side. ♦ *v* **4** sew. **in stitches**
Informal laughing uncontrollably. **not
a stitch** *Informal* no clothes at all.

stoat *n* small mammal of the weasel
family, with brown fur that turns white
in winter.

stock *n* **1** total amount of goods
available for sale in a shop. **2** supply
stored for future use. **3** financial shares
in, or capital of, a company. **4** liquid
produced by boiling meat, fish, bones,
or vegetables. **5** *pl* **6** *Hist* instrument of
punishment consisting of a wooden
frame with holes into which the hands
and feet of the victim were locked.
♦ *adj* **7** kept in stock, standard. **8**
hackneyed. ♦ *v* **9** keep for sale or
future use. **10** supply (a farm) with
livestock or (a lake etc.) with fish.
stockist *n* dealer who stocks a
particular product. **stocky** *adj* (of a
person) broad and sturdy.
stockbroker *n* person who buys and
sells stocks and shares for customers.
stock car car modified for a form of
racing in which the cars often collide.
stock exchange, market institution
for the buying and selling of shares.
stockpile *v* **1** store a large quantity of
(something) for future use. ♦ *n* **2**
accumulated store. **stock-still** *adj*
motionless. **stocktaking** *n* counting

and valuing of the goods in a shop.

stockade n enclosure or barrier made of stakes.

stocking n close-fitting covering for the foot and leg.

stodgy adj **stodgier, stodgiest 1** (of food) heavy and starchy. **2** (of a person) serious and boring. **stodge** n Brit, Aust & NZ heavy starchy food.

stoep [**stoop**] n S Afr verandah.

stoic [**stow**-ik] n **1** person who suffers hardship without showing his or her feelings. ♦ adj **2** (also **stoical**) suffering hardship without showing one's feelings. **stoically** adv **stoicism** [**stow**-iss-izz-um] n

stoke v feed and tend (a fire or furnace). **stoker** n

stole[1] v past tense of STEAL.

stole[2] n long scarf or shawl.

stolen v past participle of STEAL.

stolid adj showing little emotion or interest. **stolidly** adv

stomach n **1** organ in the body which digests food. **2** front of the body around the waist. **3** desire or inclination. ♦ v **4** put up with.

stomp v Informal tread heavily.

stone n **1** material of which rocks are made. **2** piece of this. **3** gem. **4** hard central part of a fruit. **5** unit of weight equal to 14 pounds or 6.350 kilograms. **6** hard deposit formed in the kidney or bladder. ♦ v **7** throw stones at. **8** remove stones from (a fruit). **stoned** adj Slang under the influence of alcohol or drugs. **stony** adj **1** of or like stone. **2** unfeeling or hard. **stony-broke** adj Slang completely penniless. **stonily** adv **Stone Age** prehistoric period when tools were made of stone. **stone-cold** adj completely cold. **stone-deaf** adj completely deaf. **stonewall** v obstruct or hinder discussion. **stoneware** n hard kind of pottery fired at a very

high temperature.

stood v past of STAND.

stooge n **1** actor who feeds lines to a comedian or acts as the butt of his jokes. **2** Slang person taken advantage of by a superior.

stool n **1** chair without arms or back. **2** piece of excrement.

stool pigeon n informer for the police.

stoop v **1** bend (the body) forward and downward. **2** carry oneself habitually in this way. **3** degrade oneself. ♦ n **4** stooping posture.

stop v **stopping, stopped 1** cease or cause to cease from doing (something). **2** bring to or come to a halt. **3** prevent or restrain. **4** withhold. **5** block or plug. **6** stay or rest. **7** n **8** stopping or being stopped. **9** place where something stops. **10** full stop. **11** knob on an organ that is pulled out to allow a set of pipes to sound. **stoppage** n **stoppage time** same as INJURY TIME. **stopper** n plug for closing a bottle etc. **stopcock** n valve to control or stop the flow of fluid in a pipe. **stopgap** n temporary substitute. **stopover** n short break in a journey. **stop press** news item put into a newspaper after printing has been started. **stopwatch** n watch which can be stopped instantly for exact timing of a sporting event.

store v **1** collect and keep (things) for future use. **2** put (furniture etc.) in a warehouse for safekeeping. **3** stock (goods). **4** Computers enter or retain (data). ♦ n **5** shop. **6** supply kept for future use. **7** storage place, such as a warehouse. ♦ pl **8** stock of provisions. **in store** about to happen. **set great store by** value greatly. **storage** n **1** storing. **2** space for storing. **storage heater** electric device that can accumulate and radiate heat generated by off-peak electricity.

storey *n* floor or level of a building.

stork *n* large wading bird.

storm *n* **1** violent weather with wind, rain, or snow. **2** strongly expressed reaction. **3** *v* **4** attack or capture (a place) suddenly. **5** shout angrily. **6** rush violently or angrily. **stormy** *adj* **1** characterized by storms. **2** involving violent emotions.

story *n, pl* **-ries 1** description of a series of events told or written for entertainment. **2** plot of a book or film. **3** news report. **4** *Informal* lie.

stoup [stoop] *n* small basin for holy water.

stout *adj* **1** fat. **2** thick and strong. **3** brave and resolute. ♦ *n* **4** strong dark beer. **stoutly** *adv*

stove¹ *n* apparatus for cooking or heating.

stove² *v* a past of STAVE.

stow *v* pack or store. **stowaway** *n* person who hides on a ship or aircraft in order to travel free. **stow away** *v* hide as a stowaway.

straddle *v* have one leg or part on each side of (something).

strafe *v* attack (an enemy) with machine guns from the air.

straggle *v* go or spread in a rambling or irregular way. **straggler** *n* **straggly** *adj*

straight *adj* **1** not curved or crooked. **2** level or upright. **3** honest or frank. **4** (of spirits) undiluted. **5** *Slang* heterosexual. **6** *adv* **7** in a straight line. **8** immediately. **9** in a level or upright position. **10** *n* **11** straight part, esp. of a racetrack. **12** *Slang* heterosexual person. **go straight** *Informal* reform after being a criminal. **straighten** *v* **straightaway** *adv* immediately. **straight face** serious facial expression concealing a desire to laugh. **straightforward** *adj* **1** honest, frank. **2** (of a task) easy.

strain¹ *v* **1** cause (something) to be used or tested beyond its limits. **2** make an intense effort. **3** injure by overexertion. **4** sieve. **5** *n* **6** tension or tiredness. **7** force exerted by straining. **8** injury from overexertion. **9** great demand on strength or resources. **10** melody or theme. **strained** *adj* **1** not natural, forced. **2** not relaxed, tense. **strainer** *n* sieve.

strain² *n* **1** breed or race. **2** trace or streak.

strait *n* **1** narrow channel connecting two areas of sea. ♦ *pl* **2** position of acute difficulty. **straitjacket** *n* strong jacket with long sleeves used to bind the arms of a violent person. **strait-laced, straight-laced** *adj* prudish or puritanical.

straitened *adj* **in straitened circumstances** not having much money.

strand¹ *v* **1** run aground. **2** leave in difficulties. ♦ *n* **3** *Poetic* shore.

strand² *n* single thread of string, wire, etc.

strange *adj* **1** odd or unusual. **2** not familiar. **3** inexperienced (in) or unaccustomed (to). **strangely** *adv* **strangeness** *n*

stranger *n* person who is not known or is new to a place or experience.

strangle *v* **1** kill by squeezing the throat. **2** prevent the development of. **strangler** *n* **strangulation** *n* strangling. **stranglehold** *n* **1** strangling grip in wrestling. **2** powerful control.

strap *n* **1** strip of flexible material for lifting, fastening, or holding in place. ♦ *v* **strapping, strapped 2** fasten with a strap or straps. **strapping** *adj* tall and sturdy.

strata *n* plural of STRATUM.

stratagem *n* clever plan, trick.

strategy *n, pl* **-gies 1** overall plan. **2** art

of planning in war. **strategic** [strat-**ee**-jik] *adj* 1 advantageous. 2 (of weapons) aimed at an enemy's homeland. **strategically** *adv* **strategist** *n*

strathspey *n* Scottish dance with gliding steps.

stratosphere *n* atmospheric layer between about 15 and 50 kilometres above the earth.

stratum [**strah**-tum] *n, pl* **strata** 1 layer, esp. of rock. 2 social class. **stratified** *adj* divided into strata. **stratification** *n*

straw *n* 1 dried stalks of grain. 2 single stalk of straw. 3 long thin tube used to suck up liquid into the mouth. **straw poll** unofficial poll taken to determine general opinion.

strawberry *n* sweet fleshy red fruit with small seeds on the outside. **strawberry mark** red birthmark.

stray *v* 1 wander. 2 digress. 3 deviate from certain moral standards. ♦ *adj* 4 having strayed. 5 scattered, random. ♦ *n* 6 stray animal.

streak *n* 1 long band of contrasting colour or substance. 2 quality or characteristic. 3 short stretch (of good or bad luck). ♦ *v* 4 mark with streaks. 5 move rapidly. 6 *Informal* run naked in public. **streaker** *n* **streaky** *adj*

stream *n* 1 small river. 2 steady flow, as of liquid, speech, or people. 3 schoolchildren grouped together because of similar ability. ♦ *v* 4 flow steadily. 5 move in unbroken succession. 6 float in the air. 7 group (pupils) in streams. **streamer** *n* 1 strip of coloured paper that unrolls when tossed. 2 long narrow flag.

streamline *v* 1 make more efficient by simplifying. 2 give (a car, plane, etc.) a smooth even shape to offer least resistance to the flow of air or water.

street *n* public road, usu. lined with buildings. **streetcar** *n US* tram. **streetwise** *adj* knowing how to survive in big cities.

strength *n* 1 quality of being strong. 2 quality or ability considered an advantage. 3 degree of intensity. 4 total number of people in a group. **on the strength of** on the basis of. **strengthen** *v*

strenuous *adj* requiring great energy or effort. **strenuously** *adv*

streptococcus [strep-toe-**kok**-uss] *n, pl* -**cocci** bacterium occurring in chains, many species of which cause disease.

stress *n* 1 tension or strain. 2 emphasis. 3 stronger sound in saying a word or syllable. 4 *Physics* force producing strain. ♦ *v* 5 emphasize. 6 put stress on (a word or syllable). **stressed-out** *adj Informal* suffering from tension.

stretch *v* 1 extend or be extended. 2 be able to be stretched. 3 extend the limbs or body. 4 strain (resources or abilities) to the utmost. ♦ *n* 5 stretching. 6 continuous expanse. 7 period. 8 *Informal* term of imprisonment. **stretchy** *adj*

stretcher *n* frame covered with canvas, on which an injured person is carried.

strew *v* strewing, strewed, strewed *or* strewn scatter (things) over a surface.

striated *adj* having a pattern of scratches or grooves.

stricken *adj* seriously affected by disease, grief, pain, etc.

strict *adj* 1 stern or severe. 2 adhering closely to specified rules. 3 complete, absolute. **strictly** *adv* **strictness** *n*

stricture *n* severe criticism.

stride *v* striding, strode, stridden 1 walk with long steps. ♦ *n* 2 long step. 3 regular pace. ♦ *pl* 4 progress.

strident *adj* loud and harsh. **stridently** *adv* **stridency** *n*

strife *n* conflict, quarrelling.

strike v **striking, struck 1** cease work as a protest. **2** hit. **3** attack suddenly. **4** ignite (a match) by friction. **5** (of a clock) indicate (a time) by sounding a bell. **6** enter the mind of. **7** afflict. **8** discover (gold, oil, etc.). **9** agree (a bargain). **10** n **11** stoppage of work as a protest. **striking** adj **1** impressive. **2** noteworthy. **strike camp** dismantle and pack up tents. **strike home** have the desired effect. **strike off, out** v cross out. **strike up** v **1** begin (a conversation or friendship). **2** begin to play music.

striker n **1** striking worker. **2** attacking player at soccer.

string n **1** thin cord used for tying. **2** set of objects threaded on a string. **3** series of things or events. **4** stretched wire or cord on a musical instrument that produces sound when vibrated. ♦ pl **5** restrictions or conditions. **6** section of an orchestra consisting of stringed instruments. ♦ v **stringing, strung 7** provide with a string or strings. **8** thread on a string. **stringed** adj (of a musical instrument) having strings that are plucked or played with a bow. **stringy** adj **1** like string. **2** (of meat) fibrous. **pull strings** use one's influence. **string along** v deceive over a period of time. **string up** v Informal kill by hanging. **stringy-bark** n Australian eucalyptus with a fibrous bark.

stringent [**strin**-jent] adj strictly controlled or enforced. **stringently** adv **stringency** n

strip[1] v **stripping, stripped 1** take (the covering or clothes) off. **2** take a title or possession away from (someone). **3** dismantle (an engine). **stripper** n person who performs a striptease. **striptease** n entertainment in which a performer undresses to music.

strip[2] n **1** long narrow piece. **2** Brit, Aust & NZ clothes a sports team plays in. **strip cartoon** sequence of drawings telling a story.

stripe n **1** long narrow band of contrasting colour or substance. **2** chevron or band worn on a uniform to indicate rank. **striped, stripy, stripey** adj

stripling n youth.

strive v **striving, strove, striven** make a great effort.

strobe n short for STROBOSCOPE.

stroboscope n instrument producing a very bright flashing light.

strode v past tense of STRIDE.

stroke v **1** touch or caress lightly with the hand. ♦ n **2** light touch or caress with the hand. **3** rupture of a blood vessel in the brain. **4** blow. **5** action or occurrence of the kind specified, e.g. a stroke of luck. **6** chime of a clock. **7** mark made by a pen or paintbrush. **8** style or method of swimming.

stroll v **1** walk in a leisurely manner. ♦ n **2** leisurely walk.

strong adj **1** having physical power. **2** not easily broken. **3** great in degree or intensity. **4** having moral force. **5** having a specified number, e.g. twenty strong. **strongly** adv **stronghold** n **1** area of predominance of a particular belief. **2** fortress. **strongroom** n room designed for the safekeeping of valuables.

strontium n Chem silvery-white metallic element.

strop n leather strap for sharpening razors.

stroppy adj **-pier, -piest** Slang angry or awkward.

strove v past tense of STRIVE.

struck v past of STRIKE.

structure n **1** complex construction. **2** manner or basis of construction or organization. ♦ v **3** give a structure to.

structural *adj* **structuralism** *n* approach to literature, social sciences, etc., which sees changes in the subject as caused and organized by a hidden set of universal rules. **structuralist** *n, adj*

strudel *n* thin sheet of filled dough rolled up and baked, usu. with an apple filling.

struggle *v* **1** work, strive, or make one's way with difficulty. **2** move about violently in an attempt to get free. **3** fight (with someone). ♦ *n* **4** striving. **5** fight.

strum *v* **strumming, strummed** play (a guitar or banjo) by sweeping the thumb or a plectrum across the strings.

strumpet *n Old-fashioned* prostitute.

strung *v* past of STRING.

strut *v* **strutting, strutted** **1** walk pompously, swagger. ♦ *n* **2** bar supporting a structure.

strychnine [**strik**-neen] *n* very poisonous drug used in small quantities as a stimulant.

stub *n* **1** short piece left after use. **2** counterfoil of a cheque or ticket. ♦ *v* **stubbing, stubbed** **3** strike (the toe) painfully against an object. **4** put out (a cigarette) by pressing the end against a surface. **stubby** *adj* short and broad.

stubble *n* **1** short stalks of grain left in a field after reaping. **2** short growth of hair on the chin of a man who has not shaved recently. **stubbly** *adj*

stubborn *adj* **1** refusing to agree or give in. **2** difficult to deal with. **stubbornly** *adv* **stubbornness** *n*

stucco *n* plaster used for coating or decorating walls.

stuck *v* past of STICK². **stuck-up** *adj Informal* conceited or snobbish.

stud¹ *n* **1** small piece of metal attached to a surface for decoration. **2** disc-like removable fastener for clothes. **3** one of several small round objects fixed to the sole of a football boot to give better grip. ♦ *v* **studding, studded** **4** set with studs.

stud² *n* **1** male animal, esp. a stallion, kept for breeding. **2** (also **stud farm**) place where horses are bred. **3** *Slang* virile or sexually active man.

student *n* person who studies a subject, esp. at university.

studio *n, pl* **-dios** **1** workroom of an artist or photographer. **2** room or building in which television or radio programmes, records, or films are made. **studio flat** *Brit* one-room flat with a small kitchen and bathroom.

study *v* **studying, studied** **1** be engaged in learning (a subject). **2** investigate by observation and research. **3** scrutinize. ♦ *n, pl* **studies** **4** act or process of studying. **5** room for studying in. **6** book or paper produced as a result of study. **7** sketch done as practice or preparation. **8** musical composition designed to improve playing technique. **studied** *adj* carefully practised or planned. **studious** *adj* **1** fond of study. **2** careful and deliberate. **studiously** *adv*

stuff *n* **1** substance or material. **2** collection of unnamed things. **3** *v* **4** pack, cram, or fill completely. **5** fill (food) with a seasoned mixture. **6** fill (an animal's skin) with material to restore the shape of the live animal. **stuffing** *n* **1** seasoned mixture with which food is stuffed. **2** padding.

stuffy *adj* **stuffier, stuffiest** **1** lacking fresh air. **2** *Informal* dull or conventional.

stultifying *adj* very boring and repetitive.

stumble *v* **1** trip and nearly fall. **2** walk in an unsure way. **3** make frequent mistakes in speech. ♦ *n* **4** stumbling. **stumble across** *v* discover accidentally. **stumbling block** obstacle or difficulty.

stump n 1 base of a tree left when the main trunk has been cut away. 2 part of a thing left after a larger part has been removed. 3 *Cricket* one of the three upright sticks forming the wicket. ♦ v 4 baffle. 5 *Cricket* dismiss (a batsman) by breaking his wicket with the ball. 6 walk with heavy steps. **stumpy** adj short and thick. **stump up** v *Informal* give (the money required).

stun v **stunning, stunned** 1 shock or overwhelm. 2 knock senseless. **stunning** adj very attractive or impressive.

stung v past of STING.

stunk v a past of STINK.

stunt[1] v prevent or impede the growth of. **stunted** adj

stunt[2] n 1 acrobatic or dangerous action. 2 anything spectacular done to gain publicity.

stupefy v -**fying, -fied** 1 make insensitive or lethargic. 2 astound. **stupefaction** n

stupendous adj very large or impressive. **stupendously** adv

stupid adj 1 lacking intelligence. 2 silly. 3 in a stupor. **stupidity** n **stupidly** adv

stupor n dazed or unconscious state.

sturdy adj -**dier, -diest** 1 healthy and robust. 2 strongly built. **sturdily** adv

sturgeon n fish from which caviar is obtained.

stutter v 1 speak with repetition of initial consonants. ♦ n 2 tendency to stutter.

sty n, pl **sties** pen for pigs.

stye, sty n, pl **styes, sties** inflammation at the base of an eyelash.

style n 1 shape or design. 2 manner of writing, speaking, or doing something.

3 elegance, refinement. 4 prevailing fashion. 5 v 6 shape or design. 7 name or call. **stylish** adj smart, elegant, and fashionable. **stylishly** adv **stylist** n 1 hairdresser. 2 person who writes or performs with great attention to style. **stylistic** adj of literary or artistic style. **stylize** v cause to conform to an established stylistic form.

stylus n needle-like device on a record player that rests in the groove of the record and picks up the sound signals.

stymie v -**mieing, -mied** hinder or thwart.

styptic n, adj (drug) used to stop bleeding.

suave [swahv] adj smooth and sophisticated in manner. **suavely** adv

sub n 1 subeditor. 2 submarine. 3 subscription. 4 substitute. 5 *Brit informal* advance payment of wages or salary. ♦ v **subbing, subbed** 6 act as a substitute. 7 grant advance payment to.

sub- prefix used with many main words to mean: 1 under or beneath, e.g. *submarine*. 2 subordinate, e.g. *sublieutenant*. 3 falling short of, e.g. *subnormal*. 4 forming a subdivision, e.g. *subheading*.

subaltern n British army officer below the rank of captain.

subatomic adj of or being one of the particles which make up an atom.

subcommittee n small committee formed from some members of a larger committee.

subconscious adj 1 happening or existing without one's awareness. ♦ n 2 *Psychoanalysis* that part of the mind of which one is not aware but which can influence one's behaviour. **subconsciously** adv

subcontinent n large land mass that is a distinct part of a continent.

subcontract n 1 secondary contract

by which the main contractor for a job puts work out to others. ♦ *v* **2** put out (work) on a subcontract. **subcontractor** *n*

subcutaneous [sub-cute-**ayn**-ee-uss] *adj* under the skin.

subdivide *v* divide (a part of something) into smaller parts. **subdivision** *n*

subdue *v* **-duing, -dued 1** overcome. **2** make less intense.

subeditor *n* person who checks and edits text for a newspaper or magazine.

subject *n* **1** person or thing being dealt with or studied. **2** *Grammar* word or phrase that represents the person or thing performing the action of the verb in a sentence. **3** person under the rule of a monarch or government. ♦ *adj* **4** being under the rule of a monarch or government. ♦ *v* (foll. by *to*) **5** cause to undergo. **subject to 1** liable to. **2** conditional upon. **subjection** *n* **subjective** *adj* based on personal feelings or prejudices. **subjectively** *adv*

sub judice [sub **joo**-diss-ee] *adj Latin* before a court of law and therefore prohibited from public discussion.

subjugate *v* bring (a group of people) under one's control. **subjugation** *n*

subjunctive *Grammar* ♦ *n* **1** mood of verbs used when the content of the clause is doubted, supposed, or wished. ♦ *adj* **2** in or of that mood.

sublet *v* **-letting, -let** rent out (property rented from someone else).

sublimate *v Psychol* direct the energy of (a strong desire, esp. a sexual one) into socially acceptable activities. **sublimation** *n*

sublime *adj* **1** of high moral, intellectual, or spiritual value. **2** unparalleled, supreme. ♦ *v* **3** *Chem* change from a solid to a vapour without first melting. **sublimely** *adv*

subliminal *adj* relating to mental processes of which the individual is not aware.

sub-machine-gun *n* portable machine gun with a short barrel.

submarine *n* **1** vessel which can operate below the surface of the sea. ♦ *adj* **2** below the surface of the sea.

submerge *v* put or go below the surface of water or other liquid. **submersion** *n*

submit *v* **-mitting, -mitted 1** surrender. **2** put forward for consideration. **3** be (voluntarily) subjected to a process or treatment. **submission** *n* **1** submitting. **2** something submitted for consideration. **3** state of being submissive. **submissive** *adj* meek and obedient.

subordinate *adj* **1** of lesser rank or importance. ♦ *n* **2** subordinate person or thing. ♦ *v* **3** make or treat as subordinate. **subordination** *n*

suborn *v Formal* bribe or incite (a person) to commit a wrongful act.

subpoena [sub-**pee**-na] *n* **1** writ requiring a person to appear before a lawcourt. ♦ *v* **2** summon (someone) with a subpoena.

subscribe *v* **1** pay (a subscription). **2** give support or approval (to). **subscriber** *n* **subscription** *n* **1** payment for issues of a publication over a period. **2** money contributed to a charity etc. **3** membership fees paid to a society.

subsection *n* division of a section.

subsequent *adj* occurring after, succeeding. **subsequently** *adv*

subservient *adj* submissive, servile. **subservience** *n*

subside *v* **1** become less intense. **2** sink to a lower level. **subsidence** *n* act or process of subsiding.

subsidiary *adj* **1** of lesser importance.

♦ *n, pl* **-aries 2** subsidiary person or thing.

subsidize *v* help financially. **subsidy** *n, pl* **-dies** financial aid.

subsist *v* manage to live. **subsistence** *n*

subsonic *adj* moving at a speed less than that of sound.

substance *n* **1** physical composition of something. **2** solid, powder, liquid, or paste. **3** essential meaning of something. **4** solid or meaningful quality. **5** wealth. **substantial** *adj* **1** of considerable size or value. **2** (of food or a meal) sufficient and nourishing. **3** solid or strong. **4** real. **substantially** *adv* **substantiate** *v* support (a story) with evidence. **substantiation** *n* **substantive** *n* **1** noun. ♦ *adj* **2** of or being the essential element of a thing.

substitute *v* **1** take the place of or put in place of another. ♦ *n* **2** person or thing taking the place of (another). **substitution** *n*

subsume *v* include (an idea, case, etc.) under a larger classification or group.

subterfuge *n* trick used to achieve an objective.

subterranean *adj* underground.

subtitle *n* **1** secondary title of a book. ♦ *pl* **2** printed translation at the bottom of the picture in a film with foreign dialogue. ♦ *v* **3** provide with a subtitle or subtitles.

subtle *adj* **1** not immediately obvious. **2** having or requiring ingenuity. **subtly** *adv* **subtlety** *n*

subtract *v* take (one number or quantity) from another. **subtraction** *n*

subtropical *adj* of the regions bordering on the tropics.

suburb *n* residential area on the outskirts of a city. **suburban** *adj* **1** of or inhabiting a suburb. **2** narrow or unadventurous in outlook. **suburbia** *n* suburbs and their inhabitants.

subvention *n* Formal subsidy.

subvert *v* overthrow the authority of. **subversion** *n* **subversive** *adj, n*

subway *n* **1** passage under a road or railway. **2** underground railway.

succeed *v* **1** accomplish an aim. **2** turn out satisfactorily. **3** come next in order after (something). **4** take over a position from (someone). **success** *n* **1** achievement of something attempted. **2** attainment of wealth, fame, or position. **3** successful person or thing. **successful** *adj* having success. **successfully** *adv* **succession** *n* **1** series of people or things following one another in order. **2** act or right by which one person succeeds another in a position. **successive** *adj* consecutive. **successively** *adv* **successor** *n* person who succeeds someone in a position.

☑ **SPELLING TIP**
The Bank of English evidence shows that people are able to remember the double s at the end of **success** more easily than the double c in the middle.

succinct *adj* brief and clear. **succinctly** *adv*

succour *v, n* help in distress.

succulent *adj* **1** juicy and delicious. **2** (of a plant) having thick fleshy leaves. ♦ *n* **3** succulent plant. **succulence** *n*

succumb *v* **1** (foll. by *to*) give way (to something overpowering). **2** die of (an illness).

such *adj* **1** of the kind specified. **2** so great, so much. ♦ *pron* **3** such things. **such-and-such** *adj* specific, but not known or named. **suchlike** *pron* such or similar things.

suck *v* **1** draw (liquid or air) into the mouth. **2** take (something) into the mouth and moisten, dissolve, or roll it around with the tongue. **3** (foll. by *in*)

draw in by irresistible force. ♦ *n* **4**
sucking. **sucker** *n* **1** *Slang* person who
is easily deceived or swindled. **2** organ
or device which adheres by suction. **3**
shoot coming from a plant's root or
the base of its main stem. **suck up to**
v Informal flatter (someone) for one's
own profit.

suckle *v* feed at the breast. **suckling** *n*
unweaned baby or young animal.

sucrose [**soo**-kroze] *n* chemical name
for sugar.

suction *n* **1** sucking. **2** force produced
by drawing air out of a space to make
a vacuum that will suck in a substance
from another space.

sudden *adj* done or occurring quickly
and unexpectedly. **all of a sudden**
quickly and unexpectedly. **suddenly**
adv **suddenness** *n* **sudden death**
Sport period of extra time in which the
first competitor to score wins.

sudorific [syoo-dor-**if**-ik] *n, adj* (drug)
causing sweating.

suds *pl n* froth of soap and water,
lather.

sue *v* **suing, sued** start legal
proceedings against.

suede *n* leather with a velvety finish on
one side.

suet *n* hard fat obtained from sheep
and cattle, used in cooking.

suffer *v* **1** undergo or be subjected to.
2 tolerate. **sufferer** *n* **suffering** *n*
sufferance *n* **on sufferance** tolerated
with reluctance.

suffice [suf-**fice**] *v* be enough for a
purpose.

sufficient *adj* enough, adequate.
sufficiency *n* adequate amount.
sufficiently *adv*

suffix *n* letter or letters added to the
end of a word to form another word,
such as *-s* and *-ness* in *dogs* and
softness.

suffocate *v* **1** kill or be killed by

deprivation of oxygen. **2** feel
uncomfortable from heat and lack of
air. **suffocation** *n*

suffragan *n* bishop appointed to assist
an archbishop.

suffrage *n* right to vote in public
elections. **suffragette** *n* (in Britain in
the early 20th century) a woman who
campaigned militantly for the right to
vote.

suffuse *v* spread through or over
(something). **suffusion** *n*

sugar *n* **1** sweet crystalline
carbohydrate found in many plants
and used to sweeten food and drinks.
♦ *v* **2** sweeten or cover with sugar.
sugary *adj* **sugar beet** beet grown
for the sugar obtained from its roots.
sugar cane tropical grass grown for
the sugar obtained from its canes.
sugar daddy *Slang* elderly man who
gives a young woman money and gifts
in return for sexual favours. **sugar
glider** common Australian phalanger
that glides from tree to tree feeding on
insects and nectar.

suggest *v* **1** put forward (an idea) for
consideration. **2** bring to mind by the
association of ideas. **3** give a hint of.
suggestible *adj* easily influenced.
suggestion *n* **1** thing suggested. **2**
hint or indication. **suggestive** *adj* **1**
suggesting something indecent. **2**
conveying a hint (of). **suggestively**
adv

suicide *n* **1** killing oneself intentionally.
2 person who kills himself
intentionally. **3** self-inflicted ruin of
one's own prospects or interests.
suicidal *adj* liable to commit suicide.
suicidally *adv*

suit *n* **1** set of clothes designed to be
worn together. **2** outfit worn for a
specific purpose. **3** one of the four sets
into which a pack of cards is divided. **4**
lawsuit. ♦ *v* **5** be appropriate for. **6** be

acceptable to. **suitable** *adj* appropriate or proper. **suitably** *adv* **suitability** *n* **suitcase** *n* portable travelling case for clothing.

suite *n* **1** set of connected rooms in a hotel. **2** matching set of furniture. **3** set of musical pieces in the same key.

suitor *n* Old-fashioned man who is courting a woman.

sulk *v* **1** be silent and sullen because of resentment or bad temper. ♦ *n* **2** resentful or sullen mood. **sulky** *adj* **sulkily** *adv*

sullen *adj* unwilling to talk or be sociable. **sullenly** *adv* **sullenness** *n*

sully *v* **-lying, -lied 1** ruin (someone's reputation). **2** make dirty.

sulphate *n* salt or ester of sulphuric acid.

sulphide *n* compound of sulphur with another element.

sulphite *n* salt or ester of sulphurous acid.

sulphonamide [sulf-**on**-a-mide] *n* any of a class of drugs that prevent the growth of bacteria.

sulphur *n* Chem pale yellow nonmetallic element. **sulphuric, sulphurous** *adj* of or containing sulphur.

sultan *n* sovereign of a Muslim country. **sultana** *n* **1** kind of raisin. **2** sultan's wife, mother, or daughter. **sultanate** *n* territory of a sultan.

sultry *adj* **-trier, -triest 1** (of weather or climate) hot and humid. **2** passionate, sensual.

sum *n* **1** result of addition, total. **2** problem in arithmetic. **3** quantity of money. **sum total** complete or final total. **sum up** *v* **summing, summed 1** summarize. **2** form a quick opinion of.

summary *n, pl* **-ries 1** brief account giving the main points of something. ♦ *adj* **2** done quickly, without formalities. **summarily** *adv*

summarize *v* make or be a summary of (something). **summation** *n* **1** summary. **2** adding up.

summer *n* warmest season of the year, between spring and autumn. **summery** *adj* **summerhouse** *n* small building in a garden. **summertime** *n* period or season of summer.

summit *n* **1** top of a mountain or hill. **2** highest point. **3** conference between heads of state or other high officials.

summon *v* **1** order (someone) to come. **2** call upon (someone) to do something. **3** gather (one's courage, strength, etc.). **summons** *n* **1** command summoning someone. **2** order requiring someone to appear in court. ♦ *v* **3** order (someone) to appear in court.

sumo *n* Japanese style of wrestling.

sump *n* **1** container in an internal-combustion engine into which oil can drain. **2** hollow into which liquid drains.

sumptuous *adj* lavish, magnificent. **sumptuously** *adv*

sun *n* **1** star around which the earth and other planets revolve. **2** any star around which planets revolve. **3** heat and light from the sun. ♦ *v* **sunning, sunned 4** expose (oneself) to the sun's rays. **sunless** *adj* **sunny** *adj* **1** full of or exposed to sunlight. **2** cheerful. **sunbathe** *v* lie in the sunshine in order to get a suntan. **sunbeam** *n* ray of sun. **sunburn** *n* painful reddening of the skin caused by overexposure to the sun. **sunburnt, sunburned** *adj* **sundial** *n* device showing the time by means of a pointer that casts a shadow on a marked dial. **sundown** *n* sunset. **sunflower** *n* tall plant with large golden flowers. **sunrise** *n* **1** daily appearance of the sun above the horizon. **2** time of this. **sunset** *n* **1**

daily disappearance of the sun below the horizon. **2** time of this. **sunshine** n light and warmth from the sun.

sunspot n **1** dark patch appearing temporarily on the sun's surface. **2** *Aust* small area of skin damage caused by exposure to the sun. **sunstroke** n illness caused by prolonged exposure to intensely hot sunlight. **suntan** n browning of the skin caused by exposure to the sun.

sundae n ice cream topped with fruit etc.

Sunday n first day of the week and the Christian day of worship. **Sunday school** school for teaching children about Christianity.

sundry adj several, various. **sundries** pl n several things of various sorts. **all and sundry** everybody.

sung v past participle of SING.

sunk v a past participle of SINK.

sunken v a past participle of SINK.

sup v supping, supped **1** take (liquid) by sips. ♦ n **2** sip.

super adj Informal excellent.

super- prefix used with many main words to mean: **1** above or over, e.g. superimpose. **2** outstanding, e.g. superstar. **3** of greater size or extent, e.g. supermarket.

superannuation n **1** regular payment by an employee into a pension fund. **2** pension paid from this. **superannuated** adj discharged with a pension, owing to old age or illness.

superb adj excellent, impressive, or splendid. **superbly** adv

superbug n Informal bacterium resistant to antibiotics.

supercharged adj (of an engine) having a supercharger. **supercharger** n device that increases the power of an internal-combustion engine by forcing extra air into it.

supercilious adj showing arrogant

pride or scorn.

superconductor n substance which has almost no electrical resistance at very low temperatures. **superconductivity** n

superficial adj **1** not careful or thorough. **2** (of a person) without depth of character, shallow. **3** of or on the surface. **superficially** adv **superficiality** n

superfluous [soo-**per**-flew-uss] adj more than is needed. **superfluity** n

superhuman adj beyond normal human ability or experience.

superimpose v place (something) on or over something else.

superintendent n **1** senior police officer. **2** supervisor. **superintend** v supervise (a person or activity).

superior adj **1** greater in quality, quantity, or merit. **2** higher in position or rank. **3** believing oneself to be better than others. ♦ n **4** person of greater rank or status. **superiority** n

superlative [soo-**per**-lat-iv] adj **1** of outstanding quality. **2** Grammar denoting the form of an adjective or adverb indicating most. ♦ n **3** Grammar superlative form of a word.

superman n man with great physical or mental powers.

supermarket n large self-service store selling food and household goods.

supermodel n famous and highly-paid fashion model.

supernatural adj of or relating to things beyond the laws of nature. **the supernatural** supernatural forces, occurrences, and beings collectively.

supernova n, pl -vae, -vas star that explodes and briefly becomes exceptionally bright.

supernumerary adj **1** exceeding the required or regular number. ♦ n, pl -ries **2** supernumerary person or thing.

superpower *n* extremely powerful nation.

superscript *n, adj* (character) printed above the line.

supersede *v* replace, supplant.

☑ **SPELLING TIP**

Although there is a word 'cede', spelt with a *c*, the word **supersede** must have an *s* in the middle.

---

supersonic *adj* of or travelling at a speed greater than the speed of sound.

superstition *n* **1** belief in omens, ghosts, etc. **2** idea or practice based on this. **superstitious** *adj*

superstore *n* large supermarket.

superstructure *n* **1** structure erected on something else. **2** part of a ship above the main deck.

supervene *v* occur as an unexpected development.

supervise *v* watch over to direct or check. **supervision** *n* **supervisor** *n* **supervisory** *adj*

supine *adj* lying flat on one's back.

supper *n* light evening meal.

supplant *v* take the place of, oust.

supple *adj* **1** (of a person) moving and bending easily and gracefully. **2** bending easily without damage. **suppleness** *n*

supplement *n* **1** thing added to complete something or make up for a lack. **2** magazine inserted into a newspaper. **3** section added to a publication to supply further information. ◆ *v* **4** provide or be a supplement to (something). **supplementary** *adj*

supplication *n* humble request. **supplicant** *n* person who makes a humble request.

supply *v* **-plying, -plied 1** provide with something required. ◆ *n, pl* **-plies 2** supplying. **3** amount available. **4**

Economics willingness and ability to provide goods and services. ◆ *pl* **5** food or equipment. **supplier** *n*

support *v* **1** bear the weight of. **2** provide the necessities of life for. **3** give practical or emotional help to. **4** take an active interest in (a sports team, political principle, etc.). **5** help to prove (a theory etc.). **6** speak in favour of. **7** *n* **8** supporting. **9** means of support. **supporter** *n* person who supports a team, principle, etc. **supportive** *adj*

suppose *v* **1** presume to be true. **2** consider as a proposal for the sake of discussion. **supposed** *adj* presumed to be true without proof, doubtful. **supposed to 1** expected or required to, e.g. *you were supposed to phone me.* **2** permitted to, e.g. *we're not supposed to swim here.* **supposedly** *adv* **supposition** *n* **1** supposing. **2** something supposed.

suppository *n, pl* **-ries** solid medication inserted into the rectum or vagina and left to melt.

suppress *v* **1** put an end to. **2** prevent publication of (information). **3** restrain (an emotion or response). **suppression** *n*

suppurate *v* (of a wound etc.) produce pus.

supreme *adj* highest in authority, rank, or degree. **supremely** *adv* extremely. **supremacy** *n* **1** supreme power. **2** state of being supreme. **supremo** *n* *Informal* person in overall authority.

surcharge *n* additional charge.

surd *n* *Maths* number that cannot be expressed in whole numbers.

sure *adj* **1** free from uncertainty or doubt. **2** reliable. **3** inevitable. **4** *adv, interj* **5** *Informal* certainly. **surely** *adv* it must be true that. **sure-footed** *adj* unlikely to slip or stumble.

surety *n, pl* **-ties** person who takes

responsibility, or thing given as a guarantee, for the fulfilment of another's obligation.

surf n **1** foam caused by waves breaking on the shore. ♦ v **2** take part in surfing. **3** move quickly through a medium such as the Internet. **surfing** n sport of riding towards the shore on a surfboard on the crest of a wave. **surfer** n **surfboard** n long smooth board used in surfing.

surface n **1** outside or top of an object. **2** material covering the surface of an object. **3** superficial appearance. ♦ v **5** rise to the surface. **6** put a surface on.

surfeit n excessive amount.

surge n **1** sudden powerful increase. **2** strong rolling movement, esp. of the sea. ♦ v **3** increase suddenly. **4** move forward strongly.

surgeon n doctor who specializes in surgery. **surgery** n **1** treatment in which the patient's body is cut open in order to treat the affected part pl **-geries) 2** place where, or time when, a doctor, dentist, etc. can be consulted. **3** Brit occasion when an elected politician can be consulted. **surgical** adj **surgically** adv

surly adj -**lier**, -**liest** ill-tempered and rude. **surliness** n

surmise v, n guess, conjecture.

surmount v **1** overcome (a problem). **2** be on top of (something). **surmountable** adj

surname n family name.

surpass v be greater than or superior to.

surplice n loose white robe worn by clergymen and choristers.

surplus n amount left over in excess of what is required.

surprise n **1** unexpected event. **2** amazement and wonder. **3** v **4** cause to feel amazement or wonder. **5** come upon, attack, or catch suddenly and unexpectedly.

surrealism n movement in art and literature involving the combination of incongruous images, as in a dream. **surreal** adj bizarre. **surrealist** n, adj **surrealistic** adj

surrender v **1** give oneself up. **2** give (something) up to another. **3** yield (to a temptation or influence). ♦ n **4** surrendering.

surreptitious adj done secretly or stealthily. **surreptitiously** adv

surrogate n substitute. **surrogate mother** woman who gives birth to a child on behalf of a couple who cannot have children.

surround v **1** be, come, or place all around (a person or thing). ♦ n **2** border or edging. **surroundings** pl n area or environment around a person, place, or thing.

surveillance n close observation.

survey v **1** view or consider in a general way. **2** make a map of (an area). **3** inspect (a building) to assess its condition and value. **4** find out the incomes, opinions, etc. of (a group of people). ♦ n **5** surveying. **6** report produced by a survey. **surveyor** n

survive v **1** continue to live or exist after (a difficult experience). **2** live after the death of (another). **survival** n condition of having survived. **survivor** n

susceptible adj liable to be influenced or affected by. **susceptibility** n

sushi [**soo**-shee] n Japanese dish of small cakes of cold rice with a topping of raw fish.

suspect v **1** believe (someone) to be guilty without having any proof. **2** think (something) to be false or questionable. **3** believe (something) to be the case. ♦ adj **4** not to be trusted. ♦ n **5** person who is suspected.

suspend v **1** hang from a high place. **2**

cause to remain floating or hanging. **3** cause to cease temporarily. **4** remove (someone) temporarily from a job or team. **suspenders** pl n **1** straps for holding up stockings. **2** US braces.

suspense n state of uncertainty while awaiting news, an event, etc.

suspension n **1** suspending or being suspended. **2** system of springs and shock absorbers supporting the body of a vehicle. **3** mixture of fine particles of a solid in a fluid. **suspension bridge** bridge hanging from cables attached to towers at each end.

suspicion n **1** feeling of not trusting a person or thing. **2** belief that something is true without definite proof. **3** slight trace. **suspicious** adj feeling or causing suspicion. **suspiciously** adv

suss out v Slang work out using one's intuition.

sustain v **1** maintain or prolong. **2** keep up the vitality or strength of. **3** suffer (an injury or loss). **4** support. **sustenance** n food.

suture [**soo**-cher] n stitch joining the edges of a wound.

suzerain n state or sovereign with limited authority over another self-governing state. **suzerainty** n

svelte adj attractively or gracefully slim.

SW southwest(ern).

swab n **1** small piece of cotton wool used to apply medication, clean a wound, etc. ♦ v **swabbing, swabbed 2** clean (a wound) with a swab. **3** clean (the deck of a ship) with a mop.

swaddle v wrap (a baby) in swaddling clothes. **swaddling clothes** long strips of cloth formerly wrapped round a newborn baby.

swag n Slang stolen property. **swagman** n Aust hist tramp who carries his belongings in a bundle on his back.

swagger v **1** walk or behave arrogantly. ♦ n **2** arrogant walk or manner.

swain n Poetic **1** suitor. **2** country youth.

swallow[1] v **1** cause to pass down one's throat. **2** make a gulping movement in the throat, as when nervous. **3** Informal believe (something) gullibly. **4** refrain from showing (a feeling). **5** engulf or absorb. ♦ n **6** swallowing. **7** amount swallowed.

swallow[2] n small migratory bird with long pointed wings and a forked tail.

swam v past tense of SWIM.

swamp n **1** watery area of land, bog. ♦ v **2** cause (a boat) to fill with water and sink. **3** overwhelm. **swampy** adj

swan n **1** large usu. white water bird with a long graceful neck. ♦ v **swanning, swanned 2** Informal wander about idly. **swan song** person's last performance before retirement or death.

swank Slang ♦ v **1** show off or boast. ♦ n **2** showing off or boasting. **swanky** adj Slang expensive and showy, stylish.

swanndri [**swan**-dry] n ® NZ weatherproof woollen shirt or jacket (also **swannie**).

swap v **swapping, swapped 1** exchange (something) for something else. ♦ n **2** exchange.

sward n stretch of short grass.

swarm[1] n **1** large group of bees or other insects. **2** large crowd. ♦ v **3** move in a swarm. **4** (of a place) be crowded or overrun.

swarm[2] v (foll. by up) climb (a ladder or rope) by gripping with the hands and feet.

swarthy adj **-thier, -thiest** dark-complexioned.

swashbuckling adj having the exciting behaviour of pirates, esp. those depicted in films.

swashbuckler n

swastika n symbol in the shape of a cross with the arms bent at right angles, used as the emblem of Nazi Germany.

swat v **swatting, swatted 1** hit sharply. ♦ n **2** sharp blow.

swatch n sample of cloth.

swath [**swawth**] n see SWATHE.

swathe v **1** wrap in bandages or layers of cloth. ♦ n **2** long strip of cloth wrapped around something. **3** (also **swath**) the width of one sweep of a scythe or mower.

sway v **1** swing to and fro or from side to side. **2** waver or cause to waver in opinion. ♦ n **3** power or influence. **4** swaying motion.

swear v **swearing, swore, sworn 1** use obscene or blasphemous language. **2** state or promise on oath. **3** state earnestly. **swear by** v have complete confidence in. **swear in** v cause to take an oath. **swearword** n word considered obscene or blasphemous.

sweat n **1** salty liquid given off through the pores of the skin. **2** Slang drudgery or hard labour. **3** v **4** have sweat coming through the pores. **5** be anxious. **sweaty** adj **sweatband** n strip of cloth tied around the forehead or wrist to absorb sweat. **sweatshirt** n long-sleeved cotton jersey. **sweatshop** n place where employees work long hours in poor conditions for low pay.

sweater n (woollen) garment for the upper part of the body.

swede n kind of turnip.

sweep v **sweeping, swept 1** remove dirt from (a floor) with a broom. **2** move smoothly and quickly. **3** spread rapidly. **4** move majestically. **5** carry away suddenly or forcefully. **6** stretch in a long wide curve. ♦ n **7** sweeping. **8** sweeping motion. **9** wide expanse.

10 sweepstake. **11** chimney sweep. **sweeping** adj **1** wide-ranging. **2** indiscriminate. **sweepstake** n lottery in which the stakes of the participants make up the prize.

sweet adj **1** tasting of or like sugar. **2** kind and charming. **3** agreeable to the senses or mind. **4** (of wine) with a high sugar content. ♦ n **5** shaped piece of food consisting mainly of sugar. **6** dessert. **sweetly** adv **sweetness** n **sweeten** v **sweetener** n **1** sweetening agent that does not contain sugar. **2** Brit, Aust & NZ slang bribe. **sweetbread** n animal's pancreas used as food. **sweet corn** type of maize with sweet yellow kernels, eaten as a vegetable. **sweetheart** n lover. **sweetmeat** n Old-fashioned sweet delicacy such as a small cake. **sweet pea** climbing plant with bright fragrant flowers. **sweet potato** tropical root vegetable with yellow flesh. **sweet-talk** v Informal coax or flatter. **sweet tooth** strong liking for sweet foods.

swell v **swelling, swelled, swollen** or **swelled 1** expand or increase. **2** (of a sound) become gradually louder. ♦ n **3** swelling or being swollen. **4** movement of waves in the sea. **5** Old-fashioned slang fashionable person. ♦ adj **6** US slang excellent or fine. **swelling** n enlargement of part of the body, caused by injury or infection.

swelter v feel uncomfortably hot.

sweltering adj uncomfortably hot.

swept v past of SWEEP.

swerve v **1** turn aside from a course sharply or suddenly. ♦ n **2** swerving.

swift adj **1** moving or able to move quickly. **2** n **3** fast-flying bird with pointed wings. **swiftly** adv **swiftness** n

swig n **1** large mouthful of drink. ♦ v **swigging, swigged 2** drink in large mouthfuls.

swill v **1** drink greedily. **2** rinse (something) in large amounts of water. ◆ n **3** sloppy mixture containing waste food, fed to pigs. **4** deep drink.

swim v **swimming, swam, swum 1** move along in water by movements of the limbs. **2** be covered or flooded with liquid. **3** reel, e.g. *her head was swimming*. ◆ n **4** act or period of swimming. **swimmer** n **swimmingly** adv successfully and effortlessly. **swimming pool** (building containing) an artificial pond for swimming in.

swindle v **1** cheat (someone) out of money. ◆ n **2** instance of swindling. **swindler** n

swine n **1** contemptible person. **2** pig.

swing v **swinging, swung 1** move to and fro, sway. **2** move in a curve. **3** (of an opinion or mood) change sharply. **4** hit out with a sweeping motion. **5** *Slang* be hanged. **6** n **7** swinging. **8** suspended seat on which a child can swing to and fro. **9** sudden or extreme change.

swingeing [**swin**-jing] adj punishing, severe.

swipe v **1** strike (at) with a sweeping blow. **2** *Slang* steal. **3** pass (a credit card or debit card) through a machine that electronically reads information stored in the card. ◆ n **4** hard blow. **swipe card** credit card or debit card that is passed through a machine that electronically reads information stored in the card.

swirl v **1** turn with a whirling motion. ◆ n **2** whirling motion. **3** twisting shape.

swish v **1** move with a whistling or hissing sound. ◆ n **2** whistling or hissing sound. ◆ adj **3** *Informal* fashionable, smart.

Swiss adj **1** of Switzerland or its people. ◆ n, pl **Swiss 2** person from

Switzerland. **swiss roll** sponge cake spread with jam or cream and rolled up.

switch n **1** device for opening and closing an electric circuit. **2** abrupt change. **3** exchange or swap. **4** flexible rod or twig. ◆ v **5** change abruptly. **6** exchange or swap. **switchback** n road or railway with many sharp hills or bends. **switchboard** n installation in a telephone exchange or office where telephone calls are connected. **switch on, off** v turn (a device) on or off by means of a switch.

swivel v **-elling, -elled 1** turn on a central point. ◆ n **2** coupling device that allows an attached object to turn freely.

swizzle stick n small stick used to stir cocktails.

swollen v **a** past participle of SWELL.

swoon v, n faint.

swoop v **1** sweep down or pounce on suddenly. ◆ n **2** swooping.

swop v **swopping, swopped,** n same as SWAP.

sword n weapon with a long sharp blade. **swordfish** n large fish with a very long upper jaw. **swordsman** n person skilled in the use of a sword.

swore v past tense of SWEAR.

sworn v **1** past participle of SWEAR. ◆ adj **2** bound by or as if by an oath, e.g. *sworn enemies*.

swot *Informal* ◆ v **swotting, swotted 1** study hard. ◆ n **2** person who studies hard.

swum v past participle of SWIM.

swung v past of SWING.

sybarite [**sib**-bar-ite] n lover of luxury. **sybaritic** adj

sycamore n tree with five-pointed leaves and two-winged fruits.

sycophant n person who uses flattery to win favour from people with power

or influence. **sycophantic** *adj*
sycophancy *n*

syllable *n* part of a word pronounced as a unit. **syllabic** *adj*

syllabub *n* dessert of beaten cream, sugar, and wine.

syllabus *n, pl* **-buses, -bi** list of subjects for a course of study.

syllogism *n* form of logical reasoning consisting of two premises and a conclusion.

sylph *n* **1** slender graceful girl or woman. **2** imaginary being supposed to inhabit the air. **sylphlike** *adj*

sylvan *adj Lit* relating to woods and trees.

symbiosis *n* close association of two species living together to their mutual benefit. **symbiotic** *adj*

symbol *n* sign or thing that stands for something else. **symbolic** *adj*
symbolically *adv* **symbolism** *n* **1** representation of something by symbols. **2** movement in art and literature using symbols to express abstract and mystical ideas.
symbolist *n, adj* **symbolize** *v* **1** be a symbol of. **2** represent with a symbol.

symmetry *n* state of having two halves that are mirror images of each other.
symmetrical *adj* **symmetrically** *adv*

sympathy *n, pl* **-thies 1** compassion for someone's pain or distress. **2** agreement with someone's feelings or interests. **sympathetic** *adj* **1** feeling or showing sympathy. **2** likeable or appealing. **sympathetically** *adv*
sympathize *v* feel or express sympathy. **sympathizer** *n*

symphony *n, pl* **-nies** composition for orchestra, with several movements.
symphonic *adj*

symposium *n, pl* **-siums, -sia** conference for discussion of a particular topic.

symptom *n* **1** sign indicating the presence of an illness. **2** sign that something is wrong. **symptomatic** *adj*

synagogue *n* Jewish place of worship and religious instruction.

sync, synch *Informal* ♦ *n* **1** synchronization. ♦ *v* **2** synchronize.

synchromesh *adj* (of a gearbox) having a device that synchronizes the speeds of gears before they engage.

synchronize *v* **1** (of two or more people) perform (an action) at the same time. **2** set (watches) to show the same time. **3** match (the soundtrack and action of a film) precisely. **synchronization** *n*
synchronous *adj* happening or existing at the same time.

syncopate *v Music* stress the weak beats in (a rhythm) instead of the strong ones. **syncopation** *n*

syncope [**sing**-kop-ee] *n Med* a faint.

syndicate *n* **1** group of people or firms undertaking a joint business project. **2** agency that sells material to several newspapers. **3** association of individuals who control organized crime. ♦ *v* **4** publish (material) in several newspapers. **5** form a syndicate. **syndication** *n*

syndrome *n* **1** combination of symptoms indicating a particular disease. **2** set of characteristics indicating a particular problem.

synergy *n* potential ability for people or groups to be more successful working together than on their own.

synod *n* church council.

synonym *n* word with the same meaning as another. **synonymous** *adj*

synopsis *n, pl* **-ses** summary or outline.

syntax *n Grammar* way in which words are arranged to form phrases and sentences. **syntactic** *adj*

synthesis *n, pl* **-ses 1** combination of objects or ideas into a whole. **2** artificial production of a substance.

synthesize *v* produce by synthesis.
synthesizer *n* electronic musical
instrument producing a range of
sounds. **synthetic** *adj* **1** (of a
substance) made artificially. **2** not
genuine, insincere. **synthetically** *adv*
syphilis *n* serious sexually transmitted
disease. **syphilitic** *adj*
syphon *n, v* same as SIPHON.
syringe *n* **1** device for withdrawing or
injecting fluids, consisting of a hollow
cylinder, a piston, and a hollow
needle. ♦ *v* **2** wash out or inject with a
syringe.

syrup *n* **1** solution of sugar in water. **2**
thick sweet liquid. **syrupy** *adj*
system *n* **1** method or set of methods.
2 scheme of classification or
arrangement. **3** network or assembly
of parts that form a whole.
systematic *adj* **systematically** *adv*
systematize *v* organize using a
system. **systematization** *n* **systemic**
adj affecting the entire animal or body.
systole [**siss**-tol-ee] *n* regular
contraction of the heart as it pumps
blood. **systolic** *adj*

T t

t tonne.

T *n* **to a T 1** in every detail. **2** perfectly.

t. ton.

ta *interj Informal* thank you.

TA (in Britain) Territorial Army.

tab *n* small flap or projecting label.
keep tabs on *Informal* watch closely.

TAB (in New Zealand) Totalisator
Agency Board.

tabard *n* short sleeveless tunic
decorated with a coat of arms, worn in
medieval times.

Tabasco *n* ® very hot red pepper sauce.

tabby *n, pl* **-bies,** *adj* (cat) with dark
stripes on a lighter background.

tabernacle *n* **1** portable shrine of the
Israelites. **2** Christian place of worship
not called a church. **3** *RC Church*
receptacle for the consecrated Host.

tabla *n, pl* **-bla, -blas** one of a pair of
Indian drums played with the hands.

table *n* **1** piece of furniture with a flat
top supported by legs. **2** arrangement
of information in columns. ♦ *v* **3**
submit (a motion) for discussion by a
meeting. **4** *US* suspend discussion of (a
proposal). **tableland** *n* high plateau.
tablespoon *n* large spoon for serving
food. **table tennis** game like tennis
played on a table with small bats and
a light ball.

tableau [**tab**-loh] *n, pl* **-leaux** silent
motionless group arranged to
represent some scene.

table d'hôte [**tah**-bla **dote**] *n, pl*
tables d'hôte, *adj* (meal) having a set
number of dishes at a fixed price.

tablet *n* **1** pill of compressed medicinal
substance. **2** inscribed slab of stone etc.

tabloid *n* small-sized newspaper with
many photographs and a concise, usu.
sensational style.

taboo *n, pl* **-boos 1** prohibition
resulting from religious or social
conventions. ♦ *adj* **2** forbidden by a
taboo.

tabular *adj* arranged in a table.
tabulate *v* arrange (information) in a
table. **tabulation** *n*

tachograph *n* device for recording the
speed and distance travelled by a
motor vehicle.

tachometer *n* device for measuring
speed, esp. that of a revolving shaft.

tacit [**tass**-it] *adj* implied but not
spoken. **tacitly** *adv*

taciturn [**tass**-it-turn] *adj* habitually
uncommunicative. **taciturnity** *n*

tack¹ *n* **1** short nail with a large head. **2**
long loose stitch. ♦ *v* **3** fasten with
tacks. **4** stitch with tacks. **tack on** *v*
append.

tack² *n* **1** course of a ship sailing
obliquely into the wind. **2** course of
action. ♦ *v* **3** sail into the wind on a
zigzag course.

tack³ *n* riding harness for horses.

tackies, takkies *pl n, sing* **tacky** *S
African informal* tennis shoes or
plimsolls.

tackle *v* **1** deal with (a task). **2** confront
(an opponent). **3** *Sport* attempt to get
the ball from (an opposing player). ♦ *n*
4 *Sport* act of tackling an opposing
player. **5** equipment for a particular
activity. **6** set of ropes and pulleys for
lifting heavy weights.

tacky¹ *adj* **tackier, tackiest** slightly
sticky.

tacky² *adj* **tackier, tackiest 1** *Informal*
vulgar and tasteless. **2** shabby.

taco [**tah**-koh] *n, pl* **tacos** *Mexican
cookery* tortilla fried until crisp, served

with a filling.

tact *n* skill in avoiding giving offence.
tactful *adj* **tactfully** *adv* **tactless** *adj*
tactlessly *adv*

tactics *n* art of directing military forces
in battle. **tactic** *n* method or plan to
achieve an end. **tactical** *adj*
tactician *n*

tactile *adj* of or having the sense of
touch.

tadpole *n* limbless tailed larva of a frog
or toad.

TAFE *Aust* Technical and Further
Education.

taffeta *n* shiny silk or rayon fabric.

tag¹ *n* **1** label bearing information. **2**
pointed end of a cord or lace. **3** trite
quotation. ♦ *v* **tagging, tagged 4**
attach a tag to. **tag along** *v*
accompany someone, esp. if uninvited.

tag² *n* **1** children's game where the
person being chased becomes the
chaser upon being touched. ♦ *v*
tagging, tagged 2 touch and catch in
this game.

tagliatelle *n* pasta in long narrow
strips.

tail *n* **1** rear part of an animal's body,
usu. forming a flexible appendage. **2**
rear or last part or parts of something.
3 *Informal* person employed to follow
and spy on another. ♦ *pl* **4** *Informal* tail
coat. ♦ *adj* **5** at the rear. ♦ *v* **6** *Informal*
follow (someone) secretly. **turn tail**
run away. **tailless** *adj* **tails** *adv* with
the side of a coin uppermost that does
not have a portrait of a head on it.
tailback *n Brit* queue of traffic
stretching back from an obstruction.
tailboard *n* removable or hinged rear
board on a truck etc. **tail coat** man's
coat with a long black split into two
below the waist. **tail off, away** *v*
diminish gradually. **tailplane** *n* small
stabilizing wing at the rear of an
aircraft. **tailspin** *n* uncontrolled

spinning dive of an aircraft. **tailwind**
n wind coming from the rear.

tailor *n* **1** person who makes men's
clothes. ♦ *v* **2** adapt to suit a purpose.
tailor-made *adj* **1** made by a tailor. **2**
perfect for a purpose.

taint *v* **1** spoil with a small amount of
decay, contamination, or other bad
quality. ♦ *n* **2** something that taints.

taipan *n* large poisonous Australian
snake.

take *v* **taking, took, taken 1** remove
from a place. **2** carry or accompany. **3**
use. **4** get possession of, esp.
dishonestly. **5** capture. **6** require (time,
resources, or ability). **7** assume. **8**
accept. **9** *n* **10** one of a series of
recordings from which the best will be
used. **take place** happen. **taking** *adj*
charming. **takings** *pl n* money
received by a shop. **take after** *v* look
or behave like (a parent etc.). **take
away** *v* remove or subtract.
takeaway 1 *n* **2** shop or restaurant
selling meals for eating elsewhere. **3**
meal bought at a takeaway. **take in** *v*
1 understand. **2** deceive or swindle. **3**
make (clothing) smaller. **take off** *v* **1**
(of an aircraft) leave the ground. **2**
Informal depart. **3** *Informal* parody.
takeoff *n* **takeover** *n* act of taking
control of a company by buying a
large number of its shares. **take up** *v*
1 occupy or fill (space or time). **2**
adopt the study or activity of. **3**
shorten (a garment). **4** accept (an
offer).

talc *n* **1** talcum powder. **2** soft mineral
of magnesium silicate. **talcum
powder** powder, usu. scented, used to
dry or perfume the body.

tale *n* **1** story. **2** malicious piece of
gossip.

talent *n* **1** natural ability. **2** ancient unit
of weight or money. **talented** *adj*

talisman *n, pl* **-mans** object believed

to have magic power. **talismanic** *adj*

talk *v* **1** express ideas or feelings by means of speech. **2** utter. **3** discuss, e.g. *let's talk business.* **4** reveal information. **5** (be able to) speak in a specified language. ♦ *n* **6** speech or lecture. **talker** *n* **talkative** *adj* fond of talking. **talk back** *v* answer impudently. **talkback** *n NZ* broadcast in which telephone comments or questions from the public are transmitted live. **talking-to** *n Informal* telling-off.

tall *adj* **1** higher than average. **2** of a specified height. **tall order** difficult task. **tall story** unlikely and probably untrue tale.

tallboy *n* high chest of drawers.

tallow *n* hard animal fat used to make candles.

tally *v* **-lying, -lied 1** (of two things) correspond. ♦ *n, pl* **-lies 2** record of a debt or score.

tally-ho *interj* huntsman's cry when the quarry is sighted.

Talmud *n* body of Jewish law. **Talmudic** *adj*

talon *n* bird's hooked claw.

tamarind *n* **1** tropical tree. **2** its acid fruit.

tamarisk *n* evergreen shrub with slender branches and feathery flower clusters.

tambourine *n* percussion instrument like a small drum with jingling metal discs attached.

tame *adj* **1** (of animals) brought under human control. **2** (of animals) not afraid of people. **3** meek or submissive. **4** uninteresting. ♦ *v* **5** make tame. **tamely** *adv*

tamer *n* person who tames wild animals.

Tamil *n* **1** member of a people of Sri Lanka and S India. **2** their language.

tam-o'-shanter *n* brimless wool cap with a bobble in the centre.

tamp *v* pack down by repeated taps.

tamper *v* (foll. by *with*) interfere.

tampon *n* absorbent plug of cotton wool inserted into the vagina during menstruation.

tan *n* **1** brown coloration of the skin from exposure to sunlight. ♦ *v* **tanning, tanned 2** (of skin) go brown from exposure to sunlight. **3** convert (a hide) into leather. ♦ *adj* **4** yellowish-brown. **tannery** *n* place where hides are tanned.

tandem *n* bicycle for two riders, one behind the other. **in tandem** together.

tandoori *adj* (of food) cooked in an Indian clay oven.

tang *n* **1** strong taste or smell. **2** trace or hint. **tangy** *adj*

tangata whenua [tang-ah-tah fen-noo-ah] *pl n NZ* original Polynesian settlers in New Zealand.

tangent *n* **1** line that touches a curve without intersecting it. **2** (in trigonometry) ratio of the length of the opposite side to that of the adjacent side of a right-angled triangle. **go off at a tangent** suddenly take a completely different line of thought or action. **tangential** *adj* **1** of superficial relevance only. **2** of a tangent. **tangentially** *adv*

tangerine *n* small orange-like fruit of an Asian citrus tree.

tangible *adj* **1** able to be touched. **2** clear and definite. **tangibly** *adv*

tangle *n* **1** confused mass or situation. ♦ *v* **2** twist together in a tangle. **3** (often foll. by *with*) come into conflict.

tango *n, pl* **-gos 1** S American dance. ♦ *v* **2** dance a tango.

taniwha [tun-ee-fah] *n NZ* mythical Maori monster that lives in water.

tank n 1 container for liquids or gases. 2 armoured fighting vehicle moving on tracks. **tanker** n ship or truck for carrying liquid in bulk.

tankard n large beer-mug, often with a hinged lid.

tannin, tannic acid n vegetable substance used in tanning.

Tannoy n ® Brit type of public-address system.

tansy n, pl -**sies** yellow-flowered plant.

tantalize v torment by showing but withholding something desired. **tantalizing** adj **tantalizingly** adv

tantalum n Chem hard greyish-white metallic element.

tantamount adj **tantamount to** equivalent in effect to.

tantrum n childish outburst of temper.

tap¹ v **tapping, tapped** 1 knock lightly and usu. repeatedly. ♦ n 2 light knock. **tap dancing** style of dancing in which the feet beat out an elaborate rhythm.

tap² n 1 valve to control the flow of liquid from a pipe or cask. ♦ v **tapping, tapped** 2 listen in on (a telephone call) secretly by making an illegal connection. 3 draw off with or as if with a tap. **on tap 1** Informal readily available. 2 (of beer etc.) drawn from a cask.

tape n 1 narrow long strip of material. 2 (recording made on) a cassette containing magnetic tape. 3 string stretched across a race track to mark the finish. ♦ v 4 record on magnetic tape. 5 bind or fasten with tape. **tape measure** tape marked off in centimetres or inches for measuring. **tape recorder** device for recording and reproducing sound on magnetic tape. **tapeworm** n long flat parasitic worm living in the intestines of vertebrates.

taper v 1 become narrower towards one end. ♦ n 2 long thin candle.

taper off v become gradually less.

tapestry n, pl -**tries** fabric decorated with coloured woven designs.

tapioca n beadlike starch made from cassava root, used in puddings.

tapir [**tape**-er] n piglike mammal of tropical America and SE Asia, with a long snout.

tappet n short steel rod in an engine, transferring motion from one part to another.

taproot n main root of a plant, growing straight down.

tar n 1 thick black liquid distilled from coal etc. ♦ v **tarring, tarred** 2 coat with tar. **tar-seal** n NZ tarred road surface.

taramasalata n creamy pink pâté made from fish roe.

tarantella n 1 lively Italian dance. 2 music for this.

tarantula n large hairy spider with a poisonous bite.

tardy adj **tardier, tardiest** slow or late. **tardily** adv **tardiness** n

tare n 1 type of vetch plant. 2 Bible weed.

target n 1 object or person a missile is aimed at. 2 goal or objective. 3 object of criticism. ♦ v **-geting, -geted** 4 aim or direct.

☑ **SPELLING TIP**

Lots of people put an extra *t* into *targetting* and *targetted*, but they are wrong: the words are **targeting** and **targeted**.

---

tariff n 1 tax levied on imports. 2 list of fixed prices.

Tarmac n 1 ® mixture of tar, bitumen, and crushed stones used for roads etc. 2 (t-) airport runway.

tarn n small mountain lake.

tarnish v 1 make or become stained or less bright. 2 damage or taint. ♦ n 3 discoloration or blemish.

tarot [**tarr**-oh] n special pack of cards used mainly in fortune-telling. **tarot card** card in a tarot pack.

tarpaulin n (sheet of) heavy waterproof fabric.

tarragon n aromatic herb.

tarry v **-rying, -ried** Old-fashioned **1** linger or delay. **2** stay briefly.

tarsus n, pl **-si** bones of the heel and ankle collectively.

tart¹ n pie or flan with a sweet filling.

tart² adj sharp or bitter. **tartly** adv **tartness** n

tart³ n Informal sexually provocative or promiscuous woman. **tart up** v Informal dress or decorate in a smart or flashy way.

tartan n **1** design of straight lines crossing at right angles, esp. one associated with a Scottish clan. **2** cloth with such a pattern.

tartar¹ n **1** hard deposit on the teeth. **2** deposit formed during the fermentation of wine.

tartar² n fearsome or formidable person.

tartare sauce n mayonnaise sauce mixed with chopped herbs and capers, served with seafood.

tartrazine [**tar**-traz-zeen] n artificial yellow dye used in food etc.

TAS Tasmania.

task n (difficult or unpleasant) piece of work to be done. **take to task** criticize or scold. **task force** (military) group formed to carry out a specific task. **taskmaster** n person who enforces hard work.

Tasmanian n, adj (person) from Tasmania. **Tasmanian devil** small carnivorous Tasmanian marsupial. **Tasmanian tiger** same as THYLACINE.

tassel n decorative fringed knot of threads.

taste n **1** sense by which the flavour of a substance is distinguished in the mouth. **2** distinctive flavour. **3** small amount tasted. **4** brief experience of something. **5** liking. **6** ability to appreciate what is beautiful or excellent. ◆ v **7** distinguish the taste of (a substance). **8** take a small amount of (something) into the mouth. **9** have a specific taste. **10** experience briefly. **tasteful** adj having or showing good taste. **tastefully** adv **tasteless** adj **1** bland or insipid. **2** showing bad taste. **tastelessly** adv **tasty** adj pleasantly flavoured. **taste bud** small organ on the tongue which perceives flavours.

tat n Brit tatty or tasteless article(s).

tattered adj ragged or torn. **in tatters** in ragged pieces.

tattle v, n Brit, Aust & NZ gossip or chatter.

tattoo¹ n **1** pattern made on the body by pricking the skin and staining it with indelible inks. ◆ v **-tooing, -tooed** make such a pattern on the skin. **tattooist** n

tattoo² n **1** military display or pageant. **2** drumming or tapping.

tatty adj **-tier, -tiest** shabby or worn out.

taught v past of TEACH.

taunt v **1** tease with jeers. ◆ n **2** jeering remark.

taupe adj brownish-grey.

taut adj **1** drawn tight. **2** showing nervous strain. **tauten** v make or become taut.

tautology n, pl **-gies** use of words which merely repeat something already stated. **tautological** adj

tavern n Old-fashioned pub.

tawdry adj **-drier, -driest** cheap, showy, and of poor quality.

tawny adj **-nier, -niest** yellowish-brown.

tax n 1 compulsory payment levied by a government on income, property, etc. to raise revenue. ♦ v 2 levy a tax on. 3 make heavy demands on. **taxable** adj **taxation** n levying of taxes. **tax-free** adj (of goods, services and income) not taxed. **taxpayer** n **tax relief** reduction in the amount of tax a person or company has to pay. **tax return** statement of personal income for tax purposes.

taxi n 1 (also **taxicab**) car with a driver that may be hired to take people to any specified destination. ♦ v **taxiing, taxied** 2 (of an aircraft) run along the ground before taking off or after landing. **taxi meter** meter in a taxi that registers the fare. **taxi rank** place where taxis wait to be hired.

taxidermy n art of stuffing and mounting animal skins to give them a lifelike appearance. **taxidermist** n

taxonomy n classification of plants and animals into groups. **taxonomic** adj **taxonomist** n

TB tuberculosis.

tbs., tbsp. tablespoon(ful).

tea n 1 drink made from infusing the dried leaves of an Asian bush in boiling water. 2 leaves used to make this drink. 3 Brit, Aust & NZ main evening meal. 4 Chiefly Brit light afternoon meal of tea, cakes, etc. 5 drink like tea, made from other plants. **tea bag** small porous bag of tea leaves. **tea cosy** covering for a teapot to keep the tea warm. **teapot** n container with a lid, spout, and handle for making and serving tea. **teaspoon** n small spoon for stirring tea. **tea towel, tea cloth** towel for drying dishes. **tea tree** tree of Australia and New Zealand that yields an oil used as an antiseptic.

teach v **teaching, taught** 1 tell or show (someone) how to do something. 2 give lessons in (a

subject). 3 cause to learn or understand. **teaching** n

teacher n person who teaches, esp. in a school.

teak n very hard wood of an E Indian tree.

teal n kind of small duck.

team n 1 group of people forming one side in a game. 2 group of people or animals working together. **teamster** n US commercial vehicle driver. **team up** v make or join a team. **teamwork** n cooperative work by a team.

tear[1], **teardrop** n drop of fluid appearing in and falling from the eye. **in tears** weeping. **tearful** adj weeping or about to weep. **tear gas** gas that stings the eyes and causes temporary blindness. **tear-jerker** n Informal excessively sentimental film or book.

tear[2] v **tearing, tore, torn** 1 rip a hole in. 2 rip apart. 3 rush. 4 n 5 hole or split. **tearaway** n wild or unruly person.

tease v 1 make fun of (someone) in a provoking or playful way. ♦ n 2 person who teases. **teasing** adj, n **tease out** v remove tangles from (hair etc.) by combing.

teasel, teazel, teazle n plant with prickly leaves and flowers.

teat n 1 nipple of a breast or udder. 2 rubber nipple of a feeding bottle.

tech n Informal technical college.

techie Informal ♦ n 1 person who is skilled in the use of technology. ♦ adj 2 relating to or skilled in the use of technology.

technetium [tek-**neesh**-ee-um] n Chem artificially produced silvery-grey metallic element.

technical adj 1 of or specializing in industrial, practical, or mechanical arts and applied sciences. 2 skilled in technical subjects. 3 relating to a particular field. **4** according to the letter of the law. **5** showing technique, e.g. *technical brilliance.* **technically** *adv* **technicality** *n* petty point based on a strict application of rules. **technician** *n* person skilled in a particular technical field. **technical college** higher educational institution with courses in art and technical subjects.

Technicolor *n* ® system of colour photography used for the cinema.

technique *n* **1** method or skill used for a particular task. **2** technical proficiency.

techno *n* type of electronic dance music with a very fast beat.

technocracy *n, pl* **-cies** government by technical experts. **technocrat** *n*

technology *n* **1** application of practical or mechanical sciences to industry or commerce. **2** scientific methods used in a particular field. **technological** *adj* **technologist** *n*

tectonics *n* study of the earth's crust and the forces affecting it.

teddy *n, pl* **-dies 1** teddy bear. **2** combined camisole and knickers. **teddy bear** soft toy bear.

tedious *adj* causing fatigue or boredom. **tediously** *adv* **tedium** *n* monotony.

tee *n* **1** small peg from which a golf ball can be played at the start of each hole. **2** area of a golf course from which the first stroke of a hole is made. **tee off** *v* make the first stroke of a hole in golf.

teem¹ *v* be full of.

teem² *v* rain heavily.

teenager *n* person aged between 13 and 19. **teenage** *adj*

teens *pl n* period of being a teenager.

teepee *n* same as TEPEE.

tee-shirt *n* same as T-SHIRT.

teeter *v* wobble or move unsteadily.

teeth *n* plural of TOOTH.

teethe *v* (of a baby) grow his or her first teeth. **teething troubles** problems during the early stages of something.

teetotal *adj* drinking no alcohol. **teetotaller** *n*

TEFL Teaching of English as a Foreign Language.

Teflon *n* ® substance used for nonstick coatings on saucepans etc.

tele- *combining form* **1** distance, e.g. *telecommunications.* **2** telephone or television, e.g. *teleconference.*

telecommunications *n* communications using telephone, radio, television, etc.

telegram *n* formerly, a message sent by telegraph.

telegraph *n* **1** formerly, a system for sending messages over a distance along a cable. ♦ *v* **2** communicate by telegraph. **telegraphic** *adj* **telegraphist** *n* **telegraphy** *n* science or use of a telegraph.

telekinesis *n* movement of objects by thought or willpower.

telemetry *n* use of electronic devices to record or measure a distant event and transmit the data to a receiver.

teleology *n* belief that all things have a predetermined purpose. **teleological** *adj*

telepathy *n* direct communication between minds. **telepathic** *adj* **telepathically** *adv*

telephone *n* **1** device for transmitting sound over a distance along wires. ♦ *v* **2** call or talk to (a person) by telephone. **telephony** *n* **telephonic** *adj* **telephonist** *n* person operating a telephone switchboard.

telephoto lens *n* camera lens producing a magnified image of a distant object.

teleprinter n Brit apparatus like a typewriter for sending and receiving typed messages by wire.

telesales n selling of a product or service by telephone.

telescope n 1 optical instrument for magnifying distant objects. ♦ v 2 shorten. **telescopic** adj

Teletext n ® system which shows information and news on television screens.

television n 1 system of producing a moving image and accompanying sound on a distant screen. 2 device for receiving broadcast signals and converting them into sound and pictures. 3 content of television programmes. **televise** v broadcast on television. **televisual** adj

telex n 1 international communication service using teleprinters. 2 message sent by telex. ♦ v 3 transmit by telex.

tell v telling, told 1 make known in words. 2 order or instruct. 3 give an account of. 4 discern or distinguish. 5 have an effect. 6 Informal reveal secrets. **teller** n 1 narrator. 2 bank cashier. 3 person who counts votes. **telling** adj having a marked effect. **tell off** v reprimand. **telling-off** n **telltale** n 1 person who reveals secrets. ♦ adj 2 revealing.

tellurium n Chem brittle silvery-white nonmetallic element.

telly n, pl -lies Informal television.

temerity [tim-**merr**-it-tee] n boldness or audacity.

temp Brit informal ♦ n 1 temporary employee, esp. a secretary. ♦ v 2 work as a temp.

temp. 1 temperature. 2 temporary.

temper n 1 outburst of anger. 2 tendency to become angry. 3 calm mental condition, e.g. I lost my temper. 4 frame of mind. ♦ v 5 make less extreme. 6 strengthen or toughen (metal).

tempera n painting medium for powdered pigments.

temperament n person's character or disposition. **temperamental** adj 1 having changeable moods. 2 Informal erratic and unreliable. **temperamentally** adv

temperate adj 1 (of climate) not extreme. 2 self-restrained or moderate. **temperance** n 1 moderation. 2 abstinence from alcohol.

temperature n 1 degree of heat or cold. 2 Informal abnormally high body temperature.

tempest n violent storm. **tempestuous** adj violent or stormy.

template n pattern used to cut out shapes accurately.

temple¹ n building for worship.

temple² n region on either side of the forehead. **temporal** adj

tempo n, pl -pi, -pos 1 rate or pace. 2 speed of a piece of music.

temporal adj 1 of time. 2 worldly rather than spiritual.

temporary adj lasting only for a short time. **temporarily** adv

temporize v 1 gain time by negotiation or evasiveness. 2 adapt to circumstances.

tempt v entice (a person) to do something wrong. **tempt fate** take foolish or unnecessary risks. **tempter, temptress** n **temptation** n 1 tempting. 2 tempting thing. **tempting** adj attractive or inviting.

ten adj, n one more than nine. **tenth** adj, n (of) number ten in a series.

tenable adj able to be upheld or maintained.

tenacious adj 1 holding fast. 2 stubborn. **tenaciously** adv **tenacity** n

tenant n person who rents land or a building. **tenancy** n

tench *n, pl* **tench** freshwater game fish of the carp family.

tend[1] *v* **1** be inclined. **2** go in the direction of. **tendency** *n* inclination to act in a certain way. **tendentious** *adj* biased, not impartial.

tend[2] *v* take care of.

tender[1] *adj* **1** not tough. **2** gentle and affectionate. **3** vulnerable or sensitive. **tenderly** *adv* **tenderness** *n* **tenderize** *v* soften (meat) by pounding or treatment with a special substance.

tender[2] *v* **1** offer. **2** make a formal offer to supply goods or services at a stated cost. ♦ *n* **3** such an offer. **legal tender** currency that must, by law, be accepted as payment.

tender[3] *n* **1** small boat that brings supplies to a larger ship in a port. **2** carriage for fuel and water attached to a steam locomotive.

tendon *n* strong tissue attaching a muscle to a bone.

tendril *n* slender stem by which a climbing plant clings.

tenement *n* (esp. in Scotland or the US) building divided into several flats.

tenet [**ten**-nit] *n* doctrine or belief.

tenner *n Brit informal* ten-pound note.

tennis *n* game in which players use rackets to hit a ball back and forth over a net.

tenon *n* projecting end on a piece of wood fitting into a slot in another.

tenor *n* **1** (singer with) the second highest male voice. **2** general meaning. ♦ *adj* **3** (of a voice or instrument) between alto and baritone.

tenpin bowling *n* game in which players try to knock over ten skittles by rolling a ball at them.

tense[1] *adj* **1** emotionally strained. **2** stretched tight. ♦ *v* **3** make or become tense.

tense[2] *n Grammar* form of a verb showing the time of action.

tensile *adj* of tension.

tension *n* **1** hostility or suspense. **2** emotional strain. **3** degree of stretching.

tent *n* portable canvas shelter.

tentacle *n* flexible organ of many invertebrates, used for grasping, feeding, etc.

tentative *adj* **1** provisional or experimental. **2** cautious or hesitant. **tentatively** *adv*

tenterhooks *pl n* **on tenterhooks** in anxious suspense.

tenuous *adj* slight or flimsy. **tenuously** *adv*

tenure *n* (period of) the holding of an office or position.

tepee [**tee**-pee] *n* cone-shaped tent, formerly used by Native Americans.

tepid *adj* **1** slightly warm. **2** half-hearted.

tequila *n* Mexican alcoholic drink.

tercentenary *adj, n, pl* **-naries** (of) a three hundredth anniversary.

term *n* **1** word or expression. **2** fixed period. **3** period of the year when a school etc. is open or a lawcourt holds sessions. ♦ *pl* **4** conditions. **5** mutual relationship. ♦ *v* **6** name or designate.

terminal *adj* **1** (of an illness) ending in death. **2** at or being an end. ♦ *n* **3** place where people or vehicles begin or end a journey. **4** point where current enters or leaves an electrical device. **5** keyboard and VDU having input and output links with a computer. **terminally** *adv*

terminate *v* bring or come to an end. **termination** *n*

terminology *n* technical terms relating to a subject.

terminus *n, pl* **-ni, -nuses** railway or bus station at the end of a line.

termite *n* white antlike insect that destroys timber.

tern *n* gull-like sea bird with a forked tail and pointed wings.

ternary *adj* consisting of three parts.

Terpsichorean *adj* of dancing.

terrace *n* 1 row of houses built as one block. 2 paved area next to a building. 3 level tier cut out of a hill. ♦ *pl* 4 (also **terracing**) tiered area in a stadium where spectators stand. ♦ *v* 5 form into or provide with a terrace.

terracotta *adj, n* 1 (made of) brownish-red unglazed pottery. ♦ *adj* 2 brownish-red.

terra firma *n Latin* dry land or solid ground.

terrain *n* area of ground, esp. with reference to its physical character.

terrapin *n* small turtle-like reptile.

terrarium *n, pl* **-raria, -rariums** enclosed container for small plants or animals.

terrazzo *n, pl* **-zos** floor of marble chips set in mortar and polished.

terrestrial *adj* 1 of the earth. 2 of or living on land.

terrible *adj* 1 very serious. 2 *Informal* very bad. 3 causing fear. **terribly** *adv*

terrier *n* any of various breeds of small active dog.

terrific *adj* 1 great or intense. 2 *Informal* excellent.

terrify *v* **-fying, -fied** fill with fear. **terrified** *adj* **terrifying** *adj*

terrine [terr-**reen**] *n* 1 earthenware dish with a lid. 2 pâté or similar food.

territory *n, pl* **-ries** 1 district. 2 area under the control of a particular government. 3 area inhabited and defended by an animal. 4 area of knowledge. **territorial** *adj* **Territorial Army** (in Britain) reserve army.

terror *n* 1 great fear. 2 terrifying person or thing. 3 *Brit, Aust & NZ informal* troublesome person or thing.

terrorism *n* use of violence and intimidation to achieve political ends. **terrorist** *n, adj* **terrorize** *v* force or oppress by fear or violence.

terry *n* fabric with small loops covering both sides, used esp. for making towels.

terse *adj* 1 neat and concise. 2 curt. **tersely** *adv*

tertiary [**tur**-shar-ee] *adj* third in degree, order, etc.

Terylene *n* ® synthetic polyester yarn or fabric.

tessellated *adj* paved or inlaid with a mosaic of small tiles.

test *v* 1 try out to ascertain the worth, capability, or endurance of. 2 carry out an examination on. ♦ *n* 3 critical examination. 4 Test match. **testing** *adj* **test case** lawsuit that establishes a precedent. **Test match** one of a series of international cricket or rugby matches. **test tube** narrow round-bottomed glass tube used in scientific experiments. **test-tube baby** baby conceived outside the mother's body.

testament *n* 1 proof or tribute. 2 *Law* will. 3 (**T-**) one of the two main divisions of the Bible.

testator [test-**tay**-tor], (*fem*) **testatrix** [test-**tay**-triks] *n* maker of a will.

testicle *n* either of the two male reproductive glands.

testify *v* **-fying, -fied** give evidence under oath. **testify to** be evidence of.

testimony *n, pl* **-nies** 1 declaration of truth or fact. 2 evidence given under oath. **testimonial** *n* 1 recommendation of the worth of a person or thing. 2 tribute for services or achievement.

testis *n, pl* **-tes** testicle.

testosterone *n* male sex hormone secreted by the testes.

testy adj **-tier, -tiest** irritable or touchy. **testily** adv **testiness** n

tetanus n acute infectious disease producing muscular spasms and convulsions.

tête-à-tête n, pl **-têtes, -tête** private conversation.

tether n **1** rope or chain for tying an animal to a spot. ♦ v **2** tie up with rope. **at the end of one's tether** at the limit of one's endurance.

tetrahedron [tet-ra-**heed**-ron] n, pl **-drons, -dra** solid figure with four faces.

tetralogy n, pl **-gies** series of four related works.

Teutonic [tew-**tonn**-ik] adj of or like the (ancient) Germans.

text n **1** main body of a book as distinct from illustrations etc. **2** passage of the Bible as the subject of a sermon. **3** novel or play studied for a course. **4** text message. ♦ v **5** send a text message to (someone). **textual** adj **textbook** n **1** standard book on a particular subject. ♦ adj **2** perfect, e.g. a textbook landing. **text message** message sent in text form, esp. by means of a mobile phone.

textile n fabric or cloth, esp. woven.

texture n structure, feel, or consistency. **textured** adj **textural** adj

thalidomide [thal-**lid**-oh-mide] n drug formerly used as a sedative, but found to cause abnormalities in developing fetuses.

thallium n Chem highly toxic metallic element.

than conj, prep used to introduce the second element of a comparison.

thane n Hist Anglo-Saxon or medieval Scottish nobleman.

thank v **1** express gratitude to. **2** hold responsible. **thanks** pl n **1** words of gratitude. ♦ interj **2** (also **thank you**)

polite expression of gratitude. **thanks to** because of. **thankful** adj grateful. **thankless** adj unrewarding or unappreciated. **Thanksgiving Day** autumn public holiday in Canada and the US.

that adj, pron **1** used to refer to something already mentioned or familiar, or further away. ♦ conj **2** used to introduce a clause. ♦ pron **3** used to introduce a relative clause.

thatch n **1** roofing material of reeds or straw. ♦ v **2** roof (a house) with reeds or straw.

thaw v **1** make or become unfrozen. **2** become more relaxed or friendly. ♦ n **3** thawing. **4** weather causing snow or ice to melt.

the adj the definite article, used before a noun.

theatre n **1** place where plays etc. are performed. **2** hospital operating room. **3** drama and acting in general. **theatrical** adj **1** of the theatre. **2** exaggerated or affected. **theatricals** pl n (amateur) dramatic performances. **theatrically** adv **theatricality** n

thee pron Obs objective form of THOU.

theft n act or an instance of stealing.

their adj of or associated with them. **theirs** pron (thing or person) belonging to them.

✅ **SPELLING TIP**

Do not confuse **their** and **theirs**, which do not have apostrophes, with **they're** and **there's**, which do because letters have been missed out where two words have been joined together.

---

theism [**thee**-iz-zum] n belief in a God or gods. **theist** n, adj **theistic** adj

them pron refers to people or things other than the speaker or those addressed. **themselves** pron

emphatic and reflexive form of THEY *or* THEM.

theme *n* 1 main idea or subject being discussed. 2 recurring melodic figure in music. **thematic** *adj* **theme park** leisure area in which all the activities are based on a single theme.

then *adv* 1 at that time. 2 after that. 3 that being so.

thence *adv* 1 from that place or time. 2 therefore.

theocracy *n, pl* **-cies** government by a god or priests. **theocratic** *adj*

theodolite [thee-**odd**-oh-lite] *n* surveying instrument for measuring angles.

theology *n, pl* **-gies** study of religions and religious beliefs. **theologian** *n* **theological** *adj* **theologically** *adv*

theorem *n* proposition that can be proved by reasoning.

theory *n, pl* **-ries** 1 set of ideas to explain something. 2 abstract knowledge or reasoning. 3 idea or opinion. **in theory** in an ideal or hypothetical situation. **theoretical** *adj* based on theory rather than practice or fact. **theoretically** *adv* **theorist** *n* **theorize** *v* form theories, speculate.

therapy *n, pl* **-pies** curing treatment. **therapist** *n* **therapeutic** [ther-rap-**pew**-tik] *adj* curing. **therapeutics** *n* art of curing.

there *adv* 1 in or to that place. 2 in that respect. **thereby** *adv* by that means. **therefore** *adv* consequently, that being so. **thereupon** *adv* immediately after that.

☑ SPELLING TIP

Do not confuse **there**, which is closely connected in meaning and in spelling with 'here', and **their**, which means 'belonging to them'.

---

therm *n* unit of measurement of heat.

thermal *adj* 1 of heat. 2 hot or warm. 3 (of clothing) retaining heat. ♦ *n* 4 rising current of warm air.

thermodynamics *n* scientific study of the relationship between heat and other forms of energy.

thermometer *n* instrument for measuring temperature.

thermonuclear *adj* involving nuclear fusion.

thermoplastic *adj* (of a plastic) softening when heated and resetting on cooling.

Thermos *n* ® vacuum flask.

thermosetting *adj* (of a plastic) remaining hard when heated.

thermostat *n* device for automatically regulating temperature. **thermostatic** *adj* **thermostatically** *adv*

thesaurus [thiss-**sore**-uss] *n, pl* **-ruses** book containing lists of synonyms and related words.

these *adj, pron* plural of THIS.

thesis *n, pl* **theses** 1 written work submitted for a degree. 2 opinion supported by reasoned argument.

Thespian *n* 1 actor or actress. ♦ *adj* 2 of the theatre.

they *pron* refers to: 1 people or things other than the speaker or people addressed. 2 people in general. 3 *Informal* he or she.

thiamine *n* vitamin found in the outer coat of rice and other grains.

thick *adj* 1 of great or specified extent from one side to the other. 2 having a dense consistency. 3 *Informal* stupid or insensitive. 4 *Brit, Aust & NZ informal* friendly. **a bit thick** *Informal* unfair or unreasonable. **the thick** busiest or most intense part. **thick with** full of. **thicken** *v* make or become thick or thicker. **thickly** *adv* **thickness** *n* 1 state of being thick. 2 dimension through an object. 3 layer. **thickset** *adj* stocky in build.

thicket *n* dense growth of small trees.

thief *n, pl* **thieves** person who steals.
thieve *v* steal. **thieving** *adj*

thigh *n* upper part of the human leg.

thimble *n* cap protecting the end of the finger when sewing.

thin *adj* **thinner, thinnest** **1** not thick. **2** slim or lean. **3** sparse or meagre. **4** of low density. **5** poor or unconvincing. ♦ *v* **thinning, thinned** **6** make or become thin. **thinly** *adv* **thinness** *n*

thine *pron, adj Obs* (something) of or associated with you (thou).

thing *n* **1** material object. **2** object, fact, or idea considered as a separate entity. **3** *Informal* obsession. ♦ *pl* **4** possessions, clothes, etc.

think *v* **thinking, thought** **1** consider, judge, or believe. **2** make use of the mind. **3** be considerate enough or remember to do something. **thinker** *n* **thinking** *adj, n* **think-tank** *n* group of experts studying specific problems. **think up** *v* invent or devise.

third *adj* **1** of number three in a series. **2** rated or graded below the second level. ♦ *n* **3** one of three equal parts. **third degree** violent interrogation. **third party** (applying to) a person involved by chance or only incidentally in legal proceedings, an accident, etc. **Third World** developing countries of Africa, Asia, and Latin America.

thirst *n* **1** desire to drink. **2** craving or yearning. ♦ *v* **3** feel thirst. **thirsty** *adj* **thirstily** *adv*

thirteen *adj, n* three plus ten. **thirteenth** *adj, n*

thirty *adj, n* three times ten. **thirtieth** *adj, n*

this *adj, pron* **1** used to refer to a thing or person nearby, just mentioned, or about to be mentioned. ♦ *adj* **2** used to refer to the present time, e.g. *this morning.*

thistle *n* prickly plant with dense flower heads.

thither *adv Obs* to or towards that place.

thong *n* **1** thin strip of leather etc. **2** skimpy article of underwear or beachwear that covers the genitals while leaving the buttocks bare.

thorax *n, pl* **thoraxes, thoraces** part of the body between the neck and the abdomen. **thoracic** *adj*

thorn *n* **1** prickle on a plant. **2** bush with thorns. **thorn in one's side, flesh** source of irritation. **thorny** *adj*

thorough *adj* **1** complete. **2** careful or methodical. **thoroughly** *adv* **thoroughness** *n* **thoroughbred** *n, adj* (animal) of pure breed. **thoroughfare** *n* way through from one place to another.

those *adj, pron* plural of THAT.

thou *pron Obs* singular form of YOU.

though *conj* **1** despite the fact that. ♦ *adv* **2** nevertheless.

thought *v* **1** past of THINK. ♦ *n* **2** thinking. **3** concept or idea. **4** ideas typical of a time or place. **5** consideration. **6** intention or expectation. **thoughtful** *adj* **1** considerate. **2** showing careful thought. **3** pensive or reflective. **thoughtless** *adj* inconsiderate.

thousand *adj, n* **1** ten hundred. **2** large but unspecified number. **thousandth** *adj, n* (of) number one thousand in a series.

thrall *n* state of being in the power of another person.

thrash *v* **1** beat, esp. with a stick or whip. **2** defeat soundly. **3** move about wildly. **4** thresh. **thrashing** *n* severe beating. **thrash out** *v* solve by thorough argument.

thread *n* **1** fine strand or yarn. **2** unifying theme. **3** spiral ridge on a screw, nut, or bolt. ♦ *v* **4** pass thread through. **5** pick (one's way etc.).

threadbare adj **1** (of fabric) with the nap worn off. **2** hackneyed. **3** shabby.

threat n **1** declaration of intent to harm. **2** dangerous person or thing. **threaten** v **1** make or be a threat to. **2** be a menacing indication of.

three adj, n one more than two. **threesome** n group of three. **three-dimensional, 3-D** adj having three dimensions.

threnody n, pl **-dies** lament for the dead.

thresh v beat (wheat etc.) to separate the grain from the husks and straw. **thresh about** move about wildly.

threshold n **1** bar forming the bottom of a doorway. **2** entrance. **3** starting point. **4** point at which something begins to take effect.

threw v past tense of THROW.

thrice adv Lit three times.

thrift n **1** wisdom and caution with money. **2** low-growing plant with pink flowers. **thrifty** adj

thrill n **1** sudden feeling of excitement. ♦ v **2** (cause to) feel a thrill. **thrilling** adj

thriller n book, film, etc. with an atmosphere of mystery or suspense.

thrive v **thriving, thrived** or **throve, thrived** or **thriven 1** flourish or prosper. **2** grow well.

throat n **1** passage from the mouth and nose to the stomach and lungs. **2** front of the neck. **throaty** adj (of the voice) hoarse.

throb v **throbbing, throbbed 1** pulsate repeatedly. **2** vibrate rhythmically. ♦ n **3** throbbing.

throes pl n violent pangs or pains. **in the throes of** struggling to cope with.

thrombosis n, pl **-ses** forming of a clot in a blood vessel or the heart.

throne n **1** ceremonial seat of a monarch or bishop. **2** sovereign power.

throng n, v crowd.

throstle n song thrush.

throttle n **1** device controlling the amount of fuel entering an engine. ♦ v **2** strangle.

through prep **1** from end to end or side to side of. **2** because of. **3** during. ♦ adj **4** finished. **5** (of transport) going directly to a place. **through and through** completely. **throughout** prep, adv in every part (of). **throughput** n amount of material processed.

throve v a past tense of THRIVE.

throw v **throwing, threw, thrown 1** hurl through the air. **2** move or put suddenly or carelessly. **3** bring into a specified state, esp. suddenly. **4** give (a party). **5** Informal baffle or disconcert. **6** n **7** throwing. **8** distance thrown. **throwaway** adj **1** done or said casually. **2** designed to be discarded after use. **throwback** n person or thing that reverts to an earlier type. **throw up** v vomit.

thrush¹ n brown songbird.

thrush² n fungal disease of the mouth or vagina.

thrust v **thrusting, thrust 1** push forcefully. ♦ n **2** forceful stab. **3** force or power. **4** intellectual or emotional drive.

thud n **1** dull heavy sound. ♦ v **thudding, thudded 2** make such a sound.

thug n violent man, esp. a criminal. **thuggery** n **thuggish** adj

thumb n **1** short thick finger set apart from the others. ♦ v **2** touch or handle with the thumb. **3** signal with the thumb for a lift in a vehicle. **thumb through** flick through (a book or magazine).

thump n **1** (sound of) a dull heavy blow. ♦ v **2** strike heavily.

thunder n **1** loud noise accompanying

lightning. **2** v **3** rumble with thunder. **4** shout. **5** move fast, heavily, and noisily. **thunderous** adj **thundery** adj **thunderbolt** n **1** lightning flash. **2** something sudden and unexpected. **thunderclap** n peal of thunder. **thunderstruck** adj amazed.

Thursday n fifth day of the week.

thus adv **1** therefore. **2** in this way.

thwack v, n whack.

thwart v **1** foil or frustrate. ♦ n **2** seat across a boat.

thy adj Obs of or associated with you (thou). **thyself** pron Obs **emphatic form of** THOU.

thylacine n extinct doglike Tasmanian marsupial.

thyme [time] n aromatic herb.

thymus n, pl **-muses, -mi** small gland at the base of the neck.

thyroid adj, n (of) a gland in the neck controlling body growth.

tiara n semicircular jewelled headdress.

tibia n, pl **tibiae, tibias** inner bone of the lower leg. **tibial** adj

tic n spasmodic muscular twitch.

tick[1] n **1** mark (✓) used to check off or indicate the correctness of something. **2** recurrent tapping sound, as of a clock. **3** Informal moment. ♦ v **4** mark with a tick. **5** make a ticking sound. **tick off** v **1** mark with a tick. **2** reprimand. **tick over** v **1** (of an engine) idle. **2** function smoothly. **ticktack** n Brit bookmakers' sign language.

tick[2] n tiny bloodsucking parasitic animal.

tick[3] n Informal credit or account.

ticket n **1** card or paper entitling the holder to admission, travel, etc. **2** label, esp. showing price. **3** official notification of a parking or traffic offence. **4** Chiefly US & NZ declared policy of a political party. ♦ v **-eting,** **-eted 5** attach or issue a ticket to.

ticking n strong material for mattress covers.

tickle v **1** touch or stroke (a person) to produce laughter. **2** itch or tingle. **3** please or amuse. ♦ n **4** tickling. **ticklish** adj **1** sensitive to tickling. **2** requiring care or tact.

tiddler n Informal very small fish.

tiddly[1] adj **-dlier, -dliest** tiny.

tiddly[2] adj **-dlier, -dliest** Informal slightly drunk.

tiddlywinks n game in which players try to flip small plastic discs into a cup.

tide n **1** rise and fall of the sea caused by the gravitational pull of the sun and moon. **2** current caused by this. **3** widespread feeling or tendency. **tidal** adj **tidal wave** large destructive wave. **tide over** v help (someone) temporarily.

tidings pl n news.

tidy adj **-dier, -diest 1** neat and orderly. **2** Brit, Aust & NZ informal considerable. ♦ v **-dying, -died 3** put in order. **tidily** adv **tidiness** n

tie v **tying, tied 1** fasten or be fastened with string, rope, etc. **2** make (a knot or bow) in (something). **3** restrict or limit. **4** score the same as another competitor. ♦ n **5** long narrow piece of material worn knotted round the neck. **6** bond or fastening. **7** drawn game or contest. **tied** adj Brit (of a cottage etc.) rented to the tenant only as long as he or she is employed by the owner.

tier n one of a set of rows placed one above and behind the other.

tiff n petty quarrel.

tiger n large yellow-and-black striped Asian cat. **tiger snake** n highly venomous brown-and-yellow Australian snake. **tigress** n **1** female tiger. **2** Informal fierce woman.

tight adj **1** stretched or drawn taut. **2** closely fitting. **3** secure or firm. **4**

cramped. **5** *Brit, Aust & NZ informal* not generous. **6** (of a match or game) very close. **7** *Informal* drunk. **tights** *pl n* one-piece clinging garment covering the body from the waist to the feet. **tightly** *adv* **tighten** *v* make or become tight or tighter. **tightrope** *n* rope stretched taut on which acrobats perform.

tiki *n NZ* small carving of a grotesque person worn as a pendant.

tikka *adj Indian cookery* marinated in spices and dry-roasted.

tilde *n* mark (˜) used in Spanish to indicate that the letter 'n' is to be pronounced in a particular way.

tile *n* **1** flat piece of ceramic, plastic, etc. used to cover a roof, floor, or wall. ♦ *v* **2** cover with tiles. **tiled** *adj* **tiling** *n* tiles collectively.

till¹ *conj, prep* until.

till² *v* cultivate (land). **tillage** *n*

till³ *n* drawer for money, usu. in a cash register.

tiller *n* lever to move a rudder of a boat.

tilt *v* **1** slant at an angle. **2** *Hist* compete against in a jousting contest. ♦ *n* **3** slope. **4** *Hist* jousting contest. **5** attempt. **at full tilt** at full speed or force.

timber *n* **1** wood as a building material. **2** trees collectively. **3** wooden beam in the frame of a house, boat, etc. **timbered** *adj* **timber line** limit beyond which trees will not grow.

timbre [**tam**-bra] *n* distinctive quality of sound of a voice or instrument.

time *n* **1** past, present, and future as a continuous whole. **2** specific point in time. **3** unspecified interval. **4** instance or occasion. **5** period with specific features. **6** musical tempo. **7** *Brit, Aust & NZ slang* imprisonment. ♦ *v* **8** note the time taken by. **9** choose a time for. **timeless** *adj* **1** unaffected by time. **2** eternal. **timely** *adj* at the appropriate

time. **time-honoured** *adj* sanctioned by custom. **time-lag** *n* period between cause and effect. **timepiece** *n* watch or clock. **timeserver** *n* person who changes his or her views to gain support or favour. **time sharing** system of part ownership of a holiday property for a specified period each year. **timetable** *n* plan showing the times when something takes place, the departure and arrival times of trains or buses, etc.

timid *adj* **1** easily frightened. **2** shy, not bold. **timidly** *adv* **timidity** *n* **timorous** *adj* timid.

timpani [**tim**-pan-ee] *pl n* set of kettledrums. **timpanist** *n*

tin *n* **1** soft metallic element. **2** (airtight) metal container. **tinned** *adj* (of food) preserved by being sealed in a tin. **tinny** *adj* (of sound) thin and metallic. **tinpot** *adj Informal* worthless or unimportant.

tincture *n* medicinal extract in a solution of alcohol.

tinder *n* dry easily-burning material used to start a fire. **tinderbox** *n*

tine *n* prong of a fork or antler.

ting *n* high metallic sound, as of a small bell.

tinge *n* **1** slight tint. **2** trace. ♦ *v* **tingeing, tinged 3** give a slight tint or trace to.

tingle *v, n* (feel) a prickling or stinging sensation.

tinker *n* **1** travelling mender of pots and pans. **2** *Scot & Irish* Gypsy. ♦ *v* **3** fiddle with (an engine etc.) in an attempt to repair it.

tinkle *v* **1** ring with a high tinny sound like a small bell. ♦ *n* **2** this sound or action.

tinsel *n* decorative metallic strips or threads.

tint *n* **1** (pale) shade of a colour. **2** dye for the hair. ♦ *v* **3** give a tint to.

tiny *adj* **tinier, tiniest** very small.

tip¹ *n* **1** narrow or pointed end of anything. **2** small piece forming an end. ◆ *v* **tipping, tipped 3** put a tip on.

tip² *n* **1** money given in return for service. **2** helpful hint or warning. **3** piece of inside information. ◆ *v* **tipping, tipped 4** give a tip to. **tipster** *n* person who sells tips about races.

tip³ *v* **tipping, tipped 1** tilt or overturn. **2** dump (rubbish). ◆ *n* **3** rubbish dump.

tipple *v* **1** drink alcohol habitually, esp. in small quantities. ◆ *n* **2** alcoholic drink. **tippler** *n*

tipsy *adj* **-sier, -siest** slightly drunk.

tiptoe *v* **-toeing, -toed** walk quietly with the heels off the ground.

tiptop *adj* of the highest quality or condition.

tirade *n* long angry speech.

tire *v* **1** reduce the energy of, as by exertion. **2** weary or bore. **tired** *adj* **1** exhausted. **2** hackneyed or stale. **tiring** *adj* **tireless** *adj* energetic and determined. **tiresome** *adj* boring and irritating.

tissue *n* **1** substance of an animal body or plant. **2** piece of thin soft paper used as a handkerchief etc. **3** interwoven series.

tit¹ *n* any of various small songbirds.

tit² *n Slang* female breast.

titanic *adj* huge or very important.

titanium *n Chem* strong light metallic element used to make alloys.

titbit *n* **1** tasty piece of food. **2** pleasing scrap of scandal.

tit-for-tat *adj* done in retaliation.

tithe *n* esp. formerly, one tenth of one's income or produce paid to the church as a tax.

Titian [**tish**-an] *adj* (of hair) reddish-gold.

titillate *v* excite or stimulate pleasurably. **titillating** *adj* **titillation** *n*

titivate *v* smarten up.

title *n* **1** name of a book, film, etc. **2** name signifying rank or position. **3** formal designation, such as Mrs. **4** *Sport* championship. **5** *Law* legal right of possession. **titled** *adj* aristocratic. **title deed** legal document of ownership.

titter *v* **1** laugh in a suppressed way. ◆ *n* **2** suppressed laugh.

tittle-tattle *n, v* gossip.

titular *adj* **1** in name only. **2** of a title.

tizzy *n, pl* **-zies** *Informal* confused or agitated state.

TNT *n* trinitrotoluene, a powerful explosive.

to *prep* **1** indicating movement towards, equality or comparison, etc., e.g. *walking to school; forty miles to the gallon.* **2** used to mark the indirect object or infinitive of a verb. ◆ *adv* **3** to a closed position, e.g. *pull the door to.* **to and fro** back and forth.

toad *n* animal like a large frog.

toad-in-the-hole *n Brit* sausages baked in batter.

toadstool *n* poisonous fungus like a mushroom.

toady *n, pl* **toadies 1** ingratiating person. ◆ *v* **toadying, toadied 2** be ingratiating.

toast¹ *n* **1** sliced bread browned by heat. ◆ *v* **2** brown (bread) by heat. **3** warm or be warmed. **toaster** *n* electrical device for toasting bread.

toast² *n* **1** tribute or proposal of health or success marked by people raising glasses and drinking together. **2** person or thing so honoured. ◆ *v* **3** drink a toast to.

tobacco *n, pl* **-cos, -coes** plant with large leaves dried for smoking.

tobacconist n person or shop selling tobacco, cigarettes, etc.

toboggan n 1 narrow sledge for sliding over snow. ♦ v **-ganing, -ganed 2** ride a toboggan.

toby jug n Chiefly Brit mug in the form of a stout seated man.

toccata [tok-**kah**-ta] n rapid piece of music for a keyboard instrument.

today n 1 this day. 2 the present age. ♦ adv 3 on this day. 4 nowadays.

toddler n child beginning to walk. **toddle** v walk with short unsteady steps.

toddy n, pl **-dies** sweetened drink of spirits and hot water.

to-do n, pl **-dos** Brit, Aust & NZ fuss or commotion.

toe n 1 digit of the foot. 2 part of a shoe or sock covering the toes. ♦ v **toeing, toed 3** touch or kick with the toe. **toe the line** conform.

toff n Brit slang well-dressed or upper-class person.

toffee n chewy sweet made of boiled sugar.

tofu n soft food made from soya-bean curd.

tog n unit for measuring the insulating power of duvets

toga [**toe**-ga] n garment worn by citizens of ancient Rome.

together adv 1 in company. 2 simultaneously. ♦ adj 3 Informal organized.

toggle n 1 small bar-shaped button inserted through a loop for fastening. 2 switch used to turn a machine or computer function on or off.

toil n 1 hard work. ♦ v 2 work hard. 3 progress with difficulty.

toilet n 1 (room with) a bowl connected to a drain for receiving and disposing of urine and faeces. 2 washing and dressing. **toiletry** n, pl

-ries object or cosmetic used to clean or groom oneself. **toilet water** light perfume.

token n 1 sign or symbol. 2 voucher exchangeable for goods of a specified value. 3 disc used as money in a slot machine. ♦ adj 4 nominal or slight. **tokenism** n policy of making only a token effort, esp. to comply with a law.

told v past of TELL.

tolerate v 1 allow to exist or happen. 2 endure patiently. **tolerable** adj 1 bearable. 2 Informal quite good. **tolerably** adv **tolerance** n 1 acceptance of other people's rights to their own opinions or actions. 2 ability to endure something. **tolerant** adj **tolerantly** adv **toleration** n

toll[1] v 1 ring (a bell) slowly and regularly, esp. to announce a death. ♦ n 2 tolling.

toll[2] n 1 charge for the use of a bridge or road. 2 total loss or damage from a disaster.

tom n male cat.

tomahawk n fighting axe of the Native Americans.

tomato n, pl **-toes** red fruit used in salads and as a vegetable.

tomb n 1 grave. 2 monument over a grave. **tombstone** n gravestone.

tombola n lottery with tickets drawn from a revolving drum.

tomboy n girl who acts or dresses like a boy.

tome n large heavy book.

tomfoolery n foolish behaviour.

Tommy gun n light sub-machine-gun.

tomorrow adv, n 1 (on) the day after today. 2 (in) the future.

tom-tom n drum beaten with the hands.

ton n unit of weight equal to 2240 pounds or 1016 kilograms (**long ton**) or, in the US, 2000 pounds or 907 kilograms (**short ton**). **tonnage** *n* weight capacity of a ship.

tone *n* **1** sound with reference to its pitch, volume, etc. **2** *US* musical note. **3** *Music* (also **whole tone**) interval of two semitones. **4** quality of a sound or colour. **5** general character. **6** healthy bodily condition. ♦ *v* **7** harmonize (with). **8** give tone to. **tonal** *adj Music* written in a key. **tonality** *n* **toneless** *adj* **tone-deaf** *adj* unable to perceive subtle differences in pitch. **tone down** *v* make or become more moderate.

tongs *pl n* large pincers for grasping and lifting.

tongue *n* **1** muscular organ in the mouth, used in speaking and tasting. **2** language. **3** animal tongue as food. **4** thin projecting strip. **5** flap of leather on a shoe.

tonic *n* **1** medicine to improve body tone. **2** *adj* **3** invigorating. **tonic water** mineral water containing quinine.

tonight *adv, n* (in or during) the night or evening of this day.

tonne [**tunn**] *n* unit of weight equal to 1000 kilograms.

tonsil *n* small gland in the throat. **tonsillectomy** *n* surgical removal of the tonsils. **tonsillitis** *n* inflammation of the tonsils.

tonsure *n* **1** shaving of all or the top of the head as a religious or monastic practice. **2** shaved part of the head. **tonsured** *adj*

too *adv* **1** also, as well. **2** to excess. **3** extremely.

took *v* past tense of TAKE.

tool *n* **1** implement used by hand. **2** person used by another to perform unpleasant or dishonourable tasks.

toot *n* **1** short hooting sound. ♦ *v* **2** (cause to) make such a sound.

tooth *n, pl* **teeth 1** bonelike projection in the jaws of most vertebrates for biting and chewing. **2** toothlike prong or point. **sweet tooth** strong liking for sweet food. **toothless** *adj* **toothpaste** *n* paste used to clean the teeth. **toothpick** *n* small stick for removing scraps of food from between the teeth.

top¹ *n* **1** highest point or part. **2** lid or cap. **3** highest rank. **4** garment for the upper part of the body. ♦ *adj* **5** at or of the top. ♦ *v* **topping, topped 6** form a top on. **7** be at the top of. **8** exceed or surpass. **topping** *n* sauce or garnish for food. **topless** *adj* (of a costume or woman) with no covering for the breasts. **topmost** *adj* highest or best. **top brass** most important officers or leaders. **top hat** man's tall cylindrical hat. **top-heavy** *adj* unstable through being overloaded at the top. **top-notch** *adj* excellent, first-class. **topsoil** *n* surface layer of soil.

top² *n* toy which spins on a pointed base.

topaz [**toe**-pazz] *n* semiprecious stone in various colours.

topee, topi [**toe**-pee] *n* lightweight hat worn in tropical countries.

topiary [**tope**-yar-ee] *n* art of trimming trees and bushes into decorative shapes.

topic *n* subject of a conversation, book, etc. **topical** *adj* relating to current events. **topicality** *n*

topography *n, pl* **-phies** (science of describing) the surface features of a place. **topographer** *n* **topographical** *adj*

topology *n* geometry of the properties of a shape which are unaffected by continuous distortion. **topological** *adj*

topple *v* **1** (cause to) fall over. **2** overthrow (a government etc.).

topsy-turvy *adj* **1** upside down. **2** in

confusion.

toque [**toke**] *n* small round hat.

tor *n* high rocky hill.

Torah *n* body of traditional Jewish teaching.

torch *n* **1** small portable battery-powered lamp. **2** wooden shaft dipped in wax and set alight. ♦ *v* **3** *Informal* deliberately set (a building) on fire.

tore *v* past tense of TEAR².

toreador [**torr**-ee-a-dor] *n* bullfighter.

torment *v* **1** cause (someone) great suffering. **2** tease cruelly. ♦ *n* **3** great suffering. **4** source of suffering. **tormentor** *n*

torn *v* past participle of TEAR².

tornado *n, pl* **-dos, -does** violent whirlwind.

torpedo *n, pl* **-does** **1** self-propelled underwater missile. ♦ *v* **-doing, -doed** **2** attack or destroy with or as if with torpedoes.

torpid *adj* sluggish and inactive. **torpor** *n* torpid state.

torque [**tork**] *n* **1** force causing rotation. **2** Celtic necklace or armband of twisted metal.

torrent *n* **1** rushing stream. **2** rapid flow of questions, abuse, etc. **torrential** *adj* (of rain) very heavy.

torrid *adj* **1** very hot and dry. **2** highly emotional.

torsion *n* twisting of a part by equal forces being applied at both ends but in opposite directions.

torso *n, pl* **-sos** **1** trunk of the human body. **2** statue of a nude human trunk.

tort *n* Law civil wrong or injury for which damages may be claimed.

tortilla *n* thin Mexican pancake.

tortoise *n* slow-moving land reptile with a dome-shaped shell.
tortoiseshell *n* **1** mottled brown shell of a turtle, used for making

ornaments. ♦ *adj* **2** having brown, orange, and black markings.

tortuous *adj* **1** winding or twisting. **2** not straightforward.

torture *v* **1** cause (someone) severe pain or mental anguish. ♦ *n* **2** severe physical or mental pain. **3** torturing. **torturer** *n*

Tory *n, pl* **Tories** **1** member of the Conservative Party in Great Britain or Canada. ♦ *adj* **2** of Tories. **Toryism** *n*

toss *v* **1** throw lightly. **2** fling or be flung about. **3** coat (food) by gentle stirring or mixing. **4** (of a horse) throw (its rider). **5** throw up (a coin) to decide between alternatives by guessing which side will land uppermost. ♦ *n* **6** tossing. **toss up** *v* toss a coin. **toss-up** *n* even chance or risk.

tot¹ *n* **1** small child. **2** small drink of spirits.

tot² *v* **totting, totted. tot up** add (numbers) together.

total *n* **1** whole, esp. a sum of parts. ♦ *adj* **2** complete. **3** of or being a total. ♦ *v* **-talling, -talled** **4** amount to. **5** add up. **totally** *adv* **totality** *n*

totalitarian *adj* of a dictatorial one-party government. **totalitarianism** *n*

tote¹ *v* carry (a gun etc.).

tote² *n* short for TOTALIZATOR.

totem *n* tribal badge or emblem. **totem pole** post carved or painted with totems by Native Americans.

totter *v* **1** move unsteadily. **2** be about to fall.

toucan *n* tropical American bird with a large bill.

touch *v* **1** come into contact with. **2** tap, feel, or stroke. **3** affect. **4** move emotionally. **5** eat or drink. **6** equal or match. **7** *Brit, Aust & NZ slang* ask for money. ♦ *n* **8** sense by which an object's qualities are perceived when they come into contact with part of the body. **9** gentle tap, push, or caress. **10** small amount. **11** characteristic style. **12** detail. ♦ *adj* **13** of a non-contact version of particular sport, e.g. *touch rugby.* **touch and go** risky or critical. **touched** *adj* **1** emotionally moved. **2** slightly mad. **touching** *adj* emotionally moving. **touchy** *adj* easily offended. **touch down** *v* (of an aircraft) land. **touchline** *n* side line of the pitch in some games. **touch on** *v* refer to in passing. **touch-type** *v* type without looking at the keyboard.

touché [**too**-shay] *interj* acknowledgment of the striking home of a remark or witty reply.

touchstone *n* standard by which a judgment is made.

tough *adj* **1** strong or resilient. **2** difficult to chew or cut. **3** firm and determined. **4** rough and violent. **5** difficult. **6** *Informal* unlucky or unfair. ♦ *n* **7** *Informal* rough violent person. **toughness** *n* **toughen** *v* make or become tough or tougher.

toupee [**too**-pay] *n* small wig.

tour *n* **1** journey visiting places of interest along the way. **2** trip to perform or play in different places. ♦ *v* **3** make a tour (of). **tourism** *n* tourist travel as an industry. **tourist** *n* person travelling for pleasure. **touristy** *adj Informal, often derogatory* full of tourists or tourist attractions.

tour de force *n, pl* **tours de force** *French* brilliant stroke or achievement.

tournament *n* **1** sporting competition with several stages to decide the overall winner. **2** *Hist* contest between knights on horseback.

tourniquet [**tour**-nick-kay] *n* something twisted round a limb to stop bleeding.

tousled *adj* ruffled and untidy.

tout [rhymes with **shout**] *v* **1** seek

business in a persistent manner. **2** recommend (a person or thing). ♦ *n* **3** person who sells tickets for a popular event at inflated prices.

tow¹ *v* **1** drag, esp. by means of a rope. ♦ *n* **2** towing. **in tow** following closely behind. **on tow** being towed. **towbar** *n* metal bar on a car for towing vehicles. **towpath** *n* path beside a canal or river, originally for horses towing boats.

tow² *n* fibre of hemp or flax.

towards, toward *prep* **1** in the direction of. **2** with regard to. **3** as a contribution to.

towel *n* cloth for drying things. **towelling** *n* material used for making towels.

tower *n* tall structure, often forming part of a larger building. **tower of strength** person who supports or comforts. **tower over** *v* be much taller than.

town *n* **1** group of buildings larger than a village. **2** central part of this. **3** people of a town. **township** *n* **1** small town. **2** (in S Africa) urban settlement of Black or Coloured people. **town hall** large building used for council meetings, concerts, etc.

toxaemia [tox-**seem**-ya] *n* **1** blood poisoning. **2** high blood pressure in pregnancy.

toxic *adj* **1** poisonous. **2** caused by poison. **toxicity** *n* **toxicology** *n* study of poisons. **toxin** *n* poison of bacterial origin.

toy *n* **1** something designed to be played with. ♦ *adj* **2** (of a dog) of a variety much smaller than is normal for that breed. **toy with** *v* play or fiddle with.

toy-toy *S Afr* ♦ *n* **1** dance of political protest. ♦ *v* **2** perform this dance.

trace *v* **1** track down and find. **2** follow the course of. **3** copy exactly by drawing on a thin sheet of transparent paper set on top of the original. ♦ *n* **4** track left by something. **5** minute quantity. **6** indication. **traceable** *adj* **tracer** *n* projectile which leaves a visible trail. **tracery** *n* pattern of interlacing lines. **tracing** *n* traced copy. **trace element** chemical element occurring in very small amounts in soil etc.

traces *pl n* strap by which a horse pulls a vehicle. **kick over the traces** escape or defy control.

trachea [track-**kee**-a] *n*, *pl* **tracheae** windpipe. **tracheotomy** [track-ee-**ot**-a-mee] *n* surgical incision into the trachea.

track *n* **1** rough road or path. **2** mark or trail left by the passage of anything. **3** railway line. **4** course for racing. **5** separate section on a record, tape, or CD. **6** course of action or thought. **7** endless band round the wheels of a tank, bulldozer, etc. ♦ *v* **8** follow the trail or path of. **track down** *v* hunt for and find. **track event** athletic sport held on a running track. **track record** past accomplishments of a person or organization. **tracksuit** *n* warm loose-fitting suit worn by athletes etc., esp. during training.

tract¹ *n* **1** wide area. **2** *Anat* system of organs with a particular function.

tract² *n* pamphlet, esp. a religious one.

tractable *adj* easy to manage or control.

traction *n* **1** pulling, esp. by engine power. **2** *Med* application of a steady pull on an injured limb by weights and pulleys. **3** grip of the wheels of a vehicle on the ground. **traction engine** old-fashioned steam-powered vehicle for pulling heavy loads.

tractor *n* motor vehicle with large rear wheels for pulling farm machinery.

trade *n* **1** buying, selling, or exchange of goods. **2** person's job or craft. **3** (people engaged in) a particular industry or business. ♦ *v* **4** buy and sell. **5** exchange. **6** engage in trade. **trader** *n* **trading** *n* **trade-in** *n* used article given in part payment for a new one. **trademark** *n* (legally registered) name or symbol used by a firm to distinguish its goods. **trade-off** *n* exchange made as a compromise. **tradesman** *n* **1** skilled worker. **2** shopkeeper. **trade union** society of workers formed to protect their interests. **trade wind** wind blowing steadily towards the equator.

tradition *n* **1** body of beliefs, customs, etc. handed down from generation to generation. **2** custom or practice of long standing. **traditional** *adj* **traditionally** *adv*

traduce *v* slander.

traffic *n* **1** vehicles coming and going on a road. **2** (illicit) trade. ♦ *v* **-ficking, -ficked 3** trade, usu. illicitly. **trafficker** *n* **traffic lights** set of coloured lights at a junction to control the traffic flow. **traffic warden** *Brit* person employed to control the movement and parking of traffic.

tragedy *n*, *pl* **-dies 1** shocking or sad event. **2** serious play, film, etc. in which the hero is destroyed by a personal failing in adverse circumstances. **tragedian** [traj-**jee**-dee-an], **tragedienne** [traj-jee-dee-**enn**] *n* person who acts in or writes tragedies. **tragic** *adj* of or like a tragedy. **tragically** *adv* **tragicomedy** *n* play with both tragic and comic elements.

trail *n* **1** path, track, or road. **2** tracks left by a person, animal, or object. ♦ *v* **3** drag along the ground. **4** lag behind. **5** follow the tracks of.

trailer *n* **1** vehicle designed to be towed by another vehicle. **2** extract from a film or programme used to advertise it.

train v **1** instruct in a skill. **2** learn the skills needed to do a particular job or activity. **3** prepare for a sports event etc. **4** aim (a gun etc.). **5** cause (an animal) to perform or (a plant) to grow in a particular way. ♦ n **6** line of railway coaches or wagons drawn by an engine. **7** sequence or series. **8** long trailing back section of a dress. **trainer** n **1** person who trains an athlete or sportsman. **2** sports shoe. **trainee** n person being trained.

traipse v Informal walk wearily.

trait n characteristic feature.

traitor n person guilty of treason or treachery. **traitorous** adj

trajectory n, pl **-ries** line of flight, esp. of a projectile.

tram n public transport vehicle powered by an overhead wire and running on rails laid in the road. **tramlines** pl n track for trams.

tramp v **1** travel on foot, hike. **2** walk heavily. ♦ n **3** homeless person who travels on foot. **4** hike. **5** sound of tramping. **6** cargo ship available for hire. **7** US, Aust & NZ slang promiscuous woman.

trample v tread on and crush.

trampoline n **1** tough canvas sheet attached to a frame by springs, used by acrobats etc. ♦ v **2** bounce on a trampoline.

trance n unconscious or dazed state.

tranche n portion of something large, esp. a sum of money.

tranquil adj calm and quiet. **tranquilly** adv **tranquillity** n

tranquillize v make calm. **tranquillizer** n drug which reduces anxiety or tension.

trans- prefix across, through, or beyond.

transact v conduct or negotiate (a

business deal).

transaction n business deal transacted.

transatlantic adj on, from, or to the other side of the Atlantic.

transceiver n transmitter and receiver of radio or electronic signals.

transcend v **1** rise above. **2** be superior to. **transcendence** n **transcendent** adj **transcendental** adj **1** based on intuition rather than experience. **2** supernatural or mystical. **transcendentalism** n

transcribe v **1** write down (something said). **2** record for a later broadcast. **3** arrange (music) for a different instrument. **transcript** n copy.

transducer n device that converts one form of energy to another.

transept n either of the two shorter wings of a cross-shaped church.

transfer v **-ferring, -ferred 1** move or send from one person or place to another. ♦ n **2** transferring. **3** design which can be transferred from one surface to another. **transferable** adj **transference** n transferring. **transfer station** NZ depot where rubbish is sorted for recycling.

transfigure v change in appearance. **transfiguration** n

transfix v **1** astound or stun. **2** pierce through.

transform v change the shape or character of. **transformation** n **transformer** n device for changing the voltage of an alternating current.

transfusion n injection of blood into the blood vessels of a patient. **transfuse** v **1** give a transfusion to. **2** permeate or infuse.

transgress v break (a moral law). **transgression** n **transgressor** n

transient adj lasting only for a short time. **transience** n

transistor n **1** semiconducting device

used to amplify electric currents. **2** portable radio using transistors.

transit n movement from one place to another. **transition** n change from one state to another. **transitional** adj **transitive** adj Grammar (of a verb) requiring a direct object. **transitory** adj not lasting long.

translate v turn from one language into another. **translation** n **translator** n

transliterate v convert to the letters of a different alphabet. **transliteration** n

translucent adj letting light pass through, but not transparent. **translucency, translucence** n

transmigrate v (of a soul) pass into another body. **transmigration** n

transmit v -mitting, -mitted **1** pass (something) from one person or place to another. **2** send out (signals) by radio waves. **3** broadcast (a radio or television programme). **transmission** n **1** transmitting. **2** shafts and gears through which power passes from a vehicle's engine to its wheels. **transmittable** adj **transmitter** n

transmogrify v -fying, -fied Informal change completely.

transmute v change the form or nature of. **transmutation** n

transom n **1** horizontal bar across a window. **2** bar separating a door from the window over it.

transparent adj **1** able to be seen through, clear. **2** easily understood or recognized. **transparently** adv **transparency** n **1** transparent quality. **2** colour photograph on transparent film that can be viewed by means of a projector.

transpire v **1** become known. **2** Informal happen, occur. **3** give off water vapour through pores. **transpiration** n

transplant v **1** transfer (an organ or tissue) surgically from one part or body to another. **2** remove and transfer (a plant) to another place. ♦ n **3** surgical transplanting. **4** thing transplanted. **transplantation** n

transport v **1** convey from one place to another. **2** Hist exile (a criminal) to a penal colony. **3** enrapture. ♦ n **4** business or system of transporting. **5** vehicle used in transport. **6** ecstasy or rapture. **transportation** n **transporter** n large goods vehicle.

transpose v **1** interchange two things. **2** put (music) into a different key. **transposition** n

transsexual, transexual n person of one sex who believes his or her true identity is of the opposite sex.

transubstantiation n Christianity doctrine that the bread and wine consecrated in Communion changes into the substance of Christ's body and blood.

transuranic [tranz-yoor-**ran**-ik] adj (of an element) having an atomic number greater than that of uranium.

transverse adj crossing from side to side.

transvestite n person who seeks sexual pleasure by wearing the clothes of the opposite sex. **transvestism** n

trap n **1** device for catching animals. **2** plan for tricking or catching a person. **3** bend in a pipe containing liquid to prevent the escape of gas. **4** stall in which greyhounds are enclosed before a race. **5** two-wheeled carriage. **6** Brit, Aust & NZ slang mouth. ♦ v **trapping, trapped 7** catch. **8** trick. **trapper** n person who traps animals for their fur. **trapdoor** n door in floor or roof. **trap-door spider** spider that builds a silk-lined hole in the ground closed by a hinged door of earth and silk.

trapeze n horizontal bar suspended

from two ropes, used by circus acrobats.

trapezium n, pl **-ziums, -zia** quadrilateral with two parallel sides of unequal length. **trapezoid** [**trap**-piz-zoid] n **1** quadrilateral with no sides parallel. **2** Chiefly US trapezium.

trappings pl n accessories that symbolize an office or position.

Trappist n member of an order of Christian monks who observe strict silence.

trash n **1** anything worthless. **2** US & S Afr rubbish. **trashy** adj

trauma [**traw**-ma] n **1** emotional shock. **2** injury or wound. **traumatic** adj **traumatize** v

travail n Lit labour or toil.

travel v **-elling, -elled 1** go from one place to another, through an area, or for a specified distance. ♦ n **2** travelling, esp. as a tourist. ♦ pl **3** (account of) travelling. **traveller** n **travelogue** n film or talk about someone's travels.

traverse v move over or back and forth over.

travesty n, pl **-ties** grotesque imitation or mockery.

trawl n **1** net dragged at deep levels behind a fishing boat. ♦ v **2** fish with such a net.

trawler n trawling boat.

tray n **1** flat board, usu. with a rim, for carrying things. **2** open receptacle for office correspondence.

treachery n, pl **-eries** wilful betrayal. **treacherous** adj **1** disloyal. **2** unreliable or dangerous. **treacherously** adv

treacle n thick dark syrup produced when sugar is refined. **treacly** adj

tread v **treading, trod, trodden** or **trod 1** set one's foot on. **2** crush by

walking on. ♦ n **3** way of walking or dancing. **4** upper surface of a step. **5** part of a tyre or shoe that touches the ground. **treadmill** n **1** Hist cylinder turned by treading on steps projecting from it. **2** dreary routine.

treadle [**tred**-dl] n lever worked by the foot to turn a wheel.

treason n **1** betrayal of one's sovereign or country. **2** treachery or disloyalty. **treasonable** adj

treasure n **1** collection of wealth, esp. gold or jewels. **2** valued person or thing. ♦ v **3** prize or cherish. **treasury** n **1** storage place for treasure. **2** (T-) government department in charge of finance. **treasure-trove** n treasure found with no evidence of ownership.

treasurer n official in charge of funds.

treat v **1** deal with or regard in a certain manner. **2** give medical treatment to. **3** subject to a chemical or industrial process. **4** provide (someone) with (something) as a treat. ♦ n **5** pleasure, entertainment, etc. given or paid for by someone else. **treatment** n **1** medical care. **2** way of treating a person or thing.

treatise [**treat**-izz] n formal piece of writing on a particular subject.

treaty n, pl **-ties** signed contract between states.

treble adj **1** triple. **2** Music high-pitched. ♦ n **3** (singer with or part for) a soprano voice. ♦ v **4** increase three times. **trebly** adv

tree n large perennial plant with a woody trunk. **treeless** adj **tree kangaroo** tree-living kangaroo of New Guinea and N Australia. **tree surgery** repair of damaged trees. **tree surgeon**

trefoil [**tref**-foil] n **1** plant, such as clover, with a three-lobed leaf. **2** carved ornament like this.

trek n **1** long difficult journey, esp. on foot. **2** S Afr migration by ox wagon.

♦ v **trekking, trekked 3** make such a journey.

trellis n framework of horizontal and vertical strips of wood.

tremble v **1** shake or quiver. **2** feel fear or anxiety. ♦ n **3** trembling. **trembling** adj

tremendous adj **1** huge. **2** Informal great in quality or amount. **tremendously** adv

tremolo n, pl **-los** Music quivering effect in singing or playing.

tremor n **1** involuntary shaking. **2** minor earthquake.

tremulous adj trembling, as from fear or excitement.

trench n long narrow ditch, esp. one used as a shelter in war. **trench coat** double-breasted waterproof coat.

trenchant adj **1** incisive. **2** effective.

trencher n Hist wooden plate for serving food. **trencherman** n hearty eater.

trend n **1** general tendency or direction. **2** fashion. **trendy** adj, n Informal consciously fashionable (person). **trendiness** n

trepidation n fear or anxiety.

trespass v **1** go onto another's property without permission. ♦ n **2** trespassing. **3** Old-fashioned sin or wrongdoing. **trespasser** n **trespass on** v take unfair advantage of (someone's friendship, patience, etc.).

tresses pl n long flowing hair.

trestle n board fixed on pairs of spreading legs, used as a support.

trevally n, pl **-lies** Aust & NZ any of various food and game fishes.

trews pl n close-fitting tartan trousers.

tri- combining form three.

triad n **1** group of three. **2** (T-) Chinese criminal secret society.

trial n **1** Law investigation of a case before a judge. **2** trying or testing. **3**

thing or person straining endurance or patience. ♦ pl **4** sporting competition for individuals.

triangle n **1** geometric figure with three sides. **2** triangular percussion instrument. **3** situation involving three people. **triangular** adj

tribe n group of clans or families believed to have a common ancestor. **tribal** adj **tribalism** n loyalty to a tribe.

tribulation n a cause or state of suffering or distress.

tribunal n **1** board appointed to inquire into a specific matter. **2** lawcourt.

tribune n people's representative, esp. in ancient Rome.

tributary n, pl **-taries 1** stream or river flowing into a larger one. ♦ adj **2** (of a stream or river) flowing into a larger one.

tribute n **1** sign of respect or admiration. **2** tax paid by one state to another.

trice n **in a trice** instantly.

triceps n muscle at the back of the upper arm.

trichology [trick-**ol**-a-jee] n study and treatment of hair and its diseases. **trichologist** n

trick n **1** deceitful or cunning action or plan. **2** joke or prank. **3** feat of skill or cunning. **4** mannerism. **5** cards played in one round. ♦ v **6** cheat or deceive. **trickery** n **trickster** n **tricky** adj **1** difficult, needing careful handling. **2** crafty.

trickle v **1** (cause to) flow in a thin stream or drops. **2** move gradually. ♦ n **3** gradual flow.

tricolour [**trick**-kol-lor] n three-coloured striped flag.

tricycle n three-wheeled cycle.

trident n three-pronged spear.

triennial *adj* happening every three years.

trifle *n* **1** insignificant thing or amount. **2** dessert of sponge cake, fruit, custard, and cream. **trifling** *adj* insignificant. **trifle with** *v* toy with.

trigger *n* **1** small lever releasing a catch on a gun or machine. **2** action that sets off a course of events. ♦ *v* **3** (usu. foll. by *off*) set (an action or process) in motion. **trigger-happy** *adj* too quick to use guns.

trigonometry *n* branch of mathematics dealing with relations of the sides and angles of triangles.

trike *n* Informal tricycle.

trilateral *adj* having three sides.

trilby *n, pl* **-bies** man's soft felt hat.

trill *n* **1** Music rapid alternation between two notes. **2** shrill warbling sound made by some birds. ♦ *v* **3** play or sing a trill.

trillion *n* **1** one million million, 10¹². **2** (formerly) one million million million, 10¹⁸.

trilobite [**trile**-oh-bite] *n* small prehistoric sea animal.

trilogy *n, pl* **-gies** series of three related books, plays, etc.

trim *adj* **trimmer, trimmest 1** neat and smart. **2** slender. ♦ *v* **trimming, trimmed 3** cut or prune into good shape. **4** decorate with lace, ribbons, etc. **5** adjust the balance of (a ship or aircraft) by shifting the cargo etc. **6** *n* **7** decoration. **8** upholstery and decorative facings in a car. **9** trim state. **10** haircut that neatens the existing style. **trimming** *n* **1** decoration. ♦ *pl* **2** usual accompaniments.

trimaran [**trime**-a-ran] *n* three-hulled boat.

trinitrotoluene *n* full name for TNT.

trinity *n, pl* **-ties 1** group of three. **2** (T-) Christianity union of three persons, Father, Son, and Holy Spirit, in one God.

trinket *n* small or worthless ornament or piece of jewellery.

trio *n, pl* **trios 1** group of three. **2** piece of music for three performers.

trip *n* **1** journey to a place and back, esp. for pleasure. **2** stumble. **3** Informal hallucinogenic drug experience. **4** switch on a mechanism. ♦ *v* **tripping, tripped 5** (cause to) stumble. **6** (often foll. by *up*) catch (someone) in a mistake. **7** move or tread lightly. **8** Informal experience the hallucinogenic effects of a drug. **tripper** *n* tourist.

tripe *n* **1** stomach of a cow used as food. **2** Brit, Aust & NZ informal nonsense.

triple *adj* **1** having three parts. **2** three times as great or as many. ♦ *v* **3** increase three times. **triplet** *n* one of three babies born at one birth. **triple jump** athletic event in which competitors make a hop, a step, and a jump as a continuous movement.

triplicate *adj* triple. **in triplicate** in three copies.

tripod [**tripe**-pod] *n* three-legged stand, stool, etc.

tripos [**tripe**-poss] *n* final examinations for an honours degree at Cambridge University.

triptych [**trip**-tick] *n* painting or carving on three hinged panels, often forming an altarpiece.

trite *adj* (of a remark or idea) commonplace and unoriginal.

tritium *n* radioactive isotope of hydrogen.

triumph *n* **1** (happiness caused by) victory or success. ♦ *v* **2** be victorious or successful. **3** rejoice over a victory. **triumphal** *adj* celebrating a triumph. **triumphant** *adj* feeling or showing triumph.

triumvirate [try-**umm**-vir-rit] *n* group

of three people in joint control.

trivet [**triv**-vit] *n* metal stand for a pot or kettle.

trivial *adj* of little importance. **trivially** *adv* **trivia** *pl n* trivial things or details. **triviality** *n* **trivialize** *v* make (something) seem less important or complex than it is.

trod *v* past tense and a past participle of TREAD.

trodden *v* a past participle of TREAD.

troglodyte *n* cave dweller.

troika *n* **1** Russian vehicle drawn by three horses abreast. **2** group of three people in authority.

troll *n* giant or dwarf in Scandinavian folklore.

trolley *n* **1** small wheeled table for food and drink. **2** wheeled cart for moving goods. **trolley bus** bus powered by electricity from an overhead wire but not running on rails.

trollop *n* Old-fashioned promiscuous or slovenly woman.

trombone *n* brass musical instrument with a sliding tube. **trombonist** *n*

troop *n* **1** large group. **2** artillery or cavalry unit. **3** Scout company. ◆ *pl* **4** soldiers. ◆ *v* **5** move in a crowd **trooper** *n* cavalry soldier.

trope *n* figure of speech.

trophy *n, pl* **-phies 1** cup, shield, etc. given as a prize. **2** memento of success.

tropic *n* **1** either of two lines of latitude at 23½°N (**tropic of Cancer**) or 23½°S (**tropic of Capricorn**). ◆ *pl* **2** part of the earth's surface between these lines.

tropical *adj* **1** of or in the tropics. **2** (of climate) very hot.

trot *v* **trotting, trotted 1** (of a horse) move at a medium pace, lifting the feet in diagonal pairs. **2** (of a person) move at a steady brisk pace. ◆ *n* **3** trotting. **trotter** *n* pig's foot. **trot**

out *v* repeat (old ideas etc.) without fresh thought.

troth [rhymes with **growth**] *n Obs* pledge of devotion, esp. a betrothal.

troubadour [**troo**-bad-oor] *n* medieval travelling poet and singer.

trouble *n* **1** (cause of) distress or anxiety. **2** disease or malfunctioning. **3** state of disorder or unrest. **4** care or effort. ◆ *v* **5** (cause to) worry. **6** exert oneself. **7** cause inconvenience to. **troubled** *adj* **troublesome** *adj* **troubleshooter** *n* person employed to locate and deal with faults or problems.

trough [**troff**] *n* **1** long open container, esp. for animals' food or water. **2** narrow channel between two waves or ridges. **3** *Meteorol* area of low pressure.

trounce *v* defeat utterly.

troupe [**troop**] *n* company of performers. **trouper** *n*

trousers *pl n* two-legged outer garment with legs reaching usu. to the ankles. **trouser** *adj* of trousers.

trousseau [**troo**-so] *n, pl* **-seaux, -seaus** bride's collection of clothing etc. for her marriage.

trout *n* game fish related to the salmon.

trowel *n* hand tool with a wide blade for spreading mortar, lifting plants, etc.

troy weight, troy *n* system of weights used for gold, silver, and jewels.

truant *n* pupil who stays away from school without permission. **play truant** stay away from school without permission. **truancy** *n*

truce *n* temporary agreement to stop fighting.

truck¹ *n* **1** railway goods wagon. **2** large vehicle for transporting loads by road. **trucker** *n* truck driver.

truck² *n* **have no truck with** refuse to be involved with.

truculent [**truck**-yew-lent] *adj* aggressively defiant. **truculence** *n*

trudge *v* 1 walk heavily or wearily. ♦ *n* 2 long tiring walk.

true *adj* **truer, truest** 1 in accordance with facts. 2 genuine. 3 faithful. 4 exact. **truly** *adv* **truism** *n* self-evident truth. **truth** *n* 1 state of being true. 2 something true. **truthful** *adj* 1 honest. 2 exact. **truthfully** *adv*

truffle *n* 1 edible underground fungus. 2 sweet flavoured with chocolate.

trug *n Brit* long shallow basket used by gardeners.

trump¹ *n, adj* 1 (card) of the suit outranking the others. ♦ *v* 2 play a trump card on (another card). ♦ *pl n* 3 suit outranking the others. **turn up trumps** achieve an unexpected success. **trumped up** invented or concocted.

trump² *n Lit* (sound of) a trumpet.

trumpet *n* 1 valved brass instrument with a flared tube. ♦ *v* **-peting, -peted** 2 proclaim loudly. 3 (of an elephant) cry loudly. **trumpeter** *n*

truncate *v* cut short.

truncheon *n* club carried by a policeman.

trundle *v* move heavily on wheels.

trunk *n* 1 main stem of a tree. 2 large case or box for clothes etc. 3 person's body excluding the head and limbs. 4 elephant's long nose. 5 *US* car boot. ♦ *pl* 6 man's swimming shorts. **trunk call** *Chiefly Brit* long-distance telephone call. **trunk road** main road.

truss *v* 1 tie or bind up. ♦ *n* 2 device for holding a hernia in place. 3 framework supporting a roof, bridge, etc.

trust *v* 1 believe in and rely on. 2 consign to someone's care. 3 expect or hope. ♦ *n* 4 confidence in the truth, reliability, etc. of a person or thing. 5 obligation arising from responsibility. 6 arrangement in which one person administers property, money, etc. on another's behalf. 7 property held for another. 8 *Brit* self-governing hospital or group of hospitals within the National Health Service. 9 group of companies joined to control a market. **trustee** *n* person holding property on another's behalf. **trustful, trusting** *adj* inclined to trust others. **trustworthy** *adj* reliable or honest. **trusty** *adj* faithful or reliable.

truth *n* see TRUE.

try *v* **trying, tried** 1 make an effort or attempt. 2 test or sample. 3 put strain on, e.g. *he tries my patience.* 4 investigate (a case). 5 examine (a person) in a lawcourt. ♦ *n, pl* **tries** 6 attempt or effort. 7 *Rugby* score gained by touching the ball down over the opponent's goal line. **try it on** *Informal* try to deceive or fool someone. **trying** *adj Informal* difficult or annoying.

tryst *n* arrangement to meet.

tsar, czar [**zahr**] *n Hist* Russian emperor.

tsetse fly [**tset**-see] *n* bloodsucking African fly whose bite transmits disease, esp. sleeping sickness.

T-shirt *n* short-sleeved casual shirt or top.

tsp. teaspoon.

T-square *n* T-shaped ruler.

tsunami *n, pl* **-mis, -mi** tidal wave, usu. caused by an earthquake under the sea.

TT teetotal.

tuatara *n* large lizard-like New Zealand reptile.

tub *n* 1 open, usu. round container. 2 bath. **tubby** *adj* (of a person) short and fat.

tuba [**tube**-a] *n* valved low-pitched brass instrument.

tube *n* 1 hollow cylinder. 2 flexible cylinder with a cap to hold pastes.

the tube underground railway, esp. the one in London. **tubing** n **1** length of tube. **2** system of tubes. **tubular** [**tube**-yew-lar] adj of or shaped like a tube.

tuber [**tube**-er] n fleshy underground root of a plant such as a potato. **tuberous** adj

tubercle [**tube**-er-kl] n small rounded swelling.

tuberculosis [tube-berk-yew-**lohss**-iss] n infectious disease causing tubercles, esp. in the lungs. **tubercular** adj **tuberculin** n extract from a bacillus used to test for tuberculosis.

TUC (in Britain and S Africa) Trades Union Congress.

tuck v **1** push or fold into a small space. **2** stitch in folds. ♦ n **3** stitched fold. **4** Brit informal food. **tuck away** v eat (a large amount of food).

tucker n Aust & NZ informal food.

Tudor adj of the English royal house ruling from 1485–1603.

Tuesday n third day of the week.

tufa [**tew**-fa] n porous rock formed as a deposit from springs.

tuffet n small mound or seat.

tuft n bunch of feathers, grass, hair, etc. held or growing together at the base.

tug v **tugging, tugged 1** pull hard. ♦ n **2** hard pull. **3** (also **tugboat**) small ship used to tow other vessels. **tug of war** contest in which two teams pull against one another on a rope.

tuition n instruction, esp. received individually or in a small group.

tulip n plant with bright cup-shaped flowers.

tulle [**tewl**] n fine net fabric of silk etc.

tumble v **1** (cause to) fall, esp. awkwardly or violently. **2** roll or twist, esp. in play. **3** rumple. ♦ n **4** fall. **5** somersault. **tumbler** n **1** stemless drinking glass. **2** acrobat. **3** spring catch in a lock. **tumbledown** adj dilapidated. **tumble dryer, drier** machine that dries laundry by rotating it in warm air. **tumble to** v Informal realize, understand.

tumbril, tumbrel n farm cart used during the French Revolution to take prisoners to the guillotine.

tumescent [tew-**mess**-ent] adj swollen or becoming swollen.

tummy n, pl -mies Informal stomach.

tumour [**tew**-mer] n abnormal growth in or on the body.

tumult n uproar or commotion. **tumultuous** [tew-**mull**-tew-uss] adj

tumulus n, pl -li burial mound.

tun n large beer cask.

tuna n large marine food fish.

tundra n vast treeless Arctic region with permanently frozen subsoil.

tune n **1** (pleasing) sequence of musical notes. **2** correct musical pitch, e.g. she sang out of tune. ♦ v **3** adjust (a musical instrument) so that it is in tune. **4** adjust (a machine) to obtain the desired performance. **tuneful** adj **tunefully** adv **tuneless** adj **tuner** n **tune in** v adjust (a radio or television) to receive (a station or programme).

tungsten n Chem greyish-white metal.

tunic n **1** close-fitting jacket forming part of some uniforms. **2** loose knee-length garment.

tunnel n **1** underground passage. ♦ v -**nelling, -nelled 2** make a tunnel (through).

tunny n, pl -nies, -ny same as TUNA.

tup n male sheep.

turban n Muslim, Hindu, or Sikh man's head covering, made by winding cloth round the head.

turbid adj muddy, not clear.

turbine n machine or generator driven by gas, water, etc. turning blades.

turbot *n* large European edible flatfish.

turbulence *n* **1** confusion, movement, or agitation. **2** atmospheric instability causing gusty air currents. **turbulent** *adj*

tureen *n* serving dish for soup.

turf *n*, *pl* **turfs, turves 1** short thick even grass. **2** square of this with roots and soil attached. ♦ *v* **3** cover with turf. **the turf 1** racecourse. **2** horse racing. **turf accountant** bookmaker. **turf out** *v Informal* throw out.

turgid [**tur**-jid] *adj* **1** (of language) pompous. **2** swollen and thick.

turkey *n* large bird bred for food.

Turkish *adj* **1** of Turkey, its people, or their language. ♦ *n* **2** Turkish language. **Turkish bath** steam bath. **Turkish delight** jelly-like sweet coated with icing sugar.

turmeric *n* yellow spice obtained from the root of an Asian plant.

turmoil *n* agitation or confusion.

turn *v* **1** change the position or direction (of). **2** move around an axis, rotate. **3** (usu. foll. by *into*) change in nature or character. **4** reach or pass in age, time, etc., e.g. *she has just turned twenty*. **5** shape on a lathe. **6** become sour. ♦ *n* **7** turning. **8** opportunity to do something as part of an agreed succession. **9** direction or drift. **10** period or spell. **11** short theatrical performance. **good, bad turn** helpful or unhelpful act. **turner** *n* **turning** *n* road or path leading off a main route. **turncoat** *n* person who deserts one party or cause to join another. **turn down** *v* **1** reduce the volume or brightness (of). **2** refuse or reject. **turn in** *v* **1** go to bed. **2** hand in. **turning point** moment when a decisive change occurs. **turn off** *v* stop (something) working by using a knob etc. **turn on** *v* **1** start (something) working by using a knob etc. **2**

become aggressive towards. **3** *Informal* excite, esp. sexually. **turnout** *n* number of people appearing at a gathering. **turnover** *n* **1** total sales made by a business over a certain period. **2** small pastry. **3** rate at which staff leave and are replaced. **turnpike** *n Brit* road where a toll is collected at barriers. **turnstile** *n* revolving gate for admitting one person at a time. **turntable** *n* revolving platform. **turn up** *v* **1** arrive or appear. **2** find or be found. **3** increase the volume or brightness (of). **turn-up** *n* **1** turned-up fold at the bottom of a trouser leg. **2** *Informal* unexpected event.

turnip *n* root vegetable with orange or white flesh.

turpentine *n* (oil made from) the resin of certain trees. **turps** *n* turpentine oil.

turpitude *n* wickedness.

turquoise *adj* **1** blue-green. ♦ *n* **2** blue-green precious stone.

turret *n* **1** small tower. **2** revolving gun tower on a warship or tank.

turtle *n* sea tortoise. **turn turtle** capsize. **turtledove** *n* small wild dove. **turtleneck** *n* (sweater with) a round high close-fitting neck.

tusk *n* long pointed tooth of an elephant, walrus, etc.

tussle *n*, *v* fight or scuffle.

tussock *n* tuft of grass.

tutelage [**tew**-till-lij] *n* **1** instruction or guidance, esp. by a tutor. **2** state of being supervised by a guardian or tutor. **tutelary** [**tew**-till-lar-ee] *adj*

tutor *n* **1** person teaching individuals or small groups. ♦ *v* **2** act as a tutor to. **tutorial** *n* period of instruction with a tutor.

tutu *n* short stiff skirt worn by ballerinas.

tuxedo *n*, *pl* **-dos** *US & Aust* dinner jacket.

TV television.

twaddle n silly or pretentious talk or writing.

twain n Obs two.

twang n 1 sharp ringing sound. 2 nasal speech. ♦ v 3 (cause to) make a twang.

tweak v 1 pinch or twist sharply. ♦ n 2 tweaking.

twee adj Informal too sentimental, sweet, or pretty.

tweed n 1 thick woollen cloth. ♦ pl 2 suit of tweed. **tweedy** adj

tweet n, v chirp.

tweeter n loudspeaker reproducing high-frequency sounds.

tweezers pl n small pincer-like tool.

twelve adj, n two more than ten. **twelfth** adj, n (of) number twelve in a series.

twenty adj, n two times ten. **twentieth** adj, n

twenty-four-seven, ²⁴/₇ adv Informal all the time.

twerp n Informal silly person.

twice adv two times.

twiddle v fiddle or twirl in an idle way. **twiddle one's thumbs** be bored, have nothing to do.

twig¹ n small branch or shoot.

twig² v twigging, twigged Informal realize or understand.

twilight n soft dim light just after sunset.

twill n fabric woven to produce parallel ridges.

twin n 1 one of a pair, esp. of two children born at one birth. ♦ v twinning, twinned 2 pair or be paired.

twine n 1 string or cord. ♦ v 2 twist or coil round.

twinge n sudden sharp pain or emotional pang.

twinkle v 1 shine brightly but intermittently. ♦ n 2 flickering brightness.

twirl v 1 turn or spin around quickly. 2 twist or wind, esp. idly.

twist v 1 turn out of the natural position. 2 distort or pervert. 3 wind or twine. ♦ n 4 twisting. 5 twisted thing. 6 unexpected development in the plot of a film, book, etc. 7 bend or curve. 8 distortion. **twisted** adj (of a person) cruel or perverted. **twister** n Brit informal swindler.

twit¹ v twitting, twitted poke fun at (someone).

twit² n Informal foolish person.

twitch v 1 move spasmodically. 2 pull sharply. ♦ n 3 nervous muscular spasm. 4 sharp pull.

twitter v 1 (of birds) utter chirping sounds. 2 n 3 act or sound of twittering.

two adj, n one more than one. **two-edged** adj (of a remark) having both a favourable and an unfavourable interpretation. **two-faced** adj deceitful, hypocritical. **two-time** v Informal deceive (a lover) by having an affair with someone else.

tycoon n powerful wealthy businessman.

tyke n Brit, Aust & NZ informal small cheeky child.

type n 1 class or category. 2 Informal person, esp. of a specified kind. 3 block with a raised character used for printing. 4 printed text. ♦ v 5 print with a typewriter or word processor. 6 typify. 7 classify. **typist** n person who types with a typewriter or word processor. **typecast** v continually cast (an actor or actress) in similar roles. **typewriter** n machine which prints a character when the appropriate key is pressed.

typhoid fever n acute infectious feverish disease.

typhoon n violent tropical storm.

typhus n infectious feverish disease.

typical *adj* true to type, characteristic. **typically** *adv* **typify** *v* **-fying, -fied** be typical of.

typography *n* art or style of printing. **typographical** *adj* **typographer** *n*

tyrannosaurus [tirr-ran-oh-**sore**-uss] *n* large two-footed flesh-eating dinosaur.

tyrant *n* **1** oppressive or cruel ruler. **2** person who exercises authority oppressively. **tyrannical** *adj* like a tyrant, oppressive. **tyrannize** *v* exert power (over) oppressively or cruelly. **tyrannous** *adj* **tyranny** *n* tyrannical rule.

tyre *n* rubber ring, usu. inflated, over the rim of a vehicle's wheel to grip the road.

tyro *n, pl* **-ros** novice or beginner.

U u

ubiquitous [yew-**bik**-wit-uss] *adj* being or seeming to be everywhere at once. **ubiquity** *n*

udder *n* large baglike milk-producing gland of cows, sheep, or goats.

UFO unidentified flying object.

ugly *adj* **uglier, ugliest 1** of unpleasant appearance. **2** ominous or menacing. **ugliness** *n*

UHF ultrahigh frequency.

UHT (of milk or cream) ultra-heat-treated.

UK United Kingdom.

ukulele, ukelele [yew-kal-**lay**-lee] *n* small guitar with four strings.

ulcer *n* open sore on the surface of the skin or mucous membrane. **ulcerated** *adj* made or becoming ulcerous. **ulceration** *n* **ulcerous** *adj* of, like, or characterized by ulcers.

ulna *n, pl* **-nae, -nas** inner and longer of the two bones of the human forearm.

ulterior *adj* (of an aim, reason, etc.) concealed or hidden.

ultimate *adj* **1** final in a series or process. **2** highest or supreme. **ultimately** *adv*

ultimatum [ult-im-**may**-tum] *n* final warning stating that action will be taken unless certain conditions are met.

ultra- *prefix* **1** beyond a specified extent, range, or limit, e.g. *ultrasonic.* **2** extremely, e.g. *ultramodern.*

ultrahigh frequency *n* radio frequency between 3000 and 300 megahertz.

ultramarine *adj* vivid blue.

ultrasonic *adj* of or producing sound waves with a higher frequency than the human ear can hear.

ultraviolet *adj, n* (of) light beyond the limit of visibility at the violet end of the spectrum.

ululate [**yewl**-yew-late] *v* howl or wail. **ululation** *n*

umber *adj* dark brown to reddish-brown.

umbilical *adj* of the navel. **umbilical cord** long flexible tube of blood vessels that connects a fetus with the placenta.

umbrage *n* **take umbrage** feel offended or upset.

umbrella *n* **1** portable device used for protection against rain, consisting of a folding frame covered in material attached to a central rod. **2** single organization, idea, etc. that contains or covers many different organizations, ideas, etc.

umpire *n* **1** official who rules on the playing of a game. ♦ *v* **2** act as umpire in (a game).

umpteen *adj Informal* very many. **umpteenth** *n, adj*

UN United Nations.

un- *prefix* **1** not, e.g. *unidentified.* **2** denoting reversal of an action, e.g. *untie.* **3** denoting removal from, e.g. *unthrone.*

unable *adj* **unable to** lacking the necessary power, ability, or authority to (do something).

unaccountable *adj* **1** unable to be explained. **2** (foll. by *to*) not answerable to. **unaccountably** *adv*

unadulterated *adj* with nothing added, pure.

unanimous [yew-**nan**-im-uss] *adj* **1** in complete agreement. **2** agreed by all. **unanimity** *n*

unarmed *adj* without weapons.

unassuming *adj* modest or unpretentious.

unaware *adj* not aware or conscious. **unawares** *adv* **1** by surprise, e.g. *caught unawares.* **2** without knowing.

☑ **WORD TIP**
Note the difference between the adjective *unaware,* usually followed by *of* or *that,* and the adverb *unawares.*

unbalanced *adj* **1** biased or one-sided. **2** mentally deranged.

unbearable *adj* not able to be endured. **unbearably** *adv*

unbeknown *adv* **unbeknown to** without the knowledge of (a person).

unbend *v Informal* become less strict or more informal in one's attitudes or behaviour. **unbending** *adj*

unbidden *adj* not ordered or asked.

unborn *adj* not yet born.

unbosom *v* relieve (oneself) of (secrets or feelings) by telling someone.

unbridled *adj* (of feelings or behaviour) not controlled in any way.

unburden *v* relieve (one's mind or oneself) of a worry by confiding in someone.

uncalled-for *adj* not fair or justified.

uncanny *adj* weird or mysterious. **uncannily** *adv*

unceremonious *adj* **1** relaxed and informal. **2** abrupt or rude. **unceremoniously** *adv*

uncertain *adj* **1** not able to be accurately known or predicted. **2** not able to be depended upon. **3** changeable. **uncertainty** *n*

un-Christian *adj* not in accordance with Christian principles.

uncle *n* **1** brother of one's father or mother. **2** husband of one's aunt.

unclean *adj* lacking moral, spiritual, or physical cleanliness.

uncomfortable *adj* **1** not physically relaxed. **2** anxious or uneasy.

uncommon *adj* **1** not happening or encountered often. **2** in excess of what is normal. **uncommonly** *adv*

uncompromising *adj* not prepared to compromise.

unconcerned *adj* lacking in concern or involvement. **unconcernedly** *adv*

unconditional *adj* without conditions or limitations.

unconscionable *adj* **1** having no principles, unscrupulous. **2** excessive in amount or degree.

unconscious *adj* **1** lacking normal awareness through the senses. **2** not aware of one's actions or behaviour. ♦ *n* **3** part of the mind containing instincts and ideas that exist without one's awareness. **unconsciously** *adv* **unconsciousness** *n*

uncooperative *adj* not willing to help other people with what they are doing.

uncouth *adj* lacking in good manners, refinement, or grace.

uncover *v* **1** reveal or disclose. **2** remove the cover, top, etc., from.

unction *n* act of anointing with oil in sacramental ceremonies.

unctuous *adj* pretending to be kind and concerned.

undecided *adj* **1** not having made up one's mind. **2** (of an issue or problem) not agreed or decided upon.

undeniable *adj* unquestionably true. **undeniably** *adv*

under *prep, adv* **1** indicating movement to or position beneath the underside or base. **2** less than. **3** subject to.

under- *prefix* **1** below, e.g. *underground.* **2** insufficient or insufficiently, e.g. *underrate.*

underage *adj* below the required or standard age.

underarm adj 1 Sport denoting a style of throwing, bowling, or serving in which the hand is swung below shoulder level. 2 adv 3 Sport in an underarm style.

undercarriage n 1 landing gear of an aircraft. 2 framework supporting the body of a vehicle.

underclass n class consisting of the most disadvantaged people, such as the long-term unemployed.

undercoat n coat of paint applied before the final coat.

undercover adj done or acting in secret.

undercurrent n 1 current that is not apparent at the surface. 2 underlying opinion or emotion.

undercut v charge less than (a competitor) to obtain trade.

underdog n person or team in a weak or underprivileged position.

underdone adj not cooked enough.

underestimate v 1 make too low an estimate of. 2 not realize the full potential of.

underfoot adv under the feet.

undergarment n any piece of underwear.

undergo v experience, endure, or sustain.

undergraduate n person studying in a university for a first degree.

underground adj 1 occurring, situated, used, or going below ground level. 2 secret. ♦ n 3 electric passenger railway operated in underground tunnels. 4 movement dedicated to overthrowing a government or occupation forces.

undergrowth n small trees and bushes growing beneath taller trees in a wood or forest.

underhand adj sly, deceitful, and secretive.

underlie v 1 lie or be placed under. 2 be the foundation, cause, or basis of. **underlying** adj fundamental or basic.

underline v 1 draw a line under. 2 state forcibly, emphasize.

underling n subordinate.

undermine v weaken gradually.

underneath prep, adv 1 under or beneath. ♦ adj, n 2 lower (part or surface).

underpants pl n man's undergarment for the lower part of the body.

underpass n section of a road that passes under another road or a railway line.

underpin v give strength or support to.

underprivileged adj lacking the rights and advantages of other members of society.

underrate v not realize the full potential of. **underrated** adj

underseal n Chiefly Brit coating of tar etc. applied to the underside of a motor vehicle to prevent corrosion.

underside n bottom or lower surface.

understand v 1 know and comprehend the nature or meaning of. 2 realize or grasp (something). 3 assume, infer, or believe. **understandable** adj **understandably** adv **understanding** n 1 ability to learn, judge, or make decisions. 2 personal interpretation of a subject. 3 mutual agreement, usu. an informal or private one. ♦ adj 4 kind and sympathetic.

understate v 1 describe or represent (something) in restrained terms. 2 state that (something, such as a number) is less than it is. **understatement** n

understudy n 1 actor who studies a part in order to be able to replace the usual actor if necessary. ♦ v 2 act as an understudy for.

undertake v 1 agree or commit oneself to (something) or to do (something). 2 promise. **undertaking** n 1 task or enterprise. 2 agreement to do something.

undertaker n person whose job is to prepare corpses for burial or cremation and organize funerals.

undertone n 1 quiet tone of voice. 2 underlying quality or feeling.

undertow n strong undercurrent flowing in a different direction from the surface current.

underwear n clothing worn under the outer garments and next to the skin.

underworld n 1 criminals and their associates. 2 Greek & Roman myth regions below the earth's surface regarded as the abode of the dead.

underwrite v 1 accept financial responsibility for (a commercial project). 2 sign and issue (an insurance policy), thus accepting liability.

underwriter n person who underwrites (esp. an insurance policy).

undesirable adj 1 not desirable or pleasant, objectionable. ♦ n 2 objectionable person.

undo v 1 open, unwrap. 2 reverse the effects of. 3 cause the downfall of. **undone** adj **undoing** n cause of someone's downfall.

undoubted adj certain or indisputable. **undoubtedly** adv

undue adj greater than is reasonable, excessive. **unduly** adv

undulate v move in waves. **undulation** n

undying adj never ending, eternal.

unearth v 1 reveal or discover by searching. 2 dig up out of the earth.

unearthly adj 1 ghostly or eerie. 2 ridiculous or unreasonable.

uneasy adj 1 (of a person) anxious or apprehensive. 2 (of a condition) precarious or uncomfortable. **uneasily** adv **uneasiness** n **unease** n 1 feeling of anxiety. 2 state of dissatisfaction.

unemployed adj out of work. **unemployment** n

unequivocal adj completely clear in meaning. **unequivocally** adv

unerring adj never mistaken, consistently accurate.

unexceptionable adj beyond criticism or objection.

unfailing adj continuous or reliable. **unfailingly** adv

unfair adj not right, fair, or just. **unfairly** adv **unfairness** n

unfaithful adj 1 having sex with someone other than one's regular partner. 2 not true to a promise or vow. **unfaithfulness** n

unfeeling adj without sympathy.

unfit adj 1 unqualified or unsuitable. 2 in poor physical condition.

unflappable adj Informal not easily upset. **unflappability** n

unfold v 1 open or spread out from a folded state. 2 reveal or be revealed.

unforgettable adj impossible to forget, memorable.

unfortunate adj 1 unlucky, unsuccessful, or unhappy. 2 regrettable or unsuitable. **unfortunately** adv

unfrock v deprive (a priest in holy orders) of his or her priesthood.

ungainly adj -lier, -liest lacking grace when moving.

ungodly adj 1 Informal unreasonable or outrageous, e.g. an ungodly hour. 2 wicked or sinful.

ungrateful adj not grateful or thankful.

unguarded adj 1 not protected. 2 incautious or careless.

unguent [ung-gwent] n Lit ointment.

unhand v Old-fashioned or lit release

from one's grasp.

unhappy adj **1** sad or depressed. **2** unfortunate or wretched. **unhappily** adv **unhappiness** n

unhealthy adj **1** likely to cause poor health. **2** not fit or well. **3** morbid, unnatural.

unhinge v derange or unbalance (a person or his or her mind).

uni n Informal **short for** UNIVERSITY.

uni- combining form of, consisting of, or having only one, e.g. unicellular.

unicorn n imaginary horselike creature with one horn growing from its forehead.

uniform n **1** special identifying set of clothes for the members of an organization, such as soldiers. ♦ adj **2** regular and even throughout, unvarying. **3** alike or like. **uniformly** adv **uniformity** n

unify v -fying, -fied make or become one. **unification** n

unilateral adj made or done by only one person or group. **unilaterally** adv

unimpeachable adj completely honest and reliable.

uninterested adj having or showing no interest in someone or something.

union n **1** uniting or being united. **2** **short for** TRADE UNION. **3** association or confederation of individuals or groups for a common purpose. **unionist** n member or supporter of a trade union. **unionize** v organize (workers) into a trade union. **unionization** n **Union Jack, Flag** national flag of the United Kingdom.

unique [yoo-**neek**] adj **1** being the only one of a particular type. **2** without equal or like. **uniquely** adv

---

☑ **WORD TIP**
Because of its meaning, avoid using unique with modifiers like very and rather.

---

unisex adj designed for use by both sexes.

unison n **1** complete agreement. **2** Music singing or playing of the same notes together at the same time.

unit n **1** single undivided entity or whole. **2** group or individual regarded as a basic element of a larger whole. **3** fixed quantity etc., used as a standard of measurement. **4** piece of furniture designed to be fitted with other similar pieces. **unit trust** investment trust that issues units for public sale and invests the money in many different businesses.

Unitarian n person who believes that God is one being and rejects the Trinity. **Unitarianism** n

unitary adj **1** consisting of a single undivided whole. **2** of a unit or units.

unite v **1** make or become an integrated whole. **2** (cause to) enter into an association or alliance.

unity n **1** state of being one. **2** mutual agreement.

universe n **1** whole of all existing matter, energy, and space. **2** the world. **universal** adj **1** of or typical of the whole of mankind or of nature. **2** existing everywhere. **universally** adv **universality** n

university n, pl -ties institution of higher education with the authority to award degrees.

unkempt adj **1** (of the hair) not combed. **2** slovenly or untidy.

unknown adj **1** not known. **2** not famous. ♦ n **3** unknown person, quantity, or thing.

unleaded adj (of petrol) containing less tetraethyl lead, in order to reduce environmental pollution.

unless conj except under the circumstances that.

unlike adj **1** dissimilar or different. ♦ prep **2** not like or typical of.

unlikely *adj* improbable.

unload *v* **1** remove (cargo) from (a ship, truck, or plane). **2** remove the ammunition from (a firearm).

unmask *v* **1** remove the mask or disguise from. **2** (cause to) appear in true character.

unmentionable *adj* unsuitable as a topic of conversation.

unmistakable, unmistakeable *adj* not ambiguous, clear. **unmistakably, unmistakeably** *adv*

unmitigated *adj* **1** not reduced or lessened in severity etc. **2** total and complete.

unmoved *adj* not affected by emotion, indifferent.

unnatural *adj* **1** strange and frightening because not usual. **2** not in accordance with accepted standards of behaviour.

unnerve *v* cause to lose courage, confidence, or self-control.

unnumbered *adj* **1** countless. **2** not counted or given a number.

unorthodox *adj* **1** (of ideas, methods, etc.) unconventional and not generally accepted. **2** (of a person) having unusual opinions or methods.

unpack *v* **1** remove the contents of (a suitcase, trunk, etc.). **2** take (something) out of a packed container.

unparalleled *adj* not equalled, supreme.

unpick *v* undo (the stitches) of (a piece of sewing).

unpleasant *adj* not pleasant or agreeable. **unpleasantly** *adv* **unpleasantness** *n*

unprintable *adj* unsuitable for printing for reasons of obscenity or libel.

unprofessional *adj* contrary to the accepted code of a profession. **unprofessionally** *adv*

unqualified *adj* **1** lacking the necessary qualifications. **2** total or complete.

unravel *v* **-elling, -elled 1** reduce (something knitted or woven) to separate strands. **2** become unravelled. **3** explain or solve.

unremitting *adj* never slackening or stopping.

unrequited *adj* not returned, e.g. *unrequited love.*

unrest *n* rebellious state of discontent.

unrivalled *adj* having no equal.

unroll *v* open out or unwind (something rolled or coiled) or (of something rolled or coiled) become opened out or unwound.

unruly *adj* **-lier, -liest** difficult to control or organize.

unsavoury *adj* distasteful or objectionable.

unscathed *adj* not harmed or injured.

unscrupulous *adj* prepared to act dishonestly, unprincipled.

unseat *v* **1** throw or displace from a seat or saddle. **2** depose from an office or position.

unsettled *adj* **1** lacking order or stability. **2** disturbed and restless. **3** constantly changing or moving from place to place.

unsightly *adj* unpleasant to look at.

unsocial *adj* **1** (also **unsociable**) avoiding the company of other people. **2** falling outside the normal working day, e.g. *unsocial hours.*

unsound *adj* **1** unhealthy or unstable. **2** not based on truth or fact.

unstable *adj* **1** lacking stability or firmness. **2** having abrupt changes of mood or behaviour.

unsuitable *adj* not right or appropriate for a particular purpose. **unsuitably** *adv*

unsuited *adj* not appropriate for a

particular task or situation.

unswerving adj firm, constant, not changing.

unthinkable adj out of the question, inconceivable.

untidy adj messy and disordered. **untidily** adv **untidiness** n

untie v 1 open or free (something that is tied). 2 free from constraint.

until conj 1 up to the time that. ♦ prep 2 in or throughout the period before. **not until** not before (a time or event).

untimely adj 1 occurring before the expected or normal time. 2 inappropriate to the occasion or time.

unto prep Old-fashioned to.

untold adj 1 incapable of description. 2 incalculably great in number or quantity.

untouchable adj 1 above reproach or suspicion. 2 unable to be touched. ♦ n 3 member of the lowest Hindu caste in India.

untoward adj causing misfortune or annoyance.

untrue adj 1 incorrect or false. 2 disloyal or unfaithful. **untruth** n statement that is not true, lie.

unusual adj uncommon or extraordinary. **unusually** adv

unutterable adj incapable of being expressed in words. **unutterably** adv

unvarnished adj not elaborated upon, e.g. the unvarnished truth.

unwieldy adj too heavy, large, or awkward to be easily handled.

unwind v 1 relax after a busy or tense time. 2 slacken, undo, or unravel.

unwitting adj 1 not intentional. 2 not knowing or conscious. **unwittingly** adv

unwonted adj out of the ordinary.

unworthy adj 1 not deserving or worthy. 2 lacking merit or value. **unworthy of** beneath the level

considered befitting (to).

unwrap v remove the wrapping from (something).

unwritten adj 1 not printed or in writing. 2 operating only through custom.

up prep, adv 1 indicating movement to or position at a higher place. ♦ adv 2 indicating readiness, intensity or completeness, etc., e.g. warm up; drink up. ♦ adj 3 of a high or higher position. 4 out of bed. ♦ v upping, upped 5 increase or raise. **up against** having to cope with. **up and** Informal do something suddenly, e.g. he upped and left. **ups and downs** alternating periods of good and bad luck. **what's up?** Informal what is wrong? **upward** adj 1 directed or moving towards a higher place or level. ♦ adv 2 (also **upwards**) from a lower to a higher place, level, or condition.

upbeat adj 1 Informal cheerful and optimistic. ♦ n 2 Music unaccented beat.

upbraid v scold or reproach.

upbringing n education of a person during the formative years.

update v bring up to date.

upend v turn or set (something) on its end.

upfront adj 1 open and frank. ♦ adv, adj 2 (of money) paid out at the beginning of a business arrangement.

upgrade v promote (a person or job) to a higher rank.

upheaval n strong, sudden, or violent disturbance.

uphill adj 1 sloping or leading upwards. 2 requiring a great deal of effort. ♦ adv 3 up a slope. ♦ n 4 S Afr difficulty.

uphold v 1 maintain or defend against opposition. 2 give moral support to. **upholder** n

upholster v fit (a chair or sofa) with

padding, springs, and covering.
upholsterer n

upholstery n soft covering on a chair or sofa.

upkeep n act, process, or cost of keeping something in good repair.

upland adj of or in an area of high or relatively high ground. **uplands** pl n area of high or relatively high ground.

uplift v **1** raise or lift up. **2** raise morally or spiritually. ♦ n **3** act or process of improving moral, social, or cultural conditions. **uplifting** adj

upload v transfer (data or a program) from one's own computer into the memory of another computer.

upon prep **1** on. **2** up and on.

upper adj **1** higher or highest in physical position, wealth, rank, or status. ♦ n **2** part of a shoe above the sole. **uppermost** adj **1** highest in position, power, or importance. ♦ adv **2** in or into the highest place or position. **upper class** highest social class. **upper-class** adj **upper crust** Brit, Aust & NZ informal upper class. **upper hand** position of control.

uppish, uppity adj Brit informal snobbish, arrogant, or presumptuous.

upright adj **1** vertical or erect. **2** honest or just. ♦ adv **3** vertically or in an erect position. ♦ n **4** vertical support, such as a post. **uprightness** n

uprising n rebellion or revolt.

uproar n disturbance characterized by loud noise and confusion. **uproarious** adj **1** very funny. **2** (of laughter) loud and boisterous. **uproariously** adv

uproot v **1** pull up by or as if by the roots. **2** displace (a person or people) from their native or usual surroundings.

upset adj **1** emotionally or physically disturbed or distressed. ♦ v **2** tip over. **3** disturb the normal state or stability of. **4** disturb mentally or emotionally. **5** make physically ill. ♦ n **6** unexpected

defeat or reversal. **7** disturbance or disorder of the emotions, mind, or body. **upsetting** adj

upshot n final result or conclusion.

upside down adj **1** turned over completely. **2** Informal confused or jumbled. ♦ adv **3** in an inverted fashion. **4** in a chaotic manner.

upstage adj **1** at the back half of the stage. ♦ v **2** Informal draw attention to oneself from (someone else).

upstairs adv **1** to or on an upper floor of a building. ♦ n **2** upper floor. ♦ adj **3** situated on an upper floor.

upstanding adj of good character.

upstart n person who has risen suddenly to a position of power and behaves arrogantly.

upstream adv, adj in or towards the higher part of a stream.

upsurge n rapid rise or swell.

uptake n **quick, slow on the uptake** Informal quick or slow to understand or learn.

uptight adj Informal nervously tense, irritable, or angry.

up-to-date adj modern or fashionable.

upturn n upward trend or improvement. **upturned** adj facing upwards.

uranium n Chem radioactive silvery-white metallic element, used chiefly as a source of nuclear energy.

Uranus n **1** Greek myth god of the sky. **2** seventh planet from the sun.

urban adj **1** of or living in a city or town. **2** denoting modern pop music of African-American origin, such as hip-hop. **urbanize** v make (a rural area) more industrialized and urban. **urbanization** n

urbane adj characterized by courtesy, elegance, and sophistication. **urbanity** n

urchin n mischievous child.

urethra [yew-**reeth**-ra] *n* canal that carries urine from the bladder out of the body.

urge *n* **1** strong impulse, inner drive, or yearning. ♦ *v* **2** plead with or press (a person to do something). **3** advocate earnestly. **4** force or drive onwards.

urgent *adj* requiring speedy action or attention. **urgency** *n* **urgently** *adv*

urine *n* pale yellow fluid excreted by the kidneys to the bladder and passed as waste from the body. **urinary** *adj* **urinate** *v* discharge urine. **urination** *n* **urinal** *n* sanitary fitting used by men for urination.

URL uniform resource locator: a standardized address of a location on the Internet.

urn *n* **1** vase used as a container for the ashes of the dead. **2** large metal container with a tap, used for making and holding tea or coffee.

ursine *adj* of or like a bear.

us *pron* **objective case of WE.**

US, USA United States (of America).

use *v* **1** put into service or action. **2** take advantage of, exploit. **3** consume or expend. ♦ *n* **4** using or being used. **5** ability or permission to use. **6** usefulness or advantage. **7** purpose for which something is used. **user** *n* **user-friendly** *adj* easy to familiarize oneself with, understand, and use. **usable** *adj* able to be used. **usage** *n* **1** regular or constant use. **2** way in which a word is used in a language. **use-by date** *Aust, NZ & S Afr* date on packaged food after which it should not be sold. **used** *adj* second-hand. **used to** *adj* **1** accustomed to. ♦ *v* **2** used as an auxiliary to express past habitual or accustomed actions, e.g. *I used to live there.* **useful** *adj* **usefully** *adv* **usefulness** *n* **useless** *adj* **uselessly** *adv* **uselessness** *n*

usher *n* **1** official who shows people to their seats, as in a church. ♦ *v* **2** conduct or escort. **usherette** *n* female assistant in a cinema who shows people to their seats.

USSR (formerly) Union of Soviet Socialist Republics.

usual *adj* of the most normal, frequent, or regular type. **usually** *adv* most often, in most cases.

☑ SPELLING TIP

The Bank of English shows that it's very common to write *usualy*, forgetting the double *l* of **usually**.

---

usurp [yewz-**zurp**] *v* seize (a position or power) without authority. **usurpation** *n* **usurper** *n*

usury *n* practice of lending money at an extremely high rate of interest. **usurer** [**yewz**-yoor-er] *n*

ute [**yoot**] *n Aust & NZ informal* utility truck.

utensil *n* tool or container for practical use, e.g. *cooking utensils.*

uterus [**yew**-ter-russ] *n* womb. **uterine** *adj*

utilitarian *adj* **1** useful rather than beautiful. **2** of utilitarianism. **utilitarianism** *n Ethics* doctrine that the right action is the one that brings about the greatest good for the greatest number of people.

utility *n* **1** usefulness. **2** *pl* **-ties)** public service, such as electricity. ♦ *adj* **3** designed for use rather than beauty. **utility room** room used for large domestic appliances and equipment. **utility truck** *Aust & NZ* small truck with an open body and low sides.

utilize *v* make practical use of. **utilization** *n*

utmost *adj, n* (of) the greatest possible degree or amount, e.g. *the utmost point; I was doing my utmost to comply.*

Utopia [yew-**tope**-ee-a] *n* any real or

imaginary society, place, or state considered to be perfect or ideal. **Utopian** *adj*

utter[1] *v* express (something) in sounds or words. **utterance** *n* **1** something uttered. **2** act or power of uttering.

utter[2] *adj* total or absolute. **utterly** *adv*

uttermost *adj, n* same as UTMOST.

U-turn *n* **1** turn, made by a vehicle, in the shape of a U, resulting in a reversal of direction. **2** complete change in policy, e.g. *a humiliating U-turn by the Prime Minister.*

UV ultraviolet.

uvula [**yew**-view-la] *n* small fleshy part of the soft palate that hangs in the back of the throat. **uvular** *adj*

uxorious [ux-**or**-ee-uss] *adj* excessively fond of or dependent on one's wife.

V v

V volt.

v. 1 versus. **2** very.

vacant *adj* **1** (of a toilet, room, etc.) unoccupied. **2** without interest or understanding. **vacantly** *adv* **vacancy** *n, pl* -**cies 1** unfilled job. **2** unoccupied room in a guesthouse. **3** state of being unoccupied.

vacate *v* **1** cause (something) to be empty by leaving. **2** give up (a job or position). **vacation** *n* **1** time when universities and law courts are closed. **2** *Chiefly US* holiday.

vaccinate *v* inject with a vaccine. **vaccination** *n* **vaccine** *n* substance designed to cause a mild form of a disease to make a person immune to the disease itself.

vacillate [**vass**-ill-late] *v* keep changing one's mind or opinions. **vacillation** *n*

vacuous *adj* not expressing intelligent thought. **vacuity** *n*

vacuum *n, pl* **vacuums, vacua 1** empty space from which all or most air or gas has been removed. **2** *v* **3** clean with a vacuum cleaner. **vacuum cleaner** electrical appliance which sucks up dust and dirt from carpets and upholstery. **vacuum flask** double-walled flask with a vacuum between the walls that keeps drinks hot or cold. **vacuum-packed** *adj* contained in packaging from which the air has been removed.

vagabond *n* person with no fixed home, esp. a beggar.

vagary [**vaig**-a-ree] *n, pl* -**garies** unpredictable change.

vagina [vaj-**jine**-a] *n* (in female mammals) passage from the womb to the external genitals. **vaginal** *adj*

vagrant [**vaig**-rant] *n* **1** person with no

settled home. ♦ *adj* **2** wandering. **vagrancy** *n*

vague *adj* **1** not clearly explained. **2** unable to be seen or heard clearly. **3** absent-minded. **vaguely** *adv*

vain *adj* **1** excessively proud, esp. of one's appearance. **2** bound to fail, futile. **in vain** unsuccessfully.

vainglorious *adj Lit* boastful.

valance [**val**-lenss] *n* piece of drapery round the edge of a bed.

vale *n Lit* valley.

valedictory [val-lid-**dik**-tree] *adj* (of a speech, performance, etc.) intended as a farewell. **valediction** *n* farewell speech.

valence [**vale**-ence] *n* molecular bonding between atoms.

valency *n, pl* -**cies** power of an atom to make molecular bonds.

valentine *n* (person to whom one sends) a romantic card on Saint Valentine's Day, 14th February.

valerian *n* herb used as a sedative.

valet *n* man's personal male servant.

valetudinarian [val-lit-yew-din-**air**-ee-an] *n* **1** person with a long-term illness. **2** person overconcerned about his or her health.

valiant *adj* brave or courageous.

valid *adj* **1** soundly reasoned. **2** having legal force. **validate** *v* make valid. **validation** *n* **validity** *n*

valise [val-**leez**] *n Old-fashioned* small suitcase.

Valium *n* ® drug used as a tranquillizer.

valley *n* low area between hills, often with a river running through it.

valour *n Lit* bravery.

value *n* **1** importance, usefulness. **2** monetary worth. **3** *pl* **4** moral

principles. ♦ *v* **valuing, valued 5**
assess the worth or desirability of. **6**
have a high regard for. **valuable** *adj*
having great worth. **valuables** *pl n*
valuable personal property. **valuation**
n assessment of worth. **valueless** *adj*
valuer *n* **value-added tax** *Brit & S Afr*
see VAT. **value judgment** opinion
based on personal belief.

valve *n* **1** device to control the
movement of fluid through a pipe. **2**
Anat flap in a part of the body
allowing blood to flow in one direction
only. **3** *Physics* tube containing a
vacuum, allowing current to flow from
a cathode to an anode. **valvular** *adj*

vamp¹ *n Informal* sexually attractive
woman who seduces men.

vamp² *v* **vamp up** make (a story, piece
of music, etc.) seem new by inventing
additional parts.

vampire *n* (in folklore) corpse that rises
at night to drink the blood of the
living. **vampire bat** tropical bat that
feeds on blood.

van¹ *n* **1** motor vehicle for transporting
goods. **2** railway carriage for goods,
luggage, or mail.

van² *n* short for VANGUARD.

vanadium *n Chem* metallic element,
used in steel.

vandal *n* person who deliberately
damages property. **vandalism** *n*
vandalize *v*

vane *n* flat blade on a rotary device
such as a weathercock or propeller.

vanguard *n* **1** unit of soldiers leading
an army. **2** most advanced group or
position in a movement or activity.

vanilla *n* seed pod of a tropical
climbing orchid, used for flavouring.

vanish *v* **1** disappear suddenly or
mysteriously. **2** cease to exist.

vanity *n, pl* **-ties** (display of) excessive
pride.

vanquish *v Lit* defeat (someone)

utterly.

vantage *n* **vantage point** position
that gives one an overall view.

vapid *adj* lacking character, dull.

vapour *n* **1** moisture suspended in air
as steam or mist. **2** gaseous form of
something that is liquid or solid at
room temperature. **vaporize** *v*
vaporizer *n* **vaporous** *adj*

variable *adj* **1** not always the same,
changeable. ♦ *n* **2** *Maths* expression
with a range of values. **variability** *n*

variant *adj* **1** differing from a standard
or type. ♦ *n* **2** something that differs
from a standard or type. **at variance**
in disagreement.

variation *n* **1** something presented in a
slightly different form. **2** difference in
level, amount, or quantity. **3** *Music*
repetition in different forms of a basic
theme.

varicose veins *pl n* knotted and
swollen veins, esp. in the legs.

variegated *adj* having patches or
streaks of different colours.
variegation *n*

variety *n, pl* **-ties 1** state of being
diverse or various. **2** different things of
the same kind. **3** particular sort or
kind. **4** light entertainment composed
of unrelated acts.

various *adj* of several kinds. **variously**
adv

varnish *n* **1** solution of oil and resin,
put on a surface to make it hard and
glossy. ♦ *v* **2** apply varnish to.

vary *v* **varying, varied 1** change. **2**
cause differences in. **varied** *adj*

vascular *adj Biol* relating to vessels.

vas deferens *n, pl* **vasa deferentia**
Anat sperm-carrying duct in each
testicle.

vase *n* ornamental jar, esp. for flowers.

vasectomy *n, pl* **-mies** surgical
removal of part of the vas deferens, as

a contraceptive method.

Vaseline n ® thick oily cream made from petroleum, used in skin care.

vassal n 1 *Hist* man given land by a lord in return for military service. 2 subordinate person or nation. **vassalage** n

vast adj extremely large. **vastly** adv **vastness** n

vat n large container for liquids.

VAT *Brit & S Afr* value-added tax: tax on the difference between the cost of materials and the selling price.

Vatican n the Pope's palace.

vaudeville n variety entertainment of songs and comic turns.

vault¹ n 1 secure room for storing valuables. 2 underground burial chamber. **vaulted** adj having an arched roof.

vault² v 1 jump over (something) by resting one's hand(s) on it. ♦ n 2 such a jump.

vaunt v describe or display (success or possessions) boastfully. **vaunted** adj

VC 1 Vice Chancellor. 2 Victoria Cross.

VCR video cassette recorder.

VD venereal disease.

VDU visual display unit.

veal n calf meat.

vector n 1 *Maths* quantity that has size and direction, such as force. 2 animal, usu. an insect, that carries disease.

veer v change direction suddenly.

vegan [**vee**-gan] n 1 person who eats no meat, fish, eggs, or dairy products. ♦ adj 2 suitable for a vegan. **veganism** n

vegetable n 1 edible plant. 2 *Informal* severely brain-damaged person. ♦ adj 3 of or like plants or vegetables.

vegetarian n 1 person who eats no meat or fish. ♦ adj 2 suitable for a vegetarian. **vegetarianism** n

vegetate v live a dull boring life with no mental stimulation.

vegetation n plant life of a given place.

vehement adj expressing strong feelings. **vehemence** n **vehemently** adv

vehicle n 1 machine, esp. with an engine and wheels, for carrying people or objects. 2 something used to achieve a particular purpose or as a means of expression. **vehicular** adj

veil n 1 piece of thin cloth covering the head or face. 2 something that masks the truth, e.g. *a veil of secrecy*. ♦ v 3 cover with or as if with a veil. **take the veil** become a nun. **veiled** adj disguised.

vein n 1 tube that takes blood to the heart. 2 line in a leaf or an insect's wing. 3 layer of ore or mineral in rock. 4 streak in marble, wood, or cheese. 5 feature of someone's writing or speech, e.g. *a vein of humour*. 6 mood or style, e.g. *in a lighter vein*. **veined** adj

Velcro n ® fastening consisting of one piece of fabric with tiny hooked threads and another with a coarse surface that sticks to it.

veld, veldt n high grassland in southern Africa. **veldskoen, velskoen** n *S Afr* leather ankle boot.

vellum n 1 fine calfskin parchment. 2 type of strong good-quality paper.

velocity n, pl **-ties** speed of movement in a given direction.

velour, velours [vel-**loor**] n fabric similar to velvet.

velvet n fabric with a thick soft pile. **velvety** adj soft and smooth. **velveteen** n cotton velvet.

venal adj 1 easily bribed. 2 characterized by bribery.

vend v sell. **vendor** n **vending machine** machine that dispenses goods when coins are inserted.

vendetta n prolonged quarrel between families, esp. one involving revenge killings.

veneer n **1** thin layer of wood etc. covering a cheaper material. **2** superficial appearance, e.g. *a veneer of sophistication*.

venerable adj worthy of deep respect. **venerate** v hold (a person) in deep respect. **veneration** n

venereal disease [ven-**ear**-ee-al] n disease transmitted sexually.

Venetian adj of Venice, port in NE Italy. **Venetian blind** window blind made of thin horizontal slats that turn to let in more or less light.

vengeance n revenge. **vengeful** adj wanting revenge.

venial [**veen**-ee-al] adj (of a sin or fault) easily forgiven.

venison n deer meat.

venom n **1** malice or spite. **2** poison produced by snakes etc. **venomous** adj

venous adj Anat of veins.

vent¹ n **1** outlet releasing fumes or fluid. ♦ v **2** express (an emotion) freely. **give vent to** release (an emotion) in an outburst.

vent² n vertical slit in a jacket.

ventilate v **1** let fresh air into. **2** discuss (ideas or feelings) openly. **ventilation** n **ventilator** n

ventral adj relating to the front of the body.

ventricle n Anat one of the four cavities of the heart or brain.

ventriloquist n entertainer who can speak without moving his or her lips, so that a voice seems to come from elsewhere. **ventriloquism** n

venture n **1** risky undertaking, esp. in business. ♦ v **2** do something risky. **3** dare to express (an opinion). **4** go to an unknown place. **venturesome** adj daring.

venue n place where an organized gathering is held.

Venus n **1** planet second nearest to the sun. **2** Roman goddess of love. **Venus flytrap** plant that traps and digests insects between hinged leaves.

veracity n habitual truthfulness. **veracious** adj

verandah, veranda n open porch attached to a house.

verb n word that expresses the idea of action, happening, or being. **verbal** adj **1** spoken. **2** of a verb. **verbally** adv **verbalize** v express (something) in words.

verbatim [verb-**bait**-im] adv, adj word for word.

verbena n plant with sweet-smelling flowers.

verbiage n excessive use of words.

verbose [verb-**bohss**] adj speaking at tedious length. **verbosity** n

verdant adj Lit covered in green vegetation.

verdict n **1** decision of a jury. **2** opinion formed after examining the facts.

verdigris [**ver**-dig-riss] n green film on copper, brass, or bronze.

verdure n Lit flourishing green vegetation.

verge n grass border along a road. **on the verge of** having almost reached (a point or condition). **verge on** v be near to (a condition).

verger n C of E church caretaker.

verify v -ifying, -ified check the truth or accuracy of. **verifiable** adj **verification** n

verily adv Obs in truth.

verisimilitude n appearance of being real or true.

veritable adj rightly called, without exaggeration, e.g. *a veritable feast*. **veritably** adv

verity *n, pl* **-ties** true statement or principle.

vermicelli [ver-me-**chell**-ee] *n* fine strands of pasta.

vermiform *adj* shaped like a worm. **vermiform appendix** *Anat* same as APPENDIX.

vermilion *adj* orange-red.

vermin *pl n* animals, esp. insects and rodents, that spread disease or cause damage. **verminous** *adj*

vermouth [**ver**-muth] *n* wine flavoured with herbs.

vernacular [ver-**nak**-yew-lar] *n* most widely spoken language of a particular people or place.

vernal *adj* occurring in spring.

vernier [**ver**-nee-er] *n* movable scale on a graduated measuring instrument for taking readings in fractions.

veronica *n* plant with small blue, pink, or white flowers.

verruca [ver-**roo**-ka] *n* wart, usu. on the foot.

versatile *adj* having many skills or uses. **versatility** *n*

verse *n* **1** group of lines forming part of a song or poem. **2** poetry as distinct from prose. **3** subdivision of a chapter of the Bible. **versed in** knowledgeable about. **versification** *n* writing in verse.

version *n* **1** form of something, such as a piece of writing, with some differences from other forms. **2** account of an incident from a particular point of view.

verso *n, pl* **-sos** left-hand page of a book.

versus *prep* **1** in opposition to or in contrast with. **2** *Sport, Law* against.

vertebra *n, pl* **vertebrae** one of the bones that form the spine. **vertebral** *adj* **vertebrate** *n, adj* (animal) having a spine.

vertex *n, pl* **-texes, -tices 1** *Maths* point on a geometric figure where the sides form an angle. **2** highest point of a triangle.

vertical *adj* **1** straight up and down. ♦ *n* **2** vertical direction.

vertigo *n* dizziness, usu. when looking down from a high place. **vertiginous** *adj*

vervain *n* plant with spikes of blue, purple, or white flowers.

verve *n* enthusiasm or liveliness.

very *adv* **1** more than usually, extremely. ♦ *adj* **2** absolute, exact, e.g. *the very top; the very man.*

vesicle *n* *Biol* sac or small cavity, esp. one containing fluid.

vespers *pl n* *RC Church* (service of) evening prayer.

vessel *n* **1** ship. **2** *Lit* container, esp. for liquids. **3** *Biol* tubular structure in animals and plants that carries body fluids, such as blood or sap.

vest *n* **1** undergarment worn on the top half of the body. **2** *US & Aust* waistcoat. ♦ *v* **3** (foll. by *in* or *with*) give (authority) to (someone). **vested interest** interest someone has in a matter because he or she might benefit from it.

vestibule *n* small entrance hall.

vestige [**vest**-ij] *n* small amount or trace. **vestigial** *adj*

vestments *pl n* priest's robes.

vestry *n, pl* **-tries** room in a church used as an office by the priest or minister.

vet[1] *n* **1** short for VETERINARY SURGEON. ♦ *v* **vetting, vetted 2** check the suitability of.

vet[2] *n* *US, Aust & NZ* military veteran.

vetch *n* climbing plant with a beanlike fruit used as fodder.

veteran *n* **1** person with long experience in a particular activity, esp. military service. ♦ *adj* **2** long-serving.

veterinary *adj* concerning animal health. **veterinary surgeon** medical specialist who treats sick animals.

veto *n, pl* **-toes 1** official power to cancel a proposal. ♦ *v* **-toing, -toed 2** enforce a veto against.

vex *v* frustrate, annoy. **vexation** *n* **1** something annoying. **2** being annoyed. **vexatious** *adj* **vexed question** much debated subject.

VHF very high frequency: radio frequency band between 30 and 300 MHz.

VHS ® Video Home System: format for recording on video.

via *prep* by way of.

viable *adj* **1** able to be put into practice. **2** *Biol* able to live and grow independently. **viability** *n*

viaduct *n* bridge over a valley.

Viagra [vie-**ag**-ra] *n* ® drug used to treat impotence in men.

vial *n* same as PHIAL.

viands *pl n Obs* food.

vibes *pl n Informal* **1** emotional reactions between people. **2** atmosphere of a place. **3** short for VIBRAPHONE.

vibrant [**vibe**-rant] *adj* **1** vigorous in appearance, energetic. **2** (of a voice) resonant. **3** (of a colour) strong and bright.

vibraphone *n* musical instrument with metal bars that resonate electronically when hit.

vibrate *v* **1** move back and forth rapidly. **2** (cause to) resonate. **vibration** *n* **vibrator** *n* device that produces vibratory motion, used for massage or as a sex aid. **vibratory** *adj*

vibrato *n, pl* **-tos** *Music* rapid fluctuation in the pitch of a note.

Vic Victoria.

vicar *n C of E* member of the clergy in charge of a parish. **vicarage** *n* vicar's house.

vicarious [vick-**air**-ee-uss] *adj* **1** felt indirectly by imagining what another person experiences. **2** delegated. **vicariously** *adv*

vice¹ *n* **1** immoral or evil habit or action. **2** habit regarded as a weakness in someone's character. **3** criminal immorality, esp. involving sex.

vice² *n* tool with a pair of jaws for holding an object while working on it.

vice³ *adj* serving in place of.

vice chancellor *n* chief executive of a university.

viceroy *n* governor of a colony who represents the monarch. **viceregal** *adj*

vice versa [**vie**-see **ver**-sa] *adv Latin* conversely, the other way round.

vicinity [viss-**in**-it-ee] *n* surrounding area.

vicious *adj* cruel and violent. **viciously** *adv* **vicious circle, cycle** situation in which an attempt to resolve one problem creates new problems that recreate the original one.

vicissitudes [viss-**iss**-it-yewds] *pl n* changes in fortune.

victim *n* person or thing harmed or killed. **victimize** *v* **1** punish unfairly. **2** discriminate against. **victimization** *n*

victor *n* person who has defeated an opponent, esp. in war or in sport.

Victoria Cross *n Brit* highest award for bravery in battle.

Victorian *adj* **1** of or in the reign of Queen Victoria (1837–1901). **2** characterized by prudery or hypocrisy. **3** of or relating to the Australian state of Victoria.

victory *n* winning of a battle or contest. **victorious** *adj*

victuals [**vit**-tals] *pl n Old-fashioned* food and drink.

vicuña [vik-**koo**-nya] *n* **1** S American

animal like the llama. **2** fine cloth made from its wool.

video n, pl **-os 1** short for VIDEO CASSETTE (RECORDER). ♦ v **videoing, videoed 2** record (a TV programme or event) on video. ♦ adj **3** relating to or used in producing television images. **video nasty** horrific or pornographic film, usu. made for video. **videotext** n means of representing on a TV screen information that is held in a computer.

video cassette n cassette containing video tape. **video cassette recorder** tape recorder for recording and playing back TV programmes and films.

video tape n **1** magnetic tape used to record video-frequency signals in TV production. **2** magnetic tape used to record programmes when they are broadcast. **videotape** v record (a TV programme) on video tape. **video tape recorder** tape recorder for vision signals, used in TV production.

vie v **vying, vied** compete (with someone).

view n **1** opinion or belief. **2** everything that can be seen from a given place. **3** picture of this. ♦ v **4** think of (something) in a particular way. **in view of** taking into consideration. **on view** exhibited to the public. **viewer** n **1** person who watches television. **2** hand-held device for looking at photographic slides. **viewfinder** n window on a camera showing what will appear in a photograph.

Viewdata n ® videotext service linking users to a computer by telephone.

vigil [**vij**-ill] n night-time period of staying awake to look after a sick person, pray, etc. **vigilant** adj watchful in case of danger. **vigilance** n

vigilante [vij-ill-**ant**-ee] n person, esp. as one of a group, who takes it upon himself or herself to enforce the law.

vignette [vin-**yet**] n **1** concise description of the typical features of something. **2** small decorative illustration in a book.

vigour n physical or mental energy. **vigorous** adj **vigorously** adv

Viking n Hist seafaring raider and settler from Scandinavia.

vile adj **1** very wicked. **2** disgusting. **vilely** adv **vileness** n

vilify v **-ifying, -ified** attack the character of. **vilification** n

villa n **1** large house with gardens. **2** holiday home, usu. in the Mediterranean.

village n **1** small group of houses in a country area. **2** rural community. **villager** n

villain n **1** wicked person. **2** main wicked character in a play. **villainous** adj **villainy** n

villein [**vill**-an] n Hist peasant bound in service to his lord.

vinaigrette n salad dressing of oil and vinegar.

vindicate v **1** clear (someone) of guilt. **2** provide justification for. **vindication** n

vindictive adj maliciously seeking revenge. **vindictiveness** n **vindictively** adv

vine n climbing plant, esp. one producing grapes. **vineyard** [**vinn**-yard] n plantation of grape vines, esp. for making wine.

vinegar n acid liquid made from wine, beer, or cider. **vinegary** adj

vino [**vee**-noh] n Informal wine.

vintage n **1** wine from a particular harvest of grapes. ♦ adj **2** best and most typical. **vintage car** car built between 1919 and 1930.

vintner n dealer in wine.

vinyl [**vine**-ill] n type of plastic, used in mock leather and records.

viol [**vie**-oll] *n* early stringed instrument preceding the violin.

viola[1] [vee-**oh**-la] *n* stringed instrument lower in pitch than a violin.

viola[2] [**vie**-ol-la] *n* variety of pansy.

violate *v* 1 break (a law or agreement). 2 disturb (someone's privacy). 3 treat (a sacred place) disrespectfully. 4 rape. **violation** *n* **violator** *n*

violence *n* 1 use of physical force, usu. intended to cause injury or destruction. 2 great force or strength in action, feeling, or expression. **violent** *adj* **violently** *adv*

violet *n* 1 plant with bluish-purple flowers. ♦ *adj* 2 bluish-purple.

violin *n* small four-stringed musical instrument played with a bow. **violinist** *n*

VIP very important person.

viper *n* poisonous snake.

virago [vir-**rah**-go] *n, pl* **-goes, -gos** aggressive woman.

viral *adj* of or caused by a virus.

virgin *n* 1 person, esp. a woman, who has not had sexual intercourse. ♦ *adj* 2 not having had sexual intercourse. 3 not yet exploited or explored. **virginal** *adj* 1 like a virgin. 2 *n* 3 early keyboard instrument like a small harpsichord. **virginity** *n*

virile *adj* having the traditional male characteristics of physical strength and a high sex drive. **virility** *n*

virology *n* study of viruses.

virtual *adj* 1 having the effect but not the form of. 2 of or relating to virtual reality. **virtual reality** computer-generated environment that seems real to the user. **virtually** *adv* practically, almost.

virtue *n* 1 moral goodness. 2 positive moral quality. 3 merit. **by virtue of** by reason of. **virtuous** *adj* morally good. **virtuously** *adv*

virtuoso *n, pl* **-sos, -si** person with impressive esp. musical skill. **virtuosity** *n*

virulent [**vir**-yew-lent] *adj* 1 very infectious. 2 violently harmful.

virus *n* 1 microorganism that causes disease in humans, animals, and plants. 2 *Computers* program that propagates itself, via disks and electronic networks, to cause disruption.

visa *n* permission to enter a country, granted by its government and shown by a stamp on one's passport.

visage [**viz**-zij] *n Lit* face.

vis-à-vis [veez-ah-**vee**] *prep* in relation to, regarding.

viscera [**viss**-er-a] *pl n* large abdominal organs.

visceral [**viss**-er-al] *adj* 1 instinctive. 2 of or relating to the viscera.

viscid [**viss**-id] *adj* sticky.

viscose *n* synthetic fabric made from cellulose.

viscount [**vie**-count] *n* British nobleman ranking between an earl and a baron.

viscountess [**vie**-count-iss] *n* 1 woman holding the rank of viscount in her own right. 2 wife or widow of a viscount.

viscous *adj* thick and sticky. **viscosity** *n*

visible *adj* 1 able to be seen. 2 able to be perceived by the mind. **visibly** *adv* **visibility** *n* range or clarity of vision.

vision *n* 1 ability to see. 2 mental image of something. 3 foresight. 4 hallucination. **visionary** *adj* 1 showing foresight. 2 idealistic but impractical. ♦ *n* 3 visionary person.

visit *v* **-iting, -ited** 1 go or come to see. 2 stay temporarily with. 3 (foll. by *upon*) *Lit* afflict. ♦ *n* 4 instance of visiting. 5 official call. **visitor** *n*

visitation n **1** formal visit or inspection. **2** catastrophe seen as divine punishment.

visor [**vize**-or] n **1** transparent part of a helmet that pulls down over the face. **2** eyeshade, esp. in a car. **3** peak on a cap.

vista n (beautiful) extensive view.

visual adj **1** done by or used in seeing. **2** designed to be looked at. **visualize** v form a mental image of. **visualization** n **visual display unit** device with a screen for displaying data held in a computer.

vital adj **1** essential or highly important. **2** lively. **3** necessary to maintain life. **vitals** pl n bodily organs necessary to maintain life. **vitally** adv **vitality** n physical or mental energy. **vital statistics 1** statistics of births, deaths, and marriages. **2** Informal woman's bust, waist, and hip measurements.

vitamin n one of a group of substances that are essential in the diet for specific body processes.

vitiate [**vish**-ee-ate] v spoil the effectiveness of.

viticulture n cultivation of grapevines.

vitreous adj like or made from glass.

vitriol n **1** language expressing bitterness and hatred. **2** sulphuric acid. **vitriolic** adj

vituperative [vite-**tyew**-pra-tiv] adj bitterly abusive. **vituperation** n

viva[1] interj long live (a person or thing).

viva[2] n Brit examination in the form of an interview.

vivace [viv-**vah**-chee] adv Music in a lively manner.

vivacious adj full of energy and enthusiasm. **vivacity** n

viva voce [**vive**-a **voh**-chee] adv **1** by word of mouth. ♦ n **2** same as VIVA[2].

vivid adj **1** very bright. **2** conveying images that are true to life. **vividly**

adv **vividness** n

vivisection n performing surgical experiments on living animals. **vivisectionist** n

vixen n **1** female fox. **2** Brit, Aust & NZ informal spiteful woman.

viz. (introducing specified items) namely.

vizier [viz-**zeer**] n high official in certain Muslim countries.

vizor n same as VISOR.

vocabulary n, pl -aries **1** all the words that a person knows. **2** all the words in a language. **3** specialist terms used in a given subject. **4** list of words in another language with their translation.

vocal adj **1** relating to the voice. **2** outspoken. **vocals** pl n singing part of a piece of pop music. **vocally** adv **vocalist** n singer. **vocalize** v express with or use the voice. **vocalization** n **vocal cords** membranes in the larynx that vibrate to produce sound.

vocation n **1** profession or trade. **2** occupation that someone feels called to. **vocational** adj directed towards a particular profession or trade.

vociferous adj shouting, noisy.

vodka n (Russian) spirit distilled from potatoes or grain.

voetsek interj S Afr offens expression of rejection.

vogue n **1** popular style. **2** period of popularity.

voice n **1** (quality of) sound made when speaking or singing. **2** expression of opinion by a person or group. **3** property of verbs that makes them active or passive. ♦ v **4** express verbally. **voiceless** adj **voice mail** electronic system for the transfer and storage of telephone messages, which can be dealt with by the user at a later time. **voice-over** n film commentary spoken by someone off-camera.

void adj **1** not legally binding. **2** empty.

♦ *n* **3** empty space. ♦ *v* **4** make invalid. **5** empty.

voile [**voyl**] *n* light semitransparent fabric.

vol. volume.

volatile *adj* **1** liable to sudden change, esp. in behaviour. **2** evaporating quickly. **volatility** *n*

vol-au-vent [**voll**-oh-von] *n* small puff-pastry case with a savoury filling.

volcano *n, pl* **-noes, -nos** mountain with a vent through which lava is ejected. **volcanic** *adj*

vole *n* small rodent.

volition *n* ability to decide things for oneself. **of one's own volition** through one's own choice.

volley *n* **1** simultaneous discharge of ammunition. **2** burst of questions or critical comments. **3** *Sport* stroke or kick at a moving ball before it hits the ground. ♦ *v* **4** discharge (ammunition) in a volley. **5** hit or kick (a ball) in a volley. **volleyball** *n* team game where a ball is hit with the hands over a high net.

volt *n* unit of electric potential. **voltage** *n* electric potential difference expressed in volts. **voltmeter** *n* instrument for measuring voltage.

volte-face [volt-**fass**] *n* reversal of opinion.

voluble *adj* talking easily and at length. **volubility** *n* **volubly** *adv*

volume *n* **1** size of the space occupied by something. **2** amount. **3** loudness of sound. **4** book, esp. one of a series. **voluminous** *adj* **1** (of clothes) large and roomy. **2** (of writings) extensive. **volumetric** *adj* relating to measurement by volume.

voluntary *adj* **1** done by choice. **2** done or maintained without payment. **3** (of muscles) controlled by the will. ♦ *n, pl* **-taries 4** organ solo in a church service. **voluntarily** *adv*

volunteer *n* **1** person who offers voluntarily to do something. **2** person who voluntarily undertakes military service. ♦ *v* **3** offer one's services. **4** give (information) willingly. **5** offer the services of (another person).

voluptuous *adj* **1** (of a woman) sexually alluring through fullness of figure. **2** sensually pleasurable. **voluptuary** *n* person devoted to sensual pleasures.

volute *n* spiral or twisting turn, form, or object.

vomit *v* **-iting, -ited 1** eject (the contents of the stomach) through the mouth. ♦ *n* **2** matter vomited.

voodoo *n* religion involving ancestor worship and witchcraft, practised by Black people in the West Indies, esp. in Haiti.

voracious *adj* **1** craving great quantities of food. **2** insatiably eager. **voraciously** *adv* **voracity** *n*

vortex *n, pl* **-texes, -tices** whirlpool.

vote *n* **1** choice made by a participant in a shared decision, esp. in electing a candidate. **2** right to this choice. **3** total number of votes cast. **4** collective voting power of a given group, e.g. *the Black vote.* ♦ *v* **5** make a choice by a vote. **6** authorize (something) by vote. **voter** *n*

votive *adj* done or given to fulfil a vow.

vouch *v* **vouch for 1** give one's personal assurance about. **2** provide evidence for.

voucher *n* **1** ticket used instead of money to buy specified goods. **2** record of a financial transaction, receipt.

vouchsafe *v* *Old-fashioned* give, entrust.

vow *n* **1** solemn and binding promise. ♦ *pl* **2** formal promises made when marrying or entering a religious order. ♦ *v* **3** promise solemnly.

vowel *n* **1** speech sound made without obstructing the flow of breath. **2** letter representing this.

vox pop *n Brit* interviews with members of the public on TV or radio.

vox populi *n* public opinion.

voyage *n* **1** long journey by sea or in space. ♦ *v* **2** make a voyage. **voyager** *n*

voyeur *n* person who obtains pleasure from watching people undressing or having sex. **voyeurism** *n*

vs versus.

V-sign *n* **1** offensive gesture made by sticking up the index and middle fingers with the palm inwards. **2** similar gesture, with the palm outwards, meaning victory or peace.

VSO (in Britain) Voluntary Service Overseas.

VSOP (of brandy or port) very superior old pale.

VTOL vertical takeoff and landing.

VTR video tape recorder.

vulcanize *v* strengthen (rubber) by treating it with sulphur.

vulgar *adj* showing lack of good taste, decency, or refinement. **vulgarly** *adv* **vulgarity** *n* **vulgarian** *n* vulgar (rich) person. **vulgar fraction** simple fraction.

Vulgate *n* fourth-century Latin version of the Bible.

vulnerable *adj* **1** liable to be physically or emotionally hurt. **2** exposed to attack. **vulnerability** *n*

vulpine *adj* of or like a fox.

vulture *n* large bird that feeds on the flesh of dead animals.

vulva *n* woman's external genitals.

vying *v* present participle of VIE.

W w

W 1 watt. **2** West(ern).

WA Western Australia.

wacky *adj* **wackier, wackiest** *Informal* eccentric or funny. **wackiness** *n*

wad *n* **1** small mass of soft material. **2** roll or bundle, esp. of banknotes. **wadding** *n* soft material used for padding or stuffing.

waddle *v* **1** walk with short swaying steps. ♦ *n* **2** swaying walk.

waddy *n, pl* **-dies** heavy wooden club used by Australian Aborigines.

wade *v* **1** walk with difficulty through water or mud. **2** proceed with difficulty. **wader** *n* **1** long-legged water bird. ♦ *pl* **2** angler's long waterproof boots.

wadi [**wod**-dee] *n, pl* **-dies** (in N Africa and Arabia) river which is dry except in the wet season.

wafer *n* **1** thin crisp biscuit. **2** thin disc of unleavened bread used at Communion. **3** thin slice.

waffle[1] *Informal* ♦ *v* **1** speak or write in a vague wordy way. ♦ *n* **2** vague wordy talk or writing.

waffle[2] *n* square crisp pancake with a gridlike pattern.

waft *v* **1** drift or carry gently through the air. ♦ *n* **2** something wafted.

wag *v* **wagging, wagged 1** move rapidly from side to side. ♦ *n* **2** wagging movement. **3** *Old-fashioned* humorous witty person. **wagtail** *n* small long-tailed bird.

wage *n* **1** (often *pl*) payment for work done, esp. when paid weekly. ♦ *v* **2** engage in (an activity).

wager *n, v* bet on the outcome of something.

waggle *v* move with a rapid shaking or

wobbling motion.

wagon, waggon *n* **1** four-wheeled vehicle for heavy loads. **2** railway freight truck.

wahoo *n* food and game fish of tropical seas.

waif *n* young person who is, or seems, homeless or neglected.

wail *v* **1** cry out in pain or misery. ♦ *n* **2** mournful cry.

wain *n Poetic* farm wagon.

wainscot, wainscoting *n* wooden lining of the lower part of the walls of a room.

waist *n* **1** part of the body between the ribs and hips. **2** narrow middle part. **waistband** *n* band of material sewn on to the waist of a garment to strengthen it. **waistcoat** *n* sleeveless garment which buttons up the front, usu. worn over a shirt and under a jacket. **waistline** *n* (size of) the waist of a person or garment.

wait *v* **1** remain inactive in expectation (of something). **2** be ready (for something). **3** delay or be delayed. **4** serve in a restaurant etc. ♦ *n* **5** act or period of waiting. **waiter** *n* man who serves in a restaurant etc. **waitress** *n fem*

Waitangi Day *n* February 6th, the national day of New Zealand commemorating the Treaty Of Waitangi in 1840.

waive *v* refrain from enforcing (a law, right, etc.)

waiver *n* act or instance of voluntarily giving up a claim, right, etc.

waka *n NZ* Maori canoe.

wake[1] *v* **waking, woke, woken 1** rouse from sleep or inactivity. ♦ *n* **2** vigil beside a corpse the night before the

funeral. **waken** v wake. **wakeful** adj
wake² n track left by a moving ship. **in the wake of** following, often as a result.
walk v 1 move on foot with at least one foot always on the ground. 2 pass through or over on foot. 3 escort or accompany on foot. ♦ n 4 act or instance of walking. 5 distance walked. 6 manner of walking. 7 place or route for walking. **walk of life** social position or profession. **walker** n **walkabout** n informal walk among the public by royalty etc. **walkie-talkie** n portable radio transmitter and receiver. **walking stick** stick used as a support when walking. **walk into** v meet with unwittingly. **Walkman** n ® small portable cassette player with headphones. **walkout** n 1 strike. 2 act of leaving as a protest. **walkover** n easy victory.
wall n 1 structure of brick, stone, etc. used to enclose, divide, or support. 2 something having the function or effect of a wall. ♦ v 3 enclose or seal with a wall or walls. **wallflower** n 1 fragrant garden plant. 2 (at a dance) woman who remains seated because she has no partner. **wallpaper** n decorative paper to cover interior walls.
wallaby n, pl **-bies** marsupial like a small kangaroo.
wallaroo n large stocky Australian kangaroo of rocky regions.
wallet n small folding case for paper money, documents, etc.
walleye n fish with large staring eyes (also **dory**).
wallop Informal ♦ v **-loping, -loped** 1 hit hard. ♦ n 2 hard blow. **walloping** Informal ♦ n 1 thrashing. ♦ adj 2 large or great.
wallow v 1 revel in an emotion. 2 roll in liquid or mud. ♦ n 3 act or instance

of wallowing.
wally n, pl **-lies** Brit slang stupid person.
walnut n 1 edible nut with a wrinkled shell. 2 tree it grows on. 3 its wood, used for making furniture.
walrus n, pl **-ruses, -rus** large sea mammal with long tusks.
waltz n 1 ballroom dance. 2 music for this. ♦ v 3 dance a waltz. 4 Informal move in a relaxed confident way.
wampum [**wom**-pum] n shells woven together, formerly used by Native Americans for money and ornament.
wan [rhymes with **swan**] adj **wanner, wannest** pale and sickly looking.
wand n thin rod, esp. one used in performing magic tricks.
wander v 1 move about without a definite destination or aim. 2 go astray, deviate. 3 n 4 act or instance of wandering. **wanderer** n **wanderlust** n great desire to travel.
wane v 1 decrease gradually in size or strength. 2 (of the moon) decrease in size. **on the wane** decreasing in size, strength, or power.
wangle v Informal get by devious methods.
want v 1 need or long for. 2 desire or wish. ♦ n 3 act or instance of wanting. 4 thing wanted. 5 lack or absence. 6 state of being in need, poverty. **wanted** adj sought by the police. **wanting** adj 1 lacking. 2 not good enough.
wanton adj 1 without motive, provocation, or justification. 2 Old-fashioned (of a woman) sexually unrestrained or immodest.
WAP Wireless Application Protocol: a system that allows mobile phone users to access the Internet and other information services.
war n 1 fighting between nations. 2 conflict or contest. ♦ adj 3 of, like, or caused by war. ♦ v **warring, warred** 4

conduct a war. **warring** adj **warlike** adj **1** of or relating to war. **2** hostile and eager to have a war. **war crime** crime, such as killing, committed during a war in violation of accepted conventions. **war criminal** person who has committed war crimes. **warfare** n fighting or hostilities. **warhead** n explosive front part of a missile. **warmonger** n person who encourages war. **warship** n ship designed and equipped for naval combat.

waratah n Australian shrub with crimson flowers.

warble v sing in a trilling voice.

warbler n any of various small songbirds.

ward n **1** room in a hospital for patients needing a similar kind of care. **2** electoral division of a town. **3** child under the care of a guardian or court. **warder** n prison officer. **wardress** n fem **ward off** v avert or repel. **wardroom** n officers' quarters on a warship.

warden n **1** person in charge of a building and its occupants. **2** official responsible for the enforcement of regulations.

wardrobe n **1** cupboard for hanging clothes in. **2** person's collection of clothes. **3** costumes of a theatrical company.

ware n **1** articles of a specified type or material, e.g. silverware. ♦ pl **2** goods for sale. **warehouse** n building for storing goods prior to sale or distribution.

warlock n man who practises black magic.

warm adj **1** moderately hot. **2** providing warmth. **3** (of a colour) predominantly yellow or red. **4** affectionate. **5** enthusiastic. ♦ v **6** make or become warm. **warmly** adv

warmth n **1** mild heat. **2** cordiality. **3** intensity of emotion. **warm up** v **1** make or become warmer. **2** do preliminary exercises before a race or more strenuous exercise. **3** make or become more lively. **warm-up** n

warn v **1** make aware of possible danger or harm. **2** caution or scold. **3** inform (someone) in advance. **warning** n **1** something that warns. **2** scolding or caution. **warn off** v advise (someone) not to become involved with.

warp v **1** twist out of shape. **2** pervert. ♦ n **3** state of being warped. **4** lengthwise threads on a loom.

warrant n **1** (document giving) official authorization. ♦ v **2** make necessary. **3** guarantee. **warranty** n, pl **-ties** (document giving) a guarantee. **warrant officer** officer in certain armed services with a rank between a commissioned and noncommissioned officer.

warren n **1** series of burrows in which rabbits live. **2** overcrowded building or part of a town.

warrigal Aust ♦ n **1** dingo. ♦ adj **2** wild.

warrior n person who fights in a war.

wart n small hard growth on the skin. **wart hog** kind of African wild pig.

wary [**ware**-ree] adj **warier, wariest** watchful or cautious. **warily** adv **wariness** n

was v first and third person singular past tense of BE.

wash v **1** clean (oneself, clothes, etc.) with water and usu. soap. **2** be washable. **3** flow or sweep over or against. **4** Informal be believable or acceptable, e.g. that excuse won't wash. ♦ n **5** act or process of washing. **6** clothes washed at one time. **7** thin coat of paint. **8** disturbance in the water after a ship has passed by. **washable** adj **washer** n ring put under a nut or bolt or in a tap as a seal. **washing** n clothes to be washed. **washing-up** n (washing of) dishes and cutlery needing to be cleaned after a meal. **wash away** v carry or be carried off by moving water. **washout** n Informal complete failure. **wash up** v wash dishes and cutlery after a meal.

wasp n stinging insect with a slender black-and-yellow striped body. **waspish** adj bad-tempered.

waste v 1 use pointlessly or thoughtlessly. 2 fail to take advantage of. ♦ n 3 act of wasting or state of being wasted. 4 anything wasted. 5 rubbish. ♦ pl 6 desert. ♦ adj 7 rejected as worthless or surplus to requirements. 8 not cultivated or inhabited. **waste away** (cause to) decline in health or strength. **wastage** n 1 loss by wear or waste. 2 reduction in size of a workforce by not filling vacancies. **wasteful** adj extravagant. **wastefully** adv **waster, wastrel** n layabout. **wastepaper basket** container for discarded paper.

watch v 1 look at closely. 2 guard or supervise. ♦ n 3 portable timepiece for the wrist or pocket. 4 (period of) watching. 5 sailor's spell of duty. **watchable** adj **watcher** n **watchful** adj vigilant or alert. **watchfully** adv **watchdog** n 1 dog kept to guard property. 2 person or group guarding against inefficiency or illegality. **watch for** v be keenly alert to or cautious about. **watchman** n man employed to guard a building or property. **watchword** n word or phrase that sums up the attitude of a particular group.

water n 1 clear colourless tasteless liquid that falls as rain and forms rivers etc. 2 body of water, such as a sea or lake. 3 level of the tide. 4 urine. ♦ v 5

put water on or into. 6 (of the eyes) fill with tears. 7 (of the mouth) salivate. **watery** adj **water buffalo** oxlike Asian animal. **water closet** Old-fashioned (room containing) a toilet flushed by water. **watercolour** n 1 paint thinned with water. 2 painting done in this. **watercourse** n bed of a stream or river. **watercress** n edible plant growing in clear ponds and streams. **water down** v dilute, make less strong. **waterfall** n place where the waters of a river drop vertically. **waterfront** n part of a town alongside a body of water. **water lily** water plant with large floating leaves. **watermark** n faint translucent design in a sheet of paper. **watermelon** n melon with green skin and red flesh. **water polo** team game played by swimmers with a ball. **waterproof** adj 1 not letting water through. ♦ n 2 waterproof garment. ♦ v 3 make waterproof. **watershed** n 1 important period or factor serving as a dividing line. 2 line separating two river systems. **watersider** n NZ person employed to load and unload ships. **water-skiing** n sport of riding over water on skis towed by a speedboat. **watertight** adj 1 not letting water through. 2 with no loopholes or weak points. **water wheel** large wheel which is turned by flowing water to drive machinery.

watt [wott] n unit of power. **wattage** n electrical power expressed in watts.

wattle [wott-tl] n 1 branches woven over sticks to make a fence 2 Australian acacia with flexible branches formerly used for making fences

wave v 1 move the hand to and fro as a greeting or signal. 2 move or flap to and fro. ♦ n 3 moving ridge on water. 4 curve(s) in the hair. 5 prolonged spell of something. 6 gesture of

waving. **7** vibration carrying energy through a medium. **wavy** *adj*
wavelength *n* distance between the same points of two successive waves.
waver *v* **1** hesitate or be irresolute. **2** be or become unsteady. **waverer** *n*
wax¹ *n* **1** solid shiny fatty or oily substance used for sealing, making candles, etc. **2** similar substance made by bees. **3** waxy secretion of the ear. ♦ *v* **4** coat or polish with wax. **waxen** *adj* made of or like wax. **waxy** *adj*
waxwork *n* **1** lifelike wax model of a (famous) person. ♦ *pl* **2** place exhibiting these.
wax² *v* **1** increase in size or strength. **2** (of the moon) get gradually larger.
way *n* **1** manner or method. **2** characteristic manner. **3** route or direction. **4** track or path. **5** distance. **6** room for movement or activity, e.g. *you're in the way.* **7** passage or journey. **wayfarer** *n Lit* traveller. **waylay** *v* lie in wait for and accost or attack. **wayside** *adj, n* (situated by) the side of a road.
wayward *adj* erratic, selfish, or stubborn. **waywardness** *n*
WC water closet.
we *pron* (used as the subject of a verb) **1** the speaker or writer and one or more others. **2** people in general. **3** formal word for 'I' used by editors and monarchs.
weak *adj* **1** lacking strength. **2** liable to give way. **3** unconvincing. **4** lacking flavour. **weaken** *v* make or become weak. **weakling** *n* feeble person or animal. **weakly** *adv* feebly. **weakness** *n* **1** being weak. **2** failing. **3** self-indulgent liking.
weal *n* raised mark left on the skin by a blow.
wealth *n* **1** state of being rich. **2** large amount of money and valuables. **3** great amount or number. **wealthy** *adj*

wean *v* **1** accustom (a baby or young mammal) to food other than mother's milk. **2** coax (someone) away from former habits.
weapon *n* **1** object used in fighting. **2** anything used to get the better of an opponent. **weaponry** *n* weapons collectively.
wear *v* **wearing, wore, worn 1** have on the body as clothing or ornament. **2** show as one's expression. **3** (cause to) deteriorate by constant use or action **4** endure constant use. ♦ *n* **5** clothes suitable for a particular time or purpose, e.g. *beach wear.* **6** damage caused by use. **7** ability to endure constant use. **wearer** *n* **wear off** *v* gradually decrease in intensity. **wear on** *v* (of time) pass slowly.
weary *adj* **-rier, -riest 1** tired or exhausted. **2** tiring. ♦ *v* **-rying, -ried 3** make or become weary. **wearily** *adv* **weariness** *n* **wearisome** *adj* tedious.
weasel *n* small carnivorous mammal with a long body and short legs.
weather *n* **1** day-to-day atmospheric conditions of a place. ♦ *v* **2** (cause to) be affected by the weather. **3** come safely through. **under the weather** *Informal* slightly ill. **weather-beaten** *adj* worn, damaged, or (of skin) tanned by exposure to the weather. **weathercock, weathervane** *n* device that revolves to show the direction of the wind.
weave *v* **weaving, wove** *or* **weaved, woven** *or* **weaved 1** make (fabric) by interlacing (yarn) on a loom. **2** compose (a story). **3** move from side to side while going forwards. **weaver** *n*
web *n* **1** net spun by a spider. **2** anything intricate or complex, e.g. *web of deceit.* **3** skin between the toes of a duck, frog, etc. **the Web** short for WORLD WIDE WEB. **webbed** *adj*

webbing n strong fabric woven in strips. **webcam** n camera that transmits images over the Internet. **webcast** n broadcast of an event over the Internet. **weblog** n person's online journal (also **blog**). **website** n group of connected pages on the World Wide Web.

wed v **wedding, wedded** or **wed 1** marry. **2** unite closely. **wedding** n act or ceremony of marriage. **wedlock** n marriage.

wedge n **1** piece of material thick at one end and thin at the other. ♦ v **2** fasten or split with a wedge. **3** squeeze into a narrow space **wedge-tailed eagle** large brown Australian eagle with a wedge-shaped tail.

Wednesday n fourth day of the week.

wee adj Brit, Austral & NZ informal small or short.

weed n **1** plant growing where undesired. **2** Informal thin ineffectual person. ♦ v **3** clear of weeds. **weedy** adj Informal (of a person) thin and weak. **weed out** v remove or eliminate (what is unwanted).

weeds pl n Obs widow's mourning clothes.

week n **1** period of seven days, esp. one beginning on a Sunday. **2** hours or days of work in a week. **weekly** adj, adv **1** happening, done, etc. once a week. ♦ n, pl **-lies 2** newspaper or magazine published once a week. **weekday** n any day of the week except Saturday or Sunday. **weekend** n Saturday and Sunday.

weep v **weeping, wept 1** shed tears. **2** ooze liquid. **weepy** adj liable to cry. **weeping willow** willow with drooping branches.

weevil n small beetle which eats grain etc.

weft n cross threads in weaving.

weigh v **1** have a specified weight. **2** measure the weight of. **3** consider carefully. **4** be influential. **5** be burdensome. **weigh anchor** raise a ship's anchor or (of a ship) have its anchor raised. **weighbridge** n machine for weighing vehicles by means of a metal plate set into the road.

weight n **1** heaviness of an object. **2** unit of measurement of weight. **3** object of known mass used for weighing. **4** heavy object. **5** importance or influence. ♦ v **6** add weight to. **7** slant (a system) so that it favours one side rather than another. **weightless** adj **weightlessness** n

weighting n Brit extra allowance paid in special circumstances.

weighty adj **weightier, weightiest 1** important or serious. **2** very heavy. **weightily** adv

weir n river dam.

weird adj **1** strange or bizarre. **2** unearthly or eerie.

☑ **SPELLING TIP**

The pronunciation of **weird** possibly leads people to spell it with the vowels the wrong way round. The Bank of English shows that *wierd* is a common misspelling.

---

weirdo n, pl **-dos** Informal peculiar person.

welch v same as WELSH.

welcome v **-coming, -comed 1** greet with pleasure. **2** receive gladly. ♦ n **3** kindly greeting. ♦ adj **4** received gladly. **5** freely permitted.

weld v **1** join (pieces of metal or plastic) by softening with heat. **2** unite closely. ♦ n **3** welded joint. **welder** n

welfare n **1** wellbeing. **2** help given to people in need. **welfare state** system in which the government takes responsibility for the wellbeing of its citizens.

well[1] *adv* **better, best 1** satisfactorily. **2** skilfully. **3** completely. **4** intimately. **5** considerably. **6** very likely. ♦ *adj* **7** in good health. **8** *interj* **9** exclamation of surprise, interrogation, etc.

well[2] *n* **1** hole sunk into the earth to reach water, oil, or gas. **2** deep open shaft. ♦ *v* **3** flow upwards or outwards.

wellbeing *n* state of being well, happy, or prosperous.

well-disposed *adj* inclined to be friendly or sympathetic.

wellies *pl n Brit & Aust informal* wellingtons.

wellingtons *pl n Brit & Aust* high waterproof rubber boots.

well-meaning *adj* having good intentions.

well-spoken *adj* speaking in a polite or articulate way.

well-worn *adj* **1** (of a word or phrase) stale from overuse. **2** so much used as to be affected by wear.

welsh *v* fail to pay a debt or fulfil an obligation.

Welsh *adj* **1** of Wales. ♦ *n* **2** language or people of Wales. **Welsh rarebit, rabbit** dish of melted cheese on toast.

welt *n* **1** raised mark on the skin produced by a blow. **2** raised or strengthened seam.

welter *n* jumbled mass.

welterweight *n* boxer weighing up to 147lb (professional) or 67kg (amateur).

wen *n* cyst on the scalp.

wench *n Facetious* young woman.

wend *v* go or travel.

went *v* past tense of GO.

wept *v* past of WEEP.

were *v* **1** form of the past tense of **be** used after *we, you, they,* or a plural noun. **2** subjunctive of BE.

we're we are.

weren't were not.

werewolf *n* (in folklore) person who can turn into a wolf.

west *n* **1** (direction towards) the part of the horizon where the sun sets. **2** region lying in this direction. **3** (W-) western Europe and the US. ♦ *adj* **4** to or in the west. **5** (of a wind) from the west. ♦ *adv* **6** in, to, or towards the west. **westerly** *adj* **western** *adj* **1** of or in the west. ♦ *n* **2** film or story about cowboys in the western US. **westernize** *v* adapt to the customs and culture of the West. **westward** *adj, adv* **westwards** *adv*

wet *adj* **wetter, wettest 1** covered or soaked with water or another liquid. **2** not yet dry. **3** rainy. **4** *Brit informal* (of a person) feeble or foolish. ♦ *n* **5** moisture or rain. **6** *Brit informal* feeble or foolish person. **7** *v* **wetting, wet** *or* **wetted 8** make wet. **wet blanket** *Informal* person who has a depressing effect on others. **wetland** *n* area of marshy land. **wet nurse** woman employed to breast-feed another's child. **wet suit** close-fitting rubber suit worn by divers etc.

whack *v* **1** strike with a resounding blow. ♦ *n* **2** such a blow. **3** *Informal* share. **4** *Informal* attempt. **whacked** *adj* exhausted. **whacking** *adj Informal* huge.

whale *n* large fish-shaped sea mammal. **have a whale of a time** *Informal* enjoy oneself very much. **whaler** *n* ship or person involved in whaling. **whaling** *n* hunting of whales for food and oil.

wharf *n, pl* **wharves, wharfs** platform at a harbour for loading and unloading ships. **wharfie** *n Aust* person employed to load and unload ships.

what *pron* **1** which thing. **2** that which. **3** request for a statement to be repeated. ♦ *interj* **4** exclamation of anger, surprise, etc. ♦ *adv* **5** in which way, how much, e.g. *what do you care?* **what for?** why? **whatever** *pron* **1** everything or anything that. **2** no matter what. **whatnot** *n Informal* similar unspecified things. **whatsoever** *adj* at all.

wheat *n* **1** grain used in making flour, bread, and pasta. **2** plant producing this. **wheaten** *adj* **wheatear** *n* small songbird.

wheedle *v* coax or cajole.

wheel *n* **1** disc that revolves on an axle. **2** pivoting movement. ♦ *v* **3** push or pull (something with wheels). **4** turn as if on an axis. **5** turn round suddenly. **wheeling and dealing** use of shrewd and sometimes unscrupulous methods to achieve success. **wheeler-dealer** *n* **wheelbarrow** *n* shallow box for carrying loads, with a wheel at the front and two handles. **wheelbase** *n* distance between a vehicle's front and back axles. **wheelchair** *n* chair mounted on wheels for use by people who cannot walk. **wheel clamp** immobilizing device fixed to one wheel of an illegally parked car.

wheeze *v* **1** breathe with a hoarse whistling noise. ♦ *n* **2** wheezing sound. **3** *Informal* trick or plan. **wheezy** *adj*

whelk *n* edible snail-like shellfish.

whelp *n* **1** pup or cub. **2** *Offens* youth. ♦ *v* **3** (of an animal) give birth.

when *adv* **1** at what time? ♦ *conj* **2** at the time that. **3** although. **4** considering the fact that. ♦ *pron* **5** at which time. **whenever** *adv, conj* at whatever time.

whence *adv, conj Obs* from what place or source.

where *adv* **1** in, at, or to what place? ♦ *pron* **2** in, at, or to which place. ♦ *conj* **3** in the place at which. **whereabouts** *n* **1** present position. ♦ *adv* **2** at what place. **whereas** *conj*

but on the other hand. **whereby** *pron* by which. **wherefore** *Obs* ♦ *adv* **1** why. ♦ *conj* **2** consequently. **whereupon** *conj* at which point. **wherever** *conj, adv* at whatever place. **wherewithal** *n* necessary funds, resources, etc.

whet *v* **whetting, whetted** sharpen (a tool). **whet someone's appetite** increase someone's desire. **whetstone** *n* stone for sharpening tools.

whether *conj* used to introduce an indirect question or a clause expressing doubt or choice.

whey [way] *n* watery liquid that separates from the curd when milk is clotted.

which *adj, pron* **1** used to request or refer to a choice from different possibilities. ♦ *pron* **2** used to refer to a thing already mentioned. **whichever** *adj, pron* **1** any out of several. **2** no matter which.

whiff *n* **1** puff of air or odour. **2** trace or hint.

Whig *n* member of a British political party of the 18th–19th centuries that sought limited reform.

while *conj* **1** at the same time that. **2** whereas. ♦ *n* **3** period of time. **whilst** *conj* while. **while away** *v* pass (time) idly but pleasantly.

whim *n* sudden fancy. **whimsy** *n* **1** capricious idea. **2** light or fanciful humour. **whimsical** *adj* unusual, playful, and fanciful.

whimper *v* **1** cry in a soft whining way. ♦ *n* **2** soft plaintive whine.

whin *n* Brit gorse.

whine *n* **1** high-pitched plaintive cry. **2** peevish complaint. ♦ *v* **3** make such a sound. **whining** *n, adj*

whinge *Brit, Aust & NZ informal* ♦ *v* **1** complain. ♦ *n* **2** complaint.

whinny *v* **-nying, -nied 1** neigh softly.

♦ *n, pl* -**nies 2** soft neigh.

whip *n* **1** cord attached to a handle, used for beating animals or people. **2** politician responsible for organizing and disciplining fellow party or caucus members. **3** call made on members of Parliament to attend for important votes. **4** dessert made from beaten cream or egg whites. ♦ *v* **whipping, whipped 5** strike with a whip, strap, or cane. **6** *Informal* pull, remove, or move quickly. **7** beat (esp. eggs or cream) to a froth. **8** rouse into a particular condition. **9** *Informal* steal. **whip bird** *Aust* bird with a whistle ending in a whipcrack note. **whiplash injury** neck injury caused by a sudden jerk to the head, as in a car crash. **whip-round** *n Informal* collection of money.

whippet *n* racing dog like a small greyhound.

whirl *v* **1** spin or revolve. **2** be dizzy or confused. ♦ *n* **3** whirling movement. **4** bustling activity. **5** confusion or giddiness. **whirlpool** *n* strong circular current of water. **whirlwind** *n* **1** column of air whirling violently upwards in a spiral. ♦ *adj* **2** much quicker than normal.

whirr, whir *n* **1** prolonged soft buzz. ♦ *v* **whirring, whirred 2** (cause to) make a whirr.

whisk *v* **1** move or remove quickly. **2** beat (esp. eggs or cream) to a froth. ♦ *n* **3** egg-beating utensil.

whisker *n* **1** any of the long stiff hairs on the face of a cat or other mammal. ♦ *pl* **2** hair growing on a man's face. **by a whisker** *Informal* only just.

whisky *n, pl* -**kies** spirit distilled from fermented cereals. **whiskey** *n, pl* -**keys** Irish or American whisky.

whisper *v* **1** speak softly, without vibration of the vocal cords. **2** rustle. ♦ *n* **3** soft voice. **4** *Informal* rumour. **5**

rustling sound.

whist *n* card game in which one pair of players tries to win more tricks than another pair.

whistle *v* **1** produce a shrill sound, esp. by forcing the breath through pursed lips. **2** signal by a whistle. ♦ *n* **3** whistling sound. **4** instrument blown to make a whistling sound. **blow the whistle on** *Informal* inform on or put a stop to. **whistling** *n, adj*

whit *n* **not a whit** not the slightest amount.

white *adj* **1** of the colour of snow. **2** pale. **3** light in colour. **4** (of coffee) served with milk. ♦ *n* **5** colour of snow. **6** clear fluid round the yolk of an egg. **7** white part, esp. of the eyeball. **8** (W-) member of the race of people with light-coloured skin. **whiten** *v* make or become white or whiter. **whiteness** *n* **whitish** *adj* **white-collar** *adj* denoting professional and clerical workers. **white elephant** useless or unwanted possession. **white flag** signal of surrender or truce. **white goods** large household appliances such as cookers and fridges. **white-hot** *adj* very hot. **white lie** minor unimportant lie. **white paper** report by the government, outlining its policy on a matter.

whitebait *n* small edible fish.

whitewash *n* **1** substance for whitening walls. **2** *v* **3** cover with whitewash. **4** conceal or gloss over unpleasant facts.

whither *adv Obs* to what place.

whiting *n* edible sea fish.

Whitsun *n* Christian festival celebrating the descent of the Holy Spirit to the apostles.

whittle *v* cut or carve (wood) with a knife. **whittle down, away** *v* reduce or wear away gradually.

whizz, whiz *v* **whizzing, whizzed 1**

make a loud buzzing sound. **2** *Informal* move quickly. ♦ *n, pl* **whizzes 3** loud buzzing sound. **4** *Informal* person skilful at something. **whizz kid, whiz kid** *Informal* person who is outstandingly able for his or her age.

who *pron* **1** which person. **2** used to refer to a person or people already mentioned. **whoever** *pron* **1** any person who. **2** no matter who.

whodunnit, whodunit [hoo-**dun**-nit] *n Informal* detective story, play, or film.

whole *adj* **1** containing all the elements or parts. **2** uninjured or undamaged. ♦ *n* **3** complete thing or system. **on the whole** taking everything into consideration. **wholly** *adv* **wholefood** *n* food that has been processed as little as possible. **wholehearted** *adj* sincere or enthusiastic. **wholemeal** *adj* **1** (of flour) made from the whole wheat grain. **2** made from wholemeal flour. **whole number** number that does not contain a fraction.

wholesale *adj, adv* **1** dealing by selling goods in large quantities to retailers. **2** on a large scale. **wholesaler** *n*

wholesome *adj* physically or morally beneficial.

whom *pron* **objective form of** WHO.

whoop *v, n* shout or cry to express excitement.

whoopee *interj Informal* cry of joy.

whooping cough *n* infectious disease marked by convulsive coughing and noisy breathing.

whopper *n Informal* **1** anything unusually large. **2** huge lie. **whopping** *adj*

whore [**hore**] *n* prostitute.

whorl *n* **1** ring of leaves or petals. **2** one turn of a spiral.

whose *pron* of whom or of which.

why *adv* **1** for what reason. ♦ *pron* **2** because of which.

wick *n* cord through a lamp or candle which carries fuel to the flame.

wicked *adj* **1** morally bad. **2** mischievous. **wickedly** *adv* **wickedness** *n*

wicker *adj* made of woven cane. **wickerwork** *n*

wicket *n* **1** set of three cricket stumps and two bails. **2** ground between the two wickets on a cricket pitch.

wide *adj* **1** large from side to side. **2** having a specified width. **3** spacious or extensive. **4** far from the target. **5** opened fully. ♦ *adv* **6** to the full extent. **7** over an extensive area. **8** far from the target. **widely** *adv* **widen** *v* make or become wider. **widespread** *adj* affecting a wide area or a large number of people.

widgeon *n* same as WIGEON.

widow *n* woman whose husband is dead and who has not remarried. **widowed** *adj* **widowhood** *n* **widower** *n* man whose wife is dead and who has not remarried.

width *n* **1** distance from side to side. **2** quality of being wide.

wield *v* **1** hold and use (a weapon). **2** have and use (power).

wife *n, pl* **wives** woman to whom a man is married.

wig *n* artificial head of hair.

wigeon *n* duck found in marshland.

wiggle *v* **1** move jerkily from side to side. ♦ *n* **2** wiggling movement.

wigwam *n* Native American's tent.

wild *adj* **1** (of animals) not tamed or domesticated. **2** (of plants) not cultivated. **3** lacking restraint or control. **4** violent or stormy. **5** *Informal* excited. **6** *Informal* furious. **7** random. **wilds** *pl n* desolate or uninhabited place. **wildly** *adv* **wildness** *n* **wild-goose chase** search that has little chance of success.

wildcat *n* European wild animal like a large domestic cat. **wildcat strike** sudden unofficial strike.

wildebeest *n* gnu.

wilderness *n* uninhabited uncultivated region.

wildfire *n* **spread like wildfire** spread quickly and uncontrollably.

wildlife *n* wild animals and plants collectively.

wiles *pl n* tricks or ploys. **wily** *adj* crafty or sly.

wilful *adj* **1** headstrong or obstinate. **2** intentional. **wilfully** *adv*

will¹ *v, past* **would** used as an auxiliary to form the future tense or to indicate intention, ability, or expectation.

will² *n* **1** strong determination. **2** desire or wish. **3** directions written for disposal of one's property after death. ♦ *v* **4** use one's will in an attempt to do (something). **5** wish or desire. **6** leave (property) by a will. **willing** *adj* **1** ready or inclined (to do something). **2** keen and obliging. **willingly** *adv* **willingness** *n* **willpower** *n* ability to control oneself and one's actions.

will-o'-the-wisp *n* **1** elusive person or thing. **2** pale light sometimes seen over marshes at night.

willow *n* **1** tree with thin flexible branches. **2** its wood, used for making cricket bats. **willowy** *adj* slender and graceful.

willy-nilly *adv* whether desired or not.

willy wagtail *n Aust* black-and-white flycatcher.

willy-willy *n Aust* small tropical dust storm.

wilt *v* (cause to) become limp or lose strength.

wimp *n Informal* feeble ineffectual person.

wimple *n* garment framing the face, worn by medieval women and now by nuns.

win *v* **winning, won 1** come first in (a competition, fight, etc.). **2** gain (a prize) in a competition. **3** get by effort. ♦ *n* **4** victory, esp. in a game. **winner** *n* **winning** *adj* **1** gaining victory. **2** charming. **winnings** *pl n* sum won, esp. in gambling. **win over** *v* gain the support or consent of (someone).

wince *v* **1** draw back, as if in pain. ♦ *n* **2** wincing.

winch *n* **1** machine for lifting or hauling using a cable or chain wound round a drum. ♦ *v* **2** lift or haul using a winch.

wind¹ *n* **1** current of air. **2** hint or suggestion. **3** breath. **4** flatulence. **5** idle talk. ♦ *v* **6** render short of breath. **windy** *adj* **windward** *adj, n* (of or in) the direction from which the wind is blowing. **windfall** *n* **1** unexpected good luck. **2** fallen fruit. **wind instrument** musical instrument played by blowing. **windmill** *n* machine for grinding or pumping driven by sails turned by the wind. **windpipe** *n* tube linking the throat and the lungs. **windscreen** *n* front window of a motor vehicle. **windscreen wiper** device that wipes rain etc. from a windscreen. **windsock** *n* cloth cone on a mast at an airfield to indicate wind direction. **windsurfing** *n* sport of riding on water using a surfboard propelled and steered by a sail.

wind² *v* **winding, wound 1** coil or wrap around. **2** tighten the spring of (a clock or watch). **3** move in a twisting course. **wind up** *v* **1** bring to or reach an end. **2** tighten the spring of (a clock or watch). **3** *Informal* make tense or agitated. **4** *Slang* tease.

windlass *n* winch worked by a crank.

window *n* **1** opening in a wall to let in light or air. **2** glass pane or panes fitted in such an opening. **3** display area behind the window of a shop. **4** area on a computer screen that can be manipulated separately from the rest of the display area. **5** period of unbooked time in a diary or schedule. **window-dressing** n **1** arrangement of goods in a shop window. **2** attempt to make something more attractive than it really is. **window-shopping** n looking at goods in shop windows without intending to buy.

wine n **1** alcoholic drink made from fermented grapes. **2** similar drink made from other fruits. **wine and dine** entertain or be entertained with fine food and drink.

wing n **1** one of the limbs or organs of a bird, insect, or bat that are used for flying. **2** one of the winglike supporting parts of an aircraft. **3** projecting side part of a building. **4** faction of a political party. **5** part of a car body surrounding the wheels. **6** Sport (player on) either side of the pitch. ♦ pl **7** sides of a stage. ♦ v **8** fly. **9** wound slightly in the wing or arm. **winged** adj **winger** n Sport player positioned on a wing.

wink v **1** close and open (an eye) quickly as a signal. **2** twinkle. ♦ n **3** winking. **4** smallest amount of sleep.

winkle n shellfish with a spiral shell. **winkle out** v Informal extract or prise out.

winnow v **1** separate (chaff) from (grain). **2** examine to select desirable elements.

winsome adj charming or winning.

winter n **1** coldest season. ♦ v **2** spend the winter. **wintry** adj **1** of or like winter. **2** cold or unfriendly. **winter sports** open-air sports held on snow or ice.

wipe v **1** clean or dry by rubbing. **2** erase (a tape). ♦ n **3** wiping. **wipe out** v destroy completely.

wire n **1** thin flexible strand of metal. **2** length of this used to carry electric current. **3** Obs telegram. ♦ v **4** equip with wires. **wiring** n system of wires. **wiry** adj **1** lean and tough. **2** like wire. **wire-haired** adj (of a dog) having a stiff wiry coat.

wireless n Old-fashioned same as RADIO.

wireless adj **1** (of a computer network) connected by radio rather than by cables or fibre optics. ♦ n **2** Old-fashioned same as RADIO.

wisdom n **1** good sense and judgment. **2** accumulated knowledge. **wisdom tooth** any of the four large molar teeth that come through usu. after the age of twenty.

wise¹ adj having wisdom. **wisely** adv **wiseacre** n person who wishes to seem wise.

wise² n Obs manner.

wisecrack Informal ♦ n **1** clever, sometimes unkind, remark. ♦ v **2** make a wisecrack.

wish v **1** want or desire. **2** feel or express a hope about someone's wellbeing, success, etc. ♦ n **3** expression of a desire. **4** thing desired. **wishful** adj too optimistic. **wishbone** n V-shaped bone above the breastbone of a fowl.

wishy-washy adj Informal insipid or bland.

wisp n **1** light delicate streak. **2** twisted bundle or tuft. **wispy** adj

wisteria n climbing shrub with blue or purple flowers.

wistful adj sadly longing. **wistfully** adv

wit n **1** ability to use words or ideas in a clever and amusing way. **2** person with this ability. **3** (sometimes pl) practical intelligence. **witless** adj foolish.

witch n **1** person, usu. female, who practises (black) magic. **2** ugly or wicked woman. **witchcraft** n use of magic. **witch doctor** (in certain

societies) a man appearing to cure or cause injury or disease by magic.
witch-hunt n campaign against people with unpopular views.

witchetty grub n wood-boring edible Australian caterpillar.

with prep indicating presence alongside, possession, means of performance, characteristic manner, etc., e.g. *walking with his dog; a man with two cars; hit with a hammer; playing with skill.* **within** prep, adv in or inside. **without** prep not accompanied by, using, or having.

withdraw v **-drawing, -drew, -drawn** take or move out or away. **withdrawal** n **withdrawn** adj unsociable.

wither v wilt or dry up. **withering** adj (of a look or remark) scornful.

withers pl n ridge between a horse's shoulder blades.

withhold v **-holding, -held** refrain from giving.

withstand v **-standing, -stood** oppose or resist successfully.

witness n **1** person who has seen something happen. **2** person giving evidence in court. **3** evidence or testimony. ♦ v **4** see at first hand. **5** sign (a document) to certify that it is genuine.

witter v Chiefly Brit chatter pointlessly or at unnecessary length.

wittingly adv intentionally.

witty adj **wittier, wittiest** clever and amusing. **wittily** adv **witticism** n witty remark.

wives n plural of WIFE.

wizard n **1** magician. **2** person with outstanding skill in a particular field. **wizardry** n

wizened [**wiz**-zend] adj shrivelled or wrinkled.

WMD weapon(s) of mass destruction.

woad n blue dye obtained from a plant, used by the ancient Britons as a body dye.

wobbegong n Australian shark with brown-and-white skin.

wobble v **1** move unsteadily. **2** shake. ♦ n **3** wobbling movement or sound. **wobbly** adj

wodge n Informal thick lump or chunk.

woe n grief. **woeful** adj **1** extremely sad. **2** pitiful. **woefully** adv **woebegone** adj looking miserable.

wok n bowl-shaped Chinese cooking pan, used for stir-frying.

woke v past tense of WAKE¹. **woken** v past participle of WAKE¹.

wold n high open country.

wolf n, pl **wolves** **1** wild predatory canine mammal. ♦ v **2** eat ravenously. **cry wolf** raise a false alarm. **wolf whistle** whistle by a man indicating that he thinks a woman is attractive.

wolverine n carnivorous mammal of Arctic regions.

woman n, pl **women** **1** adult human female. **2** women collectively. **womanhood** n **womanish** adj effeminate. **womanly** adj having qualities traditionally associated with a woman. **womanizing** n practice of indulging in casual affairs with women. **womanizer** n **Women's Liberation** movement for the removal of inequalities between women and men (also **women's lib**).

womb n hollow organ in female mammals where babies are conceived and develop.

wombat n small heavily-built burrowing Australian marsupial.

won v past of WIN.

wonder v **1** be curious about. **2** be amazed. ♦ n **3** wonderful thing. **4** emotion caused by an amazing or unusual thing. ♦ adj **5** spectacularly successful, e.g. *a wonder drug.*

wonderful adj 1 very fine. 2 remarkable. **wonderfully** adv **wonderment** n **wondrous** adj Old-fashioned wonderful.

wonky adj **-kier, -kiest** Brit, Aust & NZ informal shaky or unsteady.

wont [rhymes with **don't**] adj 1 accustomed. ♦ n 2 custom.

won't will not.

woo v 1 try to persuade. 2 Old-fashioned try to gain the love of.

wood n 1 substance trees are made of, used in carpentry and as fuel. 2 area where trees grow. 3 long-shafted golf club, usu. with wooden head. **wooded** adj covered with trees. **wooden** adj 1 made of wood. 2 without expression. **woody** adj **woodbine** n honeysuckle. **woodcock** n game bird. **woodcut** n (print made from) an engraved block of wood. **woodland** n forest. **woodlouse** n small insect-like creature with many legs. **woodpecker** n bird which searches tree trunks for insects. **woodwind** adj, n (of) a type of wind instrument made of wood. **woodworm** n insect larva that bores into wood.

woof¹ n cross threads in weaving.

woof² n barking noise made by a dog. **woofer** n loudspeaker reproducing low-frequency sounds.

wool n 1 soft hair of sheep, goats, etc. 2 yarn spun from this. **woollen** adj **woolly** adj 1 of or like wool. 2 vague or muddled. ♦ n 3 knitted woollen garment.

woomera n notched stick used by Australian Aborigines to aid the propulsion of a spear.

woozy adj **woozier, wooziest** Informal weak, dizzy, and confused.

wop-wops pl n NZ informal remote rural areas.

word n 1 smallest single meaningful unit of speech or writing. 2 chat or discussion. 3 brief remark. 4 message. 5 promise. 6 command. ♦ v 7 express in words. **wordy** adj using too many words. **wording** n choice and arrangement of words. **word processor** keyboard, microprocessor, and VDU for electronic organization and storage of text. **word processing**

wore v past tense of WEAR.

work n 1 physical or mental effort directed to making or doing something. 2 paid employment. 3 duty or task. 4 something made or done. ♦ pl 5 factory. 6 total of a writer's or artist's achievements. 7 Informal full treatment. 8 mechanism of a machine. ♦ adj 9 of or for work. ♦ v 10 (cause to) do work. 11 be employed. 12 (cause to) operate. 13 (of a plan etc.) be successful. 14 cultivate (land). 15 manipulate, shape, or process. 16 (cause to) reach a specified condition. **work-to-rule** n protest in which workers keep strictly to all regulations to reduce the rate of work. **workable** adj **worker** n **workaholic** n person obsessed with work. **workhorse** n person or thing that does a lot of dull or routine work. **workhouse** n (in England, formerly) institution where the poor were given food and lodgings in return for work. **working class** social class consisting of wage earners, esp. manual workers. **working-class** adj **working party** committee investigating a specific problem. **workman** n manual worker. **workmanship** n skill with which an object is made. **workshop** n room or building for a manufacturing process. **worktop** n surface in a kitchen, used for food preparation.

world n 1 the planet earth. 2 mankind. 3 society of a particular area or period. 4 sphere of existence. ♦ adj 5 of the whole world. **worldly** *adj* **1** not spiritual. **2** concerned with material things. **3** wise in the ways of the world. **world-weary** *adj* no longer finding pleasure in life. **World Wide Web** global network of linked computer files.

worm *n* **1** small limbless invertebrate animal. **2** *Informal* wretched or spineless person. **3** shaft with a spiral thread forming part of a gear system. **4** *Computers* type of virus. ♦ *pl* **5** illness caused by parasitic worms in the intestines. ♦ *v* **6** rid of worms. **worm one's way 1** crawl. **2** insinuate (oneself). **wormy** *adj* **worm-eaten** *adj* eaten into by worms. **worm out** *v* extract (information) craftily.

wormwood *n* bitter plant.

worn *v* past participle of WEAR.

worry *v* **-rying, -ried 1** (cause to) be anxious or uneasy. **2** annoy or bother. **3** (of a dog) chase and try to bite (sheep etc.). ♦ *n, pl* **-ries 4** (cause of) anxiety or concern. **worried** *adj* **worrying** *adj, n*

worse *adj, adv* comparative of BAD *or* BADLY. **worst** *adj, adv* **1** superlative of BAD *OR* BADLY. ♦ *n* **2** worst thing. **worsen** *v* make or grow worse.

worship *v* **-shipping, -shipped 1** show religious devotion to. **2** love and admire. ♦ *n* **3** act or instance of worshipping. **4** (W-) title for a mayor or magistrate. **worshipper** *n* **worshipful** *adj* worshipping.

worsted [**wooss**-tid] *n* type of woollen yarn or fabric.

worth *prep* **1** having a value of. **2** meriting or justifying. ♦ *n* **3** value or price. **4** excellence. **5** amount to be had for a given sum. **worthless** *adj* **worthy** *adj* **1** deserving admiration or respect. ♦ *n* **2** *Informal* notable person. **worthily** *adv* **worthiness** *n* **worthwhile** *adj* worth the time or

effort involved.

would *v* used as an auxiliary to express a request, describe a habitual past action, or form the past tense or subjunctive mood of WILL¹. **would-be** *adj* wishing or pretending to be.

wouldn't would not.

wound¹ *n* **1** injury caused by violence. **2** injury to the feelings. ♦ *v* **3** inflict a wound on.

wound² *v* past of WIND².

wove *v* a past tense of WEAVE. **woven** *v* a past participle of WEAVE.

wow *interj* **1** exclamation of astonishment. ♦ *n* **2** *Informal* astonishing person or thing.

wowser *n* Aust & NZ slang **1** puritanical person. **2** teetotaller.

wpm words per minute.

wrack *n* seaweed.

wraith *n* ghost.

wrangle *v* **1** argue noisily. ♦ *n* **2** noisy argument.

wrap *v* **wrapping, wrapped 1** fold (something) round (a person or thing) so as to cover. ♦ *n* **2** garment wrapped round the shoulders. **3** sandwich made by wrapping a filling in a tortilla. **wrapper** *n* cover for a product. **wrapping** *n* material used to wrap. **wrap up** *v* **1** fold paper round. **2** put warm clothes on. **3** *Informal* finish or settle (a matter).

wrasse *n* colourful sea fish.

wrath [**roth**] *n* intense anger. **wrathful** *adj*

wreak *v* **wreak havoc** cause chaos. **wreak vengeance on** take revenge on.

wreath *n* twisted ring or band of flowers or leaves used as a memorial or tribute. **wreathed** *adj* surrounded or encircled.

wreck *v* **1** destroy. ♦ *n* **2** remains of something that has been destroyed or badly damaged, esp. a ship. **3** person in very poor condition. **wrecker** n **wreckage** n wrecked remains.

wren n **1** small brown songbird. **2** Australian warbler.

Wren n Informal (in Britain) member of the former Women's Royal Naval Service.

wrench v **1** twist or pull violently. **2** sprain (a joint). ♦ n **3** violent twist or pull. **4** sprain. **5** difficult or painful parting. **6** adjustable spanner.

wrest v **1** twist violently. **2** take by force.

wrestle v **1** fight, esp. as a sport, by grappling with and trying to throw down an opponent. **2** struggle hard with. **wrestler** n **wrestling** n

wretch n **1** despicable person. **2** pitiful person.

wretched [retch-id] adj **1** miserable or unhappy. **2** worthless. **wretchedly** adv **wretchedness** n

wrier adj a comparative of WRY. **wriest** adj a superlative of WRY.

wriggle v **1** move with a twisting action. **2** manoeuvre oneself by devious means. ♦ n **3** wriggling movement.

wright n maker, e.g. wheelwright.

wring v wringing, wrung **1** twist, esp. to squeeze liquid out of. **2** clasp and twist (the hands). **3** obtain by forceful means.

wrinkle n **1** slight crease, esp. one in the skin due to age. ♦ v **2** make or become slightly creased. **wrinkly** adj

wrist n joint between the hand and the arm. **wristwatch** n watch worn on the wrist.

writ n written legal command.

write v writing, wrote, written **1** mark paper etc. with symbols or words. **2** set down in words. **3** communicate by letter. **4** be the author or composer of. **writing** n **writer** n **1** author. **2** person who has written something specified. **write-off** n Informal something damaged beyond repair. **write-up** n published account of something.

writhe v twist or squirm in or as if in pain.

wrong adj **1** incorrect or mistaken. **2** immoral or bad. **3** not intended or suitable. **4** not working properly. ♦ adv **5** in a wrong manner. ♦ n **6** something immoral or unjust. ♦ v **7** treat unjustly. **8** malign. **wrongly** adv **wrongful** adj **wrongfully** adv **wrongdoing** n immoral or illegal behaviour. **wrongdoer** n

wrote v past tense of WRITE.

wrought [rawt] v **1** Lit past of WORK. ♦ adj **2** (of metals) shaped by hammering or beating. **wrought iron** pure form of iron used for decorative work.

wrung v past of WRING.

wry adj wrier, wriest or wryer, wryest **1** drily humorous. **2** (of a facial expression) contorted. **wryly** adv

wt. weight.

WWW World Wide Web.

wych-elm n elm with large rough leaves.

X x Y y Z z

X 1 indicating an error, a choice, or a kiss. **2** indicating an unknown, unspecified, or variable factor, number, person, or thing.

xenon *n Chem* colourless odourless gas found in very small quantities in the air.

xenophobia [zen-oh-**fobe**-ea] *n* fear or hatred of people from other countries.

Xerox [**zeer**-ox] *n* **1** ® machine for copying printed material. **2** ® copy made by a Xerox machine. ♦ *v* **3** copy (a document) using such a machine.

Xmas [**eks**-mass] *n Informal* Christmas.

X-ray, x-ray *n* **1** stream of radiation that can pass through some solid materials. **2** picture made by sending X-rays through someone's body to examine internal organs. ♦ *v* **3** photograph, treat, or examine using X-rays.

xylem [**zy**-lem] *n* plant tissue that conducts water and minerals from the roots to all other parts.

xylophone [**zile**-oh-fone] *n* musical instrument made of a row of wooden bars played with hammers.

Y2K *n Informal* name for the year 2000 AD (esp. referring to the millennium bug).

ya *interj S Afr* yes.

yabby *n, pl* -**bies** *Aust* **1** small freshwater crayfish. **2** marine prawn used as bait.

yacht [**yott**] *n* large boat with sails or an engine, used for racing or pleasure cruising. **yachting** *n* **yachtsman, yachtswoman** *n*

yak[1] *n* Tibetan ox with long shaggy hair.

yak[2] *v* **yakking, yakked** *Slang* talk continuously about unimportant matters.

yakka *n Aust & NZ informal* work.

yam *n* tropical root vegetable.

yank *v* **1** pull or jerk suddenly. ♦ *n* **2** sudden pull or jerk.

Yankee, Yank *n Slang* person from the United States.

yap *v* **yapping, yapped 1** bark with a high-pitched sound. **2** *Informal* talk continuously. ♦ *n* **3** high-pitched bark.

yard[1] *n* unit of length equal to 36 inches or about 91.4 centimetres. **yardstick** *n* standard against which to judge other people or things.

yard[2] *n* enclosed area, usu. next to a building and often used for a particular purpose, e.g. *builder's yard*.

yarmulke [**yar**-mull-ka] *n* skullcap worn by Jewish men.

yarn *n* **1** thread used for knitting or making cloth. **2** *Informal* long involved story.

yashmak *n* veil worn by a Muslim woman to cover her face in public.

yaw *v* (of an aircraft or ship) turn to one side or from side to side while moving.

yawl *n* two-masted sailing boat.

yawn *v* **1** open the mouth wide and take in air deeply, often when sleepy or bored. **2** (of an opening) be large and wide. ♦ *n* **3** act of yawning. **yawning** *adj*

yd yard.

ye [**yee**] *pron Obs* you.

year *n* **1** time taken for the earth to make one revolution around the sun, about 365 days. **2** twelve months from January 1 to December 31. **yearly** *adj, adv* (happening) every year or once a year. **yearling** *n* animal between one and two years old.

yearn *v* want (something) very much.

yearning n, adj

yeast n fungus used to make bread rise and to ferment alcoholic drinks. **yeasty** adj

yebo interj S Afr informal yes.

yell v 1 shout or scream in a loud or piercing way. ♦ n 2 loud cry of pain, anger, or fear.

yellow n 1 the colour of gold, a lemon, etc. ♦ adj 2 of this colour. 3 Informal cowardly. ♦ v 4 make or become yellow. **yellow belly** Aust freshwater food fish with yellow underparts. **yellow fever** serious infectious tropical disease. **yellowhammer** n European songbird with a yellow head and body. **Yellow Pages** ® telephone directory which lists businesses under the headings of the type of service they provide.

yelp v, n (give) a short sudden cry.

yen¹ n, pl yen monetary unit of Japan.

yen² n Informal longing or desire.

yeoman [yo-man] n, pl -men Hist farmer owning and farming his own land. **yeoman of the guard** member of the ceremonial bodyguard of the British monarchy.

yes interj 1 expresses consent, agreement, or approval. 2 used to answer when one is addressed. **yes man** person who always agrees with their superior.

yesterday adv, n 1 (on) the day before today. 2 (in) the recent past.

yet conj 1 nevertheless, still. ♦ adv 2 up until then or now. 3 still. 4 now.

yeti n same as ABOMINABLE SNOWMAN.

yew n evergreen tree with needle-like leaves and red berries.

Yiddish adj, n (of or in) a language of German origin spoken by many Jews in Europe and elsewhere.

yield v 1 produce or bear. 2 give up control of, surrender. 3 give in. 4 n 5 amount produced. **yielding** adj 1 submissive. 2 soft or flexible.

YMCA Young Men's Christian Association.

yob, yobbo n Slang bad-mannered aggressive youth.

yodel v -delling, -delled sing with abrupt changes between a normal and a falsetto voice.

yoga n Hindu method of exercise and discipline aiming at spiritual, mental, and physical wellbeing. **yogi** n person who practises yoga.

yogurt, yoghurt n slightly sour custard-like food made from milk that has had bacteria added to it, often sweetened and flavoured with fruit.

yoke n 1 wooden bar put across the necks of two animals to hold them together. 2 frame fitting over a person's shoulders for carrying buckets. 3 Lit oppressive force, e.g. the yoke of the tyrant. 4 fitted part of a garment to which a fuller part is attached. ♦ v 5 put a yoke on. 6 unite or link.

yokel n Offens person who lives in the country and is usu. simple and old-fashioned.

yolk n yellow part of an egg that provides food for the developing embryo.

Yom Kippur n annual Jewish religious holiday.

yonder adj, adv (situated) over there.

yonks pl n Informal very long time.

yore n Lit of yore a long time ago.

Yorkshire pudding n baked batter made from flour, milk, and eggs.

you pron refers to: 1 the person or people addressed. 2 unspecified person or people in general.

young adj 1 in an early stage of life or growth. ♦ pl n 2 young people in general. 3 offspring, esp. young animals. **youngster** n young person.

your adj **1** of, belonging to, or associated with you. **2** of, belonging to, or associated with an unspecified person or people in general. **yours** pron something belonging to you. **yourself** pron

youth n **1** time of being young. **2** boy or young man. **3** young people as a group. **youthful** adj **youthfulness** n **youth club** club that provides leisure activities for young people. **youth hostel** inexpensive lodging place for young people travelling cheaply.

yowl v, n (produce) a loud mournful cry.

yo-yo n, pl **-yos** toy consisting of a spool attached to a string, by which it is repeatedly spun out and reeled in.

yttrium [**it**-ree-um] n Chem silvery metallic element used in various alloys.

yucca n tropical plant with spikes of white leaves.

yucky adj **yuckier, yuckiest** Slang disgusting, nasty.

Yule n Lit Christmas (season).

yuppie n **1** young highly-paid professional person, esp. one who has a materialistic way of life. ♦ adj **2** typical of or reflecting the values of yuppies.

YWCA Young Women's Christian Association.

zany [**zane**-ee] adj **zanier, zaniest** comical in an endearing way.

zap v **zapping, zapped 1** Slang kill (by shooting). **2** change TV channels rapidly by remote control.

zeal n great enthusiasm or eagerness. **zealot** [**zel**-lot] n fanatic or extreme enthusiast. **zealous** [**zel**-luss] adj extremely eager or enthusiastic. **zealously** adv

zebra n black-and-white striped African animal of the horse family. **zebra crossing** pedestrian crossing marked by black and white stripes on the road.

zebu [**zee**-boo] n Asian ox with a humped back and long horns.

Zen n Japanese form of Buddhism that concentrates on learning through meditation and intuition.

zenith n **1** highest point of success or power. **2** point in the sky directly above an observer.

zephyr [**zef**-fer] n soft gentle breeze.

zeppelin n Hist large cylindrical airship.

zero n, pl **-ros, -roes 1** (symbol representing) the number 0. **2** point on a scale of measurement from which the graduations commence. **3** lowest point. **4** nothing, nil. ♦ adj **5** having no measurable quantity or size. **zero in on** v **1** aim at. **2** Informal concentrate on.

zest n **1** enjoyment or excitement. **2** interest, flavour, or charm. **3** peel of an orange or lemon.

zigzag n **1** line or course having sharp turns in alternating directions. ♦ v **-zagging, -zagged 2** move in a zigzag. ♦ adj **3** formed in or proceeding in a zigzag.

zinc n Chem bluish-white metallic element used in alloys and to coat metal.

zing n Informal quality in something that makes it lively or interesting.

Zionism n movement to found and support a Jewish homeland in Israel. **Zionist** n, adj

zip n **1** fastener with two rows of teeth that are closed or opened by a small clip pulled between them. **2** Informal energy, vigour. **3** short whizzing sound. ♦ v **zipping, zipped 4** fasten with a zip. **5** move with a sharp whizzing sound.

zircon n mineral used as a gemstone and in industry.

zirconium n Chem greyish-white metallic element that is resistant to corrosion.

zither *n* musical instrument consisting of numerous strings stretched over a flat box and plucked to produce musical notes.

zodiac *n* imaginary belt in the sky within which the sun, moon, and planets appear to move, divided into twelve areas, called signs of the zodiac, each named after a constellation.

zombie, zombi *n* **1** person who appears to be lifeless, apathetic, or totally lacking in independent judgment. **2** corpse brought back to life by witchcraft.

zone *n* **1** area with particular features or properties. **2** one of the divisions of the earth's surface according to temperature. ♦ *v* **3** divide into zones as for different uses or activities. **zonal** *adj*

zoo *n, pl* **zoos** place where live animals are kept for show.

zoology *n* study of animals. **zoologist** *n* **zoological** *adj* **zoological garden** zoo.

zoom *v* **1** move or rise very rapidly. **2** make or move with a buzzing or humming sound. **zoom lens** lens that can make the details of a picture larger or smaller while keeping the picture in focus.

zucchini [zoo-**keen**-ee] *n, pl* **-ni, -nis** *US & Aust* courgette.

Zulu *n* **1** member of a tall Black people of southern Africa. **2** language of this people.

zygote *n* fertilized egg cell.

WRITE FOR LIFE

Supplement

TABLE OF CONTENTS

WRITE FOR LIFE

INTRODUCTION

Throughout life you often need to communicate your thoughts and feelings in writing. Writing concise and effective letters, speeches, and emails is easy, once you know exactly what you want to say. This supplement covers the basic rules of style and form to follow, whether you are writing a business letter or a text message to a friend. Whatever you need to write, however, the two most important rules for expressing yourself through language are simple, but often ignored:

✔ Be clear

Choose words that occur to you naturally and convey exactly what you mean. If you have a choice between a basic word and a showy one, choose the basic one. Do not repeat yourself, exaggerate, or stray from your main topic. To find the best words to express your thoughts, particularly on difficult or complex subjects, refer to this dictionary and a good thesaurus. Check that each sentence flows easily, and sends a clear message.

✔ Think of your audience

When writing to or for someone, think of that specific person's position, interests, and relationship to you. What information does he or she need from you? How can you persuade him or her to do what you ask? What language would this person best understand? When writing to strangers or business contacts, write in a polite and formal style. When writing to close friends, you are free to use more casual and personal language, including slang. People always respond better to letters that show regard for who they are and what matters to them.

This guide outlines everything you should need to know to communicate effectively and clearly through writing in all areas of life. It shows examples of good letters for work, school, money matters, and social situations. It covers basic rules of etiquette for emails, and text messaging language. It also includes advice for writing and delivering confident and memorable speeches.

Every section of this supplement provides practical answers to frequently asked questions (FAQs) about the format and words required for a particular situation. This guide also suggests useful phrases that you might include in your writing. For each topic and situation, it gives useful tips and examples, and advice regarding how and when to approach a particular subject.

Think through what you want to say. Then use this supplement to write it down in a style that will smoothly communicate your message to your audience.

JOB APPLICATIONS

FAQ

Q. *Should my letter be typed or handwritten?*
A. It should be typed on A4 paper. Only the signature should be handwritten.

Q. *To whom should I address my letter?*
A. If you do not know the name of the person who would deal with your application, call the company to find out their name.

Q. *Is it OK to send out the same letter to all those companies I'm interested in?*
A. No. Try to avoid generalisable letters. Find out as much as you can about the company, and tailor your letter accordingly.

Q. *Should I mention salary in my accompanying letter?*
A. It is usually best not to touch on the subject of salary at this stage, unless requested in the advertisement.

Useful phrases

First of all, identify the job you are applying for:
- I would like to inquire as to whether there are any openings for junior telesales operators in your company.
- I am writing to apply for the post of senior marketing manager.
- I would like to apply for the position of online learning co-ordinator, as advertised on your website.
- I am writing to apply for the above post, as advertised in *the Guardian* of 8 August 2005.

Next, give some examples of personal achievements:
- I have gained experience in several major aspects of publishing.
- I co-ordinated the change-over from one accounting system to another.
- I developed designs for a new range of knitwear.
- I have supervised a team of telesales operators on several projects.
- I contributed to the development of our new database software.

Then outline your personal qualities:
- I see myself as systematic and meticulous in my approach to work.
- I am a fair and broad-minded person, with an ability to get on well with people from all walks of life.
- I am hardworking and business minded, and I tend to thrive under pressure.

Explain why you want this job:
- I am now keen to find a post with more responsibility.
- I now wish to find a more permanent full-time position.
- I would like to further my career in the field of production.
- I feel that your company's activities most closely match my own values and interests.

Express your willingness to attend an interview.

WRITE FOR LIFE

● Application for an advertised post

☑ When applying for an advertised post, ensure that you head the letter with the exact name of the post, quoting any reference number given.

45 Fairways
Little Fordnam
Northumberland
N21 3RS

30 June 2006

Mrs F Reid
Recruitment Officer
Affinity Development Projects
3 Albion Court
Newcastle
N4 7JS

Dear Mrs Reid

application for post of Community Development Officer: post no: 513/6

I am writing in response to your advertisement in the June edition of Community Now, and am enclosing my CV for your review.

As you will see, I have gained valuable experience in working with Black and Asian communities, and have a strong understanding of community development. I am self-motivating, and can work as an effective leader of a team.

In my current position at the Northumberland Renewal Programme, I have initiated a strategic framework for obtaining funding and attaining targets.

I am at present completing a distance-learning course on Equality and Diversity Policy Development, and am now looking for a post which gives me an opportunity to use my new skills.

I look forward to having the opportunity to discuss this further with you.

Yours sincerely

Brian Hanlan

Brian Hanlan

● A speculative job application

✓ When applying for a job on a speculative basis, try to speak to the person responsible for recruitment in the appropriate department beforehand. This way, you will have a specific person to write to, as well as having established a relationship with them.

34 St Dunstan's Way
Vancouver
V6G 7D7

19 July 2006

Ms D Wallis
Youngs Accountancy and Finance
19 Lockwood Road
Vancouver
V9P 8K1

Dear Ms Wallis

post of software development co-ordinator

Thank you very much for taking the time to speak to me yesterday about the possibility of a position as software development co-ordinator with your company.

Please find attached a CV which highlights my prior professional experience, and the qualities which I feel make me suited to this position. You will see that I have a strong interest in, and knowledge of, staff management, and have gained extensive experience in handling large development projects and meeting deadlines.

I see myself as being well-organized and self-motivated, and have excellent communication skills. I am keen to develop my career with Youngs Accountancy and Finance, and so would very much appreciate the opportunity to discuss further my suitability for the post.

Please feel free to contact me, either by email: dgormanl@netserve.com, or by leaving a message on (604) 473 5522. I look forward to speaking to you soon.

Yours sincerely

D Gorman

Deborah Gorman

WRITE FOR LIFE

FAQ

Q. *How should a CV be presented?*
A. It should be constructed on a word-processor, well laid out and printed on a good quality printer. Do not use too many different font types and sizes. Use bullets or similar to start sub-sections or lists.

Q. *I usually send the same CV out to all potential employers. But should I be tailoring it to different jobs?*
A. Yes, you should. Consider carefully how your skills, education, and experience compare with the skills that the job requires. Ask for more detail if needed. Spend time researching the employer - their structure, products and approach.

Q. *What details do I need to include in my CV?*
A. You should include the following:
personal details: name, home address, phone number, email address, URL of your own web page if you have one, date of birth.
education: Give places of education where you have studied, with most recent first.
work experience: List your most recent experience first. Give the name of your employer, job title, and what you actually did and achieved in that job. Make sure all time periods are accounted for.
interests: If you are just entering the work force, and have little employment experience, an employer will be particularly interested in activities where you have leadership or responsibility, or which involve you in relating to others in a team.
skills: Ability in other languages, computing experience, or possession of a driving licence should be included.
references: Usually give two names. Make sure that referees are willing to give you a reference. If you do not wish to name them on your CV, it is perfectly acceptable to write 'on request'.

Q. *How long should my CV be?*
A. Keep it as short and relevant as possible. One page is ideal. It should not normally be longer than three pages.

Q. *I've heard people talk about writing a 'personal objective statement' at the top of a CV. Is this expected/appropriate?*
A. It can be a good idea to start with a personal objective statement. This is a short overview of your skills, qualities, hopes and plans. If you are replying to a specific job advertisement, review what key words and tasks were used. Which of these words apply to you? Use these words in your statement. But if you do not feel confident about doing this, there is no obligation to include one.

● Basic graduate CV

CV

Name	Kate Maxwell
Date of birth	29.02.75
Address	19, The Poplars Bristol B10 2JU
Telephone	0117 123 4567
Email	katemaxwell@atlantic.net
Nationality	British

Education

1994–1998	**BA Hons in Modern Languages, University of Exeter** (final grade 2.1)
1992–1994	**Clifton Road Secondary School**: 3 'A' levels - French (A) German (A) History (B)
1987–1992	**Clifton Road Secondary School**: 8 GCSEs including Maths and English

Employment history

1994–1995	**Sales Assistant, Langs Bookshop, Bristol** I was responsible for training and supervising weekend and holiday staff.
1995–1996	**English Assistant, Lycée Benoit, Lyons** I taught conversational English to pupils aged 12-18, preparing the older students for both technical and more academic qualifications. I organized an educational trip to the UK for fourth-year pupils.

Positions of responsibility held

1995–1996	**Entertainments Officer for University Student Social Society** I organized and budgeted for entertainment for a student society with over 1000 members.
1994 – present	**Captain of the university women's netball team** I was in charge of training, organizing and motivating the women's team from 1995 to date.

Other skills

Fluent French and German
Extensive knowledge of Microsoft Word, Excel and Access
I hold a clean driving licence

References

on request

● **CV for experienced candidate**

CV

Andrew Baird
134 Newton Road, Lincoln, LI5 6HB
tel: 01453 678234
email: abaird@coms.net
date of birth: 8 September 1965

Work experience

1995 to present
Coogan and Kidd Web Design Ltd, Lincoln – Website Developer
- Development of company website
- Responsible for team of 8 staff
- Project management: have led several projects providing web design and support for a number of leading insurance companies
- Training: overseeing development of technical training programmes
- Customer support: following up and advising customers on website management
- Quality assurance
- Information architecture

1990–1995
Centaur Software Development, Cambridge – Computer Programmer
- programming
- database design: set up database for network of travel companies
- software design: assisted in the design of financial management application for use by financial advisers

Programming languages

C, C++, Java, Perl, Visual Basic, VBScript, JavaScript

Applications

Visual Interdev, Dreamweaver

Servers

Apache, IIS

Other skills

clean driving licence held

Education

1999 – Microsoft Certified Systems Engineer+Internet
1990 – MSc Multimedia Design
1988 – BSc Computer Science (2.1)

References

on request

WRITING FOR BUSINESS

● Writing business letters

> **FAQ**
>
> **Q.** *Is there a particular style I should use?*
> **A.** Most companies have their own way of doing things. They have a 'house style' for layout and punctuation so if you are unsure or new to a company, look back in the filing to find out which style has been used as the house style.
>
> **Q.** *What do I need to include in a business letter?*
> **A.** You should include: the company letterhead; the letter reference; date; addressee's name and address; salutation(opening); subject heading; body of the letter; subscription (closing); signature or signatory.

 Tips

- Keep letters short and to the point.
- The subject heading indicates the subject of the letter for quick reference and should only be two or three words.
- Make sure you open with a statement of intent and close with a request or promise of action.
- Avoid using ambiguous words or phrases. If there is any chance of a misunderstanding, find an alternative way to say it.
- Think out your letter before you start to compose it. Make notes if it helps to organize the information in a logical order.
- Remember that the standard method of closing before the signature depends on the opening at the start of the letter. If you opened with 'Dear Sir', you should close with 'Yours faithfully', if you opened with 'Dear Mr....' you should close with 'Yours sincerely'.
- All parts of a letter are designed to give important information. If your letters give accurate information, you will increase efficiency.
- If you can amend a standard or similar letter to say what you need to say, do so. It will save you time.
- If the sender is not available to sign, the letter can be signed *per procurationem* ('for and on behalf of') by another person (the signatory). This is indicated by the abbreviation 'pp' written or typed before the signatory.
- Always proofread your letters for spelling errors and other details. Don't rely on your computer spell-check facility.
- If the letter has been marked 'Personal', 'Private' or 'Confidential', ensure that the envelope has been marked in the same way. Private means personal, confidential means sensitive.

Useful phrases

- Thank you for your letter/email …
- With regard to … I am writing to …
- Further to our recent telephone conversation …
- Further to your recent email …
- If you require further information please don't hesitate to get in touch.

Ms R. Aitchison
124, Raven Road
HARROGATE
HG2 8OP

27th January, 2005

Dear Ms Aitchison

I am writing to thank you for coming down to Oxford yesterday so that we could discuss the possibility of our company taking over responsibility for publishing The Big Book of Yo-Yos. This is an exciting opportunity for us and I hope that we are able to reach a mutually beneficial agreement.

I will present this title to my sales and marketing team at our regular meeting midweek, and will then take the proposal to the more formal acquisitions meeting early next week. I have sounded my marketing director out already and he is as enthusiastic as I am to publish your book, so I am not anticipating too many problems getting a positive response from the sales team.

I will also look at the financial side of the project, and you are kindly going to send me a copy of your current contract, detailing royalty rates. I have requested a copy of our standard author contract from the legal department and will forward this to you as soon as it arrives.

I enjoyed meeting you on Friday and hope that this is the start of a fruitful relationship. I will of course keep you up to date with progress.

Yours sincerely

James Nichols

James Nichols
Publishing Manager

● Writing memoranda

> **FAQ**

Q. *What is a memorandum?*
A. A memorandum (or memo) is a short letter or note sent to a particular in-house member of staff or circulated to groups of people.

Q. *Can I send a memo to someone in another company?*
A. Memos are not usually sent out of house.

Q. *What information does a memo usually contain?*
A. A memo usually contains: the sender's name and department; the addressee's name and department; date; and the subject.

Q. *Can memos be used for confidential information and do they need a signature?*
A. They are not normally used for confidential information, but if they are they should be placed in a sealed envelope marked 'Confidential'. Memos are not usually signed, but if they contain financial information it may be usual for the sender to add initials as confirmation.

Q. *Do I need to keep a copy?*
A. Always keep and file copies of all memoranda, as with other forms of correspondence.

To: Amy Wall
Publishing Production

From: Lorna Gilmour
Editorial Department

23/01/05

THE BIG BOOK OF YO-YOS
TEXT PRINTING COPY

Amy,
With regard to passing the book for press, I enclose the text printing copy:
– complete set of text pages, with book pages marked and margins ruled up for all prelims.
– pagination and margins list.
– sheet showing book pages and their content.
Please pass this and request a full set of proofs from the printer for checking.
Cover copy for this edition already passed.

Thanks,
Lorna

● Writing business reports

> *FAQ*
>
> **Q.** *How do I start?*
> **A.** You will find it much easier to write if you have a clear idea in your mind of the line of argument you want to take before you begin to write. Begin by making a note of all the evidence you have amassed and decide on a line of argument. Group together the evidence under various headings and gradually the argument will begin to take shape.
>
> **Q.** *What should a report contain?*
> **A.** Reports should include: a heading; a reason for the report; an argument; and a conclusion or recommendation.
>
> **Q.** *How do I persuade the reader to accept my proposal?*
> **A.** The golden rule is to find out what the priorities of your reader are, and then write the report from that point of view.

 Tips

- Aim to be accurate, concise and brief.
- Never use words that you don't understand. Keep jargon to a minimum, but use technical words accurately.
- Reports on meetings should be written in the third person: 'It was decided', 'A proposal was put forward'. Individual reports can be written in the first person: 'I looked into the cost of …'
- Think about whether or not you need to include graphics or illustrations (such as pie charts, bar graphs, line graphs or flow charts) in your report and choose the ones that are best suited to your purpose.
- Decide whether you want to use paragraph numbering or headings. Paragraph numbering is often much clearer than using headings and allows you to refer back and forward to specific paragraphs by number. It also reduces the need for page numbering. If you do decide to use headings, make sure that the hierarchy is consistent.
- Also think about the general layout. Do you want the text to be justified or unjustified? Where are you going to position the page numbers, if you use them? Are you going to include footnotes and a bibliography?
- To make sure you've included everything, ask yourself four questions:
  – Have I included all the information that may be needed for the reader to make a decision?

- Have I covered all the possible options and made a convincing case for the alternative that I am recommending?
- Have I explained my proposal adequately and proved that it is better than alternatives?
- Have I successfully put myself in the reader's shoes, and presented the problem and the solutions with his or her priorities in mind?

● Always pay attention to:
  - consistency in headings or numbering.
  - accuracy of information in graphics, tables, footnotes, etc.
  - spelling, punctuation and grammar.
  - overall order of the argument.
  - length: is the report too long?

● Asking for increased salary

FAQ

Q. *Isn't this usually done verbally?*
A. Yes, but you may be asked to follow up in writing. The advantage of putting your request in writing is that it enables you to set down your thoughts clearly, and gives your supervisor something concrete to use when negotiating with upper management on your behalf.

Q. *Is it a good idea to threaten to leave as a way of getting a pay increase?*
A. Generally not. Your boss is likely to call your bluff, and you may have problems further down the line if you need to ask him or her for a reference. However, if you have genuinely been offered another job with a higher salary, but are reluctant to leave your current job, it may be worth mentioning this.

Q. *Whom should I address my letter to?*
A. Check with your supervisor, but it is a good idea to address it to your supervisor, and to copy in his or her manager and the human resource manager if there is one.

 Tips

- Open by telling your recipient how much you enjoy being a part of the team at your company, mentioning specific skills that you have.
- Let your recipient know how valuable you are to them, by listing some accomplishments, especially in terms of revenue you have brought in to the company or money saved.
- Finish off by saying that you would like to continue being a valuable asset to the firm and that you appreciate their serious

WRITE FOR LIFE

consideration of your request for an increase.
- Be realistic in the amount that you ask for: find out how much others make in comparable jobs.
- You could also attach an updated copy of your CV, which should show all of your accomplishments in your current position as well as those for your previous jobs.

Useful phrases

- I am writing to ask if you could consider the question of my salary.
- I enjoy my work with ... very much.
- Since joining PGL, I have greatly enjoyed being a member of the I.T. department.
- During my time with PGL I have made several valuable contributions to the company's success: ...
- Many responsibilities have been added to my work over the last year.
- I am therefore requesting a salary increase of £... per annum.
- I would like to continue being a valuable asset to the firm and I appreciate your serious consideration of my request.
- Please find attached an updated copy of my CV, which details my skills and accomplishments.
- I should appreciate the opportunity to discuss this with you further.
- If you would like to discuss this matter further, please do not hesitate to contact me to arrange a meeting at your convenience.

WRITE FOR LIFE

48 Ashgate Drive
Sydney
NSW 2001

14 April 2006

Mr A Williamson
Head of I.T.
Planet Insurance Ltd
Henderson Way
Sydney
NSW 2004

Dear Mr Williamson

request for increased salary

In the six years that I have been working for Planet Insurance, I
have greatly enjoyed being a member of the I.T. department,
combining my programming knowledge with my
communication and people skills.

I feel that during this time, I have not only benefitted greatly
from the experience, but that I have also made certain
accomplishments that have been of benefit to the company. In
2001, for example, I wrote a computer program which greatly
reduced the time spent on certain backup procedures, and in
July 2002 I was responsible for the successful introduction of the
online account management system.

With these points in mind, I would like to request a salary
increase of $2000 per annum.

I am very keen to continue being a valuable asset to the firm
and I appreciate your serious consideration of my request.

Please find attached an updated copy of my CV, which details
my skills and accomplishments, both in my current work at
Planet Insurance and in my previous jobs.

If you would like to discuss this matter further, please do not
hesitate to arrange a meeting at your convenience.

Yours sincerely

Patrick Evans

Patrick Evans

WRITE FOR LIFE

● Giving notification of maternity leave

✅ You are required by law to give your employer 21 days' notice in writing of your intention to take maternity leave. You must tell them the date you intend to stop work, the week the baby is due, and whether you intend to return to your job. This protects your right to maternity pay and return to work. **You must give at least 21 days' notice, in writing, of the date on which you intend to return to work.**

6 Dudley Avenue
Livingston
Edinburgh
EH14 5TY

15 July 2006

Mr C McLeod
Cardrona Housing Association
3 Victoria Road
Edinburgh EH3 5WD

Dear Mr McLeod

maternity leave notification

I am writing to notify you that I am pregnant, the expected date of delivery being 24 September 2006. Please find attached a copy of form MAT B1, which confirms this date. I plan to begin my maternity leave on 27 August 2006.

I intend to return to work in April 2007, and will give you at least 21 days' notice of the exact date of my return.

Yours sincerely

Linda Allen

Linda Allen

6 Dudley Avenue
Livingston
Edinburgh
EH14 5TY

15 July 2006

Mr C McLeod
Cardrona Housing Association
3 Victoria Road
Edinburgh EH3 5WD

Dear Mr McLeod

notification of return to work

I am writing to notify you that I intend to return to work on 4 April 2007.

I am looking forward to taking up my post with you again after maternity leave.

Yours sincerely

Linda Allen

Linda Allen

● Asking for holiday entitlement

☑ It may not be necessary to write a letter when asking for holiday entitlement. An email is often considered satisfactory.

Dear George

I would like to take two weeks of my holiday entitlement from 25 April 2006–7 May 2006.

I have checked schedules, and feel confident that my work on the first stage of the current web project will be completed by then.

I hope these dates will be convenient.

Kind regards
Jack Lyons

● Asking for unpaid leave

Dear George

I would like to request permission to be absent from work from 6–10 June 2006. My mother will be undergoing an operation on 3 June, and she will be requiring assistance with daily chores on her return home.

I hope you will give my request consideration. I realize that I would not be paid for this week's leave.

Kind regards

Sandra Greene

Sandra Greene

● Writing a letter of resignation

 Tips

- Keep it simple.
- If giving your reason for leaving, try to avoid indirectly criticizing the company or your co-workers: you may wish to use your employer as a reference at a later date.
- Thank the recipient for any help or support you feel they have given you during your time at the company.
- Show that you are willing to make the transfer as easy as possible.

Useful phrases

- I have decided that it is time to move on and I have accepted a position elsewhere.
- This is to inform you that an opportunity has presented itself that will enable me to work in the area of …
- Please accept this letter as my formal resignation as Systems Administrator for DAL publishing, to become effective as of …
- I am tendering my resignation from your company and wish to advise you that … will be my last day of employment.
- As required by my contract of employment, I hereby give you 4 weeks' notice of my intention to leave my position as …
- I am confident that my new role will help me to move towards some of the goals I have for my career.
- I believe this position will offer me more opportunity for advancement, and allow me to broaden my own experience and knowledge.
- I want to take this opportunity to thank you for your time and

efforts in my training and advancement during the past three years.
- The support shown by you and the rest of the management team has been greatly appreciated.
- My experience with FTL has been very rewarding.
- Thank you for your time and consideration, and I wish you all the best in the future.
- Please be assured that I will do all I can to assist in the smooth transfer of my responsibilities before leaving.

16 Lonsdale Crescent
Betchworth
Surrey
RH10 7KM

4 April 2005

Mr K Robertson
Managing Director
Geode Publishing
3-5 Guildford Road
Dorking
Surrey
RH7 4GL

Dear Keith

resignation

I am writing to inform you that I have decided it is time to move on, and I have accepted a position at Topline Publishing in Croydon, starting on 5 April 2005. I believe this position will offer me more opportunity for advancement, and allow me to broaden my own experience and knowledge.

I want to take this opportunity to thank you for your time and effort in my training during the past three years, and wish you all the best for continued success in the future.

Please be assured that I will do all I can to assist in the smooth transfer of my responsibilities before leaving.

Yours sincerely

James Payne

James Payne

SCHOOL-RELATED CORRESPONDENCE

FAQ

Q. *Whom should I address my letter to?*

A. For straightforward matters such as homework and absences, write to your child's class teacher. For more serious issues or complaints, address your letter to the headteacher. If you are not satisfied with the response, you local education authority will be able to tell you whom to contact next.

Q. *How can I find out about legal issues regarding bullying, truancy, exclusion, etc?*

A. The Advisory Centre for Education (ACE) publishes booklets outlining your rights on these matters. The material can also be read on their website.

● Explaining a child's absence from school

16 Newstead Road
Invercargill
9501

12 Jan 2005

Dear Mr Dobson

Stephen was unable to attend school yesterday as he was suffering from a 24-hour stomach bug. He seems to be well enough to come in today.

Please advise us of any work he should be doing to make up for lost time.

Thank you.

Yours

Lesley Allen

● Excusing a child from school

☑ Your letter is more likely to receive a positive response if you phrase it as a request rather than as a *fait accompli*.

Ensure that the educational value of the arrangement is stressed.

Express willingness to make up for any missed work.

39 Kayside Cottages
Perth
PE2 5GK
16 Jan 2005

Mrs H Ross
Headteacher
St Mary's High School
Perth
PE3 5RA

Dear Mrs Ross

request for absence from school

On 1 Feb 2005, my employer, the NHS, will be observing 'Take your child to work day'. The purpose of this event is to introduce children aged 8 to 16 to the world of work, and to encourage them to consider a career in medicine. The programme will include many educational activities, including workshops, tours and demonstrations. I feel sure that the experience will prove to be rewarding for all children concerned.

I am therefore writing to request that my daughter, Isobel, be excused from school that day. She will, of course, make every effort to catch up on any vital school or homework that she will be forced to miss.

I look forward to hearing from you. If you wish to discuss the matter further, please do not hesitate to call me on 01252 568356.

Yours sincerely

Irene Marchant

Irene Marchant

● Notifying school of bullying

☑ Attach a report giving details of exactly where and when the incident(s) took place, who was responsible, what happened, and how your child was affected by this.

Be sure to ask for details of the school's anti-bullying strategy. (The headteacher must by law have measures in place to deal with bullying among pupils.)

Useful phrases

- I wish to inform you of a serious situation involving ...
- I am writing to express my deep concern about ...
- My daughter has recently been experiencing ...
- I have spoken to ... but the situation has not improved.
- He has spoken to his class teacher, who has reprimanded those concerned. However, ...
- My daughter is usually able to look after herself, but ...
- As you can imagine, this problem is causing him great anxiety.
- I am anxious to resolve this problem as soon as possible.
- Please find attached a report of the series of incidents in question.
- I would like to request a meeting to discuss a resolution to this problem.

19 Fairfield Drive
Toronto
Ontario
N59 6YS

25 March 2006

Mr D Fitzgerald
Headteacher
Hornslea Primary School
Toronto
Ontario
N55 7XG

Dear Mr Fitzgerald

For the last three days my daughter, Hannah Moore, has been arriving home in tears, due to continual name-calling from a small group of girls in her class. I have mentioned it to her class teacher, who has spoken to those concerned, but it has only made the problem worse. As you can imagine, this problem is causing Helen great anxiety, and now she is becoming fearful of going to school.

I understand that the school and the LEA have a duty of care towards my child, and so I would like to request a meeting at your earliest convenience to discuss this.

I look forward to hearing from you.

Yours sincerely,

Katherine Moore

Katherine Moore (Mrs)

56 Holmes Drive
Reigate
Surrey
RH2 5GD

25 February 2006

Mr R Thomson
Headteacher
Croydon High School
Selsdon Road
Croydon
SE14 6YE

Dear Mr Thomson

change of school

I would like to inform you that my daughter, Emma Dixon, will be leaving Croydon High School at the end of this term.

My husband has taken a new job in Scotland, and we will therefore be moving to Edinburgh at the end of April. Emma has a place at James Gillespie's School in Marchmont, which I am told has an excellent academic record.

I would like to take this opportunity to thank you for all the help and encouragement you and your staff have given Emma over the last three years.

Yours sincerely

Pauline Dixon

Pauline Dixon

WRITE FOR LIFE

SCHOOL-RELATED CORRESPONDENCE

● Excusing a child from religious instruction

67 Langley Avenue
Crawley
W. Sussex
RH8 3FX

12 July 2005

Mrs J Wilson
Langley Green Secondary School
Langley Drive
Crawley
RH8 4WA

Dear Mrs Wilson

religious instruction

My son, Aashir, will be attending your school from the beginning of next term, and I am writing to ask that he be excused from religious education classes.

He is being raised in the Muslim faith, and receives his religious instruction outside school.

Thank you very much for your understanding.

Yours sincerely

Mahira Pandit

Mahira Pandit (Mrs)

● Non-completion of homework

Dear Mr Mitchell
John was unable to finish his essay that was due to be handed in today, as he was suffering from a severe migraine for most of yesterday evening.
He will make every effort to complete it tonight and hand it in tomorrow.
Thank you for your understanding.
Yours sincerely
Helen Maxwell

DOMESTIC MATTERS

● To a landlord concerning outstanding repairs

✅ In the first instance, simply list the repairs required, and ask the landlord to contact you so that a time may be arranged for them to be carried out.

56 Kayside Close
Redditch
Worcs.
RD14 7NX

4 April 2005

Dear Mr Fairchild

I am writing to notify you that the following repairs to 56 Kayside Close require attention:

There are several loose tiles on the roof.
The kitchen tap is leaking.
The sealant round the bath needs replacing.

I would appreciate it if you would contact me as soon as possible to arrange a time to have these problems taken care of. Thank you very much.

Yours sincerely

Matthew Chalmers

Matthew Chalmers

✅ If repairs are not forthcoming within a reasonable amount of time, write again, once more itemizing the repairs, and reminding the recipient how long you have been waiting. This time you might want to give the landlord a deadline, and show that you are aware of your rights in law.

Useful phrases

- Further to my previous correspondence, the following repairs to the above address remain outstanding: …
- I have been waiting for a considerable amount of time to have these repairs completed.
- By law, a landlord is responsible for providing and maintaining residence in a good state of repair.
- Please contact me immediately so that we may resolve this problem.
- I would be glad if you could see that the matter is resolved as soon as possible.

WRITE FOR LIFE

56 Kayside Close
Hawkes Bay
4230

1 May 2005

Dear Mr Fairchild

In my previous correspondence to you I requested repairs to be completed to 56 Kayside Close. The following items remain outstanding:

There are several loose tiles on the roof.
The kitchen tap is leaking.
The sealant round the bath needs replacing.

I have been waiting for a considerable amount of time to have these repairs completed. I would ask you to take care of this matter within one week of receipt of this letter.

I remind you that by law, a landlord is responsible for providing and maintaining residence in a good state of repair, and for complying with housing and maintenance standards.

Please contact me immediately so that we may resolve this problem.

Yours sincerely

Matthew Chalmers

Matthew Chalmers

DOMESTIC MATTERS

● Letter to a housing advice centre regarding unfair rent

☑ If your landlord/landlady is trying to put the rent up and you don't agree to the increase, it may be worth negotiating with them. They may agree to a lower rent increase in return rather than having to relet the property. Alternatively, they may agree to increase the rent in stages over a period of time.

45 Victoria Street
Headley
Northants.
NO3 7FS

16 April 2005

The Rents Adviser
Headley Housing Advice
4 The Row
Headley
Northants.
NO2 4TY

Dear Sir/Madam

unfair rent query

I am writing to request your advice on an issue regarding what I consider to be an unfair increase in rent.

My landlord has recently increased my rent from £300 a month to £360 a month. Not only do I find this amount unreasonable, but I am also having difficulty sustaining the payments. Furthermore, there are several outstanding repairs to be attended to in the house.

I would be grateful if you could inform me of my rights, and let me know what, if anything, I can do to challenge this increase. I look forward to hearing from you.

Yours faithfully

Katherine Gulliver

Katherine Gulliver

DOMESTIC MATTERS

● Letter to a housing advice centre regarding eviction

☑ Most private tenants can only be evicted if their landlord gets a possession order from the court. If your landlord has evicted you without following the correct procedure this may be illegal.

34 Tadworth Court
Ducksbury
Berkshire
RD7 4GN

3 June 2005

Dear Sir/Madam

eviction query

I am writing to request advice from you regarding a matter of urgency.

My landlord has just issued me with an eviction notice, due to come into force on 4 July 2005. His justification for this action is that I have not paid my rent for the last two months.

I am a single mother with two young children, and I have been unable to pay the rent due to the fact that my ex-husband has not kept up regular maintenance payments over the last four months.

Could you please inform me of my rights, and advise me on how I should proceed?

I look forward to hearing from you. If you wish to speak to me directly, please call me on 01456 783219.

Thank you in advance.

Yours faithfully

Sally Nettles

Sally Nettles

● letter to planning authority inquiring as to whether planning permission is needed

✓ Some minor developments (such as certain extensions to domestic property, or changes in the way a building is used) may not need express planning permission. With buildings that are listed for preservation, it is generally best to consult with the local planning authority before any changes are made.

If you are unsure as to whether or not your development requires planning permission, you should contact your local planning authority.

---

19 Limes Avenue
Cambridge
CB12 4LA
tel: 01356 721673

17 June 2005

The Planning Department
Cambridge District Council
University Road
Cambridge
CB2 7KS

Dear Sir/Madam

inquiry re. necessity of planning permission

I am writing to inquire as to whether I will need to apply for planning permission for a proposed development I wish to undertake at the above address.

The specifications of the development are as follows:

description:
garage
location:
side of property
use:
car storage
dimensions:
floor surface area: 6m x 3.5m
height: 2.5m

If you require any further information, please do not hesitate to contact me at the telephone number above. I look forward to hearing from you.

Yours faithfully

Harriet Yates

Harriet Yates (Mrs)

● Objecting to a planning permission application

FAQ

Q. *What sort of objection is considered valid, and what is not?*
A. Objections should be confined to such issues as:
> design, appearance and general impact
> significant overlooking or overshadowing
> traffic impact
> noise, smell or other pollutants
> harm to local landmarks or public views

Objections which cannot normally be considered include:
> loss of a personal view from a particular property
> loss of property value

 Tips

- Write to the Director of Planning at your local district council.
- Refer to the application number and the site address.
- Clearly outline the reasons why you wish to object to the proposal.

Useful phrases

- I wish to object to the above planning permission application for …
- I am writing to register my objection to the planning application detailed above.
- I am seriously concerned that the noise and the smell from the plant would be detrimental to my health.
- The increase in traffic caused by the development would significantly affect the character of the area.
- This building would significantly affect my family's quality of life.
- I request that you take this into account when considering this application.
- I urge you to give my objection serious consideration.
- I urge you to reject this application.

WRITE FOR LIFE

7 Fallowfield Terrace
Fordham
Hants
SO12 5AZ

19 May 2005

The Director of Planning and Technical Services
Fordham District Council
Riverside House
Fordham
Hants
SO13 5HB

Dear Sir/Madam

Planning application no: 00006721 45793

I wish to object to the above planning permission application for 5 Fallowfield Terrace.

This extension, if constructed, would significantly affect the amount of light reaching the back rooms of my house, as well as compromising my family's privacy and quality of life.

I request that you take this into account when considering this application and urge you to reject it.

Yours faithfully

Malcolm Skinner

Malcolm Skinner

● Objecting to the proposed erection of a mobile phone mast

FAQ

Q. *To whom should I address my letter?*

A. Write to the council's planning department and copy it to your local councillor and the landowner. You could also write to your MP about the application and contact the local press.

Q. *How should I formulate my objection?*

A. Some ideas for formulating your objection are:
Have the regulations been followed? To find out the details of

regulations affecting mobile phone masts, visit your local library, or find an appropriate site on the World Wide Web.
Is it necessary?
Are there alternative sites, and if so, is the application accompanied by evidence that they were considered?

 Tips

- Identify the deadline date for objections.
- Different regions have different policies on the erection of mobile phone masts.
- Find out what your council's policy is before writing your letter.

45 Hopetoun Gardens
Hopetoun, West Lothian
LV4 7NX

3 April 2005

Mr R. McKinnon
Chief Planning Officer
Hopetoun District Council
Hopetoun, West Lothian
LV2 4GY

Dear Mr McKinnon

Re: planning application no. 39100921/000128

I am writing in objection to the proposed erection of a telecommunication mast on land situated at Hopetoun Park, West Lothian. My objection is based on the following grounds:

As you will be aware, there are a large number of conflicting academic reports on the dangers of irradiation emitted from base stations. The proposed mast would be situated only 30 metres away from a residential area. With no clear evidence showing that such masts are safe, particularly with regard to children's health, I feel that this is proximity is unacceptable.

The mast is unnecessary, since the signal for the network concerned is adequate in this area.

With these points in mind, I urge you to reject this application.

Yours sincerely

Roger Hall

Roger Hall

WRITE FOR LIFE

MONEY-RELATED CORRESPONDENCE

● **letter to a lender advising of difficulty in mortgage payment**

 Tips

- Identify the deadline date for objections.
- If you are having trouble with your mortgage payments, or if you can see that you are going to have problems, contact your lender as soon as possible.
- In your letter, show that you are willing to negotiate with the lender. Most will help you explore your options.
- Make it clear to your lender that you are keen to keep paying as much as you can afford.

Useful phrases

- I am writing to inform you that I am anticipating having some difficulty in continuing to meet my mortgage payments.
- I am currently finding it hard to meet all my financial commitments.
- My employers went into liquidation two months ago.
- I have recently been made redundant.
- I am suffering from a long-term illness, and am no longer entitled to sickness pay.
- I was wondering if it would be possible to reduce my monthly payments.
- I would like to request that my mortgage payments be reduced from July.
- I am keen to continue paying as much as possible.
- I would be pleased to come into your office and discuss this matter further with you.
- Would it be possible to arrange an interview with you, so that we may come to some sort of arrangement?
- I do hope that you will give sympathetic consideration to my situation, and look forward to hearing from you.

WRITE FOR LIFE

12 Darwin Road
Canberra
2605

15 May 2006

Mr J McVee
Senior Credit Controller
Castle Building Society
17 Martyn Place
Canberra
2602

Dear Mr McVee

request for reduction in mortgage payments

I am writing to inform you that, due to my recent redundancy, I am anticipating having some difficulty in continuing to meet my mortgage payments.

I am making every attempt to find work elsewhere, but if I am unsuccessful, I would like to request that my mortgage payments be temporarily reduced from July, and the terms of my mortgage extended accordingly.

I am keen to continue paying as much as possible, and am currently in consultation with my financial adviser to calculate how much money I can reasonably afford each month.

Would it be possible to arrange an interview with you, so that we may come to some sort of arrangement?

I do hope that you will give sympathetic consideration to my situation, and look forward to hearing from you.

Yours sincerely

Jack Everett

Jack Everett

WRITE FOR LIFE

● **letter to an insurance company advising of an accident**

Ken Howland
2 Rowlands Ave
Birmingham
B6 7PL

25 July 2006

The Claims Officer
Hotline Insurance
3 Castle Court
London
W1 5HT

Dear Sir/Madam

Policy No: 0000931 45621

I am writing to notify you that I wish to make a claim under the provisions of the insurance policy detailed above.

The loss came about on 12 July 2006 as a result of an accident between the insured vehicle and another vehicle at the intersection of Channel Street and Caddonfoot Road in Pitlochry, Perthshire. As a result, the insured vehicle suffered damage to the rear bumper and the lights.

Please contact me at the address shown above, so that a formal claim according to your company's procedures may be made. Thank you for your attention to this matter.

Yours faithfully

Kenneth Howland

Kenneth Howland

- **letter to an insurance company advising of a home burglary**

Patrick Norton
23 Lucas Rd
Kingston-Upon-Thames
Surrey
KT6 2PL

25 July 2006

The Claims Officer
UK Assured Ltd
6 West Gorton Rd
Lincoln
LI4 9TZ

Dear Sir/Madam
Policy No: 12409745 000002

I am writing to inform you that I have suffered a loss to the above-named property, insured with you, and I would like to make a claim under the provisions of the insurance policy named above.

The loss came about on 23 July 2006, as a result of a burglary. I sustained losses of jewellery believed to have a value of £2000, a television with a value of £350, and damage to the home which will cost £500 to repair.

I would be grateful if you could contact me at the address shown above, so that a formal claim according to your company's procedures may be made.

Thank you for your attention to this matter.

Yours faithfully

Patrick Norton

Patrick Norton

LETTERS OF COMPLAINT

FAQ

Q. *Is it OK to send a complaint by email?*

A. On the whole, it is advisable to send your complaint in the form of a letter, rather than an email.

Q. *To whom should I address the letter?*

A. For a large company, direct your letter in the first instance to the Customer Relations Manager.
For a small company, you should write directly to the Managing Director.

Q. *What is the best way to ensure a speedy reply and get the desired result?*

A. Collect together all the relevant facts, then calmly set them down in a logical sequence. If you have a reference number that will help to identify the purchase or invoice in question, quote this in the subject heading of the letter. Show that you are a reasonable person by making reference to positive aspects of your contact with the company. Finally, specify a time limit (usually 14 days) within which you expect to hear from the company, stating the action you wish to be taken.

Q. *What sort of tone should I use? Is an angry tone more likely to get results?*

A. A letter that is polite and firm, and that sticks to the facts is far more effective than one written in a fit of temper.

Q. *What do I need to know about my legal rights?*

A. It often helps if you know the basics of the Sale of Goods Act, and to make this fact known to your recipient. Unless you are really sure about particular laws, though, it is best just to suggest that you know your legal rights and will use them if reasonable action is not taken.

Q. *How should I respond if I just get a bland, non-committal reply?*

A. Contact the managing director of the company, explaining your problem again. If you still do not get results, try contacting a Citizens' Advice Bureau to get legal help.

Useful phrases

- I am writing to express my dissatisfaction with the service I received from your …
- At the time of booking it was agreed that …
- However, on our arrival, we discovered that …
- I recently bought …(include colour, model and price) in your shop in …
- When I tried to use this item, I discovered that …
- I have contacted you by telephone three times and each time you have promised to visit and put the faults right.
- To date these problems have not been resolved.

- Under the terms of your guarantee, I would like to request a full reimbursement of the amount paid.
- I am withholding payment of the above invoice until I have heard your response to the points outlined above.
- Under the Goods and Services Act 1982, I am entitled to expect work to be carried out using due care and skill.
- If I do not hear from you within 14 days, I will have no choice but to take the matter further.
- Because of these faults I now consider you to be in breach of contract.

• letter of complaint regarding unsatisfactory holiday accommodation

WRITE FOR LIFE

16 Hopeside Crescent
East Sussex
EG13 6HJ

24 August 2005

The Customer Relations Manager
Sunkiss Holidays
58-60 East Preston Street
Manchester
M2 9LP

Dear Sir

Re. booking reference number 610004367

I am writing to express my dissatisfaction at the standard of holiday accommodation my family and I were forced to accept at the above holiday apartment in Ibiza last week.

At the time of booking, I requested a three-bedroomed apartment with living room and fully-equipped kitchen.

However, on our arrival, we discovered that the third 'bedroom' consisted of a sofa-bed in the living area, and the kitchen was small, dirty and in a very bad state of repair. I enclose photos.

Under the Supply of Goods and Services Act 1982, I am entitled to expect the accommodation provided to be of a satisfactory standard, and for it to be as described in your brochure. I look forward to an offer of compensation within 14 days.

Yours faithfully

Charles MacLennan

Charles MacLennan (Mr)

LETTERS OF COMPLAINT

● **letter of complaint regarding a faulty appliance**

41 Selwood Avenue
Kingston-upon-Hull
East Yorks
HU7 4DS

4 May 2005

Ms Jane Andrews
Customer Relations Officer
Stewarts Electrics
Electra House
Foxton High Road
London
SW3 6BZ

Dear Ms Andrews

Re: faulty appliance: Giolaggio Express A261

I recently bought a chrome 'Giolaggio Express' A261 espresso
machine (£129.99) from your store in Middleham. When I tried
to use it, I discovered that the element was faulty, and that the
resulting coffee was lukewarm.

I have returned to your store in Middleham on several
occasions, firstly requesting a replacement appliance, and
subsequently, due to an extended delay, requesting a refund.
The latter has not been forthcoming, and I have been advised by
the shop manager to take my complaint to you.

Under the Sale of Goods Act 1979, purchased items should be of
satisfactory quality and fit for their purpose. Since neither of
these criteria are met, I would like to request a full
reimbursement of the amount paid.

I look forward to your reply within 14 days, and hope this
matter can be resolved quickly.

Yours sincerely,

A. Fraser

Anne Fraser (Mrs)

WRITE FOR LIFE

● Complaining about public transport

☑ If your letter of complaint is triggered by a series of problems that have been experienced in relation to a particular service, it is important that your letter should not become a long and verbose essay. It can be easy to get carried away with all the negative implications of each error, in the misguided belief that you will arouse your recipient's sympathy. Instead, list your complaint clearly and succinctly. If you are using a computer, you could separate the items with bullet points.

WRITE FOR LIFE

35 Fairways Drive
Penicuik
Midlothian
EH17 4KC

4 October 2005

The Customer Relations Manager
Scotbus
Burns House
McGowan Road
Glasgow
G4 7JY

Dear Sir/Madam
Re: Route 95, Penicuik to Edinburgh, 2 October 2005
I am writing to complain about the bus journey I undertook yesterday on the number 95 bus from Penicuik to Edinburgh. I had scheduled a meeting for lunchtime, and gave myself ample time, choosing to take the 11.15 service. I was dissatisfied with the service in the following ways:

The bus arrived 20 minutes late.

The bus finally left the bus station 30 minutes late.

The temperature inside the bus was about 35 degrees Centigrade. I asked the driver if he could turn the heating off, but he explained that it had to be switched on, as it formed part of the bus's cooling system.

Being nearly 7 months' pregnant, I found this journey very uncomfortable, and by the end, quite distressing.

I would be interested to hear your comments on this, and any offer of compensation you may consider appropriate.

Yours faithfully
P. Holmes
Patricia Holmes

● Shoddy workmanship

 Tips

- Discuss the problem with the tradesperson first, and give them a chance to put it right. If this doesn't work, put your complaint in writing giving a deadline. Send it to the head office if there is one.
- Keep copies of all letters sent and received and make a note of conversations.
- If you chose a contractor that belongs to a trade association, they may offer a conciliation or arbitration service to settle your dispute.

---

77 Bishop Road
Newport
Gwent
NP3 5NQ

31 October 2005

The Customer Services Manager
L. Smart & Co. Contractors
17 Trevellyan Road
Cardiff
CA4 5GT

Dear Sir/Madam

Re: estimate 700003412

I am writing to express my dissatisfaction with the service I received from one of your builders recently.

Before accepting your estimate for the job, I was assured that the work would be completed by 10 October. Three weeks later, the work is still incomplete. Moreover, the work that has been done is defective. The new door that was fitted is not flush with the frame, and the lock is consequently very stiff.

If the work is not completed and the defect rectified within 14 days, I shall consider our contract to be at an end. I shall then instruct another firm to complete the work, and deduct the cost from your original price.

Yours faithfully

Douglas Fairburn

Douglas Fairburn

● Complaining to a health authority

 Tips

- Address your letter to the Complaints Manager of the Local Health Authority
- Give name of doctor, GP or practitioner concerned.
- Give a brief background to case.
- State the problem. If your complaint consists of a catalogue of errors, itemize them clearly and succinctly.
- Note that it is one of the NHS's officially stated core principles that it is committed to shaping its services around the needs and preferences of individual patients, their families and carers.

7 Oaklands
Horley
RH6 2QT

17 November 2005

The Complaints Manager
East Surrey Local Health Authority
5 Market Street
Redhill
RH1 4GA

Dear Sir

I am writing to express my concern about the treatment that my elderly mother, Mrs Grace Harding, is currently undergoing. Her GP is Dr Middleton at the Longwood Surgery, Horley.

In 2001, my mother was diagnosed as suffering from shingles. Since that time she has experienced continual pain down the sides of her body.

However, she recently received a letter informing her that she would no longer be able to attend the pain clinic. She has been given no explanation as to the reasons for this decision from the health authority or from her doctor.

Since it is one of the NHS's officially stated core principles that it is committed to shaping its services around the needs and preferences of individual patients, I feel that you have a duty to ensure that she enjoys this later period of her life.

I would be glad to hear your comments on this case.

Yours faithfully

G. Glover

Gillian Glover

LETTERS OF COMPLAINT

● Complaining about financial services

 Tips

- You must complain to the firm before you go to the ombudsman.
- Remember to include important details like your customer number or your policy or account number. Put these details at the top of your letter.
- Remember to enclose copies of any relevant documents that you believe back up your case.
- Keep a copy of any letters between you and the firm. You may need to refer to them later.

---

4 Crow Lane
Wagga Wagga
2650

24 October 2005

The Customer Relations Manager
Castle Building Society
Short Street
Wagga Wagga
2650

Dear Sir/Madam

Complaint: savings acc. no. 9450001992

I wish to register my dissatisfaction with the service that I have received from the staff at your Brighton branch.

I opened a savings account, and arranged for a monthly standing order of $200 a month to be made from my current account, held at another bank. However, the last time I asked for a mini-statement, I noticed that there had not been a credit to my savings account for the previous two months, despite the fact that the money had been debited from my current account. Enclosed are copies of both the relevant statements.

I am therefore appealing to you for a thorough investigation into this matter, and look forward to hearing from you.

Yours faithfully

Patrick Horton

Patrick Horton

● Formal invitations

 Tips

- Use good quality stationery that reflects your personal style, and the nature of the occasion.
- Issue your invitation well in advance of the occasion, so that the recipient will be able to make space in his or her calendar for your event.
- Include details of the nature of the event, the address, date and time, and indicate whether or not food and drink will be provided if the time is near to a usual meal time. If a dress code or special parking arrangements are required, give these details in as clear and brief a manner as possible.
- Include the line "RSVP" with a telephone number or address, so that guests can tell you whether or not they will be able to attend. You may want to include an RSVP card for the recipient's use.

● A wedding invitation

> John and Angela Shaw
> *are delighted to invite*
> Jeremy Kempton and Kay Whitcroft
> *to the wedding of their daughter*
> Catharine
> *to*
> Matthew Tibbits
> *on Saturday 5th April 2005*
>
> *at 2pm*
> *at Hemel Methodist Church, Bristol*
> *and afterwards to a*
> *Reception*
> *at Austen Place, Keynsham*
>
> RSVP
> Cathy Shaw
> 89 Caird Drive
> Brighton
> BN1 9TQ

SOCIAL CORRESPONDENCE

● Refusing invitations

 Tips

- Begin by thanking the person for the invitation.
- Then show regret and give reasons.
- Finally, express desire to see them at a future date.

Useful phrases

- Thank you so much for the invitation to …
- Many thanks for your invitation to …
- I'm afraid I'm not going to be able to come.
- Unfortunately we're not going to be able to make it.
- Unfortunately I already have something arranged for that day.
- It's our 30th wedding anniversary, and we're going out for a meal that night.
- It's the day we get back from our holiday, so I don't know if we'll be home in time.
- Harry's got his school concert that night.
- What a shame!
- I'm really sorry, as I'd have loved to see you all.
- I hope we can get together soon, though.
- I hope you all have a really great time.

● Declining a formal invitation to a wedding

 Use the same style as that used in the invitation.

> 25 Dean Avenue
> Yeovil
> Somerset
> YO3 8LR
>
> 23 March 2005
>
> Mr and Mrs K Forbes thank Mr and Mrs O'Neill for their kind invitation to their daughter's wedding, and to the reception afterwards, but regret that a prior engagement prevents them from attending.

● **Declining a formal invitation to dinner**

8 Holmes Close
Eskbank
Midlothian
EH16 3BV

14 May 2005

Dear Caroline

Many thanks for your kind invitation to dinner on 1st August.
Unfortunately, Jeff is away on business that week, and I've
arranged to go and visit Jackie and the children, so I'm afraid
we won't be able to be with you.

We are both very sorry, and hope to see you soon.

Thank you again.

Fiona

● **An informal letter or email declining an invitation**

67 Hawthornevale
Gosforth
Newcastle
N7 5GD

24 April 2005

Dear Nicola
Thanks ever so much for the invitation to Gordon's party,
but I'm afraid I'm not going to be able to make it. It's our
30th wedding anniversary that day, and we're going out for
a meal in the evening. What a shame! I hope we'll be able to
get together again soon.

Hope you all have a great time.

love,

Teresa
xxx

● Writing a letter of apology

 Tips

- Make it clear from the start that you are apologizing, and state what you are apologizing for.
- Explain how the mistake came about, accepting responsibility if you are at fault.
- Think about how you can put the problem right, and suggest your solution tentatively.
- At the end of the letter, reiterate your apology.

Useful phrases

- I am writing to apologize for …
- I've just realized that …
- I can't tell you how sorry I am.
- I am sorry that …
- Due to …, I was unable to …
- I know it's no excuse, but …
- Unfortunately …
- I hope you will accept …
- Can I suggest …?
- Would you agree to …?
- Again, please accept my apologies (for …).
- In the meantime, many apologies again.

● Letters wishing a speedy recovery

FAQ

Q. *What sort of tone should I use?*
A. It is acceptable to use a fairly informal tone if you know that the person will recover quickly. If the illness is serious, you will need to use a slightly more formal tone.

Q. *Should I send a card or a letter?*
A. For informal wishes, a card is most appropriate. For more formal wishes, or if the illness is serious, you may like to write a letter.

● Informal wishes (card)

Useful phrases

- Hoping you get well very soon.
- Wishing you a speedy recovery.
- Sorry to hear you're not well. We're thinking of you.

SOCIAL CORRESPONDENCE

● **Formal wishes (letter)**

Useful phrases

- I was very sorry to hear of …
- Please accept my sympathies …
- … and best wishes for a speedy recovery.
- It must be an anxious time for you.
- You have our deepest sympathy.
- Is there any way in which we can help?
- If there's anything I can do, please don't hesitate to let me know.
- We hope and trust you will soon be better.
- We are feeling for you.

● **Formal letter wishing someone a speedy recovery**

Upper Steading, 17 June, 2006

Dear Mr Grierson

We were very sorry to hear of your wife's sudden illness. Please accept our sympathies and give her our best wishes for a speedy recovery.

It must be a very anxious time for you. If there's anything we can do, please don't hesitate to let us know. In the meantime, we are thinking of you both.

Yours sincerely

Mary Fawkes

✓ If the recipient is unlikely to make a full recovery, it is unwise to suggest that this might be the case.

● **Letters of condolence**

FAQ

Q. *What form should a letter of condolence take?*
A. A letter of condolence should normally be handwritten. However, you need to use your own discretion, depending on your relationship with the recipient.
Q. *I never know what to say at such times. Don't letters of condolence require flowery language and literary turns of phrase?*
A. No. Try to express yourself simply, and speak from the heart.
Q. *Should I make reference to God and religion?*
A. Only if you know that your recipient shares your beliefs.

SOCIAL CORRESPONDENCE

 Tips

A simple and effective structure for a condolence letter might be as follows:

- Express your shock or regret and the person's death.
- Briefly point out the deceased's qualities, and any achievements you may want to mention.
- Say how much the deceased will be missed.
- Offer any help that you are genuinely willing to give.

• An informal letter of condolence

Useful phrases

- We were very sad to hear of …'s death.
- It came as a terrible shock to us all.
- Everyone who knew him found him a warm and affectionate person.
- She was such a good friend to us.
- We will all miss him terribly.
- We're thinking of you all.
- Please don't hesitate to call on us at any time.
- Is there anything we can do to help?

Littleton, 24 March 2006

Dear Pat,

We were terribly sad to hear the tragic news of Ken's death. It 's been a great shock, and we want you to know that you are in our thoughts.

Everyone who knew Ken found him an exceptional person, with his great talent for painting and his kindness and warmth. We will miss him greatly.

You know that you can call on us any time. Please don't hesitate if there is anything we can do to help.

All our love

Leonie and Andrew

SOCIAL CORRESPONDENCE

● **A more formal letter of condolence**

- I was deeply saddened to hear of …'s death last …
- I have just heard of the sad death of …
- It has come to us as a great shock.
- Please accept my sincerest condolences.
- I am sure you know how much he was liked and respected by everyone.
- We will all miss him greatly.
- He will be greatly missed.
- It must be a comfort to you to know that …

Taunton, 14 April 2005

Dear Mrs Morrison

I was very sad to hear of your husband's death last week, and I write to offer sincere condolences to you and your family.

I am sure you know how much Mr Morrison was liked and respected in the community. We will all miss him greatly.

If there is anything I can do to help, please don't hesitate to get in touch.

Kindest regards

Yvonne Tullis

WRITING SPEECHES

● Writing your speech

 Tips

- When writing your speech, if you're unsure of what to say, look at other people's speeches in books and on websites. Reading what others have said can help you decide what's appropriate for you.
- Think about who will be in the audience. What would *they* appreciate? How formal is the setting? What kind of jokes are likely to go down well?
- Brainstorm on topics.
- Select topic(s).
- Gather your material.
- Organize your material.
- Draft your speech.
- Practise your delivery.

● Delivering your speech

FAQ

Q. *Is it OK to read my speech or should I try to memorize it?*
A. It's best not to trust everything to memory. Try to thoroughly familiarise yourself with your speech and then reduce it to a set of brief notes on cue cards. This way your speech will not sound as if it is being read word for word.

Q. *Should I practise my speech, or might too much practice make it sound contrived?*
A. You should rehearse it, then rehearse it again. And then again, until you have had enough of it. Get a friend or family member to help by listening and ask them to tell you honestly how your voice sounds.

Q. *I tend to gabble when I'm nervous. How can I avoid this?*
A. Always pause to let your points sink in and wait for the laughs you want. Take your time. What will seem like an age to you will really only be a few seconds to your audience. Use pauses to gather your thoughts, glance at your notes and breathe in and out. Don't give in to the urge to speed up.

Q. *Is it advisable to have a few drinks beforehand?*
A. Don't drink too much before speaking. You might think it helps, but your audience won't.

Q. *How can I give an impression of confidence, even when I'm nervous?*
A. When delivering your speech, be conscious of your body language from the start. Stand with your weight equal on both feet, and look around at your audience for a few seconds before you start to speak. Try to make eye contact with the audience. Try to make everyone feel included.

WRITE FOR LIFE

WRITING SPEECHES

● Wedding speeches

There are three main speeches that are usually given at a wedding reception. They are:
- the bride's father's speech
- the bridegroom's speech
- the best man's speech

Other speeches are possible. For example, the bridegroom's father may give a short speech of thanks to the host and hostess for the occasion, or the bride may wish to give a speech. Here, though, we will look at the three principal speeches.

 Tips

- Once you have completed all the formalities, you may wish to expand your speech a little. When drafting your speech, start by considering some of the following points:
- When did you first meet the bride/groom?
- Who brought you together? (for bridegroom only)
- How did she/he come across to you then?
- Can you remember anything unusual that happened when you first met?
- What are her/his best qualities?
- Think of three words describing the way you feel about him/her.
- Do you have any plans or wishes for your future together? (for bridegroom only)

● The bride's father

The bride's father is called upon by the best man to propose a toast of health and happiness to the bride and bridegroom.

Before doing so, he should welcome the groom's parents, and the relatives of both families. He should say a few words about his daughter, and then the groom, welcoming him into the family.

Useful phrases

- On behalf of (name of wife) and myself, I would like to start by saying what a pleasure it is to welcome, on this very happy occasion (names of groom's parents), (named close relatives), together with all relatives and friends of both families.
- As father of the bride, it is my privilege to make the first speech, and I would like to start by …
- First I would like to welcome everybody here today to join (bride) and (groom) on this special day.
- To (name of officiator), our thanks for officiating at the ceremony,

and to his 'boss' for keeping the weather at bay.

- I know some people have travelled quite some distance, and I would like to express our gratitude and thanks for the effort they have made.
- I would like to thank (bride) and (groom) for organizing such a splendid occasion. I am sure you will agree that it is a tremendous success.
- I'd like to take this opportunity to thank especially, (wife), for not only being a tolerant wife but more importantly an outstanding mother.
- (Groom) is attentive, caring, hard-working, intelligent, and informed on most subjects, except football (he supports ......). I am very pleased and proud to welcome him as a son-in-law.
- During the time we've known him, we've come to realize how special he is to her. I would like to welcome my new son-in-law into our family.
- (Bride's name) and (groom's name),

  Here's to the past

  Here's to the present

  And here's to the future, for all that you can look forward to together.
- Ladies and gentlemen, please be upstanding, and raise your glasses to (bride) and (groom).
- The bride and groom.
- Thank you.
- It is now my pleasant duty to propose a toast to the happy couple. Please join me in wishing them a long and happy life together. Ladies and Gentlemen fill your glasses and join in the toast to the happy couple, (bride) and (groom).

● The bridegroom

The bridegroom replies on behalf of himself and his bride, thanking his parents for their love and care, and for the start they gave him in life. He will also take this opportunity to thank all those present for their gifts. Any members of the family who could not attend the wedding because of illness should be mentioned and wished a speedy recovery. He would normally then say a few words about his new wife. The bridegroom should propose a toast to the bridesmaids, and thank them for doing such a good job.

WRITING SPEECHES

> *Useful phrases*

- I'd like to thank (bride's father) for those kind words, I am very proud to be your son-in-law; I hope I can live up to your expectations.
- I would sincerely like to thank you and (bride's mother) for welcoming me into your family.
- Thank you again to (bride's father) and (bride's mother) for your daughter's hand. Julia is the most special person I've ever known, and I promise I'll take good care of her.
- To our parents, thank you for your love and support over the years, for the advice you have given us, for putting up with us and pointing us in the right direction.
- On behalf of my new wife and myself, I would like to say thank you to a few people:
- Firstly, to (bride)'s parents and to my own parents … We could never thank you enough for all your very generous help and the tremendous love and support you've always given us, but in particular in the last few months.
- To our two lovely bridesmaids for taking such good care of (bride) and getting her to the church on time.
- To my ushers, (names), for looking after me so well today.
- To (name of Master of Ceremonies), for keeping us all in line today as Master of Ceremonies.
- To my best man (name), for calming my nerves on the run-up to the wedding and for looking after me so well today.
- To everybody for all your cards, kind thoughts and presents. We've been quite staggered by your generosity.
- I would like to say thanks very much for all of you for sharing this special day with us.
- It's been an amazing day and having you all here has helped to make this the most memorable and happiest day of our lives.
- In conclusion, I would also like to thank my best friend for agreeing to marry me today.
- The one person in this room to which I owe the most thanks is (bride), my wife. I am sure you will all agree how stunning she looks today.
- She is beautiful, intelligent, hard-working – the list is endless, but unfortunately I can't read her handwriting …

● The best man

It is the best man's duty to respond to this toast on behalf of the bridesmaids. His speech should be light-hearted and fun.

WRITING SPEECHES

Useful phrases

- Firstly on behalf of the bridesmaid(s), (names), I'd like to thank (groom) for his kind words. I'm sure you'd agree with me that they look beautiful and that they have done an excellent job today.
- Firstly on behalf of the bridesmaid(s), (bridesmaids' names), I would like to thank (groom) for his kind words.
- I am sure you will all agree she does/they do look marvellous.
- The bride, well, we all agree how wonderful she looks today, and (groom) scrubs up well himself …
- I must say she is one of the nicest people you could ever wish to meet.
- On a serious note, can you all be up standing and charge your glasses while I propose a toast:
- To the bride – may she share everything with her husband, including the housework!
- To the bride and groom – may the roof above you never fall in and may you both never fall out!
- Please stay upstanding and join me in a toast to the bride and groom's parents … and those who were sadly unable to be here today.
- It gives me great pleasure to invite you to all stand and raise your glasses in a toast for (bride) and (groom). We wish them well for the future and hope they enjoy a long and happy marriage together.

● Writing a eulogy

FAQ

Q. *What sort of tone should I adopt when writing a eulogy?*

A. Generally, a eulogy should be written in an informal, conversational tone. Humour is acceptable if it fits the personality of the deceased. When delivering your eulogy, talk to the audience as though you were talking to a friend.

Q. *Should I just speak about my own experiences of the deceased, or should I try to include other people's experiences?*

A. A eulogy should convey the feelings and experiences of the person giving it. Don't try to objectively summarize the person's life or speak for all present. Having said that, it can be a good idea to write about memories that the audience can remember, and to get the audience involved in what you are saying.

Q. How long should I speak for?

A. Keep it brief. Five to ten minutes is the norm, but it's a good idea to verify that with the officiator.

WRITING SPEECHES

 Tips

- Be yourself.
- Be honest, and focus on the person's positive qualities.
- You may want to include the deceased's favourite poems, book passages, scripture verses, quotes, expressions or lines from songs.
- You could interview family and friends when preparing your draft.
- Some of the simplest thoughts are deeply touching and easy for those congregated to identify with. For example, 'I'll miss her laughter' is just as good as 'I admired her courage.'
- Here are some questions to ask yourself:
- How did you and the deceased become close?
- Is there a humorous or touching event that represents the essence of the deceased?
- What did you and others love and admire about the deceased?
- What will you miss most about him or her?

Useful phrases

- When I think of …, I think of laughter and love.
- I can remember …ing with …
- One time …
- … even made it into the newspaper about it.
- … taught me how to …
- … was involved in so many activities; she/he was very popular.
- I can see her/him now: …ing, …ing and …
- … was like a ray of sunshine.
- … gave me so much wisdom.
- She/he always showed loyalty, courtesy and consideration for others.
- I am so lucky to have had … as a friend.
- And in spirit she/he joins us today.
- I will miss her/him very much.

WRITING SPEECHES

● Leaving and retirement speeches

 Tips

- Remember that your approach may be slightly different depending on whether the employee is leaving under happy or more regrettable circumstances.
- Make sure you get your facts right, for example how long the employee has been working for the company.
- Remember that your main aim is to thank the employee and to praise them for any achievements you want to mention.
- On the whole, this kind of speech should be short, as people are usually standing at such occasions.
- Even if your relationship with the employee was not very warm, try to concentrate on their good points.
- Try to think of at least one anecdote, humorous if possible, that you can recount about the person who is leaving.

Useful phrases

- This is both a time to look back and a time to look forward.
- Some people here may remember the time when ...
- When Jack first arrived at the company, there was ... Now, there are ...
- Thank you for all your hard work, especially ...
- You have certainly made my job easier.
- The company has a lot to thank you for.
- We respect the decision you have made, and wish you all the best in your future career.
- We are sorry you had to leave under these circumstances, but we wish you every success in the future.
- Your future is looking very exciting, and we wish you great happiness in your new job.
- We are all going to miss you very much, and hope that the rest will do you the good your deserve.
- Everyone joins me in wishing you well.
- Please accept this gift as a mark of our respect and gratitude for all you have done.

WRITE FOR LIFE

Tips

The rules of polite behaviour for email conversation are known as 'netiquette'.

Some rules of netiquette are:

- Do not write in capital letters. This is considered to be the equivalent of shouting in speech.
- Use asterisks (*) before and after a word if you want to emphasize it.
- Be careful about using irony or sarcasm. Readers cannot see facial expressions or hear the tone of voice, and so statements intended as jokes may be taken seriously.
- Jokes can be shown by using a 'smiley' or 'emoticon' such as :-). On the other hand, do not use too many of these.
- Avoid 'flames'. A flame is an angry response to a message, especially on a newsgroup. An exchange of flames or a 'flame war' can be very annoying for other newsgroup readers.
- Always include the subject of a message in the subject line.
- Messages should be relatively short and to the point.
- Do not forward other people's messages without the author's permission.
- Include the parts of the message being responded to in new emails or posts to newsgroups.

● Emoticons

Emoticons or 'smileys' are often used to indicate tone. These symbols are read with the head tilted on the left shoulder. The basic smiley is :-). It may mean 'I'm happy to hear from you', or it may be used after a jokey statement. Tongue-in-cheek remarks might use a winking smiley ;-). Below is a list of emoticons in common use, both in email and text messaging:

o:-)	angel
;/	confused
>:-)	devil
:-%	Get lost!
:-s	I'm not making sense.
:-p	naughty
:@)	pig
:-(	sad
:-O	shouting
:o	surprised
:-@!	swearing
;&	tongue-tied

WRITE FOR LIFE

● Net abbreviations

Net abbreviations have developed to shorten messages and speed up typing. It is best to avoid using them if you are not sure that your recipient will understand them. Some of the more common ones are:

AFK	away from keyboard	IMHO	in my humble opinion
BAK	back at keyboard	IOW	in other words
BTW	by the way	NRN	no reply necessary
FAQ	frequently asked question(s) (or a web page containing frequently asked questions)	OTOH	on the other hand
		ROFL	rolling on the floor laughing
FWIW	for what it's worth	RSN	real soon now (often used ironically)
FYI	for your information		
FUA	frequently used acronym	SITD	still in the dark
IAE	in any event	TIA	thanks in advance
IMO	in my opinion	TIC	tongue in cheek
IMCO	in my considered opinion	TLA	three letter acronym

Useful phrases

Generally, email avoids the use of the more formal opening and closing conventions used in traditional letter writing. Below are the most common ones used:

more formal

Dear George
Dear Mr Thomas

All the best
Best wishes
Kind regards
Regards

more informal

Hi Jenny
Jenny
Hi there!

See you soon
All the best
Best wishes
Take care
Love
Lots of love

WRITE FOR LIFE

● An informal email

To: jennymartin@viking.net
Cc:
Bcc:
Subject: Friday night
Attachments:

Hi Jenny

How're things? Hope all's well, and that you had a riveting time last night at the committee meeting ;-)

I was wondering what you and Will are up to on Friday? We're thinking of going out for something to eat – maybe an Indian. Do you fancy coming too?

BTW, I've just heard that Kate's taken that new job. IMHO it's not going to be an easy job, but good for her anyway.

Let us know what you think about Friday night.

Lots of love

Tamsin xxx

● A more formal email

To: frankcollins@planet.co.uk, viviankaye@planet.co.uk
Cc: robertwestwood@planet.co.uk
Bcc:
Subject: sales review meeting
Attachments: salesfigures_jan_to_march2005.doc

Dear Frank, Vivian

I've just been looking at the sales figures for the last quarter, and I think it would be beneficial for us all to get together to discuss them.

I'm attaching a copy of the document, and would be grateful for any comments you may have, especially with regard to the post-Christmas sale period.

Would Thursday afternoon suit you both, say, 2.30pm? Please let me know if this is not convenient. Thanks.

Regards

Brian

● Response to an informal email

To: tforbes@pgl.com
Cc:
Bcc:
Subject: Re: Friday night
Attachments:

Hi Tamsin

You wrote:

>Hope all's well, and that you had a riveting time last night at the >committee meeting ;-)

I nearly died of boredom, as you can well imagine!

>I was wondering what you and Will are up to on Friday? We're thinking of going out for >something to eat – maybe an Indian. Do you fancy coming too?

Sounds great! I'll have been paid by then, so I'll be up for a big night :-)

>BTW, I've just heard that Kate's taken that new job. IMHO it's not going to be an easy >job, but good for her anyway.

I'm amazed, but I suppose our Kate's always up for a challenge. Rather her than me though …

Looking forward to seeing you. Will give you a ring about meeting up on Friday.

Love

Jenny

xx

WRITE FOR LIFE

● Text messaging

Since most mobile phones do not have keyboards, senders of messages have to key through the letters marked on the numeric keypad. This can be tedious, and so text messages tend to be short, using a large number of short cuts. As with email, emoticon are also used. Some of the more common abbreviations are listed below:

1CE	once	NETHING	anything
2DAY	today	NO1	no one
2MOR	tomorrow	NP	no problem
2NITE	tonight	OIC	oh, I see
ASAP	as soon as possible	OMG	oh, my God
B	be	PLS	please
BCNU	be seeing you	PPL	people
BRB	be right back	R	are
BTDT	been there, done that	RTFM	read the flippin' manual
BTW	by the way	RU	are you
C	see	RUOK	are you okay
CID	consider it done	SOZ	sorry
COZ	because	STFU	shut up
CU	see you	SUM1	someone
DA	the	THANQ	thank you
EZ	easy	THX	thanks
F2T	free to talk	TMB	text me back
FOTFLOL	falling on the floor, laughing out loud	TTYL	talk to you later
		TXT BAC	text back
GAL	get a life	TYVM	thank you very much
GR8	great	U	you
GTG	got to go	W/O	without
H8	hate	WAN2	want to
K	okay	WBS	write back soon
L8	late	WIV	with
L8ER	later	WKND	weekend
LOL	laughing out loud or loads of love	WUD?	what you doing?
		XLNT	excellent
LV	love	Y	why
M8	mate	YR	your
MMFU	my mate fancies you	YYSSW	yeah yeah sure whatever
NE	any		
NE1	anyone		